An Indonesian-English Dictionary

AN
Indonesian-English
Dictionary

By JOHN M. ECHOLS

and HASSAN SHADILY

Second Edition

Cornell University Press

ITHACA, NEW YORK

PREFACE TO THE FIRST EDITION

An Indonesian-English Dictionary is intended to be a practical, comprehensive dictionary of modern Indonesian with English equivalents for the use of those who wish to read contemporary Indonesian materials. A large number of technical terms have been included, but no attempt has been made to be exhaustive. This dictionary should also be useful to Indonesians who wish to learn the English equivalent of an Indonesian utterance. It departs from the usual bilingual dictionary in one respect: it provides illustrative phrases and sentences, whereas the usual bilingual dictionary is an index of word equivalents. We hope that the inclusion of illustrations for a large number of the entries and subentries may provide the English-speaking student with examples of usage in context, thereby giving some indication of the range of meaning of the items.

A further word should be said about the illustrative phrases and utterances. Any attempt to present illustrative material involves problems of usage, of what is standard and what is substandard. Present-day Indonesian is fairly fluid, and this dictionary makes no attempt to be prescriptive (this is the prerogative of Indonesians); it merely presents the words and idioms found in print and in the speech of educated Indonesians.

Indonesian, the Malay-based national language of Indonesia, is undergoing rapid development, and its effort to become a vehicle adequate in all spheres of knowledge has placed tremendous pressure on its users to supply the necessary terms. The Komisi Istilah has done great service over the past few years in deciding on such new terms and in affirming those already existing.

Since the primary aim of this dictionary is practical utility, no attempt has been made to give etymologies. A number of Western words which would be obvious to the user have been omitted. Some obsolete and obsolescent words as well as dialectal words have been included, but there has been no intention to cover this area completely.

During the work on this project seven Indonesians assisted at various times and on certain, not all, sections of the dictionary. They were all well-educated men and women but in no sense specialists in the Indonesian language. Virtually all were from places outside Jakarta but had lived for varying periods in the capital. In education and background they represented Madura, central Java, west Java, Jakarta, and the Minangkabau and Batak areas. We checked many entries and illustrative examples with Indonesians other than those assisting us on the project, and to these, as well as to the many others who, knowingly and unknowingly, contributed to whatever merits the book may possess, deep appreciation is extended.

Thanks are expressed to Hilman Adil, Samiati Alisjahbana, Harsja Bachtiar, Idrus Nazir Djajadiningrat, Kismadi, Julia Shadily, and Odjahan Siahaan for their assistance at various stages in the dictionary's growth. Without their help publication would have been delayed much longer.

A word of appreciation should also go to the Program on Oriental Languages of the American Council of Learned Societies and to the Southeast Asia Program at Cornell University for financial aid and moral support.

Last, but by no means least, we owe a great debt of gratitude to Mrs. Nancy D. Echols and to Mrs. Tazu Warner, secretary in the Department of Far Eastern Studies, for typing two complete drafts of this book. Without their unstinted assistance this volume would never have reached publication.

We are aware of the limitations of this dictionary in spite of our efforts to make it as comprehensive as the resources available to us permitted. We would, therefore, be most grateful if users would supply us with any corrections or comments that might make a later edition more useful and accurate. Although assistance was received from many sources, we assume full responsibility for all deficiencies and for the arbitrary decisions necessary when the contributors could not reach an agreement.

JOHN M. ECHOLS
HASSAN SHADILY

Ithaca, New York, and Jakarta, Indonesia
March 1960

PREFACE TO THE SECOND EDITION

THE opportunity to prepare a revised edition of this dictionary presented itself far earlier than we would ever have expected. Although we are grateful for the opportunity, it has come at a period when, for various reasons, we could not devote full time to the task.

We have received much assistance from a number of scholars and interested friends, among whom we wish to mention Professors Denzel Carr and Rufus Hendon, Dr. Anthony Johns, Messrs. Valentine Ostrovsky and A. Ed. Schmidgall-Tellings, Drs. Soebardi, Mr. Renaldi Tedjasukmana, Professors A. Teeuw and Gerald Williams, and Sir Richard O. Winstedt, to all of whom we are indebted for their constructive, often detailed criticisms and suggestions for improvement. Any number of other individuals provided assistance here and there, and we are grateful for their interest and help.

In contrast to our practice in the first edition we have, at the insistence of many users, included a rather substantial number of the Western loanwords that are to be found in the Indonesian language of 1962.

We are grateful to the Program on Oriental Languages of the American Council of Learned Societies and to the Southeast Asia Program of Cornell University for financial assistance and support. Mrs. Nancy D. Echols assisted in the preparation of the manuscript and to her we express our heartfelt thanks.

Since the response to our earlier request for comments was excellent, we extend the invitation once again in the hope that each succeeding edition (by us or by others) will be a distinct improvement over the previous one.

JOHN M. ECHOLS
HASSAN SHADILY

Ithaca, New York, and Jakarta, Indonesia
May 1962

CONTENTS

INTRODUCTION

Arrangement

1.   Since the dictionary is designed primarily for Western users who are familiar with a certain alphabetical arrangement and since Indonesians are acquainted with Western alphabetization, it seemed practical to follow the English alphabetical arrangement. All the bilingual Indonesian dictionaries consulted use a Western alphabetical arrangement, but the more advanced student of the Indonesian language who uses the monolingual dictionaries will discover that those of Harahap and Poerwadarminta have the following arrangement: *a,b,ch,d,dj,e,f,g,h,i,j,k,l,m,n,ng,nj,o,p,r,s,sj,t,tj,u,(v),w,z.*

2.   The arrangement is according to entry and subentry. The entries are arranged in alphabetical order as stated in (1), regardless of whether a given entry consists of one word or more. This dictionary follows the traditional arrangement of citing the *base* as the main entry with the affixed forms as subentries. Since affixed forms are common and since bases frequently undergo modification when certain prefixes are attached, it is necessary to recognize these modifications in order to locate the affixed forms under the proper base. The following constitutes a list of prefixes and suffixes in Indonesian:

Prefixes	*Examples*
be-	bepergian
bel-	beladjar
ber-	berada, berasa (from *rasa*)
di-	dibuka
ke-	keterangan
me-	(used with bases beg. with *j,l,m,n,ng,nj,r,w*) mejakinkan, melaporkan, memainkan, menanti, mengerikan, menjanjikan, merata, mewudjudkan.
mem-	(used with bases beg. with *b,f,v,p* [which disappears]) membatja, memfitnahkan, memvéto, memotong (from *potong*).
memper-	memperdalam

men-	(used with bases beg. with *d,dj,tj,t* [which disappears]) menduduk, mendjadi, mentjari, menonton (from *tonton*).
meng-	(used with bases beg. with a vowel, *g,h,k* [which disappears]) mengadakan, menggosok, mengharap, mengarang (from *karang*).
menj-	(used with bases beg. with *s* [which disappears]) menjapu (from *sapu*).
pe-	(undergoes same changes as *me-*, etc.)
pel-	peladjar
per-	pertemuan
ter-	terbuka

Suffixes	*Examples*
-an	aturan
-i	memenuhi
-kan	membawakan
-lah	sudilah
-nja	achirnja

A word beginning with *mem-* plus a vowel offers three possibilities: a base beginning with *m* or *p*, or *mem-* as part of the base. Statistically one should look first under a base with initial *p-*. Similarly a word with initial *men-* plus a vowel may be located under a base with initial *n-*, *t-*, or *men-*. The most common is *t-*. For words with *meng-* plus a vowel there are four possibilities: the base may begin with a vowel, *ng-*, *k-*, or *meng-*. One should look under *k-* first and next under the vowel. A word with initial *menj-* should be sought under bases beginning with *nj-* and *s-*. The latter is by far the more common.

3.   Subentries are arranged as follows (the prefixed forms in alphabetical order):

be-an	ke-an	mem-kan
ber-(-)	ke- -²an	me-m-²kan
ber-(an)	kepe-an	memper-
ber- -²(an)	kese-an	memper- -²
ber-kan	me-	memper-i
berke-an	me- -²	memper-kan
berpe-an	me-ani	men-
bersi-	me-i	men- -²
di-	me-kan	men-i
di-an	me- -²kan	men-kan
di-i	mem-	meng-
di-kan	mem- -²	me-ng-²
ke-	mem-i	meng-i

me-ng-^{2}i	pen-	se-nja
meng-kan	pen-an	se- -^{2}nja
me-ng-^{2}kan	peng-	ter-
menge-i	peng-an	ter- -^{2}
menge-kan	penge-	ter-i
menj-	penge-an	ter-kan
menj-i	penj-	terke-
menj-kan	penj-an	-an
menje-	per-	-^{2}an
menje-kan	per-an	-nja
pe-	perse-an	-^{2}nja
pe-an	se-	-^{2}
pem-	se-an	- (in compounds)
pem-an	se- -^{2}(an)	

4.　Words with the same spelling are generally incorporated in one entry regardless of etymology. For example:

aki 1 grandfather. 2 storage battery.

5.　Indonesian abbreviations and geographical names have been incorporated into the text rather than listed separately in appendixes.

Spelling

1.　Perusal of the major monolingual and bilingual Indonesian dictionaries will show that Indonesian, like many other languages, has variant spellings, for example, **tolong** and **tulung**. Usually only one is illustrated and the variants are cross-referenced.

2.　It is customary to indicate in textbooks and dictionaries for foreigners the distinction between /ə/ and /e/. This is shown by writing e and é respectively.

3.　It should be noted that Indonesian language materials printed as late as 1947 use the Dutch spelling oe for the sound represented in present-day Indonesian by the letter u, e.g., boekoe: buku. Many personal names still retain the older spelling.

4.　For the past few years the Indonesians and Malayans have discussed the possibility of unifying the orthography of the two versions of Malay, but as of May 1962 no agreement had been reached in this matter. A comparison of the two alphabets, the Indonesian based on Dutch orthography and the Malay on English, indicates that four major changes are needed to bring about uniformity. Comparison with the proposed "reform alphabet" reveals the possibility of the following changes in both orthographies: c for Indonesian tj and Malay ch; ŋ for ng; ñ for nj and ny; ŝ for sj and sh.

Indonesian Alphabet	Malay Alphabet	Reform Alphabet
a	a	a
b	b	b
tj	ch	c
d	d	d
e	ě	e
é	e	é
f	f	f
g	g	g
h	h	h
i	i	i
dj	j	j
k	k	k
l	l	l
m	m	m
n	n	n
ng	ng	ŋ
nj	ny	ñ
o	o	o
p	p	p
r	r	r
s	s	s
sj	sh	ŝ
t	t	t
u	u	u
v	v	v
w	w	w
x	x	x
j	y	y
z	z	z

The Sounds of Indonesian (Phonemes)

Symbol	Description of Sound	Indonesian Spelling	Examples
1.	**Vowels.**		
/i/	Approximately like *ee* in *see*, but shorter and without off-glide. Sounds more like *i* in *pit* in closed syllable.	i	itu /itu/ 'that' pagi /pagi/ 'morning' inti /inti/ 'nucleus'

		Indonesian	
Symbol	Description of Sound	Spelling	Examples

/e/	Like the *a* in *make* but shorter.	e	sen /sen/ 'signal'
/ɛ/	Like the *e* in *pet*.	e	sen /sɛn/ 'cent'
/a/	Like *a* in *father* but much shorter.	a	apa /apa/ 'what' tanda /tanda/ 'sign'
/ə/	Approximately like *a* of *sofa*.	e	ke /kə/ 'to' empat /əmpat/ 'four'
/o/	Like the *o* in *coat* but shorter.	o	kopi /kopi/ 'copy'
/ɔ/	Like the *aw* in *law* but shorter.	o	kopi /kɔpi/ 'coffee'
/eu/	Approximately like *er* in *her* but with lips rounded.	eu	peujeum /peujeum/ 'fermented cassava with yeast'
/u/	Approximately like the *oo* in *food*.	u	susu /susu/ 'milk' minum /minum/ 'to drink' tuan /tuan/ 'sir'

2. Diphthongs.

/aj/	Something between the *ie* in *pie* and the *ay* in *pay*.	ai	pandai /pandaj/ 'clever' lantai /lantaj/ 'floor'
/aw/	Roughly equivalent to *ou* in *house* or *ow* in *now*.	au	tembakau /tembakaw/ 'tobacco' kalau /kalaw/ 'if'
/oj/	Similar to *oy* in English *boy*.	oi	amboi /amboj/ 'well!'

3. Consonants.

/b/	Similar to *b* in *rub*.	b	batu /batu/ 'stone' habis /habis/ 'finished'
/p/	Similar to *p* in *lip*. Without puff of air.	p	pukul /pukul/ 'to strike' asap /asap/ 'smoke'
		b	bab /bap/ 'chapter'
/d/	Similar to *d* in *red*.	d	duduk /duduq/ 'to sit'
/t/	Similar to *t* in *let*. Without puff of air.	t	tudjuh /tudjuh/ 'seven' mulut /mulut/ 'mouth'
		d	abad /abat/ 'century'
/g/	Similar to *g* in *dog*.	g	gadji /gadji/ 'wage' tiga /tiga/ 'three'
/k/	Similar to *k* in *like*. Without puff of air.	k	kabar /kabar/ 'news' makan /makan/ 'to eat'
		g	bedug /beduk/ 'drum'
/dj/	Similar to *j* and *dg* in *judge* but without the 'zh' sound.	dj	djalan /djalan/ 'road' médja /medja/ 'table'
/tj/	Similar to *ch* in *church* but without the 'sh' sound.	tj	tjari /tjari/ 'to seek' tjutji /tjutji/ 'to wash'

Symbol	Description of Sound	Indonesian Spelling	Examples		
/f/	Similar to f in fan.	f	fihak	/fihaq/	'side'
			safar	/safar/	2nd month of Moslem year
		v	vak	/faq/	'subject'
/m/	Similar to m in maim.	m	minta	/minta/	'to want'
			malam	/malam/	'evening'
/n/	Similar to n in noon.	n	nama	/nama/	'name'
			dan	/dan/	'and'
/nj/	Similar to ny in canyon.	nj	njanji	/njanji/	'to sing'
			tanja	/tanja/	'to ask'
/s/	Similar to s in send.	s	sumur	/sumur/	'well'
			masa	/masa/	'time'
			malas	/malas/	'lazy'
/sj/	Similar to sh in shoot.	sj	sjukur	/sjukur/	'thanks'
			tamasja	/tamasja/	'scene'
/z/	Similar to z in zeal.	z	zat	/zat/	'substance'
			azas	/azas/	'principle'
/ng/	Similar to ng in singer, not the ng in finger. The latter is represented in Indonesian by ngg.	ng	dengan	/dəngan/	'with'
			ngeri	/ngəri/	'to shudder'
			uang	/uang/	'money'
/w/	Ranges between v in vane and w in wane.	w	wasit	/wasit/	'referee'
			lawan	/lawan/	'opponent'
/l/	Approximates l in leave. Tongue more advanced than English l in lee or hill.	l	lima	/lima/	'five'
			boléh	/boleh/	'may'
			dalil	/dalil/	'proof'
/r/	Similar to r in British very or tt in butter. Not American r in rule. Sometimes trilled strongly.	r	roda	/roda/	'wheel'
			kiri	/kiri/	'left'
			atjar	/atjar/	'pickles'
/j/	Similar to y in you.	j	jang	/jang/	'who'
			saja	/saja/	'I'
/h/	Similar to h in hope. Occurs at end of words in Indonesian.	h	hal	/hal/	'thing'
			Tuhan	/tuhan/	'God'
			sudah	/sudah/	'already'
/ch/	Voiceless velar spirant similar to the sound made by a mild clearing of the throat.	ch	achir	/achir/	'end'
/q/	Produced by holding one's breath for a fraction of a second and then suddenly releasing it. Glottal stop.	k	baik	/baiq/	'fine'
			tundjukkan	/tundjuqkan/	'point!'
		'	ra'jat	/raqjat/	'people'

Materials Consulted

In preparing this dictionary the following monolingual and bilingual dictionaries have been consulted:

Harahap, E. St. *Kamus Indonēsia.* Tjētakan jang kesembilan. Bandung: G. Kolff & Co., 1951.

Korigodsky, R. N., O. N. Kondrashkin, and B. I. Zinov'ev. *Kamus Bahasa Indonesia — Rusia.* Moscow: Badan Negara Penerbit Kamus² Bahasa Asing dan Nasional, 1961.

Pino, E., and T. Wittermans. *Kamus Inggeris, Part II: Indonesian-English.* Groningen/Djakarta: J. B. Wolters, 1953.

Poerwadarminta, W. J. S. *Kamus Umum Bahasa Indonesia.* Tjetakan 3. Djakarta: Dinas Penerbitan Balai Pustaka, 1961.

Poerwadarminta, W. J. S., and A. Teeuw. *Indonesisch-Nederlands Woordenboek.* Tweede, bijgewerkte druk. Groningen/Djakarta: J. B. Wolters, 1952.

Winstedt, R. O. *Kamus Bahasa Mĕlayu.* Singapore: Marican & Sons, 1960.

Winstedt, R. O. *An Unabridged Malay-English Dictionary.* 3rd ed. Singapore: Marican & Sons, 1959.

Wojowasito, S., W. J. S. Poerwadarminta, and S. A. M. Gaastra. *Kamus Bahasa Indonesia-Inggeris.* Amsterdam/Djakarta: W. Versluys N.V., 1958.

Zain, Sutan Mohammad. *Kamus Moderen Bahasa Indonesia.* Djakarta: Jajasan Dharma, [1955].

A number of smaller and more specialized dictionaries were also examined as were the lists and the several *Kamus Istilah*'s of the Komisi Istilah in Jakarta. Some of the new entries and subentries as well as a number of illustrative examples were taken from current newspapers, magazines, books, and pamphlets, but the overwhelming majority of the illustrative phrases and sentences were supplied by contributors. Only time and usage will decide whether the neologisms will survive and become an integral part of the Indonesian vocabulary.

Symbols

–   indicates the main entry, e.g., under **ada:** **ber–** represents *berada.* Under **rumah:** *– baru* represents *rumah baru.*

∼   refers back to the nearest *affixed* form; thus under the entry **ada,** subentry **ke–an,** one finds the illustrative sentence ∼ *baik,*

The situation is good. **meng–kan** is followed by the illustrative phrase $\sim$ *pidato* to deliver a speech. The symbol $\sim$ may also refer back to a reduplicated form without affixation, e.g., $-^2$.

[2] the raised numeral two indicates reduplication of all the material back to the hyphen, if there is one. For example, under **abah**: $-^2$ signifies *abah²*, or *abah-abah*. Under **kali**: *se-* $-^2$ is equivalent to *se-kali²*, or *sekali-kali*, whereas *se–²* is equivalent to *sekali²*, or *sekali-sekali*. Under **pudji**: *me-m–²* equals *memudji mudji*.

( ) indicates that the portion within the parentheses may or may not occur with the remainder of the item without changing the sense. For example, under **agak**: **ter–(–)** 'to long for' means that either *teragak* or *ter-agak²* may be used without any difference in meaning. Similarly under **ahli**: – *(men)didik* may occur as *ahli didik* or *ahli mendidik* with the same sense.

see indicates a cross reference: **tulung** see TOLONG.

Abbreviations

abbrev.	abbreviation	kpd	kepada (to)
admin.	administration	lg.	language
anat.	anatomy	math.	mathematics
arith.	arithmetic	med.	medicine
attrib.	attributive	mil.	military
auto.	automobile	o.	one
beg.	beginning	o's	one's
bhw.	bahwa (that)	o.s.	oneself
blm.	belum (not yet)	pd	pada (to, on)
bus.	business	phon.	phonetics
dgn	dengan (with)	phot.	photography
dlm	dalam (in)	pl.	plural
elec.	electricity	sdh.	sudah (already)
e.o.	each other	s.o.	someone
fem.	feminine	s.t.	something
geog.	geography	sw	southwest
geol.	geology	tgl	tanggal (date)
gram.	grammatical	tlh	telah (already)
jg	jang (who, which)	ttg	tentang (concerning)
k.o.	kind(s) of	utk	untuk (for)

An Indonesian-English Dictionary

A

A.A. [*Asia-Afrika*] Asia-Africa.

A.B. [*anggaran belandja*] budget.

aba[2] order, command (in calisthenics, drill practice, etc.). *Ia memberi – utk berbaris*, He gave the command to line up, fall in.

abad century. *pd – ini* in this century. **ber- –**[2] for centuries. *– pertengahan* the Middle Ages.

abadi eternal, lasting, enduring. **ke-an** 1 durability, permanence. 2 eternity. **memper-, meng-kan** to immortalize. *Tugu itu ∼ djasanja*, The monument immortalizes his service.

abah direction. **meng-** to aim at. *∼ ke* to head for, steer toward. *–*[2] *kuda* harness. *–*[2] *tenun* weaving loom.

abai meng-kan 1 to ignore, disregard. *Pegawai itu ∼ perintah madjikannja*, The employee ignored his boss's order. 2 to underestimate s.t. or s.o. 3 to make light of s.t. 4 to break a promise or agreement. **peng-** careless, indifferent person. **peng-an** 1 carelessness, indifference. 2 slovenliness. **ter-** slighted, ignored.

abang 1 older brother. 2 form of reference for older males. 3 form of address by wife to husband regardless of latter's age. **-an** see ORANG. **–**[2] form of reference for market vendors. *– bétjak* pedicab driver. *– tua* maroon, dark red.

abar meng- 1 to impede, hinder. *Pertempuran*[2] *∼ djalannja perundingan*, Clashes impeded the progress of negotiations. 2 to remove. *Obat baru itu ∼ keadaan pajah pasién*, The new drug brought relief to the patient. 3 to lessen. *∼ keadaan bahaja perang* to lessen the danger of war.

abdas ablutions before prayer.

abdi servant. *– negara* servant of the state. **meng-** to serve. *Ia ∼ tanah air*, He serves his fatherland. **meng-kan** *diri* to devote o.s. *Ia ∼ diri kpd partainja*, He devotes himself to the party. **peng-an** 1 service. 2 servitude, submission.

abdjad alphabet. **meng-** to alphabetize.

abésé [*a.b.c.*] the alphabet.

abid see ABADI.

abis see HABIS.

ABN [*Anggaran Belandja Negara*] national budget.

abolisi abolition.

abonemén subscription (to magazine, etc.). **ber-** to subscribe. *Ia ∼ bioskop*, He bought a monthly book of movie tickets.

abrit–abritan running helter-skelter.

absah 1 valid, legal, legitimate. 2 see SAH. **meng-kan** 1 to endorse, approve. 2 to legalize. **peng-an** 1 endorsement, approval. 2 legalization.

absén meng- to call the roll.

absorpsi absorption.

absténsi abstention.

abstrak abstract.

abstraksi abstraction.

abu 1 dust. 2 ashes. **ber-** dusty. **ke- –**[2]**an** grayish. **meng-i** to spray earth on s.t. *∼ mata* to deceive s.o. *Ia selalu ∼ mata madjikannja*, He's always deceiving his boss. **peng-an** *mata* camouflage. **per-an** container for cremation ashes. *–*[2] gray. *– gosok* scouring sand.

abuh 1 swollen. 2 swelling.

abuk fine powder. *– gergadji* sawdust.

accu see AKI 2.

achir end, finish. *pd – minggu ini* at the end of this week. *– ini* recently. **ber-** to end. *Pertemuan itu ∼ pd djam 2*, The meeting ended at 2. **ber-kan** to end in. *Pemogokan itu ∼ damai*, The strike ended peacefully. **meng-i** to end, close. *Ia ∼ pidatonja dgn utjapan terima kasih*, He ended his speech with an expression of thanks. **meng-kan** 1 to place last. *Adiknja di–kan*, His younger brother was placed last. 2 to set s.t. back. *Ia ∼ djamnja*, He set his watch back. **peng-an** end(ing). **ter-** the latest, last, final. *Ini kabar ∼ malam ini*, This is the latest news this evening. **-an** suffix. **-nja** finally. *–*[2] *ini* of late,

1

lately. *Ia tak kelihatan ~ ini*, He hasn't been seen lately. - *minggu* weekend.

achirat the world hereafter.

achirulkalam in conclusion. - *saja uraikan bhw...* In conclusion I wish to explain that...

achlak character, morals. **ber-** *tinggi* to be of good character.

achlas see ICHLAS.

activir **meng-** to activate.

A.D. 1 [*Angkatan Darat*] army, ground forces. 2 [*Anggaran Dasar*] statutes.

ada 1 there is, are. - *andjing disini*, There's a dog here. *Dia sdh -?* Is he here already? 2 to be. *Saja - di New York*, I'm in New York. 3 to have *Saja - uang*, I have some money. 4 do, does, did. *Ia - menerima uang itu*, He did receive the money. 5 to be in. *Ia tidak -*, He isn't in. 6 existing. *menurut ketentuan² jg -* according to existing stipulations. 7 to chance, happen to. - *punja péna?* Do you happen to have a pen? **ber-** 1 to be. *Ia ~ di New York*, He's in New York. 2 well-to-do. *Ia anak seorang ~* , He's from a well-to-do family. **ber-** –² to have a hidden motive. *Tentu ia ~ utk memberikan uangnja begitu sadja*, He must have a hidden motive for giving his money away like that. **ke-an** 1 situation, state. *~ negeri itu kurang baik*, The state of the country isn't good. 2 condition. *Bagaimana ~mu?* How are things with you? *~ bahaja* emergency. *~ (ter)paksa* emergency situation. **meng-** –² to invent (stories, etc.). **meng-kan** 1 to organize, arrange. *Ia ~ perajaan besar*, He organized a big celebration. 2 to give, hold, make, deliver. *Ia ~ tjeramah*, He gave a lecture. 3 to create, make. *Tuhan ~ bumi dan langit*, God created heaven and earth. 4 to launch. *Ia ~ bantahan*, He launched a protest. 5 to cause (a catastrophe, etc.). 6 to establish, institute, carry out (measures, etc.). **se-** –²**nja** as o. finds it. *Apa saudara mau makan ~ ?* Would you like to share potluck with us? **-nja** 1 presence. *~ disini* his presence here. 2 situation. *Demikian ~*, Such is the situation. –² incredible. *~ sadja* 1 it's always s.t. *Kalau adik saja datang ~ sadja jg ditjeritera-kannja*, When my youngest brother comes there's always s.t. for him to relate. 2 there's always s.t. (the matter). 3 nonsense. *~ sadja! Kalau mau pulang, pulanglah!* Nonsense! If you want to go home, go! **-kah** do(es). *~ andjing berékor?* Does a

dog have a tail? **-kalanja** sometimes, at times. *~ ia sakit*, Sometimes he's sick. **-lah** 1 am, is, are. *Ia ~ seorang kaja*, He's a rich man. 2 there is, was. *~ seorang radja...*, Once upon a time there was a king... **-pun** as for, well... *~ begini agaknja*, Well, it's s.t. like this. *~ tjeritera itu tidak dpt diteruskan*, It so happens, the story cannot be continued. *dlm ke-an demikian* under such circumstances.

adab 1 courtesy. 2 culture. 3 polite, well-mannered. *Anak itu kurang betul -nja thd orang tua*, That child is very impolite toward his elders. **ber-** 1 polite. 2 cultured, civilized. *Bangsa itu ~ betul*, That nation is very civilized. **ke-an** politeness, refinement, good breeding. **memper-kan** to civilize s.o. or s.t. **per-an** culture, civilization.

adan see AZAN.

adang **meng-** to block. *Pohon ~ didjalan*, A tree blocks the road. **meng-** –² to hold up, waylay s.o. **peng-** 1 obstacle. 2 robber, highwayman. **peng-an** ambush.

adapun see ADA.

adaspula sari fennel.

adat 1 custom, tradition. *Ia tahu -*, He's well-mannered. 2 behavior, action. **ber-** 1 to do s.t. in a traditional way (a wedding, etc.). 2 well-mannered. **meng-kan** to institute s.t. as a custom. *Meréka ~ kebiasaan jg tlh didjalankan turun-temurun*, They instituted a custom which has been practiced for generations. *Ter- lambat laun ~ djuga kebiasaan itu*, Gradually the habit became a custom. - *bahasa* good form. - *-istiadat* customs and traditions. - *lembaga* old customs and institutions. - *resam* customs and traditions. *kurang -* rude, impolite, ill-mannered. *Kalau menemui tamu tidak memakai djas dinamai kurang -*, Receiving guests without wearing a coat is considered rude. *pd -nja* usually.

adegan scene, act in a play.

adekan see ADEGAN.

adem 1 cool, calm. 2 tasteless.

adik 1 younger brother or sister. 2 form of address to younger brother or sister and to younger people. - *hendak kemana?* Where are you going? **ber--berkakak** to be brother and sister. *Ali dan Sitti ~* , Ali and Sitti are brother and sister. **memper-** to regard as a younger brother or sister. *Ia ~ saja*, He regards me as younger.

adil just, fair, legal. *Ia orang -*, He's a just man. **ke-an** justice, right. *~ sosial* social justice. **ketidak-an** injustice. **mengi–i** 1 to hear, try, a case. *Siapa jg ~ dlm perkara itu?* Who's presiding over that case? 2 to administer justice. **peng–an** 1 the court. 2 trial. 3 session. 4 jurisdiction. *~ negeri* court of first instance. *~ tentara* court martial. *~ tinggi* appellate court. **per–an** justice.

adinda you (form of address and reference to younger sibling, to wife, to younger person; more intimate and affectionate than *adik*).

adja see SADJA. *Sdh –, mari pulang,* Let's quit and go home.

adjaib 1 miraculous. 2 astonishing. **ke–an** miracle. **meng–kan** amazing, miraculous. *Kedjadian itu sangat ~ ,* That incident was truly amazing.

adjak meng– 1 to invite, ask. *Ia ~ saja pergi dgn dia,* He invited me to go with him. 2 to persuade. *Ia ~ orang² bekerdja keras,* He persuaded the people to work hard. 3 to urge. 4 to challenge, invite. *Ia rupa²nja ~ berkelahi,* It seems he challenged s.o. to a fight. **peng–** inducement. **–an** 1 invitation. 2 challenge. 3 stimulus.

adjal predestined hour of death, end. *Tak ada dokter jg dpt tolong lagi, karena tlh sampai –nja,* No doctor can be of any further help because his hour has arrived.

Adjam Iran, Persia.

adjar bel– 1 to study. *Ia ~ peladjarannja,* He's studying his lesson. 2 to learn. *Ia ~ bahasa Perantjis,* He's learning French. *~ sopir* learning to drive. *~ kenal* to make s.o's acquaintance. *Saja ingin ~ kenal dgn saudara,* I'd like to introduce myself. *~ pd* to study under (s.o.). **mempel–i** to study carefully, diligently. **meng–** 1 to teach. *Ia ~ bahasa Indonésia,* He teaches Indonesian. 2 to give s.o. a lesson he won't forget. *Pengchianat di– oléh kawan²nja,* The traitor was given a lesson by his friends. **meng–i** 1 to train. *Ia ~ anak² berbaris,* He trains the children to do close order drill. 2 to reproach s.o. **meng–kan** to teach s.t. **pel–** student. **pel–an** lesson, course. **peng–** instructor, teacher. **peng–an** 1 education, instruction. 2 doctrine. *~ Monroe* the Monroe Doctrine. **terpel–** educated, learned. *Ia termasuk golongan ~ ,* He belongs to the educated class. **–an** 1 teachings. 2 theory. 3 doctrine. 4 tenet.

adjé see SADJA. *Diputar –,* Just turn it around.

adjéktip adjective.

adji spell, charm. **meng–** to read, recite formulas.

adjidan see ADJUDAN.

adju meng–kan 1 to file, submit. *Ia ~ protés,* He filed a protest. 2 to submit, offer. *Sebuah topi di–kan sebagai bukti,* A hat was submitted as evidence. 3 to send, submit. *Lamaran harus di–kan kepadanja,* The application must be sent to him. 4 to propose, put a motion.

adjudan 1 adjutant. 2 chief petty officer. *– djénderal* adjutant general.

adjuk meng– 1 to observe, estimate. *Inilah waktu jg baik utk ~ hatinja,* This is a good time to observe her character. 2 to imitate, parrot, mock. *Murid jg nakal itu ~ gurunja,* The naughty pupil imitated his teacher.

adjun meng– to intend to, plan. *Ajah ~ berangkat hari ini,* Dad plans to leave today.

adjun(g) adjunct.

adm. [*administrasi*] administration.

administrasi administration. *– negara* public administration. *– niaga* business administration.

adon meng– to knead. **–an** batter, dough.

adperténsi advertisement.

adpis advice.

adpisir adviser.

adpokat lawyer.

adrés address. **meng–kan** to address.

ADRI [*Angkatan Darat Républik Indonésia*] the Indonesian Army.

adu ber– 1 to collide. *Mobil ~ dgn grobak,* The car collided with a cart. 2 to compete. *Cornéll ~ dgn Princeton,* Cornell competes with Princeton. 3 to sleep (of royalty). *~ lengan* to compete in strength. *~ tindju* 1 to box. 2 to have a fist fight. **meng–** 1 to confront. *Hakim ~ dua saksi itu utk mengetahui siapa jg benar,* The judge confronted the two witnesses to find out which was right. 2 to bump s.t. *Ia ~ kepalanja dgn témbok,* He bumped his head against the wall. 3 to have s.t. or s.o. fight. *Orang Bali suka ~ ajam,* The Balinese like to have cocks fight. 4 to contest. *Dua pudjangga itu ~ kepandaian,* The 2 scholars are matching their wits. 5 to complain. *Guru ~ kpd orang tua murid²,* The teacher complained to the pupils' parents. *~ lidah* to quarrel. *Djangan ~ lidah kalau ternjata salah,* Don't argue if you're clearly wrong. *~ tuah* to take a chance. *~ untung* to try o's luck. *Biarlah saja ~ untung ikut bermain loteré,* Let me try my luck at playing the lottery. **meng– -dombakan** to incite against e.o. **peng–** informer. **peng–an** accusation, complaint, **per–**

an royal bed. **-an** 1 fight. ~ *sapi* bullfight. 2 competition. ~ *sepuluh* decathlon. - *djotos* to box. - *gulat(an)* wrestling match.

aduh 1 ouch! ow! 2 alas. **meng-** to lament.

aduhai see ADUH.

aduk meng- 1 to stir. *Ia* ~ *téhnja,* He stirred his tea. 2 to beat batter, etc. 3 to mix s.t. ~ *téh tjina dgn téh djawa* to mix Chinese tea with Javanese tea. **peng-** a stirring spoon. **peng-an** *semén* cement mixer. **-an** mixer, beater. ~ *telor* eggbeater.

adun dress, finery. **ber-** to dress up. see ADON.

aestétika aesthetics.

afal see APAL.

'afiat health. **meng-kan** to make healthy. see WAL'AFIAT.

aga see RAGA.

agah ber-an to look at e.o. defiantly. **meng-** to look at s.o. in a defiant manner.

agak rather, somewhat. *Ia* - *besar utk umurnja,* He's rather large for his age. - *mudik* not far upstream. **ber-** to intend. *Ia* ~ *pergi ke Indonésia,* He intends to go to Indonesia. **ber-** -² 1 to ponder, consider s.t. 2 to hesitate. **meng-(-)** to guess correctly, rightly. *Ia* ~ *bhw tidak ada orang dirumah,* He guessed correctly that no one was at home. **meng- -agihkan** 1 to blame. 2 to look after everything. **se-** of the same mind. *Si Ali* ~ *dgn saja akan naik hadji,* Ali and I are of the same mind about going on the pilgrimage to Mecca. **ter-(-)** to long for. *Sdh* ~ *benar saja kpd ibu,* I greatly long for my mother. *tidak* ~ unexpectedly. *Tidak* ~ *akan berdjumpa dgn kamu disini,* I didn't expect to meet you here. **-nja** 1 presumably, probably. ~ *ia tak akan datang,* Presumably he isn't coming. 2 actually, really. *Apa* ~ *maksudmu?* What do you actually mean? -² careful. ~ *berdjalan malam,* Be careful about going out in the evening.

agam 1 male. 2 physically strong, virile.

agama religion. **ber-** 1 to have a religion. *Ia* ~ *Islam,* He's a Moslem. 2 to be religious. **ke-an** 1 religious matters. 2 religious. - *Bahai* Bahaism. - *Buda* Buddhism. - *Hindu* Hinduism. - *Hindu Bali* Balinese Hinduism. - *Islam* Islam. - *Jahudi* Judaism. - *Keristen* Christianity (Protestantism). - *Nasrani* Christianity (Catholicism).

agamawan religious person.

agan ber- to intend, plan. **meng- -²i** to plague, tease.

agar in order to. *Saja selalu berlatih* - *menang,* I always practice in order to win. -² a gelatin made of seaweed. - *supaja* in order to.

agén 1 agency, branch. 2 agent. - *polisi* policeman. **ke-an, per-an** agency. - *surat kabar* local newspaper distributor.

aggrégat electric generator.

agih meng-(kan) to distribute, share.

agitasi agitation.

agraria agrarian affairs.

agrési aggression.

aguk locket.

agung impressive, exalted, high, noble. - *benar kelihatannja pembesar itu,* That prominent person looks very impressive. **ke-an** 1 greatness, nobleness. ~ *Sultan Djokjakarta utk memberikan istananja utk gedung sekolah tinggi tak akan dilupakan,* The greatness of the Sultan of Djokja in giving his palace for a university building will not be forgotten. 2 sublimity. 3 grandeur. 4 majesty. **meng-kan** 1 to glorify. 2 to praise s.o. or s.t. ~ *diri* 1 to boast. 2 to be proud of.

agus see BAGUS 5.

Agustus August.

Ahad Sunday. **meng-kan** to unite in marriage. - *palem* Palm Sunday.

ahangkara egotism.

ahli 1 expert. 2 skilled, competent. **ke-an** skill, expertise. **meng-kan** *diri* to specialize in s.t. *Ia* ~ *diri dlm pelajaran,* He is specializing in navigation. - *bahasa* linguistic expert. - *bedah* surgeon. - *bintang* astronomer. - *bius* anaesthetist. - *bumi* geologist. - *djiwa* 1 psychologist. 2 psychiatrist. - *fakih* expert in canon law. - *filsafat* philosopher. - *firasat* physiognomist. - *gunung berapi* vulcanologist. - *hikmat* wizard. - *hukum* legal expert, lawyer. - *ilmu bangsa²* ethnologist. - *ketjantikan* beautician. - *kimia* chemist. - *(men)didik* educationist. - *mesin* expert machinist. - *negara* 1 political scientist. 2 politician. - *nikah* in-laws. - *nudjum* astrologer. - *obat* pharmacist. - *pembukuan* certified public accountant. - *penggunaan tanah* soil scientist. - *pengetahuan* scholar, scientist. - *pidato* orator, speaker. - *pikir* philosopher. - *ragam* musical composer. - *rias* make-up artist. - *rumah* housemates. - *sastera* man of letters. - *sedjarah* historian. - *sihir* 1 hypnotist. 2 sorcerer. - *sunah,* - *sunat* observer of the traditional law. - *tafsir* annotator, commentator. -

tanah agronomist. – *tarich* 1 genealogist. 2 historian, chronicler. – *tenung* fortune-teller. – *tjeritera* storyteller. – *ukur tanah* surveyor. – *waris* (joint) heirs. *jg* – professional.

ahmak 1 fool. 2 foolish. 3 stupid.

aib 1 shame, disgrace, scandal. 2 error, mistake. **ke–an** 1 humiliation, disgrace. 2 shame. **meng-kan** 1 to humiliate, bring disgrace upon s.o. 2 to blame, reprimand.

AIB [*Ambtenaar Inlandsch Bestuur*] 1 official of the Netherlands Indies Government. 2 junior government official.

aidilfitri see IDULFITRI.

air 1 water. 2 juice. 3 liquid. **ber–** 1 to have water. *Sungai ini tak ~ dlm musim kering,* This river has no water during the dry season. 2 juicy. *Buah ini sangat ~ ,* This fruit is very juicy. **ke–an** flooded, inundated. *Rumahnja ~ ,* His house was flooded. **meng–** to become water. *És itu ~ ,* The ice has become water. **meng-i** to irrigate, water s.t. *Petani itu ~ sawah,* The farmer irrigates the wet rice field. **peng-an** irrigation. **per-an** 1 territorial waters. 2 waterworks. – *abu* lye. – *aki* battery acid. – *alas* brackish water. – *anggur* 1 wine. 2 grape juice. – *api* hydrochloric acid. – *bah,* – *bandjir* flood, inundation. – *batu,* – *beku* ice. – *belanda* soda water. – *bena* tidal wave. – *besar* 1 flood. 2 night soil, feces. – *buah* fruit juice. – *djeruk* orange juice and other citrus drinks. – *galian* ground water. – *hidup* running water. – *kaku* hard water. – *kapur* lime water. – *kelapa* coconut milk. – *kelonjo* eau de cologne. – *kentjing* urine. – *keras* (hydrochloric) acid. – *lebah* honey. – *lédéng* piped in, running water. – *liur,* – *ludah,* saliva, spittle. – *madu* honey. – *mani* sperm, seed. – *mas* fluid for gilding. – *masin* salt water. – *mata* tears. – *mati* 1 bay, inlet. 2 creek. – *mawar* rose water, perfume. – (*me*)*lata* 1 waterfall. 2 mountain stream. – *mentah* fresh water. – *muka* 1 facial expression, countenance. – *mukanja kelihatan marah,* He looks angry. 2 surface. – *mukabumi* surface water. – (*me*)*mantjur* 1 fountain. 2 small waterfall. – *murni* pure water. – *nanas* pineapple juice. – *pajau* brackish water. – *pasang* high tide. – *pérak* silver zinc. – *perbani* neap tide. – *ra*(*k*)*sa* quicksilver. – *rebusan* water left over after boiling. – *ruang* bilge water. – *sadah* hard water. – *sebak* flooding. – *seléra* saliva. –

sembahjang water for ritual ablutions. – *seni,* – *siau* urine. – *serani* water for baptismal purposes. – *suling* distilled water. – *sumur* well water. – *surut* low tide. – *susu* mother's milk. – *sutji* holy water. – *tadahan* captured rain water. – *talkin* water sprinkled on grave. – *tanah* ground water. – *tapai* arrack. – *tawar* 1 fresh water. 2 unboiled water. – *téh* tea (drink). – *tepung tawar* magic potion. – *terdjun* water-fall. – *timah* tin coating. – *tomat* tomato juice. – *ukup* perfumed holy water. – *wangi* perfume, scent. – (*w*)*udu* water for ritual ablutions. – *zamzam* water from the well at Mecca.

aj. [*ajat*] paragraph.

ajah father. – *bunda* parents. – *tiri* stepfather. **meng-i** to father.

ajahanda father (respectful form of address).

ajak sieve, strainer. **meng–** to sift. *Koki ~ tepung,* The cook sifted the flour. **peng-(an)** sieve, sifter. –² k.o. spider.

ajal 1 slow. 2 hesitating.

ajam chicken. –²**an** 1 weathercock. 2 wild hen, snipe. – *aduan* fighting cock. – *babon* laying hen. – *belanda* turkey. – *betina* hen. – *bugil* featherless chicken. – *dara* pullet. – *djago,* – *djantan* cock, rooster. – *itik* poultry. – *kasi* capon. – *katik* short-legged Bantam chicken. – *kebiri* capon. – *kukus* steamed chicken. – (*pe*)*laga,* – *sabungan* fighting cock. – *singgang* roast chicken. – *teruna* cockerel.

ajat 1 Koranic verse. 2 paragraph.

ajo come on! –, *pulang,* Come on, let's go home. –*lah* well then; come on then.

ajoh see AJO.

aju 1 pretty, beautiful. 2 see RADÉN.

ajuh see AJO. –*lah duluan,* Go ahead first.

ajuhai hey you!

ajun **ber–** –² to rock, sway. **meng–** 1 to rock, sway. 2 to go down (sun). **meng-kan** 1 to rock (cradle, baby). 2 to move s.t. ~ *kepal* to shake o's fist. 3 to swing, wield. ~ *tjangkul pertama* to break ground, wield the first spadeful of earth (for a building, etc.). **peng-an** *tjangkul pertama* ground breaking. –**an** 1 swing. 2 cradle.

ajunda form of address to older sister (frequent in correspondence).

akad 1 contract. 2 agreement. – *bawah tangan* private agreement. – *djual beli* sale agreement. – *nikah* marriage contract.

akadémi 1 academy. 2 college.

akadémis academic.
akadémikus academician.
akal 1 mind, intellect, brains. *Ia tadjam sekali –nja*, He has a very keen mind. 2 way, tactics. *Ia mentjari – utk menangkap pentjuri itu*, He's seeking a way to capture the thief. 3 advice, instruction. **ber–** intelligent, smart. *Ia seorang* ∼ , He's a smart person. **meng–i** to deceive, double-cross s.o. **meng–kan** to work s.t. out. *Bagaimana* ∼ *supaja dia bisa datang kesini?* How can we work it out so he can come here? *– budi* common sense, intelligence. *– bulus* 1 cunning mind. 2 sly trick. *– kantjil* 1 ruse, artifice, prank. 2 shrewd, clever. *– keling* very shrewd. *– laba²* trickster. *– melintas* a sudden thought, inspiration. *– péndék* 1 narrow-minded. 2 shortsighted. 3 stupid. *– tjerdik* brain wave. *–nja pandjang* tricky, crafty.
akan 1 will (future idea). *Nasi ini – dimakan nanti*, This rice will be eaten later. 2 about. *Ia lupa – djandjinja*, He forgot about his promise. 3 for. *Minjak ini – pembakar kaju*, This oil is for burning wood. 4 in. *Saja tidak pertjaja – dia*, I have no confidence in him. 5 of. *Ia bangga – anaknja*, He's proud of his son. 6 to. *– mendapat kepertjajaannja tidak mudah*, To gain his confidence isn't easy. *kemampuan – membajar* the ability to pay. 7 as for. *– saja* as for me. **ke–an** the future. **meng–** to strive, aim for. **meng–kan** to suppose. **–an** horizon. **se– –²** as if, as though. *Ia terus bekerdja* ∼ *tak mendengar temannja*, He kept on working as if he didn't hear his friend. *– tetapi* 1 but, however. *Anak itu ketjil – tetapi kuat*, The child is small but strong. 2 yet, still. *Walaupun dia lapar sekali, – tetapi dia tidak mau makan*, Though he was very hungry, still he didn't want to eat. *selama – kau suka tinggal disini* as long as you want to stay here.
akar 1 root. *– pohon waringin* the root of the banyan tree. *– kata 'menerima' ialah 'terima,'* The root of the word *'menerima'* is *'terima.'* 5 *adalah – persegi dari 25*, 5 is the square root of 25. 2 root, source. *Uang adalah – segala kedjahatan*, Money is the root of all evil. **ber–** 1 to have roots in. *Adat ini* ∼ *kpd kepertjajaan kuno*, This custom is rooted in an old belief. 2 to take root. *Bibit ini mulai* ∼ , The seed is beginning to take root. *– (ber)gantung* aerial root. *– bulu* radical root. *– gigi* root of a tooth. *– pangkat dua* square root.

– parsi asparagus. *– serabut* root hairs. *– umbi* tuber.
akas clever, handy, skillful. **ke–an** skill.
akasa see ANGKASA.
akbar great(est). *mesdjid – a* great mosque.
Akbp [*Adjung komisaris besar polisi*] adjunct chief commissioner of police.
akékah ritual shaving of baby's head for the first time, usually on the seventh day after birth.
aki 1 grandfather. 2 storage battery.
akibat result, consequence. *–² besar* far-reaching consequences. **ber–** *dgn* to result in. **meng–kan** to result, end in. *Tindakan itu* ∼ *amarah ajahnja*, That act resulted in his father's anger. **–nja** finally, as a consequence.
akik see BATU.
akil-balig(h) 1 legally responsible. 2 of age, grown up (from 15 on).
akir see ACHIR.
akontan see AKUNTAN.
akrab intimate, close. *Hamid teman – saja*, Hamid is my close friend. **ke–an** intimacy.
aksara letter of the alphabet.
aksén accent.
aksép an I.O.U., promissory note.
aksi 1 action. 2 to take action. 3 to act in a bragging way. **ber–** 1 to be in action. *Polisi* ∼ *memberantas pengatjau*, The police are in action against the insurgents. 2 to show off. *Lihatlah si Amat sedang* ∼ *memakai katjamata hitam*, Look at Amat showing off his dark glasses.
akta see AKTE.
akte 1 official document. 2 diploma, certificate. *– guru* teacher's certificate. *– lahir* birth certificate. *– notaris* notarial document.
aktentas brief case.
aktif 1 active, energetic. 2 functioning. **meng–kan** to activate.
aktip see AKTIF. **ke–an** activity.
aktipité activity.
aktir actor.
aktiv see AKTIF. **ke–an** activity.
aktiva assets.
aktivitas activity.
aktivitét see aktipité.
aktris actress.
aktuil recent, topical, current.
aku 1 I (familiar). *– katakan kepadamu*, I told you. 2 see AKI 1. **ber–** to use the familiar form with s.o. **ke–an** egoism. **meng–** 1 to confess, admit. *Ia* ∼ *salah*, He admitted he was wrong. 2 to consider as o's own. *Djangan* ∼ *djasa orang lain*, Don't consider another's achievements as your own. 3 to claim to be. *Ia* ∼

ahli hukum, He claims to be a legal expert. **meng-i** 1 to acknowledge. *Ia ~ bhw kelambatan itu disebabkan oléhnja,* He acknowledged that he was the cause of the delay. 2 to confess, admit. 3 to recognize, acknowledge. *Ia ~ kekuasaan pemerintah,* He recognized the authority of the government. **(peng)-an** 1 acknowledgment. 2 confession. 3 creed. 4 recognition. *-ku jg kedua* my alter ego.

akulturasi acculturation.

akuntan certified public accountant.

akuntansi accountancy.

akur 1 to agree. *Ia – utk pergi dgn saja,* He agreed to go with me. *- (déh),* Agreed! 2 to be in harmony. *Mérah dan biru tidak – dlm perhiasan ini,* Red and blue clash in this decorative scheme. 3 to be at peace. *Laki-isteri jg tadi berkelahi itu sekarang rupanja tlh – lagi,* The husband and wife who were fighting just now seem to be at peace again. **ke-an** harmony, peace. **meng-i** to agree with. **meng-kan** 1 to reconcile s.o. *Agén itu ~ dua orang itu,* The policeman reconciled the two men. 2 to check s.t. *Ia ~ turunan itu dgn jg asli,* He checked the copy against the original. 3 to harmonize s.t. *~ warna² to harmonize the colors.

akustis acoustic.

akut acute, critical. **peng-an** crisis, acute situation.

a.l. [*antara lain*] among other things.

ala in the. *- Barat* in western style.

alah 1 defeated, beaten, conquered. 2 see KALAH. **ber-an** to end in a draw. **ke-an** loss, defeat. **meng-** to concede, admit, yield, give in. *Saja ~ karena saja merasa kasihan kepadanja,* I gave in because I felt sorry for him. **meng-kan** to beat, defeat. *Perkumpulan kami ~ meréka,* Our team defeated them. **peng-an** 1 victory. 2 concession, admission. **per-an** victory, conquest. *- -meng-(i)* to adjust to e.o. *Orang harus tahu ~ ,* People must know how to adjust to e.o.

alaihissalam On whom be peace.

alaikum salam Peace be unto you.

alalbihalal to ask and give forgiveness. *Pd hari Lebaran orang² mengadakan – ,* On Lebaran people ask and give forgiveness. see HALALBIHALAL.

alam 1 world, realm. 2 nature. **ber-peng-an** to have experience, be experienced. **ke-an** nature, character. **meng-i** to experience s.t. **peng-an** experience. **se-** of the same nature. *Irian ~ dgn Australia,* New Guinea has the same type of nature as Australia. *- arwah* the world of spirits. *- baka* eternity. *- barzach* period be-

tween death and judgment. *- dunia* the world. *- fana* perishable world. *- malakut* the world of spirits. *- Minangkabau* the Minangkabau world. *- nasut* mankind. *- pikiran* view, philosophy, way of thinking. *- samar* the invisible world. *- sekeliling, - sekitar* environment, surroundings. *- semésta* the universe. *- terbuka* open-air. *réstoran - terbuka* open-air restaurant. *- tumbuh²an* plant kingdom.

alamat 1 address. *Tjoba tulis -nja disini,* Please write the address here. 2 sign, indication. *Itu -nja bhw ia sakit,* That's a sign he's sick. 3 target. 4 title. *Apakah - buku jg kaubatja itu?* What's the title of the book you're reading? **ber-** 1 to have an address. *Surat itu tidak ~ ,* That letter has no address. 2 to indicate. *Angin teduh biasanja ~ datangnja angin tofan,* A calm wind usually indicates the coming of a typhoon. 3 to be titled. **meng-kan** 1 to address. *Ia ~ surat² undangan itu,* She addressed the invitations. 2 to indicate, foretell. *Angin sedjuk ~ hudjan,* A cool wind indicates rain. **si-** the addressee.

alami(ah) natural, concerned with nature.

alan² comedian, jokester.

alang 1 crosswise, diagonal. 2 crossbeam, bar. **ber-an** to be hindered, handicapped. **meng-** 1 to lie athwart, across. *Pohon ~ didjalan,* A tree blocks the road. 2 to prevent. *Ia ~ saja pergi,* He prevented me from going. **meng-i** to prevent, hamper. *Ia ~ supaja saja tidak lulus udjian,* He prevented me from passing the exam. **meng- -²i** to obscure, cut off. *Pohon rimbun ~ pemandangan indah itu,* A leafy tree cut off the beautiful view. **peng-** hindrance, stumbling block. **-an** hindrance, obstacle. *Apa ~ utk tidak datang pd pésta itu?* What kept you from coming to the party? **-²(an)** indifferent, neither here nor there. **-²** tall grass. *- kepalang* insufficient, inadequate, trifling. *Hanja sedikit itu? - kepalang!* Only that little bit? Not worth bothering with! *rumah - kepalang* wooden partition. *bukan - kepalang* extremely, very. *Kawan saja bukan - kepalang kajanja,* My friend is extremely rich.

alangkah how. *- énaknja!* How tasty!

alap meng- to pick fruit. **-²** 1 hawk. 2 thief. 3 kite.

alas 1 layer, lining. *Kain ini utk - badju saja,* This material is for the lining of my jacket. 2 base, foundation. – *bunga ini hidjau warnanja*, The color of the flower pot is green. 3 sheet, linen. *Dimana – kasur itu?* Where's the sheet for the mattress? **ber–(an)** to have a foundation. *Uraiannja tidak ~* , His explanation is without foundation. **ber–kan** to be based on. *Tuduhan korupsi ~ bukti² jg sah*, The accusation of corruption is based on valid evidence. **meng–i** 1 to cover. *Ibu ~ médja dgn alas baru*, Mother covered the table with a new cloth. 2 to lay a base, foundation. **meng–kan** to found, lay the foundation of s.t. **-an** 1 reason, motive. *Apa ~nja dia tidak datang?* What was his reason for not coming? 2 layer, basis, foundation. *– kata* introduction. *– médja* table cloth. *– perut* breakfast. *– tilam* sheet. *– tjangkir*, *– tjawan* saucer.

alat 1 instrument, tool, device. 2 organization, organ. 3 guest. **ber–** to celebrate at a feast. **memper–** to use (as a tool), manipulate. *Ia ~ saja utk mentjapai maksudnja*, He used me to achieve his purpose. **memper–i** to equip s.t. *Ia ~ rumahnja*, He equipped his house. **memper–kan** to give a celebration for s.o. **meng–i** to equip. **meng–kan** to use as a tool. **per–an** 1 equipment, tools. 2 feast, celebration. **-²** *kantor* office equipment. **-²** *olahraga* sporting goods. *– besar* heavy equipment. *– bitjara* microphone. *– gésék* string instrument. *– hubungan semésta* mass communications media. *– kebesaran* insignia of state. *– kelamin* sex organs. *– keradjaan* insignia of royalty. *– lauk* feast held 8 days after a wedding to introduce bride and groom to relatives. *– mesin tenun* power loom. *– napas* respiratory organs. *– negara* instrument of the state. *– pelampung* lifeboat. *– pemanas hawa* radiator. *– pembajaran luar negeri* foreign exchange. *– pembesar* enlarger. *– pemetik* mechanized picker. *– pemindjah atom* atom smasher. *– pemotrét* camera. *– pemutar lampu* light switch. *– pengempelas* 1 scrub rag. 2 abrasive. *– pengeras suara* loudspeaker. *– penghembus hawa* air vent. *– pentjakar tanah* steam shovel. *– pentjernaan* digestive organs. *– penukar*, *– petukar*, *– pertukaran* medium of exchange. *– pernapasan* respiratory tract. *– perumahan* furniture, household furnishings. *– rias* make-up equipment. *– Röntgen* X-ray equipment. *– sendjata* armament.

aldjabar algebra.

Aldjairah Algeria.

Aldjazair Algiers.

aléfon allophone (phon.).

alem spoiled (of a person).

alfabét alphabet.

algodjo 1 executioner. 2 bully.

alhamdulillah Praise be to God.

alhasil 1 eventually. *– ia pergi djuga*, He eventually went anyway. 2 result. *–, kami tak djadi pergi*, The result was... we didn't go after all. 3 to make a long story short.

ali meng– *-²* to sling s.t., hurl. **(peng)** *-²* slingshot. 2 catapult, sling.

alias 1 alias. 2 same as. 3 otherwise called. *Ali – Samin* Ali, alias Samin.

alif first letter of the Arabic alphabet (a vertical line). *– bata* alphabet. *mulai dari – bata* to start from the beginning, from scratch. *Sekalipun tlh berumur 80 ia masih berdiri tegak seperti –*, Though 80 he still stands straight as a ramrod.

Alifuru the Alfurese.

alih ber– to change. *Zaman ~*, Times change. *~ fikiran* to change o's mind. *~ rumah* to move from one house to another. *~ tjakap* to change the subject. **meng–(kan)** to shift, change. *Djawatan Pengairan ~ djalan sungai*, The Irrigation Works changed the river's course. **per–an** 1 transfer, change, shift. *~ pemerintahan* transfer of rule. 2 transition. *~ zaman* change of the times. **-(kan)** 1 on the other hand. 2 ...let alone...

alik see ULANG.

alim 1 learned. 2 pious, religious, devout. 3 religious scholar. **ke–an** 1 learning, scholarship. 2 piety. *– ulama* religious scholar.

aling meng–i to shelter, cover. *Ia ~ isterinja dari peluru*, He sheltered his wife from the bullets. **meng–kan** to hide s.t. *Ia ~ bukunja dari mata saja*, He hid his book from my eyes. **-an** 1 screen, protection. 2 concealing. **-²an** hide and seek.

alir ber–an to have a tendency, ideology. *Perkumpulan itu ~ radikal*, That group has a radical tendency. **meng–** 1 to flow. *Sungai ~ dibelakang rumah*, The river flows behind the house. 2 to well up. *Air matanja ~* , His tears welled up. 3 to pour, stream. *Ribuan orang ~ ketanah lapang*, Thousands of people poured into the square. **meng–i** to flow through. *Sungai Donau ~ Austria*, The Danube River flows through Austria. **meng–kan** 1 to channel s.t. *Pak tani ~ air itu kesawahnja*, The farmer channels the water into his wet rice field. 2 to siphon. *Ia ~ tjuka dari botol*, She siphoned vinegar from a bottle. 3 to aim, point. *Kemana Perantjis sekarang ~ politiknja?* Where is France aiming its policy now? **peng–an** 1 flow, stream, drift. 2 trend, drift. **–an** 1 current. ~ *listerik* electric current. 2 current, trend, ideology. 3 conduit, wiring. 4 school. ~ *Praha* Prague school (of linguistics). 5 pipeline. 6 brook. ~ *darah* circulation of the blood.

alis eyebrow. *–nja melengkung,* She has curved eyebrows.

alkissah 1 the story. 2 once upon a time. see KISAH.

Al-kitab the Bible.

Alkur'an the Koran.

Allah God. **ke–an** 1 the Godhead. 2 divinity, deity.

alm [*almarhum*] the late.

almahdi the Messiah.

almanak almanac.

almarhum the late. – *Dr. Sutomo* The late Dr. Sutomo.

almarhumah the late (fem.). – *Ibu Kartini* the late Kartini.

almari see LEMARI.

al-Masih the Messiah.

almenak see ALMANAK.

Al-Nabi the Prophet Mohammed.

alokasi allocation.

alon[2] slowly.

alot 1 tough (of meat). 2 heavy.

alpa neglectful, inattentive. *Ia – akan kewadjibannja,* He's neglectful of his duties. **ke–an** 1 shortcomings, omission. *Harap dimaafkan segala ~ saja,* Please forgive all my shortcomings. 2 neglect. **meng–kan** to neglect s.t.

Al-Qur'an the Koran.

ALRI [*Angkatan Laut Républik Indonésia*] the Indonesian Navy.

alu rice stamper.

alum faded, withered, wilted. **meng–** to wither, fade.

aluminium aluminum.

alun wave, swell. **ber–** to heave, roll, pitch. *Dari tepi pantai kelihatan laut ~ ,* From the shore you can see the pitching sea. **ber– –**[2] to wave. *Tanaman padi ~ ditiup angin,* The paddy plants wave in the breeze. **meng–** to pitch, heave. *Lautan Teduh ~ ,* The Pacific Ocean is heaving. **–**[2] village town or city square used for playground, sports, military drill, parades, and mass meetings. **–an** wave in hair.

alur gully, channel, groove. **ber–** to have a groove. 2 to discuss. *Meréka ~ sebelum mengambil keputusan,* They held a discussion before making a decision. **meng– –**[2] to be able to count o's ribs. ~ *dadanja,* He was so thin his ribs were sticking out. *menurut –an adat* fitting, proper.

alus see HALUS.

am general, ordinary. *Ia seorang –,* He's an ordinary man. **di–kan** announced, made public.

ama 1 small insects. 2 plant disease. 3 see HAMA. **ber–** to be diseased, blighted. – *tikus* rat plague.

amal 1 deed, work. *banjak – sedikit berbitjara* much work little talk. 2 good deed. *Ia suka berbuat –,* He likes to do good deeds. 3 charity. **ber–** 1 to do a good deed. 2 to pray. *Ia ~ kpd Tuhan,* He prays to God. **meng–kan** 1 to put into practice, apply. *Ia ~ ilmunja utk masjarakat,* He puts his knowledge to use for society. 2 to carry out with devotion. *Ia ~ niatnja,* He carried out his intention with devotion. **peng–an** 1 the doing of good deeds. 2 sincerity in doing s.t. 3 implementation. **–an** 1 good deed. 2 habit. – *baik* good deed, good turn, good works. – *saléh* pious deed.

aman 1 peaceful. – *sekali keadaan dinegeri ini,* The situation in this country is very peaceful. 2 safe, secure. *Saja merasa – dikota ini,* I feel safe in this town. **ke–an** 1 safety, security. *Déwan ~* Security Council. 2 peacefulness, tranquillity. **meng–kan** 1 to pacify, render safe. *Polisi Negara tlh ~ daérah ini,* The State Police have rendered this area safe. 2 to hand over for safekeeping. *Kakak saja ~ harta bendanja kpd ibu,* My sister handed over her valuables to mother for safekeeping. 3 to reassure s.o. **peng–** 1 safeguard. 2 pacifier. **peng–an** pacification. – *sedjahtera* peaceful and tranquil.

amanat 1 trusteeship, mandate. 2 instruction, commission, mandate. – *ajahnja* his father's instruction or mandate. 3 peace. 4 message. – *présidén* the president's message. **ber–** to instruct, order. *Djéndral itu ~ kpd anak buahnja supaja bertahan hingga darah penghabisan,* The general ordered his men to resist to the end. **meng–kan** 1 to instruct, order. *Opsir itu ~ budi pekerti,* The officer ordered good conduct. 2 to dedicate. *Ajahnja ~ segala harta bendanja kpd jajasan,* His father dedicated all his fortune to the foundation. 3 to commit. entrust to s.o. – *Penderitaan Rakjat* Message of the People's Suffering.

amandel 1 almond. 2 tonsil.

amar order, command.

amarah(an) see MARAH.

amat very. *Gedung itu – besar,* That building is very large. **memper–(kan)**

to intensify. *Polisi* ~ *pendjagaan*, The police intensified the patrol. **meng–(–)i** 1 to watch closely. *Ia* ~ *tingkah laku orang itu*, He watched that man's behavior closely. 2 to guard. *Ia* ~ *gedung ini*, He's guarding this building. 3 to inspect. **peng–** 1 caretaker. 2 observer, inspector. **peng–an** 1 supervision. 2 survey. ~ *pembatja* readership survey. **ter–** very. – *sangat* extremely.

amatir amateur.

amatirisme amateurism.

ambah trade, handicraft.

ambai a scoop net. **meng–** to scoop up in a net. –² an ocean crab.

ambal carpet. **ber– –²an** 1 in throngs. 2 in procession. **–²an** troupe, crowd.

ambang 1 threshold, doorstep. 2 window sill. 3 railroad tie. **meng–** to float. *Majat itu* ~ , The corpse was floating. – *pintu* door frame.

ambar 1 amber. 2 insipid, tasteless (food, remarks). – *hati* despondent, discouraged.

ambasadur ambassador.

ambek angry. **ng–** to sulk. **–an** breath. *Ia makan terlalu banjak hampir tak bisa* ~ , He ate so much he could hardly breathe.

ambelas 1 to sink in mud, etc. *Mobilnja – ditengah sawah*, His car sank in the middle of the rice field. 2 to disappear. *Rumahnja – kebakaran*, His house burned to the ground.

amberuk 1 to collapse, sag. *Rumahnja – karena gempa bumi*, His house collapsed from the earthquake. 2 to be destroyed. – *keséhatannja*, His health is declining. *Perusahaannja –*, His firm is bankrupt.

ambil meng– 1 to take. *Siapa jg* ~ *buku saja?* Who took my book? 2 to get, fetch. *–lah pajung saja*, Go get my umbrella. 3 to subtract. *100 di–20 mendjadi 80*, 100 minus 20 is 80. ~ *langkah seribu* to flee, scram. **meng–i** 1 to keep taking s.t. *Ia* ~ *kué hingga habis*, He kept taking the cookies till they were all gone. 2 to take, steal. **meng–kan** to get s.t. for s.o. *Ia* ~ *isterinja uang*, He took his wife some money. **peng–** taker. **peng–an** 1 removal, withdrawal. 2 interpretation, understanding. *menurut* ~ *saja dari peraturan ini...* according to my interpretation of this regulation... ~ *alih* expropriation. ~ *bagian* participation. ~ *oper* taking over, assuming. ~ *suara* vocal recording. **–an** the take. *Tidak banjak* ~*nja bulan ini*, His take wasn't much this month. – *anak* to adopt a child.

– *angin* to get a breath of air. – *bagian* to participate. – *berat* to take s.t. seriously. *Ia – berat kesalahan bawahannja itu*, He takes his subordinates' mistakes seriously. – *dihati* to take into serious consideration. – *gampang* to take s.t. lightly. – *hati* to be in favor with s.o. *Ia datang pagi² kekantor utk – hati madjikannja*, He comes to the office early to be in favor with his boss. – *hawa* to take an airing. – *kias* to draw a moral from s.t. – *marah* to be angry. *Djangan – marah perbuatan saja*, Don't be angry at what I did. – *muka* to be praised, flattered. *Murid itu suka meng– muka pd gurunja*, The pupil likes to be praised by his teacher. – *oper* to take over. – *pusing* to worry over. *Djangan – pusing perkataannja itu*, Don't worry about what he said. – *rantang* 1 to supply food in multiple-unit containers. 2 to subscribe to meals delivered in containers. – *ringkas* to put it briefly. *Di– ringkas, tjeriteranja begini*, To put it briefly, his story was like this. – *sumpah* to administer an oath. – *tahu* to find out about s.t. – *tjontoh* to take as a model. *Ia meng– tjontoh kpd ajahnja*, He took his father as a model. – *upah*. 1 to work for wages. 2 to accept a bribe.

ambin strap, sling, rope. **ber–** *lutut* to squat while the knees are tied with a strap. **meng–** to carry things on the back. *Di Djawa Tengah biasanja orang perempuan* ~ *bakulnja*, In Central Java the women usually carry their baskets in a sling on their backs. **–an** 1 knapsack, pack. 2 a load carried on the back.

ambing udder.

ambisi ambition.

amblas see AMBELAS.

ambles see AMBELAS.

amboi hey! (expresses surprise or sympathy).

Ambon Ambon, Amboina.

ambruk see AMBERUK.

ambu² tunafish.

ambul meng– to bounce, rebound, bob up and down. *Bolanja tidak* ~ , The ball doesn't bounce.

ambulans ambulance.

ambung meng– 1 to toss, throw up (baby, ball, etc.). 2 to kiss. **meng–kan** to toss, throw up. *Si Ali* ~ *bola utk adiknja*, Ali threw the ball up for his little brother. **meng– –²** to flatter, praise. **meng– –²kan** to toss up and down. *Perahu itu di– –²kan oléh ombak*, The boat was tossed up and down by the waves.

amé see SAMA.

améndemén amendment.

Amérika America(n). - *Serikat* the United States of America.

amil mosque official who collects the *zakat.*

amin amen. meng- to say amen, concur. meng-i, meng-kan to approve of s.t. *Semua orang* ∼ *usulnja,* All approved of his proposal.

amir leader.

amis odor of fish.

ammaba'dahu and furthermore (used in correspondence and speeches).

amnésti amnesty.

amoniak ammonia.

ampai slim, slender. meng- to hang over, on. *Ada ular mati* ∼ *dipagar,* There's a dead snake hanging on the fence. meng-kan to hang out to dry. -an clothesline. -² jellyfish.

ampas 1 waste, dregs. 2 molasses. - *kopi* coffee dregs. - *minjak* oil waste. - *tebu* cane pulp.

ampat see EMPAT.

ampé see SAMPAI.

ampelas 1 fig tree. 2 sandpaper. meng-i to rub with sandpaper, to polish.

ampelop envelope.

ampér ampere.

ampo red clay.

ampu meng- 1 to prop up. *Rumah tua itu di-,* The old house was propped up. 2 to reign, govern. *Tlh 50 tahun radja itu* ∼ *negerinja,* For 50 years the king has reigned over his country. peng- 1 support. 2 means of support. *Abu* ∼ *ibunja,* Abu is his mother's means of support. - *kaki* big toe. - *tangan* thumb.

ampuh 1 talented. 2 invulnerable. ke-an invulnerability. meng- to flood, inundate.

ampul meng- 1 to swell, expand. *Katjang tanah kalau ditaruh dlm air* ∼ , If you put peanuts in water they will swell. 2 to thrive, do well.

ampun 1 pardon, forgiveness. *Ia minta - kpd ajahnja,* He asked his father's pardon. 2 mercy. 3 apology. ke-an 1 pardon, forgiveness. 2 amnesty. 3 reprieve. meng-i to forgive s.o. meng-kan to forgive s.t. *Sesungguhnja kamu harus* ∼ *dosa itu,* You must really forgive that sin. peng- o. who will forgive. peng-an pardon, forgiveness. *Ajahnja memberi* ∼ *kepadanja,* His father forgave him.

amril sandpaper.

amtenar government official.

amuba amoeba.

amuk ber- to have a fight. *Kedua ajam itu* ∼ *hébat sekali,* Those two

chickens had a terrific fight. meng- to go berserk, run amuck. meng-kan to incite s.o. to violence. *Ia* ∼ *anak buahnja,* He incited his men to violence. peng- o. who goes berserk. peng-an running amuck, fury, raging. -²an a fight. *berkelahi* ∼ to have a knockdown, drag-out fight.

amunisi ammunition.

a.n. [*atas nama*] in the name of.

anachoda see NACHODA.

anai² termite, white ant.

anak 1 child. 2 son. 3 daughter. 4 young, offspring. 5 to be a native of. *Ia - Malang,* He's a native of Malang. ber- 1 to have children. *Ia* ∼ *tiga,* He has 3 children. 2 to bear, give birth to. 3 together with the children. *Amat tiga* ∼ *berkeliling negeri,* Amat and his two children toured the country. 4 to get interest. *Uangnja* ∼ , His money is increasing through interest. ke- -²an childish, childlike. memper-kan 1 to bear, give birth to. *Ia* ∼ *seorang laki²,* She gave birth to a boy. 2 to treat as o's own child. *Ia* ∼ *saja dirumahnja,* He treated me like his own son. memper- -²kan to treat like a little child. *Guru itu* ∼ *murid²nja,* The teacher treats his pupils like little children. mempertirikan, meng-tirikan to treat like a stepchild. *Pemerintah selalu* ∼ *daérah itu,* The government always treats that area like a stepchild. per-an 1 half-breed, half-caste. 2 Indo (European father and Indonesian mother). 3 uterus, womb, native of. *Ia seorang* ∼ *kota Malang,* He's a native of Malang. -an 1 interest (monetary). 2 doll. -²an doll. -² 1 children. 2 a child. - -ber- 1 for generations. 2 with all the children. *Perempuan itu pergi* ∼ *dari satu rumah kerumah jg lain,* That woman went from one house to another with all her children. - *Adam* human being. - *adjaib* prodigy. - *ajam* baby chick. - *andjing* puppy. - *angkat* adopted child. - *babi* shoat, young pig. - *badju* undershirt. - *bangsawan* 1 member of nobility. 2 actor in a folk play. - *batu tulis* slate pencil. - *bawang* 1 insignificant person. 2 young child whom the older children take into the game but disregard. *Ia mendjadi - bawang dikeluarga itu,* He doesn't count in that family. - *bedil* bullet. - *belasan* teen-ager. - *bini* the entire family (wife and family). - *buah* 1 member. - *buah pasukan Siliwangi tak pernah kenal pajah,* The members of the Siliwangi Division never knew fatigue. 2 crew member. 3 loyal follower, faithful

adherent. – *bukit* hill. – *bungsu* youngest child. – *busur* arrow. – *dapat* foundling. – *dara* 1 virgin, unmarried girl. 2 bride. – *dara sunti* a girl approaching puberty. – *Djakarta* a Jakartan. – *djentera* wheel spoke. – *djudul* subtitle. – *domba* lamb. – *duit* interest on money. – *gadis* virgin, unmarried girl. – *gampang* bastard, illegitimate child. – *gindjal* adrenal. – *genta* bell clapper. – *gugur* premature baby. – *halal* legitimate child. – *haram* illegitimate child. – *jatim* orphan. – *jg terbelakang ketjerdasannja* retarded child. – *kalimat* subordinate, dependent clause. – *kambing* young of a goat. – *kandung* o's own flesh and blood. – *kapal* crew member. – *kolong* bastard. – *kembar* twins. – *kembar tiga* triplets. – *kemenakan* nephew, niece. – *kentjing* illegitimate child. – *komidi* member of stage cast. – *kualon* stepchild. – *kuda* colt. – *kuntji* key. – *kutjing* kitten. – *laki*[2] 1 son. 2 boy. – *lembu* calf. – *lidah* uvula. – *limpa* gall bladder. – *lontjéng* bell clapper. – *mana?* Where're you from? *Saja – Surabaja,* I'm a Surabayan. – *mas* favorite child. – *mata* pupil of eye. – *médja* table or desk drawer. – *mérah* newborn baby. – *muda* young adult. – *murid* pupil, school child. – *negeri* a subject of a state. – *obat* 1 a patient. 2 child raised largely on medicine. – *orang* another's child. – *orok* a baby. – *panah* arrow. – *pandji* banner, pennant, streamer. – *patju* jockey. – *pénak* descendants. – *perahu* sailor, member of crew. – *perawan* virgin, unmarried girl. – *perempuan* 1 daughter. 2 girl. – *perusahaan* affiliated firm. – *piara* foster child. – *piatu* orphan. – *pinak* descendants. – *pungut* foster, adopted child. – *rambut* 1 lock of hair. 2 man's receding hairline. – *remadja* adolescent, teen-ager. – *roda* wheel spoke. – *saku* small pocket. – *sapi* calf. – *semang* 1 boarder. 2 employee. – *sétan* 1 Dammit. 2 you s.o.b. – *sulung* oldest child. – *sumbang* bastard. – *sungai* tributary. – *susuan* unweaned child. – *tangan* 1 finger. 2 apprentice. – *tangga* 1 ladder rung. 2 (stair)step. – *tanggung* adolescent, teen-ager. – *tanggungan jg berwali* ward. – *tari* dancer. – *taruhan* favorite child. – *tekak* uvula. – *telinga* tympanum (of ear). – *teruna* youth. – *timbangan* weights of scales. – *tiri* stepchild. – *tjutju* 1 children and grandchildren. 2 descendants. – *tonil* member of stage cast. – *torak* bobbin. – *tunggal* only child. – *zina* bastard.
anakanda 1 child (formal speech). 2

familiar form of address to young people. – *hendak kemana?* Where are you going, child?
analis analyst.
analisa analysis. **meng–** to analyze.
analisir meng– to analyze.
analysa see ANALISA.
anam see ENAM.
anarki anarchy.
anasir element, substance, component.
a.n.b. [*atas nama beliau*] in his name.
anda you (used especially in advertisements). *Inginkah – menonton pertandingan itu?* Do you wish to see the contest? *Tahukah – bhw...* Do you know that...
andahan transition.
andai ber- –[2] 1 to discuss, consult e.o. *Meréka sedang ∼ ttg usul itu,* They are discussing the proposal. 2 to assume. **meng–kan** to suppose s.t. **se–nja, –kan, –kata** supposing that. **–**[2] supposition.
andak meng– 1 to take in, lower (a sail). 2 to limit to. *Ia ∼ djam bitjaranja dua djam,* He limits his office hours to 2 hours. **meng–kan** to reef down, take in sails.
andal meng–kan to rely on s.t. *Ia ∼ kepandaiannja utk lulus udjian,* He relied on his ability to pass the exam. **–an** 1 mainstay. 2 security, pledge.
Andalas Sumatra.
andam karam irretrievable. *Rumahnja – karam dimakan api,* His house was completely destroyed by fire.
andang[2] 1 yardarm. 2 mole (on the skin).
andapita dainty, tidbit.
andeng[2] 1 see ANDANG[2]. 2 barrier, screen.
andépi see ANDÉWI.
andéwi endive.
andi title of nobility in Macassar.
andil share, stock.
andja ber–(–) spoiled (of a person).
andjak ber– to budge, move. *Setapakpun ia tak mau ∼ ,* He won't budge a step. **meng–** to transplant s.t.
andjal meng– 1 to bounce, rebound. 2 elastic, resilient, springy.
andjangsana house-to-house campaign.
andjar anchor.
andjing dog. – *air* 1 otter. 2 uninvited guest. – *betina* bitch. – *galak* ferocious dog. – *geladak* stray dog. – *gila* mad dog. – *hutan* wild dog. – *laut* seal. – *pemburu* hunting dog. – *tanah* mole cricket.
andjir fig.
andju an attempt.
andjung extension, annex. **meng–**

(kan) 1 to hold s.t. up. *Ia ~ baji,* He held the baby up. 2 to praise. *~ diri* to boast. -an 1 extension, annex. 2 ship's bridge. -²an 1 praise. 2 raised platform at stern.

andjur meng- 1 to stick out, protrude. *Potlotnja ~ dari kantongnja,* His pencil is sticking out of his pocket. 2 to move on, toward. *Pagi² benar orang² desa tlh ~ kepasar,* Very early the villagers moved on to the market. *~ diri kebelakang* to retreat, withdraw. *~ surut* to withdraw, order a retreat. meng-kan 1 to propose, put forward. *Ia ~ pertanjaan,* He proposed a question. 2 to suggest, propose. *Ia ~ bhw saja lebih baik pulang sadja,* He suggested that I'd better go home. 3 to extend, protrude. *Penumpang² tidak boléh ~ badannja keluar djendéla,* Passengers may not lean out the window. 4 to hand over, pass. *Teman saja ~ koper kedalam keréta,* My friend passed the suitcase into the coach. peng- 1 leader. 2 promoter, propagandist. *~ perang* warmonger. peng-an proposal. -an 1 proposal, suggestion. 2 recommendation.

andong four-wheeled carriage used as taxi in Jogja and Solo. meng- to ride in an *andong. Kami ~ ke Djokja,* We rode to Jogja in an *andong.*

anduh meng- 1 to bind together. *Saja ~ lidi,* I bind the palm leaf ribs together. 2 to hold. *Tangan di-karena djatuh,* His hand's in a sling from a fall. peng- (*kaju*) splint. -an 1 support, prop. 2 sling.

anduk towel. - *mandi* bath towel. meng- to wipe with a towel. *Ia ~ adiknja,* She wiped her sister with a towel.

andun to go to another place. *Meréka - makan dirumah Ali,* They went to Ali's house to eat.

andung grandmother.

anéh strange, odd, queer, peculiar. - *benar kedjadian itu!* What a strange thing that is! ke-an oddity, peculiarity. *Kedjadian itu ialah suatu ~ ,* That incident was really a peculiar thing. meng-kan to be strange, peculiar. *Sungguh ~ mengapa dia tidak datang,* It's really strange that he hasn't come. -²an oddity.

anéka various, all sorts of. ber- to be multicolored, varied. *Bendéra itu ~ warna,* The flag is multicolored. ke-warnaan miscellany, variety.

anémer contractor.

anémi anemia.

angah ter- 1 excited, nervous, upset. 2 gasping for breath. *Anak itu ~*

karena ketakutan, The child was gasping for breath from fear.

angan intention, purpose. *Mémang - saja utk berdjumpa dgn kamu,* It has been my intention to meet you. ber- -² 1 to daydream, imagine. *Ia tak bekerdja, ~ sepandjang hari,* He doesn't work, he just daydreams all day. 2 to hope, want to. *Ia ~ pergi ke Éropah,* He hopes to go to Europe. meng-(-)kan 1 to reflect on s.t. *Ia ~ waktu masih muda,* He reflected on his youth. 2 to hope, desire. *Meréka ~ supaja perang lekas selesai,* They hope the war will soon be ended. 3 to imagine. per-an imagination. ter- -² to be hoped. *~ oléhnja utk me-lihat² kota Roma,* He was hoping to see Rome. -an idea. -² 1 aspiration, ideal. 2 thought, idea, mind. *Keinginan itu hanja dlm ~ sadja,* The desire was merely in the mind. 3 illusion, fancy. *Ini bukan suatu ~ sadja,* This isn't just an illusion. *~ hati* heart's desire. *tidak masuk -* impossible.

angé see HANGAT. *Semangatnja itu -² tjirit ajam sadja,* His enthusiasm doesn't last long.

anget see HANGAT.

angg. [*anggota*] member.

anggal 1 light. *Serangan malarianja tlh -,* His malaria attack was light. 2 with light ballast. 3 slack, light. *Musim panas adalah masa jg - dipertjétakan,* Summer is a slack season at the printing shop. ber- -²an to invite e.o. meng-i, meng-kan to lighten s.t.

anggap meng- 1 to believe, think, consider, deem. *Meréka ~ itu salah,* They think it wrong. 2 to invite s.o. *Saja ~ kepala kampung hadir diperkawinan anak saja,* I invited the village chief to my daughter's wedding. -an opinion, belief, notion. *~ umum* 1 public opinion. 2 invitation. - *sepi* to ignore. *Duta besar itu - sepi duta besar jg lain,* The ambassador ignored the other ambassador.

anggar fencing. ber- *lidah* to debate, argue. ber- *pikiran* to exchange views. meng- 1 to estimate, plan. *~ belandja sukar betul,* To estimate expenses is quite hard. peng-an, peng-belandjaan budgeting. -an 1 estimate. 2 shed, hangar. 3 quay. *~ belandja* budget. *~ burung* perch in bird cage. *~ dasar* statutes. *~ rumah tangga* rules.

anggauta see ANGGOTA.

anggerik orchid.

anggit meng- 1 to lace, thread, string. *Ia ~ sepatunja,* He laced his shoes.

2 to compose, draft. *Siapa jg ~ musik itu?* Who composed that music? **–an** composition (music, written).

angglap to steal.

anggota 1 member. *Ia mendjadi – pengurus,* He became a member of the board. 2 limb, member. *Ia merasa lemah pd –nja,* He felt weak in his limbs. 3 part, member. *Keréta api itu terdiri dari 5 –,* The train consists of 5 parts. **ber–** to have as members. **ber–kan** to be a member of. **ke–an** membership. *– kehormatan* honorary member.

angguk a nod. **meng–** to nod. *Ia ~ menjatakan setudju,* He nodded confirming the agreement. *~ kepala* to nod the head. **meng– –²** to keep nodding.

anggul meng– to raise, tip upward. *Kidang ~ kepalanja,* The deer raised its head. **ter– –²** to bob up and down. *Perahu itu ~ diatas gelombang,* The boat bobbed up and down on the waves.

anggun 1 neat, well-dressed, nice. – *betul kelihatannja dgn pakaian baru itu,* He looks very neat in his new suit. 2 proud, haughty. **ke–an** pride, haughtiness.

anggung meng–kan to lift s.t.

anggur 1 wine. 2 slip, cutting of a plant. **meng–** 1 to be unemployed. *Ia ~ bulan ini,* He's out of work this month. 2 to transplant. **peng–** an unemployed person. **peng–an** unemployment. *– kering* raisin, currant.

anggut meng– 1 to nod. 2 to pitch (of a ship).

angin 1 wind. 2 air. 3 opportunity. *Sebaiknja saja menunggu – baik,* It's best I wait for a good opportunity. 4 flatus, breaking wind. 5 rumor. **ber–** 1 to have air circulating. *Bilik ini hampir tidak ~ ,* This room has almost no air circulating. 2 windy. **ber– –²** to get some fresh air. *Marilah kita duduk diserambi ~ ,* Let's sit on the front porch and get some fresh air. **ke–an** 1 wind-blown. 2 rumored about. 3 to come in contact with air. *Minjak wangi ini tidak boléh ~ ,* This perfume mustn't come in contact with air. **meng–i** to air s.t. *Pagi² kami ~ kamar,* In the mornings we air the rooms. **meng–(–)kan** 1 to expose to the air. *Babu ~ tjutjian supaja lekas kering,* The maid exposed the laundry to the air so it would dry quickly. 2 to air, depict. *Ia ~ keuntungan² dari perusahaan bersama itu,* He depicted the advantages of the joint enterprise. **per–an** 1 airy

spot. 2 balcony. **ter–** 1 blown away. 2 noticeable. **–²** rumors. *– badai* storm, gale. *– baik* windfall, good luck. *– beralih* shifting wind. *– buritan* tail wind. *– ékor dujung* wind coming from several directions. *– gila* shifting wind. *– gunung²an* a big storm. *– haluan* head wind. *– kentjang* strong wind. *– langkisau* whirlwind. *– laut* sea breeze. *– mati* calm, dead wind. *– paksa* favorable wind. *– pasar* trade wind. *– pantjaroba* shifting, changeable wind. *– pujuh, – puting beliung* whirlwind, cyclone. *– ributt* storm. *– sakal* head wind. *– salah* ill wind. *– selembubu* whirlwind. *– sepoi², – silir semilir* soft breeze. *– sorong (buritan)* tail wind. *– timba ruang* strong side wind. *– turutan* tail wind.

angit smell of burnt rice.

angka 1 figure, numeral. 2 mark, grade. *– saja utk sedjarah tidak baik,* My history grade isn't so good. 3 number. *– sial* unlucky number. **meng–kan** 1 to mark, grade (exams, etc.). 2 to mark. *Ia sedang ~ peti² jg akan dikirim,* He's marking the boxes to be sent. **per–an** statistics. **–²** figures, statistics. *– dua* symbol ² (used to indicate doubling of a word or part of a word). *– kelahiran* birth rate. *– kematian* death rate. *– pandai* school grades. *– penundjuk* index number. *– permautan* death rate. *– rumawi* Roman numeral. *– tipis* narrow margin.

angkar see ANGKER.

angkara 1 cruel, wild. *Djangan berbuat – thd sesama manusia,* Don't be cruel to fellow humans. 2 greedy. 3 insolent, arrogant. 4 selfish, jealous. **ke–an** 1 greed. 2 insolence. **ke–murkaan** greed. *– murka* greedy.

angkasa 1 sky. 2 atmosphere. 3 heaven, firmament. **ke–an** *luar* outer space. **meng–** to fly into the sky. *– luar* outer space.

angkat generation. *Keluarga itu sdh 4 – ada disana,* The family has been there for 4 generations. **ber–** to leave, depart, go, set out. *Tadi pagi ia ~ ke New York,* He left this morning for New York. **ber–nja** departure. **ke–an** appointment to a position. **keber–an** departure. **member–kan** to dispatch, send. *Kepala setasiun ~ trém itu lebih dulu daripada mestinja,* The stationmaster dispatched the train earlier than he should have. *Pesuruh itu diber–kan segera,* The messenger was dispatched immediately. **meng–** 1 to lift up, raise s.t. *Ia ~ batu itu,* He lifted that stone. 2 to appoint, nominate. *Ia di– mendjadi kepala daérah,* He was appointed regional head. 3 to promote. *Djurutulis itu di– mendjadi sékretaris,* The clerk was promoted to secretary. 4 to take away. *Perampok² itu ∼ segala barang² kami,* The bandits took all our things away. 5 to start, take up. *Tak lama lagi murid² itu ∼ njanjiannja,* Before long the pupils began to sing. *∼ bahu* to shrug o's shoulders. *∼ langkah seribu* to flee, run. *∼ makanan* 1 to serve food. *Makanannja sdh di–, silahkan makan,* The food is served, please eat. 2 to clear the table. *Sesudah tamu² selesai, makanan di–,* After the guests had finished, the table was cleared. *∼ sembah* to make the *sembah* or fold the hands as a sign of obeisance. *∼ sendjata* to present arms. *∼ sumpah* 1 to take an oath. *Ia memberi keterangan itu dgn ∼ sumpah,* He gave the information under oath. 2 to swear in. *Présidén ∼ duta besar baru itu,* The president swore in the new ambassador. **meng-i** to lift repeatedly. *Kerdja kuli itu ∼ batu sungai,* The coolie's job is to keep picking up the river stones. **meng-kan** 1 to lift s.t. up. 2 to roll up. *Ia ∼ lengan badjunja,* He rolled up his shirt sleeves. **meng- –²** to praise. **peng-** 1 supporter. *Tongkat ini utk ∼ barang,* This cane is for supporting things. 2 opportunist. **peng-an** appointment to s.t. **per-an** equipment. *∼ nikah* wedding attire. **seper-(an)** a set. *pakaian ∼ lengkap dgn perhiasannja* a suit of clothes complete with accessories. **-an** 1 task force. *∼ Amérika dikirim keperairan asing,* An American task force was sent to foreign waters. 2 branch of armed forces. 3 appointment. *Kakaknja menerima ∼ utk mendjadi kepala djawatan,* His brother received an appointment to become division head. 4 generation *∼ '45* the Generation of '45. *∼ darat* ground forces. *∼ laut* navy. *∼ muda* the younger generation. *∼ negara* appointed government office. *∼ perang* armed forces. *∼ udara* air force. *– besi* weight lifting. *– bitjara* to begin to speak. *Siapa jg pertama – bitjara?* Who began to speak first? *– hakim* judicial decision, indictment. *– kaki* to flee. *Pentjuri itu – kaki waktu polisi datang,* The thief fled when the police arrived. *– rumput* to weed. *– sendjata!* Present arms! *– suara* 1 to begin to speak. 2 to raise o's voice, speak louder. *Para pendengar me-*

minta supaja jg berbitjara – suara, The listeners asked the speaker to talk louder. *– tangan!* Hands up! *– barang, tuan?* Take your bag, sir? **angker** 1 anchor. 2 motor armature. 3 haunted. *rumah –* haunted house.

angkét 1 inquiry, poll. 2 questionnaire.

angkin waistband made of cloth and worn by women.

angkit meng- to remove cooking utensils from the stove.

angklung Sundanese musical instrument made of bamboo.

angkong 1 k.o. rickshaw. 2 k.o. blackjack card game.

angkuh 1 arrogant, conceited. 2 form, appearance. **ke-an** 1 arrogance, conceit. 2 vanity.

angkup tweezers. **meng-** to hold with tweezers, pinch. **ter- –²** open and closed continuously. *Lukanja ∼ ,* His wound was constantly opening and closing. *–²* valve.

angkut meng- 1 to carry, transport. *Motor grobak ∼ barang² kepelabuhan,* The truck transports the goods to the harbor. 2 to carry away, transport. *Air sungai itu ∼ kotoran,* The river carries the refuse with it. 3 to collect, gather. *∼ sampah* to collect the garbage, trash. 4 to contain. *Bengkak ∼ darah,* The swelling contains blood. **peng-** 1 transport, carrier. 2 transporter, truck, van. *Besar sekali pesawat ∼ itu,* That transport plane is quite large. **peng-an** transportation, transport. *∼ antarpulau* interisland transportation. **-an** 1 load. 2 transport. *–²* wasp.

anglap see ANGGLAP.

anglo charcoal brazier.

angon meng- to herd, graze. *Anak itu ∼ sapinja dihutan,* The boy grazes his cattle in the forest. **-an** cattle.

angot to talk deliriously.

angsa goose.

angsur ber- 1 to continue to be (for better or worse). *Sesudah suntikan itu keséhatannja ∼ baik,* After the inoculation his health continued to be better. 2 to move up. *∼lah kemuka,* Please move up. **ber-(–)** 1 little by little, gradually, by degrees. *Orang datang ∼ ketanah lapang,* The people gradually came to the open field. 2 in instalments. *Saja tak dpt membajar kontan. Boléhkah saja membajar ∼ ?* I can't pay cash. May I pay it in instalments? **meng-** 1 to pay in instalments. *Ia ∼ utangnja,* He's paying off his debt in instalments. 2 to do s.t. gradually. 3 to move s.t. *Siapa ∼ potrét ini?* Who moved this picture? *–lah kemuka,* Please move forward. **meng–i** 1 to pay. *Saja tak dpt ∼ padjak saja,* I can't pay my taxes. 2 to pay in instalments. 3 to proceed slowly with s.t. **meng–kan** 1 to order s.o. forward. *Ketua rapat ∼ para hadirin kemuka,* The chairman ordered all present to move forward. 2 to pass, hand over. *Tjobalah ∼ korsi itu kemuka!* Please pass the chair up front! **per–an** 1 a shifting of s.t. 2 shift, move, exodus. *Ada ∼ penduduk Kebajoran,* There is an exodus of inhabitants from Kebajoran. **–an** instalment (payment).

angus 1 burnt, scorched. *Nasinja –,* The rice is burnt. *Rumahnja – terbakar,* The house has burned down. 2 singed. **ke–an** burnt. *Saja membau ∼ didapur,* I smell s.t. burning in the kitchen. **meng–kan** 1 to roast until burnt. *Kopi harus di–kan sebelum dpt didjadikan bubuk,* Coffee must be roasted before being made into a powder. 2 to burn, singe, scorch s.t. *∼ hati* to make s.o. angry. *Djangan suka ∼ hati orang,* Don't make s.o. mad. *–² hati* to become jealous. *Ia merasa ∼ hati,* He became jealous.

angut meng– to doze. *Djangan duduk ∼ ; pergilah minum kopi,* Don't sit and doze; go get some coffee. **peng–** an indolent person.

ani warp for weaving. **meng–** to arrange warp on a loom. **peng–** spool rack. **–an** warp. **–²** knife for cutting rice stalks.

aniaja 1 injustice. 2 tyranny, oppression. 3 ill treatment. 4 unjust. 5 tyrannical. **meng–(i)** 1 to maltreat, torture. *Radja itu ∼ rakjatnja,* The king maltreated his subjects. 2 to tyrannize, persecute. **peng–** oppressor, tyrant. **peng–an** tyrannical treatment, oppression, cruelty. **ter–** molested, maltreated. *Anak itu ∼ ,* The child was maltreated. *mati ∼* murdered in a terrible manner.

anis anisette.

anjam meng– to plait, weave. **–an** 1 braid. 2 plait, tress. 3 basketry. *∼ rambut* braided hair, pigtail. **––meng–** 1 plaiting. 2 basketry.

anjang raw-meat dish with spices.

anjar new(ly). *negara² jg – merdéka* newly independent countries.

anjelir carnation.

anjir 1 with strong fish odor, rancid. 2 moist appearance.

annémer see ANÉMER.

anonimitét anonymity.

Ant. [*Antara*] Indonesian News Agency.

antah 1 rice chaff. 2 see ENTAH. 3 see NEGERI.

antam see HANTAM.

antamér see ANTAMIR.

antamir meng– to undertake, tackle.

antan wooden polelike rice pestle.

antap 1 massive. 2 solid. 3 calm, quiet. 4 see ANTEP.

antar meng–(kan) 1 to introduce. *Ketua itu ∼ pembitjara itu,* The chairman introduced the speaker. 2 to bring. *Ibu tiap hari ∼ anak² kesekolah,* Mother brings the children to school every day. 3 to see off. *Saja ∼ ibu kelapangan terbang,* I saw my mother off at the airfield. 4 to lead, accompany. *Paman ∼ tamu²nja kepintu,* Uncle accompanied his guests to the door. 5 to deliver s.t. to the house. **meng–i** to send s.t. *Selama ditawan ahli rumahnja ∼ makanan kepadanja,* During his internment his family kept sending him food. **peng–** 1 companion. 2 messenger, courier. 3 escort. 4 introduction. *∼ ékonomi* introductory economics. *∼ chajal* prologue. 5 conductor (of elec.). *∼ kalam* preface, foreword. *∼ koran* newspaper boy. *∼ pos , ∼ surat* postman. **– -meng–** to send to o. another. **–an** delivery. *∼ pos* postal delivery. **–²** rotor. **–** *benua* intercontinental. **–** *diri* interpersonal. **–** *djawatan* interoffice. **–** *golongan* interracial. **–** *negara* international. **–** *planit* interplanetary. **–** *pulau* interisland. **–** *waktu* interim.

antara 1 between. *Djarak – Ithaca dan Syracuse kl 50 mil,* The distance between Ithaca and Syracuse is about 50 miles. 2 among. *Ali jg terpandai – teman²nja,* Ali is the brightest among his friends. 3 distance, gap. *Berapa méter –nja dari rumah kesungai?* How many meters' distance is it from the house to the river? 4 in, about (of time) – *lima hari pesanannja akan selesai,* The order will be ready in about 5 days. 5 not far from. *Kapal berlabuh – Semarang,* The ship anchored not far from Semarang. 6 in the meanwhile. **ber–** 1 at intervals. *Meriam berdentum ∼ tiga detik,* The guns boomed at 3-second intervals. 2 to have an intermediary. *Tamu² harus ∼ ; tak dpt bertjakap dengannja dgn langsung,* The guests must have an intermediary; they cannot talk with him directly. **di–** among, between. **meng–** to mediate. *PBB ∼ dlm perselisihan dua negara itu,* The

UN mediated in the conflict between the two countries. **meng–i** to separate, divide. **peng-, per-** 1 mediator, go-between. 2 agent. ~ *pertanggungan* insurance agent. **per–an** 1 intermediary, mediation. 2 middleman. 3 relationship. ~ *dgn madjikannja rupanja baik,* The relationship with his employer apparently wasn't too good. 4 intervention. *dgn* ~ via, by means of. *Pengumuman itu diberikan dgn* ~ *radio,* The announcement was made via radio. **-nja** among others. – *itu* 1 thereafter. *Pentjuri keluar tak lama – itu,* The thief came out not long thereafter. 2 at that moment. *Pd – itu djuga ia merasa salah,* At that very moment he felt guilty. – *lain* among other things.

anteng 1 calm, quiet. *Ia – sadja sekalipun isterinja marah²,* He remained calm even during his wife's fury. 2 undisturbed. *Ia – bekerdja dari djam 8 hingga djam 5 soré,* He works undisturbed from 8 to 5.

antep heavy. **meng–i** 1 to believe in. *Segala orang* ~ *perkataannja,* Everyone believed him. 2 to be faithful to s.o. *Pegawai itu sangat* ~ *madjikannja,* The employee is very faithful to his boss. 3 to permit, let. *Ia* ~ *orang² mengédjéknja,* He let people make fun of him.

anteré see ANTRÉ.

antéro whole, all. **se-** whole, all, entire. **se–nja** everything, entirely.

anti anti. – *perang* antiwar.

antih **meng-** to spin. **peng–an** spinning machine, spinning wheel.

antik antique.

anting **meng-** to swing, dangle. *Kera* ~ *diranting pohon,* A monkey is swinging on a tree branch. **–²** 1 pendant, earring. 2 pendulum of antique clock. – *neratja* weight of pair of scales.

antisipir **meng-** to anticipate.

antjak bamboo stand or container for offerings. **–²** nonchalant.

antjam **meng-** to threaten. *Ia* ~ *akan memanggil polisi,* He threatened to call the police. **di-** liable to. *Ia* ~ *dgn denda,* He's liable to a fine. **meng–kan** to threaten s.t. *Kaum buruh* ~ *pemogokan,* The labor group threatened a strike. **(peng)–an** threat. ~ *bahaja* threat of danger.

antjang **meng- –²** 1 to run, take a run. *Ia* ~ *sebelum melompat,* He ran a little before jumping. 2 to make preparations. *Ia* ~ *perdjalanannja keluar negeri,* He's making preparations for his trip abroad.

antjer target.

antjuk **ber-** to copulate. **di-** dammit! (to hell with you.)

antjur see HANTJUR.

antré 1 line. 2 to stand in line, queue. – *beras* to queue for rice. – *kartjis keréta api* to queue for railway tickets. – *minjak tanah* to queue for kerosene. – *tekstil* to queue for textiles.

antri see ANTRÉ.

antuk **ber- –²an** to collide, hit against e.o. *Giginja* ~ , His teeth were chattering. **meng-** 1 to strike against, bump. *Kakinja* ~ *dgn batu,* He bumped against a rock. 2 to be sleepy, drowsy. *Saja* ~ *karena tidak tidur tadi malam,* I'm sleepy because I didn't sleep last night. **peng-** sleepyhead. **ter-** to be bumped. *Kakinja* ~ *pd korsi,* He bumped his foot against a chair.

antul **meng-** to bounce, spring.

antung² a hanging holder for earthen jugs, etc.

antusias enthusiastic.

anu 1 so and so, an unknown person. *Ia mendapat surat dari si–,* He got a letter from s.o. or other, from Mr. So-and-So. 2 s.t. or other. 3 unknown quantity in mathematics. 4 see SI.

anugerah 1 a gift from God, mercy. 2 a gift from a person of higher status to one of lower. *Madjikan kami memberi – kpd segala pekerdjanja,* Our boss gave a gift to all his employees. **meng–i** to give a present to s.o. **meng–kan** to give s.t. as a present. **peng–an** bestowal, presentation.

anulir **meng-** to annul, cancel.

anumerata posthumous(ly). *djénderal* – posthumously appointed general.

anut attentive, meek, pliant. *Anak itu – sekali kpd naséhat² orang tuanja,* The child is very attentive to his parents' advice. **meng–(i)** 1 to follow, submit to. *Ia* ~ *naséhat² gurunja,* He followed his teacher's advice. 2 to profess s.t. *Meréka* ~ *agama Kristen,* They profess the Christian religion. **peng-** 1 follower, adherent. *Ia* ~ *agama baru itu,* He's an adherent of the new religion. 2 a meek person. *Ia seorang* ~ ; *tak pernah membantah,* He's a meek person; he never argues. **–an** 1 adherence. 2 conviction.

a.p. [*atas perintah*] at the order of.

apa 1 what. – *ini? Ini –?* What's this? 2 what, which. *Bunga – ini?* What flower is this? *Matjam –?* What kind? *Hari – sekarang?* What's today? 3 (question indicator.) – *saudara sdh makan?* Have you eaten?

4 or. *Bisa tinggal disini – tidak?* Can you live here or not? **ber–** 1 how much? ∼ *harga buku ini?* How much is this book? 2 how many? ∼ *djam lamanja ke New York naik mobil?* How many hours does it take to New York by car? **meng–** why. ∼ *ia menangis?* Why is she crying? *Tidak* ∼ , No matter. **meng–(–)i** to do s.t. to s.o. ∼ *ia padamu?* What did he do to you? *Ia tidak* ∼ , He didn't do anything. **meng–kan** to do s.t. to s.o. *Di–kan adikmu hingga ia menangis?* What did you do to your little brother to make him cry? **–²an?** What sort of thing is this? ∼ *ini! Saja disuruh datang kerumahnja tapi waktu saja sampai disana ia bepergian,* What's going on? I was told to come to his house but when I arrived he had left. **–²** *(sadja)* anything. *Kalau sampai disana djangan mengatakan* ∼ *(sadja),* When you get there don't say anything. ∼ *sadja dimakannja kalau lapar,* He eats anything when he's hungry. **–bila** when. ∼ *ia datang?* When's he coming? *Katakan kpd saja* ∼ *ia datang,* Tell me when he's coming. **–(kah)** whether. *Ditanjakan* ∼ *ia pernah pergi ke Bali,* He was asked whether he'd ever gone to Bali. **–kala** 1 when. ∼ *ia merajakan hari ulang tahun...* When he celebrates his birthday... 2 if. ∼ *kedinginan pakailah djas,* If you're cold put on a coat. **–lagi** 1 above all, especially. *Semua gembira waktu adik datang,* ∼ *ibu,* Everyone was happy when brother came, especially mother. 2 even less. *Saja tidak pertjaja,* ∼ *dia,* I didn't believe it, even less did he. 3 moreover, besides. 4 much less. *Kelakuannja tak dpt saja benarkan,* ∼ *béla,* I couldn't approve of his behavior, much less defend it. **–lah** please. **–nian** whatever. **–nja?** Which one? **–pun** *djuga* regardless, irrespective of, whatever. *Warganegara² mengambil bagian didalam kebudajaan bangsa,* ∼ *djuga asal-keturunannja,* Citizens participate in the national culture regardless of descent. **–** *djuga* anything. **–** *djuga baik,* Anything will do. **–** *sadja* 1 everything. **–** *sadja disumbangkan kpd korban bandjir itu,* Everything was contributed to the flood victims. 2 what all. **–** *sadja jg dibitjarakan tadi?* What all was discussed just now? **–mu** *jg kena?* Where were you hit? **–** *akal?* What'll we do? *ada* **–²nja** to have s.t. behind it. *Ia terlampau baik pd saja hari ini; tentu ada* ∼ , He's very nice to me today; there must be s.t. behind

it. *Tidak –(–),* It's nothing. (It doesn't matter. Think nothing of it. It's all right.) *Saja tidak* **–²,** I don't mind. *Tidak djadi* **–,** It doesn't matter. *Tidak meng–,* It's all right. **–** *boléh buat?* What's to be done? **–** *kata?* What can I say?

apabila see APA.

apak musty. *Badjunja* **–,** His clothes are musty.

apal to know by heart. *Ia sdh* **–** *peladjarannja,* He knows his lesson by heart. **meng–(kan)** to learn s.t. by heart. **–an** material to be learned by heart. *Saja ada* ∼ *utk bésok,* I have s.t. to memorize for tomorrow. ∼ *Kor'an* recitation of the Koran from memory.

apalagi see APA.

apam rice fritter.

aparatur apparatus.

apas 1 tough luck. 2 elegant.

apati apathy.

apatis apathetic.

apdéling division, section.

apek 1 see APAK. 2 see APIK.

apel apple. **–** *mus* applesauce.

apél 1 appeal. 2 roll call. **meng–** to appeal, enter an appeal. *Ia* ∼ *ke Mahkamah Agung,* He appealed to the Supreme Court. **–** *besar* grand roll call.

apermut oatmeal.

apes unfortunate, too bad.

api 1 fire. **–** *masih menjala,* The fire's still going. 2 light. **ber–** 1 to have fire. *Gunung* **–** *adalah gunung* ∼ , A volcano is a mountain with a fire. 2 to be on fire. *Rumahnja jg terbakar itu* ∼ *karena angin keras,* The burning house is raging from the strong winds. 3 fiery, fervent. **ber–** **–²** furious, raging. *Guru* ∼ *dikelas tadi,* The teacher was furious in class this morning. *Pidatonja* ∼ , His speech was fiery. **memper–kan** to broil s.t. **meng–** **–²kan** 1 to stir a fire. 2 to incite, start a quarrel. 3 to warm s.o. up to s.t. *Ia* ∼ *saudaranja supaja membeli mobil baru,* He warmed his brother up to the idea of buying a new car. **per–an** 1 oven, open stove. 2 furnace. 3 range. **–²** 1 match. 2 firefly. **–** *lantjip* 1 pilot light on a gas stove. 2 flame of a blowpipe or torch. **–** *luka* erysipelas. **–** *mengangah* a fire of coals. **–** *unggun* campfire.

apik neat and nice. **–** *benar rumahmu,* Your house is really nice and neat. **meng–kan** to straighten up. *Ibu* ∼ *kamar duduk,* Mother is straightening up the living room.

apit pinched. **ber–** 1 to be close to e.o. *Anak² itu duduk* ∼ , The children sat close to e.o. 2 to be between two things. *Ia duduk ∼ timbunan beras,* He sat between heaps of rice. 3 jammed, stuck. **memper-kan** to move s.o. or s.t. close together. *Supir ∼ penumpang² supaja jg lain bisa duduk djuga,* The driver moved the passengers close together so others could sit down. **meng-** 1 to flank. *Dua pendjaga ∼ pendjahat itu,* Two guards flank the criminal. 2 to press, squeeze. *Ia ∼ tebu supaja keluar airnja,* He pressed the sugar cane to get the juice. 3 to press, hold. *Ia ∼ pajung itu dgn lututnja,* He held the umbrella between his knees. 4 to staple s.t. *Ia ∼ kertas,* He stapled the paper. **peng-** 1 paper clip. 2 flanker. *Dua polisi ∼ mobil radja,* Two policemen flank the king's car. 3 hemmed in. **per-** hemmed in. **ter-** surrounded, hemmed in. *Pentjuri itu ∼ diantara orang² kampung,* The thief was surrounded by the village people.

apiun opium.

apkir rejected for military service. **meng-** 1 to reject. *Dokter ∼ ia masuk tentara,* The doctor rejected him for enlistment in the army. 2 to condemn a building. 3 to prohibit, ban s.t. **-an** 1 rejection. 2 rejected individual or article.

aplos applause. **meng-** to applaud.

aplus 1 relieved, changed. 2 redeemed. 3 applause. **meng-** to relieve. *Pendjaga baru ∼ jg lama,* New guards relieved the old ones.

apokat 1 see ADPOKAT. 2 avocado.

apoték pharmacy.

apotéker pharmacist.

apotik see APOTÉK.

appél see APÉL.

A.P.R. [*Amanat Penderitaan Rakjat*] Mandate of the People's Suffering.

APRI [*Angkatan Perang Républik Indonésia*] the Indonesian Armed Forces.

April April.

apukat see ADPOKAT.

apung 1 to float. 2 floating. **meng-** to float. *Kaju² ∼ kelaut,* Pieces of wood are floating to the sea. **meng-kan** to float s.t. *Anak² ∼ perahunja ditelaga,* The children are floating their boats on the lake. **peng-** buoy, float. **ter-** **-²** floating, drifting around. **-²** 1 floating object. 2 life buoy, float.

apus see HAPUS.

ara see BUAH.

arab 1 Arab. 2 Arabic.

arah 1 direction, course. *Jg dinamai kiblat ialah - ke Mekkah,* 'Kiblat' means the direction toward Mecca. 2 aim, direction. *Kemana -nja pem-*

bitjaraan itu? Where's the discussion headed? **ke-** toward. **ke-an** direction. **meng-** 1 to aim, direct. *Ia ∼ langkahnja kedjurusan itu,* He pointed his steps in that direction. 2 to aim at s.t. *Ia ∼ bola itu, tapi tak kena,* He aimed at that ball, but missed. 3 to manage, direct, administer. **meng-kan** 1 to direct, aim, point at. *Pemburu itu ∼ bedilnja kekidang itu,* The hunter aimed his gun at that deer. 2 to mean, intend. *Mémang ia ∼ supaja ia datang dirumahnja,* He surely meant that he would come to his house. **meng-** **-²i** 1 to resemble. *Tingkah lakunja ∼ pemain tonil,* His attitude resembles that of an actor. 2 to observe carefully. *Ia ∼ penumpang²,* He observed the passengers carefully. **peng-** manager, director. **∼ laku** stage director. **-²** to resemble. *Rupanja ∼ bapaknja,* He looks like his father.

arak 1 rice wine, arrack. 2 brandy. 3 gin. **ber-(-)** to go in a procession. *Anak² sekolah ∼ menudju istana présidén,* The school children went in procession to the president's palace. **meng-** to accompany in a procession. *Banjak orang didésa ∼ tjalon hadji itu,* Many of the village people accompanied the future hadji in the procession. **peng-** participant in a procession. **peng-an** 1 an arrack distillery. 2 procession. **per-an** procession. **-²an** procession, review.

aral hindrance, obstacle. *Kalau tak ada - saja akan datang bésok,* If nothing happens, I'll come tomorrow. *- melintang* obstacle. *Saja sdh siap utk pergi tapi lalu ada -,* I was ready to go, but then s.t. happened.

aram-temaram twilight.

arang 1 charcoal. 2 coal. **meng-** to burn charcoal, to char. **per-an** charcoal furnace. *- besi* 1 coke, slag. 2 cinders. *- dimuka* 1 shame. *Dia membunuh diri utk menghilangkan - dimuka,* He committed suicide to remove his shame. 2 insult, affront. *- kaju* charcoal. *- pagu, - para* soot.

arangesemén arrangement (music).

aransemén see ARANGESEMÉN.

ararut arrowroot.

aras to checkmate (in chess). *Radja di-,* The king was checkmated.

Arba Wednesday.

arbei strawberry.

are 100 square meters.

arék son, boy. *- Surabaja* people hailing from Surabaya.

arén sugar palm.

ari² 1 abdomen. 2 afterbirth.

aria title of nobility.

arif 1 capable. 2 wise, clever. *Ia terkenal sebagai orang* -, He's known as a wise man. 3 energetic, go-getting. **ke–an** 1 learning, wisdom. 2 ability. **meng–i** to understand, see. **meng–kan** to realize, understand. – *bidjaksana* wise and intelligent.

arih meng–kan to hold out s.t. *Ibunja* ∼ *tangan kepadanja utk memeluk,* His mother held out her hands to embrace him.

arik insomnia.

aring 1 odor of wine. 2 a trap, snare. 3 lasso. 4 to stink.

ario see ARIA.

arip 1 see ARIF. 2 sleepy.

aris hem.

arisan see DJULO².

arit 1 sickle. 2 rubber tapping knife. 3 grass knife. **meng–** to cut the grass.

arkip see ARSIP.

arlodji a watch. – *kantong* pocket watch. – *tangan* wrist watch.

arnal hairpin.

arpus 1 catgut. 2 wood glue.

arsip archives, files. – *negara* state archives. **ke–an** archival matters.

arsiték architect.

arti 1 meaning. *Apa –nja?* What's its meaning? *$1000 tak ada –nja bagi seorang kaja seperti dia,* $1000 means nothing to o. as rich as he. 2 sense. *dlm – sempit* in the narrow sense. **ber–** 1 to mean. *Apa* ∼ *'what,'* 'Apa' means 'what.' 2 to be significant, be of value. *Ia memberi uraian jg tak* ∼ *kpd rapat,* He gave a useless explanation to the meeting. **mengkan** to understand, interpret. **–an** 1 meaning. 2 idea, concept. **–nja** i.e. – *kiasan* figurative sense.

artikel 1 article, column. 2 article, clause. – *karét* a clause subject to various interpretations.

artja statue, image.

aruh see PENGARUH.

arun meng– to stir, beat up.

arung meng– to wade across, cross. *Mari kita* ∼ *sungai ini,* Let's wade across this river. *Kapal baru itu* ∼ *segara,* The new ship crossed the ocean. **meng–i** 1 to cross. *Meréka* ∼ *padang pasir itu 40 hari lamanja,* They crossed the desert for 40 days. 2 to sail, navigate. 3 to ford, wade across. **–an** 1 the crossing, ford. 2 trough of the waves. 3 the shallows.

arus 1 see HARUS. 2 current. *Diantara Bali dan Djawa ada – jg kuat,* There's a strong current between Bali and Java. – *bolak-balik* alternating current. – *gelombang panas* Gulf Stream. – *listerik* electric current. – *olak* eddy, current (electricity). –

olak(an) rolling waves. – *searah* direct current.

arwah soul. **meng–kan** to hold a memorial service in honor of the deceased.

a.s. [*alaihissalam*] Peace be with him.

A.S. [*Amérika Serikat*] U.S.A., the United States of America.

asa hope. **–²an** ever hoping. – *sia²* vain hope.

asabat 1 nerve. 2 sinew, muscle.

asah meng– 1 to sharpen. *Ia* ∼ *pisau,* He sharpened the knife. 2 to file. *Ia* ∼ *gigi anaknja,* He filed his child's teeth. 3 to polish up. *Ia* ∼ *intannja,* She polished up her diamond. 4 to plane. *Papan itu di– sebelum dipelitur,* The board is planed before it is varnished. **peng–** 1 grinder, hone. 2 (knife) grinder. **peng–an** 1 sharpening, grinding. 2 whetstone, hone. **–an** 1 shavings. ∼ *kaju* wood shavings. 2 dust. *Ia pandai sekali meng– hati orang,* He's very clever at persuading people.

asai to rot away. *Dinegeri panas banjak matjam kaju lekas –,* In tropical countries many kinds of wood rot away quickly.

asak ber– to move, budge. *Sekalipun orang lainnja mengongsi, orang tua itu tidak* ∼ , Although other people were evacuating, the old man wouldn't budge. **ber–(an)** to jam, crowd. *Pd habis minggu penumpang* ∼ *ditrém,* On weekends passengers crowd into the streetcars. **meng–(i)** 1 to cram, jam in. *Ia* ∼ *peti itu dgn beras,* He crammed the box with rice. 2 to insist. *Ia* ∼ *pamannja supaja mendjual saham karétnja,* He insisted that his uncle sell his rubber stock. 3 to move. *Ia* ∼ *pohon itu ketempat jg lebih subur,* He moved his tree to a more fertile spot. 4 to replace, supplant. 5 to push onward. 6 to corner. **ter–** 1 to be compelled. *Ia merasa* ∼ *utk mendjual tanahnja,* He felt compelled to sell his land. 2 to be moved. *Tiba² ia mengetahui bhw ia* ∼ *ketempat jg lain,* He suddenly realized he was being moved to another place.

asal 1 origin, source. *Dimana – sungai itu?* What's the source of that river? 2 parentage, descent. *Ia seorang anak désa jg tak ketahuan –nja,* He's a villager whose parentage is unknown. 3 provided (that), only if. *Ia boléh kebioskop, – ada uang,* He may go to the movies, provided he has the money. 4 derivation. **ber–** 1 to come from, hail from. *Barang² ini* ∼ *Djepang,* These goods come from

Japan. *Darimana dia* ~ *?* Where does he come from? 2 to be from a good family. **meng–kan** to trace the origin of. *Ahli sedjarah* ~ *kesenian Borobudur,* The historian traced the origin of the art of the Borobudur. ~ *kpd* to reduce s.t. to (math.). se-related. **–kan,** – *sadja* provided that. ~ *makan sadja tentu ia lekas sembuh,* He will surely recover right away provided he eats. **–nja** originally. **– –ber–** to be of good family. – *djasad* organic. – *kata* base, stem. – *mula* origin, the very beginning. – *usul* 1 pedigree, descent, origin. 2 history, origin. *Bagaimana* – *usul penjakit itu?* What's the history of that disease?

asam 1 sour. *Tjuka* –, Vinegar is sour. *Mukanja* –, He has a sour look. 2 acid. 3 tamarind. **meng–** to wash with acid. **meng–i** 1 to pickle. 2 to spice with tamarind. **meng–kan** 1 to pickle. 2 to can, preserve. **–an** pickle. **–²an** 1 acids. 2 all k.o. pickles. – *arang* carbon dioxide. – *belirang* sulphuric acid. – *djawa* tamarind. – *garam* 1 spice. 2 hydrochloric acid. – *limau* citric acid. – *samak* tannic acid. – *semut* formic acid. – *sendawa* nitric acid.

asap 1 smoke. 2 steam, vapor. **ber–** to smoke. **meng–i** 1 to smoke out. *Ia* ~ *njamuk,* He smoked out the mosquitoes. 2 to steam s.t. **meng–kemenjani** to praise. *Ia suka* ~ *mertuanja,* He loves to praise his father-in-law. **peng–an** fumigation. **per–an** 1 fumigation. 2 incense container. – *air* vapor.

asar 1 afternoon prayer (4 p.m.). 2 period between 3 and 5 p.m. – *rendah* late in the afternoon. – *tinggi* early afternoon.

asas 1 principle, basis. 2 foundation, base. – *rumah itu dibuat dari besi,* The foundation of this house is made of iron. **ber–(kan)** 1 to be based on. *Negara Pakistan* ~ *keislaman,* Pakistan is based on Islam. 2 to have principles. *Perkumpulan ini* ~ *sosial,* This association has social principles. **meng–kan** to found, base. *Ia* ~ *peladjarannja kpd tjita² Islam,* He founded his teaching on Islamic ideals. **peng–** founder. *Pd –nja ia salah,* Fundamentally he's wrong.

asasi fundamental, basic. *hak* – basic right.

asbak ash tray.

asbés asbestos.

aseli see ASLI.

asép bill of payment.

asi care. **meng–** to pay attention to, care for. *Anak itu sama sekali tidak*

~ *perkataan ajahnja,* The child didn't pay any attention to what his father said.

asih see KASIH. *Maha-* – All Loving.

asik see ASJIK.

asimilasi assimilation.

asin 1 salty. *Supnja terlalu* –, The soup is very salty. 2 salted, briny. **meng–i** 1 to salt s.t. 2 to pickle. **meng–kan** 1 to salt s.t. *Ia* ~ *ikan,* He salted the fish. 2 to pickle. **–an** salted vegetable. **–²an** pickle. – *garam* full of worries, problems.

asing 1 strange, foreign, alien. *Saja merasa* – *disini,* I feel strange here. 2 odd, queer. *Agak* – *matjam pakaian orang itu,* That man's wearing a rather odd kind of clothing. 3 remote, isolated. *Rumah itu sangat* – *tempatnja,* That house is very isolated. 4 unusual, foreign. *Kedjadian seperti itu mémang tidak* – *disana,* Events like that aren't unusual there. **ber–** isolated. *Anak itu selalu* ~ *seorang diri,* That child's always going off by himself. **ke–an** 1 strange. *Ia akan merasa* ~ *disini,* He'll feel strange here. 2 strangeness. 3 oddness. **mem-per–kan** 1 to alienate s.o. 2 to isolate s.t. 3 to confine, intern s.o. **meng–** to isolate. *Teman saja itu selalu* ~ , That friend of mine is always isolating himself. **meng–kan** 1 to exile s.o. 2 to isolate. *Pemerintah* ~ *orang sakit lépra kepulau ketjil,* The government isolated the lepers on a small island. **peng–an** 1 place of exile. 2 internment. 3 isolation, exile. ~ *suatu virus* isolation of a virus. 4 estrangement. **per–an** exile, isolation. **ter–** 1 isolated, out of the way. *Orang itu hidup* ~ *diatas gunung,* That man lives isolated up in the mountains. 2 exotic, very foreign.

asistén assistant. – *ahli* university lecturer. – *wedana* subdistrict head. **ke–an** assistantship. **–an** subdistrict.

asjik 1 passionate(ly). *Ia* – *mentjintai kekasihnja,* He passionately loves his sweetheart. 2 to be in love, be infatuated. *Ia* – *sekali kpd gadis itu,* He's very much in love with that girl. 3 busy, occupied. *Ia sedang* – *makan siang,* He's busy eating lunch. 4 zealous, eager, absorbed. *Ia* – *beladjar bahasa Indonésia,* He's absorbed in studying Indonesian. **ke–** **–²an** 1 very passionately. 2 anxious. **meng–kan** attractive. – *akan* to have a passion for s.t. *Ia* – *akan perangko,* He has a passion for stamps. – *berahi* infatuated. *Ia* – *berahi akan perempuan itu,* He's infatuated with that woman. – *dan maksjuk* deeply in love with e.o.

Asjura the 10th day of Muharram; celebrating Hasan and Husein Day or Day of Atonement.

asli 1 original. *Inilah surat keterangan* –, This is the original certificate. 2 genuine, authentic. *Ini laporan – ttg keadaan,* This is an authentic report of the situation. 3 indigenous, autochthonous. 4 of noble descent. 5 primitive. **ke–an** 1 originality. 2 authenticity, genuineness.

asmara love. *– berahi* erotic.

aso meng– to take a break. *Sdh 4 djam kita bekerdja; marilah ~ sebentar,* We've been working for 4 hours; let's take a break. **peng–an** resthouse, rest spot.

aspal asphalt. **meng–** to asphalt s.t.

asperdjis asparagus.

aspirasi aspiration.

asrama 1 dormitory. 2 barracks. 3 boardinghouse. **meng–kan** to station in a barracks.

assalam alaikum Peace be unto you (greeting).

assumsi assumption.

astaga God forgive me.

astagfirullah God forgive me.

astakona 1 octagon. 2 polygon.

astana see ISTANA.

astronot astronaut.

astronotik astronautics.

asuh meng– 1 to take care of, rear, bring up. *Ia ~ tiga anak jatim,* He brought up three orphans. 2 to educate. 3 to train, prepare. *Opsir itu harus ~ tentera²nja,* The officer must train his soldiers. **peng–** 1 caretaker, nurse. 2 guardian. 3 trainer. **–an** 1 education. 2 upbringing. 3 direction, leadership.

asung see ASUT.

asuransi insurance. **meng–** to insure. **peng–** insurer. **per–an** system of insurance. *jg di–kan* the insured.

asut meng– 1 to incite, stir up. *Djangan ~ andjing,* Don't get the dog aroused. 2 to instigate, incite. *Ia ~ buruh minjak supaja mogok,* He incited the oil refinery workers to strike. **peng–** agitator, provocateur. **peng–an** instigation, provocation. **–an** instigation.

AT [*Asia Tenggara*] Southeast Asia.

atap 1 roof. 2 thatched roof of palm leaves. **ber–(kan)** roofed. **meng–i** to roof s.t. *Ia ~ rumahnja dgn idjuk,* He put a palm fiber roof on his house. *– langit* in the open air. *– séng* corrugated roof.

atas 1 on, upon, on top of. *Dari – bukit itu lihat laut,* From the top of that hill I see the sea. *Jg tersebut di– tidak benar,* What was mentioned above is not correct. 2 upper. *Pintu itu rusak dibagian –,* The upper section of the door is damaged. *Sebelah – médja itu ditjat kuning,* The upper side of the table is painted yellow. 3 above, superiors. *Ia mendapat peringatan dari – bhw pekerdjaannja tidak bérés,* He received a warning from above that his work was not in order. 4 for. *– kebaikanmu itu saja utjapkan terima kasih,* I thank you for your kindness. 5 because of, thanks to. *– usaha teman² saja...* Thanks to the efforts of my friends... 6 in(to). *Buku itu terbagi – 3 bagian,* The book is divided into 3 parts. 7 at, upon. *Saja datang disini – undangan ajahmu,* I came here at your father's invitation. 8 upstairs, second floor. *Djl. Braga 132 (–)* 132 Braga St. (2nd floor). **ber– –²an** to excel o. another. **di–** 1 on, upon, on top of. *~ médja ada buku,* There's a book on top of the table. 2 above. *Tinggi ~ telaga Cayuga terletak Universitas Cornéll,* High above Lake Cayuga lies Cornell University. 3 over, above. *Lampu bergantung ~ médja,* A lamp hangs over the table. *Pesawat itu terbang ~ Bangkok,* A plane flew over Bangkok. 4 rather than, over. *binasa ~ ditindas* annihilation over tyranny. **ke–** 1 up, over. *Anak² umur 10 tahun ~ mesti bajar penuh,* Children 10 and up must pay full fare. 2 upward. *Balon² itu ditiup angin ~,* The balloons were blown upward by the wind. **meng–** 1 to rise, go upward. *Debu ~ karena tiupan angin,* The dust rose because of the wind. 2 to aspire, rise. *Tjita²nja selalu ~,* His ideals are always rising. 3 to appeal. *Ia ~ kpd kepala sekolah,* He appealed to the principal of the school. **meng–i** 1 to surpass. *Ajahnja kaja, tapi ia masih ~nja,* His father is wealthy, but he still surpasses him. 2 to overcome, surmount. *Ia dpt ~ kesukaran² itu,* He was able to overcome the difficulties. **meng–kan** 1 to lift up. *Ibu ~ ampaian,* Mother lifted up the clothesline. 2 to favor s.o. *Ia selalu ~ bangsanja,* He's always elevating his own people. **meng–namakan** to authorize, do s.t., in the name of s.o. *Ia ~nja tanpa izin,* He authorized it without permission. **–an** higher. *Golongan ~pun hidupnja sangat sederhana,* The higher group too live very modestly. *Pendidikan ~ blm dpt dibentuk,* Higher education cannot be arranged yet. **– –meng–** to go up and up. **– –meng–i** to excel o. another. **–mu** you should, it's obligatory for you.

tak dpt di–i insurmountable. – *nama perkumpulannja* on behalf of his organization.
atasé attaché.
atau or. –...– either...or.
atéis atheist.
Aténa(i) Athens.
ati[2] to be careful. –, Be careful. *Ia – mentjutji piring itu,* She's very careful in washing the dishes. **ber-** –[2] to be careful. see HATI.
atjak meng- wild, without rules, chaotic. *Permainan sépak bola itu ∼,* The soccer game was a wild one. –[2]**an** confusion, chaos. –[2] hurry. *Mengapa ∼ pulang? Hari baru pukul 7,* Why hurry home? It's only 7.
atjap 1 to get into s.t. deeply. *Roda mobil itu – dilumpur,* The car was stuck deep down in the mud. 2 to be under water. *Seluruh kota – karena bandjir,* The whole city was flooded by the rising waters. **meng-i** to soak s.t. *Ibu ∼ tjutjian dlm air sabun,* Mother soaked the laundry in soapy water. –[2] 1 often. 2 fast. – *kali* often.
atjar 1 pickles. 2 vegetable dish with pickles.
atjara 1 program, agenda. *Apakah – rapat nanti malam?* What's on the agenda for tonight's meeting? 2 judicial procedure. 3 jurisdiction. 4 ceremony. **ber-** 1 to sit, be in session (of a court, etc.). 2 to have on the agenda. *Pembitjaraan itu akan ∼ tiga soal,* The discussion will have three matters on the agenda. 3 to be in litigation. **meng-** 1 to hand down. *Hakim ∼ hukuman pendjara 5 tahun,* The judge imposed a sentence of 5 years' imprisonment. 2 to administer justice. **meng-kan** 1 to bring up s.t. *Ia ∼ itu kpd hakim,* He brought it up with the judge. 2 to place s.t. on the agenda. *PBB ∼ soal itu sebagai – pertama,* The UN placed that problem first on the agenda. **peng-** lawyer, attorney.
atji tapioca flour. **meng-** –[2]**kan** 1 to suppose. 2 to imagine. –[2]**an** 1 imagination. 2 supposition. –[2]**nja** supposing, assuming. *∼ ia benar, pasti sadja ia datang sendiri kemari,* Assuming that he was right, he'd come here himself.
atjo meng- 1 to talk incoherently. *Ia ∼ karena panasnja terlalu tinggi,* He talked incoherently because his fever was very high. 2 to lie, tell a falsehood. 3 to be confusing. *Keterangannja sangat ∼ ,* His statements were very confusing. 4 to be incorrect. *Arlodji saja ∼ ,* My watch is incorrect. – *bélo* nonsense chatter.

atju ready. *Ia sdh – utk berangkat,* He's ready to leave. **meng-** 1 to strike a threatening posture. 2 to direct, aim, point. *Ia ∼ bedilnja utk menémbak kidang,* He aimed his gun at a deer. **meng-kan** 1 to stick s.t. out, point. *Ia ∼ tombaknja kpd saja,* He stuck out his spear at me. 2 to plan, advocate. *Ia ∼ pemberantasan buta huruf dgn besar[2]an,* He planned a literacy campaign on a large scale. 3 to refer. *Utk keterangan jg lebih djelas ia ∼ kpd tjeramahnja kemarén,* For a clearer statement he referred to his lecture yesterday. 4 to tune. *Meréka lebih dulu ∼ gitarnja kpd biola itu,* They first tuned their guitar to the violin. **meng-** –[2] to plan. *Sdh lama kami ∼ utk pergi ke Miami,* For a long time now we have planned to go to Miami. **se-** from the same mold. *Ia ∼ dgn ajahnja,* He looks like his father. **–an** 1 form, model. *∼ kué* cake pan, baking pan. 2 mold, shoe last.
atjuh care. *Ia – sekali kpd tanamannja,* He gives his plants a great deal of care. **meng-kan** to care about, be concerned about, be attentive to. *Murid itu ∼ benar segala perkataan gurunja,* The pupil was very attentive to the teacher's words. – *tak* – to act unconcerned, be indifferent. *Ia – tak – waktu saja menanja mau ikut apa tidak,* He acted unconcerned when I asked him whether he wanted to go along or not.
atjum meng- to incite, instigate, provoke s.o. *Ia selalu ∼ tetangganja,* He was always inciting his neighbors against e.o.
atjung meng-(kan) 1 to hold up o's hand. *Ia ∼ utk mendjawab pertanjaan itu,* He held up his hand to answer the question. 2 to raise o's hand in greeting. 3 to point. *Senapan di-kan kebawah,* The rifle was pointed downward.
atlét athlete.
atlétik athletics.
atlit see ATLÉT.
Atmil [*Atasé Militér*] military attaché.
atom atom.
atop belching.
atos hard. – *benar bola ini,* This ball is very hard.
atraksi attraction.
atrét to back up, go in reverse.
atur ber- to be arranged. *Segala ∼ baik[2],* All has been arranged carefully. **meng-** 1 to get, put in order. *Saja akan ∼ dapur dulu,* I'll put the kitchen in order first. 2 to regulate. *Agén polisi itu ∼ lalu lintas,* The

policeman regulated the traffic. 3 to arrange, settle. *Saja akan ~ urusan saja dulu,* I'm going to arrange my affairs first. 4 to string s.t. *Gadis itu ~ mutiara didjadikan kalung,* The girl strung pearls into a necklace. *~ sikap* to come to o's attention. **meng–kan** 1 to offer. *Bersama ini kami –kan dgn hormat kpd Tuan...* We herewith respectfully offer you... 2 to hand over s.t. **peng–** arranger. *Siapa ~ pésta itu?* Who arranged that festival? *~ lalu lintas* traffic policeman. **peng–an** co-ordination. *~ langkah* co-ordination of steps. **per–an** regulation, ordinance. *~ pemerintah* government regulation. *~ penguasa perang* war administration regulation. **ter–** 1 orderly, in order. *Keamanan tlh ~ kembali,* Peace has been restored. *Meréka berdjédjér dgn ~,* They stood side by side in orderly fashion. 2 regular, arranged. *Pengadjaran diberikan dlm waktu jg ~,* Teaching is done at regular periods. **–an** 1 arrangement, setup. *Gedung ini baik benar ~nja,* This building has quite a nice arrangement. 2 regulation. 3 manner, behavior. *Rupanja ia tak tahu ~,* He doesn't seem to have any manners. 4 routine (of a household, etc.). *~ tertib* rules of proper conduct. *~nja* 1 according to the regulations. *~nja tiap kelahiran harus didaftarkan,* According to regulations all births must be recorded. 2 in fact, as a matter of fact. *~ ia harus sdh disini sebelum saja datang,* Actually he should have been here before I came.

audisi audition.

aum 1 roaring, bellowing. *Apa kaudengar – harimau?* Did you hear the tiger's roar? 2 raging storm. **meng–** 1 to roar, bellow. 2 to buzz. **me-ng–²kan** to boast of s.t.

aur 1 bamboo (pole). 2 see AWUR.

aurat 1 nakedness. *– lelaki ialah dari pusat kelutut,* The 'aurat' of a man is from the navel to the knees. 2 genitals.

AURI [*Angkatan Udara Républik Indonésia*] the Indonesian Air Force.

aus 1 see HAUS. 2 worn-out, shabby. **meng–i** to wear s.t. out. *– tanah* erosion.

Australi Australia.

autarki autarchy.

autonomi see OTONOMI.

avontir see AVONTUR.

avontirir adventurer.

avontur adventure.

awak 1 I. *– tak dpt pergi,* I can't go. 2 my, our. *Banjak sekali orang bangsa – di New York,* A great many of our countrymen are in New York. 3 people from Minangkabau. 4 body. *Asap kelihatan daripada – kapal itu,* Smoke was seen coming from the body of the ship. *Saja merasa tidak énak –,* I don't feel well. **peng–an** figure, shape. **per–an** 1 figure. *gadis tjantik dgn ~nja jg ramping itu* the pretty girl with the slender figure. 2 build. *–ku (-mu, -nja)* I (you, he, she). *Mengapa -ku harus sakit disini?* Why must I be sick here? *– kabin* cabin boy. *– kapal* crewman. *Djanganlah malu, kita hanja – sama –,* Don't be shy; we're among friends.

awal 1 beginning. *– tahun ini* the beginning of this year. 2 beginning, initial. *Hudjan – tlh djatuh,* The first rain has fallen. 3 first, early. *Lebih baik datang – daripada achir,* It's better to come first than last. **meng–(i)** 1 to head, be first. *Ia ~ teman²nja memberi sumbangan,* He was the first of his friends to give a contribution. 2 to precede. *Dialog itu di–i dgn musik,* The dialogue was preceded by music. **peng–** pioneer. *Alif ~ huruf alfabét,* Alif is the first letter of the alphabet. **–an** prefix.

awam 1 common, general. 2 nonexpert, layman. **meng–kan** 1 to announce, promulgate. *Pemerintah ~ undang² baru,* The government announced a new edict. 2 to propose s.t. 3 to advocate s.t. **peng–** propagandist, advocate.

awan cloud. **ber–** cloudy, overcast. **meng–** to climb into the sky. *Pesawat udara itu ~,* The plane climbed into the sky.

awang **meng–** 1 to go up into the air. 2 to indulge in fancies. *Djanganlah selalu ~,* Don't always be indulging in fancies. **per–an** *tjita²* castles in the air. *–² 1* air, atmosphere. 2 in the air, far-off, uncertain. *Persetudjuan masih di~,* An agreement is still far off.

awas 1 careful. *Kita harus – kalau naik keréta api,* We must be careful if we go by train. *–, keréta api sdh datang, djangan dekat² rél²,* Be careful, the train's coming. Don't get too near the tracks. 2 to see clearly. *Matanja tidak – lagi,* His eyes aren't good anymore. 3 magical, sharp. *Ia terkenal sebagai ahli nudjum jg –,* He's known as a sharp astrologer. **ber–(–)** 1 to be careful. *Kita harus ~ djika berbitjara dgn penipu itu,* We must be careful when talking with that fraud. 2 to control, check. **meng–i, meng–kan** 1 to supervise.

Siapa jg ~ *pekerdjaan ini?* Who's supervising this work? 2 to supervise, look after. *Ia* ~ *anak²*, She looked after the children. **peng–** 1 supervisor, superintendent, overseer. 2 caretaker, keeper. **peng–an** supervision, care. – *kalau kamu tidak mau bajar utangmu,* Don't pay your debt and see what happens. – *waspada* to be on the alert, be careful.

awét durable, lasting. *Sepatu ini – sekali,* These shoes are very durable. **ke–an** 1 life, durability (of washing machine, car, etc.). 2 preservation. **meng–** to can, put up, preserve fruits, vegetables. **meng–kan** to make s.t. last. *Apakah jg* ~ *warna batik itu?* What has made the color of the batik last? **peng–** preservative. **peng–an** conservation. **–an** preserves. – *muda* to stay young. *Ia – muda karena hidupnja selalu senang,* He stayed young because he always led a happy life.

awit see AWÉT.

awur meng– to do s.t. at random. *Pesawat musuh itu* ~ *sadja membom kota,* The enemy plane bombed the city at random. **meng–i** to spread. *Gadis* ~ *bunga dimakam,* The girl

spread flowers on the grave. **meng–kan** to spread, circulate s.t. **–²an** at random.

azab 1 torment. 2 punishment. – *Allah* God's punishment. **meng–** to torment s.o. – *sengsara* torment and misery, suffering.

azal see ADJAL.

azali ancient. *masa* – time immemorial.

azam 1 greatly respected. *Nama Allah adalah nama* –, God's name is greatly respected. 2 intention. **meng–kan** to intend. *Ia* ~ *akan berangkat bésok,* He intends to leave tomorrow.

azamat see AZMAT.

azan call to prayer. **meng–kan** to call to prayer.

azas see ASAS.

azasi see ASASI.

azimat amulet, charm.

aziz respected (person).

azmat 1 enormous, great. *Kota itu memperlihatkan perhatian jg – thd rombongan tari Bali,* The city showed enormous interest in the Balinese dance group. 2 bustling, loud, noisy. *Sorak penonton² itu sangat* –, The applause of the spectators was extremely loud.

B

B [*Bekasi*] 1 district of Greater Jakarta. 2 telephone exchange.

ba' 1 like. *Serupa betul dua saudara itu,* – *dua titis air,* Those brothers look as much alike as two drops of water. 2 abbrev. of Jav. *bakju* (form of address to older sister or older woman). *Apakah – sdh dengar ttg kabar itu?* Have you heard the news?

bab 1 chapter of a book. 2 subject, topic of conversation.

baba Indonesian-born Chinese.

babad 1 history, chronicle. – *Tanah Djawa* Chronicle of Java. 2 tripe (food).

babah see BABA.

babak 1 act of play. 2 round (boxing). *Louis mengalahkan lawannja dlm – ke-4,* Louis defeated his opponent in the fourth round (used also of other sports). 3 phase, stage. *Perang itu mentjapai – terachir,* The war has

reached the final stage. **–an** 1 set (in tennis). 2 act of play. 3 round, period. ~ *waktu* periodization. – *belur* black and blue (from a beating or accident). – *penjisihan* elimination round.

babang a gaping mouth, wound, abyss.

babar mem–kan 1 to spread, unfurl. *Tak lama lagi perahu* ~ *lajarnja,* Before long the boat unfurled its sails. 2 to lay out. *Pendjual itu* ~ *barang² dagangannja dipinggir djalan,* The vendor laid out his merchandise at the roadside. 3 to explain s.t. *Penaséhat itu* ~ *pendapatnja ttg rentjana baru itu,* The advisor explained the new project. 4 to extend, spread. *Radja itu* ~ *kekuasaannja,* The king extended his sway.

babas ter– 1 to be driven off course, drift off course. *Karena udara djelék* *kapal terbang ke New York* ∼ *ke Washington,* Because of bad weather the plane for New York had to land in Washington. 2 carried away, swept away (in a drift, flood, etc.). 3 washed out (of a road). 4 to go by mistake. *Karena disangka hotél banjak orang* ∼ *kerumah itu menanja kamar penginapan,* Because it was thought to be a hotel, many came to that house looking for a room.

babat 1 tripe (food). 2 group. *Dlm pergaulan masjarakat orang mentjari sama —nja,* In social intercourse one looks for his own kind. **mem–** to clear away, cut through. *Utk membuka djalan orang harus* ∼ *dulu,* In opening up a road one must first clear away the jungle. ∼ *rumput* to mow the lawn. **se–** of the same kind.

babi pig, hog, swine. **mem–** *buta* 1 to storm, rage. 2 raging. 3 demonic, titanic. 4 to act blindly, at random. – *alu* tapir. – *asap* 1 bacon. 2 ham. – *dujung* sea cow, manatee. – *hutan* wild boar. – *laut* sea urchin. – *lu!* You're a pig! – *rusa* babirusa.

babil quarrelsome. **ber–** to squabble. *Meréka* ∼ *ttg warisan,* They were squabbling over the inheritance. **per–an** squabble, row.

babit **mem–(kan)** to involve, implicate s.o. in s.t. *Ia* ∼ *saja dlm pertikaiannja,* He involved me in his argument.

babon laying hen.

babtis see BAPTIS.

babu maid, housemaid, domestic servant. **memper–** to treat s.o. as a *babu.* – *anak* children's maid. – *dalam* maid. – *masak* female cook. – *téték* wet nurse. – *tjutji* laundress.

babut rug.

bachil stingy. *Si –* The Miser.

bachsjis tip (money).

bada after. *Kami berangkat – makan malam,* We left after dinner. *tidak ter– –²* 1 indescribable. 2 irrepressible. *amarah jg tak* ∼ irrepressible anger.

badai storm, hurricane. **mem–** to rage, storm about. *Ia* ∼ *dikantor, sebab pegawai² datangnja terlambat,* He was in a rage at the office because the employees came late. **ter–** to stretch out. *Ia* ∼ *didipan,* He stretched out on the sofa.

badak rhinoceros. – *sungai* hippopotamus.

badal representative. *Pak Aflus mendjadi – rombongannja,* Aflus became the representative for his group.

badam almond. – *hidjau* pistachio.

badan 1 body. *Saja merasa sakit diseluruh –,* I feel sick all over. 2 body, group, agency. – *pengawas* supervisory group. 3 committee. – *pekerdja* working committee. 4 corporation. **ber–** to have a body. *Pemuda jg* ∼ *séhat lebih disukai bekerdja,* A healthy youth is preferred for the job. ∼ *dua* to be pregnant. **pem–an** embodiment. – *bulat* stripped to the waist. – *hukum* corporate body. – *pemeriksa* investigating committee. – *pengelola* executive body. – *penjelidik* investigative agency. – *perantaraan* liaison board. – *perwakilan* parliament, council, assembly. – *usaha* 1 committee. 2 executive branch.

badang sieve, strainer.

badani(jah) physical.

badar 1 sea and fresh-water fish. 2 dish, course. *Berapa matjam – makan malam nanti?* How many dishes are we having this evening? 3 full moon.

badi contagious matter.

badik small dagger.

badja 1 steel. 2 armor. 3 fertilizer, manure. 4 mixture of oil and burnt coconut shell for blackening the teeth. **mem–** 1 to harden, toughen, strengthen. *Kepertjajaan rakjat tlh* ∼ *thd pemimpin itu,* The confidence of the people in that leader has been strengthened. 2 to become steel. *Karena panas api jg keras itu besi mudah* ∼ , Because of the intense heat iron easily becomes steel. **mem–i** 1 to harden into steel. 2 to fertilize (a field). 3 to blacken. *Ia* ∼ *giginja supaja kuat,* He blackened his teeth to make them strong. **mem–kan** to steel. ∼ *semangat* to steel the spirit.

badjak plow. **mem–** 1 to plow. 2 to carry on piracy, plunder. **pem–an** piracy. – *laut* pirate.

badjan frying pan.

badjang an evil spirit believed to bewitch pregnant women.

Badjau sea nomads off the east coast of Borneo.

badji wedge. **mem–** to split a tree with a wedge.

badjik good, wholesome. **ke–an** 1 well-being, welfare. 2 benefit.

badjing squirrel. **–an** scoundrel, thief, gangster.

badju 1 jacket. 2 blouse. **mem–i** to dress s.t. *Sarinah* ∼ *anak²annja,* Sarinah dressed her doll. – *bébé* woman's Western-style dress. – *belah dada* jacket with open front. – *besi* armor. – *blus* blouse. – *bodo* woman's dress of south Celebes. – *dalam* 1 undershirt. 2 underwear. – *djadi* ready-made jacket. – *djas* coat. – *kaos* undershirt. – *kelepak* k.o. jacket.

– *kurung* long shirt for Sumatran women. – *kutang* bodice. – *lasak* daily dress. – *mandi* bathing suit. – *maskat* vest. – *monjét* 1 coveralls. 2 one-piece child's play suit. – *perang* battle attire. – *rok* woman's Western-style dress. – *sika* close-fitting blouse. – *teluk belanga* collarless coat or jacket. – *tidur* nightgown. – *tjina* pajamas. *Ia mentjabik – dadanja*, He disclosed his own secret.

badjul 1 crocodile. 2 scoundrel, pickpocket. – *buntung* s.o. who annoys or molests women.

Badui 1 an aboriginal group in west Java. 2 Bedouin.

badut clown. **mem-** to act as a clown.

bag. [*bagian*] part, section.

bagai 1 kind. *tiga – mobil* three types of cars. 2 equivalent, peer. *Gunung itu indah sekali; tak ada –nja*, That mountain is very pretty; it has no peer. 3 like. *Penerangan dikamar ini terang, – siang*, The illumination in this room is bright, like daylight. **ber-(-)** various, all sorts of. ~ *bahasa terdapat dikota itu*, All k.o. languages are found in that city. **mem-kan** to humiliate, insult. *Djangan ~ orang miskin karena kemiskinannja*, Don't humiliate a poor person because he's poor. **memper-kan** to treat as o. pleases. *Tiap opsir ~ anak buahnja*, Every officer treats the soldiers as he pleases. **se-** 1 like. *Ia ~ burung disangkar emas*, He's like a bird in a gilded cage. 2 as. ~ *saja katakan tadi...* As I said just now... *Ia memimpin pasukan itu ~ kaptén*, He led his troops as captain. *dan ~nja* and so forth, and so on, etc. *buku², potlot² dan ~nja* books, pencils, etc. *tidak ber-* incomparable, without equal. *Pengaruhnja didalam DPR tidak ~* , His influence in parliament has no equal.

bagaikan as if. *Ia tak melihat kpd saja, – tak dengar panggilan saja*, He didn't look at me, as if he didn't hear me call.

bagaimana 1 how. 2 how so, how's that? – *dia sekarang*? How's he now? – *kabarnja*? How are things? **di-kan** to be done with. *Mau ~ daging ini, digoréng ataukah direbus*? What's to be done with this meat, fry it or boil it? **se-** as, like. *Kerdjakanlah ~ saja tlh uraikan tadi*, Do as I just explained. **-(pun)** *djuga* however it may be, somehow, in any case. ~ *djuga tak boléh ia kasar thd ibunja*, However that may be, he isn't permitted to be rude to his mother.

bagan 1 draft, sketch, blueprint. 2 skeleton, frame. *Lihatlah – rumah terbakar*, Look at the skeleton of the burned house. 3 program, schedule. *Kami membuat – perdjalanan ke Éropah*, We've worked out a program for our trip to Europe. 4 chart.

bagar kambing a dish with mutton as a base.

bagas 1 robust. *badan jg – a robust body*. 2 strong. *angin – a strong wind.*

bagasi 1 baggage, luggage. 2 baggage car. 3 baggage rack. – *lebih* excess baggage. – *tjuma²* free baggage allowance. **meng-kan** to check baggage.

bagi 1 for. *Korsi itu – ibu saja*, That chair is for my mother. 2 concerning. – *soal ini, lupakanlah dulu*, With regard to this matter, just forget it. 3 part. *Dua – diberikan kpd ajahnja*, Two parts were given his father. **ber-(-)** 1 to divide. 2 to fork (of a road). 3 to share. **ke-an** to get o's share. *Banjak orang tidak ~*, Many people did not get their share. *Pesan sekarang supaja ~* , Order now and get yours. **mem-** 1 to divide by (*dgn*). *Ia ~ 30 dgn 5*, He divided 30 by 5. 2 to divide into (*atas*). 3 to distribute. *Ia ~ makanan kpd penduduk*, He distributed food to the inhabitants. ~ *berékor* long division. **mem-kan** 1 to divide. *Ia ~ daging itu dlm beberapa potong*, He divided the meat into several pieces. 2 to allot, allocate s.t. **mem-(-)kan** to distribute. *Ia ~ bukunja diantara teman²nja*, He distributed his books among his friends. **pem-** divisor (in arith.). ~ *persekutuan terbesar* largest common denominator. **pem-an** 1 distribution. 2 division (in arith.). 3 division, allotment. *Kita harus mengadakan ~ waktu jg baik*, We must arrange a good division of time. ~ *koték* long division (in arith.). ~ *rezeki* sharing of spoils. ~ *wewenang* delegation of authority. **se-an** a part. *Penduduk kota itu ~ miskin ~ kaja*, A part of the population is poor, a part rich. ~ *besar* the majority. **-an** 1 part. 2 share. *Berapa ~ saja dlm keuntungan ini*? How much is my share of this profit? 3 part, participation. *Ia tidak mengambil ~ dlm pembitjaraan itu*, He didn't participate in the discussion. 4 section, department, division. ~ *Ilmu Persoalan Timur Djauh* Department of Far Eastern Studies. ~ *peralatan*, ~ *perbekalan* supply dept. *tak ter-indivisible. Djumlah ini tak ~* , This amount is indivisible.

bagia see BAHAGIA.

baginda His Majesty (title in certain areas of Sumatra's West Coast).

bagong 1 big and heavy, cumbersome. *Itu perahu –* , That's a cumbersome boat. 2 wild boar. 3 clown in a wajang play.

bagor coarse weave of palm leaves.

bagur oversized (of persons or animals).

bagus 1 nice, kind. *Ia – sekali*, He's very nice. 2 nice, splendid. *– benar kalau ia dpt datang*, It will be nice if he can come. 3 handsome. *Pemuda itu – rupanja*, That young man looks very handsome. 4 beautiful. *– sekali tjuatja hari ini*, The weather is beautiful today. **ke–an** 1 beauty. 2 splendor. **mem– –²kan** to flatter. **memper–kan** 1 to make happy. 2 to improve in looks, beautify. *Ia ~ rumahnja*, He improved the appearance of his house. 3 to touch up (a photograph).

bah 1 inundation. 2 see BABAH.

bah. [*bahasa*] language.

bahadur 1 bold. 2 knight, hero.

bahaduri heroic, chivalrous.

bahagi see BAGI.

bahagia 1 luck. 2 happiness. 3 welfare. 4 happy. *kabar – good news.* **ber–** 1 to be happy. *Rupanja sangat ~*, He looks very happy. 2 to be fortunate. *Ia sangat ~ mendapat rumah di Djakarta*, He was very lucky to find a house in Jakarta. **ke–an** happiness, well-being. **mem–kan** to make s.o. happy. *Surat itu tlh ~ ibunja*, That letter made his mother happy.

bahaja 1 danger. 2 threat, hazard. 3 crisis. **ber–** 1 dangerous, hazardous, risky. *Djalan ini ~* , This road is dangerous. 2 vulnerable (in bridge). **mem–i** to endanger. **mem–kan** 1 to endanger, threaten. *Serangan musuh ~ pembélaan kita*, The enemy's attack endangered our defenses. 2 to risk. *Ia ~ keselamatannja*, He risked his safety. 3 dangerous. *– bandjir* flood danger. *– kelaparan* threat of starvation, famine. *– rugi* risk. *Orang harus berani menanggung – rugi*, One must run risks.

bahak burst of laughter. **ter– –²** to roar with laughter.

bahala disaster, calamity.

baham molar tooth. **mem–** to chew with mouth closed.

bahan 1 (raw) material. 2 chips, wood splinters. 3 matter. 4 ingredient. **mem–** to shape wood into boards, plane wood. **–²** ingredients. *– bakar* fuel. *– baku* basic material(s).

– buangan waste matter, material. *– hidup* provisions. *– letupan, – letusan* explosives. *– makanan* foodstuffs. *– pakaian* clothing material. *– peledak, – peletus* explosives. *– pembungkus* packaging. *– penambah* extra material. *– pengadjaran* teaching material. *– pokok* basic commodity. *– tahan api* fire resistant material.

bahana 1 sound, noise. 2 echo. 3 sonorous. **ber–, mem–** 1 to sound. 2 to echo, reverberate.

bahar 1 weight (375 lbs.). 2 load. 3 large river. 4 sea.

bahari 1 antique, ancient. *Itu kepertjajaan –*, That's an ancient belief. 2 pretty, charming.

baharu see BARU.

bahas 1 research, investigation, study. 2 criticism. **ber–** to discuss, debate. *Meréka ~ ttg peraturan baru itu*, They discussed the new regulation. **mem–** 1 to discuss s.t. 2 to criticize s.t. *Kaum kiri ~ politik pemerintah*, The leftist group criticized government policy. 3 to investigate. *Polisi ~ ketjelakaan itu*, Police investigated the accident. **pem–** discussant, panelist. **pem–an** discussion, criticism. **per–an** discussion. **–an** 1 criticism. *Ia marah karena ~ jg tadjam itu*, He got angry at the sharp criticism. 2 discussion. 3 investigation. *~ polisi* police investigation.

bahasa 1 language, speech. 2 good manners. *Ia adalah seorang jg baik budi –nja*, He's a person of good manners. 3 that. *Ia mengatakan – ia tak datang*, He said that he isn't coming. **ber–** 1 to talk, speak. *Ia ~ Arab*, He speaks Arabic. 2 well-mannered. *Ia seorang jg ~* , He's well-mannered. **mem– Indonésiakan** to put s.t. into Indonesian. **mem–kan** 1 to express. *Ia tak dpt ~ apa jg disaksikan itu*, He couldn't express what he'd actually witnessed. 2 to call, address. *Ia ~ anak pd saja*, He called me 'son.' 3 to show respect. *Ia ~ tamunja utk duduk dimuka sekali*, He showed his guest respect by having him sit in the front row. **per–(an)** 1 proverb. 2 good manners. 3 a little, slightly. *Badjunja basah ~ terkena hudjan*, His suit was slightly wet from the rain. *– daérah* local language, vernacular. *– dalam* language used at the court. *– dunia* international language. *– kawi* Old Javanese language. *– kebangsaan* national language. *– pasar* the market language, simplified form of a language used as lingua franca. *– pasaran* slang. *– pengantar, – perantaraan*

medium of instruction. - *sulung* the first words of a child when he is beginning to talk.
bahasi see BAGASI.
bahath see BAHAS.
bahela old-fashioned.
baheula see BAHELA.
bahgia see BAHAGIA.
bahkan 1 moreover, furthermore. *Ia mengetahui, - ia sendiri jg mengatakan bhw korsi itu tidak baik,* He knew, moreover, he said, that the chair wasn't any good. 2 on the contrary, in fact. *Ia tidak miskin; - terkaja dikota itu,* He isn't poor; in fact, he's the richest person in town. 3 yes... indeed. -, *tuan, mémang benar apa jg tuan bilang itu,* Yes, sir, what you said is indeed true.
bahna 1 see BAHANA. 2 owing to.
bahtera ship, sailboat, prow.
bahu 1 shoulder. 2 see BAU 3. **mem**- 1 to shoulder, support with the shoulder. *Ia ~ tiang,* He supported the pole with his shoulder. 2 to carry on the shoulder. *Ia ~ kerandjang jg berat itu,* He carried that heavy basket on his shoulder. - **-mem**- 1 shoulder to shoulder. *Meréka berdiri ~ ,* They stood shoulder to shoulder. 2 to support e.o.
bahubahasa multilingualism.
bahwa that. *Ia mengatakan - harga daging naik,* He said that the price of meat was going up.
bahwasanja 1 see BAHWA. 2 truly, indeed.
ba'id distant (of relatives).
baiduri 1 opal. 2 quartz.
baik 1 good, nice. *Ia orang -,* He's a good man. *Pekerdjaannja -,* His work is good. 2 well. *Saja tak bisa melihat -,* I can't see well. 3 nice. *Guru - sekali kpd saja,* The teacher was very nice to me. 4 well (of health). *Apa ia sdh - lagi dari penjakitnja?* Has he recovered from his illness? 5 yes, all right. -, *tuan, saja mau pergi,* All right, sir, I'll go. 6 better. - *kita tunggu,* We'd better wait. 7 favorable (of weather). **ber-(-an)** to be on good terms. *Sesudah berkelahi dua adik saja itu ~ lagi,* After quarreling, my younger brothers are on good terms again. **ke-an** *(hati)* goodness, kindness. **mem-kan** to treat well, do well by s.o. **memper-i** 1 to correct. *Murid² itu ~ salahnja,* The pupils corrected their mistakes. 2 to repair. *Djawatan Pekerdjaan Umum ~ djembatan itu,* The Department of Public Works repaired the bridge. 3 to improve s.t. 4 to reform. **per-an** 1 repair. ~

djalan road under repair. 2 improvement. *Adakah ~ ?* Is there any improvement? ~ *sosial* social rehabilitation. **se-** as soon as. *Seluruh negeri berduka ~ kabar diterimanja,* The whole country was in mourning as soon as it received the news. **se-nja** better, best, preferable. ~ *kita pergi lebih dulu,* It's best that we go first. **se- -²nja** 1 as well, as good as possible. 2 however good. ~ *orang, tak ada jg melebihi ajahnja,* No one, however good, can surpass his father. **-an** better. **-²** carefully, well. *Bungkuskan barang² itu ~ ,* Wrap those things carefully. **-...-** both...and. - *dia - saja suka makanan jg énak,* Both he and I like good food. - *buruknja* quality. *Ia menanjakan - buruknja mobil itu,* He asked about the quality of that car. - *hati* good-natured. - *...maupun* 1 both...and. 2 neither...nor. - *ini maupun itu dia tak suka,* He liked neither this nor that. -...- *tak* neither...nor. - *dia - saja tak mempunjai uang,* Neither he nor I have any money. - *rasinja* to be lucky. *tidak* **teper-i** unlucky. **-lah** all right. ~ *kalau begitu* very well then. **-²** *lo!* Be careful! Take care of yourself! **-²** *nak, ja!* Please be careful, child!
bait 1 house. 2 couplet, stanza. **ber**- to recite verse.
baitul-mal treasury.
baitulmukaddis 1 Jerusalem. 2 the temple in Jerusalem.
baja age. *Ia seorang jg tlh -,* He's an old man. *setengah -* middle-aged. **se**- of the same age. *Ia ~ dgn guru saja,* He's the same age as my teacher.
bajak fat, corpulent, obese, stout. **ke-an** potbellied, obese. *Orang itu kuatir ~ ,* That man was afraid he'd become overly fat.
bajam spinach.
bajan 1 parakeet. 2 clear, distinct. **mem-kan** to explain.
bajang ber- reflected. *Pohon besar itu ~ diair,* The large tree was reflected in the water. **ber- -²** to hover, be in o's mind. *Selama ia sakit ajahnja selalu ~ didalam fikirannja,* During his illness his father was always in his thoughts. **mem**- to reflect. *Évaluasi ini ~ keadaan sebenarnja,* This evaluation reflects the true situation. **mem-i** 1 to shade. *Pohon itu ~ rumahnja,* The tree shades his house. 2 to overshadow s.t. **mem- -²(kan)** 1 to figure out s.t., imagine. *Dapatkah kamu ~ betapa girang ibumu nanti?* Can you imagine how

happy your mother will be? 2 to give o. to understand, hint. *Ia ~ kepadanja bagaimana baiknja kalau ia pergi dgn dia*, He gave him to understand how good it would be if he went with him. **pem-an** 1 imagination. 2 estimate. 3 idea. *~ udara* mirage. **per-an** imagination. **-an** 1 shadow. 2 imagination. 3 estimate. **-²** 1 shadow. *~ pohon tlh pandjang*, The shadows of the trees are already long. 2 image. *Lihat ~ saja ditjermin itu*, Look at my image in the mirror.

bajar ber- paid. *Ia hutangnja blm ~* , He hasn't paid his debt yet. **mem-** 1 to pay. *Ia ~ 5 rupiah*, He paid 5 rupiahs. *Saja mau ~ dimuka*, I want to pay in advance. 2 to pay for s.t. 3 to fulfill. *Ia ~ niat*, He fulfilled his promise. **mem-kan** to pay out. *Ajah saja ~ separuh gadjinja*, My father paid out half of his salary. **pem-** payer. **pem-an** payment. **-an** 1 payment. *Berapa ~ mendjaga anak² satu djam?* How much is baby-sitting per hour? 2 salary. *Bolèhkah saja mem- dibelakang?* May I pay C.O.D.?

bajat mem- to initiate. **pem-an** initiation.

bajem see BAJAM.

baji baby. *- mèrah* newborn baby.

bajonèt bayonet.

baju 1 wind. 2 storm. 3 slave, servant. 4 rotten, putrefied. *Makanannja tlh -, buang sadja*, The food is rotten, throw it away. 5 stale (of food). **ke-an** (food) kept too long. **-an** 1 rotten food. 2 food kept too long.

bak 1 basin, vessel. 2 mold (for gelatin). *- mandi* bathtub. *- potrèt* photo-developing basin.

baka 1 eternal, lasting. *persahabatan jg -* lasting friendship. 2 hereditary. *Puteri itu membuang - utk menikah dgn orang biasa*, The princess renounced her heritage to marry a commoner. **ke-an** eternity. **mem-kan** to immortalize.

bakal 1 (raw) material. 2 future, prospective, candidate. *Ia - prèsidèn*, He's a candidate for president. 3 for. *Pantji ini - memasak nasi*, This pan's for cooking rice. **mem-(kan)** to plan, design. *Merèka ~ utk membuat djalan baru*, They are making plans to build a new road. *- badju* material for clothes. *- buah* ovary. *- guru* student teacher. *- menantu* future son-in-law. *- rumah* material for a house.

bakar ke-an a fire. **mem-** 1 to burn, set on fire. 2 to bake, roast s.t. *~ arang* to make charcoal. *~ bata* to make bricks. *~ hati* to make s.o. angry, to mortify. *Ia ~ hati tetang-*

ganja, He made his neighbor mad. *~ rokok* to light a cigarette. **mem-i** to burn up. *Ia sibuk ~ surat²nja*, She's busy burning up her letters. **pem-** burner (of a lamp). *Pakailah kertas ini utk ~* , Use this paper as a burner. *Anak ini ~ hati ajahnja*, This child made his father mad. **pem-an** 1 burning. *~ djenazah di Bali sangat mahal*, Cremation in Bali is very expensive. 2 ignition. 3 stove, oven. *~ kapur* limekiln. **ter-** 1 on fire. *Rumahnja ~* , His house is on fire. 2 burned down.

bakat 1 trace, trail. 2 sign, omen. *Mèga mendung adalah - hudjan*, Cloudiness is a sign of rain. 3 talent, aptitude. *Ia ada - menggambar*, She has a talent for drawing. 4 (foot)print. *Ada - kaki harimau dihalaman*, There's a tiger's footprint in the yard. 5 crest, head. *- ombak* the crest of the waves. 6 scar. 7 faculty, ability. **ber-** 1 marked, scarred. *Mukanja ~ tjatjar*, His face is pock-marked. 2 talented. *pemuda jg ~* a talented youth. **mem-** to indicate. *Sunji senjap dilaut ~ datangnja angin ribut*, Calm at sea indicates a storm is coming.

bakau *(djangkar)* mangrove.

bakda see BADA. *- subuh* period just after early morning prayer (5-6 A.M.).

baki 1 tray. 2 eternal. 3 remainder, balance. *Dari uang saja 100 dolar itu masih ada -nja 15 dolar*, Of my $100, there's still a balance of $15. 4 foreign exchange.

bakiak wooden clog.

bakik pepper vine. (The leaves are used with betel nut and other ingredients for chewing.)

bakju 1 older sister. 2 form of address to older sister and older women.

bakmi Chinese noodles. *- baso* noodles with Chinese meatballs. *- kuah* boiled noodle dish.

bako 1 all the relatives on the father's side. *Karena banjak teman jg baik² ia merasa dirumah induk ~* , Because of his many good friends he felt quite at home. 2 see TEMBAKAU.

bakti 1 homage, devotion. 2 service. *Merèka masuk tentara utk berbuat - kpd negara*, They entered the army to serve their country. 3 faith, loyalty. *Ia melupakan - kpd orang tuanja*, She forgot her loyalty to her parents. **ber-** to be loyal, serve devotedly. *Ia ~ kpd ibunja*, She's loyal to her mother. **ke-an** 1 religious service, worship. 2 loyalty, devotion. **mem-kan** 1 to dedicate, devote. *Ia ~ tenaganja kpd tanah air*, He dedicated his energies to his country. 2 to be at

o's disposal. **pem–an** 1 worship. 2 devotion. ~ *kpd tanah air* devotion to o's country. 3 loyalty, faithfulness.
baku 1 full-fledged. *guru* – a full-fledged teacher. 2 basic. *harga* – the basic cost. *karja* – standard work.
bakul basket. – *kerau* bamboo basket.
bakup red and swollen. *Matanja – karena menangis*, Her eyes were red and swollen from crying.
bal 1 ball. 2 bag, bale.
bala 1 troops, army. 2 disaster, catastrophe. – *bantuan* reinforcements. – *bentjana* distress, emergency. – *Keselamatan* Salvation Army. – *tentara* army.
balah argument, quarrel. **ber–** to argue, quarrel. **mem–** to oppose, argue against. *Semua anggota* ~ *andjuran itu*, All members opposed the proposal. **pem–an** argument against s.t. **per–an** argument.
balai 1 hall. – *lélang* auction hall. 2 building. – *perguruan tinggi* university building. 3 office. – *penerangan* information office. **–²** 1 couch. 2 bamboo cot. – *agung* town hall, municipal building. – *angin* vacation cottage or bungalow. – *bendul* reception hall for royal guests. – *dagang* chamber of commerce. – *derma* charitable institution. – *désa* village council hall. – *istirahat* resthouse. – *keséhatan* medical clinic. – *kota* town, city hall. – *penghadapan* reception hall. – *pengobatan* medical clinic. – *peranginan* vacation bungalow. – *perpustakaan* library. – *pertemuan* meeting hall. – *Pustaka* Government Publishing House (formerly called the Bureau for Popular Literature). – *rendah* House of Commons. – *senirupa* art gallery. – *tinggi* House of Lords. – *wartawan* press room.
balam k.o. wood pigeon. **ber–, mem–** to be unclear. *Karena kabut itu penglihatan sangat* ~ , Because of the fog, visibility was extremely poor.
balang 1 long-necked bottle. 2 two-masted prow. 3 spotted. *sapi* – spotted cow.
balap racing. **pem–** runner, racer. **–an** 1 race. 2 race track. ~ *kuda* horse race.
balar 1 albino. 2 with white spots.
balas ballast. **ber–** 1 to respond. *Kebaikannja tak* ~ , His kindness had no response. 2 to reverberate, echo, respond. *Dlm sumur itu suara* ~ *riuh*, In the well a sound reverberated loudly. **ber–²an** to correspond. *Meréka* ~ *surat*, They correspond with e.o. **mem–** 1 to answer, reply. ~ *surat tuan tgl 3 Maret...* In reply

to your letter of March 3rd... *Ia blm* ~ *surat saja*, He hasn't answered my letter yet. 2 to repay, reward. *Ia* ~ *kebaikan kpd temannja*, He repaid his friend with kindness. 3 to avenge, take revenge. *Ia disakiti oléh orang itu dan hendak* ~ , He was hurt by that person and wants revenge. 4 to retaliate. ~ *dendam* to take revenge. ~ *djasa* to return, repay a service. ~ *guna* to render service. **pem–** 1 avenger. 2 response. *Inilah* ~ *dia kpd segala kebaikan ibunja*, This is his response to all his mother's kindness. 3 o. who replies. *Siapakah* ~ *surat itu?* Who replied to that letter? **pem–an** 1 reply. 2 response. 3 counter-. *Pd tengah malam musuh mengadakan serangan* ~ , At midnight the enemy launched a counter-attack. **–an** 1 answer, reply. 2 response. – **-ber–** mutual. *kebaikan jg* ~ mutual kindness. – **-mem–** 1 to reply to o. another. *Sdh 2 tahun meréka* ~ *berkiriman surat*, They've been corresponding for two years. 2 to avenge e.o. – *budi* gratitude. – *dendam* revenge. –*kata* reply, rejoinder.
balatentara 1 army. 2 see BALA.
balau see KATJAU
balé see BALAI. **–²** bamboo cot. ~ *mota* canvas cot.
baligh see AKIL.
balik 1 the reverse, the contrary. *Ia bertindak – hukum*, He acted against the law. 2 the other side, the back side. *Ia berdiri di– médja*, She was standing behind the table. 3 to return. *Ia blm – dari Éropah*, He hasn't returned from Europe yet. 4 again. *Setelah 3 hari sepi, maka pasar itu – ramai*, After 3 days of quiet the market is busy again. **ber–** 1 to turn over, upside down. *Mobilnja* ~ *dlm ketjelakaan itu*, His car turned over in the accident. 2 to change, take another course. *Perkataannja* ~ , His words took another course. *Ia* ~ *pikiran*, He changed his mind. 3 to turn around. *Ia* ~ *melihat isterinja*, He turned around to look at his wife. 4 to turn back. *Kedengkian itu akan* ~ *kpd dirinja sendiri*, That cruelty will turn back on him. 5 to return. *Ia sdh* ~ *dari perdjalanannja*, He has returned from his trip. 6 to reflect. *Sinar matahari jg* ~ *dari katja itu sangat kuatnja*, The sunlight reflected from that glass was very strong. 7 retrograde. **ke–an** the contrary, the reverse. *Musim dingin* ~ *dari musim panas*, Winter is the opposite of summer. **mem–** 1 to turn around. *Ia* ~

menghadap kearah saja, He turned in my direction. 2 to turn s.t. over. − *ikan itu supaja lekas masak,* Turn the fish over so it will cook quickly. 3 to deflect, ricochet. *Ia luka kena peluru jg ∼ dari tiang besi,* He was struck by a bullet which ricocheted from an iron pole. 4 to turn over, capsize. *Perahunja ∼ karena angin ribut,* The storm capsized the boat. 5 to reverse, change s.t. *Ia ∼ perintah madjikannja,* He reversed his boss's order. **mem–i** 1 to return to. *Ia ∼ isteri jg tua,* He returned to his former wife. 2 to repeat. *Ia ∼ permintaannja,* He repeated his request. **mem–kan** 1 to turn s.t. *Ia ∼ médja tulisnja menghadap pintu,* He turned his desk so it faced the door. 2 to place upside down. *Ia ∼ botol itu diatas médja,* He placed the bottle upside down on the table. 3 to return. *Meréka selalu dpt ∼ serangan musuh,* They could always return the enemy's attacks. 4 to change. *Ia selalu ∼ perkataannja,* He was always changing his words. **mem– –²** 1 to turn over and over. *Ia ∼ kotak itu sebelum membelinja,* He turned the box over and over before buying it. 2 to alter repeatedly. **pem–an** inversion. **se–nja** on the contrary, the other way around. **ter–** 1 to be upside down. *Bis jg djatuh didjurang itu ∼ ,* The bus which fell into the ravine was upside down. 2 the reverse, the other way around. *Buku ini ∼ ,* This book was the other way around. 3 inside out. *Pijamanja ∼ karena ia ter-buru² memakainja,* His pajamas were inside out because he put them on in such a hurry. − *adab* ill-mannered. − *belah* upside down. − *bokong* reverse. − *kerak* to remarry o's divorced wife. − *mata* to pretend not to know. *Ia − mata thd kesalahan²nja,* He pretended to be unaware of his mistakes. − *sadar* to return to consciousness. *di− awan* like walking on air, being in a cloud. −*! Kanan!* Rightabout-face!

baling ber– to turn. *Roda ∼ tjepat sekali,* The wheel turned very fast. **–²** 1 weathercock. 2 propeller. *∼ angin* fan. *hati bagai ∼ diatas bukit* vacillating.

balkon 1 balcony. 2 most expensive section of theater.

balok 1 beam (of wood). 2 epaulet.

balon balloon. **–²an** soap bubbles. − *lampu,* − *listrik* light bulb. − *sabun* soap bubbles.

balong 1 pond, pool. 2 puddle, mudhole.

balu widow(er).

baluarti fortress, bastion.

baluh(an) 1 wooden frame for seat on elephant. 2 wooden frame for drum.

balui a draw, tie (in sports).

balun mem– 1 to beat with a stick. *Ia ∼ kentongan itu dgn kerasnja,* He beat the drum very loudly. 2 to fold, roll up. *Ia ∼ lengan badjunja utk bekerdja,* He rolled up his sleeves for work.

balung 1 bone. 2 cockscomb. − *sumsum* marrow. *Dia seorang romantikus sampai ke− sumsum,* He's a romanticist to his very marrow.

balur 1 crystal. 2 dried meat. 3 rawhide. **mem–(kan)** to crystallize.

balut 1 bandage, dressing, wrapping. 2 red and swollen (of eyes). **mem–(kan)** 1 to dress, bandage. 2 to wrap, roll. *Ia ∼ tembakonja,* He rolled his tobacco. *Ia ∼ bukunja dlm kain hidjau,* He wrapped his book in green cloth. **pem–** 1 bandage. 2 wrapping. *Ini kertas ∼ ,* Here's wrapping paper. **–an** 1 bandage. 2 parcel, package. − *luka* bandage. − *rokok* cigarette wrapper.

bam 1 crossbeam on a ship's rudder to hold rudder. 2 to indicate sound of a big drum. *Sesudah djénderal meninggal maka oléh tentara itu terasa patah kemudi dgn −nja,* After the general died, the army lost all hope.

bambang vast, extensive. *Tanah − meluas dibalik gunung itu,* A vast flat area lies behind the mountain. **berse–an** 1 to act big. 2 extended. **ter–** 1 to extend. *Lapangan jg luas ∼ diantara dua gunung itu,* A vast plain extended between the two mountains. 2 to be displayed. *Pandji² memuat sembojan² ∼ disepandjang djalan,* Banners were displayed along the road.

bambu bamboo. − *runtjing* bamboo spear.

bami see BAKMI.

ban 1 tire. − *mati* a solid tire. 2 ribbon, band. *Ia memakai − hitam,* He wore a black band. **ber–** to have a ribbon or band on. − *angin* pneumatic tire. − *dalam* inner tube. − *djalar* conveyor belt. − *kipas* fan belt. − *luar* tire, casing. − *pengangkut* conveyor belt. − *pinggiran putih* white sidewall tire. − *tanpa − dalam* tubeless tire.

BANAS [*Badan Nasionalisasi*] Nationalization Board.

banat mem– to whip, thrash, defeat.

band see BAN.

bandar 1 harbor, port. 2 pool, watercourse. 3 branch manager. 4 banker in gambling. *Siapa mendjadi − sekarang?* Who's the banker now? **ber–**

to pool (of water). **mem–** 1 to trade.
Ia ~ sebagai penghidupannja, He
trades for a living. 2 to be a banker
in gambling. **mem–kan** to lead s.t.
Ia ~ air hudjan kesawahnja, He led
the rain water into his wet rice fields.
~ air kebukit to be unsuccessful.
per–an harbor office. **–an** *air* ground
reservoir. *– sampah* junk yard.
bandel obstinate, stubborn. **mem–** to
be stubborn.
bandeng k.o. seafish raised in brackish
water. *– kaléngan* canned *bandeng*.
banderék ginger drink served hot.
bandering slingshot.
banderol tax stamp (on packages of
cigarettes, etc.).
banding 1 equivalent, equal. *Ia pandai sekali, tak ada –nja*, He's very
clever, he has no equal. 2 consideration. *Ia ingin minta – lagi kpd hakim
jg lebih tinggi*, He wanted to request
consideration from a higher judge.
ber– proportionate, in proportion to.
Gadjinja ~ dgn ketjakapannja, His
salary was in proportion to his ability.
ber– *sebagai* in the ratio of. *~
sebagai 5:7* in the ratio of 5 to 7.
ber–an 1 to match, be congruent, in
harmony. *Warna rambutnja ~ dgn
warna pakaiannja*, Her hair matched
the color of her dress. 2 in accordance.
*Itu tidak ~ dgn kedjadian jg sebe-
narnja*, That was not in accordance
with the facts. **mem–** to appeal. *Ia
~ perkaranja ke Mahkamah Agung*,
He appealed his case to the Supreme
Court. **mem–i** to equal, counterbalance. *Ia mentjoba utk ~ saudaranja hidup dgn méwah*, He tried to
counterbalance his brother's extravagant living. **mem(per)–kan** to compare
s.t. **per–an** 1 comparison. 2 example.
*Ia mentjeriterakan pengalamannja se-
bagai ~* , He related his experience
as an example. 3 an appeal (legal).
~ berat specific gravity. **se–** proportional. *Kekuatannja ~ dgn bentuk
badannja*, His strength is proportional
to his body.
bandit 1 bandit. 2 scoundrel. **mem–**
to commit petty crimes.
bandjar 1 line, row, series. 2 train of
events. **ber–** to form a line. *Pohon² ~
dikanan kiri djalan*, Trees line both
sides of the road. **mem–kan** to line
s.t. up. *– pulau* series of islands.
bandjir 1 to flood, overflow. *Sungai
–*, The river overflowed. 2 flood. *Ada
– besar sesudah hudjan itu*, There was
a big flood after the rain. **ke–an**
flooded by. *Negeri Belanda ~ air laut*,
Holland was flooded by the sea.
mem–i to flood. *Barang² ini ~ pasar*

Djakarta, These goods are flooding
Jakarta's markets.
bandot 1 billy goat. 2 old goat,
roué. 3 ladies' man.
bandul 1 pendulum. 2 hanger. **mem–**
1 to swing. *Tentara pajung²an ~
dilangit*, The paratroopers were swinging in the air. 2 to hang. *Ada sarang
~ diranting pohon itu*, A nest is
hanging on that tree branch. **–an** 1
pendulum. 2 hanger.
bandung pair, set, duo. **se–** 1 a twin.
Ia ~ dgn saudaranja, He's one of
twins. 2 a pair, set. *~ permata dimuat
ditjintjin mas*, A pair of jewels was
mounted in a gold ring.
bandut a cord, string. **mem–** to hang
by tying two pieces together. **pem–**
strap, belt.
bang 1 bank. 2 see ABANG. **per–an**
banking. *– bétja* pedicab driver. *–
gelap* illegal bank. *– tabungan* savings
bank.
bangai **ter–** 1 neglected, abandoned.
Rumahnja ~ , Her house was neglected. 2 given up, abandoned. *Pekerdjaannja ~ karena kekurangan
ongkos*, His work was given up because of lack of funds.
bangar odor of s.t. rotten, stinking.
bangat 1 fast, quick. 2 soon. **mem–
kan** 1 to quicken. *Ia ~ langkahnja*,
He quickened his steps. 2 to step,
speed s.t. up.
bangau long-legged bird similar to
heron or stork.
banget very.
bangga 1 pride. 2 proud, stubborn.
Ia – sekali akan anaknja, He's very
proud of his son. **ke–an** 1 pride. 2
boasting. **mem–kan** 1 to make o.
proud. *Anak itu ~ ajahnja*, The
child made his father proud. 2 to
boast of, be proud of. *Ia dpt ~
kudanja*, He can boast of his horses.
bangka tough and stiff.
Bangkahulu Bencoolen.
bangkai carcass, corpse. *Ia mendjemur
– keatas bukit*, He exposed his own
shortcomings. *Ia bertjermin – karena
tindakan saudaranja itu*, He was
exposed to shame because of his
brother's action.
bangkang **mem–** to protest. **(pem)–an**
protest. **ter–** unfinished, abandoned
(work).
bangkar tough and stiff, rough. **mem–**
to become tough.
bangkas yellow with light-brown and
white dots (of a chicken).
bangk(e)rut bankrupt. **ke–an** bankruptcy. **mem–kan** to bankrupt s.o.
bangkit 1 to rise, get up. *Ia – dari
duduk*, He got up from a sitting

position. 2 to arise. – *perasaan bentji thd gurunja,* A feeling of dislike toward his teacher arose. 3 attack (of illness). **ber–** 1 to rise, get up. 2 to break out (of a disease). **ke–an** 1 resurrection. 2 resurgence, rise. ∼ *negeri*[2] *Asia* the resurgence of the countries of Asia. **mem–** 1 to raise s.t. *Ia* ∼ *tangannja,* He raised his hand. 2 to arouse, inspire. ∼ *ketakutan* to arouse fear. 3 to dig up, harvest. *Ia* ∼ *kentang dari dlm tanah,* He dug up potatoes from the ground. **mem-kan** 1 to raise, resurrect. *Salah satu mu'djizad Nabi Isa ialah bhw ia pernah* ∼ *orang jg tlh mati,* One of the miracles of Jesus is his resurrection of a man from the dead. 2 to arouse. *Andjuran*[2] *itu* ∼ *perasaan bersatu,* The proposals aroused a feeling of unity. 3 to encourage. 4 to generate (electr.). 5 to give rise to s.t. **mem–** –[2]**(kan)** to dig up s.t. *Apa guna* ∼ *hal jg tlh liwat?* Why dig up the past? **pem–** 1 generator. ∼ *tenaga listerik* electric generator. 2 motivator. **pem–an** construction. **–an** 1 harvest. 2 story that has been dug up from the past.

bangku seat, bench. – *taman* park bench.

banglas vast, extensive (of a view).

bangsa 1 nation, people. 2 race. 3 nationality. *Ia* – *Indonésia,* He's Indonesian. 4 family, category, sex. *Héwan jg menggigit itu* – *kutjing,* The animal that did the biting was a feline. 5 social class, group. *Ia bukan dari* – *jg tinggi dimasjarakatnja,* He was not from one of the higher classes in his society. 6 type. *pesawat terbang* – *pelémpar bom* airplane of the bomber type. 7 kind. *Kami diberi makanan* – *és krim sebagai pentjutji mulut,* We were given a k.o. ice cream for dessert. 8 breed. **ber–** 1 of noble birth. 2 to have a nationality. *Orang Djawa dan Sunda* ∼ *satu,* The Javanese and Sundanese are of one nationality. 3 to be related to. *Ia* ∼ *kpd isterinja,* She's related to his wife. **ke–an** 1 nationality. 2 national. *lagu* ∼ national anthem. 3 nationalism. 4 nationalist. *pergerakan* ∼ nationalist movement. **se–** 1 of one nationality. *Meréka adalah* ∼ *dan setanah air,* They are fellow nationals. 2 of the same kind. *Padi adalah* ∼ *rumput,* The rice plant is of the same kind as grass. – *jg sedang membangun* developing nations. – *kerdil* pygmy. – *terbelakang* underdeveloped nations.

bangsai 1 rotten. *Kajunja* –, The wood is rotten. 2 fragile, brittle.

bangsal 1 shed, warehouse. 2 hall. – *pertemuan* meeting hall. 3 emergency housing, lean-to.

bangsat 1 scoundrel, rascal. 2 bedbug. **ke–an** criminality.

bangsawan 1 noble. 2 nobility. 3 theater, stage. **ke–an** aristocracy.

bangsi flute. **ber–** to play the flute.

bangun 1 to wake up. *Ia* –; *tak dpt tidur,* He woke up; he couldn't sleep. 2 to get up. *Ia duduk dan* – *lagi,* He sat down and got up again. 3 to rise (of dough). 4 structure. *Indah sekali* – *rumah itu,* The structure of that house is very beautiful. 5 model, type. *Mobil ini* – *1958,* This is a 1958 model. 6 shape, form. – *mukanja seperti orang barat,* The shape of his face was like that of a Westerner. 7 a fine. *Ia membajar* –, He paid a fine. **ke–an** 1 awakening. ∼ *bangsa*[2] *djadjahan* the awakening of the colonial peoples. 2 insurrection, uprising. 3 revival. ∼ *rohani* spiritual revival. **mem–** 1 to build, construct. *Ajah* ∼ *rumah,* Dad built a house. 2 to develop. ∼ *industri nasional* to develop a national industry. 3 to rise. *Asap* ∼ *kelangit,* The smoke rose to the sky. 4 constructive. *ketjaman* ∼ constructive criticism. 5 to pay. *Kedjahatan tidak* ∼ , Crime does not pay. **mem–kan** 1 to wake s.o. up. 2 to build up (a country). 3 to raise, lift s.t. or s.o. 4 to restore. *Meréka* ∼ *rumah jg roboh itu,* They restored the dilapidated house. 5 to shape, fashion. *Ia* ∼ *anak*[2]*an dari tanah liat,* She fashioned a doll of clay. 6 constructive (criticism). 7 to (re)construct. *Ia* ∼ *gedung raksasa di-tengah*[2] *kota itu,* He constructed a gigantic building in the center of the city. **pem–** builder, constructor, founder. *Ezra Cornéll adalah* ∼ *Universitas Cornéll,* Ezra Cornell was the founder of Cornell University. **pem–an** 1 (re)construction. 2 development. 3 foundation. ∼ *perkumpulan ini dipelopori oléh pemuda,* The initiative to set up this association was taken by the youth. **ter–** to awake suddenly. *Ia* ∼ *pd tengah malam,* He was awakened suddenly in the middle of the night. **–an** 1 building. 2 installation. ∼ *militér* military installation. 3 scaffolding. **–**[2]**an** 1 buildings. 2 scaffolding.

bani 1 sons of. – *Israél* sons of Israel, Jews. 2 people of.

banjak 1 many. *Disini ada* – *buku,* There are many books here. 2 much. *Oto* – *dipakai disini,* The car is much used here. 3 amount. *–nja uang adalah*

3 dolar, The amount of money was 3 dollars. **4** a lot, a great deal. *Ia – menangis,* She cries a lot. **5** number. *–nja orang ditoko itu kira² 20,* The number of people in the shop was about 20. **ber- –²** in great numbers. *Orang kota ~ pergi kedésa mentjari makanan,* City people went to the village in great numbers in search of food. **ke–an 1** for the greater part, majority. *Orang² dinegeri Amérika ~ mempunjai mobil,* The majority of Americans have cars. **2** too much. *~ tidur tidak baik,* Too much sleep isn't good. **3** common. *Ia adalah dari keluarga orang ~ sadja,* He's from just an ordinary family. **mem-i** to increase. **memper-** 1 to multiply. *Murid itu ~ tudjuh dgn sepuluh,* The pupil multiplied 7 by 10. **2** to increase. *Paberik itu ~ produksinja,* The factory increased its production. **3** to reproduce. *Dapatkah tjeramah itu diper–?* Can the lecture be reproduced? **memper-i** to increase, raise. *~ upah* to raise wages. **memper–kan 1** to multiply. **2** to increase. **per–an** multiplication. **se–** as much as, amounting to. *Uangnja ~ itu,* His money amounted to that. **se- –²nja** as much, as many as possible. **ter-** 1 more. *~ disini daripada disana,* There are more here than there. **2** the greater part. *~ dari penduduk kota itu* the greater part of the city's inhabitants. **3** the majority. *Ia dipilih mendjadi ketua dgn suara ~ ,* He was elected chairman by a majority vote. **–nja 1** quantity, amount. **2** number. *~ pengongsi tlh lebih dua djuta,* The number of evacuees already exceeds 2 million. **–** *duit* wealthy. **–** *kali* often, frequently. **–** *mulut* too much talk. *Djangan* **–** *mulut,* Don't talk too much. **–** *orang* many people. **–** *pikiran* much worry. **–** *sedikitnja* amount, extent. **–** *sedikitnja kerusakan* the extent of the damage. **–** *terima kasih* many thanks. *diper–* *terima kasih* much obliged. **–** *tjingtjong* much ado or talk.

banjol 1 clown. **2** joke. **mem-** to tell jokes. **pem-** joker. **–an** joke.

bank see BANG.

bantah quarrel, conflict. **ber-** to quarrel. *Tetangga kami ~ sepandjang hari,* Our neighbors quarrel all day long. **mem-** 1 to argue, contest, deny. *Ia ~ kebenaran kabar itu,* He contested the accuracy of the news. **2** to oppose, protest. *Ia ~ keinginan ajahnja utk beladjar hukum,* He protested his father's wish that he study law. **3** to contradict. *Kabar ini ~ kabar tadi*

pagi, This news contradicts this morning's news. **mem-i 1** to argue. **2** to oppose. **3** to contradict. **mem–kan 1** to discuss. **2** to argue over s.t., quarrel. **3** to debate. **memper–kan** to discuss, argue over. *Meréka ~ soal politik,* They discussed political matters. **pem-** 1 opponent. **2** debater. **per–an 1** quarrel. **2** conflict. **3** debate. **–an 1** protest. *Meréka mengadakan ~ jg keras,* They launched a strong protest. **2** contradiction. **–** *bentoh* squabble, hassle, wrangle. *Ia tak dpt di- lagi mendjadi nomor satu dikelas,* He was indisputably number one man in his class.

bantai meat of a butchered animal. **mem-** to slaughter, butcher. **pem-** butcher. **pem–an 1** slaughterhouse. **2** butchering. **3** butchery, slaughter. *Inilah ~ dimana orang² désa ini dibunuh oléh musuh,* This is the scene of the butchery in which the villagers were killed by the enemy. **–an 1** meat block in a butcher shop. **2** cattle for slaughter.

bantal pillow. **ber-** 1 to use a pillow. *Ia tidur ~ lengannja,* He used his arm as a pillow. **2** to sleep anywhere. **–an 1** underpinning. **2** (pin)cushion. **3** railroad tie. **–** *guling* bolster, Dutch wife. **–** *kembung* round pillow. **–** *peluk* bolster, Dutch wife. **–** *peniti* pincushion. **–** *pipih* flat pillow. **–** *téko* tea cosy. **–** *tikar* belongings.

bantat not well done, partially done. *Itu roti –,* That's not well-done bread.

banténg wild buffalo.

banter fast, quick. *Air itu – djalannja,* The water ran quickly. *Paling – ia akan meliwati 100 mil dgn ban jg sdh tua itu,* At the most he will cover 100 miles with that old tire.

banteras see BERANTAS.

banting ke–an to be struck, hit. *Ia ~ batu,* He was hit by a rock. **mem-** 1 to throw, fling. **2** to beat. *Babu ~ tjutjiannja pd batu,* The maid beat the wash on a stone. **3** to turn. *Ia ~ setir kekanan ketika melihat anak lari didjalan,* He turned the wheel to the right when he saw the child running in the street. **~** *harga* to lower prices. **~** *kaki* to click o's heels. **~** *pintu* to slam the door. **~** *tulang* to do all in o's power, to exert oneself. *Meréka ~ tulang utk menjekolahkan anaknja,* They did everything in their power to send their child to school. **mem–kan** to throw down, smash. *Ia sangat marah dan ~ piring itu,* He was very angry and smashed the plate. **mem- –²** to keep tossing up and down. *Karena ombak besar kapal*

~ , Because of the big waves the ship kept tossing up and down. **-an** 1 beating, smashing, hitting. 2 (sudden) shock. 3 reduction (in price).

bantjang mem– to tether an animal.

bantji 1 transvestite. 2 hermaphrodite. 3 Chinese or Hindu census. 4 k.o. big ax. 5 see BENTJI. – *lu!* You're a sissy!

bantjih mixed (up), confused. *Tempat duduk ini –,* These seats are mixed up. **mem–(kan)** to mix, beat up s.t. ~ *kartu* to shuffle cards.

bantu 1 help, assistance. 2 relief. **mem–** 1 to help, assist. *Saja akan ~ ajah,* I'm going to help my father. 2 to support, promote. *Kita harus ~ pemerintah,* We must support the government. 3 to contribute. *Saja ~ dgn karangan² péndék kpd suratkabar itu,* I contributed short essays to the newspaper. **memper-kan** to offer the services of s.o. *Pemerintah ~ seorang ahli ékonomi kpd panitya itu,* The government had an economist assist the committee. **pem–** 1 helper, assistant. 2 contributor, correspondent. *Ia ~ dari New York Hérald,* He's a contributor to the New York Herald. ~ *suratkabar* newspaper correspondent. ~ *jg setia* faithful lackey. ~ *létnan* ensign. ~ *létnan I* chief warrant officer. ~ *létnan II* warrant officer. ~ *tenaga* 1 assistance. 2 assistants. **pem-an** 1 assistance, help, support. 2 co-operation. **-an** 1 support. ~ *uang* financial support. 2 help, assistance. – *tenaga* 1 assistance. 2 assistants.

bantun mem– 1 to weed. 2 to pull out, extract. *Dokter gigi ~ giginja,* The dentist extracted her tooth. **mem-i** 1 to pull out one by one. 2 to weed thoroughly.

bantut mem– to hinder, oppose, block. *Sénsur jg keras itu ~ perkembangan persuratkabaran,* The severe censorship hindered the development of the newspaper industry. **ter–** 1 stopped up. *Got ini ~ karena kotoran,* This gutter was stopped up with dirt. 2 hindered. 3 backward.

bapa see BAPAK.

bapak 1 father. 2 protector. *Ia seorang – rakjat,* He's a people's leader. 3 form of address to an older man. – *Sudirman terkenal sebagai pahlawan kemérdékaan,* Bapak Sudirman is known as a hero of independence. 4 see PAK. **ber–** 1 to have a father. *Anak ini jatim; ia tak ~ lagi,* This child is an orphan; he no longer has a father. 2 to call father. *Ia ~ kpd*

pamannja, He called his uncle father. – *angkat* foster father. – *gedé* grandfather. – *ketjil* uncle (younger brother of father or mother). – *kualon,* – *tiri* stepfather. – *tjilik* younger brother of father or mother. – *tua* uncle (older brother of father or mother).

bapét worthless.

baptis baptism. **mem–(kan)** 1 to baptize. 2 to christen. **pem-an** 1 baptism. 2 christening.

bara live coals, embers. **mem–** 1 to be aglow. 2 to char. **pem-an** brazier. – *api* live coals. – *bahara* ballast.

barah boil, swelling (with pus). **mem–** to fester. *Lukanja ~ ,* His wound festered.

barak 1 barracks. 2 quarantine, quarters. **mem–** to quarantine. *Penumpang kapal itu di– seminggu lamanja,* The ship's passengers were quarantined for a week.

baran swampy forest.

barang 1 things, goods, commodities. 2 luggage. 3 baggage. 4 a wish. – *luluslah ia dlm udjiannja itu,* May he pass his exams. 5 matter. *Berhutang adalah – jg biasa bagi orang itu,* Accumulating debts was a common matter for that man. 6 see BARENG. **se(m)–** any. *Bukan ~ orang diundang kpd pertemuan itu,* Not just anyone was invited to that meeting. **–²** 1 things, goods, commodities. 2 baggage. ~ *amanat,* ~ *bersjarat konsinjasi* goods on consignment. – *apa* anything, whatever. – *apa jg ditjeriterakannja selalu benar,* Anything he said was true. – *bahan* raw material. – *bahari* antiquities. – *batjaan* reading matter. – *bergerak* movable goods. – *besi* ironware. – *bila* whenever. – *bila ia ingin pergi selalu djatuh hudjan,* Whenever he wanted to go it always rained. – *buatan badja* steel products. – *dagangan* articles, commodities. – *dimana* wherever. – *dimana kita pergi...* Wherever we go... – *djadi* readymade goods. – *gedjos* a fake object. – *gelap* contraband goods. – *jg berlebihan* surplus goods. – *kala* whenever. – *kataja* whatever he says. *Djangan pertjaja segala – katanja,* Don't believe all he says. – *kelontong* household utensils. – *kemana* to wherever. – *kodian* 1 mass-produced item. 2 poor-quality product. – *kumango* 1 earthenware. 2 small wares. – *kuno* antiquities. – *ledak* explosives. – *lélangan* auctioned goods. – *letupan* explosives. – *makanan* foodstuffs. – *méwah* luxury items. – *muatan* cargo. – *orang* anyone. –

orang pergi kesana mesti dirampoknja, Anyone going there was sure to be robbed. – *pakaian* clothing. – *pemakaian dapur* kitchen utensils. – *pemakaian rumah tangga* household utensils. – *pemakaian sehari* things for daily use. – *petjah belah* dinnerware, china. – *petjahan* 1 dinnerware, china. 2 earthenware, ceramics. – *pindahan* furniture to be moved. – *purbakala* archaeological pieces, antiquities. – *pusaka* heirloom. – *sedikit* a little. – *seni* art objects. – *sesuatu* anything, everything. – *sesuatu jg dibawanja mesti diperiksa oléh polisi,* Everything he brought had to be inspected by the police. – *siapa* anyone, whoever. – *siapa mau masuk kepaberik itu mesti membawa keterangan,* Anyone who wants to enter the factory must have a permit. – *sudah* manufactured goods, finished products. – *tadahan* stolen goods. – *tambang* minerals. – *tanah* earthenware. – *tangkapan* confiscated goods. – *tentu* a positive fact. *Bhw ia seorang kaja, itu sdh – tentu,* That he is a rich man is a positive fact. – *tenun* textiles. – *tetap* immovable goods. – *tiga* about three. – *tiruan* imitation goods. *Awas – tiruan,* Beware of imitations. – *tjair* liquid. – *tjétak(an)* printed matter. – *tuangan* cast-iron articles. – *satu sénpun tak ada,* There isn't a single cent. *Minumlah obat ini – dua tiga mangkok tiap hari,* Take 2 or 3 cups of this medicine every day.

barangkali perhaps, maybe. – *ia sdh datang,* Maybe he's already come.

baras leprosy.

barat 1 west. 2 western, occidental. **ke–an** the West. **ke– –²an** westernized. *Ia fikirannja ~ ,* His thoughts are westernized. **mem–** to go westward. *Pesawat terbang itu ~ ,* The plane went westward. **mem–kan** *diri* to westernize o.s. – *daja* southwest. – *laut* northwest.

barbur 1 to splash, spill. *Orang mandi – diair,* The bathers were splashing in the water. 2 to waste. *Ia – dgn uangnja,* He was wasting his money.

bareng with, together with. *Ia pergi – ibunja,* He went with his mother. **ber–(an)** together. *Mari kita ~ ,* Let's go together. **mem–i** to accompany s.o. **pem–an** synchronization.

barét 1 beret. 2 laceration.

bargas barge, launch.

bari² banana fly.

barik² 1 grain of wood. 2 veins in marble. **ber– –²** veined, striped.

baring ber– to lie down. *Ia ~ dibawah pohon waringin,* He was lying under

a banyan tree. **mem–kan** to put down, lay down. *Wanita itu ~ anaknja ditempat tidur,* The woman put her child down on the bed. ~ *diri* to lie down. **pem–an** a place to lie down and rest. **ter–** stretched out, lying. *Orang tua itu ~ ditanah,* The old man lay stretched out on the ground.

baris 1 row. *Tempat saja ada dipertama,* My place was in the first row. 2 line. *Mulailah – baru supaja mudah membatjanja,* Please begin with a new line so it will be easy to read. 3 line, queue. *Pagi² sdh ada – jg pandjang,* In the morning there was already a long line. 4 rank. **ber–** 1 to march. *Meréka ~ kerumah djénderal,* They marched to the general's house. 2 to line up, form a queue. *Meréka ~ membeli kartjis,* They formed a queue to buy tickets. 3 to drill. *Meréka ~ dilapangan,* They were drilling on the field. **mem–** to form a line, line up. *Pengungsi² ~ dimuka Kantor Palang Mérah,* The evacuees lined up in front of the office of the Red Cross. **mem–kan** 1 to line up. *Wasit itu ~ kesebelasan²,* The referee lined up the soccer teams. 2 to drill. *Opsir² itu ~ pasukannja,* The officers drilled the troops. **–an** 1 line, row. 2 troops. 3 formation, column. ~ *belakang* 1 rear echelon. 2 home front. ~ *depan* front line. ~ *kehormatan* guard of honor. ~ *pengawal* escort platoon. – **-ber-** in formation.

barkat see BERKAT.

barong name of a character in a Balinese play. **-an** giant doll, puppet, or dragon carried by s.o. inside it.

baru 1 new, recent, modern. *Ia masih – disini,* He's still new here. 2 just. *Ia – kemarén datang disini,* He just arrived here yesterday. – *terima* just received. 3 not until, only then. *Sesudah kata itu ditulis – ia mengerti maksudnja,* Not until the word was written down did he understand the meaning. *Petanghari – pulang,* She didn't return until the afternoon. *Kalau ada anggota parlemén jg mengantarkan – boléh,* You may go only if you are accompanied by a member of parliament. 4 clear, unused. 5 fresh. *daging –* fresh meat. **ke–an** 1 being new. *Karena ~nja ia tak tahu apa jg dikerdjakan lebih dulu,* Because he was new he didn't know what to do first. 2 novelty. **mem–i** 1 to renew. *Ia ~ kontraknja,* He renewed his contract. 2 to modernize. *Ia ~ pendapatnja sesudah datang dari Éropah,* He brought his views up to date after his return from Europe.

memper–i 1 to repair. 2 to renovate. 3 to reform. 4 to modernize. **pem–** 1 reformer. 2 innovator. **pem–an** 1 renewal. ~ *nomer mobil harus berdjalan sebelum tgl 31 Djanuari,* Renewal of auto licenses must take place before January 31. 2 renovation. 3 reform. 4 modernization. 5 innovation. –² *ini* recently.

baruh lowlands.

barung² 1 cottage, hut. 2 stall, stand. 3 temporary dwelling.

barusan just, just now. *Kapan disini?* –. When did you come? Just now. *Ia – pergi,* He just left. – *ini* recently.

barut bandage, dressing. **mem–** 1 to dress a wound. 2 to scrub, clean, wipe. *Tiap hari ia ~ lantai rumahnja,* She scrubs her floors every day. **pem–** bandage, dressing. **pem–an** 1 bandaging, dressing of wounds. 2 dressings.

bas 1 boss. 2 bass (sound).

basa 1 see BAHASA. 2 language. 3 good manners. *Ia tak tahu –,* He doesn't know the proper etiquette. **memper–kan** 1 to entertain. 2 to invite. **per–an** 1 ceremony. 2 compliments. – *-basi* 1 customs. 2 good manners.

basah 1 wet. *Tangannja –,* His hands are wet. 2 damp, moist. *Hawanja –,* The weather is damp. 3 red-handed, in the act. *Pengédar uang palsu tertangkap –,* A counterfeiter was caught red-handed. **ber–** –² soaking wet. *Meréka ~ karena hudjan,* They were soaking wet from the rain. **ke–an** *udara* humidity. **mem–i** to wet, dampen. *Ia ~ saputangannja,* He wet his handkerchief. **mem–kan** to wet, make wet. *Air hudjan ~ ladang jg kering itu,* Rain water made the dry field wet. **–an** 1 work-. *pakaian* ~ work clothes. 2 loincloth. – *kujup,* – *letjap* soaking wet.

basal 1 erysipelas. 2 swelling, tumor.

basi 1 rotten, spoiled. *Nasinja sdh* –, The rice is spoiled. 2 out of date, stale, not topical. *Kabar itu sdh* –, The news is stale. 3 overtime, extra. 4 bowl, plate. 5 serving dish. – *sup* soup tureen.

basil germ, bacillus.

baskom washbasin.

basmi **mem–** 1 to exterminate (rodents, weeds, etc.). 2 to wipe out, eradicate. *Polisi ~ pelatjuran,* The police wiped out prostitution. 3 to burn off, clear by burning. *Meréka ~ hutan utk didjadikan ladang,* They burned off the jungle to turn it into fields for cultivation. 4 to cremate.

pem– eradicator. **pem–an** 1 extermination. 2 cremation, burning.

baso Chinese meatball.

basuh **mem–** 1 to wash. *Ia ~ tangannja,* He washed his hands. 2 to do the dishes. **pem–** 1 washing material. *air ~ tangan* water for washing the hands. 2 a dishwasher (in a restaurant). ~ *désa* offering to cleanse village of sin. ~ *mulut* dessert. ~ *tangan* bribe.

bata brick. **ke–** –²**an, ter–** –² hesitant, vacillating. *Meréka ~ mentjeriterakan keadaan jg sesungguhnja,* They were hesitant to tell the true story. – *emas* gold bars. – *garam* salt bricks. – *genting* cinder block.

batak 1 Batak (people of north-central Sumatra). 2 hobo, vagabond. **mem–** to rob, plunder. *Ia hidupnja* ~ , He makes a living by plundering. **pem–** robber.

batal 1 canceled, null and void. *Perdjalanannja* –, His trip was canceled. 2 in vain. 3 invalid. *Puasanja –setelah ia terpaksa minum,* His fasting was invalid after he was forced to drink. **mem–kan** 1 to cancel, abrogate. *Ia ~ penerbangannja,* He canceled his flight. ~ *persetudjuan* to abrogate an agreement. 2 to revoke, rescind (a law). *Ia ~ kontraknja,* He revoked his contract. *Idjazah sopirnja di–kan,* His driver's license was revoked. 3 to renounce, withdraw. *Meréka ~ tuduhan² itu,* They withdrew the accusations. **pem–an** 1 cancelation, abrogation. 2 abolition. 3 renouncement. 4 disqualification.

bataljon battalion.

batang 1 stem, stalk. – *padi* rice stalk. 2 stick, pole. 3 stalk, blade. *se–* *rumput* blade of grass. 4 used with oblong, cylindrical objects. *dua* – *potlot* two pencils. 5 bar, ingot. *se–* *sabun* a bar of soap. 6 stem, handle. – *pajung* umbrella handle. 7 frame (of a bicycle). **se–** *kara* 1 all alone. 2 without relatives. **–an** 1 crossbeam. 2 barrier. 3 frame. 4 to go stag. –² to go stag. – *air* river. – *api²* matchstick. – *dajung* oar. – *hari* 1 noon. 2 main stream of river. – *hidung* bridge of nose. – *kaju* tree trunk. – *kaki* leg. – *léhér* nape of the neck. – *lengan* upper arm. – *nadi* aorta. – *palang* crossbeam. – *penggerak* lever. – *pohon* tree trunk. – *sepéda* bicycle frame. – *tenggorok* trachea. – *tjendawan* mushroom stem. – *tubuh* torso, trunk. *Ia membangkit – terendam,* He mentioned matters long forgotten.

batara 1 deity, lord. 2 title of a monarch.
batari goddess.
batas 1 limit. – *ketjepatan* speed limit. 2 border, boundary. *Pagar ini – halaman saja*, This hedge is the boundary of my yard. *buku ini sangat* be limited. *Persediaan buku ini sangat ∼ ,* The supply of this book is very limited. 2 to border on. *Désa ini ∼ pd ladang pasir,* This village borders on the desert. **ber-an** *dgn* to border on. *Negeri Birma ∼ dgn Negeri Muangthai,* Burma borders on Thailand. **mem–** to divide, separate. *Pegunungan jg tinggi ini ∼ daérah itu dlm bagian timur dan barat,* This high mountain range separates that region into an eastern and a western section. **mem-i** 1 to border, fence. *Ia ∼ halamannja,* He fenced in his yard. 2 to limit, restrict. *Ia ∼ pengeluarannja,* He limited his expenses. **memper-kan** to limit, restrict. **pem-an** 1 restriction. 2 definition. *∼ kelahiran* birth control. **per-an** border, division. *Itu daérah ∼ ,* That's border territory. **ter-** limited, restricted. *Pendjualan kartjis itu sangat ∼ ,* The sale of tickets was very limited. **-an** 1 border, boundary. 2 limitation, restriction. *– kota* city limits. *– saldju* snow line. *– waktu* 1 time limit. 2 deadline.
baterai 1 dry-cell battery. 2 artillery battery.
bateré see BATERAI.
bathin see BATIN.
bathiniah spiritual.
batih family.
batik batik, batik work. **mem–** to do batik work. **pem–** o. who works on batik. **pem-an** 1 batik work. 2 workshop for batik.
batil 1 plate. 2 copper bowl. 3 tray. 4 incorrect, invalid. 5 see BATAL.
batin 1 inner, internal, spiritual. 2 mind. *Dlm -nja ia mentjurigai kawannja itu,* In his mind he suspected his friend. 3 head, chieftain. **ber-** to deliberate to o.s. **ke-an** 1 mysticism. 2 related to o's inner self. **mem-kan** to keep to o.s., keep secret. *lahir dan -* 1 internal and external. 2 entire, whole, complete(ly). *Meréka menjatakan setia lahir dan - kpd perdjuangan nasional,* They declared their complete loyalty to the national struggle. *membatja - to read to o.s. membatja - orang* to read o's mind.
batja **mem–** to read. *Ia suka ∼ buku,* He likes to read books. *Ajahnja selalu ∼ do'a,* His father always says grace. *∼ dlm hati* to read to o.s.

mem-kan to read (to), for s.o. *Ia ∼ suratkabar kpd ajahnja,* He reads the paper to his father. **pem–** reader. **pem-an** 1 lecture. 2 reading. *∼nja kurang djelas,* His reading isn't too clear. 3 literature, reading. **-an** 1 literature, reading. 2 reading. *∼ kitab itu djelas sekali,* The reading of the book was very clear. *buku ∼* reader, reading text. *tak* **ter-** illegible.
batjar mulut garrulous, talkative.
batjin odor of s.t. rotten.
batjok **mem–** 1 to chop, cut up, cleave. 2 to stab. *Ia ∼ lawannja dgn pisau,* He stabbed his opponent with a knife.
batjul without spirit.
batok 1 coconut shell. 2 approx. one liter. *– kepala* skull.
batu 1 stone, rock, boulder. 2 milestone. 3 chessman. **mem–** 1 to become hard as a rock. *Kuéhnja ∼ ,* The cookies became hard as a rock. 2 to freeze. *Air disungai ∼ ,* The river froze over. 3 to petrify. *Didaérah ini banjak terdapat pohon ∼ ,* In this region many petrified trees are to be found. 4 to be adamant, unwilling to budge. *Dia ∼ sampai terpaksa saja menilpon pulisi,* He refused to budge so I was forced to call the police. **mem-i** 1 to pave, lay with stones. *Meréka ∼ djalan itu sebelum diaspal,* They laid stones before asphalting the street. 2 to stone. *Orang² itu ∼ andjing,* The people stoned the dog. *– akik* agate. *– ambar* amber. *– anggur* tartar. *– anting* hanger. *– api* 1 flint. 2 firebrand, instigator. *– apung* pumice. *– arang* coal. *– asah(an)* grindstone. *– bara* coal. *– bata* brick. *– baterai* flashlight battery. *– belanda* imitation diamond. *– berani* magnet. *– bersurat* stone inscription (inscribed stone). *– besi* granite. *– datjin* weight(s). *– delima* ruby. *– duga* sounding lead. *– empedu* gallstone. *– firus* k.o. turquoise. *– gamping* limestone. *– gerétan* flint. *– giling* millstone. *– gindjal* kidney stone. *– gragal* gravel. *– hampar* flagstone. *– kapur* limestone. *– karang* coral. *– karang lingkaran* atoll. *– kawi* bituminous coal. *– kelikir* gravel. *– kepala* skull. *– kerikil* gravel. *– kisaran* millstone. *– kolar* pebble. *– ladung* sinker on fishing rod. *– lontjatan* stepping stone. *– mérah* brick. *– nilam* sapphire. *– paras* sandstone. *– pelinggam* marble. *– penarung* 1 stumbling block. 2 obstacle. *– pengasah* grindstone. *– pertama* cornerstone. *– pualam* marble. *– sandungan* obstruc-

tion, obstacle. – *sarawak* antimony. –
sendi 1 cornerstone. 2 foundation. –
sontokan stumbling block. – *tahu*
gypsum. – *témbok* brick. – *timbang(an)*
weight(s). – *timbul* pumice. – *tjanai*
grindstone. – *tjatur* chessman. – *tulis*
slate. – *ubin* floor tile. – *udjian* 1
touchstone. 2 criterion.
batuk 1 a cough. *Ia sakit* –, He's
suffering from a cough. 2 to cough.
ber– to cough. **mem–kan** to cough up.
Ia ~ darah, He coughed up blood.
ter– –² to cough and cough involuntarily. – *ketjil* to clear o's throat.
– *lelah* asthma. – *redjan* whooping
cough.
bau 1 smell, scent, odor. 2 unpleasant odor, stench. 3 7096.5 sq. meters.
ber– to smell. *Masakannja ~ énak
sekali*, The cooking smelled delicious.
mem–i 1 to smell, sniff. *Anak gadis
itu ~ bunga mawar*, The girl smelled
the rose. 2 to be on the track, scent
of. *Polisi ~ pembunuh*, The police
are on the track of the murderer.
se– 1 of the same odor. 2 in harmony
with s.t. **ter–** 1 smelled, sniffed, detected. *~ oléhnja asap kebakaran*,
He smelled smoke. 2 known, detected.
rahasia ~ a secret which was detected. **–²an** perfume. – *busuk* ill-
smelling. – *harum* fragrance, pleasant
odor.
bauk fuzzy hair between chin and
neck. **ber–** bearded.
baun see BAU.
baur mixed. **ber–** 1 to mix with.
tepung ~ dgn gula flour mixed with
sugar. 2 to mix, associate. *Ia suka ~
dgn orang*, He likes to mix with people.
mem–kan to mix s.t. *Ia ~ tepung
beras dgn tepung gandum*, She mixed
rice flour with wheat flour. **per–an**
1 mixing. *Disekolah itu ada ~ laki
dan wanita*, At that school there is
a mixing of boys and girls. 2 association, intercourse. *~nja dgn pentjuri
itu mendjadikan ia pentjuri djuga*,
His association with the thief made
him a thief too. 3 marriage. **–an**
mixture.
bausastra dictionary.
baut 1 bolt. 2 bully, strong-arm man,
bouncer.
bawa ber–an to match. *Tjelananja
~ dgn djasnja*, His trousers and coat
match. **berpem–an** 1 to have talent,
ability. *Ia ~ menggambar*, He has a
talent for drawing. 2 to have a background. **mem–** 1 to bring, carry, take.
Saja tidak ~ uang waktu pergi ketoko,
I didn't take any money when I went
to the store. 2 to bring, transport,

deliver. *Motor grobak ~ barang² dari
pelabuhan kekota*, A truck brought
the goods from the harbor to the
city. 3 to bring, take along. *Ia ~
andjingnja kesekolah*, He took his dog
along to school. 4 to bring about,
cause. *Siaran itu ~ akibat kebi-
ngungan diantara pendengar²*, That
broadcast caused confusion among
the listeners. 5 to check. *Barang² ini
saja mau – bagasi, satu koper saja
mau – sendiri*, I want to check this
baggage, one bag I'll take with me.
~ adat well-mannered. *~ agama* to
be converted. *~ aturan sendiri* to do
as o. likes. *~ berat* to be pregnant.
~ bulan to menstruate. *~ diri*
to get along with others. *~ dirinja*
1 to go, betake o.s. *Ia ~ dirinja ke
London*, He went to London. 2 to
flee, escape. *Ia ~ dirinja ketika musuh
datang*, He fled when the enemy arrived. *~ djalan* to guide, show the
way. *~ kakinja* to go anywhere. *~
lagu* to sing. *~ maut* mortal. *~
mobil* to drive a car. *~ nasib* to try
o's luck. *~ njawa* to seek safety.
~ salah to misunderstand. *~ sendjata
api* to carry firearms. *~ serta* to
accompany. *~ suara* to make a
speech. *~ untung* to try o's luck.
mem–kan 1 to bring s.t. (*utk*) for s.o.
Ajah ~ air minum utk adik, Father
brought some water for my younger
brother. 2 to bring, cause. *Pendjualan
itu ~ untung besar kepadanja*, The
sale brought him a big profit. 3 to
present, give. *Dia ~ prasaran*, He
presented a working paper. *~ lagu*
to lead the singing. *~ langkahnja*
to do as o. pleases. **mem–** –² to involve, mention. *Djangan ~ nama
saja dlm soal itu*, Don't involve my
name in that matter. **pem–** bearer,
carrier. *~ surat ini namanja Amat*,
The bearer of this letter is called
Amat. *~ barang* deliveryman. *~
berita* correspondent. *~ pos* postman.
(pem)–an 1 transport. *~ bahan
makanan dikerdjakan dgn hélikoptér*,
The transport of food was done by
helicopter. 2 gift. 3 brought. *Barang²
ini ~ saja dari Hong Kong*, These
things I brought from Hong Kong.
4 talent, ability. 5 attitude. 6 result. 7 background. *~ pendidikannja
memuaskan*, His educational background was satisfactory. **ter–** 1
brought, taken (accidentally). *Kuntji
rumahnja ~ kekantor*, His house key
was accidentally taken to the office.
2 involved. *Ia ~ dlm perkara itu*,
He was involved in that matter. 3

because of, influenced by. ~ *tabi'at
ibunja jg ramahtamah itu iapun mendjadi baik tabi'atnja*, Because of his
mother's friendly nature he too became a man of good character. –
kabur 1 to flee. 2 to take away.
Harta itu di– kabur oléhnja, The effects
were taken away by him.
bawab door- or gate-keeper, guard.
bawah below, under, beneath, under-
neath, bottom. **di–** 1 under. *Buku
itu ada ~ médja*, The book is under
the table. 2 on the floor. *Ia duduk ~*,
He's sitting on the floor. 3 as follows.
Utjapannja adalah sebagai ~ ini,
What he said is as follows. ~ *tanah*
underground. ~ *tangan* underhanded.
~ *umur* underage. **dike–kan** to be
lowered. *Bendéranja ~ , kalau matahari sdh terbenam*, The flag is lowered
at sunset. **ke–** 1 downward. *Ia turun
dari atas ~ gunung*, He came down
from the mountain. 2 under, beneath.
Andjing itu lari ~ médja, The dog
ran under the table. 3 and under.
umur 17 tahun ~ 17 years old and
under. **mem–** to be subordinate to,
serve under s.o. *Ia ~ pd opsir itu*,
He was subordinate to that officer.
mem–i 1 under, beneath. *Pesawat
pengebom itu terbang ~ méga*, The
bomber flew beneath the clouds. 2 to
be inferior. *Kedudukannja tidak ~*,
His position is not inferior. **mem–kan**
1 to supervise. *Mandur itu ~ 30
orang pekerdja*, The foreman supervises 30 men. 2 to have, be in charge
of. *Gubernur itu ~ daérah jg luas
sekali*, The governor is in charge of a
vast area. **ter–** 1 lowest. *Sepatu saja
ada dirak ~ ,* My shoes are on the
lowest shelf. 2 under the command
of. *Pasukan gerilja ini ~ oléh kaptén
Ali*, The guerrilla troops were under
the command of Capt. Ali. **terke–** the
lowest. *Meréka termasuk golongan
jg ~ ,* They belong to the lowest
stratum of society. **–an** subordinate(s).
Ia sangat baik kpd ~nja, He's very
kind to his subordinates.
bawak see BAWA.
bawang onion. – *atjar* pickled onion.
– *Bombai* large yellow onion. – *mérah*
shallots. – *perai* leek. – *putih* garlic.
– *tjina* white onion.
bawasir hemorrhoids.
bawel 1 tedious. 2 meddlesome.
b.d.b. [*bébas dari béa*] duty-free.
Bdg. [*Bandung*] Bandung.
bdgk [*bandingkan*] cf., compare.
béa 1 tax, excise, duty, toll. 2 cost,
expenses. **mem–** to tax. *Pemerintah
~ segala barang keméwahan*, The gov-

ernment is taxing all luxury goods.
pe–an customs office. – *dan tjukai*
customs duties. – *keluar* export duty.
– *masuk* import duty. – *meterai* tax
stamps. – *pemasukan* import duty. –
warisan inheritance tax.
béaja expenses, cost. **mem–i** to finance, pay for. *Berat sekali utk ~
anaknja bersekolah*, It's very hard to
finance his son's schooling. **mem–kan**
to spend. *Ia ~ segala simpanannja
utk menjekolahkan anaknja*, He spent
all his savings to send his son to
school. – *perang* war expenditures.
– *perdjalanan* travel expenses.
béasiswa scholarship, fellowship.
bebal stupid. **ke–an** stupidity.
beban 1 load (in vehicles or on shoulder). 2 responsibility. *Ia merasakan
– jg berat itu*, He felt the heavy responsibility. 3 burden. **mem–i** 1 to
pack. *Ia ~ mobilnja dgn beras*, He
packed his car with rice. 2 to burden.
Ia ~ rakjat dgn ber-matjam² padjak,
He burdened the people with various
taxes. **mem–kan** to place upon s.o.
*Ajah ~ kewadjiban jg berat itu kpd
kami*, Father placed the heavy responsibility upon us.
bebang stillborn. **ke–an** strangled in
course of birth.
bebar **ber–an** spread, scattered. *Bukunja ~ di-mana²*, His books were
scattered everywhere. **ter–** spread,
scattered. *Kabarnja ~ bhw ia akan
ke Éropah*, The news spread that he
was going to Europe.
bébas 1 free, unhampered. *Meréka
boléh bertanja dgn –*, They may ask
questions freely. *Ia membuka pintu
dgn tangan jg masih – itu*, He opened
the door with his still free hand. 2
freed, independent. *Negeri itu sdh –
dari pendjadjahan*, The country has
been freed from colonialism. 3 released. *Sesudah ditahan 3 minggu
lamanja ia – kembali*, After being detained for 3 weeks he was released.
4 exempted. *Karena anggauta diplomatik ia – dari béa pendjualan*, Because he is a member of the diplomatic
corps, he is exempted from any sales
tax. 5 acquitted, set free. 6 clear
(of debt, etc.). **ke–an** freedom, liberty.
Disini ada ~ berbitjara, Here there's
freedom of speech. **mem–kan** 1 to
release. *Kaptén itu ~ tahanan*, The
captain released the prisoner. 2 to
liberate. *Tentara sekutu ~ Asia*,
Allied troops liberated Asia. 3 to
exempt. *Pemerintah ~ bahan makanan
dari béa*, The government has exempted all foodstuffs from duty.

mem–tugaskan to discharge o's duty. **pem–** liberator. **pem–an** 1 release. 2 liberation. 3 acquittal. 4 exemption. 5 emancipation. ∼ *padjak* tax holiday.

bebat bandage, dressing. **mem–** to bandage, dress. **pem–(an)** bandage, dressing.

bébé 1 dress. 2 BB [*Binnenlandsch Bestuur*] Dutch East Indies Civil Service. – *dalam* lingerie, ladies' underwear.

bébék duck. **mem–** 1 to quack. 2 to parrot, imitate. **pem–** mimic, imitator.

bébér **mem–kan** 1 to unfold, unroll. *Njonja* ∼ *pajung*, The lady unfolded an umbrella. 2 to explain, announce. *Ia* ∼ *rentjananja*, He explained his plan. **mem–bentang(kan)** to explain in detail, disclose. **pem–an** explanation.

beberapa 1 several, some, a few. – *buku* several books. 2 several, a few. *Ia berdiri disana – menit lamanja,* He stood there for a few minutes. see BERAPA.

béda difference. *Apakah –nja antara dua orang itu?* What's the difference between those two men? **ber–** to be different, differ, diverge. *Ini* ∼ *dari itu,* This is different from that. **ber–an** 1 to be different from o. another. 2 to be different from (*dgn*). **ber– –²** to vary, be different. *Uraiannja* ∼ *tapi maksudnja sama,* The explanations differ, but the meaning is the same. **mem–(-)kan, memper–kan** 1 to discriminate, show discrimination. *Negara itu masih* ∼ *orang itu dan orang ini,* That state still discriminates between those people and these. 2 to treat differently. *Ia* ∼ *anak tiri dan anak kandungnja,* She treats her stepson differently from her own son. 3 to distinguish, tell apart. *Ia tak dpt* ∼ *jg mana kudanja,* He couldn't tell which horse was his. **pem–an** 1 discrimination. ∼ *ras* racial discrimination. 2 distinction. *Ditentara harus diadakan* ∼ *antara pradjurit dan opsir,* In the army there must be a distinction between enlisted personnel and officers. 3 division, classification. *Dibeberapa daérah* ∼ *warna mendjadi dasar* ∼ *golongan dlm masjarakat,* In some areas the color distinction became the basis for group division in the society. **per–an** 1 difference. ∼ *paham* difference of opinion. 2 distinction. ∼ *warna* color distinction.

bedah surgical operation. **mem–** to operate on. *Dokter* ∼ *pradjurit,* The doctor operated on a soldier. **pem–an** 1 surgical operation. 2 dissection. – *majat* autopsy.

bedaja Javanese court dancer.

bedak (face) powder. **ber–** 1 to powder o.s. 2 powdered. *Mukanja* ∼ *putih,* Her face is white with powder. **mem–i** to powder. – *talek* talcum powder.

bedal **mem–** 1 to whip, thrash. *Ia* ∼ *tawanannja,* He whipped his prisoner 2 to run wild, bolt (of a horse).

bedawi Bedouin.

bedebah 1 misery, distress. 2 wretched. 3 wretch. *si–* a stinker.

bédék see BIDIK.

bedél surgical operation. **mem–** 1 to operate on. *Ia tlh di–,* He's been operated on. 2 to lance, operate on. *Kaki jg bengkak itu di–,* His swollen foot was lanced.

bédéng 1 shed, barracks. 2 dike. 3 bed for flowers and vegetables. **–an** dike.

bedil gun, rifle. **mem–** 1 to shoot s.t. or s.o. 2 to use a rifle. **mem–i** to shoot at. *Ia* ∼ *matjan,* He shot at a tiger. – *buluh* bamboo gun.

bedjana 1 cask, barrel. 2 tank. 3 tray. – *pasir* sandbox.

bedjat 1 to limp, walk with a limp. *Ia – kena témbak pahanja,* He limped from a bullet in the thigh. 2 unstable. *Médja ini –,* This table is unstable. 3 damaged, corrupted. *Fikirannja –,* His mind became corrupted. – *gendi* smashed jar. – *kerandjang* torn basket. **ke–an** corruption, crookedness.

bedol désa entire village with government offices.

bedug see BEDUK.

beduk large drum such as is used at the mosque at prayer time.

bedung diaper. **mem–** to put a diaper on a baby.

béga **ber–** to circle (of a bird). **mem–** to circle around. *Burung élang itu* ∼ *dilangit,* The hawk circled around in the sky.

begadring meeting.

bégal robber. **mem–** to rob. **pem–** robber. **pem–an** robbery.

begap sturdy and solid.

begar 1 confirmed, inveterate, hardened. *pemabuk jg –* confirmed drunkard. 2 rude, callous.

bégar **ber–** to circle around. **mem–** to circle around, pivot.

begini thus, like this. – *tjeriteranja,* The story goes like this. – *besarnja,* It's this large. **mem–kan** to treat, manage, handle s.o. like this. *Gurunja* ∼ *dia,* His teacher treated him like

this. **se–** like this, as... as. ∼ *banjaknja* as much as this.

begitu 1 like that. *–lah keadaannja sesudah ditinggal oléh isterinja,* Such was his situation after his wife left him. *Djangan – kalau membutuhkan pertolongan,* Don't act like that if you need help. 2 so. *Rumahnja – besar,* His house is so big. *Adiknja tidak – pandai,* His younger brother isn't so clever. 3 how. *– bagus rumahnja!* How beautiful his house is! **di–kan** to be treated like that. *Saja tidak mau* ∼ , I don't want to be treated that way. **se–** like that. ∼ *banjaknja* as many as that. **–pun** 1 likewise, and so, also. *Ia kaja* ∼ *pamannja,* He's rich and so is his uncle. 2 in spite of. ∼ *pergi djuga kerumahnja,* In spite of it, he went to his house anyway. *–lah kira²,* Possibly so. (That's about the way it is.) *– sadja* just like that.

beguk 1 goiter. 2 below the mandibles.

béha bra.

bék 1 head of an area. 2 back (in soccer). **mem–** to play the back position.

béka ber– –² to chat.

bekakas see PERKAKAS.

bekal stock, supplies, provisions. **ber–** to carry a supply of s.t. *Ia* ∼ *nasi dlm perdjalanan itu,* He took a supply of rice on the trip. **mem–i** to provide, supply. ∼ *makanan* to provide food. ∼ *obat²an* to supply medicines. **mem–kan** to give as provisions. *Ia* ∼ *roti dan telor kpd anaknja,* He supplied his son with bread and eggs. **pem–an** supply, provisioning (of the army, etc.). **per–an** provisions, supplies. *orang jg tjukup –nja* a person of sufficient means.

bekam bruise. **mem–** 1 to pinch. 2 to seize. *Harimau* ∼ *mangsanja,* The tiger seized its prey. 3 to bleed s.o.

bekas 1 print, trace. *Ia memakai kaus tangan sehingga tak ada –nja pd lemari besi itu,* He wore gloves so that there would be no prints on the safe. 2 used, secondhand. 3 result, consequence, as the result of. *Ia mati – pukulan halilintar,* He died from a stroke of lightning. 4 ex-, former. *Ia – guru,* He's a former teacher. *Dia – saja,* She's my ex-girl friend. 5 remnant, remainder(s). 6 extinct. *– kawah* extinct crater. **ber–** 1 to have a print. *Tangannja tidak* ∼ , There's no print of his hands. 2 to leave an imprint. *Kesusahannja tiada* ∼ *pd parasnja,* Her worries left no imprint on her face. 3 to have results. *Usahanja tiada* ∼ , His efforts were without results. **mem–kan** to cause, leave behind. *Pengadjarannja* ∼ *perasaan bersatu jg kuat,* His teaching left behind a strong feeling of unity. **–an** secondhand. *piano* ∼ a secondhand piano. *– djari* fingerprint. *– kaki* footprint. *– luka* scar. *– tangan* 1 handwriting. 2 signature. 3 handiwork. *– tinta* inkwell. *– tubuh* secondhand clothes.

bekel see PERBEKEL.

béker 1 alarm clock. 2 loving cup. 3 cup.

bekléding upholstery or covering of car, chair, wall.

békot boycott. **mem–** to boycott. **pem–an** boycott. **–an** s.t. boycotted.

beku 1 frozen, solid. *Airnja –,* The water's frozen. *Uangnja dibang –,* His bank account is frozen. 2 rigid, inflexible. *Pikirannja –,* He's rigid in his thinking. 3 dull, slow. 4 coagulated. **ke–an** freezing. **mem–** 1 to freeze over. *Semua sungai* ∼ *semalam,* All rivers froze over last night 2 to clot. *Darah* ∼ , The blood clotted. 3 to congeal. *Agar²* ∼ , The jelly congealed. **mem–kan** to freeze s.t. *Hawa dingin* ∼ *air,* Cold weather froze the water. *Pemerintah* ∼ *segala pembajaran pd bank itu,* The government froze all payments at that bank. **pem–an** freezing. ∼ *keuangan* freezing of accounts.

bekuk **mem–** 1 to break in two. *Ia* ∼ *kaju itu,* He broke the stick in two. 2 to arrest. *Polisi* ∼ *pendjudi²,* The police arrested the gamblers. 3 to swindle. *Toko itu* ∼ *pembeli²,* That shop swindled the customers. *– lulang* 1 fold of the skin. 2 curved zinc roof.

bél bell.

bela **mem–** 1 to care for. *Djururawat itu* ∼ *orang jg sakit,* The nurse took care of the patient. *Ia* ∼ *ibunja,* He takes care of his mother. 2 to protect. **pem–** 1 protector. 2 supporter. *Ia* ∼ *ibunja,* He supports his mother. **pem–an** 1 care. 2 protection.

béla 1 sacrifice. 2 sacrificial victim. 3 o. who sacrifices himself. 4 a suicide. **mem–** 1 to follow s.o. in death. 2 to avenge. *Ia* ∼ *anaknja jg terbunuh itu,* He avenged his murdered son. 3 to defend. *Ia* ∼ *ibunja,* He defends his mother. **pem–** 1 defender. 2 nurse, attendant. **pem–an** 1 defense. 2 care. 3 revenge. *– sungkawa* condolence, sympathy.

beladau k.o. bolo knife.

beladjar see ADJAR.

belado dish with red pepper.

belah 1 crack, gap, crevice. *Ada – ditémbok itu*, There's a crack in the wall. 2 half, cut in half. *seperti pinang – dua* like betel nut cut in half, identical. 3 replica, exact image. 4 side. **dise–** 1 beside. *~ rumah itu ada pohon apel*, Beside the house is an apple tree. 2 on the other side. 3 on the side. *~ sini* on this side. **mem–** 1 to split, cut in two. 2 to part. *Ia ~ rambutnja*, He parted his hair. **menje–** 1 to side, take sides. *Ia ~ kpd negeri² Arab*, He sided with the Arab countries. 2 partial, biased, one-sided. *Hakim itu sangat ~*, The judge was extremely biased. **menje-i** to side with. **menje-kan** to shunt aside. **pem–an** cleavage. **se-** a half, one of several. *Sandal saja hilang ~nja*, One of my sandals has disappeared. *~ matahari mati* the West. **se- -menje–** 1 side by side. *Rumah saja ~ dgn rumah kawan saja*, My house is beside that of my friend. 2 neighbors. *Rumah kami ~*, We are neighbors. 3 on both sides. *~ djalan itu terdapat pohon²*, On both sides of the street there are trees. 4 opposite. *Meréka duduk ~*, They sit opposite e.o. **ter–** split, cracked. *Tanah ~ karena gempa bumi*, The ground was split by an earthquake. **–an** 1 split, crack, cut. *~ ditémbok* a crack in the wall. 2 splinter, fragments. *~ gelas* glass fragments. 3 slice, cut. *~ buah semangka* slice of watermelon. 4 half. *dibagian ~ utara* in the northern half. 5 a relative. *~ dekat* a close relative. *~ diri* 1 sweetheart. 2 wife. *~ djiwa* 1 wife, better half. 2 sweetheart. *– paru* lobe of the lung.

belahak mem– to produce a rattling sound in the throat.

belai mem– 1 to flatter. 2 to caress. **–an** flattery.

belajar see LAJAR.

belak grain of wood.

belaka 1 entirely, completely. *Djandjinja palsu –*, His promise was entirely false. 2 pure. *Gelang itu terbuat dari pérak –*, The bracelet was made of pure silver. 3 quite. *Mempelai itu masih muda –*, The bride was still quite young. 4 only. *Ia – jg datang*, He was the only o. who came.

belakang 1 back, backside. *Saja gatal di-*, My back itches. 2 behind, back of. *– rumah* behind the house. *Musuhnja datang dari –*, The enemy approached from the rear. 3 later. *Ambillah barang² itu dulu, bajarannja*

urusan –, Take the goods now; payment can be arranged later. **ber– –²an** back to back. *duduk ~ to* sit back to back. **di–** 1 behind. *Ia berdiri ~ pintu*, He's standing behind the door. 2 after. *~ pidatonja ada njanjian lagu kebangsaan*, After the speech the national anthem is sung. 3 later. *Bangsa Indonésia jg ~ akan mengalami kemadjuan negeri*, Generations of Indonesians to come will experience the country's development. 4 on the back, reverse side. *Ia luka ~ tangannja*, He was wounded on the back of his hand. **ke–** 1 to the back, to the rear. *Ia pindah ~*, He moved to the back. 2 behind. *Ia pergi ~ rumah*, He went behind the house. 3 to the rest room. *Ia pergi ~*, He went to the rest room. *Permisi ~ sebentar*, Excuse me while I go to the rest room. **keter–an** backwardness, underdevelopment. **mem–** 1 to be, stay, behind. *Mengapa ia selalu ~ ?* Why is he always behind? 2 to be backward. *Kalau dpt, saja lebih baik duduk ~*, If possible, I'd better sit facing backward. **mem-i** 1 to turn o's back on s.o., give s.o. the cold shoulder. *Ia ~ anaknja*, He turned his back on his child. 2 to have o's back to. *Ia duduk ~ papan tulis*, He sat with his back to the blackboard. 3 to neglect, ignore. *Meréka ~ kesopanan*, They ignored decent behavior. **mem–kan** 1 to postpone, put off. *Meréka ~ rapat itu*, They postponed the meeting. 2 to neglect. *Ia ~ hal keduniaan*, He has neglected worldly matters. 3 to put off till later. **menge-kan** 1 to move back. *Ia ~ lajar putih itu supaja gambarnja lebih djelas*, He moved the screen back so the pictures would be clearer. 2 to turn, move back. *Ia ~ arlodjinja*, He turned his watch back. 3 to neglect. *Tak lama lagi ia ~ ibadatnja*, Before long he neglected his religious duties. **ter–** 1 last. *Ia duduk ditempat jg ~*, He sat in the last seat in the rear. 2 latest. *Kabar jg ~ mengatakan bhw ia selamat*, The latest news stated that he was safe. **terke–** 1 to be left behind. *Kalau berdjalan kaki ia selalu ~*, When walking he was always left behind. *Dikelas ia selalu ~*, In class he was always left behind. 2 backward, underdeveloped. *negeri ~* underdeveloped countries. 3 to be in the background, be put in the shade. *Ia merasa ~*, He felt he had been pushed into the background. 4 neglected. *Peladja-*

rannja ∼ , His studies were neglected.
-an 1 later. *Saja pergi* ∼ *sadja*,
I'll just go on later. 2 eventually.
Mula² tidak ada harapan, ∼ *ichti-*
arnja berhasil, Initially there was no
hope, but eventually his effort was
crowned with success. 3 later on.
∼ *ia mengaku bhw ia salah,* Later on
he admitted he was wrong. ∼ *ini*
recently, lately. ∼ *ini ia menjurat*
kpd saja, Recently he has been
writing me. *jg* ∼ *ini* the latter. *Dia*
lebih besar daripada jg ∼ *ini,* He's
larger than the latter. – *hari* future,
in days to come. *Ia menjimpan uang*
utk – hari, He has saved money for
the future. – *tangan* back of the hand.
belalai 1 trunk of an elephant. 2
proboscis of an insect.
belalak mem- to open wide. *Ia* ∼
matanja, He stared wide-eyed. **mem-**
kan 1 to open widely. *Ia* ∼ *matanja,*
He opened his eyes wide. 2 to look
with big eyes at s.o. **ter-** 1 surprised.
2 distended.
belalang locust, grasshopper. – *ka-*
tjung, – *sentadu* praying mantis. –
kerit² cricket.
belam 1 a fire which is kept burning
in order to make another fire. 2 dusk,
twilight. **mem-** 1 to burn. *Api* ∼ ,
The fire is burning. 2 to become dusk,
turn dark. *Mari kita pulang, sdh* ∼ ,
Let's go home, it's getting dark. **ter-**
to become dark.
belan mem- to bar.
belanda Dutch. *Ia seorang* –, He's
a Dutchman. **ke-** –²**an** too Western-
minded, Westernized. **mem-kan** 1
to put s.t. into Dutch. *Ia* ∼ *Kitab*
al-Qur'an, He translated the Koran
into Dutch. 2 to treat s.o. as Dutch.
Pemerintah itu ∼ *meréka jg memin-*
tanja, The government conferred
European status upon those who
requested it. – *hitam* 1 Indonesians
with Dutch citizenship. 2 Indonesians
who felt and acted like Dutch. –
Indo Dutch Eurasian. – *témpé* Dutch
Eurasian (pejorative in tone). – *totok*
full-blooded Dutchman.
Belandanisasi Hollandization.
belandja 1 expenses, expenditures.
Berapa – *se-hari²?* How much are
the daily expenses? 2 cost, expense.
3 pay, salary. *Berapa* – *babu itu?*
How much is the maid's salary?
ber- 1 to shop, go shopping. *Banjak*
orang ∼ *di Toko Hsien,* Many people
shop at Hsien's store. 2 to buy,
purchase. ∼ *buah²an* to buy fruit.
mem-i to finance, defray the cost.
Pemerintah ∼ *perdjalanannja,* The
government financed his trip. **mem-**

kan to spend. **pem-** customer, client.
pem-an, per-an 1 expenses, (national)
budget. 2 financing. **-an** items purchased, shopping goods. – *dapur*
kitchen expenses. – *mati* fixed expenses. – *negeri* government expenses.
– *pasar* household money.
belandong lumberjack. **-an** 1 timber.
2 lumberjacking.
belang 1 spot, stain. *Harimau me-*
nundjukkan –nja, The tiger showed
his spots. 2 blemished, spotted. –
tjetjak spotted marks.
belanga earthen cooking pot.
belangkas 1 k.o. horseshoe crab. 2
k.o. small bolo knife.
belangkin 1 asphalt. 2 black shoe
polish.
belantara jungle.
belantik 1 javelin used in hunting
game. 2 broker, middleman.
belas 1 mercy, pity. 2 tens, teens
(used in the numbers from 11 through
19). *dua* – twelve. **ber-** *kasihan* to
pity, have pity. *Ia* ∼ *kasihan kpd*
saja, She had pity on me. – *kasihan*
pity, mercy, sympathy. **se-** eleven.
-an 1 between 10 and 20. 2 teen-
ager. – *teran* bastard.
belasah mem- to whip, thrash s.o.
bélasungkawa sympathy, condolence.
belasut a growl, snarl. **mem-** to
growl, snarl, spit (of a cat).
belat 1 bamboo screen. 2 fish trap.
3 splint. **mem-** to put in splints.
Dokter ∼ *lengan jg patah itu,* The
doctor put the broken arm in splints.
– *belit* underhanded. *Mulutnja* –
belit, He was underhanded.
belati a small daggerlike knife.
belatjan shrimp or fish paste used as
an ingredient in several Indonesian
dishes.
belatju unbleached cotton.
belau 1 blue. 2 glitter. **ke-** –²**an** 1
bluish. 2 glittering.
Belawan Déli the port of Medan.
beldu see BELEDU.
belebas 1 lath. 2 ruler, measuring
stick.
beledu velvet.
belék mem- to operate on.
bélék inflamed. *Matanja* –, His eyes
are inflamed. **mem-** to peer at,
watch, spy on.
beléng ber- to turn around. **mem-**
to turn s.t. around. *Ia* ∼ *kepalanja,*
He turned his head. **mem-** –²**kan**
to rotate.
belenggu handcuffs, fetters, shackles
of wood or iron. **mem-** to put s.o. in
chains or in irons, shackle.
beléngkét mem- to stick, cling,
adhere. **mem-kan** to paste to, stick

s.t. on. *Ia ~ pengumuman itu kpd papan pengumuman,* He pasted the announcement on the bulletin board.

beléngkok 1 to turn. 2 bent. **mem-** to bend. *Sungai ini ~ kekanan,* The river bends to the right. **-an** a curve, turn.

beléngsét inside out. *Matanja -,* Disease had caused his lower eyelid to turn inside out.

belérang sulphur. **mem-** 1 to treat with sulphur. 2 to fumigate s.t.

Belgia Belgium.

beli 1 a purchase. 2 proceeds from sale of s.t. **ber-(-)an** to do some shopping. **mem-** to buy s.t. *Saja sdh ~ oto,* I've bought a car. **mem-kan** to buy for. *Ia ~ anaknja main²an,* He bought his son some toys. *Ia ~ uangnja (kpd) sebidang tanah,* He bought a tract of land with his money. **pem-** buyer. **pem-an** purchasing. *~ tanah dilarang bagi orang asing,* Foreigners are forbidden to purchase land. **ter-** 1 for sale. *Mobil itu ~* , That car's for sale. 2 bribed, bought. **-an** merchandise, purchases. *Apa ~nja di New York?* What did you buy in New York?

beliak mem-(kan) to open wide (eyes). **ter-** wide open.

beliau 1 he, she (respectful form of address or reference). *Menlu tidak dpt datang; - sakit,* The minister of foreign affairs could not come; he was ill. 2 the honorable.

belibis small wild duck.

belik see BELÉK.

beliku bend, curve (in road, etc.).

belimbing k.o. fruit tree with tasty fruit (*Averrhoa belimbi*). Used in making candy and other sweets.

belindjo a tree bearing edible seeds from which *emping* is made.

beling 1 porcelain. 2 glass, chinaware fragments.

belingkang ter- sprawling. *Ia djatuh ~* , He fell sprawling.

belintang ber- to lie across, athwart. *Bis jg terbalik itu ~ didjalan,* The overturned bus lay across the road. **ber-an** to lie spread over. *Pohon² jg ditebang itu ~* , The felled trees lay spread all over. **mem-kan** to place, lay across s.t.

belirang see BELÉRANG.

belit ber- 1 to wind, twist. *Sungai ini ~ dipegunungan,* This river winds through the mountains. 2 complicated, involved. **ber-** -² 1 to wind in and out. 2 complicated. *Soal ini ~* , This matter is complicated. 3 to be involved with. *Soal ini ~ dgn pembunuhan djanda,* This matter

is involved with the murder of a widow. **mem-** 1 to wind. *Djalan itu ~ digunung,* This road winds in the mountains. 2 to curve, wind around s.t. 3 to bind, wrap together. **mem-i** to wind, veer. **mem-kan** 1 to wind, wrap s.t. on. *Roda itu di-i dgn rantai besi,* The wheels were fitted with chains. **mem-kan** to wind s.t.

belitu bent, crooked. *Pakunja -,* The nail's bent.

Belitung Billiton.

beliung hatchet, pickax.

bélok a curve, bend. **ber-** to turn. *Mobil itu ~ kekanan,* The car turned to the right. **ber-** -² 1 to have curves. *Djalan itu ~* , That road has many curves. 2 to zigzag. **mem-** to turn, veer. **mem-kan** 1 to turn. *Ia ~ mobilnja kekanan,* He turned his car to the right. 2 to divert, distract. *Ia ~ perhatian pendengar²,* He diverted the attention of the listeners. **pem-an** 1 a curve, bend. 2 twist. *Apakah arti ~ itu?* What does this change, twist, mean? -² to tack (of a sailing vessel).

belon = BELUM.

belongkang barge, river freighter.

bélot 1 turncoat, traitor. 2 accomplice. **mem-** to desert to the enemy.

belu-belai chatter.

belubur a large barrel, earthen pot, or small shed in which rice is stored.

beludar round cakes.

belukar thicket, underbrush.

beluku plow.

belulang 1 tough, dry. 2 callous (of hands or feet). 3 rawhide. **ber-** to have a callus. *~ sapi* dry cowhide.

belum not yet. *Ia - besar,* He isn't big yet. *Apa saudara sdh melihatnja? -,* Have you seen him? No, not yet. **ke-déwasaan** immaturity. **se-** before. *~ perang* before the war. *~ pergi, makanlah dulu,* Eat first before you go. *~ dan sesudahnja* in anticipation. *~ waktu* premature(ly). **se-nja** previously, formerly. *- lagi* not yet. *Sdh djam 4, ia - lagi datang,* It's 4 and he hasn't come yet. *- lama ini* just recently, not so long ago. *Saja melihat dia ditoko - lama ini,* I just saw him in the shop a little while ago. *- pernah* never (in the past). *Saja - pernah melihat film 3D,* I've never seen a 3-D film. *- tahu* never. *Saja - tahu kesana,* I've never gone there.

belun = BELUM.

belundjur stretched out. *Ia duduk -,* He sat with legs outstretched.

beluntas a k.o. shrub often used for hedges.

belus 1 loose-fitting. 2 blouse.
belut eel.
bembam mem– 1 to roast in hot ashes. 2 to toast.
bémo [*bétjak bermotor*] motorized pedicab.
bena mem–kan 1 to clear away (of dishes). 2 to make, put in order. *Ia ~ tempat tidurnja,* She made the bed.
béna 1 particular(ly), very. *Ia tak – besarnja,* He's not particularly large. 2 care, attention. *Andjing ini tak mendapat – dari pemiliknja,* This dog did not receive much care from its owner. mem–kan to care for. *Ia tak begitu ~ pekerdjaannja,* He doesn't care so much for his job. *– tak –* to be indifferent.
benah see BENA. mem–i to fix, get s.t. ready (beds, etc.) $-^2$ to get ready. *Saja segera ~ utk tidur,* I got ready for bed right away.
benak marrow. *tak* ber– very stupid.
benalu 1 parasite. 2 sponger.
benam ber– to disappear, to hide. *Dimana kau~ ?* Where have you been? mem–kan 1 to drown, immerse. *Anak² itu ~ andjing disungai,* The children drowned the dog in the river. 2 to suppress, abolish. *Ajahnja ~ tuduhan² anaknja kpd tetangganja,* The father suppressed his son's accusations of his neighbors. 3 to scuttle. ter– 1 to disappear, go down. *Matahari ~ dibarat,* The sun sets in the west. 2 to be buried. *Rumah² itu ~ dibawah saldju,* The houses were buried in the snow. *Ia ~ dlm hutang,* He's flooded with debts.
benang thread, yard. mem– 1 to string along, be interminable. *Tjeriteranja ~ ,* His story strings along, has no end. 2 stringy. se– a little bit. *– arang* thread stained with a mixture of soot and oil the imprint of which on timber provides the carpenter a line along which to cut the wood. *– radja* rainbow. *– sajét* knitting wool. *– salib* cross wires. *– sari, – serbuk* stamen. *– sela* thread with several strands. *Ia mendirikan – basah,* He did an impossible task.
benar 1 correct. *Taksiran itu –,* That estimate is correct. 2 right, honest, true. *Ia berpegang kpd pedoman jg –,* He keeps to the true course. 3 just, honest. *Ia terkenal sebagai hakim jg –,* He's known as a just judge. 4 true, not false. *keadaan jg – the true situation. 5 sincere, true. *Ia mendjalankan kewadjiban dgn hati jg –,* He carried out his task with

sincerity. 6 valid. *Surat perdjandjian itu tidak –,* The certificate of agreement is not valid. 7 truthful. *Berkatalah jg –,* Tell the truth. 8 right. *– ia tidak membajar harga buku itu,* He was right not to pay the price of the book. 9 very, quite, really. *Film itu bagus –,* The picture was very good. ber– 1 to be sincere. 2 to state candidly, admit frankly. ke–an 1 correctness, rightness. 2 truth. 3 honesty. 4 by accident, coincidentally. *~ saja akan pergi ke Chicago djuga,* By chance I'm going to Chicago too. 5 proof, acknowledgment. *Inilah ~ jg menjatakan bhw saja berhak pd tanah itu,* This is the proof that I am entitled to that land. mem–kan 1 to correct. *Ia ~ kesalahannja,* He corrected his mistakes. 2 to confirm. *Ia ~ kabar itu,* He confirmed the news. 3 to approve (of). *Ia ~ perkawinan itu,* She approved of the marriage. 4 to acknowledge. *Ia ~ penerimaan uang,* He acknowledged receipt of the money. 5 to permit. *Polisi tidak ~ mobil berdjalan malam,* The police do not permit cars to run at night. 6 to arrange, fix. *~ rambut* to arrange the hair. pem–an 1 correction. 2 confirmation, acknowledgment. 3 approval. se–nja 1 in fact, as a matter of fact, actually. *~ ia takut,* As a matter of fact, he was afraid. 2 proper, fitting. *Sdh ~ kalau ia menjokong ibunja,* It was proper that he should support his mother. 3 true. *Keadaan jg ~ ialah seperti ini,* The true situation is like this. $-^2$ seriously. *Peladjari keadaan itu ~ ,* Study the situation seriously.
benara laundryman.
benatu laundryman.
benda thing, inanimate object, article. ber– wealthy. ke–an 1 matter. 2 materialism. per–an 1 stock, supply of goods. 2 matters concerning goods. $-^2$ *padat* solid matter (in physics). *– buang* dirt, manure. *– hidup* livestock. *– letupan* explosives. *– mati* goods, things.
bendahara treasurer. per–an 1 treasury. 2 financial. *soal –* financial matters. 3 equipment, valuable items. *~ kata* vocabulary. *~ negara* state finances. *Kantor Pusat ~* General Accounting Office.
bendaharawan treasurer.
bendahari treasurer.
bendaniah material (attrib.).
béndel file (of documents). mem– to bind books, papers.
bendéra flag. *– kebangsaan* national

flag. – *mérah putih* the red and white flag of Indonesia.

benderung empty space between two buildings.

béndi a gig, two-wheeled carriage.

bendjol lump, bump, bruise. **ber- –²** black and blue.

bendul crossbeam. – *pintu* threshold. *si–* numskull.

bendung 1 dike. 2 dam. **mem–** 1 to dam (up). *Orang² ~ sungai itu,* People dammed up the river. 2 to dam, stem, check. *Meréka ~ serangan musuh,* They stemmed the enemy attack. **mem-i** to dam up. **–an** 1 dike. 2 dam. *tidak* **ter–** irresistible.

bengal 1 stunned. *Ia – karena kepalanja kepukul kepintu,* He was stunned from hitting his head on a door. 2 stubborn, obstinate. 3 forward, impertinent. **ke–an** stubbornness.

bengang 1 ringing in the ears. 2 wide open. **ber–** to ring in the ears. **ter–** 1 wide open. *Mulutnja ~ ,* His mouth was wide open. 2 surprised. *Ia ~ melihat suaminja datang,* She was surprised to see her husband coming.

bengap 1 dull (of color or sound). 2 mumbling, stuttering, incoherent (from embarrassment, shyness, or hesitation).

bengawan river, rather large stream. – *Solo* Solo River.

bengék 1 asthma. 2 asthmatic.

Benggala Bengal.

Benggali Bengali.

benggil bump, bruise. *Mukanja benggal– –,* His face was black and blue.

bénggol 1 2½ cent coin. 2 bump, bruise. **–an** 1 leader of a criminal gang (highwaymen, smuggling ring, etc.). 2 chief culprit.

bengik see BENGÉK.

bengis 1 cruel. 2 strict, severe. *Guru itu sangat –,* The teacher was very strict. 3 harsh, hard, rude. *Anak itu – kpd adiknja,* The boy was harsh to his younger brother. 4 sharp, harsh. *Perkataannja –,* His words were harsh. 5 penetrating, pungent. *Baunja –,* The odor is penetrating. 6 angry. *Mengapa ia mendjadi –?* Why did he become angry? **ke–an** 1 cruelty. 2 severity, harshness. **mem–** to be angry. *Ia ~ kpd adiknja,* He became angry with his little brother. **mem-i** 1 to be angry with s.o. *Ia ~ adiknja,* He was angry with his little brother. 2 to be cruel to. *Pendjaga itu ~ tawanan,* The guards were cruel to the prisoners.

bengkak 1 swollen. *Kakinja –,* His foot is swollen. 2 swelling, tumor.

mem– to swell. *Kakinja ~ ,* His foot swelled.

bengkal ke–an to choke, swallow the wrong way. *Anak itu ~ djarum,* The child accidentally swallowed a needle. *Ia ~ air,* He choked on the water.

bengkalai mem-kan to leave s.t. unfinished. *Ia ~ pekerdjaannja,* He left his work unfinished. **ter–** unfinished.

bengkang 1 crooked. 2 curve. – *bengkok* zigzagging. – *bengkung* curved. *Djalan ini – bengkung,* This road has many curves.

bengkar mem– 1 to expand. *Djagung ini ~ kalau digoréng,* This corn expands when fried. 2 to be in bloom, to bloom. *Bunga mawar ~ ,* The rose was in bloom.

bengkarak 1 skeleton. 2 bones.

bengkarung k.o. scaly lizard.

béngkél 1 workshop. 2 repair shop. – *kerdja* workshop. – *kerdja sastera* literary workshop. – *mobil* auto repair shop, garage. – *roti* bakery.

béngkéng irritable, touchy, irascible. **mem-i** to tease, nag s.o.

bengkok with a goiter.

béngkok 1 crooked, bent. *Tiang itu –,* The pole is bent. 2 crooked, sly. *Hatinja –,* He has a cunning mind. *Maksudnja –,* His intentions are crooked. **mem–** 1 to turn, make a turn. 2 to bend. *Tongkatnja ~,* The cane bent. **mem-kan** to bend, lean over. *Ia ~ badannja,* He leaned over.

bengkol bent.

béngkong 1 crooked, bent. 2 o. who performs circumcisions.

Bengkulu Bencoolen (sw Sumatra).

bengkung 1 bent, crooked. 2 girdle band for women often worn after giving birth; made of several yards of cotton.

bengong dazed, stupefied (from desperation, grief, astonishment).

béngot slanting, sloping.

bengu stale (air).

benguk 1 angry, surly, sulking. 2 downhearted. **mem–** to be angry. *Ia kelihatannja ~ sadja,* He looks angry all the time.

benian strongbox, jewelry box.

benih 1 seed(ling). – *padi* rice seedling. 2 semen. 3 germ. – *penjakit tjatjar* smallpox germ. 4 cause, origin. *Itu – perselisihan,* That was the cause of the conflict. 5 origin, descent. *Ia adalah – radja²,* He's a descendant of kings. **mem-kan** to germinate. **pem-an** substratum for bacteria, bacilli, virus, etc.

bening clear, transparent. **mem-kan** to purify (water).

benjai soggy, mushy. *Nasinja –,* The rice was mushy.

bénjék soft (of fruit).

bénjot slanting, sloping, leaning.

bénkap leggings.

bénsin gasoline.

bentak **mem-** to snap at s.o. or s.t. *Ia ~ orang tua itu,* He snapped at the old man. **-an** growling, snapping.

bentan to have a relapse. *Djagalah supaja sembuh samasekali, djangan sampai –,* Be sure to recover completely lest you have a relapse.

bentang **mem-kan** 1 to spread out s.t. *Ia ~ babut,* He spread out a rug. 2 to explain s.t. *Ia ~ pendapatnja,* He explained his views. *~ segala maksudnja* to lay all o's cards on the table. 3 to spread, extend. *Daérah ini ~ kepantai itu,* This area extends to the shore. **mem-bébérkan** to explain, unfold s.t. **ter-** 1 to be spread out. *Peta Asia ~ ,* A map of Asia was spread out. 2 extending outward. **-an** taut, tight. *~ langit* the firmament.

bentar **se-** 1 for a moment. *Saja mau singgah disini ~ ,* I want to stop in here for a moment. 2 a moment. *Tunggu ~ ,* Wait a moment. 3 very soon. *Tunggulah ~ ; ~ dia akan datang,* Please wait a moment; he will be coming very soon. *~ ini* a moment ago, just now. *Saja berdjumpa dgn dia ~ ini,* I met him a short while ago. *~ lagi* 1 a little longer. *Tunggulah ~ lagi,* Please wait a little longer. 2 in a few minutes. *Ia akan berangkat ~ lagi,* He will be going in a few minutes. *~ soré* this evening. **se-–²** 1 frequently, again and again. *~ ia datang utk minta uang pd ajahnja,* He frequently came to ask money of his father. 2 for a few moments. *Ia kalau datang hanja ~ sadja,* If he came he only stayed for a few moments. *Lampu itu ~ mati ~ hidup,* The light went off and on.

béntar **ber-(-)** 1 to turn, revolve. *Dunia ~ ,* The earth revolves. 2 to turn off, *Ia mengambil djalan ~ ,* He took a detour. **mem-i** to circle. *Harimau itu ~ mangsanja,* The tiger circled its prey.

bentara 1 herald. 2 see BINTARA.

béntéh **ber-** to trip up.

bénténg 1 fortress. 2 fortification, entrenchment. 3 bulwark, stronghold. 4 goal. **ber-** to be fortified. **mem-i** to fortify s.t. **(per)-an** fortification. **-an** a wall.

bentét to burst open.

bentil nipple, teat. *- susu* udder, teat, nipple.

bentjah swamp. **ber-(-)** swampy, marshy.

bentjana disaster, calamity, catastrophe. **ke-an** doom. **mem-i** 1 to disturb, cause trouble. 2 to deceive, swindle s.o. **mem-kan** 1 to disturb. *Radio jg dikeraskan waktu malam itu ~ tetangga,* The radio which was on so loud in the evening disturbed the neighbors. 2 to endanger s.o. or s.t. 3 dangerous. *- alam* natural disaster, catastrophe. *Ia selalu dlm –,* He's always in danger.

bentjat stunted in growth.

bentji hate, dislike, aversion. *Ia - kpd orang itu,* He hates that person. **ke-an** 1 hate, hatred. 2 dislike, aversion. **ke- -²an** vindictive. **mem-(i)** to hate, dislike, despise. *Ia ~ temannja,* He hates his friend. **pem-hater.** *Ia ~ perempuan,* He's a woman hater.

bentok **ke-** to hit against. *Lengannja ~ témbok,* His arm hit the wall.

bentrok **mem-kan** 1 to collide, bump against. *Ia ~ mobilnja kpd pohon,* His car collided with a tree. 2 to bring s.o. into conflict. *Ia ~ ajahnja dgn gurunja,* He brought his father into conflict with his teacher. **per-an** 1 conflict, dispute. 2 collision. **-an** *dgn* 1 to collide with. *Mobil itu ~ dgn keréta api,* The car collided with a train. 2 a quarrel.

bentuk 1 shape, form, type. *Saja suka - rumah,* I like the shape of the house. 2 bend, curve. 3 used with round or curved objects. *satu - tjintjin* a ring. *satu - roda* a wheel. **ber-** 1 to have the form of. *Negara kami ~ républik,* Our government has the form of a republic. 2 to have the shape of. *Kapal itu ~ ikan,* That boat has the shape of a fish. **mem-** 1 to form. *Dapatkah kamu ~ kata dari tiga huruf ini?* Can you form a word from these three letters? 2 to compose, form. *Perdana Menteri itu ~ kabinét,* The Prime Minister formed a cabinet. 3 to curve, bend. *Ia ~ tjintjin,* He bent the ring. *Élok sekali dahan itu ~ !* How nicely that branch curves! **pem-** prime-minister-designate. *~ kabinét baru* prime-minister-designate of the new cabinet. **pem-an** formation, establishment. **-an** 1 form. 2 formed. *kabinét ~ kaum kiri* cabinet formed of the leftists. 3 derivative.

bentur **ber-an** to collide. *Dokar dan mobil ~ ,* A horse cart and a car collided. **ke-** 1 to collide with, strike against. *Mobil* ~ *pohon,* A car collided with a tree. 2 failed. **mem**- to bend, bow. *Pohon²* *itu* ~ *karena angin jg keras,* The trees bent from the strong wind. **ter**- 1 to collide with. 2 to fail. *Ia selalu* ~ *dgn rentjananja,* He's always failing in his plans. **-an** collision.

benua 1 continent. 2 country.

benum mem- to appoint s.o. **-an** appointment.

béo myna bird. **mem**- to parrot, imitate.

Béograd Belgrade.

berabé 1 nuisance. – *kalau mesinnja rusak,* It's a nuisance when the engine breaks down. 2 annoying. *Wah, itu kan* –, Oh, it's too much trouble.

berahi 1 in love, infatuated. 2 passionate. 3 passion, lust. **ke–an** passion. ~*nja kpd kuda membangkrutkan orang itu,* His passion for horses ruined the fellow. **mem–kan** 1 to charm, enchant. *Penari itu* ~ *penontonnja,* The dancer charmed the spectators. 2 to get a kick out of s.t.

berai mem- -²kan to spread, scatter. *Ia* ~ *kabar bhw harga kopi akan naik,* He spread the news that the price of coffee would rise.

bérak night soil, feces. **ber**- to defecate, have a move. **mem**- to defecate. **mem–i** 1 to discharge on. *Andjing kami* ~ *kasur,* Our dog discharged on the mattress. 2 to disgrace, dishonor. *Ia* ~ *nama keluarganja,* He dishonored his family's name. **ter**- to have an accidental discharge. – *air* diarrhea. – *darah* dysentery. *Ia tak bisa – dan tak bisa kentjing,* He can't defecate or urinate.

beram liquor made of fermented rice or tapioca.

beranda 1 veranda, porch. 2 station platform.

berandal rascal, scoundrel.

berandang striking, noticeable.

berang –an otter. –² 1 arsenic. 2 rat poison. 3 otter.

bérang 1 angry, furious. 2 anger. 3 short sword. **mem**- to be furious. *Ia* ~ , He was furious. **mem–i** to be angry with s.o. *Ia* ~ *isterinja,* He was angry with his wife. **pem**- hothead.

berangsang mem- to be very angry. *Mengapa dia* ~ *?* Why was he so angry? **mem–kan** 1 to make s.o. angry. *Édjékannja* ~ *temannja,* His ridicule made his friend angry. 2 to encourage s.o. **pem**- hothead.

berangus 1 muzzle. 2 bridle. **mem**- 1 to muzzle (a dog). 2 to control, bridle, muzzle (the press). **pem–an**

control. ~ *pihak oposisi* muzzling of the opposition.

berani 1 brave, plucky, valiant. *Ia seorang* –, He's a brave man. 2 to dare. *Ia* – *mengatakan itu kpd ajahnja,* He dared say it to his father. **ke–an** bravery, courage, valor. **mem–kan** to encourage. *Ia* ~ *anaknja pergi sendirian,* He encouraged his son to go alone. ~ *diri* to gather courage. **pem**- 1 courageous person. 2 daredevil. 3 hero. – *buka – bajar* to pay the piper. – *lalat* pretend to be brave. – *mati* to have contempt for death, be very brave. – *sumpah* to dare swear. – *sumpah saja tidak mentjuri arlodji itu,* I swear I did not steal the watch. – *tjandang* 1 reckless, foolhardy. 2 bold. – *udang* to be scared.

berantakan 1 chaos, disorder, in a mess. *Pekerdjaannja* –, His work's in a mess. 2 to fall to pieces, be dilapidated (of a car, etc.).

berantas mem- 1 to fight against, combat s.t. 2 to abolish. **pem–an** combating of s.t. ~ *buta huruf* the fight against illiteracy. ~ *hama* pest control.

berapa 1 how much. – *harga buku ini?* How much does this book cost? 2 how many? – *orang datang kerumahmu?* How many people came to your house? 3 how. – *ketjil rumah itu?* How small is the house? – *lama saudara tinggal disini?* How long have you lived here? – *djauh rumahmu dari sini?* How far is your house from here? 4 see APA. **be**- several, some, a few. ~ *buku* several books. *Ia berdiri disana* ~ *menit lamanja,* He stood there for a few minutes. **ber**- to have how many. **se**- if, insofar as. ~ *boléh kuda itu djangan dipakai lagi hari ini,* If possible that horse shouldn't be used any more today. *tidak* ~ not so much. *Ia tak* ~ *tjapai,* He's not so tired. – *lama* no matter how long. – *lama ditjarinja uangnja tak terdapat djuga,* No matter how long he searched for the money, it couldn't be found. – *lagi* the more so, especially. *Kamar ini dingin,* – *lagi kalau pintunja dibuka,* This room is chilly, especially when the door is opened. – *sadja* any amount whatsoever. *tidak* – not so much. *Bédanja tidak* –, There isn't so much difference.

berarakan spread, scattered. *Bukunja* – *dikamarnja,* His books are scattered all over the room.

beras hulled rice. – *djagung* rice mixed with corn. – *giling* milled rice. – *kepala* highest quality rice. – *ketan* sticky rice. - *kuning,* - *kunjit* yellow rice (used on ceremonial occasions such as weddings, etc.). - *menir* finely ground rice. - *petas* all k.o. rice. - *pulut* sticky rice. - *retjak²* cracked rice. - *tumbuk* pounded rice. *Itu* - *basah,* That's useless.

berat 1 heavy. *Batu ini* -, This stone's heavy. *Kewadjibannja* -, His responsibility is heavy. 2 serious, severe. *Ia luka* -, He was seriously injured. *Ia dihukum* -, He was severely punished. 3 difficult. *Peladjaran ini sangat* -, This lesson is extremely difficult. 4 weight. *Berapa* - *barang ini?* What's the weight of this article? (How much does this article weigh?) **berke–an** to have objections. *Ia ∼ mendjalankan perintah itu,* He objected to carrying out that order. **ke–an** 1 overloaded. *Motor grobak itu rupanja ∼* , The truck appears to be overloaded. 2 objection. 3 burden, load. 4 too heavy. **mem–i** 1 to load s.t. 2 to weigh on. *Apakah jg ∼ fikiranmu?* What's weighing on your mind? **mem–kan** 1 to load s.t. with ballast. 2 to aggravate, stiffen, strengthen s.t. *Ia ∼ tuduhannja dgn bukti² njata,* He strengthened his accusations with factual proof. 3 to stress, emphasize. *Meréka ∼ pertahanan negeri dlm pembitjaraan perbelandjaan itu,* They stressed national defense in the budget discussions. **–nja** weight. *Oto itu ∼ 2 ton,* That car weighs 2 tons. - *bersih* net weight. - *dibongkarkan* weight delivered. - *dimuatkan* weight shipped. - *djenis* specific gravity. - *hati* 1 to suspect. *Ia - hati kpd orang itu,* He suspected that man. 2 heavyhearted. *Ia - hati utk meninggalkan anaknja,* She was heavyhearted over leaving her child. - *(i)ni!* This is quite a job! *Apakah saja mesti mendjaga dimuka rumah sepandjang malam?* - *'ni!* Do I have to guard the house all night long? That's quite a job! - *kaki* lazy. - *kepala* dull, slow mentally. - *kotor* gross weight. - *mulut* taciturn. - *pd mata* to be respected. *Ia - pd mata teman²-nja,* He's respected by his friends. - *sebelah* one-sided, biased. - *tangan* lazy. - *sama dipikul, ringan sama didjindjing* sharing the good and the bad.

berdjuis bourgeois.
berdus obese, fat, potbellied.
berédél **pem–an** censorship.
beremban crossbeam.
berenang see RENANG.
beréndi brandy.

berenga maggot.
berengos thick mustache.
berengut **mem–** to look sullen.
berenti see HENTI.
bérés 1 in order, well done. *Pekerdjaannja* -, His work is in order. *Pikirannja kurang* -, His thoughts are befuddled. *Semua pekerdjaannja tanggung* -, All his work is certain to be well done. 2 cleared away, finished. *Sdh* -, It's taken care of. **ke–an** order, neatness, tidiness. **mem–kan** 1 clear up, settle s.t. *Polisi ∼ kekatjauan itu,* The police settled the disturbance. 2 to put in order. *Ia ∼ pekerdjaan jg katjau balau itu,* He put the chaotic work in order. *∼ tempat tidur* to make a bed. **pem–an** settlement (of conflict, debt). *Tahu –!* Leave it to me!
berésok see BÉSOK.
bérét exacting, demanding.
beréwok hairy, shaggy.
bergedél 1 meat ball. 2 hamburger.
berguk a dress covering the entire body except the face and hands; used by Moslem women on the pilgrimage to Mecca.
berhala idol.
berhenti see HENTI.
beri **mem–** 1 to give. *Ia ∼ izin,* He gave permission. *Ia ∼ hadiah,* He gave a gift, or a reward. 2 to let. *Ia ∼ dia lari,* He let him escape. 3 to offer, put up. *Meréka ∼ perlawanan jg sengit,* They put up stiff resistance. 4 to put on, paint. *Ia ∼ warna hidjau kpd dinding kamar duduk itu,* He painted the living room wall green. *∼ hati* 1 to make happy, cheer up. 2 to encourage. *Ia ∼ hati kpd saja utk menerima tugas itu,* He encouraged me to accept the task. 3 to give in to s.o.'s whims. *Bapaknja selalu ∼ hati kpd anaknja,* His father is always giving in to his son's whims. *∼ hormat* 1 to extend regards. *Ia ∼ hormat kpd kawannja,* He extended his regards to his friends. 2 to present arms (mil.) *∼ ingat* to remind s.o. of s.t. *∼ isjarat* to signal with the hands. *∼ leta* to despise s.o. *∼ malu* to shame s.o. *∼ pindjam* to lend s.t. to s.o. *∼ rezeki* 1 to make a living. 2 to bring luck. *∼ salam* to greet s.o., say hello. *Ia ∼ salam kpd temannja,* He said hello to his friend. *∼ suara* to vote for s.o. *∼ tanda* to signal with the hands. *∼ telinga* to listen, lend an ear. **mem–kan** 1 to give, hand over. *Ia ∼ uangnja kpd adiknja,* He gave his money to his brother. 2 to bid, offer a bid. **mem–tahu** to

report, inform. *Ia* ~ *suratkabarnja*, He informed his newspaper. **mem-tahukan** to announce, report. *Ia* ~ *perkawinannja*, She announced her marriage. **pem-** giver, donor. **pem-an** 1 gift, present. 2 distribution, act of distributing. 3 issue. *tempat* ~ place of issue. 4 delegation. ~ *kuasa* delegation of authority. 5 giving, extension. ~ *izin* licensing. ~ *krédit* extension of credit. **pem-tahuan** announcement, notice. ~ *pengangkutan* notice of shipment. **-an** gift, present. **- -mem-** give and take. *Ia memtjelaan kpd teman²nja*, He disgraced his friends. *Di- betis hendak paha*, Give s.o. an inch and he'll take a mile.
béri² illness caused by inadequate diet. *- kering* dry scurvy.
beringas wild, savage. *mata -* fierce eyes.
beringin banyan tree.
berisik 1 noisy, tumultuous. 2 uproar, noise.
berita 1 news (report). 2 announcement, report. **be(r)-** to have, bring news. **mem-kan** to report, inform. *Ia* ~ *dari Tokyo bhw ajahnja sampai dgn selamat*, He reported from Tokyo that his father had arrived safely. **pem-** reporter, news correspondent. **pem-an** 1 news release, announcement, report. 2 communication(s). *- bulanan* monthly announcement, *- dalam negeri* home news. *- dengkul* secondhand rumors. *- hawa* weather report. *- kilat* bulletin. *- negara* official government gazette. *- rapat* minutes (of a meeting, etc.). *- sepekan* weekly news. *- udara* weather report.
beritahu see BERI.
berkah see BERKAT.
berkas bundle, bunch. *se- kaju bakar* a bundle of firewood. **mem-** to bind, put in sheaves. *- tjahaja* a shaft of light.
berkat 1 blessing, favor. *Ia meminta - orang tuanja*, He asked for his parents' blessing. *Usahanja tak ada -nja*, His efforts have been unsuccessful. 2 thanks to. *- do'a ibuku* thanks to my mother's prayers. 3 owing to, due to. *- usahanja* owing to his efforts. 4 profitable. *Perdagangannja -*, His business is profitable. 5 a small portion of a meal taken home after the ceremony. **mem-i** 1 to bring s.o. happiness, make s.o. happy. *Pengairan ini* ~ *penduduk désa ini*, This irrigation work makes the villagers happy. 2 to bless s.o. or s.t. **pem-an** blessing.
berlian polished diamond.
bernas 1 filled out. *Lihatlah buah*

apel jg - rupanja, Look at the filled-out apple. 2 promising. *Tanamannja - sekali rupanja*, His plants look very promising. 3 pithy, terse. *Ia mengadakan pidato jg -*, He delivered a terse speech.
bero fallow.
berondong mem- to fire a volley. **-an** a salvo, volley of gunfire.
berongsong to flare up, explode in anger.
berontak revolt, rebellion. **mem-** to rebel, revolt. *Meréka* ~ *thd peraturan baru itu*, They rebelled against the new regulation. **pem-** rebel, insurgent. **pem-an** uprising, insurrection, revolt, rebellion.
bersih 1 clean. *Piring² ini -*, These plates are clean. 2 innocent, pure. *Ia - dlm hal itu*, He was innocent in that matter. 3 pure, unadulterated. *Didésa itu masih terdapat adat-istiadat jg -*, In that village pure customs and traditions still exist. 4 neat. *Tulisannja - sekali*, He has a very neat handwriting. 5 net. *penghasilan - net* income. **ke-an** 1 cleanliness, tidiness. 2 purity. ~ *hati* purity of heart. **mem-kan** 1 to clean, wash. *Ia* ~ *tangannja*, He washed his hands. 2 to clean up s.t. *Ia* ~ *kamarnja*, He cleaned up his room. **pem-an** 1 cleaning, cleansing. ~ *rumah* house cleaning. 2 purification (of soul, water). 3 purge (political). 4 mopping up. *gerakan* ~ mopping-up operations. 5 raid, roundup.
bersil mem- to protrude.
bersin to sneeze.
bersit to protrude, stick out. **mem-kan** to whip out. *Ia* ~ *péstolnja*, He whipped out his pistol.
bersut mem- to glare at.
bertih roasted rice kernels.
beruang 1 a bear. 2 see UANG.
berudjul small plowshare.
berudu tadpole.
beruk k.o. monkey.
berumbun to loom up. *Gedung besar - dimuka pemandangan kami*, A large building loomed up before our eyes.
berumbung tubular, cylindrical.
Berunai Brunei. *Kota -* Brunei Town.
berungut mem- to grumble, gripe. **mem-i** to grumble about, have a gripe against. *Ia* ~ *kakaknja*, He had a gripe against his older brother.
beruntus -an pimple, rash (prickly heat, etc.).
bésan relationship of parents whose children are married to e.o., in-laws. *Amin dan saja adalah -*, Amin is related to me as father of my son-in-

law. **ber–** to be related as parents-in-law. **per–an** connubium. **–an** = – .

besar 1 big, large. *Ia orang –*, He's a large man. 2 big, great. *Ia orang –*, He's a great man. 3 tall. *Badannja –*, He's tall. 4 adult, grown. **ke–an** 1 too large. *Sepatu ini ∼* , These shoes are too large. 2 amount, volume. *∼ béaja itu tidak disetudjui oléh rapat,* The amount of the cost was not agreed upon by the meeting. 3 state, pomp, ceremony. 4 greatness, grandeur. *∼ keradjaan Roma* the grandeur of the Roman Empire. 5 might, power. *∼ hati* pride. **mem–** 1 to expand. *Saja melihat balon itu ∼* , I saw the balloon expanding. 2 to grow up. **mem–kan** 1 to revere. *Ia ∼ sedjarah negerinja,* He speaks with reverence about his country's history. 2 to make great. *Kemenangan²nja ∼ negerinja,* His victories made his country great. 3 to enlarge, increase, expand. *Ia ∼ lampu,* He turned the light on brighter. 4 to raise, bring up. *Dia di–kan di Malang,* He was brought up in Malang. *∼ diri* to boast. *∼ hati* 1 to encourage. 2 to please. 3 encouraging. *Situasi ékonomis itu ∼ hati,* The economic situation is encouraging. **mem– –²kan** to exaggerate s.t. **memper-(kan)** 1 to enlarge, expand. *Kawan saja ∼ perusahaannja,* My friend expanded his business. 2 to increase. *Madjikannja ∼ gadjinja,* His boss increased his salary. 3 to extend. *Radja itu ∼ pengaruhnja,* The king extended his influence. 4 to rear, bring up. **pem–** 1 an official, authority. 2 big shot, prominent person. **pem–an** 1 enlargement. 2 expansion, increase. **–²an** large, largish. *Ia mengadakan perajaan itu setjara ∼* , He celebrated on a large scale. *– hati* 1 proud. *Ia – hati mendengar anaknja lulus udjian,* He was proud to hear that his son had passed the examination. 2 happy, pleased. *– kepala* 1 stubborn, obstinate. 2 conceited. *– lambung* greedy. *– lengan* powerful, influential. *– mulut* proud, arrogant. *– perkataan* conceited, boastful. *– terak* quite large. *– tjita* ecstasy, rapture.

bések covered square basket made of thin bamboo slats.

beséro see SÉRO.

besét mem– to skin, flay s.t.

besi iron. **mem–tuakan** to turn s.t. into scrap iron. *– badja* steel. *– berani* magnet. *– beton* iron bars for concrete. *– buruk, – tua* scrap iron. *– dadur timah* tin-plated iron. *– galbani* gal-

vanized iron. *– gubal* pig iron. *– lantai, – lémpéng* sheet iron. *– lantak* iron bars. *– lunak* nonmagnetic iron. *– papan* iron plate. *– putih* tin plate. *– sadur séng* zinc-plated iron. *– tempa* wrought iron. *– tjor* cast iron.

beskit cooky.

beslah seizure. **mem–** to seize, confiscate s.t. **pem–an** seizure, confiscation.

beslit 1 governmental decree. 2 letter of appointment. *– kenaikan gadji* decree for pay raise. *– (peng)angkatan* decree of appointment.

bésok 1 tomorrow. 2 later on, in the future. *Anak ini – akan mendjadi orang jg terpeladjar,* This boy will be a scholar later on. 3 later. *Ia akan pergi – bulan Djuni,* He will go later in the month of June. *– lusa* day after tomorrow, sometime in the future. *– malam* tomorrow night. *– pagi* tomorrow morning. *– paginja* the next morning. *– soré* tomorrow afternoon.

bestari 1 expert, skilled. 2 bright, clever.

bésték steak.

bestél 1 an order. 2 ordered. *Apakah Tuan sdh –?* Have you already ordered, Sir? **mem–** to order s.t. **–an** 1 an order, s.t. ordered. *∼nja sdh datang,* The order has arrived. 2 package.

bestir 1 government. 2 administration. 3 board of directors.

besut mem– to flow, gush (of blood).

béta 1 I. *– melihat setasiun itu,* I see the station. 2 me. 3 my, mine. *Buku itu punja –,* That book is mine. **mem–** to use *béta.*

betah 1 to stand, endure. *Ia – menahan perasaan sakit,* He can stand pain. 2 to like, adjust to. *Saja baru – tinggal disini sesudah anam bulan ini,* I began to like it here only after 6 months. **mem– –²kan** to endure, put up with.

betapa 1 how. *– girangnja orang itu mendjumpai anaknja lagi,* How happy he was to see his child again. 2 as. *Kerdjakanlah ini – biasa,* Do this as usual. *– lagi* the more so, even more, even less. *Ia kaja – lagi ajahnja,* He's rich and his father even more so. *Ia tak berani berdjalan sendirian, – lagi isterinja,* He didn't dare go alone and even less did his wife.

betas 1 torn. *Badjunja –,* His jacket is torn. 2 loose. *Kelimannja –,* The hem was loose.

Betawi 1 Batavia (now Jakarta). 2 Batavian.

bétét parakeet.

béti proof, evidence. **ter–** proved.
betik 1 papaya. 2 red spot. **ter–** to
be announced. *Kabar ~ bhw buruh
akan mogok*, It was announced that
the workers would strike. –² irritated
(heat rash, etc.).
betina female of animals. – *djelita*
pretty female. *kuda* – mare.
beting shoal, sandbank. **ter–** run
aground on a shoal.
betis calf (of leg).
bétja(k) 1 pedicab, tricycle. 2 DC-3
plane.
betjak see BÉTJAK.
bétjak 1 muddy. 2 dirty. 3 dots. –²
1 dirty, filthy, soiled. *Kertasnja
djatuh dilumpur ~*, The sheet of
paper fell in the mud and got dirty.
2 spotted, dotted. *Tjitanja ~*, The
material has a dotted design.
bétjék muddy.
betjus *tidak* – 1 not smart. 2 un-
satisfactory. *Kelakuannja tak –*, His
behavior leaves much to be desired.
betok etched.
beton concrete.
betot **mem–** 1 to pull with force.
2 to take s.t. off.
betul 1 right, correct. *Ini alamat jg
–*, This is the right address. 2 true,
right. *Ini tjeritera jg –*, This is a
true story. 3 exact, right. *Médja ini
– di-tengah² kamar itu*, This table is
right in the middle of the room.
4 very, really. *Rumahnja besar –*,
His house is very large. 5 exactly.
Ja, –, Yes, exactly. **ber–an** *dgn* to
coincide with. *Perkawinannja ~ dgn
udjiannja*, His wedding coincided
with his exams. **berke–an** *dgn* to
coincide with. **ke–an** 1 by chance,
accidentally. *Ia ~ mau pergi djuga
sehingga kami dpt pergi ber-sama²*,
Just by chance he was going too so
we were able to go together. 2 to
happen to. *Saja ~ tahu ttg soal itu*,
I happen to know about that matter.
3 lucky, just right. *~ sekali kamu
datang*, It was lucky you came. (You
came at just the right time.) **mem–**
to be true, straight. *Kaju tua ~
tinggi*, An old tree stood straight and
tall. **mem-i** 1 to repair. 2 to correct.
3 to aim for. *Kapal itu ~ pelabuhan
jg terdekat*, The ship headed for the
nearest port. 4 to fulfill. *Ia ~ harapan
anaknja*, He fulfilled his son's wish.
5 to coincide with. *Usul itu ~
angan² saja*, The proposal coincides
with my wishes. **mem-kan** 1 to repair, fix. *Ia ~ sepédanja*, He repaired
his bicycle. 2 to correct. *Ia ~ salahnja*, He corrected his mistake. **pem–an**
1 repair. 2 improvement. 3 correc-

tion. **se–nja** actually, in fact, as a
matter of fact. *~ saja sdh tjapé*, As
a matter of fact I'm tired. –² sincerely.
Ia pertjaja ~ kpd orang itu, He
sincerely believed in that man. *Jg –
sadja dong*, Be reasonable.
betung large bamboo tree. *Dlm
urusan itu ia membelah –*, In that
matter he was biased.
betutu 1 boned chicken. 2 k.o. river
fish.
béwok beard, whiskers.
bg. [*bagian*] section, division.
BH [*béha*] bra(ssière).
bhakti see BAKTI.
bhg. [*bahagian*] section, part. see
BAGIAN.
bhs [*bahasa*] language.
bhw [*bahwa*] that.
b.i. [*bulan ini*] this month.
B.I. [1 *Bahasa Indonésia*. 2 *Bank
Indonésia*.] 1 Indonesian language.
2 Bank of Indonesia.
bia see BÉA.
biadab 1 ill-mannered, impolite, rude.
2 uncivilized, savage, primitive.
Disini ada suku bangsa jg masih –,
Here one will find a still savage tribe.
ke–an 1 impertinence, rudeness, insolence. 2 primitiveness, paganism.
biadi thread or hair worm.
biaja see BÉAJA. **pem–an** financing.
– *makelar* brokerage. – *pelabuhan*
harbor dues, dock charges, wharfage.
– *penundaan* towage. – *sampan*
lighterage.
biak fertile. **ber–** to multiply, increase. *Pemberantasan buta huruf ~ *,
Literacy campaigns are flourishing.
mem– to flourish, multiply. **mem-kan**
to grow, breed, rear. *Ia ~ ikan
tambak*, He breeds fresh-water fish.
pem– *ikan* fish breeder. **pem–an**
breeding, cultivation. **–an** 1 breeding, raising. 2 cultivated, reared,
bred. *ikan ~* cultivated fish. – *dara*
parthenogenesis.
biang 1 mother (of animal), parent
species (of plants). – *ajam* mother
hen. 2 origin, source. – *penghidupan*
a source of income. 3 essence. – *tjuka*
essence of vinegar. – *keladi* 1 basic
cause. 2 ringleader of criminals, out-
laws. – *keringat* prickly heat. – *roti*
leaven. – *tangan* thumb.
bianglala rainbow.
biar 1 to let, permit. – *saja pergi
sekarang*, Let me go now. – *dia
menangis; itu tidak apa*, Let him
cry; it doesn't matter. *Lepaskan
talinja – dia lari*, Let go of the rope
so he can run. 2 so that, in order that.
Beri makan banjak – lekas besar,
Give him a lot of food so that he'll

grow fast. 3 (al)though. – *ketjil ia
berani*, Although small, he's brave.
4 better. – *mati daripada kalah*, It's
better to die than lose. 5 that's
enough. **mem–kan** 1 to let, permit,
allow. *Ia ~ andjingnja tidur*, He let
the dog sleep. 2 to neglect, let go.
Ia ~ segala kewadjibannja, He neglected all his responsibilities. 3 to
connive. *Ia ~ orang mentjuri garam
pemerintah*, He connived with people
in stealing government salt. –² in-
testinal worm. – *bagai manapun* be
that as it may. – *begitu* 1 nonetheless,
yet. 2 nevertheless. – *dahulu*, Leave
it as it is. – *datang*, Let (him) come.
– *lah*, That'll do. (Never mind.) –**pun**
although. – *saja urus*, Leave it to
me. – *putih tulang djangan putih
mata*, Better death than disgrace.
biara 1 monastery. 2 nunnery. 3
Buddhist wat.
biarawan monk.
biarawati nun.
bias mem– to be adrift. *Perahu
itu ~ dari djalan biasa*, The boat
was adrift from its usual course.
ter– to be cast adrift.
biasa 1 to be used to, accustomed to.
Ia – pergi kesana, He's accustomed
to going there. 2 usual, customary.
Ia makan seperti –, He ate as usual.
jg – the usual. 3 ordinary, common.
Disini tinggal banjak orang –, Many
ordinary people live here. **ke–an** 1
usage. 2 habit, custom. **mem–kan** to
become accustomed to s.t. *Meréka
~ pemakaian mesin*, They became
accustomed to the use of the machinery. *~ diri kpd* to adjust oneself
to s.t. *Meréka ~ diri kpd keramaian
dikota*, They adjusted themselves to
the noise of the city. **ter–** habitual.
–nja usually. *Itu – sadja*, Nothing
at all.
biawak iguana. **mem–** to creep like
an iguana, on all fours.
biawas k.o. guava.
bibi(k) 1 aunt. 2 form of address to
older women.
bibir 1 lip. 2 hem. 3 edge. **pem–an**
labialization. – *atas* upper lip. –
bawah lower lip. – *émbér* edge of a
basin. – *hutan* edge of a forest. –
mata eyelid. *Ketjelakaan itu terdjadi
di– mata saja*, That accident took
place right in front of my very eyes.
– *sumbing* harelip. – *tangan* side of
the hand. *Hanja di– sadja ia berdjandji akan menolong*, He was just
talking when he promised to help.
–nja *seperti delima merekah* full,
well-shaped lips.
bibit 1 seedling. 2 seed, semen, germ.

3 germ, bacteria. 4 cause, origin. 5
prospective, future, candidate. *Ia –
guru*, He's a future teacher.
bibliografi bibliography.
bidadari 1 fairy. 2 beautiful woman.
bid'ah 1 lie. 2 liar. 3 heretical, false.
4 heresy, Islamic modernism. 5 free-
thinking.
bidai 1 bamboo or rattan screen.
2 basketwork. 3 splint. 4 base (in
sports such as baseball). **mem–** to
put in splints. *Meréka ~ lengan jg
patah itu*, They put the broken arm
in splints.
bidak pawn in chess.
bidal 1 proverb, maxim. 2 thimble.
bidan midwife. **mem–i** to be a midwife. *Siapakah jg ~ pd kelahiran itu?*
Who was midwife at the birth?
bidang 1 plane, level, surface. 2
spacious, broad. *Bahunja –*, His
shoulders are broad. 3 piece, plot,
patch. *Ia mempunjai se– tanah*, He
owns a piece of land. 4 field. –
pengadjaran field of education. 5
sector. **mem–kan** to extend, expand.
Ia ~ dadanja, He puffed out his
chest. **pem–an** a tenter or stretcher
for cloth. – *pertjobaan* experimental
stretch (of road, etc.).
bidas mem– 1 to penetrate, pierce.
Barisannja ~ djauh didaérah musuh,
His troops penetrated far into enemy
territory. 2 to fly from, shoot away.
Batu ~ dari pelanting, The rock
flew from the slingshot. **pem–** lance.
bidik mem– 1 to peer. *Ia ~ dlm
gelap gulita*, He peered into the
darkness. 2 to aim, take aim. *Ia
~ benar² sebelum memasang*, He
aimed carefully before shooting.
mem–kan *kpd* to aim at s.o. or s.t.
Meréka ~ bedilnja kpd rusa itu,
They aimed their guns at the deer.
pem–an firing, shooting.
bidjak 1 able, smart, experienced. 2
witty, fluent in conversation. **ke–an**
intelligence, wisdom.
bidjaksana 1 wise, astute, shrewd.
Ia mengambil tindakan jg –, He took
wise measures. 2 prudent, tactful.
ber– to be wise. **ke–an** 1 wisdom,
prudence. 2 wise guidance, policy.
3 insight.
bidjan sesame seed.
bidji 1 seed, kernel, stone. – *djeruk*
orange seed. 2 grade. *Ia mendapat –
jg baik sekali dikelasnja*, She got very
good grades in her class. 3 used
with small round objects. *tiga – bola*
three balls. **ber–** *sabak* to cry, weep.
mem– to give a grade. *Guru itu tak
pernah ~ banjak*, That teacher never
gives very high marks. –²**an** cereals.

- *mata* 1 eyeball, pupil. 2 darling, sweetheart. - *pala* nutmeg.

bidjih ore. - *besi* iron ore.

biduan singer, vocalist.

biduanita female vocalist.

biduk small craft, k.o. canoe. **ber-(-)** to go boating. *Saja bersatu - dgn dia,* We are colleagues in the same shop.

bidur block of approx. 2 lbs, formerly used as a weight.

bihara see BIARA.

bihun thin noodles. - *kuah* noodle soup.

bikang k.o. cooky. **pem-an** baking pan.

bikin **di-** -² farfetched, strained. **mem-** to make. *Ia ~ rumah,* He built a house. **pem-an** manufacture, construction. **-an** 1 product. 2 produced, made. *~ mana mobil ini?* Where is this car made? 3 fib. *Itu hanja ~ sadja, tidak mungkin benar,* That's just a fib, it can't be true. -² to pretend, make up. *pertundjukan jg ~* a made-up performance. - *basah* to wet, dampen. - *besar* to enlarge. *Ia - besar rumahnja,* He enlarged his house. - *betul* to repair. *Ia - betul mobilnja,* He repaired his car. - *lembék* to melt. - *sembuh* to cure. - *takut* to frighten.

biksu Buddhist priest.

biku 1 serrated, toothed. 2 Buddhist monk. **ber-(-)** 1 to curve, zigzag. *Djalannja ~ ,* The road zigzags. 2 toothed.

bila 1 when. - *kamu akan pergi?* When are you going? 2 when, if. *Bawalah buku ini - saudara pergi,* Take this book when you go. *Selesaikanlah sekarang - mungkin,* Finish it now if possible. -² now and then. *~ ia mengeluarkan saputangannja,* Now and then he would take out his handkerchief. -(-) *sadja* any time. *Datanglah dirumah - sadja,* Come and see me any time.

bilah 1 lath. 2 chip of wood. 3 knife blade. 4 used with knives, swords, etc. *tiga - pisau* three knives.

bilai 1 hem, border, edge. 2 addition. **mem-** 1 to lengthen. *Ia ~ pipa tjelananja,* He lengthened his trouser leg. 2 to fill teeth. *Dokter gigi itu ~ gigi dgn mas,* The dentist filled the tooth with gold. 3 to add. *Ia bekerdja malam djuga utk ~ penghasilannja,* He worked at night too to add to his income.

bilal muezzin, o. who summons to prayer.

bilamana when(ever). *Saja pergi - saja selesai,* I'll go when I'm ready. - *djuga* anytime.

bilang 1 to say. *Apa dia -?* What did he say? 2 every. - *hari* every day. **ber-** 1 to say. 2 some, a few, several. *Ia akan bepergian ~ hari lamanja,* He'll be away for several days. *~ kali* several times. **ke-an** prominent, well-known. *Dinegerinja ia termasuk orang jg ~ ,* In his country he belongs among the prominent people. **mem-** *ramal* to predict. **mem-(kan)** 1 to say. *Ia ~ apa?* What did he say? *Dinegeri itu boléh di- tak ada pengemis,* In that country one may say there are no beggars. 2 to mention. *Ia tidak ~ nama saja,* He didn't mention my name. 3 to count. *Ia ~ uangnja,* He counted his money. *Ia ~ dari 1 hingga 100,* He counted from 1 to 100. 4 to consider, take into account, *Ia hanja ~ pembesar² sadja,* He paid attention to the big shots only. **pem-** numerator (arith.). **pem-an** counting. **se-** every. *~ hari* every day. *~ waktu* each, every time. **ter-** 1 to be calculated. *Banjaknja korsi ini ~ seratus buah,* The number of these chairs was calculated at 100. *Tak ~ banjaknja orang dilapangan itu,* There were an incalculable number of people in the square. 2 to be regarded as. *Ia ~ orang kaja,* He was regarded as a rich man. 3 eminent, prominent. **-an** 1 number, amount. *dlm ~ jg besar* in large numbers. 2 numeral, number. *~ satu sampai seribu* the numbers 1 to 1000. 3 area, district, territory. *Ini termasuk ~ negarabagian New York,* This is included in the area of New York State. 4 calculation. 5 fate. *Kalau masih bukan ~nja orang tak mudah mati,* If o's number hasn't come up yet, it isn't easy to die. 6 group, sphere. *Ia masuk ~ orang terpeladjar,* He belongs to the intellectual group. 7 mention. 8 pronunciation. *~ bulat* round number. *~ gandjil* odd number. *~ persepuluhan* decimals. *~ petjahan* fraction (arith.). *~ utuh* round numbers.

bilas **mem-** to rinse, wash off.

bilik 1 room. 2 plaited bamboo slats used for walls. *Rumahnja berdinding -,* His house has bamboo walls. **ber-** to have a room. - *djantung* ventricle. - *muka* front room.

bilis bloodshot and burning (of the eyes).

biljar billiards.

biljun billion.

billahi by God! - *saja tidak mengambil barang² itu,* I swear by God that I didn't take those things.

bilur welt, wound caused by a whip-lash. **ber-** –² to be hurt by a lashing.
bimbang 1 to hesitate, be dubious about. *Ia – akan pergi atau tidak,* He hesitated whether to go or not. 2 worried, anxious. *Ia – memikiri ajahnja jg sakit,* He was worried over his sick father. 3 anxiety. **ke-an** 1 worry, anxiety. 2 doubt, hesitation. 3 in doubt. **mem-kan** 1 to cause hesitation. *Kabar itu ~ hatinja utk pergi atau tidak,* The news caused him to hesitate about whether to go or not. 2 to be anxious about s.o. *Kabar itu ~ ajahnja ttg anaknja,* That news made the father anxious about his son.
bimbing ber- 1 to go hand in hand, hold on to. *Ia ~ pd lengan anaknja,* He held on to his son's arm. 2 to find guidance. *Ia ~ pd Kitab Indjil,* He found guidance in the Bible. 3 to lead. *Ia ~ tangan anaknja,* He led his child by the hand. **mem-** 1 to lead, guide. *Présidén ~ rakjat,* The president leads the people. 2 to conduct, lead. *Ketua itu ~ rapat,* The chairman led the meeting. *~ keluar* to show to the gate or exit. 3 to introduce s.t. *Mata peladjaran baru di– oléh guru,* The teacher introduced a new course. **pem-** 1 guide. *~ pembatja* reader's guide. 2 leader. 3 introduction, preface. *kata ~* preface. **-an** leadership, guidance.
bimbit mem- 1 to carry s.t. in the hand. *Ia ~ tas buku,* He was carrying a brief case. 2 to lead s.o. by the hand.
bin son of. *Ali – Amar* Ali, son of Amar.
bina building, construction. **mem-** 1 to build, found. *Ia ~ negara,* He founded a state. 2 to develop, cultivate, construct. *Ahli bahasa itu ~ bahasa,* That linguist developed a language. **pem-** founder, builder. *Ia ~ bahasa Indonésia,* He's the builder of the Indonesian language. **pem-an** creation, construction. *~ kembali* construction, restoration. *~ sesuatu negara* the creation of a state.
binal 1 obstinate, rebellious (of a child). 2 disobedient. 3 wild, untamed.
binar bright. *tjahaja jg –* bright light. **ber-** –² to be very bright. *Penglihatannja ~,* He was blinded, saw stars.
binasa destroyed, wiped out. *Kota itu – karena bom atom,* That city was wiped out by an atom bomb. **ke-an** destruction, annihilation. **mem-kan** 1 to destroy, annihilate. 2 to ex-

terminate. **pem-** destroyer, eradicator. **pem-an** 1 utter destruction. 2 extermination.
binatang animal, beast. **ke-an** bestiality, brutality. *– berkantung* kangaroo. *– buas* wild animal, beast. *– djinak* tame animal. *– kerat, – mengerat* rodent. *– melata* amphibian. *– menjusui* mammal. *– timangan* pet.
binatu laundryman.
bindeng 1 to talk through the nose. 2 nasal (of speech).
bindu lathe. **mem-** to work with a lathe.
bingas short-tempered, irascible.
bingit 1 ill at ease, uncomfortable. 2 jealous, envious.
bingka k.o. cooky.
bingkah bit, lump, fragment, chunk. **ber-** –² in bits, in fragments. **mem-i** to smash s.t. to bits, into chunks. **-an** *tanah* a lump of clay.
bingkai brim, rim, fringe, edge. *– mata* rim of the eye. *– roda* rim of a wheel. **mem-(kan)** to frame s.t. *Ia ~ gambarnja,* He framed his picture.
bingkas 1 resilient, elastic. 2 elasticity. **ber-** to bounce, rebound. **mem-** 1 to bounce, rebound. *Bola ténis ~,* The tennis ball bounces. 2 to bounce, jump up. *Ia ~ dari duduknja,* He jumped up from his seat.
bingkis mem- to send a gift. **-an** 1 gift, present. 2 souvenir. 3 parcel, package.
bingung confused, upset, bewildered. *Ia – sekali,* He was very confused. **ke-an** 1 confusion. 2 panic. 3 confused. **mem-kan** 1 to confuse, bewilder. *Peraturan ini ~ rakjat,* This regulation confuses the people. 2 confusing, bewildering. *Peraturan ini ~,* This regulation is confusing.
bini wife. **ber-** 1 to marry. *Ia pulang kedésa mau ~,* He returned to the village to marry. 2 to have a wife. *Ia ~ orang asing,* He has a foreign wife. *Ia ~ dua,* He has two wives. 3 to be a married man. *Ia sdh ~,* He's a married man. **ber-kan, mem(per)-kan** to marry s.o. off. *Ia ~ anaknja jg sulung,* He married off his oldest son. **-an** 1 to want to marry. *Ia suka ~,* He wants to marry. 2 mistress. *Ia bukan –nja, ~ sadja* She's not his wife, but s.o. he's playing around with. *– adji* concubine. *– gahara, – jg terang* legal wife. *– muda* second wife. *– tua* first wife.
bintang 1 star. 2 star, fate, luck. *–nja naik,* His star is rising. 3 medal,

decoration. **ber–** 1 starry. *malam*
~ a starry night. 2 to be lucky.
Hidupnja tak ~ , He's unlucky.
ber– –² 1 starry. *langit terang jg* ~ a
clear sky with many stars. 2 starry-
eyed. 3 with stars before the eyes.
4 to shine through, glitter. **ber-**
gelap to have bad luck. **ber–** *terang*
to have good luck. *Ia* ~ *terang*
selama ada dinegeri asing, He had
good luck while abroad. **mem–i** to
star in (a movie, etc.). **per–an** 1
astronomy. 2 astrology. 3 horoscope.
se– to agree. *Saja* ~ *dgn dia,* I agree
with him. **–an** constellation. **–²an**
imitation star. **–²** spotted, dotted.
– *beralih* meteor, shooting star. –
berasap comet. – *berédar* planet. –
berékor, – *berkoték* comet. – *biduk*
Big Bear. – *djadi* Capricorn. – *djasa*
service medal, medal for meritorious
conduct. – *djohar* Venus. – *djung*
Big Bear. – *gugur* falling star. –
keberanian medal of valor. – *kedjora*
Venus. – *kehormatan* military or
civilian decoration. – *kemintang dila-*
ngit the starry host, the stars in the
firmament. – *ke(r)tika* Pleiades. –
musjtari Jupiter. – *pari* Southern
Cross. – *pengandjur,* – *pengarak siang*
morning star. – *pilem* movie star.
– *sandiwara* stage star. – *sapu*
comet. – *siang* morning star. – *siarah*
planet. – *timur* Venus, morning star.
– *tjorat-tjorét* meteor, falling star. –
tohok Southern Cross. – *utara* North
Star. – *waluku* star propitious for
plowing.
bintara noncommissioned officer.
binti daughter of. *Salimah* – *Saléh*
Salimah, the daughter of Saleh.
bintik dot, speck. **ber– –²** to be
spotted, have spots.
bintil small pimple.
bintit a sty in the eye.
bintjang ber– to discuss, deliberate.
ber– –² to discuss. *Meréka* ~ *hingga*
djauh malam, They discussed until
late at night. **mem(per)–kan** to discuss, talk about s.t. *Ia* ~ *soal kea-*
manan, He discussed the problem of
security. **per–an** 1 discussion. 2 conference.
bintjul lump, bump.
bintul a pimple caused by a mosquito bite.
bintur a trap for crabs.
biografi biography.
biokimia biochemistry.
biola violin.
bioskop movie theater. *Ke–lah se-*
kali², Go to the movies once in a
while.
bir beer. – *tongan* draft beer.

birahi see BÉRAHI.
birai 1 low wall, balustrade. 2 banister. 3 curb, edge, border. 4 lodge.
birat scar around the mouth.
biri² 1 sheep. 2 beriberi disease.
birih see BIRAI.
biring rusty yellow. – *peluh* prickly
heat.
Birma Burma.
biro office, bureau. – *Perantjang Na-*
sional National Planning Bureau.
birokrasi bureaucracy.
birsam pleurisy.
biru 1 blue. 2 fold, hem, pleat. **ber–**
to have a hem. **ber– –²** pleated.
ke– –²an bluish. **mem–** to become
blue. *Bibirnja* ~ *karena dingin,* His
lips turned blue from the cold.
mem–kan to paint or dye s.t. blue.
– *tjutji* blueing.
bis 1 bus. 2 (mail)box. 3 tube. **mem–**
kan 1 to mail s.t. *Ia* ~ *dua surat,*
He mailed two letters. 2 to send by
bus, load on a bus. *Ia* ~ *barang²,* He
sent the goods by bus. – *surat* mailbox.
bisa 1 to be able. *Ia tidak* – *datang,*
He can't come. 2 poison injected
through a wound (snake bite, etc.).
3 to be poisonous. **ber–** poisonous.
ke–an 1 ability. 2 poisoned. *Kambing*
itu mati ~ , The goat died from
poisoning. **se–nja** where possible.
Pd tiap sadjak ~ *disebutkan sumber,*
The source for every poem is given
wherever possible. **se– –²nja** 1 as
much as possible. 2 to the fullest
extent. – *djadi* possible. – *djadi ia*
tak datang, It's possible he won't
come.
bisik ber– –² 1 to whisper. *Ia* ~
kpd temannja, He whispered to his
friend. 2 to conspire. *Meréka* ~ *utk*
membékot madjikannja, They con-
spired to boycott their boss. **mem–i**
to whisper to. *Ia* ~ *kawannja supaja*
pergi, He whispered to his friend to
go. **mem–kan** 1 to whisper. *Ia* ~
perintahnja, He whispered his order.
2 to inspire, prompt, suggest. *Kedja-*
dian itu ~ *rentjana jg tetap kepadanja,*
The incident suggested a definite plan
to him. *Ada jg* ~ *bhw saja harus*
tinggal disini, Something tells me I
should stay here. **pem–** 1 prompter.
2 whisperer. **–an** 1 a whisper. 2
whispering. 3 suggestion.
bising 1 noise, uproar, hullabaloo.
Ia berbuat –, He caused an uproar.
2 rushing, murmur of a stream. 3
rustling, swishing of a dress. 4 dazed,
stunned. *Ia* – *karena bunji bom,*
He was dazed from the noise of the
bomb. **ber–** 1 to make a noise. 2
to be dazed. **ke–an** noise, uproar.

mem–kan to deafen, daze. *Bunji itu ~ telinga,* The noise deafened his ear.
biskit cracker.
biskwik cracker.
biskwit cracker.
bislah see BESLAH.
bismillah in the name of God.
bisték steak.
bistik beefsteak.
bisu 1 dumb. 2 stupid. **mem–** to keep quiet, say nothing. *– tuli* deaf and dumb.
bisul 1 tumor. 2 boil, abscess. 3 ulcer. *– benta* small abscess on upper lip. *– djerawat* pimple on the face. *– sabut* carbuncle.
bit beet.
biti see BÉTI.
bitjara 1 to speak. *Ia – bahasa Perantjis,* He speaks French. 2 to talk. *Ia – keras sekali,* He talks loudly. *Djangan banjak –,* Don't talk so much. 3 busy, occupied. *Sedang –,* The line's busy. 4 opinion. *Apa –mu ttg keadaan itu?* What's your opinion about that situation? **ber–** 1 to speak. *Ia ~ bahasa Inggeris,* He speaks English. 2 to talk. *Ia ~ dgn ajahnja,* He's talking with his father. 3 to discuss. *Ia ~ ttg perbelandjaan negara dgn présidén,* He discussed the government budget with the president. 4 speech. *kemerdékaan ~ freedom* of speech. **mem–kan** to discuss, deliberate over. *Dlm rapat itu meréka ~ pembélaan negeri,* In that meeting they discussed national defense. **pem–** 1 speaker. 2 adviser, spokesman. 3 lawyer. **pem–an** 1 discussion, deliberation. 2 conversation.
bitju² a jack for lifting s.t.
biuku turtle.
bius 1 unconscious, drugged. 2 stupefied. *Ia – tak ingat pula,* He was stupefied and couldn't remember any more. 3 narcotic. **mem–i** 1 to drug, anesthetize. 2 to calm, appease. *Naséhat itu ~ hatinja jg kuatir,* That advice calmed down his anxiety. **mem–kan** 1 to drug, anesthetize. 2 to calm down, appease s.o. **pem–an** anesthetization.
B.L. *[Barat Laut]* northwest.
blandong lumberjack, woodcutter.
blangkon male Javanese batik headdress.
blanko 1 blank. *Kertasnja –,* The sheet is blank. 2 form to be filled in. 3 abstention in voting. *– wésél* postal money order blank.
blatju see BELATJU.
Bld. *[Belanda]* 1 Dutch. 2 Holland.
blék tin(can).

blesek crammed, chockful. **ke–** crammed, chockful. **mem–i** to cram, jam with. *Trém penghabisan itu di–i dgn pekerdja²,* The last streetcar was jammed with workers.
bl(n). *[bulan]* month.
blok 1 roll. *satu – tjita* one roll of material. 2 block. *satu – rumah* a block of houses. 3 bloc. 4 street block.
blokir mem– to blockade.
blumkol cauliflower.
blus 1 blouse. 2 see BADJU.
B'masin *[Bandjarmasin]* Bandjermasin.
B.M.K.N. *[Badan Musjarawat Kebudajaan Nasional]* National Cultural Council.
Bn. *[Bataljon]* battalion.
bobok 1 to sleep. 2 fixing, inserting. **mem–** 1 to insert, fix s.t. *Pipa listerik di– ditémbok,* An electric rod was inserted in the wall. 2 to pierce, bore through. **mem–kan** to put to sleep.
bobol ter– crushed, smashed.
bobos wide breach, crack. *Témboknja –,* There's a crack in the wall. **mem–** to pierce, penetrate. *Peluru itu ~ témbok,* The bullet penetrated the wall.
bobot heavy.
bobrok 1 dilapidated, rickety. *Rumahnja –,* His house is dilapidated. 2 rotten, degenerate. *Masjarakatnja –,* The society was degenerate. **ke–an** collapse.
bodo 1 see BODOH. 2 see BADJU.
bodoh 1 stupid, dull. 2 foolish. **ke–an** stupidity. **mem–kan** to cheat s.o. *Djangan ~ orang tua,* Don't cheat an old man. **memper–** 1 to cheat, take s.o. in. 2 to keep in a state of ignorance. *Kadang² pemerintah pendjadjahan mentjoba ~ djadjahannja,* A colonial government sometimes tries to keep its colony in ignorance. *~ diri* to act ignorant. *Ia ~ diri mengenai soal itu,* He acted as if he were ignorant of the matter. *Masa –,* I don't care. *Ia tahu bhw temannja tjelaka, tapi ia masa – sadja,* He knew his friend had had an accident, but he simply didn't care.
bodok a type of leprosy.
bodor clown, comedian.
bogem mentah a blow in the face.
Bogor Buitenzorg.
bohlam 1 electric light bulb. 2 arc lamp.
bohong 1 lie, falsehood. *Ia berkata –,* He tells lies. 2 to lie. *Djangan –,* Don't lie. **ber–** to lie, tell a lie. **ke–an** lie, falsehood. **mem–i** to lie to. *Ia ~*

saja, He lied to me. **mem–kan** 1 to deny s.t. *Ia ~ segala tuduhan² itu,* He denied all the accusations. 2 to consider s.t. as untrue. **pem–** liar. **pem–an** lying.

boikot 1 boycott. 2 see BÉKOT.

bojak 1 tasteless, insipid. *Téh ini –,* This tea is tasteless. 2 boring, tiresome. *Kehidupan ditempat ketjil mémang –,* Life in a small place is certainly boring. **ke–an** boredom, tediousness.

bojong ber– 1 to move. *Ia sdh ~ ketempat jg baru,* He's moved to a new place. 2 to emigrate, settle. **pem–an** emigration, settling. **–an** moving, removal. *Apakah engkau sdh ~ ?* Have you already moved?

bok 1 form of address and reference to an older woman of lower status. 2 see MBOK(MAS).

bokék 1 rejected, unfit. 2 destitute.

bokong 1 buttocks. 2 hind part first, the wrong way round. 3 back. *memikul beban di–* to carry a load on o's back. **mem–** 1 to attack from the rear. 2 secretly, on the sly. *Ia menangis ~ ,* She cried secretly. **pem–an** treacherous attack.

bokor copper or silver bowl with wide rim.

bola 1 ball. 2 globe. *– baskét* basketball. *– bulutangkis* shuttlecock. *– bumi* terrestrial globe. *– kerandjang* basketball. *– lampu* light bulb. *– mata* eyeball. *– sodok* billiards. *– tampél, – ténis* tennis ball. *– ténis médja* ping-pong ball. *– turut bunji* resonator.

bolak-balik 1 to and fro, back and forth. *Bis ini tiap hari pergi kekota Washington –,* This bus goes to Washington and returns every day. *Berapa harga kartjis – ke Syracuse?* How much is the round-trip ticket to Syracuse? 2 frequently. *Ia – pergi kekantor imigrasi,* He frequently goes to the immigration office. 3 contradictory. *Uraiannja –,* His explanation was contradictory. 4 to go up and down. **mem–kan** 1 to turn back and forth. *Ia ~ kertasnja,* He was turning his paper back and forth. 2 to twist. *Ia pandai ~ perkataannja,* He's clever at twisting his words.

boléh 1 to be permitted, may. *Meréka – berumah disini,* They are permitted to live here. 2 to be able, can. 3 likely. **mem–kan** to permit, allow. *~ membatja* to allow to read. **memper–kan** to permit, allow. *Se-kali² tidak diper–kan masuk,* One is not permitted to enter. **se– –²nja** as well as o. can. **–lah** all right. *~ kalau*

begitu, Very well then. *– djadi* possibly, probably. *– djadi ia sdh datang,* Perhaps he's already come. *Tak – djadi,* It's impossible. (It can't be.) *– djuga.* 1 fair, not too bad. *– djuga pekerdjaanmu itu,* Your work isn't too bad. 2 maybe, not impossible. *– djuga ia ikut ajahnja,* It's not unlikely that he went with his father. *tak – tidak* can't avoid, have to. *Ia tak – tidak harus pergi,* He can't avoid going. *Apa – buat kalau uangku sdh habis?* What can I do now that my money's gone? *Mana – ia akan datang sekarang karena kemarin ia masih sakit?* How could he come now when he was still sick yesterday? *Seberapa – pekerdjaan ini harus diselesaikan bésok,* If possible this job must be finished tomorrow.

bolong perforated, pierced. **ber– –²** pierced, perforated. *– melompong* completely empty. *Buah ini – melompong,* This fruit is completely empty. *Ia tiba pd tengah hari –,* He arrived at noon.

bolos 1 penetrated, broken through. *Garis pertahanan –,* The defense line was broken. 2 to desert, go A.W.O.L. 3 to play hooky. 4 to escape from captivity. **mem–** to cut class, play truant. **pem–** a truant, deserter.

bolot mem– to wrap s.t. up together.

bolsak a mattress.

bolu k.o. sponge cake.

bom 1 bomb. 2 boom at customs barrier. **mem–i** to bomb s.t. *Musuh ~ kota,* The enemy bombed the city. **menge–** to bomb. **pem–an, penge–an** bombing. **penge–** bomber, bomb thrower. *– atom* atom bomb. *– (pem)bakar* incendiary bomb. *– kambang* sea mine. *– laut* depth charge. *– waktu* time bomb.

bombardir mem– 1 to bombard, shell s.t. 2 to appoint. *Ia ~ adiknja mendjadi menteri pertahanan,* He appointed his younger brother to be defense minister. 3 to bombard, shower. *Ia ~ kawannja dgn pertanjaan,* He bombarded his friend with questions.

bon 1 ration coupon. 2 voucher for payment. 3 bond. 4 check, bill. *Kasi –,* Give me the check. 5 account(s). **menge–** to buy s.t. on a charge account. *Ia selalu ~ ,* He always charges it. *–² candy. – utang* charge slip.

bonda see BUNDA.

bondjol 1 lump. 2 projection. 3 to protrude.

bondong group, throng, crowd. **ber– –²** in throngs, droves.

bonéka 1 doll. 2 puppet. **mem(per)-kan** to use as a puppet. *Negara itu ~ pemerintah,* That country used the government as a puppet.
bongak 1 stupid. 2 proud, arrogant.
bonggol 1 lump, hump. 2 outgrowth. 3 knot in a tree.
bongkah lump, nugget, hunk. *se-mas* a gold nugget.
bongkak 1 proud. 2 insolent, arrogant.
bongkar **ke-an** to be broken into, burglarized. *Semalam rumahnja ~ ,* His house was burglarized last night. **mem-** 1 to force open. *Ia ~ pintu,* He forced the door open. 2 to break in. *Meréka mentjuri barang itu dgn ~ ,* They stole it by breaking in. 3 to demolish. *~ rumah* to demolish a house. 4 to disclose, expose. *Ia ~ rahasia,* She disclosed the secret. 5 to unload, discharge. *Orang² buruh ~ kapal,* The workers unloaded the ship. 6 to open up a crate, large box. 7 to unpack trunks, suitcases, etc. 8 to dig up. *~ tanah* to dig up the ground. *~ hal² jg sdh dilupakan orang* to dig up long-forgotten matters. 9 to take apart (a bicycle, etc.). **mem- -bangkir** to spread, scatter s.t. **pem-** demolisher. *~ kapal* stevedore. **pem-an** 1 demolished goods. 2 discharged goods. **ter-** uncovered, disclosed, bared. *Komplotan itu ~ ,* The plot was bared. **- -bangkir** scattered, spread about.
bongkok see BUNGKUK.
bongkong stupid.
bongkot 1 tree stump. 2 cabbage stalk.
bongsang fruit basket.
bonjok soft consistency as of overripe fruit.
bonjor overripe (of fruit).
bontak chubby, bulging. *Pipinja -,* His cheeks are chubby.
bontjéng **mem-** 1 to get a lift, a ride. *Boléhkah saja ~ pulang?* May I get a lift home? 2 to sponge on s.o. *Ia selalu ~ kpd ajahnja,* He's always sponging on his father. **pem-** sponger. **-an** 1 to ride tandem. *Dua saudara itu tiap hari ~ kesekolah,* Every day the two brothers ride a tandem bike to school. 2 carrier on a bicycle.
bopéng pock-marked.
bopét buffet, counter, side table.
bopo(k) damaged, worn out, in bad shape.
bopong **mem-** to carry in the arms. *~ anak* to carry a child in o's arms.
bor drill. **mem-(kan)** to drill, bore. **pem-an, penge-an** drilling, boring. *- listrik* electric drill.

borak 1 Mohammed's horse; a winged horse with human head which carried Mohammed to heaven. 2 borax.
bordél **mem-** to embroider. **-an** embroidery.
bordjuis bourgeois.
boréh yellow-colored perfumed mixture of powder and a fluid used as ointment or liniment.
borék see BURIK.
borgol handcuffs, manacles. **mem-** to handcuff.
borhan proof.
boroh security, guaranty. **mem-i** to provide security, guarantee a loan.
borok 1 ulcer, boil. 2 bad, rotten. *Ia - hatinja,* He's very bad. **mem-** to fester.
borong whole, entire, all together. **mem-** 1 to buy wholesale. *Ia ~ barang² itu,* He bought the whole stock. 2 to do an entire job. *Perusahaan itu ~ segala pembangunan,* The firm contracted to do the entire construction job. **mem-kan** 1 to sell wholesale. *Ia ~ barang²nja kpd pembeli,* He sold the goods wholesale to the buyer. 2 to give the entire contract. *Ia ~ pembangunan rumahnja kpd pem- itu,* He gave the entire contract for the construction of his house to the contractor. **pem-** 1 contractor. 2 supplier. **pem-an** 1 letting out of a contract. 2 wholesale buying or selling. 3 chartering. **-an** 1 wholesale. 2 taking over s.t. completely. *~ pekerdjaan* contracting to do the entire job.
boros 1 to get loose. *Kudanja -,* The horse got loose. 2 wasteful, extravagant. *Ia sangat - tak bisa menjimpan uang,* He was very wasteful and couldn't save money. **ke-an** waste. **mem-kan** to waste, squander. *Ia ~ uang pemerintah,* He was wasting the government's money. **pem-** squanderer. **pem-an** waste.
bortél carrot.
bortol carrot.
bos bunch, bundle. *satu - kaju bakar* one bundle of firewood.
bosan bored, fed up. *Ia - mendengar perkataan itu,* He was fed up with those words. *Ia - makan,* He's bored with eating. **ke-an** boredom, weariness, satiation. **mem-kan** 1 to bore. *Mukanja ~ saja,* His face bores me. 2 boring.
bosen see BOSAN.
bosman boatswain.
bosor pierced.
botak bald-headed.
botjah young boy.

botjor 1 leak. *Ia menambal* –, He plugged the leak. 2 to leak. *Atapnja* –, The roof leaks. *Rahasianja* –, The secret leaked out. 3 to urinate frequently. 4 leak (in a tire or tube). **ke–an** 1 leaked through. *Kamarnja basah karena* ∼ , The room is wet from leaking. 2 leaked out. ∼ *rahasia itu merugikan pemerintah*, The leaking out of the secret hurt the government. **mem–kan** to puncture, cause a leak. **-an** 1 leak. 2 leakage. *air* ∼ leaking water. – *mulut* garrulous, talkative.

botok a dish made of coconut and fish wrapped in a banana leaf and steamed.

botol bottle.

BP [1 *Balai Pustaka*. 2 *Badan Pusat*] 1 government publishing house. 2 central board.

BPN [*Biro Perantjang Nasional*] National Planning Board.

BPS [*Biro Pusat Statistik*] Central Bureau of Statistics.

BPU [*Badan Pimpinan Umum*] General Management Board.

br– see BER–.

brambang shallot.

brankar stretcher, litter.

brankas a safe.

brantam = BERHANTAM. see HANTAM.

brantas see BERANTAS.

Brasilia Brazil.

brédél bridle, curb. **mem–** 1 to check, curb. 2 to muzzle (press, etc.).

breidél see BRÉDÉL.

brétel suspenders.

brigadir djénderal brigadier general.

brigdjén [*brigadir djénderal*] brigadier general.

Brigmob see MOBRIG.

brompit motor bike.

bros crisp, brittle.

brosur brochure. **mem–kan** to put into the form of a brochure.

Brt [*Barat*] West.

Brunai see BERUNAI.

bt. [*binti*] daughter of.

bto. [*bruto*] gross.

bu 1 form of address to a mother or other older woman (abbrev. of *ibu*), used in addressing women teachers, etc. 2 maid servant (abbrev. of *babu*).

buah 1 fruit. 2 result. *Usahanja tak ada –nja*, His efforts are fruitless. – *perundingan* result of the discussions. 3 used with nonhuman objects. *se-rumah* one house. *dua – rumah* two houses. *tiga – negeri* three countries. **ber–** 1 to bear fruit. *Pohon ini* ∼ , This tree bore fruit. 2 to bear fruit, be successful. *Usahanja* ∼ , His

efforts have borne fruit. **mem–i** to impregnate. *Lebah* ∼ *bunga jg mekar*, The bee impregnated the blossom. **mem–kan** to produce, result in, yield. *Beladjar* ∼ *kepandaian*, Study produces ability. **menje–kan** to make one, make a whole. **pem–an** 1 impregnation, insemination. 2 fertilization. **-²an** 1 fruit, all k.o. fruit. 2 imitation fruit. ∼ *tjampur* 1 fruit cocktail. 2 mixed fruits. – *anggur* grape. – *ara* fig. – *badam* almond. – *badju* button. – *betis* calf of the leg. – *bibir* subject of conversation. – *dada* female breast, bust, bosom. – *dam* draftsman. – *datjin(g)* weights. – *geli (geli)* kidneys. – *hati* 1 heart. 2 sweetheart. – *kalam* essay, composition. – *karya* literary work. – *kerindjal* kidney. – *keringat* the result of o's efforts. – *kérsen* cherry. – *kotak* capsule. – *lengan* biceps. – *mimpi* a dream. – *mentéga* avocado. – *mulut* subject of conversation. – *pala* nutmeg. – *peladjaran* 1 subject of study. 2 result of study. – *pelir* testicle. – *pembitjaraan* subject, topic of conversation. – *péna* essay, composition. – *pikiran* idea, thought. – *pinggang*, – *punggung* kidneys. – *sawo* sawo (fruit roughly similar to a peach). – *tangan* 1 a gift brought back from a trip or presented when visiting s.o. 2 literary work, creation. – *tasbih* prayer bead. – *timbangan* weights. – *tjatur* chessman. – *tutur* topic of conversation. – *undi* dice.

buai **ber–** -² to swing. *Anak itu* ∼ *diudara*, The child was swinging in the air. **mem–** to swing. **mem–kan** to swing, rock. *Ia* ∼ *anaknja*, He rocked his child in his arms **-an** 1 cradle, swing. 2 pendulum.

buaja 1 crocodile. 2 villain, scoundrel. 3 impostor. **mem–** 1 to creep, crawl. 2 to cheat, deceive. *Ia hidupnja* ∼ , He makes his living by dishonest means. **mem–i** 1 to cheat, deceive. *Ia* ∼ *madjikannja*, He deceived his employer. 2 to scare, bully s.o. – *darat* rascal, a Don Juan. – *pasar* pickpocket.

bual 1 bubbling. – *sumber* bubbling of the well. 2 boasting, big talk. *Saja bentji mendengar – orang itu*, I'm tired of hearing that man boast. **ber–(–)** 1 to bubble up, to fizz, foam. 2 to boast, talk big. *Ia* ∼ *kpd teman²nja*, He boasted to his friends. **mem–** 1 to bubble up. 2 to boast. **mem–kan** 1 to spout, expel. *Sumber itu* ∼ *air panas*, The well spouted forth hot water. 2 to give forth, spout. *Ia* ∼ *tjeritera jg tidak²*, He spouted forth nonsense. 3 to brag, boast. 4 to exaggerate. **pem–** braggart. – *basung* nonsense.

buana earth, universe.

buang mem– 1 to throw, cast. *Ia ~ bola kpd saja,* He threw the ball to me. 2 to throw away. *Ia ~ pakaian jg tlh sobék,* He threw away his torn clothes. 3 to exile. *Pemerintah ~ orang hukuman,* The government exiled the convicts. *~ adat* to be ill-mannered. *Kalau ada orang tua djangan ~ adat,* If parents are present, don't be ill-mannered. *~ air* to discharge, relieve o.s. *Ia ~ air disungai,* He relieved himself in the river. *~ air besar* to defecate. *~ air ketjil* to urinate. *~ aksi* to pose. *~ angin* to pass gas, flatulate. *~ arang muka* to remove shame. *~ belakang* to flee, escape. *~ bini* to divorce s.o. *~ diri* 1 to commit suicide. 2 to isolate o.s., go into seclusion. *~ langkah* 1 to flee, escape. 2 to execute steps in fencing, *silat,* etc. *~ lelah, ~ letih* to take a break, a rest. *~ malu* 1 to take revenge. 2 to circumcise. *~ mata* to look at, glance around. *~ muka* 1 to avert o's eyes. *Ia ~ muka melihat temannja jg miskin itu,* He turned away upon seeing his impoverished friend. 2 to dislike. *~ mulut* to talk unclearly, vaguely. *~ nama* to disgrace o's name. *~ njawa* 1 to die. 2 to risk o's life, be reckless. *~ pandang* to glance, look at. *~ peluru* to put the shot (track and field event). *~ pukulan* to parry a blow. *~ sikap* 1 to remove, get rid of, an attitude. *Ia ~ sikap jg tjongkak itu,* He's got rid of his boasting attitude. 2 to act (walk, talk, etc.) in an affected manner. *~ sipat* to do s.o. bodily harm. *~ témpo* to waste time. *~ undi* 1 to shoot dice. 2 to draw lots. *~ waktu* 1 to waste time. 2 to give up time for or to. *Kami girang bhw tuan suka ~ waktu utk urusan kami ini,* We are delighted that you are willing to give up time for our affair. **mem–kan** 1 to throw. 2 to exile, banish. **mem–** –² to waste. *Djanganlah ~ waktunja,* Don't waste your time. *~ mata* to look s.t. over carefully. **pem–an** exile. **ter–** expelled. **–an** 1 cast off, discarded. *Pakaian ini ~ dari tentara,* These clothes were discarded by the army. 2 exile, o. sent into exile. *Banjak ~ ditempatkan di Boven Digul,* Many exiles were placed at Boven Digul. 3 exile. *Dimana tempat ~ ?* Where was the place of exile? –² *air* diarrhea.

buani universal.

buar extravagant, wasteful. **pem–** spendthrift, lavish spender.

buas 1 wild. *Apa binatang itu –?* Is that animal wild? 2 cruel. *Itu perbuatan jg –,* That's a cruel deed. **ke–an** cruelty, ferocity. **mem–** to be or become wild.

buat 1 for – *apa? – saja,* What for? For me. 2 in order to. **ber–** 1 to do, carry out. *Ia tak ~ apa²,* He doesn't do anything. *Ia jg ~ ,* He's the perpetrator. 2 to make, build. *Ia ~ rumah,* He's building a house. *~ djahat* to do wrong. *~ olah* to be tricky. **di–(–)nja** feigned, pretended. *Kesusahan itu ~ sadja,* That sadness was merely feigned. **mem–** 1 to make. *Kami ~ salah,* We made a mistake. 2 to do. *Akan ~ apa kalau sdh begini?* What are we going to do if it's like this? 3 to make, cause. *Ia ~ anaknja takut,* He frightened his son. *~ gawé* to cause trouble. *~ muka* to be kind. *~ negeri* to found a colony. **memper–** 1 to make, build. 2 to do. **pem–** 1 maker, producer. 2 framer (of constitution, etc.). **pem–an** 1 production. 2 manufacture. **per–an** 1 action, deed. 2 performance. 3 conduct, behavior. *~ melanggar hukum* torts. **–an** 1 make, brand. *~ luar negeri* foreign made. *~ mana djam itu?* What's the clock's make? 2 product. *~nja baik,* His product is good. 3 artificial. *gigi ~* false teeth. *pupuk ~* commercial fertilizer. 4 pretense. *Itu hanja ~ sadja,* It was just pretense. 5 deed. *Apa ~nja dia satu hari dirumah?* What was he doing at the house the whole day?

bubar 1 dispersed, spread, scattered. *Tiga empat orang – karena kedatangan tentara,* Three or four people dispersed upon arrival of the army. 2 ended, finished, broken up. *Rapat itu – djam 7,* The meeting broke up at 7. 3 to resign. *Kabinét –,* The cabinet resigned. **mem–kan** 1 to disperse, break up. *Polisi ~ orang² jg berkumpul dimuka kantor itu,* The police broke up the group in front of the office. 2 to discharge, dissolve. *Meréka ~ perusahaannja,* They dissolved their firm. **pem–an** 1 dissolution (of a firm, association, cabinet, etc.). 2 resignation (of cabinet, etc.). 3 disbandment, abolition. *~ tentara sukaréla* disbandment of the volunteer corps. 4 abrogation (of a treaty or agreement). –! Dismissed!

bubu basket trap for fish.

bubuh mem–(i) to put, place s.t.

Ia ∼ *gambar pd dinding,* He hung a picture on the wall. *Ia* ∼ *tanda tangan pd surat itu,* He affixed his signature to the letter. *Ia* ∼ *pendjelasan pd uraian itu,* He provided clarification for the explanation. **mem-kan** to add. *Ia* ∼ *titik pd kalimat itu,* He added a period to the sentence. **pem-an** placing. ∼ *tanda lalu lintas* placing of traffic signs. **-an** 1 addition. 2 affix.

bubuk 1 powder. 2 woodworm. **mem-** 1 to pulverize, become dust. *Kapur itu* ∼ *karena kehudjanan,* The lime turned into dust from exposure to the rain. 2 to grind. *Ibu* ∼ *kopi,* Mother grinds coffee. – *beras* 1 rice powder. 2 rice bug. – *besi* iron dust. – *kopi* coffee powder. – *sabun* soap powder.

bubul ulcer on feet of humans or animals. **mem-** 1 to repair. *Ia* ∼ *djala,* He repaired a net. 2 to blaze. *Apinja* ∼ *keatas,* The fire blazed upward. 3 to swarm up. *Burung²* ∼ , The birds swarmed upward. 4 to heave (of the ground, earth).

bubun² fontanel.

bubung 1 ridge, top. 2 ridgepole. **mem-** to rise, go upward. *Pesawat terbang* ∼ , The plane rose. *Harga kopi* ∼ , The price of coffee rose. **mem-kan** to raise considerably, increase. *Ia* ∼ *harga,* He raised the price considerably. **memper-kan** to raise. **-an** ridge, top. ∼ *rumah* the roof top of the house.

bubur porridge. *Nasi sdh djadi -,* There's no use crying over spilt milk. **mem-** 1 to become porridge. 2 to make porridge. *Ibu* ∼ *ketan,* Mother made sticky rice porridge. – *katjang idjo* small green-pea porridge. – *kaju* wood pulp. – *ketan* sticky rice porridge.

bubus **mem-** to swarm out. *Semut* ∼ *dari lobang,* Ants swarmed out of the hole.

bubut **mem-** 1 to operate a lathe. 2 to pull out. *Ia* ∼ *rumput,* He pulled out the grass. **pem-** 1 lathe worker. 2 lathe. **pem-an** lathe work. **-an** stay of a sailing vessel.

Buda Buddha.

budaja 1 cultural. *antropologi* – cultural anthropology. 2 cultural, civilized, cultured. *Ia mempunjai djiwa jg -,* He has a cultured mind. **ke-an** culture, civilization. *Kementerian Pengadjaran, Pendidikan dan* ∼ Ministry of Education and Culture.

budajawan a person of culture.

budak 1 lad, lass. *Ia* ∼ *nakal,* He's a naughty boy. 2 servant. 3 slave.

ber- **-²an** childish. *Ia tingkah lakunja masih* ∼ , His actions are still those of a child. **ke-** **-²an** childish. **mem-** 1 to become a slave. 2 to enslave. **memper-** 1 to treat as a slave. *Radja itu* ∼ *rakjatnja,* The king treated his subjects as slaves. 2 to enslave. **per-an** slavery, servitude. – *belian* bought slave. – *djogét* dancing girl. – *gembala* herdsman, shepherd. – *pelari* a boy who is playing hooky.

budek anonymous. *surat* – an anonymous letter.

Budhis Buddhist.

budi 1 mind, insight. 2 levelheadedness. 3 character. *Ia baik -,* He's of good character. 4 trick, cunning. *Ia mentjari -,* He looked for a trick (which would help him). *Ia ketahuan -,* His evil intentions were known. **ber-** 1 wise, reasonable, rational. 2 of good character, honest. 3 well-behaved, nice. **memper-kan** to fool, deceive s.o. **se-** *akal* 1 by all possible means. 2 to the utmost. *Ia mengerdjakan tugasnja* ∼ *akal, tapi tak hasil djuga,* He carried out his task to the utmost, yet failed. – *bahasa* good manners, nice behavior. – *bitjara* common sense, intelligence. – *manusia* human intelligence. – *pekerti* character.

budiman wise, prudent, sensible.

budjal protruding, bulging.

budjang 1 single, unmarried. 2 bachelor. 3 servant. 4 widow(er). **mem-** 1 to be single. *Ia masih* ∼ , He's still single. 2 to work as a servant. *Ia* ∼ *pd keluarga,* He works as a servant for a family. **-an** bachelor. **pem-an** celibacy. – *bertjerai* divorcee. – *mati lakinja* widow. – *talang* childless widow(er).

budjangga 1 poet, man of letters, writer. 2 scholar. 3 hermit. 4 disciple. 5 see PUDJANGGA. **ke-an** literary, poetic. *dunia* ∼ the literary world.

budjuk 1 flattery, smooth words. – *dan tipunja tak berhasil,* His intrigues and flattery were of no avail. 2 coaxing, cajoling, 3 deceit. **mem-** 1 to flatter. 2 to persuade, coax, induce. 3 to deceive, cheat. **pem-** 1 deceiver. 2 flatterer. **-an** flattery. – *-raju* gentle persuasion, coaxing.

budjur 1 length. 2 lengthwise. 3 straight. 4 stroke of luck, a fluke. **mem-** to stretch out, lie alongside. *Ia tidur* ∼ *ditanah,* He slept stretched out on the ground. *Pohon jg djatuh itu* ∼ *rumah,* The fallen tree lay alongside the house. **mem-kan** to lay s.t. alongside. – *barat* west longitude. - *sangkar* 1 rectangle. 2 rectangular, quadrilateral. - *sirih*, - *telur* oval-shaped. - *timur* east longitude.

budu a k.o. salted fish.

buduk covered with sores and repulsive in appearance.

bugil naked, bare. **ke-an** nakedness.

Bugis Buginese (South Celebes).

buhul knot of rope or string. **mem-(kan)** to tie, make a knot.

bui 1 prison. 2 shackles. **mem-** to imprison.

buih foam. **ber-** to foam. *Mulutnja* ∼ , He foamed at the mouth. **mem-** to foam, froth.

Buitenzorg Bogor (city in west Java).

bujar 1 to run (like ink on blotting paper), spread. 2 scattered, dispersed. *awan* - scattered clouds.

bujung 1 narrow-necked, big-bellied earthenware jug. 2 boy, youth.

bujut 1 great-grandfather. 2 great-grandmother. 3 sacred place. 4 old, ancient. **(ke)-an** doddering (of old people). *Orang itu sdh* ∼ *kok masih naik sepéda*, That man is doddering, yet he still rides a bicycle.

buka 1 to open. *Toko ini - djam 7*, This shop opens at 7. 2 width. - *djalan* the width of the road. 3 breaking of the fast. *Djam berapa - hari ini?* What time is the fast over today? *Ibu memasak -*, Mother is cooking for the breaking of the fast. **ber-** to break the fast. ∼ *puasa* to break the fast. **mem-** 1 to open. *Ia* ∼ *pintu*, He opened the door. *Ketua itu* ∼ *rapat*, The chairman opened the meeting. *Ajahnja* ∼ *toko*, His father opened a shop. 2 to launch, open. *Musuhnja* ∼ *serangan*, The enemy launched an attack. 3 to clear. *Petani* ∼ *tanah*, The farmer cleared the land. 4 to remove, take off. *Ia* ∼ *katja matanja*, He removed his glasses. *Ia* ∼ *sepatu*, He took off his shoes. 5 to unveil. ∼ *patung* to unveil a statue. 6 to disclose, expose. *Ia* ∼ *rahasia*, She disclosed a secret. 7 to begin, start. *Isterinja* ∼ *bitjara*, His wife began to speak. *Ia* ∼ *kata*, He began to talk. 8 to unfurl sails. 9 to unfasten a rope, safety pin, etc. 10 to pioneer. *Ia* ∼ *djalan*, He paved the way. 11 to found. *Ia* ∼ *negeri*, He founded a colony. ∼ *mulut* to talk. ∼ *nudjum* to consult the stars. ∼ *puasa* to break the fast. **mem-** -² to leaf through. ∼ *madjalah* to leaf through a magazine. **mem-i** 1 to open to. *Ia tidak di-i pintu*, The door wasn't opened to

him. 2 to open s.t. for s.o. *Ia* ∼ *kopernja utk pegawai douane*, He opened his suitcase for the customs official. **mem-kan** 1 to open s.t. (especially the eyes). 2 to open s.t. for s.o. ∼ *perasaan* to bare, disclose o's feelings. **pem-** *akal* broadener of the mind. *Hitungan adalah* ∼ *akal*, Arithmetic is a broadener of the mind. ∼ *kata* preface, introduction. **pem-an** 1 opening, preface. *Nama lagu* ∼ *apa?* What's the name of the theme song? *Banjak terima kasih atas kata* ∼ , Many thanks for the words of introduction. 2 preamble. **ter-** 1 open. *Pintunja* ∼ , The door's open. *dgn tangan* ∼ open-handed. 2 public, open. *rapat* ∼ public meeting. *tak* ∼ can't be opened. **-an** *botol* bottle opener, corkscrew. ∼ *kaléng* can opener.

bukan 1 not, no. *Dia - orang Inggeris, dia orang Amérika*, He's not an Englishman, he's an American. 2 isn't it? aren't you? etc. *Ini bukumu, -?* This is your book, isn't it? **mem-kan** to deny. *Ia* ∼ *kakaknja sebagai radja jg sjah*, He denied that his older brother was the legitimate king. **-kah** isn't it? ∼ *orang jg pakai topi itu pamanmu?* Isn't the man with the hat your uncle? **-nja** not. *Ia* ∼ *malas melainkan bodoh*, He isn't lazy, but stupid. **-tah** isn't it? **-²** 1 nonsense. 2 impossibility. *Ia mengharapkan hal jg* ∼ *buatan*, He expected the impossible. 3 improper. 4 very. *Ramainja* ∼ *buatan*, It was very crowded. - *barang tentu*, It's not likely. - *buatan* very, extraordinary. *Beratnja - buatan*, The weight was tremendous. - *karena* it's not that... - *kepalang* very, extraordinary. - *main* extraordinary. - *pd tempatnja* improper, not fitting. - *pd tempatnja kalau tidak mengundang dia pd perajaan itu*, It won't be proper if we don't invite him to the celebration. - *sadja...tetapi djuga* not only...but also. - *tidak* not true. *Ia - tidak mau akan tetapi ia berhalangan*, It's not that he doesn't want to but that he simply can't. -...- neither...nor. - *Amat dan - Dul jg berani memikul tanggung djawab, akan tetapi si Slamat jg menerimanja*, Neither Amat nor Dul dared assume the responsibility; it was Slamat who did.

bukat dirty, muddy. - *likat* thick mud.

bukit 1 hill. 2 mountain. **ber-** -² hilly, mountainous. **mem-** 1 to pile up. *Buah kelapanja* ∼ , The coconuts

piled up. 2 to form a hill. *Pasirnja*
~ , The sand formed a mound. 3 to
climb a hill. *Sdh 3 djam kami* ~ , *blm
sampai djuga*, We've been climbing
for 3 hours and haven't got there
yet. **mem- --²** hilly. - *bukau* wilderness.

bukti proof, evidence. **ber-** to have
proof. **mem-kan** to prove s.t. - *saksi*
1 evidence. 2 testimony. - *njatadiri*
identification card.

buku 1 book. 2 knuckle, joint. 3
knot. 4 grain of salt, sand, etc.,
pellet. *garam dua* - two lumps of
salt. *tanah se-* one lump, clod of
earth. 5 gist, substance. *Apa --nja
tjeritera itu?* What's the gist of that
story? **ber-** 1 to have joints, jointed.
2 to clot. *Darahnja* ~ , His blood
clotted. **mem- --²** 1 to clot. 2 to
well up. *Ia merasa hatinja* ~ , He
felt his anger welling up inside him.
mem-kan 1 to enter in a book.
2 to put into book form. **mem-
hitamkan** to black-list s.o. **pem-an**
1 entry. 2 bookkeeping. ~ *muatan*
cargo booking. **per-an** foundation,
cornerstone. - *atjara* program. -
batjaan reader, reading book. -
benang bobbin. - *djari* knuckle. *Ia
mengadu - djari*, He boxes. - *gerédja*
prayer book. - *harian* 1 diary. 2
journal. - *hitam* blacklist. - *hukum
siksa* penal code. - *kaki*, - *lali* ankle.
- *kas* ledger. - *kenang²an* commemorative volume. - *léhér* cervical vertebra. - *nilai* teacher's grade book.
- *pegangan* 1 handbook. 2 guidebook.
- *peringatan* 1 memorial volume. 2
diary, notebook. - *peta* atlas. -
petundjuk télpon telephone directory.
- *plontjo* school annual, students'
yearbook. - *Putih* White Paper (of
government). - *sabun* cake of soap.
- *sebaran* pamphlet. - *simpanan*
bank savings book. - *tahunan* an
annual. - *tela'ah* exegesis. - *tjatatan*,
- *tulis* notebook.

bukung 1 tailless. *andjing* - a tailless
dog. 2 woman's short hairdo.

bulai albino.

bulak-balik 1 frequently. 2 to and
fro. see BOLAK-BALIK.

bulan 1 month. 2 moon. **ber-** for a
month. *Ia tinggal* ~ *disana*, He
stayed there for a month. **ber- --²**
for several months. **-an** monthly.
madjallah ~ a monthly. **-²an** target.
- *kesiangan* pallid moon in daylight.
- *madu* honeymoon. - *Maret* March.
- *mati* new moon. - *perbani* crescent.
- *purnama* full moon. - *sabit* crescent.
- *susut* waning moon. - *tiga persegi*

12th day of the month. - *timbul*
crescent, waxing moon, new moon.

bulang 1 wrapper, headdress. 2 tape,
ribbon, etc., for fastening spur to
cock's foot in cockfighting. **ber-** 1 to
wear a headdress, turban. 2 to wind,
wrap. *Ia* ~ *kain putih pd pinggangnja*,
He wrapped a white cloth around
his waist. 3 to wear a spur. **mem-**
1 to wear, wrap around. 2 to tie
on. - *baling* 1 propeller, whirligig. 2
small mill. - *hulu* headdress, turban.

bular cataract of the eye.

bulat 1 circle. 2 ball. 3 spherical,
round. 4 circular. 5 complete. 6
unanimous. *pendapat* - unanimous
opinion. 7 over-all. *rentjana* - over-
all plan. **ber-an** concentric. **ke-an**
1 roundness. ~ *bumi* roundness of
the earth. 2 unanimity. 3 completeness. ~ *fikiran* decision. ~ *hati*
frankness, sincerity. ~ *suara* unanimity. **mem-** 1 to become round.
2 to become unanimous. **mem-i** to
adopt in full. **mem-kan** 1 to complete s.t. 2 to round s.t. off. *Ia* ~
bilangan, He rounded off the figures.
~ *hati* 1 to concentrate. *Ia* ~ *hati
dlm peladjarannja*, He concentrated
on his studies. 2 to make a decision.
Ia ~ *hati utk mengalahkan musuhnja*,
He made a firm decision to defeat his
opponent. ~ *ingatan* to concentrate.
~ *mufakat* to arrive at an agreement.
~ *pikiran* to concentrate. ~ *suara*
to come to an agreement. ~ *tindju*
to clench o's fist. **pem-an** 1 rounding off. 2 integration. ~ *bilangan*
the rounding off of figures. ~ *fikiran*
decision. ~ *suara* agreement. **-an**
circle. - *budjur* oval. - *buluh* cylindrical. - *bumi* globe, earth. - *hati* 1
resolute, determined. 2 frankness, sincerity. - *kata* 1 agreement. 2 resolution. 3 conclusion. - *lipir* round and
flat. - *mata* eyeball. - *pandjang*
elliptical. - *pipih* round and flat. -
tekadnja definite decision. - *telor*
oval-shaped. - *tjekung* concave. -
tjembung convex. - *torak* 1 cylinder.
2 cylindrical. *dgn suara* - unanimously. *Saja mengutjapkan selamat
kepadamu dgn se- --² hati!* Heartiest
congratulations!

bulbul nightingale.

Buléléng the port of Singaradja,
Bali.

buli² small jug.

bulir 1 ear of corn. 2 sheaf of paddy,
etc.

bulu 1 body hair. 2 feathers, plum-
age, down. 3 wool. **ber-** hairy,
feathery. ~ *mata melihat* to hate to

look. **mem–i** 1 to pluck feathers. 2 to
dress. *Ibu* ∼ *ajam,* Mother dressed
a chicken. –² plume. – *ajam* 1 chicken
feathers. 2 feather duster. – *babi*
hog bristles. – *balik* feathers of fowl
turned wrong way. – *dahi* 1 horse's
mane. 2 hair on brow. – *domba*
wool. – *kalong* down. – *kambing* wool.
– *kapas* soft, fluffy feathers. – *katja*
glass wool. – *kempa* felt. – *kening*
eyebrows. – *ketiak* underarm hair. –
lebat shaggy. – *mata* eyelash. –
ramang, – *roma* body hair. – *suak*
hair at nape of neck. – *tampél,* –
tangkis badminton. – *tengkuk* mane.
buluh bamboo (generic name). **pem–**
tube, duct, conduit. ∼ *darah* blood
vessel. ∼ *kentjing* urinary passage.
∼ *kerongkongan* larynx, esophagus.
∼ *makanan* alimentary canal. ∼
mekar varicose veins. ∼ *nadi* artery.
∼ *napas* respiratory tract. –² tube,
pipe, hose. – *perindu* 1 sound produced by blowing. 2 aeolian harp. –
sasak bamboo wattle for fences. –
sumpit(an), – *temiang* blowpipe.
bulukan moldy, mildewed.
bulur overpowering hunger. **ke–(an)**
overpowered by hunger.
bulus 1 smooth, bald, bare. *Kepa-*
lanja –, His head is bald. 2 to pierce,
penetrate. 3 to be struck by a blow,
e.g., in boxing.
bulutangkis see BULU.
bumban wreath, garland.
bumbu mixture of spices for use in
foods. **mem–i** to spice, flavor, season.
Ia ∼ *pidatonja dgn lelutjon,* He
spiced his speech with jokes. *Ia* ∼
daging utk gulai, He spiced the meat
for the stew. –² seasoning.
bumbun 1 shady, shadowy. 2 shelter. 3 heap, pile. – *beras* a pile of
rice. 4 heaping up. *Piringnja – dgn*
nasi, Rice was piled high on his
plate. **mem–** 1 to pile up, store. *Ia*
∼ *bahan makanan utk musim dingin,*
He stored up food supplies for winter.
2 a heaping. *satu séndok kopi* ∼ a
heaping spoonful of coffee.
bumbung 1 bamboo cylinder intact
at one end; used as a container. 2
tubing. – *pengembun* tubing for condensation. **–an** ridge of a roof.
bumel local (train).
bumi earth, land. **mem– -anguskan**
to carry out a scorched earth policy,
reduce to rubble. **menge–kan** to
bury, inter. – *angus* scorched earth.
bagai – dgn langit as different as
day and night.
bumiputera a native.

bunda mother (respectful).
bundar round, globular. *Mukanja –,*
His face is round. *Médja Bundar*
The round table. **mem–** 1 to form
a circle. 2 to circle. **mem–kan** to
make s.t. round. **–an** 1 circle. 2
hoop. – *telur* oval.
bundjai edge, fringe.
bundung liver rot in cattle.
bung 1 you (popular and familiar
form of address among men). *Ajo*
pulang, –! Let's go home, fellow!
2 brother. – *Karno* President Soekarno (form of reference to popular
and highly respected individuals).
3 comrade. 4 used also as form of
address to waiters, peddlers, salesmen, pedicab drivers, etc., when name
is not known.
bunga 1 flower. 2 flower, heart.
Pemuda – bangsa, Youth are the
flower of the nation. 3 blossom. 4
floral design. 5 interest (in money).
6 tire tread. **ber–** 1 to be in bloom,
flower. *Pohonnja* ∼ , The tree is in
bloom. 2 to bear interest. *Uangnja*
∼ , His money is bearing interest.
3 to succeed. *Andjurannja* ∼ , His
suggestion is succeeding. **ber– –²** to
dress o.s. up. **mem–** to flower. **mem–**
–²i to strew, decorate with flowers.
2 to lay a wreath. **memper–kan** to
invest, lend at interest. **pem–an** 1
flowering, blossoming. 2 investing.
–²an 1 flowers. 2 artificial flowers.
3 floral decoration. – *api* 1 fireworks.
2 spark. – *badan* reddish skin (skin
disease). – *bakung* lily. – *barah* a
rash of small white spots often
initial symptom of yaws, leprosy, etc.
– *bibir* flattery, sweet words. – *désa*
village belle. – *karang* coral sponge.
– *katjapiring* gardenia. – *kuku* cuticle.
– *kundai* flower in a hair bun. – *kusta*
leprosy markings. – *latar* prostitute.
– *mawar* rose. – *matahari* sunflower.
– *melati,* – *melur* jasmine. – *modal*
capital interest. – *pala* mace. – *puru*
white spots on skin. – *raja* 1 hibiscus.
2 prostitute. – *rampai* 1 anthology.
2 bunch, bouquet of flowers. – *sanggul*
hair ornament. – *sedap malam* tuberose. – *serunai* bell-mouthed chrys-
anthemum. – *tahi* dirty words. –
taluki pink carnation. – *tanah humus*
topsoil. – *teratai* lotus.
bungkah lump, piece.
bungkal 1 lump, piece. 2 leaden
weight, sinker. 3 measure of weight
for gold. **ber– –²** in chunks, hunks.
bungkam quiet, silent. **mem–** to gag,
silence. **mem–kan** to have s.o. keep
quiet.

bungkang laid out like a corpse. - *-bangking* lying stretched out.
bungkil peanut oil cake. - *kelapa* coconut oil cake.
bungkuk crooked, bent, humped. *Badannja –*, His back is bent. (He's hunchbacked.) **mem–** to stoop, duck. **mem– –²** 1 to bow several times. 2 to humble o.s. - *sabut* bent with old age. - *udang* a slouchy, droopy posture.
bungkul knob on end of umbrella handle, walking stick, etc.
bungkus 1 parcel, package. 2 package. *se-* rokok a package of cigarettes. **ber–** wrapped up. **mem–** to wrap. *Ia ~ buku ini*, He wrapped up this book. **pem–** 1 wrapping. *~ majat* shroud. 2 wrapping paper. 3 wrapper, packer. **pem–an** packing. **–an** parcel, package. - *bingkis* all k.o. packages.
bunglon 1 chameleon. 2 o. who vacillates as the wind blows. 3 opportunist.
bungsu youngest. *si* – the youngest son or daughter in the family. *hudjan* – the last rain of the season.
bungur tree with pink and purple blossoms.
bunji 1 sound, note. 2 sound. *–nja begitu*, It sounds like that. 3 contents. *Bagaimana – surat itu?* How does the letter read? *–nja*, It goes as follows. **ber–** 1 to sound. *Suaranja ~ keras*, His voice sounds loud. 2 to sound, read. *Surat itu ~ begini*, His letter goes as follows. 3 to explode, go off. *Bomnja tidak ~ ,* The bomb didn't go off. **mem–kan** 1 to sound, ring. *Siapa jg ~ bél?* Who rang the bell? 2 to click. *~ lidah* to click the tongue. 3 to beat, sound. *~ tong kosong* to beat on an empty drum. 4 to blow, honk. *~ klakson* to honk the horn. 5 to read aloud. *~ surat itu* to read the letter aloud. 6 to pronounce, sound. *~ kata* to pronounce words. **se–** 1 of the same sound. 2 a true copy of a document, letter, etc. **–²an** 1 music. 2 orchestra. - *djanggal* discord. - *gésér* spirant. - *kembar* diphthong. - *kerap* a creaking sound. - *letus* a stop sound. - *pepet* sound of the unstressed *e* in Indonesian. - *sengau* a nasal sound. - *serangkap* diphthong. - *tjina karam* very noisy.
buntak short and stout.
buntal swollen, bloated.
buntang 1 tense. 2 staring. *Matanja –*, His eyes were staring. 3 stiff (of a carcass). **mem–** 1 to stretch out stiffly. *Majat orang tenggelam itu ~ ,* The corpse of the drowned man

stretched out stiffly. 2 to emerge, pop up. *Kapal silam ~ dimuka mata kami*, A submarine emerged before our very eyes. **mem–kan** to stretch s.t. out. *Ia ~ tjutjiannja dipanas matahari*, He stretched out his laundry in the sunshine.
buntat gallstone. - *hendak djadi gemala*, He has absurd pretensions.
buntel (cloth) bundle. **mem–** to wrap, bundle. *Ia ~ pakaiannja*, He wrapped his clothes together. **–an** bundle.
buntil knapsack.
bunting pregnant (of animals; sarcastic or rude if applied to humans). *Andjing itu –*, The bitch is pregnant. **mem–** *padi* to have the shape of a fully formed rice grain. *Betisnja ~ padi*, Her calves are beautifully formed. **mem–kan** 1 to make pregnant. *Siapa jg ~ gadis itu?* Who got the girl pregnant? 2 to be pregnant. *Ia sering sakit waktu ~ anaknja*, She was often ill during her pregnancy. **pem–an** fertilization, impregnation. **–an** gestation. - *besar*, - *sarat* advanced pregnancy. - *ketjil* early stage of pregnancy.
buntjah disturbed, uneasy, upset. *Pikirannja –*, He's upset. **ke–an** disturbance, trouble. **mem–(kan)** to upset, disturb s.o. or s.t.
buntjis beans. - *mérah* kidney beans.
buntjit distended, bloated. *Perutnja –*, His abdomen is distended. **mem–kan** 1 to blow up, puff out. 2 to cram. **–an** 1 last. *Dimana nomor ~ ?* Where's the last issue? 2 final.
buntu 1 blocked, clogged up. *djalan* – blind alley. 2 deadlocked. **ke–an** deadlock. *~ djalan keluar* no way out. **mem–kan** 1 to cause a deadlock. 2 to block s.t. (alley, road, etc.). - *akal* 1 a dead end. 2 to be at a loss, at the end of o's wits.
buntung 1 used of s.t. lopped off (arm, tail, tree branch, etc.). 2 bad luck, misfortune.
buntut 1 end, tail, hind part, rear. *pd – bulan ini* at the end of this month. 2 aftermath, consequence. *Kedjadian itu pasti ada –nja*, There will surely be an aftermath to that incident. 3 trailing after. *Ia selalu mendjadi – saudaranja*, He's always trailing after his brother. **ber–** to have a tail. **ber– –²** one after the other. *Meréka datang ~ ,* They came one after the other. **mem–** 1 to follow. *Ia selalu ~ ajahnja*, He's always following after his father. 2 to follow at the rear. *Mari kita ~ arak²an ini*, Let's follow this procession at the rear. **mem–i** 1 to

follow, trail. *Ia ∼ pentjuri*, He
trailed the thief. 2 to put a tail
on s.t. *Ia ∼ andjing²an*, He put a
tail on his toy dog. – *andjing* dog's
tail. – *kapal* ship's stern. – *kuda*
ponytail (hairdo).

bunuh ber-(–)an to kill o. another.
mem– 1 to kill, murder s.o. 2 to
cross, cancel out. *Ia ∼ kalimat*, He
crossed out a sentence. 3 to blow
out, extinguish. *Ia ∼ lampu*, She
blew out the light. *Suaminja ∼ api*,
Her husband extinguished the fire.
pem– killer, murderer. **pem-an** murder. – **-mem**– to kill o. another.
– *diri* suicide.

bupati regent. **kabupatén** regency.

bupét 1 buffet, sideboard. 2 refreshment bar. 3 to serve a buffet.

bura mem– 1 to spit, spew out.
Ular itu ∼ bisa, The snake spit out
poison. 2 to make a mistake, slip.
Hilanglah dia kalau ∼ , He'll be
lost if he makes a mistake.

burai ber– to protrude. **mem**– to
spill. *Beras ∼ dari kantong jg terkojak*,
Rice spilled from the torn bag. **ter**-
hanging out. *rambut ∼ oléh angin*
hair disheveled by the wind.

buram blueprint, design, plan. –
naskah manuscript copy.

buras 1 chitchat, conversation. 2 k.o.
rice cake wrapped in banana leaves.
3 damaged, spoilt. **mem**– 1 to discuss. 2 to coax, soothe by making
small talk. **mem-kan** to talk to make
conversation. *Ia ∼ kudanja*, He
talked about his horse (just to have
s.t. to say).

burdjuis see BORDJUIS. **ke-an** bourgeoisie.

bureng hazy, unclear, dim. **pem-an**
fog.

burhan evidence, clear proof.

burik 1 pock-marked. 2 dotted,
speckled (of feathers, skin, etc.).

burit posterior, rear, behind, der-
rière. **mem**– to commit sodomy.
-an ship's stern.

burokrasi see BIROKRASI.

buron(an) a fugitive from justice,
wanted. **pem**– fugitive.

bursa exchange.

bursuasi bourgeoisie.

buru ber– 1 to hunt, pursue. 2 to
go hunting. **ber**– –² to chase, pursue.
Ia ∼ pentjuri itu, He chased the
thief. **mem**– 1 to hunt. *Ia ∼ kidang*,
He hunts deer. 2 to hurry to. *Ia
segera ∼ kami*, He immediately
hurried over to us. **mem**– –²**kan** to
urge s.o. on, speed s.o. up. *Ia ∼
adiknja bekerdja*, He urged his younger
brother to work. **pem**– hunter. **pem**-

an hunt, pursuit, chase. **per-an** 1
fugitive, the hunted one. 2 prey,
game. **ter**– *nafsu* to be in a great
hurry. *Ia ∼ nafsu utk mendjumpai
pamannja*, He was in a great hurry
to meet his uncle. **ter**– –² in a hurry,
in great haste. *Ia ∼ pulang*, He was
in a hurry to go home. **-an** 1 game,
prey. 2 fugitive, a hunted person.
–² in a hurry.

buruh worker, laborer. **mem**– to
work as a laborer. *Ia ∼ pd paberik
itu*, He worked as a laborer at the
factory. **per-an** labor. *Kementerian
∼* Ministry of Labor. **-an** wages,
salary. – *kasar* unskilled, manual
labor. – *postel* post-office worker. – *tani*
farm worker.

buruk 1 old, worn out, dilapidated,
decayed. *Badjunja* –, His jacket is
worn out. *Giginja* –, His teeth are
decayed. 2 rotten. *Kajunja tlh* –,
The wood is rotten. 3 bad. *Ia berbuat*
–, He does bad things. *Ia mempunjai nama* –, He has a bad name.
4 foul. **ke-an** evil, wickedness.
mem(per)-kan 1 to worsen, make
worse, aggravate. *Tindakan itu ∼
perhubungan diantara dua negeri itu*,
That action aggravated the relationship between the two countries. 2
to slander. *Ia ∼ tetangganja*, He
slandered his neighbor. *tidak ada
–nja* 1 not to do harm. *Tak ada ∼
kalau saja minta diri dulu dari ajah*,
It won't do any harm if I take leave
from my father first. 2 no bad ones.
Telor ini baik semua; tak ada ∼ ,
All these eggs are good; there aren't
any bad ones.

burung 1 bird. 2 euphemism for male
organ. –²**an** artificial toy bird. –
bangau egret. – *buas* bird of prey.
– *dara* pigeon, dove. – *déwata* bird of
paradise. – *djalak* starling. – *djendjang*
crane. – *elang* hawk. – *gerédja* sparrow. – *hantu* owl. – *kenari* canary.
– *kepudang* golden oriole. – *kesturi*
parakeet. – *lajang²* swallow. – *lang*
hawk. – *manjar* weaverbird. – *merak* peacock. – *murai* magpie. – *nilam*
golden oriole. – *pegar* pheasant. –
pelatuk woodpecker. – *pingai* white
crow. – *pujuh* quail. – *serak* owl.
– *simbang* sea gull. – *suangi* owl. –
tjelutut snipe. – *udang* beach bird.
– *undan* pelican. – *unta* ostrich. –
upik gray stork.

burut rupture, hernia.

bus = BIS.

busa foam, lather. – *sabun* soap
lather. **ber**– to foam, lather. *Sabun
∼* , The soap lathers. *laut ∼* the
foaming sea. **mem**– 1 to foam, lather.

2 to blow. *Ia ~ debu dimédja,* He blew dust on the table. 3 to pant. **mem–kan** 1 to blow up (a balloon, etc.). 2 to blow out, spray (as water, etc.). **pem–** *api* bellows operator.
busah see BUSA.
busar see BUSUR.
busét an exclamation expressing wonder, surprise, etc. (used by the common people in Jakarta). –, *apa betul ia berbuat demikian?* My word (really), did he do that?
busi spark plug.
busuk 1 putrid, rotten, bad. *Dari mana datang bau – itu?* Where's that putrid odor coming from? *Napasnja –,* His breath smells foul. 2 decay. *Ia mendjaga bangkai daripada –,* He preserved the corpse from decay. 3 low, depraved, corrupt. *Hatinja –,* He's depraved. *Niatnja –,* His intentions are bad. **ke–an** 1 decay, corruption. 2 perversion. **mem–** *rabu* to possess a strong odor. **mem–kan** 1 to disgrace, defame s.o. *Ia ~ keluarganja,* He disgraced his family. 2 to slander. 3 to putrefy. *Kutu² ~ daging,* Worms putrefied the meat. **pem–an, per–an** 1 putrefaction, decay. 2 disgrace, defamation.
busung 1 bloated, distended. *sakit –* dropsy. 2 on a high elevation. *Disitu ada tanah –,* There's hilly ground over there. 3 bulging, packed. *Sakunja –,* His pockets are bulging. **mem–** to be distended, bloated. *Perutnja ~ ,* His belly is distended. *Dadanja ~ ,* He feels proud. **mem–kan** 1 to boast. 2 to inflate a tire. *– air* dropsy. *– dada* 1 proud. 2 conceited. *– kelaparan* dropsy caused by malnutrition. *– lapar* malnutrition, undernourishment.
busur 1 arch. 2 arc. 3 archer's bow. 4 cotton gin. **mem–** 1 to shoot with

bow and arrow. 2 curved. *Alisnja ~ ,* Her eyebrows are curved. 3 to clean. *Ia ~ kapas,* He cleaned cotton. *– tjahaja* arc of light.
busut 1 anthill. 2 mound, hillock. *– betina* large rounded anthill. *– djantan* small pointed anthill.
but² see HATI.
buta 1 blind. 2 giant. 3 blank. *dinding –* a blank wall. **ke–an** blindness, darkness. **mem–** 1 to be blind to s.t. 2 to act blindly, recklessly. **mem–** *tuli* to act recklessly. **pem- -tuli** a reckless person. **mem–kan** to blind s.o. **–²an** wildly, recklessly, at random. *Pesawat itu mengebom kota itu ~ ,* The plane bombed the city at random. *– ajam* 1 nearsighted. 2 twilight blindness. *– belalang* blind stare. *– hati* cruel, harsh. *– huruf* illiterate. *– kaju* complete illiteracy. *– malam* night blindness. *– perut* 1 inability to tell one taste from another. 2 eating forbidden food by mistake or pretended mistake (e.g., eating of pork by Moslems). *– pitjak* blind through loss of eye. *– sebelah* blind in one eye. *– tjémér* incurably blind. *– warna* color-blind.
butang button.
butek thick, turbid.
butir 1 grain, particle, pellet. *– padi* grain of rice. 2 used with round objects. *tiga – telur* three eggs. *empat – mangga* four mangoes. 3 small, fine object. *Dgn perkakas itu orang bisa melihat –²nja pd bagian bulan,* With that instrument one can see small objects on parts of the moon.
butuh 1 need (for: *akan, dgn, kpd, pd*). *Ékonomi itu – pd pertolongan,* The economy has need of help. 2 penis. **ke–an** need, necessity, wants. **mem–i, mem–kan** to need.
butul(an) side entrance.
butut worn out, threadbare.

C

cassa 1 cashier's window. 2 box office (of theater, etc.).
C.C. [*Céntral Comité*] central committee.
cg. [*centigram*] centigram.
chabar see KABAR.

chadam slave, servant.
chaid menses, menstruation.
chaimah see KÉMAH.
chajal 1 fancy, vision, imagination. *Semua itu – belaka,* They were all visions. 2 imaginary. **ber–** 1 to see

visions. 2 to indulge in fancies.
meng-kan to vision, imagine. **(peng)–
an** 1 fancy, imagination, hallucination, fantasy. 2 image, vision.
chajali 1 imaginary. *Dimana musuh
jg – ?* Where's that imaginary enemy?
2 intoxicated, in a trance. *Ia sedang
–,* He was intoxicated.
chalaik see CHALAJAK.
chalajak 1 creature. 2 multitude, the
public. – *pembeli* the buying public.
– *ramai* the public.
chali empty, unoccupied. *Ia tiada –
bekerdja,* He works all the time.
chalifah caliph.
chalik Creator.
chalikah 1 creation. 2 situation, nature, character, behavior.
chalis pure, genuine.
chalwat solitude, retirement from the
world, seclusion. **ber–** to retire from
the world, meditate.
chamar 1 wine. 2 liquor.
Chamis see KEMIS.
chas special, exclusive, for private
use. *Ia mempunjai mobil utk keperluan –,* He owns a car for special use.
ke–an specific character. **meng-kan**
to reserve for special use. *jg –* characteristic.
chasiat special virtue, peculiarity.
meng-i to scrutinize closely, investigate minutely (for details).
chatam 1 seal, signet ring. – *Suleiman* Solomon's seal. 2 final, last.
Ia nabi jg –, He's the last prophet.
3 finished, ready. *Ia – koran,* He's
finished reading the newspaper.
meng-kan to finish reading. *Ia ∼
bukunja dlm satu hari,* He finished
reading his book in one day. **–an**
ceremony of completion of first reading of the Koran.
chatan circumcision. **ber–** to be
circumcised. **meng–** to circumcise.
meng-kan to have s.o. circumcised.
Ia ∼ anaknja, He had his child
circumcised.
chatib 1 anyone, religious official or
layman, who delivers the Islamic
sermon. 2 mosque official.
chattulistiwa equator.
chawatir 1 anxious, uneasy, worried.
Djangan –, Don't worry. 2 afraid.
Ia – suratnja tidak sampai, He was
afraid his letter wouldn't arrive.
ke–an fear, worry, anxiety. **meng-i**
to fear, be afraid. *Ia ∼ bannja akan
petjah,* He feared his tire would blow
out. **meng-kan** to disturb, alarm,
upset, worry. *Keadaan politik ∼
kami,* The political situation worried
us.

chazanah 1 treasury, treasure chamber. 2 library. 3 treasure.
chéwan see HÉWAN.
chianat treason, treachery, betrayal.
Ia berbuat –, He committed treason.
ber– to betray. *Ia ∼ kpd tanah air,*
He betrayed his country. **meng-(i)**
to betray. *Anaknja ∼ negerinja,*
His son betrayed his country. **peng-**
traitor, betrayer. **peng-an** betrayal,
treason.
chidmat 1 respect, duty. *Ia tunduk
kepala dgn –,* He dutifully bowed his
head. 2 humility, submission. **ber–**
1 dutiful, respectful, obliging. *Ia ∼
kpd perintah,* He carried out orders
loyally. 2 to serve. *Ia ∼ kpd negerinja,* He served his country.
chilaf 1 (to make a) mistake, error,
slip. 2 to be uncertain. *Saja – ttg
tanggalnja,* I'm uncertain about the
date. **ke–an** mistake, error, slip. –
dan alpa mistakes and oversights.
Chili Chile.
chitan see CHATAN. **peng-an** circumcision.
chodja(h) 1 title of religious and
wealthy merchant class. 2 merchant,
trader.
chotbah sermon. **ber–** to preach, deliver a sermon. **peng–** o. who delivers
a sermon.
chotib see CHATIB.
chulak divorce initiated by the wife
by returning wedding gifts.
chusjuk 1 devoted, humble before
God. 2 deeply absorbed, engrossed
in. *Ia – membatja koran,* He was
deeply absorbed in reading the newspaper.
chusu 1 devotion, humility. 2 conscientious.
chusus 1 special, specific. *Itu peladjaran jg –,* That's a special course.
2 particular. **ke–an** specification.
meng-kan to specialize, deal with
exclusively. **peng-an** *usaha* specialization. **ter–** especially, particularly,
specifically. *pd –nja* in particular,
especially.
CIAD [*Corps Intendan Angkatan
Darat*] army quartermaster corps.
combi microbus, Volkswagen bus.
comité committee.
corps corps, body.
COWAD see KOWAD.
crossboy male juvenile delinquent.
crossgirl female juvenile delinquent.
c.s. [*cum suis*] 1 with his friends,
companions, associates. 2 with affiliates.

D

D [*Danau*] lake.

d/a [*dengan alamat*] in care of, c/o.

dabung ber– to file teeth (for aesthetic or religious reasons).

dabus awllike dagger with which participants in mystical ceremonies, after reaching a state of trance, inflict wounds upon themselves. **ber–** to use the *dabus*.

dachil 1 inner life. 2 intimate. *Persahabatan meréka – benar*, They are on very intimate terms.

dada chest, breast, bosom. **ber– –²an, men–** to do hand-to-hand fighting. – *bidang* broad-chested. – *burung* pigeon-breasted. – *lapang* phlegmatic. *–nja lapang*, He's phlegmatic. – *lega* relieved. *–nja lega setelah membatja surat itu*, He was relieved after reading that letter. – *manuk* pigeon-breasted.

dadah medicinal herb. **pe–** small container for medicinal herbs.

dadak men– suddenly. *Hudjan turun dgn* ∼ , It suddenly began to rain. ∼ *sontak* very suddenly.

dadar see TELUR.

dadih curd. – *darah* coagulated blood of cattle prepared in cakes.

dadjal 1 deceiver, swindler. 2 Antichrist.

dadu 1 die, dice. 2 cube. 3 pink. *pipi berwarna* – rosy cheeks. **ber–** to shoot dice.

daduh see DADUNG.

dadung men– to sing s.o. to sleep. *Ia* ∼ *anaknja sehingga tidur*, She sang her child to sleep.

daéng title of nobility among the Buginese of Celebes.

daérah 1 territory, region. 2 environs, vicinity. 3 area. **ke–an** local, regional, provincial. *Kedjadian itu hanja bersifat* ∼ , That was only a local incident. **se–** local, regional. – *antar* 1 interregional. 2 postal zone. – *batja* reading public. – *chattulistiwa* tropical, equatorial area. – *djadjahan* colony. – *hawa panas* tropics. – *hawa sedang* temperate zone. – *istiméwa* special region (Jogjakarta and Solo). – *minus* low food-producing zone. – *negara* national territory. – *pedalaman*

hinterland. – *pengaruh* sphere of influence. – *perwalian* trust territory. – *pinggiran* 1 borders. 2 periphery. – *plus* surplus-producing area. – *seberang* overseas territory. – *swapradja* principality. – *takluk* dependency. – *tatapradja* regional administrative unit. – *terdjepit* enclave. – *tidak bertuan* no man's land.

daftar list, roster. **men–kan** 1 to register, record. 2 to enroll, enlist. ∼ *diri* to register o.s. *Saja* ∼ *diri dikantor tatausaha*, I registered at the administration office. **pen–an** registration. **ter–** registered. – *buku* book list, catalogue. – *darab* multiplication table. – *gadji* payroll. – *hadir* roll, attendance list. – *harga* price list. – *hitam* blacklist. – *kali²an* multiplication table. – *kematian* mortality table. – *makanan* menu. – *nama* 1 roll, list of names. 2 nomenclature. – *penundjuk* index. – *perdjalanan* schedule, timetable. – *pertanjaan* 1 application form. 2 questionnaire. – *usaha* program, schedule.

daga see DAHAGA.

dagang 1 trade. 2 foreign. *Ia adalah orang –*, He's a foreigner. **ber–** 1 to trade. *Ia* ∼ *emas*, He trades in gold. 2 to roam abroad. *Ia tlh lama* ∼ , He's been roaming abroad for a long time. ∼ *diri* to go abroad. *Ia meninggalkan kampungnja dan* ∼ *diri*, He left his village and went abroad. **mem(per)–kan** to deal in s.t. *Kita dilarang* ∼ *uang pérak*, We are forbidden to deal in silver. **pe–** 1 merchant. 2 trader. 3 salesman. **pen–** shoulder pole. **per–an** trade, commerce. **–an** 1 merchandise. 2 load. – *gelap* smuggling trade. – *senteri* strangers.

dagelan 1 joke. 2 group of clowns or comedians.

dagi men– to put up resistance. **pen–** rebel, insurgent.

daging 1 meat. 2 flesh. **ber–** 1 fat, stout. *Orang itu sungguh* ∼ , That man is really fat. 2 rich. **men–** to put on weight. *Bapak* ∼ , Dad's putting on weight. **pen–an** *dari nafsu² dan keinginan²* materialization of desires and wants. **ter-** to make a deep impression. *Nasihatnja tlh ∼ padaku,* His advice has made a deep impression upon me. *– ajam dan – sapi* chicken and beef. *– anak sapi* veal. *– asap* smoked beef. *– babi* pork. *– berteduh* fillet. *– darah* o's own flesh and blood. *– domba* mutton, lamb. *– has* fillet of beef. *– kain* unprocessed material to be woven into cloth. *– kantjing* muscle. *– lembusir* shoulder. *– mati* meat of an animal not ritually slaughtered. *– sapi* beef. *– sapi digiling* hamburger. *– sapi panggang* roast beef.

dagu chin.

dah abbrev. of SUDAH.

dahaga thirsty. **ber–** *(akan)* to thirst (for). **ke–an** thirst. **men–kan** to thirst for s.t. *Ia sangat ∼ pendidikan,* He is thirsting for education very much.

dahak phlegm, sputum. **men–** to spit.

daham a cough. **ber–** to clear the throat.

dahan tree branch.

dahar to eat.

dahi forehead. *– sehari bulan* a well-shaped forehead.

dahsjat 1 horrifying, terrifying, appalling. *Pertempuran itu –,* The fight was terrifying. *Dentuman meriam –,* The rumble of the guns was appalling. 2 enormous, mighty. *Di New York banjak gedung² jg –,* In New York there are many enormous buildings. 3 fear, awe. **ke–an** awe, horror. **memper–** to grow worse. **men–** to become terrifying. *Angin taufan itu makin ∼ ,* The typhoon became more and more terrifying. **men–kan** to terrify s.o. *Pertumpahan darah itu ∼ hati saja,* The bloodshed terrified me.

dahulu 1 formerly. *– ia tinggal disini,* He formerly lived here. 2 former. *Pd zaman – blm ada mobil,* In former times there were no cars. 3 first. *Makanlah – sebelum engkau pergi,* Eat first before you go. 4 before, prior. *– dari pd surat ini kami tlh mengirim surat jg lain,* Prior to this letter we sent you another o. 5 for the time being. *Duduklah – , tuan,* Sit down for now, sir. 6 a moment. *Tunggulah –,* Wait a moment. 7 see DULU. **ber– –²an** to race e.o., try to be first. *Anak² itu ∼ menduduki korsi² dlm bioskop itu,* The children raced e.o. to occupy seats in the theater. **ke–an** 1 origin. 2 to be preceded by. *Saja tlh ∼ orang lain, tempat duduk saja tlh hilang,* S.o. else preceded me and I lost my seat.

men–i 1 to be ahead of s.o. *Ia ∼ saja,* He's ahead of me. *Djangan datang ∼ waktunja,* Don't come ahead of time. 2 to precede. *kata jg ∼* the preceding word. 3 to overtake. *Mobilnja ∼ mobil saja,* His car overtook mine. **men–kan** to give precedence, priority. *Orang muda harus ∼ orang tua,* Young people should give precedence to old people. *Kewadjiban harus di–kan,* Duty comes first. **pen–an** 1 preface. 2 introduction. *pemeriksaan² ∼* preliminary investigations. **ter–** 1 first. 2 earlier. **–(–)nja** formerly. **– –men–i** to race o. another. *– kala* long ago.

daif 1 weak. *Alasannja itu –,* His argument is weak. 2 lowly born. 3 humble. *abdi tuan jg –* your humble servant. 4 incompetent. *Ia – menandatangani surat itu karena ia mabuk,* He was incompetent to sign that letter because he was intoxicated. **ke–an** 1 weakness. *∼ alasannja* the weakness of the argument. 2 incompetence. **men–kan** to look down on s.o. *Djangan ∼ orang miskin,* Don't look down on poor people.

daim 1 eternal, everlasting. 2 fast (of colors).

daing dried fish or meat.

daja 1 power, energy. 2 influence. *– kebudajaan barat* the influence of Western civilization. 3 effort(s). *Tiada berhasil segala –nja,* All his efforts were in vain. 4 wit, strength. *Ia sdh habis segala –nja,* He's at his wit's end. (He's at the end of his rope.) **ber–** powerful. *Saja sangat lelah, hampir tidak ∼ lagi,* I'm very tired and have almost no strength left. **ber–guna** efficient. **memper–i** 1 to deceive s.o. 2 to tempt s.o. **memper–kan** to fool, deceive s.o. **men–kan** to endeavor. **men–upajakan** to endeavor. *Indonésia ∼ supaja mentjapai kemakmuran,* Indonesia is endeavoring to achieve prosperity. **pe–an** 1 deceit, trick. 2 influence. 3 a way out, expedient. **per–an** trick, fraud. **se–upaja** utmost. *Ia berusaha ∼ ,* He does his utmost. **teper–** taken in. *Saja ∼ karena kata²nja jg manis itu,* I was taken in by his nice words. *– angkat* lifting capacity. *– angkut* transport. *– atom* atomic energy. *– batin* inner strength. *– bekerdja* work capacity. *– beli* purchasing power. *– berat* gravity. *– bertahan* stamina. *– chajal* imaginative power, vision. *– gaib* supernatural power. *– gerak* thrust. *– guna* 1 productivity. 2 efficiency. 3 life (span). *– hasil* productivity. *– hisap* absorptive capacity. – *karya*, – *kerdja* work efficiency, work capacity. – *kuda* horsepower. – *lenting* flexibility. – *listerik* electric power. – *maknit* magnetic force. – *muai* expansive power. – *penarik* power of attraction. – *pendjiwa* power of inspiration. – *penggerak* motive power. – *pesona* personal magnetism. – *pikul* carrying capacity. – *surut* retroactive. *Peraturan ini berlaku dgn – surut hingga 1 Djan. 1962*, This regulation is retroactive to January 1, 1962. – *tahan* 1 resistant. 2 resistance. – *tarik* power of attraction. – *tembus* transparency. – *tempuh* stamina, endurance. – *tjipta* creativity. – *upaja* efforts. *Apa –?* What can be done?

dajah wet nurse.

Dajak Dayak (name of a tribe in central Kalimantan).

daju **men–** 1 to rumble softly. *Suara guruh jg ∼ kedengaran dari djauh*, The soft rumbling of thunder was heard from afar. 2 to moan.

dajuh **ter–** moved, touched.

dajung 1 oar, paddle. 2 fin of a fish. **ber–** to row. *Ia pergi ∼ dilaut*, He went out to row on the sea. **men–** 1 to row a boat. 2 to pedal. **pen–** 1 oar. 2 oarsman. – *gébéng* paddle made of a blade nailed to the end of a handle. – *kebas* paddle with long, narrow blade. – *majung* all k.o. blades.

daka lid of a Moslem coffin.

daka'ik intricate questions.

dakap **ber–** to embrace. *∼ tangan* with arms folded. **ber– –²an** to embrace e.o. **men–** to embrace s.o. **sepen–an** an embrace. *Pohon itu besarnja ∼* , That tree is as large as one can encircle with o's arms.

dakar 1 stubborn. 2 reckless. 3 penis.

daki fine dirt on the body, on clothing and furniture. **men–** to climb, ascend. *Ia ∼ gunung*, He climbed the mountain. **men–kan** 1 to raise. *Ia ∼ lampu*, He raised the lamp. 2 to cause to or have climb. *Ia ∼ keranja keatas pohon*, He made his monkey climb a tree. 3 to appeal (to a higher court). *Ia ∼ perkaranja*, He appealed his case. **pen–an** 1 pass. *∼ Kaiber* Khyber Pass. 2 steps cut out of the soil along a slope. 3 ascent. **-an** slope, incline. – *dunia* filthy lucre.

daktur editor.

daku 1 I. 2 me (generally used when the preceding word ends in an *n*). *Ma'afkan –* , Pardon me.

dakwa 1 accusation. 2 claim, demand. **ber–** to litigate. *Ia sedang ∼* ,

He's engaged in litigation. **men–** 1 to accuse s.o. *Ia ∼ saja mentjuri bukunja*, He accused me of stealing his book. 2 to sue s.o. **men–i** to claim, lay claim to. *∼ hak²* to claim o's rights. **memper–kan, men–kan** to bring a case to court. **pen–** complainant, plaintiff. **(pen)–an** accusation, charge. **ter–** the defendant, the accused.

dalal mediator, go-between.

dalalah 1 deviation. 2 see DALIL.

dalam 1 in. *Ada banjak tamu – rumah*, There are a lot of people in the house. 2 in, within, inside. – *sedjam kita akan sampai di Djakarta*, We'll arrive in Jakarta in an hour. 3 deep. *Samudera itu sangat –*, The ocean is very deep. 4 deep, profound. *pengetahuan jg –* profound knowledge. 5 court, palace. *Ia pergi ke– radja*, He went to the king's court. **ber–** –² to deepen, worsen. *Perselisihan itu ∼* , The quarrel has worsened. **di–** inside. *Meréka ada ∼ rumah*, They're inside the house. **ke–an** depth, profundity. **men–** 1 deep-rooted. *Kedjahatan tlh ∼* , The criminality is deep-rooted. *Kebudajaan Hindu sangat ∼ di Indonésia*, Hindu civilization is very deep-rooted in Indonesia. 2 profound. *Pertjintaan meréka sangat ∼* , Their love was very profound. **men–i** to steep o.s. in s.t. *Ia ∼ ilmu bintang*, He has steeped himself in astronomy. **memper–, men–kan** to deepen s.t. *∼ parit* to deepen a ditch. **pe–an** hinterland, interior. **-an** bowels, entrails. **-nja** depth. *∼ sungai 20 métér*, The depth of the river is 20 meters. – *negeri* 1 inland, interior. 2 home affairs. 3 domestic. *produksi – negeri* domestic production. – *pd itu* in the meantime, meanwhile. *Bekerdjalah giat, tetapi – pd itu keséhatan harus selalu didjaga*, Work hard, but meanwhile always take care of your health. – *hati* to o.s., in o's own mind. *membatja – hati* to read to o.s.

dalang 1 puppeteer, narrator, and manipulator of Javanese and Sundanese shadow plays. 2 mastermind. *Siapakah jg mendjadi – komplotan itu?* Who was the mastermind behind that plot? **ber–, men–** to perform a puppet play. **men–i** to mastermind. *Ia dituduh ∼ pemberontakan itu*, He was accused of masterminding the rebellion. **men–kan** to manipulate the puppets in a shadow play. **pe–an** 1 place of the *dalang*. 2 act of narration by *dalang*.

dalih excuse, subterfuge. **ber–** to look

for an excuse. **ber- -²an** to blame e.o. *Meréka ~ mengenai kerugian meréka,* They blamed e.o. for their losses. **men–kan** to feign, pretend.

dalil 1 argument based on the Koran to prove s.t. 2 proof, proposition. 3 axiom, thesis, theorem. **-²** *ilmu ukur* geometrical theorems. **ber-** to be valid. *Pendiriannja itu tak ~ ,* His views aren't valid. **men–kan** to defend an opinion. **- -al-hajat** a memento indicating that o. is still living.

dalu overripe. **ke–an** overripe.

dam 1 checkered design. 2 sound of a drum. **-²an** checkers.

damai 1 peace. 2 agreement. 3 peaceful. **ber-** 1 to make peace. *Kedua negeri itu tlh ~ ,* The two countries have made peace. 2 to arrive at, come to an agreement. *Meréka ~ ttg harga itu,* They agreed on the price. **ke–an** *rochani* peace of mind. **memper–kan** 1 to reconcile. *Saja mentjoba ~ pendirian meréka,* I tried to reconcile their opinions. 2 to pacify. **men–kan** to bring peace, pacify. *~ kedua negeri itu* to bring peace between the two countries. **per–an** peace.

damak dart used with blowpipe.

damar 1 resin. 2 oil lamp. 3 torch. **men-** to collect resin. **men–i** to illuminate an area with a torch. **pen-** resin tapper. **pe–an** 1 torch. 2 area where resin can be found. **- batu** hard resin.

damba *(pd)* to long for s.o. or s.t. *Saja - padanja,* I long for her. **(ke)–an** longing. **men-** to embrace s.o. **men–kan** to desire, covet. *Ia ~ kedudukan jg paling tinggi baginja,* He coveted the highest position for himself. *~ diri* to collapse. *Ia pingsan dan ~ dirinja,* He fainted and collapsed. **per–an** desire, covetousness.

dambin 1 see DAMBUN. 2 clumsy. **ber-** to produce a thud. *Batu besar djatuh ~ ditanah,* The large rock fell on the ground with a thud. **- dambun** a series of thuds.

dambun 1 thud. 2 boom. **ber- -²** to boom. *~nja bedug mesdjid* the booming of the mosque drum.

damik **men-** *dada* to beat o's breast.

dampak **men-** to bump, collide (with). *Sepédanja ~ mobil saja,* His bicycle collided with my car.

dampar **men-** 1 to break (of waves). 2 stranded. **men–kan** to strand. *Ombak² tlh ~ perahu itu pd batu karang,* The waves stranded the boat on a coral reef. **ter-** 1 washed ashore. *Sisa² kapal itu ~ kepantai,* The wreckage of the ship was washed ashore. 2 to run aground, be stranded. *Kapal itu ~ pd karang itu,* The ship ran aground on a coral reef.

dampil **ber-** to lean closely against o. another.

damping intimate. *Si Amat sahabat - saja,* Amat is an intimate friend of mine. **ber–an** 1 side by side. *Meréka duduk ~,* They sat side by side. *~ meréka menghadapi musuh,* Side by side they faced the enemy. 2 adjacent. *Djérman ~ dgn Perantjis,* Germany is adjacent to France. 3 in connection. *~ dgn hal ini saja ingin menanjakan beberapa hal,* In connection with this matter I'd like to ask some questions. **ke–an** 1 closeness. *~nja kpd keluarganja mengharukan,* His closeness to his family is touching. 2 loyalty. **men–i** 1 to stand next to. *Wakil présidén ~ présidén,* The vice president stood next to the president. 2 to flank. *Orang tuanja ~ pradjurit jg menerima Bintang Gerilja,* The parents flanked the soldier who received the Guerrilla Medal. **se- -²nja** the most closely related.

damprat abuse, scolding. **men-** to scold, reproach. *Ia ~ saja dgn tidak ada alasan,* He scolded me without any reason. **-an** = DAMPRAT.

D.A.M.R.I. [*Djawatan Angkutan Motor Républik Indonésia*] Indonesian Motor Transport Office.

Damsjik Damascus.

dan 1 and, plus. *bapak - ibu* father and mother. 2 well... then? *Sekarang bagaimana -?* Well, and now what?

dana 1 donation, alms. 2 fund. *- piatu perang* a war orphan fund. **ber-** to donate. *Ia suka ~ ,* He likes to give donations. **ke–an** generosity. **men–kan** to donate s.t.

danau lake.

dandan clothes, clothing, outfit. **ber-** 1 to dress up. *Ia lagi ~ ,* She's dressing up. 2 adorned, attired. *Ia ~ indah,* She was beautifully attired. *Karangannja itu ~ kata² jg indah,* His article was adorned with pretty words. **men–i** 1 to attire, adorn s.o. or s.t. *Pengantin itu di–i ibunja,* The bride was attired by her mother. 2 to equip. *Para kelasi ~ kapal silam itu,* The sailors equipped the submarine. 3 to repair. *Tukang djam ~ djam saja,* The watchmaker repaired my watch. **-an** 1 clothing, outfit. 2 make-up, adornment.

dandang 1 bronze bottom part of rice steamer for holding water. 2 rice steamer. 3 dugout canoe. 4 a crow.

dandi 1 k.o. lute. 2 spotted, striped like a tiger. **ber-** to play a *dandi*.

dangau a small hut located in the field to guard against damage by birds, cattle, or wild hogs; usually on stilts and occupied during the day by children who serve as guards.

dangir men- to hoe the ground.

dangka see SANGKA.

dangkal 1 shallow. *Kali itu –*, The river is shallow. 2 superficial. *pengetahuan jg* – superficial knowledge. 3 hard (of fruit). **ke-an** 1 shallowness. 2 superficiality. **men-kan** 1 to make shallow. *Ia ~ sumur itu dgn tanah*, He made the well shallow by filling it with dirt. 2 to consider s.t. trivial.

dangkap see DAKAP.

dangkung a disease closely resembling leprosy.

dangsa Western-style dancing. **ber-** to dance Western-style.

danguk ber-, men- to sit with chin in hands and stare.

dansa see DANGSA. *– pergaulan* social dancing.

dansa-dansi dancing.

dansanak kin, relative. *– kandung* sibling.

danta ivory.

danur liquid emitted by putrefying cadaver.

dapat 1 can, be able, possible. *Ia – membatja sadja*, He can only read. *– mengemudi mobil* to be able to drive a car. *– djuga ia tak kembali lagi*, It's quite possible he won't return. 2 may. *-kah saja datang?* May I come? 3 to get. *– kenaikan pangkat* to get a promotion. *– perbesar modalnja* to succeed in increasing o's capital. *– penghinaan* to be humiliated. 4 to meet, find. *Walaupun diperiksa se-teliti²nja kesalahan dlm buku kas tak – djuga*, Although the ledger was checked thoroughly, the mistake still could not be found. 5 to have, get. *Saja harap kau– djawaban jg menjenangkan*, I hope you'll have a favorable reply. 6 to catch, get. *Ia – ikan besar*, He caught a big fish. (He bought a big fish. He got a big fish as a present.) 7 to achieve, get. *Moga² kau– apa jg diperdjuangkan*, I hope you'll achieve what you are fighting for. **ber-** adequate, sufficient. *Kalau harganja ~ saja akan djual mobil ini*, If I get a decent offer, I'll sell this car. **ber-an** to meet. *Anggauta² ~ dirumah saja*, The members met at my house. **ke-an** found, discovered. *Pentjuri itu ~ oléh polisi*, The thief was found by the police. *Ia ~ menerima suap*, He was found taking bribes. *~ budi* to discover o's bad intentions. *Ia tlh ~ budi oléh saja*, I discovered his bad intentions. **memper-** 1 to reach, obtain, get. *~ persetudjuan setelah lama berunding* to reach an agreement after long negotiations. 2 to agree on s.t. *~ harga barang itu* to agree on the price after extensive bargaining. **men-** 1 to get. *Ia ~ teguran*, He got a warning. 2 to receive, get. *~ kabar* to receive news. 3 to find. *~ pisau lipat didjalan* to find a pocketknife in the street. 4 to meet, see. *~ dia dirumahnja* to see him at home. 5 to meet with. *~ ketjelakaan* to meet with an accident. *~ nama* to become famous. *~ rezeki* to have luck. **men-i** 1 to find out, discover. *Polisi ~ béngkél pemalsu uang*, Police found a counterfeiter's workshop. 2 to meet. *Ia ~ adiknja distasiun*, He met his brother at the station. **men-kan** 1 to get, obtain. *Ia ~ pekerdjaan bagi saja*, He got me a job. 2 to visit, see. *~ anaknja dirumah sakit* to visit o's child at the hospital. 3 to (on letters). *~ Tuan Ali* to Mr. Ali. 4 toward. *~ Hari Natal* toward Christmas. 5 shortly before. *~ djam lima* shortly before five o'clock. 6 to discover, invent. *Edison ~ lampu listerik*, Edison invented the light bulb. **pen-** 1 opinion, judgment. *pd ~ saja* in my opinion. 2 inventor. **pen-an** 1 income. 2 opinion, view. 3 solution. *Berapakah ~ soal aldjabar itu?* What's the solution to that algebra problem? 4 invention. 5 discovery. *~ jg menggelikan* a weird discovery. 6 yield, output, produce. *~ sawah* yield of wet rice fields. 7 product, result (in math.). 8 catch. *Apa ~ pemburuanmu?* What did you bag in your hunting? 9 revenue. 10 acquisition. **se-** upon getting. *~ surat ini* upon receipt of this letter. **se- -²nja** as well as possible. *Kerdjakanlah itu ~ ,* Do that as well as possible. **sepen-** of the same opinion. *Ia ~ dgn saja*, He's of the same opinion as I am. **ter-** to be found. *Kera tak ~ di Amérika*, The monkey isn't found in America. *– balik* reversible. *– hati* 1 to take courage. 2 to like (be happy). 3 to have o's way. *– kain kotor* to menstruate. *– larut* soluble. *tak – tidak* 1 it can't avoid being, can't be otherwise. *Tak – tidak dialah jg bersalah*, It must be his fault. 2 without fail. *–pun...*

takkan even though... won't. *-pun demikian takkan saja berubah pendirian,* Even though that's the case, I won't change my mind.

daptar see DAFTAR.

dapur 1 kitchen. 2 furnace. – *arak* distillery. – *leburan* blast furnace. – *matahari* solar oven. – *umum* public, community kitchen.

dar 1 place, location. 2 region, territory, abode. *-u'lbaka* the hereafter. *-u'lfana* this world of ours. *-u'l Islam* abode of Islam.

dara 1 virgin. 2 girl. 3 virginity. – *laut* tern.

darab a heavy blow. *Hal itu sebuah – baginja,* That was a heavy blow for him.

daradjat see DERADJAT.

darah blood. **ber–** 1 to bleed. *Hidungnja ~ ,* His nose is bleeding. 2 to have blood. *Ia ~ Tionghoa,* He has Chinese blood. 3 bloody, bloodied. *Pakaiannja itu ~ ,* His clothes are bloodstained. 4 of noble descent. *~ dingin* cold-blooded (of animals). *~ hangat* warm-blooded. **men–** *daging* to become a habit. *~ sumsum* integrated, deeply rooted. *Adat itu sdh ~ sumsum,* That custom has become deeply rooted. **per–an** hemorrhage. – *daging* 1 blood relative. 2 second nature, habit. *Kebiasaan itu tlh mendjadi – dagingnja,* That habit has become second nature for him. *Marilah membéla tanah air kita dgn – daging kita,* Let's defend our country with our lives. – *dingin* phlegmatic, imperturbable. *Ia tak pernah gugup, ia sangat dingin –nja,* He never gets upset, he's imperturbable. – *hidup* fresh blood, gore. – *kotor* menstrual blood. – *lintah* thick, sticky. *Kopi itu seperti – lintah sadja,* The coffee is too thick. – *mati* congealed blood. – *nifas* 1 postnatal hemorrhage. 2 afterbirth. – *panas* hotheaded. – *putih* 1 white corpuscles. 2 of noble descent.

daras **men–** 1 to recite Koranic texts. 2 to examine, investigate thoroughly. *Ia ~ kelakuan murid²nja,* He examined his students' behavior.

darat 1 land. 2 shore. 3 inshore, inland. **men–** to land. *Kapal terbang ~ dilapangan terbang,* The plane landed on the airfield. *Perahu ~ dipelabuhan,* The boat landed at the island. *Pasukan ~ di Palau,* Troops landed on Palau. **men–i** to set foot on. *Orang blm pernah ~ pulau ini,* Nobody has ever set foot on this island. **men–kan** to put s.t. ashore. *Kapal itu ~ muatannja,* The ship

put its cargo ashore. **pen–** means for landing. **pen–an** 1 landing, disembarkation. 2 landing place. 3 pier, jetty, landing. **–an** 1 mainland. 2 landing. *~ darurat* emergency landing.

dar-dur rattling of guns.

dari 1 from. *Saja datang – Indonésia,* I come from Indonesia. 2 than. *Besar saja – kamu,* I'm bigger than you. 3 of. *dasawarsa – sekolah itu* the decennial of the school. 4 out of. *Sabun ini dipakai oléh 9 – 10 bintang pilem,* This soap is used by nine out of ten film stars. se– since. *~ masa ketjilnja ia sdh sakit sadja,* He's been sickly since childhood. – *itu* therefore. *Saja lapar, – itu saja mau makan,* I'm hungry, therefore I want to eat. **–mana** 1 from where. *~ dia datang?* Where does he come from? 2 Who's calling? *~ tahu?* How do you know? **–pada** 1 than. *Ia lebih pandai ~ saja,* He's smarter than I am. 2 of. *Médja itu dibuat ~ kaju,* The table is made of wood.

darimana see DARI.

daripada see DARI.

darma duty.

darmasardjana fellowship, grant.

darmasiswa scholarship, fellowship.

darmatamu leader grant.

darmawisata 1 excursion, outing. 2 field trip. **ber–** 1 to go on an outing. 2 to make a field trip.

darun **se–** in unison. *"Pembohong!" meréka berteriak ~ ,* "Liar!" they shouted in unison.

darurat emergency. *Dlm keadaan –, panggillah polisi,* In an emergency call the police. *Negara ada dlm keadaan –,* The country is in a state of emergency. *undang² – emergency* laws. **men–kan** to compel. *Perang ~ kita memobilisir tentara kita,* The war compelled us to mobilize our army.

darwis(j) dervish, fakir.

das a shot, bang of a gun.

dasa– ten. – *lomba* decathlon. – *sila* ten principles. – *warsa* decennial.

dasar 1 background. – *lukisan itu biru,* The background of the painting is blue. *Apakah – pendidikannja?* What's his educational background? 2 base, foundation, basis. *Saling hormat menghormati adalah – persahabatan,* Mutual respect is the basis of friendship. 3 principle. *Itu bertentangan dgn – démokrasi,* That's contrary to the principles of democracy. 4 bottom. *pd – laut* at the bottom of the sea. *Pd –nja ia orang baik,* Basically, he's a good fellow. 5 floor. – *rumah itu tanah,* The house

has a dirt floor. 6 nature. *Itu mémang sdh —nja,* That's his nature. 7 foundation of a building. **ber-** 1 to have as a background. *Kebajanja ~ mérah,* Her jacket has a red background. 2 to have as a basis. *Pendapatnja itu sama sekali tak ~ ,* His opinion has no basis whatever. **berkan** to be based on. *Negara kita ~ azas démokrasi,* Our country is based on the principles of democracy. **men-i** to provide the basis for. *gagasan jg ~ malam sastera* an idea which provided the basis for a literary evening. **men-kan** to base. *Ia ~ dakwaannja itu atas hasil penjelidikannja,* He based his accusation on the result of his investigations. − *kepandaian* talent, aptitude. − *mudasir* always the case. − *mudasir anak tolol,* He's always been a dull child. − *pelantjongan* nothing but a drifter. − *tengkorak* base of skull.
dasariah basic.
dasi necktie. **ber-** to wear a tie. − *djepitan* tie clip. − *kupu*² bow tie. − *péndék* a short tie worn by teen-agers.
dasun k.o. garlic. *Hidungnja bagai − tunggal,* He had a well-shaped nose.
DASWATI [*Daérah Swatantra Tingkat*] autonomous region. As of 1962 *DASWATI I* is the equivalent of a former province, *DASWATI II* of a former regency.
datang 1 to come. *Ia − dari Éropah,* He came from Europe. 2 to arrive. *Kapan Saudara − ?* When did you arrive? **ber-** *sembah* to approach reverently. **ke-an** 1 arrival. 2 attacked, invaded. *Kota itu ~ musuh semalam,* The city was attacked last night. 3 to be afflicted by a disease. *~ maut* to die. **men-** 1 to come suddenly. *Malam ~ ,* Night fell. *Hal itu ~ pd fikiran saja,* It flashed across my mind. 2 to occur, happen suddenly. *Akibat jg ~ itu menginsjafkan dia akan kesalahannja,* The unexpected circumstance made him realize that he had made a mistake. **men-i** 1 to visit, pay a call. *Polisi ~ kantornja,* The police visited his office. *Ia ~ Garut ditahun 1936,* He visited Garut in 1936. 2 to attack, invade. *Kampung itu di-i musuh,* The village was attacked by the enemy. 3 to attach an affix. *Kata itu di-i awalan 'ke,'* The prefix 'ke' is attached to that word. **men-kan** 1 to import s.t. 2 to bring about, cause. *Kelalaiannja itu ~ kerugian,* His negligence caused a loss. 3 to summon. *Polisi ~nja,* The police summoned him. 4 to bring. *Ia ~*

otonja, He brought his car. −² 1 suddenly, all of a sudden. *~ ia menjalahkan saja,* All of a sudden he threw the blame on me. 2 to drop by. *~lah kemari!* Do drop by again! 3 to keep coming, come repeatedly. *Apa kerdja orang itu? Ia ~ sadja kemari,* What does that fellow want? He keeps coming here. *jang akan −* next, future. *Ia akan pergi minggu jg akan −,* He's going next week.
datar 1 flat, level. *Permukaan laut itu −,* The surface of the sea is smooth. 2 superficial. *Pengetahuannja −,* His knowledge is superficial. **men-** 1 to be level, smooth. *Djalan itu ~ ,* The road is level. 2 horizontal. **men-kan** to level, make smooth. *~ tanah jg tak rata itu* to level uneven land. **pe-an** 1 plateau. 2 plain. **-an** 1 a plain. *~ rendah* lowland plain. *~ tinggi* upland, plateau. 2 shelf. *~ Sahul* Sahul shelf.
datjin(g) 1 a bar hinged at a point near the end to which the object to be weighed is attached. The measuring weight slips on the longer arm of the bar and can be moved back and forth. 2 unit of weight.
datu 1 shaman. 2 herb doctor.
datuk 1 grandfather. 2 head (oldest male) of the family clan. 3 headman. 4 honorific term. *Apa kabar, −?* How are you, sir? 5 k.o. title for persons in high position. − *bendahara* the king's treasurer. 6 epithet for a tiger. *Bawalah bedilmu, kalau² bertemu dgn − dihutan,* Take your gun along in case you meet up with a tiger in the jungle. 7 idols in a Chinese temple. 8 guardian genie. −², − *nénék* ancestors.
Daud David.
daulat hail. −, *tuanku!* Yes, milord. (lit., Hail to thee, milord.) **bersovereign.** *pemerintah jg ~* a sovereign government. **ke-an** sovereignty. **men-(kan)** 1 to kidnap s.o. 2 to murder s.o. 3 to rob, appropriate. *Kaum pemberontak ~ harta benda penduduk,* The rebels appropriated the property of the inhabitants. 4 to oust, deprive forcibly of authority. *Kolonél itu tlh di− anak buahnja sendiri,* The colonel has been forcibly relieved of his authority by his own men. 5 to fire s.o. **pen-** 1 murderer. 2 kidnaper. 3 plunderer. 4 o. who ousts or fires s.o. **pen-an** 1 kidnaping. 2 murder. 3 plundering. 4 ousting, firing.
daun 1 leaf of a tree. 2 playing card(s). **ber-** to have leaves, be leafy. **men-** to be like a leaf. *Penonton*

jg berkumpul di alun[2] ∼ *kaju*, Many spectators were assembled in the square. ∼ *kunjit* to be useless. **-an** foliage. – *bawang* spring onion, leek. – *bunga* petal. – *dajung* oar. – *hidup* touch-me-not plant. – *lindung* calyx or sepal. – *médja* table leaf. – *neratja* scales for weighing. – *pandan* pandanus leaf often used in cooking. – *penumpu* stipule. – *penutup* sepal or calyx. – *(kertas) rokok* cigarette paper. – *rompong* truncated leaf. – *salam* bay leaf. – *selada* lettuce. – *telinga* auricle. – *tjeki* small Chinese playing cards.

daur cycle. – *besar* 120-year cycle. – *ketjil* cycle of eight years.

da'wa see DAKWA.

dawai wire.

dawat ink.

db [*dibawah*] below, under.

dbp [*dibawah pimpinan*] under the leadership (of).

debah exposed, uncovered. **men-kan** to expose. *Ia* ∼ *pakaian*, He undressed. ∼ *sarong* to take off o's sarong. **ter-** 1 wide-open. *Djendéla itu* ∼ *sadja*, The window is wide-open. 2 exposed. *Dadanja* ∼ , His chest is exposed.

debak ber- to make a thud. *Buku itu* ∼ *kelantai*, The book fell to the floor with a thud.

debap 'plop.'

debar ber- to throb, beat, palpitate. *Hati saja* ∼ , My heart is throbbing. **ber-** –[2] to pound. *Hatinja* ∼ *ketakutan*, His heart pounded from fear. **-an** palpitation. – *djantung* pulse.

débat debate. **ber-(-)** to debate. *Meréka* ∼ *selama 2 djam*, They debated for 2 hours. **memper-kan** to debate about s.t. **per-an** 1 a debate. 2 debating.

debik men- to pat, slap, whack with the open hand.

debu dust. **ber-** dusty. *Djalan itu* ∼ , The road's dusty. **men-** dustlike, powdery. *Ia menumbuk kopi itu sampai* ∼ , He pounded the coffee until it was like dust.

debuk see DEBAK.

debur with a big splash (of s.t. large falling into the water). **ber-** to roar (of waves). **men-kan** to make s.t. splash. **-an** beating (of waves, heart).

debus 1 whistling, howling of the wind. 2 see DABUS.

dedah ter- opened wide.

dedai ber- –[2] in droves. *Orang datang* ∼ *melihat présidén*, People came in droves to see the president.

dedak bran.

dedau men- to scream.

dedaunan leafy edibles.

dédél men- to cut open the seam of a dress. **men-i** to cut s.t. open.

dedemit ghost.

dédés 1 musk. 2 civet cat. **men-** to slice s.t. **se-** a slice.

defilé parade. **ber-** to parade. *Rakjat* ∼ *didepan istana présidén*, The people paraded in front of the president's palace.

définisi definition.

deg –[2]**an** to pound, beat. *Hati saja* ∼ , My heart was pounding.

degan young coconut.

degap sturdy. *Ia* –, He's sturdy. **ber-** –[2] to pound. *Hatinja* ∼ *karena ia ketakutan*, His heart pounded with fear. –[2]**an** pounding.

degil obstinate, stubborn. **ke-an** obstinacy.

deging ber- to persevere through thick and thin.

déh colloquial abbrev. for SUDAH.

deham see DAHAM.

dék 1 deck. 2 blanket.

dékadénsi decadence.

dekah ber- –[2] to roar with laughter. *Ia tertawa* ∼ , He roared with laughter.

dekak 1 see DEKAH. 2 abacus, counting frame.

dekam ber-(-) to seclude o.s. *Gadis itu* ∼ *sadja dirumahnja*, The girl secluded herself in her home. **men-** to crouch ready to leap.

dekan an insect that feeds on bamboo.

dékan dean of a university faculty.

dekap see DAKAP.

dékar men- to fence (a sport). **pen-** 1 fencing master. 2 champion, advocate of a cause.

dekat near, close by. *Rumah saja* – *dari kantor pos*, My home is near the post office. *Hari Natal sdh* –, Christmas is near. **ber-** to be near. **ber-** –[2] to be close to e.o. *Djangan* ∼ *dgn anak*[2] *jg nakal*, Don't mix with bad boys. **ber-an** adjacent. *Sekolah kami* ∼ *dgn bioskop*, Our school is beside the theater. *Meréka duduk* ∼ , They sat close to e.o. **ke-an** 1 nearness, propinquity. 2 too close, near. *Itu* ∼ *dari sini*, That's too close to here. **memper-kan** to reconcile s.o. **men-** to draw near, approach. *Hari Natal sdh* ∼ , Christmas is drawing near. **men-i** to approach s.o. or s.t. *Ia* ∼ *saja*, He approached me. *Kami sdh* ∼ *tudjuan kami*, We're approaching our destination. **men-kan** to bring closer. *Ibu* ∼ *médja kedinding*, Mother brought the table closer to the wall.

pen–an approximation. **per–an** affinity. **ter–** nearest. **ter–i** to be approached. *Ia susah sekali* ~ , He's very hard to approach.

dekih men–(–) to snicker, chuckle.

dekil dirty, filthy.

deking 1 a cover. 2 reserve, covering funds.

déklamasi declamation.

déklarasi 1 declaration (customs). 2 voucher.

dékolonisasi decolonization.

dékrit decree. **men–kan** to decree.

deku men– to kneel down.

dekur men– to coo.

dekus ber– to hiss, spit. *Kutjing itu selalu* ~ , The cat is always spitting. **men–** to hiss at s.t.

dekut see DEKUR.

delapan 8. *–belas* 18. *–puluh* 80.

délégasi delegation.

déleman 2-wheeled horse-drawn carriage.

delep men– *–²kan* to be unfaithful to s.o. in marriage.

delik men– 1 to be dilated, wide-open. *Mata saja* ~ *karena ketakutan*, My eyes popped from fear. 2 to glare. *Ia* ~ *pd saja*, He glared at me.

délik offense. *Daktur suratkabar itu kena –*, Legal proceedings were instituted against the editor.

delima 1 pomegranate. 2 ruby. *– merekah* ripe pomegranate. *Bibirnja seperti – merekah*, She has beautiful lips.

délman see DÉLEMAN.

delong men– sunken (of eyes).

deluang see DJELUANG.

dem garbage dump.

demah warm compress. **men–** to apply a warm compress.

demam fever. *Ia –*, He has a fever. *–² pujuh* to pretend to be ill. *– berselang, – selang-seling* intermittent fever. *– dingin* to have a fever. *– (ke)pialu* high fever. *– kura²* malaria. *– pujuh* light fever. *– selésma* influenza, flu.

deman to like. *Saja – mangga*, I like mangoes.

demang chief of a district in Sumatra.

demap greedy, voracious.

démarkasi demarcation.

demek moist.

demen see DEMAN.

demés flat (of a nose).

demi 1 by. *Saja bersumpah – Allah bhw itu tidak benar*, I swear by Allah that it isn't true. *satu – satu* one by one. 2 when. *– dilihatnja bhw rumah itu terbakar ia memanggil polisi*, When he saw that the house was on fire, he called the police. 3 after.

gelas – gelas glass after glass. *– kepentingan* for the sake of.

demik see DAMIK.

demikian 1 thus. *–lah achir tjerita ini*, Thus ended this story. 2 such. *Saja ingin badju jg – ini*, I want such a shirt. *Sdh – lamanja ia tak menulis saja*, He hasn't written me in such a long time. *se– like that. Laki² ~ itu tak dpt dipertjajai*, A man like that can't be trusted. *– djuga* likewise. *– djuga engkau harus bertindak*, You should act likewise. *dgn – thus*, so.

démisionér dismissed (from cabinet or administration).

démo 3-wheeled motorcar.

démobilisan a demobilized soldier.

démokrasi democracy.

démokratis democratic.

démokratisasi democratization.

démoralisasi demoralization.

dempak 1 broad and flat. *Atap rumah itu –*, The house roof is broad and flat. 2 stocky. *Tubuh orang itu –*, The man is stockily built.

démpét stuck together. *Kedua pisang itu –*, The two bananas are stuck together. **ber– –²(an)** to be packed together. *Rumah ~ dlm kota ini*, The houses are packed together in this city. **men–kan** to press s.t. together.

dempok ter– to bump against s.t. *Saja ~ médja*, I bumped against a table.

dempol see DEMPUL.

dempuk see DEMPOK.

dempul glazier's putty.

dén abbrev. of the title *radén* and used as form of address to young men of the upper class. *"–, tadi pagi orang menilpon," kata babu*, "Someone called you this morning, sir," said the maid.

déna see DINA.

dénah 1 sketch. 2 blueprint. 3 ground plan. *– vokal* vowel pattern.

denai trail, track (of big game).

denak decoy (used in hunting birds and animals).

denda fine. *– 50 rupiah* a 50-rupiah fine. **men–(i)** to fine s.o. **–an** the act of fining s.o.

dendam 1 revenge, vengeance. 2 grudge, resentment. *Ia menaruh – pd saja*, He bears me a grudge. **ber–an** to have hard feelings toward e.o. **men–(i)** to bear s.o. a grudge. **men–kan** to resent s.t. *Ia ~ kata² saja*, He resented my words. **pen–** s.o. who bears a grudge. **– –men–** to hate o. another. *– bentji* grudge and hatred. *– berahi* passionate love. *–*

kasemat enmity, rancour. *Saja ingin membalas –*, I want to take revenge.
dendang raven.
déndang song, chant. **ber–** to sing gaily, happily. *Gadis² memotong padi sambil* ~ , The girls sang gaily while cutting the rice. **men–** to sing, chant. *Meréka* ~ *njanjian baru*, They sang new songs. **men–kan** to sing for s.o. ~ *pantun* to recite pantuns. *Meréka mengerdjakan pekerdjaan meréka dgn –*, They did their jobs in good spirits.
déndéng spiced dried meat. *– babi* seasoned dried pork. *– belado* hotly seasoned dried meat.
dengak bent forward.
dengan 1 with. *Ia pergi – ajahnja*, He went with his father. *Ia menulis – potlot*, He writes with a pencil. 2 and. *Siti – Amat akan datang bésok*, Siti and Amat will come tomorrow. 3 by. *datang – keréta api* to come by train. 4 in. *– alamat* in care of. *Kirimlah surat itu – alamat sekolahnja*, Send the letter in care of his school. *– nama Tuhan* in the name of God. *– begitu* thus. *– djalan* 1 by means of. *– djalan menipu ia mentjapai kedudukan jg tinggi*, By means of cheating he reached a high position. 2 by way of. *Ia datang ke Amérika – djalan Éropah*, He came to America by way of Europe. *– hormat* Dear Sir, Madame (used in correspondence). *– kadarnja* to the best of o's ability. *– lisan* verbal(ly). *– sekaligus* 1 simultaneous(ly). *Ia menjudahkan dua pekerdjaan – sekaligus*, He finished two jobs simultaneously. 2 promptly. *– sekaligus musuh menduduki kota itu*, The enemy promptly occupied the city. 3 all together. *Meréka datang – sekaligus*, They all came together. *– sendirinja* 1 automatically. *Radio itu akan mati – sendirinja*, The radio will turn off automatically. 2 obvious. *Sdh – sendirinja ia susah ketika ia tidak lulus udjiannja*, It was obvious that he was unhappy when he failed his exam. *– sepatutnja engkau meminta maaf*, In such a case you should offer your apologies. *– tiada (– tidak)* without. *Ia pergi – tiada izin*, He went without permission. *– tjara bagaimana* how. *– tjara bagaimana ia melamar utk pekerdjaan itu?* How did he go about applying for that job? *– tulisan* in writing, written.
dengap **ber–** 1 to pound, beat (of the heart). 2 to pant, gasp.
dengar **ber–** to be obeyed. *Perintahnja* ~ , His orders were obeyed.

ke–an audible. *Suara* ~ *dari sini*, His voice is audible from here. **memper–kan** to let s.o. hear, have s.o. listen. *Penjanji itu* ~ *suaranja jg merdu itu*, The vocalist sang beautifully. **men–** to hear. *Orang itu tidak dpt* ~ *lagi*, That man can't hear any more. **men–kan** to listen to. *Ia* ~ *radio*, He listens to the radio. **men– –²kan** 1 to listen to. *Djangan* ~ *akan budjukan orang itu*, Don't listen to that man's tempting proposition. 2 to hear partially. *Saja* ~ *sadja*, I just heard bits of it. 3 to listen in. *Tak usah ikut* ~ *; ini bukan mengenai kamu*, You don't have to listen; this doesn't concern you. **pen–** 1 listener, hearer. 2 auditor in a class. 3 telephone receiver. ~ *tengah* middle ear. **pen–an** (sense of) hearing. *–²an* 1 obedient. *Kita harus* ~ *kpd Tuhan*, We must obey God. 2 hearsay.
denging **men–(–)** to ring. *Telinga saja* ~ , My ears are ringing.
dengkang **ber–** to croak (of frogs). **ber– –²** to laugh uproariously.
déngkang-déngkol bent and bowed.
déngkél dry, not succulent.
dengki maliciously jealous. **ke–an** jealousy.
dengking a squeal, yelp. **ber–**, **men–** to squeal, yelp (of a dog).
déngkol 1 crooked, bent (of arms). 2 impediment of speech.
dengkul 1 knee. 2 see DÉNGKOL.
dengkur a snore. **ber–**, **men–** to snore.
dengkus see DEKUS. **ber–** to snort.
dengu see DUNGU. **ber–** to breathe audibly.
dengung a drone, wail, buzz. **ber– –²** 1 to drone. *Kapal terbang itu* ~ , The plane droned. 2 to wail. *Siréne* ~ , The siren wailed. 3 to resound. *Tepuk sorak* ~ *dlm gedung itu*, The building resounded with cheers and hand clapping. **men–kan** to reverberate, resound. **men– –²kan** 1 to emit a loud sound. *Harimau* ~ *suaranja dihutan*, The tiger's roar filled the jungle. 2 to propagandize in a bombastic way. 3 to boast. **–an** 1 wail. 2 drone. 3 propaganda.
dengus see DEKUS.
dengut **ber– –²** to ring out. *Bunji burung pujuh* ~ , The sound of a quail rang out.
denjar a flash. *– kilat* a flash of lightning.
denjut a throbbing. **ber–** to throb, palpitate. *– djantung* heartbeat. *– nadi* pulse.
dentam see DENTUM.

dentang a clang. **ber–** to clang.

denting a jingle. **ber–** to jingle.

dentjing see DENTING.

dentum **ber–** to boom. *Meriam² itu* ~ , The cannons boomed. **–an** a boom(ing).

dentur **ber–** to crack. *Senapan² itu* ~ , The rifles cracked.

dép **di–** 1 to be suppressed (of a controversial document, etc.). 2 to be shelved (a question, etc.).

Dép. [*Départemén*] department, ministry.

depa fathom (distance from finger tips to finger tips when arms are stretched sideways). **men–** to measure in fathoms. **men–kan** *tangan* to spread out the arms sideways.

depak clip-clop (of horses' hoofs). **ber–** **–²** 1 to smack o's lips. 2 to go clip-clop (of horses). **men–kan** *lidah* to make a clacking sound with the tongue.

dépak a kick. **men–** 1 to kick. *Ia* ~ *bola*, He kicked the ball. 2 to fire, kick out. *Ia* ~ *pegawainja jg malas itu*, He fired his lazy employee.

depan 1 front. *Di– rumah ada pohon*, In front of the house is a tree. *Ia berdjuang digaris –*, He fought on the front line. 2 up ahead. *Itu dia di–*, That's it up ahead. 3 coming, next. *bulan –* next month. **ber–an** to face o. another. *Rumahnja* ~ *dgn rumah saja*, His house faces mine. **menge-kan** to place s.t. forward, propose. *Ia* ~ *médja*, He placed the table forward. *Ketua* ~ *usulnja*, The chairman submitted his proposal. **ter–** 1 foremost, front. *Ia duduk dibangku jg* ~ , He sat on the front bench. 2 in the lead (in contests, etc.).

depang **ber–** 1 to stretch out both arms sideways. 2 to form a cross by stretching the arms sideways. **men–** to block o's way.

Déparlu [*Départemén Luar Negeri*] Department, Ministry of Foreign Affairs.

départemén department, ministry.

Dép DNOD [*Départemén Dalam Negeri dan Otonomi Daérah*] Ministry of Internal Affairs and Regional Autonomy.

DÉPERINDRA [*Départemén Perindustrian Rakjat*] Ministry of People's Industry.

Dépernas [*Déwan Perantjang Nasional*] National Planning Council.

Dépertan [*Déwan Pertahanan Nasional*] National Defense Council.

dépisen foreign exchange.

Dépkes [*Départemén Kesehatan*] Department of Health.

dépo(t) a k.o. refreshment stand, shop.

DÉPPEN [*Départemén Penerangan*] Ministry of Information.

déprési depression.

déprésiasi depreciation.

depun a hem. **men–** to hem a dress, etc.

dera a whipping. **men–** to whip s.o.

deradjat 1 degree. *Panasnja 98 –*, It's 98°. 2 level. *– pengetahuan* level of knowledge. 3 standard, level. *– penghidupan* standard of living. 4 prestige. **se–** of the same degree, level. *Pengetahuanku* ~ *dgn pengetahuanmu*, My knowledge is on the same level as yours. *– busur* degree of a circle. *– panas* temperature.

derai **ber–** 1 in drops. *Hudjan –*, The rain patters down. 2 granulated. *tanah berisi emas* ~ *sand* containing gold particles. *Hatinja remuk* ~ , His heart was torn to pieces. **ber–** **–²** in droves. *Penonton²* ~ *datang dipekan raya*, Spectators arrived at the fair grounds in droves. **men–kan** *air mata* to shed tears.

derak **ber–** to crackle, creak. *Dahan² kering itu* ~ , The dry branches creaked. **ber–** **–²** to squeak. *Pérnja* ~ , The springs kept squeaking. **men–** **–²kan** to gnash. *Ia* ~ *giginja*, He gnashed his teeth.

deram **ber–** **–²**, **men–** to rumble. *Guruh* ~ , The thunder rumbled. *Aum harimau* ~ *dari djauh*, The roar of a tiger rumbled in the distance.

derang **ber–** ruffling (of a drum). ~ *siang* daybreak, ca. 5:30 A.M. *Hari hampir* ~ *siang*, It's almost daybreak. **men–** to ruffle.

derap 1 see DERAK. 2 a trot. *Kuda itu berlari –*, The horse trots. **ber–** to trot. **–an** rapping, rattling.

deras 1 fast. *Larinja sangat –nja*, He runs very fast. *Kali itu – arusnja*, The river has a fast current. *Hudjannja sangat –*, The rain came down in buckets. 2 speed, swiftness. **ber–** to rustle. **men–** 1 fast-flowing. *Kali itu sangat* ~ , The river flows fast. 2 energetic. *Pemuda* ~ *tentu madjunja*, Energetic youth will surely get ahead. **men–kan** to increase speed. *Ia* ~ *larinja*, He ran faster. **pen–an** rapids, cataract.

derau see DERAI.

dérék 1 see DERAK. 2 see DÉRÉT. **–²** derrick.

derél salvo. men– to execute by a firing squad.

dérés men– to tap a tree. pen– a tapper.

dérét row, line. *dua – tanaman* two rows of plants. ber– in rows. *Meréka duduk ~* , They sat in rows. ber– –² to be lined up. *Orang² ~ sepandjang djalan*, The people lined up along the road. memper–kan to line s.o. up. men–i to line s.t. *Sungai itu di–i dgn pohon²*, The river was lined with trees. men–kan to line up. *Ia ~ murid²nja*, He lined up his pupils. –an row, line. *– hitung* arithmetical progression. *– ukur* geometrical progression.

deretak ber– –² to rattle (of machinery).

derhaka see DURHAKA.

derik see DERAK.

deril 1 strong twilled cotton. 2 see DERÉL.

dering see DERANG. ber– 1 to trumpet (of an elephant). 2 to chirp. *Djangkrik itu ~* , The cricket chirped.

derit ber– to creak. *Lantai papan ~ dibawahnja*, The flooring creaked under him.

derita men– to suffer. *Ia ~ sakit*, He suffers from an illness. *~ kekalahan* to suffer defeat. *~ kemiskinan* to suffer from poverty. pen– 1 sufferer. *Ia ~ penjakit paru²*, He's afflicted by tuberculosis. *~ tjatjad* the physically handicapped. 2 object (in grammar). (pen)–an suffering(s). *tiada* ter– unbearable.

derma 1 alms. 2 donation. 3 fund. ber– 1 to give alms. 2 to make donations. men–kan to donate s.t. pen– 1 generous, charitable. *Ia amat ~* , He's very generous. 2 donor. *~ darah* blood donor.

dermaga 1 quay, pier. 2 breakwater.

dermawan generous person. ke–an philanthropy, charity. *– darah* blood donor.

dersik sighing (of the wind).

deru men– to roar, howl (of the wind).

derudji trellis.

derum men– 1 to kneel. *Gadjah itu ~* , The elephant knelt. 2 to rumble. *Guruh itu ~* , The thunder rumbles. 3 to buzz (of bees). se– all together. *Meréka datang ~* , They came all together.

derup-derap sound of many footsteps.

derwis(j) see DARWIS(J).

Dés. [*Désémber*] December.

désa village. ke–an rural. pe(r)–an 1 pertaining to the *désa*. *Djawatan*

~ Office of Village Affairs. 2 village settlement. *– keputihan* sacred village; village of religious people, usually free of village tax or other obligations.

desah men– to rustle softly (leaves).

desak ber– to crowd e.o. ber– –²kan to jostle o. another. men– 1 to push. *Ia ~ saja kedinding*, He pushed me to the wall. 2 to urge, press, insist. *Ibu ~ saja supaja kawin*, Mother urged me to get married. 3 urgent, pressing. *Waktu sdh ~* , Time is pressing. *Ini adalah soal ~* , This is an urgent matter. 4 to creak (of a board, etc.). men–kan to impose s.t. *Ia ~ kemauannja pd saja*, He imposed his will on me. *~ diri* to impose, thrust o.s. on s.o. pen–an ousting of s.o. –an pressure.

desar ber–, men– to sizzle (in cooking).

desas-desus 1 rumors. 2 whispering of voices. men–kan to spread rumors.

desau see DESAR.

Désémber December.

déséntralisasi decentralization.

désérsi desertion.

desik men– to rustle (of papers).

desing ber–, men– to whistle. *Taufan itu ~* , The typhoon whistled. *Peluru ~ disekitar saja*, Bullets whistled around me.

desir ber– to swish (of wind-blown sand). men– –² soft swishing. –an swishing.

destar Javanese head covering.

desuk see DESAK.

desur see DESAR.

desus ber– to rustle (of the wind).

Dét. [*Détasemén*] detachment (mil.).

detak ber–, men– 1 to throb, beat (of the heart). 2 to tick (of a clock, watch). men–kan to click (the tongue). *– djantung* heartbeat. *– hati* impulse.

détasemén detachment.

detik second. *Satu menit adalah 60 –*, One minute is 60 seconds. ber– to tick. –an throb, palpitation. *– detak* tidings. *Kami tidak mendengar – detaknja lagi*, We don't hear anything from him any more. *– djantung* palpitation of the heart.

detjap ber– –² to smack o's lips.

detjéh see DETJAP. men– –² to make a clicking sound.

detjit ber–, men– 1 to squeak (of a mouse). 2 to chirp (of a bird).

detjur men– to spurt. *Air sumber ~ dari birai*, Well water spurts from the ledge.

detup see DETUS.

detus ber– to crack. *Senapan itu ~* ,

The rifle cracked. ∼ *hati* suspicious. *Dgn ∼ hati ia memasuki rumah itu,* Full of suspicion he entered the house. **-an** cracking, popping (of a rifle, firecracker, etc.).

Dév. [*Dévisa*] foreign exchange.

dévaluasi devaluation. **men-** to devaluate.

dévisa foreign exchange.

dévizen see DÉVISA.

déwa god, idol. **ke-an** divine. *kekuatan* ∼ divine powers. **memper-kan, men-kan** to idolize s.o. or s.t. *Ia ∼ isterinja,* He idolized his wife. **pen-an** idolization. ∼ *diri* self-worship.

déwala stone wall.

déwan 1 council. 2 board. − *niaga* board of trade. − *gerédja* synod. − *Keamanan* Security Council. − *menteri* cabinet council, ministerial cabinet. − *penaséhat* advisory council. − *pengawas* 1 supervisory council. 2 inspectorate. − *Perwakilan Rakjat* Parliament. − *Perwakilan Rakjat Daérah* Provincial Assembly. − *pimpinan* board of directors. − *rakjat* people's council. − *redaksi* editorial board.

déwangga special cloth design. − *raja* firmament of heaven.

déwasa 1 time. *Sdh datang −nja utk bekerdja giat,* The time has come to work hard. 2 adult. *Ia sdh −,* He's an adult. **ke-an** 1 adulthood. 2 maturity. − *dulu* formerly. − *ini* nowadays, at the present time.

déwata see DÉWA. **ke-an** 1 home of the gods. 2 divine.

déwék o's own.

déwi 1 goddess. 2 darling. − *Sri* the Goddess of Rice (fertility goddess). − *pertiwi* earth goddess.

dg [1 *désigram* 2 *dengan*] 1 decigram. 2 with, by.

Dg. [*Daéng*] (a title in South Celebes).

dgn [*dengan*] with, by.

d.h. [*dengan hormat*] Dear Sir, Madam.

d/h [*dahulu*] formerly.

dharma bakti volunteer work for o's country.

D.I. [*Daru'l Islam*] fanatical Moslem group in West Java.

di 1 in. −*dapur* in the kitchen. 2 at. −*rumah* at home. 3 on. − *Djawa* on Java. see also ANTARA, ATAS, BAWAH, BELAKANG, DALAM, DEPAN, LUAR, SAMPING, SANA, SEBELAH, SEBERANG, SINI, SITU, TENGAH.

dia 1 he, she. − *lagi makan,* He's (She's) eating. 2 him, her. *Saja lihat −,* I see him (her). 3 it. − *saja taruhkan disini,* I put it here. 4 his,

her. *nama* − his (her) name. **men-kan** to refer to s.o. as *dia. Djangan ∼ présidén,* Don't use *dia* with the president. *si−* boy or girl friend, sweetheart. *Saléh, saja bertemu dgn si−mu tadi,* Saleh, I just ran into your girl friend.

diagnosa diagnosis.

diaklas jointings (geol.).

dialéktika dialectic.

dialéktis dialectical.

dialog dialogue.

diam 1 silent, taciturn, quiet. *Ia − sadja, tidak berkata apa²,* He was silent and said nothing. *Keadaan dikampung itu − sadja,* It was quiet in the village. −*!* Quiet! 2 to keep silent. 3 motionless. *Bola itu tidak bergerak; tinggal − sadja,* The ball didn't move; it remained motionless. 4 idle. *Ia tak pernah −, selalu ada jg dikerdjakan,* He was never idle but was always busy doing s.t. **(ber)−** to live, dwell, reside. *Meréka ∼ dikota,* They live in town. **ber-(kan)** *diri* to keep quiet. *Ia ∼ diri,* He kept quiet. **ke-an** residence, domicile. **memper-kan, men-kan** 1 to silence s.o. 2 to stop. *Ia ∼ apa jg tlh dilihatnja itu,* He kept quiet about what he had seen. 3 to leave s.o. alone. *Semendjak kita bertengkar ia ∼ saja,* Since our quarrel he has ignored me. **men-i, menge-i** to reside, live at. **pen-** a taciturn person. **ter-** 1 quietest. 2 to become speechless. *Ia ∼ mendengar berita itu,* He became speechless on hearing the news. 3 tongue-tied. −² quietly, secretly. *Meréka kawin dgn ∼ sadja,* They were married secretly. ∼ *ubi,* Still waters run deep.

dian 1 candle. 2 kerosene lamp. **men-i** to illuminate with a candle or kerosene lamp.

diang ber- to warm s.o. **men-** 1 to roast. 2 to warm, heat s.t. 3 the late. ∼ *Tuan A.* the late Mr. A. **pen-an** hearth, fireplace.

diar see BIAR.

diat compensation for bodily injury or manslaughter. **men-kan** to pay compensation.

diatas see ATAS.

didih ber-, men- 1 to boil. *Air itu sdh ∼ ,* The water's boiling. 2 to boil, rage, seethe. *Darahnja ∼ ,* He was raging mad. (He was boiling over).

didik men- 1 to educate s.o. 2 to bring up. *Orang tua ∼ anaknja,* The parents bring up their children. **pen-** educator. **pen-an** education.

~ *masjarakat* mass education. **ter-**
educated. **-an** 1 upbringing. 2 education. 3 pupil, disciple.
didis see DÉDÉS. **ber-** to delouse.
men- to slice (cake, etc.).
difinisi see DÉFINISI.
Digul place of exile in Western New
Guinea. **men-kan** to send into exile
at Boven Digul (a river).
DIJ [*Daérah Istiméwa Jogjakarta*] the
Special District of Jogjakarta.
dik see ADIK.
dikau see ENGKAU.
dikir ber-, **men-** to recite, repe-
titiously, short Moslem religious
phrases praising the Lord. **pen-** o.
who recites these phrases.
dikit ber- $-^2$ 1 little by little. 2 to
be thrifty. *Asal* ~ *sadja tjukuplah
gadjihmu itu*, If you are thrifty your
salary will suffice. **se-** a little, few.
Ia hanja makan ~ *sadja*, He only
ate a little. *Disini hanja* ~ *orang*,
Only a few people are here. ~ *demi*
~ little by little, gradually. **se- -²nja**
at least. *Engkau harus beladjar* ~
sedjam sehari, You should study at
least an hour a day.
diko 1 see DUKO. 2 see TUKANG.
dikrit see DÉKRIT.
diktator dictator.
dikté dictation. **men-kan** to dictate
s.t. **-an** 1 dictation. 2 dictated.
dim inch.
dimana see MANA.
dimpit see DÉMPÉT.
dina see HINA DINA.
dinamika dynamics.
dinamis dynamic. **pen-an** dynamism.
dinamit dynamite.
dinas 1 office, department. *Ia bekerdja utk suatu* – *pemerintah*, He
works for a government office. 2
service, agency, department. – *Penerangan Amérika Serikat* U.S. Information Service. 3 length of service. – *saja sdh 10 tahun*, I have
served 10 years. 4 to be on duty.
Ia sedang –, He's on duty. 5 official.
utk – for official use. **ke-an** service. ~
umum public service. – *kepanduan*
pilot service. – *penjelidik* intelligence
service. – *tentara* military service.
dinda see ADINDA.
dinding wall, partition. **ber-** 1 to
have walls. 2 partitioned. **men-** to
form a wall. **men-i** to wall s.t. in.
Ia ~ *kebunnja*, He walled in his
garden. **men-kan** to use s.t. as a wall.
~ *tangan* to shade the eyes or cup
the ears. **pen-** partition, screen.
ter- partitioned, screened.
dines see DINAS.

dingin cold, cool, chilly. – *hari ini*,
It's cold today. *Ia diterima dgn* –,
He was received coolly. **ber-** $-^2$ to
enjoy the coolness. **ke-an** 1 to feel
cold, be chilled. *Ia merasa* ~ , He
felt cold. 2 too cold. **men-** to become cold. *Malam mulai* ~ , The
evening is getting cold. **men-kan** to
refrigerate, make cold. **pen-** 1 a
cooler, refrigerator. *sistim* ~ cooling
system. 2 o. who feels cold all the
time. **pen-an** refrigeration. $-^2$ *panas*
feverish. – *hati* indifferent, cool. –
kepala coolheaded. – *tertulang* very
cold, chilled to the bones.
dingkelik see DINGKLIK.
dingkik men- to watch, spy on.
dingklik settee.
dinihari dawn.
dipan divan, sofa.
diplomasi diplomacy. **ber-** diplomatic.
diplomat diplomat.
diplomatik diplomatic.
diréksi management.
diréktorat directorate.
diréktur director.
dirgahaju long live!
diri self, oneself. *Ia membunuh* –, He
killed himself. *Djagalah* –*mu*, Take
care of yourself. **ber-** 1 to stand.
Ia ~ *dipintu*, He's standing at the
door. 2 to stand, exist. *Negara kita
tlh* ~ *be-ratus² tahun*, Our country
has existed for hundreds of years.
~ *azamat* to stand in a respectful
position. 3 standing room. ~ *sendiri*
1 to be on o's own. *Sedjak saja
déwasa saja* ~ *sendiri*, Since I've
been grown I have been on my own.
2 independent. *Negara kita sekarang*
~ *sendiri*, Our country is now
independent. **berpen-an** to be of the
opinion. *Ia* ~ *bhw kita harus mentjegah
perang*, He's of the opinion that we
must prevent war. **men-kan** 1 to
build, erect. *Ia* ~ *sebuah gedung*,
He erected a building. 2 to found,
establish. *Ia* ~ *perusahaan*, He
established a business. ~ *bulu roma*
to stand o's hair on end. ~ *kémah* to
pitch a tent. **pe-** subject (person).
pen- founder. **pen-an** 1 erection,
building. ~ *tugu ini* erection of this
monument. 2 establishment, founding. ~ *negara kita* founding of our
country. 3 standpoint. 4 proposition.
sepen- the height of a man. **ter-** *atas*
or *dari* to consist of. *Pengurus* ~
dari 3 orang, The board consists of
3 persons. – *sendiri* 1 o.s. *Djika
tidak hati² -mu sendiri akan rugi*, If
you don't watch out, you yourself
will be the loser. 2 confidentially,

between us. *antara kita - sendiri* just among us, confidentially between us. **sen–an** alone.

diris men– to water plants. **pen–** refreshments.

dirus see DIRIS.

disértasi dissertation.

disiplin discipline.

diskriminasi discrimination.

diskusi discussion. **men–kan** to discuss.

dislokasi dislocation.

distorsi distortion.

distribusi distribution.

distrik district.

diterdj. [*diterdjemahkan*] translated.

Div. [*Divisi*] division.

diversifikasi diversification.

dj [1 *djam* 2 *djilid*] 1 o'clock. 2 volume.

djabal mountain. **men–** 1 to rob, steal. 2 to loom large. **(pen)–an** rubber band.

djabang-baji newborn baby.

djabar almighty. **men–kan** to reduce a fraction to its lowest terms, simplify s.t. ~ *petjahan* to simplify a fraction.

Djabar [*Djawa Barat*] West Java.

djabat ber–(an) *tangan* to shake hands. *Bapak dan saja ~ tangan,* Father and I shook hands. **men–** 1 to seize, grasp. *Ia ~ tangan saja,* He seized my hand. 2 to occupy a post, hold an office. *Ia ~ tiga kedudukan,* He occupies three posts. *Ia ~ kepala kantor pos,* He occupies the post of head of the post office. *Ia ~ walikota Bandung,* He is the mayor of Bandung. **pe–** functionary, official. **pen–** 1 official. ~ *negeri* government official, officeholder. 2 employee. **se–** colleague. **-an** 1 function. ~*nja ialah melajani tamu luar negeri,* His function is to take care of foreign visitors. ~ *gindjal adalah...* The function of the kidney is to... 2 office. ~ *djaksa agung* the office of the attorney general. 3 post.

djabir ber– –² slovenly, sloppy. *Pakaiannja ~ ,* His clothes were sloppy.

djabung resin.

djadah 1 see DJUADAH. 2 see HARAM.

djadam a strong laxative.

djadi 1 finished, accomplished. *Pekerdjaan itu sdh –,* That job is accomplished. 2 as a result. *Saja – lihat gambar hidup,* I did get to the movies. 3 so, therefore, thus, hence. *– kalau begitu, saja pulang sadja,* So, if that's the case, I might as well go home. 4 outcome. *Begitulah –nja kalau tidak hati²!* That's what hap-

pens if you aren't careful! *Saja tidak tahu apa –nja anak itu kelak,* I don't know what will happen to that boy. *Bagaimana –nja?* How did it end? 5 ready. *Télpon itu blm –,* The telephone call isn't ready yet. 6 *tidak –* didn't work (out). 7 to become, get. *– pemandian* to turn into a bathing place. *– kering* to get dry. 8 to be, serve as. *Ia – dokter dirumah sakit,* He serves as a doctor at a hospital. 9 to take place, come off, happen. *Udjian tak –,* An exam isn't going to be held. *–lah terang,* Let there be light. **ke–an** 1 creation. ~ *bumi* creation of the world. 2 to happen. *Hal demikian itu blm pernah ~ di Indonésia,* Such a thing has never happened in Indonesia. 3 incident, event. ~ *alam* natural phenomenon. **men–** 1 to become. *Si Amin ingin ~ serdadu,* Amin wants to become a soldier. 2 into. *Kota itu dibagi ~ tiga bagian,* The town is divided into three sections. 3 as. *Ia dipilih ~ lurah,* He was chosen as village chief. ~ *karun* to become rich. ~ *pengantin* to marry. 4 to be. *Nénék mojangnja ~ radja,* His ancestors were kings. 5 to succeed, to go through (with), to win out. *Sekali ini ~ rentjananja,* This time his plan succeeded. **men– –²** 1 to increase. *Hutangnja ~ sadja,* His debts have increased. 2 to get worse. *Penjakitnja ~ sadja,* His illness gets worse and worse. **men–kan** 1 to make. *Ia ~ saja sebagai wakilnja,* He made me his deputy. *Présidén ~ dia perdana menteri,* The president made him prime minister. 2 to finish s.t. *Saja ~ pekerdjaan saja,* I finished my work. 3 to create. *Tuhan ~ bumi ini,* God created the world. 4 to cause, bring about. *Kemalasannja ~ kemarahan bapaknja,* His laziness brought about his father's anger. 5 to turn s.t. into. ~ *daérah ini men– sawah* to make this area into a wet rice field. ~ *periksa* to be apprised. *Demikian agar spj sdr. ~ periksa,* The foregoing is so that you will be apprised (of this matter). **men– –²kan** to make worse. *Tindakannja ~ kebentjian rakjat padanja,* His behavior made the people hate him more and more. ~ *hati* 1 grievous. 2 to embitter. **pen–** developer, doer. **pen–an** 1 outbreak ~ *penjakit* outbreak of a disease. 2 development. **se– –²nja** as much, as hard, as possible. *Ia bekerdja ~ ,* He worked as hard as possible. **ter–** 1 to happen. *Apa jg tlh ~ tak dpt ditiadakan,* What's done can't be undone. 2 to consist. *Pengurus itu ~ dari dua orang,* The committee consists of two persons. *~ dgn* to become of. *Apa ~ dgn buku jg baru itu?* What's become of the new book? *–²an* 1 ghost, apparition. 2 imitation. *Bunga ~ itu dibuat dari kertas,* Those imitation flowers are made of paper. **–nja** consequently, hence. *– lah!* All right! (It's O.K.) *– landas* to serve as a scapegoat.

djadja ber–, men– to peddle. *Ia ~ berkeliling kota,* He peddled around town. **men–kan** to peddle s.t. *Ia ~ és krim,* He is peddling ice cream. **pen–** peddler. **–an** merchandise which is peddled.

djadjag men–i to measure the depth of s.t.

djadjah to have traveled widely. *Ia sdh – di Éropah,* He has traveled all over Europe. **men–** 1 to colonize s.t. 2 to dominate. *Ia di– oléh isterinja,* He is dominated by his wife. **men–i** to traverse. *Ia ~ seluruh dunia,* He traversed the whole world. **pen–** 1 colonizer. 2 despot. **pen–an** colonial domination. **–an** 1 colony. 2 territory. *~ seberang lautan* overseas territory.

djadjak men– to probe, take soundings.

djadjal men– to try, test.

djadjan a sweet. **(ber)–** to eat sweets purchased from peddlers.

djadjar row, line. **ber–** 1 in a row. *Anak² duduk ~ ,* The children sat in a row. 2 next to e.o. *Saja duduk ~ isteri saja,* I sat next to my wife. **ber–an** in rows. **men–** to plow. **men–kan** 1 to put in a row. 2 to place next to o. another. 3 to make parallel. *Ia ~ dua papan itu,* He laid the two planks parallel. 4 to pull. *Kerbau ~ beluku,* The water buffalo pulls a plow. **menje–kan** 1 to place s.o. on a par. *Saja ~nja dgn Toto,* I place him on a par with Toto. 2 to equate. *Peraturan baru ~ pangkat komisaris polisi dgn pangkat létnan kolonél,* The new regulation equates the rank of police commissioner with that of lieutenant colonel. **perse–an** parallelism. **se–** parallel. *Dua djalan ini ~ ,* These two roads run parallel. **ter–** 1 placed in rows. *Buku² ~ rapi dlm almari,* The books are neatly arranged in the bookcase. 2 dragged, thrown backward. **–an** 1 row, line. 2 furrows. *– géndjang* parallelogram.

djadwal a time schedule indicating the hour of sunrise and sunset during the fasting month. *– logaritma* logarithmic table(s).

djaga 1 to wake up. *Ia – dari tidurnja,* He woke up. 2 Watch it! (Look out!) 3 guard, watchman. *– malam* night watchman. 4 to guard. **ber–** to stand guard. *Peradjurit ~ didepan istana,* A soldier stands guard in front of the palace. **ber– –²** 1 to be on o's guard. *Meréka ~ menghadapi musuh,* They were on their guard against the enemy. 2 to be careful. *~ sedikit membawa piring itu,* Be careful carrying those plates. **ke– –²an** sleepless. *Ia ~ 24 djam lamanja,* He was sleepless for 24 hours. **men–** 1 to guard s.o. or s.t. 2 to keep watch. *Ia ~ ibunja jg sakit itu,* He kept watch over his sick mother. 3 to look after, baby-sit. *Siti ~ adiknja,* Siti looked after her younger brother. 4 to prevent. *Tindakan ini diambil utk ~ bahaja kebakaran,* This measure was taken to prevent the danger of fire. **men–i** to guard. *Ia ~ djalan kegua,* He guarded the way to the cave. **men–kan** to wake s.o. up. **pen–** guard, watchman. *~ anak* baby sitter. *~ dada* chest protector (baseball). *~ tempat* usher. **pen–an** 1 a guard. 2 prevention. *~ penjakit* disease prevention. 3 care. *~ baji* care of babies. **ter–** 1 to be awakened. 2 guarded. *Pendjara itu tak ~ ,* That prison is not guarded. 3 controlled. *Anak itu tak ~ ,* That child can't be controlled. *–lah kebersihan,* Keep (Indonesia) tidy.

djagabaja village constable.

djagal butcher. **ber–** to run a small business. **men–** to butcher, slaughter. *Djagal ~ sapi,* The butcher butchers a beef. *Tentara ~ musuhnja,* The army slaughtered its enemy. **pen–an** 1 abattoir. 2 slaughter (of animals). **–an** 1 merchandise. 2 abattoir.

djagang pole used for reinforcement (of wall, etc.).

djagat world. **se–** world-wide, international. *fédérasi buruh ~* international labor federation. *– buana, – raja* the entire world.

djago 1 cock, rooster. 2 leader, champion. *Ali selalu mendjadi – anak² itu,* Ali has always been the leader of those boys. *Dialah jg mendjadi – dlm kelasnja,* He is tops in his class. 3 cock of the walk. *Tingkahnja seperti dia sendirilah jg paling –,* He behaves as if he were

cock of the walk. **men–i** to take the
lead in. *Ia* ∼ *Grand Prix de l'Indonésie,* He took the lead in the
Grand Prix de l'Indonésie. **men–kan**
to champion, back, sponsor. **–an** 1
gamecock. 2 leader, champion. **–²an**
reckless. *Ia selalu* ∼ *naik motornja,*
He always drives his car recklessly.
– *berenang* swimming champ. – *bola*
football player. – *gelut* wrestler. –
makan inveterate eater. – *menonton*
inveterate moviegoer. *si– mérah* the
fire. *Si– mérah mengamuk,* The fire
raged. – *tindju* boxer.

djagung corn. **men–** 1 to sprout.
Padi sdh ∼ *disawah,* The rice is
sprouting in the rice fields. 2 to appear. *Gigi anak saja* ∼ , My child's
tooth is coming out. *Penjakitnja* ∼ ,
The initial symptoms of his disease
have appeared.

djagur robust, sturdy, big for o's age.
Si– name of the sacred cannon in
Jakarta.

djahanam 1 hell. 2 accursed! scoundrel! damned! *–! Pergilah!* Damn
you! Go! **men–kan** to curse, swear at.
Ia ∼ *anaknja jg menentangnja itu,*
He put a curse on his child who
opposed him.

djahat bad, wicked, evil, malicious.
Ia selalu berbuat –, He's always doing
bad things. **ber–** 1 to sin. 2 to do
wrong. **ke–an** 1 badness. ∼*nja itu
tak bisa diperbaiki lagi,* His badness
cannot be cured any more. 2 crime.
3 sin. **men–i** 1 to wrong s.o. *Ia* ∼
orang tuanja sendiri, He wronged his
own parents. 2 to seduce. *Ia* ∼ *anak
gadis,* He seduced a girl. **men–kan** 1
to make o. look bad. *Ia* ∼ *nama
orang tuanja,* He gave his parents a
bad name. 2 to think badly of s.o.
Djangan ∼ *semua orang,* Do not
think badly of everyone. **pen–** criminal.

djahé ginger.

djahid an ascetic, hermit.

djahil ignorant of the teachings of
Islam. **ke–an** ignorance.

Djahiliah Age of Ignorance (pre-
Islamic era in Arabia).

djahit **men–** to sew. **pen–** 1 tailor. 2
seamstress. 3 sewing needle. **(pen)–
an** sewing. *Apakah ada* ∼ *jang harus
dikerdjakan hari ini?* Is there any
sewing to be done today? ∼ *ini
kurang kuat,* This sewing is not
strong enough. **–²an** sewn goods. –
-men– needlework.

djail rascal. **men–i** to nag, pick (on
s.o.). *Si Amat selalu* ∼ *adiknja,*
Amat is always nagging his brother.

djaja victory. **ber–** 1 victorious, tri-
umphant. 2 glorious. *Indonésia* ∼
glorious Indonesia. **ke–an** 1 glory,
fame. 2 prosperity, wealth. **men–kan**
1 to glorify, make famous. *Kita
harus* ∼ *negara kita,* We must glorify
our country. 2 to be successful.

Djaja see DJAYA.

Djajakatera see DJAKARTA.

djak jug.

djaka bachelor.

Djakarta Jakarta (prior to independence known as Batavia), capital of
Indonesia.

djakat see ZAKAT.

djakét 1 morning or cutawat coat.
2 leather jacket of motorcyclists.

djaksa public prosecutor. **ke–an** 1
office of the counsel for the prosecution. 2 office of the public prosecutor. 3 judiciary. ∼ *tentara* military
tribunal. – *agung* attorney general. –
panitera secretary to the prosecutor.
– *tinggi* chief public prosecutor. –
umum public prosecutor.

djala (casting) net. **men–** to fish
with a net. **pen–** fisherman who uses
a net. **–²** 1 net. ∼ *rambut* hair net.
2 hair net. – *kerap* a small mesh
casting net.

djalak 1 bold. *orang jg* – a bold
man. 2 starling.

djalal most holy, supreme. *Allah jg*
– The Supreme God, God Almighty.

djalan 1 road, path. 2 street. *Dia
tinggal di* – *Kijai Madja,* He lives
on Kijai Madja Street. 3 way, manner. *dgn* – by means of. *Bagaimana
–nja membuat bom atom?* What is
the process for making an atom bomb?
4 course. *–nja pemeriksaan lambat,*
The course of the investigation was
slow. 5 to be going on, approaching.
Ia sdh – *10 tahun,* He's going on 10.
6 lineal family relation. *Menurut* –
bapak saja berasal dari Sumatera, On
my father's side I come from Sumatera. 7 to pass. *Minta –, tuan,* May
I get by, Sir? 8 route. – *niaga* trade
route. **ber–** 1 to walk. *Djangan*
∼ *ditengah –,* Don't walk in the
middle of the road. 2 to run (of an
engine). *Tutuplah penutup radiator
sambil mesin* ∼ , Close the radiator
cap while the engine is running. 3
to run, go smoothly. *Pekerdjaannja*
∼ *dgn lantjar,* His work is going
along smoothly. 4 to work. *Itu hanja*
∼ *di-negara² industriil,* It only
works in industrial countries. ∼
béngkok to follow the crooked path.
∼ *dahulu* 1 to precede s.o. 2 to die
ahead of s.o. ∼ *darat* to go overland.

∼ *dari pintu belakang* to be dishonest. ∼ *kaki* to go on foot. ∼ *lurus* to follow the straight and narrow path. **ber-** –² 1 to take a walk, stroll. 2 to take a pleasure trip. *Ia* ∼ *ke Amérika,* He took a pleasure trip to America. **men–i** 1 to use, walk on, traverse. *Djangan* ∼ – *itu,* Don't use that road. 2 to endure, accept. *Ia* ∼ *hukumannja,* He accepted his punishment. 3 to undergo, endure. *Ia* ∼ *pembedahan,* She underwent an operation. 4 to travel around in. *Ia diundang akan* ∼ *Djepang,* He was invited to travel around in Japan. **men–kan** 1 to make go. *Ia* ∼ *kudanja kentjang,* He made his horse go fast. 2 to drive. *Ia* ∼ *mobilnja,* He drove his car. 3 to carry out, do. *Ia* ∼ *kewadjibannja dgn baik,* He carried out his responsibility very well. 4 to serve. ∼ *hukuman* to serve a sentence. ∼ *uang* to circulate money. **pe–** *kaki* pedestrian. **pen–** driver. **per–an** 1 trip. 2 course. ∼ *bintang²* the course of the stars. ∼ *darah* circulation of the blood. **se–** 1 parallel. *Garis² itu* ∼ , Those lines are parallel. 2 in accordance. *Kelakuannja tidak* ∼ *dgn kedudukannja,* His behavior is not in accordance with his position. 3 in line, in compliance. ∼ *dgn permintaannja* in compliance with his request. ∼ *djadi* of the same mother. **–an** road, track. **–nja** to behave, act. *Bagaimana* ∼ *radio Anda?* How's your radio behaving? –² to go for a walk. *Mari* ∼ , Let's take a walk. (Let's go out somewhere.) – *air* watercourse. – *angin* exhaust pipe. – *bahasa* idiom. – *besar* highway. – *buntu* 1 dead end, blind alley. *Dilarang masuk.* – *buntu!* Do not enter. Dead end! 2 deadlock, impasse. – *keluar* exit. – *lepas* way out. – *masuk* entrance. – *mati* dead end. – *memintas* short cut. – *napas* 1 respiratory tract. 2 trachea. – *péndék* short cut. – *pikiran* train of thought. – *raja* highway. – *sérong* cunning ways. – *singkat* short cut. *tak dpt* – out of commission. – *tambak* roadway, embankment. *Itu tidak pd –nja,* That's not proper.

djalang wild, undomesticated (of animals). **ke–an** wildness. **men–** 1 to return to a state of nature. 2 neglected.

djalar **ber–an** to spread. **men–** 1 to crawl. *Ular* ∼ , A snake crawls. 2 to spread. *Penjakit* ∼ *ke-mana²,* The disease spread everywhere. 3 to climb. *tanaman* ∼ a climbing plant,

creeper. **men–i** to penetrate into. **pen–an** 1 creeping. 2 spreading. 3 pole or stick to which a creeper can be attached.

djalin **ber–** stuck together. *Papan² itu* ∼ , The planks are stuck together. **ber–** –² complicated, intricate. *Perkara itu sungguh* ∼ , That is quite an intricate case. **memper–** to weave together. **men–** 1 to braid. ∼ *rambut* to braid o's hair. 2 to plait. ∼ *tikar* to plait a mat. 3 to compose. ∼ *tjerita* to compose a story. **men–kan** to weave in. **ter–** tied in. ∼ *rapat dgn* closely tied in with. **–an** 1 texture. 2 wickerwork.

djalu 1 cock's spur. 2 male, masculine. **men–** to play a dirty trick on s.o.

djalur 1 strip, stripe. 2 space between 2 rows of plants. 3 a column between 2 lines. **ber–** 1 striped. 2 in columns, in rows spaced evenly apart (of plants). – *suara* sound track.

djam 1 o'clock. – *berapa?* What time is it? – *dua* two o'clock. 2 hour. *dua* – two hours. 3 watch, clock. **ber–** –² for hours. ∼ *ibu menantikan kedatangan bapak,* For hours mother waited for dad's arrival. – *bitjara* office hours. – *dinding* wall clock. – *karét* not on time (expandable, elastic time). *–nja selalu* – *karét,* He's always late. – *malam* curfew. – *pasir* hourglass. – *peladjaran* period of a lesson. – *pér karét* never late, always on time. – *saku* pocket watch. – *tangan* wrist watch.

djama'ah 1 parish. 2 community, assembly. – *hadji* group of pilgrims going to Mecca.

djamah touch. **men–** 1 to touch, feel. 2 to stain, sully. **–²an** maidservant and also concubine.

djamak 1 plural. 2 ordinary, normal. *Hal itu bukanlah suatu perkara jg –,* That is not an ordinary case. **se–nja** proper. *Sdh* ∼ *bhw kita menghormati orang tua kita,* It is only proper that we should show respect to our parents.

djaman 1 period, age, era. 2 see ZAMAN. **pen–an** periodization. **se–** current. *keadaan jg* ∼ current situation. – *Batu Lama* Old Stone Age. – *langgeng* eternity.

djamang diadem. **se–** a moment. *Tunggulah* ∼ *dahulu,* Please wait a moment.

djambak 1 tuft. *Rambutnja tinggal se– sadja,* He had only one tuft of hair left. 2 bunch. *Saja memetik beberapa* – *bunga,* I picked several bunches of flowers. **men–** 1 to pull o's hair. *Adik* ~ *rambut ibu,* Kid brother pulled Mother's hair. 2 to seize by the forelock.

djamban toilet, rest room. – *kentjing* urinal.

djambang(an) vase, pot.

djambar 1 shelter, temporary hut. 2 tray, serving. **se–** one serving of food. *Kedua anak makan* ~ *itu,* The 2 children ate one helping of food.

djambatan bridge. **men–i** to bridge. *Pemerintah tlh* ~ *semua sungai²,* The government has bridged all the rivers. – *angkat* drawbridge. – *darurat* temporary bridge. – *djungkatan* drawbridge. – *gantung* suspension bridge. – *tarik* drawbridge.

djambel 1 tramp. 2 prostitute.

djamblang a sweet-sour and puckering fruit dark purple in color and about the size of an olive.

djamboré jamboree.

djambrét men– 1 to snatch. *Ia* ~ *saputangan saja dari kantong saja,* He snatched my handkerchief out of my pocket. 2 to plagiarize. *Amat* ~ *karangan kawannja,* Amat plagiarized his friend's composition. **–an** plagiarism.

djambu k.o. fruit. **–²** tuft, tassel. – *bidji,* – *lambo* guava. – *monjét* cashew nut.

djambul 1 tuft, plume. 2 front wave in hair.

djamdjam see ZAMZAM. – *durdja* facial expression.

djamin men– to guarantee. *Saja* ~ *djam ini tahan air,* I guarantee that this watch is waterproof. **pen–** guarantor. **pen–an** a warrant. **–an** 1 guarantee. 2 warrant. ~ *hak* patent. ~ *hak tulis* guarantee of copyright. ~ *haritua* old-age pension. ~ *hukum* legal guarantee.

djampé see DJAMPI.

djampi magic formulas. **men–(kan)** to utter magic formulas. **–an** = –.

djampuk k.o. owl.

djamrud emerald.

djamu 1 guest. 2 medicinal herbs. **ber–** 1 to call on. *Bapak* ~ *kerumah guru saja,* Father called on my teacher. 2 to have, receive visitors. **memper–, men–** 1 to entertain. 2 to give medicinal herbs. **men–i** to entertain guests. *Présidén* ~ *tamu luar negeri,* The president entertains the foreign visitor. **men–kan** to serve (to guests). *Ibu* ~ *minuman pd tetamu,* Mother served drinks to the guests. **per–an** 1 reception, banquet. 2 a party. 3 a call, visit. **–an** dishes and

drinks offered to guests. ~ *minum* a party at which drinks are served (sometimes used for a cocktail party). – *makan* banquet. – *sutji* Holy Communion.

djamur 1 fungus. 2 mushroom. – *nasi* edible mushroom. – *padi* edible mushrooms cultivated on the ashes of paddy bran. 3 mold. – *karang* 1 moss growing on coral. 2 coral polyps. **–an** covered with mildew.

Djan. [*Djanuari*] January.

djanabah impure, ceremonially unclean. *Orang* – *tidak boléh masuk mesdjid,* Defiled people may not enter the mosque.

djanat see DJANNAH.

djanda 1 widow. 2 widower. 3 divorcee. – *berhias* childless widow. – *blm berlaki* a girl left by her lover after being seduced. – *kembang* childless widow.

djandjang 1 ladder. 2 pole for climbing plants. **ber–** by ladder.

djandji 1 promise, agreement. *Djangan lupa –mu,* Do not forget your promise. 2 to agree. *Meréka* – *utk bertemu lagi,* They agreed to meet again. 3 condition. *Kau boléh bersekolah lagi dgn* – *kau akan bekerdja keras,* You may return to school on condition that you will work hard. 4 delay. *Ia minta* – *seminggu,* He asked for a week's delay. 5 dying hour. *Sdh sampai –mu!* Your last hour has struck! 6 engagement, appointment. **ber–** to promise. *Ia* ~ *tidak akan mentjuri lagi,* He promised not to steal again. **men–kan** to promise. *Ia* ~ *saja arlodji,* He promised me a watch. **per–an** 1 agreement. 2 last will and testament. ~ *Baru* the New Testament. ~ *dagang* business deal. ~ *Lama* the Old Testament. ~ *sosial* social contract. – *keling* false promise.

djangak profligate, dissolute, debauched. **men–** to live a life of profligacy, of dissoluteness. *Setelah dia mendjadi kaja, kehidupannja selalu* ~ *sadja,* After he got rich he led a life of profligacy.

djangan 1 do not, don't. – *pergi,* Don't go. 2 should not. *Kita* – *patah hati,* We shouldn't be discouraged. 3 vegetable soup. **–kan** let alone, much less. ~ *dpt berdjalan, dudukpun ia tak dpt,* He can't even sit, let alone walk. **–²** 1 if not. 2 maybe, perhaps. ~ *ia datang nanti malam,* Maybe he'll come tonight, I fear. ~ *tuan akan lupa* otherwise you'll forget. – *sampai* lest, that. *Hati²* – *sampai djatuh,*

Be careful you don't fall. – *tidak must. Engkau – tidak datang nanti malam,* You must come tonight.

djangat 1 skin. 2 rind. 3 bark. **men**– to skin, flay.

djanggal 1 awkward, clumsy. *Bunji kalimat itu –,* That sentence sounds awkward. *Tingkah laku anak itu – kelihatannja,* That child's behavior seems clumsy. 2 discordant, out of tune. 3 peculiar. *Bukankah perkara itu agak –?* Isn't that case rather peculiar? **ke-an** 1 awkwardness, clumsiness. 2 peculiarity.

djanggi 1 Ethiopian. 2 Negro. 3 exotic. *hal² jg* – exotic matters.

djanggut beard. **ber**– bearded.

djangir 1 Balinese dancing girl. 2 k.o. Balinese dance and music.

djangka 1 a pair of compasses. 2 period of time. *dlm – satu tahun* within a period of one year. 3 measurement. 4 phase. *Perdjuangan kita mentjapai – baru,* Our struggle has arrived at a new phase. **ber**– 1 to measure. *Djalan ini lébarnja ∼ lima métér,* This road measures 5 meters in width. 2 to be spaced. *∼ lama* long-term. **men-(kan)** 1 to measure off. 2 to plan. *Pemerintah ∼ tindakan jg akan dilakukan,* The government plans the steps to be taken. *– pandjang* long-term. *Itu rentjana – pandjang,* That is a long-term program. *– péndék* short-term. *tidak ada* **–nja** unlimited.

djangkah step, stride. **men**– to step over s.t., clear without touching.

djangkang **men**– to walk with legs far apart.

djangkap even, not odd.

djangkar 1 aerial roots like that of the mangrove. 2 anchor. **ber**– to anchor. *Kapal ∼ dipelabuhan,* The ship anchored in the harbor.

djangkau **men**– to reach out. *Bapak ∼ memetik bunga,* Father reached out to pick a flower. **se**– within arm's length. **ter**– within reach. *Tjita² itu pasti ∼ oléhmu,* Such ideals are certainly within your reach.

djangkih see DJANGKIT. *– mangkih* scattered around. *Pakaiannja tersebar – mangkih dikamar,* His clothes were scattered all around the room.

djangkit **ber**– 1 to spread. *Penjakit itu ∼ ke-mana²,* The disease spread everywhere. 2 contagious. *Koléra adalah penjakit ∼ ,* Cholera is a contagious disease. **ke**– contaminated. **ke-an** to become infected, catch a disease. **men-i** to infect, contaminate. **men-kan** to spread s.t. around. *Lalat ∼ penjakit,* A fly spreads

disease. **pen-an** spread of a disease. *∼ penjakit pés* the spread of plague.

djangkrik see DJENGKERIK.

djangkung 1 k.o. heron. 2 tall (of a person). **-an** stilts.

djanin fetus.

djannah paradise.

djantan 1 male, masculine (of animals). *ajam* – rooster. 2 he-man. *Tarzan adalah benar² seorang –,* Tarzan is a real he-man. 3 valiant, dashing, bold. *Seorang kesatria selalu bersifat –,* A knight should always be valiant. *utjapan jg* – bold statement. **ke-an** 1 manliness, masculinity. 2 courage, valor. **men-i** to copulate (of animals).

djantera see DJENTERA.

djantung heart. *– betis* calf (of the leg). *– hati* sweetheart. *– paha* thigh. *– pisang* banana blossom. *– tangan* the ball of the thumb.

djantur 1 juggling trick. 2 spell. *Puteri itu kena – dukun djahat itu,* The princess was caught under the spell of the evil sorcerer. 3 magic. **men**– 1 to perform juggling tricks. 2 to conjure, bewitch. **-an** narration in Javanese shadow play by the puppeteer.

Djanuari January.

Djapen [*Djawatan Penerangan*] Information Office.

Djapendi [*Djawatan Penerangan Daérah Istiméwa*] Special Region Information Office (Jogjakarta).

Djapenka [*Djawatan Penerangan Kabupatén*] Regency Information Office.

Djapenko [*Djawatan Penerangan Kota*] Municipal Information Office.

Djapenpro(p) [*Djawatan Penerangan Propinsi*] Provincial Information Office.

djara small drill, auger. **men**– 1 to bore, drill. 2 to plow.

djarah see ZARRAH. **men**– to plunder s.t. *∼ rajah* to plunder and pillage. **pen**– plunderer, robber. **-an** plundered loot.

djarak 1 distance. 2 radius of a circle. 3 castor-oil plant. **ber**– to be at a distance from. *Pohon ∼ 3 métér dari rumah,* The tree is 3 meters from the house. **men**– to put distance between, move away from. *Anak² dibaris depan ∼ sedikit,* Children in the front row moved a bit away from e.o. **men-kan** to separate. *Wasit ∼ kedua petindju itu,* The referee separated the two boxers. *– baris berganda* double margin. –

dekat a short distance. - *djauh* a long distance.

djaram **men**- 1 to dab. *Ia ~ dahi orang jg sakit itu*, He dabbed the forehead of the sick man. 2 to apply a compress. **pen**- compress.

djarang 1 wide apart. *Gadis itu giginja -*, The girl's teeth are spread wide apart. 2 rare. *Mutiara sematjam itu - ada*, A pearl like that is rare. 3 rarely, seldom. *Ia - datang kemari*, He rarely comes here. 4 sparse, thin. *Bapak rambutnja -*, Father's hair is sparse. *Daérah itu berpenduduk -*, That area is sparsely populated. 5 transparent. **memper-**, **men-kan** 1 to thin out. *Petani ~ tanaman dikebunnja*, The farmer thins out the plants in his garden. 2 to dilute, water down. **pen-an** thinning out.

djaras 1 bunch of long objects. *bawang perai se-* a bunch of leeks. 2 wicker basket. **men-** to tie in a bundle.

Djarék [*Djalannja Révolusi Kita*] March of Our Revolution.

djari 1 finger. 2 toe. $-^2$ radius of a circle. 2 spoke of a wheel. 3 grating, latticework, etc. - *ampai* horsewhip. - *hantu* middle finger. - *kaki* toe. - *kelingking* little finger. - *malang* middle finger. - *manis* ring finger. - *mati*, - *pandjang* middle finger. - *rimpang* fingers or toes wide apart. - *telundjuk* index finger. - *tengah* middle finger.

djaring net. **men-** to fish with a net. *~ angin* useless activity. **-an** network, fabric. *~ ikat* connective tissue. *~ djalan*² highway network. *-²* (mesh) net. *~ bahu* thoracic region below the shoulders.

djaro bamboo lath.

djarum 1 sewing needle. 2 hypodermic needle. 3 hand of a clock or watch. **ber-** 1 to have an injection. 2 thorny, with nettles. **men-** 1 to pin s.t. 2 to have an injection. 3 to give an injection. 4 to sew by hand. **pen-** = DJARUM. **pen-an** 1 a procurer. 2 matchmaker, intermediary. 3 seam (of clothing). **-an** 1 intrigue. 2 go-between, marriage broker. 3 procurer. 4 needlework. *halus* ruse, sly trick. - *neratja* balance needle. - *pandjang* minute hand. - *péndék* hour hand. - *radjut* knitting needle. - *tjotjok* awl.

djas coat. - *buka* open jacket with lapels. - *dingin* overcoat. - *hudjan* raincoat. - *luar* overcoat, topcoat. - *mandi* bathrobe. - *tutup* jacket with stiff high collar and no lapels.

djasa 1 merit. 2 service. *Ia banjak* - *thd tanah air*, He has rendered his country many services. 3 favor. **ber-** to be meritorious, render a person a service. - *baik* favor.

djasad 1 body. 2 organism. - *renik* microorganism.

djasadi bodily, physical.

djasmani 1 body. *dlm* - *jg séhat terdapat rochani jg séhat* a sound mind in a sound body. 2 physical, material. *kebutuhan* - physical needs. **ke-an** materialism.

djasmaniah physical.

djatah quota, allotment, allocation. - *gula utk Djabar tahun ini ialah 500 ton*, This year's sugar quota for West Java is 500 tons. **pen-an** 1 alloting. 2 distribution, allocating.

Djateng [*Djawa Tengah*] Central Java.

djati teakwood, teak tree. **kese-an** genuineness. **se-** 1 true. *Ia seorang kawan ~ *, He is a true friend. 2 genuine. *Ia adalah seorang Amérika ~ *, He is a genuine American.

Djatim [*Djawa Timur*] East Java.

Djatinegara 1 formerly Meester Cornelis (southern section of Jakarta). 2 telephone exchange in Jakarta.

djatmika polite. **ke-an** politeness.

djatuh 1 to fall. *Ia - dari atap*, He fell from the roof. *Ia - kasih*, He fell in love. *Ia - sakit*, He fell ill. - *ketangan* to fall into the hands, clutches of s.o. 2 to lead to. *Djalan ini - ke Tjandi Mendut*, This road leads to Tjandi Mendut. 3 to reach, arrive. *Kapal pendjeladjah - dipelabuhan Médan*, The cruiser arrived at the harbor of Medan. 4 to flunk, fail. *Ia - dlm udjian ilmu pasti*, He failed his math exam. 5 related. *Kau apa -nja dgn Tomo?* How are you related to Tomo? **ber-an** to fall. *Buah² kastanje ~ kedalam truck*, The chestnuts poured into the truck. **ke-an** 1 fall, downfall. *~ kabinét menimbulkan krisis*, The fall of the cabinet caused a crisis. 2 hit by a falling object. *Kepalanja ~ kelapa*, He was hit on the head by a coconut. *~ bulan* to have a windfall. *Ia ~ untung*, Good fortune befell him. 3 to come down with s.t. *Ia ~ penjakit*, He came down with an illness. **men-i** 1 to fell s.t. *Ia ~ rusa dgn sebuah batu*, He felled the deer with a rock. 2 to impose. *~ hukuman* to impose sentence on s.o. **men-kan** 1 to let fall. *Dia ~ diri*, He let himself fall. 2 to cause to fall, topple. *Djénderal itu ~ présidén dari kedudukannja*, The general toppled the president from his position. 3 to drop s.t.

Kapal terbang ~ *bom,* The plane dropped a bomb. 4 to ruin s.t. or s.o. *Korupsi* ~ *perusahaan jg besar itu,* Corruption ruined that large business enterprise. ~ *hukuman* 1 to pass, impose sentence. 2 to pass judgment. *Publik itu* ~ *hukuman,* The public passed judgment. ~ *kesalahan* to blame s.o. ~ *talak* to divorce o's wife by repudiation. **pen–an** *hukuman* pronouncement of sentence. **ter–** to be overthrown. – *bangun* to fall and rise again, persevere. – *diatas tilam* 1 to have a lucky break. 2 to get off easy. – *hati kpd* 1 to fall in love with s.o. 2 to feel sorry for s.o. – *hudjan* rainfall. – *keatas* to be lucky. *Ia selalu* – *keatas,* He's always lucky. – *mérek,* – *nama* to lose o's good name. *Karena kelakuannja itu ia* – *mérek,* Because of his behavior he lost his good name. – *miskin* to be impoverished. – *pd* to fall for. *Kita tak akan* – *pd tipu-muslihatnja,* We won't fall for his tricks. – *tjoloknja* degraded, debased.

djauh 1 far, distant, remote. *Indonésia* – *dari Amérika,* Indonesia is far from America. 2 (by) far. *Lukisan ini* – *lebih bagus dari pd jg lain,* This painting is far better than the others. **ber–an** to be far apart. *Meskipun kita* ~ *kita tak akan saling melupakan,* Although we are far apart, we will not forget e.o. **ber– –²an** to keep apart. *Meréka duduk saling* ~ , They sat down, away from e.o. **ke–an** 1 too far (away). *Médja itu* ~ *dari saja,* The table is too far away from me. 2 distance. **men–** to go (get, draw) farther away. *Kapal itu makin* ~ *dari pantai,* The ship drew farther and farther away from shore. **men–i** 1 to avoid. *Ia selalu* ~ *saja,* He always avoids me. 2 to fail s.o. **men–kan** to keep s.o. away from s.t. *Orang tua selalu* ~ *anaknja dari bahaja,* Parents always keep their children away from danger. ~ *diri dari* to refrain from. – *ditjari* exaggerated. – *malam* late at night. – *umur* advanced in age. *Ia mati sesudah* – *umur,* He died at an advanced age. –² *asal selamat,* It doesn't matter how far, provided it's safe.

djauhar 1 jewel. 2 fetus, embryo.

djauhari 1 jeweler. 2 expert.

Djaw. [*Djawatan*] office, division.

Djawa 1 Java. 2 Javanese. **ke–an** Javaneseness, Javanism.

djawab 1 a reply, answer, response. 2 an accounting. **ber–** 1 to answer, reply. "*Tidak,*" *ia* ~ , "No," he replied. 2 answered. **men–** to reply,

answer, respond. ~ *perdjamuan* to return a call. **men–i** to answer s.o. or s.t. **(pen)–an** response, reply, answer. – *kedua* rejoinder.

djawatan government office, department, service. – *béa dan tjukai* customs and excise service. – *distribusi* rationing office. – *imigrasi* immigration service. – *keréta api* Indonesian railways. – *luar negeri* foreign service. – *pelajaran* navigation service. – *penerangan* information service. – *penerbangan* aviation service. – *purbakala* archaeological service. – *rahasia* secret service. – *tera* bureau of standards. see DJABAT.

djawawut millet.

djawi 1 ox. 2 cow. 3 term used in Malaya to designate Malay in Arabic script. **men–kan** to translate into Malay. – *pekan* of mixed Malay and Ceylonese (Tamil) blood.

Djaya [*Djakarta Raya*] Greater Jakarta.

djazirah peninsula.

djebah broad in the lower part of the face.

djebak trap. **men–** to trap, snare. *Pemburu* ~ *matjan dlm –,* The hunter traps the tiger in a trap. **pen–** trapper. **ter–** to be tricked, taken in. **–an** trap, snare.

djebat musk. **men–i** to anoint. **–²an** perfumes.

djeblok mud. **ke–** 1 to be stuck in the mud. 2 to get into trouble.

djeblos **ke–** 1 to fall, step (into a hole). ~ *dlm lumpur* to get stuck in the mud (of a vehicle, etc.). 2 to fall into a trap. *Ia* ~ *oléh pihak musuh,* He fell into a trap his enemy had set for him. **men–kan** 1 to throw s.t. ~ *batu* to throw a rock. ~ *pendjahat kedalam pendjara* to throw a criminal into jail. 2 to deceive s.o. **ter–** = KE–.

djebol broken down. **men–** 1 to break s.t. down. ~ *pintu* to break down a door. 2 to penetrate. ~ *pertahanan musuh* to penetrate the enemy's defenses. ~ *dan membangun* to tear down and rebuild. **pen–an** demolition.

djebrol to eject, push out. **men–** to eject, erupt. *Lahar* ~ *dari mulut gunung berapi,* Lava erupted from the mouth of the volcano. **men–kan** to produce, bring forth. *Sapi tlh* ~ *anaknja,* The cow had calves. *Tukang sunglap* ~ *telur dari mulutnja,* The magician produced eggs from his mouth.

djeda rest, respite. *Ia bekerdja tak ada –nja,* He worked without respite.

djeding bathroom. *bibir* – curled lips.

djedjak 1 trail, track (of an animal). 2 footsteps. 3 wake of a ship. 4 footprint. **ber–** to step, tread on. *Rambutnja ∼ bahu,* Her hair is shoulder length. **men–** to set foot on s.t. *Saja blm ∼ Amérika,* I have not set foot in America. **men–kan** *kaki* to set foot – *bara* almost touching the ground. – *djari* fingerprint. – *kaki* footprint.

djedjaka 1 youth, young man. 2 not yet married, bachelor.

djedjal **ber–** to crowd, jam. *Tetamu ∼ diserambi muka,* The front room was jammed with people. **men–(i)** to stuff, plug. *∼ bantal dgn kapok* to stuff a pillow with kapok. *Ia ∼ lobang didjendéla dgn kertas,* He plugged the hole in the window with paper. **men–kan** to stuff, cram.

djedjamu see DJAMU.

djedjas 1 lacerated. 2 laceration. 3 to be injured. *Ia djatuh tetapi ia tidak – sedikit djuapun,* He fell but he was not injured at all.

djedjek stable. *masjarakat jg – a* stable society. **ke–an** stability.

djedjenang 1 superintendent. 2 referee. 3 adjutant.

djédjér series, row. **ber–** in a row. **–an** in rows.

djegog **men–** to bark at.

djegung place on a ship for the storage of rigging, sails, etc.

djéksi see INDJÉKSI. **men–** to give an injection.

djél jail.

djéla **ber–(–)** to dangle, swing (to and fro). *Udjung tali itu ∼ ditiup angin,* The end of the rope was swinging in the wind.

djeladjah **men–(i)** 1 to explore. *Perintis itu pergi ∼ Kutub Selatan,* The pioneer went to explore the South Pole. 2 to cross. *Saja ingin ∼ seluruh benua Éropah,* I would like to cross the entire continent of Europe. **pen–** explorer.

djelaga soot.

djelai 1 jam, jelly. 2 Job's tears.

djelak to be tired of. *Saja – akan makanan itu,* I am tired of that food. **ter–** to be satiated with food. *Saja sdh ∼,* I am stuffed (with food).

djelang **men–** 1 to visit, pay a call on s.o. *Ia ∼ saja,* He called on me. 2 to pay o's respects. *Pd Hari Tahun Baru setiap orang berkesempatan ∼ présidén,* On New Year's Day everyone has the opportunity to pay his respects to the president. 3 around, toward. *Saja akan datang ∼ sendja,* I will come around sundown. 4 approaching, imminent. 5 to... (used to address mail). *∼ tn.* to Mr.

djelangak **men–** to look up.

djelantah coconut oil which has been used to fry s.t.

djelas 1 clear, plain. *Perkara itu sdh mendjadi –,* The case has become clear. 2 settled, resolved. **member–** to clarify, explain s.t. **men–i** to look into a matter, seek clarification or an explanation. **men–kan** to explain, clarify. *Guru ∼ tjara bekerdjanja mesin uap,* The teacher explained how a steam engine works. **pen–an** explanation, clarification, elucidation.

djelata common, of the masses.

djelatang stinging nettle.

djelatik paddybird.

djelék 1 ugly. *Rumah itu –,* That house is ugly. 2 bad, evil. *Pikirannja selalu – sadja,* He always has bad thoughts. **ke–an** 1 ugliness. 2 badness. **men–kan** 1 to make ugly. 2 to tarnish. *Perbuatan djahatmu itu akan ∼ nama bapakmu,* Your misdeeds will tarnish your father's name.

djelempah **men–** scattered. *Bukunja ∼ di-mana² dlm kamarnja,* His books were scattered all about his room.

djelentik barely touch.

djelepok **men–** to fall (flat on o's back).

djelik see DJELÉK.

djelilitan to look around confusedly.

djelimet hairsplitting.

djeling **men–** to ogle s.o.

djelir **men–** projecting, sticking out. **men–kan** *lidah* to stick out o's tongue.

djelita 1 graceful, charming. 2 beautiful, sweet.

djelma incarnation. **men–** 1 to assume a new form, transform o.s. *Tukang sihir itu ∼ mendjadi seékor burung,* The wizard transformed himself into a bird. 2 to incarnate. *Sesudah mati ruh kita akan ∼ lagi,* After death our soul will be reincarnated. **men–kan** 1 to create. *Tuhan ∼ langit, bulan dan bintang²,* God created the sky, the moon, and the stars. 2 to realize, bring about. *∼ tjita²nja* to realize o's ideals. 3 to transform. **pen–an** 1 incarnation. 2 creation. 3 personification. 4 realization, materialization. 5 metamorphosis. 6 an actor's role, part. **–an** 1 transformation. 2 incarnation.

djeluak **men–** to vomit.

djeluang bark cloth.

djeludjur **men–** to stitch loosely. **men–i** to stitch on.

djeluk deep (of plates and cups).

djelungkap **men–** to spring loose.

djelunut men- to stick.
djelus jealous. **men-kan** to cause jealousy.
djelutung k.o. rubber tree.
djema'ah see DJAMA'AH.
djemala 1 head. 2 skull.
djemang se- moment.
djemari finger. see DJARI.
djemawa 1 conceited. *Si Amat sungguh* –, Amat is really conceited. 2 meddlesome. **ke-an** conceit.
djemba a measure of length (2 fathoms). **men-** to reach out for, grab s.t. *Ia ∼ rambut pengemis*, He grabbed the beggar's hair. **-an** = –.
djembak men- to flutter. **ter-** –² to wave. *Rambutnja ∼ kena angin*, Her hair was fluttering in the wind.
djembalang gnome, goblin (often in the shape of a horned animal).
djembatan see DJAMBATAN.
djémbél poor, shabby.
djembiah dagger.
djempalik to turn a somersault.
djemparing arrow.
djempol thumb. **-an** 1 champion. 2 first rate. *kwalitét ∼ first-rate quality.*
djemput men- 1 to meet. *Ia datang ∼ saja kesetasiun*, He came to pick me up at the station. 2 to call for. *Saja pergi ∼ dokter karena ibu sakit*, I went to call for the doctor because Mother was ill. 3 to invite. *Bapak ∼ walikota utk menghadiri perkawinan saja*, Father invited the mayor to be present at my wedding. 4 to pick up (with the fingertips). *Ia ∼ koran dari djalan*, He picked up a paper from the street. 5 to adapt. *Ia ∼ sandiwara itu dari sebuah roman*, He adapted that play from a novel. **se-** a pinch of s.t. *∼ garam* a pinch of salt. **-an** 1 invitation. 2 proposal (to a man). 3 dowry.
djemu 1 to be bored. *Saja merasa – hari ini*, I feel bored today. 2 to be sick of s.t. or s.o. *Saja – mendengarkan kamu*, I'm sick of listening to you. 3 to be fed up. *Kami – dgn kelakuannja*, We're fed up with his behavior. **ke-an** boredom. **men-kan** boring, tiresome, monotonous. *tidak –²nja* tirelessly. *Ia bekerdja tidak ∼ ,* He worked tirelessly. *– djelak* to be fed up, tired to death, with. *– hidup* tired of living.
djemuas filthy, covered with dirt, stained, soiled.
djemudju caraway seed.
djemur sun bath. **ber-** –² to sun (bathe), sit in the sun. **men-** to dry s.t. in the sun. **pen-an** 1 clothesline. 2 place for drying. **-an** 1 things being dried. 2 the wash. *Bapak*

memasukkan ∼ padinja kedalam lumbung, Father put the dried rice in the barn. *Djangan kena – badju sutera itu*, Don't expose the silk dress to the sunlight.
djenak se- a moment.
djenaka funny, comical, humorous. **ber-** to joke. **ke-an** humor, fun.
djenang 1 doorframe. 2 porridge. 3 k.o. taffy. **men-i** 1 to supervise. *Dukun ∼ djalannja upatjara*, The shaman (witch doctor) supervised the ceremony. 2 to lead. *Lurah ∼ pekerdjaan itu*, The village chief leads the work. 3 to referee. *Orang jg tertua didésa harus ∼ segala perselisihan*, The oldest villager has to referee all conflicts. **pen-** 1 supervisor. 2 foreman. 3 referee. 4 master of ceremonies. 5 adjutant.
djenangau rice insect.
djenazah corpse, mortal remains. **men-kan** to bury, lay to rest.
djén(d). [*djénderal*] general (mil.).
djendal-djendul bumpy.
djendéla window. *– atap* skylight.
djénderal general (title). *– major* major general.
djendjang 1 ladder, scale, 2 slender, long (of neck). **ber-** terraced. *Diléréng gunung sawah² ∼ ,* On the hill slope the rice fields are terraced.
djendol 1 bump. *Ia dipukul dan mendapat – dikepalanja*, He was hit and received a bump on his head. 2 bumpy. *Bola itu tidak bulat benar; agak – sedikit*, The ball is not well rounded; it is somewhat bumpy. **-an** bump, hump, knob.
djéndral see DJÉNDERAL.
djendul see DJENDAL.
djeneng 1 name. 2 status.
djénéng slanting. *Atap rumah itu –*, The roof of the house slants. **men-kan** to slant, tilt s.t.
Djenéwa Geneva.
djenéwer Dutch gin.
djengah 1 shy. 2 embarrassed.
djengat 1 skin. 2 bark. 3 rawhide rope. see DJANGAT.
djengék men-i to ridicule s.o. **men-** –² to mock, make fun of s.o. *Djangan ∼ orang tjatjad*, Don't make fun of deformed people. **-an** mockery, ridicule.
djenggar-djenggur overgrown, exceptionally big for o's age.
djénggot beard.
djenggul see DJENDOL.
djengit ber- to look startled. *∼ getir* to look sour. **men-** to be startled. *Ia ∼ ketika pintu terbuka se-konjong², He was startled when the door suddenly opened. **men-** –² to bob up

and down. *Ékor kutjing itu* ~ ,
The cat's tail bobbed up and down.

djengkal span (of the hand). **men-**
to measure s.t. in spans. ~ *dada*
to be modest about o's abilities.
Meskipun dia pandai sekali, ia hanja
~ *dada sadja*, Although he is very
smart, he's modest about his abilities.
~ *muka* to do s.t. useless. *Pekerdjaan
itu seperti* ~ *muka sadja*, To do that
work is useless. ~ *kepandaian orang*
to underestimate s.o.'s knowledge.

djengkang ke- to fall backward.
men- 1 to fall backward. 2 to lie
on o's back. *Orang sakit itu* ~ , The
sick man lay flat on his back. **ter-**
to topple over, fall backward. *Ia
djatuh* ~ *dari kudanja*, He fell backward from his horse. *Badjingan itu
sdh lama* ~ , That scoundrel died a
long time ago.

djéngkang ber- to lift a leg. *Ia
duduk* ~ , He sits with one leg drawn
up. – *djéngkot* to limp. *Ia* – *djéngkot
djalannja*, He limps when he walks.

djengkau see DJANGKAU.

djéngkék ber- -² 1 to leap with joy.
Ia ~ *mendengar berita jg menggembirakan itu*, He leaped with joy
on hearing the happy news. 2 to
skip, hop.

djengkel men- to upset, capsize.
-an capsizing, spill.

djéngkél to be annoyed, irritated. –
saja mendengarkan keluh kesahnja, I
am annoyed at listening to his complaints. **ke-an** 1 annoyance, irritation, vexation. 2 vexed, annoyed.
men-kan 1 annoying, irritating. 2
to annoy s.o. *Pekerdjaan ini* ~ *betul²*,
This work is really annoying.

djéngkéng 1 see DJÉNGKÉT. 2 see
DJENGKING. **ber-an** to stick out in
all directions.

djengkerik cricket.

djéngkét ber-, berse-, bersi-, men-
to walk on tiptoe.

djéngki 1 foreign, strange. 2 blue
jeans.

djengking men- with the buttocks
up. *Anak baji tidur* ~ , The baby
slept face down, knees doubled up,
and buttocks up.

djengkit men- to stand upright.
Ékor andjing ~ , The dog's tail stood
upright.

djéngkol edible but malodorous fruit.

djengkolét men- to capsize, tumble
over or down into the water.

djéngkot ber-, men- 1 to limp. *Ia
berdjalan* ~ , He limps when he
walks. 2 lame.

djenguk men- 1 to look, observe
with head thrust forward. *Ia* ~ *dari*

djendéla, He stuck his head out of
the window to look. 2 to visit, pay
a call. *Ia datang* ~ *kawannja jg sakit
itu*, He visited his sick friend.

djengul men- to protrude. *Matanja*
~ , His eyes protrude. **men-kan** to
stick out. *Ikan itu* ~ *kepalanja dari
air*, The fish stuck its head out of
the water.

djeni 1 genius. *Ia seorang* – , He is a
genius. 2 detachment of army engineers.

djenis 1 kind, sort. *Dia mendjual
berbagai* – *dagangan*, He sells different
k.o. merchandise. 2 variety. *Dlm
kebun itu terdapat bermatjam* – *bunga²*,
A variety of flowers can be found in
the garden. **ber-** all k.o. ~ *orang
terdapat disekolah ini*, There are all
k.o. people in this school. **men-kan**
to sort, separate. **se-** of one kind.
Tidak ada lagi kain ~ *ini*, There is
no more cloth of this kind. *Kembang
itu adalah* ~ , Those flowers are
of the same kind. **pen-an** grouping.
– *bangsa* race. – *kelamin* sex, gender.
– *ubah* variety.

djénmaj. [*djénderal major*] major general.

djentera 1 wheel. 2 mill. 3 spinning
wheel. **ber-** 1 on wheels. 2 motorized.

djentik men- 1 to pinch. 2 to rap
with the fingers, to snap, to flick.
-² mosquito larvae.

djenuh to be satisfied, satiated.
*Djangan tambah makanan lagi, saja
sdh* -, Don't add any more food,
I've had enough.

Djepang Japan(ese). **men-kan** to
Japanize.

djepit ke- 1 to be squeezed. *Ia* ~
diantara orang banjak itu, He was
hemmed in by the crowd. 2 in a fix.
men- to squeeze, pinch. **-an** 1
squeezing. 2 tweezers, 3 clothespin.
~ *kertas* paper clip.

djeprét men- to let fly, to shoot
away (like a rock with a slingshot,
etc.). **-an** slingshot.

Djepun Japan(ese). see DJEPANG.

djeput see DJEMPUT. **se-** a handful.
~ *hari* all day long.

djera to be afraid, discouraged.
Setelah mengalami ketjelakaan, ia –
mengemudi mobilnja, After the accident he was afraid to drive his car.
men-(kan) to discourage. *Ketjurian
itu* ~ *dia tidak menguntjikan pintu
kamarnja*, After the burglary he was
afraid to leave the door of his room
unlocked. **ter-** dismayed.

djerabai see DJUMBAI. **ber-** frayed.

djerah 1 abundant. *Buah mangga*

tahun ini sangat –, The mangoes are really abundant this year. 2 prevalent (of a disease, etc.). – *djerih* tired, exhausted.

djerahak ter– unfinished, abandoned (of work, a problem, etc.).

djerahap men– 1 to bend over. 2 to lie on o's stomach, lie prone. **ter**– to fall, trip headlong, prostrate with arms thrown out.

djerait ber-(an) grown together. *Kedua tanaman itu* ∼ , The two plants have grown together. *Tjotjok sanggul* ∼ *pd djala rambut*, The hairpin got caught in the hair net.

djeram rapids. **men**– to take a cold shower. *Sungguh énak* ∼ *badan kalau hari panas*, It is nice to have a cold shower when the day is hot.

djeramah men– to fall upon, seize. *Harimau* ∼ *rusa*, The tiger fell upon the deer.

djerambah k.o. terrace used for drying the wash, washing dishes, etc. **men**– 1 to use as a *djerambah*. 2 to treat (a wife, woman) like a drudge.

djerambai see DJUMBAI.

djerambang will-o'-the-wisp.

djerami stubbles (dried paddy stalks).

djerang men-kan 1 to heat. 2 to put s.t. on the fire, stove, etc. ∼ *air* to boil water.

djerangkang ber– to stick up, project upward. *Tiang bendéra* ∼ *sepandjang djalan*, Flagpoles were sticking up all along the road. *Meréka berbaring dipantai dgn kaki* ∼ , They were lying on the beach with their feet in the air.

djerat 1 a snare. 2 loop. 3 lasso. **men**– 1 to snare (animals). 2 to trick, deceive s.o. 3 to entice (of merchants). **se**– a bunch. ∼ *bunga* a bunch of flowers.

djerau bright red. **men**– to glitter, shine, sparkle.

djeraus sprightly, nimble. *Dgn* – *ia melompati segala rintangan*, He nimbly leaped over all obstacles. **men-kan** to make o. active. *Gerak badan* ∼ *serta menjéhatkan dia*, Physical exercise made him active and healthy.

djerawat pimple, blackhead.

djerdjak 1 lath. 2 lattice.

djerékét stuck, glued together. *Halaman*[2] *buku itu* –, The pages of the book were stuck together.

djerembab men-kan to cause s.o. to fall headlong. **ter**– to fall headlong.

djerémbét see DJERÉPÉT.

djerépét ber– 1 linked together. *Mata rantai itu* ∼ , The links of a chain are joined together. 2 grown together.

djeri 1 to be scared. – *saja masuk kekamar itu*, I am afraid to enter that room. 2 to waver. *Musuh* –, *lalu mundur*, The enemy wavered, then retreated. **men-kan** fearsome.

djeridji 1 finger. 2 trellis, lattice. – *kaki* toe.

djerih tired. *Saja sangat* –, I am very tired. **ke-an** 1 weariness, fatigue. 2 tired. **men-kan** 1 tiring. 2 to tire. – *lelah* exertion. – *pajah* exertion, effort. *Segala* – *pajahnja tak berguna*, All his efforts were of no avail. – *penat* very tired.

djering see DJÉNGKOL.

djerit 1 a scream. 2 strong complaint. **men**– to scream. **pen**– 1 screamer, yeller. 2 siren. – *rakjat* the clamoring of the people. **-an** = –.

djerkah snarl. **men**– to snarl, snap at s.o.

djermal a fish trap ending in a large net.

Djérman German(y).

djernih 1 clear. *Air itu* –, The water is clear. *Mata anak itu* –, The child has clear eyes. 2 pure. **ke-an** 1 clarity. 2 purity. **men-kan** 1 to make clear, explain. 2 to purify. **pen-an** purification. ∼ *air* water purification. **per-an** clarification.

djeroan intestines and tripe of slaughtered animals.

djerodjol men-, ter– to protrude. *Dompétnja* ∼ *dari kantongnja*, His wallet protruded from his pocket.

djerubung awning.

djerudji 1 trellis. 2 lattice.

djeruk citrus fruit. – *bali* shaddock. – *garut*, – *kepruk* tangerine. – *manis* orange. – *nipis* lime. – *siam* sweet orange.

djerumat men– to darn, mend s.t. **pen**– darning needle.

djerumbai see DJUMBAI.

djerumun 1 shelter, hide-out. 2 lair of a wild boar.

djerumus men-kan to cause to fall, to trip. *Ia* ∼ *saja dlm lobang itu*, He made me fall into that hole. *Ia* ∼ *gadis itu dlm kesengsaraan*, He ruined the girl. **ter**– to fall flat on o's face.

djerung large shark.

djét jet. – *ber-baling*[2] jetprop. – *niaga* commercial jetliner. – *pantjargas* turbojet.

djéwér men– 1 to pull o's ear. *Ibu* ∼ *anaknja jg nakal itu*, Mother pulled her naughty son's ear. 2 to reprimand. *Dia sering* ∼ *bawahannja jg malas*, He often reprimands his lazy subordinates. **-an** reprimand, scolding.

djiarah see ZIARAH. **ber–** to make a visit to a sacred place. **pen–an** a pilgrimage to a sacred place (grave, etc.).

djidar 1 rule(r). 2 line.

djidat forehead.

djidjik 1 hideous. *Luka itu –*, The wound is hideous. 2 to be disgusted. *Saja – melihat kotoran itu*, I felt disgusted at seeing that filth. **ke–an** 1 filthiness. 2 disgust. **men–kan** 1 loathsome. 2 disgusting. 3 to abhor s.t.

djidjit see DJINDJIT.

djidwal see DJADWAL.

djihad holy war. **ber–** to wage a holy war. *Kaum Muslimin ∼ melawan kaum kafir*, The Moslems waged a holy war against the infidels.

djihin see DJIN.

djika(lau) 1 when. *– engkau mendjadi déwasa, engkau harus bekerdja*, When you grow up, you have to work. 2 if, in the event that. *– kauperkenankan, saja mau pulang*, If you will permit me, I want to go home. *– kiranja* 1 supposing. 2 if, by any chance. *– kiranja itu benar, saja girang sekali*, If by chance it were true, I would be very glad. *– ...sekalipun* even if. *– benar sekalipun, saja tak pertjaja padamu lagi*, Even if it were true, I would never trust you again.

djilam see DJILAT.

djilat **men–** 1 to lick. *Andjing itu ∼ kaki saja*, The dog licks my foot. 2 to flatter s.o. *∼ pantat* 1 to fawn over s.o. 2 to butter s.o. up, to flatter excessively. *∼ air liur* to praise s.t. previously despised. *∼ pantat kepalanja* to flatter o's boss to excess. **pen–** flatterer.

djilid 1 volume. *dua – * 2 volumes. 2 the binding of a book. **men–** *buku* to bind a book. **pen–** bookbinder. **pen–an** 1 (book) bindery. 2 bookbinding. **–an** a bound volume.

djilma see DJELMA.

djima(k) sexual intercourse. **men–** to have sexual intercourse.

djimat charm, mascot, talisman, fetish, amulet.

djin 1 evil spirit. 2 gin.

djinah see ZINA.

djinak 1 tame. *matjan – * a tame tiger. 2 gentle. 3 domesticated (of animals). **ber– –²an** to be on intimate terms with s.o. **men–i** to be close to s.o., chum up with s.o. *Ia ∼ saja karena ia membutuhkan pertolonganku*, He chummed up with me because he needed my help. **men–kan** to tame an animal. **–² merpati** to be hard to get on intimate terms with, although

seemingly easily approachable (of a woman).

djindjang 1 see DJENDJANG. 2 leader of a group. 3 necromancer.

djindjing **men–** to carry s.t. light in o's hand. **–an** handle.

djindjit **ber– –²** to walk on tiptoe, to tiptoe. **men–** 1 to carry in o's hand. 2 to pull (out). *∼ telinga* to pull s.o.'s ear. 3 to undress.

djingau **men–** to peer at.

djingga orange (color).

djingkat see DJÉNGKÉT.

djingkik **ber–(–)** to hop along. *Anak ketjil itu berdjalan ∼* , The small child hopped along.

djingkrak **ber– –²** to jump up and down.

djinsom ginseng.

djintan 1 k.o. parsley. 2 caraway seed.

djip jeep.

djiplak **men–** 1 to copy. 2 to cheat during an exam, crib. 3 to plagiarize. 4 to imitate. **pen–** 1 duplicating machine. 2 plagiarist.

djiran 1 kin. 2 neighbor. **ber–** adjacent. *Rumah saja ∼ dgn rumahmu*, My house is next to yours.

djirat 1 grave. 2 see DJERAT.

djirus pointed. *Pinsil itu –*, That pencil is pointed. **men–** to water (flowers). **–an** effusion.

djisim body.

djitak **men–** to pat s.o. on the head.

djitu correct, exact. *Djawabannja itu –*, He gave a correct answer. **men–kan** to make s.t. correct.

djiwa 1 soul. 2 spirit. **ber–** 1 to be alive. *Selama masih ∼* , *djanganlah putus asa*, Never give up as long as you live. 2 animated. **ke–an** 1 spiritual. 2 psychological. **men–i** 1 to endow s.t. *Tudjuan komersil di–i dgn tudjuan kulturil*, The commercial aim was endowed with a cultural aim. 2 to inspire, be the soul of. *Ia ∼ pemberontakan itu*, He was the inspiration of the uprising. *–ku* my beloved. *–nja melajang*, He died. *– budak* slavish spirit. *– ksatria* warrior spirit. *– raga* body and soul.

Djkt [*Djakarta*] Jakarta.

Dj(l) [*Djalan*] street, road. *– Toko 3* 3 Toko St.

djml. [*djumlah*] amount.

djoang see DJUANG.

djoblos see DJEBLOS.

djobong a prostitute.

djodjol palisade to dam a river, creek, etc. **men–** to protrude. *Pistolnja ∼ dari kantongnja*, His gun protruded from his pocket.

djodo(h) 1 marriage partner. 2 to

match. *Tjelana ini tak – dgn djas itu*, These pants don't match that coat. 3 to suit. *Harganja tak –*, The price doesn't suit him. **ber–** to be married. *Ia sdh ~* , He is already married. **memper–kan** 1 to marry s.o. off. 2 to marry. *Ia ~ djanda itu*, He married the widow. **men–kan** to marry s.o. off. *Ia ~ anaknja*, He married his daughter off. **per–an** 1 wedding. 2 marriage. 3 matrimony, wedlock. **se–** 1 a pair. *~ burung* a pair of birds. 2 twosome, couple. *~ jg indah* a handsome couple. *~ bagai tjintjin* a well-matched couple. *sdh –nja* o's fate to marry s.o.

djogét 1 dance. 2 dancing girl. **ber–** to dance.

djohan 1 young man. 2 honorific title. *– arifin* brilliant man. *– pahlawan* hero.

djok seat (of car, pedicabs, etc.). *– muka* front seat.

Djokja Jogja(karta).

djolak ber–, men– to blaze. *Api itu ~* , The fire blazed. **–an** *api* sea of fire.

djoli 1 palanquin. 2 team of horses. **se–** a couple. **–²** k.o. dinghy.

djolok men– 1 to poke, prod. *Ia ~ buah itu dgn tongkat*, He poked at the fruit with a stick. 2 to interrogate, investigate. *Polisi ~ dia beberapa djam lamanja*, The police interrogated him for several hours. *~ sarang tabuhan* to undertake a dangerous venture deliberately, stick o's hand in a hornet's nest.

djolong for the first time. *Pohon ini – berbuah*, For the first time this tree bore fruit. **–²** 1 first-born. 2 the first to be or to do s.t.

djombang beautiful, pretty.

djompak ber– to rear, prance (of a horse, etc.).

djompo old, decrepit. *pemeliharaan –* care of the aged.

djompong pe–an 1 name of reservoir and area in Jakarta. 2 rallying place.

djondjot to pull apart. **men–** *kapas* to pull a ball of cotton apart. *– kapas* a small ball of cotton wool.

djongang protruding (of teeth).

djongét curving upward of upper lip.

djongkang 1 k.o. sailboat. 2 protruding (of teeth). *– -djangking* sticking out right and left.

djongkar(-djangkir) see DJONGKANG-DJANGKING.

djongkat-djangkit to wobble, bob up and down.

djongkok ber– to squat. **ber– –²** to cringe before. *Ia selalu ~ thd ata-*

sannja, He always displays a cringing attitude toward his superiors.

djongkong dugout, canoe.

djongos 1 houseboy. 2 waiter.

djor –²an o. after the other, continuously.

djoran fishing rod. *– ampai* divining rod.

Djordania Jordan.

djori team of horses.

djorok 1 slovenly. *Pekerdjaannja –*, His work was slovenly. 2 dirty. *Anak itu – benar*, That child is very dirty. **ke–an** 1 slovenliness. *~ bahasa surat kabar* the slovenliness of newspaper language. 2 dirtiness. 3 shabbiness. **men–** to stick out, protrude. *Tanah itu ~ kelaut merupakan semenandjung*, The land sticks out into the sea to form a peninsula. **pen–** dirty person.

djorong oval-shaped.

djotos ber– to box. **–an** 1 a blow with the fist. 2 boxing match.

djua 1 nothing but, nobody but. *Meskipun dia bekerdja keras sekali, umpatan – jang diterimanja*, Although he worked very hard, he got nothing but scoldings. *Semuanja sdh datang, si Amat – jg harus datang terlambat*, Everybody has arrived and nobody but Amat has to come late. 2 (stresses preceding word or phrase). *Apa – jg diperbuatnja, orang tuanja tidak puas*, Regardless of what he did, his parents were not satisfied. *Bagaimana – ditjobanja, ia tidak berhasil*, However much he tried, he did not succeed. **–pun** even. *Tak seorang ~ datang kerumah saja*, Not even one person came to my house.

djuadah 1 delicacy made of rice. 2 foodstuffs, provisions.

djuak ber– to compete with. **men–** to incite, instigate. *Ia ~ adiknja supaja berkelahi*, He incited his younger brother to fight. **pen–** instigator. *~ perang* warmonger.

djual on sale. **ber–** to be in business. *Penghidupannja dari ~ sepéda*, He earns his living selling bicycles. *~ beli* to trade. *Indonésia ~ beli dgn India*, Indonesia trades with India. **ber–an** to live by peddling. **memperbelikan** to trade in s.t. *~ karét* to trade in rubber. **men–** to sell. *~ akad* 1 to pawn, hock. 2 to sell under certain conditions. *~ aksi* to show off. *~ bangsa* to betray o's country. *~ kepala* 1 to enlist in a mercenary army. 2 to enslave o.s. *~ lélang* to auction off. *~ lepas* to sell unconditionally. *~ merugi* to sell at a loss. *~ mutlak* to sell unconditionally. *~*

nama to trade on. *Anak itu* ∼ *nama ajahnja,* The boy trades on his father's name. ∼ *tampang* to show off. **men–i** to sell. *Ia* ∼ *permatanja satu persatu,* She sold her jewels one by one. **men-kan** to sell s.t. for s.o. *Saja* ∼ *sepatunja utk dia,* I sold his shoes for him. **pen–** seller, dealer. ∼ *besar* wholesaler. ∼ *étjéran* retail dealer. **pen–an** sale, turnover. **ter–** out of stock, sold out. *Buku itu habis* ∼ , That book is sold out, out of print. **–an** merchandise, goods. – *beli* trade.

djuang ber– to fight, struggle. *Meréka* ∼ *utk kemerdékaan,* They fought for freedom. **memper–kan** to strive, fight for. *Tiap² bangsa berhak* ∼ *kemerdékaannja,* Every nation has the right to strive for its independence. **pe(r)–** fighter, soldier. **per–an** fight, strife, struggle. ∼ *hidup* struggle for life. ∼ *sutji* crusade.

djuar a k.o. shade tree.

djuara champion. **ke–an** championship. ∼ *dunia* world championship. – *dunia* world champion. – *kedua* runner-up.

djubah robe, cloak (used by Arabs, priests, judges, etc.). **ber–** to wear a *djubah.*

djubal ber–(–) to crowd. *Orang* ∼ *disana,* People were crowding there.

djubel see DJUBAL.

djubin floor tile.

djubir [*djurubitjara*] spokesman.

djubit see TJUBIT.

djublek men– to stare.

djubur 1 anus. 2 buttock.

Djudah Jiddah.

djudas 1 slanderous. 2 mean, cruel, vicious.

djudes see DJUDAS. *Dia –,* She's a bitch.

djudi game of dice. **ber–** 1 to play dice, shoot craps. 2 to gamble. **men–kan** to gamble away. *Ia tlh* ∼ *segala kepunjaannja,* He has gambled away all his holdings. **pen–** gambler. **pen–an** 1 gambling place. 2 gambling.

djudjat slander, insult, abuse.

djudju see TUDJU.

djudjuh ber– –² incessantly. *Anak itu menangis* ∼ *sepandjang hari,* That child cried incessantly the whole day.

djudjur 1 honest, on the level. 2 dowry to be given to the bride's parents by the bridegroom. **ke–an** honesty. **men–i** to present a dowry to. *Ia* ∼ *bakal mertuanja itu lima ékor sapi,* He gave his future parents-in-law 5 cows as a dowry.

djudjut men– to pull at, draw. *Ia* ∼ *tali itu,* He pulled at the rope.

djudul 1 title. 2 caption. 3 credits (in movie or on TV). **ber–** to have the title of. – *tambahan* subtitle.

djuga 1 also, too. *Saja – mau makan,* I want to eat too. *Ia – mendjadi menteri,* He is also a minister. 2 see DJUA. 3 rather. *Berat – kerusakannja,* The damage was rather heavy. 4 anyway. *Walaupun ia bersalah, saja menolongnja –,* Though he was wrong, I helped him anyway. *baik –* quite all right, rather good. *Inikah jg kau pilih? Baik –,* Is this the one you are going to take? That's all right with me. (That suits me.)

djuih curled (of lips).

djuita sweet, lovely, beautiful.

djuk see TJUK.

djukung see DJONGKONG.

djulai 1 twig (a slender end of the stem of a creeper). 2 runner (of strawberry plants, etc.). **ber– –²** to dangle.

djulang men– 1 to soar. *Gunung itu* ∼ *sampai kelangit,* The mountain soared up to the skies. *Api* ∼ *tinggi,* The flames soared high. 2 to carry on the shoulder. *Bapak* ∼ *anaknja itu,* Father carried his child on his shoulder. 3 to hold in high esteem. *Rakjat sangat* ∼ *présidénnja,* The people hold their president in high esteem. 4 to hurl upward.

Djuli July.

djuling cross-eyed.

djulita see DJELITA.

djulo lottery by neighborhood wives. **ber– –²** to raffle off. **–²** see ARISAN.

djulukan nickname, alias.

djulung o. who is always unlucky. **–²** k.o. fresh-water fish.

djulur men– to stick out. *Ia men–kan lidahnja,* He stuck out his tongue. **–** *djalar* to go in and out all over the place. *Semut – djalar ditempat gula,* Ants were crawling all over the sugar bowl.

Djuma'at see DJUM'AT.

Djum'ah see DJUM'AT.

djumantara atmosphere.

Djum'at 1 Friday. 2 week. *Ia tinggal disana tiga –,* He stayed there for three weeks. 3 see DJEMA'AH.

djumbai 1 fringe. 2 tassel. **ber– –²** 1 fringed, frayed. 2 to flutter. *Daun² kering itu* ∼ *ditiup angin,* The dry leaves fluttered in the breeze.

djumbuh identical.

djumbul ter– –² to bob up and down. *Itik itu* ∼ *diatas air,* The duck bobbed up and down on the water.

djuml. [*djumlah*] amount.

djumlah 1 sum, amount. 2 number, quantity. 3 total. **ber–** to number.

Bunga dlm kebun ini ∼ *ratusan,* There are hundreds of flowers in the garden. **men–** to add. *Adik beladjar* ∼ *disekolah,* My little brother learns to add at school. **men–kan** to count up, add up. **pen–an** addition. **se–** to the amount of, as much as. *Hutangnja* ∼ *5000 dolar,* His debts amount to $5,000. ∼ *besar* a large number (of). ∼ *besar penduduk mati kelaparan,* A large number of the population starved to death. ∼ *ketjil* a small number. **ter–** 1 added up. *Semua angka²nja sdh* ∼ , All his marks were added up. 2 to be considered among. *Ia* ∼ *anak jg pandai dlm kelasnja,* He is considered one of the bright children in his class. **–nja** in the amount of. – *dan mutu* quantity and quality.

djumpa ber– (*dgn*) to meet, run into, come across. *Saja* ∼ *dgn si Ali didjalan,* I met Ali on the street. **memper–kan** 1 to bring together. *Siapa* ∼ *kedua orang itu?* Who brought those two people together? 2 to reconcile. *Meréka mentjoba* ∼ *pendapatnja jg berlainan itu,* They tried to reconcile their different opinions. **men–i** to meet with. *Ia* ∼ *seékor harimau dihutan,* He met with a tiger in the jungle. *Ia* ∼ *ketjelakaan ditengah djalan,* On his way he met with an accident. **per–an** meeting. **ter–** to be found. *Singa tak* ∼ *dinegeri kita,* Lions are not native to our country.

djumpluk pile, mop. *se– rambut putih* a mop of white hair.

djumput men– to pick up, meet. see DJEMPUT.

djunam men– 1 to dive. *Kapal terbang itu* ∼ , The plane dived. 2 to shoot down (of a flying eagle on its prey, etc.).

djundjung men–(kan) 1 to carry on the head. *Ibu* ∼ *kendi,* Mother carried a water jar on her head. 2 to respect deeply, idolize. *Rakjat* ∼ *radjanja jg budiman itu,* The people deeply respected their noble king. ∼ *tinggi* to hold in high esteem. *Ia di– tinggi,* He was held in high esteem. ∼ *uban* to be very old. **–an** 1 master, lord. 2 pole for climbing plants.

djung Chinese junk.

djungat bow or stern tilted upward.

djungkang men– to bob up. – –*djungkit.* to bob up and down, go up and down.

djungkat men– tilted surface. *Lantai itu* ∼ , The floor slants. – *djangkit* to bob, go up and down.

djungkel ter– toppled over. *Ia*

djatuh ∼ *dari kursinja,* He toppled from his chair.

djungkir men–, ter– to tumble. **men–balikkan** to turn s.t. upside down. – *balik* 1 to turn somersaults. 2 upside down. **pen–balikan** 1 an upset. 2 somersault.

djungkung see DJONGKONG.

djungur 1 snout, beak, 2 muzzle.

djungut mountain spur.

Djuni June.

djuntai ber–, ter– dangling. *Ia duduk dgn kakinja* ∼ , He sat with his legs dangling. **men–kan** to let dangle. *Kalau duduk djanganlah* ∼ *kakimu,* If you sit down don't let your feet dangle.

djunub ritually impure (e.g., after coitus, after giving birth, after menstruation, etc.).

djuragan 1 skipper. 2 master.

djurai bunch. *Ia memetik bunga se–,* She picked a bunch of flowers. **ber–(–)** to hang down in fringes.

djuran see DJORAN.

djurang ravine, gully.

djuri jury.

djuri'at descent, generation.

djurnalis journalist, reporter.

djuru an expert, trained worker. **ke–an** vocational. – *arsip* file clerk. – *bahasa* interpreter. – *batu* 1 marine pilot. 2 boatswain. – *berita* reporter. – *bitjara* spokesman. – *buku* bookkeeper. – *dapur* cook. – *gendang* drummer. – *indjil* evangelist. – *kamera* cameraman. – *kerah* village messenger. – *ketik* typist. – *kira* certified public accountant. – *kuasa* proxy. – *kuntji* 1 janitor. 2 in last place, in the cellar (of athletic teams). – *lélang* auctioneer. – *masak* cook. – *mesin* locomotive engineer. – *mudi* helmsman. – *obat* pharmacist. – *penerang* information specialist. – *potrét* photographer. – *pustaka* librarian. – *rawat* nurse. – *selam* diver. – *Selamat* the Saviour. – *sita* process server, bailiff. – *sténo* stenographer. – *suara* sound man (film and TV). – *tafsir* commentator. – *ték* typist. – *télpon* telephone operator. – *teluh* utterer of magic formulas. – *tenun* weaver. – *tenung* fortuneteller. – *terbang* plane pilot. – *tik* typist. – *tulis* clerk. – *tulis bantu* assistant clerk. – *uang* cashier. – *ukur* surveyor. – *ulas* commentator. – *warta* reporter.

djurus straight. **ber– –²** again and again, repeatedly. ∼ *anak sakit itu minta air,* Again and again the sick child asked for water. **men–** to go in a certain direction. *Ia* ∼ *kebarat,* He went westward. **men–kan** 1 to direct, aim at. 2 to guide, direct s.o.

pen– directive. **se–** a moment. *Tung-gulah* ∿ , Wait a moment. **-an** 1 direction. 2 field, subject (academic). 3 line, route (of a bus, streetcar).

djus 1 part of the Koran. *Qur'an itu terbagi dlm 30 –*, The Koran is divided into 30 parts. 2 sound of a steam locomotive.

djusta see DUSTA.

djust(e)ru exactly, precisely, just. – *pd saat itu ia tidak beruang sama sekali*, Just at that moment he had no money at all. *Itu tidak benar, melainkan – kebalikan dari kenjataan*, That is not true, but is exactly the opposite of the truth.

djuta million. **ber–** –[2] millions (of). **-an** by the millions.

djutawan millionaire.

D.K. [*Daja Kuda*] horsepower.

DKA [*Djawatan Keréta Api*] Indonesian Railways.

d.k.k. [*dengan kawan*[2]] and friends.

Dkt. [*Djakarta*] Jakarta.

dll. [*dan lain*[2]] et cetera, and so forth.

dl(m). [*dalam*] in.

dls. [*dan lain sebagainja*] et cetera, and so forth.

DN [*Dalam Negeri*] Interior, Home Affairs.

Dng [*Djatinegara*] a district in Jakarta.

dng. [*dengan*] with, by.

doa prayer. **ber–, men–** to pray, say prayers. **men–kan** to pray for s.o. or s.t. – *selamat* a blessing, grace.

doane customs.

doang(an) only. *Ia memberikan saja sepérak –*, He gave me only one rupiah.

dobel double(s). – *pria* men's doubles (in tennis). – *putri* women's doubles. – *tjampuran* mixed doubles.

dobi laundryman.

doblé gold-plated. *Séndok itu ber-lapis –*, The spoon is gold-plated.

dobol torn. *Karung itu –*, The sack has a hole in it.

dobrak **men–** to batter down. *Meréka* ∿ *pintu itu*, They battered the door down. **pen–** 1 batterer. 2 destroyer. **pen–an** 1 battering. 2 break through.

dodét **men–** to rip s.t.

dodol k.o. sweet cake.

dodor **ke–an** shabby, ill-fitting. *Pakaiannja* ∿ , His clothes were shabby.

dodos **men–** to plane (a plank).

dodot k.o. sarong worn with ceremonial dress.

dogél tailless, featherless.

dogér k.o. dance, entertainment for the lower class.

dogol 1 stupid. 2 without horns.

Kambing itu – , That goat has no horns. **ke–an** stupidity.

dojan to be fond of, like. *Saja tidak – makan mangga*, I don't like mangoes.

dojong leaning. *menara – Pisa* the leaning tower of Pisa. **men–** to lean (over). *Menara itu –*, The tower leans.

dokar dogcart. **ber–** 1 to go by dogcart. 2 to use a dogcart.

dokoh 1 see DUKUH. 2 pendant.

dokter doctor, physician. **ke–an** medical. *fakultas* ∿ faculty of medicine. ∿ *gigi* dentistry. – *anak* pediatrician. – *djaga* doctor on duty, call. – *djawa* prewar Indonesian doctor who received his education in Java. – *djiwa* psychiatrist. – *gigi* dentist. – *héwan* veterinarian. – *mata* oculist.

doktor o. who holds a doctorate. – *ékonomi* Ph.D. in economics.

doktorandus candidate for doctor's degree who has completed all work but the dissertation.

dokumén document.

dokumentasi documentation. **men–kan** to document. **pen–an** system of documentation.

dol 1 k.o. drum. 2 screw with thread stripped. 3 loose, worn off. *Skrupnja –*, The thread is worn loose on the screw.

dolar dollar.

domba sheep. – *Allah* Christ.

dominasi domination.

dominé pastor, minister (of Protestant faith).

dompak **men–** to rear. *Kuda itu* ∿ , The horse reared.

dompét purse.

donasi donation.

donat doughnut.

dondang **men–(kan)** to rock. *Ia* ∿ *anaknja sampai tertidur*, She rocked her child to sleep. **-an** cradle, swing.

dong (a word used in the sense of 'please,' 'you bet,' etc.). *Djangan begitu –*, O, please (don't be so silly). (Don't do that, will you please?) *Saja kira mémang begitu –?* That's how I see it, don't you? *Apa kabar? Baik sadja –*, How are you? Quite well, as usual. *Kasi – sedikit*, Please give me some, will you?) *Kamu turut pergi?* Are you coming along? *Ja –!* You bet!

dongak **men–** with head up. **men–kan** to cock o's head.

dongéng 1 story. 2 fairy tale. **men–** to tell a story, a fairy tale. **men–kan** to relate, narrate. *Ia* ∿ *semua pengalamannja kpd kita*, He related all his adventures to us. **pen–** storyteller, narrator. **-an** 1 tall tale. *Itu*

~ *belaka*, That is just a tall tale. *Itu hanja* ~ *sadja*, That is just your story. 2 myth. – *sasakala* legend.

dongkol 1 irked. *Saja – menantikan dia sekian lamanja*, I was irked waiting for him for such a long time. 2 hornless. *kerbau* – water buffalo without horns, water buffalo with horns turned downward. **ke-an** annoyance. *Dlm* ~ *ia mengutjapkan kata² jg pedas*, In his annoyance he uttered sharp words. **men-** annoyed. **men-kan** irksome. *Menunggu lama adalah* ~ , To wait for a long time is irksome.

dongkrak automobile jack. **men-** to jack up. *Ia* ~ *mobilnja*, He jacked up his car.

dongok 1 rotund, plump. *Orang itu – tubuhnja*, That man is plump. 2 stupid, dumb. 3 see DUNGU.

dop hubcap.

dorna agitator. **men-i** to incite, egg s.o. on.

dorong men- 1 to push. *Saja* ~ *mobil*, I pushed the car. *–!* Push! 2 to urge. *Ia* ~ *saja utk meneruskan peladjaran saja*, He urged me to continue my studies. **pen-** 1 promoter. ~ *pergerakan perburuhan* promoter of the labor movement. 2 incentive. **pen-an** stimulus. **ter-** 1 pushed. *Ia* ~ *kedinding*, He was pushed to the wall. 2 pressed. *Karena* ~ *waktu ia bekerdja siang dan malam*, Because he was pressed for time he worked day and night. 3 rash. *Kata²nja jg* ~ *itu menjakitkan hati saja*, His rash words hurt me. **–an** 1 pushing. *Karena* ~ *kami mobil itu berdjalan*, Because of our pushing the car started. 2 urging. *Ia kawin atas* ~ *ibunja*, He married as a result of his mother's urging. 3 incentive, inducement. 4 thrust.

dos small box, carton.

dosa 1 sin. 2 crime. **ber-** 1 to sin. *Ia* ~ *thd agama*, He sinned against religion. 2 to be guilty. *Dia tidak* ~ , He isn't guilty. **ke-an** sinfulness.

dosén lecturer (at a university).

dosin dozen.

dot nipple of a nursing bottle.

dozén see DOSÉN.

d/p *[dengan perantaraan]* via.

Dp *[Dépok]* telephone exchange in Jakarta.

DPA *[Déwan Pertimbangan Agung]* Supreme Deliberative Council.

DPLAD *[Dinas Peralatan Angkatan Darat]* Army Supply Corps.

DPN *[Déwan Perantjang Nasional]* National Planning Council.

DPP *[Déwan Pimpinan Pusat]* Central Management Board.

DPR *[Déwan Perwakilan Rakjat]* Parliament.

DPRD *[Déwan Perwakilan Rakjat Daérah]* Provincial Assembly.

DPR(D)GR *[Déwan Perwakilan Rakjat (Daérah) Gotong Rojong]* (Regional) Mutual Aid Parliament.

dpt *[dapat]* be able.

DPUT *[Départemén Pekerdjaan Umum dan Tenaga]* Department of Public Works and Energy.

dr. *[dari]* from, of.

DR *[Djakarta Raya]* Greater Jakarta.

dr *[1 dokter 2 doktor]* title used for holders of (1) doctor of medicine, (2) doctor of philosophy.

dr- see DER-.

dra *[doktoranda]* title of woman who holds this degree (between master's and doctor's).

drama drama. **pen-an** dramatization.

dramatisasi dramatization.

dramawan dramatist.

dramawati female dramatist.

drastis drastic.

drél see DERÉL.

dria senses.

dril see DERIL.

drs *[doktorandus]* title of man who holds this degree (between master's and doctor's).

dsb. *[dan sebagainja]* et cetera.

dsl. *[dan selandjutnja]* et cetera.

dst. *[dan seterusnja]* et cetera.

Dt. *[Datuk]* (a title).

d.t.o. *[ditandatangani oléh]* signed by.

dua 2. **ber-** both. *Meréka* ~ *pergi*, Both of them went. **ber-(-)** in twos, 2 by 2. ~ *kami* the 2 of us. ~ *hati* 1 to hesitate. 2 to doubt. **ber-an** confidentially, between us. **ke-** 1 second. *Itu buku jg* ~ , That's the second book. 2 two. *Itu* ~ *buku*, Those are the 2 books. ~ *belah* both. ~ *belah pihak* both sides. ~ *belah tangan* both hands. *di*~ *belah pinggir djalan* on both sides of the road. **ke-(-)nja** both of them. **ke-kalinja** for the second time. **memper-(kan)** 1 to duplicate, double. 2 to halve, divide into halves. ~ *sawah* to let s.o. till a rice field the crop of which is divided between the land-owner and the tiller. **men-** 1 to become two. *Tongkat patah* ~ , The stick broke in two. 2 twofold. *Maksudnja* ~ , It has a dual purpose. 3 to trot (of a horse). ~ *hati* 1 to hesitate. 2 to be dishonest. **men-hatikan** to arouse doubt. **men-i** to take a second wife. **men-kan** to double, duplicate. ~ *Allah* to be a polytheist. ~ *isteri* to take a second wife. ~ *laki* to commit bigamy (by a woman). **men–kalikan** to double s.t. **pen–** 1 branch. 2 additional, reserve. **pen–an** method of sharecropping. **per–** half. **seper–** a half. ~ *umur* middle-aged. –² both. – *belas* 12. – *mingguan* bimonthly. – *puluh* 20. – *sedjoli* married couple.

duane customs.

Dubes [*Duta Besar*] ambassador.

dubilah God forbid!

dubur 1 anus. 2 buttock.

duda widower. – *kembang* childless widower.

dudu men– to follow o. after the other.

duduk 1 to sit (down). *Ia – dikorsi*, He sat on a chair. 2 situation. *Bagaimana – perkara itu?* What are the facts of the case? *Kota –nja disebelah selatan*, The city is situated in the south. 3 sediment, dregs. **ber–** 1 to have a seat (in parliament). 2 to be seated (in a car). ~ *dgn* to be wedded to. **berke–an** 1 to be located, reside. *Ia ~ di Rangoon*, He's located in Rangoon. 2 to hold the position of. *Ia ~ daktur surat kabar*, He's editor of a newspaper. **ke–an** 1 situation. ~ *perkara itu sdh djelas*, The state of affairs regarding the case is now clear. 2 position. ~ *negara itu sangat penting*, The country's position is very important. ~*nja dlm pemerintahan* his position in the government. ~ *penjangga* buffer position. 3 status. ~ *sumurung* privilege. **kepen–an** 1 residence, residential affairs. *Bagian ~* Residential Division. 2 citizenship. **men–i** 1 to occupy, hold, possess. *Ia ~ kursi itu*, He was occupying the chair. *Musuh sdh ~ kota itu*, The enemy has already occupied the city. 2 to inhabit. *Pulau itu tiada di–i orang*, The island is uninhabited. **men–kan** 1 to put, place. 2 to marry off. **pen–** inhabitant. *Djumlah ~nja tidak banjak*, The population isn't great. **pen–an** occupation. ~ *Djérman* the German Occupation. **ter–** to settle. *Bubuk téh tlh ~* , The tea leaves have settled. – *berdjuntai* to sit with legs dangling. – *bersanding* to sit close together. – *dgn* 1 to marry. 2 to be engaged. – *kokol* to sit hunched over. – *perut* pregnant. – *simpuh* to sit with o's feet behind o. (of women).

duga men– 1 to fathom. *Ia ~ dalamnja laut*, He took soundings of the sea's depth. *Saja tidak dpt ~ hatinja*, I cannot fathom his mind.

2 to take soundings. 3 to guess. ~ *djawaban* to guess the answer. 4 to presume. *Meréka ~ bhw saja akan datang hari ini*, They thought that I would come today. **pen–** a gauge. **–an** 1 guess. ~ *saja salah*, My guess was wrong. 2 assumption. ~*nja itu berdasarkan berita² jg terachir*, His assumption was based on the latest reports. *tidak ter–* –² 1 unfathomable. 2 unexpected.

dugal nausea, nauseous. *Saja merasa – dan hendak muntah*, I felt nauseated and wanted to vomit. **men–kan** nauseating.

dugang supporting rope. **men–** to support with ropes.

duhai 1 see ADUHAI. 2 Oh!

duilah ouch, my gosh (exclamation of surprise or astonishment). – *apa betul begitu?* My gosh! Is that so?

duit 1 money. *Berapa – harganja ini?* How much does this cost? 2 coin. **ber–** wealthy.

dujun ber– –² to throng, flock. *Meréka datang ~ hendak melihat gambar hidup*, They came flocking to watch the movie.

dujung manatee. **men–** to hover.

duka grief, sorrow. **ber–(-tjita)** 1 to grieve. *Ia ~ karena anaknja meninggal*, He grieved over his child's death. 2 to mourn. *Seluruh negara ~ ketika radja meninggal*, The whole country mourned when the king died. **ke–an** 1 distress. 2 grief. 3 distressed. **men–kan** 1 to distress s.o. *Djangan ~ orang tuamu*, Don't distress your parents. 2 distressing. **men–tjitakan** to mourn, grieve over s.o. – *nestapa* grief and sorrow. – *tjita* sorrow, grief, sadness.

dukana sensual.

dukatjita see DUKA.

duko men– to apply Duco to.

duku k.o. fruit.

dukuh hamlet. **pe–an** pertaining to the hamlet or village. **–an** village.

dukun shaman, medicine man, healer, sorcerer. **ber–** *kpd* to ask the help of a *dukun*. – *beranak* midwife.

dukung ber– to carry on the back. *Anak ~ dipunggung ibunja*, The mother carries the child pickaback. **men–** 1 to carry on o's back or hip. *Ia ~ anaknja*, She carried her child on her back. 2 to support. *Ia ~ orang tuanja*, He supported his parents. **–an** support.

dulang tray. **men–** 1 to feed (a child). *Ibunja harus ~ dia*, His mother has to feed him. 2 to pan for gold.

duli dust. – *baginda* your majesty. – *tuanku* your lordship.

dulu see DAHULU. **men–i** to precede. **–an** first, prior. *Kami dpt memilih ~*, We get first choice. *Ajuhlah ~*, Go ahead first. **–nja** previously.

dungkul 1 hornless. 2 with horns growing downward. 3 powerless. *Orang itu sdh hilang kekuasaannja, ia sdh –*, He has lost his power, he is powerless. see DONGKOL.

dungu stupid, retarded. **ke–an** stupidity.

dunia world. **ke–an** 1 worldly. 2 earthly. *kesenangan ~* earthly pleasures. **men–kan** to secularize, make profane. **pen–an** worldliness, secularization. **se–** 1 the whole world. *manusia seluruh ~* people of the whole world. 2 international. *féderasi mahasiswa ~* the international students' federation. – *achirat* the world hereafter. – *perdagangan* the business world.

duniawi earthly. *kekajaan –* earthly riches. **ke–an** worldly.

dup di– to be baptized.

dupa incense. **men–i** 1 to burn incense for. 2 to hold s.t. over burning incense. **pe–an** incense burner.

dupak see DEPAK.

duplo men– to duplicate. *Ia ~ surat itu*, He duplicated the letter.

dur pearl.

dura hati worried, anxious. *Ia – hatinja memikirkan anaknja*, He was worried about his child.

durdja countenance.

durdjana 1 evil, bad. 2 evildoer, criminal. **ke–an** evil.

durén see DURIAN.

durhaka 1 insubordinate, rebellious. 2 revolt, uprising. 3 sinful. **ber–** 1 to commit treason. *Ia ~ thd tanah airnja*, He committed treason against his country. 2 to rebel. *Ia ~ kpd pemerintah*, He rebelled against the government. 3 to commit an act of insubordination. *Ia ~ thd opsirnja*, He committed an act of insubordina-

tion toward his (superior) officer. **ke–an** rebelliousness. **men–** 1 to betray. *Ia ~ bangsanja*, He betrayed his people. 2 to sin, rebel. *Djangan ~ pd ajah dan ibu*, Don't sin against your father and mother. **men–i** to rebel, sin against. **pen–** 1 traitor. 2 rebel. **pen–an** 1 treachery. 2 rebellion.

duri 1 thorn. 2 fishbone. 3 prickle. **ber–** 1 thorny. 2 prickly.

durian fruit with pungent smell and taste.

dus 1 carton, cardboard box. 2 so, consequently.

dusin dozen. **men–** 1 to be awake. *Ia ~ sebentar lalu tertidur lagi*, He was awake for a while then fell asleep again. 2 to be aware of. *Ia tidak ~ maksudnja*, He was not aware of his intentions.

dusta a lie, falsehood. **ber–** to lie. **ke–an** lie, falsehood. **men–i** to lie to s.o. *Ia ~ saja*, He lied to me. **men–kan** to deny. *Ia ~ segala desas[2] itu*, He denied all the rumors. **pen–** liar. **pen–an** lying.

dusun village. **ke–an** rusticity. **pe–an** countryside.

duta 1 envoy. 2 minister of legation. **ke–an** legation. *~ besar* embassy. **pen–** envoy. **per–an** mission, legation. – *besar* ambassador. – *keliling*, – *pengembara* ambassador-at-large. – *pribadi* personal envoy (of the president, etc.).

dutawati ambassadress.

DUVRI [*Départemén Urusan Vétéran Républik Indonésia*] Ministry of Veteran's Affairs.

dwi two. *–bahasa* bilingualism. *–ganda* duplicate. *–kewarganegaraan* dual citizenship or nationality. *–lingga* reduplication. *–tunggal* 1 twosome, duumvirate. 2 President Soekarno and former Vice-President Hatta of Indonesia. *–warna* Indonesia's red and white flag. *–wulanan* bimonthly (every two months).

E

ebam oval tureen.

éban meng- to throw away.

ebang call to prayer. *Tiap petang kedengaran – dari mesdjid itu*, Every afternoon the call to prayer can be heard from the mosque.

ébék 1 awning. 2 sunshade.

ébéng meng- to dance with a dancing girl, without touching o. another.

ébi dried shrimp.

ebom see BOM.

ebon see BON. meng- 1 to buy on credit. 2 to subscribe to s.t.

ébro 4-wheeled hackney carriage.

édan 1 crazy, wild, frantic. 2 insane. – *keasmaraan* to fall madly in love.

édar ber-, meng- 1 to turn, revolve. *Bumi* ∼ , The earth revolves. 2 to wander, roam. *Kapal silam itu tlh ber-bulan²* ∼ *dilautan*, The submarine had been roaming the ocean for months. 3 to circulate. *Banjak uang palsu* ∼ *selama perang itu*, Much counterfeit money circulated during the war. meng-i 1 to revolve, turn, rotate, circle. *Bumi* ∼ *matahari*, The earth rotates around the sun. 2 to travel over, traverse. meng-kan to circulate, send around, pass around. -*kan maklumat itu*, Send the announcement around. peng- distributor (of magazines, etc.). per-an 1 circulation. 2 rotation. 3 revolution (of a wheel). 4 orbit. ∼ *darah* circulation of the blood. ∼ *dunia* the way of the world, life's ups and downs. ∼ *udara* ventilation, air circulation. -an cycle.

édja meng- to spell. *Bagaimana dikata ini?* How is this work spelled? meng-kan to spell out. -an spelling, orthography.

édjah see ÉDJA.

edjan meng- to exert abdominal pressure.

édjék meng- to mock, ridicule, deride. meng-kan 1 to ridicule. 2 scornful, mocking. -an mockery, derision, ridicule.

é-é to defecate (children's term).

éfék effect.

éfféktip effective.

éfféktiv see ÉFFÉKTIP. ke-an effectiveness.

éfféktivitas effectiveness.

éfféktivitét see ÉFFÉKTIVITAS.

éfisién efficient.

egah glory, fame. meng-kan *diri* to boast, brag.

égah meng- to walk with long steps and with each step thrust a shoulder forward.

égol meng-i to jerk, shake (loose).

égos meng-i 1 to make way, get out of the way. 2 to get around s.t. *Dia* ∼ *sénsor Inggeris*, He got around the British censor. meng-kan 1 to avoid. 2 to have s.o. stand aside.

éjang grandparent.

ékamatra unidimensional.

ékéh ter- -² panting.

ékonomi 1 economy. 2 economic(al). 3 economics. ber- to economize. ke-an economic. per-an 1 economy. 2 economic affairs. – *berantjangan*, - *berentjana* planned economy. – *terpimpin* guided economy.

ékonomis economic(al).

ékor 1 tail (of an animal). 2 rear. – *pasukan itu diserang dari udara*, The rear of the forces was attacked from the air. 3 result, consequence. 4 used with animals. *dua – kuda* two horses. ber- to have a tail. ber- -² o. after the other. meng- 1 to hang like a tail. 2 to follow obediently. meng-i to follow, tail. peng- follower. – *kuda* 1 a horse's tail. 2 a frayed piece of cloth. – *mata* outer corner of eye. – *pulau* end of an island. *Kurang –!* The devil!

éks. [*éksemplar*] example.

éksak exact.

éksekutip executive.

ékséntrik eccentric.

ékspansi expansion.

ékspér expert.

éksploitasi exploitation. meng- to exploit.

éksplorasi exploration.

éksponén exponent.

ékspor export. peng- exporter.

éksprési expression.

éksprésionis expressionist.

éksténsi extension.

éksténsip extensive.
ékstérn external.
ékstrim extreme.
ékwivalén equivalent.
élah –an 1 excuse, pretext. 2 evasion.
élak meng– to evade, avoid, dodge.
meng–kan 1 to evade, dodge. *Ia ~ pukulan itu,* He dodged the blow. *Ia ~ pertanjaan itu,* He evaded, dodged, the question. 2 to avoid. *Ia ~ tempat jg berbahaja itu,* He avoided that dangerous place. **ter–kan** avoidable, avoided. *tak ~* unavoidable.
elang 1 hawk. 2 eagle.
élastis elastic.
élastisitas elasticity.
éléktrifikasi electrification.
éléktrisir meng– to electrify.
élo unit of measure (68 cm. or a yard). –an yardstick.
élok 1 beautiful, lovely, fine. *Rupanja sangat –,* She's very beautiful. 2 good. *Tidak – itu,* It's no good. **ke–an** beauty, loveliness, splendor.
elon meng– to lie down with a child to induce it to sleep.
elu meng–kan to welcome, meet s.o. (at the station, etc.). *~ kepala* to stretch out o's neck to look.
elus meng–(–) 1 to caress. 2 to coax. –an 1 caress. 2 coaxing.
émail enamel.
emak mother.
emang uncle.
émang see MÉMANG.
émansipasi emancipation.
emas gold. **ke–an** 1 gilded. 2 golden. **meng–** to become, turn golden. *Padinja ~ ,* The rice turned golden. **meng–i** 1 to gild. 2 to bribe. *– djuita* sweetheart. *– kawin* dowry. *– kerdjang* tinfoil. *– kertas* gold leaf. *– kodok* platinum. *– lantak* gold ingot. *– lantjung, – liplap* imitation gold. *– muda* gold of low alloy. *– pasir* gold dust. *– putih* platinum. *– tua* gold of high alloy. *– urai* gold dust. see MAS.
emat checkmate!
embah grandparent.
embalau shellac.
emban 1 breastband. 2 waistband. 3 nurse (for children).
embara meng–(i) to wander, roam about. *Ia ~ Éropah,* He roamed over Europe. **peng–** 1 wanderer, vagabond. 2 nomad. **peng–an** wandering, roaming, roving, rambling.
embarau palisade at the edge of the sea or along a riverbank.
embat meng– to lash s.o. with a strip of bamboo, piece of rope, etc.
embatjang a mango with pungent smell.

embel swamp.
émbél[2] 1 a small, unimportant addition. 2 appendage. *Sebagai ~ ia ditambahkan pd rombongan pengantar présidén,* He's been added to the president's entourage as an appendage.
émbér pail, bucket.
embih lass.
embik meng– to bleat (like a goat).
émbrat large watering can.
embuh to want, wish, like. *Sdh ber-tahun[2] ia sakit, mati tak –,* He has been ill for years, but he does not want to die.
embun 1 dew. 2 vapor, steam. **ber–** 1 to have vapor. 2 to be covered with dew. 3 to spend the night in the open. 4 to leave s.t. in the open overnight. **meng–** to condense, turn into steam or vapor. **meng–i** to wet drop by drop. *Mukanja di–i air mata,* Her face was wet with tears. **meng–kan** to expose to vapor. **peng–** condensation. *– betina* small drop of dew. *– djantan* large drop of dew. *– pagi* dew. *– rintik* small drop of dew. *kering –* about 7 A.M.
embus aspirated. *p –* aspirated 'p.' **ber–, meng–** 1 to blow, breathe. 2 to pant, puff. **meng–kan** 1 to blow away. 2 to blow out. *~ napas penghabisan* to die. **peng–** bellows. *~ angin* windstorm. –an 1 pair of bellows. 2 suggestion.
embut meng– to rise up and down (like the chest of a sleeping person).
emis see KEMIS. **meng–** to beg. **peng–** beggar.
emoh unwilling. *Negeri itu – ikut SEATO,* That country is unwilling to join SEATO.
emong meng– to care for, look after. **peng–** o. who looks after s.o.
émosi emotion.
empal sliced pieces of meat, about one-half inch thick, seasoned and fried.
empang 1 fishpond. 2 dam. **meng–** to dam up, block, bar. **peng–** dam. **ter–** blocked, barred. *Tiada ~ peluru oléh lalang,* The wish of an authority cannot be blocked. –an 1 fishpond. 2 dam. *~ djalan* road barricade.
émpang see EMPANG.
émpar meng– to be off course (of a ship, etc.). *Trém ~ ,* The streetcar was derailed.
empas meng– to lash. *Ombak ~ dipantai,* The waves lash the shore. **meng–kan** to throw, dash, fling. *Ia ~ dirinja kelantai,* She flung herself on the floor. –an surf, breakers.
empat 4. **ber–** to be 4. *Kami ~*

pergi, The 4 of us went. **ber- -²** by 4's. *Pradjurit²* berbaris ~ , The soldiers lined up in rows of 4. **member-** to divide into 4 equal parts. **per-** quarter. *seper- djam* a quarter of an hour. **per-an** crossroad, intersection. – *belas* 14. – *dasawarsa* 40th anniversary. – *kali tiga* 3333 (used in telephone call). – *pendjuru alam* the 4 points of the compass. – *puluh* 40. – *segi* square. – *tepas dunia* the 4 points of the compass.

empatpuluh 40. **meng–** *hari* to hold a religious ceremony involving the offering of prayers followed by a meal on the fortieth day after a person's death.

empedal gizzard.

empedu bile, gall.

empelas sandpaper. **meng–(i)** to scour, scrub. **peng–** abrasive.

empelop envelope.

émpér 1 veranda, porch. 2 that part of the roof covering a veranda, porch, etc.

emping seeds of *Gnetum gnemon* pounded flat, dried, and fried to make a crisp chip.

émplasemén emplacement.

émpoh to flood. **ke–an** flooded, inundated. **meng–i** to flood, inundate. **peng–an** inundation.

empok 1 older sister. 2 form of address to a woman.

empos **meng–i** 1 to breathe, blow on. 2 to prompt, instigate, instill. *Ia ~ Amat supaja membentji Ali,* He set Amat against Ali. 3 to smoke green fruit in order to accelerate ripening (mainly bananas). **–an** fruit ripened by smoking.

empu 1 master craftsman. (In Hindu-Javanese literature a form of address for those who attained high distinction, e.g., in literature, philosophy, craftsmanship, as in the art of forging creeses, etc.) 2 armorer. – *djari* thumb. – *kaki* big toe.

empuk 1 soft. *Kasur itu –,* That mattress is soft. 2 tender, well-done. *Saja suka makanan jg –,* I like tender food. 3 worn-out, frayed. *Disini ada pakaian jg sdh –,* Here are some worn-out clothes. 4 pleasant. *Suaranja –,* His voice is pleasant (to listen to). **ke–an** softness. **meng–kan** to soften. **bikin –** to tenderize.

empulur the pith or soft core of a palm tree.

empunja owner. see PUNJA.

émulsa emulsion.

énak 1 nice, tasty, delicious. *Makanan ini – sekali,* This food is delicious. 2 nice, pleasant. *njanjian jg*
– a nice tune. 3 wonderful, pleasant. *Sdh lama saja tak dengar tjeritera jg –,* I haven't heard a really good story in a long time. 4 well, pleasant, nice. *Perasaan saja tak –,* I don't feel well. **ke–an** to o's heart's content. ~ *kamu kalau saja berikan ini kepadamu,* You'll be only too happy if I give this to you. **meng–kan** to put s.o. at ease. **se--²nja** at will, when suitable. ~ *sadja* at will, as o. wishes, according to o's whim. *Ia menuduh orang dgn ~ sadja,* He accused people at will. **–²an** sweets.

enam 6. – *belas* 16. – *puluh* 60.

enau k.o. palm tree. (Its flower stalk yields liquid which can be made into palm wine, vinegar, and brown sugar.)

endal **meng–** 1 to stuff, push (s.t. in a bag, etc.). 2 springy, elastic.

endap **meng–** 1 to settle, precipitate. *Kopi itu ~ ,* The coffee settled. 2 to approach in a crouching position. **meng– -²** to stalk, steal upon s.o. **meng–kan** to embezzle. **–an** sediment. ~ *darah* blood precipitation. **–²** dregs.

enderia 1 organ of sense. 2 perception.

endjak **meng–** to step on.

endjal **meng–** 1 to stuff. 2 springy.

endjut **meng–** to tug, jerk.

endon **meng–** to stay. *Ia ~ dirumah pamannja selama dua hari,* He stayed with his uncle 2 days. **–an** guest for several days.

endus 1 to sniff. 2 to begin to know (understand).

enek 1 nauseous. 2 nauseating.

engah **meng– -²** to pant. **ter– -²** in a hurry.

engak dazed.

engap tight in the chest. **–²an** to be in o's death throes.

enggak 1 no. 2 not.

enggan 1 to dislike. *Saja – mempunjai teman seperti itu,* I dislike having such a friend. 2 to have an objection. *Saja tak – pergi kebioskop,* I have no objection to going to the movie. 3 to be averse to. **ke–an** 1 dislike. 2 unwillingness. 3 stubbornness. **meng–kan** 1 to refuse. 2 to dislike. – *djikalau* lest.

enggang hornbill.

enggih see TUKANG.

enggil **ber–** toothed, serrated.

énggokan turn in the road.

engkang **meng–** to walk with legs wide apart.

engkau 1 you (fam.). *Apa – sdh dengar tentang kabar itu?* Have you heard the news? 2 your (fam.).

ber- to use *engkau,* be on familiar terms with s.o.
éngko ber- to be in partnership (in business) with s.o.
engko(h) used when addressing an older person (mainly used by Chinese Indonesians).
éngkol crank of a machine.
engkong grandfather.
engku 1 prince. 2 title of high rank or nobility. **ber-** to be called *engku.*
éngsél 1 handle. 2 hinge.
enjah 1 to go away, flee. 2 to be off. **meng-kan** 1 to chase away. 2 to wipe away. **peng-an** 1 fleeing. 2 abolition. *-lah engkau dari sini!* Go away!
enjak meng- to stamp, press hard (of loose earth into a solid mass). **meng-kan** *diri* to let o.s. fall with a thud. ~ *diri dikursi* to drop o.s. into a chair.
énsiklopédi(a) encyclopedia.
entah 1 I don't know. - *betul – salah, saja tidak tahu,* I don't know whether it's true or false. 2 who knows. **ber-** to say no. *Ia* ~ *!* He says no! **ber-** *--²* extremely. ~ *sulitnja soal ini,* This problem is extremely complicated. *--²* maybe, perhaps. *- -ber-* unutterable. ~ *banjaknja tamu jg datang itu,* Heaven knows how many guests came.
entak meng- 1 to pulsate. 2 to stamp o's feet. 3 to thrust, stab a knife, lance, etc., into s.t. **peng-** pestle. **-an** stamping of the feet.
entar malam tonight.
énténg 1 light in weight. 2 easy. **ke-an** 1 lightness. 2 ease. **meng-kan** 1 to alleviate. 2 to lighten.
entimun cucumber.
entjék title used in addressing a full-blooded Chinese.
entjér meng- to watch, observe. *Polisi* ~ *dia,* The police are keeping an eye on him. **peng-an** watching, observing, observation.
éntjér 1 liquid. 2 weak, thin, watery. *Kopi itu -,* The coffee is weak. 3 smart, intelligent. **meng-kan** to dilute, thin. **peng-an** dilution. **-an** thinning, act of diluting.
entjik 1 Mr. 2 Mrs. 3 Miss.
entjit uncut cloth, material, fabric.
éntjok 1 stiff, rheumatic. 2 rheumatism. 3 gout.
éntjot lame.
éntré to stand in line, to queue. *Orang - membeli kartjis,* People were standing in line to buy tickets.
epah meng-kan to take a lease on, buy a concession (e.g., to exploit a mine, etc.).

épok a bag to hold the ingredients for betel-nut chewing.
épos an epic.
érak ber- 1 to uncoil (of a snake). 2 to fall apart. **meng-** 1 to unroll, uncoil (a rope, etc.). 2 to fall apart. **meng-kan** to loosen, separate.
eram meng- 1 to hatch, brood. 2 to kneel down (of an elephant, a camel, etc.), crouch low (of a tiger set to pounce on its prey). 3 to stay at home, hide. *Djangan* ~ *sadja; kebioskoplah sekali-kali!* Don't stay home all the time; go to the movies once in a while. **meng-i** to sit on eggs. **meng-kan** to hatch. **peng-an** a brood.
erang groaning, moaning. **meng-** to groan, moan. **-an** moaning.
érang 1 dark blue. 2 black. *- -érot* zigzag.
erat 1 tight, firm. 2 close. *Kami mempunjai persahabatan jg -,* We have a close friendship. **memper-, meng-kan** 1 to tighten. 2 to strengthen.
éréng leaning, sloping. *- géndéng* things that conflict with the mores of an area.
érét meng- to drag along. **peng-an** 1 luggage, cargo truck (at ports, railway station, etc.). 2 s.o. who is clever at winning a person's favor for personal gain. **-an** s.t. dragged along. ~ *sungai* river ferry which moves along a guide rope.
erik meng- 1 to scream, shout. 2 to trumpet (of an elephant).
ering bird of prey.
Éropah Europe(an).
érot distorted, wry (of face or mouth). **ber-** in a row. *- bénjot* zigzag.
erti see ARTI. **meng-** to understand. *Saja tidak* ~ *,* I don't understand. *Ia* ~ *akan maksud surat itu,* He understands the meaning of the letter. *Apakah soal itu dimeng-?* Was the problem understood? **meng-kan** to explain. *Saja* ~ *kpd ibu maksud surat itu,* I explained the purpose of the letter to Mother. **peng-an** 1 understanding. 2 explanation, interpretation. 3 conception. ~² *umum* generalizations.
értjis peas.
és ice. **di-** to be cooled off with ice. *- batu* ice cube. *- kopi* iced coffee. *- krim* ice cream. *- lilin* popsicle. *- loli* lollypop. *- perongkol* ice cube. *- téh* iced tea.
esa 1 one. 2 only. *Jg Maha -* God. **ke-an** oneness. **meng-kan** *Allah* to accept that there is but one God. **-²an** lonely.

esah 1 legal, legitimate. 2 see SAH.
meng–(kan) to legalize. peng-an 1
legalization. 2 ratification.
ésak meng– to sob.
esang meng– to blow o's nose.
ései essay.
ésok 1 tomorrow. 2 see BÉSOK. ber-
tomorrow. ke–annja, ke–an *harinja*
the next morning. meng–kan to postpone until the next day. –nja the
next morning. – *hari* tomorrow. –
lusa day after tomorrow.
ésot meng– to push, shove.
éstafétte see LARI.
éstétis aesthetic.
étalase 1 show window. 2 window
display.

éték aunt.
étik ethics.
étikad belief, creed.
étikét label on a bottle, etc. berto be labeled.
étjé meng– to make a fool of. -an
fooling.
étjék apparently. (ber)- –² to pretend. *Ia ~ tidur*, He pretended to
be asleep.
étjér meng– to sell s.t. retail. peng-
retailer. –an 1 retail. *Ia pendjual ~ ,*
He is a retailer. 2 issue (of a periodical, etc.).
étos ethos.
évaluasi evaluation.
éxpl [*éksemplar*] example, copy.

F

fa'al 1 good conduct, good deed.
Orang itu kurang baik –nja, That
man's conduct isn't so good. 2 function, action of living organisms. 3
prophecy. *Ia membuka –*, He made a
prophecy. memf–kan to prophesy.
Ajah saja ~ achir perang, My father
prophesied the end of the war.
fabrikasi manufacture.
fadihat disgrace, shame, ignominy.
Itu adalah – jg besar sekali bagi kami,
That was a great disgrace for us.
memf–kan to disgrace, humiliate.
fadil prominent, eminent, famous.
fadjar dawn. – *merekah* daybreak.
– *menjingsing*, The day is (It is)
dawning. – *siddik* daybreak.
faédah use, benefit, profit, advantage. *Kedatangannja kemari ada –nja
djuga*, There's an advantage in his
coming here. ber– useful, advantageous. *Peraturan sematjam ini akan
sangat ~ ,* Such a regulation will be
very useful. *~ utk rambut* good for
the hair.
faham see PAHAM.
fak. [*fakulta(s)*] department or school
of a university, faculty.
fakih an expert in Moslem law.
fakir 1 poor, destitute. *Ia orang –*,
He's a poor man. 2 a poor person.
3 Moslem or Hindu religious ascetic
or mendicant. ke–an poverty. –
miskin the poor and needy.
fakta fact.

fakulta(s) a department or school of a
university, faculty. – *Sastera* faculty of
literature.
fakultét a department or school of a
university, faculty. – *Hukum* faculty
of law.
falak celestial sphere.
falsafat philosophy. see FILSAFAT.
falsafi philosophical.
famili 1 relative. 2 related.
fana 1 transitory, perishable. *dunia
jg –* this world. 2 distressed, deeply
moved (e.g., because of bad news,
etc.). ke–an transitoriness.
fanatik fanatic. ke–an fanaticism.
faradj see FARDJI.
fard obligatory, strictly prescribed.
fardji vagina.
fardu religious obligations of a
Moslem.
farmasi pharmacy.
fasal see PASAL.
fase phase.
faséh see FASIH.
fasét facet.
fasih 1 fluent. *Ia – bahasa Indonésia*,
He is fluent in Indonesian. 2 glib.
– *lidahnja* to have a ready tongue,
talk persuasively, talk fluently.
fasilita² facilities.
fasis Fascist.
fatalis fatalist.
fatihah the opening chapter of the
Koran. *membatja –* to say grace.
fatsal see PASAL.

fatwa 1 final answer on a legal interpretation by a Moslem judge. 2 instructions, guidance of an older person. *Présidén memberi - kpd tentara jg akan berangkat kemédan perang,* The president gave instructions to the troops which were leaving for the battlefield. **ber-** to give instruction, advice on religious matters. **memf-kan** to advise, give a message. *Beliau ∼ supaja semua bangsa mendjaga persatuan,* He advised that all people preserve unity.

Féb. [*Fébruari*] February.

Fébruari February.

féderasi federation.

féodal feudal.

féodalisme feudalism.

Fidji Fiji.

fihak see PIHAK.

fi'il good conduct, deed, act. *-nja baik,* His conduct is good.

fikh Moslem law.

fikir see PIKIR.

fiksi fiction.

fil(e)m 1 film. 2 film, movie. **memf-** to film. **per-an** filming.

filosofis philosophical.

filsafat philosophy. **ber-** to philosophize, theorize, speculate.

filsuf philosopher.

filter filter (in photo.).

Finlandia Finland.

FIPIA [*Fakultas Ilmu Pasti dan Ilmu Alam*] faculty of mathematics and physics.

firasat 1 ability to prophesy the future. 2 reading of o's character (by palmistry, physiognomy, etc.). 3 presentiment.

fira'un Pharaoh.

firdaus paradise.

firdausi paradisiacal.

firman saying, decree, royal or divine. – *Allah* God's decree. **ber-** to decree. **memf-kan** to decree, say.

fisika physics.

fisipén kingpin.

fitnah slander, calumny, libel. **memf-(kan)** to slander, calumniate.

fitrah an obligatory gift of a certain amount of rice given by each member of the family at the end of the fasting period. **ber-** to give the *fitrah*. **memf-kan** to give away as *fitrah*.

FKIP [*Fakultas Keguruan dan Ilmu Pendidikan*] faculty of teacher training and pedagogy.

flat apartment.

fluktuasi fluctuation.

F.N. [*Front Nasional*] National Front.

foja **ber-** -² to relax, take it easy, enjoy o.s. *Meréka ∼ di New York,* They had a good time in New York.

folan see POLAN.

foném phoneme.

fonim see FONÉM.

formatir see FORMATUR.

formatur prime-minister-designate.

formulasi formulation.

formulir see PORMULIR. **memf-** to formulate.

fosfat phosphate.

fosfor phosporus.

foto photo. *-kopi* photocopy.

fraksi faction, group (of political party in parliament, etc.).

frékwénsi frequency.

front front, cadre.

fuad (al)zakiah a pure heart.

fungsi 1 function. 2 office. *Apa -nja?* What is his position?

funksi see FUNGSI. **ber-** to function.

fusi fusion, coalition. **ber-** to be in coalition.

G

G. [1 *Gunung* 2 *Gambir*] 1 mt., mountain. 2 see GAMBIR.

gaba² garlands and other decorations made of coconut or other leaves. **meng-** -² to decorate with leaves.

gabah unhulled paddy separated from the stalks.

gabak 1 cloudy, overcast. 2 measles. **meng-** gloomy, dark. *Tjuatja ∼ ,* Dark clouds are closing in. *Tanda² ∼ bhw perang akan petjah,* Dark clouds signifying an impending war are gathering.

gabas done in a hurry (as in results of manual labor). **meng-** to hurry s.o. up in doing a job.

gabir clumsy, awkward (of walking). *Anak itu masih - ,* That child still falls easily when he tries to walk.

gabuk 1 empty. *Butir² padi itu - ,* Those rice kernels are empty. 2 sterile, incapable of conception.

gabung 1 bunch. *se- bunga* a bunch of flowers. 2 cluster. **ber-** 1 gathered. *Orang² tlh ～ di balai kota,* The people are gathered at the town hall. 2 fused. *Kedua pergerakan buruh itu ～ mendjadi satu,* The two labor movements have been fused into one. 3 associated. *Kedua perusahaan itu ～ ,* The two companies are associated. **meng-kan** 1 to bundle, make a bundle of s.t. *Ia ～ ranting² jg bersérakan itu,* He bundled the scattered twigs. 2 to fuse. *Pemerintah ～ semua partai² politik,* The government fused all political parties together. 3 to unite. *Perdjuangan kemerdékaan ～ seluruh lapisan masjarakat,* The struggle for freedom united all strata of society. *～ diri* to join. *Ia ～ diri pd perkumpulan itu,* He joined the club. **peng-an** fusion. *～ kedua perusahaan itu* fusion of the 2 companies. **per-an** 1 fusion. 2 federation. *Gerakan buruh badja adalah anggauta ～ buruh se-Indonésia,* The steel workers' union is a member of the All-Indonesia labor federation. 3 association. *～ mahasiswa Indonésia* the Indonesian students' association. 4 affiliation. **-an** 1 see PER-AN. 2 combination. *～ partai² oposisi menjerang pemerintah,* A combination of the opposition parties attacked the government.

gabus 1 pike (fish). 2 cork. *- botol* bottle cork. *Tangkai pisau itu terbuat dari -,* The knife handle is made of cork. **meng-** to sharpen. *Ibu ～ pisau,* Mother sharpened a knife. **peng-** sharpener. *- kaki* door mat.

gada club. *Ia bersendjata -,* He was armed with a club. **meng-** to hit with a club. *-²* 1 small flag, pennant. 2 weather vane. *- getah* rubber truncheon.

gadai security. *Ia memberikan djamnja sebagai - atas pindjamannja itu,* He pawned his watch. **meng-** to take in pawn. *Ia ～ sawah orang itu,* He took the man's rice field in pawn. **meng-kan** 1 to pawn. *Ia ～ tjintjin emasnja,* He pawned his gold ring. 2 to mortgage o's home or building. **pe-an** pawnshop.

gadang 1 see GEDANG. 2 k.o. sieve. **ber-** to stay up. *Ia ～ semalam sentuh,* He stayed up the whole night.

gading 1 elephant's tusk. 2 ivory.

3 ivory color. *-²* 1 hoop (of a cartwheel, barrel). 2 timber (of a wooden ship).

gadis 1 girl. 2 maiden. 3 virgin. **ke-an** virginity. **ke- -²an** to act like a young girl. *Djanda itu tingkah lakunja ～ sadja,* The widow acted like a young girl. **meng-** to stay unmarried. *Perempuan itu masih suka ～ sadja,* That woman still wants to stay single. **meng-i** to have sexual intercourse with a virgin. *- sial* a woman who can't get a man. *- tua* spinster, old maid.

gadjah 1 elephant. 2 bishop (in chess). **meng-** 1 to appear big. *Bajangan ～ ,* The shadow loomed large. 2 to put on airs, act big. *-²an* to play chess. *- mina* whale.

gadji 1 wage. 2 salary. **meng-** to employ. *Ia ～ lima orang pekerdja,* He employs 5 workmen. **-an** 1 payday. 2 wage earner. *- bermula* beginning salary. *- bersih* net wages, take-home pay. *- bulanan* monthly pay. *- buta* 1 salary that is not merited. 2 unemployment pay. *- kotor* gross wages. *- permulaan* beginning salary. *- pertjobaan* probationary salary. *- pokok* base pay.

gadjih 1 fat, grease. 2 see GADJI. **ber-** 1 fat, stout. 2 rich.

gadjus cashew tree.

gado **meng-** to sample food. *Ia ～ makanan,* He sampled the food. *-²* k.o. vegetable salad with peanut butter sauce. *～ lagu* potpourri.

gaduh 1 noisy. *Djangan -, saja mau tidur,* Don't be noisy, I want to sleep. 2 alarmed, in tumult. *Seluruh negeri - karena pemberontakan itu,* The whole country was in tumult over the uprising. **ber-** 1 to quarrel. *Kedua orang itu ～ ,* The two people quarreled. 2 to be at war. *Dua negeri itu ～ ,* The two countries are at war. **ke-an** 1 noise. 2 commotion. **meng-kan** to disturb. *Pendjahat itu ～ keamanan,* The criminal disturbed the peace. *Hal itu ～ hati saja,* That distresses me very much. **per-an** commotion.

gaduk arrogant, conceited.

gadung 1 a yam, which occasionally (if not cooked well) causes intoxication. 2 tipsy. 3 madly in love, infatuated.

gaé(k) old.

gaét see GAIT.

gaga dry rice field.

gagah 1 strong. *Ia masih - meskipun sdh tua,* He is still strong though he is old. 2 brawny. *seorang opsir jg - a* brawny officer. 3 dashing, cocky.

Sangat – kelihatannja dlm unipormnja jg baru itu, He looked dashing in his new uniform. 4 sturdy. *Pohon itu berdiri dgn –nja,* The tree stood sturdily. 5 brave. *Ia sangat – dlm peperangan,* He was very brave in battle. **ke–an** 1 courage, valor. 2 cockiness. 3 pride. **meng–** to act with firmness. *Ia ∼ thd kaum pemberontak,* He acted with firmness against the rebels. **meng–i** 1 to overpower. *Ia ∼ tentara musuh,* He overpowered the enemy army. 2 to molest. *Ia ∼ seorang gadis,* He molested a girl. **meng–kan** *diri* to encourage o.s. *Ia ∼ dirinja menghadapi bahaja itu,* He steeled himself to face the danger. *– berani, – perkasa, – perwira* courageous, brave.

gagak a crow.

gagal to fail. *Segala pertjobaannnja –,* All his attempts failed. **ke–an** failure, fiasco. **meng–kan** to foil, thwart. *Ia ∼ segala serangan musuh,* He foiled all the enemy's attacks. *–kan P,* Down with P.

gagang 1 handle. 2 stem. *– bunga* flower stem, peduncle. *– katja mata* temples of glasses. *– péna* penholder. *– senapan* rifle butt.

gagap ber–(–) hurriedly. *∼ ia berpakaian,* Hurriedly he got dressed. **meng–** 1 to stutter. 2 to grope for. *Ia ∼ mentjari pintu dlm kegelapan,* He groped for the door in the dark. **ter–(–)** 1 hastily. 2 nervously.

gagas meng– to think, have an idea. **–an** 1 idea. 2 concept.

gagau meng– to grope. *Ia ∼ dlm gelap,* He groped around in the dark. **ter– –²** to walk gropingly.

gagu mute, dumb.

gahar meng– to scrub s.t.

gahara of royal descent.

gaib 1 mysterious. *Kedjadian – itu sangat menakutkan,* The mysterious incident was very frightening. 2 invisible. *sebuah tangan –* an invisible hand. 3 to disappear. *Se-konjong² ia –,* Suddenly he disappeared. 4 magical. *tenaga² –* magical powers. 5 esoteric. **ke–an** 1 mysteriousness. 2 magic. **meng–kan** to make disappear. *Ia ∼ diri,* He made himself disappear.

gairah 1 passion, strong desire. 2 jealousy. 3 ambition. **ke–an** 1 lust. 2 rapture. **meng–kan** 1 to stir, arouse. *Perempuan itu ∼ nafsunja,* The woman stirred his desires. 2 to delight, enrapture. *Musik itu ∼ hati,* That music delights the heart. 3 alluring, enticing. *mata jg ∼* alluring eyes.

gait meng– 1 to pull, pluck (fruit, etc.), with a hook attached to a pole. 2 to wheedle (money, etc.) from a person, trick s.t. out of a person. **peng–, –an** 1 a hook. 2 point of attack. *Ketagihannja akan tjandu mendjadi ∼ bagi polisi,* His addiction to opium became a point of attack for the police.

gaja 1 energy, potential. 2 strength. 3 strong. 4 form, style. 5 manner, attitude, behavior. *– jg élok* a graceful manner. 6 attractive, charming. 7 elegant. 8 musical note. *suling ampat –* a 4-note flute. 9 melody. **ber–** 1 strong, energetic. *Ia tak ∼ lagi,* His strength was gone. 2 to have style. *gedung² jg ∼ baru* the new-style buildings. **ber– –²** 1 to show off. 2 affected. **meng–** to put on airs. **meng–i** to inspire, encourage. *Ia ∼ rakjatnja supaja berontak,* He inspired his people to revolt. **meng–kan** to lend beauty to s.t. *– air* water power. *– bahasa* style. *– bébas* free style in swimming. *– berat* gravity. *– berganti* relay race. *– bobot* gravity. *– dada* breast stroke. *– lentur* flexibility. *– pantjargas* jet propulsion. *– pegas* resilience. *– punggung* backstroke. *– tarik* pulling power. *– tegang* tension, expansibility.

gajang staggering, reeling (because of drunkenness, dizziness, etc.). **–²** a rack.

gajem meng– 1 to ruminate. 2 to chew.

gajung 1 water dipper. *Ia memakai kaléng sebagai –,* He used a tin can as a water dipper. 2 blow with the fist, weapon, etc. *Saja kena –nja,* I was hit by his blow. 3 saber stroke. *Dgn sekali – sadja putuslah dahan itu,* With just one saber stroke the branch broke. **ber–** 1 to use a water dipper. *Ia mandi ∼ ,* He bathed with a water dipper. 2 to box. 3 to fence. **meng–** 1 to strike, slash. *Ia ∼ saja,* He struck me. 2 to cast an evil spell (on s.o.). 3 to harm, kill. **meng–kan** to swing the arm to strike.

gajut ber– to hang, swing. *∼ dipohon* to swing in the tree. **meng–kan** to hang s.t. *Ia ∼ topinja pd paku,* He hung his hat on a nail. **–an** circle under o's eyes.

gala 1 resin. 2 see SEGALA. 3 ruined, destroyed. 4 see GALAH. **–²** 1 putty. 2 bee. *– lembut* tar.

galagasi 1 spider. 2 spider web.

galah 1 pole. 2 punting pole (for boats). **meng–** 1 to pole. *Ia ∼ buah,* He picked fruit with a pole. 2 to punt. *Ia ∼ perahunja kepantai,*

He punted his boat to the shore. *sepeng–* a pole's length.

galak 1 wild. *andjing* – wild dog. 2 fierce. *Matanja sangat –*, His eyes look fierce. *Dgn – ia menjerang musuhnja*, Fiercely he attacked his enemy. 3 severe. *Ia sangat – kelihatannja*, He looked so severe. **meng–** to rage. *Api kebakaran itu ~* , The flames of the fire raged. **meng–kan** to incite, stir up. *Ia ~ orang² agar memberontak*, He incited the people to revolt.

galan 1 gallant. 2 see MAIN.

galang 1 girder. – *atap* the girders of the roof. 2 see ALANG. 3 see KALANG. **meng–(i)** to support. *Ia ~ atap itu dgn batang²*, He supported the roof with steel beams. **meng–kan** 1 to rest. *Ia ~ atap itu pd tiang² badja*, He rested the roof on steel poles. 2 to put in a dry dock. *Ia ~ perahunja*, He put his boat in a dry dock. **peng–** pillar, support. *~ masjarakat* pillar of society. **ter–** supported. **–an** 1 dry dock. 2 see GALENGAN. 3 dike.

galas carrying pole. **meng–** 1 to carry with a carrying pole. 2 to peddle merchandise (carried around in containers suspended from a carrying pole). **peng–** peddler, hawker. **peng–an** 1 merchandise. 2 peddling.

galat = RALAT.

galau ber– confused. **ke–an** confusion.

galengan small dikes in rice fields.

galenika k.o. patent medicine.

gali meng– to dig. **peng–** 1 spade. 2 digger. **peng–an** excavation, digging. **–an** diggings, what is dug up. **–²an** 1 minerals. 2 tuberous plants (crop).

galib normal. **ke–annja**, *pd –nja* usually, customarily, normally. *Pd ~ kita berangkat djam enam*, Normally we leave at 6 o'clock.

galir 1 loose. *Sekrup itu –*, The screw is loose. 2 fluent. *Kata²nja jg – itu menangkap perhatian saja*, His fluent speech captured my interest.

galur furrow. **ber–** –² furrowed. *Permukaan laut nampak ~* , The surface of the sea appeared furrowed. **meng––²** to unravel. *Ia ~ sedjarah keradjaan kuno itu*, He unraveled the history of that ancient kingdom.

Gama [*Gadjah Mada*] Gadjah Mada University in Jogjakarta.

gamak meng– 1 to take s.t. in o's hand to feel its size or estimate its weight. 2 to estimate, make a guess. 3 to put o's hand threateningly on the hilt of a dagger o. is wearing. *Ia*

~ péstolnja, Threateningly he put his hand on his gun. 4 see GEMAK.

gamam see GAMANG.

gaman weapon. **ber–** armed. *Ia ~ pedang*, He was armed with a sword.

gamang 1 nervous. 2 afraid. 3 to feel dizzy from heights or at the sight of blood. **peng–** acrophobe.

Gamawan male student at Gadjah Mada University, Jogjakarta.

Gamawati girl student at Gadjah Mada University, Jogjakarta.

gamb. [*gambar*] illustration, picture.

gambang xylophonelike instrument. – *keromong* a small popular Chinese-Indonesian orchestra.

gambar 1 picture. 2 drawing. 3 illustration. 4 sketch. **ber–** 1 to have o's picture made. *Ia ~ didepan kantornja*, He had a picture made of him in front of his office. 2 illustrated. *madjallah ~* an illustrated magazine. **meng–** to draw a picture. **meng–i** to illustrate. *Ia ~ madjallah itu*, He illustrated that magazine. **meng–kan** 1 to illustrate. *Ia ~ pendiriannja itu dgn beberapa tjontoh*, He illustrated his point with some examples. 2 to describe, depict. *Ia ~ pd saja segala pengalamannja*, He described to me all his adventures. **meng–kuliti** to provide (a book) with a decorated jacket. **peng–an** 1 drafting. 2 description, depiction. **ter–** pictured. *Rupa ibunja bagai ~ dlm pikirannja*, His mother's face was pictured in his mind. **–an** 1 = *gambar*. 2 description. *Ia memberi ~ ttg apa jg tlh dilihatnja*, He gave a description of what he had seen. *tak ter–kan* beyond description. – *angan²* imaginary picture. – *bagan* 1 sketch. 2 blueprint. – *bumi* map. – *édjékan* caricature. – *hidup* motion picture, movie. – *mati* portrait, still. – *sénter* lantern slide. – *sindiran* caricature, political cartoon. – *sorot* 1 movie. 2 slide. – *témpél* poster. – *timbul* bas-relief. – *tjermin* image, reflection. – *tjorét* pen drawing, sketch.

gambir 1 ingredient used for betel-nut chewing. 2 climbing plant (its leaves when boiled produce a thick-brown sediment which after cooling off and hardening is diced; also used to tan hides). 3 cream color.

Gambir (in Jakarta) 1 name of district. 2 telephone exchange. 3 railway station.

gamblang 1 see GEMBLENG. 2 clear. 3 firm, resolute.

gamboh see GAMBUH.

gambuh Javanese male dancer.

gambus k.o. Arabian 6-stringed lute. **meng–** to perform on a harmonium accompanied by tambourines.

gamelan Javanese orchestra. – *pélog*, – *sléndro* k.o. Javanese orchestra. – *sekatén* sacred Javanese orchestra played only once a year (in the Principality of Surakarta).

gamit ber–(an) 1 to nudge, tap (s.o. on the shoulder, arm, etc.), attract o's attention. 2 to flag s.o. (to attract his attention, give a sign). *Meréka ~ saling memberi kedip mata*, They gave e.o. a sign by exchanging a wink. **meng–** 1 to nudge, tap s.o. to attract his attention. 2 to pluck, strum (a guitar, ukelele, etc.). **meng–(-)kan** to tap, pluck strings with a finger. **–²an** 1 the talk of the town, on everybody's lips, talked about. 2 the object of ridicule.

gampang easy. **ke–an** too easy. **memper–, meng–kan** 1 to make easy, alleviate. *Alat ini akan ~ pekerdjaanmu*, This tool will make your job easy. 2 to facilitate. *Perdjalanan setjara modéren ~ perhubungan antara semua negara*, Modern travel facilitates better communications among all nations. 3 to take lightly. *Djangan ~ pekerdjaanmu itu*, Do not take your work lightly. 4 to underestimate. *Ia ~ ketjerdikan musuhnja*, He underestimated his enemy's skill. **–an** easier. **–²an** easy-going. *Sikapnja selalu ~ sadja*, He is always easy-going.

gampar meng– to strike with the fist or the open hand. **–an** 1 stroke. 2 wooden clogs.

Gana Ghana.

ganas 1 savage. *Harimau itu binatang –*, The tiger is a savage animal. 2 furious. *Ia berkelahi dgn –*, He fought furiously. 3 vicious. *Dgn – dibunuhnja semua musuhnja*, Viciously he killed all his enemies. *Buaja itu binatang –*, The crocodile is a vicious animal. **ke–an** 1 ferocity. 2 cruelty. **meng–** to rage. *Peperangan ~ diseluruh dunia*, War raged over the whole world.

ganda 1 opponent of unequal strength (in a game, etc.). 2 handicap (e.g., in golf, tennis). 3 double. *Uang saja dua kali – uangmu*, I have twice as much money as you. **ber–** doubled. *Tahun ini penghasilannja ~* , This year his income doubled. **ber– –²**, **memper–kan, meng–kan** to double. *Meréka ~ hasil tanaman meréka*, They doubled their crops. **memper– –²kan** to multiply. *Kita harus ~*

hasil industri kita, We must multiply our industrial output. **peng–an** multiple. **per–an** multiplication. – **-ber–** multiplied. *Dlm tahun² jg achir ini penghasilan paberik itu tlh ~* , In recent years the factory's output has multiplied.

gandapita k.o. cake.

gandar 1 carrying pole. 2 lever, arm of weighing scales. 3 axle (of wheel). **meng–** to carry s.t. **–an** load.

gandén large mallet.

gandéng ber–(an) 1 side by side. *~ kedua pengantin baru itu memasuki hidup baru*, Side by side the newlyweds entered a new life. 2 arm in arm. *Meréka berdjalan ~* , They walked arm in arm. 3 coupled. *Kedua gerbong keréta api itu tlh ~* , The two railway coaches were coupled. 4 related to. *Persengkétaan ini ~ dgn pemberontakan itu*, This incident is related to the rebellion. *~ tangan* hand in hand. *Meréka berdjalan ~ tangan*, They walked hand in hand. **memper–kan, meng–kan** 1 to couple. *Saja ~ dua keréta itu*, I coupled the two coaches. 2 to link. *Kenasionalan ~ rakjat Indonésia*, Nationalism linked the peoples of Indonesia. **meng–** to lead s.o. by the hand. **meng–i** to accompany, go hand in hand with. **per–an** parallelism. *~ connection. ~ antara kedua kawat itu kurang kuat*, The connection between the two cables is not strong enough.

gandin see GANDÉN.

ganding see GANDÉNG.

gandjak ber– to move a bit. **meng–** to push, shove, shift. *tidak* **ter–** immovable.

gandjal prop, support. **meng–** to prop up. *Ia ~ médja jg gojang itu*, He propped up the wobbly table.

gandjar reward. **meng–** to reward. *Radja ~ abdinja jg setia*, The king rewarded his faithful servant. **ter–** 1 rewarded. *Segala usahanja achirnja ~ djuga*, His attempts were finally rewarded. 2 blessed. *Kita ~ keséhatan jg baik*, We have been blessed with good health. **–an** reward.

gandjat 1 taut. 2 spasm. 3 convulsive.

gandjel see GANDJAL.

gandjil 1 uneven, odd. *Bilangan itu –*, That is an uneven number. 2 queer, odd. *Hal itu sangat –*, That is very queer. **ke–an** 1 strangeness, peculiar nature. *~ kelakuannja itu menakutkan*, The strangeness of his behavior is frightening. 2 oddity.

meng–kan 1 to make uneven. *Ia ~ bilangan itu,* He made the number uneven. 2 strange. *Hal ini sungguh ~ ,* This is really strange. 3 conspicuous.

gandjur meng– to pull back, withdraw. *~ hari keberangkatan* to set the time of departure at a later date. *~ diri* to withdraw (for a private talk).

gandrung enamored, in love. *Ia – pd seorang gadis,* He was in love with a girl.

ganduh meng– to barter, exchange.

gandul ber–, meng– to hang. *Monjét ~ pd pohon,* The monkey hangs on a tree. **meng–kan** to hang s.t. *Ia ~ lampu itu pd paku,* He hung the lamp to a nail. **–an** 1 hanger. 2 swing.

gandum wheat.

gandung raftlike construction attached on port and starboard side of a prow, either used as an outrigger or to provide more cargo space. **–an** false. *orang ~* a false person.

gang 1 passageway. 2 alley(way). 3 narrow street. 4 hallway.

Gangga Ganges.

ganggang split, crack, cleft, space (between 2 things). *persahabatan jg tlh –* a friendship which is strained. **ber–** to warm o.s. by a fire. **meng–** to warm by a fire.

ganggu meng– 1 to tease, bother. *Djangan ~ adikmu,* Don't tease your brother. 2 to disturb. *Perampok itu ~ keamanan,* The robber disturbed the peace. 3 to bother. *Djangan ~ saja, saja lagi bekerdja,* Don't bother me, I am working. 4 to annoy. *Ia ~ gadis jg berdjalan sendirian itu,* He annoyed the girl who was walking alone. 5 to interrupt. *Tak ada sesuatupun djuga jg dpt ~ pekerdjaannja,* There was nothing which could interrupt his work. **meng–gugat** 1 to molest, bother, disturb (in an official way). 2 to violate o's rights. **(peng)–an** 1 teasing. *Ia menangis karena ~ kakaknja,* He cried because of his brother's teasings. 2 disturbance. *~ keamanan* disturbance of the peace. 3 obstacle. 4 attack, annoyance. *Gadis itu melapurkan pd polisi bhw dia mendapat ~ dari seorang orang jg mabuk,* The girl reported to the police that she had been attacked by a drunken man. 5 jamming (of broadcasts). *~ listerik* electrical defect. 6 shutdown (in industry). **peng–gugat** violator, molester. **ter–** 1 disturbed. *Pikirannja ~ karena kesakitan isterinja,* He was

upset over his wife's illness. *Keamanan ~ oléh kerusuhan itu,* Peace was disturbed by the unrest. 2 hampered. *Pekerdjaannja selalu ~ oléh kekurangan tenaga,* His work was always hampered by lack of personnel. 3 interrupted. *Pidatonja ~ oléh édjékan hadirin,* His speech was interrupted by jeers from the audience. *Ia ~ keséhatannja,* He fell ill.

gangsa 1 goose. 2 brass.

gangsal see GASAL.

gangsing see GASING.

gangsir k.o. cricket. **meng–** to undermine, dig a tunnel. *Pentjuri[2] ~ utk memasuki rumah,* The thieves dug a tunnel in the ground to get into the house.

ganjah meng– 1 to polish (with sandpaper, etc.). 2 to rub, massage vigorously. 3 to strike hard (with a fist).

ganjar tough (of uncooked tubers).

gantang k.o. measuring unit (3.1 kg.) for measuring rice, etc. **meng–** to measure by *gantang. Ia ~ beras,* She measured the rice.

gantél meng–i to hang s.t. on. *Kupingnja di–i anting[2],* Earrings hung from her ears.

ganteng handsome, dashing.

ganténg to harden, jell (candy, jelly).

ganti 1 substitute. *Ia memakai minjak sebagai – mentéga,* He used oil as a substitute for butter. 2 replacement. *Inilah – gelas jg petjah itu,* This is the replacement for the broken glass. **ber–** to change. *Kita harus ~ haluan,* We have to change our course. *Saja harus ~ keréta api,* I have to change trains. *~ kemédja* to change shirts. *~ bulu* 1 to change o's attitude. 2 to shed o's feathers. **ber– –[2]** 1 to take turns. *~ meréka mendjaga rumah itu,* They took turns guarding the house. 2 to keep on changing. *Pimpinan negara itu ~ sadja,* The country's leadership kept on changing. **meng–(kan)** 1 to change. *Ia ~ namanja,* He changed his name. 2 to replace. *Ia ~ gelas jg petjah itu,* He replaced the broken glass. *Ia ~ ajahnja,* He replaced his father. 3 to substitute. *Ia ~ mentéga dgn minjak,* She replaced butter by oil. 4 to compensate, pay for, make up. *Saja harus ~ kerugiannja,* I have to make up his losses. 5 to relieve, replace. *~ pengawal* to relieve the guard. *~ tanaman* to rotate crops. **peng–** 1 replacement. 2 substitute. 3 successor. *~ radja* the king's successor. 4 stand-by. 5 stand-in. **peng–an** 1 replacement (change). *~*

pemerintahan itu the change of government. 2 compensation. 3 substitution. ∼ *itu tidak memuaskan,* The substitution was not satisfactory. **per-an** change. *Negara itu mengalami* ∼ *jg tjepat,* The country underwent a rapid change. ∼ *alamat* change of address. ∼ *nadasuara* modulation. ∼ *pimpinan* change of management. – *kerugian perang* war reparations. – *rugi* compensation. – *skéna* scene change.

gantih meng- to spin (thread), twist (fibers into ropes).

gantjang quick, spry, alert.

gantju a pole provided with a hook (e.g., to harvest fruit on trees).

gantung ber- 1 to hang. *Lukisan itu* ∼ *pd dinding,* The painting hangs on the wall. 2 to depend. *Itu* ∼ *samasekali pd keadaan,* That depends entirely on the situation. *Itu* ∼ *padamu sendiri,* It is up to you. **ber-an** to hang. *Bél itu* ∼ *diatap,* The bell hung from the roof. **keter-an** *(thd)* dependence (upon). **memper-i** to depend on s.o. **meng-** to hang up. *Saja* ∼ *pakaian saja,* I hung up my clothes. *Polisi* ∼ *pendjahat,* The police hanged the criminal. **meng-i** to hang with. *Ia* ∼ *dinding dgn lukisan²,* He put paintings on the wall. **meng-kan** 1 to hang to s.t. *Ia* ∼ *topinja pd paku,* He hangs his hat on a nail. 2 to entrust. *Saja* ∼ *nasib saja padamu,* I entrust my fate to you. 3 to make dependent. *Ia* ∼ *keputusannja pd hasil rapat itu,* He made his decision dependent on the results of the meeting. 4 to suspend. *Hakim* ∼ *perkara itu,* The judge suspended the case. **peng-an** gallows. **per-an** support. **ter-** 1 suspended. *Lampu itu* ∼ *dari langit² kamar,* The lamp was suspended from the ceiling of the room. 2 to depend. *Nasib saja* ∼ *padamu,* My fate is in your hands. ∼ *dari* dependent upon s.o. *Suratkabar* ∼ *dari pembajaran langganan utk hidup,* A newspaper is dependent upon payment of subscriptions for its survival. **-an** 1 hanger, hook (to hang s.t. on). 2 gallows. – *diri* to hang o.s.

gaok raven. **meng-** to caw.

gapa(h) skillful, good at s.t.

gapai ber-an, meng-(-) to reach for (by stretching o's arms). *Ia* ∼ *hendak bergantung pd dahan,* He reached for a branch to hang on to.

gapak see GAPA(H).

gapil meng- to touch s.t., hold s.t. in o's hand without a particular purpose. – *mulut* quick to protest, to criticize. – *tangan* shoplifter, petty thief, s.o. who likes to get his hands on everything.

gapit tweezers, pincers. **meng-** to pick up, hold with tweezers.

gaplék dried cassava, tapioca.

gapu meng-i to reach, extend to.

gapura gate, archway.

gara 1 a rare natural phenomenon like an unseasonably heavy rain, a typhoon, earthquake, considered as an omen. 2 an undesirable event causing widespread repercussions; turmoil, confusion. 3 fun or amusement. 4 see GAHARA. **ber- -²** to have fun, romp and play. **meng-** to frighten off, drive away (of birds, etc.). **peng-** rope stretched across rice field; when rope is shaken the birds are frightened away. **-²** 1 all because of. ∼ *mobil baru* all because of a new car. 2 trouble. *Mau tjari* ∼ , *ja!* Looking for trouble, eh!

garam 1 salt. 2 chemical compounds of salt. **ber-** 1 salted. 2 experienced. *Orang tua itu sdh banjak* ∼ , That old man is very experienced. **meng-** 1 to crystallize into salt. *Air laut* ∼ , Sea water crystallizes and becomes salt. 2 to make salt. *Banjak orang Madura jg penghidupannja dari* ∼ , Many Madurese make their living from salt. **meng-i** to salt. *Ia* ∼ *ikan itu,* He salted the fish. **pe-an** 1 place to make salt. *Ditepi pantai laut banjak* ∼ , On the seashore are many places for making salt. 2 salt manufacturing. – *bata(an)* brick salt. – *dapur* kitchen salt. – *hantjur* table salt. – *inggeris* Epsom salts. – *mesiu* saltpeter, niter. – *dilaut asam digunung bertemu dibelanga* married couple with quite different origins. *membuang* – *kelaut* to carry coals to Newcastle.

garan handle. – *pisau* knife handle.

garang 1 fierce, cruel. *Ia seorang hulubalang jg –,* He was a fierce warrior. 2 vivid (of color). **ke-an** fierceness. **meng-** 1 to rage, storm. 2 to roast. *Saja* ∼ *daging,* I roasted a piece of meat.

garansi guarantee, warrant.

garap meng- to work on, at. *Ia* ∼ *pekerdjaannja,* He worked at his task. ∼ *tanah* to till the land. **-an** task, assignment. *Selesaikanlah* ∼ , Finish the task.

garas shin. **meng-** to eat, gobble up.

garasi garage.

gardu 1 guardhouse. 2 bus shelter.

garebeg religious festival. – *Besar* religious festival. – *Maulud* festival commemorating Mohammed's birth. – *Puasa* festival at the end of the Moslem fasting month.

gari 1 handcuffs. 2 sealing wax. **ter-** 1 handcuffed. 2 sealed with wax.

garib peculiar, strange.

garis line. **ber-** lined. *Kertas itu ~,* That paper is lined. **meng-(i)** 1 to draw lines on. *Ia ~ kertas itu,* He drew lines on the paper. 2 to underscore. *Ia ~ kata² jg sukar,* He underscored the difficult words. **peng-, -an** ruler. **peng-an** 1 line drawing. 2 scratching. – *achir* finish line. – *alas* base line. – *bagi* bisecting line. – *balik* tropic. – *balik sartan,* – *balik Selatan* Tropic of Capricorn. – *balik Utara* Tropic of Cancer. – *belakang* 1 rear guard of an army. 2 home front. – *berat* median (in geometry). – *besar* broad outline. *Inilah – besar rentjana kita,* These are the broad outlines of our plan. – *budjur* meridian (in geography). – *chattulistiwa* equator. – *dasar* base line. – *démarkasi* demarcation line. – *depan* front line. – *haluan* line of action. *Inilah – haluan jg harus diikuti,* These are the lines of action which should be followed. – *lintang* latitude (in geography). – *perhatian* underlining, italics. – *pilih,* – *sekat* slant line. – *silang* intersecting line. – *singgung* tangent (in geometry). – *sudut menjudut* diagonal. – *tegak* perpendicular. – *tengah* diameter. – *tinggi* 1 perpendicular (in geometry). 2 contour line. – *titik* dotted line.

garit scratch. **meng-** to scratch.

garong robber. **meng-** to rob, commit robbery. **peng-an** 1 robbery. 2 banditry.

garpu fork. **be-** to use a fork. **meng-** to pick up with a fork. – *tala* tuning fork.

garu harrow. **meng-** to harrow.

garuda 1 eagle. 2 mythical bird carrier of the god Vishnu. 3 the eagle in the official seal of the Republic of Indonesia.

garuk ber-(-) to scratch. *Monjét itu ~,* The monkey is scratching. **meng-** 1 to scratch. *Ia ~ kepalanja,* He scratched his head. 2 to scrape. *Ia ~ pantji itu,* He scraped the pan. 3 to embezzle. **meng-kan** to let scrape. *Ia ~ besi itu pd tanah,* He let the piece of iron scrape over the earth. **peng-an** 1 scraping. 2 scratching. **peng-** scraper. **-an** scratching.

garung meng- to growl.

garut see GARUK.

gas gas. **meng-** to evaporate. *Alkohol itu mudah ~,* Alcohol evaporates easily. – *air mata* tear gas. – *alam* natural gas. – *karbit* acetylene. – *ratjun* poisonous gas.

gasak ber- 1 to fight. *Kedua anak itu ~,* The 2 boys fought. 2 to rub vigorously. **meng-** 1 to strike. *Ia ~ anak itu,* He struck the boy. 2 to deal a blow. *Ber-kali² ia ~ tentara musuh,* Several times he dealt blows to the enemy army. **-an** strike, blow, a drubbing.

gasal uneven, odd. *Lima adalah bilangan –,* Five is an uneven number.

gasang lascivious.

gasing a top (toy).

gasung sandbar.

gatal to itch. *Kaki saja –,* My leg itches. – *tangan saja hendak memukul dia,* My hand itches to hit him. **ke-an** 1 itching. 2 irritation. **meng-kan** 1 to make itch. *Awas, daun itu ~,* Watch out, those leaves will make you itch. 2 irritating. *Sikapnja sungguh ~,* His attitude was really irritating. – *mulut* talkative. – *réla* wanton, lascivious. **-²** to itch all over.

gatra syntactical unit.

gaul ber- to associate. *Ia hanja ~ dgn orang² terkemuka sadja,* He only associates with prominent persons. **meng-i** to have intercourse. *Puasa membatasi kemerdékaan buat ~ isteri kita,* Fasting restricts the freedom of conjugal intercourse. **per-an** 1 association, intercourse. 2 society. *~ hidup* society.

gaun gown, dress. – *rumah* 1 housecoat. 2 dressing gown. – *tidur* nightgown.

gaung an echo. **ber-** to echo.

gawai function. **pe-** 1 employee. 2 official.

gawang 1 gate. 2 goal (in soccer). **peng-** goal-keeper.

gawat 1 critical, serious. 2 dangerous, risky. **meng-** to be critical.

gb [*gambar*] illustration.

Gbr [*Gambir*] see GAMBIR.

gebes to move s.t.

gébés 1 to shake o's head. 2 to be unwilling. 3 to move s.t.

geblek stupid. **ke-an** stupidity.

geblok bolt of cloth.

gebos meng- 1 to snarl at. 2 to reprimand. **-an** a reprimand.

gebu meng- to flare up.

gebuk 1 bundle. 2 bolt. *se- tjita* a bolt of cloth. **meng-** to beat with a stick. *Ia ~ andjing itu,* He beat the dog with a stick.

gebung 1 bundle. *se- uang ratusan* a bundle of 100 rupiah notes. 2 bolt (of cloth).

gedang large, big.

gedé big. ke-an too big. *Peti itu* ~ , That box is too big.

gedebak to throb, beat. meng-kan to stamp with the foot. *Ia ~ kakinja karena marah*, He stamped his foot in anger.

gedebok 1 trunk of a banana tree. 2 sound of heavy footsteps.

gedebuk see GEDEBAK.

gedék woven bamboo.

gédéng sheaf.

gedjala 1 symptom. *Ia memperlihat-kan —² penjinaran radio-aktip*, He showed symptoms of radiation sickness. 2 indication.

gedjolak ber- to flare up.

gedjos sizzling sound when water is poured over hot embers, etc.

gedjudju meng- to pile up (of clouds).

gedong see GEDUNG.

gedontjak ber- to beat (of the heart).

gedor meng- 1 to pound on. *Bapak ~ pintu*, Father pounded on the door. 2 to plunder. *Meréka ~ rumah itu*, They plundered that house. peng- 1 plunderer. 2 bandit. peng-an 1 plunder. 2 banditry. *(barang)* -an goods obtained through plunder.

gedung building (usually of brick or concrete). – *artja* museum. – *atjara* law court. – *bitjara* meeting hall. – *flat* apartment building. – *gadjah* museum on Medan Merdeka in Jakarta. – *instansi* 1 public building. 2 building owned by a firm. – *komidi* theater. – *pemerintah* public building. – *Putih* White House. – *saté* post office building in Bandung.

gegabah rash, insolent, reckless. *tingkah lakumu jg – itu* your rash attitude. ber- to act insolently.

gegap meng-kan earsplitting. *Bunji meriam itu ~* , The sound of the guns is earsplitting. ter- -² haltingly. *Ia berbitjara ~* , He spoke haltingly. – *gempita* 1 noisy. 2 tumult. *Seluruh negara – gempita*, The whole country was in tumult.

gegar shaking. meng- 1 to shake. 2 to rumble (of artillery, thunder). -an concussion. ~ *otak* concussion of the brain.

gegares to stuff, gorge, feed.

gegas ber- -² to hurry. *Meréka ~ kesekolah*, They hurried to school. ter- -² hurriedly. *Dgn ~ meréka berpakaian*, Hurriedly they dressed up.

gegat silverfish.

gegau ter- startled, shocked with fright.

gégép pliers.

gégér 1 commotion, tumult. *Seluruh dunia –*, The whole world is in a

tumult. 2 to be in a tumult. 3 noisy. *Anak² – dlm kelasnja*, The children were noisy in the classroom. ke-an commotion, tumult. meng-kan 1 to cause a stir. *Kedjadian itu ~ seluruh negara*, The incident caused a stir in the whole nation. 2 turbulent. *tahun² ~* turbulent years. – *otak* brain concussion.

gegetun 1 too bad, a pity. 2 surprised, touched.

geladah see GELÉDAH.

geladak 1 ship deck. 2 mongrel dog. 3 criminal.

geladir slime.

gelagah a reed the height of sugar cane.

gelagapan stuttering, speaking incoherently from nervousness.

gelagat 1 indication. *Méga adalah – hudjan*, Clouds indicate rain. 2 attitude. *Dari —nja saja lihat bhw dia lagi susah*, From his attitude I noticed that he was sad. 3 habits. *Meréka mempeladjari – musuh sebelum menjerang*, They studied the habits of the enemy before attacking.

gelajut ber- to hang down (of jowls).

gelak laughter. meng-kan to laugh at, make fun of. *Ia ~ kesengsaraan saja*, He laughed at my distress. -² heartily. *Ia tertawa ~* , He laughed heartily. – *senjum* smile. – *sétan* booming laughter. – *sumbing* sickly laugh. – *tertawa* hearty laughter.

gelambir 1 wattle (of a fowl). 2 wattlelike skin fold of cows; also skin fold under the chin of old people.

gelandang 1 loafing. 2 back (soccer). ber-an to loaf around. -an 1 loafing about. 2 loafer, loiterer. – *kanan* right back (soccer). – *kiri* left back. – *tengah* center back.

gelang bracelet. per-an *kaki* ankle. per-an *tangan* wrist. – *kaki* ankle bracelet. – *kuntji* key ring. – *panggul* pelvic region. – *raja* spindle worm. – *rantai* link. -² ring-shaped objects. – *silinder* piston ring. – *tanah* earthworm. – *tangan* bracelet.

gelanggang arena, forum. ber- to form a ring. – *bergumul* wrestling ring. – *buku* book fair. – *dagang* trade fair. – *matahari* halo around the sun. – *perang*, – *perdjuangan* battlefield. – *susu* pigmented area of the skin around the nipple. – *tindju* boxing ring.

gelangsar to slip up on an object.

gelantang meng- to bleach (of clothes).

gelap 1 dark. 2 not clear. *Hal itu masih – bagi saja*, That matter is still not clear to me. (I still do not understand the matter.) 3 secret, subversive, illegal. *perkumpulan* – secret organization. **ber-** –² to be, sit, remain, in the dark. *Pasang lampu; djangan* ∼ , Switch on the light; don't sit in the dark. **ke–an** 1 darkness, obscurity. 2 angry. 3 obscured. 4 to be caught in darkness. **ke-** –²**an** fairly dark. *kamar jg* ∼ a rather dark room. **meng-** 1 to become dark. 2 to disappear, vanish. 3 to be in a rage, run amuck. **meng–kan** 1 to cause to be, make dark. 2 to embezzle, steal. **peng–an** 1 blackout (as a precaution against enemy air raids at night). 2 embezzlement, larceny. 3 eclipse. – *buta*, – *gulita*, – *katup* pitch-dark. – *mata*, – *pikiran* to go berserk, run amuck.

gelapai meng- to fight feebly (of cocks).

gelar 1 title. 2 academic title. *Saja ingin mentjapai* – *doktor*, I want to get a doctor's degree. 3 alias. *Hassan* – *Si Kutjing* Hassan alias "The Cat." **ber-** to have a title. *Ia* ∼ *doktor*, He has the title of doctor. **meng–i** 1 to name. *Ia* ∼ *anaknja Budiman*, He named his child Budiman. 2 to give a nickname. *Anak²* ∼ *saja Si Matjan*, The children nicknamed me "The Tiger." 3 to have the title of. *Menurut adat Atjéh ulama di–i Teungku*, According to Achehnese custom the religious scholar is called Teungku. **meng–kan** 1 to bestow a title, degree. 2 to unfold, stage. **per–an** 1 unfolding, presentation, staging. 2 bestowal of degree or title. **ter–** spread out. – *pusaka* hereditary title. **–an** mat. –² *tikar* to roll out a carpet.

gelas 1 glass. 2 drinking glass.

gelatak see GELÉTAK.

gelatik paddybird.

gelatuk meng- to chatter. *Giginja* ∼ *karena kedinginan*, His teeth chattered from the cold.

gelébar ber–, ter- to flap. *Lajar* ∼ *ditiup angin*, The sail was flapping in the wind.

gelébér to hang loosely.

gelédah meng–(i) to search, raid. *Polisi* ∼ *rumah itu mentjari sendjata*, The police searched the house for weapons. *Polisi* ∼ *rumah djudi jg gelap*, The police raided an illicit gambling house. **peng–an** search.

geLédék thunder. **meng-** to thunder, rumble. *Guruh* ∼ *dikedjauhan*, The thunder rumbled in the distance. *Suaranja* ∼ *mengutjapkan pidatonja*, His voice thundered when he delivered his speech.

geleding meng- to warp.

gelegak meng- 1 to seethe. *Air laut* ∼ , The sea seethed. 2 to fizz. **mengkan** to boil, make boil.

gelegar 1 beam supporting floor boards. 2 rumbling (gunfire, thunder).

gelegata 1 athlete's foot. 2 hives.

gélék meng- 1 to roll (over). *Kuda* ∼ *dirumput*, The horse rolled over and over in the grass. 2 to run over. *Mobil grobak* ∼ *andjing*, The truck ran over a dog. 3 to roll s.t. *Ia* ∼ *lilin diantara telapak tangannja*, He rolled a piece of wax between the palms of his hands. 4 to grind, crush (e.g., of whole pepper, with a pestle in a mortar). **ter-** run down, hit (by a car, train, etc.).

gelekak meng- to peel (of skin, scabs, dry paint).

gelembung 1 bubble. 2 swollen. *Perutnja* –, His stomach is swollen. **ber-**, **meng-** to be inflated. *Bola itu* ∼ , The ball is inflated. **meng–kan** to inflate. *Ia* ∼ –*annja*, He inflated his balloon. **–an** balloon. –²**an** bubbles. ∼ *air* water bubbles. ∼ *paru* alveolus (of the lung). ∼ *sabun* soap bubbles. ∼ *udara* air bubbles.

gelembur meng- to be wrinkled. *Kulitnja* ∼ , His skin is wrinkled.

geléndong bobbin, spool.

géléng meng–(kan) *kepala* to shake o's head. *Ia hanja* ∼ *kepala sebagai djawaban*, He merely shook his head in response. *Guru* ∼ *kepalanja*, The teacher shook his head. **meng-** –²**(kan)** to shake o's head repeatedly.

gelenjar meng- to tingle. *Kaki saja* ∼ , My foot tingles. (My foot is asleep. My foot is all pins and needles.)

gelentang ber- to wallow. *Babi* ∼ *dilumpur*, The pig wallowed in the mud.

gelentar meng- to tremble. *Ia* ∼ *ketakutan*, He trembled with fear.

gelepar meng- 1 to flounder. *Ikan itu* ∼ *didalam djala*, The fish floundered in the net. 2 to flutter. *Burung itu* ∼ *ditanah*, The bird fluttered on the ground. **meng–kan** to flap. *Burung itu* ∼ *sajapnja*, The bird flapped its wings.

gelépék meng- to hang down limply (like a flag when there is no wind).

gélér see GILIR.

gelésér meng- 1 to flutter. *Burung itu* ∼ *sadja*, The bird fluttered. 2 to start turning (of wheels). *Roda itu* ∼ , The wheel started to turn.

gelétak meng- to sprawl. *Ia* ∼ *dilantai*, He sprawled on the floor.

ter– sprawled. *Korban ledakan itu* ∼ *ditanah,* The victims of the explosion lay sprawled on the ground.

geletar see GELENTAR.

geletik meng– 1 to flounder. 2 to flutter. 3 to tick. *Djam itu* ∼ , The clock ticked. 4 to throb. *Hatinja* ∼ , His heart throbbed.

geleting meng– to tinkle. *És dlm gelas itu* ∼ , The ice in the glass tinkled.

geletis meng– to squirm.

geletuk see GEMELETUK.

geli 1 amused. *Saja – melihat orang² itu,* I was amused watching those people. 2 repelled. *Saja – melihat orang² jang djidjik itu,* I was repelled at seeing those hideous people. 3 ticklish. *Djangan pegang tangan saja; saja –,* Do not touch my hand; I am ticklish. **ke–an** 1 tickled. 2 amused. *Anak* ∼ *melihat kera berdansa,* The children were amused when they saw the monkey dance. **meng–** to spur, incite, urge, encourage. **meng–kan** 1 amusing, funny, *Tjeritanja sungguh* ∼ , His story was quite amusing. 2 loathsome. *Kekotoran désa itu sungguh* ∼ , The dirt of that village is really loathsome. 3 to tickle s.o. *Lalat jg hinggap dihidung saja* ∼ *saja,* The fly which perched on my nose tickled me. **peng–** jester. ∼ *hati* 1 joke. 2 humorous. *Tjerita itu adalah tjerita* ∼ *hati,* That story is a humorous story. –² kidney. – *geman* 1 irritating, gets on o's nerves. 2 horrifying, horrid, horrible.

geliang see GELIUT.

geliat meng– to stretch o.s. *Hassan* ∼ *dan menguap,* Hassan stretched himself and yawned. **ter–** sprained. *Kaki saja* ∼ , My ankle is sprained. – *geliut* to writhe in pain.

geligis meng– 1 to tremble. *Ia* ∼ *ketakutan,* He trembled with fear. 2 to shake with cold. 3 to chatter from the cold.

gelimang ber– to be soiled, stained, covered with dirt. *Pakaiannja* ∼ *lumpur,* His clothes were covered with mud. **meng–i** to cover, smear.

gelimbir *pipi* **–(an)** sagging jowls of elderly people.

gelimpang ber–(an) to sprawl. *Korban pengeboman itu* ∼ *di-mana²,* The victims of the bombardment lay sprawled everywhere. **ter–** sprawled. *Ia djatuh* ∼ , He fell sprawling.

gelinding(an) a wheel. **ber–, meng–** to roll, turn.

gelingsir ber–, meng– to slide. *Batu itu* ∼ *dari léréng gunung,* The rock slid from the mountain slope. **meng–**

kan to let slide, make slide. *Ia* ∼ *batu itu dari léréng gunung,* He let the rock slide from the mountain slope.

gelintang meng– to sprawl. *Ia djatuh* ∼ *di-batu²,* He fell sprawling on the rocks. **ter–** to lie sprawling.

gelintir 1 pellet. 2 used with small pelletlike objects. *Saja mempunjai tiga – intan,* I have 3 diamonds. **meng–** to roll into pellets. *Ibu* ∼ *adonan itu,* Mother rolled the dough into small pellets. **se–** *orang* a small body of men.

gelintjir meng–kan to derail. *Pemberontak²* ∼ *keréta api,* The rebels derailed the train. **ter–** to slip. *Ia* ∼ *didjalan jg litjin itu,* He slipped on the slippery road. ∼ *lidah* to make a slip of the tongue. *Ia* ∼ *lidahnja dan membuka rahasianja itu,* He made a slip of the tongue and disclosed his secret.

gelintjuh ter– to stumble.

gelis see GEULIS.

gelisah 1 nervous. *Djangan –; semuanja akan berachir baik,* Don't be so nervous; everything will turn out all right. 2 restless. *Semalam tidurnja – sadja,* He had a restless sleep last night. 3 worried. *Ia – ketika anaknja tidak lekas datang kembali,* He was worried when his son did not return right away. **ber–** to worry. *Ia duduk sadja dan* ∼ , He just sat and worried. **ke–an** 1 nervousness. 2 restlessness. 3 worry. **meng–kan** 1 to worry about. *Ia* ∼ *anaknja jg pergi berperang itu,* He worried about his son who went to war. 2 to perturb, upset. *Surat itu sangat* ∼ *ibu saja,* The letter upset my mother very much.

gelitik meng– 1 to tickle. 2 to prod, encourage, incite. 3 to beat faster (of the heart, from fear or in anticipation of s.t. pleasant). *Hatiku* ∼ *waktu mendengar kabar baik itu,* My heart leaped for joy upon hearing the good news.

geliut ber– to writhe. *Ia* ∼ *kesakitan,* He writhed in pain.

gelodar meng– to squirm.

gelodjak ber– to slap (of waves against side of boat).

gelodjoh 1 gluttonous. 2 greedy. – *laki* said of a woman eager to be married.

gelogok meng– 1 to gulp down. *Ia* ∼ *air kopinja,* He drank his coffee in big swallows. 2 to spill large amounts of liquid. 3 to boil, seethe.

gelombang 1 wave. – *samudera* ocean wave. – *radio* radio wave. *Musuh* *menjerang dlm beberapa –*, The enemy attacked in several waves. 2 phase. **ber–** 1 to wave, surge. *Pertempuran ~ kian kemari*, The battle surged back and forth. 2 to fluctuate. *Harga²* ~ *naik turun*, The prices fluctuated up and down. **ber–an** to surge. **meng–** to fluctuate. **meng–kan** to release, unleash. ~ *semua tenaga* to unleash all o's energy. – *bunga lepang* foam-crested waves. – *getaran* shock wave. – *mangkuk* whirlpool, eddy. – *péndék* short wave.

gelompar meng– to jump up quickly.

gelongsong seed husk, capsule. – *djagung* cornhusk.

gelongsor to slide down, off.

gelora 1 seething, tempestuous, turbulent. *laut* – the seething sea. 2 enthusiastic. 3 boisterous, riotous. 4 violent, impassioned. **ber–** 1 to rage, seethe. *Lautnja* ~ , The sea was raging. 2 impassioned. *pidato jg* ~ an impassioned speech. **meng–** to rage, seethe. *semangat jg* ~ raging enthusiasm. **meng–kan** to whip up, stir up, incite. ~ *semangat* to arouse o's spirit to a high pitch. – *hati* impulse, passion.

gelosok meng– to rub, scrub vigorously, repeatedly.

gelotak meng– to take the hard shell off a fruit, e.g., a coconut.

gelotjak see GELODJAK.

geluduk thunder. **ber–** to thunder.

gelugut meng– 1 to shake hard from cold. 2 to chatter from cold.

gelumang ber– to be smeared. *Ia* ~ *darah*, He was smeared with blood.

gelumbang see GELOMBANG.

gelung hair knot, bun. **ber–** to knot the hair. **meng–** 1 to knot the hair. 2 to coil (a rope, etc.). **ter–** knotted, in a knot. **–an** 1 hair knot. 2 a coil (of rope, etc.).

geluntjur see GELINTJIR.

gelup to fall out (of teeth).

gelut ber– 1 to wrestle. 2 to romp, play in a rough-and-tumble fashion. **meng–** to seize, embrace in o's arms. **per–an** wrestling, wrestling match.

gema echo, reverberation. **ber–** to reverberate, echo. *Suara guruh itu* ~ *didalam lembah*, The sound of thunder reverberated in the valley. *Panggilan pemimpin negara* ~ *keseluruh pendjuru negara*, The call of the nation's leader reverberated in every corner of the country. **meng–(kan)** to echo, reflect, resound. *Ia* ~ *djeritan hati rakjatnja keseluruh dunia*, He echoed the intense suffering of his people to the whole world.

gemak meng– to feel s.t. all over.

gemal 1 bunch (of twigs, paddy), sheaf. 2 a handful. **meng–** to hold in o's hands.

gemala a stone possessing magical powers.

gemalai see GEMULAI.

geman see GELI.

gemang 1 stocky, big. 2 fearful, afraid. 3 round. **peng–** coward.

gemap ter– shocked, astonished, surprised.

gemar to be fond of. *Ia* – *akan gambar hidup*, He is fond of movies. **ber–** to enjoy o.s. *Meréka pergi dan* ~ *dipantai*, They went and enjoyed themselves at the beach. **ke–an** 1 hobby. 2 entertainment. **meng–i** to be fond of. *Ia* ~ *buah²an*, He is fond of fruit. **meng–kan** to please. *Ia selalu mentjoba* ~ *orang tuanja*, He always tries to please his parents. **peng–** 1 lover, devotee, fan. *Ia* ~ *makanan baik*, He is a lover of good food. 2 hobbyist. *Ia seorang* ~ *potrét*, He is a photography hobbyist. 3 enthusiast. ~ *perangko* philatelist. – *napal* geophagy.

gemas to dislike, malign, be indignant. *Ia* – *akan tindakan saudaranja*, He disliked his brother's actions. **meng–i** to cover, smear s.t. ~ *témbok dgn lumpur* to smear mud on a wall. **ke–an** *hati* anger. **meng–kan** to make angry. *Utjapannja* ~ *ajahnja*, His statement made his father angry.

gembala shepherd, herdsman. *Tuhan adalah* ~ *saja*, The Lord is my shepherd. **meng–(kan)** to herd, tend, look after. *Ia* ~ *sapinja*, He tends his cows. *Tuhan* ~ *umatnja*, God shepherds His flock. **peng–** shepherd. **peng–an** shepherding. – *ajam* poultryman. – *domba* shepherd. – *gadjah* elephant keeper, mahout. – *harimau* tiger tamer. – *kambing* shepherd. – *kerbau* buffalo keeper. – *kuda* horseherd. – *pintu* gatekeeper. – *radjawali* falconer. – *sapi* cowherd. *gadjah seékor* – *dua* 2 lovers of one girl.

gembar 1 see KEMBAR. 2 noise. **ber–gembor** 1 to shout, cry out, be noisy. 2 to brag. **meng–gemborkan** 1 to shout at the top of o's lungs. 2 to propagandize. *Ia hanja* ~ *ttg hal démokrasi*, He only pays lip service to democracy. – *-gembor* shouting, boastful utterances.

gembéréng see GEMBRÉNG.

gembira 1 glad. *Ia* – *melihat saja*, He was glad to see me. 2 cheerful. *Anak itu tak pernah susah; selalu* – *sadja dia*, That child is never sad; he's always cheerful. 3 enthusiastic. **ber–** to rejoice. *Meréka* ~ *ketika* *perang berachir,* They rejoiced when the war ended. **ber–ria** to be happy and gay. **ke–an** joy. *Ia ber–njanji² karena* ∼ , She sang with joy. **meng–i** to cheer s.o. up. **meng–kan** 1 to cheer up, encourage. *Ia mentjoba* ∼ *saja,* He tried to cheer me up. 2 to make glad. *Uang itu* ∼ *ibunja jg miskin itu,* The money made his poor mother happy. 3 encouraging. *kabar jg* ∼ encouraging news. 4 gratifying.

gemblang broad and clear.

gembleng ber– united, welded into one. **peng–an** union.

gembléng meng– 1 to forge. 2 to harden (the spirit). 3 to train. 4 to lead. *Présidén itu* ∼ *rakjat,* The president leads the people by welding them together. **–an** 1 highly trained, disciplined. 2 hardened. 3 indoctrination. ∼ *semangat* spiritual, ideological indoctrination.

gembok padlock.

gémbol(an) pocket. **meng–** 1 to carry in the pocket. *Ia* ∼ *sebuah mangga,* He carried a mango in his pocket. 2 to carry in a sling (of cloth).

gémbong(an) 1 champion. *Ia mendjadi – rakjat jg terlindas itu,* He became the champion of the oppressed. 2 big shot, leader, prominent member (of social or political groups). *Para –² politik bersiap menghadapi pemilihan,* The political big shots prepared themselves for the elections.

gembor see 1 GEMBAR. 2 GEMBUR.

gembos deflated. *Ban itu –,* The tire is deflated. **meng–kan** to deflate. *Ia* ∼ *ban sepédanja,* He deflated the tires of his bicycle.

gembréng 1 metal bowl. 2 Chinese gong.

gembung 1 swollen. *Perutnja – penuh air,* His stomach was swollen with water. 2 stuffed, filled. **meng–** to fill up, swell up. *Balon itu* ∼ , The balloon filled up. **meng–kan** 1 to swell up. *Ia* ∼ *dadanja,* He swelled his chest. 2 to puff. *Ia* ∼ *pipinja,* He puffed up his cheeks. **–an** swelling.

gembur 1 loose (of soil). *Tanah itu –,* The soil is loose. 2 roar (of a gun). **meng–** 1 to become loose. *Tanah* ∼ , The soil becomes loose. 2 to roar. *Meriam* ∼ , The gun roars. **meng–kan** to loosen. *Ia* ∼ *tanah,* He loosened the soil.

gemelai see GEMULAI. **meng–kan** to cause to sway.

gemelentam booming of cannon fire.

gemeletak see GEMELETUK.

gemeletap sound of tapping (of fingers on a table, on a glass pane).

gemeletuk 1 to shiver. *Ia – kedingi-*

nan, He shivered with cold. *Ia – ketakutan,* He shivered with fear. 2 to chatter. *Giginja – kedinginan,* His teeth chattered with cold.

gemelugut 1 shaking hard, shivering from cold. 2 to shudder.

gementar see GEMETAR.

gemerentjang clang. **ber–** to clang. *Pedang² itu* ∼ , The swords clanged.

gemerentjik the sound of raindrops against a windowpane.

gemerentjing 1 clanging of chains. 2 jingling of money.

gemeretuk see GEMELETUK.

gemeretup see GEMELETUK.

gemerisik 1 rustle. *– daun²* rustling of the leaves. 2 a sound produced when paper is crumpled. **ber–** to rustle. *Daun² itu* ∼ *ditiup angin,* The leaves rustled in the wind.

gemerlap shining, gleaming.

gemersik see GEMERISIK.

gemertak see GEMELETAK.

gemertjak see GEMERTJIK.

gemertjik splatter, splashing. **ber–** to splatter, to splash. *Air itu* ∼ *kemana²,* The water splattered all around.

gemertjing see GEMERENTJING.

gemertuk see GEMELETIK.

gemerutuk see GEMERTUK.

gemetar to tremble. *Ia – ketakutan,* He trembled with fear. **–an** a tremor, trembling.

gemilang 1 brilliant. *bintang² jg –* the brilliant stars. *kemenangan jg –* brilliant victory. *hasil –* brilliant results. 2 see GILANG.

gemilap 1 see GEMERLAP. 2 see GILAP.

gempa ber– to quake, shake. *Tanah itu* ∼ , The earth shook. **meng–kan** to shake. *Kedjadian itu* ∼ *seluruh dunia,* The incident shook the whole world. *– bumi* earthquake. *– kiamat* the final earthquake.

gempal 1 see GUMPAL. 2 sturdy, stout. 3 lithe.

gempar to be in an uproar, commotion. *Meréka – mendengar kabar jg tak disangka itu,* They were in an uproar when they heard the unexpected news. **ke–an** 1 uproar, commotion. 2 sensation. **meng–kan** 1 to cause a stir, a commotion. 2 sensational. *kabar jg* ∼ sensational news.

gempita see GEGAP.

gempul² panting.

gempur meng– 1 to pound on, batter. *Dia* ∼ *pintu,* He pounded on the door. *Tentara* ∼ *musuh,* The army pounded the enemy. 2 to attack. *Kita* ∼ *bénténg itu,* We attacked that fortress. *Partai opposisi* ∼ *tindakan pemerintah,* The opposition party attacked the measures taken by the government. 3 to tear to pieces. *Djaksa ~ alasan terdakwa,* The prosecutor tore the defendant's argument to bits. **peng-** attacker. **peng-an** attack.

gemuk 1 stout. *Orang itu -,* That person is stout. 2 fat. *Babi itu -,* The pig is fat. *Minjak itu dibuat dari -² tanaman,* The oil is made from vegetable fats. 3 grease. *Berilah - pd éngsél pintu itu,* Put some grease on that door hinge. 4 fertile. *Tanah itu -,* The land is fertile. 5 fertilizer. *Ia memberi - pd tanamannja,* He gave his plants some fertilizer. **ke-an** too fat, overweight. **meng-** to grease. *Ia ~ roda itu,* He greased the wheel. **meng-kan** 1 to fatten up. *Ia ~ diri,* He's trying to gain weight. 2 fattening.

gemulai 1 supple. *Gerak-geriknja -,* Her movements were supple. 2 swaying (leaves in the wind, etc.).

gemuruh thundering. *Tepuk tangan para penonton sangat -,* The applause of the audience was thundering. **ber-, meng-** to thunder. *Meriam² ~ ,* The cannons thundered. *Panggilan présidén ~ diseluruh negara,* The president's appeal thundered over the whole country.

genah 1 to be proper. *Kelakuannja tidak -,* His behavior was not proper. 2 straightened out. *Perkara itu sekarang sdh -,* That case is all straightened out now. **meng-kan** to straighten out. *Ia ~ kesalahan itu,* He straightened out the mistake. *Ia ~ pakaiannja,* She straightened out her dress. **se-nja** proper. *Sdh ~ orang muda menghormati orang tua,* It's only proper for young people to respect their elders.

genang ber-, meng- to be stagnant (of water). *Air danau itu ~ ,* The water of the lake is stagnant. *Air matanja ~ ,* Tears stood in her eyes. **meng-i** to flood, inundate. *Ia ~ sawahnja,* He flooded his rice fields. **peng-an** pond for holding water. **ter-** stagnant. **-an** 1 pool. 2 puddle.

genap 1 complete. *Seluruh kelas sdh -,* The whole class is complete. *Uangnja - sepuluh rupiah,* He has exactly 10 rupiahs. *Umurnja mentjapai - enampuluh tahun,* He reached the age of 60. *Pikirannja -,* He is quite sane. 2 even (of numbers). **meng-i** to fulfill. *Ia ~ djandjinja,* He fulfilled his promise. **meng-kan** 1 to complete. *Ia ~ pekerdjaannja,* He completed his work. 2 to make s.t. come out even. *Ia ~ bilangan itu,* He made the number even. **peng-** complement. *Undang² ini membutuhkan ~ , S.t.* must be added to this statute. **se-** 1 every. *~ warganegara* every citizen. 2 all. *~ usahanja gagal,* All his attempts failed. 3 whole. *~ tubuhnja gemetar,* His whole body trembled. *- bulannja* end of the period of pregnancy.

gendak 1 mistress. 2 paramour. **ber-** 1 to have a mistress. 2 to have a lover. **meng-i** to commit adultery.

gendala obstacle. **meng-kan** to obstruct, hamper.

gendang a drum. **ber-** to play the drum. *~ paha* to gloat over s.t., find pleasure in another's misfortune. **-an** membrane. *- hati* inspiration. *- pendengar* eardrum. *- raja* 1 big drum. 2 a mosque drum.

gendang ber-an *tangan* to hold hands.

gendeng dumb, stupid.

géndéng oblique, inclined, slanting. **meng-kan** to slant, incline.

genderang a drum.

gendi see KENDI.

gending a special melody for the gamelan.

gendir a musical percussion instrument used in the gamelan.

géndjang diamond-shaped, a parallelogram. *- géndjot* diamond-checkered.

gendjur stiff (of hair).

géndong meng- to carry on the back. *Ia ~ kerandjang,* She carried a basket on her back. *~ anak* to carry a child in o's arms (or in a sarong used as a sling). **-an** burden carried on the back.

gendut 1 corpulent. 2 potbellied. 3 pregnant. *Ia sdh - lagi,* She is pregnant again. **meng-kan** *perut* to line o's stomach. *Bir ~ perut,* Beer causes a pot belly.

généralisasi generalization.

génerasi generation.

genggam handful. *beras beberapa - several* handfuls of rice. **meng-** to hold in o's grasp. *Ia ~ uang itu erat²,* He held the money tightly in his grasp. *Ia ~ kekuasaan jg tertinggi dlm negara,* He held the highest power of the state in his grasp. **se-** a handful. *nasi ~* a handful of rice. *~ serdadu* a handful of soldiers. **ter-** held, grasped. **-an** 1 grasp. *Dlm ~nja diketemukan sebuah surat,* In his grasp was found a letter. 2 clutches, grasp. *Ia djatuh dlm ~ seorang jg memindjamkan uang,* He fell into the clutches of a moneylender. *- tangan* stingy, greedy.

genggang 1 ajar, slightly open. 2 fissure, split. **ter-** ajar.

génggang gingham.

génggong jew's-harp.

géngsi 1 descent. *Ia masih – radja²*, He is of royal descent. 2 a relative. 3 prestige. ber– to have prestige. *si – putih* the white man (race).

geni see DJENI.

genit coquettish. ke–an coquettishness.

genjot crooked, out of line.

génsi see GÉNGSI.

genta 1 church bell. 2 cowbell.

gentajangan roaming around.

gentar 1 vibration (of a plucked string), quivering. 2 fear. *Dgn tiada – ia melangkah madju*, Without fear he stepped forward. ber–, meng– to tremble, vibrate, quiver. *Meréka ∼ ketakutan*, They trembled with fear. ke–an 1 vibration. 2 fear. *Dlm ∼ meréka meréka mendjadi ribut*, In their fear they became panicky. meng–kan 1 ∼ *kawat gitar* to pluck the strings of a guitar. 2 to frighten. *Tenaga atom ∼ seluruh umat manusia*, Atomic energy has frightened the whole human race. peng– terrorist. –an shiver, vibration. *tak* – undaunted.

gentas 1 pinched off (by the thumbnail), broken off (of the stem of a flower). 2 finished, complete. *Masa peralihan blm –*, The transitional period has not passed yet. *Hatinja rasakan –*, She was brokenhearted, very sad. meng– to pinch off, break off.

géntél pill, pellet. meng-i to roll into a pill.

genténg roof tile.

genting 1 narrow, thin, slender. *bagian – dari djam pasir* the waist of an hourglass. *Ada beberapa bagian – pd tali itu*, There are several thin (frayed) spots in that rope. – *tanah Kra* the Kra Isthmus. 2 see GEN-TÉNG. 3 critical. *Keadaan sangat –*, The situation is very critical. 4 tense. ke–an 1 crisis. 2 tension. 3 emergency. meng– to become critical. *Keadaan makin ∼* , The situation became more and more critical. meng–kan to make critical, aggravate. *Tindakannja jg tak bidjaksana itu ∼ keadaan*, His unwise measures made the situation critical.

gentjat stopped, suspended. *Pemeriksaan – karena kekurangan bukti*, For lack of proof the investigation was suspended. –an *sendjata* a cease-fire.

gentjer 1 sustained, incessant, continued. *Serangan musuh jg – tidak berhasil menembus pertahanan kita*, The sustained attack of the enemy failed to penetrate our defenses. 2 swiftly, quickly. *Tukang tjopét dgn*

– *menghilang*, The pickpocket quickly disappeared.

gentjet meng– 1 to squeeze. *Ia ∼ tangan saja*, He squeezed my hand. *Ia ∼ saja pd pintu*, He had me pinned against the door. *Ia ∼ kepala ular dgn batu*, He crushed the snake's head with a rock. 2 to quell, quench. *Pemerintah ∼ pemberontakan itu*, The government quelled the uprising. 3 to pick on s.o. *Guru selalu ∼ saja*, The teacher always picks on me. ter– 1 squeezed. 2 quenched. –an 1 squeeze. 2 suppression.

géntjét grown together. *Dua djarinja –*, Two of his fingers were grown together.

géografi geography.

géografis geographic.

géologi geology.

géopolitik geopolitics.

gépéng flat. *Kué itu –*, Those cookies are flat. meng–kan to flatten.

gepok bundle of paper money.

gepuk sturdy, strong. meng– to crack (with a hammer, etc.). *Ia ∼ tempurung kelapa itu*, He cracked the coconut shell. ∼ *és* to crush ice.

gera meng– 1 to frighten, startle, terrify. 2 to chase s.t. or s.o. away. *Ia ∼ burung²*, He chased the birds away. peng– *burung* scarecrow, a device made of empty tin cans provided with clappers and set in motion by pulling a string.

gerabak meng– to cry. – *gerubuk* stomping, thumping (of heavy footsteps, falling chairs, furniture being moved).

gerabang 1 a large tear (in cloth). 2 a gaping hole (in a wall, etc.).

geragas meng– 1 to run o's fingers through o's hair, to comb out o's hair. 2 to scratch. *Kera ∼ punggungnja*, The monkey scratched his back.

geragot meng– *djagung* to nibble at corn on the cob. ∼ *tulang* to gnaw on a bone.

gerah stiflingly hot, sultry, close, muggy (of the weather).

geraham molar. – *bungsu* wisdom tooth.

gerajak robber. meng– to rob. *Pendjahat² ∼ rumah itu*, Bandits robbed the house. peng– robber. peng–an robbery.

gerajang meng– 1 to crawl (of small insects, snakes, etc.). 2 to feel, touch all over with o's fingers. ∼ *rambut* to run o's fingers through o's hair. 3 to go. *Ia ∼ seluruh Éropa*, He went all over Europe. meng-i to overrun. *Kampung itu tlh di– gerom-*

bolan bersendjata, The compound was overrun by an armed band.

gerak 1 movement. *Tarian itu mempunjai* $-^2$ *jg indah*, The dance has beautiful movements. 2 slight spasms (twitching of eyelids, etc.), taken as an omen. **ber–** 1 to move, be in motion. *Keréta api itu* $\sim$, The train moved. 2 to be active. *Ia* $\sim$ *dlm lingkungan politik*, He is active in political circles. **meng–kan** 1 to move. *Ia* $\sim$ *badannja*, He moved his body. 2 to put in motion, start. *Ia* $\sim$ *mesin itu*, He started the engine. 3 to put in action. $\sim$ *hati* to touch. *Tjerita anak itu sungguh* $\sim$ *hati saja*, The child's story really touched me. 4 to motivate. **peng–** 1 prime mover. $\sim$ *kapal terbang itu adalah empat mesin djét*, The prime movers of the plane are 4 jet engines. 2 moving spirit, driving force. *Dialah jg mendjadi* $\sim$ *-an itu*, He was the driving force behind the movement. **per–an** movement. $\sim$ *politik* political movement. **ter–** moved. *Dgn tidak sengadja buku itu* $\sim$ *oléhnja*, He accidentally moved the book. *Hati saja* $\sim$ *melihat penderitaannja*, My heart was moved at seeing all his sufferings. **–an** movement. $\sim$*nja sangat indah*, Her movements were very graceful. $\sim$ *(di)-bawah tanah* underground movement. *– badan* physical exercise. *– bangkitnja* upward movement. *– batin* impulse, intuition. *– djalan* walking race. *– gerik* movements. *– hati* impulse, intuition. *Ia mengikuti – hatinja*, He followed his impulse. *– surut* ebb tide.

geram angry. **ke–an** anger. **meng–** to growl.

geranat grenade. **meng–** to attack with grenades. *Ia* $\sim$ *kedudukan musuh*, He attacked the enemy's position with grenades. *– tangan* hand grenade.

gerangan 1 possibly, can it be (wondering, expressing doubt). *Siapa – jg datang terlambat semalam itu?* Who might it be who came late last night? *Benarkah – hal itu terdjadi*, Did it really happen? *Bagaimana – pendjahat itu dpt meloloskan diri!* How could that criminal ever have escaped! *Dimanakah – tanaman serupa itu dpt diketemukan?* Where could one possibly find a plant like that? 2 how do I know?

geranggang a sharply pointed bamboo pole, a bamboo spear.

geranjam **meng–** 1 to have a tingling sensation (when drinking soda water,

striking o's funny bone, etc.). 2 said of hot air which appears to vibrate.

gerantang 1 tumultuous noise. 2 outburst of noise to scare s.o. *– keling* to bluff, browbeat.

gerapai **meng–** to grope.

geratak **meng–** to look for. *Ia* $\sim$ *digudang utk mentjari palunja*, He looked everywhere in the storeroom for his hammer.

gerbak **meng–** to spread, pervade (of odors).

gerbang spread out, hanging down (of long hair). **meng–** to be spread out. **meng–kan** to spread out. *Burung itu* $\sim$ *sajapnja*, The bird spread its wings. $\sim$ *rambut* to let o's hair down.

gerbong train coach. *– barang* freight car, boxcar. *– penumpang* railway coach.

gerdam **meng–** to fall with a thud.

gerdum see GERDAM.

gerebeg 1 see GAREBEG. 2 see GEREBEK.

gerebek **meng–** to raid, stage a raid. *Polisi* $\sim$ *tempat pendjudian itu*, The police raided the gambling den. **peng–an** a raid.

gerédja church. *– ajam* 1 church with a weathervane. 2 the English church in Jakarta. *– Indjili* Church of the Gospel. *– Rum* Roman Catholic Church.

gerédjani ecclesiastical, church (attrib.).

geréh dried salted fish.

gérék **ber–** $-^2$ perforated. *Papan itu* $\sim$, The plank is perforated. **meng–** to drill, bore. *Tukang kaju* $\sim$ *papan*, The carpenter drilled the board. **peng–**, **–an** drill, auger.

geréndéng **meng–** 1 to strike a threatening posture (like a bull lowering its head to attack, etc.). 2 the lopsided way in which a cock sidles up to a hen as part of the courting procedure. **ter–** listing. *kapal perang* $\sim$ a listing warship (after sustaining damage).

gerenik 1 small and lovely. 2 low and uneven in volume (the sound of the recitation of prayers).

gerenjam to twinkle.

gerenjau without manners, unmannered (usually of girls).

gerénjéng grinning broadly. **ter–** $-^2$ grinning so that the gums show (like monkeys).

gerénjét twitching, spasm (of muscles).

gerénjot 1 with the corners of the mouth pulled up or down. 2 smiling.

gerentam sound of explosions. – *geranat mortir* explosions of mortar shells.

gerentang see GERENTAM.

gerépés 1 fumbling, fiddling with o's fingers. 2 uneven, not smooth, rough (surface of a board, etc.).

gerésék rustle. **ber-, meng-** to rustle.

gerét meng- to scratch. *Ia ~ katja itu*, He scratched the mirror. **mengkan** to make scratch. *Ia ~ intan itu pd katja*, He made the diamond scratch across the mirror. **-an** match(es).

gérét meng- to drag. *Ia ~ 'saja masuk kekamar*, He dragged me into the room.

gerétjok meng- to annoy, bother. **peng-** troublemaker.

gergadji saw. **meng-** 1 to saw. 2 to zigzag. 3 to tack (to sail to windward). **peng-** sawer. **peng-an** sawmill. – *membuat* coping saw. – *mesin* machine saw. – *tangan* handsaw.

gergadjul scoundrel, blackguard.

gergasi a man-eating giant.

gerham see GERAHAM.

gerhana eclipse. – *bulan* lunar eclipse. – *matahari* solar eclipse. – *mutlak* total eclipse.

geriap meng- to become smaller. *Matanja makin ~ karena mengantuk*, His eyes became smaller and smaller with sleep. *Pelita mulai ~* , The oil lamp began to dim.

geridip meng- to sparkle, glitter.

gerigi ber- toothed, serrated (a saw, etc.).

gerigik a scoop made of a bamboo cylinder provided with a handle.

gerigis ber- serrated. *pisau* – a knife with a burred, chipped edge.

gerih dried fish.

gerik see GERAK-GERIK.

gerila see GERILJA.

gerilja guerrilla. **ber-** 1 to conduct guerrilla warfare. 2 to join the guerrillas.

geriljawan guerrilla fighter.

gerimis drizzling (rain). **ber-** to drizzle.

gerinda grindstone. **meng-** to sharpen on a grindstone.

gerinding 1 k.o. jew's-harp. 2 see GÉNGGONG.

gerindjal see GINDJAL.

gerindjam 1 grindstone to file teeth. 2 ear scoop (to clean o's outer ear duct).

gering ill (used honorifically). *Radja itu -*, The king is ill. **ke-an** illness. *~ bersalin* labor pains. **peng-** 1 sickly. 2 medicine for making s.o. ill.

geringsing curly. *Rambutnja -*, His hair is curly. **ber-** 1 to curl. *Rambutnja ~* , Her hair curls. 2 to distort the face. *Mukanja ~ kesakitan*, His face was distorted with pain.

gerintjing jingle.

gerip slate pencil.

geripir clerk of the court (of justice).

gerisik rustle (of leaves, of paper, etc.). **meng-** to rustle.

gerising ber- to twist, distort o's face (with pain), make faces.

gerit meng- 1 to screech. *Gerip itu ~ diatas batu tulis*, The slate pencil screeched over the slate. 2 to nibble, gnaw. *Tikus ~ médja*, The mouse nibbled at the table.

gerita see GURITA.

geritjau loud repetitive sound (like the twittering of birds, honking of geese, chattering of monkeys or people).

gerlap meng- to flicker, sparkle.

gerling see KERLING.

gerlip meng- to twinkle, glitter.

germang meng- to stand on end (of hair). *Bulu roma saja ~* , I am goose flesh all over (my skin creeps).

germut meng-i to swarm, crowd about.

gerobak cart, wagon. – *lembu*, – *sapi* bullock cart. – *roda* wheelbarrow. – *sorong* handcart, pushcart.

gerobok 1 a bamboo cupboard for storage of food. 2 large clothes chest. **meng-** to bubble. *Air mendidih itu ~* , The boiling water bubbled.

gerodak clattering (like a stone rolling on a wooden floor), clatter, stamping (of feet). **meng-** to clatter about.

gerogot meng-i 1 to bite repeatedly. *Ia ~ djagung bakar*, He was eating roasted corn on the cob. 2 to nibble at.

gerohok hollow. **ber-** 1 to have holes. *Dinding rumah ~ setelah musuh mengadakan pemboman*, The walls of the house had big holes in them after the enemy dropped their bombs. 2 to have cavities. *Giginja ~* , His teeth have cavities.

gerombol 1 group. 2 bunch. *mangga se-* a bunch of mangoes. **ber-** to group together. *Orang² ~ didepan rumah lurah*, People grouped together in front of the headman's house. **-an** 1 group. 2 band of bandits, gang. *Perkebunan itu semalam diserang oléh ~* , The plantation was attacked by a band of bandits last night. *~ bersendjata* armed band.

geronggang-geronggong hollow (of a tree trunk, a metal statue).

geronjot twitching, spasm, contraction (of muscles).

gerontang 1 frightening. 2 booming.

geropjak ber– with a thud. *Pohon besar jg ditebang djatuh* ∼ , The big tree when felled came down with a resounding thud.

geropjok meng– 1 to raid, stage a raid. 2 to give chase, attack s.o. *Seluruh kampung* ∼ *sipembunuh,* The whole village gave chase after the killer. **peng–an** raid.

geros meng– to snore.

gerosok *bunji* **ber–** shuffling, creaking sounds.

gerotjok ber–an to foam. *air* ∼ rushing water.

gerowot meng–i 1 to undermine. 2 to destroy. **peng–an** undermining.

gersak 1 crackling (of dry leaves). 2 crunching sound.

gersang see KERSANG.

gertak 1 snarl, snap. *–nja menjakitkan hati saja,* His snapping at me hurts me. 2 to bluff. *Itu hanja kosong sadja,* That's just empty bluff. 3 threat. **meng–** 1 to snarl at. *Bapak* ∼ *saja,* Father snarled at me. 2 to make s.o. jump, startle s.o. *Temannja* ∼ *dia dgn entakan kaki,* His friend made him jump by stamping on the floor. 3 to intimidate s.o. 4 to bluff s.o. **meng–kan** 1 to spur. *Ia* ∼ *kudanja,* He spurred his horse. 2 to gnash. *Ia* ∼ *giginja,* He gnashed his teeth. **–an** 1 snarl. 2 bluff. 3 intimidation. 4 spurring. *Kuda itu menaati* ∼ *pengendaranja,* The horse obeyed his rider's spurring. **–** *gerantang, – sambal* empty bluff.

gertik meng– to grate. *Ada jg* ∼ *pd katja djendéla,* S.t. is grating against the windowpane.

gerugut grooved, furrowed.

geruh unfortunately, having bad luck. **ke–an** misfortune, bad luck. **meng–** 1 to snore. 2 to trumpet (of elephants). **–** *gerah* all k.o. misfortune.

geruit meng– to wriggle (of a snake, worm).

geruk (–gerak) 1 sound of tables, chairs, scraping across the floor. 2 thunder.

gerumit meng–i to tinker, putter at s.t.

gerumut meng–i to surround.

gerun embarrassed, frightened, uncertain, unnerved.

gerundang tadpole.

gerung meng– 1 to roar. *Singa itu* ∼ , The lion roared. *Ia* ∼ *kemarahan,* He roared with anger. 2 to trumpet. *Gadjah* ∼ , The elephant trumpeted. 3 to wail. **ter–** to burst out wailing.

gerupis meng– to tinker at s.t.

gerupuk meng–kan 1 to trip. 2 to cause the downfall of s.o. or s.t. **ter–** to stumble.

gerus meng– 1 to polish s.t. until it shines. 2 to crush, grind (in a mortar).

gerut 1 gnashing (of teeth). 2 scraping, scratching. 3 to crunch.

gerutu 1 rough, coarse (of texture). 2 grumbling. **meng–** to grumble.

gerutup rapid sequence of explosions. **–** *senapan mesin terdengar dari djauh,* In the distance the rattling of machine-gun fire could be heard.

gerutus see GERUTUP.

gesa ber– –² hurriedly. ∼ *meréka menjudahkan pekerdjaan meréka,* Hurriedly they finished their work. **keter–an** haste. **meng– –²kan** to hurry s.t. up. *Ia* ∼ *temannja berpakaian,* He had his friend dress in a hurry. **ter– –²** in a hurry. *Meréka pergi* ∼ , They went in a hurry.

gésék see GOSOK. **ber–** to scrub, scour. **ber–an** to rub against. **meng–biola** to play the violin. **per–an** friction.

gésél see GÉSÉR. **ber–** to scour s.t.

gésér fricative, spirant (phon.) **ber–** 1 to shift. *Kursi itu* ∼ *dari tempatnja,* The chair shifted from its position. 2 to rub. *Lengannja* ∼ *pd témbok,* His arm rubbed against the wall. 3 to have friction. *Ia selalu* ∼ *dgn bapaknja,* There was always friction between him and his father. **ke–an** friction, irritation. **meng–kan** 1 to rub. *Ia* ∼ *lengannja pd témbok,* He rubbed his arm against the wall. 2 to shift s.t. *Ia* ∼ *médja itu,* He shifted the table. **peng–an** rubbing, friction. **per–an** 1 mobility. 2 shift, transfer. 3 reshuffle (of cabinet). **ter–** 1 rubbed. 2 shifted. *Kursi itu* ∼ *karena gempa bumi itu,* The chair was shifted by the earthquake. 3 removed (from a job).

gesit 1 nimble, adroit. *Dgn – diélakkannja pukulan lawannja,* Nimbly he parried his opponent's blow. 2 skillful. *pendébat jg –* skillful debater. 3 skittish. *kuda jg –* skittish horse. 4 tricky. *ikan jg –* a fish very hard to catch. **ke–an** 1 nimbleness. 2 activity.

géspér (belt) buckle.

geta throne.

getah 1 tree sap. 2 resin. 3 gland secretion. **ber–** 1 to have tree sap. 2 sticky. *Buah itu* ∼ , That fruit is sticky. 3 to gather sap of rubber tree. **meng–** 1 to tap a tree. 2 to collect tree sap. *Ia pergi* ∼ *kehutan,* He went to collect tree sap in the jungle. 3 to become sticky. *Tjairan* *itu mendjadi* ~ , The solution became sticky. 4 to catch birds with glue sticks. *Ia pergi* ~ *burung*, He went to catch birds with glue sticks. – *bening* lymph. – *burung* birdlime. – *karét* rubber (tree) sap. – *lambung* gastric juice. – *pertja* gutta-percha. – *radang* exudation of inflammation of lymph.

getak-getuk the knocking of a butcher's cleaver on a cutting block.

getang cover of thin material (paper, cloth, skin) tightly drawn over an opening. – *gendang* drumhead.

getap meng– to crack, break. ~ *geraham* to gnash o's teeth. **–an** 1 quickly startled. 2 quick-tempered.

getar ber– to tremble, shake. *Ia* ~ *ketakutan*, He trembled with fear. **meng–** to vibrate. *Suaranja* ~ , Her voice vibrated. **meng–kan** to cause to tremble. *Kemarahan bapaknja* ~ *dia*, His father's anger made him tremble. **peng–** tyrant. **–an** 1 vibration. 2 tremor.

getas 1 brittle. *Kaju itu sangat –*, That wood is very brittle. 2 irritated. **ber–** *hati* easily offended, touchy, irritable. *Ia sangat* ~ *hati*, He is very easily offended.

géték small raft. *perempuan* – promiscuous woman (too independent of accepted social behavior).

getik see KETIK. **meng–** to tap lightly, flick (with o's fingers).

getil meng– to pinch, hold with two fingers.

getir bitter(ly). *Buah itu –*, The fruit is bitter. *Ia tertawa –*, He laughed bitterly. **ke–an** bitterness. ~ *hidup* life's bitterness. **meng–kan** to make bitter. *Kelakuan anaknja* ~ *kehidupannja*, His son's behavior made his life bitter.

getis fragile, brittle (of health).

getjar to shudder, tremble from fear.

getok meng– 1 to hit, knock on s.t. (with a hammer, o's knuckles, a gavel). 2 to smooth s.t. out.

getol diligent, industrious.

getu meng– to crush (e.g., a small insect) with the fingernail.

getun astonished, surprised. **ke–an** surprise, astonishment.

geulis 1 nice, lovely. 2 see KELOM.

géwang 1 mother-of-pearl. 2 small eardrop.

gi see PERGI. – *dah, nanti gua susul*, Go on, I'll join you.

GIA Garuda Indonesian Airways.

giat 1 energetic. *Ia bekerdja dgn –*, He worked energetically. 2 forceful, active. *dgn – memerangi kedjahatan* to make war on crime forcefully.

ber– to be active. *Ia* ~ *memadjukan kebudajaan nasional*, He was active in promoting national culture. *Gerombolan²* ~ *lagi dlm daérah itu*, Bands of bandits are again active in that region. **ke–an** 1 energy, ardor. 2 activity. 3 assiduity. **memper–kan, meng–kan** to encourage. *Ia* ~ *para pemuda utk meneruskan perdjoangan kemerdékaannja*, He encouraged the youths to keep on fighting for freedom. **meng–kan** *kembali* to reactivate. **peng–an** activation.

gidik ber– to shudder, shiver (because of some gruesome, weird matter). **meng–(–)** to give o. the creeps, make o's flesh creep.

gigau meng– to be delirious, rave. *Ia demam dan ia* ~ , He had a fever and was delirious.

gigi 1 tooth. 2 set of teeth. 3 tooth-like objects. – *gergadji* teeth of a saw. **ber–** 1 to have teeth. *Orang tua itu tak* ~ *lagi*, The old man no longer had any teeth. 2 toothed, serrated. *Gergadji itu* ~ , The saw is toothed. **–²** tread (on tires). – *air* water's edge. – *anak* baby teeth. – *asu* eyetooth, canine tooth, fang(s). – *benar* permanent teeth. – *buatan* false teeth. – *bungsu* wisdom tooth. – *geligi* denture. – *hutan* edge of the jungle, woods. – *manis* incisor. – *palsu, – pasangan* false teeth. – *pengiris* incisor. – *sedjati* permanent teeth. – *seri* incisors. – *sulung* baby teeth. – *taring* canine tooth.

gigih 1 see GIGIL. 2 stubborn, unyielding. *Dgn – ditolaknja segala pertolongan*, He stubbornly refused any help. 3 *Nasi masih –*, The rice is not completely cooked (said of boiled or steamed rice which still has a hard uncooked core). **ke–an** stubbornness.

gigil meng– to shiver. *Ia* ~ *kedinginan*, He shivered with cold.

gigit a bite. *Berilah saja daging se–*, Give me a small piece of meat. **ber– –²** to bite e.o. *Andjing berkelahi itu* ~ , The fighting dogs bit e.o. **ke–** bitten (accidentally). **meng–** to bite. *Ia* ~ *roti itu*, He took a bite of that bread. **ter–** bitten (accidentally). *Lidah saja* ~ , I bit my tongue. – *djari* to feel disappointed, be let down.

gila 1 mad, insane. *Orang itu –*, That man is insane. 2 to be crazy about (*pd*). *Saja – padamu*, I am crazy about you. **ber– –²** madly. ~ *dia mengeluarkan uangnja*, He spent his money madly. **ber– –²an** to fool around. *Djangan* ~ *dgn pegawai* *perempuan saja,* Don't fool around with my female employees. **ke–an** 1 insanity. 2 foolishness. *Ketjelakaan itu disebabkan ∼mu* , That accident was caused by your foolishness. **ke- –²an** to be madly in love. *Ia ∼ pd gadis itu,* He is madly in love with that girl. **memper–kan** 1 to drive s.o. insane. 2 to fool s.o. **meng–** to be crazy, mad. *Harga² itu ∼* , Those prices are crazy. **meng-i** 1 to be very fond of. *Ia ∼ makanan itu,* He is very fond of that food. 2 to be madly in love with. *Ia ∼ gadis itu,* He is madly in love with that girl. **meng–kan** 1 to drive insane. *Kesusahannja ∼ dia,* His grief drove him insane. 2 see MENG–I. **meng- –²kan** 1 to drive s.o. mad. 2 to deceive s.o. **ter- –²an** to be madly in love. *Ia ∼ dgn gadis itu,* He was crazy about that girl. **–²an** to fool around with s.o. **–²** *bahasa* slightly mad. *– hormat* to insist on an excessive amount of respect from o's subordinates. *– kebangsaan* chauvinistic. *– kekajaan* money-hungry. *– kekuasaan* power-hungry. *– pangkat* to crave a higher position.

gilang *– gemilang* 1 bright. *Bulan – gemilang,* The moon is bright. 2 brilliant. *Ia lulus udjiannja dgn hasil – gemilang,* He passed his examinations with brilliant results. 3 glorious. *Ia mentjapai kemenangan – gemilang,* He won a glorious victory. *– tjemerlang* glittering, bright.

gilap see KILAP. *– gemilap* to shine brilliantly.

gilas **meng–** 1 to pulverize, crush. *Mesin² itu ∼ bidjih besi,* Those machines pulverize iron ore. 2 to run over. *Mobil itu ∼ andjing saja,* That car ran over my dog. **peng–** pulverizer. *∼ és* ice crusher.

gili **meng- –²** 1 to tickle. *Ia ∼ baji itu,* He tickled the baby. 2 to needle. *Ia ∼ saja agar saja lebih keras bekerdja,* He needled me into working harder. **–²** 1 small dike. 2 sidewalk.

gilik **meng–** 1 to roll. *Mesin itu ∼ batang besi mendjadi lembaran²,* The machine rolled the iron bars into sheets. 2 to tickle.

giling **ber–** to turn. *Mesin paberik kini ∼ lagi,* Now the machines of the factory turn again. **meng–** 1 to mill. *Ia ∼ gandumnja,* He milled his wheat. 2 to flatten. *Peng– djalan itu ∼ djalan,* The steam roller flattens the street. 3 to run over. *Keréta api tlh ∼ seorang perempuan,* The train ran over a woman. *∼ rokok* to roll a cigarette. *∼ tebu* to press

sugar cane. **peng–** *djalan* steam roller. **peng–an, –an** mill. *∼ beras* rice mill. *∼ padi* 1 rice mill. 2 rice milling. **ter–** run over. *Andjing saja ∼ mobil,* My dog was run over by a car. **–an** *air* water mill. **–²** steam roller.

gilipir see GERIPIR.

gilir **ber–** 1 to go through cycles, alternate. *Musim hudjan ∼ dgn musin kering,* The rainy season alternates with the dry season. 2 to take turns. *Meréka ∼ mendjaga rumah itu,* They took turns guarding the house. **ber- –², ber–an** to take turns. *utk* **peng–** as an alternative... *Utk ∼* , *marilah kita berenang,* Let's swim for a change. **–an** turn.

gindjal kidney.

gindjel see GINDJAL.

gingsir see GELINGSIR.

gintir **peng–an** winding *∼ benang tenun* winding of yarn on bobbins or spindles.

gintju lipstick. **ber–** to put on lipstick. *– bibir* lipstick. *– pipi* rouge.

gips gypsum.

gir gear. *– mesin itu berputar,* The gears of the engine started turning.

girang 1 glad. *Ia – mendapat uang itu,* He was glad to get the money. 2 cheerful, merry. *Ia bernjanji dgn –,* He sang cheerfully. **ber–** (*hati*) 1 to be glad. 2 to be cheerful. **ke–an** 1 gladness, joy. 2 overjoyed. *Ia ∼ mendapat uang itu,* He was overjoyed when he got the money. **ke- –²an** overjoyed. **meng–kan** 1 to make glad. *Berita itu ∼ dia,* The news made him glad. 2 to make cheerful. *Musik itu ∼ saja,* The music made me cheerful. 3 to cheer up. *Saja mentjoba ∼ kawan saja jg susah itu,* I tried to cheer up my sad friend. **peng–** happy-go-lucky, cheerful, person.

giras coarse linen.

giring **meng–** 1 to drive (cattle). 2 to lead. *Ia ∼ orang itu kependjara,* He led the man to prison. **–an** procession.

giro clearing account. *membuka –* to open an account.

gita song.

gitar guitar.

gitu see BEGITU. **–²** so-so. *Bekerdja keraskah? Oh, ∼* , Working hard? Oh, so-so. **–²an** so, that way. *Djangan ∼ dong,* Don't do it that way.

giur **meng–kan** 1 enchanting. *Ketjantikannja ∼* , Her beauty was enchanting. 2 enticing. **ter–** enchanted, charmed, fascinated. *Ia termasuk meréka jg ∼ oléh itu,* He was among those fascinated by it.

giwang see GÉWANG.

gizi nutritive element, nutrient.

gl. [gelar] a title.

global 1 roughly. *Ia menerangkan hal itu setjara* -, He explained the case roughly. 2 over-all. *mengenai keadaan* - concerning the over-all situation.

glotal glottal.

goa see GUA.

gobah see GUBAH.

gobang bronze coin, slightly larger than U.S. half-dollar piece; issue of the former Netherlands Indies government; valued at 2½ cents.

gobar depressed. - *hati* sad.

gobék small mortar to crush a quid of betel leaves for toothless chewers.

gobernor see GUBERNUR.

goblék to get ready, succeed. *Biarlah asal* - *sadja*, Doesn't matter as long as it gets ready.

goblok stupid. ke-an stupidity.

goda 1 temptation. *Gadis itu kena* -, The girl was led into temptation. 2 mischief. meng-(i) 1 to tempt. 2 to seduce. *Ia* ~ *gadis itu*, He seduced the girl. 3 to disturb. *Ketjurigaan* ~ *hatinja*, Suspicion disturbed his mind. 4 to hinder. *Angin dan taufan* ~ *perdjalanannja*, Wind and storm hindered his voyage. 5 to tease. peng- 1 tempter. 2 seducer. 3 teaser. (peng)-an = GODA. ter- 1 tempted. *Ia* ~ *sétan*, He was tempted by the devil. 2 seduced. 3 disturbed. 4 hindered. 5 teased.

godék side whiskers.

godog (peng)-an pulling, drawing.

godok meng- to boil. *Ibu* ~ *air*, Mother boils water. -an boiled food. *mi* - boiled noodles. *telur* - boiled eggs.

gogo rice grown on dry fields.

gogoh shivering.

gogok gulping (drinks).

gohong 1 hole. 2 cave.

gojah wobbly. *Djalannja* -, His walk was wobbly. *Giginja sdh* -, His teeth are loose. ke-an instability. meng-kan to rock, shake s.t.

gojak shaking. meng- *pohon* to shake a tree.

gojang 1 unsteady. *Langkah²nja* -, His steps were unsteady. *Harga² barang masih* -, The prices of goods are still unsteady. 2 wobbly. ber- 1 to rock. 2 to sway, swing. *Dahan²* ~ *ditiup angin*, The branches swayed in the wind. 3 to fluctuate. *Harga karét* ~ , The price of rubber fluctuated. ke-an 1 uncertainty. 2 fluctuation. meng-(kan) 1 to shake. *Ia* ~ *kepalanja*, He shook his head. 2 to rock. *Ia* ~ *kursi itu*, He rocked the chair. 3 to sway s.t. 4 to make

fluctuate (market prices). 5 to make unstable (the economic or political situation). ter- 1 shaken. 2 rocked. 3 swayed. 4 fluctuated. 5 made unstable. - *kaki* to take it easy. *Semua orang sibuk tetapi ia* - *kaki sadja*, Others were busy, but he was taking it easy.

gol goal.

golak ber- 1 to seethe. *Laut* ~ , The sea seethed. *Pemberontakan* ~ *diseluruh negara*, Rebellion seethed all over the country. 2 to boil. *Air* ~ , The water is boiling. per-an turbulence, disturbance. -an 1 seething. 2 violent move, stir.

golbi fly, front in trousers.

golék puppet (usually made of wood). ber-, ber- -², meng- to roll. *Batang kaju itu* ~ , The tree trunk rolled over and over. meng-kan 1 to roll s.t. *Ia* ~ *bola itu*, He rolled the ball. 2 to lay s.t. down. *Ia* ~ *badannja*, He lay down. ter- rolled over. *Menara* ~ *oléh angin badai*, The tower toppled over from a hurricane. *Ia* ~ *ketubruk mobil*, He was knocked down when a car hit him.

goléng to tap s.o. in order to get attention.

golok machete or bolo knife. meng- to use or hit with a *golok*. -²an bolo knife play.

golong meng-kan to classify. *Ia* ~ *orang² itu menurut pekerdjaan meréka*, He classified the people according to their professions. meng- -²kan to divide into separate groups. peng-an 1 classification, grouping. 2 stratification. ter- 1 classified. *Buku ini* ~ *dlm* -an *buku terlarang*, This book is classified under the classification of forbidden books. 2 to belong to. *Ia* ~ *kaum ningrat*, He belongs to the aristocratic class. -an 1 classification. 2 group. ~ *desakan* pressure group. 3 class. *Ia termasuk* ~ *masjarakat jg tertinggi*, He belongs to the highest social class. ~ *ménak* the feudal class. ~ *menengah* the middle class. ~ *pelawan* the opposition.

gombak 1 forelock. 2 tuft, crest.

gombang 1 a giant earthenware jar, big bellied with a glazed surface. 2 pretty.

gomok fat, corpulent.

gompjok thick, luxurious growth (of hair, leaves).

gondang various k.o. snails.

gondjong tapering.

gondok 1 goiter. 2 suppressed anger. *Ia* - *karena ia tidak mendapat uang dari bapaknja*, Although he didn't show it, he was angry because he

didn't get any money from his
father. **ke–an** anger, grudge against.
~nja karena tak diundang, He holds
a grudge because he was not invited.

gondol **meng–** 1 to carry in the
mouth. *Andjing ~ daging jg ditjurinja
itu,* The dog carried away the stolen
meat. *Ia ~ kedjuaraan berenang
tahun ini,* He carried off this year's
swimming championship. 2 to embezzle. *Ia ~ uang pemerintah,* He
embezzled the government's money.
peng– *hadiah* prize winner.

gondong goiter.

gondrong used of s.o. who needs a
haircut. *Kamu sdh –, perlu ketukang
pangkas,* Your hair has grown quite
a bit; you need a haircut.

gong gong.

gonggong **ber–,** **meng–** to bark.

goni see GUNI.

gonjéh **meng–** to munch (of a toothless person).

gonta-ganti 1 mutual(ly), recipro-
cal(ly). 2 changing repeatedly.

gontai slow.

gontjang shaking fast and hard, vacillating. **ber–** to shake, move violently.
ke–an 1 shock. 2 commotion. 3 fluctuation, vacillation. **meng–** *namanja*
to trade on s.o.'s name. **meng–kan** to
shake s.o. or s.t. **per–an** 1 concussion,
shock. *~ otak* brain concussion. 2
commotion. **–an** 1 emotional shock.
2 jolt. *– otak* concussion.

gontjéng see BONTJÉNG.

gopoh **ke–an** haste, hurry. **ter–** –² in
a hurry, hastily. *Ia pergi dgn ~ ,* He
went in a hurry. *– gapah* hastily.

gordén curtain.

gordin see GORDÉN.

gorék **meng–** to scratch. *Ia ~ tangannja jg gatal itu,* He scratched his
itching hand. **meng–** –² 1 to scratch.
2 to itch. *Hatinja ~ ingin melihat
gambar hidup,* He just couldn't wait
to go to the movies. *– api* matches.

goréng 1 fried. 2 roasted. **meng–** to
fry. **peng–an** 1 frying pan. 2 cas-
serole. 3 roasting. *~ kopi* roasting of
coffee. **–an** 1 a roast. 2 s.t. roasted.

gorés 1 scratch. *Lututnja penuh –,*
His knee was full of scratches. 2 line.
Kertas itu ada –nja, The paper was
lined. **ber–** –² scratched. *Lengannja
~ ,* His arms were scratched. *Kertas
itu ~ ,* There were pencil scratches
on the paper. **ke–** to be scratched.
Mobilnja ~ , His car was scratched.
meng– 1 to scratch. 2 to line. *Ia ~
kertas itu,* He lined the paper. **meng–
kan** to scratch. *Ia ~ péna pd kertas,*
He scratched the pen over the paper.
–an = GORÉS.

gorét see GORÉS.

gorok **meng–** to cut, slash, slaughter.
Pendjahat ~ léhér korbannja, The
criminal cut his victim's throat.

gosok **member–kan,** **meng–kan** to
rub on, against, s.t. *Ia ~ sepatunja
pd lantai,* He wiped his shoes on
the floor. **meng–** 1 to rub, wipe. 2 to
polish. *Ia ~ sepatunja,* He polished
his shoes. 3 to incite, egg on. *Ia ~
adiknja agar ia memukul saja,* He
incited his brother to hit me. 4 to
brush. *~ gigi* to brush the teeth.
~ biola to play the violin. **peng–**
1 abrasive. 2 instigator. *~ sepatu*
shoeshine boy. **–an** 1 rubbing. 2
polishing. 3 instigation. *– gigi* denti-
frice.

gosong 1 sandbank. 2 burnt, singed.
Makanan itu –, The food is burnt.
meng–kan to burn. *Ia ~ masakannja,*
She burned what she was cooking.

got gutter, drain.

gotjek **meng–** to maneuver with the
foot (soccer). *Dia pintar ~ ,* His
footwork is excellent.

gotjoh **ber–** to fight. **meng–** to strike
s.o. **per–an** fist fight, scrap.

gotong **meng–** to carry a heavy burden together. *Meréka ~ lemari jg
berat itu,* They carried the heavy
cupboard. **peng–rojong** co-operator.
–an burden. *– rojong* mutual co-
operation, mutual aid. *Dgn – rojong
penduduk désa itu mendirikan mesdjid
baru,* In mutual co-operation the
village inhabitants erected a new
mosque.

gotri pellets, shot (for a shotgun).

GR [*Gotong Rojong*] mutual aid.

grad degree. *100 – Celsius* 100°
Centigrade.

gradah see GELADAH.

grafik a graph.

gragot **meng–i** to chew s.t. off.

granat 1 grenade. 2 shell. **meng–** to
throw a grenade. **peng–an** attack
with grenades. see GERANAT.

grapik see GRAFIK.

grasi pardon. *Orang hukuman mendapat –,* The convict was pardoned.

grégél to let fall from o's hand.

grimis see GERIMIS.

gripir see GERIPIR.

grombolan see GEROMBOLAN.

gropjok see GEROPJOK.

gros(s)ir 1 wholesaler. 2 distributor.

G'talo [*Gorontalo*] city in North
Celebes.

gu see REGU.

gua 1 I, me (vulgar language or
used among close friends). *– sdh
makan,* I have eaten. 2 my, mine.
3 cave, grotto. *– -gerba* womb.

gual loose, wobbly. *Giginja* –, His tooth is loose. – *gail* loose and wobbly.

guam 1 conflict, litigation. 2 mouth sore. **ber–** to be at odds with s.o. **peng–** attorney. **per–an** issue in litigation.

gubah **meng–** 1 to arrange. *Ia* ∼ *bunga*², She arranged the flowers. *Ia* ∼ *musik buat sandiwara itu*, He arranged the music for the play. 2 to compose. *Ia* ∼ *sebuah lagu*, He composed a melody. *Ia* ∼ *tjerita*² *dan sjair*², He composed stories and poems. **peng–** 1 arranger. 2 composer. 3 author. **–an** 1 arrangement. 2 composition. 3 literary work. ∼ *musik* musical arrangement.

gubel **meng–** 1 to coax, urge. 2 to cling to o's parents.

gubernemén government.

gubernur governor. **ke–an** governor's residence. – *djéndral* governor-general.

gubit **meng–** to wave at (with hand, cloth, etc.).

gubris **meng–** to pay attention, heed. *Ia tidak* ∼ *permintaan kami*, He paid no attention to our request.

gubuk 1 hut, shed. 2 shelter in rice field. 3 booth, stand at a fair.

gudang warehouse, storehouse, store-room. **meng–kan** to store, place in a warehouse. *Kuli*² ∼ *muatan kapal itu*, The dock hands stored the ship's cargo. **per–an** warehousing. – *gandum* wheat barn.

gudik 1 scabies. 2 the itch. 3 mange. **–an** to have scabies.

gué see GUA.

gugah **meng–(kan)** to wake s.o. up. **ter–** awakened. ∼*lah suatu pertanjaan*, Then a question cropped up.

gugat **meng–** 1 to accuse. *Pengadilan* ∼ *dia dgn pembunuhan*, The court accused him of murder. 2 to demand. *Meréka* ∼ *pembubaran kabinét*, They demanded the dismissal of the cabinet. 3 to claim. *Ia* ∼ *hak*²*nja*, He claimed his rights. 4 to criticize. *Meréka* ∼ *tindakan*² *pemerintah*, They criticized the steps taken by the government. 5 to protest. ∼ *wewenang* to infringe on the authority. **–an** 1 accusation. 2 demand. 3 claim. 4 criticism. 5 protest. 6 suit in court.

gugu **meng–** (*akan*) to believe in.

gugub see GUGUP.

guguk hill.

gugup panicky, excited. *Semua orang berteriak dan ia mendjadi* –, Everybody screamed and he became panicky. **ke–an** 1 panic. 2 nervousness. **meng–kan** to make panicky. **peng–** nervous, panicky person.

gugur to fall. *Daun*² *dan bunga*² –,

The leaves and the blossoms fell. *Ia* – *dlm pertempuran*, He fell in battle. **ber–an** to fall out, fall by the wayside (of a horse). **ke–an** 1 the falling (shedding) of the leaves indicating the arrival of autumn. 2 fall, killed (in battle). ∼ *létnan meréka mengamukkan serdadu*² *itu*, The death of their lieutenant enraged the soldiers. 3 to have a miscarriage. *Perempuan itu* ∼, The woman had a miscarriage. ∼ *baji* miscarriage. ∼ *tanah* erosion. **meng–kan** 1 to cause to drop. *Angin* ∼ *daun*²*an*, The wind caused the leaves to fall. 2 to kill (in battle). ∼ *kandungan* to have a miscarriage. ∼ *tachta* to topple a throne, dethrone. **peng–an** *kandungan* abortion. **–an** fall. ∼ *nuklir* nuclear fallout. – *gunung* emergency assistance. *Setjara* – *gunung désa dibangunkan kembali*, The village was rebuilt by collective effort (after having been destroyed). – *hati* enchanted, charmed. – *talak* pronouncing of divorce by the husband.

gugus **–an** group, cluster (of stars). *Di*∼ *pulau manakah terdapat 'steppe'?* On what group of islands do we find steppes? – *kata* row of words.

guha see GUA.

guit **meng–** 1 to prod, touch with the fingers or toes. 2 to affect.

gujah see GOJAH.

gul goal. *Ia menghasilkan tiga* –, He scored three goals. **meng–kan** to score.

gula sugar. **ber–** to contain sugar. *Buah itu* ∼, That fruit has sugar. **meng–** to flatter. *Ia* ∼ *saja karena ia hendak memindjam uang*, He flattered me because he wanted to borrow money. **meng–i** to put sugar in. *Ia* ∼ *kopinja*, He put sugar in his coffee. –² 1 sweets, candy. 2 sweetheart. *Ia mempunjai seorang* ∼, He had a sweetheart. – *arén* brown palm sugar. – *batu* rock candy. – *djawa* brown sugar. – *hitam* caramel. – *kelapa*, – *njiur* brown sugar. – *kembang* lump sugar. – *pasir* granulated, refined sugar. – *rawak* sugar syrup. – *sakar* caramel. – *tebu* cane sugar. – *tepung* powdered sugar.

gulai k.o. curry soup. **meng–** to cook *gulai*.

gulali sugar candy.

gulang² field shelter for person watching over crops.

gulat **ber–** to wrestle. *Kedua orang itu* ∼, The two people wrestled. **per–an** 1 wrestling. 2 struggle. ∼ *utk kemerdékaan* a struggle for freedom.

gulet see GULAT.

guli a marble.

guling bolster, Dutch wife. **ber-** 1 to sleep with a bolster. 2 to roll. *Ia ~ dilantai*, He rolled over the floor. **ber-an, ber- ‑², meng-** to roll. *Batu itu djatuh ~ dari léréng gunung*, The stone went rolling down the mountain slope. **meng-kan** 1 to roll. *Saja ~ batu itu*, I rolled the rock. 2 to down, smash. *Ia ~ lawannja dlm perkelahian itu*, He downed his enemy in the fight. *Bandung ~ regu Makassar dgn 3-1*, Bandung downed Macassar 3-1. 3 to overthrow. *Meréka ~ pemerintah*, They overthrew the government. **peng-an** overthrow. *~ kekuasaan* the overthrow of power. **ter-** 1 rolled. *Batu itu ~ dari tempatnja*, The rock was rolled from its place. 2 overthrown. *Pemerintahan itu ~ ,* The government was overthrown. 3 overturned. *Lokomotipnja ~ ,* The locomotive overturned.

gulung roll. *Saja membeli kertas beberapa ‑*, I bought several rolls of paper. **ber-, ber-an, ber- ‑²** to roll, wallow. *Kerbau suka ~ dlm lumpur*, The water buffalo likes to wallow in the mud. *Batu itu ~ dari léréng gunung*, The rock rolled down the mountain slope. **meng-** to wind. *Ia ~ benang itu pd -an*, He wound the thread around a spool. **meng-kan** 1 to roll. *Ia ~ batu itu dari puntjak gunung*, He rolled the rock from the mountain top. *~ rokok* to roll a cigarette. 2 to roll up. *Ia ~ lengan badjunja*, He rolled up his sleeves. **ter-** 1 rolled. 2 wound, reeled. *Benang kail itu sdh ~ ,* The fish line is reeled. **-an** spool, reel. *- gemulung, ‑² ombak* the rolling of the waves. *- tikar* to throw in the sponge, give up the struggle.

gulut ber-(‑) in a hurry, hastily. *Perkataan ~ diutjapkannja*, The words came tumbling out of his mouth.

gumal 1 wrinkled, creased (of cloth). 2 rumpled, crumpled (of paper). **meng-** to crumple.

gumala see GEMALA.

gumam held back, suppressed (laugh or smile). **ber-** to mutter under o's breath. **meng-** 1 to mutter. *Ia ~ beberapa perkataan*, He muttered a few words. 2 to suppress. *~ gelaknja* to suppress o's laughter.

gumpal clod, clump (of earth, clay, etc.). **ber-(‑)** in clods. **meng-(kan)** 1 to crumble. *Dgn tjangkulnja ia ~ tanah itu*, With his hoe he crumbled the soil. 2 to lump. *Ia ~ tanah liat*

mendjadi bulatan, He lumped some clay into a ball. **-an** clod, clump.

gumul ber- to wrestle. **per-an** wrestling.

guna 1 use. *Karét banjak ~nja*, Rubber has many uses. 2 purpose. *Tiap² mesin ada ~nja sendiri²*, Each machine has its own purpose. 3 for. *- kepentingan anaknja* for the sake of his son. *- nusa dan bangsa* for country and nation. 4 in order to. **ber-** useful. **ke-an** usefulness. **memper-kan, meng-kan** 1 to use, utilize. 2 to make use of, resort to. **peng-an, per-an** utilization, use, application. *‑²* black magic, voodoo. *Tak ada ~nja*, It's no use. *- apa?* What for?

gunawan virtuous, noble.

gundah depressed, anxious, restless. *Hatinja ‑*, He was depressed. **ke-an** depression, anxiety. **meng-kan** to depress. *Kematian temannja ~ dia*, His friend's death depressed him. *- gulana* depressed and melancholic.

gundal 1 notch (in wood), knot (in string) as an indicator. 2 follower, accomplice, assistant.

gundik concubine. **memper-kan** to take as a concubine. *Ia ~ perempuan itu*, He took the woman as a concubine, as a mistress. **per-an** concubinage, polygamy.

gundjai tassel, tuft.

gundjing slander. **memper-(kan)** to slander s.o.

gundu(k) 1 k.o. nut. 2 marble. **ber-** to play marbles.

gundukan 1 heap, pile. 2 hillock. 3 group.

gundul 1 bald-headed. *Kepalanja ‑*, His head was bald. 2 bare. *Tanah itu - tak bertanaman*, The land was bare and without vegetation. **meng-i** 1 to shave bald. *Tukang tjukur ~ adik saja*, The barber shaved my brother bald. 2 to scalp. *PSMS ~ Palémbang 5-0*, PSMS scalped (blanked) Palembang 5 to 0. *Pendjudian ~nja*, Gambling stripped him of everything.

gung gong. *- pelaung* gong for calling people to work, etc.

guni gunny sack, jute.

guntak a rattling.

gunting scissors. **meng-** to cut with scissors. *Tukang tjukur ~ rambut saja*, The barber cut my hair. *~ pagar* to clip, trim a hedge. *~ pakaian* to cut out a dress. **peng-an** cutting, snipping. *~ pita* snipping of a ribbon. *~ uang* monetary measure (by cutting banknotes in half). **-an** 1 cut. *Badju itu bagus ~nja*, The dress had a nice cut. 2 clipping. *~ surat kabar*

newspaper clippings. - *pagar* hedge clippers. - *rambut* haircut. *Saja mesti - rambut*, I need a haircut.
guntjang see GONTJANG.
guntung 1 blunt. 2 short. *badju* - short-sleeved shirt. *tjelana* - shorts.
guntur thunder. **meng-** 1 to thunder. 2 to boom. *Suaranja* ~ *mengisi seluruh ruangan*, His voice boomed filling the whole room.
gunung mountain. **ber-, ber-** -² mountainous. *Daérah itu* ~ , That region is mountainous. **ber-** *api* volcanic. **meng-** to become mountainous. **pe-an** mountain range, mountains. -²**an** 1 piles, heaps. ~ *kotoran* piles of dirt. 2 hill, butte - (*ber*)*api* volcano. - *sulah* a bare (deforested) mountain.
gupuh see GOPOH.
gurah ber- to rinse o's mouth. **meng-** to rinse s.t. ~ *botol* to rinse out a bottle.
guram dull, dim.
gurami fresh-water fish.
gurat a scratch, line. **meng-(kan)** to scratch, make lines. **-an** s.t. underlined. - *batu* obstinate, implacable.
gurau ber- to joke. *Meréka* ~ *dan ter-tawa²*, They joked and laughed. **memper-kan, meng-kan** 1 to joke about s.t. *Djangan* ~ *hal² keigamaan*, Don't joke about religious matters. 2 to ridicule. (**per**)-**an** joking, jest. *Orang itu penuh* ~ , He is full of jokes.
gurdi drill, auger. **meng-** to drill, bore.
gurem see GURAM.
guri earthen pot.
gurih tasty.
gurima peng- fall, disappearance.
gurinda see GERINDA.

gurindam old saying, aphorism, a two-line verse. **ber-** to recite a 2-line verse.
guris see GORÉS.
gurita 1 octopus. 2 baby garment covering chest and abdomen.
guru teacher. **ber-** 1 to be a student of. *Saja* ~ *pd - besar jg termasjhur itu*, I was a student of that famous professor. 2 to be a teacher. **ke-** -²**an** pedantic. **meng-i** to lecture s.o. **per-an** 1 education. 2 school. ~ *déwasa* adult education. ~ *menengah* secondary school. ~ *rakjat* institute of mass education. ~ *rendah* elementary school. ~ *tinggi* college. - *bantu* assistant teacher, substitute teacher. - *besar* professor. - *désa* village school teacher. - *kepala* head master, principal. - *indjil* preacher, evangelist. - *mengadjil* teacher of Koranic reading. - *puteri* woman teacher.
guruh thunder. **ber-, meng-** to thunder. *Meriam²* ~ , The cannons thundered. - *gemuruh* thundering.
gurun waste land. - *pasir* desert. - *Sahara* Sahara Desert.
gusar angry. *Ia - karena uangnja hilang*, He was angry because he lost his money. **ke-an** anger. **meng-i** to be angry with. *Ia* ~ *saja*, He is angry with me. **meng-kan** to anger. *Kemalasannja* ~ *saja*, His laziness made me mad.
gusi gum(s).
gusti 1 milord, highness. *Saja, -!* Yes, Milord. 2 aristocratic title. **ber-** to wrestle.
gusur to drag, haul.
gutik meng- to touch with the tip of o's fingers.
gutji jar. - *wasiat* a secret.

H

H. [*Hadji*] o. who has made the pilgrimage to Mecca.
ha [*héktar*] hectare.
habib God's friend (honorific for Arabs in Indonesia).
habis 1 finished. *Uang saja sdh -*, My money is all gone. (I have spent all my money. I have no money left.) 2 completely, entirely. *Rumahnja - terbakar*, His house burned down

completely. 3 over. *Pertundjukan sdh -*, The show is over. 4 completed. *Pendidikannja sdh -*, His education is completed. 5 afterward. *Kita makan - itu kita pergi kegambar hidup*, We ate; afterward we went to the movie. 6 how could I. *Mengapa kamu tidak datang? -, saja tidak diundang*, Why didn't you come? How could I, I wasn't invited. (**ber**)-²**an** to the

very end. *Rumahnja terbakar* ~ ,
His house was completely wiped out
by fire. **ke–an** 1 no more left. *Ia*
~ *uang,* He had no more money left.
Ia ~ *makanan ketika ia datang
dirumah,* There was no more food
left when he came home. 2 to be
left out. *Lekas pesan; djangan* ~ ,
Order right away; don't be left out.
~ *akal* to be at the end of o's wits.
meng– -bukukan to close out o's
books (in bookkeeping). **meng–i** 1
to end, finish. ~ *pidato* to finish a
speech. 2 to wipe out, exterminate,
finish off. *Diktator itu* ~ *semua
musuhnja,* The dictator wiped out all
his enemies. **meng–kan** 1 to finish.
Ia ~ *tjeritanja,* He finished his story.
2 to use up, exhaust. *Ia* ~ *uangnja,*
He used up his money. **peng–an** 1
last. *Siapa jg datang* ~ *disini?* Who
came here last? 2 end. ~ *tjerita itu
menggembirakan,* The story had a
happy ending. ~*nja* finally. *Apakah
jg terdjadi* ~*nja?* What happened
finally? **se–** after. ~ *kita makan kita
pergi,* After we ate we went out. **se–
-²nja** to the utmost. *Ia bekerdja*
~ , He worked as hard as he could.
–²an completely, fully. *Ia* ~ *memukuli
anaknja,* He beats his child very
severely. – *akal* at o's wit's end. –
bulan end of the month. *Pd – bulan
banjak orang berbelandja,* At the end
of the month many people go shopping. – *tenaga* exhausted. *Ia – tenaganja sesudah bekerdja begitu kerasnja,*
He was exhausted after working so
hard. *tak –²*(**nja**) endless(ly). *Ia
berbitjara tak* ~ , He talked on endlessly. – *perkara,* That's final. *Saja
tak mau memberi izin, – perkara!*
I won't give my permission, and that's
final!

hablur crystal. **meng–** to crystallize.
Tjairan itu ~ , The liquid crystal-
lized. **meng–kan** to make s.t. crystallize.

Habsji 1 Ethiopia. 2 Ethiopian.

had boundary.

hadang see ADANG.

hadap 1 front. – *rumah ada pohon,*
There's a tree in front of the house.
2 side. *satu –* one-sided, prejudiced.
unilateral (of a contract, agreement).
ber–an 1 to face. *Rumah saja* ~
dgn gerédja, My house faces a church.
2 to face, be faced with. *Ia* ~ *dgn
banjak kesukaran,* He's faced with a
number of difficulties. **ber– -²** to face
e.o. *Rumah saja dan rumahnja* ~ ,
His house and mine face e.o. **di–**
in front of. ~ *saja ada orang berdiri,*
A man was standing in front of me.

di–an next, the coming. *Minggu* ~
saja akan pergi ke Surabaja, Next
week I'm going to Surabaya. **ke–an** to
(used in correspondence). **memper-
kan** to confront s.o. *Hakim* ~ *orang
jg mengadu dgn jg tertuduh,* The judge
confronted the accuser with the accused. **meng–** 1 to face, look out on.
Rumah kami ~ *laut,* Our house faced
the sea. 2 to have an interview (talk,
audience) with s.o. 3 to call on, pay
o's respects to. *Duta besar itu* ~
présidén, The ambassador called on
the president. 4 to report. *Pradjurit
itu* ~ *kpd opsirnja,* The soldier reported to his commanding officer.
meng–i 1 to face, be up against.
Meréka ~ *banjak rintangan,* They
face many difficulties. 2 to sit at.
Ia ~ *sebuah médja tulis,* He sits at
a desk. 3 to attend. *Ia tak dpt* ~
pertemuan itu, He couldn't attend the
meeting. **meng–kan** 1 to aim s.t. *Ia*
~ *meriam itu kearah kapal musuh,*
He aimed the gun at an enemy ship.
2 to present s.o. *Pahlawan itu di–kan
kpd présidén,* The hero was presented to the president. 3 to focus.
Ia tidak dpt ~ *perhatiannja kpd
pekerdjaannja itu,* He was unable to
focus his attention on his job. 4 to
bring s.t. up. *Ia* ~ *hal itu dlm rapat,*
He brought the matter up in the
meeting. **peng–** a party to a case or
contract. **peng–an** audience hall, reception hall. **ter–** 1 about, concerning. *Ia tak peduli* ~ *tjelaan itu,* He
didn't care about the criticism. 2
toward. 3 against. **–an** front. – *...kiri!*
Left...face!

hadas ritual impurity (in Islam).

hadat council.

hadiah 1 prize. 2 reward. 3 gift,
present. **ber–** to give presents. *Pd
Hari Natal seluruh keluarga saling*
~ , On Christmas the whole family
gives presents to e.o. **meng–i** to reward, present. *Radja* ~ *abdinja jg
setia itu,* The king rewarded his
faithful servant. **meng–kan** 1 to reward s.t. *Ia* ~ *uang kpd penangkap
pembunuh itu,* He rewarded the
captor of the murderer with money.
2 to present with, make a gift of s.t.
Ia ~ *djam tangan kpd anaknja,* He
presented his son with a wrist watch.
– *kerdja* bonus. – *Lebaran* bonus on
day ending the fasting period. –
penghibur(**an**) consolation prize.

hadir to be present. *Rapat dpt di-
mulai; semuanja sdh –,* The meeting
can start; everyone is present. **ke–an**
presence, attendance. **meng–i** to attend. *Perdana menteri* ~ *rapat par-*

lemén, The prime minister attended the parliamentary session.
hadirat to (honorific form). *Ke-Paduka jg Mulia Présidén* To His Excellency, the President.
hadirin those present, audience. – *berdiri dan bertepuk tangan*, The audience stood and applauded. *Para – jg terhormat!* Ladies and gentlemen!
Hadis 1 Moslem traditions. 2 record of actions or sayings of the Prophet.
hadj pilgrimage to Mecca.
hadjar meng– to beat up (s.o.). *Kalau hal itu terdjadi lagi kau akan ku–*, If that happens again I'll give you a sound thrashing.
hadjat a wish, desire. **ber–** 1 to intend. *Dia ~ hendak pergi ke Éropah*, He intends to go to Europe. 2 to need, require. **meng–kan** to need, require. *Barang² itu di–kan benar disini*, Those things are very much needed here.
hadji o. who has made the pilgrimage to Mecca.
hadlir see HADIR.
hadlirat see HADIRAT.
hadlirin see HADIRIN.
hadrah 1 congregational service by mystics with dances, chanting, and beating of drums. 2 see HADIRAT.
hafal see APAL.
hai 1 hi!. *Ia berkata "Hai!" ketika kami bertemu*, He said "Hi!" when we met. 2 I say!
haibat see HÉBAT.
haid menstruation.
hairan see HÉRAN.
haiwan see HÉWAN.
hajal see CHAJAL.
hajali see CHAJALI.
hajat life.
hak 1 right. *Kemerdékaan adalah – tiap² bangsa*, Freedom is the right of all nations. 2 competence, qualification, right. *Deradjatnja itu memberikan dia – utk mengadjar pd sekolah menenyah*, His degree gave him the qualifications to teach at a secondary school. 3 rightful property. *Djangan mengambil apa jg bukan –mu* Don't take what is not your rightful property. 4 truth, right (as opposed to wrong). 5 heel (of shoe). **ber–** 1 to have the right to. *Présidén ~ menundjuk dan memetjat menteri*, The president has the right to appoint and to dismiss ministers. 2 to reserve the right. *Rédaksi ~ menjingkat karangan mana perlu*, The editors reserve the right to shorten an article where necessary. ~ *atas* to have the right to s.t. *Saja ~ atas separuh daripada peninggalan bapak saja*, I

have the right to half of my father's estate. **meng–kan** to give the right to. *Undang² Dasar ~ présidén menjatakan perang*, The constitution gives the president the right to declare war. *al –* the Truth. *Tuhan al –* God the Righteous One. *– bersuara* suffrage. *– kuasa bapak* patriarchate. *– kuasa ibu* matriarchate. *– memilih* the franchise. *– milik* proprietary rights. *– mutlak* absolute rights. *– penerbit* copyright (of publisher). *– pengarang, – tjipta* copyright. *– pilih* the franchise. *– purba* basic right. *– undur diri* the right to refuse to answer. *– wilajah* the right to dispose of land.
hakékat 1 truth, reality. 2 essence. 3 significance. *pd –nja* really, essentially, actually, in fact.
hakiki true, real. *pd –nja* actually, in fact.
hakim judge. **ber–** to seek justice. *Ia ~ kpd radja*, He sought justice from the king. **ke–an** 1 justice. *Kementerian ~* Ministry of Justice. 2 judicature. 3 judiciary. 4 legal. **meng–i** to pass judgment. *– ~ perkara itu*, The judge passed judgment on the case.
hal. [*halaman*] page.
hal 1 matter. *Ia memperbintjangkan – itu*, He discussed the matter. 2 case. 3 fact. *– itu membuktikan bhw...* That (fact) proved that... 4 point. *–nja ialah bhw...* The point was that... 5 thing. *Itulah – jg terpenting*, That was the most important thing. 6 situation. 7 concerning. *pidato – gerakan pembrontakan* a speech concerning the rebellion. *Bagaimana –nja dgn dia?* How are things with him? **ber–** to be engaged in a situation and prevented from doing s.t. else. **ter–** see BER–. *dlm – itu* in that case. *pd –* while, even though. *Hidupnja sangat sederhana, pd – uangnja banjak*, He lived very simply, though he was quite well off. *– apa* what. *– ihwal* 1 events, circumstances. 2 particulars. *– kewirjaan* heroism, bravery. *lain –nja apabila* it would be different if. *– mana* which. *dari –* as regards. *ada sesuatu –* there is s.t. *dgn – jg demikian itu* thus, therefore, for that matter. *– demikian itu mengakibatkan...* This resulted in...
hala direction. **ber–** in the direction of. **meng–kan** to direct, guide.
halai-balai 1 ignored, neglected. 2 in confusion.
halal 1 allowed. *Bagi orang Muslim daging sapi adalah –*, To Moslems, eating beef is allowed. 2 rightful. *Uang ini saja peroléh dgn djalan –*,

I got this money by rightful means. **meng–kan** to allow. *Agamanja ~ dia memakan daging sapi*, His religion allowed him to eat beef. *~ hutang* to remit a debt. *- -bi(1)-* to forgive e.o. on the day following the end of the fasting month of Ramadan whatever wrong each has done the other.

halaman 1 yard. 2 premises. 3 page. *- muka* 1 front page. 2 front yard. *- nama buku* title page. *- rumah* yard of house. *- rumput* lawn. *- sekolah* schoolyard.

halang meng–(–)i 1 to block, obstruct. *Pohon tumbang itu ~ lalu lintas*, The fallen tree blocked traffic. 2 to prevent. *Ia ~ saja memukul adik saja*, He prevented me from hitting my little brother. *–an* obstacle.

halat traditional ceremony. **ber–** to hold a traditional ceremony. *Ia ~ merajakan perkawinan anaknja*, He held a traditional ceremony to celebrate his daughter's wedding.

halau meng– 1 to chase (away). *Ia ~ andjing itu dari kamarnja*, He chased the dog from his room. 2 to drive. *Ia ~ sapi²nja kepasar*, He drove his cattle to the market. **peng–** driver. *~ sapi* cattle driver. *~ njamuk* mosquito repellent.

halia ginger.

halilintar 1 flash of lightning. 2 thunderbolt.

halimbubu whirlwind.

halimun mist, fog.

halintar see HALILINTAR.

halipan see LIPAN.

halte stopping place. *- bis* bus stop. *- keréta api* train stop, station.

halter dumbbell, bar bell.

haluan 1 bow (of a ship). 2 direction. *Kapal itu belajar ke– timur*, The boat sailed in an eastwardly direction. 3 course. *Kapal itu berganti –*, The boat changed its course. *Partai itu mengikuti – kiri*, The party followed a leftist course. **ber–** to follow a course. *Partai itu ~ liberal*, The party followed a liberal course. *~ sama tengah* impartial, neutral. **meng–kan** to guide, direct. **se–** to follow the same course. *Kedua partai itu ~* , The two parties are following the same course. *- hidup* life's aim. *Ia kehilangan – hidupnja*, He has lost his aim in life. *- kata* foreword, preface.

halus 1 refined, sensitive, cultured. *Bahasanja –*, His language is refined. 2 soft, delicate. *Kulitnja –*, Her skin is soft. 3 gentle, refined. *perintah – gentle hint (from above, the government, etc.). **ke–an** 1 refinement, breed-

ing. 2 gentleness. **memper–** to refine. **meng–i** 1 to cheat, deceive. 2 to treat gently. **meng–kan** to refine. *~ sawah* to cultivate a wet rice field.

halwa fruits preserved in sugar. *- belanda* chocolate bar.

hama plant disease. *- penjakit* germ (of a disease). *- sundep* rice pest. *- tanaman* plant pest. *- tikus* scourge of mice (destroying field crops).

hamba 1 servant, slave. *Ia memperlakukan –nja dgn kedjam*, He treated his servant cruelly. 2 I. *- minta maaf, tuan*, I beg your pardon, Sir. 3 humble. 4 yes. *–, Tuanku*, Yes, Milord. **ber–** to become a servant. *Ia ~ pd radja itu*, He became a servant to the king. **ke–an** humility, humbleness. **memper–kan, meng–kan** to enslave. *Meréka ~ penduduk asli negara itu*, They enslaved the natives of that country. **meng–** to serve. *Ia ~ nusa dan bangsa*, He served his country and nation. **peng–an, per–an** slavery, serfdom. *- Allah* human being. *Kita semuanja adalah - Allah*, We are all human beings. *- hukum* law enforcers, police. *- negara* servant of the state. *- radja* court attendant. *- sahaja* slave. *jg diper–* your servant. *Jg diper–, Tuanku*, Your servant, Milord.

hambar tasteless, flat. *Masakannja itu - rasanja*, Her cooking is tasteless.

hambat stop (phon.) *- glotal* glottal stop. **meng–** 1 to hamper. *Kerusakan mesin ~ perdjalanannja*, Engine trouble hampered his trip. 2 to slow down. *Débat jg ramai ~ djalannja rapat*, Noisy debates slowed down the meeting. 3 to pursue. **peng–** 1 obstructor. 2 pursuer. *faktor ~* inhibiting factor. **ter–** 1 hampered. 2 slowed down. *–an* 1 obstacle, obstruction. 2 delay.

hambur to scatter. **ber–(an)** scattered, dispersed. *Uangnja ~ dilantai*, His money was scattered on the floor. **meng–** 1 to scatter, throw. 2 to jump (into the water). *Ia ~ kedalam air*, He jumped into the water. *Matjan ~ kuda*, A tiger leaped at a horse. **meng–i** to throw o.s. into, fill up. *Semua orang ~ lobang perlindungan*, All the people filled up the shelter. **meng–kan** 1 to scatter, to throw s.t. *~ djala* to cast a net. *~ uang* to throw money away, spend recklessly. *~ air mata* to shed tears. 2 to evade, escape from, ward off. *~ pukulan musuh* to ward off the enemy's blows. *~ diri dari djendéla* to throw o.s. from the window.

hambus see EMBUS.

hamil pregnant. **meng–kan** to impregnate, make pregnant. **peng–an** 1 pregnancy, conception. 2 impregnation.

haminte municipality.

hamis see AMIS.

hampa 1 empty. *Perkataannja itu – belaka*, His words were simply nonsense. 2 ineffective, futile. **ber–** *tangan* empty-handed. **ke–an** 1 emptiness. 2 vacuum. 3 futility. **meng–kan** to empty s.t. – *udara* vacuum. *dgn tangan –* empty-handed.

hampai meng– to spread out. *– sajap* to rely on.

hampar meng–i to cover. *Ia ~ lantai itu dgn permadani*, He covered the floor with a carpet. **meng–kan** 1 to spread. *Ia ~ permadani itu diatas lantai*, He spread the carpet over the floor. 2 to explain. *Ia ~ perkara itu pd saja*, He explained the case to me. **ter–** spread. **–an** rug, carpet.

hampedu see EMPEDU.

hampir 1 close, near. *Ia duduk – dgn saja*, He sat close to me. *Hari Natal sdh –*, Christmas is near. 2 almost. *Saja – terlambat*, I was almost too late. 3 close to. *– satu abad* close to a century. **ber–an** to be near. *Rumah saja ~ dgn sekolah saja*, My house is near my school. **meng–i** to approach. *Ia ~ saja*, He approached me. **meng–kan** to move s.t. closer. *Ia ~ gelas itu padanja*, He moved the glass closer to him. **peng–an** approach. **–an** vicinity, neighbor.

hamud acid.

hamuk see AMUK.

hana empty, deserted.

handai 1 friend. 2 companion. *– taulan* friends.

handam see ANDAM.

handuk see ANDUK.

hang title for men in Hindu-Indonesian history.

hangat 1 hot. *Kabar ini –*, This is hot news. *Pikirannja – ketika ia di-maki² bapaknja*, He became hot under the collar when his father scolded him. 2 warm, cordial. *Ia diterima dgn –*, He was warmly received. 3 lukewarm. *Air itu tidak panas lagi, tetapi masih –*, The water is not hot any more but it is still lukewarm. 4 critical, acute. **ke–an** 1 heat, tenseness. *~ suasana politik* the tense political situation. *Dlm ~ kemarahannja itu ia meng-umpat²*, In the heat of his anger he cursed. 2 warmth. **meng–** to become hot, critical. *Suasana politik makin ~ ,* The political situation became more and more critical. **meng–i** 1 to warm

up. 2 to incite. **meng–kan** 1 to make hot. *Pertentangan kedua partai itu ~ suasana politik*, The animosity between the two parties heated the political atmosphere. 2 to warm up, warm over. *Ibu ~ makanan saja*, Mother warmed up my food.

hanget see HANGAT.

hanggar 1 see ANGGAR. 2 hangar.

hangit burnt smell.

hangus see ANGUS.

hanja only. *Saja – mempunjai lima rupiah*, I have only five rupiahs. *–... sadja* only, just.

hanjir see ANJIR.

hanjut 1 washed away. *Pohon itu – disungai*, A tree was washed away in the river. 2 to wander. *Ia – kenegeri asing*, He traveled to foreign countries. **ber– –²** to drift. *Meréka ~ disungai itu*, They drifted down the river. **meng–kan** to wash away. *Bandjir itu ~ banjak ternak*, The flood washed away many cattle. **peng–an** washing away. *~ tanah* soil erosion.

hansop a short-sleeved, short-legged coverall type of child's garment.

hantam 1 to crush. 2 stroke, blow. *Ia kena – saja*, I hit him. **ber–** to fight. *Meréka ~ ,* They came to blows. **meng–** to hit hard. *Ia ~ saja*, He hit me hard. *Kapal terbang ~ armada musuh*, Planes struck the enemy's fleet a severe blow. **meng–kan** to strike with. *Ia ~ kepalanja itu*, He struck his head with his fist. **–an** = HANTAM. *– kromo* to do s.t. without thinking. *Hati²lah melakukan pekerdjaan itu, djangan – kromo sadja*, Be careful in doing that task; don't just do it without thinking (don't go about it indiscriminately).

hantar see ANTAR. **ber–an** to be lying around. *majat ~* dead bodies lying all over the place. **meng–kan** 1 to bring. *Ia ~ buku itu pd saja*, He brought the book to me. 2 to see off. *Ia ~ temannja kestasion*, He saw his friend off to the station. 3 to strike down. *Gegaran granat jg meledak ~ pradjurit musuh*, The concussion of the exploding grenade struck down the enemy soldiers. **peng–** see PENGANTAR. **ter–** neglected. *Bukunja sdh lama ~ sadja*, His books have been neglected for a long time.

hantjing disagreeable odor (of urine, spoilt vinegar, etc.).

hantjur 1 shattered. *Gelas itu – sama sekali*, The glass was completely shattered. 2 dissolved. *Gula itu – dlm air*, The sugar was dissolved in the water. **ke–an** 1 destruction. 2 crash. **meng–kan** 1 to smash. *Meréka*

~ *gedung itu*, They smashed the building. 2 to dissolve. *Ia* ~ *gula dlm air*, He dissolved the sugar in water. **meng-leburkan** to crush, pulverize. **meng-luluhkan** to shatter, smash. **peng-** crusher. ~ *batu* stone crusher. **peng-an** 1 smashing. 2 dissolving. **-an** 1 debris. 2 solution. **-** *hati* crushed. **-** *hatinja mendengar isterinja tlh meninggal*, He was deeply grieved upon hearing that his wife had died. **-** *lebur*, **-** *luluh* smashed, shattered, dissolved. **-** *rembas* completely destroyed.

hantu ghost, evil spirit. **ber-** haunted. *Rumah itu* ~ , That is a haunted house. **meng-i** to haunt, obsess. *Ketakutan* ~ *pikirannja*, Fear haunted his mind. **-** *kapan* ghost. **-** *rimba* spirit of the woods, jungle spirit.

hapal see APAL. **ke-an** memorization.

hapus to expire. **meng-** to wipe off, away, to clean. *Ia* ~ *papan tulis*, He wiped off the blackboard. **meng-kan** 1 to wipe out. *Satu bom atom dpt* ~ *sebuah kota seluruhnja*, One atomic bomb can wipe out an entire city. 2 to remit, wipe out. *Ia* ~ *segala hutang saja padanja*, He remitted all my debts to him. 3 to abolish. *Meréka* ~ *perbudakan*, They abolished slavery. 4 to nullify. *Perbuatannja itu* ~ *perdjandjian kita*, That act nullified our contract. **peng-** 1 wiper. 2 mop. **peng-an** 1 wiping out. 2 remission. 3 abolition. 4 nullification, abrogation. **ter-** 1 wiped out. 2 remitted. 3 abolished. 4 nullified.

harafiah see HARFIAH.

haram 1 prohibited, forbidden by Islam. *Daging babi* **-** *bagi orang Islam*, Pork is prohibited to Moslems. 2 sacred. *Tanah* **-** *ini tak boléh diindjak kaki kafir*, This sacred soil may not be trodden by unbelievers. **meng-kan** to forbid, prohibit. 1 *Agama Islam* ~ *makan daging babi*, The Moslem religion forbids the eating of pork. 2 to abstain from. *Ia* ~ *minum rokok*, He abstained from smoking once and for all. *Selama mendjalankan tugas minum air keras di-kan*, The consumption of liquor while on duty is expressly prohibited. **-** *zadah* bastard.

harap please. **-** *lekas datang kekantor saja*, Please come to my office right away. **-** *maklum*, Please take note. **ber-** 1 to hope. *Kami* ~ *engkau akan lekas sembuh*, We hope you will get well soon. 2 to expect. *Kami* ~ *engkau akan kembali*, We expect you to come back. **ber-an** 1 to hope. *Kami tetap* ~ *bhw semuanja akan*

bérés, We surely hope that everything will be all right. 2 to expect. *Saja* ~ *engkau akan bekerdja se-keras²nja*, I expect you will work as hard as possible. **ber-kan** to hope for. **memper-kan** to cherish (idle) hopes. *Ber-tahun²* *ia* ~ *kedatangan anaknja dari peperangan*, For years she has been cherishing the hope that her son will return from the war. **meng-(kan)** 1 to hope for. *Petani²* ~ *hudjan*, The farmers are hoping for rain. 2 to expect. *Kami* ~ *kehadiran présidén pd rapat kami*, We expect the president to be present at our meeting. 3 to count on. *Djangan* ~ *pertolongan orang lain*, Don't count on the help of other people. 4 nearing, with the approach of. ~ *Hari Natal banjak orang berbelandja*, Come Christmastime many people go shopping. **peng-an** 1 hope. 2 expectation. 3 reliance. ~ *pertolongan orang lain* reliance on the help of others. **ter-** **-²** eagerly awaited. *Achirnja hari jg tlh lama* ~ *itu datang*, At last the long-awaited day arrived. **-an** 1 expectation. 2 hope. ~ *tipis* little hope. 3 chance. *Tiada* ~ , There's no chance. 4 favorite. *dgn bintang²* ~ *Anda* with your favorite movie stars. **-²** *tjemas* with fear and hope. ~ *tjemas dibukanja surat itu*, With fear and hope he opened the letter.

hardik acrimonious, tart, sharp (reply, words). **meng-** to scold. *Bapak* ~ *saja*, Father scolded me. **-an** scolding.

harfiah 1 literal, word for word. 2 verbal.

harga 1 price, cost. *Berapakah* **-** *djam itu?* How much is that watch? (How much does that watch cost?) 2 value. **ber-** 1 to be priced at cost. 2 valuable. *Buku² itu* ~ , Those books are valuable. **meng-i**, **meng-kan** 1 to appraise. *Djauhari itu* ~ *intan itu*, The jeweler appraised the diamond. 2 to appreciate, esteem. *Kita sangat* ~ *pertolonganmu*, We appreciate your help very much. **peng-an** 1 appreciation. 2 respect. ~ *saja bagimu sangat besar*, My respect for you is very great. 3 valuation. ~ *intan itu terlalu rendah*, The valuation of the diamond is too low. **se-** 1 to be the same price. *Kedua tjintjin itu* ~ , The 2 rings are the same price. 2 in the amount of. *barang²* ~ *100 rupiah* goods in the amount of 100 rupiahs. *tidak* **ter-** invaluable, priceless. **-** *baku* standard price. **-** *banderol* fixed price as indicated on the revenue stamp. **-** *bantingan* bargain price. **-** *bébas* free market price. – *beli(an)* purchase price. – *borongan* 1 wholesale price. 2 price contracted for. – *diri* self-esteem. – *djual* sale price. – *étjéran* retail price. – *EZ* [*Economische Zaken*] official price. – *gelap* black market price. – *imbangan* counter value. – *langganan* subscription fee. – *luar(an)* free market price. – *mati* fixed price. *Ini – mati tidak boléh tawar*, This is a fixed price; you are not permitted to bargain. – *paku* fixed price. – *pantas* reasonable price. – *pasar(an)* retail price. – *pasti* fixed price. – *pokok* cost price. – *resmi* official price. – *rintjih* retail price. – *satuan* unit price. – *tetap* fixed price. – *uang* rate of exchange.

hari day. **ber-** –²(an) day after day. **se-** *suntuk* the whole day. **se-** –² every day. *Apakah kerdjamu* ∼ *?* What do you do every day? **se-** –²an all day long. *Ia ber-main² sadja* ∼ , He just plays all day long. **-an** daily (newspaper). *Kita berlangganan* ∼ *Pedoman*, We subscribe to the daily *Pedoman*. ∼ *fadjar* morning paper. – *Ahad* Sunday. – *Arba* Wednesday. – *atjara* session (of court). – *baik* feast day. – *batal* expiration date. – *berlakunja* date of validity. – *besar* holiday. – *bulan* date. – *bulan apa?* What's the date? – *buruk* foul weather. – *depan* later on, (in the) future. *Mudah²an di– depan tak ada perang lagi*, Let's hope that in the future there will be no more wars. – *din* doomsday. – *gelap* dark, gloomy day. – *hudjan* rainy day. *Djangan pergi*, – *hudjan*, Don't go, it's raining. – *kebangkitan* Easter. – *kebangsaan* national day. – *(ke)djadi(an)* Christmas. – *kemerdékaan* independence day. – *kemudian* later on, in the future. – *kiamat* doomsday. – *lahir* birthday. – *libur* holiday. – *mahsjar* doomsday, resurrection. – *natal* 1 Christmas, 2 birthday. – *pahlawan* memorial day. – *peringatan* anniversary. – *raja*, – *raya* holiday. – *sabak* cloudy day. – *sardjana* graduation day. – *témpo* holiday. – *tjerah* 1 a beautiful day. 2 in broad daylight. – *tua* old age. – *ulang tahun* birthday, anniversary, commemoration. – *wafat* day of death. – *sdh djauh malam*, It's late at night. – *sdh musim hudjan*, It's the rainy season now. – *terang bulan*, It's a moonlit night.

haribaan see RIBA.

harimau tiger. **meng-i** to intimidate by bullying or browbeating. – *belang* leopard. – *buluh* panther. – *kumbang* black panther.

harini = HARI INI today.

harkah see HARKAT. – *insani* human dignity.

harkat 1 level, standard. 2 rate, value. – *uang* rate of exchange. 3 dignity. *tak sesuai dgn* – *pangkatnja* not in keeping with the dignity of his official position.

harmonika harmonica.

harta wealth. *Segala –nja habis*, He lost all his wealth. **ber-** to be rich. – *bawaan* dowry. – *benda* wealth, riches, property. – *dunia* earthly riches. – *karun* 1 ownerless property, hidden treasure. 2 a fortune easily acquired. – *milik* property, possessions. – *pendapatan* dowry. – *pusaka* estate, inherited property. – *tetap* fixed, permanent property.

hartawan 1 wealthy. 2 a wealthy man.

haru ke-an emotion, feeling, sentiment. **keter-an** 1 emotion. 2 moved, touched. **meng-birukan** to start a commotion. **meng-kan** to move, touch s.o. *Tjeritanja* ∼ *hati saja*, I was moved by his story. **peng-** mischief-maker, troublemaker, agitator. **peng-an** commotion. **ter-** moved, touched. – *-biru*, – *-hara* commotion, uproar.

harum fragrant. *Bunga mawar itu –*, The rose is fragrant. **ke-an** 1 fragrance. 2 fame. **meng-i** 1 to perfume. 2 to burn incense. **meng-kan** 1 to make fragrant. *Bunga² itu* ∼ *udara*, The flowers made the air fragrant. 2 to make famous. *Keberaniannja* ∼ *namanja*, His courage made his name famous. – *namanja* famous.

harung see ARUNG.

harus to have to, must. *Saja – beladjar*, I have to study. **ke-an** necessity. **meng-kan** to compel. *Pemerintah* ∼ *semua warganegara utk bersekolah*, The government compelled all citizens to go to school. **se-nja** 1 proper. *Sdh* ∼ *kita menghormati orang tua*, It is proper that we respect our parents. 2 properly, should. *Saja akan tolong tuan, tetapi* ∼ *tuan pergi kekantor polisi dulu*, I will help you, but you should go to the police office first. – *sudah* should have. *Ia – sdh disini sebelum saja pergi*, He should have been here before I left.

hasad jealousy, envy.

hasil 1 yield, crop. 2 product. 3 result. *Apakah – perundingan?* What are the results of the negotiations? 4 success. 5 output. **ber-** to succeed. *Ia* ∼ *memperoléh gelar*, He succeeded in obtaining a degree. 2 successful. *Usahanja tak ada jg* ∼ , None of his attempts were successful.

meng–kan 1 to produce. *Indonésia* ∼ *karét,* Indonesia produces rubber. 2 to yield. *Sawah saja* ∼ *dua panén dlm setahun,* My rice field yields 2 crops a year. 3 to make successful. *Hanja saling mempertjajai akan* ∼ *perundingan itu,* Only mutual trust will made the negotiations successful. **peng–** producer. *salah satu* ∼ *karét jg terutama* one of the main rubber producers. **peng–an** 1 production. 2 yield. 3 income. ∼ *njata* real income. 4 proceeds, revenue. 5 output. – *alam* agricultural produce. – *bagi* quotient. – *bumi* agricultural produce. – *hutan* forest produce. – *kali* product (arith.). – *mahsul* products of a country. – *padi* rice harvest. – *panén* crops. – *utama* staple crop.

hasjiah 1 edge. 2 annotation.

hasrat desire. **ber–** to desire. *Ia* ∼ *mengelilingi dunia,* He desired to travel around the world **ke–an** longing. **meng–kan** to long for. *Bapak tlh lama* ∼ *mobil baru,* Father has been longing for a new car for a long time. – *hati* motivation.

hasta cubit. *Pandjang médja itu lima* –, The table is 5 cubits long. **meng–** to measure in cubits.

hasud jealous. see HASAD.

hasut see ASUT.

hati 1 heart. 2 mind. 3 liver. 4 interest. 5 attention. **ber–** *berdjantung* sensitive. **ber–** *mutu* to be at a loss, at the end of o's rope. **ber–** *rawan* to be melancholy. **ber–** *tungau* to be a coward. **ber–** *walang* to be anxious, worried. **ber– –²** to be careful, cautious. **ke– –²an** 1 care, caution. 2 attention. **memper–kan** to pay attention, note. *Per–kanlah!* Attention, please! (Please note!) **per–an** 1 interest. *Ia menaruh* ∼ *thd soal itu,* He showed interest in that problem. 2 attention. ∼ *!* Attention, please! **se–** united, unanimous. – *beku* unhappy feeling. – *berkarat* corrupted. – *buntu* afraid, uneasy. – *but²* (Ambon) timid, frightened. – *ketjil* 1 conscience. 2 inner voice. – *nurani* heart of hearts. – *sanubari* 1 feelings. 2 inner man. *Dlm* – *sanubari saja rasa...* Deep within me I feel... – *tangan* hollow of palm. *dlm* – to o's self. *Ia membatja dlm* –, He reads to himself. *dlm* – *ketjilnja* in his heart of hearts, deep down inside. *dari* – *ke*– from o. person to another. *Jg saja katakan itu adalah dari* – *ke*–, I am telling you this in all sincerity.

hatsil see HASIL.

hatta then, thereupon. – *kawinlah ia dgn puteri itu dan meréka hidup*

berbahagia se-lama²nja, Thereupon he married the princess and they lived happily ever after.

hatur see ATUR.

haus 1 thirsty. *Saja* – , I'm thirsty. *Saja* – *pengetahuan,* I am thirsty for knowledge. 2 thirst. **ke–an** 1 to be thirsty. *Saja* ∼ , I'm thirsty. 2 thirst. **meng–kan** 1 to make thirsty. *Perdjalanan itu sangat* ∼ *saja,* The trip made me very thirsty. 2 to thirst for. *Ia* ∼ *pengetahuan,* He thirsted for knowledge. – *darah* bloodthirsty.

hawa 1 air. 2 climate. *Indonésia –nja panas,* Indonesia has a hot climate. 3 weather. *–nja panas hari ini,* The weather's hot today. 4 Eve. *Adam dan* – *adalah manusia pertama,* Adam and Eve were the first humans. **meng–** to evaporate. *Minjak wangi itu* ∼ , The perfume evaporated. – *darat* continental climate. – *laut* marine climate. – *nafsu* passion. – *panas* tropical climate. *daérah – panas* the tropics.

hay tjiah pork and shrimps in soy sauce.

hb [*hari bulan*] date.

H.B. [*Hindia Belanda*] Dutch (East) Indies.

h.b.i. [*hari bulan ini*] this date.

hc [*honoris causa*] honorary. *Dr* – honorary doctor(ate).

héban meng– to throw, fling.

hébat 1 tremendous. 2 violent, exciting. 3 sensational. 4 dreadful. 5 swell, terrific. *Pilem ini* –, This film is terrific. **ke–an** 1 excitement, sensation. 2 violence. **memper–(kan)** to intensify, aggravate. **meng–** to grow worse. *Perang itu* ∼ , The war grew worse. **meng–kan** to intensify, aggravate. **–²an** on a very large scale.

héboh 1 fuss, sensation, stir. 2 excitement. 3 consternation. **ke–an** disturbance. *berita² ttg* ∼ *di kementerian itu* reports concerning disturbances at the ministry. **meng–kan** to cause an uproar, a commotion.

hédjrah see HIDJRAH.

héktar hectare.

héla meng– to drag, haul, pull. *Kuda itu* ∼ *sebuah keréta,* The horse pulled a carriage. ∼ *napas* to draw a breath. ∼ *surut* to draw back. *Ketika ia melihat saja ia* ∼ *surut ketakutan,* When he saw me he drew back in fear. **meng–kan** 1 to pull, drag. ∼ *kambing terikat dgn tali* to pull a goat by a rope. 2 to aim. ∼ *bedilnja* to aim o's rifle. **peng–an** 1 traction. 2 pulling. **–an** traction. ∼ *nafas* breath.

helai 1 sheet. *Ia membeli kertas se*–,

He bought a sheet of paper. 2 leaf. *seratus* – 100 leaves. 3 used with paper, cloth, etc. *sepuluh* – *serbét* 10 napkins. **–an** sheet (of paper, etc.).
helat 1 trick. 2 excuse, pretext. **meng–** to trick, fool s.o.
hém 1 shirt. 2 secret.
hémat 1 thrifty, economical. 2 opinion. *Pd – saja kita harus bekerdja lebih keras*, In my opinion we should work harder. **ber–** 1 to be thrifty. 2 to be of the opinion. **ke–an** thrift. **meng–kan** to be thrifty with. *Engkau harus ~ uangmu*, You should be thrifty with your money. **peng–an** 1 economizing. 2 economy.
hembalang meng–, ter– to tumble head over heels. *Ia djatuh ~* , He fell head over heels. **meng–kan** to fling s.t. away. *Ia ~ bedilnja*, He flung his gun away.
hembus see EMBUS.
hempang see EMPANG.
hempas see EMPAS.
hémpét see IMPIT.
hendak 1 to wish, will, be willing to. *Kita semua – akan penghasilan jg tetap, bukan?* We all want a steady income, don't we? *Saja – mobil seperti ia punja*, I'd like to have a car like his. *Saja berdjandji – mendjalankannja*, I promise I'll do it. 2 to intend, to be going to. *Ia – bitjara dgn gurunja*, He is going to talk to his teacher. **ber–** 1 to wish, desire. *Djika Tuhan ~ ...* The Lord willing... *Kau mémang ~ demikian, bukan?* That's what you want, isn't it? 2 to plan, hope. *Kami ~ tinggal seminggu di New York*, We plan to stay in New York a week. **berke–** to wish, intend to. *Ia ~ mengadakan pésta*, She intends to give a party. **ke–** 1 wish, desire, will. *Segala ~ anaknja dituruti*, He gave in to all his child's wishes. *Apakah ~mu sebetulnja?* What do you really want? *~nja akan mendjadi kaja menjesatkan dia*, His desire to become rich made him go wrong. 2 intention. *Menipumu, itulah ~nja!* To cheat you, that's his intention! *atas ~ sendiri* on his own initiative. **meng–i** 1 to wish for, want, desire. *Sedjak ia masih ketjil ia ~ mengelilingi dunia*, Since childhood he's wanted to travel around the world. *Bapak ~ supaja kau mendjadi tabib*, Father wanted you to become a physician. 2 to require, demand. *Soal ini ~ penjelidikan jg teliti*, This problem requires careful investigation. *~ urat lesung* to try to get blood out of a turnip. **–lah** 1 please. *~ dikirim dgn segera*, Please send it

immediately. 2 is requested. *~ diperhatikan baik² bhw...* It is hoped that careful attention will be given to the fact that... *Supaja mendapat tempat duduk, kartu undangan ~ diperlihatkan*, In order to get a seat it is requested that an invitation be shown. 3 should. *~ dipertimbangkan lebih dahulu apakah...* Prior consideration should be given as to whether... **–nja** 1 it is desirable. *Orang jg bersangkutan ~ dipanggil*, It is desirable to summon the person concerned. *~ maklum*, Please take note. 2 let's. *~ kita tunggu dahulu*, Let's wait first. *~ djangan sampai terdjadi hal itu*, It's hoped that it won't happen. *~ dibatja lebih dulu*, (You'd) better read it first. *Kemana lagi ia pergi ~ ?* Where else could he have gone? *djangan ~ it is not to be hoped. *Djangan ~ ia tersesat didjalan*, Let's hope he didn't lose his way. *Djangan ~ kau berbuat demikian*, You'd better not do that. (I'd rather you didn't do it. Don't do it, will you? Don't do it, please.) **–pun** should like, want. *Bagaimana ~ membelinja saja tak mampu mengongkosinja*, Although I'd like to buy it, I can't afford it.
hendam karam wiped out, destroyed. *Kota jg kena bom atom itu –*, Hit by an atom bomb, the city was wiped out. *suka – hatinja* to o's heart's content.
hendap see ENDAP.
hening 1 clear. *Air telaga itu – ,* The water of the lake was clear. *Pikirannja –*, His mind was clear. 2 silent, quiet. *Malam –*, The night is quiet. 3 pure. *hati jg – a* pure heart. **ke–an** 1 clarity. *~ pikiran* clarity of thought. 2 quietness. *~ malam* the quietness of the night. 3 purity. *~ hatinja* the purity of his heart. **meng–kan** 1 to clear. *~ pikirannja* to clear o's mind. 2 to make quiet. *Kata² jg tenang itu ~ orang² dlm kamar itu*, His calm words made everybody in the room quiet. 3 to concentrate s.t. *~ tjipta* 1 to meditate. 2 to observe a moment's silence. *Meréka ~ tjipta*, They observed a moment of silence. **peng–an** concentration.
henjak see ENJAK.
hentak see ENTAK. **meng–kan** to stamp. *Ia ~ kakinja karena marah*, He stamped his foot in anger.
hentam meng– 1 to stamp o's foot. *Ia ~ kemarahan*, He stamped his foot in anger. 2 to hit, pound (mainly with o's feet). *Dgn sekuat tenaga ia ~ pintu*, He kicked the door as hard

as he could. ~ *médja dgn kepalan tangan* to pound the table with o's fist.
henti ber- to stop. *Mobil itu* ~ , The car stopped. *Meréka* ~ *bekerdja*, They stopped working. **ber–kan** to stop. ~ *lelah* to (take a) rest. **keber-an** 1 resignation (giving up a job, office, position). 2 discharge (from a job, office). **member–kan** to discharge, dismiss. **memper–kan, meng-kan** 1 to stop. *Polisi* ~ *mobil itu*, The police stopped the car. 2 to halt. *Ia* ~ *kemadjuan tentara musuh*, He halted the advance of the enemy army. 3 to discharge, fire. *Ia* ~ *pegawainja*, He discharged his employee. **pember–an** stopping. ~ *buruh* work stoppage. **pembrentian** 1 resignation. 2 discharge. **peng–an, per–an** stopping place. ~ *bis* bus stop. **ter-** 1 stopped. 2 halted.
héran 1 amazed. 2 puzzled, stumped. *Ia – melihat saja*, He was surprised to see me. **ke–an** 1 amazed. 2 amazement. *Ia ternganga mulutnja dlm* ~ , His mouth gaped in amazement. **ke– -²an** utterly amazed, dumfounded, baffled. **meng–i** 1 to surprise. 2 surprising. **meng–kan** amazing. *Kekuatannja sungguh* ~ , His strength is truly amazing.
héréng **meng–kan** to slant. *Ia* ~ *tiang itu*, He slanted the pole.
héwan 1 animal, beast. 2 livestock. **ke–an** 1 bestial. 2 pertaining to animals or cattle. *Fakultas* ~ faculty of veterinary science. – *bantai* beef cattle. – *menjusui* mammal.
héwani bestial. *Dgn nafsu – ia menjiksa tawanannja*, With bestial lust he tortured his prisoners.
hias decoration, adornment. **ber-** 1 to dress up. *Ia lagi* ~ *dlm kamarnja*, She is dressing in her room. 2 dressed up. *Mengapa engkau* ~ ? *Apakah akan ada tamu?* Why are you so dressed up? Will there be guests? 3 fancy. **ber–kan** adorned with. *Ia* ~ *kalung emas*, She was adorned with a golden necklace. **memper–i, meng–i** to decorate. *Murid² ~ kelas meréka*, The pupils decorated their classroom. **(per)–an** 1 decoration. ~ *gedung itu sangat indah*, The decorations in the building were very beautiful. 2 adornment, finery. *Ia membeli* ~ *bagi isterinja*, He bought finery for his wife.
hiba see IBA.
hibah grant. *Rumah piatu itu mendapat – dari sebuah jajasan*, The orphanage received a grant from a foundation. **meng–kan** to grant. *Jaja-*

san itu ~ *sedjumlah uang*, The foundation granted a sum of money.
hibuk see SIBUK.
hibur **meng-** 1 to entertain. *Para penari* ~ *tetamu*, The dancers entertained the guests. 2 to cheer up, comfort. *Ia* ~ *anak jg menangis itu*, He comforted the crying child. **meng–kan** to console. **peng-** entertainer. **(peng)–an** 1 entertainment. 2 recreation. 3 consolation. *tak* **ter-** disconsolate.
hidajat God's guidance.
hidam see IDAM.
hidang **meng–kan** 1 to serve. *Ia* ~ *makanan itu*, She served the food. 2 to present. *Meréka* ~ *hiburan berupa njanjian dan tarian*, They presented entertainment in the form of singing and dancing. **se–an** one serving. *Meréka makan* ~ , They ate one serving. **–an** 1 dish of food. 2 presentation. ~ *sandiwara* stage performance. 3 serving.
hidjau green. *Daun itu* –, The leaf is green. *Anak muda itu masih* –, The young man was still green. **ke– -²an** greenish. **meng–kan** to make green. *Ia* ~ *gambaran itu dgn tjat* –, He made the picture green by using green paint.
hidjrah Mohammed's flight from Mecca to Medina. **ber-** to evacuate. *Tentara kita* ~ *dari daérah itu*, Our troops evacuated that region. **meng-kan** to evacuate (troops). **peng–an** evacuation of troops.
hidmat see CHIDMAT.
hidung nose. **ke– -²an, meng-** nasal. *Suaranja* ~ , He has a nasal voice. – *belang* woman chaser. – *mantjung* sharp nose.
hidup 1 to be alive, living. *Hanja ibunja masih* –, Only his mother is still alive. 2 to thrive. *Perdagangannja* –, His business thrives. 3 life. *Tjerita –nja sangat menarik hati*, The story of his life is very interesting. 4 to run, go. *Dgn sekali putar djam itu – seminggu*, By winding it once that clock runs for a week. *Siapa jg membiarkan mesin mobilnja* –? Who left the engine of his car running? 5 to run, operate. *Selama pendudukan Djepang pabrik gula terus* –, The sugar factory continued operation during the Japanese occupation. 6 to burn. *Selama siang hari lampu ini tetap* –, During the daytime this light continues to burn. *Api dianglo masih* –, The fire in the charcoal brazier is still burning. 7 to be in the running. *Tunggu dulu,*

Kertu saja masih –, Wait, I'm still in the game. 8 to have life. *Aki masih tjukup – utk mendjalankan mesin,* There is enough power left in the battery to start the engine. 9 to go on living. – *présidén!* Long live the president! 10 fresh. *Saja beli ikan mas dan sajuran* –, I have bought fresh carp and vegetables. 11 to exist, live. *Apakah perkumpulan sépakbola itu masih* –? Does that soccer team still exist? 12 to be put in use. *Dizaman perang djalan ini – kembali,* During the war this road was used again. – *dgn* to live with, on. **ke–an** 1 life. 2 livelihood. 3 existence. **memper–** 1 to invigorate. *Ia ~ gerakan kooperasi,* He brought new life to the co-operative movement. 2 to enliven. *Dialah jg ~ suasana perdjamuan,* He was the life of the party. **meng–i** 1 to grant o. his life. *Panglima jg bidjaksana itu ~ semua musuh jg tertawan,* The able army commander granted all captured soldiers their lives. 2 to take care of, bring up, care for. *Sedjak kau ketjil kakakmu jg ~ kamu,* Since you were a child, your brother has cared for you. *Waktu engkau sakit pajah ialah jg ~ kamu,* It was she who nursed you back to life from your serious illness. **meng– kan** to bring to life ~ *orang* to revive. ~ *kooperasi* to establish a co-operative. ~ *lampu listrik* to switch on the electric light. ~ *lampu minjak (api, kompor gas,* etc.) to light the oil lamp (fire, gas stove, etc.). ~ *mesin disel* to start a diesel engine. ~ *orang mati* to resurrect the dead. **meng– suburkan** to nurture into prosperity. **peng–an** 1 income. ~ *setahun* yearly income. 2 means (of support). ~*nja adalah pénsiun negara,* His means of support is a state pension. ~*nja terlalu méwah,* He is living beyond his means. 3 subsistence. ~ *jg parah* a hard life. **se–** *semati* loyal, faithful. –² alive. *Ia dibakar* ~, He was burned alive. – *kelamin* sex life.

hikajat tale, story. **ber–** to tell stories. *Kita gemar mendengarkan* ~ *nénék,* We like to listen to grandfather's stories. **meng–kan** to tell the story of s.t. – *hidup* biography. ~*nja sekarang makan bésok tidak* to live from hand to mouth.

hikmah see HIKMAT.

hikmat 1 wisdom. *Orang tua itu banjak* –*nja,* The old man has great wisdom. 2 magical powers. **ber–** 1 to have wisdom. 2 to have magical powers. **meng–i** 1 to cast a spell over s.o. *Ia ~ puteri itu,* He cast a spell over the princess. 2 to enchant, bewitch. *Ketjantikannja ~ dia,* Her beauty enchanted him.

hilaf see CHILAF.

hilang 1 lost. *Segala miliknja – selama peperangan,* He lost all his property during the war. 2 vanished. *Kapal itu – dilaut,* The ship vanished at sea. 3 dead. *Ibunja tlh* –, His mother died. 4 missing, wanting. – *nr. 3,* No. 3 is missing. **ke–an** 1 to lose. *Indonésia tlh ~ seorang putera besar,* Indonesia has lost a great son. 2 loss. ~ *besar* a great loss. ~ *akal* to lose o's head, be desperate. *Ia ~ akalnja ketika polisi datang,* He lost his head when the police came. ~ *muka* to lose face. **meng–** to disappear. *Achirnja kapal* ~ , Finally the ship disappeared. **meng–kan** 1 to lose. *Ia ~ dompétnja,* He lost his wallet. 2 to make s.t. disappear. *Tukang sulap itu ~ saputangan,* The magician made the handkerchief disappear. 3 to leave out, omit. *Ketika ia membatja buku itu ia ~ beberapa fatsal,* When he read that book, he left out some chapters. 4 to remove, get rid of. ~ *diri* to disappear. ~ *kesan* to remove an impression. **meng– -lenjapkan** to cause to disappear. –² *timbul* flickering off and on. – *arwah,* – *semangat* unconscious, fainted. – *kedengaran* faintly audible. – *kelihatan diléréng gunung* sometimes discernible on the mountain slope. – *kelihatan dlm kabut* faintly visible in the fog. – *kikis* swept, carried away. – *lenjap* vanished, entirely lost. *Rumahnja – lenjap disapu bom,* His house was completely destroyed by bombs. – *njawa* death. – *pentjaharian* to lose o's livelihood. – *seri* to evaporate. – *timbul dipermukaan air* to bob up and down on the surface of the water. – *manis sepah dibuang* to throw away after using.

hilap see CHILAF.

hilir 1 lower course. – *sebuah sungai itu dekat laut,* The lower course of the river is near the sea. 2 downstream. *Kaju itu hanjut ke–,* The wood floated downstream. 3 late. *Malam sdh* –, The night is late. **ber–an** to stream, flow. *Keringatnja* ~ , The perspiration streamed down. **berke– an** to aim at. *Politiknja ~ perkembangan industri nasional,* His policy aims at developing national industry. **meng–** to go downstream. *mendajung*

~ to row downstream. **meng–kan**
1 to let flow away. *Ia* ~ *perahunja,*
He let his boat drift away. 2 to steer.
Ketua rapat ~ *débat kearah soal
prosedure,* The chairman of the
meeting steered the debate toward
the problem of procedure. **meng-
mudikkan** 1 to steer, direct, lead.
Njonja X. ~ *suaminja,* Mr. X
does whatever his wife says. (Mrs. X
wraps her husband around her little
finger.) 2 to treat arbitrarily. *Tentara
itu* ~ *tawanan perang,* The army
dealt arbitrarily with the prisoners of
war. – *mudik* 1 up and down. *Ia
berdjalan – mudik sadja dlm kamarnja,*
He just walked up and down his
room. 2 to and fro. *Tjeriteranja tak
tentu – mudiknja,* His story made no
sense. (I could not make head or tail
of his story.)

Himalaja Himalaya.

himbau see IMBAU.

him(m)ah see HÉMAT.

himpit see IMPIT.

himpun ber– to assemble. *Meréka* ~
dirumah saja, They assembled at
my house. **meng–kan** 1 to assemble,
gather. *Guru* ~ *murid²nja,* The
teacher assembled his pupils. 2 to
collect. *Ia* ~ *tulisan² penjair itu,*
He collected the writings of the
poet. **peng–** 1 gatherer, collector. 2
compiler. ~ *listrik* storage battery.
peng–an accumulation. **per–an** association, organization. ~ *mahasiswa*
students' association. **–an** 1 association, club. 2 collection. ~ *sjair* collection of poems.

hina 1 humble. *Ia tinggal dlm gubuk
jg –,* He lived in a humble hut.
2 contemptible. *Itu perbuatan jg –,*
That is a contemptible thing to do.
ber– *diri* to be modest. *Ia selalu* ~
diri, He is always modest. **ke–an**
1 humility. 2 humbleness, humble
circumstances. 3 meanness. **meng-
(kan)** to humiliate, insult. *Ia* ~
saja, He humiliated me. **peng–an**
1 humiliation. 2 insult. **ter–** 1 humiliated. 2 insulted. – *dina,* – *lata,*
– *papa* 1 very humble. 2 very low.
– *mulia* noble and humble.

hindar meng– to pull to the side.
Mobil itu ~ *memberi djalan kpd
mobil jg lain,* The car pulled to the
side to make way for the other car.
meng–i, meng–kan 1 to avoid. *Saja
selalu mentjoba* ~ *kesukaran,* I
always try to avoid difficulties.
2 to prevent. *Ia* ~ *saja hendak
memukul dia,* He prevented me from
hitting him. 3 to evade. **peng–an**
1 prevention, avoidance. 2 protec-

tion. 3 pulling, drawing to the side.
~ *mobilnja dari tengah ketepi djalan
meng–kan tubrukan,* By pulling his
car to the side of the road, a collision
was avoided. **ter–** 1 escaped from. *Ia
selalu* ~ *dari bahaja,* He always
escaped from danger. 2 separated.
Ia ~ *dari temannja,* He was separated from his friends.

Hindia Indies. – *Barat* the West Indies. – *Belanda* the Netherlands
East Indies.

hindu 1 see INDUK. 2 Hindu.

hingar see INGAR.

hingga 1 until. *Ia makan – kenjang,*
He ate until he had enough. 2 to,
up to, as far as. *Djarak dari New
York – ke Washington adalah lebih
dari 300 mil,* The distance from
New York to Washington is over
300 miles. *tak ada –nja* endless,
unlimited. **ber–** limited. *Keadjaiban
alam tidak* ~ , The wonders of
nature are unlimited. **memper–kan,
meng–kan** to determine, define. **per–
an** limit. **se–** 1 until. *Ia makan* ~
ia merasa puas, He ate until he felt
satisfied. 2 so that, that. *Ia begitu
sakit* ~ *ia harus masuk rumah
sakit,* He was so sick that he had to
go to the hospital. *tidak* **ter–** unlimited. – *kini,* – *sekarang* up till
now, until now. – *kini saja blm
mendapat surat dari dia,* Up till now
I have not gotten any letters from
him.

hinggap 1 to perch. *Burung – diatas
dahan,* The bird perched on the
branch. 2 to attack. *penjakit adjaib jg
tlh lama – pd meréka* the mysterious
illness from which they had suffered
for a long time. **meng–** to alight.
Burung ~ *diatas rumah,* A bird
alighted atop a house. **meng–i** 1 to
perch on, alight on. *Burung itu* ~
dahan, The bird perched on a branch.
Stoplés itu di–i lalat, A fly alighted
on the glass jar. 2 to attack (of
illness). *Ia di–i penjakit,* He was
attacked by an illness.

hinggut ter– –² 1 to rock (a cradle).
2 to shake (a tree).

hintai see INTAI.

hipokrisi hypocrisy.

hipoték mortgage. **meng–kan** to mortgage. *Ia* ~ *rumahnja,* He mortgaged
his house.

hipotése hypothesis.

hipuk see IPUK.

hirap to disappear, vanish. **meng–**
to disappear, vanish. *Pentjuri jg
ditjari* ~ , The thief who was wanted
disappeared.

hirarki hierarchy.

hirau **meng–kan** to pay attention to, heed. *Ia tidak ~ kata² bapaknja*, He ignored his father's words.

hiris see IRIS.

hiru-biru see HARU.

hiruk commotion, uproar, tumult, din, hubbub. **ke–pirukan** racket, noise, commotion. **meng–** to make noise. *Djangan ~ , saja mau tidur*, Don't make any noise, I want to sleep. **meng–kan** 1 to make a fuss about s.t. *Djangan ~ perkara seketjil itu*, Don't make a fuss about such a little thing. 2 to cause a commotion, ruckus. 3 sensational. **peng–** noise-maker. **–** *pikuk*, **–** *piruk* racket, tumult, din.

hirup **meng–** to sip, suck. *Ia ~ minumannja itu*, He sipped his drink. *~ udara* to inhale air.

hisab calculation, arithmetic. **meng–kan** to calculate, compute, take account of, take stock of. **ter–** to be considered, be counted (to belong to a certain group, etc.).

hisak **meng–** to sob. *Ia ~ dan air matanja mengalir*, She sobbed and the tears flowed.

hisap see ISAP.

historiografi historiography.

hitam 1 black. 2 dark. *Malam –*, The night is dark. **ke– –²an** blackish. **meng–** to become black. *Malam ~ ,* The night became black. **meng–(–)kan** to make black. *Ia ~ gambaran itu*, He made the picture black. *Ia ~ saja pd madjikan saja*, He blackened me with my employer. **–** *djengat*, **–** *kumbang*, **–** *legam*, **–** *lotong* pitch-black. **–** *manis* light-brown complexion. **–** *mata* pupils of the eyes. **–** *pekat*, **–** *tedas* pitch-black. **–** *putihnja blm tentu*, It can't be decided yet.

hitung **ber–** 1 to count. *Anak itu sdh dpt ~ sampai sepuluh*, The small child could already count to 10. 2 arithmetic. *Anak² beladjar ~ ,* The children study arithmetic. *~ kepala* mental arithmetic. **memper–kan** 1 to take into consideration, calculate on. *Ia lupa ~ kemungkinan pergantian politik perdagangan pemerintah*, He forgot to take into consideration the possibility of changing commercial policy in the government. 2 to count on s.o. *Ia tak dpt diper–kan*, He can't be counted on. 3 to estimate. *~ banjaknja tamu jg akan datang* to estimate the number of guests coming. 4 to compensate, cover. *Ia ~ segala hutang dgn uang jg didjandjikan oléh ajahnja*, He covered all his debts with the money prom-

ised by his father. **meng–** to count. **meng– –²** 1 to count and recount. *Ia ~ uangnja*, He counted and recounted his money. 2 to calculate. *Ia ~ berapa jg harus dikeluarkannja*, He calculated how much he would have to spend. **peng–** 1 bank teller. 2 numerator in fractions. **per–an** 1 calculation. 2 consideration. *Itu sdh masuk ~ saja*, I've taken that into consideration. *~ laba rugi* balance sheet. **ter–** 1 included. *Dlm bilangan itu blm ~ meréka jg datang terlambat*, Those who came too late were not included in that number. 2 to belong to. *Ia ~ dlm golongan itu*, He belonged to that group. *tak ~* innumerable, countless. **–an** 1 see PER–AN 2 arithmetical problem.

hiu shark.

hiung **meng–** to screech.

hiuran see IURAN.

hlm. [*halaman*] page of a book.

ho [*hongeroedém*] malnutrition, under-nourishment.

Hoakiao overseas Chinese.

hobat magic spell. **meng–kan** to cast a spell on s.o.

hojak see OJAK.

hojong see HUJUNG.

holopis kuntul baris a phrase uttered by a group when carrying or trying to move heavy objects in order to obtain extra strength.

honar see ONAR.

hondji see KANDJI.

Hongaria Hungary.

hop head, chief. *Ia mendjadi – djawatannja*, He became chief of his department. **–** *agén* police sergeant. **–** *biro* police headquarters. **–** *kantor* main office.

horas long live! (Batak).

horison horizon.

hormat 1 honor. 2 respect. 3 respectful. *Tindakannja selalu ramah dan –*, His attitude was always friendly and respectful. 4 homage. 5 regards, respects. *Sampaikanlah – saja pd bapakmu*, Please give your father my regards. **ber–** respected. *Ia adalah seorang ~ ,* He is a respected person. **ke–an** 1 honor. 2 respect. 3 honorary. *anggota ~* honorary member. 4 courtesy. *visa ~* courtesy visa. **meng–(i)** 1 to honor. *Kita harus ~ orang tua kita*, We must honor our parents. 2 to respect. *Kita harus ~ undang² negara kita*, We must respect the laws of our country. **peng–an** 1 honor. *Kita mengibarkan bendéra sebagai ~ kedatangan présidén*, We flew the flags in honor of the president's arrival.

2 homage. **ter-** 1 honored. *Ia adalah seorang warganegara jg* ~ , He was an honored citizen. 2 respected. *Ia sangat* ~ *dlm désanja*, He is highly respected in his village. *Tuan² jg* ~ Dear Sirs! – *saja* Respectfully yours. *Dengan* – Dear Sir. *dgn tidak* – dishonorably. – *dan salam (dari)* with the compliments (of).

Hosti Sutji Holy Ghost.

hotél hotel. **per–an** 1 hotel business. 2 hotel management. – *perdéo* prison.

hrs [*harus*] must, have to.

hubaja² to make sure that..., above all, by all means. *Kalau ingin berhasil* ~ *engkau bekerdja teliti*, If you want to succeed by all means work accurately. *Kami harap* ~ *hal itu tak terdjadi*, We certainly hope that that won't happen.

hubung ber- 1 connected, related. *Kedua kedjadian itu* ~ *satu sama lain*, The two incidents are related. 2 due to the fact that. ~ *dgn* 1 owing to. *Keberangkatan kami diundur* ~ *dgn keadaan udara jang buruk*, Our departure was postponed owing to bad weather. 2 with regard to. ~ *dgn pentingnja hal itu, kita harus bertindak tjepat*, With regard to the importance of that matter we have to act quickly. ~ *itu harap Tuan suka ber–an dgn Sdr. Ali*, With regard to that matter will you please get in touch with Mr. Ali. **ber–an** 1 connected, related. *Kedua kedjadian itu* ~ *satu sama lain*, The two incidents were connected. 2 to contact, get in touch with. *Saja harus* ~ *dulu dgn pemerintah saja*, I have to contact my government first. 3 to be in contact with. *Selama seluruh perdjalanannja itu ia selalu* ~ *dgn saja dgn surat*, During his whole trip he was in contact with me by letter. 4 to get in touch with. **meng–i** to contact, get in touch with. *Ia blm* ~ *kedutaan besar*, He hasn't contacted the embassy yet. **memper–kan, meng–kan** to connect. *Ia* ~ *kedua udjung tali itu*, He connected the two ends of the rope. *Keréta api itu* ~ *kedua kota itu*, That train connects those two cities. ~ *diri* to merge, ally o.s. *Partai Buruh* ~ *diri dgn Partai Sosialis*, The Labor Party merged with the Socialist Party. **peng–** operator who connects nondial with dial telephones in Jakarta. **(per)–an** 1 connection. *Antara kedua kedjadian itu ada* ~*nja*, There is a connection between the 2 incidents. 2 relationship. 3 communication. ~ *dgn kota itu sama sekali terputus*, Communications with that

city were completely cut off. 4 context. *Dipandang dlm* ~*zamannja...* Viewed in the context of his time... ~ *antarbangsa* international relations. ~ *antardiri* interpersonal relations. ~ *diplomatik* diplomatic relations. ~ *djadjar* parallel connections in electric wiring. *–an antar-kepulauan* interinsular communication. *–an internasional* international relations. *–an kalimat* context (of a sentence). *–an masjarakat* social relations. *–an timbal-balik* interaction.

hudjah 1 slander, defamation. 2 proof. **meng–** to slander, defame.

hudjan 1 rain. – *turun*, The rain fell. 2 to rain. *Kalau* – *djanganlah keluar*, If it's raining, don't go out. **ber–** –² to walk in the rain. **ke–an** to be caught in the rain. *Ia* ~ , He got caught in the rain. **meng– anginkan** to expose to the weather. **meng–i** to shower. *Meréka* ~ *saja dgn pemberian²*, They showered me with gifts. – *batu*, – *beku*, – *és* hail. – *bunut* constant drizzle. – *deras* downpour. – *gerimis* drizzle. – *lebat* downpour. – *manik* hail. – *panas* rain while sun is shining. – *peluru* hail of bullets. – *renai²*, – *renik²*, – *rintik²* drizzling.

hudjat see HUDJAH.

hudjung see UDJUNG.

hujung ter– –² to stagger. *Ia berdjalan* ~ *keluar dari kamar*, He went staggering out of the room.

hukum 1 law. 2 verdict. 3 commandment. – *jg sepuluh* the Ten Commandments. **ber–** to seek justice. *Ia pergi* ~ *kepengadilan*, He went to seek justice at court. **ke–an** legal, juridical. *sjarat²* ~ legal conditions. **meng–** 1 to punish. *Bapak* ~ *anaknja jg nakal itu*, Father punished his naughty child. 2 to sentence. *Hakim* ~ *pendjahat*, The judge sentenced the criminal. 3 to judge. *Orang terlalu mudah* ~ , People judge too easily. 4 to sentence to. *Dia di–* 5 *tahun*, He was sentenced to, given, 5 years. **peng–an** sentence, judgment. **ter–** condemned. *Orang* ~ *itu menghadapi –nja*, The condemned man faced his punishment. **–an** 1 punishment. 2 sentence. *Hakim mendjatuhkan* ~ , The judge pronounced his sentence. 3 prisoner. ~ *bersjarat* suspended sentence. ~ *gantung* sentenced to hang. ~ *kawalan* sentence of restricted freedom of movement. ~ *kerdja* sentenced to hard labor. ~ *kurungan*, ~ *pendjara*, ~ *tutupan* imprisonment. ~ *mati* 1 death sentence. 2 capital punishment. ~ *sél* solitary confinement. ~ *témbak* sen-

tence of death by firing squad. – *adat*
1 customary law. 2 common law.
– *alam* natural laws, laws of nature.
– *antargolongan* interpersonal law.
– *antar-negara* international law. –
asasi basic law. – *atjara* law of procedure. – *dagang* commercial law. –
dasar negara basic law. – *gerédja*
ecclesiastical law. – *Islam* Islamic
law. – *kisas* capital punishment for
taking a human life. – *keradal* sentenced to hard labor. – *maddi* material law. – *niaga* commercial law. –
padjak tax law. – *pendjara* imprisonment. – *perdata* civil law. – *perselisihan* law of conflict. – *pidana* criminal
law. – *sipil* civil law. – *sjarak* Islamic
canon law. – *tatanegara* constitutional
law. – *tentara* military law. – *tuntutan*
law of procedure. *jg di- déwata
karena ber-kasih²an* who, because of
their love for e.o., had been condemned by the gods.
hulam see ULAM.
hulu 1 upper end. *Ia mengetjat –
tiang itu*, He painted the upper end of
the pole. 2 handle, hilt. 3 head.
Ia sakit –nja, He had a headache.
4 upper course of a river. **meng-**
to go upstream. ~ *meréka berlajar,
menghilir meréka berdajung*, Going
upstream they sailed, going downstream they rowed. – *hati* 1 midriff.
2 pit of the stomach. 3 inward. –
kepala crown of the head.
hulubalang 1 commander. 2 (in
Acheh, North Sumatra) a district
chief.
huma 1 field for dry rice cultivation.
2 newly cleared land for agriculture.
ber- 1 to cultivate rice on dry
fields. *Karena kurang air, meréka ~
sadja*, Because of lack of water they

cultivated rice on dry fields. 2 to
clear the land for cultivation. **per-an**
1 dry rice cultivation. 2 clearing
(of field).
humbalang see HEMBALANG.
hundjam see UNDJAM.
huni ber- occupied. *Rumah itu ~ ,*
That house is occupied. **meng-** to
dwell in. *Hanja hantu² sadja jg ~
rumah itu*, Only ghosts dwell in that
house. **peng-** 1 occupant, inhabitant.
2 guardian spirit.
hunus meng- to draw (a sword).
Ia ~ pedangnja, He drew his sword.
~ *tjintjin* to slip a ring off o's finger.
huria a district in the Batak area.
huruf letter, character. – *balok* block
letter(s). – *besar* capital letter(s).
– *bunji* vowel. – *djawi* Arabic characters used for Indonesian. – *gundul*
vowelless Arabic script. – *harakah*,
– *hidup* vowel. – *kandji* Chinese
characters. – *ketjil* lower case letter.
– *madjemuk* digraph. – *mati* consonant. – *miring* italics. – *pangkal*
initial. – *pengenal* identifying letter.
– *permulaan* initial letter. – *Rumawi*
roman character(s). – *saksi* vowel
mark in Arabic script. – *tebal* boldface type. – *tjétak* printed letter(s). –
tulis script letter(s).
huruhara see HARU-HARA.
husus see CHUSUS.
hutan 1 woods, forest. 2 jungle.
ke-an forestry, silviculture. **meng-kan**
to abandon to the jungle, let the
jungle take over. **per-an** forestry
service. – *belantara*, – *belukar* dense
jungle. – *larangan* forest preserve. –
lepas, – *rimba* extensive jungle, jungle
expanse. – *tutupan* forest preserve.
hutang see UTANG. **peng-** creditor.
hydrolisterik hydroelectric.

I

ia 1 see DIA. 2 he, she. – *membatja
buku*, He's reading a book. 3 him,
her. 4 yes. **ber-(-)** 1 to agree, answer
in the affirmative. *Ia ~ sadja*, He
says yes to everything. (He's nothing
but a yes man.) 2 to discuss, negotiate, deliberate. **ber- berbukan** to
consult, negotiate. **meng-kan** to
affirm, agree, answer in the affirma-

tive. **se-** *sekata* unanimous. *Meréka ~
sekata utk menutup pertemuan*, They
agreed to adjourn the meeting.
ialah is, are. *Bahasa Indonésia –
bahasa kebangsaan*, Indonesian is the
national language.
iapunja see PUNJA.
iau meng- to meow.
I.B. [*Irian Barat*] West New Guinea.

iba 1 moved, touched. 2 moving. 3 wistful. ber- -² moving, touching, pathetic. ber- *meminta* beseechingly. ke–an emotion, nostalgia, compassion, pity. meng–kan 1 to affect, move. 2 to be nostalgic about s.t. pe(ng)–compassionate.

ibadah see IBADAT. – *dlm djema'ah* God's service performed together in a group prayer.

ibadat 1 religion. 2 religious service. ber– religious, pious. per–an the observance of religious duties.

ibarat 1 symbol. 2 parable. 3 example. 4 allegory. ber– containing a parable. meng–kan 1 to follow o's example. 2 to compare. *Dunia ini di–kan lembah kesusahan,* This world is compared to a vale of sorrows. 3 to treat. *Saja di–kannja kuda sadja,* He treated me like a work horse.

ibing see ÉBÉNG.

iblis devil, Satan.

Ibrani Hebrew.

ibu 1 mother. 2 form of address to older woman or o. in higher position, teacher, employer, etc. 3 Mrs. ber– 1 to have a mother. 2 to call 'mother.' *Saja ∼ kpd isteri kawan saja,* I call my friend's wife *ibu.* ke–an maternity, motherhood. – *akar* main root, taproot. – *angkat* foster mother. – *bapak* parents. – *djari* thumb. – *guru* form of address to woman teacher. – *kaki* big toe. – *kandung* the real mother. – *kota* capital. – *kuntji* lock. – *negeri* capital. – *panah* bow. – *pasir* pebble. – *pertiwi* fatherland. – *sungai* principal (main) river. – *suri* queen mother. – *tangan* thumb. – *tangga* banister. – *tentara* main body of the army. – *tiri* stepmother.

ibunda mother (polite).

ichlas 1 sincere. 2 willing. 3 sincerity. 4 well-intentioned. ke–an sincerity, devotion. meng–kan 1 to devote o.s. to. 2 to do s.t. wholeheartedly.

ichtiar 1 initiative. 2 free choice. 3 opinion. 4 means. ber– to try, make an effort. *Ia ∼ se-baik²nja,* He did his utmost. meng–kan 1 to try, devise. 2 to advise. 3 to arrange for. *Ia tidak mengindahkan –ku,* He didn't listen to me. *Pulang – kpd tuan,* It's up to you. *Saja akan – perdjalananmu,* I'll arrange for your itinerary.

ichtiari optional.

ichtilaf 1 difference, divergence. 2 diversity.

ichtisar 1 summary, recapitulation. – *Parlemén* Congressional Record

(Indonesia). 2 survey. 3 abstract. meng–kan to summarize, recapitulate.

ichwan 1 brothers, comrades. 2 fraternal, brotherly.

id Moslem festival day.

idah gift to establish ties of love between men and women. meng– to court by giving presents. meng–kan to offer a gift to reveal o's love (man to woman).

idam 1 craving. 2 a pregnant woman's craving for special foods. meng– to crave, long for. meng–(–)kan to crave. –²an 1 desire, craving. 2 ideal.

idap eyelash. meng–(kan) to suffer from a chronic disease, be ailing. –an chronic disease.

iddah waiting period (100 days) for a widow or divorced woman before remarriage (according to Islam).

idé idea.

idéntifikasi identification. meng–kan to identify.

idéologi ideology.

idilis idyllic.

idjab 1 bid, offer. 2 confirmation. meng–kan 1 to offer. 2 to answer a prayer. 3 to perform the wedding ceremony. – *nikah* wedding ceremony.

idjadjah see IDJAZAH.

idjadjil devil.

idjasah see IDJAZAH.

idjazah 1 certificate, diploma. 2 license, permit. ber– qualified, certified, licensed. *bidan ∼* qualified midwife.

idjin see IZIN. per–an permission.

idjma' 1 consensus of opinion of Moslem scholars. 2 agreement, approval.

idjmal résumé, summary.

idjo meng– to buy paddy while it is still green (still standing in the field).

idjtihad 1 right of individual interpretation and judgment. 2 investigation, opinion. *pd –nja* in his opinion. ber– to interpret according to o's own opinion.

idjuk black sugar-palm fiber. meng–bristly. *Kumisnja ∼ ,* His mustache was bristly. ter– abashed, embarrassed.

idulfitri Lebaran day; feast at the end of the fasting period on the first of the month of Sjawwal.

idzin see IZIN. per–an permission.

ifrit evil spirit.

iftar breaking of the fast.

iga rib. – *péndék* floating rib. – *selungkang* false rib.

igal meng– 1 to show off, strut. 2 to display its feathers (of a peacock, etc.), stand the hair, feathers, on end (of a cat, bird, etc.).

igama see AGAMA.

igau meng– 1 to talk in o's sleep, be delirious. *Apa jg saja – semalam?* What did I say in my sleep last night? 2 to walk in o's sleep. **mengkan** to dream about. **ter–** to be frightened. **–an** 1 delirium. 2 idle, small talk. **–²an** 1 to be delirious. 2 noisy.

I'gris [*Inggeris*] England.

ihram 1 consecration. 2 special dress worn during pilgrimage to Mecca.

ihsan 1 good deeds. 2 charity.

ihtilam ejaculation (during sleep).

ihtimal meng–kan to order s.o., take along s.t., transmit an order, transfer a task, letter, etc.

ihwal see HAL.

ija meng– to approve, agree with.

ijuran see IURAN.

ikab punishment.

ikal 1 curl. 2 curly, wavy. **meng–** to curl. **–an** bobbin.

ikan fish. **per–an** fishery. *Djawatan* ~ Department of Fisheries. **–²** implement to measure speed of boat. *– air tawar* fresh-water fish. *– ajam* chicken. *– asin* salted fish. *– bakar* grilled fish. *– balut* eel. *– bandeng* bandeng. *– basah* fresh fish. *– bilalang* flying fish. *– darat* fresh-water fish. *– djuhi* large squid. *– dujung* sea cow. *– gurita* octopus. *– kering* dried fish. *– limbat* catfish. *– lindung* eel. *– lodan* whale. *– lumba* dolphin. *– mua* eel. *– mudjair* a fish which feeds on larvae. *– nun* whale. *– nus* squid. *– pari* k.o. ray. *– paus*, *– raja* whale. *– salem* salmon. *– sapi* beef. *– talang* mackerel. *– tjumi²* squid. *– tongkol* tuna fish.

ikat 1 string. 2 bunch, bundle. 3 band. 4 headcloth. **ber–** tied, bound. ~ *mas* gilded. **meng–** 1 to tie, fasten. 2 to compose. *Ia* ~ *beberapa kalimat*, He composed several sentences. 3 to strike, contract. *Ia* ~ *tali persahabatan*, He struck up a friendship. 4 to set stones in rings, etc. 5 to compose poetry. 6 to conclude (an agreement). *Perbuatannja itu* ~ *hati saja*, His actions have captured my heart. *Saja tak suka perdjandjian jg* ~ , I do not like binding agreements. **meng–kan** to tie with. **peng–** binding agent. **per–an** connection, relationship. **se–** a bunch, bundle. ~ *rambutan* a bunch of rambutans. **ter–** bound, restricted. *Perbuatannja selalu* ~ *oléh perdjandjian itu*, His actions were always restricted by the agreement. **–an**

1 string, band. 2 bundle. 3 union, league, club. 4 composition. 5 leash. ~ *dines* service contract, tenure. *– duduk* seat belt. *– kolam* edge of a pond. *– pinggang* belt. *– pinggang keselamatan* safety belt.

iklan advertisement. **meng–kan** to advertise. **per–an** advertising.

iklim 1 climate. 2 zone. **ke–an** climatological. *– panas* tropical zone *– sedang* temperate zone.

ikrar 1 to promise sincerely, firmly. 2 promise. 3 confession, acknowledgment. *– Lautan Teduh* the Pacific Charter. **ber–**, **meng–** 1 to confess. 2 to promise. ~ *sumpah* to take an oath. **meng–kan** to promise s.t.

iktisad economy.

ikut 1 to follow, go along. *Saja tak akan –*, I won't be going along. *Ia – pergi*, He went along with them. 2 to participate, join (in). *Boléhkah saja – main ténnis?* Can I join your tennis game? 3 to accept. *Terimalah – berdukatjita kami*, Please accept our condolences. 4 to interfere, butt in. *Djangan –²!* Don't interfere! *Dia – terlibat dlm perkara itu*, He, too, was involved in that affair. **ber–** 1 to follow. *Disambung pd halaman jg* ~ , Continued on the following page. *Kabar itu sebagai* ~ , The news is as follows. 2 together with. ~ *uang itu saja mengirim tanda penerimaan*, I sent the receipt together with the money. *Kapal* ~ *penumpangnja binasa dlm badai*, The ship and its passengers perished in the storm. 3 next. *Siapa jg* ~ ? Who's next? **ber––²** successively, consecutively. ~ *kelintji keluar dari lobang*, One after the other the rabbits came out of the hole. **memper–kan**, **meng–kan** 1 to follow. 2 to obey. 3 to add. *Pd suratnja ia* ~ *sekedar ttg riwajat hidupnja*, He added a biographical sketch to his letter. 4 to enclose. *Ia* ~ *sebuah potrét dlm surat*, He enclosed a photograph in the letter. *Ia* ~ *puteranja dgn bis pagi*, He put his son on the early bus. **meng–** 1 to follow, obey. *Ia tak pernah* ~ *perintah saja*, He never obeys my command. 2 to behave, act, follow after. *Ia* ~ *kelakuan ibunja*, She behaved like her mother. 3 to imitate. **meng–i** 1 to follow, accompany. *Saja* ~ *ibu saja*, I accompanied my mother. 2 to take, follow. *Ia* ~ *kursus bahasa Perantjis*, He took a French course. *Ia* ~ *beberapa kuliah ttg ilmu alam*, He attended several lectures on physics. 3 to trail. 4 to keep up with.

~ *berita* to keep up with the news.
~ *djaman* to keep up with the times.
meng–sertakan to accompany. **peng–**
1 follower, participant. 2 supporter,
adherent. ~ *udjian* examinee. **ter–**
included. –²**an** rashly, without reason.
Ia ~ *sadja dlm démonstrasi itu*, He
rashly joined in the demonstration. –
bersuara to have a voice (a say) in the
matter. – *serta* to accompany, go
along. *Dlm rombongan présidén* –
serta... In the president's party were...
ilah God, deity. **ke–an** divinity. *tak*
ber– godless.
ilahi divine.
ilahiat deity.
ilai meng– 1 to neigh. 2 to laugh
uproariously.
ilam² hazy, vague.
ilas meng– to squash, mash underfoot.
iler slobber. **meng–** 1 to make the
mouth water. ~ *saja melihat mobilnja
jg indah itu*, His beautiful car made
my mouth water. 2 to slobber.
ilham divine inspiration. **meng–i** to
inspire s.o. **meng–kan** to inspire with
s.t.
ilir see HILIR.
illustratip illustrative.
ilmiawan scholar, scientist.
ilmi(j)ah scientific. **ke–an** scientific.
ilmu 1 knowledge. 2 science. 3 esoteric knowledge. **ber–, ke–an** learned,
scientific. **ke–bumian** geographical.
ke–(–)an pseudoscientific. – *achirat*
eschatology. – *achlak* science concerned with the human character.
– *adab* ethics. – *administrasi negara*
public administration. – *agama* theology. – *alam* physics. – *alat* study of
the Arabic language and related
subjects. – *aldjabar* algebra. – *alik*
mysticism. – *bahasa* linguistics. –
bajan exegesis. – *bangsa²* ethnology.
– *bangun* elementary geometry. –
bangun²an architecture. – *bangunan
kapal* naval architecture. – *batin* 1
occultism. 2 psychology. – *bedah*
surgery. – *bentuk (kata)* morphology.
– *bidan* midwifery. – *bintang* astronomy. – *bumi* geography. – *bunji*
phonetics. – *chasiat obat* pharmacology. – *didik* pedagogy. – *djaringan
tubuh* histology. – *djiwa* psychology. –
fa'al alat tubuh physiology. – *fakih*
canon law. – *falak* cosmography. –
farad Moslem law of inheritance. –
firasah physiognomy. – *gaib* mysticism, occultism. – *gaja* strength of
materials. – *gaja bahasa* stylistics. –
gajagerak udara aerodynamics. – *gizi*
nutrition. – *hajat* biology. – *handasah*
geodesy. – *héwan* zoology. – *hukum*

jurisprudence. – *iklim* climatology.
– *kalam* dogmatics, doctrinal theology. – *kebatinan* psychology. –
kebidanan obstetrics. – *kebudajaan*
cultural anthropology. – *kedokteran*
medical science. – *kedokteran kedjiwa-
ragaan* psychosomatic medicine. –
kedokteran kehakiman medical jurisprudence. – *kedokteran pentjegah* preventive medicine. – *kemasjarakatan*
sociology. – *kenegaraan* political science. – *kepradjuritan* military science.
– *keséhatan* hygiene. – *ketabiban* medical science. – *ketatanegaraan* political
science. – *ketuhanan* theology. –
keturunan genetics. – *kias* magic. –
kimia chemistry. – *kira* arithmetic. –
kufur atheism. – *kuman²* bacteriology.
– *lambang* heraldry. – *ma'ani* rhetoric.
– *makanan* dietetics. – *mantik* logic. –
masjarakat sociology. – *mékanik* me-
chanics. – *mudigah* embryology. –
nahu syntax. – *nifas* knowledge which
enables o. to be successful with
women. – *nudjum* astronomy. –
obat²(an) pharmacology. – *padi* humility of wisdom. – *panas* thermo-
dynamics. – *pasti* mathematics. –
pelajaran navigation, seamanship. –
pelikan mineralogy. – *pemerintahan*
public administration. – *pengenal*
penjakit diagnosis. – *pengetahuan*
science. – *penjakit anak²* pediatrics.
– *penjakit dalam* internal medicine. –
penjakit djiwa psychiatry. – *penjakit
kandungan* gynecology. – *penjakit
kelamin* venereology. – *penjakit kulit*
dermatology. – *penjakit sarap* neur-
ology. – *penjakit mata* ophthalmalogy.
– *penjakit telinga, hidung dan
tenggorok(an)* otorhinolaryngology. –
penjakit tumbuh²an phytopathology. –
perapuh magic which breaks the
enemy's weapon. – *perbandingan
pemerintahan* comparative government. – *perokétan* rocket science. –
pesawat mechanical engineering. –
pisah chemistry. – *politik* political
science, politics. – *purbakala* archae-
ology. – *ratjun* toxicology. – *samudera*
oceanography. – *saraf* 1 grammar. 2
morphology. – *sedjarah* history. –
sihir shamanism. – *sinar* radiology. –
suara acoustics. – *sufi*, – *sunjata*
mysticism. – *surahi* knowledge of the
Koran. – *tabib* medical science. –
tanah soil science. – *tasawuf* mysticism. – *tasjrih* anatomy. – *tatabahasa*
grammar. – *tatakata* syntax. – *tata
negara* political science. – *tatarias*
cosmetology. – *tauhid* doctrine of
divine unity. – *tjuatja* meteorology.
– *tubuh tanah* pedology. – *tumbuh²(an)*
botany. – *udara* meteorology. – *ukur*

geometry. – *ukur bidang* plane geometry. – *ukur ruang* stereometry. – *ukur segitiga* trigonometry. – *ukur sudut* goniometry. – *urai (tubuh)* anatomy. – *usaha negara* public administration. – *usul* science of the sources of Moslem law. – *wasitah* spiritualism. –² *budaja* humanities. –² *pengetahuan kemasjarakatan,* –² *sosial* social sciences.

imadjinasi imagination.

imak meng- –²i to ridicule s.o. by imitating.

imam 1 a Moslem or Catholic priest. 2 Moslem leader. 3 title of chief of an Islamic state. – *mahdi* Messiah. **ke-an** priesthood. **meng-i** to conduct prayer services at the mosque. – *agung* 1 title of principal mosque leader. 2 great Moslem leader.

iman 1 faith, belief, creed. 2 confidence (in o.s.), morale. 3 spiritually well balanced. **ber-** believing, faithful. *jg* ~ the faithful. ~*lah!* Chin up! **ke-an** belief, faith. **meng-i** to believe in.

imani religious, pious.

imbal 1 not completely round (of a circle or globe). 2 unequal, unbalanced.

imbang balanced. **ber-(an)** in balance, equal, matched. *pernikahan jg* ~ a socially well-matched marriage. *pertumbuhan* ~ balanced growth. **kese-an** 1 balance, harmony. 2 equilibrium. **memperse-kan** to equalize. **meng-i** to equal, compensate. *Negara itu bekerdja keras utk* ~ *kekuatan musuhnja,* The country worked hard to keep its strength equal to that of the enemy. **meng-kan** to balance, keep in balance, match. *Kamu harus* ~ *perbelandjaan rumah tangga dgn gadji bulanan,* You must keep your household budget within the limits of your monthly salary. **peng-, per-** equal, counterpart. **per-an** 1 balance. 2 proportion. **perse-an** equality. **se-** equal, balanced. *Kekuatan meréka* ~ , Their strength is equal. **-an** 1 balance, counterbalance. *Partai Liberal mendjadi* ~ *dlm parlemén,* The Liberal Party holds the balance in parliament. 2 proportion. 3 equivalent. **-²an** approximately equal. *Kekuatan meréka* ~ , Their strength is approximately the same.

imbas 1 air current. 2 electrical current (in physics). **meng-i** to induce electrical current. **-an** air current.

imbau meng- to call, beckon. **-an** an appeal, call.

imbuh supplement, extra, a small addition given in the bargain to please a customer. **meng-** to give s.t. extra. **-an** affix.

imigrasi immigration.

iming meng- –² to tantalize.

imlah dictation. **ber-** to do dictating. **meng-** to dictate s.t.

imlék Chinese calendar. *tahun baru* – Chinese New Year.

impas paid off (of debt). **meng-** to pay off a debt.

imperialis imperialist.

imperialisme imperialism.

impi see MIMPI. **-an** dream, wish. ~ *keinginan* wishful thinking.

impit very close together. **ber-** to be very close together. ~ *kaki* with legs pressed against o. another. **meng-** 1 to join together. 2 to hold down. ~ *kertas dgn batu* to hold down a paper with a rock (as paperweight). 3 to pin down. *Dlm ketjelakaan itu ia di-* mobilnja, In the collision he was pinned under his car. **ter-** 1 oppressed. 2 to be in a tight spot, in a jam. 3 wedged in. **-an** pressure from several sides.

impor import. **meng-** to import. **peng-** importer. **peng-an** 1 importing. 2 importation.

importir 1 importer. 2 import business.

impresionis impressionist.

impropisasi improvisation.

impropisator improviser.

impulsip impulsive.

Imsak time when fasting begins in the morning.

-in = -KAN (suffix much used in speech of Jakartans).

inai 1 henna. 2 red nail polish. **meng-** to paint o's nails red.

inang 1 wet nurse. 2 nursemaid. **meng-** to be a wet nurse or nursemaid. – *pengasuh* governess, nursemaid.

inap meng- 1 to spend the night, stay overnight. 2 to stay, put up. **peng-an** 1 lodging. 2 hotel. *Ia tinggal dirumah* ~ , He lives at a hotel.

inas carbuncle on the nape of the neck.

indah 1 beautiful, attractive. *Pemandangan itu – sekali,* That view is very beautiful. 2 precious, expensive. 3 important. *uraian jg* – an important analysis. **ke-an** beauty. **memper-(kan)** to embellish. **meng-kan** 1 to mind, pay attention to, heed. 2 to admire. **peng-an** 1 embellishment. 2 attention. ~ *akan kata² gurunja tak menambah pengertiannja,* Attention to his teacher's words did not improve his understanding (of the matter). **per-an** 1 interest, attention. *Tak* *ada* ~ *orang thd itu,* People are not interested in it. 2 appreciation. – *lemas* graceful. *tak* – *akan* to be indifferent to.

indang meng– to winnow (rice).

indekos to have room and board.

indéks index.

indén pivot. **meng–** to order s.t. by making a down payment.

indera 1 the god Indra. 2 the gods. 3 o. of the five senses. **ke–an** heaven, the abode of the god Indra. *menurut* **peng–an** *saja* as it appears to me.

indik meng– to approach in a crouching position (haunches on heels and moving on tiptoe).

individuil individual.

indjak meng– to tread, trample on. *Ia* ~ *tahun kesepuluh,* He entered upon the tenth year (of his age, in service, in his profession, etc.). ~ *beling* to step on glass. **meng–(kan)** *kaki* to step, set foot on. **–²(an)** 1 stirrup. 2 pedal. 3 running board. *Dilarang* – *rumput,* Stay off the grass.

indjéksi 1 injection. 2 priming. **meng–** to give an injection.

indjil 1 gospel. 2 New Testament. 3 Bible. **peng–** preacher, evangelist. – *Al-Kudus* Holy Gospel.

indjili see GERÉDJA.

Indo Eurasian.

indoktrinasi indoctrination.

Indonésia 1 Indonesia(n). 2 Indonesian language. *Bagaimanakah –nja?* What is it in Indonesian? **ke–an** 1 Indonesian. *tjara hidup* ~ the Indonesian way of life. 2 Indonesianized. *Orang Arab itu tlh* ~ , That Arab has adopted Indonesian customs. *menurut tjara* ~ as we are used to doing in Indonesia, as is customary in Indonesia, etc. **membahasa–kan** to put into Indonesian. **meng–kan** to Indonesianize, put into Indonesian. **peng–an** Indonesianization.

Indonésianisasi Indonesianization.

Indotjina Indochina.

induk mother (mainly for animals). **per–an** 1 concentration. 2 centralization. **seper–an** brook, nest, litter. – *ajam* mother hen. – *babi* sow. – *bako* all the relatives on the father's side. – *bangsa* stock, race. – *djari* thumb. – *kaki* big toe. – *kalimat* main clause. – *karangan* editorial. – *karbol* concentrated carbolic acid. – *madu* honeycomb. – *pipa* main pipe. – *roti* dough with yeast added. – *semang* 1 landlady. 2 female employer. 3 landlord. – *taman ternak* cattle breeding center. – *tentara* main body of an

army. – *tjuka* essence of vinegar. – *utang* principal debt.

indung mother. – *mutiara* mother-of-pearl. – *telur* ovary.

indusemén inducement.

industri industry. **meng–kan** to industrialize. **per–an** industry, industrialization, industrial affairs.

industrialisasi industrialization.

industri(a)wan industrialist.

industriil industrial.

inep see INAP.

inersi energy.

inflasi inflation.

inflatoir inflationary.

infléksi inflection.

informan 1 informant. 2 see ORANG.

informasi information.

informil informal.

inga ter– –² 1 dazed. 2 absentminded. 3 surprised.

ingar meng–i to disturb, annoy by being noisy. **meng–kan** disturbing, annoying, causing a commotion. – *bingar* noisy.

ingat 1 to remember. *Saja tak* –, I don't remember. *Saja tak* – *akan tuan,* I don't remember you. 2 careful, attentive. *Ia kurang* –, He's inattentive. **ber– –²** careful, conscientious. **memper–i** to commemorate. *Jg dilihat itu ia* ~ *dlm buku tjatatan,* He recorded what he observed in a notebook. **memper–kan** 1 to remind s.o. of a person. 2 to warn, reprimand, caution. **meng–** 1 to remember, recall, recollect. 2 to take into account, recall. ~ *hal²* *jg dikatakan kemarin...* Considering the facts discussed yesterday... ~ *hal itu...* Taking that fact into account... (In view of... Mindful of...) 3 to think of. *Anak itu* ~ *ibunja,* That child thinks of its mother. **meng–i** 1 to remind, warn, caution. *Guru* ~ *anak² djangan berenang djauh²,* The teacher cautioned the children not to swim too far out. *Ia* ~ *bapaknja akan berangkatnja bis,* He reminded his father of the departure of the bus. 2 to advise. *Temannja* ~ *dia ttg djalan jg ditempuh hendaknja,* His friend advised him on what course to take. 3 to remember, recall. *Ia selalu* ~ *kebaikan budi gurunja,* He always remembered his teacher's generosity. **per–an** 1 recollection, remembrance, memory. 2 notion, idea. 3 note, remark. 4 presence of mind. 5 memo, note. 6 warning, reprimand. **se–** *saja* as far as I remember. **ter–** 1 to enter o's mind, occur to o. ~ *pd saja,* It occurred, struck me, flashed into my mind. 2 to be reminded. *Ia ~ akan anaknja jg gugur*, He was reminded of his fallen son. **-an** 1 memory. 2 thought(s), notion, idea. *~nja tertudju hendak membunuh diri*, He was thinking of committing suicide. **-²an** souvenir. **-²** *lupa* to remember vaguely. *tiada -²* unconscious. – *akan dirinja* to regain consciousness. *Tak – akan dirinja lagi*, He completely lost control of himself (because of anger). *Ia tak – diri selama dua hari*, He was unconscious for 2 days. *Kurang – saja*, I can't recall precisely. *Ia masih – djuga*, He still remembers.

inggang-inggung staggering, tottering.

Ingg(e)ris 1 English, British. *Ia berbitjara bahasa –*, He speaks English. 2 England. *Negeri –* England. *– Raya* Great Britain.

inggu asafetida.

ingin to wish, desire. *Saja – pergi sekarang*, I want to go now. **ber-**(*akan*), **ber-kan** to long for, crave, desire. **berke-an** to have the desire. **ke-an** wish, longing, desire. *~ tahu* curiosity. **memper-i** to arouse interest in s.o. **meng-i** to desire, long for. **per-an** desire, craving. *– damai* peaceloving. *– tahu* curious. *tak di-i* undesirable.

ingkar 1 to refuse, disobey, be reluctant. 2 to deny. **ke-an** 1 denial. 2 refusal. 3 defiance. **meng-i** 1 to deny. 2 to refuse. 3 to disobey.

ingsut meng- 1 to move, edge toward. 2 to shift, shove. **meng-kan** to move, shift s.t.

ingus (nasal) mucus.

ini 1 this. *buku –* this book. *– buku*, This is a book. 2 these. 3 here. *– dia*, Here it is. (This is it.) *– dia!* That's good! *-² djuga*, Always the same thing! *– djuga* this very. *Kamu harus pergi pd waktu – djuga*, You must go this very minute (now). *– hari* today. *– itu* such and such, this and that. *Meréka mempertjakapkan – itu*, They talked about this and that. *– pula* moreover. *– pula lagi*, This again! (The same thing again!)

inkarnasi incarnation.

inkonsekwénsi inconsistency.

inna lillahi wa inna ilaihi radji'un We are truly Allah's and to Him we return (placed in obituary notices).

inplénsa influenza.

insaf 1 notion. 2 realization, awareness. 3 conviction. **ke-an** realization. *~ keadilan* sense of justice. **meng-i**

1 to realize. 2 to be aware of. **meng-kan** 1 to convince. 2 to make o. realize. *– akan* to realize, see, understand. *– akan dirinja* to realize.

insan man, human being.

insang gills.

insani human. *tubuh –* human body.

insidén incident.

insidéntil incidental.

insinjur engineer. **ke-an** engineering.

insja Allah God willing.

insjaf see INSAF.

inspéksi 1 inspection. 2 inspectorate. **meng-** to inspect.

inspéktur inspector.

inspirasi inspiration.

instalasi installation.

instansi 1 authority, organ. *– pemerintah sipil* civil administration authority. 2 institute. 3 agency. 4 business firm. see 1 GEDUNG. 2 RUMAH.

institusicnil institutional.

instruksi instruction.

intai meng- to observe carefully, surreptitiously, spy, be on the lookout. **peng-** observer, scout (in army). **peng-an** observation, reconnaissance.

intan diamond. *– mentah* rough diamond.

intégrasi integration.

intelék intellect.

inteléktuil intellectual

intelidjén intelligent.

intendan quartermaster.

inténsif see INTÉNSIP.

inténsip intensive(ly). **meng-kan** to intensify.

inténsita(s) intensity.

intergéntil interpersonal.

internasional international.

internir meng- to intern. **-an** 1 internment, internment camp. 2 internee.

interpélasi interpellation.

interpiu interview. **meng-** to interview.

interpolasi interpolation. **meng-kan** to interpolate.

interprétasi interpretation.

interupsi interruption.

inti 1 kernel, nucleus. 2 stone. *– atom* nucleus of an atom. 3 tart filling. **-an** core. *sistim ~* core system. *– pati, – sari* essence. *kabinét –* inner cabinet. *sendjata –* nuclear weapon.

intil meng- to follow s.o. like a shadow. *Kemana sadja anak itu ~ bapaknja*, The child followed his father everywhere.

intim intimate. **ke-an** intimacy.

intip meng- to spy on, peep at. **peng-an** 1 spying. 2 surveillance.

intjang-intjut zigzag, higgledy-pig-gledy. *garis* – a crisscross of lines.

intjar drill. **meng-** 1 to aim (a gun, a slingshot, etc.). 2 to peer at, spy upon, watch.

intjer **meng-** 1 to spy on. 2 to aim at, draw a bead on. 3 to be after.

intji inch.

intjik paternal aunt.

intjit Be off!

intjut see INTJANG. **ter- -²** crippled.

intonasi intonation.

introdusir **meng-** to introduce.

intuisi intuition.

invasi invasion.

invéntaris inventory.

invéntarisator inventory taker.

invéstasi investment.

ipar brother-in-law, sister-in-law.

iprit **meng-** to run away through fear.

ipuh 1 poison obtained from plants and used for poisonous weapons. 2 vicious (of a person). **ber-** poisonous.

ipuk **meng-** to grow, cultivate. **peng-an** seedbed. **-an** seedling.

Ir [*Insinjur*] title of o. who has received an engineering degree in The Netherlands or in Indonesia.

iradat will of God.

Irak Iraq.

irama 1 rhythm. 2 theme. **ber-** rhythmic(al).

iras piece. **meng-** to form 1 piece. *Patung ini nampaknja* ~ , This statue appears to have been made from a solid piece. **se-** of 1 piece (of wood, etc.).

irasionil irrational.

iri **ber-** *hati* to be jealous. **ke-an** jealousy. **meng-** to be jealous. *Ia* ~ *kpd harta benda saja*, He is jealous of my wealth. **peng-** 1 envious. 2 jealous person. – *hati* 1 jealous. 2 jealousy, spite.

Irian New Guinea. – *Barat* Western New Guinea. – *Timur* Papua and Territory of New Guinea.

irigasi irrigation. **meng-kan** to irrigate.

irik **meng-** to thresh. **peng-** a flail. **ter-** to step on s.t. by mistake.

iring **ber-** successive, consecutive. **ber- -²an** o. after the other, in a procession. **meng-i, meng-kan** to accompany, escort. **peng-** retinue, follower, escort. **peng-an** procession, escort. **se-** side by side, in a row. ~ *dgn* together with, attended by. **se-an** *kapal* convoy of ships. **-²an** escort, procession. **-an** 1 accompaniment. ~ *piano* piano accompaniment. 2 flotilla, convoy.

iris slice. **se-** *roti* a slice of bread.

meng-(kan) to slice, to cut. *Saja* ~ *roti utk ibu*, I sliced the bread for mother. **-an** section, slice.

irit 1 economical. 2 frugal. 3 see ÉRÉT. **meng-** to economize.

Irlandia Ireland.

ironis ironic(al).

isa evening prayer period (approximately 8 P.M.). – *almasih* Jesus Christ.

isak **meng-** to sob. **ter- -²** 1 sobbing. 2 asthma(tic).

isap **meng-** 1 to smoke. *Ia* ~ *pipa*, He smokes a pipe. 2 to suck. 3 to inhale. **peng-** 1 piston. 2 smoker. *Ia* ~ *serutu*, He's a cigar smoker. **(peng)-an** 1 suction. 2 absorption. 3 usury. *-an djempol* invented story. *Itu* ~ *djempolmu sadja*, You made that up. *-an darah* bloodsucker (of merchants).

isarat see ISJARAT.

isbat 1 confirmation, ratification. 2 positive. *langkah jg* – a positive step. *aliran listrik* – positive electrical current. **meng-kan** to confirm, ratify.

iseng a nuisance. **-²** 1 doing s.t. to kill time. 2 to take it easy, relax. *Mari, kita* ~ *dipantai (laut)*, Let's relax on the beach. ~ *sadja sebagai hobby* to dabble merely as a hobby. **-²an** indifference.

isi 1 contents. – *buku ini kurang baik*, The contents of this book are not good. 2 gist. 3 taken, occupied (of a taxi or bus). 4 capacity. **ber-** 1 to contain. 2 filled. 3 loaded (of a gun). 4 racy, snappy (of stories). 5 well-proportioned. **ber-kan** to contain. **meng-** to fill up, load. *-lah téng bénsin saja*, Fill my gas tank, please. ~ *aki* to charge a battery. ~ *bénsin* to take on fuel (gasoline). ~ *perut* to eat. **meng-kan** 1 to fill s.t. up. 2 to put in. *Pasir itu di-kan kedalam kaléng*, The sand was put in the can. **peng-** filling, padding. ~ *halaman* filler (on a page). ~ *podjok* columnist (newspaper or magazine) ~ *waktu* pastime. **peng-an** 1 injection (of fuel). 2 act of filling. ~ *lowongan* filling of a gap or vacancy. **ter-** filled. *Lowongan tlh* ~ , The vacancy has been filled. **se-** *kampung* the whole village, all the inhabitants of the village. – *dada*, – *hati* s.t. on o's mind. *Tjurahkanlah* – *dadamu*, Tell me what's on your mind. – *kawin* sum of money, sometimes partly in kind, which the bridegroom gives to his future in-laws (usually to contribute to wedding ceremony costs). – *murni* genuine content. – *negeri* inhabitants of a state or country. – *perut* 1 in-

testines. 2 foodstuffs. 3 excrement. –
pulau inhabitants of an island. –
rumah family, occupants of a house. –
senapan charge (of a gun).
isit mulut gums.
isja 1 evening. 2 see ISA.
isjarat 1 hint, tip, wink, gesture,
sign. 2 signal. meng–kan to beckon,
give s.o. a wink, signal (with a gesture,
nod, etc.).
Islam Islam. *Ia orang –*, He is a
Moslem. ke–an concerning Islam,
Islamic. meng–kan 1 to convert to
Islam. 2 to circumcise.
Islandia Iceland.
isolasi isolation.
isolir meng– 1 to isolate. 2 to insulate (of electricity).
Isra' Mohammed's miraculous flight
from Mecca to Jerusalem.
Isro' see ISRA'.
istal horse barn, stable.
istana palace. – *présidén* the president's residence. ber– to live in a
palace.
istanggi k.o. incense.
isteri wife. ber– to be married (of a
man). memper– to marry, take a
wife. memper–kan 1 to marry a son
off. 2 to marry. – *piaraan* mistress,
concubine.
istiadat custom. meng–kan to make
a custom of s.t. ~ *berpakaian nasional
pd pembukaan parlemén* to make it
customary to wear national dress
during the opening session of parliament.
istibra sexual continence for a woman
for three months after divorce or
widowhood.
istilah 1 (technical) term. 2 terminology. *Komisi –* Terminology Commission. meng–kan to give a term or
name to s.t. per–an system of terminology.
istiméwa 1 extraordinary, special.
sidang – special session. 2 in particular, specially. *pengarang jg – menulis
ttg roman sedjarah* an author who
specializes in writing historical novels.
ke–an 1 specialty. 2 peculiarity.
meng–kan to regard s.t. as special.
ter– 1 special. 2 extraordinary. –
lagi, – pula especially, more so.
istirahat 1 rest, break. 2 interval. 3
intermission, break, pause, recess.
ber– to rest, take a break. *Apakah
waktu utk ~ ?* Is it time for recess?

meng–kan to give a break, a rest
period. peng–an, per–an 1 leave center (a place where members of a
group are provided facilities for spending their vacation). 2 place of rest.
istiwa see CHATTULISTIWA.
Itali Italy.
itam see HITAM.
itik duck. – *manila, – surati* Manila
duck.
itikad faith, determination, conviction. ber– 1 faithful. 2 to intend to.
3 to be deeply convinced (of a creed,
moral teachings, etc.). meng–kan to
believe in.
itil clitoris.
itjak² 1 to act as if. 2 not genuine.
ber– –² to pretend, simulate. *Ia* ~
pintjang, He pretends to walk with
a limp. –²an false, pretended.
itjip meng– to taste. –*lah makanan
ini dulu,* Have a taste of this food.
ittifak agreement.
itu 1 that. *topi –* that hat. – *topi,*
That's a hat. 2 those. *topi²* – those
hats. 3 the. *Perdjandjian – ditanda-
tangani semalam,* The agreement was
signed last night. – *dia* 1 That's it,
that's right, exactly, precisely. 2
That's it, there it is. 3 There he is.
– *djuga* the very. *pd hari – djuga*
on that very day. –² those same.
djeridji ~ those same bars. ~
djuga always the same.
itulah 1 What did I tell you? –*!
Beberapa kali saja katakan kepadamu
djangan berbuat demikian,* Now look!
I told you several times not to do
that. 2 That's the way it is. – *dia!*
That's your own fault. (That's just
it.)
itupun 1 that is to say. 2 with the
understanding that... – *kalau tuan
tak berkeberatan,* That's with the
understanding that you have no objections. 3 nevertheless. – *ia menolak
bertanggung djawab,* Nevertheless he
refused to shoulder the responsibility.
iuran 1 subscription. 2 contribution.
3 collection. 4 premium (insurance,
etc.). 5 dues.
izin 1 permit, license, franchise (to
operate bus line, etc.). 2 consent.
ke–an leave, permission. meng–kan
to permit, allow. – *kembali* re-entry
permit. – *leluasa* freedom of action.
– *memburu* hunting license. *dgn se-*
with the permission of.

J

ja 1 yes. –, *saja datang,* Yes, I'm coming. 2 may I not, may he not, etc. *Saja boléh datang,* –? I may come, may I not? *Djangan marah,* –? Don't be angry, will you? *Djangan ribut,* –, Don't be noisy, please. 3 go! (in racing). – *ini* these are.

j.a.d. [*jang akan datang*] the future, coming.

jagus see PADI.

jahudi Jew, Jewish. **ke–an** Judaism. **memper–kan** to revile, treat in inferior fashion, denigrate, blacken.

jais climacteric.

jaitu that is, i.e., viz.

jajasan foundation, institute. – *Ford* Ford Foundation.

jaji younger brother or sister.

jakin 1 sure, certain, convinced. *Saja tak* –, I'm not sure. 2 sincere. – *berusaha memetjahkan soal* make sincere efforts to solve the problem. **berke–an** to be convinced. **ke–an** 1 conviction. 2 certainty. 3 firm belief. **me–i** to convince firmly. **me–kan** 1 to convince, assure. 2 to make sure. *Ia* ∼ *sendiri bhw mobilnja baik,* He himself checked to be certain that his car was all right. 3 convincing.

jakni that is, namely, viz.

jalah see IALAH.

Jaman Yemen.

jamtuan monarch, ruler.

jang 1 who, which. *Siapa – datang kesini?* Who is coming here? *Itu koper – berat sekali,* That's a very heavy trunk. 2 that, which. *Buku – saudara bawa berat sekali,* The book you are carrying is very heavy. – *ini* this one. *Saja ambil – ini,* I'll take this one. *Saja lebih suka – biru,* I

prefer the blue one. – *lalu* last. *bulan – lalu* last month. 3 what. – *kami dapati disini ialah kaum pengembara,* What we found here were nomads. 4 the. *Mau minum apa?* – *biasa,* What'll you drink? The usual. – *Mulia* His (Your) Excellency.

ja'ni see JAKNI.

jatim fatherless child. – *piatu* an orphan.

jaum day. – *uddin* doomsday. – *-ul Kiamah* Day of Judgment.

jb [*jang berikut*] next, following.

j.b.l. [*jang baru lalu*] last.

jéksi injection.

jét see DJÉT.

jg. [*jang*] which, who.

j.i. [*jaitu*] that is, namely, viz., i.e.

j.l. [*jang lain*] the other.

jl. [*jang lalu*] past, last.

j.m.d. [*jang mendjalankan djabatan*] acting.

JME [*Jang Maha Esa*] the Almighty.

jodium iodine.

jodjana distance, field of vision. **se-mata** as far as the eye can see.

joga meditation.

jogia proper, fitting. **se–nja** 1 it is self-evident, obvious. 2 proper. ∼ *kamu pergi kerumahnja,* You should have gone to his home.

jth. [*jang terhormat*] the honorable.

jts. [*jang tersebut*] mentioned.

ju 1 shark. 2 older sister. – *todak* sawfish.

Juli see DJULI.

Junani 1 Greek. 2 Greece.

juran see IURAN.

juris 1 jurist, lawyer. 2 law student.

jurisdiksi jurisdiction.

jurk dress, frock.

K

k. [*katja*] page.
K. 1 [*kali*] river. 2 [*kota*] city.
ka wood glue. see KAH.
Ka [*kepala*] head, chief.
ka' see KAKAK.
ka'abah see KA'BAH.
kab. [*kabupatén*] regency (administrative unit).
ka'bah principal Islamic shrine in Mecca.
kabal see KEBAL.
kabar 1 news. *Radio menjiarkan – hari ini*, The radio broadcasts today's news. 2 report. **ber–** 1 to tell. *Ia dpt banjak* ∼ , He can tell much. 2 to let o. hear. *Ia tak pernah* ∼ , He never sent word of himself. **meng-kan** 1 to report. *Wartawan kita* ∼ - *jg terbaharu*, Our reporter reported the latest news. 2 to inform. *Surat itu* ∼ *kita ttg kematian teman kita*, The letter informed us of the death of our friend. **per-an** news. ∼ *jg disiarkan radio* the news broadcast over the radio. **ter–** spread. *Berita pemberontakan itu tlh* ∼ *ke-mana²*, The news of the revolt has spread everywhere. **-nja** people say, they say. ∼ *engkau tlh pergi keluar negeri*, People said (I heard, etc.) that you had gone abroad. – *angin*, – *selentingan* 1 rumor. 2 whispers. *Apa –?* How are you? (How do you do?) – *baik*, I am fine. *tidak – akan dirinja* to be unconscious.
kabat see KEBAT.
kabinét cabinet. – *inti* inner cabinet.
kabir mighty. *Tuhan al* – God the Almighty.
kabu² kapok.
kabul answered (of a prayer, request). **meng-kan** 1 to consent, grant (a request, wish, etc.) *Radja* ∼ *permohonan orang itu*, The king consented to the man's plea. 2 to fulfill. *Tuhan akan* ∼ *doamu*, God will fulfill your prayers. **peng-an** 1 consent. 2 fulfillment. ∼ *doanja* the fulfillment of his prayers. **ter–** 1 granted. *Permintaan saja* ∼ , My request was granted. 2 fulfilled. *Harapannja* ∼ , His hopes were fulfilled.
kabung **ber–** to mourn. *Seluruh ne-*

gara ∼ *ketika radja meninggal*, The whole country mourned when the king died. **per-an** 1 mourning attire. 2 mourning.
kabupatén 1 residence of a head of a regency. 2 office of the head of a regency. 3 regency (administrative area in Indonesia). 4 see BUPATI.
kabur 1 hazy. *Pemandangan itu sangat –*, The view was very hazy. 2 vague. *terlihat* – vaguely visible. 3 blurred. *Pemandangannja –*, His vision was blurred. 4 to run away, flee, bolt (of horses). **meng–** to fade away. *Kapal itu* ∼ *didalam kabut*, The boat faded away in the mist. **meng-kan** 1 to make hazy. *Kabut* ∼ *pemandangan*, The mist made the view hazy. 2 to blur. *Katja mata itu* ∼ *pemandanganmu sadja*, Those glasses blur your vision.
kabus see KABUR.
kabut 1 mist. 2 haze. 3 fog. **ber–** 1 misty. 2 hazy. 3 foggy. **meng-i** 1 to spray. 2 to befog, confuse. **meng-kan** to shake, beat (a tablecloth, carpet, etc.). **peng–** sprayer.
kadal lizard.
kadaluwarsa see KEDALUWARSA.
kadang² sometimes, once in a while – *ia pergi kegambar hidup*, Once in a while he goes to a movie. *kadang kala* sometimes, once in a while.
kadar 1 see KODRAT. 2 the degree, content, value, quality, standard, level. *Tebu mempunjai – gula jg tinggi*, Sugar cane has a high degree of sugar content. **meng-kan** to destine. *Demikianlah Tuhan* ∼ , Thus has God destined. **se–** just. *Ia datang* ∼ *melihat anaknja*, She came just to see her child. *Saja* ∼ *bersenda gurau sadja*, I was just joking. *ala –nja* 1 what is available. *Makan dan minumlah ala* ∼*nja*, Eat and drink what's available. 2 modest(ly). *Pengantin perempuan itu berpakaian ala* ∼ , The bride was modestly dressed. *Pésta itu ala* ∼*nja*, The party was just so-so. 3 sufficient, appropriate. *Gadjinja tjukup utk hidup* ∼*nja*, His earnings were sufficient to lead a modest life. ∼ *perlu* (if) necessary.

Ia berbitjara hanja ∼ *perlu sadja,*
He talked only when it was necessary.
∼ *tenaga* according to o's ability.
Tolonglah ia ∼ *tenagamu,* Help him
as much as you can. *Berilah dia
barang* ∼ , Give him a little. **se–nja**
1 to the best of o's ability. *Itu akan
saja kerdjakan* ∼ , I will do it to the
best of my ability. 2 as is appropriate,
appropriately. – *badja* steel alloy. –
hamud acidity.

kadas keridas an itchy, pimply rash.
kadaster land registration office.
kader cadre.
kadét midshipman.
kadi Moslem judge.
kadim 1 eternal. 2 close (in friendship). **meng–kan** to predict. **se–** of
the same descent.
kadir almighty.
kadjanah see KAZANAH. – *kata* vocabulary.
kadjang screen (of bamboo laths or
wickerwork, etc.). **meng–i** to screen
off. *Ia* ∼ *podjok,* He screened off the
corner. **pe–an** ship's cabin. – *magun*
boat awning.
kadjat see HADJAT.
kadji knowledge, teaching. *Tersohor
–nja ttg Islam,* He is famous for his
knowledge of Islam. *Tinggi –nja,* He
is a very learned man. – *pendéta
bidjaksana itu* the teachings of the
wise sage. **meng–** to recite Koranic
verses. ∼ *agama* to study religion.
∼ *baik buruknja* to consider the advantages and disadvantages. *Ia* ∼
baik buruknja perdjandjian dagang,
He was considering the advantages
and disadvantages of the business
deal. **peng–an** 1 doctrine. 2 recital
of the Koran.
kado present, gift.
kadok betel-nut leaf.
kaédah see KAIDAH.
kafan see KAPAN.
kafarat see KEPARAT.
kafilah desert caravan.
kafir 1 unbeliever, infidel. 2 pagan.
kagak 1 no. 2 not.
kagét 1 startled. *Semuanja – mendengar kabar itu,* Everybody was
startled at hearing the news. 2 taken
aback, frightened. **meng–kan** 1 to
startle. *Témbakan senapan itu* ∼ *saja,*
The rifle shot startled me. 2 startling.
Témbakan senapan itu sangat ∼ , The
rifle shot was startling.
kagum aghast, struck with amazement, amazed. *Saja – melihat gedung²
di New York,* I was amazed at the
buildings in New York. **ke–an** 1
astonishment. 2 admiration. **meng–i**
to admire. *Ia* ∼ *keindahan lukisan*

itu, He admired the beauty of the
painting. **meng–kan** 1 astonishing.
Gedung² ini sungguh ∼ , These buildings are really astonishing. 2 admirable. *Keindahan lukisan itu sungguh*
∼ , The beauty of the painting is
really admirable. ∼ *diri* to glorify
o.s. **peng–** admirer.
kah k.o. blue, livid lime or glue.
–kah 1 an interrogative particle. *Buku
tua– itu?* Is that an old book? *Itu–
buku tua?* Is that the old book (you
were talking about)? *Tua– buku itu?*
Is that book old? 2 around here?
Dimana– setasion? Where's the station? *Dimana– hotél Shoreham?*
Where's the Shoreham Hotel? *Pergi–
engkau?* Are you going? (Were you
going? Did you go?) *Begitu–?* Is that
so?
kahar vehicle pulled by draught animal (bullock cart, horse buggy, etc.).
kahwin see KAWIN.
kaidah 1 norm, rule. – *hukum* legal
norm. 2 principle. – *Bahasa Indonésia*
Principles of Indonesian. 3 method.
kail fish hook. **meng–** to fish. *Ia
pergi* ∼ *ikan,* He went out to fish.
peng– angler, fisherman.
kain 1 cloth. – *utk badju* cloth for a
shirt. 2 sarong. **ber–** to wear a
sarong. – *badju* clothing. – *bajang*
transparent cloth. – *batik* batik cloth.
– *belatju* unbleached cotton cloth. –
bentangan banner. – *djendéla* window
curtain. – *ikat kepala* headcloth. –
kadut gunny cloth. – *kapur* starched
white cloth. – *kasa* gauze. – *katji*
white cloth. – *kotor* menstruation.
– *lajar* canvas. – *lap* duster. – *linan*
linen cloth. – *lurik* hand-woven cloth
with stripe design. – *médja* tablecloth.
– *merikan* American imported fabric,
unbleached cotton. – *mota* canvas. –
muri white calico. – *pakaian* clothing
material, cloth. – *pél* dustcloth. –
pelangi woman's scarf. – *pelékat*
kind of striped material. – *pembalut*
bandage. – *penetap* towel. – *piké*
pique cloth. – *pual* voile. – *rahap*
pall. – *rami* hemp cloth. – *randi*
ribbed silk fabric. – *sampaian* laundry.
– *sarong* rectangular piece of cloth
wrapped around the body from the
waist down. – *serkai* filtering cloth. –
sungkit embroidered cloth. – *taf*
taffeta. – *teriko* tricot, tweed cloth. –
terpal tarpaulin, canvas. – *tik* pillow
slip. – *tjap* printed cloth. – *tjemar*
menstruation. – *tjindé* dyed Javanese
fabric.
kais **meng–** to scrape around for food.
Ajam² ∼ *mentjari makan,* The chickens scraped around for food.

kaisar emperor. **ke-an** empire.

kait 1 hook. 2 catch, complication. *Hati²lah, barangkali ada –nja perdjandjian itu,* Be careful, that agreement may have some catches. **beran, ber- –²** linked together. *Saja rasa semua kedjadian itu* ∼ *satu sama lain,* I think that those incidents are related. **meng–** 1 to hook. *Ia* ∼ *buah itu dari pohon,* He hooked the fruit from the tree. 2 to crochet s.t. **peng–** a hook. **-an** hook, fastener, snap. – *dan mata* hooks and eyes.

kaja 1 wealthy, well-to-do. *Ia orang –,* He is a wealthy man. 2 to be rich. *Makanan itu – dgn zat putih telur,* The food was rich in protein. 3 like. *Tingkah lakunja – orang gila sadja,* His behavior was that of a mad man. **ke-an** 1 wealth. ∼ *alam* natural wealth. 2 power. ∼ *Tuhan* the power of the Lord. ∼ *kata²* vocabulary. **memper-i** 1 to make wealthy. 2 to enrich. ∼ *pengalaman politiknja* to enrich o's political experience. **mengkan** to make wealthy. **ter–** 1 richest. 2 enriched. – *akan* rich in. *Indonésia akan hasil bumi,* Indonesia is rich in agricultural produce. – *baru* newly rich, *nouveau riche.* – *hati* to be generous. – *raja* very rich. *Orang itu – raja,* He is very rich. *Tuhan jg –* Almighty God.

kajak as, like. see KAJA 3.

kajal see CHAJAL.

kajangan Hindu heaven.

kajap tumor, boil.

kajoman protected. **peng–** protector.

kaju 1 wood. 2 wooden. *médja –* a wooden table. **ber–** wooden. *Kapal lajar ini tidak* ∼ , This sailboat has no wooden parts. **per-an** lumber business. **-²an** trees. – *anduh* prop, support. – *api* firewood. – *ara* fig tree. – *arang* ebony. – *bakar* firewood. – *basung* light k.o. wood. – *besi* ironwood. – *djati* teak. – *gaharu* aloeswood. – *hitam* ebony. – *manis* cinnamon. – *pukul,* – *pemukul* ball bat. – *putih* cajuput. – *silang* crossbeam. – *rengat* rosewood. – *tjagak* a wooden pole forked at one end, a forked piece of wood. – *tjendana* sandalwood. – *triplex* plywood.

kajuh oar, paddle. **ber-, meng–** to row, paddle ∼ *sepéda* to cycle. **peng–** 1 oar, paddle. 2 oarsman, rower.

kak see KAKAK (used by wife to husband).

kakah ter- –² to roar (with laughter). *Ia tertawa* ∼ , He roared with laughter.

kakak 1 older brother. 2 older sister. 3 form of address for older person (male or female). – **beradik** to have younger brother(s) or sister(s).

kakaktua 1 cockatoo, k.o. parrot. 2 pair of pliers.

kakanda 1 older brother. 2 older sister. 3 polite term of address for husband (by wife).

kakang 1 older brother. 2 form of address used by wife for husband. 3 form of address for older brother or older man.

kakap a sea fish similar to sole. **meng–** to reconnoiter, patrol. **peng–** scout, spy.

kakas see KAIS.

kakatua see KAKAKTUA.

kakék 1 grandfather. 2 old man. –² very old. *Orang itu sdh* ∼ , The man was very old.

kaki 1 foot. – *saja sakit,* My foot hurts. 2 leg. 3 foot (measure). *Pandjang médja itu lima –,* The table is 5 feet long. **ber–** to lean (on). **meng–** submissive. ∼ *langit* horizontal. – *angkasa* horizon. – *buatan* artificial leg. – *datar* flat foot. – *dian* candlestick. – *langit* horizon. – *lilin* candlestick. – *lima* 1 sidewalk. 2 front step. – *tangan* accomplice, henchman. *pendjahat dan – tangannja* the criminal and his accomplice. – *tiga* tripod. – *tjelana* trouser leg.

kaku 1 stiff. *Lengannja jg patah itu –,* His broken arm was stiff. 2 stiff, unbending. *Meskipun ia – kelihatannja, ia sebetulnja sangat ramah,* Although he seems to be unbending, he is really a very friendly person. 3 clumsy. *Saja masih – sadja mendjalankan mobil stir kanan,* I'm still clumsy at driving a right-hand drive car. **ke-an** 1 stiffness. ∼ *badannja* the stiffness of his body. *Dlm suasana ramah itu* ∼*nja lekas hilang,* In the friendly atmosphere his stiffness soon disappeared. 2 rigidity. – *lidah* unable to talk easily. – *tangan* callus on hand.

kakung male.

kakus toilet.

kala time. *Pd suatu – adalah seorang radja,* Once upon a time there was a king. **ber–** 1 periodically. *Pasang dan surut datang* ∼ , Flood tide and ebb tide come periodically. 2 periodical, magazine. **ber- –²** from time to time, occasional. **-an** chronological. *ada –nja* sometimes. *pd – itu* at that time. – *djengking* poisonous scorpion.

kalah 1 defeated. *Negara itu – berperang,* The country was defeated in the war. 2 to lose. *Ia – 50 rupiah* *dlm pendjudian itu,* He lost 50 rupiahs at gambling. 3 inferior to. *Anak saja tak – dari anak² lain,* My child is not inferior to other children. **ke–an** defeat. **meng–** to give in. *Ia selalu ~ pd adiknja,* He always gives in to his younger brother. **meng–kan** to defeat, lick. *Ia ~ musuhnja,* He defeated his enemies. *tak* **ter–kan** invincible. see ALAH.

kalai meng– 1 to lie down relaxed. 2 to lean against s.t. **meng–kan** to lay s.t. or s.o. down.

kalam word. – *Ullah* God's word.

kalamun see KELAMUN.

kalang support, prop. **ber–, ter–** supported. *Atap itu hanja ~ dua tiang bambu sadja,* The roof is supported by only two bamboo poles. **ber–** *tanah* deceased. **memper–, meng–** to support. *Ia ~ atap itu dgn tiang bambu,* He supported the roof with bamboo poles. **ter–** *dimata* visualized. *Rumah orang tuanja ~ dimatanja,* He could visualize his parents' house. **–an** circle. *~ pemerintah* government circles. *~ kapal* 1 dock. 2 shipyard. – *kabut* confused, chaotic. *Keadaan – kabut,* The situation was confused.

kalap 1 possessed by an evil spirit. 2 bewildered, confused. **ke–an** 1 confusion. 2 bewilderment.

kalau 1 if. – *ia datang panggillah saja,* If he comes please call me. 2 when. – *pekerdjaanmu sdh selesai engkau boléh pergi,* When you have finished your work, you may go. 3 as for... *Kakak saja gemar melihat gambar hidup, – saja, saja lebih suka tinggal dirumah,* My brother likes to go to the movies, whereas I would rather stay home. **–pun** even though. *~ ia sakit ia pergi djuga,* Even though he was sick, he went out all the same. *–²* 1 maybe. *Tanjalah dia, ~ dia tahu,* Ask him, maybe he knows. 2 lest. *Djangan memandjat pohon itu, ~ djatuh,* Don't climb that tree lest you fall. 3 otherwise. *–... bagaimana* how about. – *Rp 100 bagaimana?* How about 100 rupiahs?

kalawarta periodical, magazine.

Kalbar [*Kalimantan Barat*] West Kalimantan.

kalbu 1 heart. 2 mind. *Keluarkanlah ap jg ada dlm –mu,* Please state what you have in mind.

kaldai see KELEDAI.

kaldu broth.

kaléng 1 tin. *atap –* a tin roof. 2 tin can. **–(–)an** canned food.

kalérek clerk.

kali 1 river. 2 time. – *ini engkau masih kumaafkan,* This time I'll forgive you. *beberapa* – several times. 3 times (in multiplication). *Dua – tiga mendjadi enam,* Two times three is six. 4 fold. *sepuluh–* tenfold. 5 = BARANGKALI. *Ja,* – Yeah, maybe. **ber–** *–²* repeatedly. *Sdh ~ engkau terlambat,* You have come late repeatedly. **meng–kan** to multiply. *Ia ~ kedua bilangan itu,* He multiplied the 2 figures. **per–an** multiplication. **se–** 1 once. *Ia baru ~ pergi ke Djakarta,* He has gone to Jakarta only once. 2 very. *Ia marah ~ ,* He was very angry. 3 at the same time. *Kalau engkau pergi keperpustakaan bawalah buku ini ~ ,* If you go to the library, take this book at the same time. *~ -banjak* mass. *produksi ~ -banjak* mass production. *~ dua hari* every other day. *~ lagi* once more. *~ ...tetap...* once...always... *~ merdéka tetap merdéka* once free always free. **se–an** 1 all. *Meréka ~ pergi kesekolah,* All of them went to school. 2 at the same time. *Kembalikanlah buku ini ~ ,* Return this book at the same time. **se–gus** all at once. *Semua pekerdjaannja diselesaikannja dgn ~ ,* He finished all his work all at once. **se–pun** although. *~ ia sakit ia pergi kesekolah djuga,* Although he was sick, he went to school anyway. **se–²** once in a while, every now and then. *~ ia pergi melihat gambar hidup,* Once in a while he goes to the movies. **se–** *–²* *tidak* never, not at all. *Pintu itu ~ tidak boléh dibuka,* The door may under no circumstances be opened. *Djangan ~ kau berani pergi dgn tiada seizin saja,* Don't you dare go without my permission. **–an** you (pl.). *utk pertama –nja* for the first time.

kalifah 1 caliph. 2 caliphate.

kalimah 1 see KALIMAT. 2 – *sahadat* confession of creed (in Islam).

Kalimantan Indonesian Borneo. – *Inggeris* British Borneo.

kalimantang 1 pennant. 2 white beam of light.

kalimat sentence, phrase. – *madjemuk* compound sentence. – *tunggal* simple sentence.

kalio ajam chicken curry with chilies.

kalis 1 dull, dim (of a surface). 2 immune to disease. 3 pure. 4 phlegmatic, unmoved.

kalkarim wall paint.

kalkulasi calculation.

kalkun turkey.

kalo 1 strainer. 2 see KALAU.

kalong flying fox.
kalor heat. – *bakar* heat released by combustion.
kalori calorie.
Kalsel [*Kalimantan Selatan*] South Kalimantan.
Kalselteng [*Kalimantan Selatan & Tengah*] South & Central Kalimantan.
Kalteng [*Kalimantan Tengah*] Central Kalimantan.
kalu see KALAU.
kalung necklace. **ber–** to have as a necklace. *Gadis Hawaii ∼ rangkaian bunga*, Hawaiian girls wear leis around their neck. **meng–i** to put on a necklace. *Orang Hawaii ∼ para musafir dgn – bunga*, The Hawaiian puts leis around the tourists' necks. – *bunga* lei.
kalut confused, chaotic. *Pikiran saja –*, My mind is confused. **ke–an** confusion. **meng–kan** to upset. *Kabar itu ∼ saja*, The news upset me. – *bin katjau* extremely confused.
kamadéan parasite.
kamar room. **ber–** to room. *Ia ∼ dihotél itu*, He roomed in that hotel. – *batja* reading room. – *bedah* operating room. – *beladjar* study room. – *bitjara* consulting room (of a physician). – *bola* 1 clubhouse, casino. 2 game room, poolroom. – *duduk* living room. – *gelap* 1 prison cell. 2 (photographic) darkroom. – *ketjil* toilet, rest room. – *makan* dining room. – *mandi* bathroom. – *mati* mortuary, the morgue. – *minum* bar. – *muka* anteroom. – *penginapan* hotel room. – *pétak* partitioned room. – *petang* darkroom. – *rias* dressing room. – *tamu* living room. – *tidur* bedroom. – *tunggu* waiting room.
kambang **meng–** to float. *Batang kaju itu ∼ diair*, The log floated in the water. **–an** float (on a fishing line).
kambeli woolen fabric.
kambing goat. **meng– –²kan** to debase. **meng– -hitamkan** to make a scapegoat of s.o. – *domba* sheep. – *hitam* scapegoat. – *kibas* fat-tailed sheep.
Kambodja Cambodia.
kambrat 1 comrade. 2 party.
Kambudja see KAMBODJA.
kambu(h) to have a relapse. – *lagi* recurrence.
kamera camera. – *ketupat* box camera.
kamhar camel's hair.
kami 1 we (excluding the person addressed). – *akan meninggalkan kamu sekalian*, We will leave you all. 2 us (excluding the person addressed). *Apakah tuan memanggil –?* Did you

call us? 3 our (excluding the person addressed). *Itu rumah –, tuan*, That's our house, sir. 4 I. – *sekeluarga* my family and I.
kamiat quantity.
Kamis Thursday. see KEMIS.
kamitua deputy village chief in central Java.
kampagne see KAMPANJE.
kampai **ber–** to lie down, stretch out. **meng–** to lay s.t. down.
kampak see KAPAK.
kampanje campaign.
kampemén military barracks.
kampil gunny sack.
kampit see KAMPIL.
kampiun champion.
kamprét bat.
kampuh 1 shawl, cover. 2 hem, seam, strip of cloth used in bookbinding.
kampung 1 village, cluster of buildings making up a large homestead or a small hamlet and including the surrounding mixed gardens. 2 quarter, area, administrative or otherwise, of a city in Indonesia. **ber–** 1 gathered. 2 together. **per–an** 1 group of kampungs. 2 spot for gathering together. **–an** country bumpkin. *Kamu ini ∼ ,* You're acting like a country bumpkin. – *halaman* 1 native village. 2 birthplace.
kamu 1 you (very fam. singular and plural). – *harus makan*, You have to eat. – *semuanja harus makan*, All of you have to eat. 2 your. *Apakah ini buku –?* Is this your book?
kamus dictionary. – *ilmu bumi* gazetteer.
kan 1 abbrev. of AKAN. *Ia tak – datang*, He will not come. 2 abbrev. of BUKAN. – *dia akan datang?* He would come, wouldn't he? – *kita sdh mempunjai kemerdékaan?* Don't we already have independence? 3 pitcher.
kanak² small child. **ke– -²an** childish(ness). **–² anjir** newly born baby.
kanan 1 right. *Tangan – saja sakit*, My right hand hurts. 2 rightist. **meng–** 1 to keep to the right. *Kendaraan selalu harus ∼ didjalan*, Vehicles must keep to the right at all times. 2 to turn to the right. *Mobil itu ∼ ,* The car turned to the right.
kanda see KAKANDA.
kandang 1 stable. 2 corral. **meng–** to lock up. *Ia ∼ ternaknja*, He locked up his cattle. *Polisi ∼ pendjahat itu*, The police locked up the criminal. **meng–i** to fence in. *Ia ∼ padang rumput sapinja*, He fenced in his cow pasture. **meng–kan** to put in

the stable. *Setiap petang ia ~ ter-naknja,* Every evening he puts his cattle in the stable. **-an** prison (cell). *- ajam* chicken house. *- andjing* dog-house. *- babi* pigpen. *- bulan* halo around the moon. *- burung* bird cage. *- merpati* pigeon loft. *- mobil* garage. *- ternak* stock pen. *pulang ke-* to return to o's original home.

kandar meng-kan to operate a ve-hicle (car, pedicab, wagon). **peng-**driver, operator.

kandas 1 to run aground. *Kapal itu - pd batu karang,* The boat ran aground on the reefs. 2 to fail. *Segala usahanja -,* All his efforts failed. **ke-an** failure. **meng-kan** 1 to strand. *Badai itu ~ banjak kapal,* The storm stranded many boats. 2 to frustrate. *Lawan² politiknja hendak ~ usahanja,* His political opponents wanted to frustrate his efforts.

kandil 1 lamp, lantern. 2 candelabra, candlestick. 3 candle.

kandjang ber-persevering, persistent.

kandjar dagger.

kandjeng form of address or reference for Javanese nobility of high rank.

kandji starch. **meng-** to starch. *Ia ~ tjutjiannja,* He starched his laundry.

kandung uterus. **meng-** 1 pregnant. *Perempuan itu ~ ,* That woman is pregnant. 2 to contain. *Buah ~ banjak pitamin,* Fruit contains many vitamins. *Peristiwa ini ~ adjaran,* This event teaches us s.t. 3 to impli-cate s.o. *~ hati* to bear s.o. a grudge. **ter-** *dlm hati* to be on o's mind. *Apakah jg ~ dlm hatimu?* What's on your mind? **-an** 1 pregnancy. 2 womb. *- kentjing* bladder. *tak -* free from.

Kanékés 1 name preferred by the Badui people of West Java. 2 One of the principal villages of these people.

kang see KAKANG.

kangen to long for. *Saja - akan tanah air,* I long for my country.

kangkang 1 legs wide apart (of a person standing). 2 crotch. **meng-** to straddle. *Ia duduk ~ ,* He sat straddling. **meng-kan** to straddle (the legs).

kangkung 1 large frog. 2 k.o. spin-ach.

kangmas 1 older brother. 2 term of address for husband, darling.

kanguru kangaroo.

kanker cancer.

kanselir chancellor.

kanta lens.

kantang mud flats.

kantin canteen, PX.

kantjah 1 large kettle, cauldron. 2 troubled situation. *- kesengsaraan* slough of despair. *- peperangan* the cauldron of war. *- politik* the politi-cal arena.

kantjana see KENTJANA.

kantjap filled to the brim. *Takaran - diisi dgn minjak,* The measuring glass was filled to the brim with oil.

kantjil mouse deer.

kantjing button. **meng-(kan)** 1 to button. *Ia ~ badjunja,* He buttoned his shirt. 2 to lock, secure (a window, door, etc., which is provided with hook and catch). **peng-** fastener, catch. *- badju* shirt button. *- djeprét* 1 snap fasteners. 2 push button. *- gigi, - mulut* lockjaw. *- léhér badju* collar stud.

kantjut loincloth, G string.

kantong see KANTUNG.

kantor office. **ber-** to have o's office. *Ia ~ didalam gedung itu,* He has his office in that building. *- angin* weather station. *- bang* bank (build-ing). *- béa* customs office. *- besar* main office. *- kawat* telegraph office. *- lélang* auction hall, auctioneer's office. *- meterai* Office of Weights and Measures. *- pabéan* customs office. *- padjak* tax office. *- pelantjongan* travel agency, tourist office. *- pen-daftar* Patent Office. *- perwakilan* branch, local office. *- polisi* police station. *- pos* post office. *- pusat* main office. *- télepon* telephone station. *- tera* Office of Weights and Measures. *- tjabang* branch office.

kantuk sleepiness. **meng-** to be sleepy. *Saja sangat ~ ,* I'm very sleepy. **peng-** sleepyhead. see ANTUK.

kantung 1 pocket. 2 bag. **meng-i** 1 to carry s.t. in the pocket. *Ia selalu ~ beberapa korék api,* He always carries some matches in his pocket. 2 to pocket s.t. **meng-kan** to put s.t. in the pocket. *Ia ~ pénanja,* He put his pen in his pocket. *- belakang* hip pocket. *- kemaluan* scrotum.

kaok ber- -² 1 to cackle. *Ajam² ~ ,* The chickens cackled. 2 to yell and shout. *Anak² ~ ,* The children yelled and shouted. **meng-i** to yell after. *Ia ~ anaknja jg pergi berlari itu,* She yelled at her child who was running away.

kaonderan subdistrict.

kaos see KAUS.

kap 1 auto hood. 2 shade. *- lampu* lampshade. *- mobil* convertible top.

kapa² awning (on a ship).

kapa(h) ter– 1 startled. 2 sobbing.
3 gasping for breath. 4 shivering
from cold.
kapai see KEPAI.
kapak adz. meng– to chop with an
adz.
kapal ship, boat. ber– to go by ship.
Ia ~ pergi ke Éropah, He went to
Europe by ship. meng–kan to ship.
Ia ~ barang dagangannja, He shipped
his merchandise. peng–an shipping.
per–an 1 shipping. 2 fleet, tonnage.
3 shipyard. 4 navigation. – *api*
steamship. – *badjak* pirate ship. –
dagang cargo vessel. – *induk* aircraft
carrier, mother ship. – *keruk* dredging
boat. – *komando* flagship. – *korék* tin
dredger. – *lajar* sailboat. – *menjusur*
coaster. – *meriam* gunboat. – *mil*
mail boat. – *mualim* pilot boat. –
muatan freighter. – *nelajan* fishing
vessel. – *pandu* pilot boat. – *pemair,*
– *pemadjar* cruiser. – *pemburu* destroyer. – *penambang* ferry. – *pendarat*
landing craft. – *pendjeladjah* cruiser.
– *penempur* battleship. – *pengangkut*
freighter, transport, cargo vessel. –
pengemas salvage vessel. – *pengiring*
escort vessel. – *penjapu randjau* mine
sweeper. – *penumpang* passenger ship.
– *perang* man-of-war. – *peronda*
pantai coast guard vessel. – *perusak*
destroyer. – *pesiar* excursion steamer.
– *rambu* tourist ship. – *rampasan*
prize. – *roda lampung* stern-wheeler.
– *selam,* – *silam* submarine. – *tangki*
tanker. – *tarik* tugboat. – *terbang,* –
udara aircraft. – *uap* steamship.
kapalan calloused. *Tangannja –,* His
hands were calloused.
kapan 1 when. – *saudara akan pergi?*
When will you leave? 2 isn't it, etc.
Djangan tanja² lagi, – *sekarang sdh*
djelas, Don't keep on asking, it's
clear now, isn't it? 3 shroud of unbleached cotton. ber– shrouded. *Majat*
itu ~ kain putih, The corpse was
shrouded in white cloth. meng–i to
shroud. *Meréka ~ majat itu,* They
wrapped the corpse in a shroud. –²
whenever. *Datanglah kemari ~ kau*
suka, Drop by whenever you like. ~
sadja any time. *Datanglah ~ sadja,*
Come any time.
kapang 1 mold. 2 small testacean
which burrows in wood.
kapar ber–an scattered. *Kotoran ~*
di-mana², Rubbish was scattered
everywhere. meng–kan to deploy,
disperse. *Ia ~ pasukannja sepandjang*
pantai, He deployed his troops all
along the beach. ter– scattered in
disorderly fashion. *Korban bandjir*

itu ~ di-mana², The flood victims
were scattered everywhere. –an 1
rubbish. 2 driftwood.
kapas 1 cotton wool. 2 cotton plant.
– *pembalut* absorbent cotton.
kapasitas capacity.
kapasitét capacity.
kaper moth.
kapi pulley block.
kapilah see KAFILAH.
kapir see KAFIR.
kapit see APIT.
kapitalis capitalist.
kapok 1 see KAPUK. 2 to be cured.
Ia tak berani lagi mentjuri, ia sdh –
semendjak ia ditangkap polisi, He
does not dare steal any more; he has
had enough since he was caught by
the police. *Saja sdh – berichtiar*
menolong orang jg tidak berterima
kasih itu, I have had my fill trying
to help that ungrateful person.
meng–kan to teach s.o. a lesson.
Dgn pukulan ia ~ anaknja, By
spanking he taught his son a lesson.
kapol cardamom.
kaporal corporal (mil.).
kapstok clothes hanger.
kapsul capsule.
kapt. [*kaptén*] 1 captain. 2 lieutenant
(navy).
kaptén 1 captain. 2 lieutenant
(navy). – *udara* air force captain.
kapuk kapok.
kapung see APUNG.
kapur 1 lime. 2 calcium. meng– to
calcify. meng–i to whitewash. meng–
kan to prepare a chew of betel.
pe–an 1 lime pit. 2 limekiln. se–
sirih a chew of betel. – *barus* camphor.
– *batu* plaster. – *belanda* writing chalk.
– *hidup,* – *kuripan* quicklime. – *mati*
slaked lime, mortar. – *mentah,* –
tohor quicklime. – *tulis* chalk.
Kapurel [*Kepala Public Relations*]
Chief of Public Relations.
kar a map.
kar. 1 [*karésidénan*] residency. 2 [*ka-*
rangan] article, essay.
karabin carbine.
karaéng title of nobility in Macassar.
karah 1 stain. 2 tartar on the teeth.
ber– 1 stained. 2 to have tartar on
the teeth.
karam 1 to be shipwrecked, founder. *Kapal itu –,* The ship sank. 2
to fail. *Segala usahanja –,* All his
attempts failed. meng–kan 1 to sink.
Kapal terbang itu ~ perahu itu, The
plane sank the boat. 2 to make fail.
Ia hendak ~ usaha musuhnja, He
wanted to make his enemy's attempts
fail.

karang 1 coral. 2 coral reef. 3 atoll. **kepeng-an** authorship. **meng-** 1 to write, compose. *Ia ∼ sebuah buku*, He wrote a book. *∼ lagu kebangsaan* to compose the national anthem. 2 to make up s.t. *Ia selalu dpt ∼ alasan apabila ia bersalah*, He is always able to make up excuses when he is wrong. 3 to arrange (flowers, setting of jewels, stringing of beads, etc.). *∼ bunga* to arrange flowers. **pe-an** 1 yard (of a house). 2 premises. *Segala gedung diatas ∼nja*, All the buildings are on his premises. **peng-** author. *∼ djantung* beloved. *∼ gigi* gums. *∼ telur* ovary. **ter-** to run aground. **-an** 1 composition. 2 written by. *Hamlet ∼ Shakespeare*, Hamlet was written by Shakespeare. 3 s.t. which has been made up. *∼ bunga* 1 flower arrangement. 2 wreath. 3 bouquet of flowers. *∼ utama* masterpiece. **-meng-** composing. *Kesukaannja adalah ∼*, Composing was his hobby.
karantina quarantine.
karar stable, peaceful.
karat 1 carat (of precious stones). 2 rust. **ber-** 1 to rust. *Keringkanlah pisau itu; nanti ∼*, Dry off that knife; otherwise it will rust. 2 rusty. **-an** rusty.
karau meng- to stir, mix (food, drink).
karbit carbide.
karbol carbolic acid. **di-** 1 to be bawled out. 2 to be cleaned with carbolic acid.
kardamunggu cardamom.
kardan differential gear.
kardus 1 cardboard. 2 cardboard box, carton.
karena 1 because. *Ia tak mau makan ∼ perutnja sakit*, He did not want to eat because he had a stomach-ache. 2 reason, cause. *Ia marah dgn tidak ada ∼nja*, He was angry without reason. 3 on account of. 4 from. *Ia lemah ∼ kelaparan*, He's weak from hunger. *∼ apa* why. *∼ apa ia menangis?* Why did he cry? *∼ itu* therefore. *Ia sakit; ∼ itu ia tidak dpt pergi kesekolah*, He was sick; therefore he could not go to school. *oléh ∼ because. Oléh ∼ ia sakit ia tidak pergi kesekolah*, Because he was sick he did not go to school. *oléh ∼ itu* therefore. **di-kan** for that reason. *Para pembatja sendiri mungkin tlh maklum bhw ∼ konstalasi politik déwasa ini tiap detik ber-obah²*, The readers will know that because of that the present political situation changes every second.
karés. [*karésidénan*] residency.
karésidénan residency (admin. unit).

karét 1 rubber. 2 elastic. *ban ∼* elastic band. 3 eraser. **ber-** rubberized. **ke-an** elasticity. *∼ alam* natural rubber. *∼ busa* 1 foam rubber. 2 a sponge. *∼ tiruan* synthetic rubber.
kari curry.
karia see KARJA.
karib 1 relative. *Ia adalah ∼ saja*, He is my relative. 2 close, intimate. *Ia adalah sahabat ∼ saja*, He is a close friend of mine. *Persahabatan kita sangat ∼*, Our friendship is very close. **ber-** 1 to be related. *Saja ∼ dgn dia*, I am related to him. 2 to be friends. *Kita sdh lama ∼*, We have been friends for a long time. **ke-an** closeness. **meng-i** to be close to. *Saja ∼ keluarga kawan saja*, I am close to my friend's family. **meng-kan** to bring closer. *Minat meréka jg sama itu ∼ meréka*, Their mutual interests brought them closer. *∼ dan ba'id* relatives and friends.
kariére career.
karih meng- to stir food or drink.
karikatur caricature.
karil [*karangan ilmiah*] scientific or scholarly paper.
karim generous, magnanimous.
karja work(s). *∼ djam* timepiece. *∼ hias* decorative work. *kabinét ∼* business cabinet. *∼ Shakespeare* the works of Shakespeare. *∼ tak berkala* occasional paper.
karjawan see KARYAWAN.
karna see KARENA.
karnaval carnival.
karpus 1 conical. 2 cap of house ridge.
karsa wish, intention. *∼ dan karya* will and work.
kartjis ticket. *∼ keréta api* railway ticket. *∼ masuk* admission ticket. *∼ nama* calling card. *∼ pulang pergi* round-trip ticket. *∼ retur* return ticket. *∼ tjatutan* scalper's ticket. *∼ undangan* free, complimentary ticket.
karton cardboard.
kartotik card file.
kartu 1 card. 2 playing cards. **pe-an** card file. *∼ kuning* citizenship card. *∼ nama* calling card. *∼ pengenal* identity card. *∼ pemilihan* ballot. *∼ penduduk* a card indicating that o. is a resident. *∼ pindahan* notice of moving. *∼ pos* post card. *∼ tamu* calling card. *∼ tandatangan* signature card. *∼ undangan* invitation.
karuan see KERUAN.
karuhun formerly, previously.
karung bag, sack, bale. *∼ anak* membrane. *∼ goni* gunny sack. *∼ rami* jute sack.
karunia gift, grant. **meng-i** to re-

ward. *Radja* ∼ *saja,* The king rewarded me. **meng-kan** to present, reward. *Radja* ∼ *uang pd saja,* The king presented me with money.

karut confused, muddled, chaotic. − *bitjaranja,* He spoke incoherently. *Ingatannja* −, His mind was confused. − *marut* completely confused. *Pikirannja mendjadi* − *marut,* He lost his head completely.

karya see KARJA.

karyawan 1 author, writer. *Shakespeare* − *Macbeth,* Shakespeare is the author of Macbeth. 2 worker. − *pérs* journalist.

karyawati female worker.

kas 1 money supply. − *kita sudah kosong,* Our money supply is exhausted. 2 cash window. *Hendaklah membajar pd* −, Please pay the cashier. − *negara* 1 government treasury. 2 government's money supply.

kasa 1 grating, wire screen. 2 see KAIN. 3 see KAWAT.

KASAB [*Kepala Staf Angkatan Bersendjata*] Chief of Staff of the Armed Forces.

kasad intention.

KASAD [*Kepala Staf Angkatan Darat*] Army Chief of Staff.

kasai lotion (cosmetic).

kasak 1 persuasion. 2 destroyed. **meng-** to persuade. − *-kisik* 1 whispering. 2 rumors. 3 persuasive. − *-kusuk* consultation, plotting.

kasakata vocabulary.

kasanah see KAZANAH.

kasap coarse, rough. *berbulu* − coarse-haired.

kasar 1 coarse. *Kain itu* −, That cloth was coarse. 2 rough. *Papan itu* −, The plank was rough. 3 crude. *minjak* − crude oil. 4 rude. *Kata²nja jg* − *itu menjakiti hati saja,* His rude words hurt me. 5 vulgar, inelegant, unrefined. **ke-an** 1 coarseness. 2 rudeness. **meng-i** to treat rudely. *Djangan* ∼ *anak itu,* Do not treat that child rudely. **meng-kan** to make rough.

kasasi appeal (judicial).

kasau rafter(s) of roof.

kasemat controversy, conflict.

kasemek see KESMAK.

kasép see KASIP.

kasi to give. *-lah itu pd saja,* Give that to me. − *saja sepiring nasi,* Give me a plate of rice. **meng-** to give. − *tahu* to let know. *Diperiksa dulu, nanti saja* − *tahu,* I'll look into it and let you know later. − *lihat* to show. − *lihat,* Show me. (Let me see it.) − *tangan* to shake hands. − *turun* to lower, let down. see KASIH.

kasiat see CHASIAT.

kasidah a religious chant in Arabic.

kasih 1 affection, love. 2 to love. *Ia* − *pd anaknja,* He loved his child. **ber-** *-²an* 1 to love o. another. 2 to make love, (pay) court. **ke-** beloved. **meng-ani** to pity. *Ia* ∼ *anak jg malang itu,* He pitied the poor child. **meng-kan** to give s.t. *Ia* ∼ *uang itu pd saja,* He gave the money to me. **pe-** love charm. **peng-** 1 love charm. 2 altruistic person. 3 gift, present. **-an** 1 pity. ∼ *tuan, saja blm makan sehari,* Have pity, sir, I have not eaten all day. 2 What a pity! 3 mercy. ∼ *akan* to pity. *Saja* ∼ *akan pengemis buta itu,* I pitied the blind beggar. − **-meng-ani** to love o. another. − *mesra* deep love. − *sajang* love and affection. see KASI.

kasim castrated. **meng-** to castrate.

kasima unnerved, upset.

kasip too late. *Ia datangnja* −, He came too late. **ke-an** lateness. ∼*nja disebabkan oléh kerusakan mobilnja,* His being late was caused by car trouble.

kasir cashier.

kasitahu see KASI.

Kasjmir Kashmir.

kaspé see UBI.

kasti k.o. softball game.

kastroli castor oil.

kasuari cassowary.

kasur mattress.

kasut sandals, slippers. − *belulang* rawhide slipper. − *kaju* wooden clogs. − *kuda* horseshoe. − *roda* rim (e.g., of a bullock-cart wheel). − *rumput* straw slippers.

kata 1 word. 2 say, says, said. **-ku,** I say (said). **-nja** he says (said), etc. ∼ *kabinét akan djatuh,* People say the government will fall. 3 so-called. *orang jg* ∼ *sakti* a person with so-called supernatural powers. **ber-** 1 to talk. *Ia tidak dpt* ∼ , He cannot talk. 2 to speak. *Ia* ∼ *dgn suara lemah,* He spoke in a soft voice. 3 to say. *Ia* ∼ *bhw ia pergi kesekolah,* He said that he would go to school. ∼ *dua* to be deceitful. *Ia selalu* ∼ *dua,* He is always deceitful. **ber-** **-²** to converse, talk to o. another. − *dlm hati* to say to o.s. **memper-kan** 1 to talk about. *Meréka lagi* ∼ *keadaan politik,* They were talking about the political situation. 2 to deliberate. ∼ *penjelesaian pertjeraian* to negotiate a divorce settlement. 3 to explain s.t. verbally. ∼ *soal jg sulit* to give an oral explanation of the difficult problem. **meng-** **-²i** 1 to scold. *Ia* ∼ *anaknja,* She scolded her child. 2 to call names, abuse. *Djangan eng-*

kau berani ~ *saja,* Don't you dare call me names. 3 to cast aspersions on s.o.'s character. **meng-kan** 1 to say. *Ia* ~ *pd saja,* He said to me. 2 to tell. *Ia* ~ *semuanja pd saja,* He told me everything. *–kan sadja dari Ali,* Just tell him Ali called. ~ *amin* to say yes, to agree. **per–an** word. – *adat* traditional proverb. – *asal* root of a word. – *batin* conscience. – *benda* noun. – *bersambungan* derivative. – *bilangan* numeral. – *bilangan pengganda* multiplier. – *bilangan pokok* basic numeral. – *dasar* root of a word. – *depan* preposition. – *djadian* derivative. – *édjékan* term of abuse, abusive language. – *ganti diri* personal pronoun. – *hati* 1 conscience. 2 sincere advice. 3 (inner) conviction. – *kerdja* verb. – *keterangan* adverb. – *kiti* 1 chitchat. 2 gossip. – *madjemuk* compound word. – *mendatang* derivative. – *menjusul* postscript. – *muradjif* synonym. – *mupakat* agreement. – *olokan* derision, mockery. – *pembimbing* preface. – *pendahuluan* author's introduction. – *pengantar* preface by publisher or author or both. – *pengetjil* a diminutive. – *pengganti nama benda* pronoun. – *penghubung,* – *penjambung,* – *perangkai* conjunction. – *pengumpul* collective numeral. – *penjerta* article (def. and indef.). – *pindjaman* loanword. – *putus* decision (to release parties to an agreement, such as an engagement, etc.). – *sambung* connective. – *sambutan* 1 foreword (by a third person). 2 welcoming speech. – *sandang* article (gram). – *searti* synonym. – *sepaham,* – *sepakat* agreement. – *seru* interjection. – *sifat* adjective. – *tambahan* adverb. *memberi* – *dua* to send (present) an ultimatum. **se–** to be of o. mind. *Semua hadlirin* ~ , All present agreed. *tiada* **ter-kan** unspeakable, indescribable. *tidak* **ter-** –² speechless, tongue-tied. *djangan di– lagi* let it alone. *Bangun sadja tak mau dia, djangan di-lagi pergi kesekolah,* He doesn't even want to wake up, let alone go to school. *sepatah* – *a few* words. *Saja hendak ber– sepatah* –, I'd like to say a few words. *Apa hendak di–?* What can be done? *Boléh di–kan bhw ia tak akan datang,* It is almost certain that he will not come.
katahati see KATA.
katai 1 dwarf, pygmy. 2 short-legged bantam chicken.
katak 1 frog, toad. 2 stocky. – *betung* k.o. bullfrog. – *dlm tempurung* narrow-minded.

katalogus catalog. – *induk* union catalog.
katam see CHATAM.
katan see CHATAN.
katang² basket plaited of leaves of palmlike plant.
katapél 1 slingshot. 2 plane-launching catapult.
katé see KATAI.
katégori category.
katék 1 armpit. 2 short, dwarfish. **meng-i** to tickle, titillate.
katés papaya.
kati unit of weight (625 gr.). **–an** a scale which weighs in *kati.*
katib see CHATIB.
katil couch.
katimumul corn (on the foot).
katir outrigger.
katistiwa see CHATTULISTIWA.
katja 1 glass. 2 mirror. 3 example. *Keasjikannja hendak mendjadi* – *bagimu,* His diligence should be an example to you. 4 page (of book, etc.). **ber–** to look in the mirror. *Gadis itu* ~ , The girl looked in the mirror. ~ *mata* to wear spectacles. **ber-** –² to shine (with tears). *Matanja* ~ , His eyes shone with tears. **ber-kan** *diri* to be reflected, mirrored. *Beringin tua* ~ *diri diair,* The old banyan tree was reflected in the water. **memper-i** 1 to convince o.s. of s.t. 2 to scrutinize, put s.t. under a magnifying glass. **meng–** to look in the mirror. – *bajangan* mirror. – *baur,* – *bening* frosted glass. – *és* ground glass. – *masir* frosted glass. – *djendéla* window(pane), glass. – *mata* spectacles, glasses. – *matja hitam* dark glasses. – *méka* mica. – *muka* mirror. – *pembakar,* – *pembesar* magnifying glass. – *piring* gardenia. – *terompong* periscope. – *toko* display window of a store.
katjak 1 dashing. 2 conceited. **berpinggang** with arms akimbo. **meng–** to determine weight or size of s.t. by holding it in the hand.
katjang 1 pea. 2 bean. 3 peanut. **ber–** to scramble after s.t. *Waktu toko mengobral barang orang* ~ *membelinja,* When the shop had a sale, people scrambled to buy s.t. **memperuang orang lain** to spend someone else's money lavishly, squander. **meng–** to divide (profits, booty, the catch of fishing, etc.). –² 1 pellets, shot (for a shotgun). 2 ball bearing. – *asin* salted peanut. – *bogor* k.o. fried peas. – *buntjis* green peas. – *djambu monjét* cashew nut. – *goréng* roasted peanuts. – *idjo* small green pea. – *kedelai* soybean. – *méndé*

cashew nut. – *mérah* kidney bean. – *miang* trouble-maker. – *pandjang* string bean, cow-pea. – *polong* sugar pea. – *rebus* boiled, steamed peanuts. – *sanghai* k.o. fried peanuts. – *tanah* peanut. –²an of the bean family.

katjapiring see KATJA.

katjapuri main building of a palace.

katjau 1 confused. *Pikirannja* –, His mind was confused. 2 in disorder, uproar, confusion. *Seluruh negara* –, The whole country was in confusion. 3 untidy. *Kamarnja* –, His room was not straightened up. **ke–an** 1 confusion. 2 disorder. 3 a mess, jumble. **ke–balauan** chaos. **memper-kan, meng–kan** 1 to confuse. ∼ *foném dgn huruf* to confuse a phoneme with a letter. 2 confusing. *Keadaan sangat* ∼ , The situation was very confusing. 3 to stir up s.t. 4 to disturb, upset. **meng–** 1 to stir s.t. 2 to stir up s.t. **peng–** 1 agitator. 2 terrorist, insurgent, rebel. 3 disturber of the peace. **peng–an** rebellion, riot. **–an** a confused mixture, bastard (mainly in language). – *balau*, – *bilau* 1 chaotic. *Keadaan* – *balau*, The situation was chaotic. 2 great confusion, disorder. *Seluruh negara* – *balau*, The whole country was in great confusion. – *pikiran* a delirious person.

katjip k.o. scissors used to cut betel nut, paper, sheet metal, etc. **meng–** 1 to cut with a *katjip*. 2 to squeeze s.t. between o's legs, e.g., a leg hold in wrestling.

katjoa(k) cockroach, water bug.

katju 1 handkerchief. 2 an ingredient used in betel-nut chewing, also used for tanning of hides (see GAMBIR). **–an** bastard. *Bahasa Melaju* ∼ bastardized Malay language.

katjung youngster, boy (of servant or socially comparable groups).

katolik Catholic.

katrol pulley. **di–** to be lifted with a pulley.

katun cotton.

katung k.o. tortoise. **ter–** –² 1 to be floating. *Banjak sampah* ∼ *disungai*, A lot of refuse was floating in the river. 2 to hover. *Ia* ∼ *diantara harapan dan ketakutan*, He hovered between hope and fear. 3 to drift, be uncertain. *Pengangkatannja masih* ∼ , His appointment is still pending.

katup a valve of a machine. **memper-kan, meng–kan** to close tightly. *Pd petang hari bunga*² ∼ *daun bunganja*, In the evening the flowers close their petals (also of door, book, mouth,

etc.). **ter–** closed, locked tightly (of door, mouth, etc.). – *aman* safety valve. – *tenggorok* epiglottis.

kau see ENGKAU.

kaul vow. **ber–** to vow. *Ia* ∼ *akan berziarah kekuburan ajahnja*, He vowed he would visit his father's grave. **meng–kan** to make a vow for the benefit of s.o.

kaula 1 I. 2 servant. **ke–an** 1 serfdom. 2 submissiveness.

kaulanegara subject (of a country). **ke–an** citizenship.

kaum 1 ethnic group (of a nation). – *Minangkabau, Batak, Menado, dll.* The Minangkabaus, Bataks, Menadonese, etc. 2 family, clan. 3 social, economic, political, community, etc., group. 4 class. *Ia termasuk – modal*, He belongs to the capitalistic class. – *tua dlm kampung itu sangat berpengaruh*, The elders in that village are very influential. **ber–** to be related. **per–an** 1 family relations. 2 group. 3 communalism. – *atasan* the upper class, group of senior officials, executives, etc. – *bangsawan* the nobility. – *bawahan* the lower classes. – *buruh* workers, wage earners. – *hartawan* the wealthy. – *hawa jg lemah* the weaker sex. – *ibu* mothers, married women. *Ini adalah madjalah bagi – ibu*, This is a magazine for mothers (housewives). – *keluarga* relatives. – *kemadjuan* progressives. – *kerabat* relatives. – *ko* collaborators, those on the Dutch side during the Dutch-Indonesian conflict. – *kolot* conservatives. – *kromo* proletariat. – *lelaki, – laki²* the men. – *lunak* the moderates. – *madjikan* employers. – *marhaén* proletariat. – *mérah* leftists, Reds, left-wingers. – *miskin* the poor. – *modal* capitalists. – *muda* youth, the younger generation. – *murba* the masses, common people. – *muslimin* Moslems. – *Nasrani* Christians. – *non* non-co-operators. – *pelantjong* tourists. – *pembangkang* conservatives. – *pemuda* youth. – *penarung* the opposition. – *penganggur* the unemployed. – *pengungsi*, – *penjingkir* refugees, evacuees. – *pénsiunan* former government officials living on a pension. – *pergerakan* active party members, the politically active. – *pertengahan* the middle class. – *pindahan* emigrants. – *prijaji* upper middle class. – *rendah(an)* the lower class, group of junior officials. – *sabot* saboteurs. – *terpeladjar*, – *tjerdik pandai*, – *tjerdik tjendekia* intellectuals. – *uang* the wealthy.

kaus sock, stocking. – *badju* under-

shirt. – *kaki* sock, stocking. – *lampu*
lampwick. – *tangan* glove.
kausa cause.
kaut meng– to scoop up.
kawah 1 cauldron. 2 crater.
kawakan 1 old. *seorang bintangpilem*
– an old film star. 2 experienced,
established.
kawal 1 guard, watch. 2 sentry,
watchman. **ber–** to stand, be on
guard. **meng–(i)** 1 to guard s.t. 2
to escort. *Kapal pendjeladjah itu*
∼ *iring²an kapal itu*, The cruiser
escorted the convoy. **peng–** guard,
sentry, watchman. – *gawang* goal-
keeper (in soccer, hockey, etc.).
peng–an 1 guard. 2 escort. ∼ *iring²an*
itu diperkuat, The convoy escort was
reinforced. ∼ *udara* air escort.
kawan 1 friend. 2 companion. *Ia*
pergi sendiri sadja tidak ada –nja,
He went all by himself and had no
companions. 3 comrade. **ber–** 1 to
have friends. *Ia* ∼ *banjak*, He has
many friends. 2 to have companions.
Ia datang sendiri sadja tidak ∼ , He
came alone and had no companions.
3 to be friends with. *Saja sdh lama*
∼ *dgn dia*, I have been friends with
him for a long time. **memper–** to
make friends with s.o. *Kita mentjoba*
∼ *murid baru itu*, We tried to make
friends with the new pupil. **meng–i**
to accompany. *Ia* ∼ *saja pergi*
kesekolah, He accompanied me to
school. **se–** 1 a herd. ∼ *gadjah* a
herd of elephants. 2 a flock. ∼
burung a flock of birds. 3 a shoal.
∼ *ikan* a shoal of fish. 4 a gang. ∼
bandit a gang of bandits. **–an** band,
group (of thieves, etc.). – *berbuat*
accomplice. – *gadis* girl friend. –
hidup partner for life. – *laki²* boy
friend. – *sekerdja* colleague. – *seper-*
djuangan comrade-in-arms.
kawanua s.o. hailing from the same
part of the country. *Saja berdjumpa*
dgn seorang –, I met a fellow who
comes from the same area as I.
kawat 1 wire. *pagar* – wire fence. 2
cable, telegram. **meng–kan** to wire.
Ia ∼ *kabar itu kpd orang tuanja*, He
wired the news to his parents. –
berduri barbed wire. – *gantung pakaian*
clothesline. – *kasa* wire netting. –
listrik electric cable. – *rambut* very
fine iron wire. – *télepon* telephone
cable.
kawatir see CHAWATIR.
kawedanan see WEDANA.
kawi see 1 BAHASA. 2 BATU. **–an**
symphony.
kawin 1 to marry. *Ia – dgn kakak*
saja, He married my sister. 2 to be

married. *Apa tuan sdh –?* Are you
married? 3 to copulate (of animals).
meng–i 1 to marry s.o. *Radja* ∼
seorang gadis désa, The king married
a village girl. 2 to copulate with.
meng–kan 1 to marry off. *Ia* ∼
anaknja pd seorang saudagar kaja,
He married off his daughter to a rich
merchant. 2 to cross. *Pohon itu di-*
kan dgn pohon ini, That tree was
crossed with this tree. **per–an** 1
marriage. 2 wedding. ∼ *pertjampuran*
mixed marriage. – *dgn keris* marriage
by proxy. – *gantung* to marry in a
simple ceremony while the consum-
mation of marriage awaits an official
and more elaborate wedding. –
mawin various weddings, wedding
ceremonies. – *paksa* forced marriage.
– *tunggu tunang* married by proxy.
kawul tinder.
kazanah treasury.
Kb(j) [*Kebajoran*] district in Jakarta.
KDH [*Kepala Daérah*] district, regional, head.
KDN [*Kementerian Dalam Negeri*]
Ministry of Home (Internal) Affairs.
ke 1 to. *Ia pergi –sekolah*, He went
to school. 2 forms an ordinal. *–atas*
upward. *–bawah* downward. *–belakang*
to the rear, to the toilet. *–dalam*
into. *–empat* fourth. *–muka* to the
front. *–pada* see PADA. *–samping* to
the side. *–sana* in that direction.
–satu first. *–sini* hither.
kebaja woman's blouse reaching below the waist.
kebajan village messenger.
Kebajoran large suburban area on
the south side of Jakarta.
kebal 1 invulnerable. *Ia – tak dpt*
dilukai, He is invulnerable and cannot be wounded. 2 immune. *Karena*
suntikan itu ia – thd penjakit itu,
Because of his vaccination he is immune to that disease. **ke–an** 1
invulnerability. 2 immunity. **meng–**
kan to immunize. *Suntikan ini akan*
∼ *manusia thd penjakit disénteri*,
This vaccine will immunize people
against dysentery.
kebam gray blue, lead color (of sky,
etc.).
kebar see KIBAR.
kebas 1 paralyzed. 2 paralysis. 3
stiff from fatigue. 4 all pins and
needles (of limbs). **meng–kan** 1 to
cause a feeling of paralysis, stiffness.
2 to shake out s.t. (a tablecloth, bed
sheet, blanket, etc.).
kebat bunch. *bunga se–* a bunch of
flowers. **meng–** to wrap, bind. *Ia* ∼
lukanja, He wrapped his wound.
meng–kan to wrap s.t. *Ia* ∼ *pembalut*

itu pd lukanja, He wrapped the bandage around his wound. **ter-** 1 wrapped. *Seléndang itu ∼ pd léhérnja,* The scarf was wrapped around her neck. 2 involved. *Ia ∼ dlm perkara itu,* He was involved in that case. – *pinggang* waistband.

kebiri castrated. **peng-an** sterilization, castration. see KEMBIRI.

kebon 1 see KEBUN. 2 gardener (form of address).

kebul see KEPUL.

kebun 1 garden. 2 plantation. – *karét* a rubber plantation. 3 estate. – *téh* tea estate. **ber-** to work in the garden. *Ia gemar ∼,* He likes gardening. **memper-i** to till, raise a garden. **per-an** 1 plantation. 2 horticulture. 3 estate. – *binatang* zoo. – *bunga* flower garden. – *karét* rubber estate. – *lada* pepper plantation. – *pertjobaan* experimental garden. – *raja* the botanical garden in Bogor. – *tebu* sugar plantation. – *tumbuh²an* botanical garden.

kebur meng- to stir up. *Topan itu ∼ samudera,* The hurricane whipped up the ocean.

keburu 1 in a hurry. *Mengapa engkau – pergi?* Why are you in a hurry to leave? 2 see BURU. – *datang* to arrive, be in time. *Ia – datang utk berangkat dgn keréta api,* He arrived in time to leave by train. – *nafsu* 1 rash, too hasty. 2 impatient. 3 irascible. *masih* – just in time. *tidak* – too late.

kebut meng-(i) to dust off (furniture, etc.). *∼ sarung didalam kelambu utk mengeluarkan njamuk* to wave a sarong back and forth inside the mosquito netting to chase mosquitoes away.

kedadak choleric diarrhea.

kedah 1 with wide-open mouth. 2 widespread (of legs).

kedai shop. **ber-** 1 to keep a shop. *Penghidupannja dari ∼,* He earns his living as a shopkeeper. 2 to shop. *Ibu pergi ∼,* Mother went to shop. **meng-kan** to display for sale. *Ia ∼ dagangannja,* He displayed his merchandise. **per-an** 1 shop window. 2 display booth, stand. **-an** showcase (in a shop). – *buah²an* fruit shop. – *kopi* coffee shop, cafe. – *nasi* restaurant. – *sajur* grocery.

kedal skin disease which produces whitish spots.

kedalam see KE.

kedaluwarsa 1 superannuated. 2 barred by statute of limitations.

kedang 1 outstretched (of arm). 2 extension (opposite of flection of limbs). **meng-kan** to stretch out.

kedap 1 tightly woven (of cloth, wickerwork). 2 watertight. – *udara* airtight.

kedar see KADAR.

kédék ter- -² to stagger, toddle (of a small child), waddle (of a fat person).

kedekut miserly.

kedelai soy bean.

kedelé see KEDELAI.

kedempung 1 a word imitating sound of s.t. falling in the water. 2 wormy, worm-eaten (of fruit).

kedengkik extremely thin, skin and bones, thin as a rail.

keder afraid, shudder with fear.

kéder to lose o's way. *Saja – waktu mentjari rumahmu,* I lost my way when I tried to find your house.

kedér see KEDER.

kedi 1 a transvestite. 2 hermaphrodite. 3 sexually immature.

kedidi sandpiper. **berse-** to skip, hop (of children).

kedik bent slightly backward (of the body). **meng-** 1 to bend o's body backward. 2 to stick out o's chest. **meng-kan** to straighten out (o's body), draw o.s. up.

kedip a wink (of an eye). **ber- -²** 1 to blink. *Ia ∼,* He blinked. 2 to flicker. *Bintang² ∼,* The stars flickered. **meng-kan** *mata* 1 to blink. 2 to wink. *Ia ∼ matanja pd saja,* He winked at me. **-an** wink.

kedjai rubber. **ber-** to stretch (after sleeping). **meng-** to stretch. *∼ kaki* to stretch o's leg.

kedjam 1 closed (of eyes). 2 cruel. 3 strict. *Polisi – sekali,* The police are very strict. **ke-an** cruelty. **meng-i** to treat s.o. with cruelty. **meng-kan** *mata* to close the eyes.

kedjamas a shampoo (commonly, water in which the ashes of paddy straw have been immersed overnight).

kedjang 1 stiff. *Badannja –,* His body was stiff. 2 to be in convulsions, seized with cramp. **ber-** to twitch, be seized with cramp. *Kakinja jg sakit itu ∼,* His aching leg twitched. **ke-an** spasm, convulsion, cramp. **meng-kan** *badan* to stretch o.s. out. – *gagau* convulsion.

kedjap wink (of the eyes). **ber- -²** 1 to blink. *Matanja ∼,* He blinked his eyes. 2 to flicker. **ber- -²an** 1 to chase e.o. *Anak² ∼ didepan sekolah,* The children were chasing e.o. in front of the school. 2 to race e.o. 3 to keep abreast of. 4 to compete (in achievement). **meng-** to wink. *Ia ∼ pd saja,* He winked at me. **meng-kan** *mata* to blink o's eyes.

se– *mata* in a wink. *Ia hilang dlm* ~ *mata*, He was gone in a wink. **–an** wink.

kedjar meng–(i) 1 to run after. *Ia* ~ *saja*, He ran after me. 2 to pursue. *Ia* ~ *tjita²nja*, He pursued his ideals. **peng–an** pursuit. **–²an** game of tag.

kedjat 1 stiff, rigid. *Ia – karena keta-kutan*, He was stiff with fear. 2 firm, tight, sturdy. *Papan – terpaku pd tiang*, The board was tightly nailed to the beam.

kedjeblos see DJEBLOS.

kedjengkang see DJENGKANG.

kedjepit see DJEPIT.

kedji despicable, shameful. *Tindakan itu sangat –*, That's a despicable deed. **ber–** *diri* to stoop low, do a low trick. **ke–an** meanness. **meng–kan** 1 to despise s.o. or s.t. 2 to abuse, vilify. 3 to condemn, denounce.

kedjip see KEDJAP.

kedjot see KEDJUT. **–an** *otot* stiffening of the muscles.

kédju cheese. *– katjang* peanut butter.

kedjudju meng– ceaselessly.

kedjur stiff, bristling (of hair, fiber, etc.).

kedjut 1 frightened, scared. 2 fright. **ber–** *telinga* to cock its ears (of animals). **ber–an** to scatter in all directions out of fear (of people, animals, etc.). **ke–an** 1 startled. 2 fright. **meng–** suddenly, without warning. **meng–i, meng–kan** to startle, surprise. *Suara itu* ~ *saja*, The sound startled me. **peng–** 1 shy. 2 coward. 3 easily frightened. **ter–** startled. *Ia* ~ *melihat saja*, He was startled when he saw me. *si–* touch-me-not (a plant).

kedok 1 mask. 2 decoy, s.t. to cover up o's real intentions. **ber–** disguised. *Dgn* ~ *muka manis ia hendak memikat hati saja*, Behind sweet smiles he tries to win my heart. **memper–** to use as a mask. *Ia* ~ *kedudukannja sebagai kepala polisi utk menutupi kedjahatannja*, He used his position as police chief to mask his crimes.

kedondong k.o. sour fruit (sometimes used to prepare a dish similar to applesauce).

keduk scoop. *beberapa – beras* several scoops of rice. **meng–** 1 to scoop. *Sekop itu gunanja utk* ~ *tanah*, A spade is used to scoop earth. 2 to nab s.o. 3 to exploit. **peng–** exploiter.

kedung 1 eddy, whirlpool. 2 center of information.

kedut 1 fold, crease. 2 ripple. **ber–** wrinkled, creased. **meng–** to take by force. **–an** nervous twitch.

kéhél ter– 1 crooked, deformed. 2

off course (of ship, airplane). 3 sprained.

kehendak see HENDAK.

kéjong see KÉONG.

kekal eternal, lasting. *persahabatan jg –* eternal friendship. **ke–an** eternity. **meng–kan** to make s.t. everlasting, perpetuate.

kekam scum, foam on surface of water.

kekang 1 bit (of a bridle). 2 rein(s). **meng–** 1 to bridle. *Ia* ~ *kudanja*, He bridled his horse. 2 to hold in the reins (stop a horse). 3 to curb. *Ia* ~ *ketidaksabarannja*, He curbed his impatience. ~ *persuratkabaran* to curb the press. **–an** control, curb. *Achirnja ia terlepas dari* ~ *orang tuanja*, At last he was freed of his parents' control.

kekar 1 open. *Kuntum bunga itu –*, The flower bloomed. 2 spread out. *padi didjemur –* paddy spread out ear by ear to dry (in the sun). **meng–** to open. *Bunga itu* ~ , The flower opened. *nasi –* fluffy rice (cooked rice whose kernels do not stick together).

kekasih see KASIH.

kekau to awaken from a nightmare.

kékéh ter– –² convulsed with laughter.

kékék to giggle, snicker.

kéker 1 binoculars. 2 telescope.

kéki 1 to feel uneasy, uncomfortable. *Murid baru masih merasa – diantara anak² lain*, The new pupil is not at ease yet with the other children. 2 to resent. *Saja – kalau ia sombong*, I can't stand it when he brags.

kékok clumsy, awkward. *Gerak-geriknja –*, His movements were awkward. *Djuru rawat baru memerlukan banjak prakték; ia masih merasa –*, The new nurse needs lots of practice; she is not yet familiar with her job.

kekudung scarf used as head covering.

kel. [*keluarga*] family.

kelabakan 1 to flounder around, be in convulsions. 2 to be deeply upset. *Pemilik rumah – melihat gedung mendjadi musnah oléh api*, The owner of the house lost his head completely when he saw the fire destroy the building.

kelabang 1 poisonous centipede. **meng–** *rambut* to braid the hair. *Ia* ~ *rambut ibunja*, She braided her mother's hair. **–an** braid (of hair).

kelabu gray. **ke–an** deception. **meng–i** (*mata*) to deceive s.o. *Dgn kata² manis ia hendak* ~ *saja*, With sweet words he tries to deceive me.

keladak dregs.

keladi taro.

kelah 1 complaint. 2 a charge. *Ia memadjukan —nja thd terdakwa,* He pressed his charges against the defendant. 3 to complain. *Ia – pd polisi,* He complained to the police. **meng-** to bring suit against.

kelahi ber- to fight with fists, etc. *Ia ~ dgn kakaknja,* He fought with his brother. **memper-kan** 1 to fight (for). *Pasukan kita ~ bénténg itu,* Our troops fought for the fortress. 2 to make fight. *Ia ~ ajam djantan itu,* He made the cocks fight. **per–an** fight. *~ tindju* boxing match.

kelak 1 later. *–, kalau saja besar, saja ingin mendjadi penerbang,* Later, when I have grown up, I want to become a pilot. 2 to tell on s.o. *Mémang saja memetjahkan gelas, tapi djangan – dong,* It's true I broke a glass but don't tell on me, please. 3 to complain. *Ia – pd polisi ttg kelakuan tetangganja,* He complained to the police about his neighbor's behavior. *di– hari, di– kemudian hari* in the future. *Mudah²an di– hari tak akan ada perang lagi,* Let us hope that there will be no more wars in the future. *– keluk* curves.

kelakar joke. **ber-** to jest.

kelalang a slender-necked earthenware bottle.

kelalap see KELELAP.

kelalawar k.o. bat.

kelam rather dark, obscure. *– penglihatannja,* He blacked out, lost consciousness. **ke–an** darkness, obscurity. **meng–kan** to darken. *Awan ~ langit,* Clouds darkened the sky. **peng–an** 1 darkening. 2 blackout (during air raids). *– kabut* foggy, murky. *– lebam, – -membelam, – pekat* pitch-dark.

kelambir coconut.

kelambit k.o. bat (animal).

kelambu mosquito net.

kelamin 1 a pair (male and female). 2 sex. *Ada dua –,* There are two sexes. **ber-** to be in pairs. *~ burung membuat sarangnja,* The birds build their nest in pairs. **meng-** to marry. **per–an** sex. *sénsasi² ~* sex sensations. *se–* 1 man and wife. 2 a pair (male and female). *~ burung* a pair of birds.

kelamun meng- to daydream. *Ia suka ~ ,* He likes to daydream. **peng-** daydreamer. **peng–an** fancy, fantasy. see LAMUN.

kelana wanderer. **ber-, meng-** to roam, wander. *Saja ingin bébas supaja dpt ~ ke-mana²,* I want to be free so that I can roam everywhere.

kelandjar see KELENDJAR. *– buntu* endocrine gland.

kélang see KILANG. *– -kélok* winding, tortuous.

kelangkan see LANGKAN.

kelangkang 1 crotch. 2 seat of trousers.

kelantang meng- to bleach s.t.

kelap ber- *kelip* 1 to sparkle. *Intan itu ~ kelip,* The diamond sparkled. 2 to twinkle. *Bintang ~ kelip,* Stars twinkled. *Lilin ~ kelip,* The candle flickered. **meng-** *mata to* blink o's eye. **ter-** dozed off.

kelapa coconut. **meng–i** to put coconut milk or grated coconut on s.t. *– gading* coconut with yellow-colored hull. *– kering* copra. *– kopjor* soft coconut meat. *– puan* coconut with soft and spongy meat. *– sawit* oil palm.

kelar 1 ready. *Makan sdh –,* Dinner is ready (is served, is cooked). *Semua sdh – utk berangkat?* Is everyone ready to leave (on a trip, etc.)? 2 a notch, nick (in wood, etc.), indentation, groove. **ber–(–)** to have indentations, grooves, etc. **meng-** to make notches, etc. **ter-** cut, indented, notched.

kelas 1 grade. *Ia duduk di– dua,* He's in the second grade. 2 class-(room). *Murid² masuk ke-,* The pupils entered the class(room). 3 class. *Ia berasal dari – ningrat,* He came from the aristocratic class. **ber- –²** divided into classes. *Masjarakat itu ~ ,* That society is divided into classes. **peng–an** classification. *– atas(an)* upper class. *– bawah(an)* lower class. *– berat* heavyweight class. *– bulu* featherweight class. *– kambing* 1 gallery, pit, cheapest seats in the movie, etc. 2 lowest stratum of society. *– lajang* lightweight class. *– menengah* middleweight class. *– rangkap* parallel class. *– ringan* lightweight class. *– satu* first-rate, first-class. *Ia pemain ténis – satu,* He is a first-rate tennis player. *– terbang* flyweight boxer.

kelasa hump (on the back of a camel).

kelasi sailor, shipmate. *– I* seaman. *– II* apprentice seaman.

kelat 1 brace, sheet (of sailing vessel). 2 long, thick rope to pull down tree which is being cut. 3 puckering (from taste). *– bahu* bracelet.

kelébat see KELIBAT.

kelébék folded at the corner or edge (dog-eared pages of a book, tucked in of edges of a bedspread, tablecloth, etc.).

kelebu 1 taking water (of a leaking

boat). 2 sunk. **meng–kan** to sink (a ship, etc.).

keledai donkey.

keledék see UBI.

kélék –²(an) 1 armpit. 2 banister.

kelekatu flying ant.

kelelap to drown. *Ia – dlm sungai*, He drowned in the river. **meng–kan** to drown s.o. *Ia ~ korbannja*, He drowned his victim.

kel(el)awar tiny bat (animal).

kelélot ber– to stick out o's tongue.

kelemajar glowworm.

kelemapih gangrene.

kelemarin see KEMARIN.

kelemba ghost depicted as a giant female with red hair.

kelembuai snail.

kelemping flabby and sagging (of breasts or belly).

kelemumur dandruff.

kelendjar gland. *– beguk* goiter. *– getah bening* lymphatic gland. *– gondok* thyroid gland. *– keringat, – peluh* sweat gland. *– léhér* tonsils.

kelénéng 1 sound of a bell. 2 small bell (e.g., of a bike, etc.). **ber–** to clang. **meng–kan** to ring. *Ia ~ lontjéng itu*, He rang the bell.

kelengar to faint. *Ia –*, She fainted, became unconscious. *– matahari* sunstroke.

kelening see KELÉNÉNG.

kelentang see KELANTANG.

kelénténg Chinese temple.

kelentit clitoris.

keléntom speech intonation.

kelepai ber–, ter– to hang down limply (of a flag, ears of a hound, etc.).

kelépak somewhat bent. *– (badju)* lapel.

kelépék 1 see KELÉPAK. 2 to flutter.

kelepit limply bent.

kelepur see GELEPAR.

kélér glass jar with lid.

kelérék clerk (in an office).

keléréng marbles. **ber–** to play marbles.

kelésa easygoing, indifferent.

keléséh-péséh to speak Dutch.

kelésék dried banana tree bark (cut in strips and used as twine for wrapping packages).

kelétah 1 coquettish. 2 affected (in manner).

keletak ber– to make a clacking sound with wooden or leather heels.

keletang jingling, tinkling (of silver coins).

keletar see GELETAR.

keletik 'tick tick.'

keléwang saber, cutlass. **meng–** to strike with a saber.

keliar ber–an 1 to loiter about, drift (from o. place to another). *Ia ~ sadja tak tentu perginja*, He loitered about going nowhere. 2 to roam about. *Banjak orang djahat ~ dlm kegelapan*, Many bad people are roaming around in the dark. 3 to swarm about. *Burung lajang² ~ diatas lapangan*, Swallows were swarming about over the field. *Semut ~ ,* Ants were swarming about. **–an** to wander about. *Anak buahnja ~ ,* Members of his troop were wandering about dispersed.

keliat see GELIAT.

kelibang ber–an to swarm around. *Laron ~ disekeliling lampu*, Flying ants were swarming around the light.

kelibat 1 paddle (with a blade at each end of the handle). 2 moment. **se–(an)** in a moment, in a flash. *Dlm ~ ia menghilang*, He disappeared in a flash.

kelih meng– to look, watch over o's shoulder.

kelik 1 see KÉLOK. 2 a curve, bend. –² poisonous ant.

kelikir 1 see KERIKIL. 2 nose ring for cattle (usually made of rattan).

keliling 1 circumference. 2 around. *Di– rumah itu ada kebun jg luas*, Around the house was a large garden. 3 surrounding(s). *Djakarta dan –nja termasuk satu Balai Kota*, Jakarta and its surroundings belong to o. municipality. **ber–** to go around. *Ia ~ mendjadjakan dagangannja*, He went around peddling his merchandise. **meng–i** 1 to surround. *Musuh ~ kota kami*, The enemy surrounded our town. 2 to travel around. *Ia ~ seluruh Éropah*, He traveled around all of Europe. **peng–** *dunia* round-the-world traveler. **se–** surrounding area. *Rumahnja dan ~ habis terbakar*, His house and the surrounding buildings were entirely destroyed by fire.

kelilip –an to get in o's eye. *Mata saja ~ ,* I got dust in my eye.

kelim hem. **meng–** to hem. *Ia ~ badjunja*, She hemmed her blouse. **–an** hem.

kelimantang see KALIMANTANG.

kelimis smooth and shining. *Mukanja – bersih*, His face was shiny and clean (after a bath, etc.). *Kepala anak – gundul*, The child's head was shaved completely bald.

kelimun a thick crowd.

kelindan 1 newly spun thread. 2 conveyor rope of the spinning wheel. 3 thread on a needle. 4 bobbin, spool.

keling 1 a Tamil. 2 rivet. **meng-** to rivet.

kelingking little finger. – *kaki* little toe.

kelinik clinic. – *bersalin* maternity clinic. – *mata* eye clinic.

kelintar ber–an to loaf, hang around. *Saja tjuriga pd orang itu, ia* ∼ *sadja sekitar kampung kami,* I am suspicious of that man; he has been hanging around our neighborhood.

kelintji rabbit.

kelip 1 the glitter(ing) of eyes, e.g., when caught in a beam of light at night. 2 5-cent coin with center hole. 3 paper clip. **ber-** –² 1 to twinkle. *Bintang* ∼ *dilangit,* Stars twinkled in the sky. 2 to flicker (of an oil lamp, etc.). **se-** *mata* a moment, twinkling of an eye. *Ia hilang dlm* ∼ *mata,* He disappeared in a moment. –² firefly.

kelir 1 screen for Javanese shadow play. 2 movie screen. 3 a cover, screen to hide s.o.'s real intentions. 4 color. –*nja mérah,* The color was red. **meng-** to color. *Ia* ∼ *gambarannja,* He colored his picture.

keliru 1 to be wrong, err. *Djawabannja* –, His answer was wrong. 2 to be mistaken. *Ia mengira saja sdh pergi tetapi ia* –, He thought that I had left, but he was mistaken. 3 to make a mistake. *Orang jg terpandaipun dpt* –, Even the smartest person can make a mistake. 4 to go astray. **ke–an** 1 mistake. 2 error. **meng–kan** 1 to be misleading. *Angka² itu* ∼ , Those figures were misleading. 2 to confuse. *hendaknja djangan dikan dgn* shouldn't be confused with. – *tulis* typographical error.

kelit ber– to zigzag, dart back and forth. **ber-** –² to dart in and out. *Badjing* ∼ *keluar masuk dari lobang didalam pohon,* The squirrel darted in and out of the hole in the tree. **meng–kan** 1 to push aside. 2 to hide quickly.

keliti helm, tiller.

kelitji marbles.

kelitjih ter– slipped, skidded.

keliwat see LÉWAT.

kelojak ber– to cast off the skin. ter– abrasion, excoriation of the skin.

kelojor see KELUJUR.

kélok 1 curve. 2 turn. **ber-** –² winding. *Djalan dipegunungan itu* ∼ , The mountain road is winding. **meng-** to turn. *Mobilnja* ∼ , His car turned. **meng–kan** to turn s.t. *Ia* ∼ *mobilnja,* He turned his car.

kelola meng–(kan) 1 to manage (a business, the government). 2 to carry out (a job, etc.). 3 to organize (a mass meeting). **peng-** manager, organizer. **peng–an** management.

kelom wooden shoes or slippers. – *geulis* a woman's dress slipper made of wood (from Bandung).

kelompok 1 cluster. – *mangga* a cluster of mangoes. 2 group. *beberapa* – *orang* several groups of people. 3 band, gang. – *gerilja* a guerrilla band. **ber-** to cluster, group, gather. *Meréka* ∼ *didepan rumah saja,* They gathered in front of my house. **ber-** –² to be in groups. **ke–an** 1 cluster. 2 clustering. **meng–kan** to group. *Guru* ∼ *murid² menurut umurnja,* The teacher grouped the pupils according to their ages. **peng–an** group(ing) **se-** *pohon* grove. **–an** = KELOMPOK.

kelon meng–i to hold s.o. (a child, etc.) close while lying down next to him.

kelongsong 1 husk. 2 a wrapper (of paper, leaf, etc.). 3 discarded outer skin of a snake. 4 cartridge. – *djagung* cornhusk.

kelonjo(r) eau de cologne.

kelontang rattle of tin cans. **ber-** to rattle. *Kaléng² kosong itu* ∼ , The empty tin cans rattled.

kelontong 1 see KELONTANG. 2 peddler, hawker.

kelop to fit, jibe, tally. *Angka² itu* – *dgn jg saja perhitungkan,* That figure tallies with the result of my calculation. **meng–kan** to make fit. *Ia* ∼ *pengeluarannja dgn penerimaannja,* He balanced his receipts and expenses.

kelopak sheath, spathe (of leaf bud). **meng-, ter-** to peel off. – *buluh* young bamboo sheath. – *bunga* sepal. – *mata* eyelid.

kélor tree whose bark and leaves are used as medicine.

kelos reel, spool, bobbin.

k(el)otjah splashing, lapping (of water, fluid, etc.).

kelotjak meng– to peel s.t.

kelu dumb, mute. **meng–kan** to remain silent, keep mum (when asked a question, either because one is unable or unwilling to answer). *Segala bukti jg disampaikan itu* ∼ *lidah terdakwa,* In the face of all the evidence introduced the defendant remained silent. **ter-** struck dumb.

keluan nose rope (for cattle).

keluang a large bat.

keluar 1 to go out (of). *Saja* – *dari kamar,* I went out of the room. 2 to come out. – *sebagai pemenang* to come out winner. 3 to leave, run off, go off. *Keréta api - dari rél,* The train left the tracks. **meng-kan** 1 to take outside. *Ia ~ andjing itu,* He took the dog outside. 2 to export. *Perusahaannja ~ karét,* His company exports rubber. 3 to publish. *Penerbitan itu ~ buku peladjaran,* The publisher published textbooks. 4 to fire. *Ia ~ pegawainja,* He fired his employee. 5 to produce. *Paberik itu ~ mesin tulis,* The factory produces typewriters. 6 to expel. *Dia di-kan dari negerinja,* He was expelled from the country. 7 to spend, expend. *~ suara* to vote. **peng-an** 1 export. 2 edition, issuance. 3 expenses. 4 dismissal, expulsion. 5 release (of film, book). **-an** 1 made in. *Djam ini adalah ~ Djérman,* This watch was made in Germany. 2 graduate. *Ia adalah ~ Universitas Indonésia,* He is a graduate of the University of Indonesia. 3 published by. *Buku ini adalah ~ penerbitan itu,* This book is published by that publishing house. *- dari kalam* to issue from the pen of. *- giginja* to cut teeth. *- tanduknja* to get angry. see LUAR.

keluarga 1 family. 2 relative. 3 genus. **ber-** 1 to have a family. *Saja seorang budjang, blm ~ ,* I am a bachelor and I do not have a family yet. 2 to be related to. *Saja ~ dgn dia,* I am related to him. **ke-an** family spirit, togetherness. *- sedarah* blood relatives. *- semenda* in-laws.

kelubung a cover. **ber-** covered. **meng-i** to cover s.t.

keluh 1 sigh, moan, whimper. 2 complaint. *Ada² sadja -nja,* He always has some complaints. **ber- -kesah** 1 to moan. 2 to complain. **meng-** 1 to moan. 2 to complain. 3 to sigh. **meng-kan** to sigh over. **-an** complaint. *- kesah* 1 sigh, moan. 2 complaints. *- mati* death rattle. *- saju* lamentation, bemoaning.

kelujur ber-an to loaf, ramble, stroll around. *Ia ~ didalam kota itu sadja,* He just loafed around the town.

keluk see KÉLOK.

kelulu 1 proper, appropriate. 2 considered (of opinion). 3 discreet (of action). *bertindak tidak -* to act without thinking (rashly, etc.).

kelumbung see KELUBUNG.

kelumit part, bit. *se- pikiran* a few thoughts.

kelumpuk see KELOMPOK.

kelumun cover(let), wrapping. **meng-i** to cover, envelop. *Kabut ~ puntjak bukit,* Fog covered the hilltop.

kelung 1 bent. 2 hollow.

kelupas meng- to peel, cast off skin.

kelupur meng- to flutter.

keluron 1 abortion. 2 miscarriage.

kelus 1 broken (of skin), abrasion. 2 reel.

kelusuh-kelasah troubled, fitful (of sleep).

kelut-melut 1 commotion, confusion. 2 complicated (of a situation). 3 slump, depression.

Kem. [*Kementerian*] Ministry.

kémah 1 tent. 2 awning (aboard ship). **ber-** to camp. *Para pandu ~ ditepi danau,* The boy scouts camped on the shore of the lake. **per-an** camp.

Kemajoran Jakarta's airport.

kemak-kemik to mumble. *Bibirnja - seakan-akan ia hendak mengatakan sesuatu,* His lips were mumbling as if he wanted to say s.t.

kemal moist. *Tangannja -,* His hand was moist.

kemala 1 precious. 2 faithful. 3 see GEMALA.

keman ber- to mumble. **meng-** to hold in the mouth (a piece of candy, tobacco, etc.).

kemana see MANA.

kemanakan 1 nephew. 2 niece.

kemarau 1 dry (of the season, of the hold of a boat after it has been cleared of water, etc.). 2 the dry season. *- keras* long dry spell.

kemarén see KEMARIN.

kemari here, hither. *Datanglah -,* Come here. *- sebentar,* Come here a minute. **meng-kan** to pass, hand. *-kanlah garam,* Please pass the salt. see MARI.

kemarin yesterday. *- dulu* day before yesterday. *- malam* last night. *-nja* the day before, the other day.

kemaruk 1 ravenous (especially after a long illness). 2 greedy.

kemas orderly, well kept (of a house, etc.), put in order, cleared away. **ber-(-)** 1 to pack. *Meréka ~ utk kepergian meréka bésok pagi,* They are packing for their trip tomorrow. 2 to clear away. *~ setelah mendjamu* to clear away things after having entertained (visitors). 3 to put in order. *~ segala surat-menjurat ajah marhumnja,* He put in order all the correspondence of his late father. **meng-i** 1 to pack s.t. *Meréka ~ pakaian meréka,* They packed their clothes. 2 to put away, clear away things. 3 to put in order. *~ diri* to dress up.

kembal small wickerwork container (of rattan or leaves of palmlike plant).

kembali 1 to return. *Ia - kenegerinja,*

He returned to his country. 2 over again. *Ia harus mulai* –, He has to start over again. 3 you're welcome. **meng–kan** 1 to return. *Ia ~ buku saja*, He returned my book. 2 to restore. *Saja harus ~ kerugiannja*, I have to restore his loss. 3 to make return. *Pendjagaan di Istana ~ kami ke kantor présidén*, The palace guard made us go back to the office of the president. **peng–an** 1 return. 2 restitution. *Ia menerima uang sebagai ~ kerugiannja*, He accepted money as a restitution of his losses. **se–nja** after o's return. *~ dia, dia terus mulai bekerdja*, After his return he started to work immediately. *Terima kasih* –, You're welcome.

kemban a breast cloth (wrapped around the upper part of a woman's body). **ber–** *sarong* using a sarong as a breast cloth.

kembang 1 flower. 2 to bloom. **ber–** 1 to bloom. *Bunga² ~* , The flowers bloomed. *Dlm masa damai kesenian akan ~* , In peacetime art will bloom. 2 to develop, expand, flourish. *Pengetahuannja ~* , His knowledge developed. 3 to rise, expand (of dough, etc.). *~ biak* to multiply. *Tanaman itu ~ biak*, The plants multiplied. *~ hati* to swell with joy. *Hatinja ~ karena kegirangan*, His heart swelled with joy. *~ -mekar* to flourish. **ber–an** 1 in bloom, flowering. 2 expanding. *lajar ~* billowing sails. **memper–kan, meng–kan** 1 to expand. *Panas akan ~ hawa*, Heat will expand air. 2 to develop. *Meréka ~ kebudajaan dan kesenian*, They developed their culture and their arts. *~ hati* to cheer s.o. up. *~ lajar* to unfurl the sails, get under way. **meng–** 1 to expand. *Karena panas hawa akan ~* , Air will expand because of heat. 2 to unfurl (sail, wings, etc.). 3 to open (an umbrella, a book). *~ bakung* of beautiful wavy hair when let down (by women). **peng–** promoter. *Ia adalah ~ pergerakan nasional*, He is a promoter of the nationalist movement. **peng–an, per–an** 1 development. 2 expansion, combustion. *– api* fireworks. *– gula* candy, sweets. *– kempis* to pant. *Ia – kempis setelah berlari itu*, He was panting after he ran. *– kuntjup* to open and shut. *– latar* prostitute. *– pala* mace.

kembar 1 twin. *Kedua anak itu* –, Those two children are twins. 2 exactly alike. *Meréka – dan pakaian merékapun – djuga*, They were twins and they also dressed exactly alike. 3 match. *Dimana –nja anting² saja?*

Where is my other earring? **ber–** to match e.o. **meng–i** 1 to match. *Saja tak dpt ~ kepandaiannja*, I cannot match his brilliance. 2 to stand up to s.o. *Siapa jg berani ~ orang perindis itu?* Who dares to stand up against the bully? **meng–kan** to pair s.t. *– lima* quintuplets. *– tiga* triplets.

kembara meng– to wander, roam. *Ia tlh ~ ke-mana²*, He has been roaming everywhere. **peng–** vagabond. **peng–an** wanderings, rovings.

kembili a small potatolike tuber.

kembira to scatter in all directions (of a fleeing army, a flock of birds when chased away, sparks, etc.).

kembiri castrated. **meng–kan** 1 to castrate. 2 to emasculate. see KEBIRI.

kembodja k.o. tree (frequently grown in graveyards in Indonesia).

kémbok(an) see KOBOKAN.

kémbol bulging (of pocket).

kembung puffed up. *Pipinja* –, His cheeks were puffed up. **meng–kan** 1 to puff up. *Ia ~ pipinja*, He puffed up his cheeks. 2 to blow up. *~ balon* to blow up a balloon. *– kempis* heaving. *Dadanja – kempis*, His chest was heaving.

kemédja shirt. **ber–** to wear a shirt. *– buka* sport shirt. *– dalam* undershirt. *– puntung* short-sleeved shirt. *– silir, – tamasja* sport shirt. *– tutup* dress shirt.

kemelut crisis, critical stage (of illness involving fever, a situation, etc.). *– naik* turn for the worse (toward a crisis). *– turun* turn for the better.

kemenakan see KEMANAKAN.

kemenjan incense.

kemenondjolan see TONDJOL.

kemeriahan see RIAH.

kemidi see KOMIDI.

kemih urine. **ber–** to urinate.

kemik dented.

kemilap see GEMILAP.

kemilau shining, glittering (of metals, jewels, velvet, etc.).

kemiri candlenut tree.

kemis meng– to beg. *Ia ~ minta makanan*, He begged for food. **peng–** beggar. **peng–an** begging.

Kemis Thursday.

Kemkes [*Kementerian Keséhatan*] Ministry of Health.

Kemlu [*Kementerian Luar Negeri*] Ministry of Foreign Affairs.

kempa meng– to press. *Mesin itu ~ katjang tanah utk membuat minjak*, The machine presses the groundnuts to make oil. *~ tangan* clenching and unclenching o's fists. *– air* hydraulic press.

kempal compact. *Tanah itu sangat –*, The soil was very compact.

kempang-kempis to pant. *Ia – setelah berlari itu,* He was panting after running.

kempelang meng– 1 to strike with the fist. *Ia ∼ saja,* He struck me with his fist. 2 to box o's ears. **-an** stroke, blow.

Kempen [*Kementerian Penerangan*] Ministry of Information.

kempés 1 deflated, flat. *Ban itu –*, The tire was flat. 2 sunken. *Pipinja –*, His cheeks were sunken. **meng–kan** to deflate. *Ia ∼ ban mobilnja,* He deflated the tires of his car.

kempis see KEMPÉS.

kempit 1 an earthen pot. 2 holding under o's arm. **meng–** to carry under o's arm. *Ia ∼ sebuah buku,* He carried a book under his arm.

kempot sunken, hollow. *Pipinja –*, His cheeks were hollow.

kempu a round, wooden box with handle and cover.

kempunan 1 to be in a quandry, nervous, desperate. 2 to long for, yearn.

kempung sunken (of cheeks).

kempungan 1 abdomen. 2 bladder.

kemu ber– to rinse o's mouth.

kemudi 1 helm, rudder. 2 steering wheel. **meng–kan** to steer, drive. *Ia ∼ kapal terbangnja,* He flew his plane. 2 to govern, lead, guide. *Partai politik itu ∼ negara kita,* That political party governed our country. **peng–** 1 helmsman. 2 driver. 3 pilot. 4 director.

kemudian 1 afterward. *Ia makan, – ia minum,* He ate; afterward he drank. 2 later. *Saja ingin masuk universitas dan – saja ingin mendjadi seorang mahaguru,* I want to enter the university and later I would like to be a professor. **meng–kan** 1 to postpone. 2 to subordinate, place s.t. second to. *Kini ia bekerdja keras dan ∼ kesenangan,* He works hard now, and pleasure comes second with him. 3 to turn back (the clock). **ter–** 1 the last. *Ia selalu datang ∼ ,* He always comes last. 2 to be neglected. *Ia selalu ∼ , segala perhatian diberikan kpd kakaknja,* He was always neglected; all the attention was given to his brother. *– ini* recently. *– ini banjak dilakukan kedjahatan,* Many crimes were committed recently. (*di*)*–hari* in the future.

kemuka see MUKA.

kemukus cubeb.

kemul blanket, coverlet. **meng–i** 1 to cover with a blanket. 2 to blanket.

Awan ∼ puntjak gunung, Clouds blanketed the mountain top. **-²** munching, chewing.

kemuntjak see PUNTJAK.

kemut² ter– -² 1 pulsating, go up and down. 2 to stagger. *Orang mabuk berdjalan ∼ ,* The drunkard staggered along.

kena 1 to be struck. *Paberik itu – bom,* The factory was struck by a bomb. *Ia – penjakit,* He was struck down by an illness. 2 to fit. *Badju itu – benar padamu,* That jacket fits you nicely. 3 to come in contact with, touch, strike. *Tangannja – tjét basah,* His hand touched the wet paint. *Sikunja – lemari,* His elbow struck the cupboard. 4 to hit (a target). *Témbakan tidak – rusa jg lari,* The shot did not hit the running deer. *Tafsiranmu mémang –*, Your analysis was accurate. 5 to be subject to. *– padjak keméwahan* subject to the luxury tax. 6 to undergo, experience, suffer. *– tampar* to get slapped. **ber-an** 1 in connection. *∼ dgn perajaan Hari Kemerdékaan présidén akan mengutjapkan pidato,* In connection with Independence Day the president will deliver a speech. 2 to agree. *Sipendjual dan pembeli ∼ ttg harga,* Seller and buyer are agreed on the price. *Meréka sdh ∼ ,* They have agreed to marry. 3 on the occasion of. *∼ dgn diundangkannja undang² no. 231* on the occasion of passing law no. 231. **ber-(-)an** to have a connection. *Soal saja selalu ∼ dgn perkara ini,* There is a continuing relationship between my problem and this matter. **meng–** to be correct. *Terkaanku ∼ ,* My guess was correct. **meng-i** 1 to hit. *Bom itu ∼ sasarannja,* The bomb hit its target. 2 to touch. *Djangan ∼ badju saja,* Don't touch my jacket. 3 in connection with, concerning. *Parlemén bersidang ∼ krisis keuangan negara,* Parliament convened in connection with the country's financial crisis. 4 to concern. *Surat itu ∼ saja sendiri,* This letter concerns me. **meng-kan** 1 to put s.t. on. *Ia ∼ badjunja,* He put his jacket on. 2 to hit s.t. *Ia ∼ sasarannja,* He hit his target. 3 to levy (taxes). *Pemerintah ∼ padjak pd pengeluaran,* The government levied taxes on exports. 4 to kick, hit, strike s.t. or s.o. *Ia ∼ tendangannja tepat pd kepala andjing,* He kicked the dog right on the head. 5 to fasten, secure. *Penumpang diwadjibkan ∼ sabuk,* Passengers are required to fasten seat belts. **meng-**

–²**kan** to cheat, swindle s.o. **peng-an** application of a rule or theory. **ter-** 1 to be attached. ~ *pd dadanja nampak sebaris bintang kehormatan,* Attached to his chest was a row of decorations. 2 hit (by a bullet, fist, razor, etc.). 3 deceived, duped. *Jg tak bersalahpun* ~ , Innocent people were also duped. 4 affected by. – **-meng-** to be connected with. *Hal ini tak* ~ *dgn hal jg kemarin,* This case has no connection with yesterday's. *tidak* ~ *akan* heedless, regardless. *Tidak* ~ *akan pengorbanan djiwa musuh terus menjerang,* Heedless of the loss of life the enemy continued to attack. – *apa?* Why? – *dakwa* to be accused. – *denda* to be fined. – *djél* to be jailed. – *djelatang* lascivious. – *emas* to be bribed. – *fitnah* to be slandered. – *hama* to be infected by a contagious disease. – *kétjoh* to be swindled, gypped. – *kitju* to be deceived. – *letjah* to have o's reputation ruined. – *marah* to be reprimanded, dressed down. – *muka* to fall into disgrace. – *peluru,* – *péstol* to be shot. – *rasuk* to be possessed. – *sakal* to be tortured. – *sangka²* to be under suspicion. – *sembur,* – *semperét* to get a scolding. – *sogok,* – *suap* to be bribed. – *témbak* to be shot. – *tjap* to be labeled, tabbed. *Ia* – *tjap kolot,* He was labeled old-fashioned. – *undi* 1 to be drafted. 2 to draw lots.

kenal 1 to know, be familiar (with handling, managing s.t.). *Saja* – *mobil ini, sdh pernah saja kemudikan,* I know this car; I've driven it before. 2 to be acquainted. *Saja* – *kepadanja,* I'm acquainted with him. **ber-an** to get to know o. another. **ke-an** 1 known. 2 discovered, recognized. **memper-kan** 1 to introduce s.o. *Boléh saja* ~ *saudara kpd ibuku?* May I introduce you to my mother? 2 to familiarize, inform s.o. of s.t. **meng-** 1 to know, be acquainted with. *Saja* ~*nja,* I know her. 2 to know, recognize. **meng-i** to know, recognize, identify. **meng-kan** 1 to let s.o. know. 2 to introduce s.o. **pemper-** introducer. **peng-** 1 recognition. *tanda* ~ sign of recognition. 2 identification. **peng-an, per-an** 1 introduction. 2 act of getting acquainted. 3 knowledge of, acquaintance with. **ter-** (well) known, famous. **-an** acquaintance. – **-meng-** to get acquainted with s.o. *tidak* – *malu* thick-skinned. *tidak* – *djerih dan pajah* indefatigable.

kenan ber- 1 to have the pleasure. *Présidén* ~ *menghadiri pertemuan*

kami, The president will be pleased to attend our meeting. 2 to agree, endorse, approve of. *Ajah* ~ *akan maksud saja utk mendjadi perwira,* Father approves of my becoming an officer. **memper-kan** to permit, allow. *Agamanja tak* ~ *pertjeraian,* His religion does not permit divorce. **per-(an)** 1 permission. 2 approval. 3 agreement. 4 willingness (to agree). **ter-** to approve of s.t.

kenang meng- to reminisce, recall. *Ia* ~ *masa kanak²nja jg bahagia itu,* He reminisced about his happy childhood. **meng-i** 1 to remember. *Kita akan selalu* ~ *djasa²nja thd tanah air,* We will always remember his services to our country. 2 to commemorate. *Tugu ini utk* ~ *meréka jg téwas dlm peperangan,* This monument is to commemorate those who gave their lives during the war. **meng-kan** 1 see MENG-. 2 see MENG-I. 3 to remind one of s.o. *Ia* ~ *saja pd bapak saja,* He reminds me of my father. ~ *kembali* to recall, recollect. **ter-** to remember. *Saja* ~ *pd tanah air,* I remembered my country. **-an** 1 reminiscence(s). 2 souvenir. *Terimalah buku ini sebagai* ~ *pd tempat ini,* Take this book as a souvenir of this place. **-²an** 1 see **-AN.** 2 memoirs.

kenanga k.o. tree.

kenantan see KINANTAN.

kenapa why? – *dgn dia?* What's the matter with him (her)? *Di-in?* What's been done to him (her, you)?

kenari 1 a tree which produces nuts in a hard shell. 2 canary. – *belanda* almonds.

kendak 1 lover. 2 mistress.

kendali reins. **meng-kan** 1 to hold the reins. *Ia* ~ *kuda itu,* He held the horse's reins. 2 to manage. *Ia* ~ *seluruh pekerdjaan itu,* He managed the whole job. **peng-** manager. **peng-an** control. ~ *bandjir* flood control. ~ *harga* price control. ~ *nafsu* moral restraint. ~ *sungai* river woman. *projéktil* – guided missile.

kendang small bass drum. **se-** a ream of paper.

kendara ber-an to have a vehicle. *Kalau saudara* ~ *boléhkah saja menumpang?* If you have a car, can I get a ride? **meng-i** 1 to drive. *Ia* ~ *mobil,* He drove a car. 2 to ride. *Ia* ~ *kuda,* He rode a horse. **meng-kan** to drive a vehicle. **peng-** 1 driver, rider. 2 horseman. **-an** 1 vehicle. 2 mount.

kendati(pun) 1 although. – *ia sakit, ia bekerdja djuga,* Although he was

sick, he went to work anyway. 2
not to mention. – *serupiah, sesénpun
saja tak punja*, Not only do I not
have one rupiah, I don't even have a
single penny.
kendi an earthenware pitcher (mostly
used for drinking water). – *bertjerat*
earthen pitcher with nozzle.
kendor see KENDUR.
kendur 1 slack. *Tali itu* –, The rope
was slack. 2 loose. *Sepatu saja* –,
My shoe's loose. 3 to slow down.
*Karena panas pekerdjaan kuli² men-
djadi* –, The heat slowed down the
work of the laborers. **ber-** –² loosely.
Ia memasang tali ~ *pd tiang*, He
wrapped the rope loosely around
the pole. **ke–an** the slowdown. *Panas
matahari menjebabkan* ~ *pekerdjaan
meréka itu*, The slowdown of their
work was caused by the heat of the
sun. **meng-** to become loose, slack.
Kulitnja sdh ~ , His skin has become
slack. **meng–kan** 1 to slacken, loosen.
Ia ~ *tali itu*, He slackened the rope.
2 to slow down. 3 to turn down (the
radio, phonograph). – *menjusut* difficult to handle (of a situation).
kenduri ritual meal. **ber-** 1 to hold
a ritual gathering involving a common meal. *Karena isterinja baru
beranak ia* ~ , Since his wife had recently had a baby, he held a ritual
gathering. 2 to take part in a ritual
gathering. – *arwah* ritual gathering
offered for the peaceful hereafter of
the deceased. – *maulud* ritual gathering on the occasion of a birthday. –
meniga ritual gathering on the third
day after the death of a person.
kenék apprentice, assistant to a carpenter, a plumber, a mason, etc.;
also of a taxi or bus driver.
kenékér marble(s). **ber-** to play
marbles.
kenés coquettish, affected (in behavior, mannerism). **ke–an** 1 vanity.
2 coquettishness.
kéngkéng **meng-** 1 to yelp (of a
dog). 2 to whimper, whine.
Kénia Kenya.
kening 1 eyebrow. –*nja hitam*, Her
eyebrows were dark. 2 brow, forehead (more often used in this meaning).
kenjal 1 tough, rubbery. *Daging itu*
–, The meat is tough. 2 elastic.
serabut – elastic fibers. **meng-** to be
spongy, rubbery.
kenjam **meng-** 1 to taste (food). 2
to experience, taste. *Buat pertama
kali meréka* ~ *kenikmatan orang jg
kaja*, For the first time they experienced the pleasures of a wealthy man.

kenjang 1 satisfied. *Ia makan hingga*
–, He ate until he was satisfied. 2
saturated. *Basahilah pasir hingga* –,
Wet this sand until saturated. 3
completely filled. *Kasur ini harus
diisi kapok sampai* –, This mattress
must be completely filled with kapok.
ke–an 1 satiation. 2 saturation. 3
too full. *Saja tak dpt makan lagi,
saja sdh* ~ , I can't eat any more;
I am too full already. **meng–kan** to
satiate, fill s.o. up. *Makanan ini tak
akan* ~ , This food will not satiate
you.
kenjat-kenjit pulsating, rising and
falling.
kenji(h) 1 overly sensitive to pain.
2 of delicate health.
kenjir (*akan*) yearning (for certain
food).
kenjit **meng-** to wink.
kenjut **meng-** to suck. *Ia* ~ *djarinja*,
He sucked his finger. **–an** rubber or
plastic nipple for milk bottles.
kenop 1 knob. *Ia menekan – itu*, He
pushed the button. 2 button (of
shirt, etc.).
kental 1 thick. *Kopi itu* –, The coffee
is thick. 2 close. *Ia sahabat – saja*,
He is my close friend. **ke–an** 1 the
property of coagulation, congealing.
2 viscosity. **meng-** to coagulate. *Susu
itu* ~ , The milk coagulated. **meng–
kan** 1 to thicken s.t. *Ia* ~ *kuah
semur ajam*, He thickened the chicken
gravy. 2 to condense.
kentang potato. – *goréng* fried potatoes. – *puré* mashed potatoes.
kentara 1 visible. *Kapal terbang itu
hampir tak* –, The plane was hardly
visible. 2 discernible, apparent. *Maksudnja jg sebetulnja – meskipun hendak
disembunjikannja*, His real purpose
was discernible though he tried to
hide it.
kentjan 1 date, appointment. 2
date. *Ia – saja*, She's my date. **ber-**
1 to date. 2 dating.
kentjana gold(en). *gelang* – gold
bracelet.
kentjang 1 fast. *Mobil itu berdjalan
dgn* –, The car ran fast. 2 taut. *Tali
itu* –, The rope is taut. 3 tight.
pegangan – tight grip. **ke–an** 1 speed.
2 tension. *Ia mengurangi* ~ *kawat
itu*, He decreased the tension of the
cable. **meng-** 1 to become faster.
Mobil itu makin ~ *larinja*, The car
ran faster and faster. 2 to become
taut. *Tali ténda itu* ~ *karena hudjan*,
The tent ropes became taut because
of the rain. **meng-i**, **meng–kan**
1 to speed up. *Ia* ~ *mobilnja*, He
increased the speed of his car. 2

to tighten. *Ia ∼ tali itu*, He tightened the rope.

kentjar ter- -² nervous, agitated, flustered.

kéntjéng concave frying pan.

kentjing 1 urine. 2 to urinate. - *manis* diabetes. - *nanah* gonorrhea. **meng–i** to urinate on. **per–an** urinary system. **ter–** to urinate involuntarily.

kéntjong crooked, awry, askew. **meng–kan** to twist (lips, words).

kentjor see KENTJUR.

kentjur root of the plant *Kamferia galanga* used to spice certain Indonesian dishes such as *petjel*. Also used for medicinal purposes.

kentut flatus. **ber–** to pass gas.

kenup 1 collar button. 2 rubber club.

kéok defeated. *Ia - dlm pertandingan gulat itu*, He was defeated in the wrestling match. **ber- -²** to cackle. *Ajam ∼* , The chickens cackled. **meng–kan** to defeat. *Ia ∼ semua musuhnja*, He defeated all his opponents.

kéong snail. - *daratan* land snail.

kep. [*keputusan*] decision, decree.

Kep. [*Kepulauan*] islands, archipelago.

kép 1 form of address to a *kaptén*. 2 percussion cap.

kepada see PADA.

kepai ter- -² 1 to flutter, fluttering (of bird, butterfly, etc.). 2 flailing (of arms or legs).

kepak wing (of a bird, fowl). **ber–** winged. **me-ng-²**, **ter- -²** to flap the wings. **–an** flapping of wings.

kepaksa see PAKSA.

kepal 1 fist. 2 lump, clod. **ber- -²** in lumps, clods. **meng–** 1 to hold in o's hand. *Ia ∼ mata uang itu kuat²*, He held the coin tightly in his hand. 2 to clench. *Ia mendjadi marah dan ∼ tangannja*, He became mad and clenched his fists. 3 to knead. *Ia ∼ tanah liat itu mendjadi bulatan*, He kneaded the clay into a ball. **se–** a handful. *tanah ∼* a handful of earth. *∼ tanah* a clod of earth. **–an** (*tangan*) fist.

kepala 1 head. - *anak itu besar*, That child's head is large. 2 leader, head. *Dimana - rombongan itu?* Where's the leader of the group? 3 chief executive. 4 the uppermost, foremost, principal part, beginnings of s.t. **ber–** *dingin* coolheaded. **meng–** to act as chief. **meng–i** to head, manage, lead. **meng–kan** to appoint as leader. **se–²** individually. - *air* the edge of flooding water. - *angin* empty-headed. - *batok* 1 stupid. 2 crew cut. - *batu* obstinate. - *berat* numskull. - *berita* news headline. -

busung hydrocephalus. - *daérah* district head. - *désa* village headman. - *dinas*, - *dines* department head. - *djaga* commander of the guard. - *dua* 1 two-headed. 2 unreliable, of changing loyalty. - *kampung* village headman. - *keréta api* locomotive. - *lakon* leading character (in a story or novel). - *negara* chief of state. - *pusing* 1 to be dizzy. 2 to be at o's wit's end. - *sarong* upper edge of a sarong. - *sekolah* principal, headmaster. - *surat* letter heading. - *surat kabar* newspaper heading, headline(s). - *susu* cream. - *susu kotjok* whipped cream. - *tahun* the beginning of the year. - *udang* very stupid.

kepalang 1 inadequate, insufficient. 2 as long as. *Sdh -*, It's too late now. *bukan -* tremendous, extraordinary. *bukan - bagusnja* exceptionally nice. - *ini* might as well.

kepam musty, stale.

képang braid. **ber–** braided, plaited. *Rambutnja ∼* , Her hair was braided. **meng–** *rambut* to braid o's hair. - *képot* crisscross, topsy-turvy.

kepanggung **menge-(kan)** to stage a play. see PANGGUNG.

keparat 1 dammit! -, *diamlah kamu sekalian!* Dammit, be quiet all of you! 2 accursed. *anak -* accursed child. 3 heathen. 4 peace offering.

kepelabuhanan see LABUH.

kepemimpinan see PIMPIN.

kependudukan see DUDUK.

képéng coin with a square hole in the middle; ⅛ of a cent.

kepengarangan see KARANG.

kepéngin see KEPINGIN.

kepépét 1 squeezed. *Dompétmu diketemukan - antara dinding dan médja tulis*, We found your wallet stuck between the wall and the desk. 2 in a tight spot, in trouble.

kepergok see PERGOK.

képét fin (of a fish).

kepialu splitting headache.

kepik 1 insect harmful to agriculture. 2 small dent, slightly dented (fender, a pan, etc.).

kepil next, beside, alongside (of a ship), close to e.o. **meng–** to go alongside. *Ia berlari ∼ kakaknja*, He ran alongside (keeping close to) his brother. *Perahu berlajar ∼ pantai*, The prow sailed hugging the coastline. **meng–kan** to place close to s.t. *Ia ∼ mobilnja pd témbok*, He parked his car close to the wall. *∼ kapal* to berth, dock a ship.

kepinding bedbug.

kepindjal flea.

keping 1 chip. - *kaju* wood chip. 2

splinter. *se– gelas* a glass splinter. 3 used with thin, flat objects. *dua – papan* two boards. **ber–** –² 1 in pieces. *Piring itu petjah* ∼ , The plate broke in pieces. 2 in rags, tatters (of flag, etc.). 3 in tresses, locks (of hair). **meng–** 1 to split. *Ia* ∼ *papan itu,* He split the plank. 2 to slice, to cut (a cake, piece of meat, etc.). **–an** = KEPING.

kepingin to long (for). *Anak ketjil itu – mainan,* The little child longed for toys. *Ia – beladjar disekolah tinggi,* She longs to study at a university. *– tahu* to want to know. *Saja – tahu apa jg terdjadi dgn kawan saja itu,* I want to know what has become of my friend.

kepiran 1 neglected. *Pekerdjaannja –,* He neglects his work. 2 disappointed, let down. *Djangan –, djemputlah saja pd djam 7,* Don't let me down, pick me up at 7.

kepit ber– *tangan* with folded arms. **meng–** 1 to carry under o's arm. *Ia* ∼ *sebuah buku,* He carried a book under his arm. 2 to clasp. *Ia* ∼ *anaknja pd dadanja,* She clasped her child to her bosom. 3 to pinch. *Sepatu baru* ∼ , The new shoes pinch. ∼ *dgn pinsét* to hold with pincers. **–an** 1 s.t. held by clasping, pinching, etc. 2 clamp, pincers, etc.

kepiting crab.

kepléset to slip. *Ia – lalu djatuh,* He slipped and fell.

kepodang 1 = KEPUDANG. 2 see BURUNG.

képok ter– pushed aside, back.

kepompong cocoon.

keponakan 1 nephew. 2 niece.

képot 1 crumpled, creased. 2 tousled, disheveled. see KEPANG.

kepruk meng– to smash. *Ia* ∼ *kelapa itu pd sebuah batu,* He smashed the coconut against a stone. *Polisi* ∼ *sarang perampok itu,* The police destroyed the bandit's hideout.

kepudang oriole.

kepuh bulging (of brief case, pocket, sails). **meng–** to bulge.

kepujuh see PUJUH.

kepujuk cockroach.

kepuk dented. **meng–** to dent.

kepul ber– –² billowing. **meng–** to billow. *Asap* ∼ *dari tjorong asap itu,* Smoke billowed from the chimney. **meng–kan** to blow, exhale, smoke. *Ia* ∼ *asap rokoknja,* He blew the smoke from his cigarette.

kepulaga cardamom.

kepundan 1 lava. 2 crater.

kepung ber– to be (sit, stand) around s.t. or s.o. *Meréka tidur* ∼ *pemim-*

pinnja, They slept with their leader in the middle. **meng–** to surround. **(peng)–an** siege. **ter–** surrounded, encircled.

kera monkey.

kerab see AKRAB.

kerabat 1 relative. *Ia adalah – isteri saja,* He is a relative of my wife. 2 the family. **ber–** to be related to. *Saja* ∼ *dgn dia,* I am related to him. **ke–an** kinship.

kerabu 1 k.o. earrings. 2 cucumber cut into pieces and prepared with salt and red pepper.

kerah collar. **ber–** 1 mobilized. 2 to wear a collar. **meng–kan** 1 to summon, assemble. 2 to mobilize, call up. ∼ *tenaga* 1 to do o's utmost. 2 to recruit, call upon the service(s) of. **peng–** person charged with recruiting, summoning, etc., of people. **peng–an** *(tenaga tentera)* mobilization. **–an** 1 summons. 2 mobilization. 3 those who have been called upon to render their services. ∼ *negeri* summons, drafting by the state for compulsory services. *– lembik* soft collar.

kerai blinds made of thin bamboo slats.

kerak crust. *– bumi* the earth's crust. *– keruk* to crack.

kerakal gravel. **meng–i** to apply a layer of gravel (to a roadbed).

keram meng– to imprison, incarcerate, lock up.

kerama curse, spell.

keramas shampoo. **ber–** to (have a) shampoo. *– kutu* hair wash to get rid of head lice.

keramat 1 sacred, holy. 2 having supernatural qualities. 3 shrine. **ke–an** holiness, sacredness.

kerambil coconut.

kerambit small sickle.

keramik ceramics.

kerampang 1 perineum. 2 crotch.

keran 1 tap, faucet. 2 brazier, portable stove.

kerana see KARENA.

keranda a frame of laths (bamboo or other wood) to cover a corpse carried on a wooden stretcher (for a Moslem burial).

kerandjang basket. *– sampah* wastebasket. **ber–** –² by the basketful.

kerang 1 shell. 2 oyster, clam, mussel. **peng–an** a pile, heap of shells (empty clam, mussel shells). **–²an** shellfish (mollusks). **–²** loose stones (rocks, bricks, etc.) arranged as a path (through muddy ground, shallow water, etc.). *– kerung* clattering (of dishes).

kerangga big red ant.
kerangka 1 see RANGKA. 2 skeleton. 3 ship's hull. **ter-** only finished in its framework (of a house, a ship, etc., which is being built). *Rentjana Lima Tahun sdh* ∼ , The Five-Year Plan was being framed.
kerangkang 1 crotch. 2 perineum.
kerangkéng(an) 1 a cage. 2 playpen.
kérang-kéroh crisscross (of lines), irregular (of shape), rambling (of a house, layout of a city).
kerani clerk.
kerap 1 close. *Kain itu - tenunannja,* The cloth was closely woven. 2 often. *Ia - datang kesini,* He came here often. 3 bull racing (on Madura). **meng-** to race bulls. **meng-i** to repeat over again. *Se-kali² boléh membuat kesalahan tetapi djangan sampai engkau* ∼ *kesalahan itu,* You may make a mistake once in a while, but don't repeat the same mistake over again. **meng-kan** to make close. *Ia* ∼ *tenunannja agar kain itu mendjadi kuat,* She tightened her weaving to make stronger cloth. **-an** bull racing. **-²** 1 grating, gnawing sound (of a dog gnawing on a bone, a squirrel nibbling on a nut, etc.). 2 often. **-** *kali* often. **-** *pati* assassination.
kerapai see GERAPAI.
keras 1 hard (of rock, steel, etc.). *Ia bekerdja -,* He worked hard. *Hudjan -,* It rained hard. 2 taut (of rope, violin string). 3 tight. *teri-kat -* tightly bound. 4 strong. *desakan jg -* strong urge. *keinginan jg -* strong desire. *minuman -* strong drink, liquor. 5 harsh, stiff. *hukuman -* harsh sentence. 6 serious. *pikiran jg terganggu -* seriously disturbed mind. 7 high. *panas -* high fever. 8 loud. *suara -* loud voice. **ber-** 1 to persist. *Ia* ∼ *pd pendiriannja,* He persisted in his opinion. 2 to be hard. *Opsir itu* ∼ *thd anak buahnja,* The officer was hard on his men. 3 to use force. ∼ *hati* 1 to persevere. *Meski-pun hampir habis tenaganja ia* ∼ *hati,* Although he was near the end of his rope, he kept on. 2 to be firm. *Ia tetap* ∼ *hati,* He remained firm. ∼ *kepala* to be hardheaded, stubborn. *Djangan* ∼ *kepala; ikutilah saja,* Don't be hardheaded; follow my advice. **ber- -²an** mutually persistent. *Kedua orang itu* ∼ *mempertahankan pendirian meréka masing²,* The 2 persons were mutually persistent in defending their viewpoints. ∼ *mulut* to have a severe quarrel. ∼ *batang léhér* obstinate. ∼ *hidung* 1 self-willed. 2 narrow-minded. ∼ *lidah*

to have difficulty in learning the pronunciation of foreign words. **bersi-** to persist. **ke-an** 1 hardness, harshness. ∼ *intan tak ada bandingnja,* The hardness of a diamond is unequaled. ∼ *guru itu menimbulkan kebentjian murid²nja,* The harshness of the teacher aroused the dislike of his pupils. 2 loudness. 3 force. *Djika perlu pergunakanlah* ∼ , If necessary, use force. 4 severity. **meng-** 1 to become hard. *Semén itu* ∼ , The cement became hard. 2 to become louder. *Suaranja* ∼ , His voice became louder. **meng-i** 1 to use force, coerce. *Djangan* ∼ *meréka; tjobalah tjara² damai dahulu,* Don't use force on them; try peaceful means first. 2 to treat harshly. **memper-, meng-kan** 1 to make hard. *Matahari* ∼ *tanah liat itu,* The sun made the clay hard. 2 to make loud(er). *Ia* ∼ *suaranja,* He made his voice louder. 3 to tighten. *Ia* ∼ *sekrup itu,* He tightened the screw. 4 to force. *Ia* ∼ *meréka supaja menjumbangkan djasa,* He forced them to contribute their services. **peng-** *suara* loudspeaker, amplifier. **peng-an** 1 amplification (of sound). 2 coercion. 3 forceful measure. **-** *hati* 1 persevering. 2 firm. *Ia - hatinja,* He was firm. ∼ *kepala* stubborn, obstinate. **-** *makas* hard as a rock. **-** *mengkas* hard and unripe (of fruit). **-** *tegas* rigorous.
kerasan to feel at home, settled (in new surroundings of residence, work, school). *Apakah engkau sdh - di New York?* Do you already feel at home in New York?
kerat 1 a slice, piece, part. *daging se-* a slice of meat. 2 part (of a house, road, town). 3 see KARAT. **ber-** *rotan (dgn)* to sever relations with (a friend, relative). **meng-** 1 to carve (meat), cut (off), amputate. *Ia* ∼ *kaju itu,* He cut the wood. 2 to nibble, gnaw. ∼ *lidah* to interrupt s.o. **-an** a slice.
keratjak 1 jumping with joy, elated. 2 making good speed (of sailing vessels).
keraton palace (of Javanese prince).
kerawai a large wasp nesting in the ground.
kerawang openwork (on cloth, embroidery, lace, wood carving, leatherwork, metal). **meng-** to make openwork. *Angan²* ∼ *kepala,* Thoughts flashed through his mind. ∼ *langit* to foster wild fantasies.
kerawat plaited band of rattan, or iron band (on handle of a knife, chisel).

kerbang 1 see GERBANG. 2 a bread fruit tree.
kerbat meng- to bind, tie up. - *mulut* to gag s.o.
kerbau water buffalo. - *djalang* water buffalo which has turned wild from a domesticated state. *Ia membeli - dipadang*, He bought a pig in a poke.
kerdak 1 dreg, sediment (of coffee, wine). 2 term of reference for o's possessions as a modest, negligible quantity or quality. *Hanja rumah inilah - saja*, This is my humble abode. 3 things of no value, junk.
kerdil dwarfish, stunted. -an petty bickering.
kerdip see KEDIP.
kerdja 1 work, labor, activity. -*nja mengetik surat*, His work was typing letters. 2 occupation, job. 3 a celebration (wedding, etc.). be- 1 to work. *Ia ∼ keras*, He worked hard. 2 to have a celebration, ceremony. 3 active (of a volcano, etc.). ∼ *rodi* to do forced labor. ∼ *sama* to co-operate. *Negara² ∼ sama mendjaga perdamaian*, The nations co-operated to preserve peace. **mempe-kan** to put to work, employ, give a job. *Ia ∼ anaknja pd perusahaannja*, He put his son to work at his factory. **meng-kan** 1 to do, carry out, execute. *Ia ∼ pekerdjaannja dgn radjin*, He did his work diligently. 2 to finish off, eliminate, kill s.o. ∼ *tanah* to till the soil. pe- 1 worker. 2 laborer. 3 employee. ∼ *hukuman* a convict put to labor. ∼ *tangan* manual laborer. pe-an 1 work, task, activity. 2 job, occupation, business, enterprise, line. 3 effect (of medicine, a chemical, liquor). 4 operation. ∼ *mesin mobil* the way in which a car engine operates. 5 celebration, feast (wedding, anniversary, etc.). 6 employment. ∼ *penuh* full employment. 7 endeavor. *lapangan ∼* field of endeavor. ∼ *médja* desk job. ∼ *rodi* forced labor. ∼ *tangan* manual labor. peng-an 1 execution, implementation. 2 processing. ∼ *bahan mentah itu* the processing of the raw material. se-, sepe-an colleague. te-kan 1 done, performed, carried out. 2 workable, can be carried out. -an work. *Saja banjak ∼* , I have lots of work. - *bakti* voluntary collective work. - *borong* contract work. - *malam* night shift, night work. - *paksa* hard labor, forced labor, penal servitude. - *radja* forced labor, statute labor. - *sama* co-operation. *Apa -mu datang dikantor pos?* What were you doing at the post office?

kerdjantara employment bureau.
kerdjap see KEDJAP.
kerdut wrinkled.
keré see KERAI.
kerédak caked, dried up dirt (clinging to people, animals, or things).
kerédép see KERDIP.
kerédong ber- wrapped in (a blanket, sarong).
kerék see KERIK.
kérék 1 pulley (block). 2 measure (in lumps) of brown palm sugar. *se-gula enau* 10 lumps of palm sugar. meng- to hoist. *Meréka ∼ bendéra meréka*, They hoisted their flag. -an pulley.
kerékot 1 crooked, twisted, misshapen, disfigured (of hands, fingers; of fingers grown together because of scar tissue). 2 rough, uneven floor. 3 very stingy, avaricious.
keremi maggot. ke-an 1 to suffer from maggots. 2 to itch around the anus.
kerempagi 1 (straight) razor. 2 pocketknife.
kerén 1 impressive. *Perwira jg muda berpakaian seragam - nampaknja*, The uniformed young officer looked impressive. - *tampangnja*, He looks handsome (or) She looks beautiful. - *benar kamu berpakaian baru*, You look natty in your new suit. 2 spirited (of a horse).
kerena see KARENA.
kerenda see KERANDA.
kereng gruff, surly, grumpy.
kerengga see KERANGGA.
kerenjam geranium.
kerenjan see KERNJAN.
kerenjit see KERNJIT.
kerénjot meng- 1 to grin. 2 to twist, distort o's mouth.
kerenjut wrinkle. ber- wrinkled. *Dahinja ∼* , His brow was wrinkled. meng-kan *dahi* to frown. *Ia ∼ dahinja*, He frowned.
kerentjang see KERNTJING.
kerentjing rattling sound of a metal chain.
kerentjung see KERINTJING.
kerépés meng- to grope about for s.t.
kerépot see KERÉSOT.
keresek rustling, crackling (of dry leaves).
kerésék see KERISIK.
keréséng 1 cracked (of skin). 2 slightly open (of mouth, perhaps because of a harelip).
kerésé pésé to speak Dutch all the time (common term in Sumatra).
kerésot wrinkled, furrowed (of forehead).
keréta 1 carriage, cart. 2 car. ber-

1 to ride in a carriage. 2 to go for a ride. ~ *angin* to ride a bicycle. *Ia ~ angin kesekolah,* He rode his bicycle to school. ~ *api* to go by train. *Ia ~ api ke Surabaja,* He went to Surabaya by train. – *anak* baby carriage. – *angin* bicycle. – *api* train. – *api bawah tanah* subway. – *api bumel* local train. – *api kilat,* – *api tjepat* fast train. – *api penumpang,* – *api tumpangan* passenger train. – *badja* armored car. – *makan* dining car. – *mati* funeral hearse. – *(pari)-wisata* sight-seeing carriage. – *pemandangan* observation car. – *pengiring* trailer. – *séwa* carriage for rent. – *tangan* pushcart. – *tidur* sleeper, sleeping car. – *tolak* handcar. – *wadja* armored car.

kerétan see GERÉTAN.

keréték 1 cigarette containing cloves (in Java). 2 see ROKOK.

keretjak see KERATJAK.

kerétjéng meng–kan *mata* to blink o's eyes.

kerétol see KERÉKOT.

keri small sickle. meng– to use a *keri.*

keriap ber–an to swarm. *Semut ~ pd makanan itu,* Ants were swarming over the food.

kerih sound of a screaming monkey. meng– 1 to scream (of a monkey). 2 to scream, groan (with pain).

kerik meng– 1 to scrape. *Ia ~ kotoran dari piring itu,* He scraped the dirt from the plate. 2 to treat a cold by inducing hyperemia of the skin of o's back by scraping it vigorously with a coin dipped in coconut oil. *Kapur tulis ~ diatas papan tulis,* The chalk scraped over the blackboard. –an 1 a scratch. 2 scrapings.

kerikil gravel, pebble. meng– to cover with gravel.

kerikit meng–i to gnaw, nibble at s.t.

kerindjal kidney.

kering 1 dry. *Badjunja –,* His shirt was dry. 2 arid. *Tanah itu –,* The earth was arid (or parched). ber– –² to ring (of a telephone, doorbell, alarm clock). ke–an 1 dryness. 2 drought. 3 too dry, arid. *Tanah ini ~ ,* This land is too dry. meng– to become dry. *Tanah itu makin ~ ,* The earth became drier and drier. meng–i to drain. meng–kan 1 to dry. *Ia ~ badjunja,* He dried his shirt. 2 to dry up. peng– drier, dehumidifier. peng–an 1 drainage, draining. 2 drying up, dehydration. – *darah(nja)* to be shocked, bewildered. – *embun* about 7:30 A.M. (when the dew has evaporated). – *kerontang* completely

dried up (of a well, creek). – *ringkai* bone-dry (of laundry in the sun).

keringat sweat, perspiration. ber– to sweat, perspire. *Setiap hari ia ~ mentjari nafkahnja,* Every day he toiled for his living. meng–kan to sweat, slave over s.t. –an perspiring.

kerinjut see KERENJUT.

kerintil ber– to hang in bunches, clusters (like grapes, flowers).

kerinting salted and dried mollusks.

kerintjing 1 tinkling, jingling sound. 2 metal rattler. ber– to jingle. *Uangnja ~ ,* His money jingled. meng–kan to jingle s.t. *Ia ~ uangnja,* He jingled his money.

kerip meng– 1 to crackle. *Kerikil ~ diindjaknja,* The gravel crackled under his feet. 2 to nibble, gnaw (of a rat, squirrel).

keripik chips of sliced fried unripe banana, cassava, or sweet potato.

keriput wrinkled, lined, furrowed.

keris creese. ber– to wear a creese. meng– to stab with a creese.

kerisik dried banana leaves. ber– to rustle. *Daun² kering ~ ,* The dry leaves rustled. meng– to peel. *Kulit saja ~ ,* My skin is peeling. –an rustling.

Keristen Christian. ke–an Christianity. meng–kan to Christianize. peng–an Christianization.

kerisut see KISUT.

kerit meng–kan *gigi* to gnash the teeth. *Ia ~ giginja karena marah,* He gnashed his teeth in anger. – *dajung* a cricket.

keritik 1 criticism. 2 critical. *Keadaan –,* The situation is critical. 3 crackling. ber– –² to crackle, sputter (of a lighted candle). meng– to criticize. *Oposisi ~ pemerintah,* The opposition criticized the government. peng– 1 critic. 2 faultfinder. –an criticism.

keriting curly, kinky (of hair). *Rambutnja –,* His hair is curly. meng–(kan) *rambut* to curl the hair.

keritjau see KITJAU.

keriuk a crowing. ber– to crow.

kerkah the crunching, cracking sound of bones, wood being broken. meng– to gnaw at, tear apart.

kerlap be–an, meng– to glitter. *Bintang² ~ ,* The stars glittered. te– to sleep a wink, doze off for a moment.

kerling meng– 1 to glance sidewise, askance at. *Ia ~ pd saja dan tersenjum,* She gave me a side glance and smiled. 2 to ogle. *Ia ~ pd gadis itu dan bersiul,* He ogled the girl and whistled. 3 to blink, twinkle (of stars). meng–kan *mata* to throw a side glance at. *Ia ~ matanja pd saja,* She threw a side glance at me. **–an** side glance.

kerlip to be in love. *Ia – pd bintang pilem itu,* He was in love with the movie star. **meng–** 1 to blink. *Matanja ~ ,* His eyes blinked. 2 to twinkle (of stars). **meng–kan** to make fall in love. *Ketjantikannja ~ saja padanja,* Her beauty made me fall in love with her. *~ mata* to blink the eyes. **se–** *mata* in a wink.

kerma see KERAMA.

kerna see KARENA.

kernai meng– to cut, chop into small pieces (of meat, vegetables).

kernét driver's assistant or apprentice (of taxicab, bus).

kernia see KARUNIA.

kernjat-kernjut creaking (of shoes, doors).

kernjau 1 a crunching sound (as when o. eats raw cucumbers). 2 hoarse (of voice).

kernjih grinning, making faces at (to express ridicule, mockery). **meng–** to grin, make faces.

kernjing meng– to bare its teeth, fangs (a vicious dog, tiger).

kernjit furrow. **meng–** to frown. **meng–kan** *alis* to frown.

kernjut 1 see KERENJUT. 2 gnashing of teeth. **be–** to pulsate (of arteries, etc.).

kéro 1 squinting, squint-eyed. 2 steel bed with spring.

kerobak 1 with a hole, holes (in s.t.). *Dinding – kena peluru mortir,* The wall had a big hole caused by a mortar grenade. 2 with a big tear (a sail, flag). 3 scarred, pock-marked. *– kerabik, – kerabit, – kerobék* 1 in tatters (a flag, sail, etc.). 2 with many scars.

kerobék 1 see KEROBAK. 2 see ROBÉK. **meng–** to tear s.t. to pieces.

kerodong see KERUDUNG.

kéroh false, deceptive, crooked, on the sly.

kerojok meng– to rush, attack, mob. *Andjing² ~ babi hutan itu,* The dogs rushed the boar. **peng–** attacker. **peng–an** attack, assault, mobbing, mob violence. **–an** rush.

kerok 1 see KERIK. 2 see KERUK. 3 currycomb. **meng–** 1 to curry, rub down (a horse). 2 to snore.

keromo 1 the polite form of the Javanese language (used by those of lower status to upper-class people). 2 the common people. *Si– hidup dlm kesengsaraan,* The common people live in misery.

keromong k.o. musical instrument.

kerongkongan 1 gullet, esophagus. 2 throat. 3 pharynx.

kerongsang brooch.

kerongsong see KELONGSONG.

kerontjong 1 clanking, jingling. 2 popular Indonesian music. 3 ankle band with small bells attached. 4 the end part (farthest from its entrance) of a fish trap. **ber–** 1 to make *kerontjong* music. 2 to jingle. *Uangnja ~ ,* His money jingled. **meng–** to round (the lips). *ikan dlm ~* beyond recovery, redemption, help. **–an** clamoring. *Perutnja ~ karena lapar,* His stomach is growling from hunger.

keropas-keropis small articles, objects of no importance. **ber–** to do odd jobs of little significance.

keropéng scab (of a wound, skin eruption, rash). **meng–** to pick scabs.

keropok 1 see KEROPONG. 2 see KERUPUK. **se–** small group.

keropong hollow.

keropos 1 rarefaction. 2 porous.

kerosang brooch.

kerosi see KORSI.

kérosin kerosene.

kerosok see KERISIK.

kerosong sloughed-off skin (of a reptile). **meng–** to slough off the skin.

kerotot grooved (of a file), pock-marked, furrowed, wrinkled (like the skin of a tangerine).

kerpai cartridge pouch.

kerpus 1 cap (headdress). 2 roof ridge. 3 guardhouse (military prison). **di–** locked up, detained in the guardhouse.

kerrén see KERÉN.

kersai crumbly, loose (of sand, cooked rice).

kersang 1 barren. *Tanah itu –,* The land was barren. 2 coarse (of hair). **ke–an** barrenness.

kersik 1 grit, gravel. 2 rustling sound (of dead leaves rubbing against e.o.). **meng–i** to cover with a layer of grit, gravel. **ter–** rustling.

kersip see KEDIP.

kertak cracking sound of a breaking branch, creaking sound of wooden stairs, etc. **meng–kan** *gigi* to gnash the teeth. *– kertuk* creaking sound (of shoes, doors).

kertang caked with (dirt, dried blood, pus). *Pembalutnja di– oléh darah beku,* The bandage was caked with dried blood.

kertas paper. *– -meng–* wastepaper. *– bertinta* carbon paper. *– bujar* 1 blotting paper. 2 tissue paper. *– bungkus* wrapping paper. *– dinding* wallpaper. *– embun, – isap, – kembang* blotting paper. *– kakus* toilet paper. *– koordinir* graph paper. *– koran* newspaper print. *– kulit* parchment. – *meterai* stamped paper. – *minjak* wax paper. – *penetap* blotting paper. – *pengering* absorbent paper. – *rokok* cigarette paper. – *saring* filter paper. – *ségel* stamped paper. – *tapis* filter paper. – *tebal* cardboard. – *telur* wax paper. – *tik* typewriter paper. – *tjétak* printing paper. – *tulis* writing paper.

kertjap **meng-(kan)** to smack the (lips). *Ia ～ bibirnja*, He smacked his lips.

kertu see KARTU.

kertus 1 cartridge (of a gun). 2 sound of paper being crumpled up.

keruan certain. *Kedatangannja blm –*, His arrival is not certain yet. *tidak – to make no sense. Karangannja itu tidak –*, His article did not make sense. *rentjana pekerdjaan jg tidak –* a confused working schedule. *Dlm kabut rumah² tidak – nampaknja*, In the fog the houses were vaguely discernible. *kegelisahan jg tidak –* extreme unrest. *kedjadian ngeri jg tidak – an indescribably weird event. – sadja* you bet, by all means.

kerubung see KERUMUN.

kerubut **meng-** to gang up on, mob. *Djangan ～ saja*, Don't gang up on me. **meng-i** to crowd about. *Murid² ～ guru meréka*, The pupils crowded about their teacher.

kerudung veil. **ber-** veiled. *Perempuan berduka tjita itu ～*, The mourning woman was veiled. **meng-i** to veil. *Kegelapan ～ malam hari*, Darkness veiled the night. – *lampu* lamp shade.

keruh 1 turbid, muddy. *Kali itu – airnja*, The water of the river was turbid. 2 disturbed. *Mukanja –*, His face was disturbed. 3 restless. *Seluruh negara –*, The whole country was restless. 4 snoring. **ke-an** 1 muddiness. 2 unrest. 3 disturbance. *～ hatinja disebabkan banjaknja pikirannja*, His troubled mind was caused by his many worries. 4 irregularity, corruption. *～ dlm pembukuan keuangan* irregularities in the bookkeeping. **meng-** to become muddy. *Air kali ～ karena hudjan*, The river became muddy from the rain. **meng-kan** 1 to make muddy. *Hudjan ～ air kali²*, The rain made the rivers muddy. 2 to disturb. *Kaum pemberontak ～ keamanan dlm negara*, The rebels disturbed the peace of the country.

keruit **ber-** 1 to wiggle the hips. 2 to wriggle (worm). 3 to wag the tail. 4 to squirm.

kerujuk 1 see KEROJOK. 2 crowing of a cock.

keruk **meng-** 1 to scrape, dredge. *Kapal itu ～ pintu pelabuhan*, The dredger scraped the entrance to the harbor. 2 to curry a horse. **peng-** 1 scraper. 2 exploiter. *～ periuk* a glutton. **peng-an** exploitation. *～ kekajaan negara* exploitation of a nation's resources.

kerukut curled up (over), warped (of wood, etc., when exposed to changing climatic conditions).

kerumit **meng-** to gnaw, nibble (of rabbits, mice).

kerumuk crumpled. **ber-** to slump, to sag. *Ia ～ dikursinja setelah dimarahi ajahnja*, He slumped in his chair after his father reprimanded him. **ter-** crumpled. *Kertas itu ～*, The paper was crumpled.

kerumun **ber-** to swarm. *Orang² ～ dilapangan*, People were swarming over the field. **meng-i** to crowd. *Meréka ～ tempat pendjualan kartjis*, They crowded the ticket office.

kerumus **meng-** 1 to embrace. *Ibu itu ～ anaknja*, The mother embraced her son. 2 to fondle, caress.

kerung concave, hollow, hollowed out (of a spoon, bowl).

kerunia see KARUNIA.

kerunjut wrinkled, shriveled, withered, wizened (face). **ber-** wrinkled. **meng-** to crumple. *Ia ～ kertas itu*, He crumpled the paper. **meng-kan** to frown. *Ia ～ dahinja*, He frowned.

keruntung 1 a piggy bank (made of a bamboo cylinder). 2 tray.

keruping see KEROPÉNG.

kerupuk shrimp chip (delicacy made of shrimp and cassava flour or of fish flakes and rice dough, cut in slices and fried to crisp chips). – *belindjo* fruit, fried and eaten as snacks or with the main course.

kerus crush (a drink such as orange crush).

kerusi see KURSI.

kerut 1 furrow, wrinkle. 2 scraping. **ber-** furrowed. *Dahinja ～*, His brow was furrowed. **meng-kan** to frown. *Ia ～ dahinja*, He frowned. – *kering* shrunken, shriveled. – *merut* 1 to be wrinkled. *Keningnja – merut*, His forehead is wrinkled. 2 disheveled, in disorder (hair, appearance).

kerutjut cone, conical paper bag. **meng-** 1 conical. *Benda itu bentuknja ～*, That object is conical in shape. 2 to pout (of lips).

kerutu see GERUTU.

kes. [*kesebelasan*] soccer team.

kesad see KASAD.

kesah 1 a moan. 2 a sigh. **meng-** 1 to moan. 2 to sigh.

késah see KISSAH.

kesal 1 to be fed up. *Saja – melakukan pekerdjaan ini,* I am fed up with this work. 2 dejected. *Ia mendjadi – setelah diinsjafinja ke-sia²an usahanja,* He became dejected when he realized the futility of his efforts. 3 peevish, rankled, cross. *Ia – karena kalah débat,* He is cross because he lost the debate. **ke–an** 1 spite. 2 dejection. **meng–kan** 1 annoying. *Kekerasan kepalanja sungguh ∼ ,* His stubbornness was really annoying. 2 to make dejected. *Segala kesukaran itu ∼ hatinja,* All those difficulties made him dejected. – *hati* = KESAL.

kesalah– see SALAH.

kesambet to be seized with a sudden illness, attributed to possession by an evil spirit.

kesambi ironwood tree used for charcoal.

kesan 1 impression. 2 a trace. – *pukulan* traces of a beating. **ber–** 1 to get the impression. *Saja ∼ bhw maksud²nja tidak djudjur,* I got the impression that his intentions were not honest. 2 to leave an impression. *Segala adjaran gurunja tak ∼ padanja,* All the teachings of his teacher left no impression on him. 3 impressive. **memper–kan, meng–kan** 1 to give an impression of s.t. 2 to leave an impression. 3 impressive. *modél jg ∼ ini* this impressive model. **meng–** to leave traces, leave an impression. *tidak* **ter–i** unimpressed.

kesana see SANA.

kesandung to hit against, bump. *Kepalanja – témbok itu,* His head bumped against the wall.

kesang to blow o's nose (using only o's fingers).

kesangsang caught, stuck. *Lajangan – dlm pohon beringin,* The kite was caught in a banyan tree.

kesap-kesip blinking (of eyes).

kesasar see SASAR.

kesat 1 stiff, rough. 2 rough and dry. *Kulitnja –,* His skin was rough and dry. **ke–an** grainy, rough texture. **meng–** to wipe. *Ia ∼ dahinja,* He wiped his brow. **peng–** *kaki* door mat.

kesateria knight.

kesebelasan see SEBELAS.

keséd(an) see KÉSÉT(AN).

késék meng– to rub with a stiff object. **–an** rubbing. see GÉSÉK.

késél meng– to rub.

keselak to choke on s.t. *Karena ia makan dgn ter-gesa² ia –,* Because he ate in a hurry he choked on his food.

keseléo to be sprained. *Kaki saja –,* I sprained my ankle.

kes(e)mak persimmon.

kesemat see KASUMAT.

kesemuanja see SEMUA.

kését(an) 1 door mat. 2 to wipe o's feet on a door mat. *Hendaklah – dulu sebelum masuk kerumah,* Please wipe your feet on the door mat before you enter the house.

kesian see KASIHAN.

kesiap ter– to be startled.

kesima ter– upset, shaken (up), unnerved.

kesini see SINI.

kesip seedless (of fruit). **ber– –²** to blink o's eyes. **meng–** to suck (on a piece of candy, a juicy fruit).

keskul begging bowl.

keslio see KESELÉO.

kesmaran to be in love.

kesohor see SOHOR.

kesomplok 1 hit, bumped into. *Dlm kegelapan kamar ia – temannja,* In the darkness of the room his friend bumped into him. 2 to be broke. – *karena main djudi* to go broke because of gambling.

késot ber– to drag o.s. along (on the floor, ground, e.g., of a small child who cannot yet walk, a wounded person who is unable to stand up).

kesturi musk, civet.

kesuari cassowary.

kesuh-kesih panting.

kesuma 1 flower. 2 beautiful. 3 beautiful woman. – *bangsa* 1 soldiers killed on the field of battle. 2 youth (as the generation of the future). – *widjaja* a glorious victory.

kesumba 1 a plant which produces red dye. 2 red. *Warna badjunja –,* Her dress was red.

kesungai see SUNGAI.

kesup meng– to suck. *Ia ∼ djarinja,* He sucked his finger.

kesusu in a hurry. *Ia – hendak pulang,* He was in a hurry to get home.

ketahu see TAHU.

ketai loser (in a card game). **ber– –²** to crumble into small pieces, decay (of a cadaver, wood, cloth). **meng– daging** to cut meat into small pieces.

ketaja a torch (made of bamboo filled with resin).

ketak wrinkle, skin fold (of a double chin). **ber– –²** to cackle (of hens).

ketam 1 tightly closed. 2 with set teeth. 3 plane (carpenter's tool). 4 a crab. **meng–** 1 to close tightly. *∼ bibir* to press o's lips tightly together, bite o's lips in anger or pain. 2 to harvest rice. 3 to plane wood. **peng–** 1 a pair of pincers. 2 a knife for harvesting rice. 3 a clamp. *∼ betina* grooving plane. ~ *pandjang* smoothing plane.

peng-an 1 rice harvest. 2 wood shavings. – *mulut* lockjaw.

ketan sticky rice. – *urap* sticky rice (with grated coconut).

ketap meng- *bibir* to press o's lips together.

ketapang a tree bearing nuts resembling almonds.

ketar 1 see GETAR. 2 tart, sour. – *rasanja buah ini*, This fruit has a tart taste.

ketara see KENTARA.

ketat firmly attached. *Tjintjin – pd djari*, The ring stuck firmly to the finger. **memper-, meng-kan** *tali sepatu* to tighten shoelaces.

ketawa see TERTAWA. –an laughter.

ketegar stubborn.

keték monkey.

kéték 1 armpit. 2 small, little. **meng-i** to tickle under the arm.

ketel 1 thick, close together, tight. 2 crowded.

kétél kettle.

ketéla plant with edible roots. – *kaju*, – *pohon* cassava. – *ubi* sweet potato.

ketemu 1 to meet. *Sampai – lagi*, So long, see you soon. *Saja – dgn dia didjalan*, I met him on the street. 2 to find. *Saja tjari dia di-mana², akan tetapi tak –*, I looked everywhere for him but couldn't find him. 3 see TEMU. **meng-i** 1 to meet. *Hasan ~ temannja dikantor*, Hasan met his friend at the office. 2 to find. *Saja ~ arlodji dibawah médja*, I found a watch under the table. **meng-kan** to find, discover.

kéténg meng-i to divide merchandise for retail selling. **meng-kan** to sell retail. *Ia ~ dagangannja dgn untung sedikit*, He sold his wares retail at a small profit. **se-** half a penny. **-an** by the piece. *Saja tak mau membeli satu bungkus, mau membeli ~ sadja*, I don't want to buy the whole pack; I just want to buy by the piece.

ketengah see TENGAH.

ketepuk ber- to click, go clickety-clack. *Suara sepatunja ~* , His shoes went clickety-clack.

ketergesaan see GESA.

kétés a drop. **meng-i** to pour by the drop.

ketétér 1 to fall behind, be unable to keep up with s.o. (in running, learning, doing a job). 2 to be on the verge of defeat, helpless.

keti se- 100,000. –² a small hornet.

ketiak armpit.

ketial ponderous, having difficulty in moving about because of obesity or gout.

ketibung the sound of splashing.

ketidak- see TIDAK.

ketiding a basket (plaited of bamboo laths).

ketik tick. **meng-** 1 to tap on. *Ia ~ pintu*, He tapped on the door. 2 to type. *Ia ~ surat*, He typed a letter. **peng-** typist. –an 1 typing. 2 s.t. typed.

ketika 1 a point of time. 2 when. – *ia pergi, isterinja datang*, When he left, his wife came. **ber-** in good time. **se-** immediately. *17 orang meninggal ~ itu djuga*, 17 people died instantly.

ketil ber- –² in very small pieces. **meng-** to slice, cut into small pieces. **se-** a tiny piece about the size of sunflower seed.

ketilang 1 thrush. 2 see KUTILANG.

ketimang buckle, clasp.

ketimpung splashing in the water.

ketimun cucumber.

keting Achilles tendon. **meng-** to hamstring.

ketip 1 a dime. 2 bite, sting of a small insect (mosquito, gnat). **ber-** –² to flicker. **meng-** to bite, sting (of a small insect).

ketipung small hand drum.

ketir² fear, anxiety.

ketis meng- to flick, flip (with the fingers), a speck of dust, etc.

ketitir(an) small wood pigeon.

ketj. [*ketjamatan*] subdistrict.

ketjai ber- –², ter- smashed (of glass, pottery, stone), torn to shreds (of cloth, paper).

ketjak ber- *pinggang* arms akimbo.

ketjam meng-(kan) 1 to criticize. 2 to investigate (consider) carefully. 3 to take s.t. to heart. *Ia ~ kata² bapaknja*, He took his father's words to heart. 4 to review a book, play, etc. **peng-** critic. (peng)-an criticism.

ketjambah sprout. **ber-** to sprout. *Katjang itu mulai ~* , The bean started to sprout.

ketjamuk ber- to rage. *Peperangan ~ dgn hébatnja*, War raged violently.

ketjandan to joke, jest. **ber-** to make jokes.

ketjap meng- 1 to smack o's lips. *Kalau makan djangan ~* , Don't smack your lips while eating. 2 to taste. *Ia ~ masakan ibunja*, He tasted his mother's cooking. *Setelah ~ banjak kenikmatan sekarang ia terpaksa hidup sangat sederhana*, After tasting many luxuries he has to live very humbly now. **peng-** sense of taste.

kétjap soy sauce.

ketjapéan see TJAPÉK.

ketjapi lute.
kétjék (chit)chat. **ber-** $-^2$ to chat. *Meréka minum kopi dan* ∼ , They drank coffee and chatted. **meng-** to chat. *Djangan* ∼ *didalam kelas,* Don't talk while in class. **meng-kan** 1 to chat about. *Meréka* ∼ *kabar²* *jg baru,* They chatted about the latest news. 2 to persuade, talk s.o. into doing s.t. 3 to deceive s.o. (by talking nicely). **peng-** a chatterbox.
ketjelé to be fooled, made a fool of. *Saja* –, I've been fooled.
kétjéng meng-(kan) *mata* to close o's eye (when aiming a rifle). **se-***mata* in a moment, in the twinkling of an eye.
ketjéwa disappointed. *Ia sangat* – *ketika bapaknja tidak datang,* He was very disappointed when his father did not come. **ke-an** disappointment. **meng-kan** 1 to disappoint. *Hasil udjiannja* ∼ *dia,* The results of his examination disappointed him. 2 disappointing. *Hasil usahanja* ∼ , The result of his efforts was disappointing. *tidak* ∼ satisfactory.
ketjik see KETJIL.
ketjil 1 small. *Rumahnja* –, His house was small. 2 little. *anak* – *itu* the little boy. 3 insignificant. *Djangan mengindahkan perkara* – *itu,* Don't pay attention to such an insignificant matter. 4 childhood. *Sedjak* –*nja ia selalu suka membatja,* Since childhood he has always been fond of reading. **(ber)-** *hati* 1 to be discouraged. *Djangan* ∼ *hati, tjobalah lagi,* Don't be discouraged, try again. 2 to be peeved, vexed. *Ia* ∼ *hati ketika permintaannja tidak diluluskan,* He was peeved when his wish was not fulfilled. **ke-an** 1 smallness. ∼ *rumahnja* the smallness of his house. 2 insignificance. *Karena* ∼*nja, perkara itu tak mendapat perhatian,* Because of its insignificance the case did not receive any attention. 3 too small. *Badju saja* ∼ , My shirt is too small. **memper-, meng-kan** 1 to make smaller. *Ibu* ∼ *badju saja jg kebesaran itu,* Mother made my overly large shirt smaller. 2 to minimize, belittle. ∼ *arti* to minimize the significance. ∼ *hati* to discourage, frighten. *Kesukaran² itu* ∼ *hatinja,* Those difficulties discouraged him. 3 to grieve, hurt, gall. ∼ *ikat pinggang* to tighten o's belt. **meng-** to become smaller. *Kapal terbang itu makin* ∼ *dan achirnja menghilang dikedjauhan,* The plane became smaller and smaller and at last disappeared in the distance. **per-an** reduction. **ter-** 1 smallest. 2

minimum. *pasangan* ∼ minimal pair. –²*an* on a small scale. *Perdagangannja hanja* ∼ *sadja,* His business was only on a small scale. $-^2$ *tjabé rawit* small but brave. – *hati* 1 to be irritated. – *hatinja waktu dia melihat perbuatan jg dilakukan oléh anak itu,* He was irritated when he saw what that child had done. 2 cowardly. 3 discouraged.
ketjimpung ber-(an) to splash. *Anak²* ∼ *dlm air,* The children were splashing in the water. *Ia* ∼ *dlm politik,* He's active in politics.
ketjandan see KETJANDAN.
ketjipak ber- to splatter. *Air* ∼ , The water splattered.
ketjit see KETJIL.
ketjiut whistling, whizzing (of bullets).
kétjoh 1 **meng-** to deceive s.o. 2 to stir, cause commotion. *Chabar angin itu* ∼ *seluruh negeri,* The rumor started a stir throughout the whole country. **peng-** swindler. **peng-an** fraud.
ketjomak-ketjimik to put too much in o's mouth at o. time.
kétju robber, bandit.
ketjuali 1 except, an exception, excepted. *Semuanja pergi kegambar hidup – saja,* Everyone went to the movies except me. *Semua pemuda masuk tentara, tak ada* –*nja,* Everyone entered the army without any exception. 2 besides, in addition, not only. – *merampok ia membunuh pula,* Besides committing robbery, he is also guilty of murder. 3 only. – *dia diantara saudaranja jg masih bersekolah,* Only he among his brothers is still studying. *tidak* **ber-** without exception. *Semua orang harus membajar padjak, tidak* ∼ , Everyone, without exception, has to pay taxes. **ke-an** exception. **meng-kan** 1 to make an exception. *Saja tidak dpt* ∼ *saudara,* I cannot make an exception for you. 2 to exempt from. *Peraturan ini* ∼ *saja dari bajar padjak istiméwa itu,* This regulation exempts me from paying the special tax. **peng-an, per-an** exception. **ter-** with the exception of. *Semua orang pergi melihat présidén,* ∼ *meréka jg sakit,* Everyone went to see the president with the exception of those who were sick. **ter-an** exception. *tidak seorangpun* **ter-kan** no o. excepted. – *djika,* – *kalau* unless. *Semua orang masuk tentara* – *djika meréka kurang séhat badannja,* Everyone entered the army unless he was physically unfit.
ketjubung 1 conical in shape. 2 da-

tura plant; poisonous plant with attractive flower.

ketjuh-ketjah to make, raise a fuss.

ketjumik ber- to mumble.

ketjup kiss. **meng-** to kiss.

ketjut 1 sour (of taste, face). 2 wrinkled, shrunken, shriveled. **ke-an** cowardice. **meng-** to shrink. *Hatinja ~ karena ketakutan*, He tightened up with fear. *Papan itu ~ karena didjemur*, The board shrank because it had been dried. **meng-kan** to scare. *Kemarahan bapaknja ~ dia*, His father's anger scared him. *~ badan, ~ hati* to make s.o. shudder, give s.o. the creeps, be gruesome. *Didalam kamar nampaklah pemandangan jg ~* , Inside the room the scene was gruesome. **peng-** coward. *-² badan* to shudder from fright. *- hati* to be afraid, frightened. *Ia - hati lalu melarikan dirinja*, He was afraid and ran away.

ketok knock. **meng-** to knock. *Ia ~ pintu*, He knocked at the door. *~ kawat* to send a telegram. *Ia ~ kawat kpd saja*, He sent me a telegram. **meng-kan** to pound. *Ia ~ palu*, He pounded the gavel. *- kadal* game with bamboo sticks, usually played by children.

ketombé see KETUMBÉ.

ketopong helmet.

ketoprak k.o. stage show (popular opera in central and east Java).

ketua 1 chairman. 2 elder, chief. **meng-i** to preside over, chair. **peng-** leader, elder. *- muda* vice-chairman.

ketuat calloused wart.

ketuk see KETOK.

ketul lump. *se- nasi* a lump of rice. *se- tanah* a clod of earth.

ketumbar coriander seed.

ketumbé dandruff.

ketumbu basket with cover.

ketumbuhan smallpox. see TUMBUH.

ketungging large black scorpion.

ketup see KATUP.

ketupat rice cooked in a fist-size container plaited of young coconut leaves.

ketupuk an owl.

ketur cuspidor. **ber-** to croak. *Katak ~* , Frogs are croaking.

ketus loudly and cantankerously. *Dgn - ia menjahut*, He replied loudly and cantankerously.

kewalahan to be at o's wit's end, at a loss what to do (because of a deluge of work, in face of an over-whelmingly superior enemy, etc.).

kewatir see CHAWATIR.

kg [*kilogram*] kilogram.

ki appellation for old (male) persons.

kiah meng-(kan) to stretch (enlarge its size, e.g., of socks, gloves). **peng-**, *- sepatu* shoehorn. *-²* to enjoy o.s.

kiai 1 appellation for a venerated scholar, teacher of Islam. 2 a teacher, scholar, leader of Islam. 3 a religious preceptor. 4 a district chief in South Borneo. 5 appellation followed by name of s.t. which is considered a sacred relic (a creese, lance, old cannon), form of reference for tiger (in superstitious awe and veneration.)

kial (ber)- -², ter- -² 1 to move convulsively and vigorously, to struggle (of a man who is trying to free himself). 2 to be convulsed with laughter. *Ia tertawa ~* , He was shaking with laughter. 3 to gesticulate.

kiamat 1 doom. *hari -* Doomsday. 2 disaster, misfortune. 3 destruction

kian 1 such, so much. *dua - twice* as much as. 2 as ... as this. *Rumahnja - besar*, His house was as big as this. **ber- -²** excessive. **ke-an** number (gram.). **kese-** the nth. **se-** such and such a. *Bulan Maret tanggal ~* March the umpteenth. *~lah*, That's all. (I have spoken.) *~ dahulu* (often used to end an informal letter or speech), That's all. *jg ~ kalinja* the nth time. *-...-...* the ... (er) the ... (er). *- lama - kaja*, He became richer and richer. *- kemari* up and down, to and fro. *Ia berdjalan - kemari*, He paced up and down. *tidak ter-* innumerable.

kianat see CHIANAT.

kias 1 simile, comparison. 2 hint, allusion. 3 analogy. **meng-** 1 to goad, needle, s.o. 2 to allude, hint at. **-an** 1 simile. 2 metaphor. 3 hint, needling. 4 lesson, moral. 5 analogy. 6 symbol. *dlm arti ~* in a figurative sense.

kiat 1 stiff, cramped (of neck, limbs, etc.). 2 trick, secret. *Djikalau tahu -nja, tentu pekerdjaan itu mudah sekali*, If you know the trick, this work is certainly easy. **meng-kan** to sprain. *Ia ~ sikunja waktu melémpar bola itu*, He sprained his elbow when he threw the ball.

kibar ber- to wave, flutter. *Bendéra² ~* , The flags fluttered. **meng-kan** to put out (a flag). *Pada Hari Kemerdékaan kami ~ bendéra*, On Independence Day we put out the flag. **peng-an** *bendéra* display of flags.

kibas meng-kan 1 to wag. *Andjing itu ~ ékornja*, The dog wagged its tail. 2 to swish (the tail). 3 to flap (ears, wings). 4 to sway to and fro (elephant's trunk).

kibir arrogant, haughty. **ke–an** arrogance.

kiblat 1 direction of Mecca. *Orang bersembahjang harus menghadap –,* One has to face in the direction of Mecca when praying. 2 direction (of the wind). **ber–** *kpd* directed toward. *Politik pemerintah ~ kpd tertjapainja perdamaian,* The policy of the government is directed toward the achievement of peace.

kiblik republic.

kibul buttocks, bottom. **meng–** to lie, tell a falsehood. *Ia selalu ~ ,* He always lies. **meng–i** to deceive s.o.

kidal left-handed.

kidang see KIDJANG.

kidemat see CHIDMAT.

kidjang small deer.

kidjing k.o. mussel.

kidjip see KEDJAP.

kidul south.

kidung a ballad. **meng–** to sing a ballad. **meng–kan** to sing s.o. a ballad. *– gerédja* hymn.

Ki(e) [*Kompi(e)*] company (mil.).

kijahi see KIAI.

kik hand loom.

kikih **ter– –²** to giggle.

kikik see KIKIH.

kikir 1 stingy, closefisted. 2 a file. **ke–an** stinginess. **meng–** to file a metal object. **–an** filings. *– kuku* nail file.

kikis **meng–(kan)** 1 to scrape off. *Ia ~ djamur itu dari kaju itu,* He scraped off the mold from the wood. 2 to erode. *Laut ~ pantai,* The sea eroded the coast. 3 to erase s.t. **peng–** scraper. **peng–an** erosion. **–an** scraper. *Ber–lah engkau dari sini!* Get out! (Go away!)

kikuk 1 clumsy. *Gerak²nja –,* His movements were clumsy. 2 awkward. *Ia merasa – diantara orang² jg tak dikenalinja itu,* He felt awkward among people he did not know. **ke–an** 1 clumsiness. 2 awkwardness.

kilaf see CHILAF.

kilah 1 a trick, deception, ruse. 2 a pretext. 3 sea snail. **ber–(–)** 1 fraudulent, deceitful. 2 spurious (of an argument). **meng– –²kan** to twist words, distort the facts, the truth.

kilan a span (of the extended hand). **se–** one span. **meng–** to measure in spans.

kilang 1 a press. 2 mill. *– minjak* oil refinery. 3 fermented drink of palm sugar. **meng–** 1 to mill. *Mesin² itu ~ tebu,* Those engines milled the sugar cane. 2 to press. *Meréka ~ tebu,* They pressed the sugar cane.

peng–an 1 refinery. 2 refining. **per–an** refining. **–an** sugar mill. *– getah* rubber mill. *– tembakau* tobacco mill.

kilap 1 shine, gloss, luster, glitter. 2 see CHILAF. **ber–, mengk–** to shine. *Sepatunja ~ ,* His shoes shone. **se–** (*mata*) in a wink. *Makanannja habis dlm ~ mata,* He finished his food in a flash.

kilas a noose (of rattan). **meng–** 1 to snare. 2 to tighten a knot. **se–** (*mata, pandang*) in the twinkling of an eye, in a wink.

kilat 1 lightning. 2 flash. 3 the shine, gleam. *– kapal terbang disinar mata hari menjakitkan mata,* The gleam of the plane in the sunlight hurts the eyes. **ber–, mengk–** to shine. *Katja itu ~ ,* The mirror shone. *Matanja ~ ,* His eyes shone. **mengk–kan** 1 to make shine, glitter. *Tjahaja matahari ~ pedang terhunus,* The sunlight made the drawn swords glitter. *~ mobil* to polish the car. 2 to hint at s.t., allude to. *~ pidato tindakan jg akan diambil* to hint in a speech at the measures which would be taken. *~ kembali* to reflect (light). **peng–** a polishing substance. **ter– dlm hati** (s.t.) flashed through o's mind, dawned on o. *– bahu* bracelet.

kilau **ber–, meng–** to sparkle. *Pisau itu ~ ,* The knife sparkled. **ber–an, ber– –²** to sparkle and glitter. *Kapal terbang itu ~ kena sinar matahari,* The plane sparkled and glittered in the sunlight. **–an** shiny. *– kemilau* shining, sparkling.

kili² 1 a nose ring (of rattan or rope, of an ox, water buffalo). 2 reel (on a fish pole). **–²** *dajung* a thole pin.

kilik **me-ng–²** 1 to tickle. 2 to incite, goad.

kilir **meng–** to whet. *Ia ~ pisaunja,* He whetted his knife. **ter–** to be sprained. *Saja ~ lengan saja,* I sprained my arm. **–an** 1 whetstone, grindstone. 2 whetting, sharpening. *~ budi* s.t. to whet o's mind on. *~ tadji* the sharpened tip of a cockspur.

kilo 1 kilogram. 2 kilometer. **meng–** to measure the weight in kilograms. *Ia ~ beras itu,* He measured the weight of the rice in kilograms. **–an** 1 by the kilogram. *Beras itu didjual ~ ,* The rice is sold by the kilogram. 2 scales.

kimbang **me-ng–²** to circle, hover (airplane). *Pesawat udara ~ diudara sedjak pagi² diatas tempat itu,* The plane has been circling over that place since early morning. **ter–** hesitating, wavering.

kimia chemistry.
kimiawi chemical. *suatu tjampuran –* a chemical compound.
kimis chemical.
kimpa solid, native (of metal). **meng-** to beat, forge (metal).
kimpus hollow, fallen, sunken (of eyes, cheeks).
kina quinine.
kinantan 1 to be all-white (of cock, horse, etc.). 2 very special.
kindja ber– to jump with joy.
kini 1 now. 2 nowadays. **ke-an** the present. *dari – keatas* from now on. *hingga –* until now.
kinjang rock crystal.
kintal see KWINTAL.
kintil see INTIL. **meng-i** to follow, tail s.o. *Dia di–i pemabok,* He was followed by a drunkard.
kintjah **meng-** 1 to rinse, wash (laundry). 2 to dress game, fowl. 3 to clean slaughtered cattle.
kintjir(an) 1 water wheel. 2 spool, reel. **ber-** *alir* to be clever, shrewd. **meng-** *pakaian* to sew clothes on a sewing machine. – *angin* 1 windmill. 2 propeller. – *mendjahit* sewing machine. – *padi* rice mill (operated by water power).
kintjit involuntary bowel movement.
kintjup small, narrow (of an opening).
kiong see KÉONG.
kios newsstand.
kipang k.o. cake.
kipar twill.
kipas 1 a fan. 2 propeller (of airplane, etc.). **ber-** 1 to use, have a fan. 2 to fan o.s. **ber-(-)** to swish (tail of a horse, cow). **meng-(i)** to fan o.s. or s.t. **meng-kan** 1 to wag (the tail), flap (the ears). 2 to parry, ward off (with hand, wing, etc.). – *angin* 1 electric fan. 2 ventilator. – *hudjan* windshield wiper. – *radiator* radiator fan.
kiper goalkeeper.
kir meng– 1 to examine. *Dokter ∼ orang² jg hendak masuk tentara,* The doctor examines those who intend to enter the army. 2 to test. – *badan* physical examination. – *mobil* automobile inspection.
kira 1 to guess. *Saja – saudara benar,* I guess you are right. 2 to suppose. *Saja – semua orang kenal padanja,* I suppose everyone knows him. meng– 1 to think. *Ia ∼ bhw saja sdh pergi,* He thought that I had already gone. 2 to guess. *Sebetulnja ia tidak tahu; ia ∼ sadja,* He really does not know; he is just guessing. 3 to estimate, calculate.

Pd saat ini saja blm dpt ∼ berapa banjak uang akan kuperlukan, At this moment I cannot yet estimate how much money I will need. **me-ng-²** 1 to guess. *Sebetulnja ia tak tahu benar, ia hanja ∼ sadja,* He doesn't really know, he's just guessing. 2 to estimate. *Ia ∼ pandjangnja halaman itu,* He estimated the length of the yard. 3 to surmise. **peng-an** guess, estimate. *∼nja ttg salah suatu hal* his idea about s.t. **per-an** estimate, calculation. *Ia mengadjukan ∼ ongkos² pembikinan djembatan itu,* He submitted an estimate of the expenses for building the bridge. **se- -²** in the neighborhood of, about. **se-nja** in case, if. *∼ engkau membutuhkan uang, datanglah pd saja,* In case you need money, come to me. **-nja** 1 please. *Sudilah tuan ∼ mengembalikan buku saja?* Would you please return my book? 2 probably. *Saja mengetok pintu, tetapi ∼ meréka tidak ada dirumah,* I knocked on the door, but they were probably not home. *Bila ∼ dpt?* When do you think it can be done? 3 however. *Saja mengetok pintu ber-kali², ∼ tak ada jg mendjawab,* I knocked on the door several times, but nobody answered. 4 yet. *Pemburu sangka témbakannja luput, ∼ rusa terkena,* The hunter thought his shot had missed but the deer had been hit. **-²** 1 approximately, about. *Pandjangnja ∼ lima kaki,* It was approximately 5 feet long. 2 estimate. *Menurut ∼nja ongkosnja akan berdjumlah seribu rupiah,* According to his estimate the expenses will amount to 1,000 rupiahs. 3 be careful. *∼ dong,* Take it easy, will you? 4 probably. *Tilponlah, ∼ ia tlh kembali kekantornja,* Please phone him; he may be back in his office. *tak ter-* 1 incalculable, indescribable. *tak ∼ banjaknja* innumerable. *tak ∼ harganja* invaluable. 2 unexpected. *Kedatangannja jg se-konjong² itu sama sekali tak ∼ ,* His sudden arrival was completely unexpected.
kirai meng– 1 to shake out (wet laundry, tablecloth). 2 to winnow (rice, pepper, to separate it from chaff or impurities). 3 to spread out (drying ears of rice). 4 to shake out its feathers, flap its wings (of fowl, birds).
kirana 1 beam of light. 2 beautiful.
kirap meng– 1 to hit (with its wings, of an angry goose, hen). 2 to flap (its wings). 3 to flutter (of a flag). 4 to disappear, vanish. *Semua*

keangkuhannja tlh ∼ , All his conceit has disappeared. **meng–kan** 1 to flap, spread (its wings, a sheet). 2 to wave, flag (with a handkerchief). **ter–** 1 spread out. 2 vanished, disappeared.

kirbat a leather container (for water, wine). – *és* ice bag.

kiri 1 left. *Tangan – saja gatal*, My left hand itches. 2 leftist. 3 awkward. *Tingkahlakunja sangat –*, His behavior was very awkward. 4 unfortunate, unfavorable. **meng–** to keep to the left. *Kendaraan harus selalu* ∼ , Vehicles must always keep to the left. **meng–kan** 1 to discard. *Ia* ∼ *barang² jg tak dpt dipergunakannja itu*, He discarded the things he could not use. 2 to put, move things to the left. – *kanan* here and there. *Ditjari – kanan bukunja ta' ketemu djuga*, He looked everywhere but could not find his books. 3 to reject, turn s.t. down. **meng–** *menganan* to waver. *Tekadnja tidak* ∼ *menganan*, His determination did not waver. – *kapal* port side.

kirim ber– *salam* to send o's regards. *Djika engkau bertemu dgn ajahmu katakanlah padanja bhw saja* ∼ *salam padanja*, If you meet your father tell him that I send him my regards. ∼ *surat* to correspond. *Ketika kami berpisah kami berdjandji akan saling* ∼ *surat*, When we parted we promised to correspond with e.o. **ber–** **–²an** *surat* to correspond with e.o. **meng–(kan)** 1 to send. *Saja* ∼ *surat padamu*, I sent you a letter. 2 to ship. *Kami* ∼ *karét keseluruh dunia*, We ship rubber all over the world. 3 to forward. **meng–(-kan)** to give for safekeeping. ∼ *mobil pd teman* to leave a car with a friend. ∼ *anak pd tetangga* to leave the children at the neighbor's. **meng–i** to send to. **pe–** gift. **peng–** sender, consignor. **peng–an** 1 shipment. 2 s.t. given for safekeeping. **–an** shipment, consignment, package (received through an intermediary). ∼ *remburs* C.O.D. shipment. – *salam,* – *tabik* to send regards.

kiruh see KERUH.

kisa a small dragnet for coastal fishing.

kisah see KISSAH.

kisai meng– 1 to sift (with a sieve). 2 to unravel (a ball of wool, tangled rope). **–an** a sieve.

kisar ber– 1 to revolve, turn. *Baling² ∼ pd pusat roda*, The spokes revolve around the wheel hub. 2 to change. *Djaman sdh* ∼ , Times have changed.

meng–kan 1 to move the hands of a clock forward or backward. 2 to change s.o.'s mind. *Saja tjoba* ∼ *pendapatnja*, I tried to change his mind. 3 to pass on. *Ia* ∼ *minuman itu kegadis disamping aku*, He passed the drink on to the girl next to me. **peng–** miller. **peng–an** 1 = –AN. 2 a change, shift (in time, space). **per–an** 1 revolution. ∼ *bulan* the revolutions of the moon. 2 change. ∼ *djaman* change of the times. 3 turn. *Pd* ∼ *abad ini banjak jg terdjadi*, Many things happened at the turn of the century. **–an** 1 a revolution (of a wheel, etc.). 2 the milling, grinding (of wheat, rice). ∼ *air* whirlpool. ∼ *angin* whirlwind, cyclone. – *kopi* coffee mill, grinder.

kisi 1 grill, lattice, trellis. 2 crack, crevice, a fissure (in a door, wall, partition). **ber–** 1 provided with bars, trellis (of a window). 2 to center. *Semua perhatian* ∼ *kpd pidato présidén*, All attention centered on the president's speech. **–²** spoke. ∼ *sebuah roda* the spokes of a wheel.

kismet destiny.

kismis 1 currant. 2 raisin.

kisruh ke–an confusion. **meng–kan** to confuse.

kissah 1 story. 2 narrative. **meng–kan** to narrate. *Ia* ∼ *segala pengalamannja pd saja*, He related all his experiences to me. **al–** so the story goes. **peng–an** narrative. – *bersambung* continued, serialized story. – *perdjalanan* travelogue.

kisut 1 wrinkled. *Mukanja –*, His face was wrinkled. 2 creased (clothes, paper).

kita 1 we (including the person addressed). 2 our (including the person addressed). *orang tua –* our parents. 3 ours (including the person addressed). *"Bukankah itu – punja?" katanja pd bapaknja*, "Isn't that ours?" he asked his father. 4 I. – *orang* we (colloq.).

kitab book. – *Sutji* the Holy Book. **peng–an** *hukum* codification of the law. – *Indjil* Scriptures. – *logat* dictionary. – *nudjum* 1 book of astrology. 2 astrological tables. 3 book of prophecy. – *undang² hukum pidana* penal code. – *usul* book containing treatise on the true nature of God. – *Wasiat Baru (Lama)* New (Old) Testament. – *Zabur* Psalms of David.

kitar ber– to turn. *Roda² mulai* ∼ , The wheels started to turn. **memperkan, meng–kan** to pull s.t. back. *Ia* ∼ *tirai*, He drew the curtain back. **meng–i** to revolve, circle.

Bulan ∼ *bumi,* The moon revolves around the earth. ∼ *bumi* to orbit the earth. **per–an** rotation, revolution. **se–** 1 around. *Di*∼ *désa itu banjak sawah,* Around the village were many rice fields. 2 surroundings. *Kota dan* ∼*nja termasuk satu kabupatén,* The city and its surroundings belong to o. district. **–an** orbit.

kitik **meng–i** to tickle.

kitiran 1 windmill. 2 propeller.

kitjak see KITJAU.

kitjang-kétjoh a swindle.

kitjap **ber–** to chirp. *Burung itu* ∼ , The bird chirped.

kitjau **ber–** 1 to warble. *Burung*[2] ∼ , The birds warbled. 2 to chatter (idle talk).

kitju(h) deceit, deception. **meng–(kan)** to deceive.

kitjut **ber–** to squeak. *Pintu karatan itu* ∼ , The rusty door squeaked.

kiut see KITJUT.

KKN [*Kepala Kepolisian Negara*] head of state police.

KKO [*Korps Komando Angkatan Laut*] shore patrol, navy police.

kl. [*kelas*] class.

k.l. [*kurang lebih*] more or less, approximately.

klakson horn (of an auto, motor bicycle). **meng(k)–** to blow the horn.

klasi see KELASI.

klasifikasi classification.

klasik classic.

klausula clause, article.

klik sound of camera shutter when taking pictures.

klilip(an) see KELILIP. *Ida –* , Ida had s.t. in her eye.

klinik see KELINIK.

klisé 1 negative (of photograph, printing, movie). 2 print, picture. **mengk–kan** to make a negative.

klobot cornhusk (of young ears, dried and used as cigarette paper).

km 1 [*kilométer*] kilometer. 2 [*kamar*] room.

K.M.B. [*Konperénsi Médja Bundar*] Round Table Conference.

kmd [*komandan*] commandant.

knalpot muffler (auto).

knop see KENOP.

KOALMIL [*Komando Angkatan Laut Militér*] Co-ordinated Army and Navy Command.

kobak 1 a three-cornered tear. *Ada – pd kemédja saja,* There is a tear in my shirt. **meng–** to peel. *Ia* ∼ *kentang,* He peeled potatoes.

kobar **ber–** to flare up, rage (of fire, flames). *Pemberontakan* ∼ *di-mana*[2], Rebellions flared up everywhere. *Pertempuran* ∼ , The battle was raging. **ber– –**[2]**(an)** 1 raging. *Api* ∼ , The fire was raging. 2 spirited. *Semangatnja* ∼ , His ardor (fervor, zeal, enthusiasm) was exuberant. **meng–kan** 1 to fan. *Angin* ∼ *kebakaran dihutan sehingga lebih tjepat mendjalarnja,* The wind fanned the forest fire so that it spread faster. 2 to arouse passions, stir up animosity, foment strife. **me-ng–**[2]**kan** 1 to stir up, arouse. 2 to stimulate.

kober to have the opportunity, chance. *Saja belon – bikin betul sepatu tuan,* I haven't had a chance to repair your shoes yet.

kobis see KUBIS.

koboi cowboy.

kobok 1 a group of people. 2 a finger bowl. **ber– –**[2] to gather in groups. **–an** finger bowl.

kodak **meng–** to take a picture. *Para musafir sibuk* ∼ *apa*[2] *jg meréka lihat,* The tourists were busy shooting everything they saw.

KODAM [*Komando Daérah Militér*] Area Military Command. *– VI Djaja* 6th Military Command Jakarta.

KODAMAR [*Komando Daérah Maritim*] Naval District.

kodi a score. *Ia membeli dua – badju,* He bought 40 shirts. **–an** 1 by the score. *Badju itu didjual* ∼ , Those shirts are sold by the score. 2 ready-made clothes.

kodifikasi codification.

kodja 1 a long-necked pitcher. 2 Ceylonese, Indian. **pe–an** that quarter of a city where Ceylonese and Indians have their shops and/or residence.

kodjoh flooded (primarily of paddy fields).

kodok 1 frog. 2 frogleg. **–**[2] a piston. *– goréng* fried froglegs. *– hidjau* frog. *– puru* toad.

kodrat 1 destiny. 2 God's will. *Bhw anakmu meninggal adalah – Tuhan,* It was God's will that your child should die. 3 nature, character of a person. **meng–kan** to destine. *Djika Tuhan tlh* ∼ *saja memikul segala penderitaanku ini rélalah saja,* If God has destined me to undergo all this suffering, I humbly accept it. *– alam* natural law.

kodrati natural.

koé see KOWÉ.

kogellaher ball bearing.

kognossemén see KONOSEMÉN.

KOGOR [*Komando Gerakan Olahraga*] Central Board for Sports.

kohir assessment list for taxation purposes.

kohong stinking (like rotten eggs).

kojak torn. *Badju dia –,* His shirt was torn. **meng–kan** to tear. *Ia ~ badju saja,* He tore my shirt. **me-ng–²kan** to tear to pieces. *Andjing itu ~ kaos kaki saja,* The dog tore my socks to pieces. **ter–** torn. *kantong jg ~* torn bag. *–²* in rags.

kojan measurement of weight (27-40 picul. 1 picul = 136 lbs).

kojo 1 nonsense. 2 see TÉMPÉL.

kojok 1 a stray dog. 2 Chinese medicinal salve.

kok *– begitu!* 1 Oh, no. 2 Why, you! *Bukan, –* , Not really. *Ja, –* 1 Oh, yes. 3 It, he, she is! *Mémang begitu –,* It's like that, really. (It happened that way really.) *Lho, – mahal sekali!* Say, that's pretty steep! *Tidak apa² –, pak,* It doesn't really matter, pop.

kokang meng– to cock a rifle for firing.

koki cook.

kokoh see KUKUH.

kokok crowing. **ber–** 1 to crow. 2 to brag about o's bravery. *– beluk* an owl.

kokol huddled, doubled up (sitting or lying down). **meng–** to double up, hunch up. **ter–(–)** shivering (with fever).

kokot 1 door clasp. 2 lid of a box. **meng–** to claw, to scratch. **ter–** badly warped (of fingers or toes by scar tissue). *– betina* eye of clasp. *– djantan* hook, clasp.

kol 1 cabbage. 2 *[kolonél]* colonel. *– kembang* cauliflower. *– putih* white cabbage.

Kol. *[Kolonél]* 1 colonel. 2 captain (navy).

kolaborasi collaboration.

kolaborator collaborator.

kolak fruit stewed with brown palm sugar. **meng–** 1 to stew fruit. 2 to buy s.t. wholesale.

kolam 1 pond. 2 tank. *– air* water reservoir. *– berenang* swimming pool. *– ikan* fishpond. *– katja* aquarium.

kolang-kaling 1 up-and-down movement. 2 sugar palm fruit used for dessert.

koléga colleague.

koléh² 1 cookies made from cassava flour. 2 tapioca.

kolék a small dinghy. **ber– –²** 1 bobbing up and down. 2 to sway, reel (of a drunken person).

koléksi collection.

koléktip collective.

koléra cholera.

kolesom Korean ginseng.

kolokan spoiled (child).

kolom printed column.

kolonél 1 colonel. 2 captain (navy).

kolong 1 pit. *Meréka menggali sebuah –,* They dug a pit. 2 coal mine pit. 3 space under a house built on stilts. *– langit* the sublunary world. *– tempat tidur* space under a bed.

koloni colony.

kolonialisme colonialism.

kolonis colonist.

kolonisasi colonialization.

kolor waistband.

kolot 1 old-fashioned. *pengertian² jg –* old-fashioned ideas. 2 conservative. *pendirian jg –* a conservative point of view. **ke–an** conservatism.

kolportir peddler, hawker.

koma comma. *– bernoktah, – titik* semicolon.

komandan 1 commander. 2 commandant.

komanditér limited partner (in a business, a person who provides part of the capital without partaking in the management).

komando command. **meng–(kan)** to command. *Ia ~ serdadu²nja utk menjerang,* He commanded his soldiers to attack.

Komando Rakjat The People's Command: 1 *Kibarkan Sang Mérah Putih di Irian Barat,* Fly the Indonesian flag in Western New Guinea. 2 *Gagalkan pembentukan "Negara Papua" oléh Belanda,* Defeat the formation of a Papuan state by the Dutch. 3 *APRI siap sedia utk se-waktu² menerima perintah bébaskan Irian Barat,* Let the Indonesian Armed Forces be ready to receive at any time the order to liberate Western New Guinea.

komat-kamit 1 mumbling, muttering. 2 with moving lips (in offering a silent prayer).

kombang see KUMBANG.

kombinasi combination.

koméng stunted in growth, dwarfish, diminutive.

komentar commentary. **meng(k)–i** to comment on s.t. *Ia ~ rantjangan undang² jg baru itu,* He commented on the new draft of the bill.

komersil commercial.

komidi 1 comedy. 2 theater. **ber–** to fool. *Djangan pertjaja orang itu, ia sering ~ sadja,* Don't trust that man; he usually plays the hypocrite. **meng–kan** to fool s.o. *– bangsawan* a stage show. *– kuda* circus. *– putar* a merry-go-round. *– setambul* touring stage show.

komik 1 comic, funny. 2 comedian. **ke–an** humor.

kominikasi communication. *– harfiah* verbal communication.

kominiké communiqué.
kominis Communist.
komis an administrative position immediately senior to that of a clerk.
komisariat police headquarters.
komisaris commissioner. – *agung* high commissioner. – *polisi* police commissioner.
komisi committee, commission. **meng-** to inspect.
komkoma turmeric.
komodor commodore. – *udara* air commodore (equivalent to brigadier general).
kompak 1 compact. 2 to work together harmoniously.
kompas compass.
kompeni 1 popular term for Dutch East India Company. 2 Dutch East Indies army.
kompénsasi compensation.
kompénsir **mengk-** to compensate.
kompi(e) company (mil.).
kompléks complex. ∼ *perasaan kurang hargadiri* inferiority complex.
komplit complete.
kompoi convoy.
komplot 1 accomplice. 2 plot. **ber-** to plot. *Meréka* ∼ *hendak menimbulkan pemberontakan,* They plotted a rebellion. **-an** 1 gang. ∼ *pendjahat* gang of bandits. 2 plot, scheme. 3 accomplice in crime, conspiracy.
kompol bed-wetting.
Kompol [*Komisaris Polisi*] police commissioner.
komponén component.
kompong 1 mutilated, mangled. 2 amputated, only a stump left (of limbs).
komponis composer.
kompor stove (burns gas, kerosene or gasoline). – *listrik* hot plate.
komposisi composition.
kompromi compromise. **ber-** to compromise.
komunis Communist.
komunisme communism.
konang see KUNANG. **-an** discovered, found out. *Ia* ∼ *waktu melompat pagar,* He was discovered when he jumped over the fence.
kondangan invitation.
kondé see KUNDAI.
kondéktur conductor (of train, streetcar, or bus).
kondisi condition.
Kondjén [*Konsulat Djéndral*] consulate general.
kondjungtur boom, upswing, favorable market.
kondor scrotal hernia.
konféksi ready-made clothing.
konflik conflict.

konfrontasi confrontation, encounter. **mengk-** to confront.
kongésti congestion.
konggrés see KONGRÉS.
kongkalikong a conspiracy, plot. **ber-** 1 to be in cahoots. *Meréka* ∼ *hendak menipu saja,* They were in cahoots to deceive me. 2 to conspire, scheme against.
kongko to chatter. **meng-i** to persuade, talk s.o. into s.t.
kongkol plotter. **ber-** to plot together, conspire. **se-** 1 coconspirator. 2 to be in cahoots.
kongkong 1 shackles. 2 stocks (instrument of punishment). **meng-** 1 to shackle. *Ia* ∼ *pentjuri itu,* He shackled the thief. 2 to imprison. 3 to bark (of a dog). **-an** 1 shackles. 2 imprisonment. 3 barking (of a dog).
kongkrét concrete. **ke-an** concreteness.
kongkrit see KONGKRÉT.
kongkurén competitor, rival.
kongkurénsi competition.
kongrés congress, convention.
kongsi commercial association. **ber-** to enter into partnership (commercial). *Ia* ∼ *dgn saudagar itu,* He entered into partnership with the merchant.
kongsol see KONSOL.
konjol 1 foolish, half-witted. – *kamu menjimpan péstol tanpa izin,* You are crazy to keep a gun without a license. 2 unsuccessful. 3 in vain, for nothing. 4 improper, bad. *Anak itu* –, That child's bad. – *ini* tough luck, too bad.
konjong se- -² 1 sudden. *Serangan jg* ∼ *itu tak dpt diélakkannja,* He could not avoid the sudden attack. 2 suddenly. ∼ *ia memukul saja,* Suddenly he hit me.
konjungtur see KONDJUNGTUR.
konkrét see KONGKRÉT.
konon 1 I wonder. *Siapa – memanggil saja tadi?* I wonder who called me just now? 2 they say. – *ia dipilih mendjadi présidén,* They say he was elected president. 3 perhaps. *Bukan itu – jg dimaksudnja,* Perhaps that wasn't what he meant. **memper-** to mislead with rumors. – *lagi* let alone. *Saja tak berani memotong ajam,* – *lagi manusia,* I don't dare kill a chicken, let alone a human being.
konosemén bill of lading.
konpéksi see KONFÉKSI.
konpénsi see KONVÉNSI.
konperénsi conference. **ber-** to hold a conference.

konpoi convoy.
konsekwén consistent.
konsékwénsi consequence(s).
konséntrasi concentration.
konsép draft, rough copy.
konsépsi concept, notion, idea.
konséptuil conceptual.
konsér concert.
konsérpatip conservative. ke–an conservatism.
konsési concession.
konsol consul. – djénderal consul general. – muda vice-consul.
konsolér consular.
konsolidir mengk– to consolidate.
konstélasi constellation.
Konstituante Constituent Assembly.
konstitusi constitution.
konstruksi construction.
konsul consul.
konsulat consulate.
konsultasi consultation.
konsumén consumer.
konsumir mengk– to consume.
konsumptip consumptive.
konsumsi consumption. meng(k)– to consume.
kontak contact. meng–kan 1 to contact. 2 to switch, turn on (a light, motor). 3 to plug s.t. in.
kontal-kantil to dangle, swing to and fro.
kontan 1 cash. Ia membajar dgn –, He paid in cash. 2 prompt. Didjawabnja pertanjaan itu dgn –, He answered the question promptly. –²an, – keras then and there, immediately.
kontang-kanting to dangle. Djam itu – pd sebuah rantai, The watch dangled on a chain.
kontelir district officer of the N.E.I. Civil Service (controleur).
kontét midget.
kontjo 1 friend, buddy. 2 companion. ber– 1 to be friends with. Saja sdh lama ~ dgn dia, I have been friends with him for a long time. 2 to have companions. Ia tiada pernah ~ kemana sadja ia pergi, He never has any companion anywhere he goes.
kontol 1 testicle. 2 round. 3 heron.
kontra– contra-.
kontradiksi contradiction.
kontrak contract.
kontraksi contraction.
kontrol supervision. meng– to supervise, check on. peng–an supervision.
konvénsi convention.
koordinasi co-ordination. mengk–kan to co-ordinate.
koordinir mengk– to co-ordinate.
Kop. [Koperasi] co-operatives.
kopah clot of blood. ber- –² in clots.

Darah ~ keluar waktu pasién batuk, When the patient coughed, blood was discharged in clots.
kopak meng– to peel. Ia ~ kentang, He peeled the potatoes.
kopeling clutch.
koper see KOPOR.
koperasi 1 a co-operative (economic enterprise). 2 co-operation. ber– to work in co-operation. peng–an, per–an 1 system of co-operation. 2 system of co-operatives.
kopét narrow (of an opening, street, passage).
kopi 1 coffee. 2 copy. 3 draft. meng– to have a cup of coffee. Meréka pergi kewarung utk ~ , They went to the coffee shop to have a cup of coffee. – bubuk ground coffee. – hitam black coffee. – pahit 1 black coffee. 2 a scolding, a bawling out. – susu coffee with cream. – tubruk coffee prepared by pouring boiling water over ground coffee without using a sieve.
kopiah k.o. cap, headdress worn by Moslems. – setambul fez.
kopjok meng– 1 to shake. 2 to gamble. –an dancing.
kopjor 1 k.o. coconut from which a cold drink is made. 2 see És. 3 see KELAPA.
kopokan to suffer from a middle ear inflammation.
kopor 1 trunk. 2 suitcase, bag.
kopra copra.
Kopra [Kota Pradja] municipality.
kopral 1 corporal. 2 petty officer 3rd class.
koran newspaper. meng–kan to spread information (usually unfavorable) about s.o. – pagi a morning paper. – soré an evening paper. – warawiri impartial newspaper.
Kor'an the Koran.
korat-karit dislocated.
korban 1 sacrifice. Déwa² menuntut –, The gods demanded a sacrifice. 2 victim. ber– to make a sacrifice. Meréka ~ pd déwa², They made a sacrifice to the gods. meng–kan to sacrifice s.t. Ia ~ segala harta kekajaannja bagi perdjuangan nasional, He sacrificed all his wealth for the national struggle. peng–an sacrifice. – djiwa, – manusia casualties (in war, accident). – kebakaran victims of a fire. – misa communion. – perang war victim.
kordén curtain.
koréh see KORÉK.
korék meng– to scrape. Andjing itu ~ tanah dgn kakinja, The dog scraped the earth with its paws. peng–

telinga earpick, ear spoon (instrument for cleaning ear of wax). – *api* matches.

koréksi correction. **mengk–** to correct. **pengk–an** correction.

koréktip corrective.

korélasi correlation.

koréng 1 spotted (cow, dog). 2 sore (an ulceration).

korés see GORÉS.

korét meng– to finish the leftovers. **–an** leftover(s).

koridor corridor.

korma see KURMA.

kornél see KOLONÉL.

kornét 1 a combination of assistant, apprentice, and companion to a taxi or bus driver in Indonesia. 2 canned corned beef.

korok an excavation, excavated tunnel. **meng–** 1 to dig. *Ia ~ sebuah lobang,* He dug a hole. 2 to snore.

korps corps.

korsi chair. – *ajunan* 1 rocking chair. 2 porch swing. – *gojang* rocking chair. – *malas* lounge chair. – *pandjang* davenport. – *ungkang-ungkit* rocking chair.

KORUD [*Komando Regional Udara*] Regional Air Command.

korup corrupt. **di–** to be corrupted.

korupsi corruption.

koruptor corruptor.

kosak-kasik fidgeting.

kosék meng– *beras* to rinse uncooked rice thoroughly before cooking. – (*kaki*) foot mat.

kosél ter– 1 to hem and haw. 2 to work in fits and starts.

kosén 1 courageous, daring. 2 window frame. **ke–an** daring, bravery.

kosong 1 empty. *Kamar itu –,* The room was empty. 2 futile. 3 bad. *tjék* – bad check. **ke–an** 1 emptiness. 2 vacancy. *Apakah ada ~ dikantor tuan?* Are there any vacancies at your office? 3 gap. **meng–kan** 1 to empty. *Ia ~ kopernja,* He emptied his suitcase. 2 to vacate. *Meréka harus ~ rumah meréka dlm satu djam,* They had to vacate their house within one hour. **peng–an** 1 evacuation, clearing (of an area). 2 depletion. – *losong* completely empty. – *melompong* idle, empty (words, promises).

kota 1 city. 2 town. **ber–** fortified. **ke–an** urbanized. **meng–i** to wall in s.t. **meng–kan** to erect a fortified town, fortress. – *besar* city with the administrative status of a regency or province (as Jakarta). – *pesiar* resort town.

Kota 1 oldest section of Jakarta.

2 telephone exchange. 3 railway exchange.

Kotabaru 1 Hollandia, West New Guinea. 2 city in north Malaya.

kotai 1 to be skin and bone, desiccated. 2 to hang by a thread.

kotak 1 compartment, cubicle. 2 box. 3 drawer. 4 sector, section (usually square or oblong, e.g., of a garden divided into flower beds, of paddy fields). **ber–** –² divided into compartments. *Peti itu ~ ,* The box was divided into compartments. **meng–ngatikkan** to move, sway, set in motion. *Angin ~ lampu² jg menerangkan djalan,* The wind swayed the lamps which lighted the street. – *katik* sign, indication of s.o.'s presence. *Barangkali ia pergi karena tidak terdengar lagi – katik,* Perhaps he's left because we do not hear him moving around any more. – *korék api* matchbox. – *pos* 1 post-office box. 2 mailbox.

kotapradja municipality.

kotbah see CHOTBAH.

koték 1 to cackle. 2 tail (plumed with a tuftlike end, e.g., of a comet). **ber–** to cackle.

koténg alone, without friends. *Ia berdjalan – sadja sepandjang hari,* He walked alone the whole day. **ter–** –² all alone. *Anak itu diketemukan ~ mengembara dihutan,* That child was found wandering all alone in the woods.

kot(e)rék corkscrew.

kotés bits of thread, lint, shred. **meng–** to remove bits of thread, lint.

kotjah-katjih 1 fussing about. 2 fussy.

kotjak 1 hilarious. *Lelutjonnja sangat –,* His jokes were hilarious. 2 smart, classy, dashing. 3 proud, haughty, conceited. **ber–** 1 to shake. *Botol itu ~ ,* The bottle shook. 2 to dim, become dull (of the expression in s.o.'s eyes). 3 to be perturbed, confused. 4 to splash, lap (of waves). **ber–** –²an with impunity, safely. **meng–kan** to shake s.t. **ter–** 1 shaken. 2 confused. *~ hati* to waver, be disheartened, lose confidence (in s.o.). **–an** joke.

kotjar-katjir see KUTJAR-KATJIR.

kotjék pocket (in clothes).

Kotji(n) Cochin (China).

kotjoh haste. **ter–** –² hurriedly, hastily.

kotjok meng– 1 to shake, mix s.t. – *dahulu baik² sebelum dipakai,* Shake well before using. 2 to shuffle. *Ia ~ kartu itu,* He shuffled the cards. 3 to incite. *Ia ~ kawan²nja agar meréka membentji murid baru,* He incited all his friends to dislike the new pupil. 4 to masturbate.

kotjong 1 a hood (covering the whole head, e.g., of a person being executed by hanging). 2 a wrap-around cover with the loose ends bundled up and tied together (e.g., white cloth wrapped around a corpse in Islamic rites). **meng-** 1 to enclose in a wrap-around cover. 2 to bind the opening of a bag or loose ends of a bundle of cloth together.

kotok short (as of pant legs).

kotong 1 cut off, only a stump remaining. 2 amputated. *Lengan kirinja* –, He has only a stump of his left arm remaining. 3 see KOTOK.

kotor 1 dirty. *Tangannja* –, His hands were dirty. 2 gross (of income, profits). *penghasilan* – gross income. **ke-an** 1 soiled. 2 filth. **meng-i, meng-kan** 1 to soil. *Ia ∼ buku saja*, He soiled my book. *Ia ∼ nama baik saja*, He soiled my good name. 2 to contaminate. **peng-** dirty fellow. *Mandilah engkau, ∼ !* Take a bath, you dirty fellow! **-an** dirt, litter, rubbish, trash. *∼ dapur* garbage.

kotum quota.

kover **meng-** to cover, include.

KOWAD [*Korps Wanita Angkatan Darat*] Women's Army Corps.

kowak **ber- -²** 1 to jabber, chatter. 2 to shout (of drunkards, people wild with joy, excitement).

kowé you (rude in Indonesian but common in the Jakarta dialect). *– djangan berani melanggar perintah saja!* Don't you dare disobey my orders!

kpd [*kepada*] to.

KPKOM [*Kepala Polisi Komisariat*] chief of police headquarters.

kpts [*keputusan*] decision, decree.

kr- see KER-.

krah collar (of a shirt, coat).

kran faucet, tap.

krandjingan to have a crush on, like s.o. terribly.

krasan see KERASAN.

kré see KERAI.

kréasi creation.

kréatif creative.

kredép **ber-an** to glitter, shine. *Matanja ∼ ,* His eyes shone.

krédit credit. **meng-kan** to sell on credit. **per-an** crediting.

kremi see KEREMI.

Krésten see KERISTEN.

kriminil criminal.

kriminologi criminology.

krisis crisis.

Kristen see KERISTEN.

kritik see KERITIK.

kritikus – *sastera* literary critic.

kritis critical.

kromo see KEROMO. **ke-an** proletarianism.

krompjang 1 sound of s.t. crashing to the floor. 2 sound of tin cans.

kronologis chronological.

krontjong see KERONTJONG.

krukas crankshaft.

krupuk see KERUPUK.

K.S. [*Kepala Staf*] Chief of Staff.

KSAD see KASAD.

KSAL [*Kepala Staf Angkatan Laut*] Navy Chief of Staff.

ksatria knight, warrior. **ke-an** chivalry. **-an** barracks (military). see KESATERIA.

KSAU [*Kepala Staf Angkatan Udara*] Air Force Chief of Staff.

KTT [*Konperénsi Tingkat (Ter)tinggi*] 1 summit conference. 2 high-level conference.

ku abbrev. of AKU.

kuah sauce, gravy. **ber-** to have sauce, gravy. **meng-i** to add sauce to s.t.

kuak **ber-** 1 to open (involving a movement in 2 opposite directions leaving an opening in the middle, e.g., the opening of a curtain, of a crowd letting an oncoming car pass, etc.). 2 to widen, enlarge (of a hole, tear, etc.), scatter. *Waktu angin mulai meniup awan ∼ ,* When the wind blew, the thick cloud dispersed. **meng-** 1 to moo. *Kerbau itu ∼ ,* The water buffalo mooed. 2 to croak (of frogs). **meng-kan** 1 to tear open. *Peluru itu ∼ pahanja,* The bullet tore his thigh open. 2 to break open (by force) a window, door, safe; to break through, force a way through (a barricade, enemy defenses, etc.). 3 to part curtains, underbrush to get through, push o's way through a crowd (by shoving people to the right and left).

kuala estuary, river mouth.

kualat 1 accursed, damned. *Ia – karena menadjiskan tempat jg keramat itu,* There is a curse upon him because he desecrated that holy place.

kuali k.o. frying pan.

kuap yawn. **meng-** to yawn.

kuar see KUAK. **me-ng-²kan** to feel around (with a stick, ladle, etc.). *Ia ∼ tongkat kedalam kolam mentjari sepatu jg djatuh diair,* He felt around with a stick to find the shoe which had dropped in the water.

kuartal quarter (of a year).

kuas 1 paintbrush. 2 shaving brush. 3 k.o. lemonade. **meng-** to brush. *– -kais* to scratch the earth (of a chicken, etc.).

kuasa 1 power. 2 authority. *Ia ber-*

tindak atas – saja, He acted on my authority. 3 might. – *Madjapahit* the might of Mojopahit. 4 attorney, proxy. 5 to be powerful, able. **ber-** 1 to hold the power. *Ia ~ dlm negara itu,* He holds the power in that country. 2 to have the authority. *Polisi ~ menangkap orang,* The police have the authority to arrest persons. 3 to be in charge. *Siapa jg ~ ?* Who's in charge? **ke-an** 1 power. 2 authority, sway. **meng-i** 1 to dominate. *Partai itu ~ seluruh negara,* That party dominates the whole country. 2 to take charge, be in command. **meng-kan** to give the authority, authorize. *Undang² dasar ~ présidén utk mendirikan suatu kabinét,* The constitution gives the president the authority to appoint a cabinet. **peng-** 1 manager. 2 o. in authority. 3 administrator. *~ perang* war administrator. **peng-an** 1 authority. 2 control, command. *– menteri* proxy for the minister. *– penuh* full power(s), power of attorney. *duta besar ber- penuh* ambassador plenipotentiary. *–* usaha 1 chargé d'affaires. 2 proxy. 3 trustee.

kuat 1 strong. *Didorongnja keréta itu dgn –,* He gave the cart a strong push. 2 forceful. 3 to be able to. *Ia – makan banjak,* He can eat a lot. *Ia – berdjalan sepandjang hari,* He can walk the whole day long. 4 loud (of voice, noise, etc.). 5 to afford. *Ia tak dpt – membajar,* He can't afford to pay. **ber-** to persist. *Ia ~ dlm pendiriannja,* He persisted in his opinion. **ke-an** 1 strength. *~ batin* spiritual force. *~ dan modal* funds and forces. *~ mendidik* educational value. *~ pelenting* resilience, elasticity. *~ tjahaja* candle power. 2 energy. 3 power (of a magnifying glass). 4 intensity (of light rays, etc.). **memper-** 1 to support. *Saja ~ mosi itu,* I support the motion. 2 to strengthen. 3 to confirm. 4 to sanction. **meng-i** 1 to violate (a woman, o's rights). *Ia ~ milik saudagar itu,* He seized the merchant's property by force. 2 to support. *Saja ~ usul itu,* I supported the proposal. 3 to coerce, use coercion against. **meng-kan** 1 to strengthen. *Meréka ~ pertahanan negara,* They strengthened the country's defense. 2 to confirm, corroborate, affirm (a statement, assertion, etc.). *~ diri* to summon up. **peng-** 1 tonic. 2 impellant. *~ suara* loudspeaker. **peng-an** strengthening. *se-suara* at the top of o's voice. *Ia berteriak ~ suaranja,* He shouted at

the top of his voice. *~ tenaga* to the utmost of o's strength. *Ia bekerdja ~ tenaganja,* He worked to the utmost of his strength.

kuatir see CHAWATIR.

Kuba Cuba.

kubak **meng-** to peel. *Ia ~ kentang,* He peeled potatoes.

kubang **ber-** to wallow in a mudhole. **-an** 1 mudhole. 2 trash dump.

kubik **meng-** to peel with the nails. *Ia ~ limau itu,* He peeled the lemon with his nails.

kubis cabbage.

kubit **meng-** to tap on arm, shoulder, to attract o's attention. **se-** a tiny bit.

kubra 1 unsuccessful, a failure. 2 undecided. **meng-kan** 1 to cause s.t. to fail. 2 to dissolve, liquidate s.t. 3 to leave s.t. undecided.

kubu 1 fortification. 2 name of a preliterate tribe in Sumatra. **ber-** to fortify o.s. *Setelah meréka mendarat meréka ~ dipantai,* After they landed they fortified themselves on the beach. **meng-i** to fortify. *Kami ~ kedudukan kami,* We fortified our position. **per-an** fortification.

kubur grave. **meng-(kan)** to bury. *Meréka ~ korban pengeboman,* They buried the victims of the bombardment. **pe-an, per-an** cemetery, graveyard. **peng-an** burial. **-an** 1 grave. 2 graveyard.

kubus cube.

kuda horse. **ber-** on horseback. *Meréka datang ~ ,* They arrived on horseback. **memper-(kan)** 1 to exploit. *Ia tak segan ~ kawannja jg terbaikpun utk mentjapai kedudukan jg tinggi itu,* He did not hesitate to exploit his best friend in order to obtain that high position. 2 to ride on a horse. **pe(r)-an** 1 stud farm. 2 stable. **-²an** 1 to ride pickaback. 2 to play horse. 3 hobbyhorse. *–²* 1 trestle. 2 vaulting horse. *– balapan* race horse. *– beban* pack horse. *– belang* zebra. *– betina* mare. *– djantan* stallion. *– képang* a horse made of bamboo plaitwork with which men perform a dance, usually in a trance. *– patju* race horse. *– sandel* horse from the island of Sumba. *– semberani* winged horse. *– (sungai) Nil* hippopotamus. *– tidji* a large, fast horse. *– tunggangan* riding horse.

kudangan favorite.

kudap **meng-** 1 to taste. *Ia ~ makanan jg lagi dimasak ibunja itu,* He tasted the food his mother was preparing. 2 to eat sweets. *Djangan terlalu banjak ~ , nanti* *hilang nafsu makanmu,* Don't eat too many sweets; you will lose your appetite. $-^2$ sweets.

kudéta *coup d'état.* **meng-** to carry out a *coup d'état.*

kudi see KODI.

kudian see KEMUDIAN.

kudis scabies. **-an** to have scabies.

kudjur 1 javelin to spear fish. 2 stiff, rigid. **se-** over the whole body. *Ia terbakar* ∼ *badannja,* He was burned over his whole body.

kudjut ber- 1 to hang o.s. 2 to commit suicide. **ber-** $-^2$ to be involved. *Baik dia maupun bawahannja* ∼ *dlm perkara penggelapan uang,* Both he and his subordinate are involved in the embezzlement. **meng-** to bind (with a rope, etc.). ∼ *léhér orang* to hang s.o. by the neck. ∼ *léhér sendiri* to hang o.s.

kudrat see KODRAT.

kudrati omnipotent. *Tuhan jg* – God the Almighty.

kudu must. *Engkau* – *bekerdja keras,* You must work hard.

kuduk nape of the neck.

kudung 1 see KERUDUNG. 2 crippled. **meng-** 1 to cut off, chop off. *Ia* ∼ *kepala musuhnja,* He chopped off his enemy's head. 2 to maim, mutilate. **peng-an** mutilation. **se-** a piece, a slice, a cut (of s.t.).

kudus holy. *Hari Natal adalah hari* –, Christmas is a holy day. **meng-kan** to sanctify. *Paus* ∼ *Jeanne d'Arc,* The Pope sanctified Joan of Arc.

kué 1 cookie. 2 cake. – *lapis* layer cake. – *andapita* pastry tidbits. – *donat* doughnut. – *lopis* cookie made of sticky rice. – *mangkuk* cupcake. – *randjang* a cake prepared especially for the Chinese New Year.

kuéh see KUÉ.

kuék noise, ado, commotion.

kufur an infidel, heathen, atheist. **meng-kan** to excommunicate.

kui a crucible (to melt gold, silver).

kuih see KUÉ.

kuil (Balinese) temple.

kuis meng-(kan) 1 to kick (s.t.) aside. 2 to scratch (the earth, e.g., of a chicken). 3 to stir up (a fire).

kuit meng- 1 to beckon (with fingers, hand, for s.o. to come nearer). *Ia* ∼ *teman²nja utk berkumpul,* He beckoned to his friends to assemble. 2 to tap, to prod (with a finger or a pencil, to attract o's attention). **meng-kan** ∼ *rakit* to row a raft (by moving a paddle repeatedly left and right sideways from the stern). – *gamit* movement of finger(s). – *kapsi* 1 to rummage, putter about.

2 to scratch (of a chicken on a dunghill).

kuja k.o. turtle.

kuju 1 anxious, frightened. 2 sad.

kujup see BASAH. $-^2$ soaking wet, soaked to the skin.

kuk 1 collar, harness. 2 yoke.

kuku 1 nail. 2 claw. 3 hoof. *tidak* **ber-** powerless. – *kaki* toenail. – *tangan* fingernail. – *tjengkam* ingrown nail.

kukuh 1 firm. *Setelah di-timbang²nja, ia mengambil pendirian jg* –, After some deliberations he took a firm stand. 2 sturdy, strong. *Rumahnja* –, His house was sturdy. **ber-** *(pd)* to stick to. *Ia* ∼ *pd pendiriannja,* He stuck to his opinion. **ke-an** 1 firmness. 2 strength. **memper-** to strengthen. *Kita harus* ∼ *pembélaan negara kita,* We must strengthen our country's defense. **meng-i** 1 to adhere, stick (to an opinion). 2 to strengthen. **meng-kan** to strengthen. **peng-an** 1 sanction, affirmation, confirmation. 2 strengthening.

kukuk ber- to cackle (of a hen).

kuku(ke)rujuk cock-a-doodle-doo.

kukul 1 k.o. pimple. 2 see KOKOL.

kukur 1 cooing (of a pigeon). 2 grater. **meng-** 1 to grate. *Ibu* ∼ *kelapa,* Mother grated a coconut. 2 to scratch. *Ia* ∼ *tangannja jg gatal itu,* He scratched his itching hand. **peng-,** **-an** grater.

kukus 1 steam. 2 vapor. 3 k.o. marten. **ber-** to steam. *Kétél itu* ∼ , The kettle steamed. **meng-** to steam s.t. *Ia* ∼ *kentang,* He steamed the potatoes. **-an** rice steamer. – *bekas* exhaust.

kul see KOL.

kulah small water basin (boxlike and made of stones or bricks and cement plaster).

kulai meng-kan *kepala* to let o's head droop. **ter-** drooping. *Bunga²* ∼ *karena kepanasan,* The flowers were drooping in the heat.

kulak 1 a cubic measure. 2 to buy goods and resell them.

kulat 1 toadstool. 2 fungus, mold. **ber-** moldy.

kuli coolie, laborer. **ber-,** **meng-** to work as a coolie. *Kehidupannja dari* ∼ , He earned his living by working as a coolie. – *arit* rubber tapper. – *minterad* 1 city employee. 2 street sweeper. – *pelat* official porter.

kuliah university lecture. **meng-kan** to lecture on a subject.

kulipah successor, deputy.

kulir trowel.

kulit 1 skin. 2 hide. – *sapi banjak gunanja,* Cowhide has many uses. 3 tree bark. 4 leather. 5 peel. *ber-badak* thick-skinned, insensitive. *Ia ~ badak tak merasakan sindiran² jg ditudjukan kepadanja,* He's thick-skinned and insensitive to the insinuations directed at him. **meng-** 1 to peel. 2 to slough off the skin. *Ular itu ~,* The snake sloughed off its skin. **meng-i** to skin, peel. *Ia ~ mendjangan itu,* He skinned the deer. *Ia ~ mangga itu,* He peeled the mango. **pe-an** tannery. **per-an** wrapping, cover, jacket. – *ari* outer skin, epidermis. – *berkikir* goose flesh. – *berwarna* colored people. – *buku* book cover. – *chatan* foreskin. – *gadjah* thick-skinned. – *gendang* drumhead. – *hitam* soccer ball. – *kaju* tree bark. – *kambing* kid (leather). – *kara* turtle shell. – *kebal* invulnerable. – *kerang* clamshell. – *léndér* mucous membrane. – *manis* cinnamon (bark). – *mati* numb, insensitive. – *muka* front cover. – *pegangan* leather strap (on bus, streetcar, train). – *penggosok* chamois cloth. – *samak* tanned (of hide, skin). – *sapi* cowhide. – *siput* snail shell. – *tanduk* 1 epidermis. 2 cornea. – *telur* eggshell. – *tiruan* artificial leather.

kulliah see KULIAH.

kulminasi culmination.

kulon west. **meng–** westward. *Ia berlajar ~,* He sailed westward.

kulturil cultural.

kuluk a truncated conelike headdress worn at the courts of Javanese princes.

kulum meng– to suck.

kulup 1 foreskin. 2 appellation for small boys. **ber-** not yet circumcised.

kuma² see KUMKUMA.

kumal rumpled, disheveled. *Badjunja –,* His clothes were rumpled. **meng-kan** to rumple. *Djangan ~ badjumu jg baru itu,* Don't rumple your new shirt.

kumala see GEMALA.

kuman 1 tiny insects like mites (cause scabies, etc.). 2 germ, microbe. 3 small particles. – *penjakit* bacteria, bacilli.

kumandang echo. **ber-** to reverberate, echo. *sorak jg ~* resounding cheers. **meng-** to reverberate. **meng-kan** 1 to reverberate. 2 to carry the voice. *Radio ~ suara présidén keseluruh pelosok negara,* The radio carried the voice of the president to all corners of the country.

kumat to have a relapse. *Penjakitnja*

itu – lagi, He had a relapse of his illness.

kumba 1 basin, bowl. 2 protuberance on the forehead of an elephant. – *majang* a basin decorated with young coconut leaves and filled with bathing water for a bride.

kumbah meng– to wash. *Ia ~ badjunja,* He washed his shirt. **–an** the wash. *Ia mendjemur ~nja,* He dried his wash.

kumbang bumblebee. **meng–** to buzz.

kumidi see KOMIDI.

kumis 1 mustache. 2 see KOMIS. **ber-** to have a mustache.

kumkuma 1 turmeric. 2 saffron.

kumpal see GUMPAL.

kumpar meng– to wind (a thread, wire, etc.) on a spool. **–an** spool, reel. *~ putar* moving coil (of radio).

kumpi 1 great-grandfather. 2 see KOMPI.

kumpul ber- to gather, assemble. *Murid² ~ dimuka sekolah,* The pupils assembled in front of the school. **meng-kan** 1 to gather, assemble. *Guru ~ murid² dimuka sekolah,* The teacher assembled the pupils in front of the school. 2 to collect. *Saja ~ perangko,* I collect stamps. 3 to concentrate. *Musuh ~ pasukannja dibelakang garis pertahanan baru,* The enemy concentrated their troops behind new defense lines. **meng-satukan** to unite, bring together. **peng-an** 1 gathering. *Polisi membubarkan ~ itu,* The police broke up the gathering. 2 collection. *Ia memperlihatkan ~ perangkonja,* He exhibited his stamp collection. **per-an** 1 club, association. *~ olahraga* athletic club. 2 meeting. *~ gelap* illegal organization. *~ kematian* organization which assists at funerals (with funds, services, etc.). **–an** collection. *~ lukisan² jg ternama* a collection of famous paintings. *~ orang* crowd. *~ sapi* herd of cattle.

kumuh dirty, base, low. **meng-kan** to soil.

kumulasi cumulation.

kumur ber- to rinse the mouth. **ber- –²** to gargle.

kunang² firefly. **ber- –²** 1 to glitter. *Bintang ~ dilangit,* Stars glittered in the sky. 2 to see stars. *Matanja ~ ketika ia kena pukulan dikepalanja itu,* He saw stars when he was hit on the head.

kundai bun, knot of hair. **meng-** to put o's hair up in a bun.

kundangan see KONDANGAN.

kundjung ber- to pay a call, visit (s.o.). *Ia datang ~ kerumah saja,*

He came to my house to pay a call.
meng-i 1 to pay a call. *Ia ~ saja,*
He paid me a call. *Ia ~
permusjawaratan itu,* He attended
the conference. 3 to visit s.o., see.
(per)-an visit. *~ kehormatan* courtesy
call. *belum – , tak –* never. *Semangat
kenasionalan meréka tak – padam,*
Their national spirit will never die.
kungkang a sloth. **meng-** to gnaw,
nibble.
kungkung see KONGKONG.
kuning yellow. **ke- -²an** yellowish.
meng- to become yellow, ripen.
Sawah tlh mulai ~ , The rice fields
have started to become yellow.
meng-kan to make yellow. *Ia ~
nasi itu dgn kunir,* He made the rice
yellow with turmeric. **-an** brass.
– langsat cream-colored (usually considered a flattering skin color). *–
mas* golden (color). *– telur* egg yolk.
kunir see KUNJIT.
kunjah **meng-** 1 to chew. 2 to digest. *Ia berichtiar ~ apa jg dinaséhati
itu,* He tried to digest the advice
he was given.
kunjit turmeric.
kunjuk 1 monkey. 2 *– lu! Mengapa
tidak awas?* You stupid ass! Why
don't you look out?
kuno 1 ancient. *Mataram adalah
keradjaan –,* Mataram is an ancient
kingdom. 2 old-fashioned. *pendirian²
–* old-fashioned ideas. **ke-an** 1 conservatism. 2 relic. 3 antiquity.
kuntal-kantil see KONTAL-KANTIL.
kuntilanak spirit of a woman who
has died in childbirth and who appears as a beautiful woman with a
hole in her back.
kuntit **meng-i** to tail. *Kemana sadja
saja pergi ia selalu ~ saja,* Wherever
I went he always tailed me.
kuntja(h) a bunch, bundle.
kuntjén the caretaker of a sacred
place.
kuntji key. *Inilah – rahasia itu,* This
is the key to that secret. **meng-(kan)**
to lock. *Ia ~ pintu itu,* He locked the
door. **peng-** 1 a lock, clasp. 2 conclusion of a book or an article. **ter-**
locked. *Pintu itu ~ ,* The door was
locked. **-²** joints (anat.). *– gantung,
– kura²* padlock. *– Inggeris* monkey
wrench. *– maling* master or skeleton
key. *– mati* 1 a closely guarded
secret. 2 an impasse, deadlock. *–
paha* groin. *– pas* open-end wrench.
– ring box wrench. *– sok* socket
wrench. *– wasiat* a secret, mystery.
kuntjit see KUTJIR.
kuntjung 1 forelock. 2 tuft, crest (of
birds).

kuntjup 1 bud (of flower, leaves). 2
closed (of flowers). **meng-** 1 to close.
*Setelah matahari terbenam, bunga²
~ ,* After the sun sets, the flowers
close their petals. 2 to contract,
shrink. 3 to cringe, be frightened.
meng-kan *pajung* to close an umbrella. *– djantung* a contraction of the
heart. *– hati* frightened, afraid.
kuntul see KONTOL.
kuntum 1 a flower bud ready to
open. 2 a budding girl. 3 used with
flowers. *se- bunga* a flower. **meng-**
to bud. *Bunga itu ~ ,* The flower
budded. **ter-** a bud beginning to open.
kuntung pigtail (of Chinese).
kunun see KONON.
kupas **mengk-** 1 to peel. *Ia ~ mangga
itu,* He peeled the mango. 2 to string.
~ buntjis to string beans. 3 to analyze. *Ia ~ soal itu,* He analyzed the
problem. 4 to criticize. 5 to strip
(of clothes). **peng-** critic. **peng(k)-an**
analysis. **-an** 1 analysis. 2 discussion. 3 commentary.
kupat-kapit dangling limply.
kupét 1 bulb (of a thermometer).
2 developing tray.
kupiah see KOPIAH.
kuping ear.
kupluk a cap.
kupon coupon.
kupu² butterfly. *– malam* prostitute.
kura spleen. **-²** turtle. *~ djendéla*
window sill. *~ kaki* instep. *~ tangan*
back of the hand.
kurai 1 grain in wood. 2 vein in
marble.
Kur'an Koran.
kurang 1 less. *Uangnja – dari lima
rupiah,* His money was less than 5
rupiahs. 2 not ... enough. *Suaramu –
keras,* Your voice is not loud enough.
3 about, almost. *Ia bekerdja disini
10 tahun –,* He has worked here for
almost 10 years. 4 lack. *Karena –
modal Rentjana Lima Tahun tak
dilaksanakan,* For lack of funds the
5-year plan was not carried out. 5 of,
to (time). *Pukul 12 – sepuluh (menit),*
It is 10 (minutes) of 12. 6 not. *Ia
– pandai dari saudaranja,* He's not so
smart as his brother. 7 to decrease.
Kegiatannja makin –, His zeal is decreasing. 8 minus, less. *Sepuluh –
empat tinggal enam,* Ten minus four
is six. 9 fault, lack, shortcomings.
Pekerdjaannja banjak –nja, There is
a great deal lacking in his work. (His
work needs a lot of improvement.)
Apa –nja mobil ini? What's wrong
with this car? **ber-** to decrease.
Setiap hari uangnja ~ , Every day

his money decreased. *Sakitnja* ~ , His sickness decreased. **ber-** -²**(an)** to keep on decreasing. **berke-an** to lack. *Meréka tidak* ~ *apa²*, They did not lack anything. **ke-an** 1 to lack. *Makanan ini* ~ *garam*, The food lacked salt. 2 shortage. *Negara itu mengalami* ~ *makan*, The country had a food shortage. 3 shortcoming, lack. 4 deficit. 5 deficiency. **ke-a-djaran** rudeness, insolence. **ke-pertjajaan** lack of confidence. **ke-puasan** dissatisfaction. **meng-i** 1 to cut, decrease. *Ia* ~ *gadjih saja*, He cut my salary. 2 to subtract. ~ *dua dari enam* to subtract 2 from 6. 3 to cut down (on s.t.). 4 to wrong, harm s.o. 5 to deprive. **meng-kan** to subtract. *Ia* ~ *sepuluh kpd seratus*, He subtracted 10 from 100. 2 to reduce s.t. **peng-an** decrease. **se--²nja** at least. *Saja membutuhkan* ~ *5 rupiah*, I need at least 5 rupiahs. **ter-** lowest, least. *angka jg* ~ the lowest grade (in examination, test, etc.). -² 1 the less. ~ *diladéninja lebih²* *ia akan merasa kesalahannja,* The less we pay attention to him the more he'll feel how wrong he is. 2 although. ~ *lantjar achirnja ia menjelesaikan pekerdjaannja,* Although it was slow going, he eventually finished the job. - *adjar* impudent, insolent, bad-mannered. *Anak itu - adjar,* That boy is impudent. - *asem nih!* dammit! - *asin* flat, insipid. - *bahasa* impolite. - *baik* bad, not good. - *dalam* shallow. - *darah* anemic. - *djadi* 1 not thrive, not do well. *Bunga mawar - djadi disini,* Roses do not grow well here. 2 to fail. *Potrét - djadi,* The photograph did not turn out well. - *djantan* weak, sissified. *Ia - djantan,* He is a bit of a coward. - *garam* inexperienced, green. - *genap* incomplete. - *hati²* 1 impudent. 2 careless. - *ingat* 1 careless. 2 forgetful. *Ia - ingat akan djandjinja,* He has forgotten his promise. - *karat* of inferior quality. - *lebih* more or less, approximately. - *makan* undernourished. - *pandai* stupid, not bright. - *periksa* to be ignorant of. *Saja - periksa akan hal itu,* I do not know about it. - *tenaga* 1 not strong enough. 2 short of personnel.

kurap 1 ringworm. *Ia sakit -,* He has ringworms. 2 scabby, covered with scabs. 3 sneaky, treacherous.

kuras a quire (in printing). **meng-** to flush a drain. **peng-an** draining.

kurban see KORBAN.

kurfa curve.

kuria(h) 1 district (in Tapanuli, Sumatra). 2 parish.

kurik speckled. *ajam* - a speckled chicken. **ber-** -² spotted, speckled.

kuring scabby, sore.

kurkuma turmeric.

kurma date (fruit).

kurnia see KARUNIA.

kurs rate (of exchange). - *bébas* free market rate. - *gelap* black market rate. - *resmi* official rate of exchange.

kursemangat 1 expression used to call s.o. who has fainted back to consciousness. 2 to welcome a newborn baby. 3 dear me! good(ness) gracious! (expressing surprise, shock).

kursi see KORSI.

kursif italics.

kursus course (of study). **di-** to be trained, given a course. **meng-kan** to offer a course. - *kilat* concentrated, intensive course.

kurtjatji 1 dwarf, gnome. 2 brownie (junior girl scout). 3 cub scout.

kurujuk to crow (of a cock).

kurun century. - *waktu,* - *zaman* period of time.

kurung 1 cage. 2 prison. 3 bracket. *Ia mentjétak kalimat itu dlm -,* He printed the sentence between brackets. 4 cabin (on a ship). **ber-** 1 to be surrounded. *Rumah itu* ~ *pagar besi,* The house was surrounded by an iron fence. 2 to be between brackets (of a word). 3 to be shut up. *Sedjak isterinja meninggal ia* ~ *dirumahnja,* Since his wife died, he's shut himself up in his house. **meng-** 1 to put into a cage. *Ia* ~ *burung itu,* He put the bird into a cage. 2 to imprison, jail. *Polisi* ~ *pendjahat itu,* The police imprisoned the criminal. 3 to surround. 4 to put between brackets. *Ia* ~ *kalimat itu,* He put the sentence between brackets. **peng-an** 1 imprisonment. 2 encirclement. - *ajam* chicken coop. - *batang* bier. - *besar* bracket(s). - *buka* opening parenthesis. - *tutup* closing parenthesis.

kurus 1 thin. *Badannja -,* His body was thin. 2 barren, infertile (land). **ke-an** 1 thinness. 2 too thin. *Engkau* ~ , You are too thin. **meng-** to become thinner. **meng-kan** to make slender, reduce. *Obat ini akan* ~ *badanmu,* This medicine will make you slender. - *kering* thin as a rail, emaciated. - *pandjang* slim, slender. - *tertulang* very thin.

kus see DEKUS.

kusal **meng-** 1 to rub, wipe (clean). 2 to roll. ~ *rokok* to roll a cigarette.

~ *segumpal adonan* to roll a lump of dough between the palms of o's hands.

kusam dull (of color).

kusau 1 confusion. - *pikirannja setelah mendengar chabar buruk itu,* He was confused after he heard the bad news. 2 tousled. *Kakak perempuan saja selalu bangun dgn rambut -,* My sister always wakes up with tousled hair.

kusir coachman.

kusta leprosy.

kusuk faithful.

kusuma flower. - *bangsa* flower of the nation, hero.

kusus see CHUSUS.

kusut 1 tousled. *Rambutnja -,* His hair was tousled. 2 tangled. *Benang itu -,* The thread was tangled. 3 rumpled. *Badjunja -,* His shirt was rumpled. 4 complicated. *Perkara itu sangat -,* The case was very complicated. *Pikiranku - sekali,* I am very confused. *Hatiku - sekali,* I am completely mixed up. **ke–an** confusion. **meng–** 1 to disentangle. *Polisi mentjoba* ~ *pembunuhan itu,* The police tried to disentangle the murder. 2 to prosecute. *Djaksa agung* ~ *perkara itu,* The attorney general is prosecuting that case. **meng–kan** to confuse. *Segala kedjadian itu* ~ *pikiran saja,* All those events confused me. - *kusau* confused. - *mangasai,* - *masai* all a tangle, tousled. - *murut,* - *musut* very confused, all tangled up, all mixed up.

kutak meng– to shake hard. **meng–ngatikkan** *orang* to boss s.o., bully.

kutang 1 brassiere. 2 chemise.

kutat ber– 1 to want, desire s.t. at all costs. 2 to refuse to give in, maintain a never-say-die attitude. 3 to struggle to the utmost for s.t. - *kutit* to vacillate.

kutet see KUTAT.

kutib see KUTIP.

kutik ber– to move slightly. *Saja mendengar tikus* ~ *dibelakang almari,* I heard a mouse move slightly behind the cupboard. *Pradjurit jg luka parah itu tak* ~ *lagi,* The mortally wounded soldier showed no further signs of life. **me-ng–²** 1 to tinker. *Ia suka* ~ *mesin mobilnja,* He likes to tinker with the engine of his car. 2 to pick. *Ia* ~ *hidungnja,* He picked his nose. 3 to look for faults, split straws, cavil. *Ia selalu* ~ *urusan orang lain,* He is always looking for faults in other people's affairs. **–an** a slight nudge, touch.

kutil wart. **meng–** to nibble. *Ia* ~

sepotong ketjil dari kué itu, He nibbled a small piece from the cake. **se–** a nibble, little bit, tiny piece.

kutilang 1 thrush. 2 see KETILANG.

kutip meng– 1 to copy. *Ia* ~ *dari bukunja,* He copied from his book. 2 to quote. *Boléhkah saja* ~ *buku tuan dlm karangan saja?* May I quote from your book for my article? 3 to pick up small bits (rice, grain, etc.). *Ia* ~ *padi itu satu per satu,* He picked up the rice grains one by one. *Dilarang* ~ , Quotation without author's consent prohibited. **–an** 1 copy. 2 quotation.

kutjai leek.

kutjak see KOTJAK.

kutjar-katjir in disorder. *Musuh lari* ~ , The enemy fled in disorder. **meng– -ngatjirkan** to scatter in disorder. *Serangan jg se-konjong² itu* ~ *musuh,* The sudden attack scattered the enemy in confusion.

kutjek me-ng–² 1 to rub with the hand. *Ia* ~ *matanja,* He rubbed his eyes with his hand. 2 to stir (tea in a cup, porridge, etc.). 3 to do the laundry.

kutjerpén [*kumpulan tjerita péndék*] collection of short stories.

kutjil meng–(kan) 1 to squeeze out (tooth paste, glue, etc.). 2 to banish, expel (from family, clan relationship, political party, etc.).

kutjing cat. - *djalang,* - *hutan* alley cat, stray cat. - *negeri* house cat. - *pekak* mousetrap. - *tapai* rabbit. **-²an** 1 calf (of leg). 2 biceps, muscles of leg or arm.

kutjir 1 pigtail. 2 tuft of hair (left on top of a child's shaved head).

kutjup see KETJUP.

kutjur ber–, meng– to gush, pour forth (of fluid). *Darah* ~ *dari luka²nja,* Blood gushed from his wounds. **meng-i** to pour. *Ia* ~ *badannja dgn air,* He poured water over his body. **meng-kan** to shed. *Ia tlh* ~ *darahnja bagi tanah air,* He has shed his blood for his country. **–an** stream. *Achirnja, dgn banjak* ~ *keringat sudahlah pekerdjaannja,* At last, after toiling hard he finished his task. - *kamu!* You're stupid!

kutu 1 louse. 2 flea. **ber–** to have lice. **ber– -²** to delouse o.s. *Ia* ~ *lalu berkeramas,* She deloused herself and had a shampoo. **ber– -²an** to delouse o. another. **meng-i** to delouse. *Ia* ~ *rambut ibunja,* She deloused her mother's hair. **se–** allied. *tentara* ~ the allied army. - *busuk* bedbug.

kutub Pole. - *Djanubi*, - *Selatan* South Pole. - *Sjamali*, - *Utara* North Pole.

kutuk curse. *Ia kena - ahli sihir djahat itu*, He was under the curse of the evil magician. **meng-i** 1 to curse. *Ia ~ nasibnja*, He cursed his fate. 2 to put a curse on s.o. *Dlm kemarahannja ia ~ désa itu*, In his anger he put a curse on the village. **ter-** accursed. *Njahlah, engkau dgn pengikutmu jg ~ itu!* On your way, you and your accursed followers! *seberas basah* worthless, useless.

kutung 1 cut off, hacked off, amputated (of limbs). 2 to have to foot the bill.

kuwung rainbow.

kw [*kwintal*] 100 kilograms.

kwalitas quality.

kwalitét quality.

kwantitét quantity.

kwarsa quartz.

kwartal see KUARTAL.

kwdj [*kilowatdjam*] kilowatt hour.

kwintal 100 kilograms.

kwitansi receipt.

kwt [*kawat*] wire, cable.

L

LAAPLN [*Lembaga Alat² Pembajaran Luar Negeri*] Foreign Exchange Institute.

laba benefit, profit, gain. *Tidak ada -nja sedikitpun djuga*, There's no benefit whatsoever. *-nja berapa persén, bung?* How much percentage of profit is there, my friend? **ber-** gainful, profitable. **me-i** to be profitable. *Mudah²an pekerdjaan itu ~* , May the work be profitable. **me-kan** to be profitable. *- rugi* profit and loss.

laba(h)² spider.

laberak me- to thrash, vent o's fury on. **-an** attack, thrashing.

laberang rigging.

labrak see LABERAK.

labu 1 gourd. 2 pumpkin. **me-** 1 swollen (of the abdomen). 2 to compress. 3 to fool, pull o's leg. *- kentjing* urinal. *- siam* squash.

labuh hanging down. **ber-** 1 to anchor, dock. *Kapal akan ~ pukul 6*, The ship will dock at 6. 2 to be at anchor. 3 to be pulled down. *Keré ~* , The blinds are pulled down. **kepe-an** harbor, port, affairs. **me-(kan)** 1 to drop, lower. *Ia ~ sauh*, He dropped anchor. 2 to give birth (of cows, buffaloes, etc.). **pe-an** 1 anchorage. 2 harbor, dock, port. *~ alam* natural harbor. *~ udara* airport.

labur ke-an pitfall. **me-** 1 to whitewash. 2 to pay laborers in kind or in money.

lada 1 pepper. 2 hot to the taste.

me-i to put pepper on s.t. *- sulah* black pepper. *- tumbuk* ground pepper.

ladam horseshoe.

ladang dry field (not irrigated). **ber-** to own a dry field. **memper-(kan)** to cultivate as a dry field. **pe-** a *ladang* farmer. **per-an** 1 dry fields. 2 regarding dry-field farming. *- padi* dry rice field.

ladén me-i 1 to wait on, serve. *Orang jg ~ ditoko itu tidak tjukup*, There aren't enough salespeople in the store. 2 to listen, respond to. *Djangan kau-i hinaannja*, Don't listen to his insults. **pe-** waiter, servant. **pe-an** service.

lading a cleaver.

ladjang unwed. *Ia orang -*, She's a young unwed woman, or He's a young unwed man. **me-** 1 to jump, kick. 2 to live as a bachelor or spinster.

ladjim see LAZIM.

ladju fast, quick. *Kapal itu - sekali*, The ship is very fast. **me-kan** to accelerate, speed s.t. up. **per-an** acceleration.

ladjur 1 row. *Se- rumah ini sama*, The row of houses is all alike. 2 strip of cloth. *kain jg ber- hidjau* the cloth with the green strips. 3 column, space between lines. 4 lane. *Djalan ini terdiri dari 4 -*, This is a four-lane highway.

ladung stagnant.

lafad see LAFAL.

lafal 1 pronunciation. 2 the right version. **me–kan** to pronounce. **pe–an** pronunciation.

laga animal fight. **ber–** 1 to fight. 2 to collide. 3 to brag, boast about. ~ *pilon* to pretend to be stupid, innocent. **me–** (*ajam*) to have a cockfight. **me(mper)–kan** to pit against. **per–an** 1 fight. 2 collision. **–²an** 1 proud. 2 boastful.

lagak attitude, manner, behavior. *–nja seperti orang pandai,* He acts as if he's an intelligent person. **ber–** 1 to be proud, put on airs. *Tidak baik* ~ , It isn't good to put on airs. 2 to pretend. *Dia pandai benar* ~ *berani,* He is very good at pretending to be brave. **me–** 1 to brag. 2 to impress. *Engkau* ~ *siapa?* Who are you trying to impress? **me–kan** to brag about. *Apa sebenarnja jg kaukan?* What are you actually bragging about? **pe–** braggart. – *bahasa* accent. – *lagu* behavior.

lagam 1 style. 2 melody. 3 horse's bit.

lagi 1 to be in the process of. *Ibu –masak,* Mother is cooking. 2 more. *Dua hari – baru akan selesai,* Two more days and it will be ready. 3 again. *Mengapa dia pulang –?* Why is he coming home again? 4 as well as. *Orang itu bagus – pandai,* That person is handsome as well as clever. 5 further. *Buku ini dibagi –...* This book is further divided... 6 still. *Sdr kenalkah saja –,* Do you still know me? 7 (with negatives) any more, any longer. **se–** 1 during. ~ *ketjil dia tinggal disini,* During his childhood he lived here. 2 as long as. 3 while, during. ~ *saja hidup, saja tidak akan berkawan kembali dgn dia,* I will never be friends with him again as long as I live. *Pentjuri itu datang* ~ *kami tidur,* The thief came while we were sleeping. – *pula,* – *pun* moreover. *dan* – moreover. *Apa –?* Anything else? *Bukannja bagus –!* It's exceedingly beautiful! *Siapa –?* Who else? (Anyone else?)

lagu 1 melody, tune, song. *Pernah dengar – kebangsaan Indonésia?* Ever heard the Indonesian national anthem? 2 way, manner. *–nja blm berubah dari dulu,* His manner hasn't changed. 3 intonation. **ber–** 1 melodious. 2 to put to music. 3 to sing. *Hatiku* ~ , My heart sings. **me–** to sing. **me–i** to compose a melody. *Siapa jg* ~ *sadjak itu?* Who composed the melody for the lyrics? **me–kan** to sing, chant. **pe–** singer. **–an** melody. – *hiburan* light music. – *lagah* boom-

ing, roaring. – *lagak* behavior. – *meresap* popular song. – *tanja* question intonation. – *tutur* intonation.

-lah (suffix of emphasis). *Duduk–,* Do sit down.

lah see TELAH.

lahad see LIANG.

lahan **per– –²** slow(ly).

lahap greedy, gluttonous. **me–** to be greedy. **me– –²** to be out of breath. **pe–** glutton, greedy person.

lahar lava. **ber–** to erupt.

laher see KOGELLAHER.

lahir 1 external, outside, outward. *–nja bagus entah didalamnja,* It's fine on the outside, but I don't know about the inside. 2 worldly. *Dia suka jg – sadja,* He just likes worldly things. 3 to be born. *Dia – di Médan,* He was born in Medan. **ke–an** 1 birth. 2 pertaining to physical, external matters. 3 to be born of, spring from. ~ *rakjat djelata* of humble origin. **me–kan** 1 to give birth to. *Ia* ~ *anaknja dirumahsakit,* She gave birth to a child at the hospital. 2 to express, utter. *Sukar baginja utk* ~ *perasaannja,* It's hard for him to express his feelings. 3 to adopt, take. *–kan sikap positip,* Adopt a positive attitude. – *dan batin* 1 physically and mentally. 2 in every way. *Maafkan – batin,* Pardon all my mistakes (said at *Lebaran*). – *mati* stillborn. **pd –nja** apparently, seemingly.

lahiriah 1 physical. 2 from all appearances, from the looks of things.

laik see LAJAK.

la ilaha illa'llah(u) There is no God but Allah.

lain 1 other. *Ada orang – disini,* There are other people here. 2 another. – *hari* another day. – *kali* another time. 3 different. *Oto itu – daripada oto kami,* That car is different from our car. 4 besides, not including. *Séwa rumah ini Rp 100, – ongkos listriknja,* This house rents for 100 rupiahs, not including electricity. **ber–** to differ. *Meréka* ~ *paham,* They have different opinions. **ber–(–)an** to be different from e.o. *Badju² itu* ~ *semua,* The dresses are all different. **ke–an** 1 difference, deviation. 2 abnormality. **me–i** to violate. *Kami* ~ *édjaan resmi itu,* We are violating the official spelling. **me–kan** but (rather). **me(mper)–kan** to discriminate. **per–an** difference. **se–** 1 besides, in addition to. ~ *daripada ongkos makanan, minuman mahal djuga,* In addition to the expense of

food, drink is also expensive. ~ *itu,*
ia masih mempunjai rumah lagi di
Bogor, Besides that, he still has a
house in Bogor. 2 except. *Ambil*
semuanja, ~ *ini,* Take everything
except this one. ~*nja* the remainder,
rest. ~*nja bukan punja saja,* The
rest isn't mine. – *daripada itu* moreover, besides. – *dulu* – *sekarang* other
times, other ways. – *halnja* a different
case, another matter. – *halnja dgn*
orang itu, It's another matter with that
man. – *tidak* that's all, nothing more.
Saja hanja mau bilang itu, – *tidak,*
I just want to tell you that, nothing
more. *tidak* – none other than. *Orang*
itu tidak – *adalah paman saja,* That
person is none other than my uncle.
Apa –*?* What else? *dan* –*²* and so
forth, etcetera, etc. *tak* – *dan tak*
bukan only, nothing else but. *Jg*
dipikirkannja tak – *dan tak bukan*
uang sadja, He thinks about nothing
but money.
lajah veil. **me–** 1 to bend over, bow.
2 to soar. **me-kan** to cover with a
veil.
lajak 1 proper, suitable, fitting. *Ia*
orang jg – *dihormati,* He's o. who
should be respected. 2 deserving.
se-nja properly. *Orang tua harus*
dihormati ~ , Parents should be
properly respected.
lajan **me-i** 1 to serve, wait on. *Ia* ~
tamu², She served the guests. 2 to
listen, respond to. *Djangan kau-i*
anak itu, Don't listen to that child.
3 to supply. *Kami –i keterangan jg*
dihendaki oléh umum, We supply
the information requested by the
public. **me-kan** to serve. *Pukul*
berapa makan malam di-kan? What
time is dinner being served? **pe–** 1
waiter. 2 waitress. 3 store clerk,
salesman. ~ *sinjal* railroad crossing
guard. **pe-an** service. **-an** service. ~
berita² dunia world news service.
lajang **me–** 1 to fly, soar, float in the
air. *Kapal udara* ~ *rendah sekali,*
The plane is flying very low. 2 to
wander, drift, *Pikirannja* ~ , His
thoughts are wandering. ~ *djiwanja*
to die. **me-kan** to release, launch, let
fly. ~ *pandang* to peer. ~ *surat* to
send a letter. **se–** *pandang* at a
glance. **ter-(–)** 1 to soar, float. 2 to
wander. *Ingatannja* ~ *ke-mana²,* His
thoughts were everywhere. *Matanja*
~ , He was asleep. **–an,** –² kite.
lajap low (close to the surface).
ber-(–)an to fly close to the ground
(of birds). **berpe-an** to travel around,
take a boat trip. **me–** to skim the
surface. **me-(–)** to sleep very lightly.

me-(–)kan to move continuously
(like wind in the trees).
lajar 1 movie screen. 2 sail. 3 blind,
curtain shade (window, door). **be(r)–**
1 to sail, go by boat. *Kami* ~ *dari*
San Francisco ke Los Angeles, We
sailed from San Francisco to Los
Angeles. 2 to have a sail. *Perahu*
itu ~ *kain putih,* The boat has a
white cloth sail. ~ *kepulau kapuk*
to go to sleep. **me-i** 1 to roam, sail
over. 2 to ship s.t. *Perahu² pengang-*
kut barang ~*nja,* Cargo vessels
carried it. **me-kan** to navigate, sail
s.t. **pe–** sailor, seaman. **pe-an** 1
voyage, trip by boat. 2 navigation.
– *gusi* mizzen (sail). – *padan* storm
sail. – *pengapuh* banner on a mast.
– *putih* movie screen, the silver
screen. – *sabang* small sail.
laju 1 withered. *Buanglah bunga jg*
– *itu,* Throw away the withered
flowers. 2 weak, pale. *Mengapa* –
sadja? Why so pale? **ke-an** wasted
away. **me–** 1 to wither. 2 see MELAJU.
–²*an* withered material.
lajuh 1 paralyzed. 2 see LAJU.
lajur **me–** to singe, scorch.
lak sealing wax. **di–** sealed.
laka lacquer.
lakab title, epithet.
lakak **me–** to hit, beat.
lakan 1 cloth. 2 felt.
lakeri sealing wax.
laki² 1 man, male. 2 husband. **ber–**
to marry, take a husband. ~ *bini*
married couple. **ke-(–)an** courage,
bravery. **le–** 1 man, men. 2 male.
pengantin ~ bridegroom. 3 brave,
manly. **memper–** to take as a husband.
memper-kan to marry off. – *bini*
man and wife. –² *djemputan* very
eligible bachelor, good catch.
lakmus litmus.
laknat a curse. **ke-an** cursing. **me-**
kan to curse s.o.
lakon 1 play, drama. 2 act. – *pertama*
the first act. 3 event. – *jg menjedihkan*
sekali a very sad event. **me-kan**
to present a play, perform, act,
write a play. **pe–** 1 actor. 2 actress.
laksa 1 10,000. 2 fine noodles similar
to vermicelli.
laksamana admiral. – *madya* vice-
admiral. – *madya udara* lieutenant
general in the Air Force. – *muda*
rear admiral. – *muda udara* major
general in the Air Force. – *tertinggi*
fleet admiral. – *udara* Air Force general.
laksana 1 quality, characteristic. *Ia*
mempunjai – *perempuan,* She has
the characteristics of a woman. 2
like, resembling. *Gedung itu ting-*

ginja – gunung, That building is as high as a mountain. **me-kan** 1 to bring about, do, cause to materialize. *Mudah²an ia dpt ~ tjita²nja,* I hope he'll be able to bring about his ideals. 2 to compare, equate. *Djangan engkau ~ dia dgn aku,* Don't compare him with me. **pe–** 1 executor, o. who brings s.t. about. 2 producer. 3 manager, director. **pe(ng)-an** 1 execution, carrying out, realization of s.t. 2 implementation.

laksanawan manager. *– tingkat tinggi* high-level executive.

laku 1 behavior, conduct, attitude. *– anak itu tidak baik,* That child's behavior isn't good. 2 manner, way. *Bagaimana –nja orang bertamu disini?* What is the manner of paying visits here? 3 valid, in effect. *Paspor saja – sampai bulan Agustus sadja,* My passport is just valid until August. 4 sold. *Barang semua sdh –,* Everything was sold. 5 popular, in demand. *Dihari panas és – sekali,* On hot days ice is very much in demand. 6 sale, demand. *-nja tidak ter-kira²,* The demand was incalculable. **ber–** 1 to be valid. 2 to happen. 3 to hold, be in force. *Peraturan ini ~ bagi seluruh daérah,* This regulation holds for the entire area. **berke-an** to have character. *~ baik* to be of good character. *~ sebagai* to act as, represent; acting. **ke-an** 1 behavior, conduct. 2 event, occurrence. **me-kan** 1 to do, carry out, execute, perform. *Ia ~ kewadjiban,* He did his duty. *Meréka ~ rantjangan,* They carried out their plan. 2 to sell. *~ barang jg mahal tidak mudah,* To sell expensive items isn't easy. 3 to make. *-kanlah per-djalanan dgn GIA!* Make your trip by GIA! *~ dinas tentara* to do military service. *~ pelanggaran kriminil* to commit a criminal offense. *~ pesanan* to place an order. *-kanlah ini utk ingat kpd Aku,* Do this in remembrance of Me. **memper-kan** to treat, handle. *Orang tua djangan kau per-kan demikian,* You shouldn't treat an older person like that. **pe–** 1 executive. 2 character (in a play, novel, movie, etc.). 3 actor, actress. *~ utama* leading man, lady. **per-an** 1- treatment. *~ tawanan* treatment of prisoners. 2 occurrence. 3 action, act. *~ perang* act of war. **se–** 1 as if, like. *Ia menangis ~ anak ketjil,* He cried like a child. 2 as. *~ anggota panitya tésis* as a member of the thesis committee. 3 on behalf of. *Saja bertindak ~ wakil ajah saja,* I act on behalf of

my father. *– hidup* behavior. *– sebagai pisang goréng* sell like hot cakes.

lakur to mix, fuse (of metal). **me-kan** to mix iron with other metals. *– baur* mixed, fused.

lalab side dish of raw greens or fruits. **me–** to eat raw vegetables.

lalah greedy, gluttonous. **me–** to chase after, run after. **pe–** glutton.

lalai careless, negligent, absent-minded. *Ia – sekali,* He's very careless. **ber– –²** to be careless, indifferent, negligent, lazy. **ke-an** indifference, carelessness, negligence. **me-kan** to neglect, forget. *~ hati* to comfort s.o. *~ waktu* to have a leisurely time. **memper-kan** 1 to put off, postpone. 2 to comfort, entertain. **pe–** 1 lazybones, sluggard. 2 an absent-minded person, indifferent person. **pe-an** neglect. **ter–** neglected.

lalang a tall grasslike weed which rapidly spreads over an area that is not regularly weeded.

lalat a fly. *– hidjau* bluebottle. *– kerbau, – kuda* horsefly. *Tak ada – langau,* There's no one around.

lalau me– to hamper, thwart, obstruct. **pe–** obstacle, hindrance. **pe-an** hindrance.

laler a fly.

lali numb. **me–** to anesthetize.

lalim tyrannical, despotic, cruel. **ke-an** tyranny, oppression. **me-i, me-kan** to oppress, tyrannize over.

lalu 1 to pass. *Dilarang – disini,* Forbidden to pass. 2 past, last. *Ia datang minggu jg –,* He came last week. 3 straight to. *Ia pergi dari sini – kesitu,* He went straight from here to there. 4 overdue. *Terlambat, semua sdh –,* It's too late, it's all overdue. 5 then. *Dia datang – pergi lagi,* He came and then went away again. **ber–** 1 past, overdue. 2 gone, passed away. 3 expired (contract). **ke-an** passed, overlooked. **keter-an** exceedingly, far too. *Kelakuannja ~ buruknja,* His behavior is exceedingly bad. **me-i** 1 to go, pass through. *Dia suka ~ pasar,* She likes to pass through the market. 2 to transgress, trespass on. *~ aturan bisa dihukum,* Infraction of a regulation is punished. 3 via. *Dia pergi ke Bandung ~ Bogor,* He went to Bandung via Bogor. **me-kan** 1 to take through, cause to pass through. *Lemari sebesar itu tidak bisa di-kan dipintu,* Such a big cupboard cannot be taken through the door. 2 to pass up, pass by. *~ keuntungan* to pass up a profit. **se–**

always, continuously. *Dia* ∼ *kerdja*, He's always working. **ter-** too, very, exceedingly. *Ia* ∼ *besar*, He's too large. – *lalang* 1 back and forth, to and fro. *Dia* – *lalang dikamarnja sepandjang hari*, He paced back and forth in his room all day. 2 scattered, dispersed. *Berbagai kendaraan – lalang didjalan*, Various vehicles were dispersed over the road. 3 untidy. – *béa* passage through customs. – *lintas* traffic. *Udjian tlh –*, The exams are over. *tidak* **ber-an** limited, restricted.

lama 1 long (of duration). – *sekali dia menunggu*, He waited a long time. 2 old. *Rumah – rupanja*, It seems to be an old house. **ber- -²** 1 prolonged period, for a long time. 2 gradually, in the long run. **ke-an** 1 too long. 2 gradually, in the long run. **me(mper)-kan** to prolong, extend (the time). **se-** during, while, as long as. ∼ *perang ia tinggal dinegeri Inggeris*, During the war he lived in England. ∼ *hajat dikandung badan* as long as I live. ∼ *ini* up till now. **se-nja** always, forever after. *Meréka hidup bahagia* ∼ , They lived happily forever after. **se- -²nja** 1 forever, eternal, always. 2 at the most. *hukum pendjara* ∼ *tiga tahun* a maximum imprisonment of three years. **-²** 1 finally. 2 gradually. – *ke-an* gradually, in the long run. *tidak – lagi* before long, shortly.

laman a yard, enclosure.

lamar me- 1 to propose to. *Jg* ∼ *dia siapa?* Who proposed to her? 2 to apply for. *Dia sdh lama* ∼ *pekerdjaan itu*, He applied for that job a long time ago. **me-kan** to volunteer. *Ia* ∼ *dirinja*, He volunteered. **pe-** 1 applicant. 2 suitor. **-an** 1 proposal. 2 application.

lambai me- 1 to wave, beckon. *Dia* ∼ *dgn saputangannja*, She waved with her handkerchief. 2 to wave. *Daun kelapa* ∼ *ditiup angin*, The coconut tree leaves wave in the breeze. **me-kan** to wave s.t. *Angin* ∼ *daun kelapa*, The wind waves the coconut leaves. **-an** waving, beckoning. ∼ *bendéra* flag waving.

lambak a disorderly heap, pile. **ber-** piled up in a disorderly manner.

lamban 1 lazy, languid, indolent. 2 clumsy. **ke-an** indolence. ∼ *pikiran* lazy thinking. **me-** 1 to be lazy. 2 to be clumsy.

lambang 1 sign, symbol. 2 badge, ribbon. *Mérah – apa?* What symbol does red represent? **me-kan** to symbolize. *Mérah* ∼ *bahaja*, Red symbol-

izes danger. **per-** heraldry. – *keluarga* coat-of-arms.

lambat 1 slow. 2 late. **ber-** 1 slow, unhurried. 2 to linger. **ke-an** 1 too late. 2 slowness, inertia. 3 delay. **keter-an** delay. **me(mper)-kan** to retard, slow down, delay. **pe-** latecomer. **se- -²nja** at the latest. *Ia datang* ∼ *hari minggu*, He'll come Sunday at the latest. **ter-** 1 too late. 2 delayed. – *bangat* much delayed. – *laun* 1 gradually, in the long run. 2 finally. 3 sooner or later.

lambuk me- to dig from the ground.

lambung 1 stomach. 2 side (of ship, person). **me-** 1 to bounce. *Bola karét ini tidak* ∼ , The rubber ball doesn't bounce. 2 to jump up. *Dia* ∼ *kegirangan*, He leaped with joy. 3 to praise, extol. *Tidak baik* ∼ *anak ketjil*, It isn't good to praise a small child too much. **me-i** to fix the side of a ship, house, etc. **me-kan** 1 to toss, pitch. 2 to praise. ∼ *dada* to boast. **pe-** pitcher. **-an** side, flank. – *kosong* with an empty stomach.

lamp. [*lampiran*] 1 supplement. 2 enclosure(s).

lampai slim, slender, thin. **me- -²** to sway, swish.

lampan me- to pan tin.

lampar ber-an to be scattered. *Buku* ∼ *didalam kamarnja*, Books are scattered in his room. **me-** to spread. *Kabar itu tlh* ∼ *ke-mana²*, The news has spread everywhere.

lampau 1 past. *pd waktu jg* – in the past. 2 past, over. *Waktu makan sdh –*, Mealtime is over. 3 too much. *Dia – banjak pelesiran*, He's going out too much. **me-** to go too far, overdo. **me-i** 1 to pass by. *Dia* ∼ *rumah saja*, He passed by my house. 2 to violate, transgress. ∼ *hukum membawa kesukaran*, Violating the law will get o. into trouble. 3 to go too far, overdo. *Djangan engkau* ∼ *batas membantah orang tuamu*, Don't go too far in arguing with your parents. 4 to overcome. *Dia* ∼ *segala kesukaran*, He overcame all his difficulties. **ter-** too, very, exceedingly. *Tempat itu* ∼ *djauh*, That place is too far. **ter-i** passed over, overlooked. *Kedua halaman ini* ∼ *tadi*, Those two pages were overlooked just now.

lampias 1 to spout, flow rapidly. 2 fast. **me-kan** 1 to make s.t. flow rapidly. 2 to release, give full rein to.

lampin 1 diaper. 2 pot holder. **me-i** to put a diaper on a baby.

lampir me-i 1 to attach, enclose. *Surat ini di-i kwitansi sebanjak $.25,*

Enclosed is a receipt for 25 cents. 2 to append s.t. **me-kan** to attach, enclose. *Djangan lupa surat jg di-kan,* Don't forget the attached (enclosed) letter. **-an** 1 enclosure. 2 attachment. 3 appendix, annex. 4 supplement.

lampu lamp. — *baterai* flashlight. — *belakang* taillight. — *beléntjong* oil lamp used for lighting puppets at shadow play. — *besar* headlights. — *gantung* hanging lamp. — *ketjil* dimmers. — *listrik* electric lamp. — *minjak tanah* kerosene lamp. — *oto* car lights. — *parkir* parking lights. — *penjorot* 1 flashlight. 2 projector. — *pétromaks* kerosene lamp with pump. — *pidjar* electric light bulb. — *sekat* panel light on car or plane. — *sén* signal light, directional signals. — *séntér* flashlight. — *sentolop* flashlight. — *sorot* searchlight. — *storemking* kerosene lamp with pump. — *témpél* wall lamp. — *téplok* oil lamp.

lampung me- to float. **pe-** 1 a float (on a fishing line). 2 float, buoy. ∼ *bénsin* gasoline gauge. ∼ *berenang* life belt, life buoy. ∼ *udara* life jacket (on plane).

lampus see MAMPUS.

lamun 1 although. — *sdh dikatakan beberapa kali, masih djuga dikerdjakannja,* Although he was told several times, he did it anyway. 2 provided that, if. *Saja mau pergi, — engkau serta,* I'll go, provided you come along with me. **ke-** overwhelmed. **me-(i)** 1 to cover. *Ombak* ∼ *pantai,* The waves cover the shore. 2 to overwhelm. *Itu di- bentjana,* It was overwhelmed with disaster. 3 to ponder, muse about. **nge-** to muse, ponder over, daydream. **pe-** o. who meditates. **-an** fantasy, daydream. see KELAMUN.

lamur night-blind.

lanau 1 mud. 2 muddy.

landa lye, alkali. **me-** 1 to run down, knock down. *Sepéda itu* ∼ *pagar kami,* The bicycle knocked down our fence. 2 to mine (tin, gold, etc.). **ter-** knocked down, run down, destroyed.

landai sloping. *Disini tanah jg -,* The land slopes here. **me-** to slope. **-an** 1 a slope. 2 hilt of a creese.

landak porcupine.

landas base, substratum. **ber-an** to be based on. **-an** 1 anvil. 2 writing pad. 3 landing strip. ∼ *kata* proof, evidence. ∼ *peluntjuran* launching pad. ∼ *terbang* runway.

landja me- to go on a visit.

landjar long and pointed. **me-** to stretch. **-an** bean pole, stick.

landjrat me- to try in court.

landjur stretched, dragged out, protracted. **me-kan** to stretch. **te-** rash, excessive, gone too far. *Sdh* ∼ *berdjandji,* I've been rash in my promise. (I've promised and feel bound by it.)

landjut 1 advanced, deep. *Sdh - malam sekarang,* It's already far into the night now. 2 long, detailed. *Tjeritanja — sekali,* It's a long story. **ke-an** 1 repercussion, result, carryover. 2 continuation. **me-** continuous. **me-kan** 1 to continue. *Dia* ∼ *sekolah,* He continued his studies. 2 to lengthen. **pe-an** continuation. **per-an** *djenis* reproduction of o's kind. **se-nja** from now on, furthermore, hereinafter. *utk* ∼ henceforth. **ter-** too far, rash. **-an** continuation. *sekolah* ∼ secondary school. — *umur* advanced in years.

landung long and lanky.

lang hawk. 1 see ELANG. 2 see SELANG.

langah be- wide-open. **me-kan** to open widely. **ter-** 1 wide-open, not closed. *Pintu djangan* ∼ *sadja,* Don't keep the door wide open. 2 flabbergasted, dumfounded. ∼ *ia mendengar berita itu,* That news dumfounded him.

langau bluebottle.

langgam 1 way, custom, style. 2 melody, tune.

langganan 1 subscriber. 2 customer. 3 supplier, caterer. **ber-** to subscribe to, take. *Kami* ∼ *madjalah Zenith,* We subscribe to *Zenith.*

langgar village mosque, prayer house. **ber-an** to collide with, be in conflict (with). *Perbuatanmu* ∼ *dgn hukum,* Your action is in conflict with the law. **ke-** hit by. ∼ *mobil* hit by a car. **me-** 1 to run over, collide with. *Oto itu* ∼ *anak ketjil,* The car ran over the small child. 2 to evade, trespass, break. *Djangan tjoba* ∼ *hukum,* Don't try to evade the law. 3 to invade. ∼ *bahasa* to violate good manners. ∼ *hukum* to break the law. *Membeli dari tukang tjatut adalah* ∼ *hukum,* Buying from a black marketeer is against the law. ∼ *pantang* to violate a prohibition. **me-i** to collide with repeatedly. **pe-** trespasser, violator, transgressor. **pe-an** 1 infraction, violation. ∼ *lalu lintas* traffic violation. 2 infraction, transgression. ∼ *aturan itu berat hukuman dendanja,* Infraction of that rule means a heavy fine. 3 accident, collision. 4 penalty (in sports). ~ *pidana* criminal offense.

langgeng eternal, imperishable. **ke–an** eternity.

langguk proud.

langir a shampoo. **ber-, me-** to shampoo. **me–i** to shampoo s.o.

langit 1 sky. 2 heaven. **me-** 1 sky-high. 2 very proud. –² 1 palate. 2 canopy, awning. ~ *kamar*, ~ *rumah*, –²an ceiling.

langka rarely, seldom. **ke–an** 1 scarcity, rarity. 2 infrequency.

langkah 1 step, stride. 2 step, action, measure. *Ia mengambil – jg lajak*, He took proper measures. **ber-** 1 to step forward. 2 to trespass. **ke–an** 1 surpassed. 2 trespassed. **me-** 1 to stride, step. 2 to overstep, trespass. **me–i** 1 to overstep, disregard, trespass. *Djangan berani ~ nasihat ibumu*, Don't you dare disregard your mother's advice. 2 to surpass. **me–kan** to make the step. **pe(r)–an** 1 transgression. 2 undertaking. – *baik* propitious circumstances. – *kanan* good luck. – *laku* behavior, conduct. – *sumbang* false step. *Ia membawa –nja*, He does as he wishes. – *sdh* **ter–kan**, What's done, is done.

langkai slim, slender.

langkan balcony, balustrade.

Langkapura Ceylon.

langkas 1 dexterous. 2 keen, diligent. 3 period between blooming and harvesting of fruit trees.

langkat in 2 days.

langkau **me–i** to overlook, skip.

langlang 1 night watchman. 2 beautiful. **me-** *buana* to roam about the world.

langsai 1 curtains. 2 paid, settled.

langsar 1 slim, slender. 2 fortunate, happy.

langsat fruit of a *duku*.

langsi 1 a shrill sound. 2 a flash. **ber-** to make a shrill sound. *Peluru ~* , Bullets screamed. **me-** to make a shrill sound.

langsing slim, slender. **me-** to become thin.

langsir **me-** 1 to shunt railroad cars. 2 to launch.

langsuir vampire.

langsung 1 direct, straight. *Ia pergi dari sini – pulang*, He went straight home from here. 2 advanced. *Hari sdh –*, It's already late. 3 to go on, take place. *Upatjara –kah?* Will the ceremony go on? **ber-** to go on, take place. *Pertundjukan wajang ~ sampai*

pagi, The puppet show went on till morning. **ke–an** 1 continuance. 2 performance, execution (of a marriage ceremony, etc.). ~ *hidup jang tertjakap* survival of the fittest. **me–kan** to perform, take place, carry out. *Perkawinan di–kan kemarén*, The marriage was performed yesterday. *Pelantikan présidén di–kan pagi ini*, The presidential inauguration takes place this morning. **me-** –² continuously, incessantly. **per–an** 1 conclusion. 2 progress. **ter-** rash.

langu rotten (smell).

langut **me-** melancholy.

lanjah muddy.

lanjak **me-** 1 to stamp on the ground, trample underfoot. 2 to insult, disparage, run down. 3 to dig at the ground with o's foot.

lanjau soft mud.

lansir see LANGSIR.

lantai floor. **me-** 1 to floor s.t. *Orang itu ~ rumah*, That man floored his house. 2 to take the floor, dance. *Sesudah makan para tamu ~* , After dinner the guests danced. – *perahu* ship's bottom. – *rumah* floor.

lantak **me-** 1 to hammer s.t. 2 to attack violently, ram into. **pe-** 1 ramrod. 2 piston rod. **–an** bar. ~ *mas* gold bar.

lantam 1 loud, clear, shrill. 2 proud, aloof. **ke–an** pride. **me–kan** 1 to speak in a strident voice. 2 to blast forth, trumpet forth. 3 to brag, boast.

lantang clear, distinct. *Dia mendjawab dgn suara –*, He answered in a clear voice. *Pemandangan dari sini –*, The view from here is clear. **ke–an** 1 clarity (of sound). 2 clothing undergoing bleaching. 3 apparatus for bleaching cloth. – *pandangan* field of vision.

lantar **me–kan** 1 to cause. *Apa lagi jg ~ dia sakit?* What else could cause his illness? 2 to pass on s.t. *Dia akan ~ usul itu dipertemuan*, He will pass on the suggestion during the meeting. 3 to mediate, decide on, adjudicate a matter. **pe-** 1 mediator, intermediary. 2 copulative (gram.). **pe–an** 1 front porch. 2 through the intermediary of, with the assistance of, via. **ter-** neglected, stranded, deserted, left high and dry. **–an** 1 cause. *Anak itu menangis ~ apa?* Why is the child crying? 2 because. *Saja tidak bisa datang, ~ tak énak badan*, I couldn't come because I wasn't feeling well.

lantas 1 straightway, right away, directly. *Sampai dirumah – dia bekerdja,*

Arriving at home he immediately went to work. 2 to, up to. *Ia pergi dari sini – kerumahnja,* From here he went to his house. 3 then. **me–** to penetrate, go straight to. *Nasihat gurunja ~ telinganja,* The teacher's advice penetrated his ears. ~ *angan* to do as o. pleases. **me–i** to penetrate into. **me–kan** to bring about, carry out, carry through. *Dia ~ apa jg dikehendakinja,* He does what he wants. – *angan* reasonable.

lantéra lamp, lantern.

lantik me– to install, inaugurate. *Pemimpin baru di– pagi ini,* A new leader is being installed this morning. **pe–an** inauguration, installation.

lanting house built on a raft. **me–** 1 to throw, toss. 2 to bounce, spring up (of a ball). 3 to dash away. **me–kan** to throw away. **pe–** catapult. **terpe–** 1 thrown away, cast away. 2 catapulted.

lantjana 1 emblem, badge. 2 insignia. see LENTJANA.

lantjang 1 bold, audacious, forward. *Ia – mulut,* He's impudent. 2 shameless. 3 yacht. **ke–an** 1 impudence. 2 audacity, boldness. –² to make stones skip along the water's surface. – *tangan* light-fingered.

lantjap smooth.

lantjar 1 smooth, fluent. *Perundingan berdjalan dgn –,* The discussion went smoothly. 2 fluent. *Dia – bahasa Inggerisnja,* He speaks English fluently. **berse–** to water-ski. **ke–an** smoothness. ~ *djalannja pemerintahan* the smooth running of government. **me–** to flash by. **me–kan, memper–** 1 to speed up, accelerate. *Dia ~ otonja sampai 80 km sedjam,* He speeds his car up to 80 kilometers an hour. 2 to promote, propagandize. 3 to launch (an attack). 4 to expedite. **pe–an** runway. – *mulut* 1 talkative. 2 boastful.

lantjing trousers.

lantjip sharp and pointed. **me–kan** to sharpen. *Dia ~ potlotnja,* He sharpened his pencil.

lantjong me– to go sightseeing, take a trip. **pe–** tourist, sight-seer. **pe–an** tourism.

lantjung 1 false, fake, imitation. *Ia memakai emas –,* She wears imitation gold. 2 treacherous. *Itu perbuatan jg –,* That was a treacherous deed. **ke–an** 1 forgery, fake. 2 treachery. **me–** 1 see LANTJONG. 2 to forge, fake. **pe–** 1 tourist, sight-seer. 2 walker. **pe–an** 1 tourism. 2 trip. 3 walk. **–an** 1 imitation, fake. 2 forged

(check, etc.). 3 impure, adulterated (of food).

lantjur me– to squirt out.

lantun me–kan to launch.

lantung penetrating odor. **me–** 1 to explode. 2 to penetrate (of an odor). –² a confusion of explosive sounds.

lantur me– to digress, ramble. *Djangan bitjara ~ ,* Don't get off the subject. **me–kan** to divert, distract s.t. *Bunji itu ~ perhatianku,* The noise distracts my attention.

laos greater galingale.

lap 1 towel. 2 rag, cloth. **me–(kan)** to wipe, clean with a cloth. – *basah* damp cloth.

lapah me– 1 to devour. *Harimau ~ kambing,* The tiger devoured the goat. 2 to skin, flay.

lapal see LAFAL.

lapan see DELAPAN.

lapang 1 open, wide, spacious. *Dia tinggal dekat tanah –,* He lives near an open field. 2 free, unoccupied. *Minggu ini saja – sedikit,* I'm not busy this week. **ber–(–)** 1 to be unburdened by financial obligations. 2 ample, sufficient. **ke–an** 1 room, space. 2 leisure. 3 opportunity, occasion. 4 relieved. **me–i** 1 to make room, clear away. 2 to assist. **me–kan** 1 to clear space for, expand, enlarge. 2 to broaden. 3 to be stimulating. *Bertjakap dgn orang itu sungguh ~ pikiran,* Talking to that person is stimulating. ~ *dada* to provide relief. ~ *djiwa* to be kind, merciful, to. **memper–** 1 to widen, open up, broaden. 2 to relieve. **–an** 1 field, square, park. *Dimana ~ sépak bola?* Where's the soccer field? 2 field. *Apa ~ pekerdjaannja?* What's his field of work? 3 occasion. ~ *perang* battlefield. ~ *rumput* lawn. ~ *ténis* tennis court. ~ *terbang* airfield, airport. – *hati* broad-minded. – *maknit* magnetic field.

lapar 1 hunger. 2 hungry. *Saja – sekali,* I'm very hungry. **ber–** to be hungry. *Saja ~ ,* I'm hungry. **ke–an** 1 hunger. 2 famine, starvation. **me–kan** to starve s.o.

lapat² 1 vague, barely visible. 2 barely audible.

lapih ber– woven. **me–** to weave, plait.

lapik 1 base. 2 lining. **ber–** to have as a base or a mat. **me–i** to line, place a lining in. **me–kan** to use as a base. *Dia ~ kertas dilemari,* He lined the cupboard with paper. – *kaki* sandal. – *médja* tablecloth. – *tiang* base of a post. – *tidur* sleeping mat.

lapis 1 layer. *- jg pertama kurang tebal,* The first layer isn't thick enough. *Saja suka kué -,* I like layer cake. 2 row. 3 lining. **ber-(-)** in layers, terraced. **ber-** *badja* armorplated. **me-** to make layers, accumulate s.t. **me-i** 1 to line, cover a chair. 2 to plate a ship. **pe-an** *kemasjarakatan* social stratification. **-an** 1 layer. 2 lining. 3 stratum, class. *Ia termasuk orang* ~ *bawah,* He is a member of the lower class. ~ *masjarakat* social stratum. ~ *pelindung* protective coating. *- legit* k.o. layer cake.

lapor **me-kan** to report, notify, inform. *Ketjelakaan harus di-kan,* Accidents must be reported. *Harap* ~ *barang²* *jg baru,* Please mention the new items. ~ *diri* to report, check in. *Dimana saja* ~ *diri?* Where do I check in? **pe-** 1 rapporteur. 2 reporter, commentator. **pe-an** reporting, commentary. **-an** report, account.

lapuk 1 moldy, putrefied, mildewed. 2 rotten. *Kaju itu -,* That wood is rotten. 3 weak. *Itu dari paham -,* That's from a weak standpoint. 4 out of date, obsolete. *peraturan jg sdh -* an out-of-date regulation. **ber-** to get moldy. **ke-an** mildew, moldiness.

lapun net for catching deer. **me-** to catch animals with a net.

lapung **ber- -²** to gobble up.

lapur see LAPOR. **ber-** to twitch (of wings).

lara sick, sad, worried. **ter- -²** constantly weeping.

larai separated. **me-kan** to separate s.o. **pe-** 1 arbiter. 2 referee.

larang **me-** to forbid, prohibit. *Dimerokok disini,* No smoking here. *Di- masuk,* No admittance. **(pe)-an** prohibition, taboo. *Tak ada* ~ *utk menanam pohon,* There's no law against planting a tree.

larap in demand. **me-kan** to slacken a rope.

laras 1 pitch, scale, key. 2 harmony. 3 straight, cylindrical. 4 rifle barrel. 5 classifier. *Pemburu itu mempunjai 3 - senapan,* The hunter owns three rifles. 6 district (in Minangkabau). **ke-an** harmony. **kese-an** 1 adjustment, adaptation. 2 harmony. **me-kan** to adjust, adapt, co-ordinate. *Pembelian harus di-kan dgn kebutuhan,* Buying should be adjusted to the need. **menje-kan** to adapt, adjust, synchronize. **peng-an** adjustment, adaptation, co-ordination. ~ *kedua pendapat itu sdh terdjadi?* Has the adjustment of the 2 opinions taken place? **penje-an** adjustment, adaptation. **se-** 1 in accordance with. *Perbuatannja itu tak* ~ *dgn apa jg didjandjikannja,* His action was not in accordance with what he promised. 2 in harmony, harmonious. *Suara kedua penjanji itu tak* ~ , The voices of the 2 singers were not in harmony. 3 melodious, tuneful.

larat increasing. *Sakitnja bertambah -,* His illness became more and more severe. **ber-** 1 to spread. 2 dragging along. 3 to wander about. **me-** 1 to spread. *Api* ~ *ke-mana²,* The fire spread everywhere. 2 to wander about. **me-kan** to draw out, protract. **memper-** to procrastinate, prolong.

lari 1 to run, flee. 2 to escape, leave. *Berapa orang - dari pendjara?* How many people fled from the prison? *Dia - dari pekerdjaannja, sebab tak suka,* She quit her job, because she didn't like it. **ber-** to run. *Dia* ~ *tjepat pulang,* He ran home fast. **ber- -²** *andjing* to trot. **ber-an** to run in a hurry. **me-kan** 1 to kidnap. *Pentjuri* ~ *anak siapa?* Whose child did the thief kidnap? 2 to cause to run. ~ *sepéda sekentjang itu tidak baik,* It isn't good to ride a bicycle that fast. ~ *diri* to escape, flee. **memper-kan** to have s.t. trot. **pe-** 1 runner, sprinter. 2 fugitive. **pe-an** 1 race. 2 race track. 3 fugitive. ~ *diri* flight, escape. *- berantai, - beranting, - berganti, - beregu, - éstafétte* relay race. *- djarak péndék* sprint. *- gawang* hurdle race. *- rintangan* obstacle race. *- tjepat* sprint. *- kentjang!* On the double!

larih **ber- -²an** to drink together. **me-** to pour out drinks. **me-i** to serve drinks.

larik row, line. **me-** 1 to arrange in rows. 2 to turn on a lathe. **per-an** 1 potter's wheel. 2 lathe.

laris popular, in demand. **ke-an** popular. **me-kan** to popularize. **peng-** selling of first article cheap early in the morning in order to stimulate further sales.

laron flying white ant.

larut 1 to dissolve. *Pil itu sdh - didalam air,* The pill dissolved in the water. 2 dissolved, fused, melted. 3 late, advanced. *Ia bekerdja - malam,* He worked far into the night. **ber-** brokenhearted. **ber- -²** 1 procrastinating. 2 endless, dragging on. **me-** to dissolve. **me-kan** to drag on endlessly. **-an** solution.

las weld, joint. **me-** to weld.

lasa paralyzed.

lasah be– to strike, hit. me–kan, memper– to work s.o. like a horse, to exploit thoroughly.

lasak 1 fretful, peevish (of children). 2 restless, uneasy. 3 impermanent, temporary (of sleeping place). – tangan incapable of keeping o's hands off s.t.

lasjkar see LASKAR.

laskar 1 soldier. 2 army, troops. ke–an military (affairs). – rakjat nonprofessional troops.

lastik 1 elastic. 2 rubber band.

lat 1 interval. – dua hari a 2-day interval. 2 late.

lata 1 ugly, dirty. 2 humble. me– to creep.

latah a k.o. female hysteria. ke–an nervousness. – mulut uttering coarse words.

latak deposit of oil or paint.

latam solid, compact. me– to cramp, stuff.

latar 1 surface, plane. 2 background. 3 front yard. pe–an 1 front yard. 2 background. ∼ parkir parking area. – belakang background.

latih accustomed, trained. ber– 1 to practice, train. Tiap hari ia ∼ main piano, He practices on the piano every day. 2 trained. me– to train, practice, exercise. pe– 1 instructor, coach. 2 trainer. ter– skilled. –an 1 exercise, training, practice. 2 rehearsal. ∼ badan physical exercise. ∼ peperangan war exercises. ∼ simak memorization exercises at school. – tertib calisthenics.

latjak me– to drag slightly (of an anchor).

latji drawer (table, dresser).

latjur 1 immoral, indecent. Ia orang –, She's a prostitute. 2 mistaken, failed. 3 prostitute. me–kan diri to prostitute o.s. pe– prostitute. pe–an prostitution.

lauk side dish. ber– to eat rice with a side dish. – pauk side dishes with the rice.

laun to linger, loiter. –² hari some days ago.

laung a loud voice, loud sound. me– to yell loudly, cry out loudly. sepe–an the distance a scream can be heard.

laut sea. me– 1 to go to sea, put out to sea. 2 sealike. me–i to ply the seas. memper– to send by sea mail. pe– sailor, seaman. –an ocean. ∼ selebu the high seas. ∼ Hindia Indian Ocean. ∼ Teduh Pacific Ocean. ∼ Tengah Mediterranean Sea. – api 1 hell. 2 sea of fire. – Djawa Java Sea. – Karang Coral Sea. – Kidul Indian Ocean (south of central Java). – Kulzum Red Sea. – lepas the open sea. – pengundak frontal sea.

lawa(h) open, wide of view. –² spider.

lawak 1 fun, banter. 2 joke, jest. pe– comedian, clown. –² 1 jokes, amusing acts. 2 trough for eating. –an 1 humor. 2 joke.

lawan 1 opponent, enemy, respondent. –nja berkelahi siapa? Who was his opponent? 2 the contrary, opposite. Apa – kata itu? What's the opposite of that word? 3 to oppose. Djangan – dia, Don't oppose him. 4 against. Sekolahmu bertanding – siapa? What school is your school competing against? 5 versus. Cornell – Harvard Cornell versus Harvard. 6 they (in bridge). ber– to contest, compete. Kepandaiannja tidak ∼ , His intelligence is incontestable. ber–an to be contrary. Hal itu ∼ dgn hukum, That's contrary to the law. me– 1 to oppose, compete against. Ia berani ∼ musuhnja, He bravely opposed the enemy. 2 to be against, contrary to. Perbuatan itu ∼ adat, That act is against customary law. me–i 1 to oppose. 2 to contradict. memper–kan to pit against, oppose. Dimana orang ∼ ajam disini? Where do people fight their cocks here? pe– 1 opponent, opposition. Berapa ∼ ada? How many opponents are there? Ia masuk partai ∼ , He joined the opposition party. 2 to be contrary. per–an 1 opposition, resistance. ∼ tidak sedikit, The opposition is quite strong. 2 reverse. 3 contrast. – asas paradox. Siapa –mu ber-tjakap²? To whom did you talk?

lawang gate. – sekéténg city gate.

lawar slices of meat or fish. me– to slice thinly.

lawas 1 long time. 2 old. ke–an scope. me– open wide (of view, sight).

lawat me– to pay a visit, take a trip. Dia ∼ keluar negeri, He is taking a trip abroad. Ia ∼ ketempat kematian, He visited the home of the deceased. pe– visitor, tourist. per–an visit, trip, expedition.

lazat 1 delicious, nice, tasty. Makanan itu rasanja –, That food tastes delicious. 2 sensual pleasure. ber– fond of women. ke–an 1 delicacy. 2 taste.

lazim 1 usual, customary, common. 2 compulsory, obligatory. ke–an custom, usage, fashion, fad. me–kan 1 to make compulsory. 2 to introduce, set up.

lazuardi azure.

LBU [*Latihan Bahaja Udara*] air raid drill.

lebah honeybee.

lebai 1 mosque official, village, mosque servant. 2 dullard. - *malang* unfortunate fellow.

lebak 1 valley. 2 family. *Ia adalah - saja*, He belongs to my family. 3 the sound of 'plop.'

lébar 1 broad, wide, extensive. *Pekarangannja - sekali*, His yard is very wide. 2 width, breadth. - *sawahnja berapa?* What is the width of his wet rice field? **me-** to expand, broaden. **me-kan** to widen, broaden s.t. **pengean** width. **per-an** expansion.

Lebaran day ending the fasting period. **ber-** to celebrate *Lebaran*. - *ketupat* a festival 7 days after Idil-Fitri at which *ketupat* is the main dish.

lebas me- to whip s.o.

lebat packed, thick, dense. *Pohon djeruk itu - buahnja*, The citrus tree is packed with fruit. *hudjan -* to rain cats and dogs, a downpour.

lebih 1 more. *Dia - besar*, He's bigger. *Sdh -, bung*. It's more than enough, friend. *Saja punja - dari perlu*, I have more than is necessary. 2 rest, remainder. *Lima masukkan disini, -nja simpan sadja*, Put 5 here and just set the rest aside. **ber-** to remain, be left, be over. *Uangnja ~ 3 rupiah*, The money is 3 rupiahs too much. *Makanan kemarén ~ banjak sekali*, There is plenty of food left over from yesterday. **ber- -²** excessive, over-abundant, too much. *Uangnja ~ barangkali*, Maybe he has too much money. **ber-an** to overdo. **ber- -²an** excessive. *Tidak ~ bila dikatakan...* It's no exaggeration to say... **berke-an** 1 superabundant. *barang jg ~* surplus goods. 2 exaggerated. **ke-an** 1 majority. *~ orang pertjaja hal itu*, The majority of people believe it. 2 excess, surplus, remainder. 3 abundance. 4 advantage. *~ penduduk* overpopulation. **me-** to overdo s.t. **me-i** 1 to exceed, surpass. *Dia ~ kepandaian adiknja*, He surpasses his brother's intelligence. 2 to excel. 3 to add to. **me- -²i, me- -²kan** to overdo, exaggerate. **me-kan** 1 to increase. 2 to prefer. **se- -²nja** at most. **ter-** 1 exceedingly. 2 most. *Siapa jg ~ dulu?* Who's the very first? *~ dulu saja mau mengutjapkan terima kasih*, First of all I want to express my thanks. 3 especially. *~ dulu* 1 first of all. 2 at the outset. **ter- -²** above all, over all. **-an** remainder. **-²** especially, the more

so. *~ kalau saja mau pergi* especially if I want to go. - *dulu* prior. - *dulu daripada perbuatan itu* prior to the deed. - *lagi* 1 much more. 2 still more. *jg* **se-nja** the remainder.

lebu dust. **ber-** to be dusty. **pe-an** Balinese place of cremation.

lebuh highway.

lebun deceit, deception, fraud. **me-** to deceive.

lebur dissolved, melted, destroyed. **ke-an** 1 abyss. 2 trap, pitfall. **me-** to melt, fuse. **me-kan** to dissolve, destroy. *~ diri* to join. *Kapan dia ~ diri kedalam partai itu?* When did he join the party? **pe-an** 1 solution. 2 fusion. **-an** solution. - *-kiamat* Doomsday.

ledak me- 1 to explode. 2 to break out. *Perang kedua ~ ,* The second war broke out. **me-kan** to cause to explode, to blow s.t. up. **(per)-an** explosion.

lédéng see AIR.

lédés inflamed, chapped.

leding me- to be warped.

ledjang swift, fleeting, fast. **me-** to kick. **me-kan** *kaki* to stretch o's legs. **se-** *terbang* 1 as fast as lightning. 2 superficially. 3 at a glance.

ledjit me- to run, flee.

lédor ke-an negligence, indifference.

ledos me- 1 to explode, burst. 2 to collapse.

lega 1 roomy, open. 2 free, not busy. **ke-an** 1 relief. 2 space. **me-kan** to relieve. - *hati*, - *pikiran* relieved.

legak-legok uneven, curved.

légar space to move around in.

legat straight.

legén unfermented palm sap.

legit sweet, nice. see LAPIS.

lego me- 1 to transfer, hand over. *~ 105 baal benang tenun* to hand over 105 bales of spinning yarn. *~ djangkar* to drop anchor.

legodjo executioner, hangman.

légong a Balinese dance.

léhér neck. - *badju* collar. - *botol* neck of bottle.

léka 1 slow. 2 negligent. 3 absorbed in s.t.

lekah a crack. **me-** to chap, crack. *Bibirnja ~ ,* His lips are chapped. *bunga ~* first blooming of a flower.

lekak-lekuk bumpy.

lekang to be loosened. **me-** to burst, split, crack. *tak ~ dari pikiran* never out of o's thoughts, thinking about s.t. continuously. *tak ~ memperhatikan* watching incessantly.

lekap me-(kan) to stick, fasten, attach.

lekar rattan stand on which round-bottomed cooking vessels are placed when taken off the fire to prevent their tipping over.

lékar small table for the Koran.

lekas 1 fast, swift, quick. *Dia djalan -*, He walks fast. 2 soon. *Dia - selesai*, He finished soon. 3 hurry. *-*, Hurry up. **ber- -²** to hurry, rush. **me(mper)-kan** to speed up, accelerate. **se-** as soon as. *Ia akan pergi ∼ mungkin*, He'll go as soon as possible. *-²!* Hurry up!

lekat ber- sticky. **me-** 1 to stick, cling. 2 attached, intimate, devoted. *Itu persahabatan jg ∼*, That's a very intimate friendship. **me-i** to stick to, stick on, attach to. *Pengumuman itu di-i didinding*, The announcement was stuck on the wall. **me-kan** 1 to stick, attach. *Siapa jg ∼ perangko ini?* Who stuck this stamp here? 2 to invest. *Modal asing banjak di-kan di-perusahaan² di Indonésia*, Much foreign capital is invested in Indonesian enterprises. 3 to put on, wear. *Dia ∼ badju barunja*, She's wearing her new dress. *∼ tangan kpd* to hit, strike s.t. **pe-** poster, placard.

LEKRA [*Lembaga Kebudajaan Rakjat*] Institute of People's Culture.

léktor university lecturer. *- kepala* senior lecturer. *- muda* junior lecturer.

léktur reading matter.

lekuk 1 hollow. 2 dent. **ber-** dented. **me-** to become hollow. **me-kan** 1 to make a dent, hollow. 2 to arch the back (of a cat). *- liku* 1 many dents, hollows. 2 many tricks. 3 ins and outs. *- lutut* bend of the knee, back of the knee. *- mata* 1 eye socket. 2 orbit.

lekum 1 throat. 2 Adam's apple.

lekung hollow, curved, bent. **me-** to curve, bend.

lekup-lekap the sound of creaking joints.

léla smart, jaunty. **ber-** to act smart, jaunty. **me-** to show off, swagger, boast, be jaunty. **me-kan** to handle, manipulate swords, arms, etc. **se- -²nja** leisurely, at will. *Dia berdjalan ∼*, He walks in very leisurely fashion.

lelabah spider.

lelah tired, weary, exhausted, worn-out. **ber-(-)** to wear o.s. out, to exhaust o.s. *Dia ∼ datang sedjauh itu*, He exhausted himself by coming that far. **ke-an** 1 fatigue, weariness, exhaustion. 2 exhausted. *Saja sdh ∼*, I am exhausted. **me-kan** tiring, exhausting, wearying. *Itu ∼ sekali*, That's very tiring. *∼ diri* to wear o.s. out.

lelai me- to droop. *Tjabang pohon itu ∼*, The tree branch is drooping. **me-kan** to bend s.t. down. *Djangan kau-kan dahan itu*, Don't bend that branch down.

lelaki see LAKI.

lélang auction, sale. **me-** to auction off. **me(mper)-kan** to sell at auction. *Tuan Achmad ∼ perkakas rumahnja*, Mr. Achmad sold his furniture at auction. **(per)-an** auction, public sale.

lelangit ceiling.

lelantjur 1 young rooster. 2 a young whippersnapper.

lelap 1 lost, gone, disappeared. 2 sound-asleep, unconscious. 3 to harden (of oil). **ter-** 1 sound-asleep. 2 unconscious.

lelas 1 smooth after polishing. 2 blisters on the skin. 3 free, wide, open. **me-** smooth after polishing. *Meréka tlh lepas - dari negeri itu*, They have absolutely no relations with that country.

lelatu spark.

léléh ber-an to trickle a lot. *Badannja ∼ peluh*, His body is covered with perspiration. **me-** 1 to trickle, drip. *Air matanja ∼*, Her tears trickled down. 2 to melt. *Lilin ∼*, The candle is melting. **me-kan** to cause to drip.

lelep ke- submerged, drowned. **me-kan** to submerge, dip.

léler ber-an to be covered with perspiration. **ke-an** neglected, careless, untidy. **me-** to trickle, slobber.

leléwa ber- to show off, put on airs.

leluasa free, unhampered, at o's discretion. **ber-** to do as o. pleases, to act at o's discretion. **berke-an** to have freedom of action. **ke-an** freedom of action.

leluhur ancestors. *negeri -* country of origin.

lelutjon 1 joke, anecdote. 2 farce. 3 humor. see LUTJU.

lém glue. **di-** glued, pasted.

lemah 1 weak, feeble. *Badannja -*, His body is weak. *alasan jg -* a weak argument. 2 soft, delicate. 3 limp, supple. 4 weak, low. *Akinja -*, His battery's low. **ke-an** weakness, impotency. **me-kan** to weaken, soften. **memper-** to weaken, enervate. *- gemulai* graceful. *- hati* meek, without will power. *- langlai* feeble, weak. *- laun* very slow. *- lembut* gentle. *- lentur* flexible, pliant, supple. *- lunglai* 1 weak, limp. 2 graceful.

lemak 1 fat, grease. 2 lard. 3 greasy. 4 sweet in speech, flattering, smooth. *- babi* bacon. *- ketam* gray. *- nasi* sticky rice cooked with coconut milk. – *tulang* marrow.

lemang me– to cook rice in bamboo.

lemari cupboard, case, wardrobe. – *besi* safe. – *buku* bookcase. – *(pen) dingin*, – *és* icebox, refrigerator. – *makan* food cupboard, kitchen cabinet. – *pakaian* wardrobe, chest.

lemas 1 choked, suffocated. 2 supple, pliant, flexible. *Kaju itu –*, That wood is flexible. 3 indolent. 4 cultured. *Bahasanja –*, His speech is cultured. 5 accommodating. **me–kan** 1 to weaken, soften. 2 to refine. 3 to accommodate. ∼ *tulang punggung* to stretch o's back (after sitting for some time).

lemau weak, soft.

lembab 1 damp, moist, humid. *Hawanja –*, The weather is damp. *Tembakau itu –*, The tobacco is moist. 2 dull. *Suara kendang itu –*, The sound of the drum is dull. 3 clumsy, indolent. **ke–an** humidity, dampness. **me–kan** to moisten, dampen, wet. – *lembut* soft (of sand).

lembaga 1 institution, league, institute, organization. – *Bahasa* Language Institute. – *Bangsa*[2] League of Nations. 2 embryo, sprout, germ. – *daun* sprout of a plant. 3 origin.

lembah valley, dale. – *kehidupan* lifetime.

lembajung 1 plant with crimson flowers. 2 crimson.

lémbak me– to boil over, run over.

lembam 1 weak. 2 tired. 3 slow, indolent, lazy. **ke–an** inertia, indolence. *memukul – mata orang* to black s.o.'s eye.

lembang 1 dent, hollow. 2 valley. **me–** to hollow out s.t.

lembar 1 thread, strand. 2 page. *Dimana – muka?* Where's the front page? 3 used with thread, hair, paper. *se– kertas* one sheet of paper. **me–kan** to twist (of a rope). **–an** 1 page. 2 sheet of paper. 3 leaf of plant. 4 issue of magazine. 5 copy. ∼ *kerdja* working paper. ∼ *ketikan* typed copy. ∼ *negara* statute book. ∼ *pembina* data sheet.

lembék 1 weak, indolent. 2 soft (of porridge, rice, mattress, etc.). **ke–an** weakness, softness. **me–kan** to soften, weaken.

lembidang edge, rim (of plate, hat, etc.).

lembik see LEMBÉK.

lembing javelin. **me–** to throw the javelin.

lembu cow. – *belang* spotted cow. – *perahan* milch cow. – *tampung* piebald bull.

lembung me– 1 inflated, swollen. 2 to bounce. **me–kan** to puff up, inflate, blow up. *Dia ∼ dada*, He's bragging. **pe–an** 1 balloon. 2 soap bubble. 3 crop, gizzard of fowl.

lembur overtime, nightwork. *kerdja –* overtime work. *upah –* overtime wages.

lembusir withers.

lembut soft, smooth. *Nasi ini terlalu –*, This rice is too soft. **ke–an** 1 softness. 2 gentleness, suppleness. **me–kan** to soften, refine. ∼ *hati* to comfort, console. – *hati* kind and gentle.

lemes see LEMAS.

lempang straight. *Barisan ini –*, This row is straight. **me–kan** to straighten. ∼ *dgn* to adjust to, co-ordinate with, bring into line with. – *hati* honest.

lémpar me– to throw, cast, toss. ∼ *peluru* to put the shot. **me–i** to pelt. *Ia ∼ andjing*, He pelted the dog. **me–kan** to throw (with). *Anak itu ∼ batu kpd djendéla*, The child threw rocks at the window. *Keritik apakah jg di–kan kepadanja?* What was the criticism that was leveled at him? **pe–** launcher, pitcher. **pe–an** 1 throw. 2 throwing. ∼ *granat disitu banjak minta korban*, The tossing of hand grenades there claimed many victims. **sepe–** *djauhnja* a stone's throw away. **–an** throwing. – *lembing* javelin throw. – *martil* hammer throw. – *peluru* shot-put. – *tjakram* discus throw.

lémpéng 1 slice. 2 plate. *se– katja* a plate of glass. 3 slab. *se– tembakau* a slab of tobacco.

lemper a croquette made of glutinous rice with meat and wrapped in a banana leaf.

lemping see LÉMPÉNG.

lempit a fold. **me–** to fold.

lempung 1 clay. 2 soft and light. *Kaju itu –*, That wood is soft and light. 3 overgentle.

léna 1 to be sound (of sleep). *Ia tidur –*, He's sound asleep. 2 absentminded. **ber–** –[2] leisurely, slowly. *Dia ∼ berdjalan kepasar*, He leisurely walks to the market. **ke–an** sleepy. **ter–** 1 to be asleep. 2 to be fascinated. *Dia ∼ dlm njanjian itu*, He's fascinated by the song.

lénan linen.

lendér mucus, phlegm.

lendir see LENDÉR.

lendung me– to have a concave shape.

lendut 1 dented. 2 bowed down (from old age). *Abu mendjadi –*, Abu was bowed down.

léngah indifferent, careless, inattentive. *Ia tidak –*, He's attentive. **ber- –²** to loiter, linger. **ke–an** negligence, indifference. **me–** to be inattentive, careless. ∼ *didjalan berbahaja*, To be careless on the road is dangerous. **me–kan** 1 to neglect, ignore. 2 to divert. **me- –²** *hati* to comfort, entertain. ∼ *waktu* to waste time. **pe–** a negligent, careless, indifferent person. **pe–an** neglect, indifference. **per- –²** *hati* diversion, entertainment. ∼ *waktu* s.t. with which to kill time. **ter–** 1 neglected, forgotten. 2 absent-minded. 3 enthralled.

lengan 1 arm. 2 sleeve. – *bawah*, – *hasta* forearm. – *pangkal* upper arm.

lengang 1 lonely, deserted. 2 quiet, slack (of business). **ke–an** 1 quietness, loneliness. 2 deserted. **me–kan** 1 to empty, clear out. 2 to give s.t. a deserted appearance.

lengar **ke–** unconscious. ∼ *mata hari* to have a sunstroke. **ter–** unconscious, senseless, stunned.

lengas 1 moist, damp, humid. 2 moisture. **ke–an** humidity. **me–** to become damp, moist. **me–kan** to moisten.

lenggak platform. **ber–** 1 to have the head raised. 2 to have a platform. **me–** to throw o's head back.

lenggang to pause for a moment. *Ia seketika – lalu katanja...* He paused for a moment, then said...

lénggang swinging, swaying. **ber–**, **me–** to swing o's hips. – *kangkung* swaying like water cress, very elegantly. – *lénggok* swinging and swaying.

lenggara **me–kan** to arrange, take care of.

lénggék floor, story. **ber- –²** to have floors, stories. **memper–kan** to pile up, arrange in layers.

lénggok sway, dancing movement. **ber–** to sway continuously. **me–** to sway continuously. **me- –²kan** *kepala* to move o's head in a swaying motion. – *lénggang* swaying with the hips.

lengit lazy.

lengkang to break, crack open.

lengkap 1 full, complete. *Tuliskanlah nama saudara jg –*, Please write down your full name. 2 equipped, ready. 3 full-fledged. *rentjana* – full-fledged plan. **ber–** to prepare, equip o.s. **ber–an** to be equipped with. **ke–an** *persediaan* dowry. **me–i** to equip, complete. **memper–i** *diri* to fit o.s. out. **me(mper)–kan** to complete, add to. **pe–** 1 conclusion of a story. ∼ *tjerita ini terbit minggu depan*, The conclusion of this story will appear next week. 2 attribute (in a compound), object. ∼ *penderita* direct

object. ∼ *penjerta* indirect object. **peng–an** equipment. **per–an** 1 supply. ∼ *djauh dari tjukup*, The supply is far from sufficient. 2 equipment, outfit. ∼² facilities. **se–** a uniform, outfit, suit of clothes. **se–nja** complete, in its entirety. – *pepak* complete.

lengkara fabulous.

léngkét **be(r)–**, **me–** to stick, cling, adhere. **me–kan** to stick. *Tjoba –kan perangko ini*, Please stick this stamp on. **pe–** glue.

lengking shrill, strident of voice. **me–** to make a shrill, strident sound.

léngkok curve, bend. **ber–** to curve, bend. **be(r)–an** a curve, bend.

lengkuas greater galingale. see LAOS.

lengkung arc, curve. **me–** curved, arched. **me–i** to surround. *daérah jg* ∼ *kota* the area surrounding the city. **me–kan** to bend. *Djangan kau–kan dahan itu*, Don't bend that branch. **–an** 1 vaulting. 2 triumphal arch. 3 arc. ∼ *bulan* crescent. ∼ *langit* curve in the sky. *djalan jg* – detour.

léngos **me–** to look away from, disregard.

léngsér to go down. *Matahari sdh –*, The sun is going down. **me–** 1 to slide, glide. 2 to smear.

lenguh **me–** 1 to pant, gasp for breath. 2 to moo, bellow.

lenguk **me–** to dream, muse.

lengung **me–** to doze, muse, daydream.

lenjah muddy.

lenjap 1 gone, vanished. *Ia – dari pandangan*, She is out of sight. 2 sound-asleep. **ke–an** disappearance. **me–kan** 1 to remove, eliminate, abolish. 2 to cause to vanish. ∼ *pilek* to get rid of a cold. **pe–an** disappearing.

lénjéh **me–** to knead.

lénong open-air folk play.

lénsa lens.

lentéra lantern, lamp, light. – *djalan* street light. – *kapal* ship's lantern. – *laut* lighthouse beacon.

lentik 1 somewhat curved. 2 elegant. **ber- –²** to crackle. **me–kan** to bend slightly.

lenting **me–** 1 sound of small metal objects hitting the floor. 2 resilient, bouncy. 3 warped.

lentjana see LANTJANA. – *djabatan* official insignia.

lentjang forming a straight line. – *kanan* forming a straight line by looking to the right (in mil. formation).

lentjing **me–** to flee.

lentjit **me–** to slip through.

lentjong me– to go astray, go wrong.
lentuk me– flexible. me–kan to bend.
∼ *léhér* to nod in respect.
lentum 1 explosion. 2 see DENTUM.
lentur 1 bend, curve. 2 deflection.
3 refraction. me– to bend. ∼ *djari*
to twiddle o's thumbs.
lépa plaster, mortar. me– to plaster.
lepas 1 free, liberated. *Burung sdh*
–, The bird is free. *Keadaan itu –*
dari bahaja, The situation is free from
danger. 2 after. – *sekolah menengah*
dia kesekolah tinggi, After high school
he's going to the university. *Ia akan*
kembali – seminggu, He'll return after
a week. 3 loose. *Ikatan itu –*, The
knot's loose. 4 apart. – *dari itu, ia*
menguraikan téorinja, Apart from
that, he explained his theory. 5 to
put down, let go. *batjaan jg takkan*
– sebelum tamat reading that can't be
put down until it's finished. 6 disregarding. – *dari saja* disregarding
me, forgetting about me. 7 finishing.
Baru sadja – lohor ia tidak bangkit²
lagi dari kursi, Having just finished
his noonday prayer, he did not get
up from his chair again. 8 released.
'p' – released *p*. ber– 1 to be loose.
2 to start. ∼ *diri* to escape, flee.
∼ *tangan* 1 to have a free hand. 2 to
work for wages only. ke–an 1 escape,
freedom, release. ∼ *tentera* demobilized. 2 holiday, leave, vacation. me–
1 to permit. 2 to discharge, separate
from, fire. ∼ *uang* to lend money
with interest. me–kan 1 to liberate,
release, free. *Ia ∼ burung dari*
sangkar, He released a bird from
its cage. 2 to fire. *Sép itu ∼ dua*
orang pegawai, The boss fired two
employees. 3 to unfasten. 4 to get
rid of. *Kita tidak dpt ∼ kesan*, We
can't get rid of the impression. ∼
bedil to shoot. ∼ *dendam* to take
revenge. ∼ *diri* to flee. ∼ *djiwa* to
die. ∼ *harapan* to abandon, give up,
hope. ∼ *hati* to give rein to o's passions. ∼ *haus* to quench o's thirst. ∼
keritik to criticize. ∼ *kesetiaan* to give
up, forswear o's allegiance. ∼ *lelah* to
(take a) rest. ∼ *nafsu* to vent o's
anger. ∼ *nazar* to carry out a promise.
∼ *niat* to carry out an intention. ∼
njawa to die. ∼ *sepatu* to remove
o's shoes. me–renggangkan to loosen.
memper–kan 1 to liberate, release.
2 to exempt. pe–, peng– *uang* moneylender. ∼ *lelah* lethargy. pe–an,
penge–an 1 discharge, dismissal. 2
anus. per–an discharge, release. se– –²
as free as possible, unhampered. ∼
mata memandang as far as the eye
can see. –an former, ex-. *Ia ∼ pra-*

djurit, He's an ex-soldier. ∼ *menteri*
ex-minister. ∼ *sekolah tinggi* alumnus,
alumna. *Ia menjetir – tangan*, She
drives with her hands off the wheel.
– *béa* duty-free. – *malu* circumcised.
lepat sticky rice wrapped in banana
leaves.
lepau food stall.
lépék 1 soaking-wet. 2 saucer.
lepér flat, shallow.
lépot ber–an smeared all over, soiled.
me–i to smear, soil.
lépra leprosy.
lepuh a blister. me– to (get a) blister.
me–kan to cause blisters.
lepuk see LAPUK.
lerai see LARAI.
lerak broken-down, crushed. me–
(kan) to break down, crush.
lérang strip, width of cloth. –² a
stretcher, litter.
léréng 1 slope, incline. 2 design of
cloth. me– to slope, incline. –an slope.
–² wheels of a bed, table, etc. – *gunung*
mountain slope.
lérét row, series. *Disini ada dua –*
bunga²an, Here are 2 rows of flowers.
ber– to be in a row. me–kan to
arrange in a row. –an row, series.
lerum booming sound of guns.
lés 1 lesson. 2 list. 3 picture frame.
4 reins. – *hitam* black list.
lesat me– to fly away.
lesau rustling noise.
lésbril reading glasses.
léset to slip away.
lesit me– 1 to rustle (of noise). 2
to spout, squirt, gush. ∼ *hidung* to
blow o's nose with o's fingers.
lestari 1 eternal, everlasting. 2 continuing. me–kan to make s.t. unchanging, everlasting.
lésterik see LIST(E)RIK.
lesu 1 weak from lack of food or
sleep. 2 sluggish. *Perdagangan –*,
Business is slow. ke–an 1 weakness.
2 apathy. me–kan tiring, wearying,
exhausting.
lesung rice mortar. – *pinang* areca-
nut crusher. – *pipi* dimple in cheeks.
lesut a swishing sound.
leta 1 base, shameful, contemptible.
2 crippled. me–kan to despise.
létai weak, exhausted.
letak 1 location, place. – *tempat itu*
tidak djauh dari sini, The location
of the place isn't far from here. 2 to
be located, lie. –*nja dimana?* Where
is it located? 3 to fit (of clothing).
4 situation. *Bagaimana –nja hal itu?*
What's the situation regarding the
matter? me–kan to put, place. ∼
djabatan to resign. ∼ *sendjata* to lay
down o's arms. pe–an *pekerdjaan*

work stoppage. **per–an** laying down of s.t. ∼ *batu pertama* laying of the cornerstone. ∼ *sendjata* armistice, truce. **ter–** 1 to be, be located. *Buku* ∼ *dilemari,* The book is in the cupboard. 2 to be placed, located. *Kesalahan* ∼ *dimana?* Where does the fault lie? *Hak mengambil keputusan tidak* ∼ *kpd saja,* The right to make a decision is not mine. – *lintang* diagonal position.

létak exhausted, weary. – *lelai* completely exhausted from hunger, sleeplessness, etc.

létda [*létnan muda*] 1 warrant officer. 2 second lieutenant.

létdjén [*létnan djéndral*] lieutenant general.

létenan see LÉTNAN.

létér type, font. **be–, me–** to chatter, rattle. **pe–** a chatterbox.

letih tired, weary, worn-out. **ke–an** 1 weariness, exhaustion. 2 overly tired. *Dia tidur sebab* ∼ , She fell asleep because she was overly tired. ∼ *otot* muscle fatigue. **me–kan** 1 to exhaust. *Pekerdjaan itu* ∼ *badan,* That work exhausts the body. 2 exhausting, tiring. – *lesu* completely exhausted.

letik see DETIK. **me–** to snap, crack, break (of glass from hot water).

letjah soaked, muddy. **ter–** 1 to get o's reputation soiled. 2 to stumble into the mud.

létjak muddy, soaked ground.

létjéh 1 sticky. *Bubur manis itu* –, The porridge is sticky. 2 untidy, unkempt. *Pakaiannja selalu* –, He's always sloppy in his dress. 3 worthless. *Saja punja buku jg* –, I have a worthless book. 4 depraved. – *budinja,* His morals are depraved. **me–** to fawn upon, flatter. *Dia pandai* ∼ , He's clever at fawning. **me–kan** to insult, despise. **pe–** flatterer.

letjek disheveled, unkempt.

létjét 1 chafed. *Kakinja – kena sepatu baru,* Her feet are chafed from the new shoes. 2 damp.

letjit me– to slip away. –² button which o. presses, a snap fastener.

letjur a blister. **me–** to blister.

letjut me– 1 to whip. *Djangan* ∼ *andjing,* Don't whip a dog. 2 to slip, get away. **me–kan** 1 to whip, apply, give the whip. *Tjambuk di–kan pd kuda,* The whip was applied to the horse. 2 to squeeze out. – *tjambuk* a whip.

létkol [*létnan–kolonél*] lieutenant colonel.

létnan 1 lieutenant. 2 lieutenant (junior grade) in Navy. – *I* first lieutenant. – *II* second lieutenant. – *djénderal* lieutenant general. – *dua zeni* second lieutenant in army engineers. – *kolonél* 1 lieutenant colonel. 2 commander (Navy). – *kolonél udara* lieutenant colonel (Air Force). – *muda* ensign. – *muda udara I* chief warrant officer (Air Force). – *muda udara II* warrant officer (Air Force). – *udara I* first lieutenant (Air Force). – *udara II* second lieutenant (Air Force).

letup me– to explode. *Balon itu* ∼ , The balloon exploded. **–an** explosion.

letus detonation, report of explosion. **me–** 1 to explode. 2 to break out, erupt (of a war, quarrel). 3 to erupt. *Gunung berapi* ∼ , The volcano erupted. **(pe)–an** explosion, eruption.

léver me– to supply (goods).

léveransir supplier.

léwat 1 via, through, by way of. *Saja kesekolah – Djalan Musi,* I go to school via Musi Street. *Kami pergi ke Bandung – Puntjak,* We go to Bandung via the Puntjak. 2 beyond, past. *Sekarang pukul 5 – seperempat,* Now it's a quarter past five. 3 past, over. *Waktu beristirahat sdh* –, The intermission is over. **ke–(an)** 1 too, excessive. 2 very, exceedingly. ∼ *besar* very big. **me–i** 1 to surpass, exceed. *Kepandaiannja* ∼ *kawan²nja,* His intelligence surpasses that of his friends. 2 to pass by. *Malam² kami sering* ∼ *kuburan,* We often pass a cemetery in the evenings. 3 to step over. *Tidak baik* ∼ *orang tidur,* It isn't nice to step over a sleeping person. **me–kan** 1 to pass by with s.t. *Pedagang²* ∼ *dagangan didepan rumah²,* The peddlers pass by the houses with their wares. 2 to pass up. *satu kesempatan jg tidak boléh di–kan* an opportunity which can't be passed up. **ter–** 1 very, exceedingly, too. *Rumah itu* ∼ *bagus,* That house is very beautiful. 2 overcome, conquered. *Kesukaran sdh* ∼ , The difficulties have been overcome. – *lembajung* ultraviolet. – *mérah* infrared. – *témponja* to expire.

lezat see LAZAT.

lh [*lihat*] see.

lho see LO.

liang 1 hole. 2 cavity, passage. **ber–renik** porous. – *hidung* nostril. – *kubur* grave. – *liuk* swaying like a drunken person. – *mata* eye socket. – *peranakan* vagina. – *renik, – roma* pore. – *telinga* auditory canal.

liar 1 wild, primitive. *Disini ada banjak binatang* –, There are many wild beasts here. 2 illegal, outlawed.

sekolah – illegal school. *barisan* – irregular troops. **berke–an** to lounge about. *Dikota banjak perampok* ~ , There are a lot of bandits hanging about in the city.

liat 1 pliable, plastic. 2 tough. *Saja suka daging jg* –, I like tough meat. 3 tough, unbeatable. *Ia djagoan jg* –, He's an unbeatable champion. 4 see LIHAT. **me**– 1 to become pliable. 2 to become tough. – *liut* winding, meandering (of a river).

libat me–(kan) 1 to bandage, wrap up. *Luka itu di– baik²*, The wound was carefully bandaged. 2 to involve. *Perang akan* ~ *semua negeri*, War will involve all countries. **ter**– 1 bandaged, wrapped up. *Bagian jg sakit sdh* ~ , The sore part has been bandaged. 2 involved. *Nanti engkau* ~ *dlm perkara itu djuga*, You may get involved in that affair too.

libur ber– 1 to be on vacation, leave. 2 to go on vacation, leave. *Tuan* ~ *kemana?* Where did you go on vacation? **–an** 1 holiday, vacation. 2 free time.

lidah 1 tongue. 2 speech, pronunciation. – *api* lead flint. – *bertjabang* two-faced. – *buaja* plant from the leaves of which a hair shampoo is made. – *keling* untrustworthy. *Ia mempunjai* – *keling*, He was not to be trusted. – *ombak* roller (of waves). – *tergalang* tongue-tied. – *tidak bertulang* o. who makes and breaks promises easily.

lidas itching, sore (esp. around mouth and tongue).

lidi palm leaf rib.

lift elevator.

liga league. – *Arab* Arab League.

ligas an ambling gait.

ligat active, in action. **me**– to spin a top.

lih [*lihat*] see.

lihai 1 shrewd, cunning. *pemimpin jg* – a shrewd, cunning leader. 2 terrific, tremendous. *Dia* – , He's terrific. **ke–an** savvy, ability. *Karena* ~ *kanan dalam itu kes. Rembang menang*, Because of the savvy of the inside right the Rembang soccer team won.

lihat ber- –²an to see e.o. **ke–an** 1 visible. *Rumahnja* ~ *dari sini*, His house is visible from here. 2 to look like, look as though, appear. *Dia* ~*nja sedih*, He looks sad. **me**– 1 to see, observe. *Orang jg* ~ *pilm tidak sedikit*, Quite a few people are seeing the movie. *Saja* ~*nja*, I saw him. 2 to sight. ~ *nudjum* to consult the stars. **me**– –² to look around a store,

shop, browse. **me–i** 1 to look at. 2 to inspect, scrutinize. *–i baik² sebelum bertjakap*, Inspect carefully before you say anything. 3 to see, visit. *Saja* ~ *teman dirumah sakit*, I saw a friend at the hospital. **me–kan** 1 to see, look at. 2 to show. **memper–kan** to show, display. *Kartjis harus diperkan sebelum masuk*, Tickets must be shown before entering. **pe(ng)**– 1 viewer, observer. 2 sense of vision. 3 seeing, sight. **peng–an** 1 sight, vision. 2 perception. 3 point of view. – **-me**– 1 to look at e.o. 2 to visit e.o.

lihay see LIHAI.

likas me– to wind, reel in. **–an** reel.

likat 1 adhesive, sticky. 2 embarrassed. **pe**– 1 adhesive. 2 k.o. woven cloth for men's wear. *bukat* – thick, muddy, troubled.

liku 1 curve, bend. – *djalan* curve in the road. 2 coil. **ber- –²** 1 winding, curving (of a road). 2 devious. – *lekuk djalan tjeritera* plot of a story.

likur se– 21. *tiga* – 23. **–an** 1 21 to 29. 2 card game (21).

likwida liquid (phon.).

likwidasi liquidation. **me**–to liquidate.

likwidir me– to liquidate.

lilin 1 candle. *Ia memasang* –, He lit up a candle. 2 wax. *Ia membatik dgn* –, She did batik work with wax.

lilit ber– to twist, wind. **me**– to wind around. *Ular* ~ *dahan kaju*, The snake wound around the tree branch. **me–kan** to wind s.t. *Benang dikannja baik²*, She winds the thread carefully. **se**– circumference.

lim glue. **menge**– to glue, paste on.

lima 5. – *belas* 15. – *puluh* 50. **–an** a 5-rupiah note, a five.

limas 1 pyramid. 2 dipper or cup made of young palm leaves for offerings, drinks, or bathing.

limau citrus fruit. – *manis* orange. – *purut* a citrus fruit and its tree. – *sundai* lime.

limbah (pe)–an garbage dump.

limbang me– 1 to loiter. 2 to wash (gold).

limbat see IKAN.

limbung 1 inner harbor. 2 dock.

limon see LIMUN.

limpa 1 spleen. 2 liver. – *ketjil* spleen.

limpah 1 superfluous. 2 abundant. 3 affluent. 4 profuse. 5 abundance. **ber- –²** in abundance. **ke–an** 1 luxury, abundance. 2 superfluity. **me**– 1 to be superfluous. 2 to overflow. *Kali itu selalu* ~ , The river is always overflowing. **me–i** to flood. *Negeri itu* ~ *Indonésia dgn ber-matjam² barang*, That country flooded Indonesia with a variety of goods. **me–kan**

1 to give abundantly. *Orang tua itu ~ anaknja dgn keméwahan,* The old man showered his child with luxury. 2 to bestow. **-an** gift, grant. *~ darah didalam otak* cerebral hemorrhage. *– méwah* luxury. *– ruah* chockful.

limpit layer. **memper-kan** to fold.

limun a bottled soft drink. **-an** invisibility. *– sekuas* lemon squash.

linang ber-(-) to trickle, flow. *Air matanja ~* , His tears flowed.

lindang to disappear. **me-kan** to run through. *Hartanja tlh di-kannja semuanja,* He ran through all his possessions.

lindap me- 1 to fade. 2 to become overcast.

lindas ke- knocked down, run over. **me-** 1 to crush. *Siapa jg ~ tjabé?* Who is crushing the red pepper? 2 to run over. *Oto itu ~ kutjing,* The car ran over a cat. **pe-** mortar.

lindes see LINDAS.

lindih me- to press firmly, crush. *Lantai tanah itu di-,* The earthen floor was pressed firmly.

lindis me- to crush. *Siapa menindas akan ter-* , Whoever oppresses will be crushed.

lindu earthquake.

lindung ber- to take shelter. *Meréka ~ dibawah pohon waktu hudjan,* They took shelter under a tree during the rain. **ke-an** sheltered. **me-** to protect, shelter. *Pajung ~ thd matahari,* An umbrella protects o. against sunlight. **me-i** to protect, give shelter. *Pohon itu ~ kamar ini dari panas,* That tree protects the room from the heat. *Hak pengarang di-i oléh undang²,* The author's rights are protected by law. **me-kan** to protect, safeguard. **memper-kan** to protect, take care of. *Perkumpulan itu ~ anak² jatim,* That association takes care of orphans. **pe-** 1 protector, patron. 2 supervisor. **per-an** 1 protection. 2 sponsorship, patronship. 3 shelter. **ter-** protected, sheltered. *Semua ~ dari bahaja,* Everyone is protected against danger.

lindur sleepwalking, talking in o's sleep. **menge-** to sleepwalk.

lingar me- restless, bewildered.

lingga 1 sign. 2 monument, statue. 3 male sex organ.

linggam red lead.

linggi bow of a ship.

linggis crowbar (used for digging). **me-** to separate with a crowbar.

lingkar 1 circle. 2 bend, coil. *Ular mengolak -nja,* The snake unwinds its coil. 3 circumference. **ber-**, **me-** to coil. **me-i** to encircle, surround. *Pagar ~ rumah kami,* A fence sur-

rounds our house. **-an** 1 circle. *Tjoba gambarkan ~* , Please draw a circle. 2 perimeter. 3 area. *~ roda* rim of a wheel. *~ kutub selatan* Antarctic Circle. *~ kutub utara* Arctic Circle.

lingkung 1 circle. 2 perimeter, circumference. **me-i** to surround, encircle. *Banjak pohon ~ rumah kami,* Many trees surround our house. **se-** around, surrounding. *Kami berdjalan ~ kota,* We walked around town. **-an** 1 circle, area. *Kabar itu dari ~ jg mengetahui,* The news is from wellinformed circles. 2 environment, sphere, domain. *~ hajat* biological environment. *~ Kemakmuran Bersama di Asia Raya* Greater Asia Co-prosperity Sphere. *~ waktu* time zone.

lingkup closed, folded. **me-i** to cover, include. *Pembitjaraan itu ~ apa sadja?* Just what do the discussions cover?

linglung 1 stunned, dazed. 2 absentminded. **me-** 1 stunning, dazzling. 2 confusing. **me-kan** to confuse.

lingsir to go down (of the sun, moon). **me-kan** to unroll, let down (sleeves, etc.).

lintah leech. *– darat* usurer.

lintang across, wide. *Kamar ini -nja 4 méter,* This room is 4 meters across. **me-** 1 to lie athwart, be in the way. *Korsi ~ dimuka pintu,* A chair is blocking the doorway. 2 to hinder, be in the way. *Saja akan datang kalau tidak ada halangan ~* , I shall come if there is nothing to hinder me. **me-i** 1 to obstruct, cross s.o. 2 to protest against, object to. *Tidak baik ~ naséhat orang tua,* It's not good to object to the advice of o's parents. **me-kan** to place s.t. diagonally. **ter-** hampered, hindered. **-an** hindrance, obstacle. *~ budjur* diagonal. *~ kedak* crisscross. *~ pukang* head over heels. *– pukang* crisscross. *– utara* north latitude.

lintas ke-an past, beaten, defeated. **me-** 1 to pass by fast. 2 to take a short cut. *Mari djalan ~ sadja!* Let's take the short cut! **me-i** 1 to rush past, pass in a hurry. 2 to overcome. *Semua kesukaran sdh ~ di-i,* All difficulties have been overcome. 3 to exceed. **per-an** 1 transition. 2 transfer. **se-** *lalu* at a glance. **ter-** 1 to cross o's mind, flash through o's mind, occur to o. *Baru ~ dipikiran saja soré ini,* It flashed through my mind just this afternoon. 2 passed. **-an** flash, trace. *~ tjahaja ditempat gelap* a flash of light in a dark place.

lintjah 1 energetic, lively, active. *Gadis itu –*, That girl is energetic. 2 unstable. *Dlm pekerdjaannja dia –*, He's unstable in his work. 3 easy, smooth. *Ia – dlm pergaulan*, He's smooth in social intercourse. **ke–an** 1 liveliness. 2 smoothness. **me– –²** to be fickle, jump from o. thing to another.

lintjir 1 smooth, slippery. 2 fluent. *pidato –* a fluent speech. **me–kan** to slide over. *– mulut* glib of tongue.

lintuh weak, soft.

linu 1 smarting, shooting pains (of teeth, nerves, etc.). 2 rheumatic pains.

liontin medallion, locket, pendant.

lipan centipede. *– sama kala* when Greek meets Greek.

lipas cockroach.

lipat fold, crease. **ber–** folded, pleated. *~ ganda* multiple. **ke–an** multiple. *~ persekutuan terketjil* least common multiple. **me–** to fold. *Djangan –*, Do not fold. **me–gandakan** to multiply. **me–kan** to fold, crease. **memper– (gandakan)** *hasil bumi* to increase the farm yield. **pe–an** 1 fold. 2 multiplication. **pe–** *lutut* hollow of the knee. **pe–gandaan** multiplication. **–an** 1 fold, crease. 2 a pack (of playing cards). *– empat* fourfold. *– ganda* multiple, manifold. *– paha* groin.

lipit **me–** to hem. **pe–** a hem.

liplap 1 derisive name for Eurasians. 2 layers of various colors.

lipur consolation, comfort. **me–** to comfort, console, entertain. **peng–hati**, *~ lara* 1 comfort. 2 entertainment, diversion, recreation.

liput **me–i** 1 to cover, envelop, wrap. *Awan ~ puntjak gunung*, The clouds cover the mountain peak. *Suasana sedih ~ rumah itu*, A sad situation envelops that house. 2 to govern, control. 3 to overwhelm.

lirik **me–** 1 to glance at stealthily, peep at. 2 to pierce, perforate, bore through. **se–** at a glance. **–an** *mata* sidelong glance.

lisah to be restless, toss and turn. see GELISAH.

lisan 1 tongue. *Ia lulus udjian –*, She passed the oral examination. 2 speech, language. *Saja suka bahasa –*, I like the colloquial language. **me–kan** to utter, recite. *dgn –* oral.

lisénsi license, permit.

lisong cigar.

list(e)rik 1 electricity. 2 electric. **ke–an** electricity. **pe–an** 1 electrification. 2 electrical department.

lisut 1 wilted, faded, withered. 2 exhausted.

litak see LÉTAK.

liter(an) liter (measure).

litjak flat, level.

litjik 1 sly, cunning. 2 cowardly. **ke–an** 1 cunning, slyness. 2 cowardice. 3 trickery.

litjin 1 slippery, slick. *diwaktu hudjan djalan –* slippery when wet. 2 cunning, sly, slick. 3 nothing left. *Rumah itu – sesudah perampokan*, Nothing was left after the robbery. **ke–an** 1 smoothness. 2 slipperiness. 3 cunning, slyness. **me–kan** to make smooth, make slippery. **me(ng)–** to press clothes. *– letjat, – litjau* very slippery. *– tandas* completely finished.

litup covered completely.

liuk **me–** to bend, bow. **me–i** to stoop to pick up s.t. *Anak itu ~ permainannja dilantai*, The child bent over to pick up his toy from the floor. **me–kan** to dodge a blow by leaning to one side. **sepe–** *djauhnja* as far as o. can reach by bending over. **ter–(–)** bent over. *Tjabang² pohon itu ~ ,* The branches are bent over. *– lampai* to wind, weave, move continuously as in dancing.

liur 1 saliva. 2 phlegm. **be(r)–** to drool. **me–** to drool. *Masakan itu menimbulkan air – saja*, The cooking makes my mouth water.

liut leathery.

liwat see LÉWAT.

l.k. *[lebih kurang]* approximately, ca.

Lk *[Létnan-Kolonél]* lieutenant colonel.

L.N. 1 *[Luar Negeri]* abroad, foreign. 2 *[Lembaran Negara]* statutes.

lo (interjection expressing surprise, astonishment). *–! Kapan datang disini?* When did you get here?

loa(k) 1 garbage can. 2 used articles.

loba greedy, selfish. **ke–an** greed. **ke–tamakan** greed, greediness. **me–kan** to covet s.t.

lobak 1 radish. 2 cabbage. *– mérah* red radish.

lobang see LUBANG. *– perlindungan* a shelter.

lodan whale.

lodéh soup of vegetables and coconut milk.

lodoh overripe (of fruits).

lodong a large bamboo tube.

logam metal. *– mulia* precious metal. *– tjampur* alloy. *– tua* scrap metal.

logaritma logarithm.

logat 1 vocabulary, dictionary. 2 accent, dialect. **ber–** *Djawa* to have a Javanese accent.

logika logic.

logis logical.

loh 1 writing tablet. 2 blackboard.

lohor 1 see SEMBAHJANG. 2 prayer from 11:50 A.M. to 2:30 P.M.

loja 1 exhausted. 2 disgusted. 3 sick.

lojang 1 brass. 2 baking dishes.

lojo 1 disgusted. 2 sickened. – *perut saja melihat makanan sebanjak itu*, I feel sickened at seeing so much food. see LOJA.

lojong me– to stagger.

lojor to saunter, lounge, loaf. ke–an to saunter.

lokal local.

lokalisir me– to localize.

lokasi location.

lokék 1 stingy. 2 miserly.

lokét ticket window.

loki Chinese prostitute.

lokio chives.

loko(motip) locomotive.

lokos bare, shorn.

lolah see KELOLA.

loléng Chinese paper lantern.

lolong me– to howl, yelp. *Andjing ~ kpd bulan sepandjang malam*, The dog howled at the moon all night long. ter– –^{2} to howl continuously.

lolos to slip off, bolt away. *Andjing kami – dari ikatan*, Our dog slipped off his leash. me–kan to release. ~ *diri* to flee, escape. *Pentjuri itu ~ diri dari pendjara*, The thief escaped from prison.

lomba a race, contest. ber–(–an), me– to race, compete in a race. pe– 1 contestant, competitor. 2 athlete. per–an 1 contest, race. 2 race track. ~ *beranting* relay race.

lombok red pepper. – *rawit* chili pepper.

lombong mine, crater. me– to dig, mine. – *batu bara* coal mine. – *gunung berapi* volcanic crater.

lompat a leap, jump. ber–an to jump in turn or jointly. *Kodok ~ disawah*, The frogs are hopping in the wet rice field. ber– –^{2} to jump, leap. me– to leap, jump. me–i 1 to jump over. *Djangan ~ pagar*, Don't jump over the fence. 2 to jump at, spring at. *Kutjing ~ tikus*, The cat sprang at the mouse. me–kan to let jump. me– –^{2} to hop up and down. pe– jumper. pe–an a jump, leap. ter– to jump out accidentally. – *djauh* broad jump. – *galah* pole vault. – *sehari* every other day. – *tinggi* high jump. *sekali – sampai kesitu* to get there in one jump.

lompong me– wide-open, full of gaps, empty. – *sagu* cookies made of sago flour and bananas.

londjak ber–kan to leap. ~ *karena kegirangan* to leap with joy. me– to jump up. *Dia ~ memetik mangga*,

He jumps up to pick a mango. me– –^{2} to leap, skip. *Dia ~ kegirangan*, She leaps with joy. ter– to jump up unexpectedly. *Dia ~ dari berbaring*, She suddenly jumped up from lying down.

londjong tapering, pointed.

londjor 1 used with soap. se– *sabun* a cake of soap. 2 see LUNDJUR. –an *kaju* timber.

lonéng me– to loaf, sit idle.

longgar 1 loose. *Ikatan itu sdh –*, The bundle is loose. *Aturan itu –*, The regulation is not so binding. 2 spacious, roomy. ke–an 1 allowance. ~ *pembajaran séwa rumah diberikan*, Allowances for the rent are given. 2 alleviation. 3 opportunity, scope, room, play. me–i 1 to loosen, slacken. 2 to make room for. me–kan to mitigate. *Untung benar waktu utk pekerdjaan itu di–kan*, Fortunately more time has been given to complete the work. memper– to mitigate, alleviate.

longgok heap, pile. – *sampah* trash heap. – *pasir* sand pile. ber–(–) piled, heaped up. *Buah²an ~ didjual orang dipasar*, Fruits are piled up for sale at the market. me–kan to pile, heap up, stack up. *Djangan kau–kan barang² itu disitu*, Don't stack the things up there. –an 1 pile, stack, heap. 2 garbage heap. 3 ore deposits.

longgor 1 to grow fast. *Anak ini – benar*, This child is really growing fast. 2 robust, strapping boy or girl.

longo me– bewildered, blank. ~ *dia melihat pertundjukan itu*, Bewilderedly he watched the show.

longok me– to stare, be in a fog.

longong me– to be astonished, completely taken in.

longsor to slide down. *tanah –* earth that has moved, as in a landslide. –an landslide.

lontar 1 palmyra palm the leaves of which are used as papyrus. 2 throwing s.t. ber–an to throw at e.o. *Anak ~ batu*, The children were throwing stones at e.o. me–(kan) to throw s.t. ~ *batu keandjing* to throw a stone at a dog. me–(i) to hurl at s.o. or s.t. pe– thrower, hurler. sepe(r)–an a throw. ~ *batu* at a stone's throw.

lonté prostitute.

lontjat me– to hop, jump around. –an 1 leap, jump, hop. 2 antics. *batu ~* jumping board. – *djauh* broad jump. – *galah* pole vault.

lontjéng 1 bell, chime. 2 clock. me– to ring the bell, play the chimes, strike (of the clock).

lontjér loose. *Sekerup –*, A screw is loose. me– to be loose.

lontjo me–(–) to loaf, loiter, roam aimlessly.

lontjor pointed.

lontok plump, squat.

lontong a package of cooked rice wrapped in a banana leaf.

lopak puddle, pool. –² woven container for tobacco.

lor north.

lorék stripe. **ber–** striped. see LURIK.

loréng stripe. **ber–(–)** striped.

lorong path, lane.

lorot me– 1 to decline, sink, become lower. *Harga sajuran* ~ , The price of vegetables is declining. 2 to deteriorate. **me–kan** to lower. *Banjak pedagang* ~ *harga barang²nja*, Many merchants are lowering the prices of their merchandise.

los 1 shed. 2 pilot (of a ship).

losin see LUSIN.

losmén inn, hotel. – *remadja* youth hostel.

loték spicy salad of raw vegetables, similar to *gado-gado*. The peanut butter sauce is mixed in prior to serving.

loténg 1 attic, top floor. 2 story. **ber–** storied. *rumah* ~ a house with more than one floor.

loteré lottery. **me–kan** to draw lots.

lotjok me– 1 to move up and down. 2 to masturbate. **pe–** piston rod.

lotjot see LUTJUT.

lotok me– easy to separate the fruit from the stone.

lotot open, staring (of eyes). **me–** to stare.

lowak see LOAK.

lowong unfilled, vacant, empty. *Pekerdjaan jg – tidak ada disini*, There's no vacancy here. *Ini mengisi jg –*, This fills a gap. **–an** 1 vacancy, opening. 2 gap, vacuum. *Itu mengisi* ~ , That fills a gap.

lt [*létnan*] lieutenant.

ltd [*létnan dua*] second lieutenant.

lts [*létnan satu*] first lieutenant.

ltt [*létnan tjadangan*] lieutenant in the reserves.

lu you (rude). – *djahat!* You're bad!

luah me– sickening.

luak 1 k.o. wildcat. 2 district in Minangkabau. 3 see LOAK. **me–** to shrink, decrease.

luang empty, vacant, free. *Saja datang pd hari jg –*, I'm coming on a free day. **berke–an** to have the time. *Kami tidak* ~ *berkundjung*, We don't have the time to pay a visit. **ke–an** 1 opportunity. 2 time. **me–kan** 1 to vacate, make space for. 2 to make time for. *Saja akan tjoba* ~ *waktu*, I'll try to find time for it.

pe– 1 opportunity. *Berikan saja* ~ , Give me an opportunity. 2 calm, tranquil. *Ini musim* ~ , This is a calm (windless) season. **ter–** empty, free, spare. *Saja akan datang kalau ada waktu* ~ , I'll come if I have the spare time. *waktu* – spare time.

luap me– 1 to overflow. *Sungai Tjitarum* ~ , The Tjitarum River overflowed. 2 to boil over. *Air* ~ *dari pantji*, The water is boiling over in the pan. 3 to flare up. *Semangatnja* ~ , His spirit flared up. **me–** –² to boil over, flare up. **me–i** to overflow. **me–kan** 1 to cause to overflow. *Hudjan lebat* ~ *sungai²*, The severe storm will make the rivers overflow. 2 to cause to boil over. *Api sebesar itu* ~ *air*, A fire that large will make the water boil over. **–an** bubbling over. ~ *semangat* a superabundance of spirit.

luar outer part, outside. **di–** outside. *Ia tinggal* ~ , He's standing outside. *Hal itu* ~ *urusan saja*, That matter is no concern of mine. **ke–** 1 to go out. *Ia* ~ *dari gedung itu*, He went out of that building. 2 see KELUAR. 3 to appear, emerge. ~ *rél* derailed. **ke–an** 1 product, graduate. *Dia* ~ *sekolah guru*, He's a teachers' college graduate. 2 issue, edition. *Buku ini* ~ *penerbit mana?* Whose publication is this book? 3 product, make. 4 exodus. **ke–biasaan** peculiarity. **me–** 1 to go outside. 2 to exceed. ~ *batas kemanusiaan* to exceed human limits. **menge–kan** 1 to take outside. 2 to issue, publish. 3 to utter, express. *Ia* ~ *banjak perkataan*, He uttered many words. 4 to spend, expend. 5 to export. 6 to exclude. 7 to dismiss. 8 to expel, fire, discharge s.o. **penge–an** 1 expenditure. 2 edition. 3 export. 4 expenditure, expenses. 5 release. ~ *tawanan* release of internees. **–an** graduate (of a school). – *batas* to be out of bounds, off limits. – *biasa* extraordinary. – *dalam* inwardly and outwardly. – *dugaan* beyond expectations. – *kepala* by heart. – *negeri* abroad. *Kementerian – Negeri* Ministry of External Affairs (Department of State, Ministry of Foreign Affairs). – *rentjana* unintended, unscheduled.

luas 1 wide, broad, extensive, vast. *Pekarangan itu –nja 300 m²*, The yard is 300 square meters. 2 broad (-minded). 3 area, extent. **ke–an** 1 extent, breadth. 2 area. 3 opportunity, leeway. 4 spaciousness. **me–** to spread, extend. *Penjakit itu* ~ *ke-mana²*, The disease spread every-

where. **me(mper)-(kan)** to expand,
extend, broaden. *Ia ~ pengalamannja*,
He broadened his experience. **pe-an,
peng-an** expansion. **per-an** expansion, extension. – *lingkungan* scope.

lubang 1 hole. 2 cavity, hollow. 3
perforation. **ber-** perforated. **me-i**
to dig a hole, burrow. 2 to pierce,
perforate (the ears, etc.). **pe-an** hole
for trapping animals. – *air* waterpipe.
– *batu bara* coal mine. – *djarum* eye
of the needle. – *hawa* ventilator,
airway. – *hidung* nostril. – *kantjing*
buttonhole. – *kepundan* crater. –
kulit skin pore. – *perlindungan* a
shelter. – *tali* eyelet.

lubér 1 to desert to the enemy.
2 to overflow.

lubuk 1 water hole. 2 deep. – *akal,
lautan ilmu* a great amount of knowledge. – *hati* subconscious.

ludah saliva, spittle. **ber, me-** to spit.
me-i 1 to spit at. 2 to spit on.
Djangan ~ ubin, Don't spit on the
floor. **me-kan** to spit out. **pe-an**
spittoon. – *sirih* betel-nut spittle.

ludes 1 crushed, shattered. 2 all gone.

lugu natural(ly).

luh see LOH.

luhur noble, glorious, sublime. *Ini
tjita² jg -*, These are noble ideals.
ke-an 1 glory, grandeur. 2 solemnity. **me-kan** to exalt, glorify. *Kami
mesti ~ nusa dan bangsa*, We must
glorify our country and nation.

luik **me-** to drip, trickle.

luju drooping.

luka 1 injury, wound. *Saja ada –
dikaki*, I have a leg injury. 2 hurt,
wounded. *Siapa jg -?* Who's wounded?
me-i to hurt, injure. *Ia ~ hatinja*,
She hurt his feelings. **me-kan** to
hurt, injure s.o. – *bakar* a burn. –
hati wounded, insulted. – *létjét* to
gall, chafe. – *memar* bruise, contusion.
– *parah* seriously injured. – *sipi* flesh
wound. – *telak* slash wound. – *tikam*
stab wound.

lukah fish trap.

lukis **me-** 1 to paint, draw, depict.
Dia pandai ~ , He knows how to
paint. 2 to do a role. **me-i** to paint,
draw. *Dinding di-i djuga*, The wall
was painted too. **me-kan** to paint,
portray, render. *Dia pandai benar ~
apa jg dilihatnja*, He's very good at
depicting what he sees. **pe-** painter,
artist. **pe-an** painting, portrayal. **-an**
1 painting, drawing, portrayal. 2
diagram, design.

luku plow. **me-** to plow.

luli spinning reel, spool. **me-** to wind
thread on a spool or bobbin.

lulu **me-** merely, exclusively. *~ utk
dinas* for official use only.

luluh **me-kan** 1 to pulverize, shatter.
2 to melt, dissolve. – *lantak* smashed,
shattered. **pe-an** assimilation. *seutas
unsur² pembédaan jg* – a bundle of
simultaneous distinctive features.

luluk mud. **ber-** muddy.

lulum **me-** to chew on, suck on.
Anak itu ~ gula², The child sucks
on a piece of candy.

lulur **me-** to swallow. – *dalam* fillet.

lulus 1 to slip through, pass
(through). *Murid itu – udjian*, The
pupil passed the examination. 2 permitted, allowed. **ke-an** abortion, miscarriage. **me-i** to take o's clothes off.
me-kan 1 to permit, allow, grant.
Ia ~ permintaan, He granted the
request. 2 to yield. *Ia tak ~ permohonan saja*, He didn't yield to my
pleas. *~ diri* to flee. **-an** 1 graduate
(of a school). 2 graduation. – *air*
permeable.

lulut **ber-** to have a massage. **me-** to
massage. **pe-** 1 masseur. 2 liniment.

lumajan 1 reasonable, moderate. 2
pretty fair, not inconsiderable. *djumlah jg* – a pretty fair amount.

lumang **ber-** soiled. **me-kan** to soil,
stain.

lumar soiled, dirty. **me-(i)** to soil s.t.

lumas **me-i** to coat, cover. **pe-an**
lubrication.

lumat 1 fine powder. 2 pulverized.
me-kan to pulverize.

lumba see LOMBA. **-²** porpoise.

lumbung rice barn, rice granary. –
désa rice barn for the whole village.

lumér fluid, melted.

lumpang 1 mortar. 2 wooden bowl
for pounding rice.

lumpia Chinese pastry filled with
meat or fish and vegetables.

lumpuh paralyzed. **ke-an** paralysis.
me-kan to paralyze. *Kekurangan
sendjata ~ kekuatan tentara*, A shortage of arms paralyzed the army.
penjakit – 1 paralysis. 2 polio(myelitis).

lumpur mud. **pe-an** mudhole. – *ketam*
mud on the shore, bank.

lumrah normal, customary, general,
usual.

lumur **ber-(an)** soiled, stained. *Lantai itu ~ darah*, The floor was stained
with blood. **me-kan** to soil, stain,
smear. **-an** stain.

lumut 1 moss. 2 mildew. **ber-an** 1
moss-covered. 2 mildewed. – *karang*
sponge.

lunak 1 soft. *Ia suka makanan -*,
She likes soft food. 2 gentle, mod-

erate, meek. *Pendiriannja –*, His
stand is a moderate one. **me–** to become soft, to soften. **me–kan** to
soften, weaken. ~ *hati* to comfort
s.o. **memper–** to soften s.t.
lunas 1 keel of a ship. 2 paid.
Utangnja sdh –, His debt has been
paid. **me–i, me–kan** to pay, settle.
*Segala utang harus di–kan sebelum
habis bulan,* All debts must be paid
before the end of the month. **pe–an**
paying off, discharging of a debt.
lundjur stretched out. **be–** with legs
stretched out. **me–kan** to stretch out.
Ia ~ kaki, He stretched out his legs.
lungkup see TELUNGKUP.
lungsin warp.
lungsur **me–** to slide down, get away.
–an discarded (clothes, etc.), hand-
me-downs.
lunjah **me–** to trample.
lunta **ter–(–)** to be in constant difficulty, suffer constantly.
luntang to loaf. **pe–** float (of a fishing line). – *lanting* to loaf. *Ia – lanting
sepandjang hari,* He loafs all day long.
luntjas to miss, fall short. *Disini ia
memukul –,* Here he hit wide of the
mark. **ke–an** error. ~ *ini dibuktikan,*
This error was proved.
luntjip pointed, tapering.
luntjung pointed, tapering. *Tikus –
muntjungnja,* A mouse has a pointed
nose. **me–kan** to point outward.
luntjur **me–** 1 to slide down into,
glide away. *Anak itu ~ kedalam air,*
The child slid down into the water.
2 to launch a ship. **me–kan** to launch
s.t. *Perusahaan kapal ~ kapal dipelabuhan,* The ship-building firm
launched a ship in the harbor. **pe–**
glider. **pe–an** 1 slip, slipway. 2 slide.
3 launching. **ter–** slipped away. *Uang
~ dari tangan saja,* The money
slipped from my hands. **–an** glide
(phon.).
luntur **me–** 1 to fade, run (of color).
Kain ini ~ , This material runs.
2 to decrease, wane. **me–kan** to
cause to fade. *Pendiriannja ~ ,* His
opinion changed.
lup 1 magnifying glass. 2 form of
address for boys on Billiton.
lupa 1 to forget. *Saja sdh –,* I've
forgotten. 2 to be forgotten. **ke–an**
forgotten. *Apa ~ bung ?* Have you
forgotten s.t.? **me–kan** 1 to forget.
Djangan kau–kan, Don't forget. 2
to cause to forget. 3 to cause to
be forgotten. **memper–kan** to cause
o. to forget. **me(nge)–i** to forget.
pe– to be forgetful. *Ia ~ ,* He's a

forgetful person. **pe–an** oblivion. **ter–**
forgotten accidentally. **–²** fish bladder
for glue. ~ *ingat* to remember
vaguely. – *akan dirinja* to be unconscious. – *daratan* 1 in the clouds.
2 snobbish.
lupuh **me–** to beat bamboo until it
is flat.
luput 1 escaped, loose, free. *Ia –
dari bahaja,* He escaped from danger.
2 wrong, in error. – *tafsiran* wrong interpretation. **me–kan** to free, release.
lurah 1 village chief. 2 ravine, gully.
3 groove. **ke–an** 1 village (administrative unit). 2 ward (administrative
unit).
lurik striped material from central
Java.
luru **me–** to chase, run after. **pe–**
bullet.
lurub(an) cloth for covering a bier.
luruh **me–** 1 to shed hair, fur. 2 to
drop (of leaves, flowers). 3 to molt
(of chickens). **pe–** *keringat* means to
promote perspiration.
lurus 1 straight. *Djalan ke Bogor
tidak begitu –,* The road to Bogor
isn't so straight. 2 straight, honest,
upright. *Ia – hati,* He's honest. **ke–an**
1 honesty, sincerity. 2 justice. **me–
kan** to straighten. **memper–kan** to
judge, evaluate. **pe–an** streamlining
of s.t. – *lempeng* straight, direct.
lurut 1 to fall off, drop off. 2 to fall
out. **me–** 1 to take off, strip. 2 to
massage. 3 to wipe off. **me–kan** *diri*
to clear out, leave, depart.
lus **me–** *kain* to iron a sarong.
lusa day after tomorrow. *bésok* – before long, shortly.
lusin dozen.
lusuh dirty, old and faded, worn-out.
lut *tidak* – invulnerable.
lutju 1 funny, amusing. 2 burlesque.
3 cute. *Kutjing ini – , ja?* Isn't
this cat cute! **ke–an** joke. **pe–** joker.
–²an joke. see LELUTJON.
lutjut **me–** 1 to slip away. 2 to skin.
me–i to disarm, take away. *Musuhnja
~ sendjata,* The enemy disarmed him.
me–kan to take off. *Dia tjepat² ~
pakaiannja,* He quickly took off his
clothes. **per–an** *sendjata* disarmament.
ter– slipped away. *Uang itu ~ dari
genggamannja,* The money slipped
away from his grasp.
lutung see LOTONG.
lutut knee. **ber–** 1 to kneel. 2 to
bow to, give in to. 3 to surrender.
luwes 1 smooth, well-mannered. 2
handsome, attractive, becoming. **ke–
an** 1 smoothness. 2 attractiveness.

M

m. 1 [*métér*] meter. 2 [*menit*] minute.
M [*Maséhi*] 1 A.D. *M 1939* A.D.
1939. 2 Christian.
ma' see MAK.
ma'ab place of return.
ma'af 1 forgive, pardon. -, *tuan*,
Pardon me, sir. 2 forgiveness, pardon.
minta - 1 to apologize. 2 to ask
permission to leave. *Pd hari Lebaran
dia minta - kpd orang tuanja*, On
Lebaran day he asks his parents for
forgiveness. **ber- -²an** forgive e.o. at
end of fasting period. **me-i** to forgive
s.o. *Tentu saja -i engkau*, Of course
I forgive you. **me-kan** to forgive s.t.
Kesalahan itu susah di-kan, It's hard
to forgive that mistake. *-kanlah
kalau ada kesalahan saja*, Forgive me
if I've done wrong. **pe-** forgiver (person or thing). **per-an** the act of for-
giving.
ma'alim 1 religious teacher. 2 mosque
personnel.
ma'ap see MA'AF.
mabok see MABUK.
mabuk 1 drunk, intoxicated. *Serdadu
itu -*, The soldier was drunk. 2 be
crazy about. *Dia - gadis tjantik itu*,
He's crazy about that attractive girl.
me-kan 1 to intoxicate. 2 intoxicating. *Minuman itu ~* , That drink is
intoxicating. **pe-** drunkard, a drunk.
- bajang to desire the impossible. *-
bunga raja* flushed from drinking. *-
(bunga) selasih* drunk and unable to
stand upright. *- chajal* lightheaded,
intoxicated. *- darah* 1 sick at the
sight of blood. 2 to run amuck at
the sight of blood. *- kepajang* 1
madly in love. 2 somewhat tipsy.
- laut, *- ombak* seasick. *- tjendawan*
madly in love. *- uang* dazed from
too much money. *- udara* airsick.
mabur to flee, run away.
machluk creature.
mach(u)dum Sir (honorific, generally
used of o. well versed in religion).
mada stupid, feeble-minded, dull.
ma'da auntie (young aunt).
madah 1 eulogy, praise. 2 stanza.
ber- 1 to praise. *Ia duduk diserambi
sambil ~* , He sits on the veranda
praising (God). 2 to recite. *Ia ~*

Qur'an, He's reciting the Koran.
me-kan 1 to express, pronounce.
Murid itu ~ terima kasih, The pupil
expresses his thanks. 2 to relate.
pe- a religious person.
ma'dan mine. *- mas* gold mine.
madarsah 1 Islamic school. 2 institution of learning. *- djamiah* university.
madat 1 opium. 2 watchtower. **ber-**
to smoke opium. **pe-** opium smoker.
pe-an 1 use of opium. 2 opium den.
maddi material rather than spiritual.
madhab see MAZHAB.
Madinah Medina.
madjakaja of one piece (of poles,
sticks).
madjal blunt, dull. *Pisau itu -*, That
knife is dull.
madjal(l)ah magazine, periodical,
journal. *- bulanan* monthly magazine.
- kedjuruan trade or professional
journal.
madjelis 1 council, committee. 2
meeting, session. 3 meeting chamber. *- gerédja* vestry. *- luhur* high
council. *- pengadilan* court of justice.
- tinggi dan - rendah House of Lords
and House of Commons.
madjemuk compound, complex. *Itu
kata -*, That's a compound.
madjenun possessed, insane, crazy.
madjikan employer, boss.
madjir barren, sterile.
ma'djizat miracle.
madjong dust cloth.
madju 1 to go forward, advance,
progress. *Djangan mundur, - terus*,
Don't back up, go forward. 2 to pass
(an exam). *Adik saja - dlm udjian*, My
younger brother passed his examination. 3 to thrive, progress. *Toko itu
- sekali rupanja*, The shop is doing
a thriving business, it seems. 4 progressive, forward-looking. **ke-an** progress, advance, development. **me-kan**
1 to advance, improve. *Ia ingin ~
bahasa Inggerisnja*, He wants to improve his English. 2 to propose,
suggest. *Apa jg di-kan dimadjelis
kemarén?* What was proposed at the
meeting yesterday? 3 to press. *Ia ~
kelahnja thd terdakwa*, He pressed

charges against the defendant. 4 to forward. *Pelamar harap* ~ *surat kpd...* Applicants please forward their letters to... 5 to promote. ~ *turisme* to promote tourism. *–! Djalan!* Forward! March!

madjuh 1 gluttonous. 2 overeager.

madjung putty.

madjusi Parsi.

madrasah see MADARSAH.

madu 1 co-wife. 2 honey. 3 very sweet (of a smile). **ber–** to have a co-wife, share o's husband with another wife. **me–i** to take another wife. **memper–kan** to cause o's first wife to have a co-wife. *Ia* ~ *isterinja*, He took an additional wife. **per–an** polygyny, polygamy.

madya 1 medium, average. 2 form of the Javanese language between *kromo* and *ngoko*.

maén see MAIN.

maésan see MÉSAN.

mafhum to know, understand, comprehend. *Ia sdh – isi buku itu*, He understands the contents of that book. **me–i** to know about.

magang 1 volunteer, candidate, apprentice. 2 clerk. 3 overripe.

magel 1 half-ripe. 2 incomplete in knowledge.

magersari tenant.

magi magic.

magrib 1 west. 2 at sunset. 3 sunset prayer.

magribi western.

magun fixed, permanent. – *angin* porthole.

mah 1 abbrev. for MAHA-. 2 (used to emphasize the preceding sentence or word. *Kalau dia – tidak berani!* He doesn't dare to, does he?

maha great, very. – *baik* very good. – *besar* very large, great.

mahadahsjat tremendous, fantastic.

Mahadéwa 1 Hindu god Siva. 2 supreme diety.

Mahadéwi Hindu goddess Batara Durga.

Mahadper [*Mahkamah Angkatan Darat dalam Perang*] wartime military court.

mahaduta ambassador.

Mahaesa God.

mahaguru professor. **ke–an** professorship.

maha-keramat most sacred or holy.

Mahakuasa the Almighty.

mahal 1 expensive, high. *Barang²* *makin –*, Things are becoming more and more expensive. 2 scarce, difficult to find. – *mentjari orang sebaik itu*, It's difficult to find s.o. as good as he. **ke–an** 1 scarcity. *Pd waktu* ~ *segala harga naik*, During periods of

scarcity prices rise. 2 very expensive. *Oléh karena* ~ *saja tidak beli barang itu*, Because it was very expensive I did not buy it. 3 too expensive. **me–kan** to raise the price. *Pendjual²* ~ *barang² meréka*, The salesmen raised the price of their merchandise.

mahalama very long (of time). *waktu jg –* a very long time.

mahalezat extremely tasty.

mahamenteri high official at older Malay courts.

mahaméru the holy mountain, seat of the gods.

mahamulia exalted, lofty, sublime, illustrious. *Jg –* His Highness.

mahap see MA'AF.

mahapenting very important.

mahar bridegroom's gift to the bride.

maharadja sovereign, overlord. **ke–an** empire.

maharadjaléla bersi– 1 to rage. *Penjakit tjatjar* ~ , Smallpox was raging. 2 to rampage, operate unchecked. *Orang² djahat* ~ *di Sukabumi*, Bandits were rampaging in Sukabumi.

maharupa extremely beautiful.

mahasajang all-merciful.

mahasiswa university student. – *pendengar* auditor. **ke–an** student affairs.

mahasiswi female university student.

Mahasutji the Most Holy.

mahatahu omniscient.

mahbub lover, sweetheart (male).

mahbubah beloved, sweetheart.

mahdi guide, leader.

mahérat see MAIRAT.

mahful stored in the mind. **me–kan** to memorize.

mahir skilled, well-versed, intelligent, clever. *Dia – sekali bahasa Indonésia*, He's very clever in Indonesian. **ke–an** skill. **me–kan, memper–** to practice, learn, acquire.

mahkamah court of justice. – *Agung* Supreme Court. – *tentara* military court. – *tinggi* high court.

mahkota see MAKOTA.

mahligai see MALIGAI.

mahluk see MACHLUK.

mahmud praised.

mahoni mahogany.

mahs(j)ar gathering place (where all the Dead are judged on the Last Day).

main 1 to play. *Dia suka – bola*, He likes to play ball. 2 to start. *Bioskop sdh –*, The movie has started. **ber–** to play. *Dia* ~ *bola*, He plays ball. ~ *muda* to be unfaithful. **ber–²** playful, all in fun. *Tidak apa; hanja* ~ *sadja*, It's nothing serious; it's all in fun. ~ *lantjang* a game of

throwing stones into the water. ~
tangan to parry with the hands. ~
tangan pandjang to be impertinent
by touching a woman playfully.
me–kan 1 to play, show. *Sandiwara
itu ~ apa?* What's playing? 2 to
play s.t. *Anak itu pandai ~ piano*,
The child plays the piano very well.
~ *peranan didalam* to play a role in.
memper–kan 1 to show, present.
*Lakon jg diper–kan semalam bagus
sekali*, The play presented last night
was very good. 2 to make fun of s.o.
Anak nakal itu suka benar ~ orang,
That naughty child likes to make
fun of people. **pe–** player, actor. *Ia
~ tengah*, He's a halfback. **per–an** 1
game. 2 performance, show. 3 acting.
~ *asmara* the courting act. **–an** toy.
–²an toy(s). **–²** *sadja* just for fun.
– *ambil rokok* to take s.o.'s cigarette
(against his will). – *anggar* to fence.
– *angin* unpredictable. – *api* to play
with fire. – *bola sodok* to shoot pool.
– *burit* to commit sodomy. – *dam* to
play checkers. – *dil* to play hockey.
– *djudi* gambling. – *gadjah* to play
chess. – *gajung* to fence. – *galan²an*
to act chivalrously. – *gila* 1 to joke,
fool. 2 to be forward, bold, arrogant.
– *kaju* unfair play. – *kartu terbuka* to
lay o's cards on the table, be frank.
– *keléréng* to play marbles. – *kerojok*
to gang up on s.o. – *komidi* 1 to act
in a play. 2 to pretend. – *mata* to
wink, flirt. – *muda* to flirt, court,
neck, pet. – *perempuan* to have an
illicit affair, chase after women. –
pukul to strike, hit at random.
*Djangan – pukul sadja; nanti kena
orang*, Don't strike at random; you
may hit s.o. – *sikut* to elbow o's way.
– *silap*, – *sulap* 1 to juggle. 2 to
conjure. – *tangan* to gesticulate. –
tedéng aling² to play hide and seek.
– *témbak* to shoot without provocation. *Tentara – témbak*, The soldier
shot him without reason. – *tendang*
to kick s.o. without reason. *Djangan
– tendang sadja!* Don't keep kicking
me! – *tjeki* to play a Chinese card
game. – *udik* children's game played
with balls or hard seeds. – *undi* to
gamble. *tak –²* not easy. *Perhatikan
tanggal –nja*, Note the date of showing.

mairat 1 ascension. – *Nabi Mohammad* the ascension of the Prophet
Mohammed. 2 to disappear, die.

mait see MAJAT.

maja illusion, hallucination. **–²** clear
and transparent.

majang spadix, palm blossom.

majapada world.

majat corpse.

major 1 major. 2 lieutenant commander. – *udara* major (Air Force).

majoritas majority.

majur 1 major. 2 see SAJUR.

mak 1 mother. 2 term of address or
reference for a woman, whether a
member of the family or not, who is
older than the speaker and who might
fittingly be called 'mother.' – *angkat*
foster mother. – *bujung* 1 procuress.
2 used teasingly to indicate a pregnant woman. – *bungsu* mother's or
father's youngest sister. – *éték* aunt.
– *ketjil* auntie. – *lung* oldest aunt. –
muda 1 auntie. 2 second wife. –
saudara aunt. – *téték* foster mother.
– *tiri* stepmother. – *tjik* aunt (youngest
sister of father or mother). – *tua* 1
first wife. 2 mother's or father's
older sister.

maka then, so. **–nja** consequently,
because of that. – *dari itu* thus,
therefore.

makam 1 grave, resting place, burial
plot. 2 residence, place of residence.
ber– 1 to lie buried. 2 to reside,
dwell, stay. **me–kan** to bury, inter.
pe–an funeral, burial. ~ *negara*
state funeral.

makan 1 to eat, devour, swallow.
Ia selalu – pisang, He's always
eating bananas. 2 to destroy, consume. *Rumah itu di– api*, The house
was consumed by fire. 3 to take,
require, consume. – *waktu tiga djam*,
It takes 3 hours. 4 to take, swallow.
Ia – pil, He took a pill. 5 to chew.
Saja blm – sirih, I haven't yet chewed
betel nut. 6 to hit, strike. *Adik saja
di– peluru*, My brother was hit by
a bullet. 7 to work, hold. *Rém otonja
tidak –*, His car brakes do not hold.
8 range. – *peluru bedil zaman dahulu
adalah terbatas*, The range of an out-
moded gun is limited. 9 to draw.
Kapal itu –nja 20 métér, The ship
draws 20 meters. **ke–an** consumed,
finished, destroyed. *Rumahnja ~ api*,
His house was consumed by fire.
me– to consume, use up. **me–i** 1 to
feed. *Ibu lagi ~ baji*, The mother is
feeding the baby. 2 to feed on, eat
up. **pe–** 1 eater. 2 consumer. ~
darah bloodsucker, o. who makes too
much profit. ~ *bawang* passionate.
ter– 1 eaten, swallowed accidentally.
Bisa itu ~ , The poison was accidentally swallowed. 2 edible. *Kedjadian itu tidak ~ akal oléhnja*,
He couldn't understand that event.
~ *disadah* 1 to look blank, foolish.
2 to feel deceived. **–an** food, provisions. ~ *baku* staple foods. ~

berpantang a diet. ~ *ketjil* hors d'oeuvres. ~ *lembu* fodder. *Lawan muda itu adalah* ~ *lembu utk dia,* The young contender was a pushover for him. *-²an* various foods. *-²* to snack. *– angin* to get some fresh air. *– bawang* to be furious. *– berpantang* to diet. *– besar* to have a big party. *– daging* carnivore. *– darah* to fret. *– dawai* very poor, impoverished. *– diri* to weaken o.s. by worry, hate, anxiety. *– duit, – emas* to take a bribe. *– gadji* to work for wages. *– garam* to have lots of experience. *Ia tlh banjak – garam dlm kehidupan,* He has savored much of life. *– hak* to trespass upon o's rights. *– hati* 1 to sadden. 2 to suffer from s.o.'s act. 3 to eat o's heart out. *– kerawat* very poor, impoverished. *– kuli* to work as a day laborer. *– lembu* fodder. *– malam* dinner, supper. *– obat* to take medicine. *– pagi* breakfast. *– péna* to live by writing. *– riba* to require high interest, profiteer. *– rumput* to graze. *– siang* lunch, noonday meal. *– siku²* to talk in an indirect way. *– sogok, – suap* to take a bribe. *– sumpah* to perjure. *– tanah* to starve. *– tangan* 1 to hit with the fist. 2 to have sudden good fortune. *– tulang* to drive o.s. hard. *– ulam* to keep a mistress as well as a wife. *– upah* 1 to work for wages, be on a payroll. 2 to be open to bribery.

makanja therefore. see MAKA.

makar 1 trick, tactics. 2 hard and tough (of fruits and vegetables). 3 unripe (of fruit).

Makara 1 cancer (a sign of the zodiac). 2 mythical Hindu-Javanese sea monster.

Makas(s)ar Macassar.

makbul 1 fulfilled, answered. 2 accepted, realized. 3 effective. *Obat itu – sekali,* That medicine is very effective. **me–kan** 1 to accept. *Madjikan itu* ~ *permintaan pegawai²nja,* The employer accepted his employees' request. 2 to fulfill, realize. *Ia bekerdja keras utk* ~ *tjita²nja,* He worked hard to fulfill his ideals.

makelar broker.

makenah white cloak covering all parts of the body except face and hands; worn by women at prayer (Islam).

maki me– to abuse s.o., use abusive language. **–an** abuse, abusive words. **–²** to abuse.

makin increasingly, the more. *Kota itu – bertambah,* The city is increasingly growing. *– ... –* the more... the more. *– lama – banjak* the longer the time the greater the amount. **se–** more and more. *Suaranja* ~ *keras,* His voice became louder and louder. ~ *... ~ ...* the ... the... ~ *banjak gadjinja* ~ *malas ia bekerdja,* The more he earned the lazier he became.

maklum 1 to know about. *Ttg hal itu saudara tentu sdh –,* You already know about that matter. 2 You know how it is. *–lah, seorang pegawai,* You know how it is with an official. **me–i** to understand, know. *Ajah dan ibu sadja jg* ~ *hal itu,* Only my parents understand that matter. **memper–kan** 1 to announce, notify. *Diper–kan dgn hormat bhw...* It is respectfully announced that... 2 to declare, proclaim. *Kapan Djepang* ~ *perang kpd negeri Tiongkok?* When did Japan declare war on China? **per–an** 1 announcement, declaration, proclamation. 2 statement.

maklumat announcement, declaration, proclamation, communiqué. **me–kan** to announce, proclaim, declare. *Kementerian itu* ~ *peraturan baru,* The ministry announced a new regulation.

makmur 1 prosperous, rich, wealthy. *Negeri itu – sekali,* That country is very prosperous. 2 luxurious. *Orang kaja itu – hidupnja,* That rich man lives luxuriously. **ke–an** prosperity. *Kementerian* ~ Ministry of Welfare. **me–kan** to make prosper. *Penduduk bekerdja keras utk* ~ *daérah itu,* The inhabitants work hard to make the area prosper. **perse–an** commonwealth.

makna 1 meaning. 2 purpose, sense. *Apa –nja bekerdja sekeras itu?* What's the purpose of working so hard? **ber–** to have a meaning, be meaningful, significant. *Tiap kata itu* ~ *,* Each word has its own meaning. **me–kan** to explain, elucidate. *Orang itu* ~ *Qur'an,* That person is explaining the meaning of the Koran.

maknawi 1 spiritual. 2 important.

maknit magnet. **ke–an** magnetism.

makota 1 crown. 2 sweetheart. **me–i** 1 to crown (a king). 2 to award, crown. *Buku ini di–i hadiah,* This book was awarded a prize.

maksimal maximal. **me–kan** to maximize.

maksud 1 purpose. *Apa –nja datang sepagi ini?* What is his purpose in coming this early? 2 intention, plan. *– saja hendak pergi kebioskop,* My intention was to go to the movie. *Apa –nja?* What's he driving at? 3 aim. *– perkumpulan itu baik,* The aims of that organization are fine. 4

meaning. *Saja tidak tahu - surat ini*, I don't know the meaning of this letter. **ber-** to intend, plan. *Saja ~ kepasar siang ini*, I plan to go to the market this afternoon. **me-kan** to have in mind, intend. *Apa jg dikannja dengan surat itu, entahlah*, I don't know what he has in mind with the letter. - *tudjuan* objective.

maktab elementary school.

maktjik see MAK.

maktub 1 recorded. 2 (*almaktub*) the Holy Book. **me-kan** to write down. **ter-** written down. *Hal itu ~ dlm bukunja*, That matter is written down in his book.

ma'kul rational, logical.

ma'kulat metaphysics.

makzul see MA'ZUL.

mala 1 disaster, misfortune, accident. 2 spot, stain, flaw, a blot on o's reputation. - *petaka* misfortune.

Maladéwa the Maldives.

malaékat see MALAIKAT.

malah on the contrary. *Setelah minum obat - men-djadi[2] sakitnja*, On the contrary, after taking the medicine he became sicker. - *begitu* precisely. **-an** 1 but rather, but. *Dia tidak berhenti main, ~ terus sadja*, He doesn't stop playing, but just keeps right on. 2 but even, even. *Djangankan engkau, ~ saja tidak*, Not only do you not, but even I don't.

malaikat angel. *-maut* angel of death.

Malaja Malaya.

malak see MALAIKAT.

Malaka Malacca.

malakama 1 ill-fated. 2 evil fate (devil if you do, devil if you don't).

malakut kingdom.

malam 1 evening, night. 2 wax, paraffin. **ber-** 1 to spend the night. *Saja ~ di Hotél Garuda*, I spent the night at the Hotel Garuda. 2 to keep overnight. *Daging itu busuk baunja karena tlh ~* , The meat smells spoiled because it was kept overnight. **ke-an** overtaken by night. *Waktu ke Bogor kami ~ didjalan*, Going to Bogor we were overtaken by night. **me-i** to spend the night at the bedside. *Sdh dua - ibu ~ dia*, Mother has spent two nights at her bedside. **me(mper)-kan** to keep overnight, leave overnight. *Supaja énak rasanja baik diper-kan dulu*, To make it taste delicious you had best leave it overnight. **pe(r)-an** overnight stop, hotel, motel. **se-** 1 last night. *Saudara ~ dimana?* Where were you last night? 2 one night. *Kami tinggal dihotél itu hanja ~ sadja*, We just

stayed at the hotel one night. ~ *suntuk* all night (long). **se- -[2]an** the whole evening or night. ~ *sepitjingpun dia tidak tidur*, He didn't sleep a wink the whole night. -[2] late at night. *Mengapa ~ datang kesini?* Why did you come here so late at night? *-nja* the night before. - *buta* pitch-black night. - *gembira* 1 a merry evening. 2 open house. - *hari* night, evening. - *Kemis* Wednesday night. *Kemis* - Thursday night. - *kemarin* 2 nights ago. *kemarin* - last night. - *pandjang* 1 Saturday night. 2 any holiday eve when o. can stay up till late.

malan to have an uneasy feeling, be anxious, concerned.

malang 1 transverse, across. 2 unlucky, unfortunate. *Sekali ini mémang - buat dia*, It's just bad luck for him this time. **ke-an** 1 bad luck, calamity, distress. 2 struck by disaster, bad luck. *Keluarga itu mendapat ~* , That family was struck by a disaster. - *melintang* 1 to lie across. *Papan - melintang didjalan itu*, A plank is lying across the road. 2 bad luck. - *mudjur* at random, haphazardly.

malap 1 dim (of light). *Lampu itu terlalu -*, That lamp is too dim. 2 smoldering. - *sebagai pelita kekurangan minjak* smoldering like a lamp that is short of oil.

malapetaka see MALA.

malar 1 continuous, more and more. 2 see MALAH. *Dia - menangiskan anaknja*, She cries continuously over her child. -[2] even, but even. *Bukan berhenti, ~ berlari lebih tjepat*, He didn't stop, but ran even faster.

malas 1 lazy, indolent. *Murid itu - sekali*, The student is very lazy. 2 not feel like, not be up to. *Saja - pergi menonton malam ini*, I don't feel up to going to the movies tonight. **ber- -[2]** to loaf, take it easy, be idle. *Hari Minggu kami sering ~* , On Sundays we often loaf. **ke-an** laziness. **me-kan** to make o. lazy. *Hawa panas ~ saja bekerdja*, The hot weather makes me feel lazy for work. **pe-** lazybones, sluggard, lazy person.

Maleman the last 10 days of the fasting month for celebration of the descent of Divine inspiration; *lailatu-'lkadar*.

maligai castle, palace.

malih changed, altered. *Ulat sdh - mendjadi kupu[2]*, The caterpillar has changed into a butterfly.

malik 1 owner, proprietor. 2 king.

malim 1 a religious person, holy per-

son, religious teacher. 2 leader, guide.
3 pilot. 4 magician.
maling 1 thief. 2 to steal. **ke-an** 1
robbed. *Saja ~ tadi malam,* I was
robbed last night. 2 theft, robbery.
*Saja tidak tahu bhw ada ~ dirumah
saudara,* I didn't know there was a
theft at your house. **me-i** to steal
from, rob. *Ia ~ kawannja,* He steals
from his friend. **pe-** thief, robber.
malis 1 faded, pale (of colors). *Warna
badjuku sdh -,* The color of my dress
has faded. 2 vague. *Bau itu masih -
tertjium dari sini,* The odor can be
vaguely smelled from here.
malu 1 shy, bashful, embarrassed.
Masuklah, djangan -, Please come in,
don't be bashful. 2 respectful. *Dia -
kpd gurunja,* She is respectful toward
her teacher. 3 humble. *- sekali orang
kampung itu kpd kijai,* The villagers
are very humble toward the religious
teacher. 4 shame. **ke-an** 1 shame. 2
ashamed. *Dia pergi, ~ ,* He went
away, ashamed. *Saja ~ betul sampai
saja tidak bisa berbitjara,* I was so
ashamed I couldn't speak. 3 privates,
genitals. **ke- -²an** very bashful.
*Murid jg nakal itu berdiri dimuka
pintu ~ ,* The naughty pupil stood
in front of the door very bashful.
me-i 1 to embarrass, shame. *Si Amat
~ ajahnja dimuka orang banjak,*
Amat embarrassed his father in front
of many people. 2 to respect. *Wali
kota kami di-i oléh banjak orang,* Our
mayor is respected by many people.
me(mper)-kan to be ashamed of.
*Djangan kau-kan rumahmu jg ketjil
ini,* Don't be ashamed of your little
house. **pe-** 1 a shy person. 2 shy,
timid. *-² bahasa* very bashful. *-²
kutjing* pretending to be shy, coy.
Maluku Moluccas.
ma'lum see MAKLUM.
ma'lumat see MAKLUMAT.
mam 1 mother, mama, mum. 2 to
eat (children's lang.).
mama see MAMAK.
mamah **me-** to chew, munch. *Sapi
~ biak,* The cow chews its cud.
me-kan to chew (for). *Ia ~ anaknja
kué jg keras,* She chewed the hard
cake for her child. **pe-** *biak* ruminant.
-an cud, chewing. *~ kué itu dimakan-
kan kpd anaknja,* The chewed cake
was fed to her child.
mamai 1 to walk in o's sleep. 2
drowsy.
mamak 1 maternal uncle. 2 maternal
aunt. *- bendahara* treasurer. *- menteri*
minister.
mamanda term of respect for MAMAK.

mamang 1 dizzy. *Sesudah djatuh dia
merasa -,* After he fell he felt dizzy.
2 frightened, confused. *Anak ketjil
itu -,* The child was frightened.
mambang ghost, spirit. *- kuning,
- soré* evening glow.
mambu smelling, stinking.
mami mother, mommy (children's
term).
mamik a bad taste. *Karena tlh
lama disimpan, kué itu sdh - rasanja,*
Because it was kept so long, the cake
does not taste good any more.
mampat 1 solid, compact, compressed. *Ban - tidak énak dipakai,*
Solid tires are not comfortable. 2
clogged up. *Saluran air itu -,* The
water pipe is clogged up. 3 excellent,
fine. *- sekali, bukan?* It's excellent,
isn't it? **me-kan** 1 to compress. 2
to stanch bleeding.
mampir to drop in, come by, call
at. *-lah kapan saudara bisa,* Drop in
whenever you can. **pe-an** stop, place
to stay. *Tokio adalah tempat ~nja
bilamana ia keluar negeri,* Tokyo is
where he stops when he goes abroad.
~ bis bus stop.
mampu 1 capable, able. *Saja tidak -
menjelesaikan pekerdjaan itu hari
ini djuga,* I cannot complete the
work today. 2 well-to-do, wealthy.
Hadji itu orang - didésanja, The
hadji is a wealthy man in his village.
3 to afford, be able. *Banjak ibu jg -
utk membeli tjatbibir jg mahal,* Many
are the mothers who can afford to
buy expensive lipstick. **ke-an** 1
ability, capability. 2 prosperity.
mampuh see MAMPU.
mampung porous (of coral, sponge).
mampus 1 (rude) to die, go west.
2 very unfortunate. *- ini, uang habis
semua,* Good gosh, all the money's
gone. *-lah kamu!* To hell with you!
ma'mur see MAKMUR.
mana 1 where. *Orang -?* Where does
he come from? *Di- dia tinggal?*
Where does he live? *Saudara mau
ke-?* Where do you want to go?
2 which. *Jg - punja saja?* Which is
mine? *Tuan lebih suka kota jg -?*
Which town do you prefer? *-² 1*
wherever. *~ itu diutjapkan* wherever
it is uttered. 2 anywhere. *Kekurangan
itu dirasakan di ~ ,* The shortage
was felt everywhere. *- bisa, - boléh!*
How could it be? (Impossible!)
*- boléh, saja bertemu dgn dia tadi
pagi,* How is it possible? I saw him
this morning. *- kala* whenever. *-
kala saja pergi* whenever I go. *- lagi*
moreover. *Dia pintar, - lagi dia*

punja uang, He's clever and, besides, he has money. – *pula* moreover. – *sadja* whichever, any. *jg – sadja kausuka* whichever you like. – *tahu* who knows. – *tahu dia seorang mata*², Who knows, maybe he's a spy. **dari–** from where, whence. *Tuan datang ～?* Where did you come from? **dike–kan** to be brought where. *～ pembunuh itu?* Where did they bring the murderer? **dike– –²kan** brought to some place or other. *di– mungkin* wherever possible. *Di–mungkin dia naik motor*, Wherever possible, he drives a car. **di– –²**, **di–pun djuga** anywhere, everywhere. *Obat itu dpt dibeli ～* , That medicine can be bought anywhere. **ke– –²** to anywhere. *Sdh saja tjari ～ , tapi tidak ketemu dia*, I have looked for him everywhere, but haven't been able to find him.

ma'na see MAKNA.

manasuka as you like it, voluntarily.

manat a firm and permanent agreement.

ma'nawi see MAKNAWI.

manda(h) 1 to want, bear. *Siapa jg – tinggal lama ditempat itu?* Who could bear to stay in that place long? 2 storage place for rice.

mandala circle, area, district.

mandam 1 drunk, intoxicated. *Awas! Serdadu –!* Be careful! A drunken soldier! 2 madly in love. *Dia – akan gadis itu*, He's madly in love with that girl.

mandarsah see MADARSAH.

mandat government pay order.

mandataris signer of government pay orders.

mandau a sword made in Borneo.

mandeg see MANDEK.

mandek 1 to stop, get stuck, stall. *Otonja – ditengah djalan*, His auto got stuck in the middle of the road. 2 to stagnate. – *pikiranku kalau kutinggal disini lebih lama*, I'll stagnate if I stay here any longer. 3 to come to a standstill. *Lalu lintas – seluruhnja*, Traffic came to a total standstill. **ke–an** a halt, standstill.

mandi to bathe, take a bath. *Dia – pagi² benar*, He takes a bath very early in the morning. **ber–** to bathe. *Dia suka ～ dibawah pantjuran*, He likes to bathe under a shower pipe. **me–kan** 1 to bathe. *Djangan kaukan anak itu sepagi ini*, Don't bathe the child this early in the morning. 2 to wash, bathe. *～ kutjing tidak baik, kata orang*, Washing a cat isn't good, people say. 3 to dip. *–kan*

pantji kotor itu didalam air agak lama, Dip the dirty pan in the water for some time. **memper–kan** to baptize. *Digerédja mana anak itu diper–kan?* In which church was the child baptized? *～ majat* to bathe a corpse according to Islam. **per–an** 1 swimming pool. 2 baptism. 3 bathing spot.

mandiang see MENDIANG.

mandiri to stand alone. **ke–an** autonomy.

mandja 1 spoiled. *Anak itu – sekali*, The child is very spoiled. 2 attached, friendly. *Anak itu – sekali kpd ibunja*, That child is very much attached to her mother. 3 confidential, intimate. *Tak ada –nja thd ajahnja*, He and his father are not close. **ber– –²** to court. *Banjak peladjar² ～ didepan sekolah*, Many of the students are courting in front of the school. **ke–an** familiarity, intimacy. **me(mper)–kan** to spoil, baby, s.o.

mandjung 1 large torch used during fishing. 2 a k.o. prow.

mandjur 1 efficacious. *Obat itu –*, That medicine is efficacious. 2 strong, effective. *Awas, itu – sekali*, Be careful, it's very strong. 3 powerful. *Doanja – rupanja*, His prayers seem powerful. **ke–an** efficacy, effectiveness.

mandor see MANDUR.

mandu opinion, standpoint, point of view, thesis.

mandul barren, sterile.

mandung rooster, cock.

mandur foreman, overseer. *Si Amat – air di Tjiawi*, Amat is foreman of the gang which supervises irrigation at Tjiawi. **me–i** to supervise. *Dia ～ pekerdja² diladang*, He supervises the workers in the field.

manfa'at 1 use, benefit. *Beladjar ada –nja*, Studying has its use. 2 profit. – *dan mudarat* 1 profit and loss. 2 advantages and disadvantages. **ber–** 1 useful. 2 profitable. *Kepergian saja ke New York ～ sekali*, My trip to New York was very profitable.

mangap 1 to gape. *Dia – melihat gedung jg besar itu*, He gaped at the large building. 2 to yawn.

mangga 1 mango. 2 please (Sundanese).

manggan manganese.

manggis mangosteen.

manggistan see MANGGIS.

mangka see MAKA.

mangkar 1 green, unripe. 2 not done, raw.

Mangkasar Macassar.

mangkat to pass away, die, depart this world. *Beliau – tahun jg lalu,*

He passed away last year. **ke-an** death, demise.

mangkel annoyed, irritated.

mangkin see MAKIN.

mangkir 1 to be absent. *Dia - disekolah seminggu*, He was absent from school a week. 2 to fail. *Dia - udjian*, He failed the examination. 3 to be missing, lack. *Satu sekerup -, saja rasa*, One screw is missing, I think.

mangkok see MANGKUK.

mangkubumi governor, administrator.

mangkuk cup.

mangkus efficacious, effective.

mangro in a dual capacity. *dlm kedudukan jg - sebagai murid* in a dual capacity as a student.

mangsa 1 prey, bait. 2 victim.

mangsai see MASAI.

mangsi ink, charcoal flour for blackening the teeth.

mangu ter-(-) 1 confused, dazed. *Waktu ditanja dia ~* , When questioned he was just confused. 2 taken aback. 3 thoughtful.

mangut 1 confused, dazed. *Mengapa -, bung?* Why are you dazed, my friend? 2 to doze.

mani sperm, seed. *pantjaran -* ejaculation of sperm. **per-an** insemination. *~ buatan* artificial insemination.

manik² beads. **ber- -²** 1 to wear a string of beads. 2 drops of water or perspiration.

manikam jewel, gem, precious stone.

Manipol [*Manifésto Politik*] Political Manifesto (President Soekarno's Independence Day address of August 17, 1959). **me- usdékkan** to reorganize, retool, in accordance with the Political Manifesto and Usdek.

manipulasi manipulation. **me-kan** to manipulate.

manis 1 sweet. *Kué itu terlalu -,* That cake is too sweet. 2 sweet, nice. *- benar gadis itu*, That girl is very sweet. 3 cute, attractive. *-ku* my sweet. **ber- -²** to use flattery. *Tjoba terus-terang sadja, djangan ~* , Please be frank, don't use flattery. **ke-an** 1 sweetness. 2 beauty. *Kesederhanaannja menambah ~nja*, Her simplicity enhances her beauty. 3 oversweet. *Kopi itu ~* , The coffee is oversweet. **me-** 1 to decorate, make s.t. look nice. *Ibu lagi ~ médja dgn bunga² utk tamu²*, Mother is decorating the table with flowers for the guests. 2 to smooth s.t. over. **me-kan** to sweeten, sound nice. *Perempuan itu ~ suaranja supaja disukai orang*, That woman makes her voice sound nice so that people will like her. **memper-** to sweeten.

Djangan diper- djuga kué itu, Don't sweeten that cake any more. **pe(r)-** 1 sweetener. 2 cosmetics. 3 decoration. **-an** candy, sweets. *~ belimbing* k.o. fruit candy. *~ tjokelat* chocolate bar, candy. *~ lebah* honey. *- hati* likable, kindly. *- muka* sweet expression.

manpa'at see MANFA'AT.

mansét 1 cuff. 2 cuff links.

mansuch 1 abolished. 2 expired, null, invalid. **me-kan** 1 to abolish. *Peraturan² lama di-kan*, Old regulations are abolished. 2 to cancel, annul. *Peraturan baru itu ~ paspor saja*, The new regulation cancels my passport.

mantap 1 resolute, steady, determined. 2 faithful. **ke-an** steadiness, firmness.

mantel coat, cloak. *- hudjan* raincoat.

mantera magic formula. **me-i** 1 to charm, cast a spell. 2 to hypnotize.

manteri 1 rank of s.o. higher than a clerk but lower than a subdistrict head. 2 see MENTERI. *- hewan* animal husbandman. *- pasar* o. who collects fees for space at market; market supervisor. *- tjatjar* vaccinator.

mantjanegara foreign countries.

mantjawarna varicolored, multicolored.

mantjung 1 sharp, pointed. 2 dry sheath of a coconut.

mantram see MANTERA.

mantri see MANTERI.

mantu see MENANTU.

manuk bird. *- déwata* bird of paradise.

manusia 1 human being, man. 2 human. **ke-an, perike-an** 1 humanity. 2 human nature. 3 humanitarianism. 4 humanism. *- angkasa* spaceman, cosmonaut. *- loka* the earth, world.

manusiawi human.

manzil a place to spend the night on a trip.

map portfolio.

mapak to meet s.o., welcome.

mapalus mutual assistance.

mara 1 danger, disaster. 2 to advance, progress, approach. *- sedikit*, Step forward a little. **ke-an** progress. **me-kan** to advance, move. *Dia ~ piring kearah saja*, He moved the plate in my direction. *- bahaja* all sorts of dangers.

marah 1 angry. 2 anger, fury. 3 to become angry. 4 A Minangkabau title (below *sutan*). **ke-an** fury, anger, rage. **ke- -²an** very angry, furious. **me-i** to reprimand, be angry at. *Guru ~ si Ali*, The teacher reprimanded Ali. **me-kan** to infuriate. *Kata²nja ~ saja*, His words infuriated

me. **pe–** hothead. **–an** not on speaking terms. *Amat dan Abu lagi ~* , Amat and Abu are not on speaking terms.
marak glow. **me–** to glow, flare up. **me–kan** to light up, brighten up. *Warna ini baik sekali utk ~ badjuku,* This color is very good for brightening up my dress. **se–** glory, pride. *~ gunung Merapi* the glory of the Minangkabau people.
maras very anxious, frightened. *Dia – mendengar anaknja blm pulang,* He was frightened at hearing his child hadn't returned.
marbut janitor of the mosque.
marem satisfied, content, complacent.
Maret March.
marga 1 district (in South Sumatra). 2 clan (Tapanuli, Batak).
margasatwa 1 wild animals, beasts. 2 fauna.
marge margin.
marhaban *lagu* – melody for praising the Prophet on Ascension day (usually read).
marhaén 1 proletarian. 2 have-nots. **ke–an** proletarianism.
marhaénisme movement to fight for interests of the have-nots.
marhum see ALMARHUM.
mari come! come here! *–lah kita pergi kebioskop,* Let's go to the movies. *– kita berangkat!* Let's go! **ke–** hither, to here. *kesana ~* here and there. *– dulu, bung,* So long.
Marich Mars.
marifat 1 knowledge. 2 the highest knowledge. **ber–** 1 to philosophize. *Ia ~ ttg ketuhanan,* He philosophizes about divinity. 2 to concentrate. *Dia ~ dlm pemudjaan Tuhan,* He concentrates on worshiping God.
Marikan American.
maritim maritime.
Marjam the Virgin Mary.
markas 1 station, office. 2 army post. *– besar* headquarters.
markis awning against sun.
markonis ship's radio operator.
marmar marble.
marmot guinea pig.
marse see MARGE.
marsekal marshal.
marsosé military police, constabulary.
martabak crispy pancake filled with onions and pieces of mutton.
martabat 1 rank, grade, status. *Orang itu tinggi –nja,* That person is high ranking. 2 prestige. 3 value. *– kemanusiaan* human values.
martil hammer. **me–** to hammer.
ma'ruf 1 known. *Itu sdh – ke-mana²,*

That's known everywhere. 2 good deeds. *Tindakan jg – tak mudah dilupakan,* Good deeds are not easily forgotten.
marwah 1 pride, dignity. 2 manliness.
mas 1 sir, brother (used to older contemporaries, including wife to husband). 2 see EMAS. 3 Javanese title below *radén*. *– belanda* 18-carat gold. *– kodok* platinum. *– terus* pure gold.
masa 1 time, period. *Pd – itu saja di Bandung,* At that time I was in Bandung. 2 during. *– saja ketjil ajah saja bekerdja dikantor pos,* During my youth my father worked at the post office. 3 phase. *– genting* critical phase. **–kah, –kan** impossible, how could it be. *Sdh dua kali diterangkan, ~ blm mengerti djuga,* It's been explained twice and you still don't understand. **di–datang** the future. **me–bodohkan** to let o. do as he pleases. **se–** during the time, at the time when. " *~ ketjil dikampung" karangan Mohammad Radjab,* "When I was young in the *kampung"* was written by Mohammed Radjab. *~ zaman Djepang dilarang keras mempergunakan bahasa Inggeris,* During the Japanese occupation the use of English was strictly forbidden. *– azali* prehistoric times. *– bodoh* to be indifferent. *Pergi atau tidak kamu, – bodoh,* Whether you go or not is immaterial to me. *– depan* future. *– kesempitan* depression, slump. *– mula* at the beginning, formerly. *– nifas* postnatal period. *– perubahan* period of transition. *– purba* antiquity. *– remadja* puberty, adolescence. *– selam* the past. *– waktu* 1 chronology. 2 periodization.
masa' see MASA 4.
masaalah see MASALAH.
masai tangled. *Rambutnja –,* His hair is tangled.
masak 1 ripe. 2 cooked, done. *Nasi sdh –,* The rice is done. 3 experienced, accustomed to. *Dia sdh – akan segala matjam keadaan,* He is accustomed to all kinds of situations. 4 mature. **me–** to cook. *Ibu ~ didapur,* Mother is cooking in the kitchen. **me–kan** 1 to cook for s.o. *Kemarén teman ~ saja sesuatu énak sekali,* Yesterday a friend cooked s.t. delicious for me. 2 to cook. **me– –²** cooking. **pe–** 1 the cook. 2 cooking utensils. **pe-an** 1 the cooking. 2 cooking utensils. **–an** 1 food, cooking. 2 cuisine, the way of cooking. *~ Perantjis* French

cuisine. 3 cooking. ∼*nja tidak énak,* His cooking does not taste good. 4 see MASAKAH, MASAKAN. –² carefully, deeply, maturely. *Pikirkan* ∼ , *baru kaudjawab,* Think it over carefully and then answer. *dgn* ∼ maturely. – -me- cooking, matters connected with cooking. – *mangsai* overripe.

masakan 1 see MASA. 2 see MASAK.

masakini the present time.

masal massive. *setjara* – on a massive scale.

masalah 1 problem, complication. 2 question. me-kan to make a problem of s.t.

masalla 1 prayer mat. 2 O God!

masam 1 sour, acid. *Mangga muda ini* – *sekali,* This young mango is very sour. 2 sullen, surly. *Djangan* – *sadja mukamu,* Don't always look so sullen. ke- –²an sourlike, rather sour. me- to become sour. *Susu itu tlh* ∼ , The milk has become sour. me-kan to make sour, pickle. *Ibu* ∼ *timun utk atjar,* Mother pickles cucumber for pickle.

masap me- to evaporate.

masarakat see MASJARAKAT.

masdar infinitive (gram.).

masdjid see MESDJID. – *Agung* the large new mosque in Kebajoran Baru, Jakarta. – *alharam* the mosque in Mecca. – *alaksa* the mosque in Jerusalem. – *djamik* principal mosque.

Maséh Jesus.

maséhi 1 Christian. 2 Protestant.

masgul 1 resentful. 2 anxious, concerned. *Hatinja* – *memikirkan keadaan orang tuanja,* He is very concerned about his parents. ke-an 1 anxiety, concern. 2 resentment. *Redakanlah* ∼*mu,* Calm down your anxiety. 3 sad, discontented. me-kan to arouse anxiety, be of concern. *Keadaan sisakit* ∼ , *dokter bilang,* The condition of the patient is of concern, the doctor says.

mashab see MAZHAB.

mashur see MASJHUR.

masih still, yet. *Dia* – *dirumah,* He's still home. *Ketika saja berangkat, ia* – *tidur,* When I left home, he was still sleeping. se- when. ∼ *saja ketjil...* When I was a child...

Masih Messiah. see MASÉH.

masin salty, briny. – *lidah,* – *mulut* talkative, verbose. *Blm tahu digaram,* He hasn't had much experience yet. *Garam kami tidak* – *padanja,* He didn't listen to what we said. -an pickles.

masing² 1 each. – *mengemukakan*

pikirannja, Each presented his own idea. 2 respective(ly).

masinis 1 ship's engineer. 2 locomotive engineer.

masir 1 granular. 2 see MESIR.

Masir see MESIR.

masja Allah the will of God (used as an exclamation of surprise, pity, etc.).

masjarakat society, community. berto form a group. ke-an social. *Ada banjak soal* ∼ , There are many social problems. – *ramai* the public. – *tembéréng* fringe society.

masjawarat see MUSJAWARAT.

masjgul see MASGUL.

masjhur well-known, famous. *Dia* – *ke-mana²,* He's famous everywhere. ke-an fame. me-kan 1 to make famous. *Perbuatan itulah jg* ∼ *namanja,* It was that deed which made him famous. 2 to spread the news. *Apakah kabar ttg agama Islam di-kan?* Is the news of the Islamic religion being spread? ter- well-known, famous.

masjrik the east.

masjuk beloved, sweetheart.

maskapai company, enterprise. – *asing banjak sekali disana,* There were many foreign enterprises there. – *kapal* ship concern. – *pengangkutan* transport firm.

maskat k.o. shirt or outer jacket.

maski see MESKIPUN.

maslahat use, benefit. ke-an use, benefit, profit.

massa mass. – *aksi* mass action. – *produksi* mass production.

mastika see MESTIKA.

masuk 1 to enter, go into. *Dilarang* –! Do not enter! *Silahkan* –, Please come in. 2 to go down. *Matahari* – *pukul 8 sekarang,* The sun goes down at 8 now. 3 to be present. *Saja rasa hari ini dia* –, I believe he'll come in today. 4 to be included. *Dua rupiah sadja. Ongkos gas sdh* –, It's only 2 rupiahs. The price of the gas is already included. 5 to be entered. *Ia tak* – *buku dlm pergaulan itu,* His position in that group is unimportant. 6 to participate, join. *Kapan dia* – *perkumpulan itu?* When did he join that organization? *Ia sdh* – *tentara,* He has joined the army. 7 to be converted. *Orang dipantai* – *Islam terlebih dulu,* The coastal people were the first to be converted to Islam. ke-an 1 possessed. ∼ *sétan barangkali,* Maybe he's possessed by a ghost. 2 entered accidentally. *Botol itu* ∼ *lalat,* A fly has accidentally entered the bottle. 3 entered. *Rumah* ∼ *pentjuri*, The house was entered by a thief. **me–i** 1 to enter. *Diam*[2] *sekali dia* ∼ *kamar itu*, Very quietly he entered the room. 2 to meddle in. *Djangan* ∼ *perkara orang lain*, Don't meddle in others' affairs. **me–kan** 1 to take. *Ia* ∼ *kuda kekandang*, He took the horse to the stable. 2 to put. *Ia* ∼ *barang kedalam lemari*, She put the things in the cupboard. 3 to import. *Perusahaan itu* ∼ *barang kedalam negeri*, The firm imported goods into the country. 4 to enter in. *Mandur itu* ∼ *buku*, The foreman entered it in the book. **pe–an** 1 registration, entering. 2 import. ∼ *uang* bringing in of money. 3 introduction. *Tugas kewadjiban djawatan itu ialah* ∼ *ber-bagai*[2] *tumbuh*[2]*an jg berfaédah kedaérah kekeringan*, The function of that division is the introduction of various useful plants to the arid regions. **ter–** included, counted, belonging to. – *akal* plausible, within reason, stands to reason. *Kedjadian seperti itu* – *akal*, Events like that are plausible. – *angin* to catch a cold. – *Belanda* to become a naturalized Dutch citizen. – *bilangan* belonging to. – *Islam* to become a Moslem. – *latihan* to enter military service. – *lima tahun* exactly 5 years. – *mendjadi* to belong to. – *sekolah* to go to school. – *serdadu* to join the army. – *tempias*, It's raining in. – *tidur* to go to sleep. – *udjian* to go in for an examination. – *ulur* to become a slave.

masup see MASUK. –*in 50 liter*, Put in 50 liters.

mata 1 eye. 2 center, core, nucleus. **me– –**[2]**i** to investigate, look into. **se– –**[2] only, merely. *Itu dusta* ∼ , It's nothing but a lie. *Perkataan*[2]*nja itu* ∼ *keluar dari hati jg tjemburu sadja*, It was sheer envy that made her talk like that. **ter– –**[2] obvious, very clear. –[2] 1 spy. 2 detective. – *air* spring, well. – *anggaran* (*belandja*) budget allocation, item. – *angin* points of the compass. – *badjak* plowshare. – *bakup* black eye. – *bedil* bead (of a gun). – *beliung* the cutting edge of an adze, hoe, ax. – *benda* valuables. – *betung* dumb, uneducated, ignorant. – *bisul* the core of the boil. – *buatan* glass eye. – *buku* knuckle. – *bulan* dimly visible moon. – *dagangan* commodities. – *datjing* the stripes on the scales. – *dekat* myopic, nearsighted. – *djala* mesh of the net. – *djalan* road observer, watchman, scout.

– *djarum* eye of a needle. – *djauh* farsighted. – *duitan* craving for money. – *gelap* amuck, in a rage. – *gunting* sharp edge of scissors. – *hati* feelings, the mind's eye. – *huruf* character, letter. – *ikan* corn on toe. – *kail* fishhook. – *kain* the design on a sarong. – *kaju* knot in wood. – *kaki* ankle. – *kepala* o's own eyes. – *kerandjang* to be lecherous. – *kérék* knots on a pulley. – *kuliah* university subject. – *kutjing* semiprecious stone. – *panah* arrowhead. – *pedoman* points of the compass. – *peladjaran* subject of instruction. – *peladjaran tambahan* minor subject. – *peladjaran utama* major subject. – *pengadjaran* subject (of instruction). – *penghidupan*, – *pentjarian* livelihood, living. – *perdagangan* commodity. – *petir* flash of lightning. – *piano* piano key. – *pisau* knife blade. – *rantai* link. – *sangkur* bayonet. – *sapi* fried egg. – *sapi balik* fried egg over. – *sasaran* bull's eye. – *sipit* slant-eyed. – *surat* writing in a letter. – *susu* nipple. – *tangga* rung of ladder. – *tjintjin* stone in a ring. – *tjipit* see – SIPIT. – *tombak* sharp point of a spear. – *uang* coin.

matahari the sun. – *berajun* approximately 3:30 P.M. – *hidup* the east. – *masuk*, The sun sets. – *mati* the west. – *naik*, The sun rises. – *tenggelam*, – *terbenam* sunset. – *terbit*, The sun rises. – *terpidjak* noontime.

mata[2] see MATA.

matang 1 ripe. *Buah mangga sdh mulai* –, The mangoes have started ripening. 2 done, cooked. *Nasi sdh* –? Is the rice done? 3 mature, adult. *Ia blm* – *benar*, He is not really mature yet. **ke–an** 1 overripe. *Djangan dibiarkan dipohon. Nanti* ∼ , Don't leave it on the tree, it will get overripe. 2 ripeness. **me–kan** 1 to cook. 2 to let ripen. *Mangga ini di–kan sendiri*, This mango was left to ripen by itself.

matari see MATAHARI.

mateng see MATANG.

materi material.

mati 1 to die, be dead. *Andjing kami* –, Our dog is dead. 2 to break up. *Perkumpulan itu* –, The organization broke up. 3 fixed. *Harga itu* –, The price is fixed. 4 numb. *Udjung djariku* –, My finger tips are numb. 5 to stop. *Djam itu* –, The clock stopped. 6 to go out (of lights, gas). **ber– –**[2]**an** to work hard at. *Ia* ∼ *menjelesaikan pekerdjaannja*, He is working hard at finishing the job. **ber–kan** *diri* to pretend to be dying. **ke–an** 1 death. 2 overtaken by death, bereft of. *Keluarga itu* ~ *anak*, The family lost a child. 3 to die down. ~ *angin*, The wind has died down. **ke- -²an** 1 with every effort. 2 to appear dead. **me-kan** 1 to kill, murder. *Siapa jg* ~ *ular itu?* Who killed the snake? 2 to extinguish, put out. *Djangan lupa* ~ *api sebelum tidur*, Don't forget to put the fire out before you go to bed. **-²an** 1 to pretend to be dead. *Dia tidak -, hanja* ~ *sadja*, He isn't dead, he's just pretending. 2 with all effort, as hard as possible. *Ia bekerdja* ~ , He works as hard as he can. - *ajam* to die, croak. - *angin* weak. - *bersebab* to die an unnatural death (murder, drowning, etc.). - *disalib* crucified. - *haid* menopause. - *kekam* neap tide. - *konjol* to die in vain. - *kumlah* to die a natural death. - *kutu* powerless, impotent. - *lelas* 1 a natural death. 2 to die in vain. - *lepur* to suffocate in mud. - *mampus* 1 to die right off. 2 To hell with you! (Go to hell!) - *modar* to be killed without ritual slaughtering. - *putjuk* impotent. - *rasa* 1 apathetic. 2 anesthesia. - *sabil* to die for a worthy cause. - *sesat* to commit suicide. - *sjahid* to die in a holy war. - *suri* suspended animation. - *tersalai* asphyxiated.

matjam 1 kind, sort, quality, type. *Ini - jg terbaik*, This is the best quality. - *apa?* What kind? 2 as, like. - *siapa anak ini?* Who does this child look like? 3 way, method. *Bukan -nja*, That's not the way. 4 model, fashion. - *radio itu saja suka*, I like that radio model. **ber- -²** various. *Ada disini* ~ *bunga*, Here there are various flowers. **memper--²kan** to treat differently. *Djangan engkau* ~ *teman²mu*, Don't treat your friends differently. **se-** 1 of the kind, sort. *Otonja* ~ *oto kenalan kami*, His car is the same kind as our friend's. 2 like, as, resembling. *Rumah itu* ~ *rumah kami*, That house resembles ours.

matjan tiger. **me-i** to frighten, intimidate. **-²an** toy tiger, plaything. - *loréng* striped royal tiger. - *tutul* panther.

matjet 1 stuck, not run smoothly. *Mesin djahit kami -*, Our sewing machine isn't running smoothly. 2 clogged, stopped up. *Saluran itu -*, The pipe is clogged up. **ke-an** jamming, sticking.

matjik see MAK.

matra 1 dimension. 2 musical measure, bar.

matu unit of weight for gold. *Itu*

emas sepuluh -, That is 24-carat gold. **me-kan** to determine the purity of gold.

mau 1 shall, will. *Dia - datang soré ini*, He will come this evening. 2 to wish. *Dia - sekali ke Amérika*, He very much wishes to go to America. 3 to want. *Tuan - apa?* What do you want? 4 wish. *Itu -ku*, That's my wish. **berke-an** to have the will. **ke-an** wish, desire, will. **me-i** to demand. **me- -²kan** to force. *Si Ali* ~ *adiknja memakan és krim*, Ali forced his younger brother to eat ice cream. **se-(-)nja** at will, as one likes. *Dia bekerdja* ~ , He works just as he likes. **-nja** would like. *Berapa buku* ~ , *pak?* How many books would you like? - *sama* - mutual liking. *Kalau - sama - artinja bukan paksaan*, When both like it, there's no saying it was forced. - *tak* - willy-nilly, whether one wants to or not. - *tak -, dia harus pergi*, He has to go whether he wants to or not. - *kemana, bung?* 1 Where are you off to, fellow? 2 How're things going?

maudjud concrete, real, tangible.

maulana 1 our Lord. 2 the honorable (title of a Moslem scholar).

maulid 1 Mohammed's birthday. 2 stories of Mohammed's birth.

maulud see MAULID.

maung stinking, disgusting. *Djangan simpan lama², - baunja nanti*, Don't keep it too long, it will smell.

maupun 1 although, in spite of the fact. *Dia pergi djuga - dilarang*, He went anyway although it was forbidden. 2 see BAIK. - ... - ... 1 either ... or ... 2 whether ... or ...

maut 1 death. 2 hour of death for humans. **pe-an** mortality.

mawar rose.

mawas orangutan.

mazbah altar.

mazhab 1 school of thought concerning Moslem law. 2 school in any subject. - *hukum* law school.

mazmur psalm.

ma'zul deposed, dethroned, dismissed. **me-kan** to depose. ~ *dirinja* to abdicate.

M. B. [*Markas Besar*] headquarters.

MBAD [*Markas Besar Angkatan Darat*] army headquarters.

mbah 1 leader, champion. 2 stronghold. *Dia adalah -nja kominis*, He's a Communist leader. 3 see EMBAH.

mbakju 1 you. 2 sis. 3 see BAKJU.

MBAL [*Markas Besar Angkatan Laut*] navy headquarters.

MBAU [*Markas Besar Angkatan Udara*] air force headquarters.

mbok(mas) form of address for older Javanese woman of humble origin.

mébel furniture.

médali medal.

médan field, plain, square. – *gaja* magnetic field. – *orang pandai*[2] society of learned people. – *peperangan*, – *perang* battlefield. – *ramai* the public.

medit stingy.

médja table. – *bola* billiard table. – *bundar* round table. – *hias* dressing table. – *hidjau* the bench, court. – *kedai* shop counter. – *makan* dining room table. – *tulis* desk, writing table.

medjam to turn, spin.

medjan see MEDJEN.

medjen dysentery.

medok 1 porous. 2 dirty, filthy. 3 done. *Makin – makin énak*, The more done it is the better it tastes.

Méester Cornélis see DJATINEGARA.

méga cloud. – *mendung* rain cloud.

megah 1 fame, glory. *–nja bertambah*, His fame is on the increase. 2 proud, aloof. **ber-** –[2] to brag. **ke–an** greatness, glory, pride. **me–kan** to brag about. *Dia selalu* ∼ *kekajaannja*, He is always bragging about his wealth.

megap[2] to gasp for breath.

megar see MEKAR.

megat to spin (of a top).

megrek 1 continuously sick. 2 emaciated.

Méi May.

Mekah Mecca.

mékanis mechanical. *Dia bekerdja setjara –*, He works mechanically.

mékanisasi mechanization. **me–kan** to mechanize.

mékanisme mechanism.

mekar 1 to open up, blossom. *Kembang melati mulai –*, The jasmines have started to blossom. 2 to rise. *Adonan kué itu –*, The cake dough is rising. **me–kan** to raise, open up. *Saja* ∼ *pajung utk adik saja*, I opened up the umbrella for my sister.

Méksiko Mexico.

mél 1 to report. *Djangan lupa – kpd madjikanmu*, Don't forget to report to your boss. 2 mile.

melainkan but, except, but rather. *Tiada jg kami dapati – ikan*, We could not get anything but fish. see LAIN.

Melaju Malay. *Ia orang –*, He's a Malay. **me–kan** to translate into Malay. – *Raja* Malaysia.

melak *dgn* –[2] openly, clearly, obviously (when cheating s.o.).

Melaka Malacca.

melambang a type of flat-bottomed boat.

melar 1 to stretch, expand, rise. *Adonan itu akan –*, The dough will rise. 2 expansion. 3 elastic.

melarat 1 poverty, misery. 2 poor, miserable. **ke–an** 1 misery, poverty. 2 disadvantage.

melati jasmine.

melék to be awake, to have o's eyes open. *Baji sdh –*, The baby is awake. – *huruf* to be literate. *Ia blm –*, He's ignorant.

melempem 1 damp, not quite dry. *Kuwé itu djangan ditinggalkan diluar, nanti –*, Don't leave the cookies out; they might get damp and soggy. 2 inactive, slow. 3 to misfire.

meléng see MELING.

melését 1 slipped. *Hati*[2], *nanti –*, Be careful; you might slip. 2 depression, slump. 3 to be wrong, be misplaced. *Kepertjajaannja tidaklah –*, His confidence is not misplaced.

melik greedy. – *pangkat tinggi* a mad desire for a high position. **ke–an** greed, craving.

meling 1 careless, sloppy, untidy. 2 to look to the side, be inattentive. *Djangan – kalau menjopir*, Don't look to the side when driving.

melit curious, inquisitive.

melodi melody.

melongo taken by surprise, bewildered.

melor a 2-wheeled carriage.

melulu exclusively, only. *Uang ini – utk uang makan*, This money is exclusively for your meals. see LULU.

melur jasmine.

mem– see under base beg. with (1) *p-*, (2) *m-*.

mémang 1 of course, certainly. 2 indeed. – *pandai anak itu*, That child is indeed clever. **se–nja** 1 indeed, of course (stronger than *mémang* alone). ∼ *bahasa itu dipakai djuga*, Of course that language is used too. 2 should. ∼ *dia harus datang dulu kerumah kita*, He should come to see us first. **–nja** 1 inherently, by nature. 2 of course. ∼ *aku ini buta?* Do you think I'm blind?

memar bruised.

memb– see under base beg. with *b-*.

memedi ghost.

mémék **ber–(–)** 1 to whimper, whine. 2 to nag.

memf– see under base beg. with *f-*.

memori pendjelasan explanatory statement, memorandum.

mempan 1 to be vulnerable. *Pahlawan itu tidak – kena sendjata*, The hero was invulnerable to weapons.

2 to be sensitive to. *Dia – dinasihati*, He is sensitive to advice. 3 to be effective. *Dia – benar dlm peker-djaannja*, He's very effective in his work. *tidak* – immune.

mempeladjari see ADJAR.

mempelai 1 bride. 2 bridegroom.

mempelam mango.

mémper to resemble. *Kok nggak – ibunja, ja?* Why, she doesn't resemble her mother, does she?

mempunjai see PUNJA.

men- see under base beg. with (1) *t-*, (2) *n-*.

mena *tidak* se- –² 1 arbitrarily, in highhanded fashion, cruelly. *Musuh membom tidak ~*, The enemy bombed without cause. 2 unfair.

ménak aristocratic, distinguished, prominent.

menang 1 to win, profit. *Siapa jg – dlm pertandingan?* Who won the contest? 2 to pass an examination. *Dia – udjian*, He passed his examination. 3 not inferior, not less. *Rumah itu – bagusnja*, That house is not inferior in beauty. **ke–an** victory, superiority. **me–i** to defeat, beat. *Perkumpulan A ~ perkumpulan B*, Club A defeated Club B. **memper–kan** 1 to help win, cause to win. *Bom atom jg ~ Amérika diperang dunia kedua*, It was the atom bomb which helped the U.S. to win the Second World War. 2 to win. *Ia ~ médali emas*, He won a gold medal. **pe–** 1 winner. 2 profit. – *dgn angka* to win on points (boxing). – *suara* elected.

menantu son- or daughter-in-law. **ber–kan** to take as son- or daughter-in-law.

menara a tower, minaret. – *air* watertower. – *api* lighthouse. – *bor* drilling rig. – *penindjau* observation tower. – *radio* radio mast.

ménat see MINAT.

menatu laundryman.

mend- see under base beg. with *d-*.

mendak 1 to sink, bow. 2 to approach bowing.

mendam drunk. **ke–an** drunkenness.

mendap 1 to sink, settle. 2 sediment, deposit.

mendéra banyan tree.

mendiang the late. – *tuan Ali* the late Mr. Ali.

mendikai small watermelon.

mending(an) 1 fairly good. *Untung djualan – djuga*, The profit from the sale is fairly good. 2 average, middling. *Keadaan disini masih –*, The situation here is still average. **–an** better, preferable.

mendj- see under base beg. with *dj-*.

mendjangan deer.

mendonan immigrant, stranger.

méndréng see MIND(E)RING.

mendung cloudy, overcast. *Hari ini –*, Today it's cloudy. **mem–i** 1 to cloud over. 2 to cast a cloud over.

mendusin to wake up from sleep, recover consciousness.

meng- see under base beg. with (1) *k-*, (2) a vowel, (3) *ng-*.

mengah ter- –² gasping, out of breath.

mengangah 1 to have fiery coals. 2 see API.

mengap to gape. –² to pant, gasp for breath.

mengapa 1 why. – *bung berangkat?* Why are you leaving? 2 doing what? 3 see APA.

mengenai see KENA.

mengepas see PAS.

mengepél see PÉL.

mengerti to understand. *Saja tidak –*, I don't understand. **di–** to be understood.

mengetahui see TAHU.

mengetjat see TJAT.

mengga complete, perfect. se- –² the whole, only. se- –²nja completely, perfectly.

ménggok to (make a) turn.

mengiang rainbow.

mengi(h) 1 asthma. 2 to pant, have difficulty in breathing.

mengkal 1 unripe (of fruit). *Buah itu –*, The fruit is unripe. 2 annoyed, irritated. *Hatinja – sekali*, He's very much annoyed. **ber–** *hati* to be irritated, annoyed. **me–kan** to annoy, irritate. *~ hati* annoying, irritating.

mengkara Cancer.

Mengkasar Macassar.

mengkelan ter– to get choked.

mengkeret 1 to shrink. *Sesudah ditjutji badjunja –*, After washing the dress shrank. 2 to make gathers (in sewing). *Dia – badjunja disatu pihak sadja*, She made gathers on one side of her dress only. 3 angry. *Djangan –, bung*, Don't be angry, my friend. 4 afraid, scared. *Pentjuri itu – sekali melihat polisi*, The thief was very afraid upon seeing the policeman. 5 to double up with pain.

mengkilap 1 to shine, glitter. 2 see KILAP.

mengkilat see KILAT.

mengking to shake with fright.

mengkirik to make o's flesh creep, shiver.

mengkis 1 to challenge. 2 to scorn, taunt.

mengkudu name of a tree whose sap is used as dye for batik.

mengot crooked, curved.

mengung see MENUNG.

meni red paint against rust.

menir 1 fine grains of rice. 2 sir, gentleman.

menit minute.

menj- see under base beg. with (1) *s-*, (2) *nj-*.

menjan see KEMENJAN.

menjesal ke–an regret. see SESAL.

menjolok *mata* see TJOLOK.

Menlu [*Menteri Luar Negeri*] Minister of Foreign Affairs.

ménstruasi menstruation.

ment- see under base beg. with *t-*.

MentAgama [*Menteri Agama*] Minister of Religion.

mentah 1 unripe, raw, uncooked. *Buah – itu asam*, The unripe fruit is sour. 2 incomplete, unfinished. *Sekolahnja masih –*, He hasn't finished school yet. *–²* 1 raw, uncooked, fresh. *Djangan makan sajuran² itu ~* , Don't eat the vegetables raw. 2 unconditional, blunt, straightforward. *Semua nasihat itu ditelannja ~* , She accepts all the advice unconditionally. 3 crude. *minjak – crude oil.* ke–an rawness, unripeness.

mental 1 to bounce off, rebound. *Bola itu – djauh sekali*, The ball bounced very far away. 2 uninjured.

méntalita mentality.

méntalitét see MÉNTALITA.

mentang² only because. *– orang kaja, dia berbuat semaunja sadja*, Only because he is rich does he act so highhandedly.

mentari = MATAHARI.

mentéga butter. me–i 1 to smear with butter. *Si Mina ~ roti*, Mina butters her bread. 2 to butter up, flatter. *Supaja dia naik pangkat, pegawai itu selalu ~ madjikannja*, In order to get a promotion that employee is always flattering his boss. *– buatan, – tiruan* margarine.

Ménténg 1 section of Jakarta. 2 telephone exchange in Jakarta.

mentera see MANTERA.

mentéréng 1 dressed up. *– begini, mau kemana?* Where are you going, dressed up like this? 2 luxurious, magnificent. *Rumah menteri itu –*, The minister's house is magnificent. ke–an luxury, magnificence.

menteri cabinet minister. ke–an ministry, department. *~ Luar Negeri* Department of State, Ministry of Foreign Affairs. *– Angkatan Laut* Secretary of the Navy. *– Angkatan Udara* Secretary of the Air Force. *–*

Dalam Negeri Secretary of the Interior. *– guru* headmaster. *– Kehakiman* Minister of Justice. *– Keséhatan* Secretary of Health. *– Keuangan* Secretary of the Treasury. *– Luar Negeri* Secretary of State, Minister of Foreign Affairs. *– muda* vice-minister, deputy secretary. *– Negara* Minister of State. *– Penerangan* Minister of Information. *– Pengadjaran* Minister of Education. *– Perdagangan dan Perusahaan* Secretary of Commerce. *– Perhubungan* Minister of Communications. *– Sosial* Minister of Social Affairs. *– ukur* surveyor. *– Urusan Agama* Minister of Religious Affairs.

mentimun cucumber.

mentj- see under base beg. with *tj-*.

mentjak see PENTJAK. **ber-** to do the sword dance. *–²* 1 to be out of sorts. *Mengapa ~ ?* Why are you out of sorts? 2 to move convulsively. *Binatang itu ~ kepanasan*, The animal moved convulsively from the heat.

mentjerét diarrhea.

mentjit mouse.

méntjok to perch (of birds).

méntjong 1 askew, aslant. 2 without any specific direction or aim.

mentua parents-in-law.

menung **ber-** to muse, ponder, meditate. *Mengapa ~ sadja?* Why are you pondering all the time? ke–an meditation. me–kan to ponder deeply. *~ apa lagi engkau sekarang?* What are you pondering about now? pe–dreamer, ponderer. per–an contemplation, musing. ter- *–²* to muse, ponder. *Dia ~ memikirkan penjakit ibunja*, He ponders about his mother's illness. –an musing.

méong 1 sound made by a cat, meow. 2 cat.

mérah red. ke- *–²*(an) reddish. me–to redden, become red. *Bunga itu ~ sekarang*, The flowers are becoming red now. me–kan to make red. *Di–kannja bibirnja sebelum berangkat*, She puts lipstick on before she leaves. pe- *bibir* lipstick. *– bungsu – bungur* purple. *– djambu* pink. *– lembajung* crimson. *– merang* scarlet. *– muda* pink. *– muka* to blush, blushing. *– padam* scarlet. *– tedas* bright red. *– telur* egg yolk. *– tua* dark red, maroon.

merak peacock. *– hati* sweet and friendly.

merang rice straw (of paddy).

mérat see MAIRAT.

merawal 1 banner. 2 the colors.

merbah thrush.

merbuk turtledove.

merdéka free, independent, liberated. *Indonésia –* free Indonesia. ke–an freedom, liberty, independence. **me-kan** 1 to liberate, release, set free. 2 to acquit, exonerate, absolve. *Pendjahat² perang sdh di-kan*, The war criminals were set free. **pe-liberator.** – *ajam*, – *bébas* completely free, free as a bird.

merdésa 1 good, beautiful, decent. *Dia mempunjai watak jg –*, He possesses a good character. 2 choosy, fussy. *Dia makan tidak –*, He's not fussy about food.

merdjan red coral beads for making necklace.

merdu melodious, sweet, clear. *Suara gadis itu –*, The girl's voice is sweet.

mérék 1 brand, stamp, trade-mark, label. *–nja ada dibagian belakang*, The stamp is on the back. 2 make. *Otonja – apa?* What is the make of his car? 3 quality. **ber-** to have a trade-mark. *Mainan ini ~ Dje-pang*, This toy has a Japanese trademark.

meréka 1 they. – *suka minum kopi*, They like to drink coffee. 2 them. *Saja melihat –*, I see them. 3 their. *Ia suka oto –*, He likes their car.

merem with closed eyes. **me-kan** to close. *Sesudah beberapa djam baru dia bisa ~ matanja*, Only after several hours could he close his eyes.

méréng see MIRING.

mérés even, level.

meriam cannon, gun. – *penangkis* antiaircraft cannon. – *penémbak tjepat* rapid-fire cannon.

meriang feverish. *Badanku merasa –*, I feel feverish.

merih throat, windpipe.

merikan American.

meritja (white) pepper. – *bulat* pep-percorns.

mérk see MÉREK.

merosot see ROSOT. 1 to fall. *Harga kain –*, The price of cloth has fallen. 2 to decrease. *Namanja sedang –*, His fame is decreasing. 3 to slip. *Saja – dari tangga tadi*, I slipped from the ladder. **ke-an** fall, decline.

merpati pigeon.

mersik 1 shrill. *Suara burung itu –*, The bird's voice is shrill. 2 crisp. *Krupuk itu –*, The shrimp flakes are crisp. 3 skinny, lean. *Anak itu kurus –*, That child is skinny.

mertja-mertjik rustling of water.

mertjapada this world.

mertjon see MERTJUN.

mertju 1 tower. 2 peak, summit. 3 treetop. – *api* lighthouse. – *gunung* mountain peak. – *suar* lighthouse.

mertjun fireworks.

mertua see MENTUA.

meruah see MARWAH.

meruap 1 to steam. 2 to bubble up.

mésan tombstone, grave marker.

mesdjid mosque. see MASDJID.

mésem to smile.

mesera see MESRA.

mesigit see MESDJID.

mesin machine, engine. – *bitjara* phonograph. – *bor* drill. – *bubut* lathe. – *dérék* derrick. – *djahit* sewing machine. – *giling* rolling machine. – *hitung* 1 calculating machine. 2 computer. – *ketik* typewriter. – *kira* calculating machine. – *las* welding apparatus. – *ngomong*, – *njanji* phonograph. – *pemetjah batu* stone crusher. – *pemotong rumput* lawn mower. – *penambah* adding machine. – *penetas* brooder. – *pengeram* incubator. – *tenaga* power machine. – *terbang* airplane. – *tik* typewriter. – *tjétak* printing press. – *tjukur listerik* electric shaver. – *tjutji pakaian* washing machine. – *tulis* typewriter.

Mesir Egypt.

mesiu ammunition.

meski(pun) 1 although. – *susah, dpt djuga*, Although it was difficult, he succeeded anyhow. 2 in spite of (the fact that) – *begitu* nevertheless.

mesra 1 absorbed, fused. – *didalam hati* absorbed in his mind. 2 intimate, very close. *Dia sahabat –*, He's a very intimate friend. 3 fond. *Ada jg masih – pd bahasa itu*, There are those who are still fond of that language. **ber-** entirely mixed. *Gula itu sdh ~ dgn air*, The sugar is entirely mixed with water. **me-kan** to absorb, assimilate. *Meréka ~ naséhatnja*, They absorbed his advice entirely. **ke-an, per-an** absorption.

méster 1 lawyer, jurist. 2 title of those holding a Dutch or Indonesian law degree. 3 teacher.

Méster Djatinegara (section of Jakarta).

mesti 1 certain, surely. *Kalau beladjar keras, – dia lulus*, If he studies hard, he'll surely pass. 2 must, have to. *Saja – berangkat hari ini djuga*, I must leave this very day. **ke-an** a must, necessity, obligation. **me-kan** 1 to compel, require. *Tiap orang di-kan beladjar membatja*, Everyone is required to learn to read. 2 to regard as certain. **se-nja** should, actually, It ought. *~ harus selesai hari ini*, It should be finished today. *Tiap penduduk dianggap sdh ~ menurut peraturan negara*, Every citizen is expected to abide by the government regulations.

mestika magic jewel, precious stone. – *hati* sweetheart.
mesum 1 dirty, filthy, polluted. *Pakaiannja tlh* –, His clothes are dirty. 2 improper, indecent. *Isi batjaan itu* –, The content of the reading is indecent. 3 immoral. *perbuatan* – *an* immoral act. **ke–an** filth, dirt, indecency, obscenity.
meta 1 mad, drunk, in a rage. 2 rutting period.
metari see MATAHARI.
métér meter. **–an** meter. ∼ *air* water meter. ∼ *gas* gas meter.
meterai postage, stamp, gauge, seal. **me–(kan)** to stamp, put a seal on. *Pegawai pos* ∼ *pospakét itu*, The postal employee stamps the package. **ter–** stamped, sealed. ∼ *didalam hati* felt in his heart. – *surat* postage stamp. – *témpél* seal on money order, checks, etc. – *upah* tax seal or stamp.
métode method.
métodis methodical.
méwah luxurious, extravagant. **ke–an** luxury, extravagance.
méwék to start to cry.
mh. [*marah*] a title (in Sumatra).
Mhd. [*Mohammad*] Mohammed.
mi noodles.
miak peeping of chickens.
miang 1 bamboo hairs which cause itching. 2 traitor, slanderer. **se–** 1 a bit. *Ia tidak barang takut* ∼ *djuga*, He wasn't a bit afraid. 2 a grain, a drop of s.t.
MIB [*Maluku Irian Barat*] Moluccas and Western New Guinea.
midar to walk about.
midju² lentils.
mihrab niche in a mosque wall facing Mecca.
mikin see MAKIN.
mikrab see MIHRAB.
mikrad see MI'RADJ.
mikropon microphone.
mil mile.
miliar see MILJAR.
milik 1 property. *Ini* – *siapa?* Whose property is this? – *adalah funksi sosial*, Property is a social function. 2 fate. *Mémang sdh* – *saja*, It's just my fate. **me–i** to possess, win. *Tiada seorangpun* ∼ *tanah ini*, No one owns this land. **ke–an, pe–an** ownership, possession. **pe–** owner, proprietor.
milimétér millimeter.
milir downstream.
milisi 1 militia. 2 military man. 3 military service.
militér military. **ke–an** military.
miliun see MILJUN.

miljar billion.
miljun million. **–an** millions.
mimbar pulpit, speaking platform, chancel, podium.
mimis small round bullet.
mimisan nosebleed.
mimpi dream. **ber–** to dream. *Tadi malam saja* ∼ *ttg adik saja*, Last night I dreamed of my brother. **me–kan** 1 to dream of, about. ∼ *sesuatu ada artinja*, Dreaming about s.t. has a significance. 2 to have great dreams. *Djangan kau–kan jg bukan²*, Don't have too great dreams. **ter–(–)** to dream continuously about s.t. *Sebab ingin sekali pergi dia* ∼ , Because he wants to go very much, he dreams about it constantly. **–an** a dream, ideal, illusion. ∼ *keinginan* wishful thinking.
mina Pisces (zodiac).
minal'aidin walfaizin congratulations expressed on Lebaran day.
minat interest, proclivity. *Ia menaruh* – *pd musik*, He is interested in music. *Dia mempunjai* – *thd (kpd) ilmu kimia*, He's interested in chemistry. **ber–** to have an interest. *Dia tidak lagi* ∼ *utk mengarang*, He no longer has any interest in writing. **me–i** to observe, be interested in. *Dia* ∼ *politik luar negeri*, He's interested in foreign policy. **pe–** 1 devotee, amateur, fan. 2 interested person.
mind(e)ring to sell on the installment plan.
minggat to flee, run away.
minggir to go on the side, go along. *Perahu itu* – *sepandjang pantai*, The prow goes along the shore.
minggu 1 week. 2 Sunday. **–an** weekly. *dua* ∼ biweekly.
minim minimum.
minit see MENIT.
minjak oil, grease, fat. **ber–** to have oil, be greasy. *Dia pandai* ∼ *air*, She's very good at giving false compliments. **me–i** to oil, grease. *Dia* ∼ *otonja*, He greased his car. **per–an** petroleum, refinery affairs. – *adas* fennel oil. – *atar* perfume. – *babi* lard. – *bakar* fuel oil. – *bumi* petroleum. – *djarak* castor oil. – *djelantah* oil left in frying pan. – *gas* kerosene. – *goréng* fat for frying. – *ikan* cod-liver oil. – *katjang* peanut oil. – *kelapa* coconut oil (for frying). – *kelonjo* eau-de-cologne. – *lintjir* lubricating oil. – *madjemuk* mixture of oils, perfumes. – *mentah* crude oil. – *njaman* 1 perfumed hair oil. 2 k.o. rubbing oil. – *pelumas* lubricating oil. – *penat* ointment. – *rambut* hair oil. – *rengas* varnish. – *samin* 1

shortening. 2 k.o. butter. - *sapi*
suet, beef fat. - *sawit* palm oil. -
semir lubricating oil. - *serai* citronella.
- *sutji* chrism. - *tanah* 1 petroleum.
2 kerosene. - *tjat* oil for paint. -
wangi perfume. - *zaitun* olive oil.

minoritas minority.

minoritét see MINORITAS.

minta 1 to ask, request, beg. *Saja -
maaf*, I beg your pardon. 2 please.
- *air, bung*, A glass of water, please.
ber- -² to beg. **me-** 1 to require,
demand. *Hal itu ~ perhatian sepenuh-
nja*, The matter requires full attention. 2 to request, ask. 3 to propose
to. *Gadis itu sdh beberapa kali di-*,
The girl was proposed to several times.
4 to claim. *Kedjadian itu ~ korban*,
The incident claimed some victims.
me-i to request s.t. *Ia di-i tolong*,
He was asked aid of. **me-kan** to ask
for s.t. for s.o. *Ia ~ adiknja badju
baru*, He asked for a new jacket for
his young brother. **pe- -²** beggar.
per-an 1 request. *atas ~nja* at his
request. 2 demand. *~ dan penawaran*
supply and demand. *~ ampun* to
beg o's pardon. - *berhenti* to tender
o's resignation. - *diri* to ask to be
excused. *"Pak, saja - diri dulu,"
katanja*, "Will you please excuse me?
I have to be going," he said. - *djalan*
to request permission to pass. -
do'a to pray. - *keramat* to ask bless-
ings on a holy place. - *lihat*, Let me
see it. - *musjawarat* to request consultation. - *njawa* to beg for mercy,
beg to be spared. - *pisah* to sue for
divorce. - *tabik* to say goodbye, take
leave. - *terima kasih* to thank. -
tjerai to sue for divorce. - *disambung
dgn...*Please connect me with... -
bitjara dgn Ali! May I speak with
Ali?

mintal see PINTAL.

minterad municipal council. *kuli -*
city employee (street sweeper).

minum to drink, absorb. *Dia suka -
kopi*, He likes to drink coffee. **me-(i)**
to drink. **me-kan** 1 to give to drink.
Ibu ~ baji susu, Mother gives the
baby milk to drink. 2 to water,
drench (animals). **pe-** drinker. **pe-
an** *obat* 1 taking of medicine. 2 s.t.
used for taking medicine. **ter-** 1
drunk accidentally. *Awas! Djangan
~ air digelas kotor itu*, Be careful
not to drink the water in that dirty
glass. 2 potable, drinkable. **-an** 1
a drink. 2 beverage. *~ keras* liquor.
- *madat* to smoke opium. - *obat* to
take medicine. - *rokok* to smoke. -
air sambil menjelam to kill 2 birds
with 1 stone.

mi'radj Mohammed's ascension to
Heaven.

mirah ruby.

miring 1 at an angle, aslant, askew.
Gambar itu -, The painting hangs at
an angle. 2 italics. *Bagian ini tjétak
-*, This part should be in italics. 3
oblique. **me-kan** to put at an angle,
make aslant. *Siapa jg ~ lemari ini?*
Who made this cupboard slant?

mirip to resemble. *Topi - topi saja*,
That hat resembles mine. **ke-an**
resemblance.

mis. [*misalnja*] for example.

misa religious mass.

misai mustache.

misal example, instance. **-nja** for
example. **me-kan** 1 to represent.
Gambar itu ~ apa? What does that
picture represent? 2 to assume. *Kita
-kan dalil ini benar*, We assume that
this rule is correct. 3 to take as an
example. *Anak itu ~ kawannja*, The
child takes his friend as an example.
pe-an 1 assumption. 2 sampling.
se- like, resembling. *Perbuatan anak
itu ~ orang déwasa sadja*, The
behavior of that child is just like an
adult's. - *kata* by way of speaking.
(di)-kan assuming, supposing that.

misan nephew or niece.

misbah lamp, light, lantern.

misih see MASIH.

miskalkulasi miscalculation.

miskin poor, needy, destitute. **ke-an**
poverty, destitution. **me-kan** to impoverish. *Padjak jg tinggi ~ penduduk*, High taxes impoverish the
population. **-²**, - *papa* very poor.

misluk(t) to be botched, badly made.

misoa vermicelli.

missa see MISA.

mistar 1 ruler, line. 2 cover, wrapper.

misti see MESTI.

mitraliur machine gun.

mitraljur see MITRALIUR.

mitsal see MISAL.

MKN [*Menteri Keamanan Nasional*]
Minister of National Security.

M/KSAK [*Menteri/Kepala Staf
Angkatan Kepolisian*] Minister/Chief
of Staff of the State Police.

mlongo see MELONGO.

Mob(b)rig [*Mobiele Brigade*] Mobile
Brigade (paramilitary branch of national police).

mobil (motor) car, automobile. -
badja armored car. - *gerobak* truck.

mobilisasi mobilization.

mobilisir **me-** to mobilize.

mobilitét mobility.

mochal see MUHAL.

modal capital (financial). **ber-** *deng-*

kul to speculate with another's capital. **ber-kan** to have s.t. as capital. ~ *keberanian* to have boldness as capital. **ke–an** capitalistic. *Perkumpulan itu bersifat* ~ , That association has a capitalistic character. **me–i** to finance. *Perusahaan itu di–i pemerintah*, The enterprise is financed by the government. **pe–** capitalist. **se–** to enter into a partnership. *Dia orang* ~ , He's a partner in the firm. – *bekerdja* working capital. – *dan poténsi,* – *dan tenaga* funds and forces. – *tetap* real estate. **per–an** capitalism.

modalwan capitalist.
mode fashion.
modél model.
modér(e)n modern. **ke–an** modernity. **me–kan, memper–** to modernize.
modérnisasi modernization.
modin o. who calls to prayers, muezzin.
modjah 1 socks. 2 stockings.
moga initiative. **pe–** initiator. **se-may,** I hope that. ~ *Tuhan mengiringimu dlm segala kesulitan,* May God be with you in trying times. –² *may,* I hope that. ~ *tjita²nja berhasil,* May his ideals be fulfilled.
mogok 1 to strike. *Pekerdja² pabrik itu* –, The laborers of that factory are on strike. 2 to stall, fail, stop, break down. *Otonja* – *didjalan,* His car stalled on the road. **me–i** to strike against. *Meréka* ~ *pabrik itu,* They struck against the factory. **pe-**striker. **pe–an** strike. – *duduk* sitdown strike. – *gindjal* anuria. – *makan* hunger strike.
mohon 1 to ask, request. *Dia* – *izin kpd madjikan,* He asked permission of the boss. 2 to implore, beseech. **ber–** to request. *Saja hendak* ~ *kpd tuan, supaja saja diberi naik gadji,* I want to ask you to please raise my salary. (**ber**)– *diri* to take leave, say goodbye. **me–** to ask, request. **pe–** 1 applicant. 2 supplicant. **per–an** request, appeal, petition.
mojang great-grandfather, great-grandparents.
molék beautiful, pretty, cute. *Gadis itu* – *betul,* That girl is very beautiful. **ke–an** attractiveness, beauty, charm.
molekul molecule.
momén moment.
momok bogeyman, ghost, spook. **me–i** to haunt.
mondok 1 fat, squat. 2 to stay, live with, board with. *Dia* – *dimana?* Where is he staying? 3 to live in a subleased room. 4 see PONDOK.
monetér monetary.

monggol knotty, gnarled.
mongkok 1 to stick out. *Batu besar* – *dipermukaan air,* A big stone protrudes above the surface of the water. 2 to tower above. *Dia* – *diantara kawan²nja,* He towers above his friends.
monjét monkey.
monopoli monopoly. **me–** to have a monopoly, monopolize.
montir mechanic.
montjong 1 snout, muzzle. 2 elephant trunk. 3 spout. **me–** to put out. *Mulutnja* ~ *kedepan,* His mouth jutted forward.
montjor 1 to flow out. *Minjak* – *dari kaléng,* The oil flows out of the can. 2 diarrhea.
montok well-built, fat, plump. **ke–an** plumpness.
montor 1 motor. 2 auto, car.
morak-marik see MORAT-MARIT.
morat-marit messy, scattered around, confused, disorganized. *Médja itu* –, The desk is messy.
mori cotton material (used for batik).
mosi motion, vote. – *tidak pertjaja* vote of no confidence.
Moskwa Moscow.
moster mustard. – *basah* prepared mustard.
mota see KAIN.
motivasi motivation.
motor 1 motor, engine. 2 motor(car), auto. **ber–** motorized. 1 *Sepédanja* ~ *sekarang,* His bicycle is motorized now. 2 to go by car. *Kami* ~ *dari Djakarta ke Bogor,* We motored, went by car from Jakarta to Bogor. **me–i** 1 to motor, go by car. 2 to provide s.o. with a car. 3 to spark, be the spark plug of. *Ia* ~ *kesebelasan itu,* He sparked the soccer team. – *pompa* fire engine.
motoris engineer, motorman.
motorisasi motorization.
motorpit motorcycle.
M.P.R.S. [*Madjelis Permusjawaratan Rakjat Sementara*] Provisional People's Deliberative Council.
m.p.s. [*menurut pendapat saja*] in my opinion.
Mr [*Meester (in de Rechten)*] a law degree; used as a title by its holder.
M'Thai [*Muang Thai*] Thailand.
M.U. [*Madjelis Umum*] General Assembly.
muafakah see MUPAKAT.
muafakat see MUPAKAT.
muai **me–** to expand, swell. **pe–an** expansion. ~ *pandjang* linear expansion.
muak 1 nauseating, revolting. 2 to

loathe (food or drink). **ke-an** nausea.
me-kan nauseating, repugnant.
mual 1 queasy. *Waktu naik kapal
saja -,* I feel queasy when I go sailing.
2 to loathe s.t. 3 to vomit. *Itu
membuat kita djadi - membatjanja,*
It makes us vomit to read it. **me-
kan** sickening, loathsome, disgusting,
revolting.
mu'alamat science.
mualim see MU'ALLIM.
mu'allim 1 (religious) teacher. 2
navigator. 3 pilot, guide.
Muang Thai Thailand.
muara estuary, mouth. **ber-** to flow,
empty into. *Kali Tjiliwung ~ di
Lautan Djawa,* The Tjiliwung River
empties into the Java Sea.
muat 1 to contain. 2 to hold. *Oto
itu - enam orang,* That car holds
6 people. 3 to place. *Tuan - adperténsi dimana?* Where did you place
the advertisement? 4 to accommodate. *Rumah ini hanja - 5 orang,*
This house accommodates only 5 persons. 5 to include. **ber-** 1 to contain.
Kapal itu ~ gula, The ship contains
sugar. 2 to be charged with. *Besi
ini ~ listrik,* This iron is charged
with electricity. **me-** 1 to hold,
contain. 2 to accommodate, be able
to hold. 3 to load (a ship). 4 to
carry (a news story). **me-i** to load.
Sdh dua hari orang ~ kapal, They've
been loading the ship for 2 days.
me-kan 1 to load. *Orang sibuk ~
barang² kekapal,* People are busy
loading the ship. 2 to place. *Sdh
berapa lama kamu ~ adperténsi itu?*
How long have you had the ad in?
ter- contained in, placed. *kabar jg ~
disurat kabar* the news contained in
the newspaper. **per-an** loading, shipment. **-an** 1 load, contents. 2 capacity.
muaz(z)in see MODIN.
mubah neutral. *Mengganggu orang
dlm bulan puasa -,* Disturbing people
during the fasting month is neither
forbidden nor permitted.
muballig preacher.
mubarak blessed.
mubut fragile, brittle. **me-kan** to
grind, crush, pound.
muchalaf heresy.
muda 1 young (in age). *Waktu perang
dia masih -,* During the war he was
still young. 2 deputy. *Ketua - dimana?* Where's the deputy chairman?
3 unripe, green. *Buah - itu masam,*
The green fruit is sour. 4 light, pale.
Saja suka warna hidjau -, I like pale
green. **ber-** *diri* to marry frequently
with young girls. **ber- -²** to enjoy

o.s. like a young person. **ke-an** youth.
ke- -²an youthful behavior. **me-kan**
to rejuvenate. *Katanja obat ini ~ ,*
They say this medicine is rejuvenat-
ing. **pe-** youth, young man. *- belia*
very young, youthful. *- léla* young
and beautiful. *- remadja* to be in the
bloom of youth.
mudah 1 easy, simple. *Pekerdjaan
itu -,* That job is easy. 2 rash, hasty.
Djangan - sadja, Don't be rash.
ber- -²an to take casually. *Bukan ~ ,*
It's tough, hard. **ke-an** 1 ease. 2
rashness. **me-kan, memper-** 1 to
facilitate, ease. 2 to take s.t. lightly.
~ petjahan to reduce a fraction.
pe- 1 easy-going. 2 o. who is easy-
going. **-²an** 1 may, I hope (that).
~ sdr akan lekas pulang, May you
return soon. 2 maybe, perhaps. *Pergilah kesekolah, ~ ada manfaatnja
bagi sdr,* Go to school, maybe it'll be
of value to you.
mudarat 1 disadvantage. *Peraturan
baru itu memberi - kpd pedagang²,*
The new regulation is disadvantageous
to the merchants. 2 to fail. *Dia -
dlm usahanja,* He failed in his efforts.
mudhorat see MUDARAT.
mudi **ke-** helm, rudder.
mudigah embryo.
mudik 1 upstream. *Berlajar - tidak
mudah,* Sailing upstream is not easy.
2 to go upcountry. *Budjang kami -,*
Our servant went home. **me-i** to sail
upstream. *Perahu itu berlajar ~
sungai,* The prow sailed upstream.
me-kan to sail s.t. upstream. *~
kapal sukar,* To sail a boat upstream
is hard.
mudjair 1 name of person who discovered a k.o. fish which lives on
malaria larvae. 2 see IKAN.
mudjarrab effective, efficacious. *Obat
itu sangat -,* The medicine is extremely
effective. **ke-an** effectiveness, efficacy.
mu'djizat miracle.
mudjtahid an expert in Moslem law
who interprets the Koran and the
Hadith independently.
mudjur 1 straight ahead, straight.
Djalan itu -, The road is straight.
2 luck. 3 lucky. *Si Ali - benar
kemarén malam,* Ali was very lucky last
night. **ke-an** luck. **pe-** a lucky fellow.
mufaham to understand. *Dia - akan
hal itu,* He understands that matter.
mufakat see MUPAKAT.
mufti religious adviser, counsel.
muhal 1 impossible, out of the question. 2 absurd. **ke-an** 1 impossibility.
2 absurdity.
muhallil an intermediary (a man
who marries a divorcee in order that

she may remarry her former husband).

Muharram the first month of the Moslem year.

muhibbah good will.

muhrim the degree of consanguinity between a man and woman that renders marriage impossible but gives them the right of association. A woman undertaking a journey must be accompanied by a man who is *muhrim* to her. The most common use of *muhrim* occurs when a woman goes on the pilgrimage to Mecca. **ke–an** possessing a *muhrim* relationship.

muka 1 face. – *anak itu serupa ibunja*, That child's face resembles its mother's. 2 front. – *lemari itu sdh petjah*, The front of the cupboard is broken. 3 page. *Buku itu berapa –nja?* How many pages does the book have? 4 surface. – *bumi* earth's surface. **ber-** –² 1 to pretend. *Ia ~ sakit*, He pretended to be sick. 2 in front of. 3 frank. 4 hypocritical. **berse-** to face e.o. **di–** 1 in advance. *Dia membajar ~* , He paid in advance. 2 in front of. *Dia berdiri ~ rumahnja*, He's standing in front of his house. 3 ahead. *Waktu berpatju lari saja djauh ~* , During the race I was way ahead of the others. **ke-** to the front, forward. *Madju ~ sedikit*, Step forward a little. **menge–kan** 1 to suggest, propose, put forward. *Siapa jg ~ hal itu?* Who suggested that? 2 to put to the front. *Dia ~ kursi itu*, He pushed the chair to the front. 3 to confront s.o. *Meréka ~ jg mendakwa dgn jg terdakwa*, They confronted the accuser with the accused. *~ diri* to thrust o.s. forward. *Dia ~ dirinja utk tjalon présidén*, He thrust himself forward as a candidate for president. **pe–** leader, promoter. **penge–an** bringing forward. **per–an** surface. *~ air* surface of the water. **se–** confronting. *Mesdjid dan kantor pos ~ menghadap ketanah lapang*, The mosque and the post office face e.o. on the square. **terke-** prominent. *orang jg ~* prominent person. –² insincere, put on. *Ia ~ sadja mengerdjakan itu*, He did his job insincerely. – *papan* impudent. *Ia akan datang minggu* –, He'll come next week.

mukadimmah introduction, preface.

mukah adultery.

mukdjidjat see MU'DJIZAT.

mukim 1 to stay at, be a resident of. *Kawan saja – dihotél Garuda*, My friend is staying at the Garuda Hotel. 2 residence, district. *Tempat –nja Djakarta*, His residence is Jakarta. **ber–** to live, reside. *Ia ~ di Éropah*, He lives in Europe.

muktamar congress, conference.

mula 1 beginning. 2 cause, reason, basis, grounds. *Apa –nja dia marah?* What was the reason for her anger? **ber–** 1 to have a beginning. *Tjerita itu harus ada ~* , The story must have a beginning. 2 first. *~ dia pergi kepasar*, First she went to the market. *Kemarén saja terima gadji saja ~* , Yesterday I received my first salary. 3 before. *Lain dari ~* , *bukan?* It's different from before, isn't it? **ber–** –² first, at the beginning. **me–i** 1 to begin, to start. *Konperénsi sdh –i*, The conference has started. 2 from, beginning. *–i tgl 15 sampai tgl 25* from the 15th to the 25th. **me–kan** to start, cause. *Jg ~ perkelahian itu bukan dia*, He didn't start the fight. **menje–kan** to start from the beginning again. *Saja ~ membatja buku ini*, I am reading this book from the beginning again. **per–an** 1 beginning, the first part. *Saja tidak dengar ~ tjerita itu*, I didn't hear the beginning of the story. 2 basis, origin. *Hal itu adalah ~ pekerdjaannja*, That is the basis of his work. *~ kalam* foreword, preface. **se–** 1 from the beginning. *Semua dilakukan dari ~* , Everything was done from the beginning. 2 since. *~ djadi* since birth. 3 formerly. *Apa jg terdjadi lain dari jg disangka ~* , What happened is different from what was formerly expected. 4 at first. *~ ia malu*, At first he was bashful. **seber–** first, at the beginning. **–nja** cause, reason. –² 1 at first, at the beginning. *~ dia tak mengerti*, At first he didn't understand. 2 since. *Dia blm bertemu orang ~ dia datang kemari*, He has not met anyone since he arrived here. 3 for the first time. *dari ketjil* – from childhood. *dari –i itu* from that time, beginning then.

mulakat meeting.

mulas slight stomach upset, pain in the stomach. – *perut* stomach upset, colic.

mulia noble, sublime, lofty. *Dia orang jg* –, He's a noble person. **ke–an** magnificence, pomp, glory. **me(mper)–kan** to glorify, exalt, honor. *Kita harus ~ nusa dan bangsa kita*, We should glorify our country and nation. **per–an** magnificence, pomp, glory. **ter–** exalted, most respected. *Dia orang jg ~ dikota ini*, He's the most respected person in this city. – *raja* supreme, honorable. *Jg* – His Excellency.

muliawan a noble person.

mulud see MAULUD.

muluk 1 high-sounding. *Djangan djandji –² kalau tidak bisa ditepati*, Don't make high-sounding promises if you can't keep them. 2 bombastic, pompous. **ke–an** pomposity.

mulur 1 elastic. *Permainan karét itu –*, The rubber toy is elastic. 2 flexible. *Orangnja –*, She's a flexible person.

mulus 1 flawless, pure. *Saldju itu putih –*, The snow is pure white. 2 sincere. *Pegawai itu –*, The employee is sincere.

mulut mouth. **ber–** 1 to have an opening. *Pipa itu ∼ besar*, The pipe has a big opening. 2 to talk, chat. *Anak itu ∼ sadja dari tadi*, The child has been talking all the time. *∼ besar* to talk big, be insolent. *–²an orang* object of gossip. *– bedil* mouth of a rifle. *– busuk* bad breath. *– gunung* crater. *– kulit* pore of the skin. *– manis* gentle in speech. *– meriam* muzzle of a rifle. *– ringan* talkative. *– sumbing* harelip. *– sungai* estuary.

mumbang young coconut.

mumet 1 headache. 2 dizzy. *Saja – sesudah djatuh*, I became dizzy after I fell. *Saja tidak ambil – apa jg dikatakannja*, I don't care what he says.

mumia mummy.

mu'min(in) the believers, the faithful.

mummi mummy.

mumpung as long as. *Dpt Anda pesan – masih ada dlm persediaan*, You can order as long as it's in stock.

munafik hypocrite. **ke–an** hypocrisy.

MUNAS [*Musjawarah Nasional*] National Deliberative Council.

mundar-mandir back and forth, to and fro, up and down. *Pengawal itu – dimuka pintu*, The guard walks up and down (patrols) in front of the door.

munding water buffalo in the Sundanese area.

mundur 1 to back up, go backward. *Oto semua disuruh –*, All the cars have to back up. 2 to decline, decrease, deteriorate. *Kepandaian anak itu makin –*, The child's intelligence is declining more and more. 3 to retreat. **ke–an** 1 decline, decrease. 2 deterioration. 3 cutback (in production). *– teratur* orderly retreat.

munggu a small hill.

mungil cute, sweet, nice.

mungkar 1 denied. *Dia – akan djandjinja*, He denied his promise. 2 ignored. *Pekerdjaannja jg – tidak*

diindahkannja, He didn't care about the work he ignored. 3 sinful. **ke–an** denial, disavowal. **me–i** 1 to deny. *Dia ∼ kewadjibannja*, He denies his responsibility. 2 to ignore. *Dia ∼ orang tuanja*, He ignores his parents.

mungkin possible. *Itu tak –*, That's impossible. *Dia berlari selekas –*, He ran as fast as possible. **ke–an** possibility. **me–kan** to enable, make possible. *Pembagian waktu itu ∼ saja beladjar*, The division of time enables me to study. *– sekali* probable.

mungkir 1 to deny, disavow. *Sekali ini djangan –*, Don't deny it this time. 2 unfaithful, disloyal. *Dia – djandjinja*, He was not faithful to his promise. 3 to fail. **me–i, me–kan** 1 to deny. *Dia ∼ tuduhan*, He denied the accusation. 2 to ignore. *Saja ∼ hal jg buruk*, I ignore the bad things. *–an* denial. *tak –* tested, positive.

mungkum convex.

mungkur stretcher, palanquin.

munkar dan nakir the two angels charged with the interrogation in the tomb.

muno to keep silent and muse.

munsji language teacher.

muntah 1 to vomit, throw up. *Dia – masuk angin*, He vomits because he has caught a cold. 2 to fade, run. *Badju itu ditjutji sekali sdh –*, The dress was only washed once and has faded already. **me–i** to vomit on. *Anak itu ∼ badju ibunja*, The child vomited on his mother's dress. **me–kan** to vomit up s.t. *Anak sakit itu ∼ segala jg dimakannja*, The sick child vomited up everything he had eaten. *–an* the vomit. *– darah* to spit up blood.

muntjrat me–kan to spray, squirt.

muntjul to emerge, appear, turn up. *Sesudah dua tahun dia – lagi*, After two years he turned up again. **ber–an** to appear. **me–kan** to show. *Dia ∼ kepandaiannja*, He showed his ability. **per–an** appearance, emergence.

muntjung snout, muzzle, beak.

muntul blunt, dull.

mupakat 1 discussion, deliberation. 2 agreement, consensus. 3 to discuss. *Baik kau – dulu dgn orang tuamu*, You'd better discuss it with your parents first. **ber–** to discuss, agree. *∼lah dulu, bung!* Discuss it first, friend! **ke–an** agreement. **me–i** to agree with. *Sesudah dibitjarakan baru meréka ∼ hal itu*, They agreed with it only after it had been discussed. **me–kan** to discuss s.t. **menje–i** to agree with. **per–an** 1 discussion, meeting. 2 agreement. 3 plot, conspiracy. **se-** 1 to be in agreement. *Kami sdh ~ hendak berangkat bésok,* We have agreed to leave tomorrow. 2 unanimously. *Kami ~ mengangkatnja sebagai ketua,* We unanimously appointed him chairman.

muqaddimah see MUKADIMMAH.

mur 1 myrrh. 2 Moor. 3 nut for a bolt. *- baut* bolt.

murad 1 intention. 2 meaning, significance.

muradjif see KATA.

murah 1 cheap, inexpensive. *Dipasar barang² lebih -,* Things are cheaper at the market. 2 easy. *Tidak - mengadjak dia pergi,* It isn't easy to take her out. 3 generous. **ber-** *hati* 1 to be generous. 2 tolerant. **ke-an** 1 cheapness, inexpensiveness. 2 generosity. *~ hati* generosity. **me-kan** to lower the price. *Sekali atau dua kali setahun saudagar² ~ harga² barang,* Once or twice a year the merchants reduce their prices. **pe-** a generous person. *- hati* generous and kind. *- mulut* gentle in speech.

murai magpie.

muram sad, gloomy, depressed. *Dia - sepandjang hari,* He's sad all day. **ber-** *durdja* to look sad. **ke-an** sorrow, gloom, dejection. **me-kan** to sadden, make sad. *Apa jg ~ dia?* What is making her sad?

murang fuse for igniting firecrackers, dynamite.

murat-marit see MORAT-MARIT.

murba common, plain, ordinary. *Meréka termasuk dlm golongan rakjat -,* They belong to the common people.

murbai mulberry.

muri 1 k.o. clarinet. 2 see KAIN.

murid pupil, student.

muring in a bad mood.

muris 1 name of a fabric. 2 greedy, closefisted.

murka 1 anger, fury. 2 angry. **ke-an** 1 fury, rage, anger. 2 greed. **me-i** to be angry with s.o. **me-kan** to infuriate s.o.

murni pure, clean, sweet. *Dia bertjita² tinggi dan -,* He has high and pure ideals. **ke-an** purity, genuineness. **me-kan** to purify, clean. *Dia sembahjang ~ hatinja,* He prays to purify his heart. **pe-** cleanser. **pe-an** 1 cleansing. 2 purge. 3 refining.

murtad apostate, renegade.

murung gloomy, depressed. **ke-an** melancholy, depression.

murup to flame, flare up. *Apinja masih -,* The fire is still flaming.

Musa Moses.

musabab see SEBAB.

musafir travel, o. in travel status.

musang *(kesturi),* *- tenggalung* a civet cat. *- djebat* muskrat.

musik music. **ber-** to play music. **-an** 1 to play. 2 musician.

musim season, period. **ber-** to be in season. *Buah²an banjak jg ~ ,* Many fruits are in season. **-²an** seasonal. *- bah* floodtime. *- bunga* spring. *- dingin* winter. *- gelora* stormy, nasty weather. *- gugur* fall, autumn. *- hudjan* rainy season. *- kemarau,* *- kering* dry season. *- panas* summer. *- pantjaroba* transition period between seasons. *- penghudjan* wet monsoon, rainy season. *- patjeklik* period of shortage before harvest. *- rendeng* rainy season. *- rontok,* *- runtuh* fall, autumn. *- semi* spring. *- tandur* planting time.

musium museum.

musjafir see MUSAFIR.

musjarakah see MASJARAKAT.

musjawarah see MUSJAWARAT.

musjawarat 1 meeting, conference. 2 discussion, deliberation. **ber-** to hold a meeting. *Kepala² sekolah ~ ttg murid²,* The school principals held a meeting about the pupils. **me-kan** to discuss, deliberate over. *Kami harus ~ hal itu dulu,* We have to discuss that matter first. **per-an** 1 discussion, conference, consultation, deliberation. 2 negotiation.

musjkil see MUSKIL.

musjrik polytheist. **ke-an** polytheism.

Musjtari Jupiter.

muskil precarious, difficult, critical. **ke-an** precariousness.

muslihat 1 trick. 2 strategy, tactics.

muslimat Moslem woman.

muslim(in) a Moslem.

musna(h) annihilated, destroyed. *Segala kertas² jg berharga tlh -,* All valuable papers were destroyed. **ke-an** annihilation, destruction, extinction. **me-kan** to annihilate, destroy.

mustadjab efficacious, effective. *obat jg -* effective medicine. **ke-an** efficacy.

mustahil incredible, impossible. *- hal itu terdjadi,* It's incredible that it could happen. **ke-an** incredibility. **me-kan** to render s.t. impossible. *Pertahanan jg kuat ~ musuh masuk,* The strong defense makes it impossible for the enemy to invade.

musta'id ready, completed, at hand. **me-kan** to prepare, complete. *Sebelum berangkat meréka ~ segala pekerdjaan,* Before leaving they completed all their work.

mustakim straightforward, sincere.

musti see MESTI.

mustika see MESTIKA.
musuh 1 enemy, adversary, foe. 2 competitor, contestant. *Barang ini tak ada −nja*, Nothing can compare with this. **ber-(an)** to be enemies, fight e.o. **me−i** to compete against. **per−an** hostility. − *dlm selimut* an enemy in disguise. − - *masah* enemies.
mu'tabar respected.
mutala'ah study. **me−kan** to study s.t.
mutalak see MUTLAK.
mu'tamar congress, conference.
mutasi transfer (of a diplomat) to a new post; (of a pupil) to a new school.
mutiara pearl.
mutlak 1 absolute, unconditional. *Dia diberi hak −*, He was given absolute rights. 2 general. **ke−an** absoluteness.
mutu 1 pearl. 2 quality, grade. 3 carat. **ber−** valuable. **ter−** dumb, dumfounded, speechless.
mutung 1 burnt, lost by fire. 2 brokenhearted, discouraged. 3 to give up.
muwarich historian.
muzhab see MAZHAB.

N

na'as see NAHAS.
nabatah vegetable world.
nabati vegetable.
nabi prophet. − *Isa* Jesus. *al-Nabi* Prophet Mohammed.
nachoda ship's captain.
nada 1 intonation. 2 tone, note. − *mineur* minor note. − *tambahan* overtone. − *utama* keynote.
nadar see NAZAR.
nadi pulse. *Dokter memeriksa −*, The doctor felt his pulse. − *bersikeras*, − *mengeras* arteriosclerosis.
nadir 1 nadir. 2 rare, unusual.
nadjis filthy, unclean. **me−kan** 1 to soil s.t. 2 to consider s.t. dirty. − *besar* feces, night soil. − *ketjil* urine.
nadzar see NAZAR.
nafakah see NAFKAH.
nafas see NAPAS. **me−i** to resuscitate, revive. *Ia di−i dgn zat asam*, He was revived with oxygen. **per−an** breathing.
nafi 1 denial, rejection. 2 negative. 3 denied. **me−kan** 1 to deny. 2 to reject.
nafiri trumpet.
nafkah 1 subsistence, a living. *Ia mentjari −*, He is making a living. 2 alimony. *Ia minta −*, She requests alimony. 3 expenses. **me−kan** to spend. − *batin* conjugal rights. − *nazir* wife's maintenance.
nafsi angry. **ber−** −² 1 individual, private. 2 egotistic, selfish.
nafsu desire, lust, passion. *Ia berhasil menahan −*, He was successful in suppressing his passion. **ber−** to be passionate, lustful, desirous. − *lawa-mah* ungodly passion (in mysticism). − *makan* appetite. − *nafsi* individual desire. − *tabi'at* instinct.
naga dragon. −²**nja** apparently, seemingly.
nah 1 well! −, *sekianlah sadja*, Well, let's stop here. 2 I told you so.
nahas unlucky, ill-omened. *sa'at jg −* unlucky moment. **me−kan** to declare s.t. to be ill-omened.
nahi 1 prohibition. 2 forbidden.
naib 1 mosque official. 2 deputy. − *kadi* deputy registrar of marriages.
naif naive.
naik 1 to climb, ascend. *Kawannja bukit*, His friend climbed the hill. 2 to ascend, mount. *Radja itu − tachta*, The king ascended the throne. 3 to go with, by. *Ia − keréta*, He went by train. 4 to ride. *Ia − kuda*, He rode horseback. 5 to go on. *Lurah itu − hadji*, The village chief went on the pilgrimage to Mecca. 6 to rise, be on the increase. *Hasilnja −*, His income is rising. *Matahari −*, The sun is rising. 7 to take off. *Kapal terbang −*, A plane took off. **ke−an** 1 increase, raise. 2 promotion. *Baru² ini ia mendapat ∼ pangkat*, He recently received a promotion. ∼ *gadji* salary increase. 3 vehicle, vessel. **me−i** 1 to climb into, on. *Anak itu ∼ pohon*, The child climbed into the tree. 2 to ride in. *Ia ∼ mobil*, He rode in a car. 3 to enter into. *Ia ∼ hotél*, He entered a hotel. **me−kan** 1 to hoist, raise. *Serdadu itu ∼ bendéra*, The soldier hoisted

the flag. 2 to advance, promote. *Ia ~ pangkatnja*, He promoted him. 3 to advance, raise. *Ia ~ harga*, He raised the price. 4 to raise. *Ia ~ tempat duduk*, He raised the seat. **pe–** climber. *~ darah* 1 hothead. 2 hot-tempered. **pe–an** 1 increase, raise. 2 advance, promotion. *– api* to catch fire. *– appél* to appeal to a higher court. *– banding* to appeal (to a higher court). *– darah* to become angry. *– darat* to go ashore. *– deradjat* to increase in prestige, be promoted. *– geram* to become excited. *– hadji* to go on a pilgrimage. *– harga* to rise in price. *– hati* 1 to be happy, glad. 2 proud. 3 boastful. *– kapal* to embark. *– kelas* to be promoted. *– kesorga* to ascend to heaven. *– kuda hidjau* to be drunk. *– marah* to get angry. *– marak* 1 to start to glow. 2 to be at her best (said of a girl). 3 to rise to fame. *– mempelai* to get married. *– nobat* to be installed as ruler. *– pangkat* to advance to a higher grade, rank. *– pasang* rising tide. *– saksi* to take the witness stand. *– tangan* to have good luck.

na'im delightful, pleasant.

najaka minister (of state).

najam plowshare.

najuban dance party. see TAJUBAN.

nak 1 = ANAK. 2 = HENDAK. *– kemana?* 1 Where are you going? 2 How're things going?

naka **ber–**[2] to sing by turns.

nakal 1 naughty, mischievous. *Anak itu –*, That child is naughty. 2 frivolous, wanton. *Ia seorang perempuan –*, She's a wanton woman. **ke–an** naughtiness.

nakir angel of death.

nakoda see NACHODA.

naluri instinct.

nam see ENAM.

nama 1 name. *–nja siapa?* What's his name? *Apa –nja?* What's it called? 2 title. 3 fame. *Ia mendapat –*, He became famous. **ber–** 1 to be called. *Ia ~ Ali*, His name is Ali. 2 well-known, famous. *Ia seorang jg ~*, He's a well-known man. **berke–an** famed, famous, known **ke–an** well-known, famous. **me–i** to call, give a name to. *Ia ~ adiknja Zainah*, He called his younger sister "Zainah." **me–kan** to call, give a name to. **pe–an** 1 naming. 2 nomenclature. **ter–** well-known, famous. *– batang tubuh* real name. *– benda* noun. *– daging* baptismal name. *– diri* proper name. *– djulukan, – édjékan* nickname, alias. *– ketjil* given name. *– panggilan* nickname. *– pédéngan*

pseudonym. *– samaran* pen name, pseudonym. *– sindiran* nickname. *– tambahan* subtitle. *– timangan* pet name. *– tubuh* baptismal name. *Atas – séf saja saja mengutjapkan terima kasih*, In the name of my boss I thank you. *dgn –* by the name of. *hanja – sadja* so-called.

nambi 1 yaws, framboesia tropica. 2 skin rash.

nampak visible, evident. *Kepandaiannja tidak –*, His ability is not evident. *Ia sdh lama tidak –*, He hasn't been seen for a long time. *Ia –(nja) susah*, He looked sad. **me–kan** to show, exhibit. *di–kan* made visible.

nampan tray.

namun 1 yet, still. *– ia tak dpt lulus djuga* yet he cannot succeed either. 2 whatever. 3 in spite of. *– apa djuga diberikannja, selalu ia menolak*, He always refused whatever was given him. *– demikian* nevertheless.

nan which, who. *dosa – samar* the invisible sin.

nanah suppuration, pus. **ber–, me–** to run, suppurate, fester.

nanap 1 amazed. 2 eyes distended, wide-open. *Matanja –*, He stared.

nanar 1 confused. 2 angry.

nanas pineapple. *– tali* sisal hemp.

nanda see ANAKANDA.

nangka jack fruit.

nanti by and by, later, presently. *Itu soal –*, That's a problem for later. *hari –* later, in the future. **ber–**[2] impatiently waiting. *~ dgn gembira* to look forward to. **me–** to wait for. **me–kan** 1 to wait for. 2 to watch for. **pe–** receptionist. **pe–an** waiting room. **ter–**[2] longing for, anxiously waiting for. *– dulu*, Wait a moment. (Just a minute.) *– malam* tonight. *– soré* this afternoon.

nantiasa see SENANTIASA.

napal edible clay.

napas 1 breath. 2 roan (of horses). **ber–** 1 to breathe. 2 to sigh. **me–kan** to exhale. *~ keluar badan* to rely more on other people. *~ pandjang* to take a deep breath. **per–an** respiration. *– lelah* short-winded. *– pandjang* 1 sigh. 2 deep breath. *– penghabisan* last breath.

napi see NAFI.

napsu see NAFSU. **me–kan** 1 to entice, lure. 2 to arouse passions.

nara pidana convicted criminal.

naraka see NERAKA.

nas thesis.

nasab lineage, descent in the male line.

nasabah relationship.

NASAKOM [*Nasionalis, Agama,*

Komunis] Nationalist, Religious, Communist.
nasarani 1 Christian. 2 Catholic.
naséhat see NASIHAT.
nasi 1 cooked, steamed, or boiled rice. 2 living. *Ia mentjari* –, He is seeking a living. – *angkatan* cooked rice at banquets. – *belantah* insufficiently cooked rice. – *berkuah laksa* rice boiled with vermicelli. – *besar* cooked rice for ceremonial purposes. – *bidji limau* insufficiently cooked, still hard rice. – *bubur* porridge. – *damai* rice for wedding parties. – *datang* rice boiled in a leaf. – *didang* rice steamed in a large copper vessel. – *djelantah* insufficiently cooked rice. – *djemah* rice boiled in water. – *goréng* fried rice. – *gurih* rice cooked in coconut cream. – *hadap²an* cooked rice at wedding parties. – *kebuli* rice boiled with chick-peas. – *kepal* clotted cooked rice. – *ketupat* rice boiled in a leaf. – *kukus* rice steamed in a large copper vessel. – *kuning* yellow rice for formal occasions. – *lemak* rice boiled in coconut milk. – *lemang* rice boiled in a bamboo vessel. – *lengat* steamed rice. – *lepat* sticky rice boiled in a leaf. – *létjék* porridge. – *mentah* insufficiently boiled rice. – *minjak* rice boiled in water to which oil is added. – *pelabur* ration of rice as food in prison, military barracks, etc. – *pulan* perfectly cooked rice. – *pulau* rice boiled in broth. – *ramas* rice and side dishes mixed in together. – *ramsum* ration of rice as food in prison, military barracks, etc. – *rawon* cooked rice with egg, meat, etc. – *sebuku* one cloth of cooked rice. – *tambah* rice served a second time. – *tanak* rice boiled in water. – *tim* steamed rice. – *tingkas* white cooked rice with a border of colored rice. – *uduk* rice boiled in coconut milk. *Ber–* *dibalik kerak*, There is s.t. behind it.
nasib fate, destiny, lot in life. *Ajahku mendjalani –nja*, My father accepted his fate. *Ia mentjoba –nja*, He tried his luck. **se–** of one destiny. *kawan* ~ a fellow sufferer, o. sharing the same fate. **–²an** at random. – *baik* to be lucky. – *bedebah*, – *ditimpa malang*, – *malang*, – *tjelaka* bad luck. *Sdh untung* –, It has been o's fate.
nasihat 1 advice, admonition. *Itu* – *dari ajah*, That's father's advice. 2 moral. *Saja suka tjeritera jg mengandung* – *jg baik*, I like a story with a good moral. **me–i** to advise s.o. **me–kan** to advise, suggest s.t. **pe–** adviser, counselor.

nasional national. **ke–an** 1 nationality. 2 nationalism.
nasionalis nationalist(ic).
nasionalisasi nationalization. **me–kan** to nationalize s.t.
nasionalisir **me–** to nationalize.
naskah 1 manuscript. 2 document, original text. 3 authorized version. 4 treaty. 5 draft. 6 bill. *se–* single copy. – *asli* minutes (of a meeting).
nasrani see NASARANI.
natar 1 basic color, background. *mérah* – *kuning* red on a yellow background. 2 see LATAR. **pe–an** yard. ~ *angkatan laut* navy yard.
n.a.t.o. [*naskah asli ditetapkan oléh*] certified to be a true copy.
naung 1 shadow, shade. 2 shelter, protection. **ber–** 1 to be in the shade. 2 to take shelter. **me–i** 1 to shade. 2 to protect, shelter. **pe–** 1 protector. 2 provider of shade. **pe–an** shelter. **–an** shelter, protection.
nautika nautical science.
nazam poem, composition. **me–kan** to compose.
nazar vow, promise. **ber–** to make a promise, make a vow. **me–kan** to vow, promise.
nda(k) 1 no. 2 see HENDAK.
nébéng to sponge off s.o.
Neg. 1 [*Negeri*] country. 2 [*Negara*] nation, state.
negara state. **ke–an** state, political. *urusan* ~ affairs of state. – *bagian* state. – *hukum* constitutional state. – *kesatuan* unitary state. – *kesedjahteraan* welfare state.
negarawan statesman.
négatip negative.
negeri country, land. **me–kan** to make state-owned. *Universitas swasta itu di–kan*, The private university was made a state one. **pe–an** making state-owned. – *antah-berantah* never-never land, fairyland. – *asing* foreign country. – *awak* native country, homeland. – *Belanda* Holland. – *dan dusun* towns and villages. – *Djakarta* city of Jakarta. – *jg baka*, – *kekal* the hereafter. – *leluhur* land of the ancestors, China. – *luaran*, – *orang* foreign country. – *Perantjis* France. – *ramal* desert. *ajam* – foreign breed of chicken, such as White Leghorn, etc.
nék see NÉNÉK.
néka see ANÉKA.
NEKAD [*Negara kita pertahankan; Ékonomi kita sosialiskan; Keamanan kita selenggarakan; Agama kita muliakan; Démokrasi terpimpin kita djalankan*] The State we'll defend; the Economy we'll socialize; the

Security we'll carry out; Religion we'll esteem; Guided democracy we'll put into operation.

nékad see NÉKAT.

nékat 1 reckless, courageous. 2 obstinate, determined. **ke–an** 1 recklessness. 2 bravery, courage. **–²an** to risk everything.

nékél nickle.

néker marbles.

nelajan fisherman.

nemu see TEMU.

nenas see NANAS.

nénda see NÉNÉNDA.

nénék 1 grandmother. 2 tiger (epithet). – *mojang* forefather, ancestor.

nénékanda see NÉNÉNDA.

nénékda see NÉNÉNDA.

nénénda grandmother (polite).

nénés **me–** to ooze out.

néng 1 girl. 2 polite form of address to a girl.

néolitis neolithic.

neraka 1 hell. 2 destruction. 3 misfortune. **me–kan** to bring ruin upon.

neratja 1 pair of scales. 2 balance. 3 balance in bookkeeping. – *kekuatan* balance of power. – *niaga* trade balance. – *pembajaran* balance of payments. – *utang piutang* balance sheet.

nerimo 1 to be passive, uncomplaining, acquiescent. 2 to be fatalistic.

nésan gravestone.

nestapa sorrow, grief. **ke–an** grief, sorrow.

nétjis neat.

nétral neutral. **ke–an** neutrality. **me–kan** 1 to permit to be neutral. 2 to neutralize.

nétralisir **me–** to neutralize.

nétralisme neutralism.

nétralitét neutrality.

nétto net. *Berapa penghasilan –?* How much is the net income?

ng– = MENG– in many cases.

ngah suspicious. *Ia – akan djongos jg baru,* He was suspicious of the new boy.

ngak-ngik-ngok 1 out of tune. 2 off beat (of music). 3 vulgar, lowgrade music.

ngalau grotto.

nganga agape. **me–** to open the mouth widely, be agape. **me–kan** to keep the mouth agape. **ter–** 1 openmouthed. 2 amazed. 3 yawning.

ngangéni custom in which a girl is indirectly asked whether she has been proposed to.

ngangut **me–** to mumble to o.s.

ngantuk see ANTUK.

ngap² to gasp for breath.

ngapa why. *–in?* What are you doing? (What'll we do?)

ngarai 1 gorge, gully, ravine. 2 chasm.

ngatjau see KATJAU.

ngatjeng to become erect (of a penis).

ngatjir to flee, run away.

ngatjo to chat. **me–** to talk at random, chat. – *bélo* to talk at random.

ngaung **me–** to moo.

ngawur to chatter, babble.

ngék² sickly.

ngelotok to burst open (of fruit).

ngelu to have a headache.

ngengap to gasp for breath, pant.

ngengat moth.

ngentot to fornicate.

ngéong **me–** to meow.

ngeram **me–** 1 to buzz. 2 see KERAM. 3 to grumble.

ngeran angry.

ngeri 1 horrible, terrible. 2 stricken with panic, terrified. **ke–an** 1 horror, terror. 2 horrified. **me–kan** terrifying, horrible.

nggak 1 no. 2 not.

ngiang **me–** 1 to whine complainingly. 2 to sparkle. 3 to buzz. **ter–** –² to whine complainingly. *si* –² whining ghost.

ngiau meow.

ngidjo(n) see IDJO.

ngik² see NGÉK².

ngiler 1 to water at the mouth. 2 to foam at the mouth. 3 to long for.

ngilu to pain, hurt, smart. *Giginja –,* His teeth hurt him. –² *kuku* lukewarm, tepid.

ngintjer see INTJER.

nglambrang to wander about.

ngobrol see OBROL.

ngomél **me–** to grumble.

ngomong to talk, converse. *Djangan banjak –,* Don't talk too much. **me–** –² to talk, converse. see OMONG.

ngompol **me–** to wet the bed.

ngotot see OTOT. **ke–an** obstinacy, stubbornness.

nguler wormlike. – *kambang* very slow.

ngutngit gnawing.

ngut² 1 to daydream, loaf. 2 nervous movement of the mouth, twitch.

niaga **ber–** to trade, carry on trade. **me–** to trade. **ke–an** marketing, trade. **me–kan** to trade s.t. **memperkan** to carry on trade in s.t. **per–an** trade, commerce. ~ *étjéran,* ~ *rintjih* retail trade.

nian 1 really, quite. *Sukar – hitungan ini,* This calculation is really difficult. 2 very, excessively. *Bagus – gambar ini,* This picture is very beautiful.

niat intention, plan, aim. **ber–** to intend. **ber–** –² to wish intensely.

me–kan to intend, plan, aim. **me–
–²kan** to wish intensely to do s.t.
ter– intended, meant. **–an** intention,
intent, aim.

nibung a palm.

nifas childbed.

ni(h) see INI. – *uangnja*, Here's
your money.

Nika [*NICA*] Netherlands Indies
Civil Administration.

nikah 1 marriage, wedding. 2 to
marry. **ber–** married. **me–** to marry.
me–i to marry to s.o. **me–kan** to
marry s.o. off. *Ia* ∼ *anaknja*, He
married off his daughter. **per–an** 1
marriage, wedding. 2 wedding reception. **–²an** to marry repeatedly.

nikmat 1 comfort, luxury. 2 delicious. 3 nice, pleasant. 4 comfortable. *rumah* – a comfortable house.
ke–an 1 bliss. 2 comfort. 3 enjoy-
ment. **me–i**, **me–kan** 1 to enjoy. *Ia*
∼ *és krim*, He enjoys ice cream.
–ilah rasa segar dimulut, Enjoy the
fresh taste in your mouth. 2 to taste.

Nil Nile.

nila blue dye, indigo.

nilai 1 price, value. 2 appraisal, estimate. 3 standard. **ber–** valuable,
precious. **me–(kan)** 1 to appraise,
evaluate, estimate. 2 to appreciate.
∼ *kembali* to re-evaluate. **pe–** ap-
praiser. **pe–an** 1 judging. ∼ *dari
djawaban²* judging from the replies.
2 evaluation. ∼ *kembali* re-evaluation.
–an estimate, valuation. *tidak* ter-
inestimable. – *beli* purchasing price.
– *gizi* nutritive value.

nilakandi 1 sapphire. 2 sapphire
blue, azure.

nilam 1 see BATU. 2 see BURUNG.

ni'mat see NIKMAT.

nina-bobo(k) lullaby. **me–kan** to lull
to sleep.

ningrat 1 nobility. 2 aristocracy. 3
cultured, aristocratic. **ke–an** aristocracy. **–²an** feudal.

nipah thatch palm.

nipis see TIPIS.

nira palm juice obtained by cutting
off palm blossoms.

nirasa apathy.

nirmala clean, pure.

nisan see NÉSAN.

nisbah family name, name descrip-
tive of origin or relationship.

nisbi relative (of humidity, etc.).

niskala abstract, immaterial. **ke–an**
abstraction.

nista 1 insult, abuse. 2 indignity. 3
base, low. 4 insult. **ke–an** 1 insult.
2 feeling of indignity. **me–** to insult.
me–i, **me–kan** to insult, humiliate,
offend.

nistjaja certainly, surely, undoubt-
edly. **ke–an** certainty.

niti policy.

nitis to incarnate.

nj. [*njonja*] Mrs.

nja = NJONJA.

-nja 1 his, her, its. *toko–* his, her,
its shop. 2 him, her. *Saja melihat–*,
I saw him, her. *Uang diambil –*, The
money was taken by him, her.

njah see ENJAH.

njai 1 concubine of a European. 2
form of address to an older woman.
3 wife of a Moslem village priest.
4 housekeeper.

njala 1 flame. 2 flaming, flaring up.
ber– to flame, flare up. **ber– –²** to
burn, flare up violently. **me–** to flame,
flare up, burn. *Lampu²* ∼ , The
lamps are on. **me–i** to ignite, light.
me–kan to set fire, ignite s.t. **me– –²**
to flame, flare up violently.

njalang open. *Matanja –*, His eyes
are open. **me–kan** to open o's eyes.

njali gall, bile. – *ketjil* weakhearted,
cowardly.

njaman 1 healthy, fresh, fit. 2 pleasant. **ke–an** 1 freshness, fit feeling.
2 pleasure. **me–kan** to make fit,
freshen up.

njampang in case, perchance, just in
case. – *kekantor pos belilah perangko
utk saja*, In case you go to the post
office, please buy a stamp for me.

njamuk mosquito.

njana to expect, presume, think. *Tak
– ia akan mentjuri*, I didn't think
he would steal. **me–kan** to expect,
suspect s.o.

njang see JANG.

njanjah **me–** to mumble.

njanjar bruised (of fruit).

njanji **ber–**, **me–** to sing. ∼ *ketjil* to
hum. **me–kan** to sing s.t. **pe–** singer.
–an song, melody. ∼ *gerédja* hymn.

njanjuk 1 childish, doting. 2 dull.

njaring 1 loud and clear, high-
pitched, piercing. 2 to be sharp (of
hearing). **me–kan** to raise o's voice.

njaris nearly, almost. *Ia – mati*, He
was almost dead.

njaru disguised. *Ia pentjuri – polisi*,
He was a thief disguised as a policeman.

njata 1 clear, obvious, evident. 2
concrete, real, tangible. *penghasilan*
– real income. **ke–an** 1 fact(s), data.
2 truth, reality. ∼*nja ialah bhw ia
seorang pembohong*, The truth (fact)
is that he is a liar. 3 to transpire.
me–kan 1 to explain, clarify,
point out. 2 to declare. *Bangsa
Djepang* ∼ *perang*, The Japanese
declared war. ∼ *diri* to manifest

itself. **per–an** 1 declaration. ∼ *perang* declaration of war. 2 expression. ∼ *terima kasih* expression of gratitude. 3 statement. ∼ *bersama* joint statement. ∼ *tjinta* marriage proposal. **ter–** obvious, evident. –² decidedly.

njawa 1 life. 2 soul. *Ia membuang –nja*, He risked his life. **ber–** to have a soul, be alive. **berse–** to agree completely, see eye to eye. **memperse-kan** to combine chemically. **perse–an** chemical combination. **se–** of o. soul, completely agreed. **se–an** union, complete mixture. *tidak ber–* lifeless. *satu – dua badan* very close friends. *Ia meminta –*, He prayed for mercy.

njedar sound-asleep.

njelonong to appear, emerge suddenly.

njenjai loosely woven.

njenjak to be sound (of sleep). see TIDUR.

njénjéh me– to whine, drawl.

njeri pain.

njilu see NGILU.

njinjir talkative, fond of chatting.

njiru basket tray, winnow.

njiur coconut palm.

njolong to steal. –² secretly.

njonja 1 Mrs., Madam. 2 lady. – *rumah* 1 hostess. 2 lady of the house. 3 housewife. – *besar* 1 Mrs., Madam. 2 old lady. 3 respected woman.

njonjong me– to protrude. *Giginja* ∼ , His teeth protrude.

nn. [*nona*] Miss.

nobat royal drum used at installation ceremonies. **me–kan** to crown, install, inaugurate. **pe–an** coronation, installation, inauguration.

noda 1 stain, spot of dirt, black spot. 2 shame, disgrace. infamy, ignominy. **ber–** stained, soiled, polluted, besmirched. **me–i** 1 to stain, soil. 2 to disgrace, *tidak ber–* immaculate.

nokta(h) 1 dot, point. 2 period.

nol nought, zero.

nombor see NOMOR.

nomer see NOMOR.

nomor number. **me–i** to number s.t. *Sdr. harus* ∼ *barang² itu*, You must number those things. **pe–an** numbering. **se–** per issue, per number. – *buntjit* 1 finally. 2 last of all. – *kembar* double issue (of magazine). – *korét* the latter, the last o. – *lepas* loose issue, a single number. – *pelat* license plate. – *perkenalan* introductory number or issue. – *urut* serial number.

non 1 = NONA. 2 non-co-operative. *kaum – dan ko* the non-co-operatives and the co-operatives.

nona miss, unmarried European, Chinese or Westernized well-to-do Indonesian girl in Western dress.

nongkrong to squat.

noni young girl, Miss.

nonja see NJONJA.

nonok female sex organ.

nonsén nonsense.

nonton see TONTON.

Nopémber November.

norma norm, standard.

normalisasi standardization.

Norwégia Norway.

not musical note.

nota 1 note. 2 statement of account. – *krédit* note of credit. – *pendjelasan* aide-memoire.

notaris notary public.

notés notebook.

novel novella.

nr [*nomor*] number.

N.R.I. [*Negara Républik Indonésia*] Republic of Indonesia.

nrimo see NERIMO.

nuansa nuance.

nudjum stars. **memper–kan** to consult the stars, to cast o's horoscope. **me–kan** to prophesy, predict. **per–an** astrology. **–an** prophecy, prediction, forecast.

Nuh Noah.

nukil 1 tradition, narrative. 2 quotation, quote. 3 summary. **me–** 1 to quote. 2 to summarize. **me–kan** to quote s.t. **–an** quotation.

nuklir nuclear.

nul see NOL.

numpang 1 see TUMPANG. 2 please. – *tanja?* May I ask you s.t.?

nun yonder. – *dibalik gunung* yonder, on the other side of the mountain.

nur (divine) light.

nuraga sympathy.

nurani 1 lustrous, illuminated. 2 pure. 3 inner.

nurbisa antidote.

nuri parrot.

nurmala see NIRMALA.

nusa island. *utk – dan bangsa* for the homeland. – *Tenggara* the Lesser Sundas (Bali to Timor).

nusantara 1 archipelago. 2 Indonesian Archipelago.

Nusra [*Nusa Tenggara*] the Lesser Sundas.

Nusrabar [*Nusa Tenggara Barat*] Western Lesser Sundas.

Nusratim [*Nusa Tenggara Timur*] Eastern Lesser Sundas.

Nuzulul Qur'an day of Koran's Descent.

N.V. [*Naamloze Vennootschap*] Inc., Ltd.

O

O. [*Otomat*] dial telephone.
obah see UBAH.
oban see UBAN.
obar see KOBAR.
obat medicine, remedy. **ber–** 1 to have treatment. *Ia ~ dirumah sakit,* He is being treated at the hospital. 2 to take medicine. *Ia ~ karena sakit perut,* He is taking medicine for his stomach-ache. **memper–kan** to treat s.o. with s.t. **meng–(i),** **meng–kan** to treat medically. *Ia ~ kakinja jg luka,* He treated his injured foot. **peng–** therapist. *~ hati* consolation. **peng–an** medical treatment, therapy. **–²an** medicines. *tak* **ter–kan** incurable. *– awét muda* medicine for preserving o's youth. *– basah* wet gunpowder. *– batuk* cough medicine. *– bedil* gunpowder. *– bius* 1 anesthetic. 2 narcotics. *– dalam* medicine to be taken internally. *– demam* quinine. *– djarum* serum. *– gosok* liniment, scouring powder. *– guna* philter, charm. *– kelantang* bleaching powder. *– ketiak* deodorant. *– kumur* mouthwash, gargle. *– lali* anesthetic. *– lelah* tip. *– luar* medicine to be applied externally. *– mata* eyedrops, eye lotion. *– njamuk* insecticide, mosquito repellent. *– peluntur* laxative. *– pembasmi lipas* cockroach exterminator. *– penguat* tonic. *– pentjakar,* *– pentjutji perut* laxative. *– perangsang* tonic. *– potrét* chemicals for photography. *– sendawa* gunpowder. *– serasi* tested medicine. *– serbuk* medicine in powder form. *– suntik(an)* serum. *– tidur* barbiturate, sleeping pills. *– tjatjing* vermifuge.
obéng screw driver.
oberal see OBRAL.
objék object.
objéktif objective.
oblak spacious.
obligasi bond, certificate for security of payment.
obor 1 torch. 2 guide. **meng–** to light with a torch. **meng–i** to give s.o. a light.
obrak **meng– -abrik** 1 to destroy, ruin. 2 to upset.
obral 1 clearance sale. 2 waste.

meng–(kan) 1 to sell out, sell cheaply. *Toko itu ~ barang² lama,* The shop sold out its old stock. 2 to waste. *Ia ~ uangnja,* He wasted his money. 3 to show off. *Gadis itu ~ badjunja,* The girl showed off her clothes. **peng–an** clearance sale. **–an** goods on sale.
obrol **meng–(kan)** to chat. **–an** 1 a chat. 2 gossip.
obros colonel.
o.c. [*opus citatum*] op. cit.
odja(h) **meng–** to encourage, incite, egg on.
odoh 1 very stupid. 2 ugly.
ogah to be averse to. *Ia – bertemu temannja,* He doesn't want to see his friend. **meng–** to shake s.t. **–²an** reluctantly.
ogak joke. **ber– -²** to joke. **peng– -²** 1 jokester. 2 clown.
oi hey there!
ojak **meng– -²** 1 to shake. 2 to chase after.
ojok **meng–** 1 to arrest. 2 to catch after chasing.
OK [*Otomat Kota*] term used in automatic dialing for Kota, a section of Jakarta.
OKD [*Organisasi Keamanan Désa*] village security organization.
oknum 1 person. 2 personality. **ke–an** 1 person. 2 personality.
oksid oxide. *– belérang* sulphuric oxide.
Oktober October.
okulasi inoculation.
olah 1 manner, way of doing things. 2 trick. *Itu banjak –,* That's tricky. **ber–** to be tricky. **meng–** 1 to be tricky. 2 to prepare food, meal, dishes. 3 to treat. *~ setjara kimis* to treat chemically. 4 to process. *utk ~ kekajaan alam* in order to process the natural wealth. **peng–** processor. **peng–an** 1 preparation, manufacture. 2 processing. **se– -²** 1 as if. 2 by way of. *Buku ini ~ merupakan essay,* This book is by way of forming an essay. **–an** 1 what is prepared. 2 fickle. 3 whim, caprice. *bukan –²* unusual, extraordinary.
olahraga 1 sport. 2 physical exercise. **ber–** to engage in sports, physical

exercise. **ke–an** 1 sports. 2 sports-manlike. **peng–** athlete.

olahragawan sportsman, athlete.

olahragawati 1 female athlete. 2 sportswoman.

olak circulation, whirling, turning. **ber–** to turn, whirl. **meng–** to stir, turn. **meng– alik** to move to and fro. **–an** whirling, eddying, turning. **–(an)** *air* whirlpool. **–** *alik* to and fro.

olanda see BELANDA.

oléh 1 by. *Ia dipukul – ajahnja,* He was struck by his father. 2 because of. *Ia diam – ketakutannja,* He kept silent because of fear. 3 to. *Njata – si Amin,* It was clear to Amin. 4 for. *Sukar – seorang isteri akan...* It is difficult for a wife to... *Tjobalah pikir sadja – tuan,* Just think. **ber–** to get, obtain, receive. *Ia ～ uang dari ajahnja,* He received money from his father. **memper–** to obtain, get. **per–an** result, achievement, gain. **–²** present, souvenir given upon return from a trip. *–mu* by you. *–nja* by him, her. **–** *karena* because, since. **–** *karena itu* for that reason, therefore. **–** *sebab* because, since.

oléng shaky. **meng– –²** to shake, rock.

olés meng– to grease, lubricate. **meng–kan** to smear, grease. *Ia ～ minjak kelapa kerambutnja,* He smeared coconut oil on his hair.

oli oil. **–** *bol* oil dumpling, k.o. fried cake.

olok² 1 caricature. 2 ridicule. **ber– –²** to jest, joke at. **memper– –²kan** 1 to mock, ridicule, deride. 2 to kid. *Engkau ～ saja,* You're kidding me. **meng– –²(kan)** 1 to joke with. 2 to ridicule, mock, deride. **–an** ridicule, mockery. **–²an** joke, jest.

om 1 uncle. 2 form of address to men by children. 3 ohm.

ombak wave. **ber–** to roll, heave. *Laut ～ ,* The sea's choppy. **ber– –²** 1 to be wavy. *Rambutnja ～ ,* Her hair is wavy. 2 in waves. *Musuh menjerang ～ ,* The enemy attacked in waves. **meng–** to wave, undulate. **–²** wavy. **–** *bunga lepang* whitecaps. **–** *galur* waves dashing against the cliffs. **–** *gemulung* rolling waves. **–** *memetjah* breakers. **–** *pengundak* frontal sea wave. **–** *selabu* rollers.

ombang-ambing meng– –ambing 1 to oscillate. 2 to drift. 3 to be uncertain. **meng– –ambingkan** to make s.t. uncertain. **–** *–ambingan* vacillation, indecision.

omél meng– to grumble, grouse. **meng–i** 1 to grumble, grouse at. 2 to reprimand, rebuke. **–an** reproof, rebuke, reprimand.

omong 1 gossip. 2 to talk. **ber–** to talk, chat. **ber– –²** to converse. **meng–** to talk, say. **meng–kan** to discuss, chat about s.t. **–an** 1 gossip. 2 talk. **–²** 1 to converse. 2 by the way, speaking of that. **–** *belanda* Dutch language. **–** *kasar* rude language. **–** *kosong* 1 nonsense. 2 chatter. 3 gossip.

ompol see NGOMPOL.

ompong toothless.

onak thorn. **–²** thorny bushes.

onani masturbation.

onar 1 noisy, loud, boisterous. 2 disbelief. **ke–an** 1 confusion, boisterousness. 2 excitement. 3 disturbance. 4 nuisance. **meng–kan** 1 to excite. 2 to confuse.

ondé(h)² ball of dough with a palm sugar center and a coating of grated coconut.

ondél² see BARONGAN.

onderdil spare part.

ondernéming estate.

ondok meng–kan to hide.

onéng² remote descendant.

onggok pile, heap. **ber– –²** in heaps, stacks, piles. **meng–** to walk with a stoop. **meng–kan** to pile up, stack. **–an** pile, heap, conglomerate.

ongkang² 1 to bungle, botch. 2 to sit with legs dangling.

ongkos cost, expenses, charges. **memper-i, meng–i** to finance, pay for. **per–an** cost, expenses. **–** *bétjak* pedicab fare. **–** *kirim* forwarding, shipping charges. **–** *makan* food expenses. **–** *pasang* cost of repairs. **–** *pindah* moving costs. **–** *tetap* 1 fixed costs. 2 overhead. *dgn –* *sendiri* on o's own account.

onjak-anjik to dawdle.

onjok meng–(kan) to force s.o. to take s.t.

ons 100 grams.

onslah dismissal.

ontjom a fermented preparation made from peanut oil cake.

oom see OM.

O.P. [*Otomat Pemerintah*] government telephone dialing system.

opas see UPAS.

op(e)lét small urban bus in Indonesia.

opén 1 attentive. 2 careful. 3 oven. **meng–i** to pay attention to.

oper 1 over. 2 to shift gears. **meng–** 1 to take s.t. over. *Ia ～ pekerdjaan temannja,* He took over his friend's job. 2 to hand over, pass over to. *Ia ～ bukunja kpd temannja,* He handed over his book to his friend. 3 to transfer. *Madjikannja ～ ia kebagian perbekalan,* His boss transferred him to the supply department.

meng–kan to transfer. *tak dpt di–kan* not transferable. **peng–an** 1 transfer. 2 delegation (of powers).

opersak transferred to another bag.

opisil official.

oplah edition.

opname shot (phot.). **meng–** 1 to shoot (with a camera). 2 to hospitalize.

opor highly seasoned baked chicken.

oposisi opposition.

OPR [*Organisasi Pertahanan Rakjat*] civil defense.

opséter supervisor.

opsir officer. – *penghubung* liaison officer. – *rendah(an)* noncommissioned officer. – *tinggi* commissioned officer.

optimisme optimism.

optimistis optimistic.

OR [*Olah Raga*] sports.

orak meng– to untie.

orak-arik cabbage mixed with eggs.

orang 1 person. *Ini –nja jg membawa surat itu*, This is the person who brought the letter. 2 human being. *Ia bukan –*, He's not a human being. 3 man. *Ia tinggal dirumah –*, He's staying at another man's house. 4 one. *Kadang² – hrs pergi*, Sometimes one has to go. **pe–an** *sipil* a civilian. **perse–an** 1 individual. 2 individually. **se–** classifier. ~ *upas* a messenger. ~ *diri* all alone, by o.s. ~ *mata* pupil of the eye. **sese–** somebody. *Ada* ~ *datang kemari tadi*, Somebody came here a while ago. **se– –²** anyone. **–²an** 1 puppet, doll. 2 image. 3 dummy. *Teman saja lima –*, My friends number five. ~ *mata* pupil (of the eye). *–nja sendiri* the person himself. *–² jg tidak punja* the havenots. – *abangan* a nonreligious person. – *ajan* epileptic. – *am* crowd, general public, the masses. – *Amérika* an American. – *antun* a dandy. – *asing* foreigner, stranger. – *awak* 1 fellow countryman. 2 a Minangkabauer. – *awam*, – *banjak* the public, crowd. – *bantji* hermaphrodite. – *baru* newcomer. – *berkuda* rider, horseman. – *besar* dignitary. – *biasa* commoner. – *bukit* a hillman. – *bumi* native. – *bungkuk* a hunchback. – *dagang* merchant, tradesman. – *datang* newcomer. – *désa* 1 villager. 2 boor. – *Djakarta* Jakartan. – *Djawa* Javanese. – *djémbél* poor man. – *gelandangan* tramp, wanderer. – *halimun*, – *(machluk) halus* genie, spirit. – *hobat(an)* sorcerer, wizard. – *hukuman* prisoner, condemned man, convict. – *hulu* country bumpkin. – *hutan* orangutan. – *informan* informant, native speaker. – *jg berpunja* well-to-do person. –

jg nguler kambang 1 o. who takes things easy. 2 reformer. – *kaja* important person. – *kampung* villager, country fellow. – *kasim* eunuch. – *keling* Indian, Tamil. – *kebanjakan* commoner. – *(kulit) hitam* a Negro. – *kurungan* prisoner. – *lain* another person. – *lasak* handy man, unskilled worker. – *luar(an)* outsider, foreigner. – *mampu* person of means. – *maséhi* Christian. – *mendatang* 1 stranger. 2 foreigner. – *muatan* passengers. – *mulia* a noble. – *ngemis* beggar. – *pasak kampung* ordinary villager. – *patut²* decent person. – *pedalaman* those living in the relatively unoccupied areas of Indonesia. – *pelantjongan* 1 traveler. 2 drifter. – *penumpang* outsider. – *péréman* civilian. – *pertandang* traveling salesman. – *perutangan* creditor. – *ramai* the public, crowd. – *rantai* convict. – *risau* disturber of the peace. – *sabun* an albino. – *sebelah* neighbor. – *sedapur* the family. – *seléwéng* meddler, busybody. – *semodal* partner in a firm. – *senegeri* fellow countryman. – *se–* an individual. – *serendjang* a personality. – *setambul* Turk. – *tahanan* prisoner, internee. – *talang* villager. – *tani* farmer, peasant. – *tawanan* internee. – *terlantar* displaced person. – *ternak* a native. – *tjatjat* an invalid. – *tua* parents. – *turutan* 1 hitchhiker. 2 fellow traveler. – *tutupan* prisoner. – *udik* country fellow. – *usiran* fugitive, exile. – *utangan* debtor. – *utas* artisan, craftsman. *Kata –*, They say.

orbit orbit. **meng–kan** to put s.t. or s.o. into orbit.

ordi order.

ordonan orderly, messenger.

org [*orang*] person.

organa organ.

organisasi organization. **ber–** to organize, be organized. **meng–(kan)** to organize. *Meréka* ~ *tjara bekerdjanja*, They organized their manner of working.

organisator organizer.

organisir meng– to organize.

oriéntasi orientation.

orisinil original.

orkés orchestra.

orok baby. **meng–** 1 to snore. 2 to cough.

orong see URUNG. **–²** cricket.

otak 1 brain. 2 brains, intelligence. **–²an** 1 boasting. 2 braggart. 3 to go off o's rocker, be off mentally. – *benak* 1 brain(s). 2 sense. – *miring* crazy.

oték loose (of teeth).

oténtik authentic.

otjéh meng– to chat. peng– chatter-box, talkative person. -an gossip, chatter.
oto 1 automobile, car. 2 baby's bib. – *gerobak* truck. – *pengangkut orang sakit* ambulance.
otobis autobus, bus.
otodidak autodidact.
otomat 1 automatic dialing. 2 auto-mat.

otomatis automatic.
otomatisasi automation.
otonomi autonomy.
otoritér 1 authoritative. 2 authori-tarian.
otot 1 muscle. 2 tendon, sinew. meng– 1 persevering, tenacious, per-sistent. 2 to persist. 3 to be obsti-nate. – *kunjah* masticatory muscle.

P

p. [*pulau*] island.
P [*pelatjur*] prostitute.
P⁴ see PPPP.
pa'al act, deed.
pabéan customs house.
pab(e)rik factory. memp– to manu-facture.
pabian see PABÉAN.
pabila see APABILA.
pada 1 at. *Ia melihat – saja,* She looked at me. *Dpt dibeli – toko² buku,* Can be bought at bookshops. 2 in. – *tahun 1900* in 1900. *Perobahan dpt dilihat – nama s.k.,* A change can be seen in the name of the paper. 3 on. – *hari Selasa* on Tuesday. 4 to. – *siapa kauberikan buku itu?* To whom did you give the book? 5 with. *Buku itu ada –nja,* The book was with him. 6 enough, sufficient. *Hatinja blm –,* He was not yet satisfied. *Sedikitpun –lah,* A little will suffice. 7 all. *Bunga² – laju,* All the flowers faded. dari– 1 from. *Ini saja dpt ∼nja,* I got this from him. 2 than. *Buku ini lebih tebal ∼ buku itu,* This book is thicker than that one. ke– 1 to. *Ia katakan ∼ saja,* He said to me. 2 from. *Ia memesannja ∼ kami,* He ordered it from us. mem–i 1 to satisfy. *Gadjinja tiada ∼ ,* His salary is not sufficient. 2 to equal. *Tak ada jg dpt ∼ ketjantikannja,* Her beauty cannot be equaled. ∼ *diri dgn* to be satisfied with. mem–kan 1 to satisfy. 2 to be content with. *dlm – itu* in the meantime, meanwhile. *Katakan –nja,* Tell him.
padah omen, warning. -an unfortu-nate result, reward. *Itulah ∼nja,* It serves him right.

padahal 1 whereas. 2 although. *Ia tak mau mengeluarkan uang, – ia kaja,* He didn't want to spend money, although he was rich. 3 besides.
padam 1 extinguished. *Njawanja –,* He died. *Lampu –,* The light was ex-tinguished. 2 cooled off. *Marahnja sdh –,* His anger has cooled off. 3 hushed, muffled. 4 quenched. mem-kan 1 to extinguish, put out. *Ia ∼ njawanja,* He killed him. 2 to sup-press, put out. *Sépnja ∼ pemberon-takan,* The leader suppressed the re-bellion. pem– *api* fire extinguisher. *Djawatan ∼ Api* fire department. pem–an extinguishing, putting out (of fire).
padan 1 equal, match. 2 border, frontier. 3 promise. 4 false. mem-to oppose. se– *dgn* 1 to suit, match. *Warna itu tak ∼ dgn dia,* The color did not suit her. 2 to match, corre-spond with. *Perbuatannja tak ∼ dgn perkataannja,* His behavior does not correspond with his words. –an 1 parable. 2 comparison.
padang plain, field. pe– 1 informa-tion. 2 clarification. – *belantara,* – *gurun* desert. – *lumut* tundra. – *mahs(j)ar* gathering place on day of resurrection. – *pasir* desert. – *pem-bidikan* rifle range. – *rumput* 1 meadow. 2 steppes. – *tandus,* – *tiah* desert.
padas rocky soil.
padasan cistern, vat.
padat 1 solid, compact. 2 dense. *Kota ini penduduknja –,* This city is densely populated. ke–an density. ∼ *penduduk* density of population. mem–kan to stuff, cram. -an solid matter (in physics).

paderi 1 Catholic priest. 2 see PERANG.

padi 1 rice plant. 2 tiny, very small. – *berat* slow-growing rice. – *gadu* wet field rice. – *gogo* dry field rice. – *jagus* k.o. high-yield rice developed by a certain Jagus. – *radin* swamp rice. – *ranap* overripe rice. – *ringan* fast-ripening rice. – *séntra* rice from experimental farm. – *tjeré* quick-ripening small-grained rice. *tak se*-not a bit.

padjak 1 tax. 2 monopoly. **ke–an** revenue. **mem–i** to pay taxes for. **pem–an** 1 taxation. 2 tax system. **per–an** taxation. – *gadai* pawnshop. – *ikan* fish market. – *kekajaan* property or capital tax. – *kendaraan* vehicle, road tax. – *negeri* government tax. – *pendapatan*, – *penghasilan*, – *pentjaharian* income tax. – *pendjualan* sales tax. – *perséroan* corporation tax. – *rumah tangga* property tax. – *sajur* vegetable market. – *tanah* land tax. – *tontonan* entertainment tax. – *upah* income tax, withholding tax. – *tjandu* public opium den.

padjang **mem–** to dress windows, display. **mem–kan** to display. **pem–an** nuptial chamber. **–an** window-dressing display.

padjar see FADJAR.

padjuh **mem–** to stuff, gorge.

padma lotus.

padri see PADERI.

padu 1 solid, compact. 2 fused. **ber–** to unite. **bersatu–** to form a solid unit. **ke–an** unity. **mem–** 1 to unite, join. 2 to forge, weld. 3 to merge. ∼ *bitjara* to consult. ∼ *djandji* to come to an agreement. ∼ *hati* to consult together, negotiate. ∼ *modal* to assemble capital. ∼ *perkataan* to compound words. ∼ *suara* to sing in harmony. **menjatu–kan** to unify. **(per)–an** 1 merger, unification, fusion. 2 synthesis. 3 blend. **–an** *suara* choir, chorus.

paduka excellency. – *Jg Mulia* His Excellency.

paédah see FAÉDAH.

pagan firm, solid.

pagar 1 fence. 2 hedge. **ber–** to be fenced in. **mem–** to make a hedge. ∼ *diri* to look after o.s. **mem–i** to fence in, put a fence around. **mem–kan** to use as a fence. – *bedil* mopping-up operation by military action. – *betis* volunteer service for combating banditry in a village. – *bulan* halo. – *djaro* hedge. – *duri*, – *kawat* barbed wire.

pager see PAGAR.

pagi morning. *Hari baru (masih)* –,

It's still early. **ke–an** 1 morning. 2 too early. *Sdr* ∼ *datangnja*, You came too early. **se–an** the entire morning. **–nja** that same morning. **–²** early in the morning. ∼ *buta* very early in the morning. – *hari* this morning. – *harinja* the following morning. – *ini* this morning. – *tadi* this morning (action already completed).

pagina page (of publication).

pagini = PAGI INI.

pagut **mem–** 1 to peck. 2 to bite (of a snake). 3 to embrace. **–an** embrace.

paha thigh.

pahala merit, reward. *Ia berbuat* –, He is doing good.

paham 1 understanding. *Ia menaruh* – *soal itu*, He shows an understanding of the problem. 2 view, concept. – *ékonomis* economic concept. 3 to understand. *Saja kurang* –, I don't quite understand. 4 to know. *Saja kurang* –, I don't know exactly. **ber–** sensible. **mem–i**, **mem–kan** 1 to understand. 2 to realize. **se–** to be of the same view. *Saja* ∼ *dgn dia*, I share his view. – *akan* to understand, know about. *Dia* – *akan bahasa Perantjis*, He understands French. – *komunis* communism, understanding of communism. *Djangan salah* –, Don't misunderstand me. – *peladjarannja* to know o's lesson. *menurut* – *saja* according to my understanding.

pahar teacart, tea wagon.

pahat chisel. **ber–** carved, chiseled. **mem–** to chisel, carve, sculpt. **–an** carving, relief. ∼ *lino* linecut.

pahit 1 bitter. 2 short drink. **ke–an** bitterness, exasperation. **ke-getiran** bitterness, unpleasantness. **mem–kan** to embitter, exasperate. – *getir* unpleasantness. – *getir penghidupan* the gloomy side of life. – *maung* 1 very bitter. 2 bitterness. – *pahang* acrimony. *se– semanis* for better or for worse.

pahlawan 1 hero. 2 patriot. **ke–an** heroism. – *setia* loyal retainer.

pai pie.

pailit bankrupt.

pair see PAJAR. – *djantung* pulse deviation.

pait see PAHIT.

paja swamp.

pajah 1 tired. 2 difficult. 3 critical. **ber–** –² to toil. **ke–an** 1 weariness, fatigue. 2 difficulty. 3 exhausted. **mem–kan** 1 to tire. 2 tiring. **me-m–²kan** to work o.s. to death.

pajang large net. **mem–** to support

s.o. in walking. **pem–** seine. **pem–an** seining.

pajar ber– –² to cruise back and forth. **mem–i** to cruise, patrol. **pem–** cruiser.

pajau salty, briny.

pajit bankrupt.

pajon shed, lean-to.

paju in demand, sought after. *sdh –* already sold.

pajung 1 umbrella. 2 parachute. **mem–i** 1 to screen. 2 to protect.

pak 1 see BAPAK. 2 package, parcel. 3 lease, rent. 4 charter, pact. – *Atlantik* Atlantic Charter. **mem–** 1 to pack, wrap up. 2 to lease, rent. **mem–kan** to lease, rent out. **penge–** packer. – *Amat* 1 Mr. Amat (form of address to elderly and respected man). 2 father of Amat. – *dé*, – *gedé* an uncle older than o's father or mother. – *lik* uncle younger than o's parents. – *guru* form of address to male school teacher. – *temurun* tenure by long lease. – *tjilik* = – LIK. – *turut* a follower. – *uda* uncle.

pakai 1 to involve the use of. 2 with, by means of. **ber–** to dress. **ber–an** dressed. **mem–** 1 to wear. *Ia ∼ badju biru*, She was wearing a blue dress. 2 to use, make use of. *Meréka ∼ médja itu*, They used that table. 3 by means of. *Ia datang ∼ mobil*, He came by car. 4 to require. *Itu ∼ modal besar*, It requires a lot of capital. **mem–kan** to put s.t. on for s.o. **pem–** 1 user, consumer. 2 wearer. **pem–an** 1 use, consumption. 2 application. *se∼* complete set of clothes. **ter–** 1 used (up). 2 canceled, void (passport, visa, etc.). 3 applied. *ilmu² pengetahuan ∼* applied sciences. *tidak ∼* without. **–an** 1 clothes. 2 dress, garment. 3 suit. 4 uniform. *∼ adat* traditional dress. *∼ angkatan* military service uniform. *∼ dalam* underwear. *∼ dinas* uniform. *∼ dinas lapangan* battle dress. *∼ kebangsaan* national dress. *∼ kebesaran*, – *lengkap* full dress. *∼ pelasak* work clothes. *∼ seragam* uniform. *∼ taruhan* Sunday clothes. *∼ tekan* pressurized suit.

pakal putty. **mem–** to calk a ship.

pakan woof. **mem–kan** to interweave with.

pakansi holiday, vacation. **ber–** to go on a vacation.

pakat 1 agreement. 2 discussion. 3 see PEKAT. **ber–** 1 to agree. 2 to discuss. **mem–i**, **menje–i** to agree on. **se–** 1 agreed. 2 unanimously, in harmony. *Meréka ∼ menolak usul itu,*

They unanimously rejected the resolution.

paké see PAKAI.

pakem **mem–** to take hold (of brakes).

pakét parcel.

pakih see FAKIH.

pakir see FAKIR.

paksa 1 force. 2 necessity. 3 compulsion. 4 favorable opportunity. **ke–** to have to. *Ia ∼ pergi*, He had to go. **mem–(kan)** 1 to force, compel. 2 to persist in. **me-m–²** troublesome. **ter–** 1 forced, compelled. 2 necessary. **–an** 1 force, coercion. 2 compulsion. 3 necessity.

paksi 1 axis. 2 pivot.

paksina north.

pakta pact.

paktjik uncle.

paktur invoice. – *konsinjasi* consignment invoice.

paku 1 nail, spike. 2 fern. **ber–** *kpd* to cling, stick to. **mem–(i)** to nail. **mem–kan** to nail down, nail up. *Ia ∼ plakat pd suatu pohon*, He nailed a placard on a tree. **ter–** *ragu* bewildered, puzzled. – *alam* princely title in Jogjakarta. – *djamur* thumbtack. – *keling*, – *sumbat* rivet. – *rebana* tack.

pakum vacuum.

pal 1 approx. 1 mile. 2 pole. **ber– –²** to tack a vessel.

PAL [*Penataran Angkatan Laut*] naval base.

pala 1 see BUAH. 2 see BUNGA. **(se)– –²** if. *∼ mentjuri, ambil semuanja*, If you are stealing, you might as well take everything.

palai **mem–** to stew until tender.

palak 1 angry. *Saja – kepadanja*, I was angry with him. 2 adventurous. 3 passionate, excited. **pem–** hothead. **–²** *dingin* lukewarm.

palam **mem–** to stop a leak. **pem–** 1 stopper. 2 cork.

palang 1 crossbar. 2 bolt. 3 barrier. **mem–i** to hamper, block, obstruct. **mem–kan** 1 to crucify. 2 to conclude with. – *Mérah* Red Cross. *Ia mendapat – pintu*, He got a scolding from his wife.

palar **mem–** to be pleased with. *Biarpun sedikit, itu saja –*, Although it wasn't much, I was pleased with it.

palawidja second crop.

paling the most. *jg – baik* the best. **ber–** to turn. **mem–(kan)** to swing round, alter course. **se–** as a whole. **–²** 1 very. *Ia ∼ pandainja*, He's very clever. 2 at the most. *∼ ia dpt menamatkan sekolah menengahnja*, At the most he was able to complete his high-school education. – *banjak* 1 the most. *Ia mempunjai jg – banjak*, He had the most of all. 2 at most. – *banjak ada lima puluh*, At most there were 50. – *sedikit* 1 the least. 2 at the least.

palis ber-, mem- 1 to turn o's eyes away. 2 to ogle. 3 to polish.

palit 1 k.o. ointment. 2 bankrupt. **ke–an** bankruptcy. **mem–** to smear, daub. **mem–kan** 1 to spread evenly. 2 to declare bankrupt. **pem–** *bibir* lipstick. **ter–** –² mixed up in a dirty business.

palka hold of a ship.

palsu false, faked, counterfeit, artificial. **ke–an** meanness. **mem–kan** 1 to adulterate food. 2 to forge documents. 3 to counterfeit, falsify s.t. **pem–** 1 forger. 2 counterfeiter. **pem–an** 1 counterfeiting. 2 adulteration. 3 forgery. 4 falsification.

paltu 1 assistant. 2 acting, temporary.

palu 1 hammer. 2 blow. 3 gavel. **ber–** –² to barter. **ber–** –²an to hit e.o. **mem–** 1 to hit, beat, strike. 2 to play an instrument. **–an** blow. – *arit* hammer and sickle. – *godam* sledge hammer. – *pimpinan* gavel.

paluh deep pool.

palun ber- –² to embrace, hug e.o.

palung 1 pool. 2 trough. 3 river bed. – *ikan* aquarium.

palut ber- wrapped. **mem–** to wrap. **pem–** 1 bandage. 2 wrapper.

paman uncle.

paméo 1 slogan. 2 saying, proverb.

pamér to show off, exhibit. **ber–** *diri* to exhibit, admire o.s. *Ia ~ diri didepan tjermin*, She admired herself before the mirror. **mem(per)–kan** 1 to model (clothes). 2 to exhibit. **–an** exhibition. *~ ilmijah* scientific exhibition. *~ sendjata* military review. *~ terapung* floating exhibition.

pamflét pamphlet.

pamili 1 family. 2 relatives. **ber–** *dgn* to be related to.

pamit farewell. **ber–an** to say goodbye. **–an** farewell. *sepatah kata ~ a* few words of farewell.

pamong 1 guardian. 2 tutor. – *désa* village administrator. – *pradja* civil service.

pampang 1 wide, broad. 2 obvious. **mem–kan** 1 to extend, widen, spread out. 2 to explain.

pampas reimbursement, indemnity. **mem–** to reimburse. **–an** reparations payment. *~ perang* war reparations.

pampat mem– to press, squeeze. **pem–** press.

pamrih 1 purpose, intent. *Apa –nja kesini?* Why's he coming here? 2 profit.

pamur 1 damascene. 2 luster.

panah bow (and arrow). **mem–(i)** to shoot at s.t. or s.o. with bow and arrow. **pem–** archer. **sepem–** the distance of a bowshot. – *kelodan* lightning. – *matahari* sun's rays.

panar stunned, dull.

panas 1 warm, hot. 2 heat. 3 critical. 4 fierce. **ber–** *diri* to sun-bathe. **ke–an** 1 too hot. 2 heat. 3 suffering from the heat. **mem–i** to heat. *–ilah air*, Heat some water. **mem–kan** to heat. **pem–an** heating. –² quite new, fresh. *~ hendak* virtually unable to restrain o.s. – *bara* quick-tempered. – *dingin* malaria. – *hati* angry, cross. – *kuku* lukewarm. – *sengangar* noonday heat. – *terik* 1 stifling, suffocatingly hot. 2 red-hot (of metal). – *tubuh* body heat.

panasaran embittered.

pandai 1 clever. *Anak itu – dikelas*, The child's clever in school. 2 capable. *Anak itu – membuat lajang²*, The child's capable of making a kite. 3 to know how. *Anak itu – menjukakan hati orang tuanja*, That child knows how to please his parents. 4 to know. *Anak itu – berbahasa Inggeris*, The child knows English. 5 smith. **ke–an** cleverness, skill. – *agak* good at guessing. – *djatuh* able to shift for o.s. – *besi* smithy. – *emas* goldsmith. *Se–* –² *orang, sekali akan membuat kesalahan djuga*, As clever as o. is, he'll still make mistakes.

pandak short. **mem–kan, mem(per)–** to shorten, abbreviate.

pandang a look. **ber–an** to view e.o. **mem–** 1 to look at, gaze at. 2 to consider. *Ia ~ hal itu sebagai biasa sadja*, He considered the case a common one. *~ hina* to look down on s.o. *~ keatas* to glance up. **pem–** spectator. **pem–an** 1 view, scenery. 2 observation. **sepem–** at a glance. **ter–** 1 visible. 2 to spot, catch sight of. 3 esteemed, highly regarded. **–an** view, opinion. *~ hidup* view of life, philosophy of life, *Weltanschauung*. – **–mem–** 1 to look at e.o. 2 to respect e.o. *sekali* – at first glance. *selajang* – a glance. *dlm selajang* – at a glance. *(dgn) tidak mem– bulu* 1 indiscriminately. 2 irrespective of persons. *tidak* – irrespective, regardless. *tidak* – *bangsa dan bahasa* irrespective of race or language.

pandemén 1 basis. 2 foundation.

pandir stupid. **ke–an** stupidity.

pandita see PENDÉTA.
pandjang 1 long. 2 length. **ber-kalam** to relate in elaborate fashion. ~ *madah* to talk a great deal. **ber-an** 1 in the long run. 2 for a long time. **berke-an** 1 continuous. 2 prolonged, protracted. **ke-an** 1 too long. 2 length. 3 duration. 4 continuation. 5 full name. **mem-** to stretch. *Didepan kami* ~ *pantai laut*, Before us stretched the seashore. **mem-kan, memper-** to extend, lengthen, prolong, stretch. *Pertundjukan itu akan diper-*, The performance will be extended. **per-an** extension, prolongation. **se-** 1 along. ~ *djalan* along the road. 2 as far as. ~ *pengetahuan saja* as far as I know. ~ *hari* all day long. ~ *pikiran saja* in my opinion. **-an** extension. – *akal* clever, witty. *Orang tua itu* – *akalnja*, That old man is very clever. – *bulat* cylindrical. – *gelombang* wave length. – *kili*² full of excuses. – *kira*² 1 intelligent, wise. 2 cautious. – *landjut* wordy, verbose. – *langkah* in a round-about way. – *lébar* elaborate, detailed. – *lidah* backbiting, slanderous. – *mata* immoral. – *napas* with stamina. – *tangan* light-fingered, thievish. – *umur* to have a long life.
pandjar cash advance.
pandjat **mem-** to climb. ~ *perkara* 1 to appeal to a higher court. 2 to give notice of appeal. **mem-kan** to cause to climb. *Ia* ~ *keranja*, He made his monkey climb up.
pandji flag, standard, banner.
pandu 1 guide. 2 boy scout. **ke-an** scouting, scout movement. **mem-** to guide. **mem-kan** to pilot, bring a ship into port. **-an** escort. – *kapal* ship's pilot.
panekuk pancake.
panembrama song of welcome.
panén(an) harvest.
Pangad [*Panglima Angkatan Darat*] Commander-in-Chief of the Ground Forces.
pangah **ter-** openmouthed.
pangan food.
Pangdam [*Panglima Daérah Militér*] territorial military commander.
pangéran 1 prince. 2 lord.
pangéstu blessing.
panggak proud of s.t. or s.o.
panggang 1 toasted. *Saja suka roti* –, I like toast. 2 roasted. 3 to bake. **mem-** 1 to toast. 2 to roast. **pem-roti** toaster. **pem-an** 1 toaster. 2 roasting spit. **ter-** seared.
panggil **mem-(kan)** 1 to call, summon, send for s.o. 2 to name. **sepem-**

as far as the voice can reach. **-an** 1 call, summons. 2 calling, vocation.
panggul 1 hip. 2 pelvis. **mem-** to carry on o's hip.
panggung 1 platform, stage, grand-stand. 2 scaffolding. 3 theater balcony. **mem-kan** to stage, put on the stage. **pem-an** staging. **-an** lookout tower, post. – *suara* sound stage.
pangkal 1 base, beginning, root, starting point. 2 cause. 3 origin. 4 pole (in elec.). **mem-kan** to unload, discharge, put ashore. **-an** 1 anchorage. 2 landing place, quay. 3 depot. ~ *udara* air base. – *bedil* rifle butt. – *bertolak* starting point. – *kaki* tarsus. – *katakerdja* infinitive. – *lengan* upper arm. – *nama* first name. – *paha* hip. – *pedang* hilt of a sword. – *pohon* foot, base of a tree. – *pokok* gist, essence. – *tjerita* main point of a story.
pangkas **ber-** to get a haircut. **mem-** to cut, trim hair. ~ *kata* to summarize, recapitulate. **pem-** barber. **pem-an** 1 barbering. 2 barbershop.
pangkat 1 rank, position. 2 floor, story. 3 step. 4 degree, power (math.). 5 platform. *empat* – *tiga* four to the third power. **ber-** to hold an important position. **mem-kan** to promote s.o. **pem-an** promotion. *di-kan tudjuh* raised to the seventh power.
pangking bedroom.
pangku lap. **ber-** *tangan* to do nothing. **mem-** 1 to take on o's lap. 2 to manage, administer, run. 3 to hold, occupy a position. ~ *djabatan ilmiah* to hold a scientific post. **pem-** 1 manager. 2 functionary. ~ *djabatan* 1 functionary. 2 acting. **pem-an** administration. **-an** lap.
pangkung **mem-** to hit with a club.
pangkur 1 pickax. 2 mattock, hoe. **mem-** to till, work the soil.
panglima commander. – *besar*, – *tertinggi* commander in chief. – *mandala* theater army commander.
pangling fail to recognize.
pangon shepherd. **-an** pasture.
pangréh pradja civil service.
pangsa segment, section.
pangsan see PINGSAN.
pangur rasp, file.
pangus dashing.
panik **ke-an** panic.
panili vanilla.
panitera 1 secretary. 2 clerk. – *pengadilan* clerk of the court. 3 registrar. **ke-an** secretariat. – *utama* chief secretary.
paniteratama chief secretary.
panitia committee. – *penaskah* draft committee. – *pengudji*, – *udjian*

examining board. — *perumus* formu-
lative committee.
panitya see PANITIA.
pantai beach, coast, seashore. — *Emas*
Gold Coast. **ber–kan** to border on.
lautan jg ∼ *sebagian kepulauan Indonésia* an ocean that borders on a
portion of the Indonesian Archipelago.
— *Gading* Ivory Coast.
pantak **mem–** to penetrate. **mem–kan**
to drive a nail in.
pantalon long trousers.
pantang 1 prohibition. 2 prohibited,
forbidden. 3 abstinence. **ber–** 1 to
abstain from. 2 to be tied down to
a regulation. **mem–** to refuse, abstain
from. **–an** an order prohibiting s.t. —
kerendahan to want to be first rate.
— *mundur* never give up or give in.
— *patah ditengah* persevering. — *ter-
singgung* easily piqued, offended. *Ia*
— *surut,* He never gave up.
pantas 1 proper, nice, suitable. *Badju
itu tak — baginja,* That dress doesn't
suit her. *perumahan* — suitable housing. 2 reasonable, fair, proper. *Itu
harga –,* That's a reasonable price.
3 alert, smart. **mem–** to dress o.s. up.
se–nja fitting, proper. ∼ *kamu harus
pergi kepadanja,* It's fitting you
should go to him. — *pangus* dashing.
— *tangan* clever at picking pockets.
pantat 1 behind, bottom, buttock.
2 base. **ber–** bottomed, to have a
bottom.
panték see PANTIK.
Pantékosta Whitsuntide.
pantes see PANTAS.
panti 1 building. 2 institution, home.
— *derma* charitable institution.
pantik **mem–** 1 to strike fire. 2 to
snap o's fingers. 3 to tap. ∼ *darah*
to bleed. 4 to drill. ∼ *sumur* to drill
a well. **pem–** *api* cigarette lighter.
panting **ter–** 1 to dart away. 2 to
fall with a thud.
pantis mascara. **mem–** to black the
eyebrows.
pantja 1 five. 2 hand. **ber–** to wrestle
by pushing o's opponent with the
hands. — *Negara Colombo* the Colombo
countries.
pantjaindera the five senses.
pantjalogi five principles.
pantjalomba pentathlon.
pantjamuka multifaceted.
pantjang 1 pole, stake, pile. 2 boundary pole, stake. **ber–kan** rooted,
implanted. **mem–** to ram, drive piles.
mem–kan to stick into, fasten. **pem–
an** marking with a stake. **ter–** 1
rooted, planted in the ground. 2

established (reputation). **–an** a stake,
marker.
pantjar **ber–** to spout, spray, squirt.
Dikaki gunung itu ∼ *air dari dlm
tanah,* At the foot of the mountain
the water spouts out. **ber–** –² scattered,
dispersed. **mem–** 1 to spout, spray,
gush. *Peluhnja* ∼ *sehingga badjunja
basah,* He perspired until his clothes
were soaked. 2 to sprout. **mem–kan**
1 to radiate. *Matahari* ∼ *sinarnja,*
The sun's rays radiate. 2 to spout.
3 to broadcast. *RRI* ∼ *siarannja
pd gelombang 120 m.,* The Indonesian
Broadcasting Co. broadcasts on a
wavelength of 120 m. **pem–** 1 transmitter. 2 fountain. 3 radiator. **se–
an** homologous. **ter–** born. **–an** 1
jet, spout. 2 flow. 3 broadcast. 4
product. 5 descent. ∼ *air* fountain.
∼ *mani* seminal discharge, ejaculation.
pantjaragam various, motley, all
kinds of.
pantjargas 1 jet. 2 see PANTJAR.
pantjaroba transition period.
Pantjasila the 5 basic principles of
the Republic of Indonesia: *Ketuhanan*
Belief in God; *Kebangsaan* National
Consciousness; *Perikemanusiaan* Humanism; *Keadilan Sosial* Social Justice; *Démokrasi* Sovereignty of the
People.
pantjawarna multicolored.
pantjawarsa 5-year period, quinquen-
nium.
pantji pan. — *email* enamelware.
pantjing 1 fishing rod. 2 fishhook.
mem– 1 to fish, angle. 2 to provoke,
start s.t. 3 to ferret out secrets. **–an**
1 provocation. 2 feint, poser, entice-
ment.
pantjit **mem–** to squirt little by little.
pantjoléng thief.
pantjung 1 train of a dress. 2 angular. 3 shirttail. **mem–** to cut off,
decapitate. **mem–kan** to make sharp
or well shaped. *Dokter bisa* ∼ *hidung
dgn potongan plastik,* The doctor can
make a nose well formed by plastic
surgery. **–an** a cut. ∼ *pedang* a cut
with a sword.
pantjur **ber–** 1 to gush, spout, spray.
2 to sprout. **mem–** 1 to spout, gush,
spray. 2 to sprout. **–an** 1 shower.
2 jet, spray. 3 tap. ∼ *air* 1 water
spout. *Ia mandi dibawah* ∼ *air,* He's
taking a bath under the waterspout.
2 spray, jet of water.
pantjut **mem–** to gush.
pantul **mem–** to bounce back, bounce
off. **–an** reflection.
pantun quatrain. **ber–(–an)** to recite

with 2 or more persons singing quatrains. **mem–kan** to express o.s. by
means of pantuns. **pem–** composer of
pantuns.

papa 1 poor, destitute. 2 daddy.
ke–an poverty, destitution. **ke–
sengsaraan** poverty, destitution. –
sengsara destitute.

papah **ber–** supported. **mem–** to support. *Orang sakit itu di–, sebab ia tak
dpt berdjalan sendiri,* The sick man
was supported, because he could not
walk by himself.

papaja papaya.

papak flat, level, smooth. **ber–** to
meet. *Saja ~ dgn dia didjalan,* I
met him on the street. **mem–** 1 to
meet. 2 to receive, welcome. **–an** 1
meeting. 2 welcome, reception.

papan 1 board, plank. 2 shelf. 3
(road) sign. **mem–** to install, place
boards. – *asbés* asbestos plate. –
hubungan switchboard. – *lontjatan*
springboard. – *tjatur* chessboard. –
tongkah a sledge for use on marshy
land. – *tulis* blackboard.

papar flat, level. **mem–kan** 1 to roll
out, flatten. 2 to explain, relate.
pem–an explanation. **–an** explanation.

papas **mem–** 1 to remove, take off.
2 to sever. 3 to resist. 4 to criticize.
Ia ~ tjeramah habis²an, He criticized
the lecture to a fare-the-well.

papiljun pavilion.

para 1 rubber. 2 collective plural. –
domba flock, congregation. – *hadlirin*
Ladies and Gentlemen. – *pelaku*
cast (of a play or movie). – *pembatja*
the readers. – *pendengar* the audience,
Ladies and Gentlemen. – *penumpang*
passengers. **–²** 1 attic. 2 rack, shelf.

paradam the deuce. **mem–** to swear
at.

paradji midwife.

paraf see PARAP.

paragraf paragraph.

parah serious (of a wound).

parak 1 interspace. 2 partition. 3
difference. *Tabi'atnja tak berapa –nja
dgn ibunja,* Her character does not
differ much from that of her mother.
mem–kan to distinguish. – *siang*
shortly before daybreak.

paramanusia human race.

paramasastera grammar.

paran 1 direction. 2 goal, aim.
mem–i to approach, go to.

parang short sword or knife. **mem–
(kan)** 1 to cut. 2 to cancel.

parap initials. **mem–** 1 to initial,
mark with initials. 2 to hammer.

paras 1 face, countenance. 2 looks,
appearance. 3 smooth. **mem–** to
make smooth, level.

parasit parasite.

parau hoarse.

pardji vulva.

parik in line, in a queue.

paripurna 1 perfect, pure. 2 complete.

parit 1 moat, ditch, trench. 2 furrow, slit, groove. **ber–** grooved.

pariwara advertisement.

pariwisata 1 tourism. 2 a tour.

pariwisatawan tourist. **ke–an** tourism.

parkir **mem–** to park.

parlemén parliament.

parleméntairisme parliamentarism.

parleméntér parliamentary.

paro(h) half. **pem–** o. who shares
half the yield of a farm. **se–** half,
a part. **–an** 1 half and half, 50-50.
Untungnja ~ , The profit was shared
50-50. 2 dividend. **–²** = **–AN**.

paroki Catholic parish.

paron anvil.

Parsi Persia(n).

partai 1 party. *Ia masuk – Nasional,*
He joined the Nationalist Party. 2
lots of. *Ia membeli se– kemédja,* He
bought a lot of shirts. **ber–** belonging
to a party. *Ia tidak ~ ,* He's nonparty.
ke–an party system, party affairs.

partikelir private. *Anaknja masuk
sekolah –,* His child entered a private
school.

paru² lungs.

paruh 1 beak. 2 half, part of. 3 see
PARO(H). **mem–** 1 to divide into
half, halve. 2 to peck at. **se–** a half,
a part. **–²** 1 half-breed. 2 half-
hearted.

parut 1 rasp, file. 2 scar, scratch,
scrape. 3 board closely set with wire
teeth on which coconut meat is
grated. **mem–** 1 to rasp. 2 to scratch.

pas 1 to fit. *Badju itut ak – baginja,*
The dress didn't fit her. 2 exact(ly).
Itu – seperti saja punja, It looked
exactly like mine. *uang –* exact
amount. **menge–** to try s.t. on. **–²**
documents. – *djalan* travel permit.

pasah divorce granted by a religious
court at the wife's request upon proof
that the husband has been derelict in
the performance of his conjugal
duties. **ter–** to land. *Dimana ~ badju
saja?* What's become of my dress?

pasak 1 pin, peg. 2 bolt. 3 pivot,
axis. 4 turning point. **mem–** to peg,
pin. **mem–kan** 1 to fasten. 2 to impress s.t. upon s.o. *besar – dari tiang*
to live beyond o's social position.

pasal 1 paragraph, section. 2 article
(legal). 3 concerning, regarding,
about. – *itu djangan chawatir,* Don't
worry about that. *Apa –nja itu
terdjadi?* How did it happen?

pasang 1 pair, set. *se– sepatu* a pair of shoes. 2 to rise, increase. *Muka laut –*, The sea level rose. **ber–an** to form a pair. **ber– –²** in pairs. **mem–** 1 to fix, install. *Ia ∼ ban*, He fixed a tire. 2 to put on. *Ia ∼ pakaiannja*, He put on his clothes. 3 to turn on. *–lah lampu itu dulu*, Please turn on the light. 4 to fit, install. *Rék itu blm di–*, The shelf has not been installed yet. 5 to fasten, pin. *Ia ∼ Bintang Gerilja didadanja*, He pinned the Guerrilla Star on his chest. 6 to put in, enter. *Ia selalu di– dlm pertandingan² penting*, He's always entered in important contests. *∼ bendéra* to hang out the flag. *∼ iklan* to insert an advertisement. *∼ lajar* to set sail. *∼ mata* to watch closely. *∼ meriam* to fire a gun. *∼ pagar* to build a fence. *∼ radio* to turn on the radio. *∼ telinga* to listen attentively. *∼ tikaman* to stake o's money. **mem–kan** 1 to install, fit. *Ia ∼ lampu listerik*, He installed an electric light. 2 to make a pair. 3 to apply. **mem–tanggalkan** *telepak ban* to put on and take off tire chains. **pem–** fitter, installer. *∼ iklan* advertiser. **(pem)–an** 1 pair, set. 2 partner, counterpart. 3 installing, assembling. 4 firing, shooting. *∼ batu mérah* brickwork, masonry. **ter–** 1 discharged, fired. 2 turned on (light, radio). *– aksi* 1 to show off. *Ia – aksi dgn mobilnja jg baru*, He showed off his new car. 2 to pose, be on o's best behavior. *– kering* ebb, low tide. *– naik* 1 high tide. 2 to increase. *– purnama* spring tide. *– surut* low tide. *Kehidupan ada – surutnja*, Life has its ups and downs.

pasanggrahan resthouse.

pasar market. **pem–an** marketing. *–an dunia* world market. *– bébas* free market. *– derma* bazaar. *– gelap* black market. *– malam* fair. *– sajur* vegetable market. *– Uang* exchange.

pasara 1 cemetery. 2 grave.

pasasir passenger. *– gelap* stowaway.

paséban audience hall.

paséh see FASIH.

pasién patient.

pasih see FASIH.

pasik 1 criminal, bad. 2 crazy. **ke–an** sin.

pasilan parasite.

pasilita facility.

pasir 1 sand. 2 beach. *– beton* sand used in preparing concrete. *– pasang* sand used in laying bricks.

pasirah village chief.

pasisir 1 see PESISIR. 2 see PASASIR.

Paska(h) Easter.

pasmén lace.

paso see PASU.

paspasan getting by, just making out. *Ia membawa uang – sadja*, He took just the amount he needed.

pasrah to surrender. *Ia – kpd nasibnja*, He surrendered to his fate. **ke–an** surrender, handing over. **mem–kan** to surrender, leave to. *∼ diri* to surrender o.s.

passi passion.

passiva liabilities.

pasta paste. *– gigi* tooth paste.

pasti definite, certain. *Ia mau djawaban jg –*, He wants a definite answer. **ke–an** 1 certainty. 2 assurance. 3 for sure. *Nanti saja kasih tahu ∼nja*, I'll let you know for sure. **mem–kan** to determine, ascertain, state. *– tidaknja* whether it is certain or not.

pasu bowl, basin. **–²** cheekbones.

pasukan 1 troops. 2 group. 3 formation. *se– kapal terbang* a formation of planes. *– berkuda* cavalry. *– djalan* infantry. *– gerilja* guerrilla troops. *– laut* navy. *– meriam* artillery. *– pemadam api* fire brigade. *– pemberontak* rebel troops. *– pembidas*, *– penggempur* shock troops. *– pengawal* guard platoon. *– sukaréla* volunteer troops. *– tjadangan* reserves, reserve troops. *– udara* air force.

Pasundan Sundanese area (West Java).

pasung prisoner's stocks. **mem–** to place in the stocks.

patah broken. **ber–** *hati* to be discouraged, dejected. *Rakjat djangan ∼ hati*, The people shouldn't be discouraged. **ke–an** breakdown. *∼ rohani* mental breakdown. **mem–kan** 1 to break. *Ia ∼ tongkat itu*, He broke the stick. 2 discouraging. **pe–** proverb, aphorism, expression. **pem–an** fracture. *se– kata* 1 one word. 2 a few words. **–an** 1 fracture. 2 broken fragment. 3 fault (geol.). *– arang*, *– batu* completely broken. *– hati* discouraged. *Ia sdh – hati*, He was discouraged. *– lesu* 1 desperate. 2 brokenhearted. *– lidah* speech impediment, defect. *– majang* wavy (hair). *– selera* to have no appetite. *– tjelana* crease in trousers. *– tulang* bone fracture. *– tumbuh hilang berganti*, No o. is indispensable.

paték frambesia, yaws.

pateri solder. **mem–(kan)** to solder. **–an** soldering. *Émbér ini rusak ∼nja*, The soldering on this bucket is damaged.

paternalistis paternalistic.

pateroli patrol.

pati 1 starch. 2 core, essence. 3 see PATIH 2. – *arak* spirits.
patih 1 meek, submissive, docile. 2 governor. 3 vice regent, senior assistant or executive officer of regent. **ke–an** 1 obedience. 2 residence or office of vice-regent. **pem–** meek.
patihah first chapter of the Koran.
patik 1 slave. 2 I, me (very humble).
patil pole, shaft. **mem–** to use a pole.
patjak 1 roasting spit. 2 skilled, experienced. **mem–** 1 to fix upon a spit. 2 to impale.
patjal slave.
patjangan 1 fiancé(e). 2 partner (boy or girl).
patjar honey, darling. **ber–an** to be in love with e.o. **ber– –²an** to have a love affair.
patjat leech. – *kenjang* oblong and thick in the middle (fountain pen, pencil).
patjé ripe *mengkudu* fruit.
patjek **mem–** to cover.
patjeklik 1 famine. 2 time of scarcity before harvest.
patjombéran 1 refuse dump. 2 cesspool. 3 drainpipe for refuse.
patju spur. **ber–** to race. ∼ *kuda* to race on horseback. **mem–** to spur on. ∼ *kuda* to ride horseback. **–an** 1 race. 2 racecourse.
patjuk see PATUK.
patjul hoe. **mem–** 1 to hoe. 2 to squeeze, press.
patok pole. **–an** 1 pole. 2 directive, standard. 3 postulate. ∼ *duga* hypothesis. ∼ *harga* fixity of prices.
pat² **gulipat** corrupt, engaged in embezzlement.
patriotik patriotic.
patrun (dress) pattern.
patuh obedient, meek, submissive. **ke–an** 1 obedience. 2 discipline. **mem–** to obey. **mem–i** to obey s.t. *Ia* ∼ *hukum negara*, He obeys the state's laws.
patuk **mem–** to peck, bite. **–an** bill, beak.
patung 1 image, statue. 2 sculpture. **pem–** sculptor. **pem–an** sculpturing. – *dada* bust (sculptured).
patut 1 proper, fitting, decent. *Ini harga –*, This is a decent price. 2 should, ought to. 3 in line with. **ber–an** *dgn* to agree with, be in accordance with. **ke–an** 1 decency, respectability. 2 view, opinion. **mem–kan** to correct, put in order, fit. ∼ *diri* to dress up. **mem– –²** 1 to dress s.t. up. 2 to take a hard look. **se–nja** proper, rightly, fittingly. – *dihukum* liable to punishment.

pauh mango.
pauk **mem–** to hook. **pem–** hook. see LAUK.
paus pope. **ke–an** papacy.
paut closely joined. **ber–** to cling to. **ber–an** *dgn* closely connected, merged. **mem–** 1 to adhere, stick to. 2 to bind. **per–an** relation, connection. **ter–** 1 involved. 2 connected. **–an** 1 base, origin. 2 home.
pav. [*paviljun*] pavilion.
paviljun pavilion.
pawai parade, procession.
pawana wind.
pawang guide with magic powers. – *pukat* expert in catching fish with a dragnet.
pawijatan school, training center.
P.B. [*Pengurus Besar*] Executive Board.
P.B.B. [*Perserikatan Bangsa²*] United Nations.
PBE [*Pasaran Bersama Éropah*] European Common Market.
P.B.H. [*Pemberantasan Buta Huruf*] literacy campaign.
pd [*pemangku djabatan*] acting.
PD & K [(*Départemén*) *Pendidikan Dasar dan Kebudajaan*] Ministry of Basic Education and Culture.
PDN [*Perusahaan Dagang Negara*] state commercial enterprise.
pebéan customs office. see BÉA.
Pébruari February.
peda salted fish. **mem–** to salt fish.
pedagang see DAGANG.
pédagogi(k) pedagogy.
pedal pedal. **mem–** 1 to step on the pedal. 2 to swallow. – *gas* accelerator.
pedalaman see DALAM.
pedang sword. **mem–** to strike with a sword. **–²an** swordplay. – *djenawi* long sword with straight blade.
pedar rancid. **ke–an** out of sorts, displeased.
pedas 1 hot, highly seasoned and spiced. *Ini – sekali*, This is very hot. 2 severe, biting. *Kritiknja –*, His criticism was severe. **ke–an** suffering from s.t. hotly spiced. **mem–kan** to prepare hot, spicy food. – *hati* to be annoyed, vexed. – *hati saja melihat dia*, I hate the very sight of him.
pedat see PADAT.
pedati cart.
pedato see PIDATO.
pédéngan 1 screen, cover. 2 pseudonym. 3 hypocrisy.
pedih 1 smarting. *Matanja –*, His eyes smart. 2 poignant. **ke–an** pain, smarting. – *hati* mortified, grieved.
pedis 1 see PEDAS. 2 see PEDIH.
pedjadjaran ghost, devil, evil spirit.

pedjal solid, firm. **mem–kan** to press down.

pedjam closed (of the eyes). **mem–kan** to close o's eyes.

pedjera foresight.

Pedjompongan see DJOMPONG.

pedju semen, sperm.

pedoman 1 compass. 2 orientation. 3 manual, directive. 4 catalogue, bulletin. **ber–** *kpd* to be guided by.

peduli (*akan*) to bother about. *Saja tidak – akan perkataannja*, I paid no attention to what he said. **memp–kan** *diri* 1 to pay attention to. 2 to mind.

Peg. [*Pegunungan*] mountains.

pegal 1 stiff. 2 listless, languid. 3 weary. 4 weariness. *Rasa – sdh lenjap*, Feelings of weariness have disappeared. 5 irritable.

pegang **ber–(an)** *pd* to stick to. **ber–** *tangan* hand in hand. **mem–** 1 to hold, take hold of. *Ia* ~ *topinja*, He is holding his hat. *Djangan* ~ *buku itu*, Don't hold on to that book. 2 to handle. *Ia blm dpt* ~ *pistol*, He is not yet able to handle a pistol. 3 to control. *Dahulu Inggeris* ~ *kekuasaan dilaut*, Formerly England controlled the seas. 4 to occupy, hold. *Siapa* ~ *djabatan itu?* Who occupied that position? 5 to keep. *Orang² harus* ~ *kanan*, You must keep to the right. ~ *buku* to keep books. ~ *kemudi* to steer. **memper–i** to stick, hold to. **pem–** 1 handle, knob. 2 the o. who holds, holder. ~ *adat* adherent, supporter of the *adat*. ~ *andil* shareholder. ~ *buku* bookkeeper. ~ *kas* cashier, teller. ~ *rékor* recordholder. ~ *séro* share-, stock-holder. **pem–an** keeping. ~ *rahasia* secrecy. **per–an** 1 handle, grip. 2 function, office. **–an** 1 handle. 2 management. 3 post, office, position. 4 control. 5 guide. ~ *tangga* banister, railing. 6 (foot)hold.

pegar pheasant.

pegas 1 spring. 2 carpetbeater. **mem–** 1 to be resilient. 2 to spring.

pegat **mem–** 1 to stop, block. 2 to intercept.

pegawai 1 official. – *rendahan* subordinate official. 2 employee, worker. 3 see GAWAI. **ke–an** 1 officialdom, civil service. 2 employee affairs. – *harian* daily wage earner. – *kantor* office employee. – *pemerintah* government employee. – *tinggi* high official.

pegel 1 see PEGAL. 2 fed up with s.t.

pegi see PERGI.

pégon Javanese written in Arabic characters.

peguam lawyer.

pegujuban see GUJUB.

péhak see PIHAK.

péhong 1 nasty. 2 k.o. venereal disease.

péka thoughtful, considerate. **ke–an** sensitivity. **mem–** 1 to consider. 2 to mind, heed.

pekak deaf. **mem–(kan)** 1 to deafen. 2 deafening. *Kami di– oléh perkataan krisis*, We were deafened by the word "crisis." – *batu* stone-deaf. – *labang* slightly deaf.

pekakak a kingfisher.

pekakas see PERKAKAS.

pekam 1 brake. 2 to brake.

pekan 1 market. 2 week. **ber– –²** for weeks. **se–** 1 weekly. 2 one week.

pekarangan yard, premises. see KARANG.

pekat 1 thick, concentrated. 2 tough. 3 strong (of coffee). 4 dark. *malam – a* dark night. **ke–an** 1 thickness. 2 concentration.

pekau a scream.

pekerti see BUDI.

pekik yell, scream. **mem–**, – *pekuk* to yell, scream. **–an** a scream.

peking **mem–** to whine, howl.

pekir rejected, unfit.

pekirim see KIRIM.

pekiwan rest room.

pekoléh efficient.

pekung foul-smelling ulceration (cancerous or syphilitic).

Pekuper [*Pelaksana Kuasa Perang*] military authority.

pekur **mem–** to muse, meditate.

pél 1 pill, tablet. 2 field. 3 see KAIN. **menge–** to mop. **–an** mopping.

pelabi 1 excuse, alibi. 2 not genuine.

pelabuhan see LABUH.

pelabur ration, portion. see LABUR.

peladjar see ADJAR.

peladjaran see ADJAR.

pelah speech impediment.

pelahan-lahan see PERLAHAN.

pélak wrong. *Dugaannja itu tak –*, His guess was right. *tak – lagi* clearly, it's obvious. *Negara itu tak – lagi dari pengaruh negara lain*, That country is clearly not free from the influence of other countries.

pelakat poster, placard.

pelaminan elaborately adorned seat for a bridal couple.

pelampang pavilion for outdoor entertainment.

pélan field. see PÉL.

pelan² 1 Slow down! (Take it easy!) 2 see PERLAHAN.

pelana saddle. **ber–** saddled.

pelanduk mouse deer (hero of a famous fairy tale cycle).

pelanél flannel.
pelang 1 plank. 2 street sign.
pelangi 1 rainbow. 2 see KAIN.
pelangki palanquin.
pelangkin tar.
pelantar(an) platform.
pelanting ber–an to roll everywhere.
ter– 1 darted off. 2 shot away. 3 to
fall with a thud.
pelas mem– to tie ropes together.
pelastik plastic.
pelasuh a lazy person.
pelat phonograph record. – arlodji
face of a watch. – nomor license plate.
pélat 1 to lisp. 2 to speak with an
accent.
pelata mackerel.
pelatah a neurotic person. see LATAH.
pelatuk trigger.
pelbagai 1 various, all sorts of. 2
see BAGAI.
pelebaja hangman, executioner.
pelekat see PELAKAT.
pelékok twisted.
pelekuh crooked.
pelempap 1 palm. 2 handbreadth.
se– a handbreadth.
pelés bottle, flask.
pelesat ter– to dart away.
pelését ter– to slip.
pelesir 1 to take a trip. 2 to go out
for pleasure. 3 pleasure, amusement.
ber– 1 to take a trip. 2 to go out
for amusement. –an pleasure, amusement.
pelesit 1 locust. 2 a spirit.
pélét mem– 1 to flatter, play up to
s.o. 2 to lick, glue.
pelétjéh flatterer. mem– to flatter.
pelétjok ter– sprained.
peleton platoon.
pelihara mem– 1 to take care of,
protect. 2 to raise, rear. 3 to keep,
maintain. mem–kan dari to guard,
protect against. ~ lidah to be careful
in what o. says, watch o's language.
pem– 1 caretaker. 2 nurseryman.
pem–an 1 care, maintenance. 2 rear-
ing, cultivation. 3 safeguarding. –an
1 things to be protected, cared for.
2 mistress.
pelik 1 peculiar. 2 remarkable. 3
complicated. ke–an peculiarity. –an
mineral.
pelinteng catapult.
pelipis(an) temple (anat.). –nja luka,
He was wounded in the temple.
pelipit hem.
pelir penis. – itik a k.o. screw.
pelisir mem– to pleat.
pelit stingy.
pelita 1 light. 2 lamp.
pelitur memp– to polish furniture.

pélo 1 to lisp, babble. 2 to have a
speech defect.
pelodjok see PELOSOK.
pélog key or pitch of the gamelan.
peloh impotent.
peloksok see PELOSOK.
pelontji freshman girl.
pelontjo 1 stupid. 2 greenhorn, freshman. 3 pledge (fraternity). memp–
to haze. per–an hazing, initiation.
pelopor 1 pioneer. 2 scout. 3 shock
troops. 4 ranger. 5 vanguard, fore-
runner. mem(p)–i 1 to crusade, pioneer, fight for. 2 to initiate.
pélor bullet. – kesasar stray bullet.
pelosok 1 outlying place, remote
spot. 2 corner. dari segala – from
every nook and cranny.
pelosot ter– 1 to fall down. 2 to go
down in price.
pélpén measurement used by bricklayer to straighten wall.
pélplés canteen, water container.
pélpolisi rural constabulary.
peluang 1 to have an opportunity.
2 quiet.
pelu(h) impotent.
peluh perspiration, sweat. ber– 1 to
perspire. 2 perspiring. ber– –² to
sweat and toil.
peluit whistle.
peluk 1 embrace. 2 fathom. ber–
–²an to embrace e.o. mem– to embrace. Ia ~ anaknja, She embraced
her child. Meréka ~ agama Islam,
They embraced Islam. pem– agama
religious adherent. sepem– of such a
circumference that it can just be
embraced by a man's arms. –an embrace. – tjium hug and kisses.
peluntur laxative.
pelupuk cover, wrapper. – mata
eyelid.
peluru 1 bullet. 2 projectile, missile.
– kendali guided missile. 3 shot-put.
peluruh emetic.
pem– see under base beg. with (1)
p–, (2) m–.
pemali sacred, forbidden, taboo.
pohon – taboo tree.
pematah see PATAH.
pematang dike between rice fields.
Rupanja sawah engkau itu se– dgn
sawah saja, Apparently your rice
field has the same dike as mine.
pemb– see under base beg. with b–.
pemberhentian see HENTI.
pembrentian see HENTI.
peméo see PAMÉO. Ada – bhw...
There's a saying that...
pemp– see under base beg. with p–.
pemrasaran see PRASARAN.
pemuda young man, youth. see MUDA.

– *pelantjongan* 1 a young drifter.
2 young wanderer, traveler.
pemudi young woman, girl.
pemudjuk see BUDJUK.
pen- see under base beg. with (1)
t-, (2) *n-*.
péna writing pen.
penad relevant.
PENAD [*Penerangan Angkatan Darat*] Army Information (Office).
penak see EMPENAK.
penaka as, for instance.
PENAL [*Penerangan Angkatan Laut*] Navy Information (Office).
penala tuning fork.
penasaran see PANASARAN.
penat tired, weary, exhausted. **ber-** –² to toil and sweat. **ke-an** 1 tired.
2 weariness, fatigue. **mem-kan** 1 to tire, exhaust. 2 wearying, exhausting. – *lelah* worn-out, exhausted.
penatu laundryman.
penatua church elder.
pend- see under base beg. with *d-*.
pendam **mem-(kan)** 1 to bury, hide away. *Ia ∼ uangnja dibelakang rumahnja*, He hid his money behind his house. 2 to hide o.s. *Ia ∼ diri selama lima tahun*, He hid himself for 5 years. **ter-** 1 hidden, buried. *Katakanlah apa jg ∼ dlm hatimu*, Please tell me what you have in mind.
2 cherished. **–an** things hidden away.
Pendam [*Penerangan Daérah Militér*] regional military information (office).
pendapa 1 front veranda, porch. 2 auditorium.
pendar fluorescence. **ber-** fluorescent.
péndar **ber-**, **me-m-²kan** to turn in all directions.
péndék short. **ke-an** 1 abbreviation.
2 shortness. 3 too short. *Kakinja ∼* , His legs were too short. **mem-kan** to abbreviate, shorten. **-nja**, – *kata* in short, in brief. – *umur* to have a short life.
pendékar advocate, champion. – *kata*, – *lidah* eloquent. – *péna* skillful at writing.
pendéta 1 clergyman, priest. 2 scholar. **ke-an** clergy, ministry. – *jahudi* rabbi.
pendj- see under base beg. with *dj-*.
pendjadan misprint.
pendjara jail, prison. **ke-an** prison affairs. **mem-** *hawa nafsu* to restrain passions. **mem-kan** to imprison.
pendjunan potter.
pendjurit see PRADJURIT.
pendjuru 1 corner. 2 angle. – *angin* points of the compass.
pendopo see PENDAPA.

peng- see under base beg. with (1)
k-, (2) a vowel, (3) *ng-*.
penganan delicacies.
pengantén see PENGANTIN.
pengantin 1 bride. 2 bridegroom. – *baru* newlyweds.
pengap close, stuffy, stale. **mem-** to close tightly. **mem-kan** oppressive.
pengar to have a hangover.
pengaruh influence. **ber-** influential.
memp-i to influence.
pengat a stewed dish.
pengeboman see BOM.
pengemukaan see MUKA.
pengeng severe headache.
pengéstu see PANGÉSTU.
pengetjatan see TJAT.
pengetjoran see TJOR.
penggal 1 piece, lump. 2 fragment.
ber- –² in pieces. **mem-** to cut off, cut to pieces. *∼ kepala* to behead.
-an piece, bit.
penghulu 1 village chief. 2 Moslem leader.
péngkar crooked (of the legs). – *kedalam* bowlegged. – *keluar* knock-kneed.
péngkol bent. **mem-** to turn, branch off. **-an** curve.
pengkor crippled.
pening 1 dizzy. 2 rattled. **ke-an** 1 dizziness. 2 feeling dizzy. **mem-kan** 1 to make dizzy. 2 dizzying.
péning badge, license (for bicycles, dogs, etc.).
peniti pin. – *tjantél* safety pin.
penj- see under base beg. with (1)
s-, (2) *nj-*.
pénjék flattened.
penjengat wasp.
penjét see PÉNJÉK.
pénjét 1 flattened. 2 squeezed, pressed. see PÉNJÉK.
penjok the screaming sound made by a plane in a dive.
penju 1 turtle. 2 tortoise shell.
Penprés [*Penetapan présidén*] presidential decision or directive.
pens- see under base beg. with *s-*.
pénsil 1 pencil. 2 brush.
pénsiun pension. **di-** pensioned off, retired. **-an** s.o. retired. *∼ guru* a retired teacher.
pent- see under base beg. with *t-*.
pental **ter-** flung away.
pentang **mem-kan** to shoot, loose (an arrow).
pentas raised platform, stage. **mem-kan** to stage, present. *Sebuah drama akan di-kan bésok*, A play will be staged tomorrow. **pem-an** 1 showing, presentation. 2 staging.
pentil teat. – *susu* nipple.

péntil valve.

penting important, significant. **ke–an** 1 importance. 2 (self-)interest. *utk* ~ for the sake of. *utk* ~ *negara* for the well-being of the nation. **mem–kan** 1 to emphasize. 2 to bring to notice, advance. 3 to consider important. 4 to pluck strings. *jg* **berke–an** interested parties. *Kpd jg* ~ , To whom it may concern.

pentj– see under base beg. with *tj–*.

pentjak a system of self-defense.

pentjar see PANTJAR. **pem–an** distribution. **–an** 1 distribution. 2 dispersion.

pentjét crushed, smashed. **mem–** 1 to crush, smash. 2 to push, press. *Tjoba di– bél,* Please press the bell.

pentjil 1 isolated, secluded. 2 desolate, remote. **ke–an** isolation. **mem–kan** to isolate, segregate. ~ *diri* to isolate o.s., withdraw. **ter–** isolated, remote, secluded.

péntjong – –*méntjong* crisscross. **mem–kan** to make slanting.

pentol knob. **–an** 1 prominent. 2 gang leader. 3 leader.

pentul see PENTOL.

pentung club. **mem–** to club. **–an** club, cudgel.

penuh full of, loaded. **ke–montokan** shapeliness. **mem–i** 1 to fill. 2 to fulfill. *Ia tak dpt* ~ *djandjinja,* He could not fulfill his promise. 3 to meet a demand. 4 to comply with a request. **pem–an** fulfillment. **se–nja** fully. *Saja setudju* ~ , I agree fully. **ter–i** complied with, fulfilled. – –*montok* shapely. – *pekak,* – *pekat,* – *pepak,* – *sesak* crammed, chock-full. – *ruah* bulging out, chock-full. – *tumpah* brimful. *dgn se– hati* with full attention.

péok lame.

péot 1 see PÉOK. 2 dented. *Mobilnja* –, His car was dented.

pepadang see PADANG.

pepaja see PAPAJA.

pepak complete, full. **se–** all of them.

pepas **mem–** to fish, angle.

pepat flattened, level, smooth. **mem–** to flatten, smooth. – *gigi* tooth filing.

pepatah see PATAH.

pépéd dead end, no way out. **ke–** trapped. *Ia merasa* ~ , He felt trapped. see PÉPÉT.

pépék vagina.

Peperda [*Penguasa Perang Daérah*] Regional War Administrator.

Peperpu [*Penguasa Perang Pusat*] Central War Administrator.

Peperti [*Penguasa Perang (Ter) Tinggi*] Supreme Military Administrator.

pépés meat or fish dish wrapped in a banana leaf and roasted.

pepet 1 see BUNJI. 2 stopped up (of nose).

pépét **ke–** driven into a corner, trapped. **mem–kan** to corner, trap. **ter–** cornered. see PÉPÉD.

pepohonan see POHON.

pepudju womb.

per per, by. – *lusin* by the dozen.

pér 1 light bulb. 2 spring. **ber–** with springs. – *rambut* very fine watch spring.

per– see also PR–.

Per. [*Perusahaan*] enterprise, firm, concern.

perabot 1 utensils. 2 tools. 3 spare parts. **memp–i** to furnish a house. **–an** = PERABOT. – *mobil* spare parts, accessories (of a car). – *rumah* furniture.

perabu monarch, sovereign. **ke–an** majesty.

perada 1 tin coating. 2 gold foil for coating. 3 review, parade. – *buku* book review.

peradjurit 1 soldier. 2 heroic. **ke–an** 1 military. 2 heroism. – *I* private 1st class. – *II* private. – *udara I* airman 1st class. – *udara II* airman 2nd class. – *udara* airman.

peraga **ber–, memp–kan** to exhibit, show. *Ia* ~ *lukisan²nja,* He exhibited his paintings. see RAGA.

peragawati mannequin.

perah **mem–** 1 to squeeze. 2 to milk. *Ia* ~ *sapi,* She milked a cow. ~ *keringat* to sweat and toil. ~ *otak* to give s.t. serious thought. **pem–sapi** milker. **pem–an** squeezing. **–an** milk.

perahu boat, prow. – *gubang* sailing canoe. – *lading* longboat. – *majang* deep-sea fishing boat. – *mantjung* prow shaped like a sheath. – *motor* motorboat. – *pendarat* landing craft. – *pesiar* pleasure craft. – *tambang* ferry boat.

perai 1 loose, apart. 2 free. *Ia mendapat* – *sehari,* He had a day off. 3 empty (of a seat). 4 unhampered. **ber– –²** scattered, dispersed. see PEREI.

pérak silver. **mem–** white as silver. *se–* one rupiah. *tigapuluh* – 30 rupiahs.

peram **ber–** to shut o.s. off from society. **mem–** 1 to brood. 2 to heat. 3 to coo. 4 to stew. 5 to age s.t. **pem–an** 1 ripening. 2 hatching, brooding. 3 hatchery.

peran 1 actor. 2 character (in novel, play, etc.). **me–kan** to play the role of. **-an** role, part. – *utama* leading man or woman.

perandjat **ter-** startled, surprised.

perang 1 war. 2 battle. **ber-** to wage war. **mem-i** to fight against. ~ *pengangguran* to fight unemployment. **pe-an** 1 battle. 2 war. **-²an** maneuvers. – *asap* mock battle. – *bersosoh* a battle. – *dunia* world war. – *gerilja* guerrilla warfare. – *kilat* blitzkrieg. – *paderi* struggle between Moslems and adherents of customary law on the west coast of Sumatra. – *sabil* holy war. – *salib* crusade. – (*urat*) *saraf* war of nerves. – *saudara* civil war. – *sinu* war of nerves. – *tanding* duel.

pérang 1 reddish color, russet. 2 light brown. 3 blond.

perangai 1 nature, disposition. 2 behavior, attitude.

peranggi see PERENGGI.

perangkat *se-* a set, pair.

perangko 1 postage stamp. 2 postage paid. **me-i** to stamp, place postage on a letter. *-ilah kiriman ini setjukupnja,* Please place sufficient postage on this letter.

peranje fringe.

peranti 1 apparatus, instrument. 2 means. 3 in order to. 4 remedy.

perantjah scaffolding.

Perantjis 1 French. 2 Frenchman. 3 France.

perapatan see PRAPATAN.

peras **mem-** 1 to press, squeeze. 2 to milk. 3 to blackmail, put the squeeze on. **pem-** 1 a press. 2 exploiter. **pem-an** 1 pressing, squeezing. 2 blackmail. 3 exploitation. **-an** distillation.

perawan 1 virgin, girl. 2 virginity. – *sunti* a girl entering puberty. – *tua* spinster.

perawira see PERWIRA.

perawis ingredients.

perbahasa see PERIBAHASA.

perbal 1 official report. 2 ticket. 3 police warrant.

perban dressing, bandage. **mem-** to dress a wound.

perbawa influence, prestige. – *-diri* self-expression.

perbégu heathenish.

perbekel village chief in Bali.

perdana principal. – *menteri* prime minister, premier.

perdata 1 court of justice. 2 civil.

Perdatam [(*Départemén*) *Perindustrian Dasar dan Pertambangan*] (Ministry) of Basic Industries and Mining.

perdéo free, gratis.

perdikan freed from payment of taxes (in villages) as a result of assuming

some burden or responsibility. see DÉSA.

perdji vulva.

perdjurit see PERADJURIT.

perdom! the devil! **di-** to be cussed out by s.o.

perduli see PEDULI.

peré see PEREI.

peredus **te-** 1 pregnant. 2 potbellied.

perei free, off. *Bésok saja –,* I'm off tomorrow.

perék To hell with you!

perekat glue.

perékik unsportsmanlike, not cricket.

peréman private, civil(ian).

perempuan 1 woman, female. 2 feminine. **ke-an** feminine, female. – *bergelandang,* – *djalang* prostitute. – *djahanam* wicked woman. – *jg masih gadis* virgin. – *P,* – *tjabul* prostitute.

perenggi 1 Frank. 2 European.

pergédél see PERKÉDÉL.

pergi 1 to go. *Kemana –nja?* Where's he gone? 2 to leave. *Ia sdh –,* He's already left. 3 to disappear. *Pentjuri itu sdh –,* The thief had disappeared. **be-an** to go on a trip, travel. *~lah dgn keréta api!* Travel by train! **ke-an** 1 departure. 2 trip, journey. 3 going, passing, death. ~ *beliau dgn mendadak,* His passing was sudden. **pem-an** a lengthy journey. – *datang* 1 to walk up and down. 2 to come and go. *Banjak orang – datang,* Many people were coming and going. – *komisi,* – *turné* to make a tour of inspection.

pergok **ke-** 1 surprised, unexpected (meeting). *Saja ~ dgn Ali di New York jg kusangka masih di Djakarta,* I unexpectedly ran into Ali in New York when I thought he was still in Jakarta. 2 to be caught red-handed. *Pentjuri ~ oléh polisi,* The thief was caught red-handed by the police. **mem i** to catch, surprise, detect. **te-** surprised, detected.

perhal see PERIHAL.

peri 1 way, manner. 2 concerning. 3 fairly. **ber-** to speak. **mem-kan** to relate, tell. *-hal* 1 concerning, re. 2 events, circumstances, *-kehidupan* life. *-kemanusiaan* 1 humanity. 2 humanitarianism. 3 humanism. – (*hal*) *laku* behavior. *tak* **ter-kan** indescribable.

peria see PRIA.

periai see PRIAJI.

perian bamboo for carrying water.

peribahasa proverb.

peribumi see PRIBUMI.

peridi fertile (of animals).

perigi well, spring.

perih see PEDIH.

periksa investigation, inspection, examination. **mem–** 1 to investigate, look into. 2 to control. 3 to inspect. 4 to cross-examine, interrogate. **pem–** 1 investigator, inspector. 2 cross-examiner. **pem–an** 1 investigation, inspection. 2 cross-examination, interrogation. 3 checkup. **–an** hearing, inquest. – *majat* post-mortem, autopsy, coroner's inquest. *Kurang –,* I don't know.

pering 1 bamboo. 2 to stink.

perintah order, command. **mem–(i)** 1 to order, command. 2 to rule, govern. **mem–kan** to order, command. **pem–(an)** 1 government. 2 administration. ~ *bonéka* puppet government. ~ *darurat* emergency government. ~ *peralihan* interim government. **ter–** subjected. – *halus* 1 gentle hint (from above). 2 indirect order.

perintji 1 to design. 2 to specify. **ter–** detailed. **–an** breakdown. *Dibawah ini ~ dibeberapa ketjamatan,* Below is the breakdown in several subdistricts.

perintjis mem–kan to specify. **–an** specification.

période period (of time).

perisai shield.

peristiwa event, incident, happening, affair. – *Madiun* the Madiun Affair. *sekali* – once upon a time.

periuk boiler, caldron, cooking pot. – *api* 1 shell. 2 bomb. 3 mine. – *belanga* earthenware.

perkakas tools, implements, apparatus. **memp–i** to provide with furniture. **–an** tools, apparatus. – *bedah* surgical instruments. – *dapur* kitchen utensils. – *makan* dinnerware. – *rumah* furniture. – *tenun* weaving loom. – *tjap* printing equipment.

perkara 1 matter, case. 2 lawsuit. **be–** to litigate. **memp–kan** to bring a case into court. *Habis –,* That's that. (That'll be all.)

perkasa 1 brave, courageous. 2 powerful. **ke–an** 1 courage. 2 power. *dgn* – with force.

perkédél ground meat, usually beef and similar to hamburger.

perkosa 1 violent. *setjara* – in a violent manner. 2 violence. **memp–** to rape, violate. **–an** rape, violation.

perkutut turtledove.

perlahan 1 slow. 2 soft of voice. **memp–kan** to slow s.t. down.

perlak 1 varnished, lacquered. 2 garden.

perlambang see LAMBANG.

perlénté 1 smart, elegant, swell, dandy. 2 loafer.

perling te– to glitter.

perlintih see PERLÉNTÉ.

perlip to fall in love. **–²an** to flirt.

perlontjo see PELONTJO.

perlop 1 leave, furlough. 2 to be on leave.

perlu necessary. *Saja pergi djika –,* I'll go if necessary. *Tidak –,* It's not necessary. **ke–an** 1 need, necessity. 2 requirement. **mem–kan** 1 to need. *Ia ~ banjak uang,* He needs a lot of money. 2 to think necessary. *Ia ~ kedatanganmu,* He thought your coming necessary. 3 to require, make compulsory. *Bahasa Inggeris di–kan disekolah menengah,* English was made compulsory in the high schools. *utk (ke)–(an)* on behalf of, for the benefit, sake, of. *Apa –nja?* What's the use? (Why?) *sangat* – be imperative.

perlus te– to fall into a hole.

permadani carpet.

permai 1 pretty, beautiful. 2 valuable. **ke–an** beauty.

permaisuri queen.

permak altered. **mem–** to alter (clothes).

perman see FIRMAN.

permata jewel, precious stone. – *nila* sapphire.

permén peppermint.

Permias [*Persatuan Mahasiswa Indonésia di Amérika Serikat*] Indonesian Students' Association of America.

permili see PAMILI.

permisi 1 permission. 2 leave. – *dulu,* I ask permission to go. *Sdh – dari dia?* Did you ask his consent? 3 excuse me. **memp–kan** to ask permission.

pernah 1 once. *Saja – pergi ke Bali,* I once went to Bali. 2 ever. *Apakah saudara – pergi ke Madura?* Have you ever gone to Madura? 3 relation(ship). *blm* – never. *Saja blm – pergi,* I've never gone. *tak (tidak)* – never. *Ia tak – senang,* He was never happy. – *apa?* What's he (she) to you?

pernama see PURNAMA.

pernis varnish.

perogol mem– to violate a woman.

peroi crumbly.

peronjok ter– crushed, crumpled.

perop 1 cork, stopper. 2 plug.

perosok ter– 1 to sink into. 2 to step on.

perosot see ROSOT.

pérot see ÉROT.

perotés a protest. **mem–** to protest.

perplantjongan see LANTJUNG.

Perprés [*Peraturan présidén*] presidential regulation.

Perpu [*Peraturan Pusat*] government regulation.

pér(r)on station platform.

pérs press.

persegi see SEGI.

persekot cash advance. **mem(p)–i** to give an advance.

perselah report, account.

persemakmuran see MAKMUR.

persén 1 per cent. 2 tip. 3 present. **ke–an** percentage. **mem–i** to reward.

perséntage percentage.

perseorangan see ORANG.

perséro 1 share. 2 shareholder, partner. **–an** company. ~ *terbatas* limited liability company, Ltd., Inc. see SÉRO.

persétan! the deuce! the devil!

persih see BERSIH.

persik peach.

persil lot, plot. **te–** to protrude, bulge.

persis exactly, precisely.

perslah see PERSELAH.

persnéling 1 gear. – *kedua* 2nd gear. 2 transmission.

personalia personnel.

personil staff, personnel.

pertal **mem–** to translate. **–an** translation.

pertama first, the first. *bab jg* – the first chapter. **di–kan** to give preference to. – *-tama* first of all. *jg* – the former (not the latter). *jg* – *sekali* the very first.

pertanda 1 execution. 2 sign.

pertiwi earth. see IBU.

pertj [*pertjétakan*] printing establishment.

pertja rag.

Pertja see PULAU.

pertjaja 1 belief, faith. 2 to trust, believe. **ke–an** 1 reliable. 2 faith, trust, confidence, belief. 3 reliance. **memp–i** to believe in, rely on. **memp–kan** to entrust s.o. with s.t. *jg dpt di–* reliable. – *angin* vain hope.

pertjik stain, spot. **ber–an** spattering. **mem–(i)** to spatter, sprinkle. **mem–kan** to splash with s.t. **–an** sprinkling.

pertjis exactly.

pertjit **mem–** to spurt forth strongly.

pertjul **te–** to dart away.

pertjuma see TJUMA.

perugul see PEROGOL.

peruk **mem–** to put s.t. in a place. **ter–** collapsed, given away.

perum plummet, sounding lead.

perun trash, garbage heap. **mem–** 1 to burn trash. 2 to burn off weeds, grass, etc., for cultivation.

perunggu bronze.

perungus fiery, hot-tempered.

perus stern, grim.

perusa **mem–** 1 to violate, rape. 2 to force, compel. 3 to annoy, disturb.

perut stomach, belly. **mem–i** to remove the entrails. – *besar* 1 stomach. 2 pregnant. – *betis* calf of leg. – *buta* appendix. – *gendut* big-bellied. – *kaki* calf. – *kapal* bulge. – *muda*, – *pandjang* intestine. *dlm* – *ibunja* in his mother's womb.

perwira 1 brave, courageous. 2 chivalrous. 3 officer. **ke–an** heroism.

pes. [*pesawat*] extension (telephone).

pés plague.

pesai **ber– –²** to fall to pieces.

pésak 1 gusset. 2 seat of the trousers.

pesaka see PUSAKA.

pesalin new suit of clothes.

pesam lukewarm (of water).

pesan 1 order. 2 order, instruction, command. 3 message. **ber–** 1 to order. 2 to instruct, give a message. **mem–** to order (goods). **pem–** buyer, customer. **pem–an** ordering (of goods). **–an** 1 order, commission. 2 message. ~ *pertjobaan* trial order. ~ *ulangan* repeat order. **–²** centipede. – *tempat* to reserve seats (at a performance or on a train). *atas pem–an* order (for).

pesangon separation. – *tiga bulan gadji* 3 months' separation pay.

pesantrén religious training center for advanced Islamic studies. see SANTRI.

pesara see PASARA.

pesasir passenger.

pesat quick, speedy, rapid. **ke–an** speed, momentum. **mem–kan** to speed up. *dgn sangat –nja* at full speed.

pesawat 1 instrument, machine. 2 telephone instrument. 3 telephone extension. – *baling²* piston plane. – *pantjar gas* jet plane. – *pelémpar bom* bomber. – *peluntjur* glider. – *pembom* bomber. – *pemburu* fighter plane. – *penempur* military plane. – *penerima* radio, radio set. – *tjapung* small single-engine plane. – *uap* steam engine. – *udara* airplane. – *wésél* railroad switch.

pesegi see PERSEGI.

pésék flat-nosed.

pésér half a cent. *tak punja uang se–pun* completely broke.

peséro see PERSÉRO.

pését see PÉSÉK.

pesiar 1 trip, journey. 2 to take a trip. 3 to go for a ride. 4 pleasure trip.

pésimisme pessimism.

pesindén woman singer with a gamelan orchestra.

pesing stench.

pesirah village chief in south Sumatra.

pesisir 1 beach, coastal area. 2 passenger. 3 customer.

pesona 1 enchantment, spell. 2 magic formula. **memp–kan** 1 to enchant, enthrall. 2 enchanting, enthralling. **ter–** spellbound.

pésong crooked. **ter–** 1 to go off course. 2 to miss the target.

pésta party, festivity. **ber–** to celebrate, have a party. **mem–kan** to celebrate. – *dangsa* a dance. – *gila* masked ball.

pestaka 1 divining manual. 2 magic formula. 3 beneficent influence. 4 see PUSTAKA.

péstol pistol, revolver. **mem–** to shoot with a pistol.

pesuk hole. **ber– –²** full of holes.

pét cap.

Peta [*Pembéla Tanah Air*] Indonesian auxiliary troops in the Japanese period.

peta 1 map. 2 chart. 3 picture. **mem–kan** to map, chart. **pem–an** 1 cartography. 2 mapping. **per–an** cartography. – *angin* weather chart. – *bagan* outline map. – *laut* nautical chart. – *timbul* relief map.

pétah lidah 1 eloquent. 2 witty.

petai a tree which produces flat beans with an offensive odor but edible either raw or cooked.

péták 1 compartment. 2 partition. 3 cabin. 4 garden-bed. 5 division of a rice field. 6 white mark, blaze. **ber– –²** compartmentalized, partitioned, sectioned.

petaka accident, disaster, misfortune.

petala 1 layer. 2 floor, story.

petam forehead band.

petang afternoon. **ke–an** 1 overtaken by nightfall. 2 secret agent. **me–m–²kan** *hari* to kill time. **se– –²an** during the afternoon. – *hari* afternoon.

petani see TANI.

petari see PATERI.

petasan firecracker.

petenah see FITNAH.

peterah see FITRAH.

peti case, chest. **mem–éskan** to freeze, shelve, put on ice. *Hal ini di–éskan,* This matter has been shelved. – *besi* a safe. – *és* refrigerator. – *majat* coffin. – *mesiu* powder keg. – *njanji* phonograph. – *pendingin* freezer. – *pengering* dehumidifier.

petik **mem–** 1 to pick flowers. 2 to fire (a gun). 3 to strum a stringed instrument. 4 to pluck (the strings of a musical instrument). 5 to snap o's fingers. 6 to quote from a book. ∼ *gitar* to play the guitar. ∼ *kumis* to twist o's mustache. ∼ *tjerutu* to smoke a cigar. **pem–** 1 picker. 2

switch. 3 trigger. **pem–an** picking, gathering. **–an** 1 quotation. 2 recapitulation. 3 excerpt. 4 playing, plucking (of a guitar). *Boléh memangin!* To hell with him! (He can go jump in the lake!)

petilan episode.

petir 1 thunderclap. 2 thunderbolt. – *tunggal* a heavy crash of thunder.

petis congealed fishpaste.

petisi petition.

petitih proverb, saying.

petjah 1 broken, smashed. 2 chapped. 3 curdled. 4 broken out (of war). 5 hatched out. **ber–** *belah* broken to pieces. **mem–(kan)** 1 to analyze. 2 to split. 3 to break. ∼ *rékor* to break a record. 4 to destroy. 5 to disperse, dissect. 6 to solve. *Ia* ∼ *soal,* He solved the problem. ∼ *angkasa* deafening. ∼ *belah* to sow discord. **pem–** a breaker. ∼ *rékor* record breaker. **pem–an** solution, answer. **per–an** dissension. **ter– –²** in pieces. **–an** 1 piece, fragment. 2 fraction. ∼ *persepuluhan* decimal fraction. ∼ *ombak* breakers. ∼ *granat* shrapnel. – *belah* crockery. – *hati* dejected, despondent. *uang* – small change.

pétjai Chinese cabbage.

pétjak 1 damaged, dented, flat. 2 blind in o. eye. **mem–kan** to flatten.

petjal see PETJEL. **mem–** to squeeze, massage.

petjat fired, discharged. **mem–(kan)** 1 to discharge. *Ia di– dari pekerdjaannja,* He was fired from his job. 2 to suspend. **pem–an** 1 discharge, dismissal. 2 suspension.

petjel k.o. vegetable salad similar to *loték.*

pétji see PITJI.

pétjok dented.

petjut whip. **mem–** 1 to whip. 2 to urge on.

petopan gambling den.

pétor district commissioner.

pétromax type of lantern or stove.

petua (religious) advice, interpretation. **ber–** to advise in religious affairs. see FATWA.

peujeum cassava sweetened by yeast.

PGT [*Pasukan Gerak Tjepat*] shock or storm troops.

pharmasi see FARMASI.

PHB 1 [*Perhubungan*] communications. 2 [*Penghubung*] liaison (officer).

piagam charter, contract, deed. – *Djakarta* the Jakarta Charter. **mem–kan** to record in a charter.

pial 1 wattle. 2 gill.

piala 1 cup, goblet. 2 loving cup. – *gindjal* pelvic region.

piama pajamas. see PIJAMA.

piano piano.
piara mem– 1 to breed. 2 to keep, raise. –an 1 domestic animal. 2 mistress, concubine. *héwan* – domestic animals. see PELIHARA.
piarit harpoon.
pias margin.
piat-piut descendants.
piatu motherless child. ke–an orphaned.
piawai skilled, capable.
pi(c)két picket.
pidana criminal.
pidato speech, address. ber– to make a speech. mem(p)–kan to declaim. – *penerimaan*, – *pengukuhan* inaugural speech (professorial). – *pelantikan* (president's) inaugural speech. – *sambutan* welcoming speech.
pidi mem– to aim, direct.
pidjak ber– to stand on. mem– to step on. mem–kan to trample. pem–*kaki* 1 pedal. 2 stirrup. –² pedals. *tempatku* ber– where I am.
pidjar blazing, red-hot, glowing. ber– –² glowing. mem–(kan) to temper steel. –² borax. see LAMPU.
pidjat mem– 1 to squeeze, press. 2 to massage. –² bedbug.
pidjit mem– 1 to press, squeeze. 2 to massage.
pigi see PERGI.
pigura 1 picture, painting. 2 figure, representation.
pihak 1 side. 2 party. ber–, mem–*kpd* to take sides, side with. *Negeri itu* ∼ *Barat*, That country sides with the West. mem–kan to isolate. ∼ *sebelah* partial. – *ibu* maternal line. – *jg berperang* belligerents. – *ketiga* 1 a third party (in contracts, etc.). 2 outsider. – *sana* opponents, the opposition. *pd* – 1 siding with, belonging with. 2 with regard to. *disatu* – ...*dilain* (–) on the one side... on the other. *di– satunja... di– lainnja* on the one side... on the other.
pihutang see PIUTANG.
pi'il 1 action. 2 nature, character.
pijama pajamas.
pik [*pikul*] 137 lbs.
pikap 1 pickup (truck). 2 pickup (phonograph).
pikat 1 gadfly. 2 hornet. 3 decoy. mem– to decoy, tempt, lure. *Perkataannja sangat* ∼ *hati*, Her words were very enticing. pem– fowler, birdcatcher. ter– *hati* charmed, enchanted. –an bait, decoy.
pikau ter– –² to gesticulate wildly.
pikep see PIKAP.
pikir 1 opinion, idea. 2 thought. ber– to think. mem–(i) 1 to think about, worry over. 2 to be aware, mindful

of. mem–kan to think about, meditate over. pem–an thinking. *masih dlm* ∼ still under consideration. se–an *dgn* to share o's opinion. –an 1 thought, idea. 2 opinion. 3 intelligence. *kurang* ∼ stupid. –² *dulu* to think twice. *Dia akan* ∼ *dulu*, He'll think twice. *kurang* – rash, thoughtless. *pd* – *saja* in my opinion. *tidak* ber–an thoughtless.
pikul 137 lbs. mem– 1 to carry on the shoulders. 2 to shoulder, bear, undertake. *Ia* ∼ *semua kesusahannja itu dgn tabah hati*, He bears all his troubles bravely. ∼ *risiko* to take the risk. mem–kan to impose upon, charge s.o. with. ter– bearable. –an 1 carrying pole. 2 load.
pikun well along in years.
pil pill, tablet.
pilek to have a cold.
pilem 1 film. 2 film, motion picture. mem(p)–kan to film, make a motion picture of s.t. – *bisu* silent film.
pilih ber– –² fastidious, squeamish, choosy. mem– 1 to choose, select. 2 to elect. 3 to vote. ∼ *bulu* to discriminate. ∼ *muka* to discriminate. pem– 1 voter. 2 particular, fastidious. pem–an 1 election. 2 poll. ∼ *umum* the general elections. ter– 1 elected. 2 selected. –an 1 choice. 2 select. ∼ *alam* natural selection. ∼ *djabatan* choice of profession or calling. ∼ *tulisan* selected works. – *kasih* partial. (*dgn*) *tidak* mem– *bulu* 1 indiscriminately. 2 irrespective of persons.
pilin ber– spiral. mem– 1 to wind. 2 to twine. 3 twined. ∼ *telinga* to pull o's ear.
Pilipina the Philippines, the Philippine Islands.
pilon 1 stupid. 2 innocent, naive.
pilsapat see FILSAFAT.
pilu 1 moved, touched, affected. 2 sympathetic. ke–an 1 sadness. 2 emotion. 3 moved. mem–kan *hati* 1 to touch o's heart, move to tears. 2 touching, moving.
pimpin ke–an leadership, management. kepem–an (moral) leadership. mem–(kan) to lead, guide. pem– 1 leader, guide. ∼ *rapat* chairman. ∼ *sidang* moderator. 2 manager. 3 manual. ∼ *paberik* factory manager. pem–an leadership. –an 1 leadership, guidance. 2 management. 3 administration. ∼ *fakultas* faculty administration.
pinang areca nut. mem– 1 to propose, ask in marriage. 2 to apply for a job. pem– 1 applicant. 2 suitor. 3 betel-nut box. pem–an 1 proposal.

2 application. **-an** proposal. – *muda*
matchmaker.
pindah 1 to move. *Apakah dia sdh
– ?* Has he already moved? 2 to
change. – *keréta* to change trains.
ber- to move, remove. ~ *kerahma-
tullah* to pass away, die. ~ *negeri*
to emigrate. **ber- –²** to infect, be
contagious. **ke–an** 1 transfer. 2 infected. **mem–kan** to move, transfer
s.t. **pem–an** removal, transfer. **pem-
-bukuan** transfer to current account.
per–an 1 transfer, removal. 2 change.
-an furniture to be moved. – *alamat*
change of address. – *kapal* to transship, reship. – *rumah* change of residence. – *tangan* change of ownership.
– *tuang darah* blood transfusion.
pindakas peanut butter.
pinding bedbug.
pindjak see PIDJAK.
pindjal flea.
pindjam mem– to borrow from.
mem–i, mem–kan to lend out, loan.
pem– borrower. **(pem)–an** loan.
pingai light yellow.
pinggan dish, plate, saucer. – *mangkuk* 1 cups and saucers. 2 china.
pinggang 1 waist. 2 loins. **pem–**
amidships. – *gunung* mountain slope.
pinggir 1 edge, seam. 2 border.
mem– to go to the edge. **pem-(an)**
boundary. **-an** coastal.
pinggul 1 hip. 2 seat, behind, rear.
pingit secluded (of a marriageable
girl). **mem–** to seclude, confine,
isolate, segregate.
pingkal see PINGKEL.
pingkau see PIKAU.
pingkel ter- –² to double up with
laughter.
pingsan 1 unconscious. 2 fainted. 3
to have a fit.
pinsil see PÉNSIL.
pinta see MINTA. **ter–** predestined,
fated. **-an** 1 request. 2 question.
pintak 1 see PINTA. 2 fate, destiny.
pintal ber- –² tangled. **mem–** to spin,
twine. **pem–** spinning wheel. **pem–an**
1 spinning. 2 spinning wheel. 3 spinning mill.
pintar 1 clever, smart. 2 able. *Ia
– berbahasa Perantjis,* He speaks
French very well. **ke–an** cleverness,
skill. – *busuk* cunning, crafty, sly.
pintas ke–an 1 overcome, sur-
mounted. 2 cut short. 3 intercepted.
mem–(i) 1 to take a short cut. 2
to intercept. 3 to interrupt, cut s.o.
short. 4 to cut off, block o's way.
Saja –i djalannja, I blocked his way.
5 to cut in (in traffic). ~ *kekanan* to
turn to the right. ~ *kesukaran* to
overcome difficulties. ~ *maksud* to

beat about the bush. **mem–kan** to cut
off. **se–** for a while. ~ *lalu* in passing,
at first glance, at a glance, cursory.
-an short cut.
pinter see PINTAR.
pintil 1 skein of yarn. 2 PÉNTIL.
pintjang 1 lame. 2 crippled. *Si Pintjang* The Cripple. **ke–an** 1 lameness.
2 defect. **se–** one-and-a-half cent.
kaki – game leg. *Mesin mobil ini
– kedengarannja,* This engine sounds
as if it isn't hitting on all cylinders.
pintjil bunch, strand.
pintjuk fruit salad.
pintu 1 door. 2 gate. 3 hatch. **ke-
kubur** to die. **se–** *rumah* a house. – *air*
sluice, floodgate, locks. – *angin* porthole, vent. – *belakang* back door. –
gerbang main entrance. – *keluar* exit.
– *kolong* trap door. – *maling* side
entrance. – *masuk* entrance. – *monjét*
folding doors. – *putar* revolving door.
– *rangkap* folding door. – *sorong*
sliding doors. – *tani* outer gate of a
palace.
pion pawn (chess).
pionir pioneer.
pipa 1 smoking pipe. 2 pipe, conduit, tube. – *kuras* drainpipe. –
minjak tanah pipeline. – *napas*
trachea. – *pembuang gas* exhaust
pipe. – *pindah* siphon. – *rokok* cigarette holder. – *tjelana* trouser leg. –
wadja steel pipe.
pipi cheek.
pipih flat, thin. **mem–kan** to flatten.
pipis to urinate. **mem–** to mash,
crush up.
pipit 1 sparrow. 2 mouthpiece of a
wind instrument. **mem–** to press.
pirai gout.
piramidal pyramidal.
pirang see PÉRANG.
pirasat see FIRASAT.
pirau dark brown.
Piraun Pharaoh.
pirdaus see FIRDAUS.
pirik mem– to rub down, pulverize.
piring plate. **-(an)** *hitam* phonograph
record. **-an** *terbang* flying saucer. –
dalam soup plate. – *makan* k.o.
shallow dish from which rice is
eaten. – *mangkuk* glassware. – *tjépér*
dinner plate.
pirus turquoise.
pisah ber– 1 to part. 2 separated.
ber–an to part from e.o. **mem–** to
separate. **mem–kan** 1 to separate, set
aside, isolate. 2 to analyze. **pem–** 1
arbiter. 2 referee. **pem–an** 1 separation, division. 2 isolation. 3 discrimination. 4 distinction. **per–an** 1 discord. 2 leave-taking, parting. **ter–**
separate (table, room). *tidak* ~

inseparable. *tak dpt* **di- -²kan** inseparable.

pisang banana. *- Ambon* large green banana. *- serai* an inferior type of banana.

pisau knife. *- kertas* letter opener. *- lipat* pocketknife. *- raut* carving knife. *- silét* safety razor. *- tjukur* razor. *- wali* small knife for wood carving.

pistol see PÉSTOL.

pita 1 ribbon. 2 tape. *- mesin* driving belt, transmission belt. *- mesin tulis* typewriter ribbon. *- suara* vocal chords. *- ukur* measuring tape.

pitam 1 dizziness. 2 fit. 3 apoplexy. 4 paralytic stroke. *- babi* epilepsy.

pitamin see VITAMINE.

pitenah see FITNAH.

piterah see FITRAH.

piting **mem–** to hold on to s.t.

pitja **mem–kan** to neglect. **ter–** careless, negligent.

pitjak see PÉTJAK.

pitji national overseas type of cap of black velvet. *- lapangan* field cap.

pitjik 1 narrow. 2 narrow-minded. **ke–an** 1 to be in a fix, stuck. 2 narrow-mindedness. **memper–** to narrow s.t.

pitjing a wink. **mem–kan** *mata* to close o's eyes. *Saja tak tidur sedjua semalam,* I didn't sleep a wink last night.

pitjis **se–** a dime. *tiga –* 30 cents. **–an** dimes. *Uangnja semuanja ~ ,* All his money consisted of dimes. see ROMAN.

pitju trigger, cock, hammer (of a gun).

pitrah see FITRAH.

pituwas 1 compensation, reward. *Apa –nja dia kerdja mati²an,* What's the reward for working o.s. to death? 2 wage.

piuh **mem–** to twist. **ter–** twisted, distorted. *- pilin* word twisting.

piun see PION.

piut descendant fifth removed.

piutang 1 credit. 2 claim. **ber–** to have money lent to s.o. else. **mem–i** to lend money to s.o. else.

P.J.M. [*Paduka Jang Mulia*] His Excellency.

pk [*pukul*] o'clock.

PK [*Partai Komunis*] Communist Party.

PKI [*Partai Komunis Indonésia*] Indonesian Communist Party.

PKUS [*Partai Komunis Uni Sovjét*] Communist Party of the Soviet Union.

pl– see also PEL–.

plagiat plagiarism.

plakségel receipt stamp.

plamir putty for painting.

planit planet.

plan² see PERLAHAN-LAHAN.

plastisitas plasticity.

platina 1 platinum. 2 distributor contact; point set (auto.).

plausibilitét plausibility.

plébisit plebiscite.

pléno full, plenary.

pléster to plaster.

Plm [*Palmérah*] telephone exchange in Jakarta.

PLM [*Panglima*] commander(-in-chief).

PLN [*Perusahaan Listerik Negara*] state electricity enterprise.

plombir **memp–** 1 to fill (a tooth). 2 to stop, plug up.

PLP [*Pendidikan Latihan Pertempuran*] combat training.

P.M. 1 [*Perdana Menteri*] prime minister. 2 [*Polisi Militér*] military police.

P.M.I. [*Palang Mérah Indonésia*] Indonesian Red Cross.

P.N. [*Perusahaan Negara*] state enterprise.

podéng pudding.

podjok 1 corner. 2 newspaper column.

P.O.G. [*Perkumpulan Orang Tua Murid dan Guru*] parent-teachers' association.

pohon 1 tree. 2 origin, cause. 3 see MOHON. **pep–an** 1 trees. 2 reforestation. **–²an** 1 trees, timber. 2 vegetable world. *- bahasa* basis of language. *- buah* fruit tree. *- durén* durian tree. *- mata* inner corner of the eye. *- segala kedjahatan* the root of all evil.

pojang old man.

pokerol see POKROL.

pokok 1 main, principal, basic, fundamental. 2 beginning. 3 trunk, root. 4 subject. 5 reason, motive. 6 base. 7 capital, stake. **ber–** *pd* 1 to be based on. 2 derived from. **ber–kan** *kpd* to be based on. *Bahasa Indonésia ~ kpd bahasa Melaju,* Indonesian is based on Malay. **mem–i** to give the capital for s.t. *Ajahnja ~ dia utk membuka perusahaan itu,* His father gave him the capital to start the business. **mem–kan** (kpd) to focus (on). **ter–** 1 to cost. *~ berapa badjumu itu?* What did your dress cost? 2 principal, main. *- amal* fund. *- atjara* main point. *- hidangan* main course, dish. *- hudjan* rain cloud. *- kaju* tree trunk. *- kalimat* subject of the sentence. *- kata* root, base of a word. *- lampu* fixture of a bulb. *- lukisan* 1 theme, dominant feature, motif.

2 draft. – *pangkal(an)* main point. – *pembitjaraan* topic of conversation. – *perselisihan* cause of conflict. – *pikiran* gist of o's thoughts.

pokrol attorney, lawyer. – *bambu* 1 unlicensed lawyer. 2 able debater. 3 cheater.

pol full.

pola 1 design. 2 pattern. – *dasar* basic pattern. – *kebudajaan* cultural pattern. **mem–kan** to pattern, fashion. ∼ *masjarakat adil dan makmur* to fashion a just and prosperous society.

polah ber– –² 1 extravagant. 2 extravagance. 3 plentiful.

polan si– Mr. So-and-so. (Mr. What's-his-name.)

Polandia Poland.

polang-paling to whirl.

polang-poléng checkered.

polémik polemic.

polentér volunteer.

polés polish. **di–, –an** polished.

polis (insurance) policy.

polisi police. **ke–an** police. *akadémi* ∼ police academy. – *lalu-lintas,* – *penjeberang* traffic police. – *perairan* 1 coast guard. 2 harbor police. – *rahasia* detective.

polisionil police (attrib.).

politicus politician.

politik 1 politics. 2 political. 3 policy. – *pintu terbuka* free-trade policy.

politisi politicians.

polmah power of attorney. *Siapa memberikan* – *kepadamu?* Who gave you power of attorney?

polok mem– to swallow, bolt down.

polong ghost, evil spirit. **–an** outlet, drainpipe.

polos 1 smooth. 2 plain material.

polowidjo see PALAWIDJA.

pompa pump. **mem–** to pump. – *air* water pump. – *bénsin* gas station.

pon pound (weight and British currency).

P.O.N. [*Pekan Olahraga Nasional*] National Sports Week.

ponakan 1 nephew. 2 niece.

pondik arrogant, conceited.

pondok 1 cottage, hut, cabin. 2 Moslem boarding school. **mem–i** to room and board with. **mem–kan** to provide lodgings. **–an** lodgings, rooming house.

pondong mem– to carry in o's arms.

poném see FONÉM.

pongah conceited, cocky. **ber–** –² to boast, brag. **ke–an** conceit, cockiness, arrogance.

poni bang, fringe of hair.

ponim see FONÉM.

ponis verdict.

pontang-panting 1 scattered. 2 in a hurry.

ponten 1 marks, grades. 2 points in a game. 3 fountain. **mem–** to grade papers.

popok diaper. **–an** ghost, spook. see MOMOK.

popor rifle butt.

populér popular. **ke–an** popularity. **memp–kan** to popularize.

porak-parik 1 a mess. 2 in disorder.

porak-peranda in disorder.

pori pore.

pormulir form, declaration. *Ia mengisi* –, He filled in the form.

pornografi pornography.

poros axis, pivot. – *halang* center half (soccer).

porselén china(ware).

porstél proposal, suggestion.

portepél portfolio. – *kehakiman* justice portfolio.

pos 1 mail. 2 item, entry. 3 post, situation. **memp–kan** to mail. **–²an** guard post. – *laut* sea mail. – *polisi* police station. – *réstan* general delivery. – *udara* airmail.

posisi position.

positip positive.

pospakét parcel-post package.

pospor phosphorus.

poswésél money order.

pot 1 pot. – *bunga* flowerpot. 2 chamber pot.

poténsi potency.

poténsiil potential.

potji bowl.

potlot pencil.

potol 1 broke, hard up. 2 cut off.

potong 1 piece. *djumlah* – *barang* number of pieces of baggage. 2 lump. 3 slice. *Saja minta se*– *roti,* I want a slice of bread. **mem–** 1 to cut (off), slice. ∼ *rambut* to get a haircut. 2 to kill, slaughter. 3 to operate. 4 to deduct wages. 5 to abbreviate a word. 6 to reduce, cut. *di–* *50%* reduced 50%. ∼ *bitjara* to interrupt. **pem–an** butchering, slaughtering. **–an** 1 deduction from wages. 2 discount. 3 model, frame. 4 cut of clothes. 5 abbreviation. ∼ *badannja bagus,* He was well built. ∼ ² *lagu* snatches of music. ∼ *plastik* plastic surgery. *Apa saja ber–an penipu?* Do I look like a deceiver? – *rambut* (to get) a haircut.

potrét 1 photograph, picture, snapshot. 2 camera. **mem–** to take a picture, photograph. **pem–** photographer. **pem–an** photography. ∼ *udara* aerial photography. – *diri* self-portrait.

p.p. [*pulang pergi*] round trip.
P.P. dan K. [*Pendidikan, Pengadjaran dan Kebudajaan*] Ministry of Education and Culture.
PPDSIDR [*Persatuan Pamong Daérah Seluruh Indonesia (tjb) Djakarta Raya*] All-Indonesia Association of Local Administrators—Greater Jakarta Branch.
P.P.N.(B). [*Pusat Perkebunan Negara (Baru)*] (new) government estates central.
P.P.P.K. [*Pertolongan Pertama Pada Ketjelakaan*] first aid.
PPPP [*Panitia Penjelesaian Perselisihan Perburuhan*] Labor Dispute Arbitration Committee.
pr- see also PER-.
pra-anggapan prejudice.
prabawa induction.
pra–bedah preoperative.
pradja the state.
pradjurit 1 see PERADJURIT. 2 a private. **ke–an** military. *latihan* ∼ military exercises.
pragaan see RAGA.
prah freight, cargo.
Praha Prague.
prahara 1 hurricane. 2 tempest.
prahoto truck.
prajodjana purpose, intention, motive.
prajoga decent, suitable.
prakata foreword.
pra-kemerdékaan preindependence.
prakira assumption.
prakték practice. **memp–kan** 1 to practice, put into practice. 2 to apply. *Di-kan kpd keperluan² lain,* It's applied to other needs.
praktis practical. **ke–an** practicality.
pralambang prediction, prophecy.
pramadara freshman (female).
pramaria freshman (at university or college).
pramugara air steward.
pramugari air hostess.
Pramuka [(*Gerakan*) *Pradja Muda Karana*] Indonesian Boy Scout movement, youth corps.
pramukawati Indonesian Girl Scout.
pranata 1 institution. 2 regulation.
prangko see PERANGKO.
prapatan crossroads.
pra-pertundjukan preview.
prarasa partiality, preference.
prasangka prejudice.
prasaran working paper. **pem–** 1 keynote speaker. 2 reader of working paper.
prasasti inscription.
prasedjarah 1 prehistory. 2 prehistorical.

pra-sekolah preschool.
prasetia firm intent.
prasjarat prerequisite.
prasmanan meal served buffet style.
pra-usul working paper.
prawarsa initiative.
prawatjana foreword, preface.
prawira see PERWIRA.
pré see PEREI.
prém plum.
préman see PERÉMAN.
prémi 1 premium. 2 bonus. – *asuransi* insurance premium.
prépéntip preventive.
présidén president. **ke–an** president's residence. **–an** presidency.
presis see PERSIS.
presmanan commencement, graduation.
préstasi achievement, performance.
pria 1 man. 2 male. 3 men.
priai official, the upper middle class.
pribadi 1 individual, personal. 2 person. **ke–an** 1 individuality. 2 personality. 3 identity. **memp–kan** to personify. **pemp–an** 1 personalization. 2 embodiment. 3 personalism.
pribumi native, indigenous.
Pries Frisian.
prigel skillful. **ke–an** skill.
prihatin 1 careful. 2 concerned, apprehensive.
prija see PRIA.
prijaji see PRIAI.
primbon divining manual.
primér primary.
prinsip principle.
prioritas priority.
prioritét priority. *memberikan – djalan* to yield the right of way.
problim problem.
produk product.
produksi production.
produktipitét productivity.
produktivitas productivity.
produsén producer.
produsir **memp–** to produce.
proféssi profession.
progréssip progressive.
projék project.
projéktil missile. – *kendali* guided missile.
proklamasi proclamation. **memp–kan** to proclaim, announce.
proklamir **memp–kan** to proclaim.
proletar proletarian.
promosi 1 promotion. 2 graduation.
prop see PEROP.
propaganda propaganda. **ber–** to propagandize. **memp–kan** to propagate.
propésor professor.
propinsi province.

prosa prose.
prosén see PERSÉN.
proséntasi percentage.
proséntuil percentagewise.
prosés process.
prostitusi prostitution. memp-kan to prostitute.
protéina protein.
protéstan Protestant.
provokasi provocation.
PRRI/PERMESTA [*Pemerintah Révolusionér Républik Indonésia/Perdjuangan Semesta*] Total Struggle of the Republic of Indonesia's Revolutionary Government.
ps [*pasal*] article (in legal documents, etc).
psikologi psychology.
psk [*pasukan*] troops.
P.T. [*Perséroan Terbatas*] Inc., Ltd.
PTIK [*Perguruan Tinggi Ilmu Kepolisian*] Police Academy.
PTIP [(*Départemén*) *Perguruan Tinggi dan Ilmu Pengetahuan*] Ministry of Higher Education and Sciences.
P'tjis [*Perantjis*] France.
PTM [*Persekutuan Tanah Melaju*] Federation of Malaya.
PTP [*Pos, Télékomunikasi (dan) Pariwisata*] Post, Telecommunications, and Tourism.
P.T.T. [*Pos, Télgrap dan Télpon*] Postal, Telegraph and Telephone Service.
PU 1 [*Pedjabat Utama*] high official. 2 [*Pembantu Utama*] secretary-general of a ministry. 3 [*Pekerdjaan Umum*] public works.
puah bah! phooey!
puak group, tribe, flock. ber- -² in groups.
puaka gnome, spirit. ber- haunted.
pualam 1 marble. 2 alabaster.
puan 1 plate for betel. 2 see PEREMPUAN. 3 see KELAPA.
puas satisfied, contented. ber- hati to be satisfied. ke-an satisfaction. mem-i to satisfy. mem-kan 1 to satisfy. 2 satisfactory. 3 satisfying. pem-an satiation. - lelas satiated.
puasa the Moslem fasting period. ber- to fast, observe the fasting period.
pubertas puberty.
publik public.
publikasi publication.
publisir memp- to publicize.
publisistik publicity.
pudar 1 pale, sallow. 2 weak, dim. mem-kan to dim s.t. ~ makna to make the meaning vague.
pudi powder, dust of precious stones. mem-kan to pound, grind.
puding 1 garden croton. 2 pudding.

pudja worship, adoration. mem- to worship. pem- worshiper. pem-an 1 place of sacrifice, temple. 2 worship. -an 1 adoration, worship. 2 idol.
pudjangga 1 man of letters. 2 poet. 3 author. ke-an literary.
pudji praise. ke-an praiseworthy. mem- to praise. mem-kan to recommend. *Buku ini sangat di-kan,* This book is strongly recommended. me-m-² to praise, extol. pem- flatterer. -an 1 praise. 2 recommendation. ~ istiméwa with honors. -²an praise.
pudjuk see BUDJUK.
pudjur profligate, dissolute.
pudjut strangulation.
pudur extinguished.
pugar mem-(i) to restore. pem-an restoration.
puing ruins, debris. memp-kan to lay in ruins.
puisi poetry.
pujan body dirt. ber- dirty.
pujeng 1 headache. 2 confused, dizzy. *Dia sdh - karena tidak bisa mendjawab pertanjaan itu,* He was confused because he couldn't answer the question.
pujuh quail.
pukal lump, block. se- mas a lump of gold.
pukang 1 crotch. 2 hook. mem- to tear apart.
pukat seine, dragnet. mem- to catch with a dragnet. pem- 1 fisherman. 2 fishing boat.
pukau anesthetic. mem- 1 to drug. 2 to deceive.
puki vulva. - mai very coarse and abusive words.
pukul 1 stroke. 2 hour. - berapa? What time is it? - tiga, It's 3 o'clock. ber- -²an to hit e.o. ke- stunned. mem- 1 to hit, strike. 2 to defeat. ~ bola to serve (in tennis). ~ kawat to send a cable. ~ mundur to repulse. mem-i to keep hitting. pem- 1 hammer. 2 o. who (that, which) strikes. -an 1 stroke. ~ dada breast stroke. 2 blow, hit. 3 drive (in golf). 4 good fortune. *Ia mendapat ~ karena mobilnja terdjual mahal sekali,* He had good luck because his car brought a high price. - -mem- to hit e.o. - besi hammer. - rata all in all. - rata dpt dikatakan, buku ini se-olah² merupakan essay, All in all it can be said this book is by way of forming an essay. salah - 1 to miss. 2 to make a mistake. sekali - with one blow.
pula 1 again. *Ia datang -,* He came again. 2 also. *Itu benar -,* It was

also true. 3 yet. *Ia blm – datang*, He
had not yet come. 4 anyway. *Siapa
– jg akan melarang saja!* Who's
going to stop me anyway! *Apa
– ini?* What's this again? *Begitulah
–*, And that was it. *Begitukah –?*
Is that so?

pulang 1 to go home. *Saja mau –*,
I want to go home. 2 to come home.
Kapan bung –? When are you coming
home? 3 to land on. **ber–** to die.
~ *kerachmat'ullah* to die, pass on.
mem–i to return to o's former wife.
mem–kan to give back, return,
bring back. **pem–an** 1 return, restitution. 2 repatriation. – *balik* 1 vice
versa. 2 to and fro. 3 round trip.
– *dulu sebentar*, Come back for awhile.
– *hari* one week later to the day. –
kealam baka, – *kehadirat Tuhan* to
pass away, die. – *maklum* left to the
reader or audience. – *pergi* round
trip. – *pokok* to make no profit, come
out even. – *pulih* full recovery. *Hal
itu – kpd tuan*, That's up to you.
Sesudah lima tahun baru ia –, He
came back only after 5 years.

pulas 1 fast asleep. 2 twisted, distorted. **ke–an** fast asleep. **mem–**
1 to twist, distort. 2 to turn. 3 to
wring. 4 to paint, varnish. 5 to have
colic. **–an** a deceptive appearance.

pulau island. **ke–an** archipelago.
mem–kan 1 to isolate, insulate. 2
to boycott. **ter–** isolated. – *Pertja
Sumatra*.

pulih 1 recovered. 2 restored. 3 repaired. **mem–kan** to repair, restore.
pem–an 1 restoration. 2 repair. 3
recovery.

pulisi see POLISI.

pulpén fountain pen.

puluh 1 decade. 2 ten. **ber– –²** in
tens. ~ *tahun jg lalu* several decades
ago. ~ *abad* dozens of centuries.
per(se)–an decimal. **se–** ten. **se–nja**
ten of them. *Berapa* ~ *?* How much
are ten of them? **–an** 1 tens, decades.
2 ten-rupiah note.

pulung pellet.

pulut 1 birdlime. 2 sticky rice.

pumpun **ber–** to flock together. **mem–**
to collect, gather. **ter–** concentrated.
–an 1 meeting place. 2 center.

pun 1 also. *Anak saja– berumur lima*,
My boy is also 5 years old. 2 even.
Seorang– tak hadir, Not a soul was
present. *Datang– ia tidak*, He didn't
even come. *Makan, melihat– tidak*,
Not only have I not eaten it, I
haven't even seen it. 3 even though.
Sekali– ia sakit ... Even though he
was ill ... 4 ever. *Kemana– ia pergi,
ia selalu membawa tasnja itu*, Where-

ever he went, he took his brief case
with him.

punah destroyed, exterminated. **ke-
an** extinction. **mem–kan** to destroy,
exterminate.

punai pigeon.

punat core of a boil.

pundak 1 shoulder. 2 neck.

pundi² purse, bag.

pundjut **mem–** to tie together.

punggah **mem–** to unload. **–an** discharge berth.

punggal **mem–** to break off the point
of s.t.

punggung back. – *kuda* bareback (on
a horse).

punggur tree trunk.

pungkah piece, lump.

pungki see PENGKI.

pungkiri see MUNGKIR.

pungkur 1 rear end, posterior. 2
residue.

pungsi function.

pungut **mem–** 1 to pick, pick up.
Djangan –! Don't pick it up! 2 to
collect. *Ia ~ padjak*, He collected the
taxes. 3 to harvest. *Ia sekarang ~
hasil pekerdjaannja*, He is harvesting
the results of his work now. 4 to
quote. *Ia ~ dari kitab jg lain*, He was
quoting from other books. **mem–
kembali** to recover s.t. ~ *suara* to
put to the vote. **pem–an** 1 harvest.
2 collection. ~ *suara* 1 vote. 2
ballot. **–an** 1 pickings, harvest. 2
quotation.

punja 1 to have, possess. *Saja –
mobil*, I have a car. (My car.) *Siapa
– ini?* Whose is this? *Itu saja –*, It's
mine. 2 after, with. *tunggu – tunggu*
after much waiting. **ber–** 1 to have
property. 2 to have an owner. 3 to
be well-to-do. **ke–an** possession, property. *Itu ~ saja*, That's mine.
memp–i to possess, have, own. *Para
penumpang harus ~ surat tjatjar*,
All passengers must have a smallpox
certificate. **–mu** yours. *jg (em)–* the
owner. *orang jg ber–* a well-to-do
person. – *kerdja* to celebrate. **ia–** 1
his. 2 her. *didalam ~ kalbu* in his
heart.

puntal **ber– –²** 1 winding round. 2
in balls. **mem–** 1 to wind round. 2
to shorten. **–an** 1 bobbin, shuttle,
spool. 2 ball of wool.

puntang-panting hurriedly, in a hurry.

puntianak 1 wailing banshee. 2 female spirit or vampire.

puntil susu nipple.

puntir **mem–** to wind, twist firmly.
–an torsion.

puntja 1 flap, tail, end. 2 beginning,
introduction, elementary. – *bahasa*

Nippon elementary Japanese. – *beliung* cyclone. – *perselisihan* cause of conflict. – *tali* the end of a rope.

puntjak 1 top, summit. 2 acme, zenith. 3 peak. 4 mount (mt.). – *Tursina* Mt. Sinai. **mem–** 1 to culminate. 2 to rise to the top. **pem–** summit, culminating point. – *gigi* crown of tooth. – *paru* upper part of lung.

puntul dull, blunt.

puntung 1 blunt. 2 butt, stub, stump. *Itu – rokok,* That's a cigarette butt. 3 maimed, crippled, mutilated. **mem–** to become blunt. **mem–kan** 1 to blunt. 2 to maim, mutilate. – *api* wood remnant still ablaze. – *berasap* an impossibility.

pupu remove, degree. *saudara se–* first cousin. *saudara dua* – second cousin.

pupuh ber– to fight. **mem–** to beat.

pupuk manure, fertilizer. **mem–** 1 to fertilize, manure. 2 to put a plaster on a cut, etc. 3 to foster, cultivate. **pem–** enricher, cultivator. **pem–an** manuring, fertilizing. – *buatan* artificial fertilizer.

pupur face powder. **ber–** to powder. **mem–kan** to put powder on o.s.

pupus 1 young leaves at top of a tree. 2 wiped out, obliterated. 3 disappeared. **mem–kan** to exterminate, obliterate, wipe out.

puput whistle. **ber–** to blow. *Angin ~ ,* The wind is blowing. **–an** pair of bellows.

pura 1 bag. 2 fund. 3 exchange. **ke– –²an** 1 dissimilation, pretense. 2 feigning. **–²** 1 to pretend. *Ia ~ tidak melihat saja,* He pretended not to see me. 2 pseudo. *lambang ~* pseudo symbol.

purba old, ancient, antique.

purbakala olden times. **ke–an** archaeological. *dinas* – archaeological service.

purbasangka prejudice. **ber–** prejudiced.

puré see KENTANG.

Purel [*Public Relations*] public relations.

puri 1 castle, royal palace. 2 town. 3 Balinese house of worship.

purna ke–an fullness, completeness.

purnama full moon.

puru 1 sore, boil. 2 ulcer. – *sembilik,* – *sembilit* piles, hemorrhoids.

puruk ter– to sink away. *Matahari ~ dibalik gunung,* The sun sank behind the mountain.

purus pen. **mem–** to suffer from diarrhea.

purut rough-skinned.

pusaka heirloom. **mem–i** to inherit. **mem–kan** to leave behind.

pusar ber–, mem– to revolve. **–an** 1 rotation. 2 handle, crank. 3 centripetal. *~ air* eddy, whirlpool. *~ angin* cyclone, whirlwind. – *kepala* crown of hair.

pusara cemetery. – *negara* reins of government.

pusat 1 navel. 2 center. *kantor* – central office. **ber–** *kpd* to center, concentrate on. **ber–kan** to have the center at. **mem–kan** to concentrate on. **pem–an, per–an** 1 concentration. 2 centralization. – *berat* center of gravity. – *roda* wheel hub. – *telur* germ in egg.

pusing 1 to whirl. 2 dizzy. *Saja – kepala,* I'm dizzy. **ber–** to turn. **mem–** to spin s.t. **mem–kan** 1 to turn round. 2 to make dizzy. 3 to puzzle, confuse s.o. **pem–** centrifuge. **per–an** 1 revolution. 2 racking of o's brain. **ter– –²** to rotate. **–an** rotation. – *kepala* 1 to be at the end of o's wits. 2 to be dizzy. *Tak usah – karena itu!* Don't worry about that!

puspa flower. – *ragam,* – *warna* variegated.

Puspen A. L. [*Pusat Penerangan Angkatan Laut*] naval information center.

pustaka 1 book. 2 divining manual. **ke–an** 1 literature. 2 library. 3 documents, bibliography. **per–an** library.

pustakawan 1 librarian. 2 bibliophile.

pusung a dreamer, dullard.

pusut awl.

putar turning. **ber–** 1 to rotate. 2 insincere, dishonest. *~ haluan* 1 to take another direction. 2 to assume another policy. **mem–** 1 to turn, revolve. 2 to wind, twist. *~ lidah* to pervert words, facts. *~ otak* to trouble o's head about s.t. *~ pertjakapan* to change the subject. *~ uang dlm* to turn over money, make productive use of money. *~ balikkan* to twist. *Ia ~ balikkan perkataan,* He twisted the words. **pem–an** *filem* showing, running of a film. **pem–balikan** *fakta* distortion of the facts. **per–an** turnover. **–an** 1 rotation, revolution. 2 crank, windlass. 3 wheel. 4 showing. *~ film* film showing. – *balik* 1 to turn around. *Ia – balik dan pulang,* He turned around and went home. 2 to swindle. – *belit* ambiguous. – *negeri* revolution, *coup d'état.*

putera 1 prince. 2 son. 3 child. *Berapa – sdr?* How many children do you have? **ber–** 1 to have a child. 2 to be confined with child. – *mahkota* crown prince.

puteri 1 princess. 2 daughter. 3 girl. **ke–an** 1 women's. 2 women's affairs. 3 womanhood.
putih 1 white. 2 pale. 3 pure. **ber– mata** 1 to be annoyed at having to wait. 2 to be disgraced. **ber–** *tulang* to die. **ke–(–)an** whitish. **mem–** 1 to turn white all over. 2 to fade. 3 to turn pale. **mem–kan** 1 to bleach s.t. 2 to whitewash. – *kuning* 1 cream-colored. 2 sweetheart. – *metah* snow white. – *telur* egg white.
putik 1 bud, pistil. 2 ovary. **ber–** beginning to bear fruit.
puting 1 handle, hilt. 2 stalk. – *beliung* 1 whirlwind. 2 waterspout. – *susu* nipple.
putjat pale. – *kuam*, – *lesi*, – *manai*, – *pasi* deathly pale.
putjuk top of a leaf, shoot, sprout. **ber–** to sprout, bud. *se–* bedil a rifle. *se– surat* a letter. – *pimpinan* 1 general management. 2 governing board, central board.
putjung heron.
putra see PUTERA.

putri see PUTERI.
putus 1 broken off, severed. 2 finished, over. 3 definite, decisive. **ber– asa** desperate. **ke–an** 1 decision. 2 conclusion. 3 sentence. 4 termination, expiration, end. **ke–asaan** despair. **mem–(i), mem–kan** 1 to decide. 2 to break off, interrupt. ∼ *tjakap* to interrupt. 3 to finish. 4 to break a promise. 5 to sever s.t. **pem–an** cutting, severance. ∼ *hubungan diplomatik* severance of diplomatic relations. (**ter–)–²** broken, interrupted. **–an** 1 decision. 2 sentence, verdict. 3 fracture, break. 4 resolution (adopted at a meeting). – *arang* irreparable. – *asa* to lose hope. *Ia hampir – asa karena balasan tidak datang*, He almost lost hope because the reply did not come. – *bitjara* to be at the end of o's wits. – *harapan* desperate. – *harapannja*, He lost hope. – *harga* fixed price. – *napas* breathless, exhausted. – *njawa* to die. – *rezeki* to lose o's livelihood. *tak –²nja* incessantly.

R

R [*Rupiah*] *R500* 500 rupiahs.
R. [*Radén*] a title.
RAB [*Rentjana Anggaran Belandja*] 1 budget plan. 2 draft budget.
raba be– –² to grope, feel o's way. **me–** 1 to feel. 2 to grope. *Orang buta* ∼ , The blind man is groping. 3 to touch. 4 to guess. *Ia* ∼ *maksud orang lain*, He guessed the other's intentions. 5 to search. *Ia* ∼ *dlm sakunja*, He searched in his pocket. **me–** –² to fondle. *Ia* ∼ *kepala anaknja*, She fondled her child's head. **pe–** organ of touch. **–an** 1 feeling. 2 touch. 3 groping with the hand. 4 guess, estimate. **–²** groping. *Itu hanja* ∼ *sadja*, – *-rubu* in a hurry.
rabak 1 a large tear, rip. 2 in tatters. **me–** to tear.
raban me– 1 to jabber. 2 to rave, be delirious.
rabbani divine.
rabbi my Lord.
rabik torn, tattered at the edges. **me–** to wear at the edges.
rabit torn. **me–** to tear.

Rabi'ul-achir fourth Arabic month.
Rabi'ul-awal third Arabic month.
rabu lungs.
Rabu Wednesday.
rabuk 1 manure, fertilizer. 2 tinderwood. 3 fungus. **me–(i)** to fertilize, manure. – *buatan*, – *garam* artificial fertilizer. – *hidjau* green fertilizer.
rabun 1 smoke. 2 smoky, hazy, dim. **me–i** to smoke out. *Ia* ∼ *rumah*, He smoked out the house. **me–kan** to burn in order to produce smoke. **pe–** material used for burning out s.t. **pe–an** place or means for making smoke. – *sendja* dusk, twilight.
rabung ridge of a house. **me–** 1 to rise. *Air laut* ∼ , The sea rose. 2 to have a ridge. **pe–(an)** ridge of a house. see REBUNG.
rabut to come undone. **me–** to pull, tug at s.o.
rachmat see RAHMAT.
rad council. – *agama* religious council.
rada rather. – *ramé* rather noisy.
radak 1 stabbing with a spear. 2 attack. **be–** to stab. **me–** 1 to stab

with a spear. 2 to break through, attack. **me-(kan)** 1 to stab with a spear, stick a spear through. *Ia ~ tombaknja kekarung pasir,* He stuck his spear through a bag of sand. 2 to stir (a fire).

radang 1 inflamed, hot. 2 excited. 3 to fly into a rage. **me-** 1 to become inflamed. *Parunja ~* , His lung became inflamed. 2 to get excited. *Hatinja ~* , He got excited. *- paru²* pneumonia, inflammation of the lungs.

radén title of nobility; prince, lord. *- adjeng* title of noble unmarried woman. *- aju* title of noble married woman. *- aria* title of nobility higher than *radén pandji. - aria adipati* title given to regents. *- bagus* title of nobility for men; slightly higher than *radén. - mas, - pandji* title of nobility higher than *radén. - tumenggung* title given to regents.

radiator radiator.

radikal radical.

radin see RADÉN.

radio radio. **me-kan** to send via radio. *- sinar* microwave.

radja sovereign, king. *Ia - sehari,* He was a bridegroom. **be-** 1 to act like a king. *Ia ~ didésanja,* He acts like a king in his village. 2 to have a king. 3 to worship. *Meréka ~ kpd uang,* They worship money. **ke-an** 1 empire, kingdom. *~ Inggeris* the British Empire. 2 royal. *tanda ~* royal insignia. *~ Serikat* United Kingdom. **me-** to be a king. **me-i** to rule over. *Singa itu ~ rimba,* The lion rules over the jungle. **me-kan** 1 to make a king. 2 to treat like a king. *Ia ~ tamu,* He treats his guests like kings. 3 to worship, consider highly important. *Ia ~ uang,* He worships money. *- badar* white cotton fabric. *- laut* rear admiral. *- makan* eater. *- minjak* oil king, oil baron. *- muda* viceroy. *- singa* syphilis. *- tidur* sleeper. *- uang* money magnate.

Radjab seventh Arabic month.

radjaberana wealthy. **ke-an** wealth, property.

radjah **me-** to tattoo.

radjakula dynasty.

radjaléla see MAHARADJALÉLA.

radjam **me-** 1 to stone to death. 2 to torture. **-an** torture, stoning.

radjang **me-** to cut into small pieces, carve. **-an** cut tobacco.

radjawali 1 hawk. 2 eagle.

radjin 1 industrious, diligent. *Ia -,* He's industrious. 2 frequently. *Ia - datang dirumah,* He frequently visited my home. **ke-an** 1 industry, diligence. 2 handicraft. *~ gadis* domestic²

science, home economics. *~ tangan* handicraft. *~ wanita* home economics. **me-kan** *diri* to do o's utmost.

radjuk **me-** to grumble. **me-i** to rebuke, reprimand. **pe-** grumbler, complainer.

radjut 1 net. 2 fish net. 3 hair net. **me-** 1 to catch with a net. 2 to make a net. 3 to crochet, knit. **pe-an** knitting. **-an** crocheting.

raga 1 rough basket. 2 body. **be-** 1 to boast, show off. 2 to play ball. **me-** 1 to boast, show off. 2 hairy. **mempe-kan** 1 to boast about, show off. *Ia ~ mobilnja jg baru,* He boasted about his new car. 2 to model (clothes, etc.). **pe-** 1 boaster. 2 show. *~ mode* fashion show. **pe-an** 1 ostentation. 2 show. 3 structure, organization. 4 modeling. *- dan djiwa* body and soul.

ragam 1 melody, tune. *- bahasa Indonésia* the melody of Indonesian. 2 way, manner. *banjak orang banjak - many people, many ways.* 3 caprice, whim. *Ia banjak -nja,* He has many whims. 4 kind, sort, type. 5 color. 6 unity, solidarity. *kehidupan jg - a unified life.* **be-** 1 to sing. 2 various. *Warnanja ~* , It's in various colors. **be- -²** various colors, sounds. **ke-an** 1 state, condition. 2 unity. 3 uniformity, homogeneity. 4 unanimity. **kese-an** uniformity. **me-** 1 to sing. 2 to color, give a tinge to. **me-kan** to unite, consolidate. **menje-kan** to make homogeneous. **se-** of one kind, one set. *pakaian ~* one suit of clothing, uniform. *~ sebau* of one mind.

ragang **me-** to climb s.t. **-an** 1 stage. 2 scaffold. 3 skeleton.

ragas **me-** to pull out. *Ia ~ rambut temannja,* She pulled out her friend's hair.

ragem **be-** agreed. **ke-an** unanimity.

ragi 1 yeast. 2 fermentation. 3 design. **be-** to ferment. *tidak ~* yeastless. **me-** to color. **me-kan** 1 to rise (of bread, etc.). 2 to add yeast. **pe-an** fermentation. **se-** of one design, of one color pattern. *badju wanita ~* dresses of one design.

ragu hesitant. **ke-(-)an** 1 hesitation, doubt. 2 in doubt. **me-** 1 to disturb. *Ia datang utk ~ sadja,* He came only to disturb. 2 to doubt. *Hatinja ~ akan pergi atau tidak,* He doubted whether he should go or not. **me-i, me-kan** to confuse, make s.o. hesitate. *Surat itu ~ saja akan pergi atau tidak,* That letter made me hesitate about going or not. **-² 1** to doubt. 2 doubtful, dubious. 3 worry.

4 worried, upset. 5 confused. 6 to hesitate. *Ia tak akan ∼ memukulnja*, He wouldn't hesitate to hit him. −²*an* in doubt. − *hati* hesitant, dubious.
ragum vise.
ragut me− to tear, pull out.
rahang jaw. − *atas* upper jaw. − *bawah* lower jaw.
rahap me− 1 to cover a corpse with a cloth. 2 to alight. *Burung ∼ diranting*, A bird alights on a twig. 3 to lie down. *Anak ∼ dekat ibunja*, The child lies down near its mother. 4 to fall face down. **pe**− outer cover of a corpse.
rahasia secret. *Ia tidak dpt menjimpan* −, He cannot keep a secret. **me−kan** to keep s.t. secret. *dgn* − confidentially, in confidence.
rahat spinning wheel.
rahib 1 monk. 2 nun.
rahim 1 womb, uterus. *didalam* − *ibunja* in his mother's womb. 2 merciful. *Al−* − the Merciful. **ke−an** mercy. **me−i** to have mercy on.
rahman compassionate.
rahmat mercy, pity. **me−i** to have mercy on.
rahmatullah mercy of God.
rahsia see RAHASIA.
raib see GAIB.
raih me− 1 to take in, gather. 2 to buy up for resale. *Ia ∼ ikan*, He bought fish for resale. *∼ dajung* to row. **me−** −² to grope for. *dgn tangannja ∼ mentjari pegangan* to grope with o's hand seeking a grip. **pe**− wholesale dealer.
rais me− to sweep off.
raja 1 greater. *Indonésia* − Greater Indonesia. *Djakarta* − Greater Jakarta. **me−kan** to celebrate. **pe−an** celebration.
rajah me− to plunder, raid.
rajan² delirious. **me−** −² to be delirious. −²*an* delirium.
rajang dizzy. **me−** to feel dizzy. **pe−an** s.t. that makes the head swim.
rajap termite. **me−** 1 to creep, crawl. *tanaman jg ∼* creeping plant. 2 to move in groups. **menge−** 1 to move stealthily and rapidly. 2 to search, prowl. *Waktu malam harimau ∼ dihutan belukar mentjari mangsanja*, At night the tiger prowls the jungle in search of its prey.
ra'jat see RAKJAT.
rajau me− to wander about, be restless.
raju 1 sad, touched, moved. 2 emotional. 3 seductive. **me−** 1 to mourn for, grieve over. 2 to flatter. 3 to seduce, deceive. 4 to persuade. −*an* sentimental song or singing.

rak shelf. − *buku* bookshelf.
raka 1 unsteady, fragile. 2 cracking sound.
raka'at 1 bowing, prostration. 2 a technical term to describe that central part of the Moslem ritual prayer which is to be repeated a specified number of times during each of the 5 daily prayers.
rakam 1 stamping, printing, impression. 2 embroidering. **me−** 1 to stamp, print. *Ia ∼ kain putih utk batik*, She stamped white cloth for batik. 2 to embroider. *Ia ∼ kain sutera dgn benang mas*, She embroidered the silk with gold thread. **me−kan** to print, embroider, s.t.
rakan see REKAN. **pe−** dealer, supplier.
rakat see REKAT.
rakét 1 racket. 2 rocket.
rakit 1 raft. 2 bamboo floor. **be−** attached alongside. **me−** 1 to make a raft. 2 to invent, devise. 3 to connect, join. **se−** a pair, set, couple.
rakjat people, the populace, public. **ke−an** 1 democracy. 2 democratic. 3 citizenship. 4 the people's. 5 national. − *djelata* the masses, the common people, proletariat. − *djémbél* the poor. − *murba* the common people, the proletariat.
raksa see AIR.
raksasa 1 giant. 2 gigantic, enormous. 3 demon.
raksi 1 perfume. 2 luck. *Ia − dlm perdjalanannja*, He was lucky on his trip. **me−** 1 to perfume, scent. 2 to mix. *Ia ∼ air dgn minjak*, He mixed water with oil. 3 to cheer s.o. up.
rakuk nick, notch, indentation.
rakus greedy. **ke−an** greed.
rakut me− 1 to spin a web, lay a snare. 2 to deceive.
ralat 1 error, mistake. 2 typographical error. 3 errata.
ralip 1 very sleepy. 2 to be addicted to. *Ia − tidur siang*, He is addicted to having his siesta. **me−** to be very sleepy. **pe−** a person who is usually very sleepy.
rama² k.o. butterfly.
Ramadan ninth month of the Arabic calendar (the fasting month).
ramah jovial, friendly, intimate. **be−tamah** 1 to hold an informal meeting. 2 to be on friendly, intimate terms. **be−** −²*an* to be informal, familiar. *Ia suka ∼ dgn bawahannja*, He likes to be on familiar terms with his subordinates. **ke−an**, **ke−** −*tamahan* friendliness, informality, joviality. **pe−** a jovial, very friendly person. − *tamah* 1 confidential. 2 jovial, genial, in-

timate, friendly. 3 informal. *Meréka mengadakan pertemuan – tamah*, They held an informal meeting.

ramai 1 crowded, busy. – *betul dipasar*, It was really crowded at the market. 2 noisy, boisterous. *Ia – kalau bitjara*, He is boisterous when he talks. 3 bustling, active (noisy and crowded). *Djakarta kota jg –*, Jakarta is a bustling town. 4 interesting. *Pertundjukan sangat –*, The show was very interesting. 5 loud. *Pertjakapannja – sekali*, His conversation was loud. 6 the public. *Ia berpidato dimuka –*, He gave a speech before the public. 7 violent, noisy. – *benar témbakan semalam*, The shooting last night was very violent. 8 festive, lively. **be– –²** to be in a noisy group. *Kami pergi ∼ kerumahnja*, We went in a noisy group to his house. **ke–an** 1 noise, bustle. 2 festivity. 3 crowd. **me–kan** 1 to enliven, cheer up. *Migrasi ∼ kota ketjil ini*, Migration enlivens this little town. 2 to liven up. *Meréka ∼ perajaan dgn musik*, They livened up the celebration with music. 3 to be busy. *Pasar tidak – hari ini*, Business is slack at the market today.

ramal me–kan to predict, prophesy, tell o's fortune. *Ia ∼ bhw perang akan petjah dlm tahun ini*, He predicts that war will break out within this year. **pe–an** forecast. **–an** 1 prediction. 2 fortunetelling. *Tuan mau di–?* Do you want your fortune told?

Ramalan see RAMADAN.

ramas me– 1 to press, knead, mold. 2 to provide with a mixture, variety. *Makanan di– diatas piring*, Food was provided with a variety of dishes on the plate. 3 to mix. *∼ perut* to be extremely sorry.

rambah me– to clear away, cut down, away. *Meréka ∼ hutan*, They cleared away the forest. *Ia ∼ pohon²*, He cut down the trees. **pe–** *djalan* pioneer, pathfinder. **–an** what is cut down or cleared away.

rambai 1 fringe. 2 tuft of hair. **–an** hairy.

rambak k.o. chips made from soft part of cow's hide. **me–** to multiply, spread in all directions.

rambang broad, wide, extensive. **me–** at random. – *mata* sensual.

rambat me– 1 to spread. *Penjakit mendjalar ∼ dgn tjepatnja*, An epidemic spreads rapidly. 2 to creep. *Tumbuhan ini ∼ ditémbok*, This plant is creeping up the wall. **–an** propagation.

rambong Siamese dancing girl.

rambu 1 fringe, tassel. 2 short pillar on quay for tying up ships.

rambut 1 hair of the head. 2 mane. 3 thread. **me–** 1 stringy. 2 to become like hair. **pe–** lower end of fishing rod. **–an** hairy fruit with juicy content. – *djangkit* bristling hair. – *keriting* curly, wavy hair. – *remang* bristling hair. *si– pandjang* a woman. *si– péndék* a man.

ramé see RAMAI. *kemédja –²* loud shirt.

rames see RAMAS.

rami hemp, jute.

rampai me–kan 1 to mix, put various things together. 2 to spread. **–²** 1 jumble. 2 medley. 3 mixed.

rampak shady. **me–** to attack, storm, rush. – *rindang* shady.

rampas me– to seize, rob, loot, carry away. **me–i** to hold up, rob. *Pendjahat itu ∼ penumpang²*, The bandit held up the passengers. **pe–** robber, bandit. **pe–an** 1 robbery, holdup. 2 expropriation. **–an** loot.

rampat me– to swing, brandish. *∼ papan* to generalize. *Ia mudah ∼ papan dan mengira bhw bangsa itu semua bodoh*, He easily arrived at the generalization that all those people were stupid.

ramping slender, thin, slightly built. **be–** side by side, next to. **me–** to be worn at the edges.

rampok me– to rob, plunder, loot. **pe–** robber, bandit. **pe–an** robbery, looting.

rampung 1 finished, settled, completed. 2 pierced (of the ears). 3 disfigured, mutilated. **me–kan** to finish, complete.

rampus indecent (of language).

ramsum see RANGSUM.

ramu me– to gather, collect. **–an** ingredients, concoction.

ramus superfluous hair. **be–** hairy.

rana long-suffering. **me–** 1 to be ailing, suffer chronically. *Ia sakit ∼* , He suffers chronically. 2 to keep worrying. *Fikirannja ∼ sebelum anaknja datang*, He kept worrying before his child came. 3 to languish, waste away. *Badannja ∼* , His body is wasting away.

ranah meadow, low-lying valley.

ranai me– to drizzle, trickle, ooze.

ranap still, quiet. **me–** to bend over and touch the ground.

randa 1 widow. 2 widower (in some areas of Indonesia). – *tua* 1 bachelor (elderly). 2 old maid, spinster.

randai me– to wade through water or high grass.

randau spicy. **me–(kan)** to spice s.t. ~ *sajur*[2] to spice vegetables.

randek **me–** to jam, stall.

randi dotted.

randjang iron bed, couch. – *baji* baby's crib. – *sakit* hospital bed.

randjau 1 mantrap, booby trap. 2 mine. – *darat* land mine. – *lapuk* hidden intrigue. – *laut* sea mine. – *pérs* restriction of the press.

randjing **ke–an** possessed (by a bad spirit, etc.).

randu kapok.

randuk hairy. **me–** to wade.

randung **me–(kan)** to violate, step on, infringe.

rang rank, position. *Apa –nja?* What's his position?

'rang see ORANG.

rangah **me–** to boast.

rangas termite.

rangda see RANDA.

rangga sharp point. – *ranggu* with sharp points.

ranggah cockscomb. **me–** to strip of all fruit. *Meréka ~ pohon mangga*, They stripped all the fruit off the mango tree.

ranggak scaffold(ing), stage. **me–(kan)** to haul ashore. *Ia ~ perahu kedarat*, He hauled his boat ashore.

ranggas 1 withered, arid. 2 leafless. **me–** 1 to wither, dry up. 2 to molt, shed. *Ajam ~ *, The chickens molt.

ranggi attractive.

ranggung with the legs apart. **me–** to sit with the legs apart.

rangka 1 framework, skeleton. 2 draft, blueprint. **me–kan** to design. *Kantor pembangunan ini ~ bangunan*[2] *dilapangan pasar malam*, This construction office designed the buildings on the fair site. – *besi* steel frame. – *dada* chest cavity. – *dasar* framework. – *lajangan* frame of a kite.

rangkai bunch, combination. **be–(–)** to be attached, tied to e.o. *Dua lajangan itu terbang ~ *, The 2 kites are flying attached to e.o. **me–(kan)** to combine, attach to e.o. *Ia ~ keréta*, He attached, hooked on, the cars. **menje–kan** to combine into o. *Ia ~ bunga mérah dan putih*, She combined the red and white flowers. **pe–** connector. **se–** connected, tied together, associated. *tiga ~* triumvirate. **–an** 1 series. 2 potpourri. 3 structure, connection, link, chain. – *hati* sweetheart.

rangkaja prominent person.

rangkak **me–** 1 to crawl on hands and knees. 2 to make slow progress. 3 to fawn. **me–i** to crawl along. ~ *dinding buta* to crawl along a blank

wall. **me–kan** to have s.t. or s.o. crawl. *Ibu ~ bajinja*, A mother lets her baby crawl. **me– –**[2] 1 to cringe. *Ia ~ dihadapan madjikannja*, He cringes in front of his boss. 2 to stumble, be clumsy. *Ia ~ pembatjaannja*, He reads haltingly.

rangkang 1 religious training center for advanced Islamic studies. 2 angle, fork for support.

rangkap 1 double, dual. 2 cluster (phon.). **be–(–)** double, in sets. **me–** 1 to trap. 2 to serve concurrently, double, as. *Perdana Menteri ~ Menteri Luar Negeri*, The prime minister also holds the position of foreign affairs. 3 to wear double. *Ia ~ badjunja*, He is wearing 2 suits of clothes. **me–kan** 1 to put s.t. over s.t. else. *Ia ~ ulas médja baru pd jg lama*, She put a new tablecloth over the old o. 2 to give s.o. a double task. *Meréka ~ pekerdjaan itu kpd saja*, They gave me a double task. **pe–** 1 trap. ~ *tikus* a mousetrap. 2 a catcher. 3 a person who holds 2 jobs. 4 pitfall. **se–** a set of s.t. **–an** s.t. double. ~ *kedua* duplicate. – *dua* 1 double, in duplicate. 2 in two layers. – *lima* in quintuplicate, in 5 copies.

rangkét **me–** to thrash, cane, beat up.

rangkok hornbill.

rangkul **me–** to hug, embrace.

rangkum **me–** to embrace, enclose. **me–i** to grasp, embrace. **menje–kan** to gather together. **se–** an armful. **–an** 1 embrace. 2 armful. 3 summary.

rangkung **me–** to squat down, crouch. **–an** throat.

rangkup 1 hollow. 2 curve, cavity. 3 cover. 4 embrace. **me–** 1 to cup the two hands together. 2 to cover. 3 to embrace.

rangrang red ant.

rangrangan plan, project.

rangsang 1 tickling, irritating. 2 exciting, stimulating. 3 pungent. **me–(kan)** 1 to irritate. 2 to titillate, excite, stimulate. *Bau minjak wangi itu ~ hidung*, The odor of the perfume titillates the nostrils. 3 to attack. ~ *hati* to excite, make angry. **pe–** 1 shock troops, attackers. 2 incentive, spur, stimulus. **pe–an** 1 excitement. 2 anger. 3 irritation. 4 incentive, stimulation. – –me– interstimulation.

rangsum ration(s). **me–** 1 to put on rations. 2 to ration out.

Rangun Rangoon.

rangup 1 fragile. 2 crisp.

ranjah nervous. **me–** to eat ahead of others.

ransum see RANGSUM.

rantai 1 chain. 2 series, train, sequence, row. 3 tie. *Ia memutuskan – perkawinan,* He broke the marriage ties. **be–** 1 to have a chain. *Itu arlodji* ~ , That is a watch with a chain. 2 in sequence. **me–kan** to chain, place in chains. **pe–an** imprisonment. **–an** series, sequence, chain. *– besi* iron chain. *– hukuman* convict's chain. *– kangkang* shackles. *– mas* gold chain. *– peristiwa* sequence of events. *– sepéda* bicycle chain.

rantang 1 dinner pail. 2 basket. 3 hamper. **me–** 1 to subscribe to meals. *Karena bekerdja ia* ~ , Because she works, she has her meals delivered. 2 to deliver food in *rantangs. Ia penghasilannja* ~ , She earns her living by delivering food in *rantangs.*

rantas broken off.

rantau 1 inlet, bay. 2 reaches (of a river). *Ia berlajar sepandjang – sungai,* He sailed along the reaches of the river. 3 abroad, foreign country. *Meréka mau beladjar di–,* They want to study abroad. **me–** 1 to go abroad. 2 to leave o's home area (especially of Minangkabaus). 3 to sail along the reaches of a river. 4 to wander about. 5 to take a trip. 6 to emigrate. **pe–** 1 wanderer. 2 a foreigner wandering about the country. 3 emigrant. 4 settler. ~ *Tionghoa* overseas Chinese. **pe–an** 1 foreign country. 2 country to which to migrate. *Tionghoa* ~ overseas Chinese. 3 settlement.

ranting branch, twig. **be–** 1 to be in a chain, sequence, series. 2 to have a twig. *Pohon ini tak* ~ , This tree has no twigs. **me–** 1 to prune, lop off, clip. *Ia* ~ *pagar,* He's clipping the hedge. 2 to stretch out, protrude. *Tangannja* ~ *keatas,* His arms stretch upward. 3 to dry out. *Pohon* ~ *karena panas,* The tree dries out from the heat. 4 to have twigs. *Pohonnja tlh mulai* ~ , The tree is beginning to have twigs. *– perkumpulan* branch of an organization.

rantjah swampy.

rantjak smart, handsome, beautiful. **me–** 1 to clip. 2 to cut into small bits. **se–** a set. ~ *gamelan* a set of gamelan instruments. **–an** stand for a set of small gongs. *– dilabuah, – dilebuh* a dandy.

rantjang stake, post. **be–** to plan, intend. *Ia* ~ *utk perbuatan itu,* He intends to carry it out. **me–** 1 to stake out, place. *Meréka* ~ *bambu*

ditanah utk menandai batas, They placed bamboo in the ground to indicate the boundary. 2 to test. 3 to plan, make a schedule. **pe–** 1 planner. 2 planning body. *Biro* ~ *Nasional* National Planning Bureau. **–an** plan, scheme, program. ~ *pola* blueprint. ~ *undang²* bill (in parliament).

rantjap 1 masturbation. 2 sharp, pointed. **me–** 1 to practice masturbation. 2 to sharpen.

rantju confused. **ke–an** 1 confusion. 2 contamination. **me–kan** to confuse.

rantjung sharp, pointed. **me–** 1 to be sharp. *Potlot* ~ , The pencil is sharp. 2 to sharpen. *Ia* ~ *potlot,* He sharpened the pencil.

ranum overripe.

RAP [*Républik Arab Persatuan*] The United Arab Republic.

rapah **me–** to trample on.

rapat 1 close, intimate, familiar. *Ia – sekali pd temannja,* He is very close to his friend. 2 dense, compact. *– penduduknja,* The population is dense. 3 meeting, assembly. **be–** to hold a meeting, a conference. **ke–an** meeting, gathering. **me–** 1 to approach. 2 to moor, tie up. 3 to close, join. **me–i** 1 to be on familiar terms with s.o. 2 to approach s.t. 3 to frequent. **me–kan, mempe–** to tighten (up). **me–kan** *barisan* to close ranks. ~ *diri* to join, chum up with. *– anjamannja* closely knitted. *– kilat* emergency meeting. *– lengkap, – pléno* plenary session. *– raksasa, – samudera* mass meeting. *Pd tiap² tanggal 17 Agustus selalu diadakan – samudera,* On the 17th of August of every year a mass meeting is held.

rapi(h) 1 in order, orderly, neat, tidy. 2 punctual. **ke–an** neatness, tidiness, order. **me–kan** to put in order.

rapor see LAPOR.

rapot see LAPOR. **me–kan** to report. **–an** report.

rapuh 1 weak. 2 fragile, brittle. *Njawanja –,* He died easily. 3 subtle. **ke–an** 1 weakness. 2 fragility. **me–kan** 1 to weaken. 2 to cause to be weak. **pe–** s.t. which causes brittleness. *– hati* 1 sensitive, tender. 2 tenderhearted. *– mulut* unable to keep a secret.

rapung see APUNG.

ras 1 rustling sound. 2 reins. *Ia memegang –,* He holds the reins. 3 race. *– diskriminasi* race discrimination.

rasa 1 feeling. *Katanja Orang Djawa mempunjai – kedaérahan kuat,* The

Javanese have a strong provincial feeling, they say. 2 opinion, notion. *pd - saja* in my opinion. 3 taste. *Makanan itu -nja énak*, That food tastes delicious. 4 to think, feel. *Saja - ...* I think ... 5 sense of feeling. **be-** 1 to feel. *Saja ~ lelah*, I feel tired. 2 to taste. *Itu ~ pahit*, That has a bitter taste. *~ aral* to feel ill at ease. **ke-an** noticeable, perceptible. *Gempa bumi ~ disini*, The earthquake was noticeable here. **me-** 1 to feel. *Saja ~ senang disini*, I feel content here. 2 to think, believe. **me-i** 1 to taste. *Ia ~ makanan jg sedap itu*, He tasted the delicious food. 2 to experience, endure. *Ia ~ kesukaran dinegeri asing*, He experienced difficulties in a foreign country. 3 to feel, touch. *Ia ~ pipinja jg halus dgn djarinja*, He felt her soft cheeks with his fingers. 4 to guess, feel. *Kami dpt ~ apa jg ia pikirkan*, We can guess what he is thinking about. **me-kan, mempe-kan** 1 to feel. *Hawa panas tlh mulai ~ diri*, The hot weather is beginning to be felt. 2 to feel. *Ia ~ pengaruh temannja didaérah ini*, He feels his friend's influence in this area. *Ia ~ énaknja ada disini*, He feels happy at being here. **me- -²** to feel, touch. *Ia ~ bonékanja dgn tangannja*, She felt the doll with her hands. **pe-** 1 sense of touch. 2 a sensitive person. *~ lidah* sense of taste. *~ tubuh* sense of touch. **pe-an** 1 opinion, feeling. *menurut ~ saja* in my opinion. 2 sentiment. 3 experience, sensation. *~ masa bodoh* indifference. **te-** felt. *Sekarang ~ oléhnja betapa kedjam temannja*, He now feels how cruel his friend is. *~ sakit dikakinja*, He feels his feet hurting. *- hati* heart, mind. *- hormat* feeling of respect. *- kehormatan* sense of honor. *- kurang* feeling of inferiority. *- malu* feeling of embarrassment. *- manis* sweet taste. *- pedih* caustic taste, biting taste. *- rendah* inferiority complex. *- séntimén* sentimental feeling. *- sutji* sanctity.

rasai **me-(kan)** to suffer a painful experience.

rasam 1 custom. 2 customary, agreeable. 3 organization. **se-** harmonious, agreeable. *Kemédjanja ~ dgn dasinja*, His shirt matches his tie. *- air keair*, Birds of a feather flock together.

rasi constellation. **me-(kan)** to consult the stars, cast a horoscope. **pe-an** 1 horoscope. 2 fate. **se-** matching, fitting, belonging together.

rasia see RAHASIA.

rasial racial.

rasialis racialist.

rasialisme racialism.

rasian 1 dream. 2 astrology. 3 fortunetelling. **be-** to dream, have a dream. **me-kan** to dream about.

rasio see RATIO.

rasionalisasi rationalization.

rasionil rational.

rasmi see RESMI.

rasuah 1 bribery. 2 corruption.

rasuk 1 crossbar, crossbeam. 2 to be possessed. *Ia kena -*, He was possessed. **ke-an** to be possessed. **me-** to enter. *Djin ~ kedalam tubuhnja*, A spirit entered his body. *Fikiran utk membudjuk temannja ~ kepadanja*, A thought of cheating his friend entered his head. **me-i** to invade, capture. *Pakaian mandi itu dgn tjepat ~ angkatan muda kita*, That bathing suit quickly captured our young people. *- keréta* axletree. *- rakit* crosspiece in a raft.

rasul 1 o. sent by God. 2 prophet. 3 apostle. 4 messenger. **ke-an** 1 apostolate. 2 attribute of a messenger of God.

Rasulu'llah the Apostle of God; the Prophet Mohammed.

rat see ERAT.

rata 1 flat, level. 2 even(ly). *Gula² itu dibagi -*, The candy was divided evenly. 3 average. **me-** 1 to be smooth. *Muka laut ~ sesudah angin ribut itu*, The sea was smooth after the storm. 2 to spread. *Pengaruh pemimpin itu tlh ~ diseluruh negeri*, The influence of the leader has spread to the whole country. **me-i** 1 to cover. *Dlm perdjalanannja ia tlh ~ seluruh kepulauan Indonésia*, In his trip he covered all Indonesia. 2 to obtain equal shares of s.t. **me-kan** 1 to make smooth. *Ia ~ djalan dimuka rumah*, He is making the road in front of his house smooth. 2 to distribute evenly, equalize. *Ia ~ bahan pakaian kpd seluruh penduduk désa*, He is distributing textile goods among the villagers. **mempe-** to level s.t. **menje-kan** to spread, spread out. **se-** 1 everywhere. 2 as flat, as even as. *~ tjermin* as flat as a mirror. *-²* 1 on an average. *Tiap anggota menerima ~ 10 sén*, Every member receives on an average 10 cents. 2 generally. *Demikianlah keadaannja ~ ,* Such was the situation generally. 3 evenly. *Orang tani memukul tanah ~ ,* The farmer worked the ground evenly.

ratah simple, plain. **me-** to eat o.

thing only. *Ia* ∼ *nasi putih*, He eats only white rice.

ratap lamentation. **me–** to lament, mourn. **me–i** to lament over, bemoan. **–an** lament. **–** *tangis* mourning, lamenting.

ratib recitation of a prayer. **me–** to recite a prayer. **me–kan** to recite a prayer for s.o. else. *Meréka* ∼ *ajahnja jg tlh meninggal sepuluh tahun jg lalu*, They recited a prayer for their father who died 10 years ago.

ratifisir **me–** to ratify.

ratio reason. *setjara* **–** in a rational manner.

ratjau delirious. **me–** to rave, be delirious.

ratjik bird snare. **me–** 1 to trap with a suspended snare. 2 to cut into thin slices.

ratjun poison taken orally. **ke–an** drugged, poisoned, intoxicated. **me–i, me–kan** to poison s.o. **pe–** poisoner. **pe–an** poisoning.

ratna gem, jewel. **–** *kendi* precious stone. **–** *mutu manikam* gems of all kinds. **–** *tjempaka* topaze. **–** *wilis* emerald.

ratu 1 king. **–** *Adil* the Just King. 2 queen. **–** *Elizabéth* Queen Elizabeth. **–** *malam* moon.

ratus hundred. *dua* **–** 200. **be–** ⁻² hundreds. *Pohon kelapanja* ∼ , He has hundreds of coconut trees. **me–** 1 in hundreds. *Tentara* ∼ *berbaris didepan ratu*, Hundreds of soldiers paraded before the king. 2 to commemorate the hundredth day of death. **se–** 100. **–an** 1 hundreds. *Pekerdjanja* ∼ , He has hundreds of workers. 2 a $100 bill or 100-rupiah note.

raun rounds, patrol duty. **me–** to go the rounds.

raung **me–** 1 to roar. 2 to moan.

raup **me–** to scoop up water with the hands.

raut make, cut. **me–** to cut, carve. **se–** a cut, a slice. **–an** slice of s.t. cut or whittled by a knife. **–** *badan* build, figure. **–** *muka* features.

rawa morass, swamp, marsh.

rawan 1 anxious. 2 emotion, tenderness. *Ia memberi* **–**, She inspired tenderness. 3 used with articles made of cord. *satu* **–** *djala* one net. **me–i** to be anxious, concerned about. **me–kan** 1 to alarm, disturb. 2 to thrill.

rawang swamp.

rawat **be–** to be treated, have treatment. *Ia* ∼ *dirumah sakit umum*, He is being treated at the general hospital. **me–(i)** 1 to take care of, look

after, attend to, nurse. 2 to resume o's original form. *Sjiwa* ∼ *kembali*, Shiva resumed his original form. **pe–** nurse. **(pe)–an** 1 treatment. 2 nursing, care.

rawi 1 narrator. 2 story writer. **me–(kan)** to narrate, tell a story.

rawit fine, small. **(ke)–an** prelude.

rawon see NASI.

raya see RAJA.

rayon area, district.

razzia 1 raid. 2 house-to-house search.

RDD [*Républik Démokrasi Djérman*] German People's Republic.

RDRK [*Républik Démokrasi Rakjat Koréa*] Korean People's Republic.

RDV [*Républik Démokrasi Viétnam*] Vietnamese People's Republic.

réak see RIAK 3.

réaksi reaction.

réaksionér reactionary.

réalis realist.

réalisasi realization. **me–kan** to realize, bring about.

réalisir **me–kan** to realize.

réalisme realism.

réalistis realistic.

réalokasi reallocation.

rebab two-string violin in Javanese gamelan orchestra.

rebah **me–** 1 to fall down. 2 to lie down. 3 to rest. **me–kan** 1 to knock over, crash into. 2 to lay down. 3 to collapse. ∼ *diri* to lie down. **–an** 1 things that are overturned. 2 a place to lie down. **–** *pingsan* to fall into a faint. **–** *rempah* to stumble along. **–** *tertumus* to fall on o's face.

rébak deep cut, wound. **me–** 1 to be deeply cut, have a bad cut. *Pahanja* ∼ , He has a bad cut on his thigh. 2 to spread (of news, rumors, illness).

reban chicken house. **me–kan** to place in the chicken house. *Waktu malam ia* ∼ *ajamnja*, He puts his chickens in the chicken house at night.

rebana tambourine. **be–** 1 to play the tambourine. 2 to have a party at which the tambourine is played.

rebas **me–** to fall into ruins.

rebat **me–** to bar, block.

rébéh **me–** to hang down loosely. *Pakaiannja* ∼ , His clothes hung loosely on him.

rébewés driver's license.

Rebo see RABU.

Rebu see RABU.

rebung bamboo shoot, sprout. **me–** to sprout.

rebus **me–** to boil. *Ia* ∼ *katjang*, She boiled peanuts. **–an** what is boiled. ∼ *djagung* corn on the cob.

rebut be– to snatch away, fight for, take by force. *Tiap partai ~ korsi diparlemén,* Every party fought for a seat in parliament. be– –[2] to struggle to be first. *Meréka ~ membeli kartjis,* They were struggling to buy tickets. be– –[2]an to struggle with e.o. *Meréka ~ pangkat,* They were vying for position. me–(kan), mempe–(kan) 1 to snatch, seize, take by force. 2 to fight for. 3 to receive a prize. 4 to break a record. *Meréka ~ piala Thomas,* They snatched the Thomas Cup. pe–an struggle, fight. –an 1 struggle, fight. ~ *jg hébat terdjadi diantara orang*[2] *itu,* A violent struggle occurred among those people. 2 object of the struggle. *Barang ini mendjadi ~ orang banjak,* This object became a matter for struggle by the crowd. ~ *kekuasaan* 1 coup d'état. 2 struggle for power. ~ *pangkat* job hunting.

red. 1 [*redaksi*] editorial staff. 2 [*redaktur*] editor.

reda abated, subsided, calmed down. *Angin tlh –,* The wind has subsided. be– 1 to take shelter. 2 to lessen, abate. me–kan to soothe, calm, pacify.

réda see RÉLA.

redaksi 1 editorial staff. 2 wording (of text).

redaktur editor.

redam 1 vague, dim, faint. 2 muffled, hushed. me–kan to deaden, muffle. pe– *letus* muffler. –an attenuation. –[2] faintly visible. *Kapal jg djauh itu kelihatan ~ ,* The ship in the far distance is faintly visible.

redap tambourine. me– to spread. *Penjakitnja ~ diseluruh tubuhnja,* The disease spread throughout his entire body.

rédja leftovers, scraps.

redjah me– 1 to dash, leap. 2 to transgress, infringe upon. pe– a boor.

redjam see RADJAM.

redjan me– to squeeze out painfully.

redjang me– to dig up, break up. pe– crowbar. se– *pemanggilan* as far as o. can shout.

rédjéh blear-eyed.

redjeki see REZEKI.

redjuk me– to jump.

redup 1 overcast, dull. 2 muffled, suppressed. me– to be overcast. me–kan 1 to dim the lights. 2 to muffle. 3 to cause an overcast.

réformis reformer.

regang tense, tight, stretched. be– to be in a tense relation. bersi– to brace o.s. ~ *mulut* to have a violent quarrel. be– –[2] 1 to stretch out. 2 to quarrel. me– 1 to stretch. 2 to intensify. ~ *badan* to have convulsive motions. ~ *njawa* to be at death's door. ~ *telinga* to teach s.o. a lesson. me–kan 1 to stretch (out). 2 to widen. pe– stretcher. ~ *tjelana* trousers stretcher. –an tension, strain.

regat short cut. me– 1 to take a short cut. 2 to stop, hold up.

regén regent. ke–an regency.

régés leafless.

regi state monopoly. – *garam* state salt monopoly.

réglemén regulation.

regu 1 gang, team, group. 2 shift. 3 detail. 4 squad. *pekerdja tiga –* 3 shifts of workmen. be– in groups, in teams. ke–an teamwise. me–kan to divide into shifts, groups.

reguk a slug, a drink.

réhabilitasi rehabilitation.

réhal bookstand for reading the Koran.

réjog spectacle with horseback riding.

réjot 1 falling to pieces. 2 oblique, slanting.

rék see RAK.

réka 1 invention, concoction. 2 trick, ruse. 3 step, action. *Kami mesti mengambil –,* We must take action. me– 1 to invent, devise, contrive. 2 to imagine things, indulge in fancies. 3 to plan, schedule. –an invention, fabrication, plan. –[2] a tale, story.

rekah cracked, split. me– to split, show a crack. ~ *fadjar* daybreak. *bibirnja ~* chapped lips.

rekam see RAKAM. me– to record. –an notes.

rekan comrade, companion, ally. be–, me– to be a comrade of, be united with. *Ia ~ gurunja,* He is a comrade of his teacher.

rékapitulasi recapitulation.

rekat me– to glue. me–kan to seal. pe– glue.

rékening bill, account. – *giro,* – *koran* current account.

rekés petition. me– to request, file a petition.

réklame 1 advertising. 2 advertisement.

rékonstruksi reconstruction. me– to reconstruct.

rékor record.

rékréasi recreation.

reksa 1 protector. 2 police.

réktor dean or head of a university.

rél rail(s), railway track.

réla 1 willing, agreeable to. *Ia – pergi dgn saja,* He is agreeable to going with me. 2 agreed to, acquiesced in. *Saja sdh – akan perginja saudara saja itu,* I have agreed to my brother's going. 3 consent, approval. **ke-an** 1 agreement, consent. 2 benevolence. **me-i** to consent, permit, approve of. **me-kan** 1 to allow, consent. *Ia ∼ anaknja dirawat dirumah sakit*, He allowed his child to be treated at the hospital. 2 to acquiesce in, agree quietly with. *Ia ∼ akan penderitaannja*, He acquiesced in his sufferings. – *hati* readily, willingly. *dgn* – 1 readily, willingly. 2 kind(ly), generous.

relai me- to crumble, fall to pieces.

relang me- to glitter, flash.

relap me- to shine, glisten.

rélasi 1 customer, client. 2 relation(s). – *dagang* business relation.

relau tin smelting furnace, smelter.

relung niche, recess, hollow. **me-dome-shaped**, hollow. **-an** = RELUNG.

rém brake. **me-**, **menge-** to put on the brakes. – *angin* air brakes. – *bahaja* emergency brake. – *kaki* foot brake. – *tangan* hand brake. – *teromol* mechanical brakes.

remadja 1 adolescent, marriageable. 2 young. **me-kan** 1 to rejuvenate. 2 to replace older persons by younger ones. *nama² pegawai jg akan di-kan* names of employees who will be replaced by younger ones. **pe-an** rejuvenation. *putera* – adolescent.

rémah crumbs, food remnants. **me--²** to crumble. **me- -²kan** to make crumbs of s.t. *Ia ∼ rotinja*, He made crumbs of his bread.

remak better, preferable. – *mati daripada hidup*, Better to die than to live.

remang cloudy, overcast. **me-** 1 to bristle up, stand on end (of hair). 2 to buzz, hum of insects. 3 to stream, flow (of perspiration, tears). *∼ api* to put out a fire. *∼ hati* to get angry.

remba a pair. **be- -²** in pairs. *Pesawat itu terbang ∼* , The planes fly in pairs.

rembah me- to drop down, flow freely. **-²** to drip, flow freely. *Air matanja ∼* , Her tears flowed freely.

rembang zenith, peak. *waktu matahari* – high noon. **be-** to be bare, open, exposed. **me-** to aim at s.t.

rembes me- 1 to ooze out, leak, filter. 2 to ooze through, penetrate. **pe-an** oozing, leakage, infiltration. **-an** 1 oozing liquid. 2 pit.

rémbét hampered, impeded, obstructed. **me-** 1 to hamper, obstruct. *Bandjir itu ∼ perdjalanan kami*, The flood hampered our journey. 2 to involve. *Perkara itu ∼ seluruh keluarganja*, That affair involved all his family. 3 to spread. *Penjakit itu tlh*

∼ diseluruh kota, The disease has spread to the whole city. 4 to creep, climb up. *Tanaman itu ∼ dipagar*, The plant is creeping up the hedge. 5 to hang down. *Buahnja ∼ ketanah*, The fruits are hanging down to the ground. **me-kan** 1 to hinder, obstruct. 2 to involve in. *Ia ∼ saja dlm perkara itu*, He involved me in the affair. 3 to let hang. 4 to let creep, climb up. 5 to spread s.t. *Meréka tak sengadja ∼ penjakit*, They unintentionally spread the disease. **pe-an** involvement.

rembih me- to drip, trickle.

rembuk be- to discuss, confer on, consult about. *Meréka ∼ ttg soal perdagangan*, They conferred on commercial problems. **me-(kan)** to discuss, confer about. **pe-an** 1 discussion, deliberation. 2 conference, consultation.

rembulan moon.

rembunai medium, average, fair. *Ia tinggi* –, He is fairly tall.

rembut be- to struggle to be first to see (in a crowd).

réméh trifling, of no importance. **ke-an** a trifle, triviality. **me-kan** 1 to belittle. 2 to take lightly. *Sjarat² UUD kita djanganlah di-kan*, The stipulations in our constitution should not be taken lightly. **me-téméhkan** to belittle. – *téméh* insignificant, trifling.

remeng see REMANG.

rémét me- 1 to dawdle, loiter. 2 to talk drivel.

rempah me-(i) 1 to spice fish, meat. 2 to embalm. **pe-** 1 o. who spices. 2 seasoner. **-²** 1 spices. 2 drugs, ingredients. – *ratus* a medicine consisting of many different items.

rempak be- in a row. **menje-** to advance together, in unison. **se-** in unison, altogether. *Meréka madju ∼* , They advanced together.

rempuh me- to bump, knock over.

remuk crushed, smashed, shattered. **ke-an** blow. **me-kan** to smash, crush, shatter. – *redam* crushed to bits.

renang be- to swim. *Ia suka ∼* , She likes to swim. *∼ kodok* breast stroke. *∼ menelentang* backstroke. **me-i** to swim over, across. *Ia ∼ sungai*, She swam across the river. **me-kan** to let swim. **pe-** swimmer. **te- -²** to keep swimming. *Ia sdh 3 djam ∼* , He has been swimming for 3 hours.

rénda lace. **me-** to crochet.

rendah 1 low. – *harganja* low in price. – *pangkatnja* low in rank. 2

low, bad. - *budi* of low character. 3 humble, modest. ke-an 1 too short. *Badannja ∼ sehingga tak diterima masuk serdadu,* He was too short to be accepted for military service. 2 lowness. *∼ galangan itu menjebabkan bandjir,* The lowness of the dike caused a flood. 3 humility, modesty. *∼ budi* bad character. *∼ hati* modesty. me- 1 to descend. *Pesawat itu ∼,* The plane descended. 2 to be modest. *Wataknja selalu ∼,* He is by nature always modest. me-kan 1 to lower, reduce. *Pendjual itu ∼ harganja,* The seller lowered his price. 2 to degrade, disparage. *Ia ∼ pangkatnja,* He disparaged his rank. 3 to lower, degrade. *Ia ∼ kwalitétnja,* He lowered its quality. 4 to humiliate. *Ia ∼ temannja,* He humiliated his friend. *∼ diri* to humble o.s. -an subordinate, of lower rank. - *hati* modest, humble.

rendam be- 1 to be submerged. *Kerbau suka ∼,* Water buffaloes like to stay submerged. 2 to remain in o. place. *Ia selalu ∼ dirumahnja,* He's always staying in his house. 3 submerged. *Lihat batu ∼,* See the submerged rock. me- 1 to soak. *Ia ∼ pakaian,* She soaks the clothes. 2 to flood. 3 to submerge s.t. te- 1 to be soaked. *Badjunja sdh satu malam ∼ diair,* His clothes have been soaked for o. night. 2 to be in hiding. *Ia selalu ∼ dirumahnja,* He's always hiding in his house. 3 submerged.

rendang 1 dish of spicy meat and coconut. 2 chanting. be- to chant. me- 1 to make *rendang.* 2 to chant. pe-an frying pan.

réndéng 1 running at e.o. 2 o. after the other. be- successively.

rendet to stall, get fouled up. ke-an a foul-up.

rendjana 1 longing. 2 in love. 3 emotion.

rendjis spot, stain. me-(kan) to sprinkle, spatter. se- *susu* a dish of milk.

rénék me- to vibrate.

rengas me- to varnish.

rengat crack, split. me- 1 to have shooting pains. 2 to crack, split, chap. 3 to ooze, trickle. 4 to erupt (volcano). - *hati* furious.

réngéh a neigh, whinny. me- to neigh, whinny.

réngék me- to whine, whimper, nag. pe- whining, whimpering, nagging.

renggang distant, spaced, wide apart. *persahabatan jg* - a distant friendship. ke-an 1 aloofness, distance. 2 estrangement. me- to be apart, spaced. me-i to avoid, withdraw from.

Mengapa ia ∼ temannja? Why did he avoid his friend? me-kan, mempekan to space s.t. *Ia ∼ korsi,* He spaced the chairs. pe- s.t. causing aloofness.

renggat yearly tree ring. pe- *waktu* obstruction, s.t. which causes delay.

rénggék see RÉNGÉK.

renggut me- to pull, tug. me- -² to be tugging at. *Ia ∼ djénggotnja sambil memikir soal jg sukar itu,* He tugged at his beard while pondering the difficult problem. me-kan to tear off. -an a jerk, tug, pull.

rengit mosquito.

rengkah cracked, torn. me- 1 to crack open. 2 to be swollen, bulge out.

rengkiang rice barn on poles.

rengkuh me- to tear, pull at.

réngréngan scheme, draft, plan.

réngsa 1 apathetic. 2 lazy. 3 obstinate, stubborn. me- 1 to feel lazy, apathetic. 2 to be obstinate, stubborn.

rengus me- sullen, unhappy. pe- a sullen person.

rengut be- to be morose. me- 1 to grumble, grouse. 2 to be sullen. pe- a sullen, grumbling person.

renik fine. be- -² 1 in drizzles. 2 dotted, speckled. *kain putih ∼ hitam* white cloth with fine black dots. me- -² 1 in drizzles. *Hudjan ∼,* It's drizzling. 2 fine(ly). *Berasnja ditumbuk ∼,* The rice is pounded up fine. 3 in fine grains. *Tjitanja mérah ∼,* The cloth is red colored with fine dots. -² fine, delicate, small of stature.

renjah 1 concentration, careful attention. 2 troublesome, requiring attention. *Itu pekerdjaan jg -,* It's a job requiring careful attention. 3 pleasant. 4 fresh (of fruit). be- to give special attention. me- 1 to give careful attention. 2 to leave in a huff. *Ia ∼ dari kamar,* He left the room in a huff. 3 to pick tidbits.

renjai to sprinkle, drizzle. be-an to be dripping (with perspiration).

renjang 1 restless. 2 to feel out of sorts.

rénjéh be-1 to be muddy. *Djalannja ∼,* The road is muddy. 2 to drizzle. me- 1 to mutter, mumble. 2 to take an angry attitude. 3 to whine, whimper.

renjek crumpled, shrunk.

renjem 1 itching. *Ia - seluruh badannja,* He itched over his entire body. 2 desperate. *Ia - pikirannja mengingat soal itu,* He was desperate whenever he thought of that problem.

renjoh see RENJUK.

renjot ke-an *bibir* curling of the lips.

renjuk crumpled (up). **me–** 1 to ruffle, crumple up. *Angin ~ pasir,* The wind stirred up the sand. 2 to grumble. 3 to pull, tug, jerk. *Angin bertiup ~* , The wind blew with a sudden gust.

renjut to knock, tap. **me–kan** to shrug lightly. *Ia ~ bahunja,* He shrugged his shoulders lightly.

renta me– –² to speak in a loud voice, raise o's voice (in anger).

rénta old, worn-out.

rentak be– to stamp. *Ia ~ kaki,* He stamped his foot in anger. **me–** 1 to stamp o's foot. 2 to tug, pull violently. *Kuda itu ~ tali ingin berlari,* The horse pulled hard at the reins in an effort to run. 3 to collide against. **se–** 1 all at once, suddenly. 2 together, in a body. **te–** pulled off.

rentan 1 predisposition to poor health, sickly. 2 to anger easily. **be–** to get angry easily.

rentang me– 1 to stretch, extend. *Ia ~ pandjang,* He drew the story out. *Mandor itu ~ djalan,* The foreman extended the road. 2 to build. *Meréka ~ djambatan,* They built a bridge. 3 to stretch. *Ia ~ tali,* He stretched the cord. **me–i** 1 to stretch s.t. *Ia ~ pintu dgn tali,* She stretched a cord over the door. 2 to hinder, prevent. *Pekerdja² itu ~ orang bekerdja,* The workers hindered the people from working. **me–kan** to lay out, construct, extend. *Perusahaan itu ~ pipa minjak hingga kelaut,* The firm constructed a pipeline to the sea. **se–** a distance, part of the way. **te–** 1 stretched out, extended. 2 hindered, obstructed.

rentap see RENTAK.

rentas me– to take a short cut.

rénte interest (monetary).

réntén interest. **me–i** to pay interest on. *Ia ~ utangnja,* He pays interest on his debt. **me–kan** to lend at interest. *Ia ~ uangnja,* He lends his money out at interest.

rénténg be–(–) o. after the other, in line.

réntét be– –² in line, o. after the other. **–an** 1 series, sequence, row. 2 volley.

rentjah me– 1 to wade through. *Ia harus ~ lumpur,* He had to wade through mud. 2 to step upon. *Kerbau ~ sawah,* The carabou tread upon the wet rice field. 3 to face. *Ia ~ bahaja,* He faced the danger. 4 to be fickle, unsteady. 5 to mix. *Ia ~ tepung dgn gula,* He mixed flour with sugar. **me– –²** to do several types of work. **pe–** (flavoring) spice.

rentjana 1 program, plan, schedule. 2 report, account, article. 3 draft, copy. **me–** 1 to plan. 2 to report. 3 to narrate, tell. **me–kan** 1 to relate, give an account, narrate. 2 to plan, project. *Meréka ~ belandja pemerintah,* They planned the governmental budget. *Ia ~ serangan,* He planned an attack. 3 to compose. *Ia ~ surat,* He composed a letter. **pe–** 1 planner. 2 planning board. **pe–an** 1 planning. 2 design. *~ rumah* house design. *– kerdja* work schedule. *– kuno* an old story. *– peladjaran* curriculum. *– rapat* 1 minutes of the meeting. 2 program of the meeting. *– surat* contents of the letter.

réntjéh see RINTJIH. **ke–an** remaining part, leftover.

réntjéng 1 slender. *– badannja,* He is slenderly built. 2 a string of s.t. *se– bunga²an* a string of flowers. **–an** a string. *~ berlian* a string of diamonds.

réntjét little by little. **be– –²**, **me–** by installments, piecemeal. *Ia membajar utangnja ~* , He is paying his debt off in installments.

rentjik see RENIK.

rentjis me– to sprinkle.

réntjong Achehnese kris.

renung me– 1 to muse, meditate, ponder. *Ia ~ akan kekasihnja jg djauh,* She was musing about her sweetheart who was far away. 2 to gaze, stare at. *Se-hari² ia duduk ~* , He sits and stares every day. **me–i**, **me–kan** 1 to meditate upon. 2 to gaze at. **pe–** (day)dreamer. **–an** meditation, reflection, contemplation.

réog 1 see RÉOK. 2 joke, jest.

réok to cackle.

réorganisasi reorganization.

réoriéntasi reorientation.

repak crisp, fragile.

repang straight, trimmed, evenly filed. *Giginja –,* His teeth are even. **me–** to file evenly, cut, trim.

réparasi repair(s). **di–** to be repaired.

repas crumbly, dry and brittle.

répék me– to whine, whimper.

répés me– 1 to fidget. 2 to waste time.

répét me– to chatter. **pe–** chatterbox.

repetisi 1 rehearsal. 2 quiz.

repih crumbly. **me–** 1 to crumble. 2 to pick, pluck. *Ia ~ bunga,* She picked flowers.

repis see REPIH. **me–** to clean up land.

répolusi revolution.

réportase reporting.

repot to report. **me–kan** to report, announce. **–an** a report.

répot 1 busy, occupied. *Ia sangat –*, He is very busy. 2 difficult, cumbersome. *Pekerdjaan ini –*, This work is difficult. 3 to be fussy about. *Djangan –*, Don't be fussy about it. (Take it easy.) **ke–an** 1 stir, bustle, rush. 2 very busy. **me–kan** 1 to cause a fuss, a bother. *Perkawinan itu tak sedikit ~ ajahnja*, The wedding has caused her father a lot of bother. 2 to cause trouble, make difficulties for. *Ia selalu ~ ibunja*, He always caused his mother a lot of trouble. 3 to make difficult, cumbersome. *Peraturan ini ~ pekerdjaan*, This regulation made the job difficult.

réproduksi reproduction.

repuh² padlock.

reput rotten, crumbling into decay.

réputasi reputation.

reribu see RIBU.

rerongkongan 1 skeleton. 2 carcass, cadaver.

rerumputan 1 shrubbery. 2 grassy.

reruntuh wreckage, debris, ruins. **–an** ruins, debris. *– dunia, – masjarakat* prostitute. *– mobil* wrecked automobile.

reruntuk see RERUNTUH.

rés. 1 [*résidén*] resident. 2 [*résimén*] regiment.

resah fidgety, restless.

resam 1 custom, ways. 2 equal to. **se–** equal to. *– tubuh* bodily constitution.

resap me– 1 to penetrate. *Naséhat² itu ~ kedalam hatinja*, That advice penetrated their hearts. 2 to ooze. *Itu ~ keluar*, That oozed out. 3 to disappear. *Ditengah hutan djalan itu ~ ketutupan daun²an*, The path, covered with leaves, disappeared into the forest. 4 to evaporate. *Embun ~ disinar matahari*, Dew evaporates in the sunshine. 5 to integrate. **me–kan** 1 to cause to penetrate, disappear. 2 to ooze.

résék me– 1 to touch, grope, feel with the hands. 2 to examine.

résénsi book review.

resép 1 recipe. 2 prescription.

resépsi reception.

resérsé detective.

resési recession.

resi 1 receipt. 2 baggage check.

résidén resident, head of a residency (an Indonesian administrative unit). **ke–an** residency.

resik pure, clean. **me–** 1 shrill. 2 to whisper.

resiko see RISIKO.

résimén regiment.

resiprositét reciprocity.

Reskrim [*Resérsé Kriminil*] criminal detective.

resmi official, legitimate. **ke–an** 1 official confirmation, official announcement. *Masih blm ada ~ apakah ia benar dinaikkan pangkat atau tidak*, There is no official confirmation yet as to whether he has really been promoted or not. 2 official character. **me–kan** 1 to make s.t. official. *Saja sebagai ketua ~ dibukanja Kongrés ini*, I, as chairman, officially declare this congress open. 2 to announce officially. **pe–an, pengr–an** 1 official announcement. 2 official appointment. 3 official ceremony.

résolusi resolution.

Ré–So–Pim [*Révolusi, Sosialisme, Pimpinan Nasional*] Revolution, Socialism, National Leadership.

réstan remainder, remnant. see POS.

réstoran restaurant.

restu 1 blessing. 2 spell. **me–i** 1 to bless. 2 to place under a spell.

restung syphilitic ulceration of the nose.

resu see RESI.

réta me– 1 to talk foolishly. 2 to talk long-windedly.

retak 1 crack. 2 cracked. **ke–an** crack. **me–** to crack, show a crack. **–²** *bulu ajam* easy to compromise. *– batu* irreparable. *– melampaui tara* a big mistake. *– menanti* prelude to disaster. *– retai* covered with cracks. *– tangan* hand lines.

retas me– 1 to rip, tear. 2 to break open, take apart. *Ia ~ dinding*, He broke through the wall. *~ djahitan* to take sewing apart by pulling out the thread. *~ djalan* to cut a road through. **pe–** 1 o. who breaks through. 2 instrument for opening s.t. *~ djalan* pioneer.

rétéh 1 to crackle (of a fire). 2 to thunder.

rétét be– to rattle, give off a rattling sound.

retih me– to crackle. *– api* crackling of a fire.

retja image, idol.

retjik spot, stain. **me–** to sprinkle, spatter. *Keringat ~ didahinja*, Perspiration covered his forehead. **pe–** spray, sprinkler.

rétjok 1 noise, uproar, fuss. 2 excitement. **ke–an** excitement, fuss, noise. **me–** to be excited, noisy. **me–kan** to excite, upset.

retjup me– to bud.

retur return. **me–** to return s.t. or s.o.

revisi revision. **me–** to revise.

révolusi see RÉPOLUSI.

révolusionér revolutionary.

réwak widespread, widely published.
me- to be spread, promulgated.
Kabar itu tlh ~ diseluruh negeri,
The news has been widely spread
throughout the whole country.

réwang me- 1 to swing s.t. *Ia ~
tongkatnja,* He was swinging his walking stick. 2 to be swinging. *Kapal
itu ~ pd tali djangkarnja,* The ship
was swinging on the anchor chain.
3 at random.

réwél 1 troublesome, annoying. *Mobil tangan kedua sering -,* A used
car is often troublesome. 2 hard to
please. *Guru ini -,* This teacher is
hard to please. 3 finicky. ke-an 1
difficulties, annoyance, trouble. 2
quarrel.

rezeki 1 livelihood. 2 luck. *Kalau
ada - tentu saja akan mendapat
pekerdjaan itu,* If I have any luck, I
will surely get that job. *Itu sdh -nja,*
That was his good fortune. *- mata*
things which are nice to look at.

rezim regime.

RFD [*Républik Féderal Djérman*]
Federal Republic of Germany.

R.I. [*Républik Indonésia*] Republic of
Indonesia.

ria 1 joy, delight. 2 gay, cheerful.
3 pride, jealous pride. 4 haughty.
be-(-) to have a good time. ke-an
joy, cheerfulness, fun. - *hati* delight,
delightful. - *riuh* merry, happy.

riah 1 grand, majestic. 2 proud,
haughty. keme-an 1 solemnity. 2
grandeur. me- 1 glorious, grand.
upatjara jg ~ a glorious ceremony.
resépsi jg ~ a grand reception. 2
cheerful. *keramaian jg ~* a cheerful
celebration.

riak 1 ripples. 2 indication, intention. *Sdh kelihatan -nja bhw ia akan
lari,* His intention to run away was
clear. 3 phlegm, mucus. 4 proud.
be- 1 to ripple, move in ripples. 2
to cough up phlegm. me- to ripple.
- *air* water ripples. - *gelombang*
wavelength. - *udara* air waves.

riam river rapids.

rian 52½ yards of yarn.

riang 1 gay, cheerful. 2 dizzy.
Badannja merasa -, He felt dizzy.
be- to be gay. *~ gembira* to be delighted. *Saja ~ gembira bhw...*I'm
delighted that... *~ hati* to be in high
spirits. ke-an joy, cheerfulness. me-
to feel dizzy. me-kan 1 to cheer up,
make happy. 2 to excite. be- a
cheerful, happy person. -² cricket.
- *gembira* cheerful and happy. - *hati*
cheerful.

riap me- to flourish, grow rapidly.

rias be-, me- to dress up, adorn o.s.
~ mata to beautify the eyes. *~
rambut* to do o's hair. -an decoration,
ornament. - *kepala* headdress.

riba 1 lap. 2 usury, interest. me- to
take on o's lap. *Ia ~ anaknja,* She
took her child on her lap. -an lap.

ribu thousand. *se-* 1,000. *tiga* - 3,000.
be- -² by the thousands, thousands
of. menje- (*hari*) to celebrate the
thousandth day of a person's death.
-an 1 a thousand. 2 in thousands, by
the thousands. 3 a $1,000 bill or
Rp1,000 note.

ribut 1 stir, bustle, commotion, excitement. *Djangan -,* Don't get
excited. *Ia - kehilangan dompétnja,*
He got excited because his purse disappeared. 2 storm, gale. 3 rowdy.
be-, me- to be stormy, storm. ke-an
stir, commotion, disturbance, riot.
me-kan to excite, incite, cause a
disturbance. pe- troublemaker.

rida see RÉLA.

ridat apostasy.

ridha see RÉLA.

ridla see RÉLA.

ridloh see RÉLA.

rigi² cog, tooth. be- -² 1 toothed,
with cogs. 2 serrated.

riil real.

rikuh embarrassed, shy. *Ia merasa -
thd mentuanja,* He feels embarrassed
toward his parents-in-law.

ril see RÉL.

rimba 1 jungle. 2 forest. me- to become a jungle or wilderness. - *belantara* great jungle. - *piatu* jungle. -
raja very large jungle. - *sawang* wilderness, jungle. *hilang tak tentu -nja*
lost without a trace.

rimbas small adz. me- to cut with
an adz.

rimbawan forester.

rimbit see RÉMBÉT. *Ia se- diantara
kawan²nja,* He was squeezed in between his friends.

rimbu see RIMBA.

rimbun 1 leafy. *Daunnja -,* Its foliage is leafy. 2 thick, dense. *Rambutnja -,* His hair is thick. *perahu jg
-* a prow with many sails.

rimpuh tired, exhausted.

rimpung me- to bind the arms and
legs.

rinai drizzle. me- to hum.

rindang 1 leafy, luxuriant. 2 shady.

rinding harmonica. me- ghastly,
creepy. me-kan terrifying.

rindis pe- bully.

rindu 1 longing, yearning, homesickness. *Ia - akan kekasihnja,* He longs
for his sweetheart. *Ia -,* He's homesick. 2 desire. *Ia -,* He's in love.

ke–an 1 longing, homesickness. 2 desire, love. **me–** 1 to become homesick. 2 to be in love. **me–i** to long for. **me–kan** 1 to yearn for. *Ia* ~ *anaknja*, She yearned for her child. 2 to awake a longing. *Njanjian itu* ~ *ajahnja pd waktu semasa ketjilnja*, That melody awoke a longing for his father when he was still a child. 3 to cause homesickness for. ~ *kampung dan halamannja* to become homesick, long for home. **pe–** 1 lover. 2 o. who complains about his fate. – *dendam* 1 longing, desire. 2 love.

ring ring. – *séher* piston ring.

ringan 1 light in weight. 2 easy, smooth, unimpeded. 3 insignificant. **ke–an** 1 too light. 2 lightness, relief. **me(mpe)–kan** 1 to lighten, alleviate. *Ia mau* ~ *muatan*, He wants to lighten the burden. 2 to make light of. *Ia* ~ *kewadjibannja jg berat itu*, He takes his heavy responsibilities easily. **pe–an** lightening of s.t. – *kepala* quick-witted, smart. – *tangan* energetic, industrious. – *tulang* active, hard-working.

ringgit 1 equivalent to 2½ rupiahs. 2 a silver coin. 3 Malayan dollar. **be–** –² toothed, notched. **me–(i)** to notch.

ringih **me–** to neigh, whinny.

ringik see RÉNGÉK.

ringis **me–** 1 to grin. 2 to have a sour look (from disappointment, etc.). **pe–an** 1 a silly grin. 2 a sour look.

ringkai dry (of leaves). **me–** to be dry, shriveled up. *Daunnja kering* ~ , The leaves are dry and shriveled up. – *ringan* dry and light.

ringkas brief, succinct, concise. *Itu laporan jg* –, That's a concise report. **ke–an** 1 résumé, abstract. 2 abbreviation. **me–kan** to shorten, make brief, condense, summarize. **–an** résumé, précis, summary, condensation. **–nja** in brief, in a word. *dgn* – briefly, in short.

ringkih weak, limp.

ringkik **me–** to neigh, whinny.

ringking **me–** to yell.

ringkuk 1 bent over, stooped. 2 shut up, confined. **me–** 1 to bend over, stoop over. *Ia* ~ *waktu berdjalan dibawah djendéla itu*, He bent over as he walked under the window. 2 to be confined. *Dua tahun ia* ~ *dlm tawanan*, He was confined to a prison for 2 years. **me–kan** 1 to cause to bend. 2 to imprison, jail, confine. **–an** 1 imprisonment. 2 stooping over.

ringkus **me–** 1 to bind feet and legs. 2 to catch. *Ia* ~ *burung*, He caught a bird. 3 to embezzle. *Meréka* ~ *uang negeri*, They are embezzling state funds.

ringsek 1 broken, in pieces. 2 destroyed.

rini ½-cent coin.

rintang 1 hindering. 2 occupied with. *Ia* – *dgn pekerdjaan*, He is occupied with his work. *Ia* – *me–mikir²*, He is absorbed in his thoughts. **me–i** to interfere with, hinder. *Ia tidak mau* ~ *perdjalanannja*, He does not want to interfere with his trip. **me–kan** to block, bar. *Orang djahat itu* ~ *balok didjalan*, The bandits barred the road with a crossbar. **me–** –² to entertain, occupy. *Ia* ~ *anak itu*, She entertained the child. ~ *hati* to enjoy. ~ *pikiran* to divert. **pe–** 1 obstacle. 2 o. who hinders. **pe–** –² entertainment, distraction, pastime. ~ *waktu* time killer. **–an** 1 hindrance, interference, obstacle. *Saja mau datang kalau tak ada* ~ , I want to come if nothing interferes. 2 barrier, restriction. 3 holdup (in count down of rocket or missile launching).

rintas see RENTAS.

rintih **me–** to groan. **pe–** mourner. ~ *séwaan* hired mourner. **–an** a groan, moan.

rintik spot, fine spot. **be–** –² 1 with fine dots. 2 falling in small drops. *Hudjan* ~ , It's drizzling. **me–** –² to drip. –² small spots, dots. – *pd kulitnja* small spots on the skin. *Hudjan* ~ , It's drizzling.

rintis **me–** 1 to clear a way, path. *Ia* ~ *hutan*, He cleared a way through the forest. 2 to do pioneering work. *Meréka* ~ *djalan dlm usaha itu*, They were doing pioneering work in this undertaking. **pe–** pioneer. **–an** 1 pioneering effort. 2 path.

rintji **me–** 1 to plan, schedule. *Meréka* ~ *keramaian resmi*, They planned an official celebration. 2 to specify, design. *Meréka* ~ *perbelandjaan dlm bagian² jg tertentu*, They designed the budget in specified sections. 3 to divide. *Ia* ~ *hartanja diantara anak²nja*, She divided the wealth among her children. **pe–an** 1 specification. 2 design, project. 3 breakdown. *Dibawah ini* ~ *dlm beberapa ketjamatan*, Below is the breakdown in several subdistricts. **terpe–** specified.

rintjih 1 small parts, thin slices. 2 details. **me–** 1 to cut into thin slices, small pieces. 2 to buy or sell retail.

rintjis **me–** 1 to specify. 2 to divide into small groups.

ripuh 1 miserable, sad. 2 in a mess.

ripuk broken, damaged.

risa a callus.

risalah see RISALAT.

risalat 1 essay, composition, treatise. 2 circular, brochure. 3 minutes (of a meeting). – *udjian* thesis, dissertation.

risau 1 restless, nervous. 2 dissipated, dissolute. **ke–an** 1 commotion, riot. 2 worry, restlessness. **me–kan** to worry, disturb. *Soal itu ~ pikiran saja*, That problem worries me. **pe–** 1 disturber of the peace, agitator. 2 tramp. **–an** disturbance, commotion.

risi sensitive.

risik confidential inquiry. **be–** 1 to inquire. 2 to stir up. 3 to be noisy. **me–** 1 to make secret inquiries, sound out. *Ia ~ dulu sebelum meminta tangannja*, He first inquired about her before asking for her hand. 2 to be noisy. *Orang² tak boléh ~ diruang rapat*, People may not be noisy in the meeting hall. *Babu itu ~ dikantongnja mentjari kuntji*, The maid jingled the contents of her pocket while feeling for the key. 3 to rustle. *Daun ~ ditiup angin*, The leaves rustle in the wind. **me–kan** to cause a rustling sound. **–an** confidential inquiry.

risiko risk. *Ia memikul –*, He took the risk.

rit(sléting) zipper.

ritjau **me–** to chatter, twitter.

ritjikan *oto* spare parts of a car.

ritju confused. **ke–an** confusion.

rituil ritual(ly).

ritul **me–** to retool, reorganize. *Tjara berpikir pemimpin² kita harus di–*, The way of thinking of our leaders must be revised.

ritus rite.

riuh 1 noise, clamor, tumult. 2 noisy. *Ia – mulutnja*, She's a noisy person. – *bunjinja*, It sounds easy. – *rendah* 1 noise, clamor. 2 disturbance. 3 noisy, boisterous.

riuk 1 twisted, distorted. 2 twisted, sprained.

riwajat 1 story, narrative, tale. 2 history. **be–** 1 to narrate, relate a story. 2 historic. *Itu kedjadian jg ~* , That's a historic event. **me–kan** to tell, narrate. – *hidup* 1 biography, life. 2 curriculum vitae. – *kerdja* career.

riwan dream.

R.K. 1 [*Rum Katolik*] Roman Catholic. 2 [*Rukun Kampung*] village association.

RMS [*Républik Maluku Selatan*] South Moluccan Republic.

robah see UBAH.

robak-rabik torn in shreds, in rags.

robék torn. **me–** to tear. **–an** s.t. torn.

roboh to collapse, cave in. *Ada banjak pohon –*, There are many fallen trees. *Gedungnja –*, The building caved in. **ke–an** 1 felled. *Ia mati ~ rumah*, He was killed by a falling house. 2 collapse. 3 ruins. **me–kan** 1 to upset, overthrow. 2 to demolish, raze. *Perusahaan itu ~ gedung itu*, The firm demolished the building. 3 to ruin. *Hal itu ~ perusahaan ajahnja*, That matter ruined his father's firm. **pe–an** 1 overthrow. 2 bankruptcy. **–an** ruins.

roch see ROH.

rochani see ROHANI.

rochanijah see ROHANIJAH.

roda wheel. **be–** wheeled. *motor grobak ~ enam* a 6-wheeled truck. **me–i** to put wheels on. – *air* water wheel. – *angin* bicycle. – *gigi* cogwheel. – *penghidupan* wheel of fortune, fate. – *stir* steering wheel. – *tiga* pedicab, trishaw.

rodi 1 forced labor. 2 command, order.

rodjol **me–** to protrude, jut out, emerge. *Kepalanja ~ dari djendéla*, His head emerged from a window.

rodok **me–** 1 to thrust upward, stab. 2 to run with neck outstretched. *Burung unta itu lari ~* , The ostrich ran with neck outstretched. 3 to dash in a hurry. *Ia ~ kekantor karena sdh terlambat*, He dashed to the office because he was late. 4 to pick o's teeth. 5 to stir a fire.

rodong **me–** to run into, meet by chance.

rogoh **me–** to grope, search. *Ia ~ didalam lubang itu*, He groped in the hole with his hand.

rogol **me–** to rape.

roh spirit, life. *Ia meniupkan – kedalam badan manusia*, He breathed life into the human body. – *al kudus* the Holy Ghost. – *djasmani* spirit which gives life to the body. – *haiwani* life spirit in animals. – *insani* spirit of man. – *rahmani* the spirit of God. – *rohani* quickening spirit of spiritual life. – *rohu'lkudus*, – *sutji* the Holy Ghost. **–nja melajang**, He died.

rohani mental, spiritual. **ke–an** spiritual(ity). – *dan djasmani* spiritual and physical.

rohanijah spiritual, mental. **me–kan** to spiritualize.

rohaniwan spiritual leader.

rojak **me–** to spread, become worse.

rojal 1 generous. 2 extravagant. *Ia*

hidupnja –, He leads an extravagant life. **be- -²** *dgn,* **me-kan** to spend extravagantly. *Ia* ∼ *uangnja,* He spends his money extravagantly. **ke-an** extravagance, extravagant spending.

rojan afterpains, cramp. **me-** to suffer a cramp. – *beranak* labor pains.

rok 1 skirt. 2 gown, dress.

rokét rocket. **pe-an** rocketing.

roki a skirt. – *dalam* lady's slip.

rokok cigarette. **me-** to smoke. **pe-**smoker. **pe-an** instrument for smoking. – *hogah* water pipe. – *kertas* cigarette paper. – *kréték* cigarette wrapped in corn leaves with ground cloves added to the tobacco. – *serutu,* – *tjerutu* cigar.

roma fine hair, down.

Roma Rome.

roman 1 figure, looks. – *tjantik* a pretty figure. – *tjilik* petite figure. 2 novel. – *pitjisan* dime novel.

romantikus romanticist.

romantis romantic.

Romawi see RUMAWI.

rombak demolished, torn down. **ke-an** ruins, debris. **me-** 1 to demolish, tear down. *Pengusaha itu* ∼ *rumah,* The contractor tore down the house. 2 to break, destroy. *Ia* ∼ *adat,* He broke the local custom. 3 to reorganize. **pe-an** 1 destruction, demolition. 2 reorganization, radical change. **-an** demolition, destruction.

rombang-rambing tattered and torn.

rombéng 1 tattered, torn. 2 rags, old clothes. 3 secondhand articles. **me-** to trade in secondhand articles. **me-kan** to sell as secondhand stuff. **-an** 1 rags. 2 trash.

rombong 1 big rice basket with cover. 2 vendor. **-an** 1 group, party. ∼ *gubernur* the governor's party. ∼ *peladjar* student group. ∼ *sandiwara* theatrical group. 2 gang. 3 troupe.

romét odd jobs. **me-** to work at odd jobs.

romok **me-** to sit quietly gazing.

rompak piracy. **me-** 1 to destroy, devastate. 2 to commit piracy. **pe-**pirate. **pe-an** piracy.

rompang-ramping tattered and torn, in shreds.

rompéng damaged on the edge. *Piring ini* –, This plate is damaged on the edge.

rompés damaged slightly, chipped on the edge. **-²** many chips on the edge.

rompi waistcoat, vest.

rompok hut.

rompong 1 cut off, mutilated. 2 broken. *Giginja* –, His teeth are broken.

3 mutilation. **me-kan** to break off, cut off.

romusha see ROMUSJA.

romusja involuntary worker for the Japanese in Indonesia. **me-kan** to work as a *romusja.*

rona 1 color. 2 beauty. **be-** to have color. **me-** to give color.

ronda 1 rounds, patrol, beat. 2 guard, watchman. **me-** to patrol, make o's rounds. **pe-** patrol, watchman. – *malam* night watchman.

ronde a round in sports.

ronéo mimeograph.

rong² see RONGRONG.

rongak discontinuous, spaced. *Giginja* –, His teeth have spaces in between.

rongga hollow space, cavity, hole. **be-**spaced, hollowed. **me-** to form a hollow space. – *dada* thoracic cavity. – *hidung* nasal cavity. – *mata* eye socket. – *mulut* oral cavity.

ronggang wide apart.

ronggéng dancing girl. **me-** to dance.

rongkok **me-** to walk stooped over.

rongkongan 1 windpipe. 2 throat. 3 gullet. 4 skeleton. **ke-** 1 windpipe. 2 throat.

rongrong **me-** 1 to tempt. 2 to gnaw at s.t. 3 to undermine. 4 to hurt, damage. *Itu dpt* ∼ *kepribadian kita,* It can harm our personality. **me-i** to disturb, upset. *Tidak akan* ∼ *pekerdjaan PBB,* It won't disturb the work of the U.N. **pe-an** undermining. **-an** temptation.

rongséng sullen, quick-tempered, peevish, quarrelsome. **me-** 1 to grumble, gripe. 2 discontented, unhappy.

rongsok damaged, worn-out. **-an** worn-out articles.

ronjéh **me-** 1 to grumble. 2 to talk drivel. **pe-** o. who mumbles.

ronjok crumpled up. **me-** to crumple up. *Ia* ∼ *kertas didjadikan bola,* He crumpled the paper into a ball.

ronta **me-** to struggle, resist. *Kuda itu* ∼ *pd talinja,* The horse struggled to free himself from the rope. **me- -²** to keep struggling to get free.

rontjét small bits.

rontog see RONTOK.

rontok **me-** to drop off, shed. **me-kan** to cause to shed, fall off. *Musim dingin* ∼ *daun pohon,* The cold weather caused the leaves of the trees to fall off.

ropak-rapik in disorder, chaotic.

rosok used up, worn-out. **me-** to feel with the hand. **-an** rubbish, junk.

rosot **me-** 1 to slip off. *Tjelananja* ∼ , His trousers slipped off. 2 to decline, sink. *Harganja* ∼ , The prices declined. **me–kan** to reduce, decrease. *Ia ~ harganja*, He reduced his price.

rotan rattan. **be–** to collect rattan. *Ia hidup ~* , He makes his living by collecting rattan. **me–** 1 to collect rattan. 2 to whip, cane. ` – ulur* strong rattan.

roti bread, a loaf of bread. *– bakar* baked bread. *– kaléng* cracker. *– kering* dry bread. *– kismis* raisin bread. *– mari* cookie. *– panggang* toast. *– tawar* sandwich bread.

rotok me– to grumble, complain.

rowa voluminous. see RUA.

royemén 1 expulsion. 2 cancellation.

Rp. [*Rupiah*] rupiah. *Rp. 5* five rupiahs.

RPA [*Républik Persatuan Arab*] United Arab Republic.

RPKAD [*Résimén Pertempuran Komando Angkatan Darat*] crack troops, storm troops.

R.R.I. [*Radio Républik Indonésia*] Indonesian Broadcasting Company.

R.R.T. [*Républik Rakjat Tiongkok*] the Chinese People's Republic.

RSU [*Rumah Sakit Umum*] the public hospital.

R.T. [*Rukun Tetangga*] neighborhood association.

ru 1 casuarina. 2 14.49 square meters.

rua broad, wide, extensive, voluminous. **me–** to expand.

ruah me– 1 to pour, spill out, empty. 2 to call, shout at. **me–kan** to empty s.t. *Ia ~ karung*, He emptied a bag. **se–** a distance extending as far as a call can be heard.

ruak me– to expand, widen.

ruam skin eruption. *– saraf* shingles.

ruang(an) 1 large room, hall. 2 space. 3 leisure. *Saja mau batja buku kalau ada – waktu*, I'll read the book if there's time available. 3 column. *– pertama* the first column. *– olahraga* sports column. 4 hold (in a ship). **–an** *djuru terbang* plane's cockpit. *– batja* reading room. *– belakang* back room. *– huruf* space between letters. *– kelas* classroom. *– kuburan* grave. *– niaga* economy class (on a plane). *– pamér* exhibition gallery. *– pariwisata* tourist class (on plane). *– pertama* first class (on plane). *– rumah sakit* hospital ward. *– siksaan* torture chamber. *– tengah* center room.

ruap me– 1 to bubble up, effervesce, fizz. 2 to evaporate. 3 to smoke. *Masakannja tlh ~* , The food is burning. *~ darah* very angry.

ruas 1 space between 2 joints. 2 vertebra. 3 the parts of an equation. **be–** to have internodes. *Tebu ~* ,

Sugar cane has internodes. **me–** to have a red spot on the skin. *Kulitnja ~* , There are red spots on his skin. *– bambu* space between 2 joints of a piece of bamboo. *– djari* knucklebone.

ruat loose (of teeth). **me–** to free from a spell.

ruba gift or present to the authorities.

rubah see UBAH.

rubrik 1 heading. 2 column.

rubu see RABA.

rubuh see ROBOH.

rubung to flow together in large quantities.

ruchsah release from responsibility to observe the fasting period.

rudin shabby.

rudjah me– to stab, poke at a fire.

rudjak a dish consisting of slices of unripe fruit with a sweet, pungent sauce made of palm sugar or fish paste. **me–** to make *rudjak*.

rudji 1 trelliswork. 2 spoke.

rudjuk reconciliation. **me–** to recall a divorced wife whose divorce is not final.

rudu 1 stooping, bowed with age. 2 drooping, hanging down.

rugi 1 loss. *– lima rupiah* a loss of 5 rupiahs. 2 disadvantage. *Ia merasa – datang disini*, He felt at a disadvantage coming here. 3 loss, harm, detriment. *– kamu tidak datang pd pésta*, It was your loss for not coming to the party. 4 injury. **be–** to suffer a loss. **ke–an** loss, harm, damage. **me–** to suffer a loss. **me–kan** 1 to damage, harm. *Perbuatan itu ~ kehormatan negara*, That action is damaging to the prestige of the state. 2 to inflict loss. *Perobahan harga itu ~ petani*, The change in price inflicts a loss upon the farmer. *tak mau ~* 1 not to want to lose. 2 not to want to spend money for nothing.

rugul see ROGOL.

ruh see ROH.

ruhani see ROHANI.

ruhban monk, friar.

ruhbanat nun, sister.

ruit bent, hook-shaped barb.

rujak see ROJAK.

ru'jat sighting of the new moon to fix the beginning of the fasting period.

rujung hardwood portion of a palm trunk.

rujup 1 heavy-eyed, sleepy. *Matanja –*, His eyes are becoming heavy. 2 setting. *Matahari –*, The sun is setting.

rukjat see RU'JAT.

ruku(k) bowing at Moslem prayer. **me–** to bow, prostrate.

rukun 1 in harmony. *Meréka hidup -,* They live in harmony. 2 pillar, foundation. *- iman* pillars of faith. **ke–an** harmony, concord. **me–kan** to appease, bring peace about. *- Islam* 5 pillars of Islam. *- kampung* 1 mutual assistance association in the kampong. 2 ward. *- sjarat* basic principle. *- tani* farmers' co-operative. *- tetangga* neighborhood association.

rum cream.

Rum Rome. *- Katolik* Roman Catholic.

rumah 1 house, dwelling. 2 building. **be–** 1 to dwell, live. *Ia ~ dikota itu,* He lives in that city. 2 married, *~ tangga* to have a family. **be– –²** to have a family. *Dgn gadji seketjil itu ia blm bisa ~,* With his salary as small as it is he hasn't been able to have a family. **mempe–kan** to marry off. *Kemarén ia ~ anak,* Yesterday he married off his son. **menje–kan** to cause (e.g., two wives) to live together in one house. **pe–an** housing. *~ ketam* crab shell. *~ milik bersama* 1 mutual home ownership. 2 communal housing. **pe–tanggaan** *désa* 1 rural economy. 2 rural household. *- api* lighthouse. *- batu* stone house. *- berhala* temple. *- beristirahat* resthouse. *- bidan* midwife clinic. *- bitjara* meetinghouse. *- bola* club (house). *- djadi* prefabricated house. *- djaga* guardhouse, sentry post. *- gadai* pawnshop. *- gadjah* the museum in Jakarta. *- gambar* exhibition hall. *- gandéngan* prefabricated Quonset-type hut. *- gedang* 1 large building, main building of a housing complex. 2 long house. *- gedang bersendi pérak* rich, noble family. *- gila* insane asylum. *- instansi* 1 government official's house. 2 building of business firm. *- jatim-piatu* orphanage. *- kantjing* buttonhole. *- kedai* small shop. *- kembar* duplex house. *- kéong* 1 shell of a land crab. 2 snail's shell. *- kit* opium den. *- kolong* pile house. *- komidi* theater, playhouse. *- kongsi* coolie house, house owned by a company. *- lélang* auction house. *- liar* squatter's house. *- loténg* a house with more than o. floor. *- madat* opium den. *- makan* restaurant. *- miskin* poorhouse. *- monjét* sentry box. *- obat* pharmacy. *- pandjang* brothel, whore house. *- panggung* grandstand. *- pangkas* barbershop. *- papak* flat-roofed house. *- pasung* police station. *- pedoman* housing for a compass. *- pelatjuran* brothel. *- pemalaman* tourist home, inn. *- penatu* laundry plant, laundry. *-*

penginapan rooming house, inn. *- peranginan* resthouse. *- perdéo* jail, prison. *- pétak* 1 tenement house. 2 row houses. 3 apartment. *- piatu* orphanage. *- potong* slaughterhouse. *- sakit* hospital. *- sakit bantu* clinic. *- sakit bersalin* maternity hospital. *- selérét* a long narrow house. *- séwa(an)* rented house. *- tangga* household. *- tinggal* dwelling. *- tumpangan* boardinghouse. *- turutan* a structure not part of main building.

Rumawi Roman.

rumbah leaves eaten with rice.

rumbai tuft, tassel. **be– –²** tasseled, fringed.

rumbing somewhat damaged.

Rumi see RUMAWI.

rumit 1 slow, unwilling to work. 2 hard, difficult. 3 complex. 4 complicated. **ke–an** 1 difficulty. 2 complication, annoyance. **me–kan** 1 to make hard to please. 2 to complicate, make difficult.

rumpang spaced. *Giginja tlh -,* His teeth have gaps between them.

rumpun stool. **be– –²** to grow, be in clusters. *Bambu tumbuh ~ dipinggir sungai,* Bamboo grows in clusters along the river's edge. **se–** 1 a stool. 2 of o. family, o. group, o. stock. *Betulkah manusia ~ dgn kera?* Is it true that men are of the same stock as apes? *- bahasa* a language family. *- bambu* bamboo cluster. *- pisang* bunch of bananas.

rumput grass. **me–** 1 to gather grass. 2 to weed. **me–i** to weed. **pe–an** 1 grassland, pasture. 2 lawn. **–an** weeds. *- air* swamp grass. *- benggala* pasture grass for cattle. *- kemaluan* sensitive plant. *- kering* hay. *embun diudjung -* impermanent, transitory.

rumus 1 abbreviation. 2 formula. **me–kan** 1 to abbreviate. 2 to formulate. **pe–an** 1 abbreviation. 2 formulation. **–an** formulation.

runding discussion. **be–** to confer, discuss. **me–** to weigh, consider. **me–kan, mempe–kan** to discuss, confer about. *Ia ~ rentjana baru,* He discussed a new plan. **pe–** negotiator. **pe–an** 1 conference, negotiation. 2 discussion. **–an** 1 discussion. 2 conference. *- -me-* to weigh, consider again and again.

rundjak **me–** to jump up to reach s.t.

rundjam **me–** to thrust, stab.

rundjang **me–** to feel around, poke, grope about. **pe–** crowbar.

rundjung conical. **be–,** **me–** conical(ly). **bentuknja ~** conically shaped.

runduk **me–** to stoop, bend, bow. *Ia ~ rendah,* He made a low bow.

rundung me– to afflict, dog, pester. *Ia di– malang,* He is dogged by bad luck.

rundu-randa to go about carrying all o's possessions.

runggas me– to pull out.

rungguh pledge, guarantee, security. me– to squat. me-kan to pledge, give as security.

rungkau me– to hang down, hang over. *Rambutnja ∼ mukanja,* Her hair was hanging down over her face.

rungkuh worn-out, decrepit, aged. ke-an dilapidated, decayed, worn-out. me– to be worn out, decayed, old.

rungkup folded up (a screen, etc.). me–(i) 1 to cover up. 2 to spread over. *Pohon jg rimbun ∼ rumahnja,* A shady tree covered his house.

rungrum me– to fondle, pet.

rungus pe– hothead, spitfire.

rungut me– to grumble, gripe.

runjam 1 difficult, complicated. *Itu pekerdjaan jg –,* That's a difficult job. 2 to fail. – *usahanja,* His efforts failed. me-kan 1 to make difficult. 2 to damage, cause to fail.

runtai me– to dangle, hang loosely. se– bunch, cluster. ∼ *anggur* a bunch of grapes.

runtas me– to pull with a jerk.

runtjing sharp, pointed. ke-an 1 emergency, urgency. 2 critical situation. me– 1 to become sharp. 2 to aggravate. 3 to become critical. *Keadaan itu ∼ ,* The situation has become critical. me-i to sharpen (a pencil, etc.). me-kan 1 to sharpen. *Ia ∼ potlot,* He sharpened the pencil. 2 to aggravate. *Kegagalan perundingan itu ∼ perhubungan,* The failure of the negotiations aggravated the relationship.

runtjit see RONTJÉT.

runtuh 1 to crash down, collapse. *Rumah tua tlh –,* The old house has collapsed. 2 to fall out. *Giginja –,* His teeth fell out. 3 destroyed. – *kekuasaannja,* His power is destroyed. ke-an 1 collapse, fall. 2 overthrow, fall. ∼ *batin* mental breakdown, collapse. me– 1 to collapse, crash down, come down. *Gedung tua itu ∼ ,* The old building collapsed. 2 to infiltrate. me-kan 1 to destroy, overthrow. 2 to destroy, ruin. *–kanlah bendéra itu!* Destroy the flag! pe– destroyer. -an ruins. – *ripuk* completely destroyed.

runtun be– –² o. after the other, in a row. me– 1 to drag, tug at, pull. *Ia ∼ tali kuda,* He tugged at the horse's reins. 2 to conquer. *Meréka hendak ∼ seluruh negeri Asia,* They intend to conquer all of Asia. me-kan to link, join together. -an 1 line, queue. 2 series, row.

runtut in harmony, harmonious.

runut trace. me–(i) 1 to trail, track, follow. *Ia ∼ pentjuri,* He trailed the thief. 2 to beg, importune. *Ia ∼ suaminja utk membeli mobil,* She begged her husband to buy a car. 3 to investigate.

rupa 1 form, shape, appearance. *Bagus –nja,* It looks nice. 2 sort, kind. be– 1 shaped, have the shape of. *Itu ∼ kambing,* It's shaped like a goat. 2 in the form of. *sumbangan ∼ uang dan barang* contributions in the form of money and goods. 3 handsome, pretty. *Randa itu muda dan ∼ ,* The widow is young and beautiful. 4 various, all kinds of. be– –² all sorts, all kinds. berse– to be exactly alike. *Ia ∼ dgn ajahnja,* He looks just like his father. kese-an uniformity. me– to appear, take the shape of. *asap ∼ singa* smoke in the shape of a lion. me-i to resemble. *Badannja besar ∼ badan pemain bola,* His large body resembles that of a football player. me-kan 1 to form, shape. *Itu ∼ sebagian besar dari pendapatannja,* This forms a large part of his income. 2 to form, re-fashion. *Ia ∼ tongkatnja ular naga,* He refashioned his cane into a dragon. 3 to constitute, form. *Seribu rupiah itu ∼ modalnja jg pertama,* The 1,000 rupiahs constitute his first capital. ∼ *diri* to appear in the form of, be reincarnated as. *Krisjna ∼ diri sebagai orang tua,* Krishna was reincarnated as an old man. menje– to appear as. *Dlm permainan itu ia ∼ pengemis,* In that play he appeared as a beggar. menje-i 1 to resemble. 2 to be as... as. *keras ∼ besi* to be as hard as iron. 3 to match, equal. *Sukar utk ∼ dia dlm keradjinannja,* It's hard to equal him in his industriousness. *Buatannja ∼ barang paberik,* His product equals that of manufactured goods. menje-kan 1 to make uniform. *Ia ∼ rentjana utk seluruh negeri,* He made the plan uniform for the whole country. 2 to place on a par, equate. *Karena baiknja ia ∼ temannja dgn malaikat,* Because of her kindness he placed his friend on a par with an angel. se– 1 similar, of o. kind. *modélnja ∼ of o.* model. *dua barang jg ∼* two things of the same type. *tjelana dan djas jg ∼* the trousers and jacket of the same type. 2 to be like. *Tingkah lakunja ∼ saudagar,* His attitude is like that of a merchant. 3 as if. ~ *dgn* to resemble. **te-** imagined. *Kalau blm melihat, barang itu tak ~ bagi saja,* Without seeing them, I can't imagine what those goods look like. **-nja** it seems, apparently. ~ *mau hudjan,* It looks like rain. **-²nja** probably, seemingly. **-²** various, diverse, all sorts. ~ *barang jg didjual,* Various kinds of articles are being sold. **-** *dan bentuk* appearance and form. **-** *muka* face, facial expression.

rupawan 1 handsome, good-looking. 2 pretty, attractive. **ke-an** beauty, handsomeness.

rupiah Indonesian monetary unit worth approximately 3 cents (1962). **me-kan** to use rupiahs, put on a rupiah basis.

rurut me- 1 to fall down. 2 to slip off. *Tjintjinnja ~* , Her ring slipped off. **-** *hati* touched, moved.

Rus Russian.

rusa deer.

rusak 1 damaged, broken. *Mobilnja -,* The car is out of order, has broken down. 2 depraved, broken down. *Moralnja -,* His morals are depraved. 3 tainted. **-** *namanja,* His name is tainted. **be-** *hati* 1 depressed. 2 to have a bad name. **ke-an** damage. *Gedung itu kena ~ besar,* The building was heavily damaged. **me-** 1 to damage, ruin, destroy. *Sebuah prahoto ~ mobilnja,* A truck damaged his car. 2 to harm, damage, spoil. *Itu ~ nama perusahaannja,* That harmed the good name of the firm. 3 damaging, destructive (criticism). **me-kan** 1 to damage, destroy. 2 to break s.t. ~ *hati* to spoil. **pe-** 1 disturber. ~ *keamanan* disturber of the peace.

2 destroyer. ~ *tanaman* destroyer of plants. **pe-an, peng-an** destruction, damage. **peng-** a destroyer, o. who destroys. **-** *hati* 1 depressed. 2 bad character.

Rusia Russia(n). **me-kan** to Russianize.

rusuh 1 unsafe, restless, disturbed. *Djalan ini masih -,* This road is still unsafe. 2 turbulent, unsettled. *Keadaan negeri -,* The situation in the country is unsettled. **be-** *hati* worried, upset. **ke-an** 1 disturbance, riot. 2 turbulence. ~ *hati* 1 worry, restlessness. 2 excitement. **me-** to incite, cause a disturbance. **me-i** to render unsafe. *Gerombolan itu selalu ~ daérah ini,* That gang is always making this area insecure. **me-kan** to cause a commotion. ~ *hati* to worry, be anxious. **pe-** rioter, rebel. **pe-an** riot, disturbance. **-** *hati* worried.

rusuk 1 side, flank. **-** *rumah* side of a house. 2 margin, side. **-** *surat* margin of a letter. **me-** 1 sideways. 2 on its side. 3 to approach from the side. **-** *badan* region of the ribs. **-** *djalan* side road.

rutine routine.

rutjah 1 common, of humble origin. 2 a mob.

rutuk me- to grumble.

RUU [*Rantjangan Undang²*] 1 draft of a law; draft legislation. 2 bill (in parliament).

ruwat see RUWET.

ruwet 1 complicated. 2 confused. 3 difficult. **be-** to be complicated. **ke-an** 1 complication. 2 confusion. **me-kan** to complicate, render difficult. **-** *-bundet* extremely complicated.

S

S. [*Sungai*] river.

sa'adat 1 bliss. 2 majesty. *Baginda* **-** His Majesty.

sa'at moment. *pd* **-** *itu* at that moment. **se-** a moment. **-** *itu djuga* at the same moment.

sabak 1 sulking, pouting. *Mukanja* **-**, He was sulking. 2 dull. *Matanja* **-**, His eyes were dull. **menj-** to wail, lament.

saban 1 each, every. **-** *hari* every day. 2 see SJA'BAN. **-²** 1 time and again, frequently. 2 whenever.

sabana plain with sparse vegetation.

sabar 1 patient. *Ia tak -,* He's impatient. **-lah,** Be patient. 2 tolerant. 3 patience. **ber-** patient, calm. **ke-an** 1 patience. 2 tolerance. **menj-kan** 1 to have patience with. 2 to calm, soothe. 3 to appease. **penj-** o. with a patient nature.

sabas 1 well done! 2 hear! hear!

sabat 1 Saturday. 2 Sabbath. **menj-i** to whip s.o.

sabda word(s) used when the speaker is referring to God, Mohammed, or an exalted personage. – *Baginda* His Majesty's words. **ber-** to speak. *Radja itu* ∼ , The king spake.

saben see SABAN.

sabit 1 sickle. 2 crescent. **menj-** to cut grass. **menj-kan** to affirm s.t.

sabot sabotage. **menj-** to sabotage.

sabotase sabotage.

Sabtu Saturday. – *malam* Saturday evening. *malam* – Friday evening.

sabuk 1 loincloth. 2 belt. 3 seat belt (plane).

sabun soap. **menj-** to lather. **menj-i** to lather s.t. *Ia* ∼ *mukanja,* He lathered his face. – *air* liquid soap. – *bubuk* soap powder. – *keringat buntet* soap for prickly heat. – *mandi* bath soap. – *tjutji* laundry soap.

sabung ber- 1 to fight. 2 to flash. *Kilat* ∼ , The lightning flashes. **menj-** to fight cocks. ∼ *njawa* to risk o's life. **menj-kan** to hammer away at s.o. **penj-** cockfighter. **per-an** 1 fight. 2 pit for cockfighting. **-an** cockfighting. – **-menj-** to fly at o. another.

sabur 1 dim, vague. 2 confused. **menj-** to disappear in the crowd. 2 to become confused. – *limbur* dim, confused.

sabut husk. – *kelapa* coconut fiber.

sadah betel lime.

sadai ber- to lie back with legs extended. **menj-kan** to beach a small boat.

sadak 1 betel lime. 2 slanting.

sadap menj- 1 to tap a tree. 2 to tap blood. **penj-** tapper. **penj-an** tapping.

sadar 1 conscious, aware. *Ia tak* – *akan soal ini,* He's not aware of this problem. 2 to come to a realization of o's evil ways (and repent). **ke-an** consciousness. **menj-i** to realize. *Jg harus kita –i ialah...* What we must bear in mind is... **menj-kan** to make s.o. realize. **penj-an** an awareness. – *akan dirinja* to regain o's consciousness. *bawah* – subconscious.

sadik honest, straightforward.

sadis sadist.

sadja 1 just, merely. *Ia masuk* –, He just came on in. *Ia bertanja* –, He just asked a question. 2 to continue. *Ia menangis* –, She was crying all the time. *Ia datang* –, He kept coming. *Ia bertanja* –, He kept on

asking questions. *Itu* –, That's all. *Sama* –, Just the same. (That's O.K.)

sadja' see SADJAK.

sadjadah prayer mat.

sadjak 1 poem, verse. 2 rhyme. **ber-** to rhyme, versify. **menj-kan** to write poetry. **penj-** poet. **per-an** poetry.

sadjarah see SEDJARAH.

sadji menj-kan 1 to serve, dish up. *Ia* ∼ *makanan jg énak,* She served delicious food. 2 to provide, supply, serve. *Mingguan itu* ∼ *tjerita²* péndék, The weekly provided short stories. *Ia* ∼ *soal² baru,* He put forward new problems. **penj-an** presentation. **-an** dish, course.

sado small 2-wheeled carriage.

sadur coating of metal. **menj-** to adapt. ∼ *emas* to gild. ∼ *pérak* to coat with silver. ∼ *tjeritera* to adapt a story. **-an** 1 adaptation. 2 metal coating.

Safar second month of the Moslem year.

sagang slanting pole used for support. **menj-** to use a pole as support or as defense.

sago sago. – *belanda,* – *betawi* arrowroot.

sagu see SAGO.

sah valid, legal. *Itu tidak* –, That's not legal. (That's invalid.) **menge-kan, mens-kan** 1 to legalize. 2 to authorize. 3 to ratify, confirm. **penge-an** 1 ratification, confirmation. 2 legalization. **pens-an** legalization.

sahabat friend. **ber-** *dgn* to be friends with. **memper-kan** to introduce s.o. *Ia* ∼ *Simin dgn Ali,* He introduced Simin to Ali. **per-an** friendship. – *kandung,* – *karib* a close, intimate friend. – *Nabi* disciples of Mohammed.

sahadat see SJAHADAT.

sahadja 1 see SADJA. 2 simple, natural. **ber-** 1 simple. *Penghidupannja* ∼ , His way of living was simple. 2 primitive. *suku jg* ∼ primitive tribe. **ke-an** simplicity. **memper-kan** 1 to do s.t. on purpose. *Itu diperkannja utk mendapat keuntungan,* He did it on purpose in order to get some benefit. 2 to simplify s.t. **per-an** simplification.

sahaja 1 see SAJA. 2 servant, domestic.

saham share on the market.

sahan large earthen plate.

sahang pepper.

sahap cover, lid. **ber-** covered. **menj-** to cover.

sahid see SJAHID.

sahifah document.
sahih valid.
sahkan 1 see USAHKAN. 2 see SAH.
sahur 1 postmidnight meal (before daytime fasting). 2 see SAUR. **ber-** to have the *saur.*
sahut menj-(i) to answer, reply. **penj-an** replying. **-an** reply.
sahwat see SJAHWAT.
Sailan Ceylon.
saing fang, tusk. **ber-** to compete. **ber-an** *dgn* to compete with. *Ia* ~ *dgn ajahnja,* He competed with his father. **menj-i** to compete with. *Ia* ~ *ajahnja,* He competed with his father. **penj-** competitor. **per-an** competition, rivalry. **-an** competitor, rival. **- -menj-** 1 to compete with e.o. 2 to bite e.o.
sa'ir, sair see SJAIR.
saja 1 I. - *mau pergi,* I want to go. 2 me. *Ia melihat -,* He saw me. 3 my. *Itu buku -,* That's my book. 4 Yes. *Apa saudara sopir? -,* Are you the driver? Yes, I am.
sajang 1 sorrow, pity. - *saja tak lihat dia,* I'm sorry I didn't see him. 2 love. *Ia sangat - kpd anaknja,* He loves his child very much. **ke-an** 1 pity, sorrow. 2 love, affection. 3 darling, favorite. **menj-i** 1 to pity. - *ilah saja ini,* Pity me. *-ilah binatang,* Be kind to animals. 2 to love, be attached to. **menj-kan** 1 to spare. *Semua bukunja dibakar; tak ada jg di-kan,* All his books were burned; nothing was spared. 2 to regret. *Kedjadian itu sangat di-kan,* The incident was deeply regretted. **penj-** charitable, merciful. **ter-** -² to be sorry. *Ia* ~ *membeli badju itu,* She was sorry she had bought the dress. - *akan* 1 to pity. 2 to love.
sajap wing. **ber-** winged. - *belakang* rear wing. - *ikan* fin of a fish. - *kiri* left wing. - *roda* 1 mudguard. 2 fender.
sajat menj- to slice. ~ *hati* heartbreaking. *Tjerita itu* ~ *hati,* The story was heartbreaking. **menj-i** 1 to cut, carve. 2 to notch. **-an** 1 slice. 2 slicing.
sajembara prize contest.
saju 1 sad, downcast. *Hatinja -,* She was downcast. 2 dull. *Matanja -,* Her eyes were dull. **ke-an** sadness, melancholy, wistfulness. **menj-kan** to touch, move s.o. - *-raju* sad, wistful.
sajup² 1 blurred, indistinct. 2 scarcely, hardly. 3 faintly heard. - *mata* as far as the eye can see. - *sampai* barely. *Bunji musik kedengaran - sampai,* A vague sound of music was heard from afar. *Tangannja - sampai*

pd buku itu, He almost reached the book with his hand.
sajur 1 vegetable. 2 a vegetable soup. **menj-** to prepare a k.o. vegetable soup. -²**an,** - -*majur* all k.o. vegetables. - *asinan* spiced raw vegetable salad. - *lodéh* vegetable soup in coconut milk.
sak 1 sack, bag. 2 pocket.
saka baka 1 tradition. 2 heirlooms.
sakal menj- 1 to strike against. 2 to torture.
sakar sugar. - *emping* maltose.
sakarat ulmaut death agony.
sakat menj-kan 1 to tease, annoy. *Ia selalu* ~ *dia,* He's always teasing her. 2 to beach a boat. **ter-** stranded. *Kapal itu* ~ , The ship was stranded.
sakedidi see SIKUDIDI.
saking on account of. *Ia tak dpt melihat apa² - gelapnja,* He couldn't see anything on account of the darkness.
sakit 1 ill, sick. *Dia djatuh -,* He fell ill. 2 sore, painful. - *apa?* What hurts you? (What's wrong?) *Apa jg -?, Mana jg -?* Where does it hurt? 3 a sick person. *si- -* the patient. **ber-** -² 1 to ail, be sickly. 2 to bend every effort. **berpenj-** to suffer from a disease. *Ia* ~ *malaria,* He was suffering from malaria. **ke-an** 1 to be ill. *Ia* ~ , He was ill. 2 illness. 3 suffering, pain, trouble. ~ *hidupnja tak terkatakan,* His sufferings beggar description. **menj-** to cause, bring about pain. **menj-i** 1 to hurt. *Ia* ~ *hatinja,* She hurt his feelings. 2 to be in labor. **menj-kan** to hurt. *Perkataannja itu* ~ , His words hurt. **pe-an** 1 prisoner. 2 sickly. **penj-** 1 disease. 2 illness. 3 abuse. ~ *ajan* epilepsy. ~ *andjing gila* rabies. ~ *bengék* asthma. ~ *berdjangkit* an epidemic disease. ~ *dalam* internal disease. ~ *gelembung* glandular disturbance. ~ *gula* diabetes. ~ *ho* malnutrition. ~ *karang* kidney stones. ~ *kegatalan* itching disease. ~ *kelamin* venereal disease. ~ *kelingsir* rupture of the scrotum. ~ *(kentjing) manis* diabetes. ~ *kotor* venereal disease. ~ *léna* sleeping sickness. ~ *lumpuh anak²* poliomyelitis. ~ *mengi* bronchial asthma. ~ *menular* contagious disease. ~ *ngelu* headache. ~ *paru²* tuberculosis. ~ *pinggang* nephritis. ~ *rabu* consumption. ~ *radja singa* syphilis. ~ *sabun* gonorrhea. ~ *saraf* nervous disorder. ~ *tampak* measles. **-an** 1 prisoner. 2 criminal. - *abuh* dropsy. - *akal,* - *angan²* insane. *Ia - akal,* He's insane. - *beranak* labor

pains. – *dada* tuberculosis. – *darah tinggi* suffering from high blood pressure. – *datang bulan* monthly menstrual period. – *gadjah²an* elephantiasis. – *gambur²* dropsy. – *gigi* toothache. – *hati* annoyed, irritated by s.o. or s.t. – *ingatan* insane, crazy. – *kepala* headache. – *keputihan* leucorrhea. – *keras* seriously ill. – *kermi* to have worms. – *kuku* foot-and-mouth disease. – *kuning* jaundice. – *mangga* swelling in the groin. – *menjebar* diffuse pain. – *meriang* feverish, unwell. – *napas* asthmatic. – *panas* 1 fever. 2 feverish. – *parah* seriously ill. – *perut* 1 stomach-ache. 2 colic. – *pinggang* kidney ailment. – *radang* inflammation. – *senéwen* 1 shell shock. 2 nervous disease. – *tampak*, – *tampek* measles. – *tjéléng* epilepsy. – *tudjuk keleling* to have dizzy spells.

saklar electric switch.

sakramén sacrament.

sakrat see SAKARAT.

saksama 1 accurate, exact. 2 conscientious. *Perkara itu diperiksa dgn* –, The case was conscientiously investigated. 3 patient, unhurried. **ke–an** accuracy, precision.

saksi 1 witness. 2 testimony. **ber–kpd** to summon o. to testify. **ke–an** testimony, evidence. **memper–kan, menj–kan** 1 to testify. 2 to witness. **penj–** *mata* eyewitness. **penj–an, per–an** evidence, testimony. – *ahli* expert witness. – *utama* principal witness.

sakti 1 with supernatural power. *Ia tak dpt luka karena –nja*, He was invulnerable because of some supernatural power of his. 2 sacred. *Keris itu adalah – bagi meréka*, The dagger was sacred to them. 3 with magic power. *Kabarnja rumah itu adalah rumah –*, They say that house has magical powers. **ke–an** supernatural power.

saku 1 bag, sack. 2 pocket. – *kerdja* workbag, brief case.

salah 1 fault. – *siapa?* Whose fault was it? 2 mistake. *Itu adalah suatu – besar*, It was a big mistake. 3 wrong. *Terdjemahan itu –*, The translation is wrong. 4 guilty. *Guru menghukum jg –*, The teacher punished the guilty one. 5 to fail. *Saja – faham*, I misunderstood. *Saja – kata*, I misspoke. 6 to be in the wrong. **ber–** 1 to be wrong. 2 to be guilty. **ber–an** 1 controversial. 2 to be at variance. ~ *paham* to have a misunderstanding. **ber– –²an** to be in conflict with e.o. **ke–an** 1 mistake, error, blunder. 2 fault. 3 accidentally. 4 to be mis-

taken. 5 to be charged with. **kefahaman** misunderstanding. **menj–gunakan, mens–gunakan** to abuse, misuse. **menj–mengertikan** to misunderstand. **menj–i** 1 to conflict with. *Itu* ~ *pendirian saja*, It was incompatible with my opinion. 2 to violate. *Itu* ~ *hukum*, That violated the law. 3 to put s.o. in the wrong. *Ia* ~ *saja*, He put me in the wrong. ~ *padan* to break o's word. **menj–kan** 1 to accuse. *Kedua negeri itu saling* ~ *sebagai negara pengandjur perang*, The two countries accused e.o. of being warmongers. 2 to deny. *Tuduhan² itu di–kan*, The accusations were denied. 3 to frustrate s.t. *Serangan itu di–kan*, The attack was frustrated. **penj–gunaan** abuse, misuse. ~ *bendéra* misuse of flag. **ter–** accidentally wrong, mistaken. –² or else, lest. *Djangan gemetar,* ~ *engkau dianggap ber– nanti*, Don't be nervous or they'll think you are guilty. – *adat* abuse, misuse. – *ambilan* to misunderstand. *Ia – ambilan dari pertjakapan saja itu*, He misunderstood from my discussion. – *angkuh* 1 indecent. 2 improper. – *arti* to misunderstand. – *bebal* mistake. – *bentuk* deformed, misshapen. – *dengar* to mishear, misunderstand. – *djalan* 1 to lose o's way. 2 to walk on the wrong side of the road. – *duga* to miscalculate. – *édjaan* misspelling. – *gunakan* to misuse s.t. – *hati* peevish, snappish. – *langkah* 1 violation, misstep. 2 misstep. – *lihat* wrong view. – *raba* to be mistaken, bark up the wrong tree. – *satu* o., s.t. or other. *Ambillah – satu*, Take o. – *semat* misunderstanding. – *seorang* s.o., o. – *seorang dari meréka berdusta*, O. of them was lying. – *silih* all sorts of mistakes. – *terima* to misunderstand. – *tjerna* indigestion. – *tjétak* typographical error. – *urat* sprained. *Apa –nja?* What's wrong with that? (So what?) *Tak ada –nja*, There's no harm in it. *tak – lagi* no doubt about it. *Tak – lagi dialah jg ber–*, There's no doubt he's the guilty o.

salai roasted. *ikan –* roasted fish. **menj–** 1 to roast. 2 to dry by fire. **–an** grill, grate.

salak a fruit. **menj–** to bark, bay. *Andjing itu* ~ , The dog barked. **menj–i** to bark at.

salam 1 peace. 2 greetings. –, *bung!* Hello! *Ia mengirim – kepadamu*, He sends you his regards. *Ia memberi –*, He gives you his regards. **ber– –²an** to exchange greetings. – *dan takzim saja* Sincerely yours. – *hangat* Warm

regards. – *taklim,* – *takzim* deep respect. *berdjabat* – to shake hands in greetings.
salap ointment, salve.
salasilah genealogy.
salat five obligatory daily prayers. **ber–** to perform the 5 daily prayers. – *magrib* sunset prayer. – *subuh* (early) morning prayer (5 A.M.).
saldju snow. **ber–** snowy.
saldo balance. – *laba* credit balance.
saléh pious, virtuous. **ke–an** piety.
salep see SALAP.
salib cross. **menj–(kan)** to crucify. **penj–an** crucifixion.
salin ber– 1 to change clothes. 2 to bear a child. **ber– –²** changing, whimsical. *Kelakuannja* ~ *sadja,* His action was whimsical. **memper–kan** to give a suit of clothes as a present. **menj–** 1 to change s.t. –*lah pakaianmu itu,* Change your clothes. 2 to copy. *Ia* ~ *surat perdjandjian itu,* He copied the contract. 3 to translate. *Ia* ~ *buku itu,* He translated the book. **penj–** 1 copyist. 2 translator. **penj–an** translating. **per–an** 1 change of clothes. 2 confinement, childbirth. ~ *peresat* Caesarean birth. 3 gift of clothes. ~ *rupa* metamorphosis. **–an** 1 copy. 2 translation.
saling o. another, e.o. *Meréka* – *menolong,* They helped e.o.
salla'llahu'alaihi wassallam(a) (*s.a.-w.*) May the Lord bless him (Mohammed) and give him peace.
salp see SALAP.
saluir salute. **ber–** to salute, greet.
salung flute.
salur menj–kan to channel, lead into. **penj–** distributor. **penj–an** distribution. **–an** 1 channel(s). ~ *diplomatik* diplomatic channels. 2 line (switchboard). 3 gutter. ~ *air* waterworks, canal. ~ *empedu* gall duct.
salut 1 cover. 2 envelope. 3 wrapping. 4 mounting (of firearms). **ber–** 1 covered. 2 mounted, plated. **menj–** 1 to cover, wrap. 2 to mount. – *surat* envelope.
sama 1 same. *Umur meréka* –, They are the same age. 2 with. *Ia pergi* – *ajahnja,* He went with his father. 3 and, together with. *Ia* – *ibunja pergi bésok,* He and his mother are going tomorrow. 4 from. *Ini lain* – *itu,* This o. is different from that o. 5 used with an object (in English). *Tanja* – *dia,* Ask him. **ber–** 1 together. *Meréka datang* ~ , They came together. 2 all together. *Ini utk kita* ~ , This is for all of us. 3 joint. *Sékertariat* ~ Joint Secretariat. ~ *dgn* with, together. ~ *dgn surat ini*

saja mengirimkan potrét saja, With this letter I enclose my picture. ~ *ini* herewith. ~ *ini saja menerangkan bhw...* I herewith declare that... **ber–** –² together. *Kita pergi* ~ , We'll go together. **ber–an** 1 coinciding. ~ *dgn pendaratan itu pihak penjerang membomi ibu negeri musuh,* Coinciding with the landing, the attackers bombed the enemy's capital. 2 to be the equal. *Tenaga militér A* ~ *dgn tenaga militér B,* The military force of A is the equal of that of B. 3 to conform. *Hal itu* ~ *fasal 30 anggaran dasar,* That is in conformity with Article 30 of the statutes. **ke–an** 1 equality. 2 similarity. ~ *perangai meréka berdua tersebut di-mana²,* The similarity of their behavior was noted everywhere. ~ *deradjat* equality. **memper–kan** 1 to place on a par with. 2 to compare with. **memper– –²kan** 1 to mistake o. for s.o. else. 2 to imagine s.t. as. **menj–i** to match, equal. *Keméwahan itu tak dpt di–i,* That luxury can't be matched. **menj–kan** 1 to compare s.t. with. *Djangan kau–kan halmu itu dgn hal saja,* Don't compare your case with mine. 2 to place on a par with. *Gadjinja di–kan dgn gadji menteri,* His salary was placed on a par with that of a minister. ~ *hak* to have the same rights. *Orang² Belanda jg mendjadi warganegara di–kan haknja dgn orang Indonésia,* Dutchmen who became Indonesian citizens were given the same rights as Indonesians. **me–nj–²** to behave like. *Ia* ~ *bintang pilem,* She behaved like a film star. **menj– –²kan** to compare with. *Keadaan disana djangan di– –²kan dgn keadaan disini,* The situation there shouldn't be compared with the o. here. **menj–ratakan** 1 to generalize. 2 to treat alike. 3 to level (a building, etc.). **penj–rataan** generalization. **per–an** 1 similarity. ~ *antara kedua bahasa itu masih diselidiki,* The similarity between the 2 languages is still being investigated. 2 comparison. 3 unanimity. 4 equality. **se–** *hidup,* ~ *manusia* fellow man. –² 1 together. *Meréka* ~ *pergi,* They went together. 2 all. *Meréka* ~ *bekerdja,* All of them were working. 3 you're welcome. – *dgn* is, are the same as. *Lima tambah lima* – *dgn sepuluh,* 5 and 5 are 10. – *djuga* it's all the same. – *kaki* isosceles. – *kuat* a tie, draw. *Pertandingan itu tlh berachir dgn* – *kuat,* The contest ended in a tie. – *kupuan* equal. – *pusat* homocentric. – *rata* even (of temperature). – *sadja* it's all

the same. - *sekali* 1 entirely. *Itu -
sekali benar*, It's completely true. 2
quite. - *sendirinja* 1 each other.
Meréka tuduh-menuduh - sendirinja,
They accused e.o. 2 to o.s. *Ia berkata
- sendirinja*, He was talking to himself. - *setentang* flush with s.t. - *sisi*
equilateral. - *tengah* 1 precisely in
the middle. 2 impartial, neutral.
Dlm perkara itu kami berdiri - tengah,
In that affair we're impartial. *di-
rendahkan* to treat all alike conde-
scendingly. - *rasa - rata* equality
and fraternity. *diantara kita - kita*
between ourselves, confidentially, *entre
nous*.
samadi meditation. **ber-** to meditate.
samak tannin. **menj-** to tan s.t.
penj- tanner. **penj-an** *kulit* tannery.
samar 1 dim, vague, indistinct. 2
obscure, hidden. 3 disguised, masked.
ke-an 1 dusk. 2 obscureness. 3 confusion. **menj-** 1 to be in disguise.
Ia ~ sebagai pradjurit, He was
disguised as a soldier. 2 to be incognito. *Radja itu pergi ~* , The
king went incognito. **menj-kan** 1
to conceal, hide s.t. *Ia ~ dirinja
diantara orang ramai itu*, He hid
himself in the crowd. *Ia ~ maksudnja*, He concealed his purpose. 2 to
camouflage. **-an** disguise. - *muka*
twilight.
samarata see SAMA.
sambal 1 hot pepper sauce. 2 spicy
condiment. **menj-** to prepare a
spicy dish. **-²an** various spicy side
dishes. - *ulek* crushed red pepper.
sambang 1 watch, guard, patrol. 2
plague. 3 empty honeycomb. **ber-**
1 to keep watch. 2 to make o's
rounds. **menj-i** to patrol.
sambar **menj-** 1 to swoop down and
seize. *Burung elang itu ~ anak
ajam*, The hawk swooped down and
seized the baby chick. 2 to strike,
hit. *Pohon itu di- halilintar*, The
tree was struck by lightning. *Anaknja
di- mobil*, The child was struck by a
car. 3 to seize. *Pisaunja di-lawannja*,
The knife was seized by his opponent.
4 to attack. *Tiba² ia di- dgn pisau*,
He was suddenly attacked with a
knife. *Rumah itu di- api*, The house
caught on fire.
sambat **ber-** to ask for help. *~
dgn* connected with, joined with.
menj- 1 to ask for help. 2 to join
s.t. *Ia ~ kedua potong tali itu*, He
joined the 2 pieces of rope. **-an** 1
request for help. 2 assistant.
sambel see SAMBAL.
sambén 1 subsidiary, branch. 2 side-
line. 3 side issue.

samber see SAMBAR.
sambil 1 while. *Ia menjanji - bermain
piano*, She sang while playing the
piano. 2 at the same time. *Ia tertawa
- menangis*, She laughed and cried
at the same time. **menj-kan** 1 to do
s.t. as a side line. *Waktu ia bepergian
keluar negeri ia ~ berdagang*, When
he was traveling abroad, he did some
business as a side line. 2 to do s.t.
at the same time. **menj- -lalukan** to
consider s.t. as of secondary importance. *Pendidikan anak dirumah
tak boléh di-lalukan*, The upbringing
of a child at home shouldn't be
regarded as of secondary importance.
ter- incidental. *pendapat ~ an*
incidental remark. *Baginja uang
adalah soal ~ sadja*, Money is no
object for him. **-an** 1 side line. 2
branch, annex. 3 pretext. - *lalu* inci-
dental(ly), in passing. *Kedatangannja
itu hanja - lalu sadja*, His coming
was only incidental. *Djika ada
disebut, maka hanjalah - lalu*, If it
was mentioned, it was only in passing. *Sambil menjelam minum air*,
Those that have get.
sambit **menj-** to throw. *Ia ~ batu*,
He threw a stone.
sambuk a whip. **menj-** to whip.
sambung **ber-** 1 continued, prolonged. 2 connected. *~ kembali* to
knit (of bones). *~ tangan* to obtain
assistance. **ber- -²** successively, in a
row. **menj-** 1 to continue. *Tjeritera
itu akan di-*, The story will be continued. 2 to connect, join. *Ia ~ tali
itu*, He connected the ropes. - *saja
dgn Penerangan*, Connect me with
Information. 3 to reply to. *~ surat
tuan jg terachir* in reply to your last
letter. *~ hidup* to keep alive. *~
silaturrahim* to strengthen a friendship. **penj-** connector, link. *~ lidah*
conveyor of a message. *~ njawa*
means of livelihood. **-an** 1 continuation, extension. 2 connection. *~
tangan* helper. *~ terachir* final installment. *Tidak* **ter-** *lagi*, The
phone is disconnected. - *tangan* help,
aid.
sambut **ber-** 1 answered. 2 parried,
intercepted. *~ pd* to fulfill requirements. **ber-an** 1 to be in accordance.
Hal itu ~ dgn apa jg dikatakannja,
It was in accordance with what he
said. 2 to take turns answering.
*Dlm soal djawab itu meréka ~ terus-
menerus*, During the debate they
took turns answering. **ber- -²an** 1
to answer e.o. *Meriam kedua belah
pihak ~* , The guns of both sides
were answering e.o. 2 continually,

incessantly. *Letusan bom kedengaran* ~ , Bomb explosions were heard continually. **menj-** 1 to welcome, receive. *Orang banjak* ~ *kedatangan présidén*, The crowd welcomed the president's arrival. 2 to accept. *Usul²* *perdamaian itu di- dgn gembira*, The peace terms were gladly accepted. 3 to parry. *Ia* ~ *tuduhan² jg dilémparkan kpd kepalanja*, He parried the accusations tossed at his head. 4 on the occasion of. ~ *ulang tahun kemerdékaan jg ke-10* on the occasion of the tenth anniversary of independence. **penj-an** reception, welcoming. **-an** 1 welcome, reception. ~ *meluap* enthusiastic reception. 2 answer. 3 agreement. 4 approval.

samin see MINJAK.

samirana breeze.

samiri Samaritan.

sampah rubbish, trash. **per-an** 1 trash heap. 2 trash can. - *masjarakat* scum of society. - *sarap* trash, refuse.

sampai 1 to, till. *Ia dpt menghitung dari satu - sepuluh*, He can count from 1 to 10. 2 till, until. *Ia bekerdja - larut malam*, He works till late at night. 3 as far as, to. *Ia berdjalan - Bogor*, He walked as far as Bogor. 4 to arrive. *Kami - pukul 6 pagi*, We arrived at 6 A.M. 5 to reach. *Saja tak dpt - pd langit² kamar itu*, I couldn't reach the ceiling of the room. 6 to succeed. *Maksudnja - djuga*, He succeeded in reaching his goal. *Angan²nja - djuga*, Her dreams came true. 7 to be sufficient, reach. *Pendapatannja tak -*, His earnings are insufficient. 8 up to, until. - *sekarang* up to now. 9 should, go so far as to. *Kalau PSSI - kalah, susah djuga*, If PSSI should lose, that would be pretty bad. **ke-an** achieved, accomplished. *Maksudnja* ~ , He achieved his goal. **menj-** to hang up to dry. **menj-kan** 1 to give, convey, extend. *Akan saja -kan salammu itu*, I'll give him your regards. 2 to hand over. *Ia* ~ *seputjuk surat*, He handed over a letter. 3 to achieve. *Ia* ~ *maksudnja*, He achieved his purpose. 4 to put on. *Ia* ~ *seléndangnja*, She put on her scarf. 5 to carry on a pole. 6 to deliver. *Djika tidak dpt di-kan...* If it cannot be delivered... ~ *wedjangan* to deliver an address. **penj-an** receipt, receiving. ~ *surat² kabar* receipt of newspapers. **-an** 1 rack, hatrack. 2 drying frame. **-kan** until. *Ia menjimpan rahasia itu* ~ *matinja*, He kept the secret until his death. **-²** 1 so ... that. *Ia asjik berdjudi* ~ *ia lupa akan anaknja*,

He was so busy gambling that he forgot about his child. 2 even. ~ *badju anaknja disita*, Even his child's clothes were confiscated. - **-menj-** to make ends meet. *Gadjinja tiada* ~ , He couldn't make ends meet. - *dgn* up to and including. - *dgn 15 Maret* up to and including March 15. - *djangka* exact, quite right. - *hati* to have the heart to. *Ia tak - hati memukul anaknja*, He didn't have the heart to whip his child. - *kpd* to reach. *Kabar itu sdh - kpd orang tuanja*, The news had already reached her parents. *djangan - lest. Beladjarlah baik² djangan - kalah dlm udjian nanti*, Study hard lest you fail your exams. - *ketemu lagi*, I'll be seeing you. (So long.) - *sana sadja dulu*, That's far enough now. - *umur* to come of age. *Bagaimana kau - dipukul?* How did you happen to get hit?

sampaikan see SAMPAI.

sampak metal band around knife handle.

sampan small boat, dugout. **ber-** to go by dugout. **ber- -²** to go by dugout for pleasure. - *tunda* towed sampan.

sampang brown varnish. **menj-** to paddle at the stern of a boat. **ter-** to be hanging out.

sampanje champagne.

sampar plague, pest.

samper menj-i 1 to call on s.o. 2 to meet s.o.

samping 1 side. *Ia duduk di- saja*, She sat beside me. 2 sarong. **ber-an** side by side. *Meréka berdjalan* ~ , They walked side by side. **di-** *itu* besides. ~ *itu ia malu*, Besides, he was bashful. **ke-** to the side. **menge-kan** 1 to put aside. *Ia* ~ *perkara itu*, He put the case aside. 2 to ignore. *Ia* ~ *perasaan isterinja*, He ignored his wife's feelings. **menj-i** 1 to put beside, next to. 2 to sit next to. **menj-kan** 1 to put, lay aside. *Ia* ~ *beberapa rupiah sebulan*, He put a few rupiahs aside monthly. 2 to place side by side. *Ia* ~ *kedua anak itu*, He placed the 2 children side by side. 3 to bypass s.t. *Ia* ~ *keinginan rakjat*, He bypassed the will of the people. **ter-** ignored. *Di-mana² ia* ~ *sadja*, He was ignored everywhere.

sampir menj-kan to hang. *Ia* ~ *djasnja pd korsi*, He hung his coat over a chair. **-an** 1 clothes rack. 2 clothes peg, hook. 3 first two lines of a pantun.

sampu 1 anemia. 2 shampoo. – *pening* epilepsy.

sampuk menj– to run into s.o., fly at.

sampul 1 cover, wrapper. 2 book wrapper, dust jacket. ber– covered, wrapped, placed in an envelope. menj–i to wrap, place in an envelope. – *bantal* pillowcase. – *buku* book cover. – *hari pertama* first-day cover. – *luar* outside cover. – *peringatan* commemorative cover. – *rokok* cigarette wrapper. – *surat* envelope.

sampur sash.

samséng gamecock, fighter.

samudera ocean.

samun bushes, shrubs. ke–an robbed. *Ia ∼ kemarin malam*, He was robbed last night. menj– to rob. menj–i to rob s.o. penj– robber. (penj)–an robbery. – *sakal* robbery accompanied by violence.

san form of address for SÉRSAN sergeant.

sana there. *Ia pergi ke–*, He went there. *Ia sedang duduk di–*, He's sitting there. *di– -sini* here and there, everywhere. dike–kan to be brought there. *Meréka sdh ∼* , They had been brought there. ke– -*kemari* to and fro, back and forth. menge–kan to expel s.o. *tidak ke– tidak kesini* impartial, neutral.

sanak relative. ber– -*saudara* to have relatives. – *saudara* relatives.

sanat Moslem year. – *Maséhi* A.D.

sandal sandal, open-toe slipper.

sandang 1 shoulder strap. 2 clothing. memper–kan to carry over o's shoulders. menj–(kan) to strap on. *Ia ∼ senapannja*, He strapped on his gun. penj– shoulder strap. – *pangan* basic necessities.

sandar ber– *pd* 1 to lean on. *Ia ∼ pd dinding*, He leaned against the wall. 2 to be dependent on. *Ia ∼ pd pendapatan isterinja*, He is dependent on his wife's income. ber–(kan) (*atas*) to be based on. *Hal itu ∼ téori lama*, That's based on an old theory. memper–i to lean on s.t. menj–i 1 to support s.o. *Orang tua itu di–i oléh anaknja kalau berdjalan*, The old man was supported by his son when he went walking. 2 to lean against. *Djangan kau–i pintu jg baru ditjat itu*, Don't lean against the newly painted door. menj–kan to rely on, trust. *Ia ∼ nasibnja pd keadilan hakim*, He entrusted his fate to the justice of the judge. –an 1 support, assistance. 2 rest, prop, back. – -menj– to depend on o. another. *Kedua negeri itu ∼* , The 2 countries were dependent on e.o.

sandel see SANDAL.

sandera 1 hostage. 2 o. who gives his service as security for a debt. 3 service. menj– to serve as hostage. penj–an service, care. ∼ *sosial* social service. – *tari* ballet.

sandi code. menj– to encode. ∼ *balik* to decode.

sandinama initial(s).

sanding 1 close, near. 2 a sharp angle. ber– 1 to sit in state on the *pelaminan* as bride and groom. 2 angular. 3 sharp, biting. *Perkataannja ∼* , Her words were sharp. memper–kan, menj–kan to place near e.o. (as bride and groom).

sandiwara 1 play. 2 theatrical troupe. 3 drama. ber– 1 to be on the stage. *Tiap malam ia ∼* , Every evening she was on the stage. 2 to pretend. *Ia biasanja ∼ sadja*, She usually just pretends. menj–kan 1 to dramatize. 2 to adapt for the stage. – *sedih* tragedy.

sandjai tall and handsome.

sandjak see SADJAK.

sandjung menj–(kan) 1 to flatter. 2 to appease, cater to. –an flattery.

sandra penj–an *sosial* social service. see SANDERA.

sandratari see SENDRATARI.

sandung pedal of weaving loom. ke– to stumble over. ter– to trip over, stumble. *Kakinja ∼ pd batu*, He stumbled over a stone.

sanéring reorganization (of fiscal situation) by halving banknotes.

sang (honorific epithet). – *atas* superiors. – *Mérah Putih* the Red and White (Indonesian flag).

sanga 1 dross (in smelting). 2 nine. *wali* – the nine saints. ter- $-^2$ nervous and in a hurry.

sangai lid, cover, top. ber– to warm o.s. menj– to warm s.t.

sangar ill-fated, brings misfortune.

sangat 1 very, extremely. *Ia – kaja*, He was very rich. *Ia – sakit*, He was critically ill. 2 burning. *soal²* – burning questions. ke–an excessive, extreme. *Hampir saja lupa karena ∼ gembira*, I almost forgot because of my excessive enthusiasm. memper– to intensify. *Itu ∼ perselisihan*, That intensified the quarrel. ter– excessive, extreme.

sangga prop, support. menj– to support. penj– support. – *bunuh* charm against death in battle. – *mara* 1 crossbar. 2 gaff (sailing vessel).

sanggah small Balinese temple. menj–1 to protest, oppose. 2 to contradict. *Ia ∼ kebenaran berita itu*, He contradicted the truth of the report.

penj– 1 opponent. 2 discussant. **–an** protest, rejoinder.

sanggama coitus. **ber–** to have coitus.

sanggamara wall or fortress to protect the cannons.

sanggar 1 small house temple. 2 atelier, studio.

sanggat to run aground.

sanggerah bloodletting. **menj–** to bleed s.o. **pe–an** rest house.

sanggit **menj–** *gigi* to gnash o's teeth.

sanggul knot of hair. **ber–** to wear o's hair in a knot. **menj–(kan)** to put o's hair up in a knot.

sanggup 1 willing. *Ia tidak – menanggung djawab,* He wasn't willing to take the responsibility. 2 able, capable. *Polisi tak – mengamankan pemberontakan itu,* The police were unable to pacify the uprising. **ke–an** 1 power, capability. *Djangan chawatir akan ∼ tentara kita,* Don't doubt the power of our forces. 2 willingness. 3 ingenuity. **–an** promise. *∼ Belanda utk merundingkan kedudukan Irian Barat diterima dgn gembira,* The promise of the Dutch to discuss the West New Guinea situation was enthusiastically received. **menj–kan** 1 to enable. *Undang[2] itu ∼ Indonésia keluar dari persekutuan itu,* The decree enabled Indonesia to break with the union. 2 to promise. *Ia ∼ utk memberi Rp. 1000,* He promised to contribute 1,000 rupiahs.

sanggurdi stirrup.

sangjang a god, deity. *– Wisjnu* the god Vishnu.

sangka 1 opinion, idea. *pd – saja* in my opinion. 2 suspicion. *– itu hendaklah dihilangkan,* That suspicion should be abandoned. **ber–** to mean, think. *Ia tiada ∼ demikian,* He didn't mean that. **menj–** 1 to think, suppose. *Saja ∼ bhw engkau tak akan datang,* I thought you wouldn't come. 2 to suspect. *Ia di– turut dlm pemberontakan itu,* He was suspected of taking part in the rebellion. **me–nj–[2]** to suppose, expect. **menj–kan** to take s.o. for, consider. *Ia di–kan orang Pilipina,* He was taken for a Filipino. **per–an, –[2]** suspicion. **ter–** 1 suspected. *Ia ∼ mentjuri,* He was suspected of stealing. 2 expected. *tak ∼* unexpected(ly). *Tak ∼ kau ada disini,* I didn't expect to see you here. *tak di– –[2]* unexpected(ly).

sangkak 1 forked, fork-shaped. 2 branch. *– kaju* tree branch. 3 nest. *– ajam* hen's nest. **menj–** 1 to be angry. *Hatinja ∼ ,* He was angry. *Ajamnja ∼ bulunja,* The chicken ruffled its feathers with anger. 2 to have goose flesh. *Bulu saja ∼ karenanja,* It made my flesh creep. **menj–i** to prevent, stop.

sangkal hammer handle. **ber–** *akan* to be unwilling. *Ia ∼ akan djandjinja,* He was unwilling to keep his promise. **menj–** 1 to deny. *Ia ∼ berita itu,* He denied the report. 2 to reject. *Ia ∼ permohonan itu,* He rejected the request. **penj–** *Allah* atheist. **penj–an** 1 contradiction. 2 denial, refusal. **–an** denial. *tak dpt di–* undeniable, there's no denying.

sangkar 1 bird cage. 2 chicken coop. 3 diagonal. **menj–kan** to cage s.t. **–an** = SANGKAR.

sangkin see MAKIN.

sangkur see MATA.

sangkut **ber– –***paut dgn* closely joined, merged with. **ber–an** to be concerned with, involved with or in. *Meréka jg ∼ dgn pemberontakan itu ditahan,* Those involved in the rebellion were arrested. *Kpd jg ∼,* To whom it may concern. **ke–** 1 to stumble over s.t. or s.o. *Kakinja ∼ batu,* His feet stumbled over a stone. 2 involved in, dragged into s.t. *Ia ∼ djuga,* He too was involved. 3 to be caught on, stuck, attached to. *Lajang[2]nja ∼ didahan kaju,* The kite was caught on a tree branch. **menj–** to relate to. *Soal ini ∼ soal itu,* This problem relates to that one. **menj–kan** 1 to hang, hook. *Ia ∼ badjunja pd –an,* He hung his coat on a peg. 2 to involve s.o. in s.t. *Ia ∼ saja dlm pembunuhan itu,* He involved me in the murder. **per–an** 1 context, connection. 2 relation. **ter–** involved. *Ia ∼ dlm perkara itu,* He was involved in the case. **–an** 1 peg, hook. 2 obstacle. 3 relation. *– –paut* 1 relation, connection. *Penahanannja itu ada – –pautnja dgn pembunuhan,* His arrest had s.t. to do with a murder. 2 strings, complications. *Perdjandjian itu tak ada – –paut,* The agreement had no strings attached.

sangsang see KESANGSANG.

sangsara see SENGSARA.

sangsekerta Sanskrit.

sangsi 1 to doubt. *Saja – apakah ia akan dpt menamatkan sekolahnja itu,* I doubt whether he'll be able to complete his studies. 2 sanction(s). **ke–an** 1 doubt. 2 suspicion. **menj–kan** to doubt. *Saja ∼ kepandaiannja,* I doubted his ability. *Kepandaiannja dpt di–kan,* His ability is doubtful. *Tak dpt di–kan lagi,* There is no longer any doubt.

sangu 1 provisions. 2 traveling funds.

sanksi see SANGSI.

santak see SENTAK.

santan coconut cream.

santap ber- to dine, partake of food (formal expression). *Radja dan putera-nja* ~ , The king and his son were dining. **menj-** to eat, partake of. **per-an** 1 meal. 2 banquet. **-an** dishes, meal. ~ *rohani* spiritual nourishment.

santen see SANTAN.

santiran spitting image. *Ia adalah – ajahnja,* He's the spitting image of his father.

santri 1 student at a traditional type of Moslem school. 2 In Java, a person consciously and exclusively Moslem.

santun 1 well-mannered, well-behaved, decent. *Ia -,* He's well-mannered. 2 good manners. *Ia tahu -,* He's well-mannered. **ke-an** good manners. **menj-i** 1 to sympathize with. *Ia ~ kesusahanku,* He sympathized with my problems. 2 to help, assist. *Ia ~ orang² terlantar,* He helps displaced persons. **penj-** benevolent, sympathetic. **penj-an** help, assistance.

sanubari see HATI.

sap 1 line, series, row. 2 penwiper. **ber- -²** in rows, lined up.

sapa see SIAPA. **ber- -²an** to address e.o. **menj-** to address, speak to. *Ia ~ saja,* He addressed me. **ter-** bewitched. **-an** *salam* greeting.

Sapar see SAFAR.

sapérsi asparagus.

sapi cow. *- bantai* a bull for slaughter. *- dara* heifer. *- (pe)djantan* bull. *- perah* a milch cow.

sapih **menj-** to wean a child.

sapta seven. *- Marga* Seven Pledges. *- Usaha Tama* Seven Basic Efforts.

sapu broom. **menj-** 1 to wipe, brush. 2 to sweep. 3 to thrash, whip. **menj-kan** to sweep, brush off. **penj-** wiper, brush. ~ *randjau* mine sweeper. **-an** *katja* windshield wiper. ~ *tjat* brushwork in painting. *- djalan* street sweeper. *- lidi* broom made of palm-leaf ribs. *- tangan* handkerchief.

sapur see SABUR.

saput cover, shroud, veil. **menj-(i)** 1 to cover. *Padang itu di- oléh saldju,* The field was covered with snow. 2 to muffle a drum. 3 to drape a flag.

saputangan see SAPU.

sara pension, support. **ber-** 1 to share. 2 pensioned. *- bara* 1 confused. 2 in disorder, disarray. *Bukunja - bara terletak dilantai,* His books were scattered all around the floor.

saraf see 1 ILMU. 2 PERANG. 3 SAKIT.

sarafi neural.

sarak separated, parted. **ber-** to separate, part. **menj-** to wean.

sarakah greedy.

saran suggestion. **menj-i** 1 to suggest. 2 to influence, manipulate. **menj-kan** to propose, suggest. **-an** 1 suggestion. 2 proposition. 3 propaganda.

sarang 1 nest. 2 web. 3 hide-out, hideaway. 4 porous. **ber-** to nest, make a nest. **ber- -²** full of bullet holes. **menj-i** to make a nest in or on s.t. *- burung* (edible) bird's nest. *- laba(h)* cobweb. *- madu* honeycomb. *- penjakit* 1 focus of disease. 2 breeding place. *- senapan mesin* machine gun nest.

sarap k.o. skin rash. **menj-** 1 to litter. *Kertas² ~ dilantai,* Papers littered the floor. 2 to put in a bottom layer. *Kopornja di- dulu diisinja dgn pakaiannja,* First he put a bottom layer in his trunk before he placed his clothes in it. 3 to have breakfast. *Adik sedang ~ ,* My brother was having breakfast. **-an** 1 bottom layer. 2 breakfast. 3 to have breakfast. *Marilah ~ dulu,* Let's have breakfast first. *- sampah* litter, trash. see SARAF.

sarat 1 loaded. *Prahoto itu sdh - berisi pasir,* The truck was loaded with sand. 2 see SJARAT. 3 laden, full. *Hati saja - dgn kesusahan,* My heart was filled with sorrow. **menj-kan** to load, cram s.t. with s.t.

sarau unfortunate.

sardén sardine.

sardjana scholar. **ke-an** scientific, scholarly. *- Hukum* law degree. *- muda* Bachelor of Arts. *- sastera* Master of Arts.

sarékat see SERIKAT. *- Islam* Islamic League.

saréngat religious law.

sargut **menj-** to rip with o's teeth.

sari 1 core, essence, nucleus, gist. 2 pollen. **menj-kan** 1 to quote, abstract from. 2 to sum up. **per-an** digest, summary. *- berita* news headlines. *- pati* essence, main point. *- pidato* the tenor of a speech. *- susu* cream. *tak -²nja* unusual, peculiar.

saring **menj-** 1 to filter, strain, sift. 2 to refine. ~ *minjak* to refine petroleum. **penj-** filter. ~ *air* water filter. **penj-an** 1 sifting. 2 refining. 3 screening. **-an** 1 sieve, strainer. 2 filter.

sarip see SJARIF.

saripati essence, core. *Apakah – pidatonja?* What was the essence of his speech? see SARI.

sarit difficult.

sarodja see SERODJA.
sarong 1 piece of cloth the ends of which have been sewn together. 2 case, container. 3 sheath. 4 wrapper. 5 holster. **menj–kan** 1 to encase. 2 to put s.t. on. 3 to sheathe. – *bantal* pillowcase. – *batik* good-quality sarong. – *djari* thimble. – *korsi* slip cover. – *pedang* scabbard. – *pelékat* sarong with printed patterns. – *tangan* glove.
sartan Cancer.
saru 1 dim, vague. 2 cypress. 3 fitting, suitable, handsome. – *benar rumah itu sesudah diperbaiki*, That house looks very nice after the repairs. **menj–** to disguise o.s. *Penjelidik itu* ~ *sebagai seorang pedagang*, The detective disguised himself as a merchant. **penj–an** disguise.
saruk menj– to win. **ter–** –² 1 to totter. 2 dilapidated.
sarung see SARONG.
sarut menj– to bite. – **-ber–** *fikirannja*, His thoughts were confused.
S.A.S. [*Serikat Afrika Selatan*] Union of South Africa.
sasa strong. *Tubuhnja tegap –*, He was well built.
sasak coarse wickerwork.
sasap see SUSUP. **menj–** to pull up weeds.
sasar 1 mad, insane. 2 dazed. **ke–**lost, strayed away. *Saja* ~ *dikota*, I lost my way in the town. *Ia kena peluru* ~ , He was hit by a stray bullet. **menj–** to aim indiscriminately. *Serangan kapal terbang itu* ~ *sadja*, The plane's attack was made indiscriminately. **ter–** lost, astray. **–an** 1 target. 2 tennis court.
sastera 1 books. 2 literature. 3 letters. *Fakultas* – faculty of letters, literary faculty. **kesu–an** literature, belles-lettres.
sasterawan man of letters.
sastrawati woman writer.
saté small pieces of barbecued meat roasted on a skewer over an open fire. **menj–** 1 to prepare *saté*. 2 to cause dissension. **per–an** dissension. – *ajam* chicken *saté*. – *babi* pork *saté*. – (*h*)*ati* liver *saté*. – *kambing* goat *saté*.
satelit satellite.
sateria see KESATERIA.
satu one. **ber–** allied, united. *Meréka* ~ *dlm peperangan itu*, They were allies during the war. **ber–an** to form a unit. **ber–padukan** to unite firmly. *Kita hendaklah* ~ *dlm menghadapi kesulitan ini*, We should be firmly united in facing this problem. **ke–an** 1 unit(s). *Beberapa* ~ *musuh ber-*

hasil mendarat, Several enemy units succeeded in landing. 2 totality. 3 unity. **ke–segian, ke–sisihan** onesidedness. **memper–kan, menj–kan** 1 to unite, join, ally. *Ia berhasil* ~ *negerinja*, He succeeded in uniting his country. 2 to join. *Ia* ~ *dirinja dgn angkatan darat*, He joined the ground forces. 3 to concentrate. *Ia* ~ *segala tenaganja utk memetjahkan soal itu*, He concentrated all his efforts toward resolving the problem. **menj–lemarikan** to place in one case. **menj– -padukan** to unite s.t. **penj–an** unification. **penj–ragaman** uniformity. **per–an** association, club, union. **–an** unit. ~ *berat* unit of weight. –² 1 o. by o. 2 some, a few. *Disana tak banjak rumah; hanja* ~ *sadja*, There weren't many houses there, just a few. **–²nja** only. *anak* ~ the only child. – *dua* a few. *Ia pergi utk* – *dua hari*, He went for a few days. – *lagi* another o. *Berikan saja* – *lagi*, Please give me an additional o. **–pun** *tidak* not even o. ~ *tidak ada bukunja jg berharga*, Not a single o. of his books had any value. – *per* – o. by o. *Meréka datang* – *per* –, They came o. by o. – *sama lain* 1 o. another. *Meréka menuduh* – *sama lain*, They accused e.o. 2 mutual, o. another. *Meréka tak setudju* – *sama lain*, They didn't agree with o. another. – *sisi* unilateral. *jg* – *lagi* the other o. *Berapa harga jg* – *lagi?* What's the price of the other o.? *alat pemer–* unifying instrument.
satwa wild animal.
Satyalantjana Indonesian award for merit.
sau rustling sound. – *angin* the rustling of the wind.
saudagar merchant.
saudara 1 brother. 2 sister. 3 relative. 4 colleague. 5 bud, say. –, *mana djalan ke kantor pos?* Bud, which is the way to the post office? 6 form of address to peer and similar age level. *Bagaimana* –? How are you? 7 afterbirth. **ber–** 1 to be related. *Saja* ~ *dgn dia*, I'm related to him. 2 to be siblings. *dua orang* ~ siblings. **memper–kan** to be friends with s.o. **per–an** 1 relationship. 2 friendship. 3 fraternity, brotherhood. – *andjing* half brother, half sister. – *daging*, – *djauh* distant relative. – *dekat* close relative. – *laki*² brother. – *perempuan* sister. – *sedjalan djadi* half brother, half sister. – (*se*)*kandung* full brother, sister. – *sepupu* cousin. – *tiri* stepbrother, stepsister.
saudari female friend, colleague.

Bagaimana chabar –*?* How are you (to a woman)?

sauh 1 anchor. *membongkar* – to weigh anchor. *membuang* – to cast anchor. 2 see SAWO. **ber**– to be at anchor.

sauk menj– 1 to dip up, scoop up. 2 to lasso. **–an** 1 bucket, scoop. 2 net. **–²** bucket, scoop. – *air mandikan diri* to stand on o's own 2 feet.

saum the fast, Lent.

saung cave, grotto.

saur 1 the last meal before daybreak during fasting period. 2 see SAHUR. **ber**– interlocking. **menj-i** to grow over densely. **ter**– to stumble.

saus 1 sauce. 2 gravy.

s.a.w. [*salla'llahu'alaihi'wassallama*] May the Lord bless him (Mohammed) and give him peace.

sawah wet rice field. **ber-, menj**– 1 to own rice fields. 2 to work the rice fields. **penj**– rice grower. **per-an** 1 rice cultivation. 2 fields for rice cultivation. – *tadahan* rice field dependent upon rain.

Sawal see SJAWWAL.

sawan 1 epilepsy. 2 fit, convulsions. – *bangkai* apoplectic stroke.

sawang 1 cobweb. 2 atmosphere. **pe(r)-an** wasteland. **-an** atmosphere.

sawar barricade, fence. **menj**– to bar.

sawat 1 k.o. of driving belt. 2 shoulder strap, sling. 3 see PE–.

sawi mustard greens.

sawo 1 a popular and very tasty fruit, zapot. 2 brown. – *mateng* dark brown. – *tua* dark brown.

S.B. [*Serikat Buruh*] labor or trade union.

S'baja [*Surabaja*] Surabaya (city in East Java).

sbb. [*sebagai berikut*] as follows.

sbg [*sebagai*] as.

schors to suspend, fire. **di**– suspended.

s/d [*sampai dgn*] up to and including.

s.d.a. [*seperti diatas*] *idem,* as above.

sdr [*saudara*] Mr., Mrs., Miss.

sdri [*saudari*] Miss, Mrs.

se– 1 all. – *-Indonésia* All-Indonesia(n). 2 one. *–menit* one minute. 3 same. *Ia –umur dgn saja,* He's the same age as I. 4 when, as soon as. *Saja akan beri kabar –terimanja balasan,* I'll let you know when the reply is received. *Kirimlah kawat –tibanja disana,* Please send a cable as soon as you arrive there. 5 as ... as. *–ketjil itu sdh pandai membatja,* As small as he is, he already reads very well.

S.E. [*Surat Édaran*] circular.

seantéro entire. *Itu didjual – dunia ini,* It is sold all over the world.

seb. [*sebelum*] before.

sebab 1 cause, motive, reason. – *mati* cause of death. *Apa –nja kaukatakan itu?* What's the reason for your saying that? 2 because. *Ia tidak pergi – ia sakit,* He didn't go because he was sick. **ber**– with reason, justly. **menj-kan** to cause. *Apa jg ~ rumah itu terbakar?* What caused that house to burn up? **ter**– caused, occasioned. *Pertengkaran itu ~ oléh salah pengertian,* The quarrel was caused by misunderstanding. – *akibat* cause and effect. – *apa?* why? – *apa ia menangis?* Why is she crying? – *karena* cause, reason. – *musabab* several reasons. *Tentu ada – musababnja maka ia mengatakan demikian,* Of course there were several reasons for his saying so. *itulah –nja* that's why. *Itulah –nja maka ia tak datang,* That's why he didn't come. *Apa –nja?* Why? *oléh* – because (of). *Oléh – ia sakit ia tak pergi,* Because he was ill he didn't go.

sebagai see BAGAI.

sebagaimana see BAGAIMANA.

sebaja of the same age, contemporary. *Saja – dgn kakaknja,* I was of the same age as his older sister.

sebak to rise (of water), overflow. *Air matanja –,* Her eyes were filled with tears.

sebal resentful. *Hatinja – ketika permintaannja tak diluluskan,* He was resentful when his wish was not granted. **ke-an** resentment. **menj-kan** 1 to resent s.t. 2 tedious, annoying. *Peladjaran itu ~ ,* The lesson was tedious.

sebaliknja see BALIK.

sebam 1 gray. 2 dark.

sebar going to sleep (of arms or legs). **menj-kan** 1 to strew, scatter. *Ia ~ benih,* He scattered seeds. 2 to spread. *Ia ~ kabar bohong,* He spread rumors. 3 to distribute. *Surat² –an di-kan,* Leaflets were distributed. **penj-an** 1 distributing, spreading. 2 dissemination. **per-an** 1 the spread. *~ kebudajaan² asing ke Indonésia* the spread of foreign civilizations to Indonesia. 2 propagation, spread.

sebarang see BARANG.

sebat quick in movement. **menj**– 1 to whip. *Anaknja di–nja dgn belebas,* He whipped his child with a ruler. 2 to steal. *Ia ~ dompét saja,* He stole my wallet.

sebaur see BAUR.

sebawahan a subordinate. *Ia baik*

kpd —nja, He's good to his subordinates.

sebelah see BELAH.

sebelas 11. **ke-an** the eleven, soccer team.

sebelum see BELUM.

seberang across, opposite. **berse-an** on both sides, opposite e.o. *di-djalan* across the road. **menj–** to cross to the other side. **menj-i** to cross. *Ia ∼ sungai,* He crossed the river. *Dilarang ∼ djalan disini,* Forbidden to cross here. **menj-kan** to take s.o. or s.t. across. *Ia ∼ saja dlm perahunja,* He took me across in his boat. **penj–** *kanal* channel swimmer. **ter–** 1 crossed. 2 to flee, escape. – **-menj–** facing, opposite e.o. *Rumah kami ∼ ,* Our houses face e.o.

seberhana a suit of clothes.

seberot menj– to rob, pick pockets.

sébet fast, quick.

sebit see SABIT.

sebrang see SEBERANG.

sebu full. *Tempat sampah itu –,* The trash can was full. **menj–** to fill, stuff. **menj-kan** to fill up, plug up.

sebuk menj– 1 to infiltrate, penetrate. 2 to enter into a conversation. **penj-an** infiltration.

sebut menj-(kan) 1 to name, mention. *–kan nama gunung² pulau Djawa,* Name the mountains of Java. *Djangan – namaku,* Don't mention my name. 2 to call. *Kertas ini di– kertas minjak,* This paper is called 'wax paper.' *Ia ∼ saja bung,* He called me 'bung.' **penj–** denominator (arith.). **ter–** 1 mentioned. *Tlh ∼ tadi bhw ...* It was mentioned earlier that ... 2 known. *Ia ∼ di-mana²,* He was known everywhere. 3 mentioned above. *Rumah ∼ tlh terdjual,* The house mentioned above has been sold. *Tlh ∼ diatas bhw ...* It has been mentioned above that ... **ter-lah** he is said to. **-an** 1 mention, statement. 2 quotation. *Bukunja itu berisi ∼² dari buku² lain,* His book is filled with quotations from other books. 3 predicate. *Jg mana ∼ kalimat ini?* Which is the predicate of this sentence? **–²an** much talked of.

sedak ke-an to choke, swallow the wrong way. *Makanlah pe-lahan²,* *nanti ∼ kamu,* Eat slowly or you'll choke on your food. *∼ hidung* nasal stoppage. **ter–** to choke, swallow the wrong way.

sédak rattan band around the top of a drum serving to keep the head taut.

sedan sob. **ter–** *–²* sobbing. *– sedu* sobbing.

sédan 1 sedan. 2 glassed-in enclosure.

sedang 1 average, moderate. *Kepandaiannja –,* He was an average person in ability. 2 sufficient. *200 dollar sebulan – baginja,* 200 dollars a month was sufficient for him. 3 while. *Kutjingnja putih – kutjing saja hitam,* His cat was white while mine was black. *– ia mengutjapkan kata²nja itu isterinja mendjerit,* While he was uttering those words his wife screamed. 4 to be in the process of, -ing. *Ia – membatja ketika saja datang,* He was reading when I came. *– bitjara,* The line is busy. *– ditjétak* in press. 5 moderately. *Setasiun – djauhnja dari rumah saja,* The station was not so far from my house. 6 to fit. *Badju itu – baginja,* The jacket fits him fine. **menj–** to try on. *Ia ∼ sepatunja,* He tried on his shoes. **me-nj–²kan** to try to make ends meet. **–kan** 1 whereas. 2 even. *Djangankan membeli rumah, ∼ membeli pakaian sadja tak sanggup dia,* He couldn't even buy clothes, let alone a house. *tidak – -menj–* insufficient. *Gadjinja tidak ∼ ,* His salary was insufficient.

sedap 1 delicious. *Makanan itu –,* The food was delicious. 2 nice, pleasing. *Bau bunga itu –,* The flower smelled nice. 3 well, refreshed. *Badan saja tak merasa – ketika itu,* I didn't feel well then. 4 pleased, amused. *Tak – hatinja mendengar perkataanmu itu,* He wasn't pleased with what you said. **ke-an** 1 pleasantness. 2 refreshed feeling. 3 flavor. **menj-kan** 1 to please. *Perkataannja itu ∼ hati,* His words were pleasing. 2 to make pleasing. *Rempah² ∼ makanan,* The spices make the food tasty. **–²an** delicacies. *– malam* tuberose.

sedar see SADAR. **penj–** *sastera* literary messenger.

sedari see DARI.

sedarun all together, in unison. *Meréka mendjawab –,* They answered all together.

sedat 1 slow. *Pikirannja –,* He thinks slowly. 2 confused.

sedekah 1 alms. 2 religious meal. **ber–** 1 to give alms. 2 to give a religious meal. **menj-i** 1 to give alms to. *Ia ∼ pengemis itu,* He gave alms to the beggar. 2 to give a religious meal for s.o. *Ia bermaksud ∼ anaknja,* He intends to give a religious meal for his son. **menj-kan** to give s.t. as alms.

sedekala see SEDIAKALA.

sedelinggam red lead.

sederhana simple, plain. *Ia selalu memakai pakaian jg* –, She always wears a plain dress. *Makanan jg dihidangkan* – *sadja*, The food which was served was quite plain. *Keramaian itu* –, The entertainment was simple, nothing fancy. **ke–an** simplicity. **menj–kan** 1 to simplify. 2 to economize. **penj–an** simplification. *Hidupnja* –, He lives modestly.

sedia 1 ready. *Ia sdh* – *utk berangkat*, She was ready to leave. *Makanan sdh* –, Dinner was ready. 2 available, ready. *Ia selalu* – *utk menolong*, He was always ready to help. 3 in stock. **ber–** to be ready, prepared. *Negeri itu sdh* ∼ *utk berperang*, The country was prepared to wage war. **ke–an** 1 readiness, willingness. 2 good will. **memper–kan, menj–kan** 1 to prepare. *Ibu sedang* ∼ *makanan*, Mother was preparing the food. 2 to make ready, have ready. *Kapal² itu sdh di–kan utk mengangkut pradjurit²*, The ships were made ready to transport the troops. 3 to furnish. *Hotél itu* ∼ *selimut*, The hotel furnished the blankets. 4 to earmark, set aside funds. 5 to equip, supply. **per–an** 1 stock, supply. *Banjak pakaian dlm* ∼ , There were many clothes in stock. 2 supply. ∼ *makanan itu tak tjukup*, The food supply was insufficient. 3 preparations. *Tlh diadakan* ∼² *utk memulai perundingan itu*, Preparations had been made to hold the conference. **ter–** in stock, on hand. *Tak ada uang* ∼ *utk itu*, There wasn't any money on hand for that. **–an** 1 preparation. ∼ *darah* blood preparation. 2 spare. *ban* ∼ spare tire.

sediakala 1 former, of old. *Kemudian ia kembali ketempatnja* –, Afterward he went back to his former place. 2 as it used to be, as usual. *Hidupnja seperti* – *sadja*, His life is just as it used to be. 3 every. – *malam is pergi*, Every night he went out.

sedianja 1 as a matter of fact. – *ia tak suka kawin*, As a matter of fact he didn't want to marry. 2 properly speaking. *Pidato jg* – *akan mulai bésok diundurkan*, The speech which, properly speaking, was to begin tomorrow has been postponed. – ... *tetapi* ... It's true ... but ...

sedih 1 sad. *Hatinja* –, He was sad. 2 tragic. *Tjeritera itu sangat* –, The story was very tragic. **ber–** *hati* to be sad. **ke–an** 1 misery, distress. 2

sorrow. **menj–kan** 1 to sadden. 2 saddening, distressing. *Tjerita itu* ∼ , The story was sad. 3 appalling. – *pedih* 1 sorrow. 2 sorrowful.

sedikit 1 a little, a bit, some. *Beri saja* –, Give me a little. 2 little, few. *Ia berkata* –, He said little. *terlalu besar* – a little too big. *murah* – rather cheap. **memper–kan, menj–kan** to stint on s.t. *Ia* ∼ *pengeluaran uangnja*, He stinted on his expenditures. **menj–i** to decrease. **–nja** at least, more or less. *Walaupun tak kaja*, ∼ *ia dpt membeli makanan se-hari²*, Though he wasn't rich, he could at least buy his daily bread. **–²** 1 a little bit. *Saja bisa berbahasa Perantjis* ∼ , I can speak French a little bit. *Ia* ∼ *sadja makan*, He eats very little. 2 little by little. *Anak itu memakan kuénja* ∼ , The child ate its cake little by little. – *hari* in a few days. *Sekolah itu* – *hari akan dibuka kembali*, The school will be reopened in a few days. – *hari lagi* in a few days, before long. – *-dikitnja* 1 at least. 2 as little as possible.

sedjahtera 1 safe. 2 prosperous. **ke–an** 1 prosperity. 2 safety.

sedjak 1 since. *Ia sakit² sadja* – *minggu jg lalu*, He's been ill since last week. 2 from. – *ketjil* since childhood. 3 see SADJAK. – *tadi* just now.

sedjaman see DJAMAN.

sedjarah history. **ber–** historic. *Hari 17 Agustus adalah hari jg* ∼ *bagi orang Indonésia*, August 17 is a historic day for Indonesians.

sedjati true, real, genuine. *pahlawan* – a true hero. see DJATI.

sedji see SADJI.

sedjoli couple (husband and wife). see DJOLI.

sedjuk 1 cool, chilly. – *benar dlm kamar ini*, It's quite cool in this room. 2 fresh. *Ia mengisap hawa* –, He breathed the fresh air. **ke–an** 1 cold, coolness. 2 numb with cold. *Anak itu* ∼ , The child was numb with cold. **menj–kan** 1 to make cool. *Ia* ∼ *kamarnja*, He cooled his room off. 2 to comfort. *Perangainja itu* ∼ *hati orang tuanja*, His behavior was a comfort to his parents. ∼ *hati* to cheer s.o. up.

sedot **menj–** 1 to suck. *Anak itu* ∼ *djempolnja*, The child sucked its thumb. 2 to inhale. **–an** a straw.

sedu 1 a sob. 2 a hiccough. 3 sad. **ter–** –², – *sedan* sobbing.

sedua **menj–kan** to lease out on a part-time basis.

seduh 1 see SEDU. **menj–** to pour boiling water on s.t. *Ia ∼ téh,* She made tea.

sedut see SEDOT.

séf see SÉP.

segah full, satiated.

segak menj– to blurt out. *"Pergi dari sini," –nja dgn tiba²,* "Go away," she suddenly blurted out.

ségak 1 recovered from illness. 2 fresh. *Mukanja – sesudah sembuh dari sakitnja,* He looked fresh after recovering from his illness. 3 clever. 4 proud.

segala 1 all, all of them. *– rumahnja sudah didjualnja,* He had sold all his houses. 2 entirely, wholly. *Ia berpakaian – mérah,* She was dressed entirely in red. – **-galanja** everything. *Barangnja habis ∼ ,* He lost everything he had. *– sedikit* a little of everything. *– sesuatu* 1 everything. *– sesuatu jg ditjeriterakannja itu tiada benar,* Everything he related was a lie. 2 all this.

segan 1 reluctant, averse to. *Saja – pergi kerumahnja,* I'm reluctant to go to his house. 2 to respect. *Murid²nja – guru itu,* The pupils respect the teacher. **ke–an** 1 reluctance, aversion. 2 respect, awe. 3 apathy. **menj–hormati** to respect. **menj–i** to respect, stand in awe of. *Ia tiada ∼ ajahnja,* He doesn't respect his father. **penj–** shy. *Ia ∼ ,* He's shy. – **-menj–i** to have mutual respect. *Meréka ∼ ,* They respect e.o. *tak –²* not hesitate. *Ia tak ∼ masuk kamar saja,* He didn't hesitate to enter my room. *–²* shy. *Djangan ∼ ,* Don't be shy. *– hati* reluctant.

segar 1 fresh. *Sajur²an itu masih –,* The vegetables were still fresh. *Saja merasa – kembali,* I feel like a new person again. 2 refreshed. *Ia blm – walaupun sdh beristirahat selama sebulan,* He didn't feel refreshed though he had been on vacation for a month. 3 refreshing. *Minuman itu –,* The drink was refreshing. **ke–an** 1 freshness. 2 health. *∼nja terbajang dimukanja,* Her face reflected her health. **memper–** *kembali* to refresh. **menj–kan** 1 to make healthy. *Hawa itu ∼ badan,* The climate makes o. healthy. 2 to refresh. 3 refreshing. *Minuman itu ∼ badan,* The drink was refreshing. **penj–** 1 means of restoring freshness, tonic. 2 stimulating. *Tidur adalah ∼ badan,* Sleep is a means of restoring freshness. *kursus* **penj–an** *(kembali)* refresher course. *– bugar* 1 safe and

sound. 2 fit, like new. *Tenaganja masih – bugar,* He's still fit, in good shape.

segara ocean. *– Kidul* Indian Ocean.

ségel 1 seal, stamp. 2 ration coupon. 3 depth of 12 meters (used in anchoring). **menj–** to seal, stamp. *Meréka ∼ surat perdjandjian itu,* They sealed the contract. *Rumahnja di– karena tak ada izin tinggal,* His house was sealed because there was no residence permit. *– témpél* receipt stamp.

segenap see GENAP.

séger see SÉHER.

segera 1 quickly, immediately. *–lah membeli!* Buy right away! 2 soon. *– kemudian iapun datang,* Soon afterward he came. 3 urgent. **ber–** to hurry. *Tak usah ∼ ,* Don't hurry. **memper–(kan), menj–kan** 1 to speed up, accelerate. *Tindakannja itu ∼ djatuhnja kabinét,* His action speeded up the fall of the cabinet. 2 to overwork s.o. **per–an** speeding up, acceleration. **se–nja** as soon as possible.

segi 1 side. *– tiga mempunjai tiga buah –,* A triangle has 3 sides. 2 angle, aspect. *Ditindjau dari – itu...,* Seen from that angle... *– empat* quadrangle. 3 sector. *– ékspor* export sector. **ber–** *tiga* triangular. **per–sided.** *∼ tiga* triangular. *empat ∼* square. *empat ∼ pandjang* rectangle. *enam métér ∼* 6 square meters.

segini 1 this much. *Dia memberikan saja –,* He gave me this much. 2 as...as this. *– besarnja* as big as this.

segitu 1 that much. 2 as... as that. *– besarnja* as large as that.

sehanja *[sehéktarnja]* per hectare.

séhat 1 healthy. *Anaknja –,* His child was healthy. *Makanan itu –,* The food was nourishing. 2 sound. **ke–an** health. **menj–kan** to make o. healthy. *Makanan itu ∼ ,* The food made o. healthy. **penj–an** sanitation. *– wal'afiat* safe and sound.

séher piston.

sehingga see HINGGA.

seia unanimous. *Meréka – membeli gedung itu,* They agreed unanimously to buy the building.

seimbang see IMBANG.

sejogia(nja) see JOGIA.

séka ber– to wash o.s. *Ia ∼ dikamar mandi,* He washes himself in the bathroom. **menj–** to rub, wipe. *Ia ∼ mukanja dgn sehelai handuk,* He wiped his face with a towel. **menj–kan** to brush away (tears), wipe with s.t.

sekadar see KADAR.

sékah hearty, dashing.

sekak chess.
sekakar stingy.
sekal scale (on map or thermometer).
sekali see KALI.
sekalian all. – meréka tertawa, They all laughed. see KALI.
sekaligus all at once. Meréka menangis –, They all cried at once. see KALI.
sekalipun see KALI.
sekam husk, chaff, hull.
sekang menj– to put a plug in s.t. ter– stuck, plugged up. – mata annoying, a nuisance.
sekap menj– 1 to lock up s.o. Pembunuh itu di– dlm pendjara, The murderer was locked up in prison. 2 to ripen with heat. Ia ∼ buah, He ripens fruit with heat. -an 1 prisoner. 2 ripe fruit.
sekar flower. – majang palm blossom. – suhun a k.o. necklace.
sekarang 1 now. Mari kita pergi –, Let's go now. 2 nowadays. – ini mudah sadja bepergian, Nowadays it's very easy to travel. – ini djuga this very moment. Kerdjakan itu – ini djuga, Do that this very moment. – kemuka from now on.
sekarat see SAKARAT. ber– to be in death's throes.
sekat 1 partition. 2 screen. ber– partitioned off. ber– –² to divide into sections. menj–(i) 1 to partition off. Kedua buah kamar itu di–, The 2 rooms were partitioned off. 2 to bar. Dipisi kedua ∼ gerakan musuh, The second division barred the enemy's movements. 3 to isolate. Ia ∼ dirinja selama setahun, She went into seclusion for a year. penj– 1 separation. 2 insulator. ter– stuck fast. Léhér kerongkongan ∼ , He has a lump in his throat. -an 1 partition. 2 screen. 3 obstruction. ∼ buku flyleaf (in a book). – rongga badan midriff, diaphragm.
sekata see KATA.
sekatén a fair and celebration held in Solo and Jogja in honor of the birthday of Mohammed.
sékdjén [sékretaris-djénderal] secretary-general.
sekedar see KADAR.
sekehendak see HENDAK.
sekelat woolen cloth.
sekelébatan see KELIBAT.
sekeliling see KELILING.
sekéma see SKÉMA.
sekerdja see KERDJA.
sekeri hinge.
sékering fuse (for electrical circuit).
sékertariat secretariat.

sékertaris secretary.
sekerup 1 screw. 2 bolt.
sekésél screen.
sekip 1 target. 2 firing range.
sekiranja see KIRA.
sekitar see KITAR.
séko 1 scout. Létnan itu mengirim tiga orang –, The lieutenant sent 3 scouts. 2 spy. – itu ditémbak mati, The spy was shot. 3 espionage.
sekolah 1 school. 2 to attend school. Ia tidak –, He's not in school. (He never went to school.) ber– to go to school. menj–kan to send to school. Ia tak ∼ anaknja, He didn't send his child to school. -an school(ing). – ambah handicrafts school. – dagang commercial school. – kedjuruan vocational school. – kepandaian puteri home economics high school. – landjutan secondary school. – menengah atas senior high school. – menengah pertama junior high school. – partikelir private school. – pelajaran navigation school. – pertukangan junior technical school. – rakjat, – rendah grammar, elementary school. – tabib medical school. – tinggi college, university. – vak vocational school.
sekon second. Semenit adalah 60 –, A minute is 60 seconds.
sekongkol 1 to be an accessory. Ia – dgn penipu itu, He was an accessory to the thief. 2 scheme, plot. ber– to scheme, plot.
sekonjong-konjong suddenly, all of a sudden.
sekopong spades (in cards).
sekores to suspend, adjourn. Rapat di– selama sedjam, The meeting was adjourned for an hour.
sekotji 1 boat, sloop. 2 bobbin, shuttle.
sékr. 1 [sékretariat] secretariat. 2 [sékretaris] secretary.
sékretariat secretariat.
sékretaris secretary. – djénderal secretary-general, undersecretary.
sekrup see SEKERUP. menj–kan to screw s.t.
seksama see SAKSAMA.
séksi 1 dissection. 2 platoon. 3 section. 4 precinct.
séksuil sexual.
séktor sector.
sekundér secondary.
sekutu 1 partner. Ali dan –nja tlh bertjerai, Ali and his partner had separated. 2 ally. 3 allied. Tentera – meninggalkan pulau itu, The allied forces left the island. 4 federal. 5 accomplice. ber– united, allied. Kedua negara itu ∼ melawan musuhnja

bersama, The 2 countries united to oppose their common enemy. *machluk* ~ a social being. ~ *dgn* to side with, join. *Dlm perang dunia kedua Amérika* ~ *dgn Rusia,* During World War II the United States and Russia joined sides. **menj–i** to join. *Dulu negeri Inggeris* ~ *Rusia,* Formerly England joined Russia. **menj–kan** to consider as an ally. **per–an** 1 federation. ~ *Tanah Melaju* Federation of Malaya. 2 partnership. 3 membership. *Ia blm masuk* ~ *itu,* He hasn't joined yet. 4 league, alliance.

sél cell. **mengs–** to put in solitary confinement. – *aku* battery cell. – *raba* taste bud. – *tilpon* telephone booth.

sela 1 crack, opening. 2 gap. 3 catch crop, auxiliary crop. 4 mixture. 5 interval. **ber–** mixed with. *nasi* ~ *djagung* rice mixed with corn. **memper–kan** to insert s.t., interpolate. **menj–** to interrupt. **menj–i** 1 to vary. 2 to interrupt. **menj–kan** to insert. – **-menj–** alternate, intermittent. – *gunung* mountain pass. *tidak* **ber–** unbroken, uninterrupted. *Pagar itu tidak* ~ , There were no interspaces in the fence.

séla 1 saddle. 2 stone. 3 squinting. **menj–kan** to throw stones.

selada salad. – *air* water cress.

seladang k.o. wild ox.

seladeri celery.

seladju ber– to skate.

selagi see LAGI.

selai jelly, jam, marmalade.

selain see LAIN.

selak 1 harbor boom. 2 bolt. **menj–** 1 to bolt s.t. 2 to push forward.

sélak menj– to open o's shirt. **menj–kan** to push aside.

selaku see LAKU.

selalu always, ceaselessly. *Ia – minta uang,* He was always asking for money. see LALU.

selam Islam. *Orang –* Indonesian Moslem. **ber–** *air* to put s.o. to a water test. **menj–** 1 to dive. *Ia* ~ *kedalam air,* He dived into the water. 2 to stay. *Ia* ~ *didalam air,* He stayed in the water. **menj–i** 1 to dive. *Ia* ~ *laut,* He dived into the sea. 2 to dive for. *Ia* ~ *mutiara,* He dived for pearls. 3 to penetrate, fathom. *Saja tak dpt* ~ *perasaannja,* I couldn't penetrate her feelings. **menj–kan** 1 to immerse. 2 to convert s.o. to Islam. **penj–** diver. **penj–an** 1 immersion. 2 conversion. – *indah* fancy diving. *tak* **ter–i** unfathomable.

selamanja see LAMA.

selamat 1 safe. *Ia datang – dari peperangan,* He returned safe from the war. 2 welfare, happiness, prosperity. *Meréka membatja doa –,* They prayed for happiness and prosperity. 3 happy, pleasant, *Meréka mengutjapkan – tahun baru,* They wished us a happy new year. 4 congratulations. *Ia mengutjap – kpd saja,* He congratulated me. 5 good luck. **ke–an** 1 happiness, welfare. 2 safety. ~ *kerdja* job safety. **menj–kan** 1 to save, rescue. *Ia* ~ *semua penumpang,* He saved all the passengers. 2 to bury. 3 to hold a *selamatan* for s.o. **penj–** redeemer, savior. **-an** religious meal. – *beladjar* Happy studying. – *berdjuang* Victory. – *datang* Welcome. – *djalan* Goodbye (to the o. leaving). (Have a nice trip.) – *hari lahir* Many happy returns of the day. – *hari lebaran* Congratulations (said at the end of fasting month). – *Hari Natal* Merry Christmas. – *hari ulang tahun* Happy birthday, Happy anniversary. – *makan* Enjoy your meal. – *malam* 1 Good evening. 2 Good night. – *minum,* Enjoy your drink. – *pagi* Good morning. – *siang* Good day (around noontime). – *soré* Good afternoon. – *tidur* Good night, Sleep well. – *tinggal* Goodbye (said to o. remaining behind). –² *sadja,* Be good. (Take care of yourself.) *Saja* ~ *sadja,* I'm just fine.

selampai scarf, kerchief. **menj–kan** to sling s.t. over the arm or shoulder.

Sélan Ceylon.

Sélandia Baru New Zealand.

selang 1 interval, break. – *beberapa hari kemudian...* After several days... 2 pause. 3 hall, lobby. 4 veranda. **ber–** 1 at intervals. ~ *3 hari* at 3-day intervals. 2 ... ago. ~ *tiga hari* three days ago. ~ **-seling** alternating, alternately. *Gadis itu memakai benang mérah dan biru* ~ **-seling** *dlm djahitannja,* The girl used red and blue thread alternately in her sewing. ~ **-tenggang** to help e.o. **memper–i** to lend s.o. s.t. **memper–kan** to lend s.t. **menj–** 1 to interrupt. *Ia selalu* ~ *pembitjaraan saja,* He's always interrupting my speech. 2 to vary, alternate. *Ia* ~ *benang mérah dgn benang biru,* She alternated red and blue thread. **menj–njelingkan** to vary s.t. – *sehari* 1 every other day. 2 after a day. – **-seling** to and fro. *Banjak motor –* **-seling** *dimuka rumah saja,* Many cars pass my house. – *seminggu* after a week. *tidak – berapa lama* not long afterward.

selangkang(an) 1 groin. 2 perineum.

selap possessed. **menj–** to have fits of fury. **menj–i** to take possession of o. by a spirit. **menj–kan** to arouse o's fury.

selaput membrane, film. **ber–** covered with a membrane. – *bening* cornea. – *dada* pleura. – *dara* hymen. – *djala* retina. – *djantung* pericardium. – *lendir* mucous membrane. – *mata* cornea. – *otak* cerebral membrane. – *pelangi* iris. – *perut* peritoneum. – *tanduk* cornea.

selar menj–(kan) 1 to brand. 2 to singe. 3 to fry.

selaras see LARAS. **menj–kan** to synchronize.

Selasa Tuesday.

selasar open veranda.

selat 1 strait(s), narrows. – *Sunda* Sunda Straits. 2 passage. **menj–** to sail through a strait. **menj–kan** to insert, thrust between.

selatan south. **ter–** southernmost. – *daja* southwest. – *menenggara*, – *tenggara* south-south-east.

selawat prayers. **ber–** to hold a prayer service.

selé jelly. see SELAI.

seléderi celery.

seledjang see LEDJANG.

selékéh stain, spot. **ber–** stained, dirty. **menj–** to smear, stain. **menj–i** to stain s.t.

selékoh bastion.

seléksi selection. **menj–** to select.

selempada ant.

selempang afraid, frightened. **menj–kan** to worry about. **ter–** to fall astraddle.

selémpang shoulder belt. **menj–** to wear s.t. over the shoulders.

seléndang shawl, stole over one shoulder. **ber–** to wear a *seléndang*. **menj–** to wear s.t. as a *seléndang*. **menj–i** to put a *seléndang* on s.o. **menj–kan** to hang, carry as a *seléndang*. ~ *tas buku* to carry a book bag as a *seléndang*.

selenggara menj–kan 1 to run s.t., take care of. *Ajahnja* ~ *kebun*, His father ran a plantation. 2 to organize. *Meréka* ~ *sebuah pésta*, They organized a party. 3 to execute, carry out. *Ia* ~ *pekerdjaannja dgn baik*, He executed his job properly. **penj–** 1 caretaker. 2 executor. 3 organizer. 4 executive. **penj–an** 1 care. 2 execution. 3 organization, preparation.

selentik menj– to snap o's fingers.

seléo see KESELÉO.

selepa cigarette case.

seléra 1 appetite. 2 body. 3 taste.

selérang skin, hide.

selésa 1 space, room. 2 opportunity, occasion. *Ia tidak –*, He had no opportunity.

selesai 1 ready. 2 finished, done. *Pekerdjaannja sdh –*, His work was finished. *Sekolahnja sdh –*, He had finished his education. **menj–kan** 1 to finish s.t. *Ia tak pernah* ~ *pekerdjaannja*, He never finished his job. 2 to solve, settle. *Meréka berichtiar* ~ *pertengkaran itu*, They tried hard to settle the dispute. 3 to discharge a debt. **penj–an** 1 arrangement. 2 settlement. *Ia tiada memikirkan* ~ *utangnja*, He never gave any thought to settling his debts. 3 solution, settlement. ~ *pertengkaran itu lama*, It took a long time to solve the dispute.

selesma, selésma a cold.

seletuk menj– to interrupt s.o.

seléwéng menj– to deviate, digress. *Apa kita sdh* ~ ? Have we digressed from the subject? **menj–kan** to divert, deflect, s.t. **penj–** 1 busybody. 2 deviationist. **penj–an** 1 deviation (from a task or duty). 2 irregularity.

sélibat celibate.

selidik 1 accurate, careful. 2 critical, observant. *Ia sangat – akan segala perkataan saja*, He paid very close attention to everything I said. **menj–i** 1 to investigate. *Ia* ~ *pembunuhan itu*, He investigated the murder. 2 to do research. 3 to search. **penj–** 1 investigator, research worker. 2 scout, spy. 3 examiner. 4 detective. **penj–an** 1 research. 2 inquiry, investigation. ~ *ilmiah* scientific research. 3 survey.

seligi javelin. **menj–** to throw a javelin.

seligit to swarm with.

selimpang menj– to deviate from the right path.

selimpat menj– to stay clear of, avoid s.t.

selimut 1 blanket. 2 camouflage, cover. **ber–** 1 covered over. 2 camouflaged. **menj–** to cover, hide s.t. *Ia* ~ *maksudnja jg djahat itu dgn kata² jg manis*, He concealed his evil intentions behind nice words. **menj–i** to cover s.t. or s.o. with a blanket. **menj–kan** 1 to hide behind. 2 to cover, blanket.

selinap menj– 1 to crawl, move stealthily. *Ular itu* ~ *kedalam semak²*, The snake crawled into the bushes. 2 to get, slip away. *Pentjopét itu dgn segera* ~ *dari polisi*, The thief immediately got away from the policeman. **menj–kan** to cause to hide.

seling ber– to take turns, alternate. *Njanjian² barat ~ dgn njanjian² timur,* Western songs alternated with eastern ones. **ber– -ganti** interchangeable. **menj–i** to vary, alternate. **–an** 1 variation(s). 2 alternation, change. 3 interlude. see SELANG.

selingkuh dishonest, corrupt.

selip to skid. *Mobilnja –,* His car skidded. **menj–kan** to slip in between. *Ia ~ sehelai kertas dibukunja,* He slipped a piece of paper into his book. **ter–** 1 enclosed. 2 inserted, slipped in. 3 to skid. *Mobilnja ~ ,* His car skidded. **~ keluar** 1 to protrude. 2 to leak out.

selir 1 mistress, concubine. 2 second wife.

selirat ber– confused.

selisih 1 difference. *Umur kami tak banjak –nja,* Our ages don't differ much. *–nja antara dua dan tiga adalah satu,* The difference between two and three is one. 2 quarrel, dispute. **ber–** to quarrel, disagree. **~ djalan** to cruise about. **memper–kan, menj–kan** to disagree over s.t. **per–an** disagreement, quarrel, dispute. **– basah** to cruise. **– faham** disagreement.

selisik menj– to investigate, get at the bottom of. *Ia ~ perkara,* He investigated the case.

selisip menj– to slip in. **menj–kan** to insert s.t. secretly.

selisir menj– to go along the coast's edge.

selit menj–kan to enclose between 2 objects. **ter–** stuck fast, pinched.

seliwir ber–an to hang around, loiter.

sélo cello.

seloka 1 short poem. 2 aphorism. **ber–** 1 to recite a *seloka.* 2 to compose a *seloka.*

selokan 1 gutter, drain. 2 sewer.

seloki a small liquor glass.

selomot menj– to fool, hoodwink.

selomprét trumpet.

selongkar menj– 1 to turn over, put in disorder. 2 to rummage through.

selongsong 1 cover. 2 muzzle (dog).

selop slipper.

seloroh 1 funny, amusing. 2 joke. **ber–** to joke, crack jokes.

selot lock. **– gantung** padlock.

seluar a pair of trousers.

selubung 1 cover, veil. 2 wrapper. 3 envelope. **ber–** to cover o.s. up. **menj–i** to cover, wrap up. **menj–kan** to use as a cloak. **– anak** caul.

seludang sheath of the inflorescence of a palm tree.

seluduk menj– to crawl under s.t. *Ia ~ kebawah médja,* He crawled under the table.

seludup menj– 1 to duck into, hide. 2 to smuggle. 3 to infiltrate. **menj–kan** to smuggle s.t. in. **penj–smuggler. penj–an** smuggling.

seluk curve, bend, coil. **ber–** twisted, winding. **~ beluk** 1 complicated. 2 related to. **menj–** to feel for. **– beluk** 1 details. 2 complications.

selulup to dive, plunge.

selumbar wood splinters.

selumur castoff snakeskin.

selundup see SELUDUP.

selupat membrane. **– telur** transparent membrane over egg.

seluruh 1 entire, whole. **– kampung itu sepi,** The entire village was quiet. 2 all. **– jg dikatakannja itu tiada benar,** Everything he said was a lie. **ke–an** totality, whole. *dlm ~nja* as a whole. **menj–** 1 to spread. *Kabar ini sdh ~ ditanah air,* This news has spread throughout our country. 2 on the whole, wholly. *Peraturan ini utk umum dan ~ ,* This regulation is in general and on the whole. **menj–i** to enclose completely. **–nja** in aggregate.

selusuh 1 to slide. 2 s.t. to ease childbirth.

selusup menj– 1 to penetrate, infiltrate. *Ia ~ kedalam daérah musuh,* He penetrated into enemy territory. 2 to slip away, disappear. *Ia ~ kedalam semak²,* He disappeared into the bushes.

selusur menj– to slide. *Anak itu ~ dari pegangan tangga,* The boy slid down the banisters.

selut mud.

sema² a cold.

semadi see SAMADI.

sémah sacrifice against demons. **menj–** to sacrifice to. **menj–kan** to sacrifice s.t. **–an** a sacrifice.

semai seedling. **menj–(kan)** to sow close together. **per–an** seedbed. **–an** seedling.

semajam ber– to be enthroned, sit. **per–an** residence.

semak bush, shrub. **menj–** 1 to be like weeds. *Bunga²an ~ dikebunnja,* Flowers grow like weeds in his garden. 2 confused. 3 entangled. *Rambutnja ~ ,* Her hair was tangled. 4 alarmed. 5 to be sad. *Ia ~ ,* She was sad. **menj–kan** to make into a wilderness. **–²** bushes, shrubs. **– belukar** underbrush. **– samun** bushes, shrubbery. *dari – kebelukar* 6 of o. and half a dozen of the other.

semakin see MAKIN.

semalam 1 last night. 2 one night. see MALAM.

semampai slender. *Badannja* –, She was slender.

seman abortive.

semangat 1 soul, spirit. 2 zest, spirit, enthusiasm. *-nja utk beladjar tak ada lagi*, He's lost all zest for study. *Ia kalah* –, He lost courage. 3 consciousness. *Ia hilang* – *selama sedjam*, She lost consciousness for an hour. *Ia pulang* –, He regained consciousness. **ber-** 1 enthusiastic. 2 zealous, active. 3 energetic. 4 conscious. *Ia tidak* ~ , He's unconscious. **menj-i** to inspire. *Rakjat hrs di-i*, People must be inspired. – *kambing* coward. – *kampung* clique-minded. – *kedaérahan* provincialism. – *pelaut* sea-minded. – *perang* warlike, militant. – *perkampungan* group loyalty.

semangka watermelon.

semangkin see MAKIN.

sémantik semantics.

sémantis semantic.

semarai 1 cracked. 2 broken, damaged.

semarak 1 shine, luster. 2 ornament. **ber-** radiant, splendid. **menj-kan** to embellish, adorn.

semasa see MASA.

semasih see MASIH.

semat pin, peg, hook. **menj-(kan)** to fasten, pin. *Ia* ~ *peniti hiasannja pd badjunja*, She fastened her brooch to her dress. **penj-** pin. **penj-an** pinning (of medals, etc.). **-an** appendix to a book.

semata-mata see MATA.

sembab swollen. *Mukanja* –, His face was swollen.

sembabat fitting, matching.

sembah 1 respectful greeting (made with folded hands, finger tips upward and touching the forehead). 2 homage, obeisance. **ber-** to address respectfully. **memper-kan, menj-kan** 1 to offer s.t. *Sebuah patung kaju diper-kan kpd présidén*, The president was offered a wooden statue. 2 to inform, report. *Ia* ~ *segala kedjadian itu kpd radjanja*, He reported on all events to his king. 3 to dedicate. *Saja per-kan buku ini kpd ibu saja*, I dedicate this book to my mother. ~ *kurban missa* to celebrate mass. **menj-** to pay homage to s.o. **penj-** worshiper. **penj-an** adoration, worship. **per-an** 1 tribute, gift. 2 dedication. *-nja*, He spoke respectfully. – *sungkem* deepest respect. *Dgn* –, *ananda*, Most respectfully, your son.

sembahjang 1 divine service. 2 to pray. **ber-** to pray, worship. **menj-i, menj-kan** to pray for, conduct

services for. **-an** praying. – *asar* afternoon prayer (3-5 P.M.). – *doha* optional Moslem prayer performed around noon. – *ghaib* prayer for the dead. – *hadjat* prayer for fulfillment of wish. – *is(j)a* evening prayer. – *lima waktu* the 5 obligatory prayers for Moslems. – *lohor* noon prayer (1 P.M.). – *magrib* sunset prayer. – *subuh* dawn prayer. – *sunat* optional prayer. – *tahadjut* optional midnight prayer. – *wadjib* the 5 obligatory prayers for Moslems.

sembam swollen. **menj-** to roast partially.

sembarang 1 see BARANG. 2 no matter who, what, which. *Ia pertjaja pd* – *orang*, He trusted anyone. **-an** 1 anything, anyone. *Tjakapnja* ~ *sadja*, He says anything. 2 at random. *Djangan ludah* ~ , Don't spit just anywhere. *Djangan* ~ *buang sampah*, Don't be a litterbug.

sembari while.

sembat menj- to lash with a whip.

sémbat menj- to whip up with a jerk. *Rotan itu* ~ , The rattan whipped up with a jerk.

sembelih menj- to slaughter, kill. *Ia* ~ *ajam*, He killed a chicken. **penj-an** slaughter, butchering. **-an** for slaughtering. *Disitu ternak* ~ , There are the cattle to be slaughtered.

sembelit constipation.

sembér a buzzing sound.

semberono frivolous, reckless. *Djangan bitjara* – *sadja*, Don't just talk frivolously. *Djangan berlaku* –, Don't act recklessly. **ke-an** 1 frivolity. 2 recklessness.

sembilan 9. – *belas* 19. – *puluh* 90.

sembilik see SEMBELIT.

sembilu knife made of bamboo.

sembojan 1 slogan. 2 motto, catchword. 3 sign, signal. **ber-** to have as a slogan. **menj-kan** to inform according to prearranged plans.

sembrono see SEMBERONO.

sembuh to recover, heal. *Ia sdh* – *dari penjakitnja*, He's recovered from his illness. **ke-an, per-an** 1 recovery (from illness). 2 cure, healing. **menj-kan** to cure s.o. *Dokter tak dpt* ~ *penjakit anak itu*, The doctor couldn't cure the child's illness. **penj-an** recovery (from illness).

sembul menj- 1 to appear, emerge. *Seékor ular* ~ *dari lubang itu*, A snake appeared from the hole. 2 to swell, bulge, protrude. *Matanja* ~ , His eyes bulged. **menj-kan** 1 to hold out. *Ia* ~ *lengannja*, He held his arm out. 2 to hold up. *Ia* ~ *kepalanja*, He held up his head.

sembunji hidden, concealed. *Ia me-*

nulis surat itu dgn −(−), She wrote the letter in secret. **ber-** to be hidden. *Ia ~ dibawah tempat tidur,* She was hidden under the bed. **menj-kan** 1 to hide. *Ia ~ uangnja,* He hid his money. 2 to conceal, suppress. *Ia ~ kesalahannja,* He concealed his faults. 3 to hoard up s.t. **per-an** shelter, hiding place. **ter-** −² stealthily. −² *pujuh* head-in-the-sand policy.

sembur 1 spittle. 2 charm. **ber-an** to sprinkle. **ber-** −²an to spray e.o. **menj-(kan)** to spray, spout, gush. **ter-** to be scolded. *~ -gelak* to roar with laughter. **-an** 1 sprinkling. 2 scolding. 3 outpouring. *~ lava* outpouring of lava.

semburit pederasty.

seméméh soiled, dirty.

semén cement. *− beton* concrete.

semena (*-mena*) *tidak −* arbitrarily. see MENA.

semenandjung peninsula.

semenda related by marriage.

semendjak since. see SEDJAK.

semendjana mediocre.

semenggah *tak −* improper, unseemly. *Kelakuannja tidak −,* He didn't behave properly.

sementang −**kan, se-** −² just because. *~ ia anak orang kaja ia tiada mau bergaul dgn kami,* Just because he's the son of a wealthy man, he doesn't want to associate with us. **-pun** although. *~ ia sakit ia pergi djuga,* Although he was sick, he went anyway. see MENTANG.

sementara 1 while. *− ia menunggu ibunja ia mendengarkan radio,* While he was waiting for his mother, he listened to the radio. 2 a while. *Ia datang utk − sadja,* He just came for a while. 3 the time being, moment. *Itu sdh tjukup utk −,* It was enough for the time being. 4 provisional. *Undang² Dasar −* provisional constitution. 5 (a) certain. *− gurubesar²* certain professors. *− golongan* a certain group. **ke-an** transitoriness. *utk − waktu* for the moment. *− itu* in the meantime. *− itu ia meninggal,* In the meantime he died.

semér see SEMIR.

semerbak 1 fragrant. *Bunga²an itu − baunja,* The flowers had a fragrant smell. 2 to pervade.

semésta 1 whole, entire. *atlas − dunia* world atlas. 2 over-all. *rentjana pembangunan −* over-all development plan. *− alam* universe.

semi young shoot. **ber-** to sprout.

semir polish. **menj-** 1 to polish. 2 to lubricate. *− oli* lubricating oil. *− sepatu* shoe polish.

semoga see MOGA.

semokel smuggling. **menj-** to smuggle.

sempadan 1 border. 2 finishing line.

sémpak chipped.

sempal **menj-** 1 to stick. *Sebatang djarum ~ dlm kerongkongannja,* A needle stuck in his throat. 2 to gag. *Ia ~ mulut saja dgn sehelai kain,* He gagged me with a piece of cloth.

sempana see SEMPENA.

sempat 1 to have time, opportunity. *Ia tak − datang,* He didn't have time to come. 2 convenient. *Kalau −, datanglah sebentar,* If it's convenient, just come for a while. **berke-an** to have an opportunity, time. *Ia tiada ~ menjelesaikan peladjarannja,* He had no opportunity to complete his studies. **ke-an** 1 opportunity. *~ kerdja* work opportunity. 2 time, opportunity. *~ utk bertanja diberikan,* Time was allowed to ask questions. **menj-** to await an opportunity. **menj-i** to find an opportunity for s.t. **menj-kan** to give o. time, an opportunity. *Ia tiada ~ saja beladjar,* He didn't give me time to study.

sempelah 1 rubbish. 2 dregs. 3 useless, of no value.

sempena **menj-kan** to bless s.t. *− hati* conscience.

semperit see SEMPRIT.

semperong 1 lamp chimney. 2 chimney. 3 telescope. 4 tube.

semperot see SEMPROT.

sempit 1 narrow. *Djalan itu −,* The street was narrow. 2 small, tight. *Badju itu − bagi saja,* The jacket was tight on me. 3 pressed, limited. *Waktu saja − sekali,* I was pressed for time. **ke-an** 1 hard-pressed. 2 narrow. 3 shortage. *~ hidup* poverty, straitened circumstances. 4 narrowness. 5 narrow-mindedness. **memper-, menj-kan** 1 to narrow. *Meréka ~ djalan,* They narrowed the road. 2 to make small, tight. *Médja itu ~ kamar saja,* The table made my room small. *− hati* a hothead. *− ketat* tight-fitting (of a dress, etc.).

sempoa abacus.

sempojongan to totter.

semprit **menj-** to blow (a whistle). **menj-i** to blow a whistle at. *Polisi itu ~ saja,* The policeman blew a whistle at me. **-an** a whistle.

semprot syringe, squirt gun. **menj-(i)** to spray. *Pompa itu ~ pohon,* The pump sprayed the tree. *Pohon itu di-i pompa,* The tree was sprayed with a pump. **menj-kan** to squirt s.t. out. **-an** syringe, squirt gun. *Ia dpt ~ ,* He got a scolding.

sempurna 1 perfect. *Pekerdjaannja selalu dikerdjakannja dgn* –, He always did his job perfectly. 2 complete. *Kalimatmu itu blm* –, Your sentence isn't complete yet. 3 purebred. **ke–an** 1 perfection. 2 completeness. **menj–kan** 1 to perfect, execute. 2 to complete. **penj–an** action of perfecting, completing, finishing (articles, products). – *umur* grown-up.

semu 1 appearance. *Negara itu mempunjai pemerintahan démokrat jg hanja – sadja*, The government of that country was democratic in appearance only. 2 deceit, trick. *Ia kena – kemarin*, He was deceived yesterday. **menj–i, menj–kan** to deceive, trick. *Ia suka ~ orang lain*, He likes to deceive others. **penj–** impostor. –² more or less, roughly like this.

semua all. – *kata²nja itu bohong belaka*, All his words were just a lie. **ke–an** totality. ~ *penjelenggaraan* total execution. **ke–nja** all of it, everything. **–nja** all of them. *Berikan dia ~*, Give him all of them.

semuka with the same appearance. see MUKA.

semula see MULA.

semur dish of stewed meat. **menj–** to stew.

semut ant. **ke–(–)an** to go to sleep, as arm or leg. *Kaki saja ~*, My foot's gone to sleep. **menj–** to swarm, teem. *Orang ~ ditanah lapang itu*, The square was swarming with people. **–an** = KE–(–)AN. – *sentada* an ant.

sén 1 cent. 2 signal, directional indicator (auto.). **–an** 1 one-cent piece. 2 by cents.

senak 1 tight, oppressed. *Napasnja* –, He had a tightness in his chest. 2 with a stuffed feeling (from overeating). **ke–an** 1 with a stuffed feeling (from overeating). 2 with an oppressed feeling. **ke– –²an** to suffer from s.t. oppressive. **menj–** to overflow, run over. **menj–kan** 1 to oppress. *Ia tak tahu apa jg ~ dadanja itu*, He didn't know what was oppressing his chest. 2 oppressive. **ter–** 1 tonguetied. 2 with a lump in the throat. *Ia ~ kata*, He couldn't utter a word.

senam 1 gymnastics. 2 indigo blue. **ber–** 1 to do physical exercises. 2 to stretch (after resting).

senandung ber– to hum.

senang 1 comfortable. *Saja – sekali*, I'm very comfortable. 2 happy, contented. 3 pleasure, entertainment. 4 calm. **ber– –²** to enjoy, have a good time. **ke–an** pleasure, contentment.

memper– to amuse. **memper–kan** to do s.o. a favor. **menj–i** to like, be contented with. **menj–kan** 1 to please. 2 pleasant. 3 interesting. 4 favorable. *djawaban jg ~ a* favorable reply. **penj–** 1 s.t. which or s.o. who gives pleasure or comfort. 2 entertainer. – *hati* contented, satisfied. *dgn – hati* with pleasure. *tak – ill* at ease.

senantiasa always, continuosly.

senapan(g) rifle, gun. – *angin* air rifle. – *kembar* double-barreled shotgun. – *mesin* machine gun.

sénapati commander in chief.

senar string.

sénat 1 faculty senate. 2 senate.

senawi passenger who is working his way.

senda – *-gurau* 1 joke, pleasantry. 2 fun. **ber–** to joke. **memper–kan** to joke with s.o.

sendal sandal. **menj–** to pilfer.

sendang well, source.

sendat to stagnate (of water). **ter–** confined, oppressed.

sendawa gunpowder.

sendél to lean against. **ber–** *bahu* shoulder to shoulder.

séndéng 1 slanting, leaning. 2 mentally off. **menj–** to lean, slant. **menj–kan** to tilt s.t. **ter– –²** to swing the hips in walking.

séndér ber– to lean. **–an** back. ~ *kursi* back of a chair.

sendi 1 base, foundation. 2 hinge, joint. **ber–** based, founded (on). **ber– –²** with joints. **memper–kan, menj–kan** to base on s.t. **per–an** 1 foundation, base. 2 joint. – *éngsél* hinge (joint).

sendiri 1 self, myself, himself, herself, themselves, ourselves. 2 own. 3 separate, apart. **ber–, menj–** 1 to be alone, apart. 2 to retire. 3 isolated, separated. **menj–kan** to isolate s.t. or s.o. **penj–** solitary. **penj–an** isolation. ~ *golongan* group isolation. **ter–** 1 alone, apart. 2 special. 3 separately. **ter– –²** individual. *Tiap² benda harus diterangkan ~*, Every article must be declared individually. **–an** alone. *dgn –(nja)* 1 automatically. 2 it is assumed, taken for granted.

sendja twilight. – *buta* late twilight. – *kala* twilight.

sendjak see SEDJAK.

séndjang asymmetrical.

sendjata 1 weapon. 2 vowel sign in Arabic script. **ber–** armed. *gerombolan ~* armed band. **memper–i** to arm s.t. **per–an** armament, arms. – *api* firearms. – *berat* heavy artillery. –

makan tuan s.t. that backfires, turns, against o.

séndok spoon. – *makan* a spoon resembling a dessert spoon and used as the principal implement for eating Indonesian-style meals.

sendorong ter– to slide off.

sendratari ballet.

senduk spoon. menj– to ladle out.

Senén Monday. *berpuasa – (dan) Kemis* to fast on Monday and Thursday. *– -kemis* precarious. *Napasnja sdh – -kemis*, He's on his last legs. *Perusahaannja hidup – -kemis*, His firm is in a precarious state.

senéwen 1 nervous. 2 to have a nervous fit.

séng zinc. *– atap* corrugated iron (used for roofing).

sengadja intentional, deliberate, purposely. di– to be done on purpose.

sengal gout. *– pinggang* lumbago. –² *napas* out of breath.

sengam menj– to eat up, consume.

sengap to hold o's tongue. **menj–** 1 to deaden (of a sound). 2 to snap at.

sengat wasp's sting. menj– to sting. **penj–** wasp.

sengau 1 to talk through the nose. 2 nasal sound. menj–kan to nasalize. **penj–an** nasalization. **ter–kan** nasalized.

séngét haunted. menj–kan to place on o's side. **ter–** slanting.

senggajut ber– to dangle.

senggak 1 calling (to take up the dance, singing). 2 to applaud, cheer.

senggama see SANGGAMA.

senggang to be free, unoccupied (of time). *Datanglah kalau ada waktu –* , Please come when you are free.

senggara see SELENGGARA.

senggeruk snuff.

sénggol menj– to nudge with the arm. **–an** push, nudge.

senggugut irregular menstrual periods.

sengguk menj–, ter– 1 to doze. 2 to hiccup.

senggulung centipede.

senggut see SENGGUK.

sengih menj–kan 1 to open o's mouth a little. 2 to smile, grin.

sengir turpentinelike. **menj–** 1 to turn up o's nose. 2 to grin.

sengit 1 a stinging insect. 2 a sharp odor. 3 violent. 4 poignant.

sengkak menj– to massage the abdomen.

sengkang 1 crossbar, beam. 2 spoke. 3 diameter of a circle. menj– to stick, get stuck.

sengkarut ber– 1 with fingers intertwined. 2 confused.

sengkeling crossing of arms or legs. **menj–kan** to cross the arms or legs.

sengkelit rope for climbing.

sengkenit tick (insect).

sengkéta 1 lawsuit, legal action. 2 quarrel, dispute. **memper–kan** to quarrel over s.t. **per–an** quarrel, dispute.

sengkilit menj– to trip up by grabbing a leg.

sengkuap 1 shed. 2 awning.

sengsai 1 wretched. 2 emaciated.

séngsai a Chinese physician.

sengsara 1 misery. 2 suffering. 3 miserable. 4 to suffer. **ke–an** 1 misery. 2 grief. 3 suffering, torment. **menj–kan** to torment s.o.

sengsé see SENGSAI.

senguk menj– to sniff.

sengut ter– –² to snivel.

seni 1 high-pitched voice. 2 art. **ke–an** art. *– bangun* architecture. *– berperan* art of acting. *– lukis* art of painting. *– mendidik* art of teaching. *– pahat*, *– patung* sculpture. *– pentjak* art of self-defense. *– reklame* advertising. *– rupa* plastic arts. *– sastera* literary arts, literature. *– suara* music. *– sungging* enameling. *– tari* dancing. *– tjétak* typography. *– tunggang* equitation.

seni- see SENI.

seniah artistic.

seniman artist. **ke–an** artistry.

Senin see SENÉN.

seniwati artist (female).

senjak see SUNJI.

senjampang 1 it's lucky that. 2 supposing that.

senjap 1 see SUNJI. 2 see LENJAP.

senjar sensation from hitting o's funny bone in the elbow.

senjawa see NJAWA.

senjum a smile. **ter–** to smile. ~ *kambing* to give an ironical smile. ~ *radja* to give a disbelieving smile. ~ *simpul* to smile subtly. **–an** a smile.

senonoh proper. *tidak –* improper.

sénsor censor.

sénsur censorship. di– censored.

sénsus census.

senta ship's keel.

sentak menj– to snap at s.o.

séntak menj–kan to pull at, jerk at. **ter–** *bangun* to wake up with a start.

sental see SINTAL. **menj–** 1 to rub, scrub. 2 to scour.

sentana 1 relative of a member of a noble family. 2 possible. *Kalau – ...* If possible ... *dgn tidak* ber– without further ado.

sentap see SENTAK.

sentara see SEMENTARA. *djangan* – ... let alone ...

sentausa see SENTOSA.

sénténg 1 in short supply, scarce. 2 to starve. 3 not all there, a little off. **ke–an** scarcity, shortage.

sénter flashlight. **menj–i** 1 to light with a flashlight. 2 to expose (in photography). – *por* center forward in soccer.

senteri see SANTRI.

sénti centimeter.

sentiasa see SENANTIASA.

sentil menj– to snap o's fingers. **ter–** to protrude a little. **–an** scolding.

séntimén sentiment.

séntiméntil sentimental.

senting see GENTING.

sentosa 1 quiet. 2 safe. 3 tranquillity. 4 safety. **ber–** 1 peaceful, safe. 2 peaceful, quiet. **ke–an** 1 rest. 2 peace. 3 safety. **menj–kan** 1 to protect. 2 to provide rest.

séntral central. – *listrik* electric power station.

séntralisasi centralization. **menj–kan** to centralize.

sentuh physical contact, touch. **ber–an** *dgn* to have contact with, get in touch with. **menj–** to touch s.t., nudge. **per–an** contact. **ter–** 1 to touch. 2 to nudge slightly.

sentung pelalai a charm which prevents a woman from obtaining a husband.

senuh full feeling from overeating.

séok ter– –² to stagger.

seorang see ORANG.

sép chief, boss. **ber–** *kpd* to serve s.o., be subordinate to.

sepada "anybody in?" (said when entering a shop or a home).

sepadan see PADAN.

sepah chewed sugar cane. **menj–** to chew. – *radja* bird of paradise.

sépah ter– in disorder, scattered around.

sepak spike, nail.

sépak kick. **menj–** to kick. ~ *silat* to kick with the inside of o's foot. ~ *singkur* to kick with the outside of o's foot. **per–bolaan** soccer affairs. – *bola* soccer. – *raga* kickball. – *terdjang* 1 to kick, ill-treat. 2 behavior, activity.

sepakat see PAKAT. **ber–** unanimous. **menj–i** to agree on s.t. **per–an** agreement.

sepakbor mudguard on car.

sepala-pala see PALA.

sepan 1 to fit exactly. 2 tight. **menj–** to fit tightly.

sepandjang see PANDJANG.

sepangkalan see PANGKALAN.

sepanjol 1 Spanish. 2 Spain.

sepantun see PANTUN.

separuh see PAROH.

sepasan see SEPESAN.

sepasi see SPASI.

sepat 1 sour. 2 acid. 3 k.o. fish.

sepatu 1 shoe. 2 boot. **ber–** shod. – (*ber*)*duri* spikes, spiked shoes. – *bola* soccer shoes. – *karét* tennis, basketball shoes. – *kuda* horseshoes. – *luar* overshoe, galosh. – *tinggi* high heels (of ladies).

sepéda bicycle. **ber–** to bike. – *kumbang* motorbike. – *motor* motorcycle. – *roda tiga* tricycle.

sepél to play. **menj–** to spell. **–an** spelling.

sepélé worthless. **–²** *sadja* nothing big. *Dia bukan orang* –, He's an important person.

sepemeluk see PELUK.

sepeninggal see TINGGAL.

seperai sheet. – *dan bantal* bedclothes.

seperti 1 like. 2 as. **–nja** 1 for example. 2 regarding.

sepesan centipede.

sepi 1 quiet, still. 2 desolate, lonely. 3 weak (market). **ke–an** 1 solitude. 2 deserted, lonely. **menj–** 1 to grow still. 2 to retire into seclusion. – *ing pamrih* free of personal desire.

sepih splintered.

sepintas-lalu see PINTAS.

sepir jailer.

sepit narrow. **menj–** to pinch, squeeze. **penj–** 1 tweezers. 2 pincers (lobster). **ter–** to be in a tight place. – *angkup* 1 pair of tweezers. 2 clothes peg.

sepoa abacus.

sepoi Indian soldier. **ber– –²** to blow softly (of a breeze). **–² *basa*** to be gentle (of wind).

sepor 1 train. 2 sport. – *balas* freight train.

Sépt. [*Séptémber*] September.

Séptémber September.

sepuh 1 dark in color. 2 old. 3 gilding material. **menj–** to gild. **penj–** gold leaf. **ter–** gilt. **–an** gilded. – *emas* gilt.

seput fast, quick, by express train.

sera ter– –² hastily, in a hurry.

serabai pancake.

serabut 1 fiber. 2 fibrous, coarse.

seragam see RAGAM.

serah ber–, menj– to surrender. *Musuh* ~ , The enemy surrendered. **menj–i** 1 to hand over, deliver. 2 to instruct, put at o's disposal. **menj–kan** 1 to surrender, hand over. 2 to transfer s.t. 3 to leave up to, relegate. ~ *diri* to give o.s. up. **penj–fatalist. **penj–an** 1 transfer. ~ *kedaulatan* transfer of sovereignty. 2

surrender. 3 delegation. ~ *kekuasaan* delegation of authority. 4 extradition. ~ *kembali* restoration, return. **ter**-as you will. ~ *padamu*, It's up to you. (I leave it to you). – *pakai* surrender for use.

sérah bright red.

serahi flask.

serai gulai citronella grass.

sérai ter- scattered, dispersed.

seraja 1 simultaneously. 2 assistant. 3 while. **menj**- to ask for help.

serak hoarse. – *serik* term for the sound made in scrubbing a floor.

sérak ber- to scatter, spread. **menjkan** to scatter. **ter**- scattered.

serakah greedy. **ke-an** greed.

seram horrible, hair-raising. **menjkan** 1 to bristle (of hair). 2 hairraising. 3 exciting, thrilling. 4 terrifying. – *kulit* goose flesh.

serambi 1 porch, veranda. 2 front yard. – *djantung* auricle of the heart.

serampang harpoon. **menj**- to harpoon s.t. **-an** at random. – *duabelas* popular Indonesian social dance.

seran stripe.

Séran Ceram.

seranah a curse.

serandang trestle. **menj**- to support.

serandung ter- to stumble.

serang boatswain. **ber**- to make larger. **menj**- to attack. **penj**- attacker, aggressor. (**penj**)-**an** attack, offensive. ~ *djantung* heart attack.

serangga insect.

seranggung ber- to sit bent forward.

serangkak barbs used to prevent s.o. from climbing a tree. – *pajung* umbrella stays.

serani Christian. *Ia masuk* –, He became a Christian. **di-kan** to be legally married. **menj-kan** to convert, Christianize.

seranta menj-kan to proclaim widely.

serap menj- 1 to absorb a fluid. 2 to pervade. (**penj**)-**an** absorption. – *mesra* intimate.

sérap 1 reserve. 2 stock. 3 spare. *ban* – spare tire. **menj-kan** to hold in reserve, lay aside.

serapah 1 curse. 2 exorcism. **menj**-1 to exorcise. 2 to curse.

serasah 1 manure, offal. 2 a printed cotton fabric from India. 3 mountain rapids.

serasi matching. see RASI. **ke-an** matching look, appearance, harmony. **menj-kan** 1 to adapt. 2 to remodel, fix up, redo. *-kanlah rumah Anda*, Remodel your home. ~ *diri* to adapt o.s.

serat 1 fiber. 2 tight, jammed. **ter**-stuck fast. – *rayon* staple fiber.

Serawak Sarawak.

serba 1 all, all sorts of. 2 fully, wholly. – *anéka* various kinds. *Barang²* – *anéka didasar ditoko itu*, Various kinds of goods are displayed in that store. – *aku* egotistic. – *banjak* abundant. – *baru* brand-new. – *bisa* all-round, versatile. – *dapat* allaround. – *déwa* polytheistic. – *dua* dualism. – *géografi* purely geographical. – *guna* multipurpose. – *hémat* quite economical. – *hitam* all-black. – *matjam* various sorts. – *menguntungkan* quite profitable. – *omongan* just idle chatter. – *roh* spiritualism. – *putih* all-white. – *rumah* furniture. – *salah* off, wrong. – *sama* homogeneous. – *sedikit* a little of everything. – *serbi* all sorts of things. – *tudju* teleology. – *zat* materialism.

serbak see SEMERBAK. **menj-kan** to spread an odor.

serban turban. *Ia sdh memakai* –, He has made the pilgrimage.

serbat 1 sherbet. 2 k.o. ginger drink.

serbét napkin.

serbu menj-, menj-kan *diri* to attack, invade. **penj**- attacker. (**penj**)-**an** attack, invasion.

serbuk 1 dust. 2 pollen. **menj**- to pulverize. **menj-kan** to pollinate. **penj-an** pollination. – *besi* iron filings. – *gergadji* sawdust.

serdadu soldier.

serdak fine dust.

serdawa a belch. **ber**- to belch.

serdih protruding (of the chest).

seré see SERAI.

seregang see REGANG. **per-an** discord.

serem see SERAM.

serempak 1 all at once. 2 all together. **menj**- to overwhelm. **ter**-overwhelmed.

serémpét ke- grazed against s.t. **menj**- to graze, brush against s.t.

seréndéng menj- to careen.

serendjang at o's full length.

seréng rocket.

serenta 1 with. 2 soon. *dgn* – 1 immediately. 2 indirectly.

serentak jointly, together.

sérep see SÉRAP.

seret 1 to be sluggish, slow-moving (of traffic, the movement of goods). 2 hard, difficult.

sérét 1 see SERET. 2 dragging, trailing behind. 3 stripe. **menj**- to drag. **ter**- carried away with compassion.

sergah menj- to snap, snarl at s.o.

sergap menj- 1 to attack, ambush. 2 to snarl at. **-an** attack, ambush.

seri 1 royal honorific. – *Paduka* His Majesty. 2 splendor. 3 light. 4 see

SARI. 5 to have a draw (in sports).
ber– to shine, twinkle (of stars).
∼ muka to blush. **ber– –²** to shine,
beam. **menj–** to suck honey. – *pang-gung* star of the stage. – *pantai* nice
at close quarters.

séri series. **ber–** in a series.

seriawan sprue. – *usus* dysentery.

seribu 1,000.

séri(e)us serious.

serigala jackal.

serigunting a k.o. blackbird.

serik frightened.

serikaja 1 sweet sop. 2 mixture of
eggs, sugar, and coconut cream.

serikat 1 united, allied. *Amérika* –
the United States of America. 2
union, league, alliance. – *Islam*
Islamic league. **ber–** united, allied.
menj–kan *Allah* to be polytheistic.
per–an organization, association,
union. **∼** *Bangsa²* the United Nations. – *Afrika Selatan* Union of
South Africa. – *buruh* labor union.

serimbit see RIMBIT.

serimpi Javanese court dancer.

serindit a parakeet.

sering 1 tight-fitting of clothes. 2
slender. 3 often. **ke–an** frequency.
menj– to plait. – *kali* often. **–nja**
perkawinan frequency of marriage.

seringai a grin. **menj–** to grin.

seriosa semiclassical and classical
music.

serit a fine-toothed comb.

serkah 1 torn. 2 broken off. **menj–**
to rip to pieces.

serkai menj– 1 to wring out. 2
to filter.

serkap cone-shaped fish trap. **menj–**
1 to catch in a *serkap*. 2 to arrest,
catch. 3 to surprise. **menj–i** to cover
with s.t. **penj–an** raid, surprise attack.

serkup menj– to seize by covering
with the hand.

serling pitfall. **ter–** to get into a
pitfall.

sernak menj– *hati* 1 to press. 2
to pinch.

séro 1 share (bus.). 2 to have a share,
an interest, in a firm or business.
3 fish trap. **pe–** shareholder. **per–an**
company, commercial firm. **∼** *terbatas*
incorporated, limited.

serobot menj– 1 to act highhandedly.
2 to steal s.t. away, pilfer. 3 to get
the upper hand, the best, of s.o. 4
to occupy illegally. **penj–an** illegal
occupancy.

serodja lotus.

sérok 1 tributary of river or creek.
2 bay, inlet. **–an** drain, gutter.

serombong pipe, tube.

serondol see SONDOL.

serondong see SONDONG.

sérong 1 askew (of road or vision).
2 squinting. 3 slanting. **ke–an** 1 insincerity. 2 disloyalty. 3 corruption.
menj– to go askew. **menj–kan** to
tilt, slant. **– –menj–** crisscross. – *hati*
1 insincere. 2 unfaithful.

seronok pleasant, agreeable.

seropot menj– to sip s.t.

serpih splinter, scale, flake. **menj–** to
splinter. – *kaju* chips, wood shavings.

serpis service (on a car). *mudah di-easy* to service.

sérsan 1 sergeant. 2 petty officer
second class. – *kadét* technical sergeant. – *kepala* sergeant first class. –
major 1 master sergeant. 2 petty officer first class. – *udara* master sergeant (air force).

sérse detective.

sérsi 1 see SÉRSE. 2 serge.

serta 1 with, along with. *Beliau* –
rombongan tiba disini, He and his
party arrived here. 2 as soon as. –
ia mendengar berita itu, ia pergi,
As soon as he heard the report, he
went. **be–** 1 along with, as well
as. *Ia mesti berangkat* **∼** *saja,*
He has to leave along with me. 2
to take part, join in. **mempe(r)–kan,**
menj–kan to enclose s.t. **menj–i**
1 to participate in. *Ia* **∼** *rapat itu,*
He participated in the meeting. 2
to accompany s.t. or s.o. **pe–** participant. **pe–an** participation. **penj–an**
enclosure, attachment. – *bunji* consonant. – *merta* immediately.

sertarasa 1 sympathy. 2 empathy.

sértipikat certificate.

sertu menj– to cleanse o.s. after
contact with unclean animals.

seru 1 call, cry. 2 sharp, violent. 3
enthusiastic. **ber–** to call, shout out.
∼ *kpd* to appeal to s.o. **menj–** 1 to
call. 2 to hail (a cab, etc.). **menj–kan**
1 to call out, proclaim (o's wares).
2 to announce, broadcast. 3 to proclaim. *Ia* **∼** *damai,* He proclaimed
peace. **penj–** announcer. **(penj)–an**
1 call, summons. 2 exclamation. 3
a toast. 4 appeal.

seruak menj– to push aside.

serual trousers.

serudi ber– cut, polished (precious
stones). **menj–** to polish.

seruduk menj– to push from a
crouching position.

seruit harpoon. **menj–** to harpoon.

seruling k.o. flute.

serumah see RUMAH.

serunai a k.o. clarinet.

serundéng see SERUNDING.

serunding dish of grated coconut.

serunting see SUNTING.

serut small plane (carpenter's tool). menj– to plane.

serutu cigar.

sesadjén offering, sacrifice.

sesah a beating. ber– bertindju to have a violent fight. menj– to wash clothing.

sesak 1 narrow, close. 2 crowded, tight. 3 to be in a fix. ber– –² to crowd. ke–an 1 oppressiveness, closeness. 2 tightness. 3 to be in a fix. menj–(kan) 1 to oppress. 2 to urge. 3 to push. ~ napas sultry, close. ter– 1 to be hard pressed, hard put to it. 2 embarrassed. – dada, – napas short-winded. – kentjing an urge to urinate.

sesal 1 regret, remorse. 2 repentance. kemenj–an regret, repentance. menj–(akan) to be sorry, regret. Saja ~ mengirim surat kepadanja, I'm sorry I wrote her a letter. menj–i 1 to blame, reproach. 2 to repent. menj–kan 1 to regret, be sorry for. Saja ~ perbuatan saja jg kasar itu, I was sorry for my rude act. 2 to blame. Ia ~ saja tentang nasibnja jg malang itu, He blamed me for his bad luck. 3 to repent. ~ diri to reproach o.s. with. penj–an 1 regret, remorse. 2 reproach. –an regret, repentance.

sesama 1 fellow. Jg diundangnja hanja – pegawai sadja, He just invited his colleagues. 2 see SAMA.

sesap an abandoned field. menj– 1 to sip, lap up. 2 to suck. Anak itu ~ susu ibunja, The baby was sucking its mother's breast. – ber–djerami abandoned field with stubble still visible.

sesar menj–kan to move, push s.t. aside. Ia ~ tutup djendéla, She moved the curtain aside.

sesat 1 to lose o's way. Ia – didjalan, He lost his way. 2 to have go astray, lose. Ia – dlm agamanja, He lost the point of his religion. 3 to deviate. anasir² nasional jg – nationalist deviationist elements. ber– 1 to be on the wrong track. 2 lost. ke–an 1 losing o's way. 2 slip, digression. 3 error. ~ pengadilan miscarriage of justice. menj–kan 1 to lead astray, mislead. 2 misleading. ter– to be lost. Kami ~ dihutan itu, We lost our way in the forest. – barat to lose o's bearings.

seseorang see ORANG.

sésér dragnet.

sesuai 1 to fit. Badju itu tak – baginja, The dress doesn't fit her. 2 to jibe, tally. Perbuatannja tak – dgn kedudukannja dlm masjarakat, His behavior did not conform with his social position. 3 to agree with. Meréka tak – dlm perundingan itu, They didn't agree in the discussion. 4 to coincide with (dgn). ber–an 1 (of pl. subject) to be in accord (with e.o.). 2 (of sing. subj.) to be in accord (dgn with). berke–an to have uniformity. ke–an uniformity, conformity. menj–kan 1 to adjust, adapt. Ia tak dpt ~ diri dlm suasana itu, She couldn't adjust to the environment. 2 to reconcile, bring into line. Meréka ~ pendapat meréka, They reconciled their opinions. penj–an adaptation, adjustment. per–an agreement, concurrence.

sesuatu see SUATU.

sesudah see SUDAH.

sesumbar ber– 1 to challenge. 2 to revile. 3 to swear. Ia ~ akan membunuh orang itu kalau ia tertipu lagi, He swore to kill that person if he was betrayed again.

sesungguhnja see SUNGGUH.

seta cubit.

setabelan artillery.

setabil stable. ke–an stability.

setagén abdominal sash worn by Indonesian women.

setahu see TAHU.

setakona octagon.

setala see TALA.

setalén quarter (coin).

setambuk 1 genealogical register. 2 roll book.

setambul 1 Istambul. 2 name of a stage show.

sétan Satan, devil. ke–an possessed. menj– to perform a daredevil act.

setandar standard.

setangga see TETANGGA.

setanggi incense.

setap staff. see STAF.

setara see TARA.

setasiun station. – keréta api railway station. – pengamatan tracking, monitoring station.

setat list, roll, statement. – gadji payroll.

setater starter. menj– to start the engine. Mobilnja di–, The car was started.

setawar dan sedingin 1 refreshment(s). 2 k.o. medicine for fever.

seték cutting, slip of a plant.

setéker see STÉKER.

setél 1 set, suit. satu – a suit of clothes. 2 to match. Tjelana dan djasnja tidak –, His trousers and coat don't match. menj– 1 to tune up, adjust. Ia pandai ~ mesin, He was good at tuning up the engine. 2 to turn on. Ia ~ radio, He turned on the radio. 3 to match. Ia pandai ~

warna, She was good at matching colors. 4 to set a clock. **se– o. set.** *pakaian* ∼ a suit of clothes. **–an** a set of s.t. *tjangkir* ∼ a set of cups. *pakaiannja* ∼ a suit of clothes. – *kartu* deck of cards.

setelah see TELAH.

setéléng exhibition. **menj–kan** to exhibit.

setéling 1 position. *Dipantai banjak – tentara,* There are many military positions along the beach. 2 to take a position. *Polisi – ditengah djalan,* Police took up a position in the middle of the street. **menj–** 1 to put s.t. in position. 2 to surround. *Polisi* ∼ *rumah djudi,* The police surrounded the gambling house.

setém 1 vote. 2 tune, in tune. *Pianonja tidak –,* The piano isn't in tune. **menj–** 1 to vote. 2 to tune. *Ia* ∼ *piano,* He tuned the piano. **–an** voting.

setempat see TEMPAT.

setémpel stamp. **menj–** to stamp s.t.

setengah see TENGAH.

seterap punishment. **menj–** to punish. *Ia di– oléh gurunja,* He was punished by his teacher. **–an** prisoner.

seterék **menj–kan** to push, press, flip on (a button, switch). – *éser* an iron.

seteria see KESATERIA.

seterik 1 hair ribbon. 2 strict.

seterika iron, flatiron. **ber–** ironed. *kemédja jg* ∼ an ironed shirt. **menj–** 1 to iron s.t. 2 to flatten, smash. *Negeri itu kita –,* We'll flatten that country. **–an** 1 iron. 2 clothes for ironing. – *listrik* electric iron.

seterimin gauze.

seterip 1 stripe, badge. 2 line.

seteru enemy, foe. **ber–** hostile. *Meréka* ∼ *kpd orang baru,* They are hostile toward newcomers. **memper-kan** 1 to dislike intensely. *Ia* ∼ *gurunja,* He disliked his teacher intensely. 2 to make an enemy of s.o. **menj–i** to dislike, be hostile toward s.o. *Ia* ∼ *tetangganja,* He assumed a hostile attitude toward his neighbor. **per–an** enmity, hostility.

seterum electric current. **ke–** to get a shock (from electricity). **menj–** 1 to induce. 2 to electrify, charge. *Ia* ∼ *aki,* He charged the battery.

seterup syrup used in preparing cold drinks.

setia loyal, faithful. **ber–** to be loyal. **ke–an** loyalty, allegiance. **ke–kawanan** solidarity.

setiap see TIAP.

setiar to do o's best.

setiawan faithful.

setik stitch. **–an** game of marbles. – *balik* a seam. – *hiasan* ornamental stitch. – *silang* cross-stitch.

setinggil audience hall.

setip eraser. **menj–** to erase.

setir 1 steering wheel. 2 bicycle handle bar. **menj–** to drive, steer. **penj–** driver. – *kiri* left-hand drive.

setiwal leggings.

setjara see TJARA.

setolop glass cover.

setop 1 to stop. 2 stewed (of fruit). **menj–** to stop. **penj–an** stopping. **–an** stop (bus, streetcar).

setopelés glass jar with stopper.

setor poured, deposited. **menj–(kan)** to deposit. *Ia* ∼ *uang dibang,* He deposited the money in a bank. **(penj)–an** deposit, payment.

setori to quarrel, bicker. *Ia selalu – dgn madjikannja,* He was always quarreling with his boss.

setrék see SETERÉK.

setrum see SETERUM.

setu a favorable influence. **menj–i** to bless.

setubuh see TUBUH.

setudén student.

setudju see TUDJU.

setum steam. **menj–** 1 to dry-clean with steam. 2 to blow off, let off steam. *Ia naik –,* He flew into a rage.

seturi see SETORI.

seturu plot, conspiracy.

séwa rent, hire. **menj–** 1 to rent. *Ia* ∼ *rumah baru,* He rented a new house. 2 to hire. **memper-kan, menj-kan** to hire out, rent out. *Ia* ∼ *mobilnja,* He hired out his car. **penj-tenant,** lessee. **penj–an** renting out. **per–an** *tanah* land rental. **–an** rented, hired articles. – *rumah* house rent.

sewadjarnja see WADJAR.

séwah dagger.

séwaka 1 tribute, homage. 2 service. 3 asylum. **ber–** 1 to pay homage, honor. 2 to serve, wait upon. see SUAKA.

sewenang-wenang see WENANG.

S.G.A. [*Sekolah Guru Atas*] normal school.

S.G.B. [*Sekolah Guru Bawah*] junior normal school.

shahadan see SJAHDAN.

shakti see SAKTI.

shalat see SALAT.

si a k.o. definite article used (1) before names (as form of reference). – *Abdul* Abdul. – *Anu* Mr. So-and-So. *Mana – Mat?* Where's that Mat? (2) before nonproper nouns. – *alamat* addressee. – *orang préman atau – militér* a civilian or military person. – *pengirim* sender. (3) before words

which describe s.o. or s.t. (especially
used as pet names). – *Kurus* the
Thin One. – *Tolol* the Stupid One.
sia² 1 in vain, futile, useless. *Usahanja – sadja*, His efforts were all in
vain. – *ia datang kemari*, It was
futile for him to come here. 2 meaningless. *Ia kira perdjandjian kita –
sadja*, He thought our promise was
meaningless. 3 indifferently. *Ia men-
tjela setjara – sadja*, He criticized in
an indifferent manner. **ber- –²** useless.
ke- –²an futility. **me-nj-²kan** 1 to
neglect. *Ia ∼ pekerdjaannja*, He
neglected his work. 2 to ignore. *Ia ∼
naséhat*, He ignored the advice. 3
to waste. *Ia ∼ uang*, She wasted
money. 4 to underestimate. *Djangan
∼ musuh*, Don't underestimate the
enemy. 5 to foil, frustrate. **ter-** 1
futile, useless, in vain. *Usahanja ∼* ,
Her efforts were in vain. 2 wasted.
waktu jg ∼ wasted time. 3 neglected.
Pekerdjaannja ∼ , His job was
neglected.
siaga ready, prepared. **ke-an** readiness. see SIAP.
siah menj– to lift up and lay aside.
Ia ∼ kelambu, She lifted up the
mosquito netting and laid it aside.
– *lajah* to sway, stagger. *Pohon itu –
lajah ditiup angin*, The trees were
swaying from the wind. *Orang mabuk
itu berdjalan – lajah*, The drunk
staggered down the way.
siak 1 mosque caretaker. 2 the poor
who depend upon mosque revenues.
ber- to pour.
sial 1 to be unlucky. *Ia orang –*,
She was an unlucky person. 2 unfortunate, unhappy. *Hari ini –
baginja*, This day was unfortunate
for him. **ke-an** bad luck. **menj-kan**
to cause bad luck. **-an** bird of ill
omen. – *dangkalan* extremely unlucky.
Ali selalu – dangkalan, Ali never has
any luck. – *kamu!* To hell with you!
Wah, – ini! Tough luck!
sialang beehive. **ber-** 1 to swarm
(of bees). 2 to gather honey.
sialat see TJIALAT.
siamang 1 gibbon. 2 wolfram, tung-
sten.
siang 1 day, daylight period. 2 period
from 11 A.M. to 3 P.M. *Sdh –*, It's late
in the morning. 3 weeded (of a garden). 4 cleaned (of a fish). **ber-** to
clean s.t. **ke-an** 1 caught by daylight.
Rupanja putjat seperti bulan ∼ ,
He looked as pale as the moon in the
daytime. 2 late, too late. *Ia ∼
ter-buru² pergi kekantor*, He was late
and hurried to the office. 3 to oversleep. *Ia ∼ terlambat pergi kekelas*,

He overslept and arrived late to
class. **menj–** 1 to clean fish. *Ia ∼
ikan sebelum menggoréngnja*, She
cleaned the fish before frying it.
2 to clear away, off. *Ia ∼ hutan utk
meladang*, He cleared away the
jungle in order to cultivate it. **menj-i**
to weed s.t. **–²** early. *Datanglah ∼
supaja dpt tempat*, Come early so
you'll get a place. – *hari* daytime.
pd – hari by day. – *malam* night and
day.
sianu see SI.
siap 1 ready. *Meréka – utk pergi*,
They were ready to go. 2 finished,
through. *Pekerdjaannja sdh –*, His
job was finished. 3 prepared. *Meréka
– menghadapi kesukaran*, They were
prepared to face difficulties. 4 attention. *–!* Attention! **ber-** 1 attention. *∼!* Attention! 2 to be
ready, prepared. *Ia ∼ utk pergi*, He
was ready to go. 3 on your mark
(in racing). **ber- –²**, ber- *-sedia* to
make preparations. *Meréka ∼ utk
pergi*, They were making preparations
to go. **ber-** *-siaga* to be prepared, be
on the *qui vive*. **ke-siagaan** preparations. **memper-kan** 1 to arrange.
Ia ∼ panitia, He arranged a committee. 2 to prepare. *Ia ∼ laporan*,
He prepared a report. *Guru ∼
murid²nja utk udjian*, The teacher
prepared his pupils for the examination. 3 to put in order, finish. *Ia
harus ∼ pekerdjaannja*, He had to
put his work in order. **menj-i** 1 to
prepare. *Ia ∼ ladangnja utk ditanami*,
He prepared his fields for planting. 2 to equip. *Rumah itu di-i utk
diséwakan*, The house was equipped
for renting out. 3 to coach. *Ia ∼
adiknja utk udjian*, He coached his
younger brother for an examination.
menj-kan to ready. *Ia ∼ barang² jg
akan dibawa*, He readied the things
he was taking along. **per-an** 1 prepa-
ration(s). 2 setup, arrangement. *∼
pengurus kumpulan itu tidak lengkap*,
The setup of the board of the association is not complete. 3 supply. **-²an**
always prepared. – *-sedia* fully prepared. – *-siaga* prepared, ready for
action.
siapa 1 who. – *itu?* Who's that?
2 what. – *namanja?* What's his
name? – *konon* whoever, who. **–²**
who(so)ever. *∼ tidak membeli kartjis
tidak boléh masuk*, Anyone who fails
to buy a ticket cannot be admitted.
bukan ∼ no o. *Jg datang bukan ∼
melainkan teman²nja jg karib sadja*,
The only ones who came were his
close friends. **-pun** *djuga* whoever.

siar ber– to be on fire. ber–(–) to stroll about. menj–kan 1 to spread. *Ia* ~ *kabar*, He spread the news. 2 to announce. *Pemerintah* ~ *peraturan baru*, The government announced a new regulation. 3 to broadcast. *Kabar itu di–kan semalam*, The news was broadcast last night. penj– 1 announcer. 2 publisher. 3 transmitter. (penj)–an 1 broadcast. 2 announcement. 3 publication, issue. 4 circulation, spread. ~ *kilat* bulletin, leaflet. ~ *radio* broadcast. – *bakar* on fire.

siasat 1 tactics. 2 strategy. – *perang* war strategy. 3 punishment. 4 method, system, policy. – *mengadjar* teaching methods. 5 consideration, thought. ber– 1 to apply strategy, be tactful. 2 to maneuver an army. 3 to be discreet. menj–(i) 1 to investigate. 2 to interrogate. 3 to apply a method, system, strategy. 4 to reconnoiter. menj–(kan) 1 to punish. 2 to ask about a person, examine s.o. *Bila kami boléh* ~ , *saudara hendak kemana?* If I may ask, where are you going? penj–an strategy.

siau 1 back to normal, cooled off. *Demamnja sdh* –, The fever is gone. 2 digestion. ber– to be back to normal (of temperature). menj– to digest. *makanan jg tak mudah di–* food difficult to digest.

sibak ber– 1 parted, separated. *rambut jg* ~ parted hair. 2 separated. *Meréka* ~ *diluar kota*, They separated outside the city. menj– to separate, part. me–nj–² 1 to delouse. 2 to part, cleave. *Perahu* ~ *gelombang*, The prow parted the waves. 3 to sift the facts.

sibir a small slice of s.t. *se– kuéh* a small slice of cake. –an a small slice. – *rulang* the apple of o's eye.

sibuk busy, occupied. *Ia – bekerdja*, She's busy working. ke–an stir, bustle, activity. menj– to spy on s.o. menj–kan 1 to stir, incite. *Bandjir itu* ~ *penduduk utk pindah*, The flood stirred the people to move. 2 to occupy, busy o.s. with. *Ia* ~ *soal temannja*, He gave a lot of thought to his friend's problems.

sibur ladle, scoop. menj– to ladle, scoop. –² dragonfly.

sida castrated. menj– to castrate. –² eunuch.

sidang 1 (single) session, meeting. 2 council, group. ber– to convene, assemble, sit in session. *Parlemén* ~ , Parliament convened. menj–kan to convene a meeting, etc. per–an 1 meeting, assembly. 2 meeting place. 3 session (over several days). – *gabungan* joint session. – *gerédja* synod. – *hakim* members of the courts. – *paripurna* plenary session. – *pembatja* members of a reading circle. – *pengarang* editorial staff. – *perang* court-martial, military council. – *pléno* plenary session. – *ramai* the public.

sidik menj– to investigate. – *djari* fingerprint. – *midik* scrutiny, close examination. – *selidik* investigation, inquiry.

sidjingkat 1 to walk on tiptoe. 2 to make off.

sifat 1 quality. – *jg baik dan buruk* a good and bad quality. 2 property, shape. –*nja bundar*, It has a round shape. 3 attribute (of God). 4 prospect, aspect. *Pekerdjaan ini baik* –*nja*, This job has good prospects. 5 characteristic. – *asli* genuine characteristic. 6 features, looks. *Ia menguraikan – andjingnja jg hilang itu*, He explained the features of his lost dog. 7 nature. – *M.I.P.I.* the nature of M.I.P.I. ber– to have the quality, character(istic) of. *Itu* ~ *bundar*, It has a round shape. *Ia* ~ *lemah*, He has a weak nature. (He's gentle.) *Ia* ~ *penakut*, He's cowardly by nature. ~ *menjerang* aggressive in nature. ~ *tetap* permanent. menj–kan 1 to describe. *Ia* ~ *pengalamannja*, He described his experience. 2 to characterize s.t., s.o. – *ber–gado²* heterogeneous. – *chas* idiom. – *kebendaan* a materialistic nature. – *kelandjutan* continuity. – *kuping* helter-skelter. – *perawakan* personal description. – *tabi'at* character. *tidak ter–kan* indescribable.

sigai a notch, peg. menj– to climb a ladder.

sigak get out! (used to dogs).

sigap 1 efficient. 2 keen, clever. 3 energetic. ber– to be in readiness. *Ia sdh* ~ *utk perdjalanan itu*, He was ready for the trip. ke–an 1 efficiency. 2 energy. 3 capability.

sigasir mole cricket.

sigi torch. menj– 1 to light with a torch. *Meréka* ~ *kodok disungai*, They went frog hunting in the river with a torch. 2 to investigate. *Ia* ~ *soal pelarian*, He investigated the problem of refugees. 3 to point at, aim at. 4 to cleanse. 5 to pick, pull out.

sigung 1 see SINGGUNG. 2 polecat.

sih an enclitic used to soften or confirm what follows. *Ada apa* –? Is there anything wrong? *Saja – tidak salah*, I'm certainly not in the wrong.

sihir 1 black magic, witchcraft. 2

witch. **menj-(kan)** to practice black magic on s.o. *Katanja ia sakit karena di- orang*, They said he was ill because s.o. had practiced black magic on him.

sikap 1 attitude. *Bagaimana - pemerintah?* What is the government's attitude? 2 posture, attitude. *-nja tegap*, He has an erect posture. **ber-** 1 to stand at attention. 2 to have a certain attitude. *Partai ini ~ kanan*, This party has a rightist attitude. **menj-** to fold the arms. *- budi* character, kind attitude. *- laku* gesture, way of acting, behaving.

sikat 1 brush. *- gigi* toothbrush. 2 comb. 3 bunch, cluster. *se- pisang* a bunch of bananas. **menj-** 1 to brush. *Ia ~ gigi*, She brushed her teeth. 2 to comb. 3 to harrow. *Ia ~ ladang itu*, He harrowed the field. 4 to steal, take away. *Ia suka sekali ~ hak orang lain*, He likes to steal other's rights. 5 to massacre, wipe out, clean out. *Meréka ~ kaum pelarian dgn témbakan*, They massacred the refugees by shooting. **-an** stolen goods.

sikeras **ber-** 1 to use force, violence. 2 with all o's might. see KERAS.

sikit see SEDIKIT.

siksa torture. **menj-(i)**, **menj-kan** to torture s.o. **-an** torture, mistreatment.

siku 1 elbow. 2 right angle. 3 curve. **ber-** to have an angle, curve. *Djalan-nja ber- -²*, The road has a lot of curves. **menj-** 1 to form a rectangle. 2 to curve, bend. *Djalan ini ~* , This road curves. 3 to elbow o's way. 4 angular. **menj-kan** to elbow o's way. *-²* a triangle used by carpenters. *- bedil* rifle butt. *- djalan* hairpin turn. *- keluang* a zigzag design. *Tidak makan -*, That's not acceptable.

sikudidi sandpiper.

sikut elbow. **menj-** 1 to elbow o's way. 2 to deceive, cheat.

sila 1 stone, foundation. 2 cross-legged. **ber-** to sit on the floor with legs crossed. *~ panggung* to sit with knees pulled up. **memper-kan** 1 to invite. 2 to call on, invite. *Ketua per-kan sdr. Hamid*, The chairman calls on Mr. Hamid (to speak). **menj-kan** to invite, ask. *Ia ~ tamunja duduk*, He invited his guest to sit down. *-kan duduk*, Please sit down. *- kehormatan* code of honor. see 1 PANTJASILA. 2 SUSILA.

silaf see SILAP.

silah 1 wrong, error. 2 see SILA.

silam 1 disappeared, gone. *Matahari*

tlh -, The sun has gone down. *Hari tlh -*, It's become dark. 2 see SELAM. 3 darkness, gloom. **menj-** to disappear. **menj-kan** 1 to scuttle, sink s.t. 2 to dazzle s.o. **ter-** caught by darkness. *Ia ~ ditengah hutan*, He was caught by darkness in the middle of the jungle.

silang crosswise, intersecting. **ber-** 1 crossed. *Ia ~ kaki*, He had his legs crossed. 2 intersecting. *djalan ~* intersecting roads. 3 thick, dense, piled up. *Korsi ~ dihalaman*, The chairs were piled up in the yard. *~ mata* to look e.o. in the eyes. *~ siur* to cross back and forth (as in heavy traffic). **memper-kan, menj-(kan)** to cross. *Ia ~ kaki*, He crossed his legs. **per-an** crossing. *~ djalan keréta api* railroad crossing. *~ ras* racial mixture. **ter-** crossed. *dgn kakinja ~* with legs crossed. **-an** crossing (of feet, legs, or hands). *Ia melepaskan kakinja dari ~* , He uncrossed his legs. *- -menj* to crisscross. *- empat* crossroads. *- selimpat* 1 complicated. 2 crumpled, rumpled. *- selisih, - sengkéta* conflict, dispute. *- siur* crisscrossing.

silap 1 furious, angry. 2 wrong, false. 3 illusion. **ber-** 1 to conjure. 2 to deceive. **ke-an** mistake, slip, error. **menj-** to cheat, deceive. **penj-** 1 a cheat. 2 conjurer. *- mata* angry, furious.

silat a k.o. fencing. **ber-** to do the *silat*. **menj-** to parry, fend off. **per-an** *kata* repartee. *- kata* to speak glibly. *- lidah* glib of tongue.

silaturrahim 1 friendship. 2 good will.

silaturrahmi friendly.

silau dazzled, blinded by the glare. *Ia - karena sinar matahari*, He was blinded by the sun. **ber-** *mata memandang* to be blinded. **ke-an** blinded. **menj-kan** to blind s.o. *Sinar matahari soré ~ sopir mobil*, The afternoon sun blinded the driver.

silét razor blade.

silih **ber-** to turn, change into. *Malam ~ dgn siang*, Night turns into day. *~ ganti* by turns, changing. **menj-** 1 to change. *Ia ~ badju*, She changed her dress. 2 to shed skin (of reptiles). 3 to molt (of poultry). 4 to indemnify, expiate. *- berganti* alternating, o. after another. *- rugi* making indemnity. *- semilih* by turns.

silik **menj-** to observe, note carefully.

silir 1 soft breeze. 2 membrane. **ber-** *-²* soft blowing of a breeze. *- semilir* soft blowing of a breeze. **-an** *angin lalu* the blowing of a passing breeze.

silsilah pedigree, genealogy.

silu 1 painful feeling. 2 timid, modest. **ber-** to be modest, shy. **menjkan** 1 shameful, embarrassing. 2 to move, affect.

siluman 1 k.o. spirit, ghost. 2 invisible.

silungkang k.o. woven cloth.

simaharadjaléla see MAHARADJALÉLA.

simak ber- to gather, group. *Meréka ~ dikamar muka,* They gathered in the front room. **menj-** 1 to gather, collect. *Ia ~ barang² jg tlh dipakai,* She gathered the used things together. 2 to listen to attentively.

simbah ber- to be drenched, bespattered. *Ia ~ darah,* He was bespattered with blood. **menj-** 1 to splash, bespatter. *Ombak ~ pesisir,* Waves splashed on the beach. 2 to break out, appear. *Keringatnja ~ dimukanja,* Sweat broke out on his face. **menj-kan** to roll up o's sleeves.

simbang ber- to toss up (a game of tossing up stones). **menj-** to toss s.t. up. *Ia ~ dadu,* He tossed the dice.

simbolis symbolic(al).

simbur ber- 1 to splash up on. *Laut ~ kepantai,* The sea splashed up on the beach. 2 to be wrapped in. *Pemandangan ~ kabut,* The view was wrapped in fog. **ke-an** to be splashed accidentally. *Ia basah ~ ,* He was splashed with water. **menj-** to throw water. *Ia ~ air kpd temannja,* He threw water on his friend. **menj-i** to sprinkle with water. *Ia ~ daun tembakau supaja basah,* He sprinkled the tobacco leaves to make them wet.

simfoni symphony.

simpai 1 band, loop. 2 monkey. **menj-(kan)** to put a band around s.t. *Ia ~ gendang,* He put a band around a drum. *- beduk* hoop on a big drum. *- besi* iron band. *- tong* barrel hoop.

simpan menj- 1 to store, lay away. *Ia ~ bahan makanan digudang,* He stored the food supplies in the storehouse. 2 to put, lay away. *Ia ~ bukunja dipeti,* He put away his books in a box. 3 to keep. *Ia ~ rahasia,* She kept the secret. 4 to save, lay away, deposit. *Ia ~ uang dibank,* He saved his money in a bank. 5 to bear, keep. *~ dihati* to bear in mind. 6 to have, bear. *Utjapan itu ~ arti jg dlm,* That saying has a deep meaning. **menj-kan** to save, lay away for s.o. *Ia ~ uang utk anaknja,* He saved money for his son. **penj-** 1 o. who saves, a depositor. 2 storage place. **penj-an** storage, depositing, laying away. **-an** 1 savings. 2 goods laid away. 3 storage place.

simpang 1 a branching off. 2 a deviation. **ber-** 1 to branch off. *djalan ~* a branch road. 2 to differ. *Meréka ~ pendapat,* They had different opinions. *~ djalan* to go separate ways. *Kami ~ djalan,* We went our own ways. *~ kata* to hold a different opinion. *~ siur* to crisscross, zigzag. **beran** to intersect. *djalan jg ~* intersecting roads. **menj-** 1 to deviate. *Ia ~ dari adat,* He deviated from the custom. 2 to depart, wander from. *Ia agak ~ dari pokok atjara,* He departed somewhat from the topic under discussion. 3 to take a side route. *Ia ~ dari djalan besar,* He avoided the main highway. 4 to get out of the way, step aside. *Ia ~ supaja tidak ditabrak temannja,* He got out of the way so he wouldn't be struck by his friend. **menj-kan** to divert, distract s.o. **penj-an** deviation, divergence. *~ dasar* standard deviation. **per-an** 1 crossroads. 2 deviation. **per-siuran** 1 zigzagging. 2 confusion, mix-up. **-an** 1 a branching off. 2 byway, side route. 3 crossroads. *- belahan* offshoot. *- djalan* crossroads. *- siur* crisscrossing, zigzagging. *- sungai* tributary.

simpati sympathy.

simpatik 1 sympathetic. 2 congenial.

simphoni see SIMFONI.

simponi see SIMFONI.

simpuh ber- to sit on the floor with the legs together and bent back beside the body.

simpul knot. **ke-an** 1 conclusion. 2 summary. 3 inference. **menj-** 1 to button clothing. 2 to form a knot. 3 to appear. *Senjum ~ dibibirnja,* A smile appeared on her lips. **menj-kan** 1 to form a knot. 2 to conclude, summarize. *Ia ~ bhw temannja tak akan membajar utangnja,* He concluded that his friend was not going to pay his debt. **ter-** 1 knotted. 2 implied, included. *Penghargaan jg tinggi ~ dlm hadiah itu,* Great esteem was implied in that gift. **-an** 1 knot. 2 act of buttoning. 3 conclusion. *- hidup* slipknot. *- mati* a firm knot. *- pulih* slipknot. *- (urat) saraf* ganglion. *Ia tersenjum -,* She gave a faint knowing smile.

simultan simultaneous(ly).

sinanaga shingles.

sinar 1 ray. 2 gleam, glitter. 3 radiance. **ber–** 1 to radiate. 2 to shine, show. *Lampu lalulintas itu ∼ mérah*, The traffic light shows red. **menj–i** to illuminate, shine upon, irradiate. *Matahari ∼ bumi*, The sun illuminates the earth. **menj–kan** to radiate, send off. *Bom itu ∼ panas*, That bomb radiates heat. **penj–an** 1 illumination. 2 radiation. **– -menj–** to glitter, radiate. *– matahari* the sun's rays, sunshine. *– seminar* glittering. *– surya* sun's rays.

sinau to sparkle, shine. **ber– -²** to glitter and sparkle. *– seminau* glittering and sparkling.

sindap dandruff.

sinder school inspector, supervisor.

sindir **menj–(kan)** 1 to hint at, allude to, intimate. *Saja tahu bhw ia ∼ saja*, I knew he was hinting at me. 2 to tease. 3 to criticize, ridicule. **penj–** a teaser. **–an** 1 allusion, hint. 2 ridicule. 3 satire. **– -menj–** to tease e.o.

sindroma syndrome.

sing a buzzing sound.

singa lion.

Singapura Singapore.

singga see SEHINGGA.

singgah to stop by, stop in, visit. *Saja mau – sebentar*, I want to stop in for a moment. **memper–(kan)** 1 to invite. *Ia ∼ temannja masuk kerumah*, He invited his friend to enter the house. 2 to ask to stop. *Ia ∼ mobil jg lalu dimuka rumahnja*, He asked the car which passed in front of his house to stop. **menj–** to stop in for a visit. **menj–i** 1 to stop in, at, by. *Ia ∼ Délhi dlm perdjalanannja ke Éropa*, He stopped at Delhi on his way to Europe. *Ia ∼ temannja dikota itu*, He stopped in at his friend's in that town. 2 to pick up. *Ia datang utk ∼ surat saja*, He came to pick up my letter. **menj–kan** 1 to stop. *Ia ∼ bis didjalan*, He stopped a bus on the street. 2 to stop to deliver. *Mobil itu ∼ kiriman orang tuanja*, The car stopped to deliver a parcel from his parents. **per–an** 1 a stopover. 2 port of call. **– -menj–** to make several stops during a visit.

singgang 1 stewed in salt and vinegar (fish, etc.). 2 roasting after spicing meat, chicken, etc. **menj–** to roast, stew, after spicing with salt and vinegar. *ajam – chicken* prepared in this way, roast chicken.

singgasana throne.

singgir **menj–** to whine.

singgul **menj–** 1 to push aside, jostle.

Ia ∼ temannja dgn siku, He pushed his friend aside with his elbow. 2 to protrude. *Potlotnja ∼ dari sakunja*, His pencil protruded from his pocket.

singgung **ber–** to touch, nudge. **ber–an** to touch, contact e.o. **menj–** 1 to touch, contact. 2 to touch on, treat (a subject, problem). 3 to offend, insult, hurt (o's feelings). **ter–** offended. *mudah ∼* easily offended, sensitive, touchy. **–an** contact.

singit 1 slanting, at an incline. *Tiang – dimuka rumah*, There was a slanting pole in front of the house. *Matahari – dibelakang méga*, The sun was just visible behind the cloud. 2 sacred, no trespassing. *Tempat itu – tak boléh orang masuk begitu sadja*, This place is sacred and may not be entered at will. **ter–** rolled back. *Selimutnja ∼ ia kedinginan semalam*, His blanket was rolled back so he was cold last night.

singkap **menj–** 1 to reveal. *Ia ∼ rahasia*, She revealed a secret. 2 to reveal, unveil. *Ia ∼ tirai*, He unveiled the monument. 3 to turn back (a blanket, sheet). **menj–kan** 1 to disclose, reveal. *Buku ini ∼ dunia baru*, This book discloses a new world. 2 to lift up, turn back (a blanket). 3 to expose (to the air, dust, etc.). **ter–** *hati* happy. *Hari tlh ∼*, It's become day.

singkat 1 brief, concise, short. *Badjunja –*, He has a short jacket. 2 narrow-minded. 3 abridged. **(ke)–an** abbreviation. **menj–kan** 1 to abbreviate, shorten. 2 to condense, summarize. *Itu di–kan dari kata pengantar*, It's been condensed from the preface. **–nja** in short, in brief. *– akal* mentally limited. *– sungu* hot-tempered. *– umur* to have a short life.

singkéh a Chinese who has recently arrived from China.

singkir **menj–** 1 to step aside. *Ia ∼ waktu mobil liwat*, He stepped aside when the car passed. 2 to evacuate, move to. *Banjak pengungsi ∼ ketempat jg aman*, Many refugees evacuated to a safe place. **menj–i** to avoid, evade s.t. *Meréka ∼ tempat jg berbahaja*, They avoided the dangerous place. **menj–kan** 1 to evacuate s.t. to (ke). *Ia ∼ barang²nja kedésa*, He evacuated his belongings to the village. 2 to remove, eliminate. *Ia ∼ buku² jg tidak dipakai*, He removed all unused books. 3 to lay aside. *Meréka ∼ perselisihannja waktu perajaan itu*, They laid aside their differences at the celebration. 4 to put s.t. away. 5 to purge. *Musuhnja semua tlh di-kan,* All his enemies were purged. **penj–an** 1 evacuation, removal. 2 elimination. 3 purge. **ter-** *dari* prevented from, safeguarded. *Ia ~ dari bahaja,* She was guarded from danger.

singkong cassava.

singkup shovel. see SEKUP.

singkur menj– to push s.o. or s.t. aside.

singlét undershirt.

singsat tight. *Badjunja –,* His clothing is tight. **menj–** to shrink. *Kemédjanja –,* His shirt shrank. **menj–kan** 1 to roll up. *Ia ~ lengan badjunja,* He rolled up his sleeves. 2 to tighten. *Ia ~ tali,* He tightened the rope. 3 to shrink s.t. *Sabun ini ~ ,* This soap made it shrink.

singsé Chinese physician.

singsing menj– to rise, lift, break clear. *Awan tlh ~ ,* The fog has lifted. *Fadjar ~ ,* The dawn is breaking. (It's daybreak.) **menj–(kan)** to roll, tuck up. *Ia ~ lengan badjunja,* He rolled up his sleeves.

sini 1 here. *Bawa –,* Bring it here. *dari –* from here. 2 there where the recipient is (in letters). **di–** here. *Ia sdh lama ~ ,* He's been here for a long time. **dike–kan** to be sent here. *Kalau ia tidak mau terima boléhlah barang itu ~ ,* If he won't accept it you may send it here. **ke–** 1 to here. 2 we for our part. *~ tidak keberatan; bagaimana sana?* We have no objections; how about the others?

sinis cynical.

sinisme cynicism.

sinjal signal.

sinjalemén description.

sinjalir mens– 1 to call attention to, point out. *Parlemén ~ bahaja inflasi,* Parliament pointed out the dangers of inflation. 2 to signal.

sinjo European or Eurasian lad (form of address).

Sinjokelas Santa Claus.

sinoman rural association for mutual assistance among the young people.

sinonim synonym.

sintal 1 well-fed. 2 fat, potbellied. 3 plump, chubby.

sintang 1 short. 2 a little cracked in the head.

sintétis synthetic.

sinting 1 see SINTANG. 2 crazy, abnormal.

sintir 1 die, gambling cube. 2 dice game.

sintuh see SENTUH.

sintuk ber– to rub o.s. with s.t.

Ia sedang ~ badan, He was rubbing his body. **menj–(kan)** to rub s.t. on. *Ia ~ minjak itu kebadannja,* He rubbed oil on his body.

sintung menj– to touch with the elbow.

sinu nerve.

sipai see SEPOI.

sipat see SIFAT. **menj–(kan)** to measure with a tape measure. *– kuping* helter-skelter. *– mata* black grease paint for eyelashes.

sipi to be just wide of the mark, a little off center. **menj–** to graze, be just off center. *Témbakannja ~ ,* His shot just missed the bull's-eye.

sipil civil(ian).

sipilis syphilis.

sipir jailer.

sipit 1 slant-eyed. 2 see SEMPIT.

sipoa abacus.

sipolan see POLAN.

sipongang echo.

sipu ke–an embarrassed, shy, bashful. *Ia mérah mukanja ~ ,* His face was flushed from embarrassment. **ter– –²** 1 embarrassed, shy, bashful. 2 in a hurry.

sipulut see PULUT.

siput a snail. *– akik* agate shell. *– memudji buntut* to praise o.s.

SIPVA [*Surat Izin Pembelian Valuta Asing*] permit for the purchase of foreign exchange.

sir 1 lust, sensual desire. *Ia – pd perempuan,* He lusts after women. 2 mystical. 3 onomatopoetic for SIRAP.

sirah red.

sirak see SERAK.

siram ber– to shower, bathe. *Ia mandi ~ air,* He took a shower. **menj–(i)** 1 to spray, sprinkle. *Ia ~ bunga²an,* She sprinkled the flowers. 2 to flush. *~ kakus* to flush the toilet. **menj–kan** to spray, sprinkle. *Anak itu ~ air ketanah,* The child sprayed water on the ground. **penj–an** spraying, sprinkling. **per–an** bathing place.

sirap 1 slightly raised. 2 see SIREP. 3 shingle. **menj–kan** 1 to raise slightly. *Angin ~ atap,* The wind lifted the roof slightly. 2 to make angry. *Perbuatan itu ~ ajahnja,* The act made his father angry. 3 to scare s.o. **ter–** shingled. *Atapnja ~ ,* The roof is shingled.

sirat 1 mesh, network. 2 bridge. *– ulmustakim* the correct path for believers. **menj–** 1 to make a knot. 2 to knit. **ter–** 1 knotted. *tali jg ~* knotted string. 2 hidden, kept. *rahasia jg ~ dlm hatinja* a secret concealed in o's heart. −²(an) space between the teeth.

siréne siren.

sirep 1 quiet, silent. 2 fallen (of temperature). **menj-(kan)** to cast a spell over s.o.

Siria Syria.

sirih a quid consisting of betel leaf, areca nut, gambier, and lime. *Ia makan* −, She chews betel. **menj-** to chew betel. **menj-i** to offer s.t. to. *Meréka ∼ tamunja*, They offered it to their guests. **menj-kan** *rokok* to offer s.o. a cigarette. − *kuning* a pretty girl. − *pulang kegagang* proper, fitting.

sirik 1 jealous, unable to take it. *Ia − pd temannja jg kaja*, He was jealous of his wealthy friend. 2 see SJIRIK.

siring 1 shrimp net. 2 hem of cloth. **ber-** to have a hem. **menj-** to scoop up carefully. *Ia ∼ minjak dari wadjan*, He scooped up oil from the frying pan.

sirip fish fin.

sirkam ornamental comb.

sirkol sauerkraut.

sirkulasi circulation.

sirkulér a circular.

sirkus circus.

sirna destroyed, disappeared. **menj-kan** to destroy, wipe out.

sirop lemon syrup.

sirsak soursop.

sisa 1 residue, remainder, rest. − *uang* the remainder of the money. 2 remnant(s). − *makanan* leftovers from a meal. − *rimah* crumbs, leftovers. **ber-** to remain, be left over. *Kalau diambil dua ∼ tiga*, If you take away 2, 3 is left. **menj-(kan)** to leave over. *Pembelian itu ∼ 2 dolar sadja*, That purchase left just 2 dollars. **ter-** left (over). *tidak* − without remainder.

sisal sisal hemp.

sisalak **ber-** to quarrel, dispute.

sisi 1 side, flank. − *rumah* side of the house. − *kanan dan kiri* right and left side. 2 edge. **ber-(-an)** side by side. *Meréka duduk ∼* , They sat side by side. **di-** beside. *Ia duduk ∼ pamannja*, He sat beside his uncle. *∼ itu* besides. **ke-** to the side. **menge-kan** to ignore. *Ia merasa dike-kan*, He felt ignored. **menj-** 1 to move aside. *Ia ∼ karena ada mobil liwat*, He moved to the side because a car was passing. 2 to go along the side, shore. *Perahu itu ∼ sepandjang sungai*, The boat went along the river's edge. **menj-kan** to move s.t. to. the side. *Ia ∼ mobilnja*

utk diparkir, He moved his car to the side to park. **penj-an** movement to the side. − *kiri kapal* portside. − *miring* hypotenuse.

sisih **menj-** 1 to give way, get out of the way. *Ia ∼ kepinggir djalan waktu ada oto liwat*, He went to the side of the road when a car passed. 2 to be separate, aloof from. *Rumahnja ∼ dari bagian ramai*, His house was separate from the busy section. **menj-kan** 1 to separate out. *Ia ∼ buah jg busuk daripada lainnja*, He separated the rotten fruit from the others. 2 to cold-shoulder, reject, ignore. *Ia ∼ murid jg tidak disukai itu*, He cold-shouldered the unpopular student. **penj-an** 1 isolation. 2 elimination. **ter-** 1 isolated, apart. 2 rejected, avoided.

sisik 1 scale(s) of a fish or snake. 2 turtle shell. **ber-** scaly. **menj-(i)** to remove scales. *Ia ∼ ikan*, He removed scales from the fish. *Ia minta ∼ limbat*, He wants the impossible.

sisip **ke-an** to get a splinter in the skin. *Tangannja ∼* , He got a splinter in his hand. **memper-kan** to insert s.t. **menj-** to penetrate. *Djarum ∼ daging*, The needle penetrated the flesh. **menj-i** 1 to darn (socks, etc.). 2 to repair. *Ia ∼ atap*, He repaired the roof. **menj-kan** to slip, insert s.t. in. *Ia ∼ penundjuk halaman dibuku*, He inserted a bookmark in the book. *Ia ∼ pistol dibawah sabuknja*, He slipped a pistol under his belt. **ter-** 1 inserted, interpolated. 2 implied. **-an** 1 insertion, interpolation. 2 infix.

sisir 1 comb. 2 harrow. 3 bunch. − *pisang* a bunch of bananas. **ber-** 1 to comb. *Ia ∼ rambut*, He was combing hair. 2 combed. *rambut ∼* combed hair. **menj-** 1 to comb. *∼ rambut* to comb hair. 2 to harrow. *∼ tanah* to harrow the ground. 3 to go, sail along the edge, bank. **pe-** beach, shore.

sistém(a) see SISTIM. − *pengendalian* guidance system.

sistématik classification.

sistématis systematic.

sister 1 nurse. 2 nun.

sistim system.

sisurut see SURUT.

siswa university student. − *mualim* navigation pupil.

sita seizure, confiscation. **menj-, mens-** to seize, confiscate. **penj-an** seizure, confiscation. **-an** confiscated goods.

sitak 1 knapsack. 2 suitcase.

sitegang see TEGANG.

sitekan see TEKAN.

sitir menj-(kan), mens- to cite, quote.

sit(t)i title for a woman of high lineage. - *Hawa* Eve. - *Mariam* Virgin Mary.

situ 1 there (position, location). 2 you. *dari* - from there. **di-** 1 there, over there (usually within sight). *Taruh* ∼ , Put it over there. 2 you, your side. *Setudjukah* ∼ *?* Do you agree? 3 then, at that moment. ∼ *baru ia mengerti*, Only then did he understand. **ke-** to that place.

situasi situation.

siuh go away!

siuk menj- to groan, moan. *Orang sakit itu* ∼ , The patient was groaning.

siul ber- to whistle. -an whistling.

siuman to sober up, recover consciousness.

siung 1 canine tooth. 2 fang(s). 3 tusk. 4 a slice. *dua - bawang putih* clove (of garlic). 5 a buzzing sound. **ber-** to whizz by. *Peluru* ∼ *didekat telinganja*, Bullets whizzed by his ears.

siur 1 see SIMPANG. **berke-an** to blow, buzz. *Angin* ∼ *sepandjang malam*, The wind blew all night.

siut a buzzing, sizzling sound. **ber-** 1 to produce a hissing, sizzling sound. *Api* ∼ *djika disirami air*, Fire gives off a hissing sound when water is poured on it. 2 to blow. *Ia* ∼ *kepedasan*, He's blowing because of the hot spices. **menj-** to singe.

SIVA [*Surat Impor Valuta Asing*] foreign exchange import permit.

sivilisasi civilization.

siwalan fruit of a fan palm.

Sja'ban eighth month of the Arabic calendar.

sjafa'at mediation, intercession.

sjafakat kindness, sympathy.

sjah 1 ruler. 2 see SAH. **penge-an** 1 approval. 2 ratification.

sjahadat 1 confession (in Islam). 2 evidence.

sjahbandar harbor master, port officer.

sjahdan then, meanwhile, furthermore. - *sampailah radja itu ditempat jg ditudjuinja*, Meanwhile the king arrived at his destination.

sjahdu 1 eminent. 2 excellent, first-class.

sjahid martyr. *Ia mati* -, He died as a martyr to Islam.

sjahwat lust, voluptuous feeling.

sjair story related in verse form using quatrains of one rhyme. **ber-** 1 to write poetry. 2 to recite poetry.

kepenj-an poetizing. **menj-kan** to compose a poem on s.t. **penj-** poet.

sjaitan see SÉTAN.

sjak 1 suspicion. 2 doubt, distrust. **mensj-** to presume. **mensj-i** to suspect. - *wasangka* 1 suspicion. 2 doubt, distrust. *Ia menimbulkan* - *wasangka*, He aroused suspicion. *menaruh* - *wasangka* to doubt, suspect. *tiada* - *lagi* no doubt whatsoever.

sjakti see SAKTI.

sjal shawl.

Sjam Syria(n).

sjamsir saber, sword.

sjara' Islamic canon law.

sjarah 1 explanation. 2 greed. 3 desire. **ber-** to expound on s.t. **-an** 1 lecture. 2 edition. ∼ *rakjat* popular edition.

sjarak see SJARA'.

sjarat 1 condition, stipulation, term(s). *Ia tak dpt memenuhi - persetudjuan itu*, He wasn't able to fulfill the terms of the agreement. 2 requirement, requisite. *Apa -nja utk ikut udjian itu?* What are the requirements for taking the exam? 3 means. *Bekerdja itu adalah salah satu - hidup*, Work is o. of the means of keeping alive. 4 compensation, condition. *Kami harus memberi sekedar - utk diterima mendjadi muridnja*, We have to pay some compensation to be accepted as his disciple. **ber-** conditional. *penjerahan jg tak* ∼ unconditional surrender. **mensj-kan** to set s.t. as a condition. **-²** qualifications. - *kawin* marriage settlement. - *mutlak* an absolute condition, *sine qua non*.

sjari'at Islamic law.

sjarif lord (title of Mohammed's descendants).

sjarikat see SERIKAT.

sjatrija see SATERIA.

Sjaw(w)al tenth month of the Arabic calendar.

sjéch 1 chief, sheikh. 2 title of a Moslem scholar.

sjétti (Indian) moneylender.

sjir(i)k polytheistic belief. **mensj-kan** to commit, be guilty of, polytheism.

sjok 1 attractive. 2 to pretend. 3 greedy.

sjor see SJUR.

sjuk see SJOK.

sjukur thank God, thanks be to God. **ber-** to thank God. ∼ *hati* to be grateful. **mensj-kan** to be grateful to s.o. *perbuatan jg di-i orang* a grateful deed.

sjur 1 advice. 2 to be fond of.

mensj–kan 1 to advise. 2 to recommend.

sjuriah advisory.

s.k. [*surat kabar*] newspaper.

skala see SEKAL.

skéna scene.

skéts(a) sketch.

SKN [*Staf Keamanan Nasional*] National Security Staff.

skor score.

S.K.P. [*Sekolah Kepandaian Puteri*] home economics high school.

skrip script.

skripsi 1 thesis. 2 term paper.

sl see also SEL–.

sléndro harmony, tune of Javanese gamelan.

slip see SELIP.

slt [*selatan*] south.

s. M. [*sebelum Maséhi*] B.C.

S.M.A. [*Sekolah Menengah Atas*] senior high school.

smir see SEMIR.

S.M.P. [*Sekolah Menengah Pertama*] junior high school.

soal 1 problem, matter. *Itu adalah – jg sukar*, That's a difficult problem. 2 question. *Meréka memadjukan banjak –² kpd pembitjara*, They asked the speaker a lot of questions. **ber–** –² 1 to discuss. 2 to argue, debate. **memper–kan** 1 to question s.t. *Kedjudjurannja diper–kan*, His honesty is questioned. 2 to ask about, discuss. *Meréka sedang ~ rentjana itu*, They were discussing the plan. **menj– to** ask, put a question. **menj–kan** to ask, set questions. *Hal jg tidak² di-kan diudjian itu*, Impossible questions were asked on that examination. **per–an** 1 discussion, debate. 2 problem. – *djawab* 1 debate. 2 conversation. 3 question-and-answer column.

sob see S.O.B.

S.O.B. [*Staat van Oorlog en Beleg*] state of war and siege. **meng–kan** to bring under military authority during a state of war and siege. *Perusahaan asing itu di–kan*, The foreign enterprise was seized by the military authority.

sobat friend. **ber–** to be friends. **menj–i** to make friends with s.o. *Ia pandai ~ orang kaja*, He's good at making friends with wealthy people. **per–an** friendship. – *kental* close friends.

sobék torn. **menj–** to tear. **–an** torn piece.

sobok alloy. **ber–** to encounter, fall in with.

SOBSI [*Séntral Organisasi Buruh Seluruh Indonésia*] All-Indonesia Federation of Labor Organizations.

soda soda. – *api* caustic soda.

sodja to bow reverently.

sodok shovel, spade. **menj–** 1 to shovel, scoop up. 2 to push, thrust. *Ia ~ dgn siku*, He pushed with his elbow. **penj–** a shovel, spade. **–an** 1 a shot in billiards. 2 thrust, push.

sodor **menj–kan** 1 to thrust forward, stretch out. *Ia ~ kakinja*, He stretched out his legs. 2 to hand, thrust s.t. on s.o. *Ia ~ surat kpd temannja*, He handed a letter to his friend. 3 to forward. *Ia ~ usulnja kpd rapat*, He forwarded his proposal to the meeting. **penj–an** offer.

soék see SOBÉK.

soga red vegetable dye used for batiks.

sogang fence, palisade.

sogok **menj–** 1 to bribe s.o. 2 to stab s.o. **penj–an** bribery. **–an** a bribe. – *suap* 1 bribe. 2 bribery.

sohor **ke–, ter–** famous.

sojak see KOJAK.

sojat see KOJAK.

sok as if, pretending. *Ia – tahu*, He pretends to know. **–²an** pretense. ~ *filosofis* philosophical pretense. **–²** stuck-up. *anak jg ~* a stuck-up child. – *-inteléktuil* pseudo-intellectual.

sokoguru pillar.

sokong prop, support. **menj–** to support, give support to s.t. or s.o. **penj–** supporter, contributor. **–an** support, contribution.

solang **menj–** to contradict.

soldadu see SERDADU.

solék well-dressed, modish, stylish. **ber–** dressed up, stylishly dressed. **pe–** a dandy.

solidarita(s) solidarity.

Solo city in central Java.

solok gift, contribution in kind. **menj–** see TJOLOK. **penj–** gift, contribution in kind.

som a hem. **mens–** to hem s.t.

somah 1 household. 2 peon. – *seperut* uterine family.

sombol **menj–** to cram food into the mouth.

sombong arrogant, conceited. **ke–an** 1 arrogance, boasting, conceit. 2 vanity. **menj–** to be arrogant, self-assertive. **menj–kan** to boast, brag about. *Ia selalu ~ kekajaannja*, He is always boasting about his wealth. **penj–** an arrogant, conceited person, a braggart.

soméng 1 offensive. 2 annoying.

sompék chipped, broken off. *Piringnja –*, The plate is chipped.

somplok see SOMPOK.

sompok ber– to run into, meet unexpectedly. **ter–** to be trapped. *Ia tak dpt lari ketika ~ polisi,* He couldn't get away when he was trapped by the police.

somprét dammit!

sondak see SUNDAK.

sondang menj– to lift, raise o's head and shoulders.

sonder without.

sondok hair hanging over the forehead.

sondol menj– 1 to charge by lowering the head, butt s.t. 2 to hit the ball with the head (soccer).

sondong menj– to fish for shrimp. **penj–** a net for catching shrimp.

sondor see SODOR.

sonebril sunglasses.

sonéta sonnet.

songar proud, arrogant.

songél menj– to protrude, jut out.

songgéng 1 to protrude. 2 to paint.

songkét see SUNGKIT. **menj–** to embroider.

songkok Indonesian hat, fezlike cap of velvet.

songong rude, coarse, ill-mannered.

songsang see SUNGSANG.

songsong 1 state umbrella. 2 against. **ber–** 1 to go against. *Ia berdjalan ~ lawanan musuh,* He went against the opposition of the enemy. 2 to carry the state umbrella. **menj–** 1 to welcome. *Rakjat ~ kedatangan présidén,* The people welcomed the arrival of the president. 2 to commemorate. *Ia memberi pidato ~ Hari Kemerdékaan,* He gave a speech commemorating Independence Day. 3 to do o's wish. *Ia pergi kemakam ajahnja ~ permintaan ibunja,* He went to his father's grave to do his mother's wish. 4 to go against. *Ia berlajar ~ angin jg keras,* He sailed against a strong wind. 5 to oppose. *Ia ~ tindakan pemerintah,* He opposed the government's action. **penj–** welcome. *sepatah kata ~* some words of welcome. **–an** welcome.

sono see SANA.

sontak torn, damaged, broken off.

sonték menj– 1 to push away, aside. 2 to copy, crib. 3 to give a shot, injection.

sontok akal 1 stupid. 2 narrowminded. 3 shortsighted. 4 see SUNTUK.

sontolojo 1 a stupid person, idiot. 2 magician's wand.

sop soup. *– ajam* chicken soup.

sopak 1 white patches on skin of hands or feet. 2 white scars of skin disease.

sopan 1 respectful. *Ia – pd orang tuanja,* He was respectful to his parents. 2 courteous, modest. *Ia – sekali dlm tingkah-lakunja,* He has a courteous approach. 3 decent, nice. *Orang jg – tak akan berbuat seperti itu,* A decent person wouldn't do anything like that. 4 good manners, civilized behavior. **ke–an** 1 good manners, decent behavior. 2 decency. 3 politeness. 4 civilization. **menj–i** to treat s.o. with respect. **menj–kan** to civilize. *~ bangsa lain* to civilize another people. *– santun* to be correct in behavior, courteous, polite. *Anak itu – santun,* The child has good manners.

sopi gin. *– manis* liqueur. *– pahit* bitters.

sopir chauffeur, driver. **menj–(i)** to drive a car. *– maut* hearse driver.

sorak applause, cheering. **ber–** to applaud, cheer. *Meréka ~ hingga suaranja habis,* They cheered until their voices disappeared. **menj–i** to cheer s.o. *Meréka ~ djuara itu,* They cheered the champion. **menj–kan** to cry, yell out. *Meréka ~ nama orang jg harus datang,* They yelled out the names of those who had to come. **penj–** sports fan. **–an** applause, cheers, yells. *– semarai, – sorai* applause, cheering, yelling.

sorang see ORANG. 2 alone. *Njonja itu datang –,* The lady came alone. *– waé, jeu?* Are you all alone?

soré 1 afternoon. 2 early evening. **–nja** the following afternoon. *Waktu pagi ia bekerdja ~ bersekolah,* He worked in the mornings and went to school in the afternoons. *– harinja* in the afternoon. *nanti –* this afternoon, evening.

soréh see SURIH.

sorék bamboo.

sorga see SURGA.

sorok 1 see SOGOK. 2 see SURUK.

sorong 1 sliding, pushing. *pintu – * sliding door. *keréta – * pushcart. 2 bribe. *Ia makan –,* He accepted a bribe. **menj–** 1 to push, slide. *Ia ~ pintu,* He slid the door back. *Ia ~ keréta,* He pushed the cart. 2 to urge, insist. *Ia ~ temannja supaja pergi kesana,* He insisted that his friend go there. 3 to bribe s.o. **menj–kan** 1 to slide s.t. forward. 2 to push s.t. *Ia ~ usul,* He pushed a proposal. **ter–** forced, compelled. *Ia ~ utk mengaku,* She was forced to confess. **–an** 1 s.t. pushed or shoved, a bolt. 2 a bribe. 3 a push, shove.

sorot beam of light, ray. **menj–(kan)** 1 to shine, gleam. *Lampunja* ～ *keluar*, The lamp shone outside. 2 to project (pictures). **menj–i** 1 to illuminate, light up. *Ia* ～ *gang dgn lampu mobilnja*, He illuminated the alley with his car lights. 2 to spotlight s.t. or s.o. ～ *tjerpén* to throw light on, elucidate a short story. **penj–** reflector, projector. **penj–an** spot lighting. **–an** 1 ray, beam. 2 radiation. ～ *balik* flash back. – *mata* look.

sortasi sorting, grading.

sortir **menj–** to sort out. **(penj)–an** sorting out (of mail, etc.).

sosial social. **ke–an** 1 friendliness. 2 social.

sosialis 1 socialist. 2 socialistic. **menj–kan** to socialize (the economy, etc.).

sosialisme socialism.

sosiawan a social-minded individual.

sosiologi sociology.

sosis sausage.

soska [*sosialis kanan*] right-wing socialist.

soski [*sosialis kiri*] left-wing socialist.

sosoh **menj–** 1 to whiten, clean rice. 2 to fight, engage in combat. **penj–an** *beras* rice mill.

sosok 1 buttonhole, eye. 2 noose. **ber–** to have the shape of. *Badannja* ～ *tinggi besar*, His body is tall and large. **menj–** 1 to lay the keel of a ship. 2 to set up the framework of a house. **pe–** eye, loop. – *tubuh* form, shape, figure.

sosong see SONGSONG.

Sospol [(*Fakultas*) *Sosial dan Politik*] social and political science faculty.

soto a k.o. meat soup or stew. **menj–** to make *soto* of s.t. *Ia* ～ *ajamnja*, He made *soto* of his chicken. – *ajam* chicken soup. – *daging* beef *soto*.

sotoh 1 loft. 2 upper story.

sotong cuttlefish.

so'un see LAKSA.

Sovjét-Uni Soviet Union.

sowan to visit, call on (of lower status to higher). *Nj. Suwarni – pd Ibu Kartini*, Mrs. Suwarni called on Mrs. Kartini.

sp– see also SEP–.

S.P. [*Sri Paduka*] His Excellency, Highness.

spanduk banner.

spanjol see SEPANJOL.

spasi space. – *rangkap* double-space(d).

spatbor fender.

spékulan speculator.

spékulatif speculative.

spéndir **mens–** to spend.

spésialis specialist.

spésialisasi specialization.

spésifikasi specification. **mengs–** to specify.

spj [*supaja*] for, in order to, so that.

spontan spontaneous.

sprei see SEPERAI.

spt [*seperti*] as, like.

S'pura [*Singapura*] Singapore.

sr– see also SER–.

S.R. 1 [*Sekolah Rakjat*] 2 [*Sekolah Rendah*] elementary, grammar school.

Sri Langka Ceylon.

sromo key money.

srt [*surat*] letter.

s.s.k. [*surat² kabar*] newspapers.

SSKAD [*Sekolah Staf dan Komando Angkatan Darat*] Army Command and Staff School.

St [*Sutan*] title of nobility above *marah* in the Minangkabau area.

st– see also SET–.

stabilisasi stabilization. **mens–kan** to stabilize.

stadion stadium.

staf staff.

stagnasi stagnation.

stalles center seat area in theater.

standardisasi standardization.

stanplat (bus) stop.

stasiun see SETASIUN.

statis static, stationary.

statistik statistics.

statuta statutes.

stéker 1 electrical plug. 2 cigarette lighter.

stélsel system.

sténo(grafi) shorthand.

sténsilan 1 a stencil. 2 stenciled, mimeographed matter.

stéréoskopis stereoscopic.

stéwal see SETIWAL.

stimulans 1 stimulant. 2 stimulus.

stir see SETIR.

S.T.K.I. [*Surat Tanda Kewarganegaraan Indonésia*] Indonesian citizenship card.

stlh [*setelah*] after.

S.T.M. [*Sekolah Téhnik Menengah*] technical high school.

stopkontak electric socket.

stratifikasi stratification.

stratosfir stratosphere.

stréng strict, severe.

struktur structure.

studén see SETUDÉN.

studi study.

studium study.

su abbrev. of BUNGSU, youngest child.

SU [*Sékretaris Umum*] general secretary.

sua **ber–** 1 to meet, run into. *Ia* ～ *dgn adiknja*, He met his younger brother. 2 to find. *Ia tak dpt* ～ *dgn* *apa jg ditjari,* He couldn't find what he was looking for. 3 to happen, occur. *Mudah²an keuntungan itu ∼ padamu,* We hope such good fortune will befall you. ∼ *muka* to meet face to face. **memper-kan, menj-kan** to bring into contact with, confront. ∼ *ajam jg mau diadu* to bring the competing cocks together. **per-an** meeting. **ter-** to meet, run into, come across.

suai see SESUAI. **ber-** fitting, appropriate.

suak 1 inlet, small bay. 2 postponement. *Saja minta -,* I request postponement. *blm pernah* - always.

suaka 1 see SÉWAKA. 2 asylum. *minta* - to request asylum. - *alam,* - *margasatwa* wildlife preserve.

sual see SOAL.

suam hot, feverish. *Badannja -,* He has a fever. −² hot, feverish. - *kuku* lukewarm.

suami husband. **ber-** to be married. *Ia blm* ∼ , She's not yet married. **ber-kan** to be married to. *Ia* ∼ *orang kaja,* She is married to a rich man. **memper-** to take a husband. *Ia tak suka* ∼ *orang itu,* She didn't want to take that man as her husband. **memper-kan** to marry a daughter off. *Ia* ∼ *anaknja,* He married off his daughter. - *isteri* married couple.

suang *tak* −² not easy. *Pintu itu tak* ∼ *dibukanja,* That door wasn't easy to open.

suangi nocturnal ghost.

suap 1 a mouthful. *se- nasi* a mouthful of rice. *Ia mentjari* ∼ *nasi,* He was looking for a living. 2 bribe. **ber-** to eat (rice) with the hands. **ber-** −²**an** to feed e.o. **menj-(i)** 1 to eat s.t. with the hand. 2 to feed s.o. by placing the food in the mouth. 3 to bribe. **menj-kan** 1 to feed s.o. *Ia* ∼ *nasi kpd jg sakit,* She fed the patient rice. 2 to bribe s.o. with. *Ia* ∼ *100 dolar kepadanja,* He bribed him with $100. **penj-an** 1 feeding with the hand. 2 bribery. **-an** 1 act of eating with the hand. 2 bribe. see SOGOK.

suar signal light, flare. **ber-** 1 to light a signal flare. 2 to signal. **menj-** to light, illuminate.

suara 1 voice. - *ramai* public voice. 2 speech. *Ia membuka -,* He made a speech, offered his opinion. 3 vote. 4 sound, tone. *njanjian jg merdu -nja* a sweet-sounding melody. **ber-** to produce a sound. **menj-kan** 1 to say, utter, sound. 2 to sing. **penj-an** declamation. **se-** unanimously. - *blanko* an abstaining vote. - *bulat*

unanimously. - *hati* conscience. - *keras* a loud voice. - *mengalun* a voice that o. now hears, now doesn't. - *pokok* fundamental tone. - *rangkap* a duet. - *terbanjak* majority vote. - *timbang rasa* vote of confidence.

suarang joint property of husband and wife acquired during marriage. **menj-kan** to acquire common property during marriage. - *diagih* division of common property in case of divorce.

suarawati female vocalist.

suargaloka abode of the gods.

suari see KESUARI.

suasa gold with special alloy mixture.

suasana 1 atmosphere. - *politik* the political atmosphere. *terbang di-* to fly in the atmosphere. 2 sphere, world. - *kanak²* children's world. 3 situation, position. - *didunia Barat* the situation in the Western world. 4 environment, milieu. **menj-i** to encompass. *Antjaman perang* ∼ *dunia,* The threat of war encompasses the world. - *djiwa* mood.

suatu 1 one. 2 see SATU. **ber-** united, unified. **memper-kan** to unify, unite. **se-** a certain. ∼ *surat kabar mengumumkan bhw* ... A certain newspaper announced that ...

subahat 1 doubt. 2 doubtful. **ber-** 1 to doubt, hesitate. 2 to suspect.

subak water-control system in Bali.

subal ugly, untidy.

suban splinter, sliver of wood.

subang a woman's earring. **ber-** to wear earrings. **menj-** to cut into slices.

subhana'llah praised be the Lord.

subjéktif subjective.

subjéktivitét subjectivity.

sublimasi sublimation.

subuh 1 dawn, daybreak. 2 early morning prayer.

subur 1 fertile. *tanah jg* - fertile soil. 2 thriving, prosperous. *Kelihatannja - dan makmur,* He looked as if he was thriving and prosperous. 3 healthy. *Badannja tinggi dan -,* He was tall and healthy. 4 rapid, fertile. *Pohon ini - tumbuhnja,* This tree was growing rapidly. **ke-an** 1 fertility. 2 prosperity. **menj-kan** 1 to make grow. 2 to make prosper, promote.

suburban automobile used for interurban passenger transportation (often a station wagon).

subversif subversive.

suda bamboo spikes sticking upward to form a mantrap.

sudah 1 already. *Ia - pergi,* He's already gone. 2 past, last. *tahun jg -*

the past year, last year. 3 ago. *100 tahun jg* – 100 years ago. 4 done, over, through. *Setelah – pergilah ia,* After it was over he left. *Pertjakapannja tak akan – djika kami blm pergi,* The discussions would never have been over if we hadn't left. 5 gone, through. *Uangnja – habis,* His money was gone. 6 enough. *–/* That's enough! 7 finished, settled. *barang²* – finished goods. 8 besides. *– pandai tjantik lagi,* Besides being bright she's also pretty. 9 bygone. *Hal jg –(-) djangan dipertjakapkan lagi,* Don't talk about bygone things. 10 after. *– itu timbul répolusi,* After that the revolution broke out. **ber-** 1 to end, close. *~lah muktamar itu dgn pidato,* The conference was closed with a speech. 2 to have an end. *Tjeriteranja tiada ~* , The story has no end. **ber- –²** to break off (relations). **berke–an** to end, conclude s.t. **ke–an** 1 conclusion. 2 end, finish. 3 result, consequence. 4 finally. 5 termination, expiration. **memper–kan** to end, finish. **menj-i** 1 to end, conclude. *Ia ~ pidatonja dgn do'a,* He ended his speech with a prayer. 2 to fulfill. *Ia ~ perintah madjikannja,* He fulfilled the orders of his boss. **menj-kan** to end, conclude. **penj–(an)** concluding, final act. **se–** after. *~ makan pagi ia bekerdja,* After breakfast she works. **se-nja** afterward, thereafter. **se- –²nja** to o's heart's content. *Ia makan ~* , He ate to his heart's content. **–nja** finally. *~ bagaimana?* How was it finally? **–²** bygone. *– telandjur* 1 nothing can be done about a thing, it's gone too far, it's too late. *Aduh, saja – telandjur mengundangnja,* Oh dear, I've already invited her; nothing can be done about it. 2 to be halfway already. *– akan* will have. *Pd ttg 1 Agustus ia – akan berdinas 30 thn,* On August 1 he will have put in 30 years' service. *– (barang) tentu* of course, indeed. *– itu* then, next. *– léwat* to expire, run out. *– pd tempatnja* fitting, proper. *– semestinja* it goes without saying. *tak –²* without end, endless.

sudara see SAUDARA.

sudi 1 willing. *–kah saudara pindah ke Djakarta?* Are you willing to move to Jakarta? 2 to like, be willing. *Ia tak – berdjumpa dgn ajahnja lagi,* He didn't like to see his father any more. 3 please. *–lah tuan duduk!* Won't you please sit down! *–lah kiranja ...* Would you please ... **ber–kan** to be willing to. **ke–an** willingness. **memper–kan** to request,

invite. *Per–kan duduk,* Please sit down. **menj-** to interrogate, examine. **menj-kan** 1 to invite, request. *Ia ~ tamu² masuk,* He invited his guests to come in. 2 to make s.o. willing. *Kedjadian itulah jg ~ ajahnja menemui dokter,* That incident made his father willing to see the doctor. *– tak – willy-nilly. – tak – ia hrs datang,* He has to come whether he likes it or not.

sudip wooden spoon used for mixing ingredients. **menj-** to stir s.t.

sudjén skewer (for meat).

sudji embroidery. **menj-** to embroider.

sudjud the act of kneeling and bowing the head to the ground in Moslem worship. **ter-** to be in the *sudjud* position.

sudu 1 goosebeak, duckbill. 2 large spoon, usually made of coconut shell. **menj-** 1 to scoop up, ladle up. 2 to pick, pluck, up. *Itik ~ ikan diair,* The duck picked up the fish in the water. **ter-** nipped, bitten by a duck or goose.

suduk see SODOK.

sudung 1 hut, hovel. 2 shelter for rice-field guards.

sudut 1 corner. *– rumah* corner of a house. 2 angle. *– 30 deradjat* a 30° angle. 3 direction. *Orang datang dari segala –,* People came from all directions. 4 point of view. *dilihat dari – itu* seen from that point of view. **ber-** to have angles, corners. **menj-** 1 to form an angle. 2 to retire to a corner. *Silahkan kemari; djangan ~* , Please come here; don't sit in a corner. *– mata* point of view. *– siku²* a right-angled triangle.

suf wool.

sufrah floorcloth or carpet used for religious meals, festivals.

sugar **menj-** to comb the hair with o's fingers.

sugi 1 toothpick. 2 tobacco quid. **ber-** 1 to use a toothpick. 2 to have a tobacco quid in the mouth. **menj-** 1 to pick o's teeth with a toothpick. 2 to wipe betel juice from o's mouth. **pe-** toothpick.

sugih wealthy.

suguh **menj-(kan)** to treat s.o. to s.t., place s.t. before a person. *Ibunja ~ nasi,* His mother treated him to rice. *Tamunja di– téh dan pisang goréng,* Tea and fried bananas were placed before the guests. **menj-i** to treat s.o. **-an** a treat. *Apa ~nja?* What was served as a treat? *– sumbangsih* a contribution in honor of s.o.

sugul 1 grumpy. 2 spiteful.
sugun 1 tangled, tousled (of hair). 2 confused. **menj–(kan)** to seize by the hair.
suhad insomnia.
suhian a brothel.
suhu 1 body temperature. 2 temperature. – *di Djakarta* the temperature in Jakarta.
suhuf Holy Scriptures.
suit ber– to whistle. **–an** a whistle, whistling.
suk see SJOK. – *tahu* eager to learn.
suka 1 happiness, joy, pleasure. 2 to like, be fond of. *Ia – pd (akan) andjingnja*, She liked her dog. 3 to be willing, would like. *Kalau tuan – datang, silahkan datang,* If you'd like to come, please do. 4 to be apt to. *Ia – lupa pd pekerdjaannja,* He was apt to forget about his work. **ber– –²** to enjoy o.s. *Meréka ~ dipantai,* They enjoyed themselves at the beach. **ber– –²an** 1 to enjoy o.s. 2 to court, make love. **ke–an** 1 joy, pleasure. 2 happiness. 3 willingness. 4 taste. **menj–i** to like, love. *Ia tak di–i temannja,* He's not liked by his friends. **menj–kan** 1 to cheer s.o. up. *Ia selalu mentjoba ~ temannja,* He's always trying to cheer up his friend. 2 to cause s.o. to like s.t. *Ia ~ anaknja kpd andjing,* She made her child like dogs. 3 to amuse. 4 to gladden. **se–** *hati,* **se– –²** as o. wishes. *Ia beladjar ~ hati,* He studies as he wishes. **–an** 1 sweetheart, darling. 2 favorite. – *dan duka* happiness and sorrow. – *hati* pleasure, delight. – *sama –* by mutual agreement. – *tak –* indifferent, averse to. **–lah** *kiranja* if you will be so kind as to.
sukamandi k.o. dark cotton cloth.
sukar hard, difficult. **ke–an** 1 difficulty. 2 trouble, worry. 3 hardship. **memper–kan, menj–kan** to cause difficulty, trouble. *Tingkah-lakunja ~ ajahnja,* His behavior caused his father difficulties.
sukaréla 1 volunteer. 2 voluntarily. **ke–an** volunteering.
sukarélawan volunteer for military duty.
sukaria 1 happy, gay. 2 delight, pleasure. **ber–** to be happy, gay, to celebrate.
sukat 4 *gantang* or 12.6 liters (a cubic measure). **ber–** measured by *sukat.* **menj–** to measure by *sukat.* **–an** cubic measure.
sukatjita 1 happy, glad, merry. 2 joy, happiness. **ber–** to be happy, glad, merry.
sukma (life) spirit, soul.

suksés success. **mens–kan** to make s.t. successful.
suku 1 leg. – *kuda* leg of a horse. – *médja* table leg. 2 ethnic group, tribe. – *Dajak* the Dyaks. – *Sunda* the Sundanese. 3 a quarter, one-fourth. – *djam* a quarter of an hour. – *tahun* a quarter (of a year). 4 extended family. **ber–** 1 to have legs. *médja ~ tiga* a 3-legged table. 2 to be rude, ignorant of the customs. 3 to be a fraction. *hitungan ~* calculus of fractions. **ber– –²** to be grouped in tribes. **ke–an, per–an** 1 tribalism. 2 syllabification. **sepe–an** of the same tribe, ethnic group. **se–** 1 half a rupiah. 2 of the same group. – *bangsa* ethnic group, tribe. – *hidup* open syllable. – *kata* syllable. – *mati* closed syllable.
sukun breadfruit.
sukur see SJUKUR.
sula 1 sharp stake, spit. **menj–** to gather fruit with a pointed stick. **menj–kan** to impale s.t. or s.o. **penj–** sharp stake, spit. **–an** sharp stake.
sulah bald, hairless.
Sulaiman Solomon.
sulalat descent.
sulam embroidery. **ber–** embroidered. *kain ~* embroidered cloth. **ber–kan** woven with. **menj–** 1 to embroider. 2 to replace dead seedlings with healthy ones. **–an** embroidery, embroidered goods.
sulang lampblack, soot. **ber–** to be dirty with soot. **ber– –²an** to give e.o. food or drink. **menj–(i)** to feed s.t. **menj–kan** to feed with s.t. *Ia ~ djagung kpd anaknja,* She fed her child corn. – **-menj–** to feed e.o. *Meréka makan ~ ,* They enjoyed having a meal together. *Meréka tjinta-mentjintai ~ ,* They were enjoying their love for e.o. – *lampu* lampblack.
sulap juggling, conjuring. **ber–** 1 to conjure, juggle. 2 to find a defect in the weaving. **menj–** to conjure, juggle. **penj–** 1 conjurer, juggler. 2 magician. **penj–an, –²an** conjuring, juggling.
sulat-salit irregular, jagged (teeth).
Sulawesi, Sulawési Celebes.
sulbi the loins.
sulih a substitute.
Sulindo [*Suluh Indonésia*] a Jakarta newspaper.
suling 1 flute. 2 whistle. 3 siren. **ber–** tossed, tumbled upside down. **menj–** 1 to play the flute. 2 to blow a whistle. 3 to distill. *~ minjak wangi* to distill perfume. **menj–kan** to turn

s.t. upside down. **penj-an** distilling, refining. **-an** distilled. *air* ∼ 1 distilled water. 2 distillate.

sulit 1 difficult, hard, complicated. *soal jg* – a difficult problem. 2 secret, hidden, secluded. *tempat jg* – a secret place. 3 critical. **ke-an** 1 difficulty, trouble. ∼ *perumahan* housing difficulties. 2 complications. 3 hardship. ∼ *hidup* life's hardships. 4 shortage, scarcity. ∼ *air* water shortage. **memper-, menj-kan** to complicate, render difficult.

Sulselra [*Sulawesi Selatan dan Tenggara*] South and Southeast Celebes.

sultan sultan. **ke-an** sultanate.

suluh 1 torch. 2 scout, searcher. 3 spy. **ber-** to use, light with, a torch. **menj-(i)** 1 to search for with a torch. ∼ *ikan* to fish by torch. 2 to inform. ∼ *rakjat* to inform the people. 3 to investigate. *Ia* ∼ *soal tanah*, He investigated the land problem. 4 to reconnoiter. **penj-** 1 investigator, scout. 2 spy. 3 instructor. **penj-an** 1 information. 2 illumination. 3 espionage. ∼ *pertanian* agricultural extension.

suluk 1 mysticism. 2 recitation of a wayang narrator. **ber-** to retreat from the world.

sulung oldest, first-born. *anak jg* – first-born child. *buah* – first fruit of the season. *gigi* – milk teeth. – *tahun* first of the year.

sulur 1 spiraling upward (of plants). 2 stamen of a flower. 3 shoots. **ber-** to spiral, climb upward. **menj-** 1 to climb, creep upward. 2 to crawl. **-an** ivy and other climbing plants. – *batang* spiral-shaped. – *bulur* confused, rambling (of speech).

sulut menj- to light, kindle, ignite.

Sulutteng [*Sulawesi Utara dan Tengah*] North and Central Celebes.

Sum. [*Sumatera*] Sumatra.

sumangat see SEMANGAT.

sumarak see SEMARAK.

sumbang 1 incest. *anak* – child of incest. – *dgn saudaranja* to commit incest. 2 incestuous. 3 against custom. – *pd adat* against the customs. 4 error, fault. 5 indecent. *lagu jg* – an indecent song. – *didengar* not nice to hear. 6 sinful, wrong. – *langkah* the wrong step, slip. **ke-an** impropriety, indecency. **menj-** 1 to contribute. 2 to help, assist. **menj-kan** 1 to contribute, support. 2 to help. 3 to do s.t. wrong or indecent. **penj-** contributor, supporter. **-an** contribution.

sumbangsih 1 contribution. 2 alms.

sumbar menj-(nj-) to boast.

Sumbar [*Sumatera Barat*] West Sumatra.

sumbat cork, stopper, plug. – *botol* cork, bottle stopper. **menj-** to stop, close up, plug. **ter-** 1 stopped up, gagged. 2 to have a lump in o's throat. 3 clogged up (of a pipe, etc.).

sumber 1 well. 2 source. – *penghasilan* source of income. – *jg boléh dipertjaja* a reliable source. 3 resource(s). –² *alam* natural resources.

sumbi a pin used in weaving. **menj-** 1 to repair the edge of s.t. damaged. 2 to fill a tooth.

sumbing 1 jagged, dented, chipped. *pisau* – a knife with a jagged edge. 2 torn.

sumbu 1 fuse. – *meriam (mertjun)* fuse of a gun (firecracker). 2 wick. – *lampu* lampwick. 3 wagon axle. 4 pivot. **pe-an** 1 place of wick or fuse. 2 touchhole of a cannon. – *kumpai* lampwick.

sumbul a basket with a lid.

sumbur menj- 1 to protrude. 2 to emerge. **menj-kan** 1 to extend o's hand. 2 to hang out, raise, the flag. 3 to stick out the tongue. 4 to stretch out o's legs. **ter-** to bulge.

sumbut worth-while, rewarding. *Hasilnja tidak* –, The results were not worth-while.

sumir short, brief, succinct. **menj-kan** to shorten a matter.

sumpah 1 oath. *Ia mengangkat* – *setia*, He took the oath of allegiance. *mengatakan dgn* – to state under oath. – *djabatan* oath of office. 2 curse. *sakit karena* – *orang tuanja* to become ill from the curse of his parents. **ber-** 1 to swear. *Ia* ∼ *bhw ia tak berdjumpa dgn temannja*, He swore that he did not meet his friend. 2 to take the oath, make a vow. 3 to take the vows. **memper-kan** 1 to declare under oath. 2 to swear in, administer the oath to, s.o. **menj-i** 1 to swear in. *Penghulu itu* ∼ *pegawai baru*, The official swore in the new employee. 2 to curse. *Ia* ∼ *anaknja*, He cursed his son. **per-an** swearing in. –² flying lizard. – *palsu* perjury. – *seranah* curses of all sorts. – *setia* oath of allegiance.

sumpal cork, stopper. **menj-** to plug, fill a gap. **menj-kan** to plug, fill up, with. *Ia* ∼ *batu kpd lobang*, He plugged the hole with a stone.

sumpel see SUMPAL.

sumping ear ornament.

sumpit chopsticks. menj– to shoot with a blowpipe. menj–kan to use as a blowpipe. –an blowpipe.

Sumsel [*Sumatera Selatan*] South Sumatra.

sumsum marrow. – (*tulang*) *belakang* spinal cord.

Sumteng [*Sumatera Tengah*] Central Sumatra.

sumur well. – *bor* artesian well. – *didjalan* prostitute. – *ditepi djalan* everybody's darling. – *mati* dry well. – *pantikan* well drilled in ground. – *digali air terbit* to exceed o's expectations.

Sumut [*Sumatera Utara*] North Sumatra.

sunah see SUNAT.

sunam menj– to infiltrate. menj–kan to smuggle s.t. in. *Ia berhasil* ∼ *obat²an dari luar negeri*, He succeeded in smuggling medicine in from abroad.

sunan prince. ke–an principality.

sunat 1 circumcision. 2 meritorious (religious term characterizing actions the performance of which is meritorious but not obligatory). ber– to be circumcized. menj–(i), menj–kan to circumcise s.o.

sunbulat Virgo (zodiac).

Sunda Sundanese, Sunda area (West Java).

sundai see LIMAU.

sundak menj– 1 to bump o's head. *Ia* ∼ *lampu*, He bumped his head against a lamp. 2 to rise. *Pasang* ∼ , The tide has come in. ter– to bump accidentally. *Pantatnja* ∼ *témbok*, He bumped his rear against a wall.

sundal 1 prostitute. 2 lewd, immoral. ber–, menj– to carry on prostitution. per–an 1 prostitution. 2 fornication. – *bolong* vampire. – *malam* a tuberose which gives off a pleasant scent in the evening.

sundel 1 see SUNDAL. 2 bastard!

sundjam head downward, diving.

sundul see SONDOL.

sundut generation, descent. ber– hereditary. menj– 1 to carry. 2 to light, kindle.

sungai river, stream. *pergi* ke– to go relieve o.s.

sungga iron ball with 4 spikes, o. pointing upward. menj– to spur, stick with a spike.

sunggi menj– to carry on the head.

sungging a painting, decoration. menj– to paint.

sunggit see SUNGKIT.

sungguh 1 true. *Perkataanmu mémang* –, What you say is true. 2 really, truly. *Ia* – *sakit rupanja*, He really seems to be sick. 3 indeed.

Kehidupan disini – *mahal*, Life here is indeed expensive. 4 seriously, earnestly. *Ia bekerdja* –, He worked earnestly. 5 actually, in fact. – *ia mengatakan itu pd saja, tetapi saja lupa*, As a matter of fact he told me so but I forgot it. ber– –² to make every effort. ke–an 1 truth. 2 seriousness. memper-i, menj–i to take s.t. seriously. *Ia* ∼ *pekerdjaannja*, He took his work seriously. (He did his utmost in his work.) menj–kan 1 to justify s.t. 2 to verify, ratify. penj–an 1 affirmation, verification. 2 serious effort. se–nja truly, as a matter of fact, in fact. *dgn se–hati* solemnly. –² seriously, earnestly. *Ia beladjar* ∼ , He studies seriously. – *mati*, I swear it. (It's as true as can be.) – *mati saja tak berdjumpa dia*, I swear I didn't meet her.

sungguhpun (al)though, even though. – *panas saja pergi djuga*, Even though it was hot, I went anyway.

sungkah menj– to devour, eat up. menj–kan to eat.

sungkal menj– to plow, dig up. – *badjak* plowshare.

sungkan averse, unwilling, reluctant. *Ia* – *melihat gurunja*, He was averse to seeing his teacher.

sungkap menj– to lift. ∼ *tirai* to lift a curtain. ter– to come loose.

sungkawa mourning. ber– to mourn. see BÉLA.

sungkem see SUNGKUM.

sungkit embroidered. menj– 1 to embroider. 2 to uncork, open (as a bottle). penj– bottle opener.

sungkum showing respect by bowing on hands and knees. menj– to pay respect by bowing on hands and knees. menj–kan 1 to place s.t. or s.o. prostrate on the ground. 2 to prop up.

sungkup a cover for s.t. ber– to be covered. *botol jg* ∼ *mangkok* a bottle covered with a cup. menj–(i) to cover with s.t. *Ia* ∼ *botol dgn telapak tangan*, He covered the bottle with the palm of his hand. menj–kan to apply s.t. as a cover. *Ia* ∼ *tangan kpd mukanja*, He covered his face with his hands. penj– 1 a cover. 2 bell jar. –an a basket for the completed washing.

sungkur spade, shovel. menj– 1 to lower the head. *Kerbau* ∼ *menjerang lawannja*, The carabao lowered its head to attack its opponent. 2 to dig up. *Babi hutan* ∼ *tanah*, A wild boar dug up the soil. ter– to fall headfirst.

sunglap 1 juggling. 2 see SULAP.

menj-kan 1 to juggle s.t. 2 to conjure with.

sungsang 1 upside down. 2 against the grain. **menj-** 1 to be upside down. *Djangan di– memegang ajam,* Don't hold a chicken upside down. 2 against the grain. **menj-kan** to place s.t., hold s.t., upside down. *– kalak* upside down.

sungsum see SUMSUM.

sungu horn. *– badak* rhinoceros horn.

sungut 1 feelers. *– djangkerik* a cricket's feelers, antennae. *– ikan* fish barbels. 2 mustache. 3 whiskers. *– kutjing* cat's whiskers. 4 tentacle. 5 antenna. **ber-** to have feelers, etc. *Kutjing* ∼ , Cats have whiskers. **ber-**−² to grumble, complain. *Ia sehari duduk* ∼ , He sat grumbling all day. *– léter* nagging, grumbling.

sunjata **ke-an** the truth in a religious sense.

sunji 1 lonely. *Ia merasa – dinegeri asing itu,* He felt lonely in the strange country. 2 quiet. *malam jg –* a quiet night. 3 deserted, desolate. *djalan jg –* a deserted road. 4 freed. *– dari dosa* freed from sin. **ber-**(–) to withdraw, retire. **ke-an** 1 loneliness. 2 quiet, solitude. **menj-** to become quiet. *– senjap* deathly still.

sunnah 1 tradition and customs of the Prophet accepted as proper conduct to be followed. 2 see SUNAT.

sunni Sunnite.

sunti knob on ginger. *– halia* ginger

suntih **menj-** to cut into small pieces.

suntik **menj-** 1 to inject, be given a shot. *Ia di– sebelum dibedah,* He was given an injection before the operation. 2 to inoculate. *Ia di– sebelum perdjalanannja keluar negeri,* He was inoculated before his trip abroad. 3 to vaccinate. ∼ *tjatjar* to vaccinate against smallpox. 4 to incite. *Ia* ∼ *pemuda² supaja melawan,* He incited the youths to fight back. **(penj)-an** 1 injection. 2 inoculation. 3 vaccination.

sunting ornament worn behind the ear. **ber-** to wear s.t. behind the ear. **memper-** 1 to place s.t. in o's hair as an ornament. 2 to adorn s.o. or s.t. 3 to have as a wife. *Untung benar ia* ∼ *isteri tjantik,* He is a very lucky fellow to have such a pretty wife. 4 to get, obtain. ∼ *ilmu dan pengalaman* to obtain knowledge and experience. **menj-kan** 1 to place, put, stick, behind the ear or in the hair. *Ia* ∼ *bunga,* She stuck a flower in her hair. 2 to insert, add. *Kini tinggal* ∼ *kata pendahuluan kpd buku-*

nja, Now there remained the preface to his book.

suntuk 1 very, too late. *waktu jg –* too late. 2 to be overtaken. *Ia lekas pulang karena takut – malam,* He hurried home because he was afraid he'd be overtaken by darkness. 3 entire length of time. *sehari –* the whole day. *semalam –* the whole night. 4 short(sighted), narrow-minded. *– akalnja* narrow-minded. **ter-** 1 to be overtaken. *Ia* ∼ *malam didjalan,* He was overtaken by darkness along the way. 2 to be late, overdue. *Trém* ∼ *datangnja,* The streetcar was late.

sunu **menj-** 1 to burn. 2 to light, kindle.

sup soup, broth.

supaja so that, in order that, in order to. *Katakan pd temanmu – ia tahu,* Tell your friend so that he'll know. *Orang itu – dibunuh,* That man is to be killed (a command).

supel smooth, flexible.

supir see SOPIR.

supit chopstick(s).

suprémasi supremacy.

Sura see ASJURA.

surabi see SERABAI.

surah a sura or a chapter in the Koran.

surai 1 hair of the head. 2 mane (of a horse or a lion). 3 coiffure, hairdress. **ber-** to break up, disperse. *Rapat* ∼ , The meeting broke up. **menj-(kan)** to break up, disperse. *Polisi* ∼ *rapat,* Police broke up the meeting.

Surakarta another name for Solo (city in central Java).

suram 1 vague, hazy. *Ingatannja tlh –,* His memory had become hazy. 2 gloomy, dark, dull. *tjuatja jg –* gloomy weather. 3 dim, dull, hazy. *tjahaja jg –* a dim light. **ke-an** 1 vagueness, indistinctness. 2 dullness. 3 darkness, gloom. **menj-** to become dark, dim, blurred. **menj-kan** to darken s.t. −² *gelap* quite dark, period of dusk.

surat 1 letter, epistle. 2 certificate. **ber-** 1 written. 2 inscribed. **menj-** to write. *Sdh lama ia tiada* ∼ , He hasn't written for a long time. **menj-i** 1 to inscribe. 2 to write to. **menj-kan** 1 to inscribe s.t. *Ia* ∼ *perdjandjiannja kpd tembaga,* He inscribed the agreement on copper. 2 to write s.t. *Ia* ∼ *kpd madjikan,* He wrote a letter to an employer. **pe(r)-an** mail service. **per-kabaran** the press. **ter-** destined. *Sdh* ∼ *rupanja bhw engkau akan mengawini dia,* It seemed to be destined for you to marry her. **-an** 1 writing. 2 fate, destiny. 3 lines of the palm of the hand. 4 manuscript. - -menj- 1 to correspond, write to e.o. 2 correspondence. - *anggota* membership card. - *angkat(an)* letter of appointment. - *angkutan* bill of lading. - *asal usul* pedigree. - *berantai* chain letter. - *berkala* periodical. - *buta* anonymous letter. - *dakwa* summons. - *djamin(an)* warrant, guarantee. - *édaran* 1 circular (letter). 2 encyclical. - *gadai* mortgage bond. - *gadén* pawnshop receipt. - *gelap* anonymous letter. - *idjazah* diploma, certificate. - *isian* form or blank to be filled in. - *izin* permit. - *izin keluar* exit permit. - *izin pengeluaran* export permit. - *kabar* newspaper. - *kaléng* anonymous letter. - *kawat* wire, cablegram, telegram. - *kawin* marriage certificate. - *keberatan* petition. - *kematian* death certificate. - *kenalan* letter of recommendation. - *kepertjajaan* credentials. - *kesanggupan* promissory note. - *keterangan* identity card, identification papers. - *kuasa* letter of attorney, authorization, warrant. - *lahir* birth certificate. - *lamaran* application (form). - *lepas* 1 discharge papers. 2 divorce certificate. - *lulusan* certificate, permit, license. - *mati* death certificate. - *mentéga* a letter of dismissal, walking papers. - *muatan* bill of lading. - *nikah* marriage certificate. - *obligasi* bond. - *paksa* warrant, writ. - *panggilan* summons. - *pas* passport. - *pemberitahuan* declaration, letter of notification. - *pemilihan* ballot for voting. - *pengantar* 1 letter of introduction. 2 a covering letter. - *ini kirimkan ke London dgn* - *pengantar jg singkat sadja,* Send this letter to London with just a brief covering letter. 3 invoice. 4 bill of lading. 5 safe-conduct. - *perdjandjian* contract, pact. - *perintah* 1 mandate, instruction. 2 commission, mission. - *perintah perdjalanan* travel orders. - *permintaan,* - *permohonan* request. - *pudji(an)* 1 letter of recommendation, testimonial. 2 attestation. - *salinan* copy. - *ségél* writ, letter on stamped paper. - *se(le)baran* circular, pamphlet. - *siaran* leaflet. - *sita* writ of execution, summons. - *suara* ballot for voting. - *tagihan* dunning letter. - *talak* divorce certificate. - *tanda* letter of identification. - *tanda hutang* contract letter of debt. - *tanda pengenal* identity card. - *tanda tammat* diploma. - *témpélan* poster, placard, bill. - *terbuka* open letter. - *tertjatat* registered letter. - *tjepat* special-delivery

letter. - *tjerai* divorce certificate. - *tuduhan* letter of accusation. - *tugas* 1 instruction, mandate. 2 mission, commission. - *tumpangan* letter enclosed with other letters. - *ukur* 1 property title. 2 map of premises. - *uleman,* - *undangan* invitation. - *undi(an)* lottery ticket. - *uraian* explanatory letter. - *usiran* eviction notice. - *utang* I.O.U. - *wasiat* will. - *wésél* bill of exchange. *dgn* - in writing. - *menjusul,* Letter follows (in telegrams).

surau religious training center for advanced Islamic students.

surga Moslem and Christian heaven. - *dunia* an earthly paradise.

suri 1 shuttle comb on a weaving loom. 2 queen. - *teladan* model, example.

surih 1 a scratch. 2 a line. **ber-** ruled, lined. **menj-** to draw lines. **menj-kan** *djalan* to give directions. ~ *pertjakapan* to change the subject.

surili k.o. monkey.

surja sun.

surjakanta magnifying glass.

surjani Syrian.

sursak see SIRSAK.

suruh **menj-(kan)** 1 to order, have done. *Ia* ~ *adiknja menulis surat,* He had his brother write a letter. 2 to send, order. *Ia* ~ *saja pulang,* He sent me home. 3 to delegate, depute. **pe-** messenger. **penj-** the o. who gives orders. **-an** 1 message, order. 2 messenger, delegate. **-²an** errand boy, messenger. - *buat* have s.t. made.

suruk **ber-** **-²an** to play hide-and-seek. **menj-** 1 to duck the head. 2 to hide. **menj-i** to creep under. *Ia* ~ *pagar,* He crept under the hedge. **menj-kan** 1 to bend down, keep down. *Ia* ~ *kepalanja,* He bent his head down. 2 to hide. *Ia* ~ *buku dibawah tempat tidur,* He hid the book under the bed. **-an** hiding place, shelter.

surung see SORONG.

surup fitting, proper, appropriate. **ke-an** possessed by a spirit.

surut 1 to withdraw, yield. *Sekali madju tak dpt - lagi,* Once it advances it cannot withdraw any more. 2 to return. *Ia - kerumahnja,* He returned home. 3 to lessen, decrease. *Anginnja tlh -,* The wind has died down. *Penjakitnja tlh -,* His illness has decreased. 4 to go out (of a fire). 5 to ebb. *air* - ebb tide. **bersi-** to withdraw. **menj-i** to diminish, decrease. **menj-kan** 1 to withdraw.

~ *pasukannja* to withdraw o's troops. 2 to decrease, lessen. ~ *djam bekerdja* to decrease the working hours. 3 to soothe, calm down. *Ia* ~ *kemarahan gurunja*, He calmed down his teacher's anger. 4 to put out, extinguish. ~ *api* to extinguish a fire. **ter–** 1 to retire. 2 to shrink back.

surya see SURJA.

susah 1 trouble. *Itu banjak* –, That's a lot of trouble, bother, a nuisance. 2 worry. *Djangan* –, *saja jg akan mengambilnja*, Don't worry, I'll get it for you. 3 grief, sorrow. *Ia* – *karena uangnja hilang*, He was unhappy because he lost a lot of money. 4 difficult, hard, bothersome. *pekerdjaan jg* – a difficult job. 5 hard to get, come by. *Uang agak* – *sekarang ini*, Money is hard to get these days. *Buku sedemikian itu* – *diketemukan*, Such a book is hard to find. **ber–** *hati* to be worried. **ber––²**, **ber–** *pajah* to make every effort. *Ia tlh* ~ *beladjar*, He's put all his efforts into his studies. **ke–an** 1 difficulty. 2 worry, grief. 3 hardship, trouble. **memper–(kan)** to render difficult. ~ *hati* to worry about s.t. **menj–i** 1 to bother, annoy. *Djangan* ~ *orang beladjar*, Don't bother s.o. who's studying. 2 to cause worry to s.o. *Ia selalu* ~ *orang tuanja*, He has always caused his parents to worry. **menj–kan** 1 to make difficult. *Djangan terlalu* ~ *pekerdjaan orang² itu*, Don't make the work of those people too difficult. 2 to cause trouble. *Perumahan masih* ~ , Housing is still causing trouble. 3 hard, difficult. *pekerdjaan jg* ~ a hard job. 4 to worry about. – *pajah* 1 great difficulty. 2 much effort, pains.

susastera see SASTERA.

susila decent, well-behaved. **ke–an** 1 ethics. 2 decency, good behavior. *polisi séksi* – morals squad.

suster 1 nurse. 2 nun.

susu 1 milk. 2 udder. **menj–(i)**, **menj–kan** 1 to suckle. 2 to let suckle. *Ia* ~ *anak itu pd botol*, She gave the baby the bottle. **penj–** wet nurse. – *beku* curdled milk. – *bubuk* powdered milk. – *éntjér*, – *kaléngan* canned milk. – *kental* condensed milk. – *tin* canned milk.

susuh cockspur.

susuhunan title of ruling prince in Solo (central Java).

susuk 1 small piece of gold often inserted in lip or chin as sign of beauty or in body to produce strength. 2 surplus change after payment.

3 a pin. 4 nail. **ber–** 1 to insert a small piece of gold. 2 to wear a hairpin. **menj–** 1 to stab with a pin. 2 to lay out. *Kota ini di– menurut modél kota modérn*, This city was laid out like a modern city. 3 to pioneer. **menj–kan** to stick, put. ~ *hidung dlm saputangan* to stick the nose in a handkerchief. – *tubuh* shape, figure.

susul **menj–** 1 to follow. *Jg satu* ~ *jg lain*, O. followed the other. *Surat* ~, Letter follows (in telegrams). 2 to join, overtake, catch up with. *Ia* ~ *temannja*, He caught up with his friend. 3 to keep up with. *Ia harus* ~ *peladjaran² waktu ia sakit*, He had to keep up with his lessons when he was sick. 4 to bring up, touch upon. *Djanganlah* ~ *hal² jg tlh lampau*, Please don't bring up past matters. 5 to refer to. ~ *surat saja bulan jg lalu*, Referring to my letter of last month. 6 to trace. *Tidak mudah* ~ *asal-mulanja tjeritera itu*, It wasn't easy to trace the origin of that story. **menj–i** 1 to accompany. *Ia* ~ *ajahnja ke Mekah*, He accompanied his father to Mecca. 2 to add s.t. *Ia* ~ *keterangan lain kpd pidatonja*, He added some other information to his speech. **menj–kan** 1 to add. *Ia* ~ *pasal baru*, He added a new paragraph. 2 to have follow. *Anaknja akan di–kan ke negeri Belanda*, His child will be sent to Holland later. **penj–** pursuer. **–an** 1 appendix, supplement. 2 continuation.

susun 1 pile, heap. *dua – buku* two piles of books. *dua – piring* two plates, o. on top of the other. 2 row, series. **ber–** 1 piled, heaped (o. on the other). *piring* ~ plates stacked o. on the other. 2 in layers. *kué* ~ layer cake. 3 in stories. *rumah* ~ a multistoried house. 4 in rows. *berdiri* ~ *lima* to have standing in 5 rows. 5 orderly arranged. *kata² jg tidak* ~ words which are not in orderly arrangement. **menj–(kan)** 1 to pile, heap up. ~ *batu* to pile up stones. ~ *piring* to stack plates o. on the other. 2 to compose. *Ia* ~ *kalimat*, He composed a sentence. 3 to compile. *Ia* ~ *kamus*, He compiled a dictionary. 4 to form. ~ *kabinét* to form a cabinet. 5 to prepare, fix. ~ *atjara* to prepare the agenda. 6 to organize, arrange. 7 to draft. 8 to construct. **penj–** 1 composer. 2 compiler. 3 drafter. ~ *huruf* compositor, typesetter. **penj–an** 1 composition. 2 compilation. 3 arrangement. **ter–** 1 heaped up. 2 composed.

-an 1 composition, compilation. 2 formation. 3 system. 4 structure. 5 arrangement, formation. ~ *kata* wording. - *-tindih* overlapping.

susup **menj-(i)** 1 to crawl, creep along. *Anak² ~ dibawah médja itu*, The children crawled under the table. 2 to penetrate, infiltrate. *Meréka ~ kedalam rimba*, They penetrated into the forest. *Sétan ~ ketubuhnja*, The devil entered his body. **menj-kan** 1 to push, shove, slip. *Ia ~ peti kebawah lemari*, He pushed the box under the cupboard. 2 to smuggle, have infiltrate. *Ia ~ pasukan kebelakang garis musuh*, He smuggled troops behind the enemy lines. **penj-an** penetration, infiltration. - *sasap* to infiltrate, creep under things.

susur 1 edge, fringe. - *bantal* edge of a pillow. - *pantai* shore's edge. - *kota* city's edge. 2 quid of tobacco. 3 margin. **menj-(i)** to go along the edge of. *berdjalan ~ pantai* to walk along the shore. - *galur* pedigree. - *tangga* banister of a staircase.

susut **menj-** 1 to decrease. 2 to shrink (of cloth). 3 to subside (of a wind, storm, swelling, etc.). 4 to investigate. *Polisi sedang ~ perkara itu*, The police are investigating the matter. **menj-i** to reduce, decrease. ~ *perbelandjaan negara* to reduce the national budget. *Ia ~* , He was reducing (in weight). **menj-kan** to reduce, limit, decrease s.t. *Obat ini ~ badannja*, This medicine reduced his weight. **penj-an** 1 investigation. 2 reduction, decrease.

sut see SUTEN.

sutan title of nobility in Sumatra. **ber-(-)** to act in a highhanded fashion.

suten **ber-** to draw lots by throwing out fingers to see who goes first.

sutera silk. - *tiruan* artificial silk.

sutil roasting spit.

sutji 1 pure, purified, clean. 2 holy. **ber-** 1 to live a pure life. 2 to cleanse o.s. **ke-an** 1 purity. 2 holiness. 3 cleanliness. **menj-kan** 1 to purify, disinfect, clean. 2 to sanctify. **penj-a** purifying agent. **penj-an, per-an** purification, cleansing. *Jg* **Ter-** His Holiness. - *hama* sterile.

sutradara movie or play director. **menj-i** to direct a movie or play. **penj-an** 1 play or movie direction. 2 directing.

suwara see SUARA.

swa- self- (prefix).

swadaja 1 innate strength or effort. 2 autoactivity. 3 self-help.

swapradja autonomous area or region.

swara see SUARA.

swarga see SURGA.

swarna 1 goldlike. 2 very pretty.

swasembada self-supporting.

swasiswa an autodidact.

swasta private. *pengusaha* - private entrepreneur. **mengs-kan** to make s.t. private. ~ *perusahaan negara* to convert a state enterprise into a private one. **pengs-an** conversion into private ownership. ~ *perkebunan* conversion of estates to private ownership.

swat. [*swatantra*] 1 autonomy. 2 autonomous.

swatantra 1 autonomy. 2 autonomous.

swawedya self-cure.

Swédia 1 Sweden. 2 Swedish.

SWI [*Sumbangan Wadjib Istiméwa*] special obligatory contribution.

Swis 1 Switzerland. 2 Swiss.

swt [*swatantra*] 1 autonomy. 2 autonomous.

T

T [*Tangerang*] telephone exchange in Jakarta.

t. [*tanpa*] without.

ta' see TAK.

ta'adjub 1 admiration. 2 astonishment. 3 astonished. **ke-an** 1 astonishment, amazement. 2 admiration. **men(t)-i** to admire. *Ia ~ kepandaian temannja*, He admired his friend's ability. **men(t)-kan** 1 to astonish. *Keindahan kota itu ~ para pelantjong*, The city's beauty astonished the tourists. 2 amazing, astonishing.

ta'alim respect, honor. *Terimalah*

salam - saja, Please accept my respectful greetings.

ta'assub fanatical.

ta'at 1 devotion, obedience (to God). 2 to obey. *Meréka - pd perintah opsir meréka*, They obeyed their officer's commands. 3 faithful. *Ia - kpd negaranja*, He was faithful to his country. **ber-** to be obedient, be faithful. **ke-an** 1 faith, devotion. 2 faithfulness. **men(t)-i** 1 to be faithful to. 2 to obey.

tabah 1 see TEBAH. 2 determined, resolute. *Ia - sekali menghadapi* *kemalangan itu*, He's very resolute in facing the misfortune. **ke–an** firmness, determination. ~ *hati* firmness, determination. **men–kan** to make firm, make determined. *Nasihat² itu ~ hati teman²nja*, The advice has made his friends feel determined.

tabak a tray.

tabal inauguration. **men–kan** to inaugurate. **pen–an** inauguration.

taban gutta-percha tree.

tabas see TEBAS.

tabé'at see TABI'AT.

tabé(k) see TABIK.

tabél table, list. – *tegakan* yield table.

tabi'at 1 character. 2 behavior.

tabib 1 physician. 2 non-Indonesian Moslem healer. **ke–an** medicine.

tabik 1 hello. 2 goodbye. 3 greeting. *Ia memberi* –, He greeted (them). **ber–** to greet. **ber–an** to greet e.o., shake hands. **men–** to greet. *Ia ~ kawannja*, He greeted his friend.

tabir curtain, partition, screen. – *asap* smoke screen. – *besi* the iron curtain. **ber–** 1 to have, use, a curtain. 2 to be in disguise. **men–i** to cover with a curtain. *Asap ~ léréng gunung itu*, Smoke covered the slope of the mountain. – *mabir* all sorts of curtains.

tablig(h) 1 an Islamic public sermon. 2 a religious meeting. **ber–** to preach.

tabok **men–** to slap. *Ia ~ saja*, He slapped me. **men–i** to spank s.o. **–an** a slap.

tabrak **ber–** to collide. **ber–an** to collide. *Kedua mobil itu ~* , The 2 cars collided. *Mobil ~ dgn grobak*, The car collided with a truck. **men–** 1 to strike, hit against. *Mobil itu ~ témbok*, The car struck the wall. 2 to attack, hit. *Pemain bola itu ~ pendjaga gawang*, The soccer player attacked the goalie. **ter–** to strike, collide with. *Mobil ~ pohon*, A car collided with a tree. **–an** collision.

tabu taboo.

tabuh 1 drum in the mosque. 2 drumbeat. 3 drumstick. **men–** 1 to beat on a drum. 2 to drum on s.t. with o's finger. *Ia ~ gamelan*, He plays the gamelan. **pen–** drummer. **–an** 1 wasp. 2 percussion instrument. ~ *meminang anak lebah²* out of proportion.

tabun **men–** 1 to rise (of smoke). *Asapnja ~ kelangit*, The smoke rose into the sky. 2 to burn. *Ia ~ sampah*, He burned the trash. **–an** the burning of rubbish.

tabung 1 cylindrical box of bamboo, a tube. 2 money box. **men–(kan)** to

save. *Ia ~ uang dibank*, She saves money in the bank. **pen–** a depositor. **pen–an** saving(s). **–an** money box. ~ *pos* postal savings. – *kimia* test tube, retort. – *madat* opium pipe. – *pekak* savings box. – *pemilihan* ballot box. – *surat* mailbox.

tabur **ber–** **–(–)an** scattered, spread. *Bintang² ~ dilangit*, Stars were scattered about in the sky. **men–** to scatter, sow. **men–i** to scatter, sow s.t. *Ia ~ tanahnja dgn bidji*, He sowed his land with seed. **men–kan** 1 to sow. 2 to scatter, spread. **pen–** 1 sower, spreader. 2 hail, shot. **–an** sowings.

tabut ark.

tachajul see TACHJUL.

tachjul superstition. **ke–an** superstition.

tachlik **men(t)–kan** to create. *Tuhan ~ alam*, God created the universe.

tachta throne. **ber–** to reign. *Ia ~ selama 10 tahun*, He reigned for 10 years. **men(t)–kan** to crown, enthrone. *Radja ~ putera mahkota*, The king enthroned the crown prince. – *Sutji* Holy See.

tadah 1 receptacle. 2 cistern, reservoir. **ber–** *amin* to say amen. **men–** 1 to catch. *Ia ~ air dgn tangannja*, He caught the water with his hands. 2 to receive stolen goods. *Ia seorang jg ~* , He is a person who receives stolen goods. **men–kan** to catch s.t. in or with. ~ *piring* to hold a plate up to receive s.t. ~ *tangannja* to receive in the hands. **pen–** 1 container, receptacle. 2 buyer of stolen goods. 3 catcher (in sports). 4 a bat (in sports). – *keringat* 1 undershirt. 2 sweat shirt. – *tjangkir* saucer.

tadbir management. **men(t)–kan** to manage, administer. **per–an** administration, management.

tadi just now, a little while ago. – *ia disini*, He was here just now. *jg tersebut* – as mentioned just now. **–nja** 1 at first. ~ *ia takut*, At first he was afraid. 2 just now. – *malam* last night. – *pagi* this morning. – *pagi ia pergi ke Bandung*, This morning he went to Bandung. – *siang* this past noon. – *soré* just this afternoon.

tadjak a hoe. **men–** to hoe, work the soil.

tadjam 1 sharp, keen. – *akalnja* sharp-witted. – *otaknja* keen, intelligent. 2 sharp (not dull). *pisau –* a sharp knife. 3 pointed. *berudjung –* sharp-pointed. 4 sharp, acute. *sudut –* a sharp corner. **ke–an** 1 too sharp. 2 sharpness. **memper–(kan)** 1 to sharpen. *Ia ~ pisaunja*, He sharpened his knife. 2 to whet. **men–kan** 1 to sharpen. *Pertentangan itu ~ hubungan antara kedua negeri itu*, The disagreement aggravated the relationship between the 2 countries. 2 to whet. – *mulutnja* sharp-tongued. – *perasaan* sensitive.

tadji metal spur for a fighting cock. **ber–** with the spur on. – *bentuk* spur with blade slightly curved. – *golok* spur with blade of fancy design.

tadjin starch. **men–** to starch s.t.

ta'djub see TA'ADJUB.

tadjuk 1 head ornament of flowers. 2 aigrette of flowers. 3 outboard projection on small craft. **ber–** step by step, in stages. **men–** 1 to protrude. 2 prominent, well-known. – *mahkota* 1 a part of a royal crown. 2 beloved, darling. – *rentjana* editorial.

taduh see TEDUH.

taf(a)kur meditation. **ber–** 1 to reflect, consider. 2 to observe silence out of respect for s.o. **men(t)–kan** to reflect on, meditate about s.t.

tafsir 1 interpretation, explanation. 2 commentary, exegesis. **men(t)–kan** 1 to explain, interpret s.t. 2 to define. **pent–** analyst, evaluator. **pen(t)–an** 1 explanation, interpretation. 2 commentary, exegesis. **–an** = TAFSIR. – *Kor'an* exegesis of the Koran.

tagal 1 large beach stone. 2 moment. **se–** a moment.

tagan contribution.

tagar thunder. **ber–** to thunder.

tagih addiction. *Ia – bekerdja*, He has an addiction to work. **ke–** addicted to. **ke–an** 1 addiction. 2 addicted to. *Ia ~ madat*, He is addicted to opium. **men–** to dun, press for payment. *Ia ~ hutangnja*, He pressed for payment of the debt. **pe–** creditor. **(pen)–an** a claim. – *tidur* coma.

tah. [*tahun*] year.

-tah 1 an interrogative suffix expressing doubt. *Siapa– jg suka bergaul dgn orang jg djahat itu?* Who would want to go around with that bad man? *Apa– nasibku kiranja?* I wonder what in the world my fate is going to be? 2 see ENTAH. – *dimana dia sekarang*, No one knows where he is now.

tahadi see TADI.

tahak a belch. **ber–** to belch.

tahan 1 to stand, endure, take. *Ia dapat – menderita*, He can stand suffering. *Badannja tak – lagi*, His body couldn't take any more. 2 to last. *Itu bisa – lima minggu*, That can last 5 weeks. 3 to be able. *Saja*

tak – tinggal lama disini, I can't stay here long. 4 to dare. **ber–** to hold out. *Musuh masih ~ didaérah itu*, The enemy held out in that area. *Kalau hémat, uangnja akan ~ 10 hari lagi*, If they're economical, their money will hold out for another 10 days. *~ diri* to defend o.s. **ber– –²** (*larat*) to hold out, last. **ke–an** endurance, stamina. **memper–kan** to defend, maintain. *Ia ~ pendiriannja*, He defended his stand. **men–** 1 to hold back, restrain. *Pendjaga ~ orang²*, The guard held back the people. *Ia ~ hawa nafsu*, He restrained his desire. 2 to hold. *Ia ~ napas*, He held his breath. 3 to hold up, stop. *Ia ~ suratnja*, He held up the letter. *Ia ~ tiang*, He held up a pole. 4 to arrest, detain. *Polisi ~ pentjuri*, The police arrested a thief. 5 to check, control. *Meréka ~ meningkatnja harga²*, They checked the rise in prices. 6 to set, place. *Ia ~ bubu*, He set a fish trap. *~ diri, ~ hati* to restrain o.s. **men–i** to control, govern, restrain. **pen–** o. who restrains, checks. **pen–an** detention, arrest. *dinding ~* restraining wall. **per–an** 1 defense. *Départemén ~* Ministry of Defense. 2 stronghold, fortress. **ter–** impeded, checked. *tak dpt ~* irresistible. **ter– –²** 1 restrained. 2 broken down (of a car). 3 to break down while speaking. 4 to catch o's breath. **–an** 1 resistance, opposition. 2 reserve. *~ makanan utk musim dingin* food in reserve for the winter. 3 arrest, detention. – *air* waterproof, watertight. – *api* fireproof. – *besi* invulnerable. – *gelombang* resistant to the beating (pounding) of waves. – *harga* 1 with self-respect. 2 stable in price. – *hati* persistent, firm. – *hina* tolerant. – *kias* able to take teasing. – *lama* durable, lasting. – *lembab* moisture-resistant, -proof. – *nafsu* with self-control. – *ombak* resistant to pounding of waves. – *palu, – pukulan* able to take a beating. – *panas* heat-resistant. – *sabar* patient. – *sesah* washable. *putih – sesah*, *hitam – serpa* unchanging, resistant to change. – *tangan* invulnerable. – *tjutji* washable. – *turut* backstay (sailing). – *udji* tested, tried. – *warna* fast (of color).

tahang 1 ravine. 2 barrel, cask. 3 tank, reservoir.

tahap(an) stage, phase.

tahbis 1 consecrated. 2 consecration, dedication. **men(t)–kan** to consecrate. **pent–an** (act of) consecration.

tahi 1 excrement, feces. 2 filth. 3

dregs. – *air* scum, residue, on water. – *angin* 1 light drifting clouds. 2 a plant used for diarrhea. – *besi* iron rust. – *bintang* meteorite. – *gergadji* sawdust, wood filings. – *gigi* tartar. – *kikir* (iron) filings. – *kuku* dirt under the nails. – *lalat* 1 birthmark. 2 freckles. – *mata* sleep, mucus, in the eye. – *minjak* oil dregs. – *telinga* wax in the ears.

tahil a measure of weight for gold and opium.

tahir pure.

tahjul see TACHJUL.

tahkik verification.

tahlil 1 the recitation of the confession of faith: *la ilaha illa'llah.* 2 to make legally possible the remarriage of a husband to a woman on whom he has pronounced *talak* three times, by her intervening marriage to and divorce from another man (called *muhallil*).

tahmid praise to Allah by repeating *alhamdulillah.*

tahta see TACHTA.

tahu 1 to know. *Saja tidak* –, I don't know. 2 soybean cake. 3 see KE-. **ber-** 1 well-informed. 2 conceited. **berpenge-an** scholarly. **ke-an** to be found out, caught, detected. *Ia mau pergi diam², tapi ~ djuga*, He wanted to go quietly, but it was found out anyway. **memper-kan** to announce s.t. **menge-i** 1 to know. *Ia blm ~ apa salahnja*, He doesn't yet know what his mistake is. 2 to detect, find out. *Ia ~ maksud jg djelék itu*, He detected his bad intention. 3 informed. *kalangan jg sangat ~* well-informed sources. 4 to know about. *Apakah jg sdr. ke-i ttg sedjarah Indonésia?* What do you know about the history of Indonesia? 5 to discern, perceive. **penge-an** 1 knowledge. 2 skill, ability. **se-** 1 as far as o. knows. *~ saja ia tak ada disini lagi*, As far as I know he's no longer here. 2 with the knowledge of. *Itu dibeli dgn ~ ajahnja*, It was bought with his father's knowledge. *Ia pergi dgn ~ saja*, He goes with my knowledge. *~nja* knowledge of. *dgn tiada ~nja* without knowing it. **-nja** knowledgeable. *Ia ada banjak ~* , He's very knowledgeable. *~ sendiri* conceited. **-²** suddenly, unexpectedly. *~ ia datang*, He came unexpectedly. *tidak – -men-* indifferent to o. another. – *ada(nja)* sure of o.s. – *adat* well-mannered, knowing the ways. – *akal* have an idea. – *balas* grateful. – *bérés* to take things for granted. –

goréng dish of fried soybeans. – *madu* to know where the profit lies. – *sama* – 1 silent agreement between two persons participating in a mutually advantageous illegal deal. 2 we know among ourselves. *Kita – sama – bhw itu tak benar, bukan?* We know it isn't true, don't we? – *tjampur* mixture of soybeans and vegetables. *tidak – diri* 1 unconscious. 2 insolent. *tidak – marah* never angry. –, *ja*, Dunno.

tahun year. **ber-** for years. **ber- -²** for many years. *Ia ~ tinggal dinegeri asing*, He lived abroad for many years. **men-** 1 to stay for some time, for years. *Ia akan ~ di Mekah*, He will stay in Mecca for some years. 2 chronic. *penjakit ~* a chronic disease. **se-** o. year. **se- -²an** the entire year. **se- -²nja** every year. **-an** 1 for years. 2 annual(ly). *rapat ~* annual meeting. *Ia membajar ~* , He pays annually. 3 anniversary. – *baru* new year. – *berikutnja* the following year. – *datang*, – *depan*, – *hadap* next year. – *djagung* approximately 3 months (from corn crop to corn crop). – *kabisat* leap year. – *kamariah* lunar year. – *padjak* fiscal year. – *peladjaran*, – *pengadjaran* academic year. – *pembukuan* fiscal year.

taik di-i mounted (on horseback, etc.). see NAIK.

taipun see TAUFAN.

tais dirty.

tajang men- to carry in o's hands. **men-kan** to present, bring. *Program itu di-kan kpd umum*, The program was presented to the public.

tajub men- to dance to gamelan music. **-an** dancing with a female partner to gamelan music.

tak see TIDAK. **-kan** it's impossible. **ke-atjuhan** indifference, apathy. **ke-sengadjaan** unintentional. – *dpt tidak* o. can't help but. *Ia – dpt tidak pergi*, He can't help but go. – *dpt tidak harus* must. – *lain – bukan* nothing other than. – *organik* inorganic. – *tahu* never. – *usah* not necessary.

takabur 1 arrogant. 2 proud. **ke-an** 1 pride. 2 conceit.

takah 1 see TAKUH. 2 notched, jagged. 3 appearance, attitude. 4 fierce. *andjing jg –* a fierce dog. 5 handy, skillful, clever.

takal tackle, pulley.

ta'kan see TAK.

takar 1 cubic measure. 2 unit of liquid measure. 3 glass jar. **ke-an** standard of living. **men-(i)** to measure out. **se-** to match. *Kepandaiannja tak ~ dgn keberaniannja*, His ability

does not match his courage. **–an**
1 measurement. 2 measurement of
capacity.

takbir recitation of the Arabic formula
Allahu Akbar (God is the greatest).
ber– to recite this formula (especially on the way to the *Hari Raya*
prayers). **ber–an** to recite this formula
repeatedly by chanting it.

takbur see TAKABUR.

takdir 1 divine decree, fate. 2 pre-
destination. **men–kan** to predestine.
Tuhan tlh ∼ ia mendjadi présidén,
God has predestined him to be
president.

takdjub see TA'ADJUB.

takel see TAKAL.

taker see TAKAR. **–an** *tjoba* trial
batch (of cement, etc.).

takik notch, incision. **men–** 1 to
tap (rubber, etc.). 2 to cut a notch,
incision. *∼ darah dibatu* to get blood
from a turnip. **pen–** *getah* rubber
tapper.

takir container made of a banana
leaf. *se–nasi* a portion of rice wrapped
in a banana leaf.

takkan will not (from *tak akan*).
Djangan perkara djika – menang,
Don't sue if you're not sure to win.

taklid unquestioning, passive acceptance of traditional religious interpretations. **ber–** *buta* to follow s.o. blindly.

takluk 1 subject. *– kpd hukum negara*
subject to the laws of the country.
2 yielding, submitting. *– kpd permintaan ajahnja* yielding to his father's request. 3 subjection. **men(t)–
kan** to subjugate, subdue. **pen(t)–an**
subjection, submission. **–an** s.t. subjected. *daérah ∼nja* conquered terri-
tories.

takorganik see TAK.

takrim veneration.

takrir evidence, proof.

taksi taxi. **men–** to drive a cab.
men–kan to use as a cab. *Ia ∼
mobilnja,* He used his car as a cab.
per–an taxi matters.

taksir 1 estimate, value. *salah –*
wrong estimate. 2 shortcoming, failure. 3 neglect. *dgn –nja sendiri*
through his own fault. **men(t)–**
1 to estimate, evaluate. 2 to desire,
want. *Ia ∼ akan rumah itu,* He
wants that house. **men(t)–kan** to
omit, neglect. **–an** estimate, evaluation.

takuh notch. *– takah* all k.o. notches.

takuk notch. **ber–** indented, jagged.
men– to cut a notch, incision. **men–
(kan)** to fix, determine. *Ia ∼ hari
berangkat,* He fixed the departure
date.

takung men– to let s.t. settle. *Ia ∼
air sungai supaja bersih,* He let the
river water settle so it would be clean.

takur see TEKUR.

takut to be afraid. *Djangan –!* Don't
be afraid! *– akan* to be afraid of.
Saja – akan singa, I'm afraid of
lions. **ber–an** to be frightened. **ke–an**
1 fear. 2 anxiety. 3 terrified, frightened. *Ia ∼ melihat gurunja,* He was
terrified upon seeing his teacher.
memper–i to intimidate s.o. **men–i** 1
to frighten s.o. 2 to respect. *Ia ∼
ajahnja,* He respects his father.
men–kan 1 to frighten s.o. 2 to be
concerned about s.t. 3 frightening.
pen– coward. **–²an** 1 bashful, shy.
2 deathly afraid. 3 nervous. **–²** *berani*
hesitatingly.

takwa devotion. **ber–** pious, devoted.

takwim 1 almanac. 2 calendar. *tahun
–* calendar year.

takzim see TA'ZIM.

tal a fan palm.

tala men– to tune an instrument.
menje–kan to tune, put in tune.
pen– tuning fork. **se–** in tune. *– suara*
voice modulation.

tala'ah men– 1 to study. 2 to de-
cipher. see TELA'AH.

talah ter– –² hastily, hurriedly.

talak 1 divorce. 2 a divorce formula:
repudiation of the wife by the
husband. **men(t)–(i)** to repudiate.
– tiga divorce made irrevocable by
uttering *talak* 3 times.

talam tray. *– dua muka* two-faced.

talang 1 broker. 2 eave, gutter. *–
kuda* horse trader. **men–** to lend
money as a profession. **pen–** *(uang)*
moneylender.

talar ber–an open, frank.

talas taro.

talén se– a quarter of a rupiah. **–an**
a quarter (coin).

tales see TALAS.

tali 1 string, cord, rope. 2 line, connection. **ber–** with a rope. **ber–an**
1 connected, related. 2 related, to
be a relative of. **ber– –²** 1 connected,
involved. *Banjak hal ∼ dgn soal
ini,* Many things are involved in this
matter. 2 continuously. *Ia menjebut-
kan namanja ∼ ,* He mentioned his
name continuously. **memper–kan** 1
to bind. *Ia ∼ kudanja kepohon,* He
bound his horse to a tree. 2 to link,
connect, join. *Rumah² baru itu ∼
désa dgn kota,* The new houses link
the village with the town. *Meréka ∼
kematiannja dgn peminuman obat
itu,* They linked his death with the
drinking of the medicine. 3 to
marry. 4 to associate with. **men–kan**

to tie s.t. or s.o. up. **pen–** 1 binder (person or thing). ∼ *kuda* rope for a horse. 2 conclusion. ∼ *permusjawaratan* conclusion of the conference. 3 definition. **per–an** 1 relation, relationship. ∼ *bahasa* relationship of languages. 2 connection. 3 alliance, union. **se–** 1 connected to o. another. 2 see TALÉN. ∼ *tiga uang* 6 of o. and half a dozen of the other. **– -ber–** continuously. ∼ *orang jg datang kelapangan itu*, People keep coming to the field. – *air* 1 small stream, creek. 2 current. 3 perineum. – *alit* string for spinning a top. – *ambin* a strap around a load. – *anak* small auxiliary rope. – *api* fuse. – *ari²* umbilical cord. – *bahu* shoulder straps of knapsack. – *barut* abdominal strap. – *batong* sash. – *bawat* brace. – *belati* rope of European hemp. – *busur* 1 bowstring. 2 chord in geometry. – *dahi* browband of a horse. – *dahi lajar* ropes serving as bridle. – *djangkar* anchor chain or rope. – *djentera* thread in process of being spun. – *djiwa* source of life, heart. – *duga* sounding line. – *dugang* supporting rope. – *gasing* string for spinning a top. – *idjuk* rope made of sugar palm fiber. – *kail* fishing line. – *kang*, – *kekang*, – *kendali* 1 reins. 2 guideline. – *kepala* straps attaching knapsack to head. – *léhér* necktie. – *lés* reins. – *njawa* heart, source of life. – *pangkal* mast rope. – *pantjing* fishing line. – *peluga* sounding line. – *pendarat* hawser. – *pengangguk* forestay. – *penjidal kain* clothesline. – *(pen)tjemat* towrope. – *perut* 1 bellyband. 2 intestines. – *pesawat* driving belt. – *pinggang* abdominal band. – *pusar* filament. – *pusat* umbilical cord. – *ruai* a thin, weak rope. – *sabut* fiber rope. – *sepatu* shoelace, shoestring. – *singkil* a belt used by women in labor. – *sipat* plumb (carpentry). – *suai* a stay rope. – *sutji* holy bonds (of matrimony). – *tandur* cords for blinds. – *temali* 1 all sorts of ropes. 2 rigging. – *tom* reins. – *tudung* chin strap for hat. – *tunda* towrope. – *umban* a sling rope.

taligram see TÉLGRAM.
ta'lim see TA'ALIM.
talipun see TÉLPON.
talkin instruction to the dead or dying; address read at the close of a funeral service to instruct the dead what to say when questioned by the angels of death. **men(t)-(kan)** to whisper instructions in the ear of the dying.

talu opening melody at wayang show. **ber– –²** continuously, incessantly.
ta'luk see TAKLUK.
talun ber– to resound. *Suara kentongan* ∼ , The sound of the tom-tom resounded.
tama per– –² first of all. See PERTAMA.
tama' 1 greed. – *menghilangkan malu*, Greed has no shame. 2 greedy, covetous. – *akan upah* eager for pay. – *kedekut* greed and avarice.
tamad(d)un culture, refinement. **ber–** cultured, refined.
tamak see TAMA'.
tamam 1 finished, ended. 2 end (of a book, etc.).
taman 1 garden, park. – *bunga* flower garden. – *sari* pleasure park, garden. 2 room, court, yard. – *bahagia* (military) cemetery. – *batjaan* reading room (open air). – *inderia*, – *kanak²* kindergarten. – *margasatwa* 1 game preserve. 2 zoo. – *pembatjaan* reading room. – *pustaka* library.
tamar hindi tamarind.
tamasja view, scene, spectacle. *Ia pergi* –, He went on an excursion, went sight-seeing. **ber–** to go on an excursion, go sight-seeing. *Karena meréka libur, meréka pergi* ∼ *kegunung²*, Because they had a vacation, they went on a trip to the mountains.
tamat see TAMMAT.
tambah 1 more. – *besar* larger. – *gadji* more wages. – *rusak* more damaged. 2 plus. *5 – 1 ada 6*, 5 plus 1 is 6. 3 additional, more. *Lima rupiah tidak tjukup; minta* –, Five rupiahs isn't enough; I want more. **ber–** to increase. *Hutangnja* ∼ , His debts increased. ∼ *banjak* increasing in number. ∼ ... ∼ more and more. ∼ *besar* ∼ *tjongkak*, He became more and more arrogant as he grew bigger. **ber– –²** 1 to increase steadily. *Kekajaannja* ∼ , His wealth increased steadily. 2 besides, in addition. *Ia sdh bingung*, ∼ *anaknja sakit*, He was upset, and besides that his child was ill. **memper–** to increase s.t. ∼ *hasil bumi* to increase o's yield. **men–** 1 to add to. *satu di-dua* 1 plus 2. 2. 2 to add (a quality). ∼ *besar* to enlarge. ∼ *tinggi* to increase in height. 3 to supplement. **men–i** to add s.t. *Ia* ∼ *garam dlm sup*, She added salt to the soup. **men–kan** 1 to increase. *Obat itu* ∼ *sakitnja*, The medicine increased the pain. 2 to add s.t. *Ia* ∼ *gula dlm téh*, She added sugar to the tea. **pen–** 1 enumerator, counter, adder. 2 additional, extra. ∼ *belandja* addition to the budget. **pen–an** increase, raise. ∼ *gadji*

salary increase. **per–an** increase, growth. ~ *pengangguran* increase in unemployment. **–an** 1 addition, acquisition. ~ *buku² baru* acquisition of new books. 2 supplement(al). 3 extra fare. 4 increase. ~ *gadji* increase in salary. – *lama – kuat*, He is steadily becoming stronger. – *malam – gelap* the later the darker. – *pula* moreover, in addition. – *pula ia sakit*, Moreover, he fell ill.

tambak 1 a dam. 2 fishpond. 3 banking, leveling off. **men–** 1 to dam up. *Meréka* ~ *sungai*, They dammed up the river. 2 to cover over, plaster. *Ia* ~ *luka*, He put a plaster on the wound. 3 to add, heighten.

tambal 1 see TAMPAL. 2 patch. **men–** 1 to patch with plaster. *Ia* ~ *lobang ditémbok*, He patched the hole in the wall with plaster. 2 to fill a tooth. *Gigi taring akan saja* –, I'll fill the tooth. **–an** patches. *Tjelananja penuh* ~ , His pants were full of patches. – *-sulam* 1 repair by patching. 2 road repairs.

tambang 1 mine. – *besi* an iron mine. 2 passenger, load. *Sopir sibuk karena banjak* –, The driver is busy because there are many passengers. 3 fare, passage. *uang* – fare. 4 thick rope. **men–** 1 to mine, dig. *Di Sumatera Tengah orang* ~ *batu bara*, In central Sumatra people mine coal. 2 to cross in a ferry. 3 to be a passenger in a taxi. 4 to fasten with a thick rope. *Ia* ~ *perahunja pd tiang*, He fastened his boat to a pole. 5 to abandon o's wife. **men–kan** to transport across. **pen–** 1 ferryman. 2 ferry. **pen–an** ferrying, transport. **per–an** mining. **–an** 1 ferrying. 2 ferryboat.

tambat tether. **ber–** tethered, tied up. **ber–an** connected with. **men–(kan)** to tether, tie up. *Ia* ~ *sapinja*, He tethered his cow. **pen–an, per–an** 1 tie, alliance, connection. 2 relation. **–an** 1 mooring buoy. 2 tether. ~ *hati* sweetheart. ~ *larat* always in o's mind.

tambera charter, deed.

tambo 1 legend, tradition. 2 history, story, annals.

tambuh **ber–** to have another serving of rice.

tambul 1 dessert. 2 refreshment. *Ia mengeluarkan* – *berupa téh dan kopi*, She offered refreshments of tea and coffee. **ber–** 1 with dessert. 2 to have refreshments. *Sebelum rapat dilandjutkan, marilah* ~ *dahulu*, Before we go on with the meeting,

let's have some refreshments. 3 to do acrobatic stunts. **men–** to do acrobatic stunts. **pen–** 1 acrobat. 2 juggler.

tambun fat, corpulent. **ber–** to be piled up. **men–** to pile up. **men–kan** to fatten up. **(per)–an** 1 heap, pile. 2 an accumulation, piling up.

tambung rude, impertinent. **men–i** to treat s.o. in an insolent fashion.

tambur drum. **ber–, men–** to beat a drum.

tambus see TIMBUS.

taméng a shield for combat.

tamjiz ability to discriminate. **men–kan** to be able to distinguish between good and bad.

tammat 1 finished, completed, graduated. *Ia sdh – sekolah*, He's already graduated from school. 2 end, conclusion. – *alkalam* end of story, book. **men–kan** 1 to finish, graduate. 2 to end, conclude. **–an** 1 graduation. 2 a graduate. – *riwajatnja* to die, pass away, pass on.

tammatu'lkalam the end (of a story, etc.).

tampa *Ia salah* –, He misunderstood. **men–** 1 to understand. 2 to suspect.

tampah winnow.

tampak 1 visible, apparent. *Gedungnja* – *dari sini*, The building is visible from here. *Engkau sdh lama tidak* –, We haven't seen you for a long time. 2 measles. **men–** to see. *Ia* ~ *gunung didjauhnja*, He saw the mountain far away. **men–kan** to show. ~ *diri* to show up, appear. *Sdh lama engkau tak* ~ *dirimu*, You haven't shown up for a long time. **–nja** apparently. *Ia sakit* ~ , Apparently he's ill. **–²** to show up, appear. *Kenapa ia tidak* ~ ·? Why doesn't he show up? ~ *apung* not readily visible. see NAMPAK.

tampal 1 patch. 2 a mend. 3 see TAMBAL. **men–** 1 to patch, mend clothes, inner tube, tire, etc. 2 to patch, plaster. *Ia* ~ *témbok*, He plastered the wall. **men–kan** to paste, glue. *Ia* ~ *gambar ketémbok*, He pasted pictures on the wall. **–an** 1 a patch, mend. 2 appendix of a book.

tampan 1 appropriate, fitting. *Ia* – *sekali mendjadi ketua*, It's very appropriate that he become chairman. 2 to fit, suit. *Pakaiannja* – *sekali*, His clothes fit well. 3 smart, stylish. **men–** to make o.s. neat. **–nja** at first sight, first blush. **–²nja** apparently, seemingly. – *muka* 1 features. 2 appearance. – *rupa* appearance, look.

tampang 1 wad, roll, slice. *se- tembakau* a wad of tobacco. 2 seed, seedling. – *katjang* bean seedling. 3 source. *Inilah – segala kedjahatan*, This is the source of all evil. 4 appearance. **men**– to cut in slices. **pen**–1 profile. 2 diameter. 3 longitudinal section. – *muka* features, profile.

tampar a blow, slap, smack (usually with the hand). **ber**– *(tangan)* to applaud. **men**–i to beat repeatedly, violently. **men**–(kan) to slap, strike. *Ia* ∼ *saja*, He slapped me. **-an** a blow, slap. ∼ *njamuk* the shoulder.

tampas **men**– to lop off.

tampél **men**– to touch (in a sport).

tampi **men**– to winnow. **pen**– winnow. **-an** 1 s.t. winnowed. *beras* ∼ winnowed rice. 2 a winnow, fan. *Djangan tumpah padinja kalau men*–, Don't overdo it. *Darahnja men*– He got angry, excited.

tampik see TEMPIK. **men**– 1 to reject. *Ia* ∼ *tawaran saja*, He rejected my offer. 2 to decline, refuse (an invitation). **pe-an, pen-an, -an** rejection, refusal. – *sorak* shouting.

tampil 1 to appear. 2 to step forward. *Ia – kemuka utk bertjeramah*, He stepped forward to give the lecture. **men**– to step forward, appear in front. **men-kan** to bring forth, forward. *Ia* ∼ *mobilnja jg baru dihalaman*, He brought his new car out in the yard.

tampin 1 a quid (of tobacco, betel nut). 2 a stake (in games). **men**– to stake.

tampuk 1 calyx (plants). 2 cover, lid. **ber**– to have power. *Pemerintah negeri ini* ∼ *diibu kota*, The government of this country has its central office in the capital. – *lampu listerik* light socket. – *negeri* government, leadership. – *pemerintah* state leadership, supreme power. – *pimpinan* 1 supreme authority. 2 central leadership.

tampung **ber**– patched. **men**– 1 to catch. *Ia* ∼ *air hudjan*, He caught rain water. 2 to intercept letters. 3 to receive. *Ia* ∼ *bekas tawanan*, He received the ex-internees (for rehabilitation). 4 to patch, mend, fix. ∼ *badju* to repair a garment. ∼ *lantai* to fix a floor. **men-kan** to intercept with. *Ia* ∼ *tangan dibawah pantjuran*, He intercepted the water under the pipe with his hand. **pen**– s.t. or s.o. who intercepts. **pen-an** reception center, receiving station.

tampur see TEMPUR.

tampus sorrel (color).

tamsil 1 parable. 2 example. 3 comparison. **men**(t)–**kan** to analogize, compare. **-an** 1 comparison. 2 analogizing.

tam-tam k.o. drum.

tamtama enlisted man, a private.

tamu 1 guest. 2 visitor. – *agung* VIP, high-ranking visitor. **ber**– 1 to visit. *Siapa* ∼ *pd ajahnja?* Who's visiting his father? 2 to be a guest. **ke-an** to be visited by. *Ia* ∼ *tiga orang pendjahat*, He was visited by 3 bandits. **men**– 1 to be a guest of s.o. 2 to entertain o. as a guest. **men**–i to visit a place or person.

tamzil see TAMSIL.

tanah 1 land. 2 country, land. 3 soil, ground. 4 fathom. 5 background. **ber**– 1 to take roots. 2 to put down roots. *Saja sdh* ∼ *disini*, I've already put down roots here. 3 to have as a background. *bunga mérah* ∼ *hidjau* red flowers with a green background. **menge-kan** 1 to haul down a flag. 2 to pull down the shades. 3 to raze a building. 4 to bury. – *air* fatherland. – *Arab* Arabia. – *datar* flat country. – *dingin* a temperate area, zone. – *Djawa* Java. – *gojang* earthquake. – *gurun* wasteland. – *hidup* cultivated land. – *kampung* communal land. – *keradjaan* land belonging to Britain or the Netherlands. – *kering* a dry, unirrigated field. – *kosong* unused, uncultivated land. – *kuripan* land in private ownership. – *lalang* wasteland covered with grass. – *lapang* 1 field, plain. 2 a square. – *liat* clay. – *longsor* landslide. – *mati* wasteland. – *Melaju* Malaya. – *(se)menandjung* peninsula. – *milik* privately owned land. – *panas* tropics. – *pekarangan* the yard around a dwelling. – *pekat* clay, loam. – *penggembalaan* pasture, meadow. – *perumahan* residential site. – *pusaka* inherited land. – *raja* continent. – *rata* level ground. – *rembang* open, exposed ground. – *seberang* 1 areas beyond Java (e.g., Sumatra). 2 Malacca (from Sumatra). – *sutji* the Holy Land. – *tersirah* recent grave. – *tumpah darah* birthplace. – *usaha* 1 hereditary landed property. 2 cultivated land.

tanahair see TANAH.

tanai **men**– to carry in o's hands.

tanak **ber**– to boil, cook. *Djangan pergi dulu, nasi sdh* ∼ , Don't go yet; the rice is cooking (invitation for dinner). **men**– to cook rice. **sepe(r)**– about 20 minutes. **-²an** playing house.

tanam **ber**– to plant. **ber- -²an** to

be occupied with planting. ∼ *kasih* to love e.o. **men–i** to plant. *Ia* ∼ *tanahnja dgn katjang,* He planted his field with peanuts. **men–(kan)** 1 to plant. *Ia* ∼ *padi,* She planted rice. 2 to invest. *Ia* ∼ *uangnja,* He invested his money. 3 to bury. *Ia* ∼ *sendjata gelap,* He buried smuggled weapons. 4 to place. *Wakil didisemua kota,* Representatives were placed in all the towns. 5 to insert, place, plant. ∼ *benih penjakit* to insert germs. ∼ *mumbang* to undertake s.t. hopeless. **pe–an** planting area. **pen–** planter. **pen–an** 1 planting. 2 plantation, estate. 3 investment. **–an** 1 plants. 2 growth, vegetation. ∼ *merambat* vine. 3 crop. **–²an** all sorts of plants. – **-men-** the planting.

tanang men– to carry in the palms of the hand.

tanbiat prophecy.

tanbih mind you! a warning of s.t. to be clarified in the following paragraph.

tanda 1 sign, token, mark. 2 signal. 3 omen. 4 characteristic. **ber–** 1 marked, labeled. *Semua mobil* ∼ *'tentara,'* All cars are marked "military." 2 to signify. *Bendéra mérah* ∼ *bahaja,* A red flag signifies danger. **men–i** 1 to mark, indicate. *Ia* ∼ *tanda kali pd kopernja,* He put a cross on all his bags. 2 to sign s.t. 3 to note, perceive. 4 to scan s.t. **men–kan** 1 to show, indicate. *Ia menguap* ∼ *bhw ia mengantuk,* He yawned indicating that he was sleepy. 2 to show, prove, give evidence. *Ia harus* ∼ *bhw ia kepala djawatan,* He must show that he's a department head. ∼ *irama* to beat, keep time. **men–tangani** see TANDATANGAN. **pen–an** signaling, giving a sign. **pe(r)–** 1 indication, sign. 2 mark. **per–an** 1 indication, sign. 2 mark. – *akar* root sign. – *alangan* dash(-). – *anggota* membership card. – *bagi* division sign. – *bahaja* danger signal. – *bakti* testimonial. – *batja(an)* punctuation mark. – *béti,* – *biti,* – *bukti* evidence. – *djasa* 1 decoration. 2 reward. – *esrar* the Sacraments. – *gambar* illustrated poster, placard. – *hadjat,* – *hidup* souvenir. – *hormat* sign of respect. – *hubung* hyphen. – *idem* ditto mark. – *kali* multiplication sign. – *kenjataan* identification card. – *kurang* minus sign. – *kurung* brackets, parentheses. – *kurung besar* brackets, braces. – *kutip* quotation mark. – *kutip pembuka* opening quotes. – *kutip penutup* closing quotes. – *masuk* admission

stub. – *mata* memento, souvenir. – *memberi hormat* token of respect. – *panah* directional arrow. – *pangkat* 1 insignia. 2 chevrons. – *penerimaan* receipt. – *penghubung,* – *penjambung* hyphen. – *(penj)seru* exclamation point. – *peringatan* monument, memorial. – *petik* quotation marks. – *sama* equals sign. – *selar* brand, stigma. – *sengkang* dash, hyphen. – *serah* legal expenses. – *silang* cross mark. – *sjah-diri* identification card. – *tambah* plus sign. – *tangan* signature. – *tanja* question mark. – *tekanan* stress, accent. – *terima* receipt. – *tjéma* evidence. – *tjerai* hyphen. – *udjar* quotation mark.

tandak Javanese female dancer. **ber–** to dance. **pen–** dancer.

tandan *se– pisang* a bunch of bananas.

tandang a visit. **ber–** 1 to visit. *Ia* ∼ *kenénéknja,* He visited his grandmother. *Ia* ∼ *kenegeri Djepang,* He visited Japan. 2 to court with pantuns. **men–i** to visit. *Ia* ∼ *ibunja,* She visited her mother. **pe(r)–** a traveler, visitor.

tandas 1 cleaned, wiped out. – *hartanja karena hutang,* Debts have wiped him out. 2 toilet, latrine (usually over a stream). 3 firm. *sikap jg* – a firm attitude. *mengatakan dgn* – to state firmly. **men–kan** 1 to spend everything, be wiped out. 2 to state firmly, explicitly.

tandatangan 1 signature. 2 autograph. **ber–** signed. *surat jg tidak* ∼ an unsigned letter. *jg* ∼ *dibawah ini* the undersigned. **men–i** to sign s.t. **pen–** the signer, signatory. ∼ *persetudjuan* the signatory to the treaty. **pen–an** 1 the signing. ∼ *persetudjuan* the signing of the treaty. 2 signature.

tandes see TANDAS 1.

tandhim work plan.

tandil foreman, overseer.

tanding 1 match, equal, counterpart. 2 pile, heap. *se– katjang* a pile of peanuts. **ber–** 1 to match. *Warna pintu itu* ∼ *dgn warna témboknja,* The color of the door matches that of the wall. 2 to be the equal of, match. *Negeri sebesar itu tak* ∼ *kekuatannja dgn negeri kami,* A country of that size doesn't compare in power with ours. 3 to compete. *Cornell* ∼ *dgn Princeton,* Cornell competed against Princeton. 4 to fight a duel. **memper–kan** 1 to compare s.t. with. 2 to put into combat. *Achirnja ia* ∼ *pasukannja,* Finally he placed his troops in combat. **men–** 1 to compare. *Ia* ∼ *negerinja dgn negeri asing itu,* He compared his country with that foreign country. 2 to pile, heap up. **men–i** 1 to equal, compare with. *Tak ada jg ~ kepandaiannja,* No o. equals his ability. 2 to stand up to, be on a par with. *Meréka bersekutu utk ~ musuhnja,* They united in order to stand up to the enemy. 3 to compete with. **men–kan** to compare. *~ kebaikan ibu dan ketegasan ajahnja* to compare a mother's kindness with a father's sternness. **per–an** 1 contest, match. 2 competition. 3 comparison. **–an** see TANDING 1.

tandjak slanting, tilting, sloping upward (as a sail). **ber–** to rise in a sloping manner. *~ kaki* to rise up on o's toes. **men–** 1 to slope. *Djalannja ~ ,* The road slopes, a sloping road. 2 to ascend, climb. *~ gunung* to climb a mountain. 3 to rise on o's toes. *Ia berdjalan ~ ,* He walks on his toes. 4 to rise to a point. *Lajarnja dipasang ~ ,* He put the sail pointing upward. **men–kan** 1 to pull up. *Ia ~ lajar,* He hoisted the sail. 2 to bring up. *~ bahan keatas gunung* to bring supplies up the mountain. 3 to cause s.t. to rise. *Ia ~ kakinja,* He stood on his toes. **pen–an** ascending, climbing. **–an** 1 slope. 2 ascent, climb.

tandjul a lasso. **men–(i)** to lasso.

tandjung cape, promontory. *– Harapan* Cape of Good Hope. **men–** 1 to look like a cape, point. *Apa nama daérah jg ~ kelaut itu?* What's the name of the area that goes off into the sea like a cape? 2 to sail along the cape. **berlajar** *~* to sail along a cape. *– Pérak* the port of Surabaya. *– Priok* the port of Jakarta.

tandjur a scoop made of coconut shell.

tandu a litter or sedan chair. **ber–** to ride in a sedan chair. **men–** to carry in a litter.

tanduk horns of an animal. *– tegak* horns vertical with points near e.o **ber–** horned. *Kambing ~ ,* The goat has horns. **men–** 1 to butt. 2 to shoot (at billiards). *– tilpon* telephone receiver. *minta – pd kuda* to expect the impossible. *seperti telur diudjung – precarious.*

tandur **men–** to plant. *~ sawah* to plant the wet rice field.

tandus 1 to lie fallow. 2 fallow land. 3 wiped, cleaned out. **ke–an** barrenness.

tang 1 tongs, pincers. 2 tank. 3 sound of falling metal. *– badja, – kakatua* tongs, pincers.

tangan 1 hand. 2 (fore)arm. **di–** owned. **men–i** 1 to tackle a problem

or job. 2 to strike with the hand. **–an** handmade product. *–²* 1 arms of a chair. 2 handle bar of a bicycle. 3 banisters of a staircase. 4 sword hilt. 5 arm of a pair of scales. *– –men–* not original, having passed through many hands. *Arlodji ini kelihatan baru; sebenarnja ia tlh ~ ,* This watch looks new; actually it has passed through many hands. *– badju* sleeves. *– besi* firm, strict. *Ia memerintah dgn – besi,* He ruled with an iron fist. *– dingin* successful. *Ia – dingin,* He's successful. *– hampa* empty-handed. *– kanan* helper, assistant. *– kemudi* helm, rudder. *– korsi* arms of a chair. *– kosong* empty-handed. *– lébar* open-handed, generous. *– panas* unlucky, a failure. *– pandjang* inclined to petty theft. *– tangga* stair rail, handrail. *– terbuka* generous. *– terkokot* clawlike hands caused by disease. *–nja berulas,* He has a good assistant.

tangap **men–** to stop, retard, hold back.

tangas vaporization. **ber–** to take a steam bath. **men–** to steam, stew s.t. **pen–** steam bath. **pen–an** steaming.

tangéh far off, away. *Masih – dari waktunja,* It's still far ahead of the time.

tangga 1 ladder. 2 staircase. 3 stairs. **ber–** with steps. **ber–²** 1 gradually, by degrees, step by step. 2 terraced, graduated. *sawah ~* terraced rice field. **se–** see TETANGGA. *– bunji, – nada* gamut, scale. *– pengait* flexible, portable ladder for climbing trees. *– pilin* winding staircase, stairs. *– sigai* portable ladder. *– sokong* a notched climbing pole.

tanggah kitchen.

tanggal 1 date. *– berapa?* What's the date? *– enam Agustus,* It's August 6. 2 to fall. *Giginja ~ ,* His teeth fell out. *Daun pohon – pd musim rontok,* The leaves fall off in the fall. **ber–** dated. *surat jg tidak ~* an undated letter. **men–i** 1 to strip s.o. *Ia ~ terdakwa,* He stripped the suspect. 2 to strip off. *Ia ~ pakaiannja,* He stripped off his clothes. 3 to dismantle, strip. *~ paberik* to dismantle a factory. **men–kan** 1 to strip, take off. *Ia ~ pakaiannja,* He took off his clothes. 2 to pull out. *Ia ~ paku,* He pulled out a nail. 3 to date. *Ia tak sempat ~ suratnja,* He had no opportunity to date his letter. **pen–an** 1 calendar, almanac. 2 dating. 3 a horrible spook. 4 stripping, discarding. *~ kewarganegaraan* discarding of citizenship. **ter–** dated. *Suratmu* ~ ... Your letter dated ... – *pengembalian buku* return due date.

tanggam dovetail (in carpentry). **ber–** dovetailed. **men–** to dovetail.

tanggang ber– to refrain from eating, sleeping. **men–** to restrain. ~ *perut* to fast. – *malam* to keep watch through the night.

tanggap men– 1 to listen carefully. 2 to note attentively. **men–i** to reply to. **-an** 1 idea, conception. 2 performance. 3 reaction.

tangguh 1 postponement, delay. 2 of integrity, strong, firm. *pemimpin jg* – a leader of integrity. **ber–** 1 to postpone, put off. *Ia* ~ *membajarnja*, He postponed paying. 2 to hesitate, waver. *Ia tidak* ~ *lagi minta perlop*, He didn't hesitate to ask for leave. **ke–an** integrity, honesty. **memper–kan** to postpone. *Ia* ~ *pembajarannja*, He postponed his payment. **men–kan** to postpone s.t. **pen–an, per–an** postponement, moratorium, delay.

tangguk small fish net. **pen–** fisherman. **men–** to fish with a small net.

tanggul 1 dike. 2 embankment. **men–** to build a dike, embankment.

tanggulang men–i to protect, defend.

tanggung 1 guaranteed. *Pekerdjaannja* – *baik*, His work is guaranteed to be good. 2 responsible. *Ia tidak* – *akan selesainja pekerdjaan itu*, He won't be responsible for the completion of the job. 3 inadequate. *Kamar ini* – *besarnja*, This room is inadequate in size. 4 ill-timed. – *sekali kedatanganmu ini*, Your arrival was ill-timed. 5 mediocre. 6 see ANAK. **ber–** **djawab** to be responsible, account to. *Menteri negara* ~ *djawab pd parlemén*, A state minister is responsible to parliament. **di–** (*déh*) sure, of course, absolutely. **memper–** **djawabkan** 1 to account for, justify. *Ia tak dpt* ~ *segala pengeluarannja*, He could not account for all his expenditures. 2 to hold s.o. responsible for s.t. *Pemerintah* ~ *keamanan dlm negeri kpd menteri dlm negeri*, The government holds the minister of interior responsible for internal security. 3 to insure. **memper–kan** to insure s.t. or s.o. **men–** 1 to guarantee. *Siapa jg* ~ *pengeluaran ini?* Who guarantees these expenses? 2 to be responsible for, assume. *Ia* ~ *ongkos kirim*, He's responsible for shipping costs. 3 to assume responsibility. *Pemerintah* ~ *keamanan negeri*, The government assumes responsibility for the coun-

try's security. 4 to suffer. ~ *rugi* to suffer loss. ~ *sakit* to suffer illness. 5 to carry, assume. ~ *muatan jg berat* to carry a heavy burden. ~ *malu* to feel ashamed. ~ *ragam* to endure tribulations. ~ *rahasia* to keep a secret. ~ *rindu* to desire, long for. **men–** **deritakan** to suffer, endure, put up with. **men–djawab** to accept responsibility. *Ia tidak berani* ~ *atas perbuatan itu*, He didn't dare accept responsibility for that deed. **men–kan** 1 to hold s.o. responsible. 2 to endure, suffer. 3 to vouch for, guarantee. **pen–** 1 security, guarantee. 2 o. who guarantees, is responsible, an underwriter. 3 sufferer. ~ *djawab* responsible (legally liable) official or agency. ~ *kebakaran* marine underwriter. ~ *varia* accident underwriter. **pen–an** trials and tribulations. **pen–an-djawab, per–an-djawab** 1 responsibility. 2 justification, accounting. **per–an** 1 responsibility. 2 guarantee, security. 3 insurance. ~ *bunga tahun* annuity. ~ *djiwa* life insurance. ~ *djiwa kumpulan* group life insurance. **ter–** 1 endurable, tolerable. 2 suffered, endured. *tidak* ~ intolerable. **-an** 1 responsibility. 2 guarantee, bail, security. *Ia memberi tjintjinnja sebagai* ~ , He gave his ring as security. *memberi* ~ *anam bulan* to give a 6 months' guarantee. 3 burden, load. *Menjekolahkan anak* ~ *berat bagi orang tua*, To send a child to school is a heavy burden for the parents. 4 insurance. ~ *djiwa* life insurance. 5 hostage. *atas* ~ *sendiri* at o's own risk. –² 1 halfway, halfhearted. *Kalau bekerdja djangan* ~ , In your work don't do things halfway. – **-men–** to be mutually responsible. – *bérés* to take care of s.t. *Dia* – *bérés*, He'll take care of it. – *bulan* broke around the end of the month. – *djawab* responsible for. *Kpd siapa ia – djawab?* To whom is he responsible?

tangis weeping. **ber–an** to weep. *Perempuan²* , Women wept. **men–** to weep. **men–i** to weep over, bemoan. *Ia* ~ *andjingnja jg mati*, She wept over her dead dog. **men–kan** 1 to weep over, bemoan. 2 to make o. weep. *Ia* ~ *adiknja*, He made his little brother cry. **pen–** a crybaby. **-an** weeping, crying.

tangkai 1 stalk, stem. – *bunga* flower stalk. 2 stock, shaft, handle. – *bedil* rifle butt. 3 used with slender objects. *se–* *bunga* a flower stalk. – *hati* sweetheart, beloved. – *kering* a miser. – *péna* penholder.

tangkal **men–** to avoid, ward off a catastrophe. **pen–** 1 preventive, antidote, prophylactic. 2 amulet, charm.

tangkap **ke–** seized, arrested. *Pembikin*[2] *uang palsu* ~ , The counterfeiters were seized. **ke–an** an apoplectic stroke. **men–** 1 to catch, seize, arrest. *Polisi* ~ *pendjahat*, The police caught the criminal. 2 to catch. ~ *bola* to catch a ball. 3 to comprehend, grasp, understand. *Ia* ~ *maksud pembitjaraan*, He understood the meaning of the conversation. ~ *angin* to miss, fail. **men–i** to seize, arrest. **pen–** 1 captor, capturer. 2 catcher. ~ *ikan* 1 fisherman. 2 fish net, trap. ~ *suara* dictaphone, recorder. **pen–an** 1 arrest, seizure, capture. 2 haul, catch (fish). **ter–** (*basah*) caught in the act. ~ *muka* to meet face to face unexpectedly. **–an** 1 capture, arrest. 2 haul, catch. 3 prisoner.

tangkas deft, adroit, skillful. **ke–an** adroitness, skill, dexterity. ~ *djasmani* physical fitness. – *lidah* quick-witted, quick at repartee.

tangki tank.

tangkil **men–** 1 to pay o's respects to s.o. 2 to arrange, place in order.

tangkis **men–(kan)** 1 to ward off, parry. ~ *pukulan* to ward off the blows. 2 to repulse. ~ *serangan* to repulse an attack. **pen–** 1 defense. 2 antidote. ~ *serangan udara* anti-aircraft defense. **–an** defense, resistance.

tangkul large net. **men–** to fish with a net.

tangkup **ber–, men–** 1 to close, fold over. *Pintunja* ~ *dan ia terkuntji*, The door closed and he was locked in. 2 to fall headlong. *Ia* ~ *ketanah*, He fell headlong to the ground. **men–kan** 1 to lay s.t. face down. 2 to fall headfirst. *Kepalanja* ~ *ketanah*, His head hit the ground face first. **men– telentangkan** to consider thoroughly. *Meréka* ~ *soal itu*, They considered the problem thoroughly. **se–** symmetrical.

tanglung paper lantern.

tangsel stuffing. **men–** 1 to stuff. 2 to insert an ad.

tangsi barracks.

tani farmer. **ber–** to carry on farming. **pe–** 1 farmer. 2 peasant. **per–an** agriculture.

tanja question. *Numpang –, bung!* May I ask a question? **ber–** to ask a question. *Boléh saja* ~ *?* May I ask a question? **ber– –**[2] to wonder, ask o.s. *Ia* ~ *dlm hatinja mengapa ajahnja tak datang*, He was wondering why

his father didn't come. **men–** 1 to ask. *Ia* ~ *temannja kemana ia akan pergi*, He asked his friend where he was going. 2 to propose. *Ia* ~ *utk kawin*, He proposed marriage. **men–i** to ask, interrogate. *Ia* ~ *temannja ttg keadaan itu*, He asked his friend about the situation. **men–kan** to ask about s.t. *Ia* ~ *soal keuangan kpd gurunja*, He asked his teacher about financial matters. **pen–** interrogator, questioner. ~ *djawab* interviewer. **per–an** question. ~ *keliling* questions from the floor. – *djawab* 1 interview, question and answer. 2 dialogue.

tanpa without. **ke–prasangkaan** without prejudice. – (*ber*)*sjarat* unconditionally. – *bobot* weightlessness. *perkelahian* without fighting.

tanpanama anonymous.

tanpanegara stateless.

tantang **men–** to defy, challenge. *Meréka akan* ~ *musuhnja*, They'll defy the enemy. **pen–** challenger. **–an** challenge, defiance.

tante aunt (form of address by children to women).

tantjap **men–(kan)** to stick, embed, plant. *Ia* ~ *tombaknja ditanah*, He stuck his spear in the ground. **ter–** embedded, stuck.

tanur furnace, oven. – *tinggi* blast furnace.

taogé bean sprout(s).

taokéh Chinese proprietor of a shop.

taola towel.

taotji a k.o. fish jelly.

taotjo soybean paste.

tapa asceticism. **ber–** 1 to live as an ascetic. 2 to be shut up, imprisoned. *Lama ia* ~ *dipendjara*, He has been imprisoned for a long time. **memperkan** to achieve through asceticism. *Ia* ~ *maksudnja*, Through asceticism he achieved his aim. **per–** hermit. **per–an** 1 hermit's abode, retreat. 2 asceticism. 3 penance. **–**[2] thin-sliced, salted, dried fish. – *sungsang* a life of asceticism on the part of one standing on his head.

tapai fermented cassava. **men–** to become fermented. *Ketéla itu* ~ , The cassava became fermented.

tapak 1 a measure of length: palm of the hand, sole of the foot. *lébarnja dua* – the width of 2 palms. 2 trail. **ber–** 1 to step, tread on. *Kakinja* ~ *kepermadani*, His feet tread on the carpet. 2 to have an underlayer. *Kakinja tidak* ~ , He was barefooted. 3 to have a firm hold. *Kekuasaannja* ~ *di–mana*[2], His power has a firm hold everywhere. **ber–(kan)** to be based on, supported. *pemerintah jg* ~

kehendak rakjat a government based on the will of the people. **men-** 1 to measure with the palm of the hand or sole of the foot. ~ *lébarnja médja* to measure the width of the table with the palm of the hand. 2 to step, tread on. 3 to follow in the footsteps of. *Ia* ~ *ajahnja*, He is following in his father's footsteps. **men-kan** to step with s.t. ~ *kakinja ketanah* to step with the feet on the ground. **se-** 1 step. ~ *demi* ~ step by step. 2 o. palm's or sole's breadth. **-an** 1 layer, foundation. 2 place of honor at a reception. **-²** slippers, sandals. - *besi* horseshoe. - *kaki* footprint. - *kasut* sole of slipper. - *kuku* horseshoe. - *rata* flat foot. - *rumah* house site. - *sepatu* shoe sole. - *tangan* palm of hand. - *tjanai* completed. - *tjatur* the squares on a chessboard. *lari putih -nja* to run very fast.

tapal a k.o. paste. - *batas* boundary. - *gigi* tooth paste. - *kuda* horseshoe.

tapang wooden bedstead.

tapelak tablecloth. **men-i** to place a tablecloth on a table.

tapi see TETAPI.

tapian see TEPIAN.

tapih a k.o. skirt.

tapis men- to filter. *Ia* ~ *air itu*, She filtered the water. **pen-** a filter, sieve. **-an** filtered material.

taplak see TAPELAK.

tapsir see TAFSIR.

taptu taps, retreat, tattoo.

tapuk 1 see TAMPUK. 2 scar, pockmark. **ber- -²** 1 heavily pock-marked. 2 to have a bad reputation. *Namanja sdh* ~ , He has a bad reputation. **men-** to slap. *Bapak* ~ *saja*, Dad slapped me.

tar 1 see TÉR. 2 sound of snapping a whip. *kué* - cake, tart.

tara 1 matching, equal. *tiada - bagusnja* unequaled in beauty. *laki bini jg* - a husband and wife on a par. 2 counterpart. 3 tare. **ber-** matching. *tiada* ~ unequaled, unmatched. **se-** 1 to be equal. *Usahanja tidak* ~ *dgn hasilnja*, His results do not equal his efforts. 2 made for e.o., suited. *dua teman jg* ~ two friends made for e.o. **ter-** = BER-.

taraf 1 standard. - *hidup* standard of living. 2 degree, level. - *peradaban* level of civilization. 3 position. *menurut - dan umur* according to position and age. 4 phase. - *perang penghabisan* final phase of the war. 5 shade. - *warna* shade of color. **menje-kan** 1 to place on a level. *Ia* ~ *negerinja dgn negeri² jg tlh madju,*

He places his country on a par with advanced countries. 2 to balance. *Ia* ~ *keperluan dgn keuangannja,* He balances his needs with his finances. **men-kan** 1 to evaluate, grade s.t. 2 to give the rank of. **se-** equal, equivalent. *Pangkatnja* ~ *dgn gubernur,* His rank is equal to that of a governor.

tarah smooth, planed. **ber-** planed. **men-** to plane. **pen-** a plane. **-an** what has been planed, smoothed off.

tarak continence, abstinence. **ber-** to be continent, abstain from. **per-an** continence, abstinence.

taram temaram dark, cloudy.

tarap see TARAF.

tarawih special evening prayers during the fasting month.

tarbijah education.

tardjamah see TERDJEMAH.

tarékat 1 a mystical order. 2 way of life, path for mystics to follow, regimen.

tari a dance. **ber-, men-** to dance. **me-n-²** to dance with joy, dance up and down. **pen-** dancer (male or female). **-²an** dances, a variety of dances. ~ *daérah* regional or folk dances. - *gambus* dance to Arabian music. - *lénso* k.o. social dance.

tarich 1 era. - *hidjrah* Moslem era. - *maséhi* Christian era. 2 chronicle, annals, calendar. - *perang Atjéh* chronicles of the Achehnese war. **men(t)-kan** 1 to date s.t. 2 to record as a historical event.

ta'rif definition. **men(t)-kan** 1 to define. 2 to announce.

tarik ber- -²an to tug, pull at s.t. *berlatih* ~ *tali* 1 tug of war. 2 to exercise with pulleys. **ke-** drawn, attracted. *Meréka mulai* ~ *pd sastera,* They're beginning to be attracted to literature. **memper-kan** 1 to drag s.t. away. 2 to stretch, strain, draw s.t. **men-** 1 to draw, pull. *Ia* ~ *keréta,* He pulled a wagon. 2 to pull, draw out. ~ *pedang* to pull out o's sword. 3 to extract. ~ *akar* to extract the root (math.). 4 to drive. ~ *mobil* to drive a car. 5 to collect. ~ *bajaran* to collect payment. 6 interesting. 7 with reference to (in letters). ~ *diri* to withdraw. *Ia* ~ *diri,* He withdrew. ~ *hati* 1 to attract, draw attention. 2 interesting. *Itu* ~ *hati,* That's interesting. 3 absorbing. 4 attractive, engaging. 5 inviting, intriguing, appealing. ~ *kembali* 1 to withdraw s.t. 2 to reverse a decision. 3 to cancel s.t. ~ *kepengadilan* to summon before court. ~ *kesimpulan* to draw a conclusion.

~ *lagu* to start a song. ~ *lajar* to unfold a sail. ~ *loteré* to hit the jack pot. ~ *minat* to attract o's attention, interest. ~ *mundur* to withdraw. ~ *napas* to breathe, inhale. ~ *napas jg terachir* to breathe o's last. ~ *napas pandjang* to sigh. ~ *njanji* to start a song. ~ *njawa* to die. ~ *ongkos* costly. ~ *otot* stubborn, obstinate. ~ *pandjang* to stretch, prolong. ~ *perhatian* ~ *hati*. ~ *suara* to start a song. ~ *surut* to withdraw s.t. ~ *undian* to win a prize. ~ *untung* to earn a profit. ~ *urat léhér* stubborn, obstinate. ~ *utang* to collect a debt. me-n-² to involve s.o. *Ia* ~ *temannja kedalam soal itu*, He involved his friend in that matter. pen– drawer, puller. ~ *bétja* pedicab driver. pen–an lottery drawing. ~ *diri* withdrawal. ter– 1 extracted. *Giginja* ~ *djuga*, His tooth was finally extracted. 2 attracted, interested. *Ia* ~ *pd gambar itu*, She was attracted by the picture. –an 1 pulling, drawing. ~ *kuda* the pulling of a horse. 2 attraction. – *muka duabelas* to be disappointed. – *tambang* tug of war.

tarikat see TARÉKAT.

taring 1 tusk. – *babi* boar's tusk. 2 canine tooth.

tarip fare, rate. – *angkutan* rate for transporting. – *bis* bus fare. – *harga* price list. – *makan(an)* menu. – *sepur* 1 railroad timetable. 2 railroad fare.

taro(k) small tarts, cakes.

tarub see TARUP.

taruh 1 stake(s). –*nja lima rupiah*, The stake was 5 rupiahs. 2 security, deposit. *gelang mas sebagai* – a gold bracelet as security. ber– 1 to bet, wager. *Saja berani* ~ *bhw ia tak akan datang*, I bet he won't come. 2 to bet s.t. ~ *5 rupiah* to bet 5 rupiahs. ~ *djiwa* to pledge. ber–kan 1 to bet s.t. 2 to entrust. *Ia* ~ *uangnja kpd temannja*, He entrusted his money to his friend. memper–kan 1 to pawn. *Ia* ~ *arlodjinja*, He pawned his watch. 2 to bet, wager. *Ia* ~ *100 dolar*, He bet $100. 3 to entrust. *Ia* ~ *barang²nja kpd orang lain*, He entrusted his goods to other people. 4 to risk. *Ia* ~ *djiwanja*, He risked his life. 5 to be at stake. *Kehormatan kitalah jg diper–kan*, It's our honor that's at stake. men– 1 to put, place. *Ia* ~ *buku dimédja*, He put the book on the table. 2 to deposit, put. *Ia* ~ *uang dibank*, He deposited the money in the bank. 3 to put, bet. *Ia* ~ *5 dolar atas kuda itu*, He put $5.00 on that horse. 4 to have, keep, main-

tain. *Ia* ~ *mobil*, He has a car. *Ia* ~ *rahasia*, She kept a secret. 5 to raise, keep. ~ *ajam* to raise chickens. ~ *hati* to be interested. *Ia* ~ *hati kpd sedjarah*, She's interested in history. ~ *kasih* to love, pity. ~ *perhatian akan* to be interested in. ~ *sjakwasangka* to suspect s.o. ~ *tjinta* to love. men–i 1 to put s.t. on s.t. *Médja itu di–i dgn buku*, The table was covered with books. 2 to bet on s.t. *Ia* ~ *ajam putih*, He bet on the white cock. pen– *perhatian* o. who is interested. pen–an a money box, strongbox. per–an 1 a bet. 2 savings. 3 articles entrusted to s.o. ~ *sendjata* a cease-fire. pe– 1 final instructions, last will and testament. 2 security. –an 1 bet, wager. *Saja berani* ~ , I'm willing to bet. 2 prize. 3 stake. – *beras dlm padi* to keep a secret well. – *kata*, –*lah* supposing. ~ *ia tak ada dirumah?* Supposing he isn't at home? – *mata* to watch, see. – *muka* to meet people.

taruk a sprout. ber– to sprout.

tarum indigo plant.

taruna see TERUNA.

tarung ber– 1 to dispute, fight. ~ *dipengadilan* to dispute before the court. 2 to fight. *Ia* ~ *dgn lawannja*, He fought with his opponent. memper–kan 1 to fight, have fight. *Ia* ~ *ajamnja*, He fought his cock. 2 to risk. *Ia* ~ *djiwanja*, He risked his life. men– to fight against, risk. men–kan 1 to have fight. 2 to risk s.t. pen–obstacle. per–an 1 fight. 2 struggle. ter– 1 to stumble. *Ia* ~ , He stumbled. 2 to bump. *Kakinja* ~ *batu*, His foot bumped against a stone.

tarup a temporary structure (for weddings, etc.). – *agung* grandstand.

tas 1 brief case. 2 woman's handbag. 3 fast. *Ia berdjalan* –, He walked fast. 4 tree. – *pandan* screw pine.

tasak styptic. men– to stanch bleeding. pen– styptic pencil.

tasalsul genealogy.

tasbih 1 a formula extolling God's perfection. 2 rosary. men–kan to extol God. pen–an praise of God.

tasik lake.

tasjhid pronouncement of the creed. ment–kan to confess.

taslim 1 obedience. 2 salutation. ment– to convey, hand over.

tasmak spectacles, eyeglasses.

tasrif conjugation of verbs. ment–kan 1 to conjugate. 2 to decline (noun). 3 to inflect.

tata order, arrangement, system. ke–laksanaan management, managing. ke–negaraan 1 political. 2 governmental. 3 constitution(al). **ke-niagaan** business administration. **ke-pradjaan** public administration. **ke-usahaan** administration. **pen-** *bahasa* grammar specialist. $\sim$ *buku* book-keeper. $\sim$ *pradja*, $\sim$ *usaha* adminis-trator. – *adab* good manners, the conventions. – *atjara* agenda. – *bahasa* grammar. – *bentuk* morphol-ogy. – *buku* bookkeeping, accounting. – *bumi* land use or utilization. – *bunji* phonetics. – *gerédja* church ritual. – *hukum* legal order. – *kalimat* syntax. – *karya* organization. – *kata* morphology. – *katja* stained glass. – *krama* good manners. – *laksana* managing. – *masjarakat* social order. – *nama* nomenclature. – *negara* 1 form of government. 2 state struc-ture. 3 public institutions. – *perdésaan* rural order. *pembangunan* – *perdésaan jg démokratis* democratic rural devel-opment. – *personalia* personnel man-agement. – *pimpinan* management. – *pradja* public administration. – *puspa* flower arrangement. – *rias* art of make-up. – *ruang* layout. – *rupa* make-up, format. – *surya* solar sys-tem. – *susila* 1 good manners, good conduct. 2 ethics. – *susunan* organi-zation, structure, hierarchy. – *tertib* discipline, order. – *tjara* customs and manners. – *usaha* administration, management. – *warna* technicolor.

tatabahasa see TATA.

tatah inlaid work. **ber-(kan)** inlaid, encrusted, studded. **men-** 1 to en-crust, set (with jewels). 2 to teach children to walk. – **an** inlaid work.

tatakan 1 a base. 2 coaster for glasses. 3 tray.

tatal wood shavings.

tatanama see TATA.

tatang men- to carry in the palm of the hand. *Ia* $\sim$ *sebuah baki*, He carried a tray.

tatap men- 1 to scan, observe in-tently. *Ia* $\sim$ *gambar ditémbok*, He examined the picture on the wall intently. *Matanja* $\sim$ *saja*, He ob-served me intently. 2 to peer at. **men-i** to examine closely. $\sim$ *buku* to examine the books closely. **-an** close observation.

tatawarna see TATA.

tatih 1 to toddle, totter. 2 unsteady, wobbly. **ber-** to toddle along.

tating see TATANG.

tatkala when. – *tuan datang ...* When you arrived ... – *itu* at that time.

tau see TAHU.

taubat 1 repentance. 2 giving up of s.t. – *daripada minum tembakau*

giving up smoking. 3 exclamation of annoyance. (Good heavens! For heaven's sake!) –, *rupanja orang ini mémang tak mau pertjaja*, Good heavens, this man apparently doesn't want to believe. **ber-** 1 to repent. *Ia* $\sim$ *atas segala dosanja*, He repented of all his sins. 2 to give up. *Ia* $\sim$ *minum madat*, He gave up opium. **men-kan** 1 to cause to repent. *Chotbah itu* $\sim$ *banjak orang*, The sermon caused many to repent. 2 to break s.o. of s.t. see TOBAT.

taufan hurricane.

taufik God's help.

taugé bean sprout(s).

tauhid the unity of God. **ber-** to acknowledge the oneness of God. **ment-kan** 1 to acknowledge God's oneness. 2 to concentrate on s.t.

tauké 1 boss. 2 employer.

tauladan model, example.

taulan friend, comrade.

taun see TAHUN.

ta'un cholera, cholera epidemic.

taurat the Old Testament (especially the Pentateuch).

taut ber- 1 to close. *Lukanja* $\sim$, The wound closed. 2 to grow to-gether, join. *Dua matjam tumbuh²an* $\sim$, The two plants grew together. 3 to fuse. *Semua aliran politik* $\sim$ *mendjadi satu perkumpulan*, All politi-cal currents fused into o. group. 4 to draw the curtains. 5 to pull the door to. $\sim$ *tangan* to shake hands. **memper-kan, men-kan** 1 to unite, combine s.t. 2 to sew up a wound. **per-an** 1 contact. 2 joining, uniting.

tautjang pigtail.

tawa see TERTAWA. **ke-an** laughing stock. *Ia mendjadi* $\sim$ *teman²nja*, He became the laughing stock of his friends.

tawadu prescribed ablutions before performing the Moslem ritual prayer.

tawak men-i to throw stones at s.o. or s.t.

tawakkal resignation, trust in God. **ber-** to place o's trust in God.

tawan men- 1 to capture, subdue. *Ia* $\sim$ *musuhnja*, He captured the enemy. 2 to captivate. 3 to intern, imprison, incarcerate. $\sim$ *hati* to captivate o's heart. **pen-** *hati* o. who captivates the heart. **ter-** 1 interned. 2 captivated. **-an** 1 prisoner. $\sim$ *djaminan* hostage. 2 internee. 3 booty. *barang* $\sim$ captured goods. $\sim$ *kota* city arrest. $\sim$ *rumah* house arrest.

tawar 1 tasteless. *roti* – unsweetened bread. – *rasanja* tasteless. 2 in-effective, innocuous. *obat jg* – in-

effective medicine. 3 indifferent.
*Mukanja - sadja melihat suaminja
kembali,* She appeared indifferent
to her husband's return. 4 normal.
Amarahnja - kembali, He's back to
normal. 5 to bargain, haggle. *Boléh
saja -?* May I bargain? **men-** 1 to
disinfect s.t. 2 to make a bid or offer,
to bargain. **men-i** 1 to neutralize. ~
ratjun to neutralize poison. 2 to
pacify, calm down. ~ *amarah temannja*
to pacify his friend's anger. 3 to
seduce, tempt. ~ *hati djanda* to seduce
a widow's heart. 4 to offer to *(kpd)*
s.o. *Ia* ~ *rumah kpd ajahnja,* He
offered a house to his father. **men-kan**
1 to discourage. *Kesepian pasar* ~
kehendak saja utk berdagang, The
quietness of the market discouraged
my wish to trade. 2 to offer for sale.
Ia ~ *rumahnja,* He offered his house
for sale. 3 to neutralize. ~ *guna²* to
neutralize the effects of black magic.
~ *ratjun* to neutralize poison. **pen-**
1 antidote. 2 disinfectant. 3
neutralizer. **pen-an** 1 offer, bid. 2
bargaining. 3 cure. 4 exorcism. 5
neutralization. 6 trade. **-an** 1 offer,
bid. 2 invitation. **-²** 1 indifferent.
Mukanja ~ *sadja menerima tamu,*
He appeared indifferent while receiving his guests. 2 moderate, average. *Perdagangan* ~ *sadja hari ini,*
Business is just average today.
--men- to bid back and forth,
bargain. - *hambar* utterly insipid. -
hati discouraged.

tawarich see TARICH.

tawas alum.

tawon 1 bee. 2 wasp.

ta'ziah sympathy, condolence.

ta'zim respect, esteem. *Ia menjampai-
kan salam -nja,* He sent his regards
and respect.

tbc [*tébésé*] tuberculosis.

tebah men- to beat. *Ia* ~ *babut,*
He beat the rug. *Ia* ~ *dada,* He
beat his breast. **pen-** a (rug) beater.

tebak ke-an guess. **men-** to guess.
pen- guesser. **-an** 1 a guess. 2 riddle.
-² *manggis,* Keep guessing.

tébak men- 1 to chop, hew. 2 to
till (the soil).

tebal 1 thick. *buku* - a thick book.
2 dense, thick. *kabut jg* - a dense
fog. 3 strong. *iman jg* - a strong
faith. 4 insensitive. 5 boldface type.
ke-an thickness. **memper-** to
strengthen, firm up. **men-** to thicken.
Kabur ~ , The fog became thick.
men-kan 1 to reinforce. ~ *kejakinan
kita* to reinforce our assurance. 2
to thicken s.t. **pen-an** *huruf* boldface
type. - *hati,* - *kulit* cruel, merciless,

pitiless. - *muka* 1 insensitive. 2
impudent. - *telinga* 1 indifferent. 2
unabashed. 3 stubborn.

tebang men- to fell (trees). **pen-**
a woodcutter. **pen-an** the felling of
trees. **-an** the felled material.

tébar ber-(an) spread around, scattered about. *Madjalah ini* ~ *diseluruh
Djawa,* This magazine is distributed
over all of Java. **memper-kan** to
spread around. ~ *kabar* to spread the
news. **men-(kan)** 1 to spread around.
~ *bau busuk* to spread a bad odor
around. 2 to spread out. *Ia* ~ *djala,*
He spread out a net. 3 to throw out.
Ia ~ *djala,* He threw out a net.
-an 1 circular, bulletin. 2 seed.

tebas men- 1 to cut, clear away.
Meréka ~ *djalan,* They cleared the
road by cutting away the under-
growth. 2 to buy up wholesale.
Ia ~ *segala beras jg ada digudang,*
He bought up all the rice in the
godown. 3 to buy up before harvested.
Tengkulak sdh ~ *padinja jg masih
hidjau itu,* The middleman bought
up the still-green rice. **men-kan**
1 to cut, clear with. *Ia* ~ *pedangnja
kepohon,* He cut into a tree with his
sword. 2 to sell wholesale. 3 to sell
before harvesting. **men-** *menebang*
to clear away all vegetation. **-an**
1 wholesale buying. 2 produce bought
before harvesting.

tebat 1 embankment. 2 fishpond.
men- to create a pond by damming
a stream.

tébéng screen. *Tempat itu tak kelihatan karena - dari bukit,* That place
isn't visible because it is screened by
the hill. **men-** 1 to put up a partition.
2 to display. ~ *buku²* to display
books. 3 to sponge on s.o. - *djendéla*
window hangings. - *topi* wide brim
of sun hat.

tébésé tuberculosis.

tebing 1 steep riverbank. - *sungai*
riverbank. 2 a hill embankment.

tébok men- to hit hard.

tebu sugar cane. **-²** joints. *dpt -
rebah* to be in luck, hit the jack pot.

tebuk men- 1 to pierce, punch, perforate. 2 to bore, dig through.

tebus men- 1 to cash, redeem. ~
wésél to cash a money order. ~
tjintjin to redeem o's ring (from a
pawnshop). 2 to ransom. ~ *djandji*
to fulfill a promise. ~ *dosa* to expiate
a sin. ~ *kata* to keep o's word. ~
malu to wipe out a disgrace. ~ *talak*
to obtain a divorce from o's husband
by returning dowry. **pen-** 1 ransom.
2 redeemer. *Sang* ~ the Redeemer

(Jesus Christ). **pen–an** redemption, act of redeeming s.t. **–an** ransom.

téchnik see TÉHNIK.

téchnis see TÉHNIS.

téchnologi technology.

tedas sharp, clear, distinct. *berkata –* to speak clearly, distinctly.

tédéng screen. **ber–(an)** to disguise, cover up. *– aling²* to hide, seek cover.

tédja the glow of sunset.

teduh 1 quiet, calm. *Angin –,* The wind has died down. *Hudjan tlh –,* The rain has stopped. 2 shelter. *Ia berenti di– djalan,* He stopped at the shelter along the street. 3 gloomy, not bright. *Matahari – sepandjang hari,* The sun has not shone brightly the whole day. **ber–** to take shelter. ∼ *dibawah pohon* to take shelter under a tree. **ber–kan** *diri* to protect o.s. **ke–an** 1 calm, quietness. 2 shelter, lee. 3 sheltered. **men–** to take shelter. **men–i** to protect s.o. from the sun. **men–kan** 1 to calm s.o. down, quiet. 2 to protect from rain, sunshine, etc. 3 to take s.t. as shelter.

téga 1 to be able to stand, have the heart to. *Ia tak – melihat orang sakit itu,* He couldn't stand to see the sick man. 2 to dare. *Ia – meninggalkan anaknja,* He dared leave his child.

tegah men–kan to forbid, prevent s.t. **pen–an** a fight.

tegak 1 upright, erect. *Ia berdiri –,* He stood upright. 2 standing. **men–tiang** to stand straight as a ramrod. **men–kan** 1 to erect, build. ∼ *rumah* to erect a house. 2 to erect, stand up. ∼ *léhér badju* to turn up the coat collar. ∼ *tiang* to erect a pole. 3 to maintain, keep. ∼ *semangat berdjoang* to maintain a fighting spirit. **pen–pendapat** holder of an opinion. **pen–an** maintenance. ∼ *haknja* the maintenance of o's rights. **se–** height of a standing man. **ter–** to stand upright. **–²** upright. *– damar* torch stand. *– tjantjang* pointed upward. *– sama tinggi duduk sama rendah* equal in all respects.

tegal(an) dry, not irrigated, field.

tegang 1 taut, tight. *Talinja –,* The rope is taut. 2 tense, strained. *perhubungan jg –* a tense situation. *– memutus* a difficult situation. **ber–** to hold on, persevere. ∼ *(urat) léhér* stubborn. **bersi–** 1 to persevere. 2 to be stubborn. **ke–an** 1 strained situation. 2 tension. 3 incident. **men–** to be tight. **men–i** to tighten. **men–kan** 1 to tighten, make taut. 2 strain. *Peristiwa itu* ∼ *hubungan kedua negeri itu,* The incident strained the

relations of the two countries. **(per)–an** tension.

tegap 1 well-built, sturdy. *Badannja –,* He's well built. 2 firm. *pimpinan jg –* firm guidance. **ke–an** 1 sturdiness. 2 firmness. **men–kan** to strengthen, emphasize.

tegar 1 stiff, strained. 2 stubborn. 3 see TAGAR. **ke–an** obstinacy. **men–kan** to harden, stiffen.

tegas 1 clear, distinct. *dgn –* clearly. 2 firm, resolute. *sikap jg –* firm attitude. *tindakan jg –* a resolute step. **ke–an** 1 firmness, resoluteness. 2 sternness, strictness. 3 emphasis. 4 explanation. **men–kan** 1 to explain, clarify. 2 to affirm, ratify. 3 to confirm. **(pen)–an** 1 affirmation. 2 confirmation. 3 emphasis. **per–an** = PEN–AN. **–nja** i.e., in other words. *– ringkas* brief but clear.

tegor see TEGUR.

teguh 1 firm, secure. *Meréka masih – pd adatnja,* They are still firm in their customs. 2 firm, dependable. *djandji jg –* a firm promise. **ber–** 1 to hold to, be firm in. 2 to strengthen o.s. **ber– –²an** to affirm mutually. ∼ *persahabatan* to affirm mutual friendship. **ke–an** firmness, strength. ∼ *iman* integrity. **memper–kan, men–kan** 1 to confirm s.t. 2 to consolidate s.t. 3 to affirm, ratify. **pen–an** 1 confirmation. 2 the act of strengthening. *– bedegap* robust, strong.

teguk a swallow, gulp. *se– air* a swallow, drink, of water. **men–i** to swallow, gulp down.

tegun ter– 1 to stop suddenly, stall. *Mobil itu* ∼ , The car stalled. 2 to get stuck, stop suddenly. *Pembitjara itu* ∼ , The speaker got stuck. 3 to stand stiffly erect. **ter– –²** to keep stopping, falter, stall.

tegur ber– –² to address o. another. **ke–an** made ill by a ghost. **men–** 1 to address, greet. *Ia* ∼ *tapi tak didjawab,* He addressed him but was not answered. 2 to admonish, warn. *Ia* ∼ *temannja supaja bekerdja,* He admonished his friend to do his work. 3 to reprimand s.o. **–an** 1 warning, admonition. 2 reprimand. 3 greeting. 4 criticism. *– sapa* 1 polite, well-mannered. *orang jg baik – sapanja* a polite and well-mannered person. 2 amiability.

téh tea. *– és* iced tea. *– susu* tea with cream.

téhnik 1 technique. 2 technology.

téhnis technical.

ték see TIK.

tékad 1 determined, firm-willed. 2 a

strong will. - *jg bulat* a very determined will. **ber-** to be determined.
tekak 1 soft palate. 2 throat. 3
stubborn, strong-willed. 4 taste. **men-**
to cleave to the palate. *manisnja* ~
very sweet. - *haus*, - *kering* a dry
throat. - *languk* a nasty taste in the
mouth.
tekan pressure. **ber-, bersi-** to lean
on. *Ia* ~ *pd tongkatnja*, He leaned
on his cane. ~ *pinggang* with arms
akimbo. **men-** 1 to press. *Ia* ~
kenop itu, She pressed the button.
2 to suppress. 3 to oppress. **men-kan**
1 to stress, emphasize s.t. 2 to press.
Ia ~ *djarinja ketémbok*, He pressed
his finger into the wall. **(pen)-an**
1 pressure. 2 emphasis, stress. 3
tension. - *udara* air, atmospheric,
pressure.
tékan see TÉKEN.
tekap cover. **ber-** to cover. *Ia* ~
mulut dgn saputangan, She covered
her mouth with a handkerchief.
men-(i) to cover. *Ia* ~ *mulut anak
jg berteriak itu*, He covered the
mouth of the screaming child. **-an**
1 cover. 2 dome, cupola.
tekat embroidery. **men-** to embroider.
tékat see TÉKAD.
teka teki 1 riddle. 2 puzzle. - *silang*
crossword puzzle. **ber-** 1 to play
riddles. 2 to ask a riddle.
tekebur see TAKABUR.
tékelék wooden clog with leather
straps.
téken signature. **men-** to sign s.t.
~ *serdadu* to sign up for military
service. **-an** 1 drawing. 2 registration. ~ *masuk serdadu* registration
for military service.
téker **men-** to light a fire.
téknik see TÉHNIK.
téknis see TÉHNIS.
téknologi technology.
téko(h) teakettle.
tékongan curve.
tekor to show a deficit. *Uangnja -
50 dolar*, He has a deficit of $50. **ke-
an** 1 deficit. 2 to be short of. *Saja*
~ *uang*, I'm short of money.
tékosi tea cozy.
téks text.
tékstil textile. **per-an** textile industry.
tékté key money.
tekuk **ber-** bent, crumpled. ~ *lutut*
1 to bend the knees. 2 to surrender.
~ *tangan* to fold o's arms across the
chest. **men-** 1 to fold. *Ia* ~ *surat
itu*, He folded the letter. 2 to defeat.
Ia ~ *lutut musuhnja*, He brought
the enemy to its knees. **-an** 1 a fold.
2 bowing of head, curtsy.
tekukur small wood pigeon.

tekun diligent. *Ia beladjar dgn -*, He
studied diligently. - *rakjat* the sincerity of the people. **ber-** 1 to be
diligent. *Ia* ~ *bekerdja*, He works
diligently. 2 to hold fast, adhere to.
~ *pd adat kuno* to hold on to archaic
customs. **ke-an, per-an** 1 diligence.
2 perseverance. **men-kan** to concentrate. *Ia* ~ *perhatian pd pekerdjaannja*, He concentrated his attention upon his work. **ter-** to be diligent, persevering.
tekur **ber-** with head bowed. *duduk*
~ to sit with bowed head. **men-**
1 to bend, bow. 2 to meditate.
men-kan *kepala* to bow the head.
Tel. [*Teluk*] 1 gulf. *Tel. Iran* the
Persian Gulf. 2 bay. *Tel. Benggala*
Bay of Bengal. 3 [*télpon*] telephone.
tela see TELA'AH. **per-an** proceedings,
report.
tela'ah 1 study, research. 2 decipher-
ment. **men(t)-** 1 to analyze, study.
2 to prophesy. **pen-an** study, research.
teladan model, example. **men-** to
follow the example of. *Ia* ~ *kakaknja
jg pandai itu*, He followed the example
of his brilliant brother. **men-i** to set
an example for. *Guru mesti* ~
muridnja, The teacher must set an
example for his pupils.
telaga 1 lake. 2 pond. 3 stagnant
pit, well. - *tahi* cesspool.
telah 1 already. *Ia - besar*, He's
already grown. 2 indicates past
action. *Ia - datang*, He has come.
men-(kan) to predict. *Kita blm dpt* ~
hasil^2 pemilihan, We can't predict
the results of the elections yet.
pen- prophesier, forecaster. **pen-an**
prophecy, prediction. **se-** after. ~
itu ia tidur, After that he went to
sleep. ~ *makan ia tidur*, After eating
he went to sleep.
telampung raft, float.
telan **men-** 1 to swallow. ~ *makanan*
to swallow food. 2 to swallow, take
(insults). 3 to require, swallow up.
Perdjalanan itu ~ *banjak ongkos*,
The trip cost a lot of money. ~
ludah to swallow (from nervousness,
anxiety, fear). **pen-an** swallowing.
ter- swallowed accidentally. - *mentah^2*
to defeat, clobber, smother (a team,
etc.). - *seperti kasuari* to swallow
whole (Amb.).
telandjang bare, naked, nude (body,
sword). **ber-** to be naked, bare.
men-i 1 to strip, undress, s.o. 2
to strip s.o. of s.t. ~ *penumpang^2
dari barang^{2}nja* to strip the passengers
of their goods. 3 to uncover, expose.
~ *rahasia* to uncover a secret. **pen-**

an stripping, undressing. - *bogél*, - *bulat* stark-naked.

telandjur 1 gone ahead, rashly. *Kalau sdh - mengetjét kuning tjétlah semuanja*, Now that you've gone ahead and painted it yellow, paint it all yellow. 2 go too far. *Djangan - mengatakan ini dan itu*, Don't let your tongue run away with you. 3 prematurely. *Ia - membeli kartjis*, He bought the tickets prematurely. *Ia - mengatakan itu*, He's already said it, unfortunately. **ke-an** exceedingly, extremely. ~ *nakalnja* extremely naughty.

telangkai intermediary for marriage.

telangkup upside down. **men-kan** to place upside down.

telantar neglected. *Meréka memberi pertolongan kpd anak*[2] -, They give aid to neglected children.

telap 1 injured. *Ia tidak* -, He's invulnerable. 2 to strike with a weapon. **men-** 1 to hit. 2 to hurt.

telapak(an) 1 palm of the hand. 2 sole of foot. 3 bottom. - *kembar* 1 dual tread. 2 two-ply.

telat 1 overdue. *Keréta api datang* -, The train was overdue. 2 too late.

telatén 1 patient. *Ia tak - menunggu*, He became impatient while waiting. 2 painstaking, punctual.

telau a spot, stain of color. **ber-** 1 bright (of color). 2 to shimmer. *kebiruan* ~ bluish in color.

télé ber- -[2] to talk nonsense.

teledék dancing girl.

teledor 1 negligent, careless. *Ia - dlm pekerdjaannja*, He's negligent in his work. 2 rascal, scoundrel. **ke-an** 1 negligence, carelessness. 2 to default to. **men-kan** to neglect s.t.

teledu otter.

télégram telegram.

télégrap telegraph.

télégrapis telegraphist.

telekan ber- to lean on s.t.

télékomunikasi telecommunications.

telekung veil or head covering worn by women when praying.

telempap breadth of hand (a measure).

téléng 1 awry, at an angle. 2 eyeball. **men-kan** *kepalanja* to hold o's head at an angle.

telentang men- to lie on o's back. *Ia* ~ *ditempat tidurnja*, He lay stretched out on his bed. **men-kan** to stretch s.o. out. *Dokter* ~ *sisakit diatas médja bedah*, The doctor stretched his patient out on the operating table. **ter-** to lie stretched out. *Ia djatuh* ~ *ditanah*, He lay stretched out on the ground.

télépisi see TÉLÉVISI.

telepuk a figured design.

télépun see TÉLPON.

télévisi television.

télgram telegram.

telik 1 perspicacious. 2 spy. **men-** to spy on.

telinga 1 ear. - *gadjah* large ears. 2 handle. - *pantji* handle of pan. - *tempajan* ears that do not hear. *masuk - kanan keluar - kiri* in o. ear and out the other.

telingkah ber- to quarrel.

teliti 1 careful, accurate, in detail. *memeriksa dgn* - to examine in detail. 2 thorough. **ke-an** 1 accuracy. 2 precision. **men-** to examine carefully. **pen-** *matahari* suntracker. **pen-an** 1 thorough, detailed, examination. 2 investigation. 3 research. 4 screening. ~ *guna* applied research.

telor see TELUR.

télor speech defect. **ke-an** *bahasa* bastardization of the language. **men-** to lisp.

télp. [*télpon*] telephone.

télpon telephone. **ber-** to talk by phone. **men-** to telephone.

teluh magical formula.

teluk 1 bay. - *Benggala* Bay of Bengal. 2 gulf. - *Iran* Persian Gulf. - *rantau* 1 district, region. 2 river bed. *djadi - ulakan air* to go round in circles.

telukup see TELUNGKUP.

telundjuk index finger. - *lurus kelingking berkait* 2-faced, treacherous. - *merosok mata sendiri* to be hoisted by o's own petard.

telungkup face downward, upside down. **men-** to lie face downward. **men-kan** to place s.t. face downward.

telur 1 egg. 2 fish roe. **ber-**, **men-** to lay eggs. *Ajam* ~ , The hen laid eggs. **men-kan** 1 to lay eggs. 2 to drop. *Kapal terbang* ~ *bom*, The plane dropped a bomb. 3 to bring forth, produce. *Ia* ~ *pendapat baru*, He brought forth a new invention. ~ *hasil* to produce results. **pen-an** egg laying, egg production. - *asin* salted egg. - *dadar* omelet, scrambled eggs. - *ikan* fish roe. - *kol* cauliflower. - *kutu* nit. - *masak setengah* soft-boiled egg. - *mata sapi* fried egg. - *rebus* boiled egg. - *terubuk* herring roe, Indonesian caviar. - *tetasan* egg for hatching. - *tjeplok* fried egg. - *diudjung tanduk* critical, delicate, precarious, on the horns of a dilemma.

telut ber- 1 to kneel down. 2 to surrender. 3 to harm. *tak - sendjata* invulnerable.

telutut men- to kneel.

téma theme. **ber–kan** to have as a theme.

tema'ah greedy.

teman 1 friend, comrade. 2 companion. **ber–** 1 with friends. *Ia datang* ~ , He came with his friends. 2 to be a friend. *Ia* ~ *dgn anak saja*, He's a friend of my son. 3 to be married. *Ia sdh* ~ , *bukan budjang lagi*, He's married and not a bachelor any more. **men–i** to accompany. *Siapa jg* ~ *ibumu?* Who's accompanying your mother? **pe–an** companionship. – *hidup* life's companion, helpmate. – *seasrama* dormitory mate. – *sedjawat*, – *sekerdja* colleague. – *sekamar* roommate. – *sekelas* classmate. – *seperdjalanan* traveling companion. – *seperdjuangan* comrade-in-arms. – *sepermain(an)* playmate. – *setanahair* fellow countryman.

temas(j)a see TAMASJA.

tembaga copper. **men–** to be copper-colored. – *kuning* brass. – *mérah* copper. – *perunggu* bronze. – *putih* pewter.

témbak men– 1 to shoot, fire. 2 to aim at, intend. **men–i** 1 to fire on. *Kapal itu di–i pesawat udara*, The ship was fired on by a plane. 2 to shell. ~ *musuh* to shell the enemy. **men–** *djatuh* to shoot s.t. down. **men–kan** to fire, shoot. *Ia* ~ *bedilnja*, He fired his rifle. *Ia* ~ *peluru penghabisan*, He shot his last bullet. **pen–** rifleman, marksman. ~ *mahir* sharpshooter, crack shot. **pen–an** 1 shelling, bombardment. 2 firing (of a missile). **ter–** 1 shot. *Ia* ~ *mati*, He was shot to death. 2 struck. *Rumahnja* ~ *petir*, His house was struck by lightning. **–an** 1 shooting. 2 shot. **–²an** shooting, rifle drill. – **-men–** shooting affray. *men– tanah digunung* to carry coals to Newcastle.

tembakau tobacco. – *belati* imported tobacco. – *djawa* native-grown tobacco. – *radjangan* cut tobacco. – *sék* shag tobacco. – *tin* tobacco in cans.

tembam puffed-up face.

tembang sung or recited Javanese poetry. **men–** to recite or sing Javanese poetry, usually accompanied by gamelan music. **pen–** male crooner with gamelan orchestra.

tembékar see TEMBIKAR.

témbél 1 sty (in the eye). 2 pimple. 3 see TAMBAL. – *ban* repair of tire. **men–(kan)** to patch, plaster. **–an** patched.

tembelang rotten (of an egg).

tembéréng 1 potsherd. 2 earthenware. 3 outer edge.

tembikai watermelon.

tembikar 1 glazed porcelain. 2 earthenware. 3 ceramics.

tembilang a spade (for digging).

témbok masonry wall. **men–(i)** to wall in. 2 to do masonry. *Ia* ~ *rumahnja*, He made his house of stone. 3 to cover batik with wax to keep off dye. **–an** a stone dam. – *beton* concrete wall. – *kering* a miser.

tembolok 1 crop, gizzard. 2 paunch.

tembuk 1 perforated. 2 hole. **men–** 1 to perforate. 2 to stab.

tembung a cudgel.

tembuni afterbirth.

tembus 1 perforated. – *kena peluru* perforated by a bullet. 2 to emerge. *Djalan ini – kepasar*, This street comes out at the market. 3 penetrated. *Pertahanan musuh tlh –*, The enemy's defense was penetrated. **ber–an** filled with holes. **men–** 1 to pierce, stab. *Ia* ~ *dada musuhnja dgn bajonét*, He pierced his opponent's chest with a bayonet. 2 to penetrate, pierce, break through. *Meréka tlh* ~ *pertahanan musuh*, They have penetrated the enemy's defense. 3 to emerge, come out. *Sungai ini* ~ *ditengah kota*, This river emerges in the center of town. *Air hudjan* ~ *ditémbok*, Rain water is penetrating the wall. **men–i** to pierce, penetrate, break through s.t. **pen–an** 1 a breakthrough, penetration. 2 infiltration. **–an** 1 thoroughfare, passage. 2 tunnel. 3 a carbon copy. ~ *bermeterai* stamped, certified copy.

temenggung 1 title of high-ranking administrative official. 2 former title of regent.

tempa dagger. – *Malaka* Malay dagger. **men–** 1 to make metal objects, manufacture. ~ *barang dapur* to make kitchen utensils. 2 to forge. 3 to make daggers, knives, etc. ~ *diri* to undergo severe discipline and training. *Ia* ~ *diri mempersiapkan utk udjian*, He underwent severe training in preparation for his examinations. **pen–** a smith. **–an** 1 made, ready-made. *barang* ~ ready-made articles. 2 made in. *barang* ~ *Bali* articles made in Bali. 3 order.

tempah men–(kan) 1 to book ahead of time. 2 to order made. **–an** an order.

tempajak larva.

tempajan water jar.

témpang see TIMPANG.

tempap see TELEMPAP.

tempat 1 place. – *utk minum kopi* a place to drink coffee. 2 whom. *Ialah – kami bertanja*, He's the o.

we asked. **ber–** 1 to live, stay at.
Sdr ~ tinggal dimana? Where are
you living? 2 to take place. *Pertemuan
ini ~ digedung bioskop,* This meeting
took place at the movie theater.
men–i 1 to occupy. *Rumah ini siap
utk di–i,* This house is ready to be
occupied. *Ia ~ djawatan jg baru,*
He occupies a new post. 2 to fill.
~ lowongan to fill a vacancy. **men-
kan** to place, put. *~ topi dimédja*
to place a hat on the table. *Penolakan
saja ~ meréka dlm keadaan sulit,*
My refusal places them in a difficult
position. **menje–kan** to localize. *~
penjakit mendjalar* to localize a
contagious disease. **pen–an** 1 appointment, placement, employment. *Djawatan ~ Tenaga* placement office.
~ tenaga staffing, placement. 2 stand.
~ sepéda bicycle stand. 3 occupancy. *idzin ~* occupancy permit. 4
placing. *~ iklan* placing an ad. **se–** 1
local. *djam 15.00 waktu ~* 3 P.M.
local time. 2 of the same place. *Ia ~
dgn saja,* He comes from the same
place I do. **se–²** localized. *Tanamannja hanja ~ jg rusak,* His plants are
damaged in some spots only. *– abu*
ash tray. *– air* water drum, container.
– beribadat place of worship. *– bertaut*
point of contact. *– buang air* rest
room, toilet. *– bunga* flowerpot, vase.
– dawat inkstand. *– garam* salt
shaker. *– gula* sugar bowl. *– hiburan*
amusement park, recreation center.
– kedudukan domicile, place of residence. *– kelahiran* place of birth.
– kotoran trash can. *– kuah daging*
gravy boat. *– lapang* a square.
– mandi 1 bathhouse. 2 bathing
place. 3 swimming pool. *– mengadji*
Koranic school. *– menjeberang* pedestrian crossover. *– minjak* oilcan,
container. *– nasi* rice bowl. *– parkir*
parking place. *– peluntjuran* launching
site. *– pemberian* place of issue. *–
pemberian suara* poll, voting booth.
– pembuangan sampah garbage dump.
– pendjudian gambling den. *– penga-
singan* 1 internment camp. 2 isolation ward. *– pengumpulan beras* rice
depot. *– pengumpulan sendjata* muni-
tions depot. *– peribadatan* place of
worship. *– rokok* cigarette case. *–
sabun* soap dish. *– sampah* trash can.
– simpan container. *– susu* milk
pitcher. *– tawanan* internment camp.
– teduh lee, shelter. *– tidur* bed. *–
tinggal* residence. *– tinta* inkwell. *–
tudjuan* destination. *– tumpah darah*
birthplace. *Sdh pd –nja,* It's fitting.
Tidak pd –nja, It's not suitable,
fitting. *di– istirahat* at ease, at rest.

tempaus k.o. perfume for flavoring
tobacco produced from tree bark.
tempé k.o. soybean cake.
témpél ber– 1 to stick, adhere.
Perangkonja tidak ~ , The stamp
doesn't stick. 2 to border. *Halamannja ~ kpd sungai,* His yard borders
on the river. **men–** 1 to stick, adhere.
Perangkonja tidak ~ , The stamp
doesn't stick. 2 to stick. *Ia ~ gambar
kpd témbok,* He stuck pictures on the
wall. 3 to stick, cling. *Anak itu
~ kpd ibunja,* That child clings to
his mother. **men–i** 1 to stick to.
~ ibunja to cling to o's mother.
2 to sponge on s.o. 3 to cover, fasten
by sticking. *~ témbok dgn gambar*
to cover the wall with pictures.
4 to bribe. **men–kan** to stick s.t. on.
~ gambar ketémbok to stick pictures
on the wall. **–an** 1 a sticker, poster.
2 attached to s.o. or s.t. 3 revenue
stamp. 4 billboard. *– kojo* to confiscate.
tempelak blame, reproach. **men–** to
reproach s.o.
tempéléng a box on the ear. **men–**
to slap s.o. on the side of the head.
pen–an boxing or striking of the ears
or face.
temperas ber–an to spread about in
disorder.
tempiar ber–(an) to scatter.
tempias 1 to sprinkle (of rain). 2
to get dust particles, etc., in the
eye from the wind.
tempik 1 cry of encouragement. 2
vagina. **ber–** to yell, shout. **–an** yell,
cry. *– sorak* shout, yell.
tempil see TAMPIL.
témpo(h) 1 time. *Ia tak ada – datang
kemari,* He's had no time to come
here. *Ada –nja ia menangis,* At
times he cries. *Sdh –nja utk pulang,*
It's time to go home. 2 period.
Ia diberi – 3 bulan, He was given a
period of 3 months. 3 when. *– saja
datang ia pergi,* When I came he
left. 4 tempo. 5 break, interruption.
waktu – tahun baru at New Year's
vacation. *Ia dpt – sehari,* He gets a
day off. 6 delay. *minta – to* ask for a
delay. *–² sometimes,* now and then.
– berlaku period of validity. *– dulu*
in olden days, formerly. *– hari*
1 the other day. 2 formerly. *tidak –*
incessantly.
tempolong cuspidor.
tempua weaverbird.
tempuh ber–² to attack e.o. **ke–an**
1 to be responsible for. *Ia ~ Rp.
1000 akan kerusakan itu,* He was
made responsible in the amount of
1,000 rupiahs for damages. 2 to be

blamed. *Saja jg ~ akan kesalahan itu,* I was the o. blamed for the mistake. **men-** 1 to attack, assail. *~ musuh* to attack the enemy. 2 to penetrate. *~ hutan jg lebat* to penetrate a thick jungle. 3 to endure, go through. *~ segala kesukaran* to endure all difficulties. 4 to take. *~ udjian* to take an examination. *~ ber-bagai² peladjaran* to take various courses of study. 5 to face, risk. *~ bahaja* to face danger. 6 against. *berdjalan ~ angin* to walk against the wind. *~ djalannja* to go o's way. *~ djarak* to cover a distance. **men-kan** to make s.o. responsible for s.t. *Ia ~ tetangganja akan kerusakan itu,* He made his neighbor responsible for the damage.

tempuling harpoon.

tempur ber- 1 to fight. *~ dgn pasukan musuh* to fight enemy troops. 2 to dash. *Ombak ~ dgn karang,* Waves dashed against the cliffs. **memper-kan** 1 to fight for. *Meréka ~ kenaikan gadji,* They fought for a salary increase. 2 to have fight. *~ pasukan persediaan* to have the reserve troops fight. **men-** to attack, assail. **pen-** assailant. **per-an** 1 battle. 2 altercation, clash. *~ darah* bloodshed.

tempurung part of a coconut shell. *- biola* body of a violin. *- kepala* cranium, skull. *- lutut* kneecap. *seperti katak dibawah -* narrow-minded.

temu ber- 1 to meet. *Saja ~ dgn dia,* I met him. (I ran into him.) *Sampai ~ lagi,* So long. (I'll be seeing you.) 2 to see. *Saja ingin ~ dgn guru saja,* I want to see my teacher. 3 to match, agree. *Perkataannja tak ~ dgn perbuatannja,* His words do not match his deeds. 4 to be found. *Mungkin itu hilang, tiada ~ lagi,* Possibly it's lost, it can't be found. **memper-kan** 1 to unite s.o. or s.t. *Pertemuan itu ~ meréka dlm djodoh,* The meeting united them in marriage. 2 to confront. *Hakim ~ saksi itu dgn bukti,* The judge confronted the witness with evidence. **men-** to find. *Apa kau barangkali -?* Did you by any chance find it? **men-i** 1 to meet, see, visit. *Ia ~ temannja,* He met, saw, his friend. *~ soal baru* to meet a new problem. 2 to find. *Ia ~ barang jg ditjarinja,* He found what he was looking for. 3 to meet with. *Ia ~ kegagalan,* He met with failure. *~ adjalnja* to die. **men-kan** 1 to find, discover. *Columbus ~ Amérika,* Columbus discovered America. *~ uang lima*

rupiah to find a 5-rupiah note. 2 to invent. **pen-** discoverer. **pen-an** 1 invention. 2 discovery. 3 finding. **per-an** 1 meeting. 2 getting together, union. 3 companionship. *- kuning, - kunjit* turmeric. *- lawak* a k.o. ginger.

temut² 1 to twitch. 2 to mumble.

tenaga 1 power. *- listerik* electric power. 2 energy. *- atom* atomic energy. 3 personnel, staff, force. **ber-** 1 powerful. 2 energetic. *~ listerik* electrified. *- ahli* expert(s). *- air* hydraulic power. *- gerak* kinetic energy. *- hidup* vitality. *- kerdja terlatih* skilled manpower. *- kuda* horsepower. *- manusia* manpower. *- pekerdja* workers, labor force. *- pembeli* purchasing power. *- pengadjar* teaching staff. *- terdidik* trained staff.

tenang 1 calm. 2 quiet, still. **ke-an** 1 calm. 2 quiet. 3 composure. **men-kan** to calm s.o. down.

tenar 1 noise. 2 known. **ke-an** noise.

ténda 1 tent. 2 awning. 3 hood of car. *- pelindung* shelter.

tendang men- to kick. **-an** a kick. *~ sudut* corner. *- teradjang* kicking and stamping. *- tumit* stamping the foot.

tendas men- to decapitate.

téner paint oil.

téng a tank. *- bénsin* gasoline tank.

tengadah men- to look up at. *Ia ~ melihat kapal terbang itu,* He looked up to see the plane. **men-kan** to lift, hold s.t. up. *Ia ~ mukanja,* He lifted his face.

tengah 1 middle, center. *di- kamar* in the middle of the room. 2 on. *Di- djalan hari hudjan,* On the way it rained. 3 among, midst. *Di- kami ada orang Amérika,* There was an American among us. 4 in the midst of, while. *- bekerdja ia merasa lapar,* In the midst of working he felt hungry. 5 to be in the process of. *Ia - makan waktu temannja datang,* He was eating when his friend came. 6 neutral, in the middle. *Ia berdiri di- sadja,* He's neutral. **ke-** forward, to the middle. *Anaknja dibawa ~ ,* His child was brought forward. **men-** 1 to intercede, mediate. *Ia akan ~ dlm soal ini,* He will mediate this problem. 2 to be neutral. *Ia akan ~ dlm soal ini,* He will be neutral in this problem. 3 to move to the center. *Dari pinggir ia ~ ,* From the edge he moved to the center. 4 middle. *sekolah ~* secondary school. *Anak jg ~ lelaki,* The middle child is a boy. 5 average. *Kepandaian anak itu ~ ,* That child's intelligence is average. 6 neutral. *politik* ~ a neutral policy. **menge–i** to intercede, mediate. *PBB* ~ *dlm pertengkaran itu,* The UN interceded in the conflict. **menge–kan** 1 to produce, set forth. ~ *bukti jg kuat* to produce strong evidence. 2 to state. *Dlm rapat itu dike–kannja apa² jg terasa oléhnja,* In the meeting he stated how he felt. 3 to subpoena, summon. **pen–** 1 mediator. 2 o. with a neutral attitude, neutralist. **per–an** 1 middle. *Abad* ~ Middle Ages. ~ *bulan* in the middle of the month. 2 middle class. ~ *djalan* halfway. 3 the average. *diambil* ~*nja,* ... on the average, ... **se–** 1 half. ~ *djalan* halfway. ~ *masak* half-done. 2 some. ~ *penduduk tak pertjaja kepadanja,* Some of the inhabitants don't believe him. ~ *empat 3½,* half past three. *kerdja* ~ *hari* part-time work. ~ *hati* half-hearted. *Kalau* ~ *hatimu, djanganlah kamu pergi,* If you feel halfhearted about it, don't go. *Meréka bekerdja* ~ , They work halfheartedly. ~ *matang* 1 half-ripe. 2 half-cocked. ~ *miring otak* half-cocked. ~*nja pulang,* Some went home. ~ *rupiah* 50 cents. ~ *tiang* half-mast. ~ *tua* middle-aged. ~ *umur* middle-aged. **–an** 50-cent piece, half-dollar, etc. **–²** in the middle. *Pohon itu berdiri* ~ *alun² itu,* The tree stands in the middle of the square. – *bulanan* semimonthly. – *dua ratus* 150. – *empat puluh* 35. – *hari* noon. – *hari rembang* high noon. – *malam* midnight. – *naik* (ca.) 9 A.M. – *tiga* half past two. *di–* –² *terang* in the bright daylight. – *turun* (ca.) 3 P.M.

tengara 1 signal. 2 sign.

tenggala plow. **men–** to plow. **pen–** plowman.

ténggang ber– 1 to find ways and means to carry on. 2 to seek aid. **ber–** –²**an** to have respect for e.o. **memper–kan** 1 to get along on, be economical. 2 to consider. **men–** respect. *Ia tahu* ~ *hati orang,* He's sensitive to others' thoughts. *Ia tidak* **ter–** *lagi,* He's at his wit's end. – **–men–** to be considerate, understanding of e.o.

tenggara southeast. *Asia* – Southeast Asia. **men–** in a southeast direction. *Angin* ~ , The wind is southeast.

ténggék ber–, men– to squat.

tenggelam 1 to sink. *Kapal* –, The ship sank. 2 to sink, set. *Matahari* –, The sun set. 3 to drown. *Anaknja* –, Her child has drowned. **men–kan** 1 to sink s.t. *Kapal selam* ~ *kapal*

pendjeladjah itu, The submarine sank the cruiser. 2 to scuttle a ship. **pen–an** sinking, torpedoing.

ténggér ber– to be perched, be on a perch. *Burung* ~ *pd dahan,* The bird was perched on a branch. **–an** a perch.

tenggiling anteater.

tenggorok(an) 1 throat. 2 larynx.

tengguli molasses.

tengik 1 rotten, rank. 2 rancid, putrid. 3 biting (words).

tengil a swelling.

tengkar 1 dispute. 2 conceited. **ber–(an)** to quarrel. **memper–kan** to dispute, argue over s.t. *Meréka* ~ *soal Irian,* They argued over the problem of New Guinea. **pen–** a conceited person. **per–an** dispute, quarrel.

téngkoh prepared opium.

tengkok see TENGKUK.

tengkorak skull, cranium.

tengku sir (title of nobility). – *mahkota* crown prince.

tengkuk 1 neck. 2 nape of neck. 3 bunch (of bananas). 4 stalk of rice.

tengkulak broker, middleman.

tengkuluk headdress.

tengkurap lying prostrate. **ber–** to lie prostrate.

téngok men– 1 to view s.t. ~ *tanaman diladang* to view the plants in the field. 2 to visit, see. ~ *teman jg sakit* to visit a sick friend. 3 to look. ~ *kekanan* to look to the right. 4 to judge from. ~ *pakaiannja ia orang asing,* Judging from his clothes he's a foreigner. **pen–** 1 visitor. 2 observer. – *kanan!* Eyes right!

tengu mite.

ténis tennis. – *médja* ping-pong, table tennis.

téntamén preliminary examination.

tentang 1 about, regarding. *Ia tak tahu suatu djuapun – itu,* He didn't know a thing about it. 2 opposite, facing. *Kantornja di– setasiun,* His office is opposite the station. 3 around, on. *Talinja diikatkan – pohon,* The rope was fastened around the tree. 4 directly above. *Matahari di– kepala,* The sun was directly overhead. **ber–** to be opposite. *Rumah-nja* ~ *dgn mesdjid,* His house is opposite the mosque. ~ *mata* face to face. **ber–an** 1 to be in contradiction. *Uraiannja* ~ *dgn kenjataan,* His explanation was in contradiction of the facts. 2 to be in conflict. *Ia selalu* ~ *dgn madjikannja,* He's always in conflict with his boss. 3 to be in contravention. 4 to face. ~ *musuh* to face the enemy. ~ *paham* to have conflicting opinions. **memper-kan** 1 to oppose. 2 to contrast. *Istilah ini diper–kan dgn istilah itu,* This term was contrasted with that term. **men–** 1 to look, gaze, at, into. ~ *muka ibunja* to look into his mother's face. ~ *matahari* to look at the sun. 2 to face. *duduk dimuka pintu* ~ *laut* to sit in front of the door facing the sea. 3 toward. *berdjalan* ~ *kota* to walk toward town. ~ *angin* against the wind. 4 to oppose. ~ *politik pemerintah* to oppose government policy. *Dua suara* ~ , Two votes were against. 5 to defy. *tindakan jg* ~ *hukum* an action which defied the law. 6 to risk, challenge. ~ *bahaja maut* to risk death. **men–i** 1 to face, oppose. ~ *musuh* to face the enemy. 2 to oppose. *Ia* ~ *usul sematjan itu,* He opposes a proposal of that kind. **men–kan** 1 to face. *Ia* ~ *pintu,* He faced the door. 2 to have s.o. face. *Ia* ~ *adiknja kepintu,* He had his brother face the door. **pen–** 1 the opposition. 2 opponent. **pen–an** resistance. **per–an** 1 conflict, controversy. 2 contradiction. 3 opposition. 4 resistance. **se–** just opposite. *Ia duduk* ~ *saja,* He sat just opposite me. *sama* ~ flush with. **ter–** 1 observed. *sinar jg tak* ~ *mata* light which can't be observed by the eyes. 2 be contradicted. *Kebenarannja tak* ~ *pula,* The truth could not be contradicted any longer. **–an** 1 resistance, opposition. 2 at stake. *Djiwa anakmu menghadapi* ~*nja,* Your child's life is at stake.

tentara see TENTERA.

ténténg men– to carry in o's hands.

tentera 1 army. 2 military. 3 troop(s). – *pajung* paratroop unit. **ke–an** 1 military. 2 military forces. **pe(r)–an** 1 military barracks. 2 garrison. 3 army base.

tenteram 1 quiet, peaceful. 2 safe. **ke–an** 1 calm, tranquillity. 2 order. **men–kan** 1 to pacify. 2 to reassure, calm.

tentu 1 fixed, definite. *tak –arahnja* no fixed direction. 2 specified. *menurut masa jg –* according to a specified time. 3 definite. *Djawabnja blm –,* His answer isn't definite yet. 4 sure, certain. *Sdh –,* That's sure. *Ia –menang,* He's certain to win. *Itu masih blm –,* That's not certain yet. **ber–** to be certain. *Ia blm* ~ *perginja,* He's not certain he's going. **ber– –²** certainly, positively. **berke–an** to be sure, certain. *tidak* ~ unsure, uncertain. **ke–an** 1 certainty. 2 stipulation. 3 provision, proviso. 4 de-

cision. **men–i** 1 to examine. *Ia* ~ *barang²,* He examined the articles. 2 to visit, call on. ~ *orang sakit* to visit a patient. 3 to pay up. ~ *utangnja* to pay up o's debts. **men–kan** 1 to determine, fix. ~ *hari berangkatnja* to determine the day of departure. 2 to secure. *Ia* ~ *pendapatan 500 dolar,* He secured an income of $500. 3 decisive, deciding. *faktor* ~ a decisive factor. 4 to decide. ~ *tempat* to locate s.t. **pen–an** 1 decision. *Bésok* ~*nja. Siapa jg beruntung?* The decision is tomorrow. Who'll be the lucky one? 2 determination. ~ *kebidjaksanaan* policy formulation. **ter–** 1 sure. *suatu hal jg* ~ a sure thing. 2 fixed. ~ *djumlahnja* a fixed amount. 3 specific. 4 most certain. 5 stipulated, specified. *– sadja* certainly.

tenuk a tapir.

tenun ber–, men– to weave. **per–an** 1 textile mill. 2 textiles. **–an** fabric, woven product.

tenung 1 fortunetelling. 2 horoscope. **ber–** to tell fortunes. **men–(kan)** to prophesy, tell fortunes. **pen–** fortuneteller. **pen–an** fortunetelling. **–an** 1 prophecy. 2 fortunetelling.

téokrasi theocracy.

téorétikus theoretician.

téorétis theoretical.

téori theory. **ber–** to theorize.

téosopi theosophy.

tép see TIK.

tepak a light slap. **men–** to slap slightly. **–an** a slap.

tépak a betel box. *– rokok* cigarette case. *– tembakau* tobacco pouch.

tepam men– 1 to slap with the palm of the hand. 2 to grasp, seize.

tepas bamboo railing. **ber–** protected by bamboo wickerwork. **men–i** to screen s.t. *empat – dunia* the 4 points of the compass.

tepat 1 exact. *perhitungan jg –* an exact calculation. 2 on the stroke of, sharp. *– djam 4* exactly 4 o'clock. 3 right. *Ia duduk – dimuka saja,* He sat right in front of me. *Ia gurubesar jg –,* He's the right professor. 4 due, directly. *utara –* due north. **berke–an** coincidentally, accidentally. *Perkawinannja* ~ *pd bulan puasa,* His marriage coincided with the fasting month. **ber–an** 1 to be a coincidence. *Itu* ~ *sadja,* It's just a coincidence. 2 to coincide. *Ia* ~ *pulang sehingga saja dpt ikut,* His return coincides so that I can go along. 3 to happen to be. *Hari berangkatnja* ~ *tgl satu,* His departure date happens to be the first. 4 to agree, concur. *Pendapatnja* ∼ *dgn pikiran saja,* His opinion agrees with my views. *bertolak* ∼ *dgn tembakan* to start at the crack of the gun. **ke–an** 1 accuracy, exactness. 2 to happen to be, coincidentally. *Ia* ∼ *ada dirumah,* He happened to be at home. **ke–gunaan** efficiency. **men–** 1 to go, lead to. *Djalan ini* ∼ *kepasar,* This road leads straight to the market. 2 to go straight. *Ia* ∼ *kerumahnja,* He went straight to his house. **men–i** 1 to head straight for. 2 to fulfill. ∼ *djandji* to fulfill a promise. **men–kan** 1 to aim, direct. *Ia* ∼ *pasangannja kerumah itu,* He directed his firing at that house. 2 to set, adjust. ∼ *djam* to set a clock. 3 to adapt. **pen–an** 1 adjustment, correction. 2 adaptation. **per–an** co-incidence. **–an** 1 place of destination. 2 guest, spare, bedroom. 3 aim, purpose. **–guna** efficient.

tepaut to be different. – *5 rupiah* with a difference of 5 rupiahs.

tepék se– lump. ∼ *gula* a lump of sugar. ∼ *mentéga* lump of butter. **ber–** soiled. **men–** to stick on.

tepékong Chinese temple.

tepekur 1 absorbed in thought. 2 meditation.

tepi 1 shore. – *laut* seashore. 2 bank, side. – *sungai* riverbank, river's edge. 3 side, edge. – *djalan* side of the road. 4 hem. – *badju* hem of jacket. 5 periphery. **ber–** to be bordered, edged. **ber–kan** to have as an edge. *kain* ∼ *mérah* cloth with a red border. **ke–** 1 peripheral. 2 to go to o. side. **men–** 1 to move to o. side. 2 to go along the edge, side (of the road, etc.). **menge–kan** 1 to ignore, neglect. ∼ *kewadjiban* to ignore o's responsibility. 2 to place s.t. at the side. ∼ *mobil* to park a car at the side of the road. **–an** 1 edge, border. 2 hem. 3 shallows (of a river). ∼ *ilmu* learned person, scholar. ∼ *mata* sweetheart. – *langit* horizon.

tepis men– 1 to skim. *Burung* ∼ *dilaut,* The birds skimmed over the sea. 2 to skim s.t. ∼ *susu* to skim the milk. **men–kan** to parry, ward off. ∼ *pukulan* to parry the blow.

tepok worn-out, run-down.

tépok lame.

tépos with big hips.

tepuk ber– (*tangan*) to clap, applaud. ∼ *sebelah tangan* to receive no love in return. **ber– –²** to splash (of waves). **men–** to beat, clap, slap. ∼ *dada* to beat o's breast. **–an** clapping, applause. – *berbalas* tit for tat. – *dada*

slapping o's breast. – *sorak,* – *tangan* applause. – *tari* dance accompanied by hand clapping.

tepung 1 flour. 2 powder. **men–** to pound into flour. ∼ *beras* to pulverize rice. ∼ *tawari* to exorcise s.t. – *ragi* baking powder. – *tawar* an antidote. – *terigu* wheat flour.

tér tar. **men–** to tar.

tera 1 stamp, seal, imprint. 2 gauge. **men–** 1 to stamp, seal. 2 to gauge. **men–kan** to print s.t. **pen–** inspector of weights and measures. **per–an** printing office. **ter–** printed. *Kegembiraannja tak* ∼ , His joy was indescribable. **–an** 1 stamp. 2 imprint.

teradjang see TERDJANG.

teradju balance, pair of scales.

terak slag. **men–** to collide with. – *api* cinders. – *dapur* kitchen rubbish. – *nasi* crust.

teral men– 1 to browbeat, bully. *Mandur itu* ∼ *kuli²nja,* The foreman browbeats his workers. 2 to incite s.o.

terali latticework. – *kapal* ship's railing.

teraling parakeet.

teram-temeram overcast.

teran to strain in childbirth. **men–** to press.

terang 1 clear, bright. 2 evident, clear. **ber– –²** bluntly, frankly. *Ia* ∼ *mengatakan segala keluhnja,* He frankly stated all his complaints. **ke–an** 1 certificate. 2 information. 3 explanation. 4 statement. ∼ *pemerintah* the government's statement. ∼ *kelakuan baik* statement of good conduct. ∼ *kerdja* grammatical object. ∼ *pabéan* customs declaration. ∼ (*tanda²*) legend (on a map). **men–** to dawn, become light. *Hari mulai* ∼ , The day has begun to dawn. **men–i** 1 to light s.t. *Lampu* ∼ *djalan,* The lamp illuminated the street. *–ilah djalan!* Light the way! 2 to weed s.t. ∼ *kebun* to weed a garden. **men–kan** 1 to explain. *Ia* ∼ *keadaan,* He explained the situation. 2 to declare, state. *Ia* ∼ *dirinja tak mampu,* He declared himself financially insolvent. 3 to ascertain, determine. ∼ *sikapnja dlm suatu perselisihan* to ascertain his attitude in a dispute. 4 to indicate. *Tanda² ini* ∼ *akan datangnja hudjan,* These signs indicate rain. 5 to enlighten, illuminate s.t. **pen–an** 1 information. *Kementerian* ∼ Ministry of Information. 2 explanation, clarification. 3 illumination. ∼ *djalan* street illumination. 4 enlightenment. **–²an** frank, open, blunt. *Saja akan* ∼ *padamu,*

I'll be very frank with you. **-nja** i.e., in other words. **-²** 1 very clear, bright. 2 frank, open, aboveboard. ~ *gelap* dusk, twilight. ~ *kain* not too clear. ~ *larat* 1 vague. 2 twilight. - *benderang* very bright, clear. - *bulan* moonlight. - *gemblang* bright and clear. - *hari* bright day. - *hati* bright, smart. - *lampu* lamplight. - *lengkap* full particulars. - *matahari* sunlight, sunshine. - *tanah* twilight. - *temerang* radiant, brilliantly clear. - *terus* transparent. - *tjuatja* a clear sky, nice weather. *utk -nja* for clarity's sake. *sdh -lah* it goes without saying.

terap 1 k.o. tree whose bark is used in making bark cloth. 2 see TIARAP. 3 arranging, applying, adjusting. 4 groove along blade of kris. **ber-** inlaid. **men-** 1 to lay brick. 2 to do inlay work. 3 to adjust, apply, arrange. **pen-an** assembling. **-an** 1 inlaid. 2 hollowed. 3 applied. *ilmu bahasa* ~ applied linguistics.

térapi therapy.

teras 1 pith, kernel. 2 essence, nucleus. 3 principal element. **men-** to take the kernel, the essence, only.

téras porch, terrace.

terasi a fish paste made from shrimp or small fish pounded fine.

teratai water lily.

teratak shed, temporary hut.

terawang ber- full of holes. **men-** to muse. ~ *langit*, ~ *udara* to daydream, build castles in the air. **-an** porous. *bahan tipis* ~ thin fleecy material.

terawih voluntary evening prayers during the fasting period.

terban to collapse.

terbang 1 to fly. *Burung - tinggi*, A bird flies high. 2 to disappear, evaporate. - *pikiran* losing o's mind. *minjak harum jg - perfume which evaporates.* **be(r)-an** to fly about. *Kertasnja* ~ *ditiup angin*, The sheets flew everywhere, blown by the wind. **men-i** to fly over. ~ *laut* to fly over the sea. **men-kan** 1 to have, let fly. *Ia* ~ *burung*, He let the bird fly. 2 to fly s.t. ~ *lajang²* to fly a kite. 3 to flee with. *Ia* ~ *uang bank*, He fled with the bank's money. **pen-** flyer, pilot. ~ *angkasa* cosmonaut. **pen-an** 1 flight. ~ *jg 5 djam lamanja* a 5-hour flight. 2 aviation. 3 flying. *djawatan* ~ flying service. - *lajang* glider flying. *pagi blm - lalat* early dawn.

terbelakang see BELAKANG.

terbis landslide.

terbit 1 to rise, emerge. *Matahari -*

di timur, The sun rises in the east. 2 to appear, come out. *Surat kabar tidak - hari ini*, The paper didn't come out today. *Madjallah itu - tiap minggu*, The magazine is published every week. 3 to arise, well up. - *keinginan utk melantjong*, A desire to travel arises. **men-kan** 1 to publish, issue. *Ia* ~ *surat kabar*, He publishes a newspaper. 2 to cause, produce. *Soal itu* ~ *kekatjauan*, That matter has caused unrest. **pen-** publisher. **pen-an** 1 publication. *Buku ini* ~ *Pertjétakan Pemerintah*, This book is a publication of the government press. 2 publishing house. 3 edition, issue. **-an** 1 publication. 2 edition, issue. 3 published, issued. *Buku ini* ~ *Bandung*, This book is published in Bandung. - *dari hati jg sutji* from the bottom of o's heart.

terbus a fez.

terdjal steep, sheer. *Léréng gunung itu -*, The mountain slope was steep.

terdjang men- 1 to attack, trample on. *Ia* ~ *orang² jg tak mau menjingkir itu*, He attacked those who wouldn't give way. 2 to kick. **men-kan** to kick with s.t. *Ia* ~ *kakinja*, He kicked with his foot. **(pen)-an** attack. - *tumit* to drive the heel into the ground for firmer support.

terdjemah ment-kan *(kedalam)* to translate (into). **pent-** translator. ~ *lisan* interpreter. **(pen)t-an** 1 translation. ~ *kpd bahasa Indonésia* a translation into Indonesian. 2 translating.

terdjun 1 to jump off, jump down. *Ia - kedalam air*, She dived into the water. 2 to disappear. *Ia tak kelihatan lagi, - diantara orang jg banjak*, He was no longer to be seen; he'd disappeared in the crowd. **men-(i)** 1 to dive, jump into. *Ia* ~ *sungai jg dlm*, He dived into the deep river. 2 to deal with s.t. *Ia* ~ *soal jg sulit itu*, He dealt with the difficult problem. **men-kan** to drop s.t. *Ia* ~ *andjingnja kedalam air*, He dropped his dog into the water. ~ *diri* to disappear in the water. **pen-** jumper.

térék miscarriage.

terém 1 tram, streetcar. 2 train.

teri k.o. small dried anchovy.

teriak scream, yell, shout. - *orang kesakitan* the scream of s.o. in pain. **ber-** to scream, shout. **ber-²** to keep shouting. *Ia* ~ *minta tolong*, He kept shouting for help. **men-i** to yell, shout at s.o. *Ia* ~ *adiknja*, He shouted at his brother. **men-kan** 1 to yell out. *Ia* ~ *tiap² kata*, He yelled out each word. 2 to show off.

Ia ~ kepandaiannja kpd teman²nja,
He was showing off his skill to his
friends. **-an** a yell, scream, shout.
terigu wheat.
terik 1 tight. 2 solid, firm. **men–kan**
to tighten s.t.
terima acceptance. **ber–** acceptable.
~ kasih to be grateful. **men–** 1 to accept. *Ia ~ segala tuduhan,* He accepted
all charges. *~ nasib* to accept o's
fate. 2 to receive. *Ia ~ surat,* He
received a letter. *Ia ~ tamu,* She
received guests. *~ baik* to agree with,
accept. *Kabinét ~ baik laporan
Menlu,* The cabinet agreed with the
foreign minister's report. *~ télpon* to
take a call. **men–kan** to hand s.t.
over. *Ia ~ suratnja kpd ajahnja,* He
handed his letter over to his father.
pen– 1 receiver, receiving set. 2 resigned, acquiescent. **pen–an** 1 acceptance. *~ anggauta baru* the acceptance
of new members. 2 reception. *~
tamu* reception of guests. 3 receipt.
~ surat receipt of a letter. 4 receipts.
– kasih thank you. *kurang – kasih*
ungrateful. *Ia masih kurang – kasih
sadja,* He's still ungrateful. *salah –*
to misunderstand. *– salah* to admit
guilt.
teripang sea cucumber.
teritis 1 narrow bridge. 2 narrow
passage over plank bridge. 3 edge
of corrugated iron roof.
terka men– 1 to suppose. *Saja sdh
~ bhw ia ada dirumah,* I'd supposed
he was at home. 2 to guess, surmise.
Ia tidak bisa ~ , He can't guess. 3
to suspect. *Djangan ~ saja,* Don't
suspect me. **pen–** 1 riddle, puzzle.
2 o. who suspects. **pen–an** 1 guess,
conjecture. 2 suspicion.
terkadang sometimes. see KADANG.
terkam men– to pounce on. *Kutjing
~ tikus,* The cat pounced on the
mouse. **-an** 1 grasp, grip. 2 might,
power.
terkup men– to fall on s.t.
terlalu 1 too, excessively. *Hawanja
– panas,* The weather is too hot.
2 very. *Ia – kaja,* He's very rich.
3 see LALU. **ke–an** excessively, overly.
Ia ~ nakalnja, He's unusually
naughty.
terlampau 1 excessively, very. *Ia –
kuat,* He's extremely strong. 2 see
LAMPAU.
termala 1 withered. 2 suffering, lan-
guishing.
términologi terminology.
térmométér thermometer.
térmos thermos bottle.
ternak 1 cattle, livestock. 2 native.
Ia – Mekah, He's a native of Mecca.

3 to reside for some time. *Ia – kpd
tempat ini,* He's lived at this place
for some time. **be(r)–** to breed cattle.
ment–kan 1 to raise, breed cattle.
2 to raise chickens. 3 to grow plants.
pe– cattle breeder. *~ unggas* poultry
breeder. **pe–an** cattle raising. *~
ajam* poultry husbandry. *– unggas*
poultry breeding.
terobos men– to break through. *Pentjuri ~ pagar,* A thief broke through
the fence. **pen–** 1 piercer. 2 burglar.
pen–an 1 a break-in, burglary. 2
breakthrough, penetration. **-an** breakthrough.
teromol 1 drum. *rém –* mechanical
brakes. 2 box. *– pos* portable post
office box.
terompah sandal. *– kuda* horseshoe.
terompét trumpet, bugle. **men–kan**
to proclaim loudly.
teropong 1 telescope, spyglass. 2
tube, pipe. **men–(i)** 1 to look through
a spyglass. *Nakoda ~ pulau,* The
captain looked at the island with
his spyglass. 2 to observe carefully,
study. *Panitia itu ~ keadaan negeri,*
The committee studied the country's
situation. **pen–an** study, close observation.
téror terror.
téroris terrorist.
terowongan tunnel.
terpa men– to pounce on, jump at.
Harimau ~ kidang, The tiger
pounced on the deer. **-an** jump, leap.
terpal see KAIN.
terpekur see TEPEKUR.
terpeladjar see ADJAR. **ke–an** intel-
lectualism.
térpentén turpentine.
tertawa 1 to laugh. 2 laugh. *– besar*
a hearty laugh. *– ketjil* a smile.
men–i to laugh at s.o. **men–kan** 1
to laugh at, ridicule s.o. 2 to make
s.o. laugh. *Ia pandai ~ orang,*
He's good at making people laugh.
-an object of ridicule. *– ter-pingkal²*
to shake with laughter.
tertib 1 order. *– hukum* legal order.
2 orderly, correct. **ke–an** 1 order.
~ umum public order. 2 correct
conduct. **men–kan** to straighten up,
put in order. *Ia ~ kamar tidur,* She
straightened up the bedroom. 2 to
control, curb. **pen–an** control, curb.
1 *– atjara* standing orders. 2 program. *– nikah* marriage ceremony.
– sopan well-mannered, decent.
terum see DERUM.
terumbu 1 cliff. 2 reef.
teruna 1 youth. 2 youthful.
terung eggplant.

terungku prison. **men–kan** to imprison.

terus 1 straight, direct(ly). *Ia pergi dari rumah – kerumah sakit*, He went from home straight to the hospital. 2 straight away, immediately. *Sampai dirumah ia – makan*, As soon as he arrived home he ate straight away. 3 continually, to keep on. *Ia bekerdja –*, He kept on working. *Ia beladjar –*, He studied continually. *Anginnja – menghébat*, There continued to be a strong wind. *Kamar ini gelap –*, This room continued to be dark. *Ia mati –*, He remained dead. 4 pure, unmixed. **ber– terang** 1 to be frank. 2 frankly. **ber– –²** continually. *Ia ∼ meminta uang pd ajahnja*, He continually asked his father for money. **ke– terangan** frankness. **men–(i)** to break through s.t. *Ia ∼ pagar*, He broke through the fence. **men–i, men–kan** 1 to continue. *Ia ∼ perdjalanan*, He continued the trip. 2 to pierce. 3 to forward, pass (on). *Ia ∼ surat kpd madjikannja*, He forwarded a letter to his boss. **pen–an** 1 continuation, sequel. 2 continuity. *∼ suara* projection of the voice. **se– nja** from now on, henceforth. *Dan ∼ meréka hidup senang*, And they lived happily ever after. *Mudah²an ia baik ∼* , Let's hope he'll be all right from now on. *dan lain² ∼* and so forth, etc. **–an** 1 continuation, sequel. *Tjeritera ini tak ada ∼nja*, This story has no sequel. 2 canal, ditch. *∼ Panama* Panama Canal. 3 channel. *∼ Inggeris* English Channel. 4 continuously. *Ia menangis ∼* , She cried continuously. **–²an** constantly. *Ia menangis ∼* , She cried constantly. **– –men–** constantly. **– –mata** clearsighted. **– terang** frank(ly), candid, straightforward. *Ia mengatakan – terang bhw ialah jg mentjuri uang*, He frankly admitted that he stole the money. *Bagaimana –nja?* How does it go afterward?

terusi hydrated sulphate of iron.

tésis thesis.

tesmak glasses, spectacles.

tetak men–(kan) to hack, chop, cut. *∼ pedangnja kepohon* to hack into a tree with a sword.

tetal dense, compact, compressed. *penduduk jg – a* dense population. **men–** to be compact, compressed. *Isinja ∼* , The contents are compact. **men–kan** to make s.t. compact. *∼ karung dgn djagung* to fill up a bag with corn.

tetampah sieve, winnowing basket.

tetamu guest.

tetangga neighbor.

tetap 1 permanent, fixed. *penduduk – permanent* resident. 2 settled, decided. *Soal itu masih blm –*, That matter hasn't been settled yet. 3 fixed, definite. *Padjaknja blm –*, The tax isn't fixed yet. 4 definitely. *Keséhatannja – baik*, His health remained good. 5 same, constant. *Keadaannja – sebagai dulu*, The situation is the same as before. 6 persistent, determined. *Meréka – tidak mau bajar*, They persisted in not paying. 7 regular. *guru – regular* teacher. **ke–an** 1 decision. 2 assessment. *∼ padjak* tax assessment. 3 firmness, resolve. 4 determination. **memper–(kan)** see MEN–KAN. **men–** 1 to reside, live, make o's home, maintain a permanent residence. *Ia ∼ dikota ini*, He's a permanent resident of this city. *Dia ∼ digua*, He lives in a cave. 2 to blot, suck up, dry up (of ink, water). **men–i** 1 to fulfill, keep. *∼ djandji* to keep a promise. 2 to comply with, carry out. *∼ peraturan pemerintah* to comply with a government regulation. **men–kan** 1 to decide, determine. *Ia ∼ bhw rumahnja akan dibuat dari kaju*, He decided that his house would be made of wood. 2 to appoint. *Rapat ∼ ia mendjadi utusan keluar negeri*, The meeting appointed him to be an overseas representative. 3 to determine, decide. *∼ kehendak utk pergi* to determine the intention to go. 4 to maintain. *Ia ingin ∼ kedudukannja diparlemén*, He wanted to maintain his position in parliament. 5 to keep, fulfill. *Ia ∼ djandji utk datang hari ini*, He kept his promise to come today. 6 to fix, determine. *Ia bertugas ∼ harga²*, He was in charge of fixing the prices. 7 to draw up. *∼ peraturan* to draw up a regulation. *∼ hati* to encourage, boost s.o. **pen–** object for blotting or absorbing s.t. **pen–an** 1 fulfillment. *∼ djandji* fulfillment of a promise or agreement. 2 fixing, determining. *∼ waktu kundjungan* fixing of visiting hours. *∼ harga* price regulation. 3 appointment. *∼ ketua panitya* appointment of a committee chairman. 4 decision, decree. *– hati* steadfast, firm, resolute. *– pd waktunja* promptly. *– pendirian* consistent.

tetapi 1 but. *Ia miskin – suka menolong orang*, He's poor but he likes to help people. 2 yet, still. *Walaupun ia miskin, – ia suka menolong orang*, Though he is poor, still he likes to help people. *murah – bagus* cheap but nice.

tetas men– 1 to break, crack open. *Ia ~ témbok*, He cracked open the wall. *Témboknja ~* , The wall cracked open. *Telornja ~* , The egg cracked. 2 to hatch. *Anak ajam blm ~* , The chick hasn't hatched yet. **men–kan** 1 to hatch (eggs). 2 to cause, produce. *kedjadian jg ~ hiru-hara* an event which caused a commotion.

téték female breast. **men–** 1 to suck the nipple. 2 to be breast-fed. **men–i, men–kan** to give the breast. *~ anaknja* to give o's child the breast. *– bengék* trifles, trifling matters. *Saja tak mau memperhatikan segala – bengék itu*, I didn't want to pay any attention to all those trifling matters.

tétés 1 a drop. 2 molasses. 3 see TITIS. **men–** to drip. *Air ~ dari médja*, Water dripped from the table. **men–i** to sprinkle. *~ luka dgn spiritus* to sprinkle spirits on a wound. **men–kan** to pour in drops. *~ obat keséndok* to pour medicine by the drop into a spoon. **–an** a drop. *~ air* a drop of water. *~ darah Napoléon* a descendant of Napoleon. *~ péna* writings.

tetirah to go somewhere for a cure. **ber–** to vacation in a cool area. *Ia ~ di Lémbang*, He's vacationing in Lembang.

tetua blackhead, pimple.

tetumbuhan plants. see TUMBUH.

Teuku see TEUNGKU.

Teungku title of religious leader in Achin.

téwas 1 to be slain, killed in action. *– dlm pertempuran* to be killed in battle. 2 to lose. *– perangnja* to lose the war. 3 defect, trouble. *Apa – mobil itu maka ia tiada dpt berdjalan?* What's the trouble with the car that it won't go? **ke–an** 1 defeat. 2 disaster, mishap. 3 bereft by death. *Ia ~ ajahnja*, His father died. **men–kan** 1 to defeat, overcome. *Ia ~ musuhnja*, He defeated the enemy. 2 to kill, slay. *Harimau ini tlh ~ 10 orang*, This tiger has killed 10 people.

tg [*tanggal*] date.

Tg. [*Tandjung*] cape, point.

Tgk [*Tengku*] sir.

Thailandia Thailand.

thd [*terhadap*] toward, to.

th(n) [*tahun*] year.

T'hoa [*Tionghoa*] Chinese.

thp [*terhadap*] toward, to.

tiada 1 not. *– besar* not large. 2 is not, are not, etc. *– orang disini*, There's no one here. 3 see TIDAK. **ke–an** 1 lack, shortage. *Ia ~ uang*, He's short of money. 2 nothingness.

hilang dlm ~ all gone. **ke- -djalan kembali** no return. **ke–mampuan** 1 impotence. 2 inability. *~ pimpinan* incapability of leadership. **memper–kan, men–kan** 1 to break off, discontinue. *~ perhubungan ketempat itu* to break off communications with that place. 2 to abolish. *~ kerdja malam* to abolish the night shift. 3 to nullify s.t. 4 to deny. *Ia ~ Tuhan*, He denies the existence of God. 5 to ignore, disregard. *Ia ~ temannja*, He ignored his friend. **pen–an** 1 negation. 2 abolition, discontinuance.

tian abdomen of a pregnant woman. **ber–(an)** pregnant. **men–i** to make pregnant. *dlm –* pregnant.

tiang 1 pole. *– bendéra* flagpole. 2 post. *– pagar* fence post. 3 pillar. *– ibu rumah* the main pillars of a house. *– tanam* house pillars implanted in the ground. *– negara* pillars of state. 4 pile. **ber–** (*kpd*) to rest on. **men–i** to provide with poles. *– agung* mainmast. *– penggantungan* gallows. *– penghidupan* main source of income. *– salib* cross. *– topang* foremast.

tiap 1 every, each. *– hari* every day. *– orang* each person. 2 key money. 3 dose, dosage. **men–** to give key money. **setiap,** *–²* each, every. *sewaktu* whenever.

tiarap ber– to lie prone. **men–** to lie face downward. **men–i** to lie face downward on s.t. *Pradjurit² itu ~ tanah jg basah*, The soldiers lay face downward on the wet ground. **men–kan** to place s.o. on his stomach. *Ia ~ adiknja jg kebanjakan minum air*, He placed his brother, who had taken too much water, on his stomach. **ter–** to lie or fall face downward. *Korban bom mati ~* , The bombing victims fell dead face downward.

tiba 1 to arrive. *Ia – di Bandung dgn selamat*, He arrived safely in Bandung. 2 to arrive, come. *Saatnja tlh –*, The moment has come. **ke- -²an** suddenness. **se–nja** upon arrival. *~ dihotél ia menélpon kerumahnja*, Upon his arrival at the hotel he telephoned home. *–²* 1 suddenly. 2 unexpectedly.

tidak 1 no. *–, ia – dpt pergi*, No, he can't go. 2 not. *– besar* not big. *Ia – ada disini*, He's not here. *Ia – makan*, He isn't eating. **ke–adilan** injustice. **ke–atjuhan** indifference. **ke–benaran** 1 absence of truth. 2 inaccuracy. 3 incorrectness. **ke–bérésan** irregularity. *Ada ~ pd kantor keuangan*, There are irregularities at the finance office. **ke–déwasaan** immaturity. **ke–djelasan** lack of clarity. **ke- djudjuran** dishonesty. **ke-**

hadliran absence. **ke–mampuan** 1 impotence. 2 incapability. **ke–merataan** inequality. **ke–merdékaan** lack of freedom. **ke–normalan** abnormality. **ke–pastian** indefiniteness. **kepertjajaan** lack of confidence. **ke–puasan** dissatisfaction. **ke–rasionalan** irrationality. **ke–rélaan** unwillingness. **ke–rukunan** dissension. **ke–sabaran** impatience. **ke–samaan** inequality. **ke–seimbangan** imbalance. **ke–senangan** discontent. **ke–senonohan** impropriety. **ke–sesuaian** discrepancy. **ke–setiaan** disloyalty. **ke–setudjuan** disagreement. **ke–stabilan** instability. **ke–tentuan** uncertainty. **ke–tepatan** 1 imprecision, inexactness. 2 inappropriateness. **ke–tenteraman** 1 a lack of quiet. 2 a lack of order. **ke–tetapan** inconstancy. **ke–tjakapan** a lack of ability. **memper–kan, men–kan** 1 to deny. 2 to reject. 3 to ignore. 4 to abolish. **se–(–)nja** 1 in any case. 2 at (the) least. $\sim$ *ia akan mengirim kartupos kpd saja*, At least he'll send me a post card. –² nonsense. *Ia mengatakan hal jg $\sim$ dirapat*, He talked nonsense at the meeting. – *boléh* – 1 no doubt. – *boléh* – *bahasa Nippon akan sangat penting di Asia*, There's no doubt that Japanese will be very important in Asia. 2 must, have to, it's inevitable. *Saja harus ikut,* – *boléh* – , I must go, I can't do otherwise. – *dpt* = – = – BOLEH –. – *lain* – *bukan* nothing else than, definitely. *Penjakit ini* – *lain* – *bukan disebabkan kurang tidur*, This illness has been caused by nothing other than lack of sleep. –*... lagi* any longer, any more. *Saja* – *tinggal lagi disini*, I don't live here any more.

tidjak see PIDJAK.

tidur to sleep. *Ia* – , He's sleeping. **ber–** –² an to lie down. *Ajah sedang $\sim$ melepaskan lelah*, Dad has lain down to take a rest. **berseke–an** to have intercourse. **ke–an** 1 bed. 2 to oversleep. *Guru tak datang dikelas karena $\sim$,* The teacher didn't come to class because she overslept. **men–i** 1 to sleep on s.t. *Ia biasa $\sim$ kasur*, He's accustomed to sleeping on a mattress. 2 to sleep with s.o. **men–kan** 1 to put to bed. $\sim$ *anaknja* to put o's child to bed. 2 to lay s.t. down. $\sim$ *tongkat* to lay down a cane. **pen–** a sleepyhead. **pe(n)–an** a place to sleep. **seke–an** sleeping together, sharing the same bed. **ter–** to fall asleep. *Ia $\sim$,* He fell asleep. –² an to lie down. – *ajam* to doze. – *léna*, – *lenjap* sound-asleep. – *membungkuk* to sleep huddled up (from cold, lack

of space). – *miring* to sleep on o's side. – *njenjak* sound-asleep. – *siang* afternoon nap. – *terbungkang* to sleep stretched out. – *terkedah* to sleep on o's back with knees spread apart.

tifa a small drum.

tiga three. **ber–** to constitute a group of 3. *Kami $\sim$ tinggal dirumah ini*, We 3 are staying at this house. **ke–** 1 third. *buku jg $\sim$* the third book. $\sim$ *dari kiri* third from the left. 2 three. $\sim$ *buku itu* the 3 books. *Meréka $\sim$ pergi kerumahnja*, The 3 of them went to his house. **ke–(–)nja** all 3, the 3 of them. **men–** *hari* to celebrate the third day of a person's death. **per–an** one-third. *mendapat hasil $\sim$* to get a third of the share. **seper–** one-third. **seper–an** *malam* last third of the night, late at night. –² nja all 3. $\sim$ *djatuh disungai*, All 3 fell into the river. – *belas* 13. – *persegi* triangular. – *puluh* 30. – *ratus* 300. – *warna* the tricolor (Dutch flag).

tik see KETIK.

tika² a skein of yarn.

tikai difference. **ber–** to differ in opinion, quarrel. **men–** to contradict. **per–an** conflict, controversy, disagreement.

tikam 1 a stab with a knife or dagger. 2 sword thrust. **ber–** –² an to stab e.o. **men–** 1 to stab. $\sim$ *musuhnja dgn pisau* to stab o's opponent with a knife. 2 to hurt o's feelings. *kata² jg $\sim$ hati* words that hurt o's feelings. 3 to strike, put up a stake in a card game, etc. **men–kan** to stab with s.t. $\sim$ *tombaknja* to stab with a spear. **ter–** stabbed. *Ia mati $\sim$ didadanja*, He died from a stab in the chest. **pen–an** a stab, stabbing. **per–an** a fight with daggers or similar weapons. –**an** 1 a stab, thrust. 2 stake in gambling. – –**men–** to stab e.o.

tikar a mat made of palm leaves. **ber–kan** to sleep on. – *bantal* bedding. – *ladang* a rough woven mat. – *sembahjang* prayer mat. – *tidur* sleeping mat.

tikung **men–** to curve, bend to the left or right. –**an** a curve.

tikus mouse, rat. –**an** a squib. –**² an** toy mouse. – *belanda* guinea pig. – *kesturi* a stink mouse. – *mondok* a mole. – *tanah* field mouse.

tilam mattress. **ber–** *pasir* homeless. *djatuh diatas* – to be in luck.

tilem–timbul up and down.

tilgram telegram. **men–** to send a telegram.

tilgrap telegraph.

tilik **men–** 1 to observe carefully,

watch. *Ia ~ mukanja dimuka tjermin,* She observed her face carefully in the mirror. 2 to consider, regard. *Ia ~ perbuatan itu sebagai perbuatan jg salah,* He regarded that act as an evil deed. 3 to distinguish s.t. *Hakim itu ~ warna dan agama,* The judge distinguished color and creed. 4 to supervise. *~ orang bekerdja, pengeluaran* to supervise workers, expenditures. 5 to prophesy, tell fortunes. *~ rupanja mabuk,* He looked drunk. 6 to pay a visit. *Ia datang ~ ibunja,* He came to visit his mother. **me-n-²** to peer. **pen-** 1 supervisor, inspector. 2 clairvoyant. **pen-an** 1 supervision, control. *dibawah ~ pemerintah* under government control. 2 opinion. *pd ~ saja* in my opinion. **-an** 1 observation. 2 examination. 3 control, supervision. *baik -nja* keen-eyed. *djahat -nja* to have an evil look. *kurang -nja* not very strict. *pd -nja* in his opinion.

tilp. [*tilpon*] telephone.

tilpon see TÉLPON.

tim pe-an pan for boiling rice.

timah tin. *- daun* tin foil. *- hitam* lead. *- sari* zinc. *- wurung* bismuth.

timang me-n-² 1 to observe by holding in the hand. *Ia ~ barang itu sebelum membelinja,* He looked at it carefully in his hand before he bought it. 2 to coddle, pet. *Ia suka ~ anaknja,* She likes to coddle her child. 3 to lull. *Ia ~ anaknja supaja tidur,* She lulled her son to sleep. **-(-)an** mother's pet.

timba 1 pail, bucket. 2 dipper. **ber-karang** to start a row. **men-** to scoop out, bail, water. **pen-** 1 a scoop, bucket for scooping s.t. out. 2 o. who scoops out water, etc. **pen-an** scooping, dipping.

timbal balancing. **ber-** 1 to be in balance. *Beratnja ~ ,* The weights are in balance. 2 to be on both sides. *Pohon² itu berdiri ~ djalan,* Trees stand on both sides of the road. *~ balik* to be on both sides. **ber-an** *dgn* to be the equal of. *Ia dipelihara ~ dgn anaknja sendiri,* He was treated like a real son. **ber- -²an** to respond to e.o. *Meréka menjanji ~ ,* They sang contrapuntally. **men-i** to counterbalance s.t. **se-** in balance. *Besarnja tak ~ ,* They are not of the same weight. **-an** (counter)balance. *- balik* 1 on both sides. *Kertas itu tertulis pd -baliknja,* This paper is written on on both sides. 2 mutual. *Meréka bersurat²an - balik,* They are carrying on a mutual correspondence.

timbang balance. **ber-** to exchange. *~ kata* to exchange words. *~ pandang* to exchange glances. *~ rasa* to be sympathetic. *~ tanda* to exchange engagement rings. **ber-an** *dgn* commensurate with. *upah jg ~ dgn djasanja* a salary commensurate with his services. **kese-an** 1 harmony, balance. 2 stability, equilibrium. **memper-kan** = MEN-KAN. **men-** 1 to consider, take into account. *~ bhw ...* considering that ... *Ia ~ perlu utk mengadakan rapat,* He considered it necessary to call a meeting. 2 to weigh. *Ia sedang ~ beras,* He's weighing the rice. **men-i** 1 to repay, counterbalance. *Utk ~ kebaikannja saja memberi uang Rp. 500 kepadanja,* To repay his kindness I gave him 500 rupiahs. 2 to be in proportion to. *Upahnja ~ usahanja,* His salary was in proportion to his efforts. **men-kan** 1 to consider, weigh. *Parlemén ~ soal itu,* Parliament is considering that matter. 2 to hand over for consideration. *Meréka ~ soal itu kpd Mahkamah Agung,* They handed that matter over to the Supreme Court for its consideration. **men-terimakan** to hand over, transfer. *~ djabatan* to hand over an office or post. **menje-kan** to harmonize, balance. **pen-** 1 pair of scales. 2 counselor. **per-an** 1 judgment, opinion. *~ nilai* value judgment. *menurut ~ saja* in my opinion. 2 consideration. *~ rochaniah* psychological consideration. 3 review. **se-** 1 in balance. *Beratnja ~ ,* The weight's balanced. 2 in proportion. *Ongkosnja ~ dgn beratnja pekerdjaan,* The cost is in proportion to the hard labor. **-an** 1 pair of scales. *~ daging* meat scales. 2 opinion, criticism. *~ buku* book review. 3 equal. *Ia bukan ~ pd suaminja jg terpeladjar itu,* She isn't the equal of her educated husband. 4 rather than. *~ diam tidak ada kerdja, dan spj tidak merasa kesal* rather than do nothing and get bored. *- -men-* to weigh, consider carefully. *- rasa* 1 sympathy. 2 confidence. *- terima* transfer. *- terima pimpinan* the transfer of command. *- tunai* C.O.D.

timbau men- to add a piece.

timbil a sty in the eye.

timbrung men- to interfere in s.o.'s affairs.

timbul 1 to rise, appear. *penulis jg baru - an* up-and-coming writer. 2 to emerge, come up. *- perasaan jg tidak énak,* An unpleasant feeling emerged. **men-kan** 1 to cause, bring about. *~ kekatjauan* to bring about chaos. 2 to lead to. *Kedjadian² itu* *dpt* ∼ *perang*, Those events can lead to war. 3 to make come to the surface. ∼ *barang jg sdh lama ditanam* to bring to the surface things that have long been in the ground. ∼ *ketjurigaan* to arouse suspicion. **pen**– mercury rubbed onto the body to produce invulnerability. – *bulan ini* the new moon. – *marah* to become angry. – *tenggelam* 1 to rise and sink, go up and down. – *-tenggelam keradjaan²* rise and fall of kingdoms. 2 to be heavily in debt. 3 unsure.

timbun heap, pile. **ber–(-)** 1 to pile up. *Bukunja* ∼ , His books were piling up. 2 to be buried under, covered with. *Djenazahnja* ∼ *pasir*, The corpse was covered with sand. **men–i** to fill s.t. up, bring s.t. over. **men–(kan)** 1 to heap, pile up s.t. ∼ *tanah* to pile up dirt. 2 to accumulate s.t. *Ia* ∼ *bahan makanan*, He accumulated food supplies. 3 to hoard. 4 to accumulate, pile up. *Hartanja* ∼ , His wealth accumulated. **pen–** a hoarder. **pen–an** 1 accumulation, piling up. 2 hoarding. **se–** a pile. ∼ *pasir* a pile of sand. ∼ *kaju* pile of wood. **ter–** 1 piled, heaped up. *Barangnja* ∼ *dimuka rumahnja*, His goods were piled up in front of his house. 2 buried under, covered with. *Badannja* ∼ *pasir*, His body was buried under sand. **–an** a pile, heap.

timbus **men–** to bury, cover over.

timpa **ber–** –² to pour in, come in stacks. ∼ *suratnja jg datang*, The letters came pouring in. ∼ *bola* to pass, throw a ball back and forth. **men–** 1 to strike, fall on. *Batu besar* ∼ *kakinja*, A big stone struck his foot. 2 to strike, hit. *Ketjelakaan* ∼ *keluarganja*, An accident struck his family. ∼ *musuhnja dgn pedang* to hit o's opponent with a sword. 3 to steal, pilfer. ∼ *barang² digudang* to pilfer goods from a warehouse. **men–kan** 1 to drop s.t. on. ∼ *batu kekakinja* to drop a stone on o's foot. 2 to blame. *Ia* ∼ *segala kekeliruan kpd temannja*, He blamed all his mistakes on his friend.

timpal see TIMBAL.

timpang 1 lame. *Kakinja –*, He's lame in the legs. 2 defective, unstable. *Médja itu –, kakinja hanja tiga*, That table is unstable; it has only 3 legs. 3 to limp. *Ia – djalannja*, He's limping. 4 biased. *pendapat jg –* a biased opinion. 5 unbalanced. *keadaan jg –* an unbalanced situation. **ke–an** 1 lameness. 2 defect. 3 partiality. **men–** to limp. *Mengapa ia* ∼ *?* Why is he limping? **men–(-)kan** to pretend to

limp. ∼ *kakinja* to cause o's leg to limp.

timpas dried up. *sumur* – a dry well.

timpuh see SIMPUH.

timpuk **men–** to throw s.t. at s.o.

timpus pointed, tapering.

timur east, oriental. **ke–an** eastern, oriental. *lagu* ∼ oriental song. **men–** to the east, eastward. – *Dekat* Near East. – *Djauh* Far East. – *laut* northeast. – *menenggara* east-southeast. – *Tengah* Middle East. – *tenggara* east-southeast.

tin can, tin. *susu* – canned milk.

tindak act, action. **ber–** 1 to take steps, measures. *Polisi* ∼ *keras thd perampok itu*, The police took harsh measures against the robbers. 2 to act. *Ia tak berani* ∼ *kalau tak ada perintah*, He wouldn't have dared act if he hadn't been ordered to. **men–kan** to carry out, practice. ∼ *kekerasan* to practice strong measures. **se–** o. step. ∼ *demi* ∼ step by step. **–an** 1 measure, step. ∼ *darurat* emergency measure. 2 action. ∼ *jg njata* a clear action. ∼ *kelandjutan* follow-up. ∼ *pelaksanaan* executive action. – *perkosa* act of God (*force majeure*). – *pidana* criminal act. – *tanduk* behavior.

tindas **men–** 1 to oppress. ∼ *rakjatnja* to oppress the people. 2 to subdue, suppress, crush. ∼ *pemberontakan* to crush a revolt. **pen–** oppressor. **pen–an** 1 oppression. 2 suppression. **–an** 1 oppression. 2 suppression. 3 copy. ∼ *surat* copy of a letter.

tindih **ber–(-)** 1 to lie on e.o. *Korban pengeboman mati* ∼ , The dead victims of the bombings lay on e.o. 2 dense, crowded. *Orang* ∼ *dipasar*, It was very crowded in the market. **ke–an** 1 pressed, caught. *Badannja* ∼ *pohon rebah*, His body was caught under a fallen tree. 2 to have a cramp. *Kakinja* ∼ , He had a cramp in his leg. **men–** 1 to press. ∼ *kertas jg kerenjut* to press a crumpled piece of paper. 2 to suppress. ∼ *perasaan hati* to suppress o's feelings. 3 to oppress. *padjak jg* ∼ *rakjat* an oppressive tax. **pen–** oppressor. ∼ *kertas* paperweight. **pen–an** 1 oppression. 2 suppression. 3 copy. **–an** 1 pressure. ∼ *jg berat* a heavy pressure. 2 oppression. 3 copy. ∼ *surat ini* a copy of this letter.

tindik **ber–** to pierce. *upatjara* ∼ *telinga* ear-piercing ceremony. **men–telinga** to pierce the ear.

tindis **men–** 1 to oppress. 2 to suppress. **pen-** bully. **(pen)-an** oppression.

tindja feces, excrement.

tindjau ber- -² to observe, be on o's guard. **men-** 1 to observe, make a study, a survey, of s.t. *Wakil pemerintah pusat ~ keadaan ditempat,* A central government representative studied the local situation. 2 to watch, observe at a distance. ~ *kapal liwat* to watch a passing ship. 3 to view, look at, consider. ~ *dari sudut ékonomi soal ini boléh disebut kurang penting,* Looking at it from an economic point of view, this problem can be called unimportant. 4 to scout, reconnoiter. 5 to guess. *Ia dpt ~ perasaan ajahnja,* He could guess his father's feelings. ~ *kembali* 1 to contemplate. 2 to reconsider. **pen-** observer. **pen-an** 1 observation. 2 consideration, contemplation. 3 reconnoitering. ~ *kembali* 1 a review. 2 revision. **-an** 1 observation. 2 contemplation. ~ *buku* book review.

tindju 1 fist. 2 boxing match, fight. *Nanti malam ada -,* There's boxing tonight. **ber-, men-** to box. **pe(n)-** a boxer. **per-an** boxing match. **ter-** a knockout.

ting a tinkling sound. -² sweetmeat. ~ *katjang* sweetmeat made of sugared peanuts.

tinggal 1 to live, stay. *Ia – di Garut,* He lives in Garut. *Saudara – dimana?* Where do you live? 2 to be left, remaining. *Sepuluh jg – akan saja kirim bésok,* I'll send the remaining 10 tomorrow. *Uangnja – berapa?* How much money do you have left? *5 diambil 3 – 2,* 5 minus 3 leaves 2. 3 to be behind. *Ia – djauh dlm peladjarannja,* He is far behind in his studies. 4 to remain, keep, stay. *Ia – diam,* He remained quiet. *Djangan – diam, ambillah tindakan,* Don't sit still, do s.t. *Teman – teman,* A friend remains a friend. 5 past, gone, receded. *Masa jg tlh – tak akan kembali lagi,* The time which has passed won't return. 6 to remain, be up to. *Sekarang – pd kamu utk menolak atau menerimanja,* Now it's up to you to reject or accept it. 7 it remains for s.o. *Kamu – menandatangani sadja,* It just remains for you to sign. *Kartjisnja sdh dibeli, kamu – berangkat sadja,* The tickets have been purchased; all you have to do is go. 8 except. *Semua sdh disini? Sdh, – engkau,* All here? All except you. **di-kan** *mati (oléh)* to be left alone by the death

(of). **ke-an** 1 remainder. ~*nja akan saja berikan lain kali,* I'll give you the remainder another time. 2 to be left out, omitted. *Dua hal jg ~ ,* Two matters were left out. *Dua kalimat ~ tidak ditik,* Two sentences were omitted in the typing. 3 to be forgotten. *Bukunja ~ dirumah,* She forgot her book at the house. 4 to be left behind, miss. *Ia ~ bus,* She missed the bus. 5 to be behind. *Negeri itu sangat ~ dlm hal téknik,* That country is very much behind in technical matters. ~ *zaman* behind the times, old-fashioned. 6 to be remiss. *Ia tak ~ meramaikan hari itu,* He wasn't remiss in celebrating that day. **men-** *(dunia)* to die, pass away. *Ia tlh lama ~ ,* He died a long time ago. **men-i** 1 to live in, stay at. *Ia sdh lama ~ rumah itu,* He's lived in that house for a long time. 2 to leave behind, bequeath. *Ia ~ anaknja sebidang tanah,* He left his son a piece of land. **men-kan** 1 to leave (behind). *Ia ~ dua anak,* He left 2 children. 2 to leave. *Ia ~ negerinja,* He left his country. *Ia ~ pekerdjaannja,* He left his job. *Kapan ia ~ rumahnja?* When did he leave his house? 3 to leave in the lurch. 4 to forget. *Ia tidak ~ adat waktu menemui mentuanja,* He didn't forget his good manners when he met his in-laws. **pen-** 1 death, passing away. 2 separation. **pen-an** 1 estate, inheritance. 2 remains (archaeological). 3 remainder, rest. **sepen-** after the departure of, in the absence of. **ter-** left (behind). *Pajung ~ dirumah,* The umbrella was left at home. **-an** 1 inheritance. 2 remainder, rest. ~ *kepopak salak* broke, on the rocks. ~ *nadi* critically ill. ~ *tulang* very thin.

tinggi 1 high. *menara – a* high tower. *pegawai –* high official. 2 tall. *berbadan –* to be tall. 3 height. *-nja 8 méter,* The height is 8 meters. 4 advanced. *umur jg tlh –* an advanced age, along in years. *peradaban jg –* advanced civilization. 5 high, expensive. *harga –* high prices. 6 higher. *perguruan –* higher education, university. **ke-an** 1 too high. *Tempatnja ~ ,* The place is too high. 2 podium. *Ia bitjara dari ~ itu,* He spoke from the podium. 3 height, elevation. 4 boastful. ~ *tjakapnja* boastful language. **memper-** 1 to heighten. 2 to enlarge. **memperkan** *diri* to boast. **men-** 1 to go higher. *Matahari makin ~ ,* The sun rose higher and higher. 2 to advance, rise (in position). 3 to boast, be boastful. *Pertjakapannja makin* ∼ , His conversation became more and more boastful. *Ia selalu* ∼ *thd teman²nja*, He was always boasting to his friends. **men–kan** 1 to raise, heighten. 2 to increase. **pe–** village headman. **pen–an** heightening, raising. ∼ *taraf hidup* raising of living standards. **ter–** highest, supreme. – *awan* sky-high. – *hari* late in the morning. – *hati* 1 proud, boastful. 2 conceited. – *rasi* to have a lucky star. – *tjakapnja* to brag.

tinggir see TÉNGGÉR.

tinggung ber– to squat.

tingkah 1 behavior, action. *Ia baik –nja*, His behavior is good. 2 caprice, whim. *gadis jg banjak –nja* a girl of many whims. 3 k.o. drum. **ber–** 1 to act foolishly, do foolish things. *Hati² dikota besar, djangan* ∼ , Be careful in a big city; don't do foolish things. 2 to be capricious. 3 to act up. *Motor itu sdh* ∼ *pula*, The engine has begun to act up again. 4 to take turns, alternate. *Meréka* ∼ *memperdengarkan piano dan gitar*, They played the piano and guitar by turns. **men–(i)** 1 to accompany. ∼ *njanjian dgn gitar* to accompany a song with the guitar. 2 to object to, contradict. ∼ *aturan pemerintah* to object to a government regulation. 3 to respond to. *Ia* ∼ *permintaan ibunja*, She responded to her mother's request. **–an** accompaniment in music. – *laku*, – *langkah*, – *perangai* behavior.

tingkal borax.

tingkalak fish trap.

tingkap small window, peephole. **–an** porthole.

tingkat 1 floor, story. *rumah tiga –* a 3-story house. 2 class. *pegawai negeri – tiga* a third-class government official. 3 level, class, degree. *kebudajaan jg tinggi –nja* a high level of civilization. 4 rung, step. *tangga sepuluh –* a 10-rung ladder. 5 ship's deck. 6 phase, stage. **ber– –²** 1 multistoried. *Rumahnja* ∼ , He has a multistoried house. 2 stratified. *masjarakat jg* ∼ a stratified society. 3 terraced. *sawah jg* ∼ terraced wet rice fields. 4 in stages, phased. *Pekerdjaan ini harus dikerdjakan* ∼ , This job must be done in stages. **men–** 1 to climb, ascend. ∼ *pohon* to climb a tree. ∼ *tangga* to ascend steps. 2 to rise, mount. *Panasnja* ∼ , The temperature rose. *Harga beras* ∼ , The price of rice went up. 3 to be promoted, advance. *Ia* ∼ *kelasnja*, He was promoted a class higher. 4 to

increase. *Hébatnja* ∼ , His violence increased. *Umurnja* ∼ , He became older. 5 to terrace. *Petani* ∼ *sawahnja*, The farmer terraced his wet rice field. **me-n–²** 1 to keep increasing. 2 to terrace. *Ia* ∼ *sawahnja*, He terraced his rice field. **men–kan** to increase s.t. ∼ *produksi* to increase production. ∼ *pemasukan* to increase income. **se–** o. level. *Ia naik* ∼ , He advanced o. level. *Kamarnja* ∼ *dgn kamar saja*, Our rooms are on the same floor. **–an** 1 floor, story. 2 class, level. 3 stage, phase. ∼ *permulaan* initial stage. ∼ *terachir* final phase. – *tiga* Third Estate (French Revolution).

tinta ink.

Tionghoa Chinese. **ke–an** Chinese. – *peranakan* Indonesian Chinese. – *totok* newly arrived Chinese in Indonesia.

Tiongkok China.

tip a tip. **ment–** to write on a typewriter.

tipar dry rice field.

tipifikasi typification.

tipis 1 thin, worn thin. *kertas jg –* thin paper. 2 slight, slim. *harapan jg –* a slight hope. *keuntungan jg –* a slight profit. 3 low, slight. *Persediaan makanan sdh –*, The food supply is running low. 4 fine (of thread). 5 sheer (of material). **men–** 1 to become thin. 2 to run low. **men–kan** 1 to make s.t. thin. *Ia* ∼ *kaju*, He thinned out the wood. 2 to thin, dilute s.t. 3 to reduce, decrease. ∼ *keinginan utk menjerang* to reduce the desire to attack. – *telinga* 1 touchy, irritable. 2 sensitive.

tipu 1 trick, stratagem, ruse. 2 deceit. **men–** to deceive, trick. **pen–** deceiver, impostor. **pen–an** deception, swindle. – *daja* deceit, trickiness. – *mata* optical illusion. – *tépok* ruse, trick.

tir tar. see TÉR.

tirah see TETIRAH. **pe–an** health resort.

tirai 1 curtain. 2 partition. – *Bambu* Bamboo Curtain. – *bantal* pillow fringe. – *Besi* Iron Curtain. – *kelambu* mosquito curtain. – *mirai* curtains of all sorts.

tirakat ber– to lead an ascetic religious life.

tiram oyster. **pe–an** oyster field or bed.

tiras ravel.

tirau gnome.

tiris to leak through. *Atapnja –*, The roof is leaking. **ke–an** 1 to get wet from a leak. *Kamarnja basah* ∼ *hudjan*, The room got wet from a leak. 2 a leak. **men–kan** to cause to leak. **–an** a leak.

tirta holy water. – *kentjana* golden water.

tiru men–(kan) 1 to imitate. ~ *tanda tangan* to imitate, copy a signature. 2 to echo. ~ *tiap kata* to echo each word. **–an** 1 imitation, copying. 2 counterfeit, forgery. – *teladan* example.

tisik men– to darn, mend. ~ *kaus jg lobang* to mend a hole in a stocking. **–an** a mend.

titah royal word, utterance. **ber–** to speak, utter. **men–kan** to command, commission, s.o.

titar ber– –² to move quickly back and forth.

titel 1 title. 2 article, column heading. **ber–** 1 to have a degree. *Ia* ~ *dokter,* He has a medical degree. 2 titled. *seorang jg* ~ titled person.

titi wooden or bamboo bridge. **men–** to cross s.t. narrow. ~ *djambatan jg sempit* to cross a small narrow bridge. ~ *batang kaju,* ~ *buih,* – *kawat* to perform a very difficult task. **–an** bridge.

titik 1 drop. 2 period, point. *mena–ruh* – *diachir kalimat* to place a period at the end of a sentence. **ber–** 1 to drip. *Darahnja masih* ~ *,* The blood is still dripping. 2 to have a period. *Kalimat ini tidak* ~ *,* This sentence has no period. **men–** 1 to drip. *Darahnja terus-menerus* ~ *,* The blood drips continuously. 2 to place a period. 3 to hammer on s.t. ~ *besi* to hammer on iron. **men–beratkan** 1 to stress, emphasize. 2 to reckon on. *Negeri itu* ~ *pem–bélaannja kpd 2 kapal perang,* That country reckoned heavily on 2 warships for its defense. **men–i** to sprinkle. ~ *luka dgn obat* to sprinkle medicine on the wound. **men–kan** to cause to drip, fall in drops. – *air mata* teardrop. – *api* focus (of a lens). – *beku* the freezing point. – *berat* 1 center of gravity. 2 heart, center. – *berat dari pembélaan negeri itu dipusatkan kpd kekuatan angkatan udara,* The heart of the country's defense was centered in the air force. – *darah penghabisan* last drop of blood. – *didih* boiling point. – *dua* colon (punctuation). – *kata* decision. – *koma* semicolon. – *lebur* melting point. – *lidah* a saying. – *mata* point of view. – *nol* zero. – *pangkal* basic stand from which to initiate a discussion. – *perubahan pokok* turning point. – *pusat* center. – *seléra* to have o's mouth water. – *tjair* the melting

point. – *tolak* point of departure. *tidak karuan* – *komanja* unfathomable, difficult to figure out.

titimangsa 1 chronicle. 2 date.

titinada musical note.

titip men–(kan) 1 to entrust to s.o. ~ *barang pd teman* to entrust s.t. to a friend. 2 to deposit. ~ *uang dibank* to deposit money in a bank. **pen–an** storage place. ~ *pakaian* cloakroom. **–an** 1 deposit. 2 deposited goods.

titir signal of an alarm. **ke–an** a pigeon. **men–** to beat a drum. **–an** 1 propeller. 2 k.o. mill.

titis a drop. **men–** 1 to drip. 2 to incarnate. **men–i** to sprinkle. ~ *luka dgn obat* to sprinkle medicine on a wound. **men–kan** to sprinkle s.t. on s.o. or s.t. **pen–an** reincarnation. **–an** (re)incarnation. ~ *péna* essay, composition. – *air* a drop of water.

titit sound made by car or motorcycle horn.

titulatur terms of address.

tituler titular. *kaptén* – o. who holds the title of captain but does not execute the functions of his military rank.

tiup 1 a fan. 2 blowing (of wind). **ber–** to blow. *Angin* ~ *sepandjang malam,* The wind blew the whole night. **men–** 1 to blow. ~ *pluit* to blow a whistle. 2 to blow s.t. up. ~ *balon²an* to blow up a balloon. 3 to blow, play. ~ *trompét* to play a trumpet. **men–i** 1 to blow on s.t. ~ *api* to blow on a fire. 2 to treat with magic, blow on. *Dukun itu* ~ *orang jg sakit,* The medicine man treated the patient with magic. **men–kan** 1 to blow glass. 2 to fan, stir up s.t. **pen–** *gelas* glass blower. **–an** blowing, blast (of wind). *kwintét* – wind quintet.

tiwas see TÉWAS.

tiwikrama ber– to do o's utmost.

tjabai red pepper. **ke–an** 1 to feel hot from eating red peppers. 2 to feel ill at ease. – *rawit* cayenne pepper. *mendapat* – *rawit* to be severely criticized, scolded. *ketjil²* – *rawit* a small but enraged person.

tjabang 1 branch. – *pohon* tree branch. *kantor* – branch office. 2 subdivision, unit. 3 wing of a house or building. **ber–** 1 to have branches. *Maskapai ini* ~ *diseluruh negeri,* This company has branches all over the country. *Pohon ini tak* ~ *,* This tree has no branches. 2 to branch off, split. *Disitu djalan itu* ~ *,* The road branches off there. **ber– –²** to have many branches, subdivisions. **men–kan** to inoculate. **per–an** branch-

ing, fork(ing). ~ *djalan* crossroads.
~ *sungai* fork of a river.
tjabar 1 insipid, flat. 2 reckless.
men–kan *hati* to discourage s.o. –
hati 1 discouraged, dejected. 2 cowardly.
tjabé see TJABAI.
tjabik torn, snagged. **men–** to tear
up. ~ *arang,* ~ *mulut* to cry out,
scream. **men–kan** *badju didada* to
disclose o's secret shame. **–an** a tear,
snag, split. **–²** in tatters, worn to
shreds.
tjabir see TJABIK. **ber–an** in shreds,
in tatters.
tjabit see TJABIK.
tjabo prostitute.
tjabuh in an uproar.
tjabuk 1 see TJAMBUK. 2 ulcer.
tjabul 1 indecent, disgusting. *sikap* –
a disgusting attitude. 2 indecent,
pornographic. *gambar* – pornographic
photo. 3 see TJÉBOL. **ber–** to rage,
prevail. *Penjakit koléra sedang* ~
disana, Cholera is raging there. **ke–an**
1 pornography. 2 obscenity. **men–i**
to violate, outrage a woman. **pen–an**
violation, outrage.
tjabur see TJEBUR. **ke–an** misery,
fear.
tjabut **ber–** drawn, extracted. **men–**
1 to draw. ~ *pistol* to draw a gun.
~ *kartu* to draw a card. 2 to pull
out, extract. ~ *gigi* to pull teeth.
~ *rumput* to pull up grass. ~ *untung*
to extract a profit. 3 to revoke,
cancel, rescind. ~ *undang²* *lama* to
revoke old laws. ~ *malu* to save o's
face. *Tuhan* ~ *njawanja,* God took
his life. **men–i** to pluck at, keep
pulling. *Sepandjang hari ia* ~ *djang-*
gotnja, All day long he plucked at his
beard. ~ *rumput* to keep pulling up
grass. **men–kan** to pull out for s.o.
Ia ~ *adiknja rumput,* He pulled up
grass for his little brother. **pen–an**
1 revocation. 2 cancellation. – *lari*
to flee, scram. *Mari kita* – *lari,*
Let's go. (Let's hit the road.)
tjadang **men–(kan)** 1 to reserve s.t.
~ *tempat duduk utk tamu* to reserve
seats for the guests. 2 to lay aside,
place in reserve. ~ *uang utk hari*
tua to lay aside money for o's old
age. 3 to nominate, propose. ~
seorang utk diréktur to nominate s.o.
as director. 4 to propose, put forward. ~ *usul* to put forward a
proposal. 5 to plan. ~ *rentjana*
baru to plan a new project. **pen–**
proposer, o. who moves adoption of a
motion. **pen–an** 1 reserve. 2 nomination. **–an** 1 reserve. ~ *emas* gold
reserves. *uang* ~ reserve fund.

pasukan ~ reserve troops. 2 proposal. ~ *perdamaian* peace proposal.
3 vote. ~ *tidak pertjaja* a vote of
no confidence. 4 project, plan. – *10*
tahun a 10-year plan.
tjadar 1 veil. 2 sheet. **ber–** veiled.
tjadas rocky area.
tjadok nearsighted.
tjaéng 400 liters.
tjagak 1 post or pillar used for
support. – *potrét* tripod for camera.
– *télpon* telephone pole. 2 crossing.
– *djalan* crossroads. **ber–** 1 branched,
forked. *djalan* ~ forked road. 2
supported. *Témbok ini* ~ *besi,* This
wall is supported by iron props.
men– to support. ~ *témbok supaja*
tidak rubuh to support a wall to
prevent it from falling. **ter–** 1 supported, on a stand. *Pemotrétan ini*
tidak akan bergerak karena ~ , This
camera won't move because it's on
a stand. 2 to rise, loom. *Gedong jg*
indah ~ *dimuka matanja,* A beautiful
building loomed before his eyes. –
hidup life annuity.
tjagar security, pledge. **men–kan** to
offer s.t. as security. **–an** 1 security.
2 guarantee. – *alam* natural preserve.
tjagut **men–** to peck, bite. *Burung*
~ *djari saja,* The bird pecked at my
finger.
tjah oh!
tjahaja 1 radiance, brilliance. 2 shine,
gleam, glow. **ber–** to gleam, shine,
radiate. **men–i** to illuminate s.t.
2 to expose (film). **men–kan** to cause
to shine, radiate. **pen–an** illumination, lighting. – *madjemuk* light consisting of component parts (physics).
– *mata* sweetheart. – *muka* complexion.
tjahar **men–** to take a laxative.
pen– purgative.
tjahari see TJARI.
tjaing² in tatters. **men– –²** to tear
to bits.
tjair 1 liquid, fluid. 2 thin, weak
(of liquids). **men–** to become liquid.
men–kan to liquefy. **pen–** solvent.
–an liquid. ~ *malam* liquid wax.
tjais rein(s).
tjaja see TJAHAJA.
tjak 1 sound of smacking the lips in
tasting food. 2 form of address used
in calling a pedicab driver. –, *bétjak*
ke Salemba berapa? Driver, how
much to Salemba?
tjakal-bakal founder of a Javanese
village.
tjakalélé war dance in East Indonesia.
tjakap 1 able, capable. *Ia* – *men-*
djalankan tugasnja, He was able to

carry out his task. 2 handsome, good-looking. *Ia - sekali rupanja*, He looked very handsome. 3 talk, language. - *Inggeris* English. 4 prattle, rubbish. **ber-** 1 to talk. *Ia pandai ~ Inggeris*, He speaks English very well. *Djangan banjak ~*, Don't talk too much. 2 to be able, capable. *Ia ~ mengalahkan musuhnja*, He was able to defeat his enemy. *~ perut* to ventriloquize. **ber- -²** to chat, chatter, talk. *Ia ~ , tidak beladjar*, He's chatting, not studying. **ke-an** 1 ability. 2 capacity to do s.t. *~²* skills. **memper-kan** 1 to discuss, talk about s.t. *~ soal politik* to discuss political matters. 2 to speak. *Ia pandai ~ bahasa itu*, He was good at speaking the language. 3 to enable. **per-an** 1 conversation. *bahasa ~* the spoken language. 2 discussion. - *angin* 1 empty talk, nonsense. 2 boasting. - *olah-alih*, - *pantjaroba* inconsequential chatter. - *tinggi* boasting.

tjakar 1 claw (of animals and birds). 2 paw. **ber-** 1 to have claws. *Garuda ~*, An eagle has claws. 2 to fight. *Ia sedang ~ dgn suaminja*, She's fighting with her husband. **ber- -²an** 1 to scratch e.o. 2 to fight, quarrel. **men-** 1 to scratch, scrape (of chickens in search of food). 2 to claw (of a lion, tiger, or cat). *~ langit* very high. **pen-** *awan*, *~ langit* skyscraper. - *ajam* poor handwriting. - *balar*, - *bara* scratches all over the body.

tjakatan see TJEKATAN.

tjakera(m) see TJAKRA(M).

tjakerawala 1 firmament, atmosphere. 2 rotation of heavenly bodies. *dibawah* - under the sky.

tjaklat 1 dammit! 2 unfortunate, too bad.

tjakra(m) discus. - *optik* optical disk.

tjakrawati **ke-an** rule, sway.

tjakup **men-** 1 to catch, grasp. 2 to scoop, ladle s.t. out. **men-kan** to scoop with s.t. **pen-** a trap. **-an** scooping.

tjal shawl.

tjalak 1 chic, stylish. 2 to walk away.

tjalar a scratch.

tjalit stain, spot. **ber-** stained, dirty.

tjalok 1 recruiter for jitneys. 2 ticket scalper.

tjalon 1 candidate, aspirant. 2 applicant. 3 recruit. **men-kan** to nominate s.o. **pen-an** 1 nomination. 2 candidacy. - *guru* student teacher. - *ibu* mother-to-be. - *opsir* cadet. - *penerbang* fledgling pilot. - *penulis*

would-be writer. - *tertanggung* prospective insured person.

tjalus 1 to slip, get away. 2 loose. **men-kan** to let get away.

tjam 1 see KETJAM. 2 interested, taken by. *Ia tak berapa - akan usul itu*, He wasn't very much interested in the proposal. **men-kan** 1 to note, observe carefully. *Ia ~ naséhat ajahnja*, He carefully noted his father's advice. 2 to criticize. *~ tindakan pemerintah* to criticize the government's actions. *~ pd* to remind s.o. of s.t. *Ia ~ pd teman²nja supaja bekerdja keras*, He reminded his friends to work hard. 3 to review.

tjamat subdistrict head (= ASSISTÉN-WEDANA). **ke-an** subdistrict (administrative unit).

tjambang side whiskers. **ber-** to have whiskers.

tjambuk a whip. **men-** to beat, strike with a whip.

tjambul see TJEMBUL.

tjambung 1 a large basin. 2 tureen.

tjampah flat, insipid.

tjampak a throw, toss. **men-(kan)** 1 to throw, toss. *~ tombak pd musuhnja* to throw a spear at o's enemy. 2 to throw out. *~ djala* to throw out a net. - *buang* javelin.

tjampin skillful, handy.

tjamping in rags, tattered.

tjampung 1 lopped off (of a tree branch). 2 clipped (of bushes). 3 see TJEMPLUNG.

tjampur mixed, blended. **ber-** mixed. *susu ~ air* milk mixed with water. *~ darah* of mixed blood. *Ia ~ darah dgn bangsa Swédia*, He also has Swedish blood. *~ baur*, *~ gaul* to associate, have social contact with. *~ tangan* to be involved in. **men-** 1 to mix. *~ air dgn minjak* to mix oil and water. 2 to mix, mingle. **men-i** 1 to participate, join in. *~ perdébatan* to participate in debating. 2 to interfere, meddle in. 3 to mix. *~ mas dgn tembaga* to mix gold with brass. **men-kan** 1 to mix, mingle, blend. 2 to confuse, mix up. **men-adukkan** 1 to mix (up). 2 to confuse. **per-an** 1 interference, meddling. 2 social intercourse. 3 mixing. **-an** 1 intervention. 2 interference, meddling. 3 intercourse. 4 alloy. 5 medley. - *aduk* 1 mixed. 2 medley. 3 confused. - *baur*, - *gaul* 1 mixed (up). *Buku² masih - baur*, The books are all mixed up. 2 to associate with. - *bitjara*, - *mulut* to enter into the conversation. - *tangan* 1 to interfere in, invade the rights of others. 2 intervention.

tjamuk **men–** to stab.

tjanai **men–** to sharpen on a grindstone.

tjanang crier's cymbal. **men–kan** to announce, proclaim. **pen–** crier. **–an** 1 summons. 2 description.

tjanda 1 joke. 2 whim, caprice. **ber–** to joke.

tjandi 1 Hindu temple. 2 shrine, monument.

tjandra moon.

tjandu 1 opium (ready for use). 2 addicted to. *Ia – main golf,* He's addicted to playing golf. **ke–an** addicted. **men–** 1 to smoke opium. 2 to become addicted to s.t. *Ia tlh ~ pd minum kopi,* He has become addicted to drinking coffee. **pe–** 1 fan, devotee. 2 addict. *~ bioskop* dyed-in-the-wool moviegoer. 3 = PEN–. **pen–** opium smoker.

tjandung a meat cleaver.

tjangak see TJONGAK.

tjangap groove.

tjanggah 1 two-pronged pitchfork. 2 great-great-grandchild.

tjanggai long fingernail (natural or artificial) as a decoration.

tjanggung 1 uneasy, insecure, unsafe. *Ia merasa – mengendarai mobil dikota jg ramai itu,* He felt uneasy driving in that busy city. 2 awkward, clumsy. *Ia – benar naik sepéda,* He is awkward on a bicycle. 3 embarrassed, bashful. *Ia selalu merasa – ber-tjakap² dgn gurunja,* He always feels embarrassed when talking with his teacher. 4 ill-mannered, improper. *Perkataannja kasar dan –,* His words were coarse and ill-mannered. 5 insufficient, inadequate. *kepandaian jg – insufficient ability. penghasilan jg –* inadequate income. **ke–an** clumsiness. **ter–** to feel lonely. *~ rasanja tinggal seorang diri,* How lonely it felt to be left by o.s.

tjangkél to be fast, stuck. **men–kan** 1 to hook on to s.t. 2 to attach conditions to s.t.

tjangk(e)long 1 k.o. bag. 2 bamboo tube.

tjangkih-mangkih to stick out in all directions.

tjangkir 1 cup. *se– kopi* a cup of coffee. 2 spur (of a bird). *– piring* china.

tjangkok see TJANGKUK.

tjangkriman riddle.

tjangkuk 1 shoot, cutting. 2 elephant's goad (of metal). **–an** false, an imitation.

tjangkul hoe. **men–(i)** to hoe the ground. **pen–an** breaking ground.

upatjara ~ ground-breaking ceremony.

tjangkum to embrace.

tjangkung **ber–** to squat.

tjantat xanthate.

tjantél **–an** hook.

tjant(e)rik pupil.

tjantik pretty, charming. *– rupanja* to have a pretty face. **ber–** –² to dress up beautifully. **ke–an** 1 beauty. 2 charm, sweetness. **men–kan** to make pretty.

tjanting a small brass pot used in batiking.

tjantjang to be standing on end. **men–kan** 1 to stand s.t. on end. 2 to fasten a rope.

tjantjut loincloth. **ber–** 1 to wear a loincloth. 2 to roll up o's sleeves. **men–kan** *lengan badjunja, – taliwondo* to roll up o's sleeves and get down to work.

tjantol hook. **ke–** to get involved, caught. *Djangan ~ , bung!* Don't get hooked (by a girl), fellow! **men–i** to attach, hook onto. *Talinja ~ kawat listerik,* The string hooked onto an electric wire. *– an* hook, hanger.

tjantum **ber–** 1 to close up, heal a wound. 2 to touch. **men–** to close, bring together. **men–kan** 1 to stitch. *~ lubang dipakaian* to stitch up a hole in a garment. 2 to carry, insert. *Harian ~ kabar baik,* The paper carried the good news. 3 to attach, stick. *Gambaran itu saja –kan didinding itu,* I stuck the poster on the wall. 4 to include. **ter–** 1 included, inserted. *Kabar itu tiada ~ lagi,* That news wasn't included again. 2 mentioned.

tjap 1 stamp, seal. *– pemerintah* government seal. 2 (trade-)mark. *– Matjan* the Tiger trade-mark. 3 to do s.t. without cause or warning. *– ambil* to take s.t. without cause. *– témbak* to shoot without cause. **men–(kan), menge–kan** 1 to stamp, place a seal on s.t. 2 to print (as batik). 3 to brand, label s.o. *Ia ~ tetangganja pentjuri ajam,* He branded his neighbor a chicken thief. **penge–an** printing office. *– batu* lithography. *– djari* fingerprint. *– djempol* thumbprint. *– lak* wax seal. *– pos* postmark.

tjapa wild camphor plant.

tjapai tired, exhausted. **ke–an** 1 weariness, fatigue. 2 fatigued, worn-out. **men–** 1 to reach. *Ia tlh ~ umur tua,* He has reached old age. *Ia ~ puntjak gunung,* He reached the mountain top. *Ia dpt ~ buah itu,* He can reach the fruit. 2 to achieve, attain. *~ maksud* to achieve o's purpose. **pen–an** achieving, attaining. **sepen–** as far as o. can reach. **ter–** reached, achieved. *tidak* ~ inaccessible, unobtainable.

tjapak men– 1 to underestimate, take s.t. lightly. 2 to neglect s.t. 3 to smack (o's lips) while eating.

tjapé(k) tired, exhausted, worn-out. *Buat apa –² mengarang?* Why wear yourself out writing? see TJAPAI.

tjap(e)lok 1 to snap at. 2 to swallow, gulp down. **men–** 1 to snatch, pilfer. ~ *tas buku* to pilfer a brief case. 2 to seize, annex. ~ *negeri jg lemah* to seize weak countries.

tjapik lame, paralyzed.

tjapil Javanese sun hat made of tobacco or palm leaves.

tjaping a metal cover. – *telinga* lobe of ear.

tjaplak a tick (insect).

tjaptjay vegetables flavored with pork and chicken.

tjapuk pockmarked.

tjapung dragonfly.

tjara 1 manner, way. *bertjakap – tjina* to talk in the Chinese way. 2 style. – *Barat* Western style. – *kerdja* procedure. – *menulis* style of writing. 3 method, way. – *mengadjar* method of teaching. **se–** 1 in a ... manner. ~ *damai* in a peaceful manner. 2 on a ... scale. ~ *besar²an* on a large scale. 3 as (if). *Ia diperlakukan* ~ *tuan besar,* He was treated like a big shot. *diterima* ~ *tamu* received as a guest. 4 according to, in accordance with. *merajakan* ~ *adat lama* to celebrate according to old customs. 5 in a manner. ~ *anumerata* posthumously. ~ *sepihak* in a unilateral fashion. ~ *tidak merata* in an unequal manner. *uraian* ~ *ringkas* a short explanation. ~ *resmi* official. – *beristirahat* at ease, parade rest. – *berpikir* 1 Weltanschauung. 2 way of thinking. – *bersiap* at attention. – *pendekatan* approach. – *pengerdjaan* operation.

tjaraka envoy. – *negara* foreign service officer.

tjari ber– –² 1 to look for e.o. 2 to play hide-and-seek. **men–** to look for, seek. *Ia* ~ *salah,* He's looking for mistakes. *Tuan – apa?* What can I do for you (in shops, etc.)? ~ *akal* to look for a way out. ~ *béla* to kill s.o. in order that his spirit will accompany the spirit of another dead person. ~ *hitungan* to solve an arithmetic problem. ~ *ichtiar* to make an effort. ~ *kutu* to look for lice. ~ *makan* to seek a living. ~ *muka* to seek praise. ~ *nafkah* to seek a living. ~ *nama* to hunt for honors. ~ *pasal*

to have a poor excuse. ~ *rezeki* to seek a living. ~ *risik* to make secret inquiries. ~ *uang* to make a living. ~ *umbut dlm batu* hopeless, impossible. **men–** –² to find fault with. *Ia hanja pandai* ~ *sadja,* He was only good at finding fault. **men–kan** 1 to look for s.t. for s.o. *Ia* ~ *adiknja bunga mérah,* He looked for a red flower for his little sister. 2 to seek. ~ *penjelesaian* to seek a solution. **pen–** searcher. ~ *nafkah* breadwinner. **pen–an** a living, livelihood. – *gampang* easygoing. *alasan jg di–* a trumpedup charge.

tjarik 1 clerk, secretary. 2 torn, ripped (of paper). 3 a piece. *sekertas* a piece of paper. 4 see TJARI. **ber–** –² in tatters. **men–** to tear, rip to pieces.

tjarter charter. **men–** to charter (a plane, ship, etc.).

tjaruk see TJERUK.

tjarut obscene, filthy (of speech). **ber–, men–** to use foul language. **ber–** *bungkang* to revile. **pen–** foulmouthed fellow. – *-marut* abusive language.

tjas-tjus(an) 1 boasting, bragging. 2 nonsense, stupid talk.

tjat paint. – *alis* eyebrow paint. **ber–** painted, colored. *rumah jg* ~ *hidjau* a green-painted house. **men–, menge–** to paint, color. **penge–an** painting. – *air* water color. – *bakar* spray paint, Duco. – *bibir* lipstick. – *dasar* first coat of paint. – *minjak* oil paint.

tjatak horsefly.

tjatat men– 1 to note down, make a note of. ~ *pemasukan barang* to make a note of incoming goods. 2 to register. *Ia dpt* ~ *keuntungan jg besar,* He was able to register a big profit. **men–kan** diri to register. *Ia* ~ *diri utk pemberian darah,* He registered as a blood donor. **pen–** registrar. **pen–an** 1 registration. ~ *djiwa* census. 2 (price) quotation. **ter–** registered. *surat* ~ registered letter. **–an** 1 note, memo. *membuat* ~ to make a note. 2 annotation, note. ~ *dikaki halaman* footnotes. ~ *sipil* vital statistics. ~ *tjatjah djiwa* census register. *dgn* ~ 1 with the endorsement. 2 with the annotation.

tjatet see TJATAT.

tjatjad 1 see TJATJAT. 2 deformity.

tjatjah ber– tattooed. ~*-djiwa* to have a population of. *Kota ini* ~*-djiwa dua djuta,* This city has a population of 2,000,000. **men–** 1 to tattoo. 2 to give an injection. 3 to chop (meat). 4 to prepare food for animals. **pen**– census taker. – *djiwa* 1 census. 2 size of population.

tjatjak upright pole, post. **men**– upright, vertical. **men–kan** to place vertically.

tjatjap a shampoo for the hair. **men**– to shampoo.

tjatjar smallpox. **men**– to vaccinate. **pen–an** vaccination. – *air* chicken pox. – *benih* vaccine. – *djeluntur*, – *tjair* chicken pox. – *ulang* revaccination, booster shot.

tjatjat 1 physical defect. 2 invalided, disabled. 3 shortcoming. **ber**– 1 disabled, infirm. 2 to have a defect. **men**– to criticize s.t. or s.o. **men–i** to injure, harm. *Dilarang* ∼ *héwan*, It is forbidden to inflict injury upon animals. ∼ *nama ajahnja* to harm o's father's name. **pen**– critic, criticizer. – *lihat* with impaired eyesight. – *logat* speech defect.

tjatjau fickle. **men**– to rave, talk incoherently.

tjatji scorn, ridicule, contempt. **ber**–²**an** to scold e.o. **men**– to scorn, jeer at s.o. **men–maki** to taunt, ridicule. **-an** derision, scorn, ridicule. – *maki* 1 taunt, scorn, ridicule. 2 to abuse terrifically.

tjatjing worm. – *gelang*² roundworm. – *gerumit* nematode. – *gulung*, – *kalung* earthworm. – *kerawit* pinworm. – *kermi* 1 worm. 2 maggot. – *mendjadi naga* from a humble beginning to power. – *perut*, – *pipih*, – *pita* tapeworm. – *tambang* hookworm. *Selagi menunggu kabar ia seperti* – *kepanasan*, She was restless while waiting for the news.

tjatu **men–kan** to ration out. **pen–an** 1 rationing. 2 allocation. **-an** 1 portion, share. 2 rationing.

tjatuk **men**– to tap on, peck at s.t. **se**– a spoonful.

tjatur chess. **ber**– 1 to play chess. 2 checkered. *tjita* ∼ cloth with a checkered design. **per–an** 1 chess game. 2 policy. *Disini* ∼ *politik terdjadi*, The game of politics takes place here. **-an** checkered design. – *Tunggal* four-in-one unit (consisting of the Army, Police, Civil Service, and the People). – *Upaja* Four Efforts. – *wangsa* caste system.

tjaturangga chessboard.

tjatus see TJETUS.

tjatut small pliers, tweezers. **men**– 1 to extract, pull. ∼ *gigi* to extract a tooth. 2 to pull out (a nail). 3 to swindle, cheat. **men–kan** 1 to sell on the black market. *Ia* ∼ *bagiannja*, He sold his portion on the black market. 2 to swindle, embezzle. **pen**–

1 swindler. 2 black marketeer. **(pen)– an, per–an** 1 black-market activities. 2 swindling, embezzling.

tjaung sunken (cheeks).

tjawak dog collar. – *pipi* dimple.

tjawan 1 Chinese teacup. 2 goblet. – *pinggan* porcelain ware.

tjawang see TJABANG.

tjawat 1 shorts. 2 loincloth. **ber**– to wear a loincloth. **men–kan** to wear as a loincloth.

tjb. [*tjabang*] branch (of firm, etc.).

tjebak **men**– to dig, mine, into the side of s.t. **-an** ore.

tjebar-tjebur to splash, splashing. – *terdengar orang mandi dikali*, The splashing of people bathing in the river could be heard.

tjebik to contract o's lips in a derisive fashion.

tjebis *se*– a piece, a small bit.

tjébok bamboo water dipper. **ber–**, **men**– 1 to dip up water. 2 to clean o.s. with water after defecation.

tjébol dwarf. *si*– *hendak mentjapai bintang* to reach for the moon, seek the impossible.

tjébong tadpole.

tjebur **men**– 1 to splash. 2 to jump into the water. **men–kan** 1 to plunge s.t. into the water. 2 to plunge into misery. ∼ *diri* to throw o.s. into o's work, play, study, etc. *Ia* ∼ *dirinja dlm kantjah politik*, He threw himself into the political arena.

tjedera 1 disagreement, conflict. 2 fault, flaw. 3 treason, faithlessness. 4 injury. 5 damage. 6 see TJENDERA. **ber**– 1 to quarrel. 2 to have a defect. **ke–an, per–an** 1 fault, flaw. 2 conflict, quarrel. 3 treason. 4 injury. 5 damage. **men**– to betray.

tjeding 1 backward. 2 small, scrubby (of plants, fruits, etc.).

tjédok **men**– 1 to scoop up (of sand, etc.). 2 to dip up (of liquids). **pen**– a scoop, dipper.

tjédong see TJÉDOK.

tjegah **men**– 1 to restrain, prevent, prohibit. *Ia* ∼ *anaknja ber-main*² *didjalan*, He prohibited his children from playing in the street. ∼ *bahaja api* to prevent the danger of fire. 2 to restrain. ∼ *makan banjak* to restrain from eating a great deal. 3 to combat, guard against. *utk* ∼ *supaja pakaian anda djangan kena tinta* to guard against getting ink on your clothes. **pen**– 1 preventative. ∼ *penghamilan* contraceptive. 2 preservative. **pen–an** 1 prevention. 2 combating, the fight (against). **-an** prohibition, prevention.

tjegak 1 upright. 2 vigorous, robust.

tjégak 1 to feel fit as a fiddle. 2 to revive.

tjegat **men–** to waylay, intercept s.o. **pen–an** interception.

tjeguk see TEGUK.

tjék 1 a check. 2 mister or sir (used in addressing China-born Chinese in Indonesia). **men–** to check, control. *– kosong* a bad check. *– perdjalanan* traveler's check.

tjekah **ber–, men–** to burst open.

tjekak short. **ber–** to fight. ∼ *Pinggang* with arms akimbo. **men–** to pinch, seize between finger and thumb. **se–** a pinch (of pepper, salt).

tjekam see TJENGKAM.

tjekap see TJEKAK.

tjekatan capable, clever, skilled, dexterous. **ke–** skill, ability, dexterity.

tjekau **men–** to seize with the hand.

tjekék see TJEKIK. **ke–** to hiccough.

tjékél stingy.

tjekih **men–** 1 to be slightly ajar (of a door). 2 to have a slight tear.

tjekik **ber–** to quarrel, fight. **men–** 1 to strangle, throttle s.o. 2 to strangle, kill. *Monopoli itu* ∼ *pedagang ketjil*, That monopoly strangled the small businessman. ∼ *napas* to stifle. **ter–** strangled. *Ia mati* ∼ , He died from strangulation. **–an** strangulation.

tjekit **men–** to take a small bite, nibble at.

tjeklik **men–** 1 sound of s.t. broken. 2 to switch s.t. on. **–an** a switch.

Tjéko Czech.

tjekokan medicine forcibly given to children and animals.

Tjékoslowakia Czechoslovakia.

tjéktjok quarrel, dispute. **ber–** to quarrel, dispute. **memper–kan** to dispute about s.t. *Meréka* ∼ *soal jg tak berarti*, They disputed over an insignificant matter. **per–an** quarrel, dispute.

tjekuk medicine given forcibly. **men–kan** to force s.t. down a child's throat.

tjekung 1 sunken (of cheeks). *mata –* hollow eyes. *Ia – rupanja*, He has a hollow-eyed look. 2 concave.

tjekup **men–** to seize with the hand.

tjela 1 defect, flaw. 2 shortcoming, failing. 3 disgrace, shame. 4 blot, stain. **ber–** 1 with shortcomings, defects. 2 shameful. *tidak* ∼ flawless. **berke–an** ignominious(ly). **ke–an** 1 shortcoming, failing. 2 fault, defect. **men–(kan)** 1 to disapprove of, condemn. ∼ *politik pemerintah* to disapprove of government policy. 2 to criticize. 3 to blame. 4 to refute. ∼ *téori* to refute a theory. **pen–** critic. **(pen)–an** 1 criticism. 2 disapproval. 3 blame. **ter–** culpable.

tjelaga tiller (of boat).

tjelah 1 gap, space. 2 rift. 3 rent, fissure. **ber–** to have space between. *– djari* space between fingers. *– gigi* space between teeth. *– suara* glottis.

tjelak mascara. **ber–** to wear mascara. **men–i** to use an eyebrow pencil.

tjélak **ber–, men–, ter–** to sparkle, gleam.

tjelaka 1 accident, misfortune. 2 bad luck. 3 damn it! darn it! *– benar, dompétku ketinggalan dirumah*, Oh, darn it, I left my wallet at home. 4 unlucky. 5 hard blow. *Kematiannja – besar bagi orangtuanja*, His death was a hard blow for his parents. **ke–an** 1 accident, mishap. 2 bad luck. **men–kan** 1 to ruin, bring misfortune to s.o. 2 to humiliate s.o. *si–* scoundrel. *– duabelas, – tigabelas* bad luck.

tjelampak **men–** to throw away, toss on the ground.

tjelam-tjelum 1 to chase in and out of s.o.'s house without regard for anyone. 2 to bang, stamp, pound.

tjelana trousers, pants. **ber–** to wear trousers. *– (be)renang* swim trunks. *– dalam* underpants, undershorts, panties. *– djéngki* blue jeans. *– kolor* trunks, shorts. *– monjét* (c)overalls. *– Napoléon* blue jeans. *– péndék* shorts.

tjelang **men–** to stare glassily.

tjelangak open (of a door).

tjelapak **ter–** astride, straddling.

tjelékéh 1 stain, blemish. 2 dirty, soiled.

tjelempung **men–** to plunge, plop (into the water).

tjéléng wild boar. **men–** *uang* to save, hoard money. **–an** 1 savings. 2 money box.

tjeléngkang-tjeléngkok 1 winding, twisting. 2 bent.

tjelep 1 dye. 2 see TJELUP. **men–** to dye. **–an** dyed goods.

tjelepak see TJELAPAK.

tjelepik 1 to tick. 2 sound of the fall of a small object.

tjelepuk to fall with a thud, plop.

tjeli keen, sharp-eyed.

tjelik **men–** 1 to open. 2 to see. **men–kan** to open s.t.

tjelotéh **ber–** to chat.

tjelung-tjelang to jingle.

tjelup **men–kan** 1 to dye s.t. 2 to dip, immerse s.t. **pen–** 1 a dye. 2 dyer. **–an** 1 dyed article. 2 dyeing.

tjelupak Javanese oil lamp.

tjelurut k.o. skunk.

tjelus 1 to penetrate, get through s.t. 2 to get loose. **men–** to slip away.

tjema **men–** to accuse, charge.

tjemar 1 dirty, soiled. 2 besmirched, filthy. *perkataan jg* – filthy words. – *namanja* besmirched name. **ber**– dirty, soiled. *Ia* ~ *lumpur,* He's covered with mud. **ke–an** 1 dirt, filth. 2 dirtiness. **men–i, men–kan** 1 to dirty, soil. ~ *kamar* to dirty up the room. 2 to besmirch, stain. ~ *nama orang* to besmirch a person's name.

tjemara 1 casuarina tree. 2 artificial hair. 3 tassel.

tjemas 1 worried, apprehensive, concerned, disturbed. *Negeri itu* – *akan serangan itu,* The country is disturbed over the attack. 2 frightened, afraid. *Ia* – *rupanja mendengar bunji meriam,* He appeared afraid at the sound of the gun. 3 pessimistic. 4 discouraged. *Ia* – *sesudah mengalami kerugian itu,* He was discouraged after experiencing that loss. **ber**– to be anxious, uneasy. *Ia* ~ *akan waktu jg akan datang,* He's anxious about the future. **ke–an** 1 alarmed, uneasy. 2 anxiety, worry. 3 concern, apprehension. 4 fear. **men–kan** 1 to alarm, disturb. *Kabar itu* ~ *penduduk,* The news disturbed the population. 2 to worry about. *Ia* ~ *temannja,* He worried about his friend. 3 to fear, be afraid. *Ia* ~ *binatang jg besar,* He feared big animals. **pen**– 1 pessimist. 2 worrier, brooder. **ter**– worried, anxious. *Ia* ~ *akan keséhatannja,* He was worried about his health. –² nearly, almost. *Ia* ~ *terlanggar mobil,* He was almost run over by a car.

tjemat **men**– to tow a ship.

tjembul a small metal box for tobacco, etc.

tjembung 1 chubby (of cheeks). 2 convex.

tjemburu 1 jealous. *Ia* – *akan tetangganja,* He was jealous of his neighbor. 2 envious. 3 suspicious. *Ia selalu* – *pd orang asing,* He's always suspicious of foreigners. 4 envy. **(ke)–an** 1 jealousy. 2 envy. 3 suspicion. **men–i** 1 to suspect s.o. *Ia* ~ *temannja,* He suspected his friend. 2 to be envious of. *Ia* ~ *mobil temannja jg baru,* He envied his friend's new car.

tjemééh see TJEMOOH.

tjemerlang 1 to sparkle, shine. 2 bright, gleaming. *tjuatja jg* – bright weather. **ke–an** 1 glitter, glow, radiance. 2 glory.

tjemeti a whip. **men**– to whip.

tjémong 1 dirty, soiled. 2 mauled.

tjemooh(an) 1 insult, taunt. 2 ridicule, scorn. **men–kan** to ridicule, deride, scorn. *Tak pantas* ~ *gurunja,* It's not proper to ridicule o's teacher.

tjempaka term used for frangipanni, for certain kinds of gardenias, etc.

tjempala quick, mobile.

tjempedak k.o. fruit tree.

tjemperling starling.

tjemping rag, piece of cloth.

tjemplung to plunge, plop. **men**– to plunge into. **men–i** to jump into. **men–kan** *diri* to throw o.s. into.

tjempoa abacus.

tjempung see TJEMPLUNG.

tjemuh see TJEMOOH.

tjemuk pod (of peas, etc.). **men**– 1 to hit with a stick. 2 to shake.

tjéna scar, mark. **ke–an** marked.

tjenajang medium (in spiritualism).

tjenangga see TJINANGGA.

tjendala 1 low, base, mean. 2 pariah.

tjendana sandalwood. see KAJU.

tjendawan 1 mushroom. 2 toadstool. 3 fungus. 4 mildew, mold. **ber**– moldy.

tjendékia 1 learned, educated. 2 clever, shrewd.

tjendékiawan 1 an intellectual. 2 the educated (class).

tjendéla see DJENDÉLA.

tjendera 1 fast asleep. 2 see TJANDRA. – *mata* souvenir.

tjenderawasih bird of paradise.

tjenderung 1 inclined. *Hatinja* – *kpd mobil jg hitam,* He was inclined toward the black car. 2 sloping, leaning. *Tiangnja agak* –, The pole leans a bit. 3 disposed toward s.o. **ke–an** 1 inclination, preference. 2 tendency. 3 sympathy.

tjéndol a syrup made of rice or sago and coconut milk.

tjenéla slipper.

tjéng molasses.

tjengam **men**– to snap at, seize with mouth or beak (as a dog, crocodile, etc.).

tjengang **(ber)**– amazed, flabbergasted. *Ia* ~ *melihat kemadjuan téhnik,* He was amazed at seeing the technical progress. **ber–an** astonished, dumfounded. **memper–kan, men(ter)–kan** 1 to amaze, astonish. *Kepandaian itu* ~ *teman²nja,* The ability astonished his friends. 2 amazing, astonishing. 3 confusing. **ter–(–)** dumfounded, amazed. *Ia* ~ *mendengar tjeritera jg anéh² itu,* He was amazed at hearing the strange stories.

tjengar tjengir to cry hard, bawl (of babies).

tjéngéng 1 to whine. 2 tearful. 3 crybaby.

tjénggér wattle (of a fowl).

tjengis loathsome, nauseating.

tjengkal unit of length (12 ft.).

tjengkam grip, squeeze. **men**– to

seize, grasp. ∼ *kekuasaan dunia* to seize world power. *Burung elang* ∼ *mangsanja,* The eagle held its prey in its grasp. **men–kan** to grip by planting the fingernails in o's skin. **–an** grip, hold.

tjengkau the middleman, broker.

tjengké(h) see TJENGKIH.

tjengkeram 1 grip, hold. 2 security, down payment. **men–** to hold firmly in o's hand (power, etc.). **–an** grip.

tjengkerama a chat. **ber–** to have a chat.

tjengkerik see DJENGKERIK.

tjengkerma see TJENGKERAMA.

tjengkih 1 clove. 2 clubs in cards. **ber–** spiced with cloves. *Rokok ini* ∼ , This cigarette has cloves in it.

tjengking yelling, squealing (of a dog). **ber–** to yap, squeal. *Andjing* ∼ *ditengah malam,* The dog yapped in the middle of the night.

tjéngkok crooked, twisted.

tjéngkong deformed, misshapen.

tjengkung 1 hollow, sunken (of cheeks, eyes). 2 dimple **–²** to yap, whine, growl (of a dog).

tjéntang **men–** to comment on. **–an** comment. **–** *-perénang* in disorder.

tjenténg guard, watchman.

tjentil see SENTIL.

tjentjang **men–** 1 to chop to bits, cut into bits. 2 to break ground. **–an** *daging* chopped up meat. ∼ *dua segeragai* to kill 2 birds with o. stone. *seperti* ∼ *air* undisturbed.

tjéntjong 1 fuss, bother. 2 fussy. *banjak* – exacting, finicky. see TJINGTJONG.

tjéntong ladle. **–** *nasi* rice ladle. **men–(kan)** 1 to scoop. 2 to serve with a ladle. *Ia sibuk* ∼ *nasi,* She was busy serving rice.

tjentung 1 lock of hair. 2 tuft, crest (of a bird).

tjenung **ter–** 1 pensive, musing. 2 flabbergasted, dumfounded.

tjepak a smacking sound. **men– –²** to make a smacking sound. *Ia makan sambil* ∼ , He made a smacking sound while eating.

tjepat 1 fast, speedy, quick. *Ia berdjalan* –, He walked fast. 2 in a hurry. *Ia – pulang,* He hurried home. 3 early, first. *Siapa – dpt dahulu,* First come first served. 4 speed. *–nja 50 mil dlm satu djam,* The speed is 50 miles an hour. **ber– –²** to hurry. *Meréka* ∼ *pulang,* They hurried home. **berse–** hastily, in confusion. **bersi–** to race. **ke–an** 1 speed, velocity. ∼*nja 50 mil sedjam,* The speed was 50 miles per hour. 2 too fast. *Mobilnja* ∼ , His car was

too fast. 3 too early. *Ia berangkat* ∼ , He started too early. ∼ *djeladjah* cruising speed. **memper–** to speed up, accelerate s.t. *Mesin ini* ∼ *produksi,* This machine speeds up production. **men–** to speed up. *Mobilnja* ∼ , The car speeded up. **men–kan** to speed s.t. up. **per–an** 1 acceleration. 2 speeding up. ∼ *pembitjaraan soal itu menguntungkan bagi semuanja,* Speeding up of the discussion was advantageous to all. **–an** *dong!* Hurry up, please! **–** *achir* final velocity. **–** *lidah,* **–** *mulut* rash, hasty. **–** *réaksi* velocity of reaction. **–** *tangan* light-fingered, a pilferer.

tjepéng half a cent.

tjépér 1 low-rimmed saucer or plate. 2 flat.

tjepit 1 see SEPIT. 2 DJEPIT.

tjeplok fried. **men–** to fry.

tjepol broken off. **men–** to strike, hit s.o.

tjepu wooden or metal betel box.

tjerabah dirty, untidy.

tjerah clear. **–** *tjuatja* clear weather. **ke–an** brightness. **men–kan** to brighten s.t.

tjerai **ber–** 1 to part, separate. *Disini djalan kami* ∼ , Our ways part here. 2 to be divorced. *Meréka sdh* ∼ , They've been divorced. ∼ *-berai* dispersed, scattered in all directions. *Pentjuri itu lari* ∼ *-berai,* The thieves ran in all directions. **memper–kan, men–kan** 1 to separate. *Ia* ∼ *orang berkelahi,* He separated those fighting. 2 to divorce. *Ia* ∼ *isterinja,* He divorced his wife. 3 to analyze. ∼ *kalimat* to analyze a sentence. 4 to divide, part. ∼ *menjusu* to wean. *Anaknja sdh di-kan menjusu,* Her child has been weaned. **men–** to part, separate. ∼ *rambutnja* to part o's hair. ∼ *-beraikan* to disperse. *Polisi* ∼ *orang² jg berkumpul,* Police dispersed the group that had gathered. **pen–an** 1 separation. 2 division, partition, splitting. **per–an** divorce, separation. **–** *-berai* dispersed, scattered. **–** *susu* weaning.

tjeramah 1 (popular) lecture. 2 talkative, garrulous. **ber–** to give a lecture. *Ia* ∼ *dua djam lamanja,* He lectured for 2 hours. **men–kan** to lecture on s.t. *Ia* ∼ *perdjalanannja ke Éropah,* He lectured on his trip to Europe. **pen–** lecturer.

tjerana a metal bowl, box, or tray for keeping articles used in betel chewing.

tjeranggah **ber–, men–** 1 forked, branched. 2 prickly, thorny.

tjerantjang **ber–(an)** prickly, thorny.

tjerap **men–** to note, observe. **–an**
salah illusion.
tjerat 1 nozzle. 2 faucet. **ber–** to
have a spout, nozzle. **men–** 1 to
pour a liquid through a nozzle or
faucet. 2 to pour via a spout.
tjeratjap cymbal.
tjeratjau **men–** to be delirious.
tjerau rustling, buzzing.
tjerawat rocket.
tjerbergam [*tjeritera bergambar*] illustrated story.
tjerbersam [*tjeritera bersambung*] continued, serialized story.
tjerdas 1 intelligent, educated. *Ia
seorang –*, He's intelligent. 2 shrewd,
clever. *Ia - berdagang*, He's shrewd
in business. **ke–an** 1 intelligence. 2
education. 3 shrewdness, astuteness.
men–kan to develop, sharpen o's
mind. *latihan utk ∼ pikiran* an exercise to sharpen o's mind. *- tangkas*
quiz contest.
tjerdik 1 smart, clever, bright. 2
cunning, shrewd. **ke–an** 1 cleverness,
intelligence. 2 shrewdness, cunning-
ness. *- pandai*, *- tjendékia* 1 intellectual. 2 brilliant.
tjérék 1 kettle. 2 watering can.
tjérét see TJÉRÉK.
tjeréwét 1 fussy, quarrelsome. *Isterinja - sekali*, His wife was very
fussy. 2 hard to please, faultfinding.
tjergas enterprising, active, energetic.
tjeria pure, cleansed. **men–kan** to
purify.
tjeriga dagger.
tjerita see TJERITERA. **pen–an** story-
telling. *- pandjang* novelette.
tjeritera 1 story, account, narrative.
- perdjalanannja account of his trip.
2 twitter of a bird. **ber–** 1 to tell,
relate. *Ia ∼ ttg pengalamannja dinegeri Turki*, He told about his
experiences in Turkey. 2 to twitter.
Dengarkanlah burung itu ∼ , Listen
to that bird twitter. **men–i** to tell,
relate to s.o. *Ia ∼ anaknja ttg perdjalanannja*, He told his son about
his trip. **men–kan** to tell, relate,
narrate s.t. *∼ kehidupan orang Inggeris* to tell the life story of an
Englishman. *- bersambung* serial, continued story. *- péndék* short story.
- silat Chinese story adapted into
Indonesian.
tjerkas see TJERGAS.
tjerkau **men–** to scratch.
tjerlang see TJEMERLANG. **ber–** to
glisten, shine.
tjerling **men–** 1 to ogle. 2 to look
at from the corner of the eye. *Ia ∼*

kpd ibunja, He looked at his mother
from the corner of his eye.
tjermat 1 accurate, careful. *membatja
buku dgn -* to read a book accurately.
2 neat, orderly. *mengatur kamarnja
dgn -* to arrange a room neatly. 3
thrifty. **ke–an** 1 neatness, orderli-
ness. 2 accuracy. **men–** to economize
on. *∼ pengeluaran uang* to economize
on expenditures. **men–i** to pay close
attention to. *∼ uraian gurunja* to
pay close attention to the teacher's
explanation. **men–kan** 1 to be accurate in s.t. *∼ pekerdjaannja* to be
accurate in o's work. 2 to be economical.
tjermin 1 mirror. *melihat di–* to look
in the mirror. 2 example. *Ia mendjadi
- bagi teman²nja*, He has become an
example for his friends. **ber–** 1 to
look in the mirror. *Lama sekali ia
∼* , She looked in the mirror a long
time. 2 to have, be provided with
mirrors. *Kamarnja ∼ lima*, Her
room has 5 mirrors. 3 to take as an
example. *Ia selalu ∼ kpd ajahnja*,
He always takes his father as an
example. *∼ -bangkai* to put to shame,
have a guilty conscience. *Daripada
hidup ∼ -bangkai lebih baik mati
berkalang tanah*, Better dead than to
live in shame. *∼ dlm hatinja* to reflect in o's heart. **men–i** 1 to hold
the mirror before s.o. *Ia ∼ ibunja*,
She held the mirror in front of her
mother. 2 to look at s.t. in the
mirror. *Ia ∼ lukanja*, He looked at
his wound in the mirror. **men–kan**
to reflect. *Ia ∼ keadaan jg sebenarnja*,
He gave a picture of the true situation. **pen–an** reflection. *∼ berbagai
kesulitan* a reflection of various difficulties. **ter–** mirrored, pictured, reflected. *Wadjah kekasihnja tetap ∼
dlm hatinja*, His sweetheart's face
was permanently mirrored in his
mind. **–an** reflection. *- mata* glasses,
spectacles.
tjerna(h) 1 digested. 2 dissolved.
men–(kan) 1 to digest, dissolve. *Obat
ini ∼ segala bagian makanan jg keras*,
This medicine digests all hard parts
of the food. *∼ rentjana besar²an* to
digest a great plan. 2 to think over,
register, take in. *∼ segala naséhat
gurunja* to think over all the teacher's
advice. **pen–an** digestion, assimilation.
tjeroboh 1 improper, indecent, immoral. *tindakan jg -* an improper act.
2 awkward, clumsy. 3 cruel, merciless. *hati jg -* a cruel heart. 4 sloppy,
slovenly, untidy. *Pekerdjaannja -*,
His work is sloppy. 5 careless. *Kabar²
ini dipilih dgn -*, This news is care-

lessly selected. **ke–an** 1 indecency. 2
awkwardness. 3 carelessness, sloppiness.
tjerobong 1 chimney. 2 funnel on a
ship. 3 smokestack.
tjeronggah see TJERANGGAH.
tjerotjok funnel, spout.
tjerpelai weasel.
tjerpén [*tjeritera péndék*] short story.
tjerpénis [*tjeritera péndék+is*] shortstory writer.
tjerpu sandal.
tjertja 1 censure, reprimand. 2 derision. 3 scorn. **men–i** 1 to deride. 2
to censure, reprimand. *Pemerintah* ∼
tindakan sematjam itu, The government censured such an action. **(pen)–
an** 1 reprimand, censure. 2 derision,
insult. 3 scorn, abuse.
tjertjak slightly pockmarked.
tjertjap **men–** 1 to flop about, squirm.
2 to produce a flapping or flopping
sound.
tjeruh cleaned (of rice). **men–** to
pound rice a second time.
tjeruk 1 hole, cleft. 2 cranny, nook.
3 incision. **men–** to dig a hole in the
side (of a mountain, etc.).
tjerut **men–** 1 to tie up, tighten.
2 to rope off.
tjerutjup 1 chimney, funnel. 2
pointed, tapering. **ber–** 1 to have a
chimney. *Rumah itu* ∼ *tinggi*, That
house has a tall chimney. 2 to project. *pagar jg* ∼ *tadjam²* a hedge
with sharp projecting points.
tjerutu cigar.
tjespleng to cure instantly, provide
instant relief. *Obat ini – utk sakit
kepala*, This medicine cures headaches instantly.
tjét see TJAT.
tjét. [*tjétakan*] edition.
tjétak **men–** 1 to print (books, bank
notes, etc.). 2 to cast, shape. ∼ *kué*
to shape, cut cookies. ∼ *roda* to
cast a wheel. 3 to produce coins. 4 to
produce, achieve. ∼ *kemenangan jg
gemilang* to achieve a glorious victory.
∼ *gol* to score. **men–kan** to print.
∼ *bukunja di Djakarta* to print o's
book in Jakarta. **men–ulang** to reprint s.t. **pen–** printer. ∼ *gol* scorer
(in soccer). **pen–an** printing. ∼ *buku
sangat mahal*, The printing of a book
is very expensive. **per–an** printing
office. ∼ *Negara* Government Printing Office. **–an** 1 publication. *Buku
ini* ∼ *Pembangunan*, This book is
published by Pembangunan. 2 printing. *Karena sukar kertas* ∼ *buku
mahal*, Due to the scarcity of paper
book printing is expensive. 3 edition, printing. ∼ *biru* blueprint. 4
mold, matrix. ∼ *kué* cookie mold.
∼ *roda* mold for casting wheels. –
batu lithoprinting, lithography. –
lepas offprint. – *ulang(an)*, – *tambahan*, – *ulang* reprint.
tjéték 1 shallow. *sungai jg* – shallow
river. 2 superficial, shallow. *pengetahuan jg* – superficial knowledge.
tjéténg **men–** to carry in o's hand.
tjéti moneylender.
tjetjah **men–(kan)** to touch s.t.
lightly. **se–** just slightly, lightly,
barely.
tjetjak see TJITJAK. **men–** 1 to pick
pockets. 2 to pinch. **pen–** pickpocket.
tjetjap **men–** to taste s.t.
tjetjar **men–** to keep after, pester,
s.o.
tjétjé great-great-grandchild.
tjétjér spilled. **ber–an** scattered
around, spilled all over. **men–(kan)**
1 to spill s.t. out. 2 to scatter s.t.
around. **ter–** 1 spilled, poured out.
2 to be left behind.
tjétjok see TJÉKTJOK.
tjetjunguk 1 cockroach. 2 spy. 3 detective.
tjétok trowel.
tjetus **men–** 1 to scratch, scrape.
∼ *korék api utk membuat api* to
scratch a match to make a fire. 2 to
flash. *Api mertjun* ∼ *dgn tiba²*, The
fire of the firecrackers flashed suddenly. 3 to carp at, find fault with.
Ia suka ∼ *ttg tetangga*, He likes to
find fault with his neighbors. **men–
kan** to light, ignite. ∼ *korék* to
strike a match. ∼ *–keluar* to ignite,
set off. **pen–** spark, impetus. **pen–an**
igniting, ignition. **–an** 1 sparks. 2 a
flash. ∼ *ketawa* a burst of laughter.
tjéwék girl, broad, dame.
tji see ENTJIK.
tjiak twittering, peeping of birds.
ber– to chirp, twitter. ∼ *miak* to
peep, chirp.
tjialat dammit!
tjiap see TJIAK.
tjibir **men–** to curl o's lip. **men–kan**
1 to turn up o's nose at, scorn. *Ia* ∼
temannja, He turned up his nose at
his friend. 2 to ridicule, mock. ∼
naséhat gurunja to ridicule the advice
of o's teacher. **–an** scorn, contempt.
tjibuk see TJÉBOK.
tjidera see TJEDERA.
tjiduk see TJÉDOK.
tjigak monkey.
tjik see ENTJIK.
tjika diarrhea. – *kedadak* cholera.
tjikalbakal 1 see TJAKALBAKAL. 2
founder.

tjikar bullock cart.

tjik(e)rak wastebasket. **ber-** **-²** to jump with joy.

tjilaka see TJELAKA.

tjilap **ter-** **-²** to flicker.

tjilat trick. **men-** to deceive.

Tjili Chile.

tjilik little, small.

tjiling see TJÉLÉNG.

Tjina 1 China. 2 Chinese. – *buta* figurehead. *seperti* – *karam* noisy.

tjinangga deformed.

tjindai a flowered sash.

tjindil baby mouse.

tjinganah **ter-** startled, surprised.

tjingkéh see TJENGKÉH.

tjingtjong 1 excuse, pretext. *Djangan banjak* –, Don't make poor excuses. 2 ado, fuss. *banjak* – much ado.

tjinta 1 love, affection. – *jg dalam* deep, profound love. – *tanah air* love for o's country. *Ia berdjuang karena* – *kpd tanah airnja*, He fought out of love for his country. 2 sorrow, regret. *Ia merasa* – *karena tiada beranak*, She felt regret at not having any children. **ber-** *akan*, **ber-kan** 1 to love. *Ia* ∼ *tanah airnja*, He loves his country very much. 2 to mourn, sorrow over. *Ia* ∼ *kematian anaknja*, He mourned the death of his child. **ke-an** 1 love, affection. 2 sweetheart, darling, apple of o's eye. *Ia* ∼ *ajahnja*, She's her father's darling. 3 worry, concern. 4 to mourn, bemoan. *Ia* ∼ *karena kemalangan itu*, He was bemoaning his bad luck. **men-** to mourn for. *Ia* ∼ *gurunja jg menemui ketjelakaan*, He was mourning for his teacher who met with an accident. **men-i**, **men-kan** 1 to love. *Ia* ∼ *kekasihnja*, He loved his sweetheart. 2 to long for. *Ia* ∼ *kampung halamannja*, He longed for his village. **pen-** 1 lover. 2 devotee. *Ia* ∼ *sépakbola*, He's a devotee of soccer. ∼ *alam* nature lover. ∼ *tanah air* patriot. **per-an** 1 love. 2 mourning, sorrow. 3 love affair. 4 longing. **ter-** dear, beloved. *Ibuku jg* ∼ Dearest Mother. – *berahi* love's desire. – *monjét* infatuation. – *rasa* affection. – *udara* air-minded.

tjintjang see TJENTJANG.

tjintjin 1 a ring. 2 washer for bolts, faucets, etc. – *berapit* ring with 2 stones. – *garam sebuku* a ring with a single stone. – *kawin* wedding ring. – *mata tiga* ring with 3 stones. – *setémpél* signet ring. – *tanda (pertunangan)* engagement ring. – *tjap* signet ring. *bagai* – *dgn permata* a perfect match.

tjintjong see TJINGTJONG.

tjintuh see SENTUH.

tjipit slanting (of eyes).

tjiplak see DJIPLAK.

tjiprat **ber-an** to spray e.o. **men-** 1 to sprinkle. 2 to splash. **men-kan** to cause to spray, shake the spray. ∼ *air dari mantel* to shake the water from a coat.

tjipta 1 creative force, power. 2 thought, concentration. **men-(kan)** 1 to create. ∼ *dunia* to create the world. 2 to concentrate on. **pen-** 1 creator, maker. 2 author. **pen-an** creation, composition. ∼ *lagu²* *baru* the composition of new songs. **ter-** created, conceived. **-an** creation, product, composition.

tjiri 1 identifying mark. 2 type. **memper-**, **men-** to type, characterize.

tjirit 1 diarrhea. 2 excrement, droppings. 3 sediment. – *bintang* meteor. – *kopi* dregs.

tjis 1 bah! 2 what a shame! –, *tak ingat pd anak-isterinja*, What a shame he forgot about his family.

tjita 1 printed cotton, cloth. 2 see TJINTA. **ber-** to desire, long. *Ia* ∼ *bepergian di Éropa*, He longed to travel in Europe. **ber-** **-²**, **men-** **-²** to have as an ideal. *Ia* ∼ *utk mendjadi dokter*, His ideal was to become a doctor. **men-(kan)** to desire, long for. *Ia mendapat segala apa jg di-*, He got everything he wanted. *Ia* ∼ *mempunjai rumah jg indah*, He longed to own an attractive home. **-²** 1 ideal, aspiration. 2 desire. 3 idea. – *rasa* taste.

tjitak see TJÉTAK.

tjitjak house lizard. – *terbang* flying lizard.

tjitjil **men-** to pay in installments. *Ia* ∼ *hutangnja*, He pays his debts in installments. **(pen)-an** installment. *Berapa* ∼*nja satu bulan?* How much is the monthly installment?

tjitjip **men-** 1 to taste s.t. 2 to cheep, twitter.

tjitjir see TJÉTJÉR.

tjitjit great-grandchild. **men-** to squeak (of a mouse).

tjium kiss. **men-** 1 to kiss s.o. 2 to smell, sniff. *Ia* ∼ *bunga*, She sniffed the flowers. 3 to sense, learn. *Ia* ∼ *kabar jg membahajakan itu*, He learned the dangerous news. **men-i** to kiss repeatedly. *Ia* ∼ *anaknja sebelum pergi*, She kissed her child repeatedly before going. **men-kan** to have s.o. sniff s.t. **pen-** (sense of) smell. *Hidung adalah alat* ∼ ,

The nose is the organ of smell. **ter–** 1 kissed accidentally. 2 learned, found out. ~ *kabar padanja...,* He came to learn... **–an** kiss.

tjiut 1 narrow. *Djalannja –,* The road's narrow. 2 thin. *buntut kuda jg* – a thin horsetail. **ber– –²**, **men– –²** 1 to squeak. *Sepatunja* ~ , His shoes squeaked. 2 to howl, whistle. *Anginnja meniup* ~ , The wind howled.

tjlik **men–** to snip. ~ *pita* to cut a ribbon.

tjoang **ber–(an)**, **men–** to protrude, stick up all over. **men–kan** to hold s.t. up.

tjoba 1 please. – *ia suruh masuk,* Ask him to come in, please. 2 look! –, *bagaimana ini?* Look, what does this mean? (What about this?) – *lihat, pekerdjaan apa ini!* Just look what he was doing! 3 if, supposing. – *ajahnja tak ada siapa jg akan membajar hutangnja?* If his father weren't there, who would pay his debt? **men–** 1 to try (out). –*lah mobil ini dulu,* Try this car first. 2 to try on. –*lah pakaian ini dulu sebelum kantjingnja dipasang,* Try this suit on first before I fix the buttons. 3 to try, attempt. *Ia* ~ *berhubungan dgn temannja,* He tried to get in touch with his friend. 4 to test, try. *Ia* ~ *kepandaian temannja,* He tested his friend's skill. *Ia* ~ *masakan isterinja,* He tested (or tasted) his wife's cooking. **men–i** to put to the test. ~ *mobil baru* to try out a new car. ~ *kesetiaan temannja* to test a friend's loyalty. **men–kan** 1 to try out, test on s.o. *Ia* ~ *kepandaiannja kpd saja,* He tried out his skill on me. 2 to try s.t. on s.o. ~ *pakaian kpd anaknja* to try a suit on o's child. **pen–an** 1 effort, attempt. 2 testing. ~ *mesin baru* testing of a new engine. **per–an** 1 test(ing). 2 trial, experiment. ~ *berlajar* trial run (of a ship). 3 specimen, trial. *nomor* ~ a specimen copy. 4 attempt. ~ *membunuh* a murder attempt. 5 trial, affliction. ~ *tjétak lepas* galley proof. ~ *tjétak halaman* page proof. **–an** 1 test. 2 trial, ordeal. **–²** 1 to attempt, try. *Ia* ~ *membuka pintu jg terkuntji itu,* He was attempting to open the locked door. 2 to try out merely. *Rupanja ia* ~ *sadja,* Apparently he was just trying it out.

tjobak-tjabik in tatters. *Badjunja –,* His clothes were in rags.

tjobék earthenware bowl used for grinding spice. **men–** to tear. **–²** in tatters.

tjoblos **men–** 1 to punch, perforate.

2 to vote by perforating the ballot. *Penduduk ta'at dan tenang* ~ , The inhabitants obediently and calmly voted.

tjodak **men–(kan)** to hold s.t. up.

tjodot a bat (mammal).

tjogan emblem. – *kata* slogan.

tjokék dance party.

tjok(e)lat 1 chocolate. 2 (dark) brown.

tjokét **men–** to take a small piece of s.t. *Ia* ~ *kué,* She broke off a small piece of cake.

tjokmar club, cudgel.

tjokol **ber–** 1 to squat. 2 to sit nearby. 3 to live, dwell. *Ia lama* ~ *di Paris,* He's lived in Paris a long time.

tjola² 1 to talk nonsense. 2 to gripe about s.t.

tjolang-tjaling in disorder.

tjolék see TJOKÉT.

tjoléng **pen–** thief.

tjolok 1 small torch. 2 piece of cloth dipped in oil and used as a light. 3 fuse, wick. **men–** 1 striking. *kelemahan jg* ~ striking weakness. 2 shocking, surprising. *angka² jg* ~ shocking figures. ~ *mata* 1 to catch o's eye. 2 obvious, conspicuous. *Kepandaiannja* ~ *mata,* His ability was obvious. 3 scandalous, shocking. *perbuatan jg* ~ *mata* a scandalous deed. **men–(i)** to illuminate with a torch.

tjolong **men–** to steal. **pen–** thief.

tjolot **men–** to jump over s.t. *Pentjuri itu* ~ *pagar,* The thief leaped the fence.

tjombér see PATJOMBÉRAN. **ke–an** rust. **–an** drainage ditch. *air* ~ rusty water.

tjombol see TOMBOL.

tjomék small hairs beneath lower lip.

tjomél 1 grumbling, nagging. *Djangan terlalu –,* Don't grumble so much. 2 dainty, exquisite. **men–i** to scold, reprimand. *Ia* ~ *anaknja,* She scolded her child. **–an** scolding, reproach. – *tjantik* extremely beautiful to look at.

tjomot grimy, dirty. *Mulutnja – dgn gula²,* His mouth was dirty from eating candy. **ber–** to be dirty, grimy, smeared. ~ *minjak* to be smeared with oil. **men–** to reach out to seize s.t. *Tangannja* ~ *utk mengambil pisau,* His hand reached out to seize the knife. – *momot* stained, soiled, smeared.

tjompang-tjamping in rags, tatters.

tjondong 1 leaning, inclining to o. side. *menara Pisa jg* – the leaning tower of Pisa. 2 inclined, sympathetic. *Ia – kepihak kiri,* He inclined toward the leftist party. 3 to set.

Matahari tlh –, The sun has set. 4 off, insane. *Pikirannja* –, He was slightly insane. **ke-an** 1 leaning, bias, sympathy. ∼ *résidén kepihak itu mendatangkan ketjurigaan,* The resident's sympathy for that side caused suspicion. 2 tendency, inclination. **men-kan** 1 to bend. 2 to incline, tend. *Penawaran sematjam itu mudah sekali* ∼ *hati,* An offer like that easily tempts one. – *ingatan* slightly crazy.

tjongak **men-** to hold o's head up. *Ia berdjalan sambil* ∼ , He walked with his head in the air. **men-kan** to lift, raise o's head.

tjongék deaf.

tjonggok **men-** to erect s.t.

tjongkah to stick out at an angle.

tjongkak 1 proud. 2 conceited, arrogant. 3 a shell sometimes used as money. **ke-an** 1 arrogance. 2 pride. – *dan ria* arrogant and haughty.

tjongkar-tjangkir protruding everywhere.

tjongkél see TJUNGKIL.

tjongk(e)lang to gallop.

tjongkol **men-kan** to project, stick out, cause to protrude. *Ia* ∼ *kepalanja membuang muka,* He stuck out his head to avoid seeing him.

tjongkong sentry box.

tjongo pickpocket.

tjongok **men-** to be upright, erect.

tjongol **men-** to protrude. *Bibirnja* ∼ , Her lips protruded.

tjongor snout.

tjonténg smear, stain, blemish. **ber-** to be smeared, smudged. **men-** to soil, dirty, smear. – *moréng* smeared and streaked.

tjonto see TJONTOH.

tjontoh 1 specimen, sample. – *barang jg mau dipesan* sample of the article to be ordered. 2 model. 3 pattern. 4 example. **memper-kan** to exemplify, give as an example. **men-** 1 to imitate, copy. *Ia* ∼ *temannja,* He imitated his friend. 2 to copy (from). *Ia* ∼ *dari buku,* He copied from a book. ∼ *karangan orang lain* to copy another's essay. **men-i** to exemplify, give an example to s.o. **men-kan** 1 to imitate. 2 to show by example. *Ia* ∼ *pd anaknja tjara membunuh lalat,* He showed his child how to kill a fly. **per-an** 1 specimen, sample. *nomor* ∼ trial number. 2 model. *désa* ∼ model village.

tjontong cone-shaped paper wrapper or container. *se- katjang* a container of peanuts.

tjop sorry, pardon me.

tjopét pickpocket. *Awas* –, Beware

of pickpockets. **ke-an** to be pilfered of s.t. *Ia* – *dompétnja dikeréta api,* His wallet was stolen on the train. **men-** to pickpocket, pilfer. **pen-** a pickpocket. **pen-an** pickpocketing, pilfering.

tjoplok to come loose, break off. *Kaki médja* –, The table leg came loose. **men-kan** to break s.t. off. *Ia* ∼ *kaki korsinja,* He broke off the leg of his chair. see TJEPLOK.

tjopot 1 dislodged. 2 broken off, loosened. *Pakunja blm* –, The nail hasn't come loose yet. *Giginja* –, The tooth fell out. **men-i, men-kan** 1 to take s.t. off. ∼ *sepatu* to take off shoes. 2 to pull s.t. out. ∼ *paku* to pull out a nail. 3 to untie. 4 to dismantle, take apart. 5 to remove, take away. *Usahanja utk* ∼ *semua kekuasaan dari radja itu blm berhasil,* Efforts to remove all authority from the hands of the king have not yet succeeded. **pen-an** removal, change. – *ban* to take a tire off a wheel.

tjor **di-** cast. **penge-an** foundry.

tjorak 1 design, motif. – *batik* batik design. 2 color. *–nja mérah,* The color is red. 3 stripe (of flag). 4 type, form. 5 feature, character(istic). *Perkumpulan itu –nja komunis,* The character of that organization is communistic. **ber-** 1 to have the design of. *kain jg* ∼ *burung dan padi* a cloth with a bird and rice-plant design. 2 striped, with bars. 3 to have the character of. *kumpulan jg* ∼ *politik* an organization with a political character. **men- -tjarikkan** to tear to bits. – *-tjarik* in tatters, in rags.

tjorang see TJURANG.

tjorat-tjarét rough draft, sketch.

tjorék scratch.

tjoréng 1 scratch, streak. 2 smear. **ber-** 1 streaked, striped. *matjan* ∼ striped tiger. 2 tattooed. **men-** to cross, scratch s.t. out. **men-kan** to streak, scrape s.t. on. *Ia* ∼ *kapur mérah ketémbok,* He scraped red chalk on the wall. **-an** 1 scratch. 2 streak. – *moréng* full of streaks and scratches.

tjorét scratch. **ber-** 1 underlined. 2 streaked. **men-** 1 to cross out (the wrong words). 2 to rule, make lines. 3 to do a pen drawing. *Ia pandai* ∼ , He's good at pen drawing. 4 to scratch, streak. ∼ *témbok dgn arang* to streak the wall with charcoal. **-an** 1 scratch, line, stripe. 2 pen drawing. – *morét* full of scratches.

tjoro cockroach.

tjorong 1 funnel. – *kapal* ship's funnel. – *utk menuang minjak* funnel for

pouring oil into s.t. 2 tube, pipe. 3
mine shaft. 4 microphone. 5 mouthpiece. **men-** 1 to shine, glare. *lampu
mobil jg* ~ glaring headlights. 2 to
radiate. **men-kan** 1 to broadcast. 2
to shine. *Ia* ~ *lampu mobilnja
ketempat itu*, He shone his headlights
on that spot. - *asap* chimney. -
bitjara megaphone. - *dengar* acoustic
duct. - *lampu* glass chimney of kerosene lamp. - *pembesar suara* loudspeaker. - *télpon* telephone receiver.
tjorot spout, mouth of a watering
can. **pen-** late-comer.
tjotjok 1 to agree, tally, jibe. *Uraiannja tidak - dgn kenjataan*, His explanation did not agree with the facts.
2 correct, exact. *Djamnja tidak -*,
The clock isn't correct. 3 to come
true. *Ramalannja -*, His prediction
came true. 4 to match. *Bunga itu -
dgn warna témbok*, The flowers match
the color of the wall. 5 to fit, be
suited. *Kuntji ini tidak - pd pintu
itu*, This key doesn't fit the door.
*Tanah itu tidak - dgn tanaman
tembakau*, This soil isn't suited for
growing tobacco. 6 to like, be agreeable. *Kalau - boléh ambil*, If you like
it you may have it. 7 pin. 8 skewer.
dua - saté two skewers of barbecued
meat. **ber-** to wear a hairpin. ~ *tanah*,
~ *tanam* to till the soil. **ke-an** agreement. **men-** 1 to pin. 2 to prick. 3
to puncture. *Duri* ~ *ban*, The thorn
punctured the tire. **men-kan** 1 to
compare, check. ~ *hasil hitungan* to
compare the results of the calculation. 2 to adjust. ~ *diri kpd iklim*
to adjust o.s. to the climate. 3 to set
right, correct. ~ *arlodji* to set the
watch right. 4 to pin. 5 to prick,
stick. ~ *djarum kebantal* to stick a
needle in the pillow. 6 to fit s.t. in
s.t. **ter-** pricked, stuck. *Kakinja* ~
paku, He stuck a nail in his foot.
pen- electric light plug. - *sanggul*
hairpin.
tjotjol men- to protrude. **men-kan**
to stick in, insert.
tjotok bill, beak. **men-** to peck.
tjuai insignificant. **men-** to despise,
hold contempt for s.o.
tjuatja 1 weather. 2 clear, bright.
terang - sesudah angin ribut semalam
a bright day after the storm last night.
tjuban reel.
tjubit men- to pinch. **men-i** to keep
pinching. *Ia* ~ *adiknja*, She kept
pinching her little sister. **-an** a pinch.
- *getil* a slight pinch.
tjubung² larva of flies.
tjuh go away! (to dogs)

tjuik see TJOBÉK. **men-** to salt and
dry fish.
tjuil men- to touch slightly, nudge.
Ia ~ *temannja mengadjak pulang*,
He nudged his friend asking him to
go home.
tjuit ber-(-), **men-(-)** to move o's
fingers excitedly. **men- -gamit** to
make nervous movements with o's
fingers. *Pembitjara itu* ~ , *tak tenang
sama sekali*, The speaker nervously
played with his fingers and was far
from calm. - *gamit* finger movements
by nervous speakers.
tjuk 1 see TJUKULÉLÉ.   2 choke
(auto). 3 mosquito larva.
tjuka vinegar.
tjukai 1 customs duty, toll, tax. -
tembakau duty on tobacco. 2 tariff.
men- to impose duty.
tjuki 1 k.o. checkers. 2 see PUKI.
ber- to play checkers. - *mai!* Dammit!
tjukil see TJUNGKIL. **-an** *kaju* etching,
woodcut.
tjukit 1 fork. 2 chopstick. - *gigi*
toothpick.
tjukulélé ukulele.
tjukup 1 enough, sufficient, adequate.
- *utk hari ini* enough for today.
persediaan jg - adequate supply.
Sdh - pandjangnja, It's long enough.
2 exactly. *Umurnja - 6 tahun*, He's
exactly 6 years old. *Uangnja - 6
rupiah*, He has exactly 6 rupiahs. 3
well-to-do, prosperous. *Ia termasuk
keluarga jg -*, He belongs to a well-
to-do family. 4 complete. *sebuah
rumah - dgn dapur dan kamar mandi*
a house complete with kitchen and
bathroom. 5 moderate. - *sadja untungnja*, The profit was moderate.
berke-an to be in moderate circumstances. *Iapun tidak* ~ , He doesn't
even have enough. **ke-an** a sufficiency,
an adequate amount. **men-i** 1 to
make up, complete, supplement. *Ia*
~ *uangnja utk membajar hutang*, He
supplemented his money to pay the
debt. 2 to fulfill. *Ia* ~ *segala sjarat²*,
He fulfilled all the requirements. 3
to be sufficient, suffice. *Gadjinja
tidak* ~ , His salary was insufficient.
4 to confirm, fulfill. ~ *permintaan
tuan* in fulfillment of your request.
men-kan 1 to make sufficient. *Ia* ~
uangnja dulu sebelum beli kartjis, He
made up the full amount before buying the ticket. 2 to make suffice, be
adequate. *Ia* ~ *gadjinja utk satu
bulan*, He made his salary suffice for
a month. **men- -²kan** to try to make
both ends meet. **se-nja** sufficient,
adequate. *Perangkoilah kiriman² pos*

~ , Please place sufficient postage on your mail. -an *sadja* just average (of a haircut). ~ *sadja untungnja*, The profit was moderate. - *bulannja* time for bearing a child, end of the period. - *lengkap* completed.

tjukur tonsure. **ber-** to shave. *Ia sedang* ~ , He's shaving. **men-** 1 to shave s.o. 2 to defeat. *Kesatuan bola Cornell* ~ *Yale*, Cornell's team beat Yale. **pen-** 1 o. who shaves. 2 a shaver (instrument). **-an** *listerik* electric shaver. - *batok* to cut hair with a soup bowl (coconut shell). - *sutji* holy tonsure.

tjula rhinoceros horn.

tjulik **men-** to kidnap. **pen-** kidnaper. **pen-an** kidnaping.

tjuma only, merely. *Kuénja tinggal - dua*, There were only two cookies left. **memper-kan** 1 to exempt. *Anak² dibawah 5 tahun diper-kan*, Children under 5 are exempted. 2 to belittle. *Ia* ~ *pengetahuan gurunja*, He belittled his teacher's knowledge. **per-** free, gratis. **-²** 1 free of charge, gratis. *Ia mendapat makan dan minum* ~ , He got food and drink free. 2 useless, in vain. ~ *ia dlm usahanja itu*, His efforts were of no use.

tjuman only that. - *begitu sadja?* Is that all?

tjumbu 1 flattery, endearment. 2 joke. **ber-** to sit sidesaddle (on a scooter). **ber-** **-²(an)** 1 to joke, banter back and forth. 2 to make love to e.o., smooch. **men-i** 1 to flatter. 2 to fondle. *Ia* ~ *anaknja*, She's fondling her child. **-(-)an** 1 jokes. 2 flattery, compliment. - *dan belai* sweet words and caresses.

tjumbul see TJEMBUL.

tjumi² 1 rabble, scum. 2 stool pigeon. 3 squid.

tjuming see TJUMA.

tjun 1 to kiss (children's term). 2 an inch.

tjunam tongs.

tjunda see TJUTJUNDA.

tjundang 1 see KETJUNDANG. 2 troublemaking. **men-** to cause trouble.

tjung see KATJUNG. lad, small boy. -, *bawalah buku ini kesana*, Boy, take this book over there.

tjungkil **men-** 1 to lift, dig out. *Ia* ~ *batu besar itu dgn kaju*, He lifted out the big rock with a piece of wood. 2 to gouge out. *Mata² itu di- matanja*, The spy's eyes were gouged out. 3 to pick. ~ *gigi* to pick o's teeth. 4 to vaccinate, inoculate. (**pen-**)- *gigi* toothpick.

tjup halt, stop!

tjupak a cubic measure (ca. 0.786 kilograms).

tjupar **men-** to twist things around.

tjupet 1 too tight, insufficient, skimpy. 2 narrow-minded. 3 shortsighted. **ke-an** 1 narrow-mindedness. 2 cramped for space.

tjuping ear lobes.

tjuplik **men-** 1 to borrow. 2 to cite. **-an** fragment.

tjupu² jewelry box.

tjura joke, jest. **ber-** 1 to joke. 2 to call s.o. names.

tjurah **men-i** 1 to pour down on. *Hudjan* ~ *sawah*, Rain poured down on the rice fields. 2 to bestow upon. *Anak itu di-i pemberian² hari natal*, The child was showered with Christmas gifts. **men-kan** 1 to pour s.t. on. ~ *air kekepala* to pour water on s.o.'s head. 2 to expend. *Ia* ~ *segala kekuatannja utk mengangkat batu itu*, He exerted all his strength to lift that stone. ~ *isi hati* to speak freely. ~ *perhatian istiméwa* to take special pains. (**pen-**)-**an** 1 outpour. 2 bestowal. ~ *pemberian* bestowal of gifts. 3 expression. 4 pouring out.

tjurai loose, detached. *Adakah uang -?* Do you have any loose change? *Ada jg diikat ada jg -*, There are bound ones and loose ones. **men-kan** 1 to loosen s.t. 2 to explain. ~ *duduknja perkara* to explain the position of the case. 3 to separate. *Ia* ~ *uang kertas daripada uang -*, He separated the bank notes from loose cash. **-an** 1 explanation. 2 separation.

tjuram steep. **men-** 1 sloping, on an incline. 2 precipitous.

tjurang dishonest, deceitful. **ke-an** 1 deceit, fraud. 2 foul (in boxing, etc.). **men-i** to deceive, mislead s.o.

tjurat spout. **men-** to gush forth.

tjuri **ke-an** 1 to have stolen. *Ia* ~ *kudanja semalam*, His horse was stolen last night. 2 robbed. **men-** 1 to steal s.t. 2 to rob s.o. (**men-**) **-²** in a clandestine way, secretly. *Ia* ~ *menemui kekasihnja*, She was meeting her sweetheart secretly. **pen-** thief. **pen-an** theft. **-an** stolen items.

tjuriah 1 talkative, garrulous. 2 chatty.

tjuriga 1 suspicious. *Ia - thd orang baru*, He's suspicious of newcomers. 2 hesitant. *Meréka - akan menerima temannja itu*, They were hesitant about receiving their friends. **ke-an** suspicion. **men-i** to suspect, distrust s.o. **men-kan** 1 to suspect, be suspicious of s.o. 2 to arouse suspicion.

Sikapnja jg gandjil itu ∼ *temannja,* His strange attitude aroused his friend's suspicion. 3 suspicious. 4 to hesitate about s.t.

tjuti leave, furlough. *Ia lagi* -, He's on leave. **ber-** to be on leave. *Ia pergi* ∼ , He left on furlough. - *dinas* official leave. - *tahunan* annual leave.

tjutja magic formula. **men-** 1 to pronounce a magic formula. 2 to scoff at s.t. or s.o.

tjutji **men-** 1 to wash. ∼ *rambut* to shampoo the hair. ∼ *tangan* to wash the hands. 2 to wash, do the laundry. ∼ *pakaian* to launder the clothes. 3 to develop a film. **men-kan** 1 to wash s.t. for s.o. *Ia* ∼ *adiknja sebuah tjita,* She washed a piece of cloth for her younger sister. 2 to have s.t. washed, send to the laundry. *Ia* ∼ *djasnja,* She sent his jacket to the laundry. **pen-** laundryman (woman). ∼ *mulut* dessert. **pen-an** *pilem* developing of film. -an 1 laundry, wash. 2 manner of washing. ∼*nja tidak bersih,* His manner of washing isn't clean. - *darah* blood purifier. - *maki* abuse, scorn. - *muka* 1 to wash o's face. 2 washstand or basin. - *perut* laxative. - *rambut* a shampoo.

tjutju grandchild. **ber-** to have grandchildren. - *Adam* humanity.

tjutjuh **men-** 1 to kindle a fire. 2 to fire a gun.

tjutjuk **men-** to pin s.t **men-kan** to sting, tickle.

tjutjunda grandchild (respectful form).

tjutjunguk 1 slave. 2 accomplice in evil deeds.

tjutjup **men-** 1 to kiss s.o. 2 to suck on s.t.

tjutjur 1 a flow, a trickle. 2 a cake made of flour, palm sugar, and coconut and fried in oil. 3 bowsprit. **ber-an** to flow, stream, gush. *Air matanja* ∼ , The tears streamed down her cheek. **men-i** to pour on, drop on. ∼ *matanja dgn tétés mata* to pour drops in o's eyes. **men-kan** 1 to drop s.t. on. ∼ *obat pd lukanja* to drop medicine on a wound. 2 to let s.t. drop on o.s. ∼ *air dikepalanja* to let water fall on o's head. -an drain. ∼ *atap* eaves. - *darah* hemorrhage.

tjutjut shark. **men-** to suck.

T.K. [*Taman Kanak*²] kindergarten.

tk [*tingkat*] 1 level. 2 floor, story.

tkw [*tidak kawin*] unmarried.

tlh [*telah*] always.

tn. [*tuan*] Mr.

to' see DATUK. - *puan* see DATUK PEREMPUAN.

tobak **men-** to cut o's nails.

tobat 1 good heavens! 2 I've had it. (That does it.) 3 regret, remorse. 4 see TAUBAT. **ber-** to regret, be sorry. **men-kan** to break, cure, s.o. of s.t.

tob(e)ros **men-** 1 to break through. *Kuda itu lari* ∼ *pagar,* The horse ran through the fence. 2 to break in (of a door), enter by force. **pen-an** 1 a breakthrough, breach. 2 penetration.

toblos see TOB(E)ROS.

toboh a group.

toch see TOH.

todak swordfish.

todjok sodjok billiards.

todjos **pen-an** punching, perforation. ∼ *tanda gambar* punching of illustrated ballot (used by illiterates).

todong **men-(kan)** 1 to point, aim. *Ia* ∼ *pistolnja kpd saja,* He pointed his pistol at me. 2 to menace, threaten s.o. -an 1 threat. 2 holdup, stick-up.

tofan see TAUFAN.

toga 1 academic robe. 2 judge's robe.

togél tailless.

togok 1 stump, trunk. 2 lamp. **ber-** to sit somewhere.

toh 1 yet, nevertheless. *Ia* - *bisa datang?* But he can come, can't he? *Saudara* - *harus selesai hari ini, bukan?* I suppose you must be ready today, mustn't you? 2 still, yet. *Ia marah, tetapi* - *datang,* He was angry, but still he came.

tohok 1 javelin. 2 ray (fish). **men-** to stab.

tohor 1 shallow, superficial. *Pengetahuannja* - , His knowledge is superficial. 2 dried up. **ber-** to dry up. ∼ *air liur* to talk a great deal. *tidak* ∼ *kaki* to work hard with no time to rest. **men-kan** to dry s.t. up. ∼ *sungai* to dry up a river.

tojor **men-** to slap s.o. in the face.

tok just, merely, only. *Berdjuang* - *dgn tidak memakai siasat, adalah ketololan besar,* Just fighting without using strategy is very foolish.

toké(k) 1 gecko or house lizard. 2 call of a gecko.

Tokio Tokyo.

toko shop, store. - *buku* bookstore, bookshop. **ber-** to have, manage, a store. **per-an** shop matters. - *emas* jewelry store. - *kelontong* variety, general, store. - *keriting rambut* beauty parlor. - *loak* secondhand shop. - *sandang-pangan* store through which basic necessities are sold at government-fixed prices. – *tukang mendjahit* tailor shop.

tokoh 1 shape, form, figure. – *badan* bodily shape. – *jg bulat* round shape. 2 style. – *Barat* Western style. 3 figure. *Ia – jg penting dikonperénsi itu,* He's an important figure at the conference. **ber–** to have the shape of. *rumah jg ~ kapal* a house in the shape of a boat. **men–** to cheat, deceive. **men–i** to run, lead (a group). **men–kan** to feature s.t. **pen–** cheater, deceiver.

tokok s.t. extra, a windfall. **men–** 1 to give s.t. extra. 2 to replenish. 3 to tap, strike, hit. *~ kawat* to wire, send a telegram.

tokong 1 tuft of hair. 2 rocky islet.

tokowan shopkeeper, store owner.

toksikosis toxicosis.

toktjer 1 to start instantly. *Mobil saja – startnja,* My car starts instantly. 2 to light instantly. *Gerétan saja –,* My lighter catches instantly.

tolak ber– to leave. *Ia ~ ke Singapura,* He left for Singapore. *~ bara* to take on ballast. *~ belakang* to separate, take leave of e.o. *Kedua teman itu ~ belakang,* The 2 friends went their separate ways. *~ pinggang* to stand with arms akimbo. *~ dari dalil*² departing from the theses, taking the theses as a point of departure. **ber– –²** 1 to accuse e.o. 2 to impose tasks on e.o. **ber– –²an** to push e.o. **men–(kan)** 1 to reject, refuse. *Permintaan saja di–,* My request was refused. 2 to push. *~ keréta* to push a handcart. 3 to parry, push aside, ward off. *~ bala* to ward off misfortune. 4 to prevent. *~ bahaja kebakaran* to prevent danger of fire. 5 to repel. *~ pukulan* to parry a blow. *~ pukulan musuh* to repel the enemy's blows. 6 to throw on s.o. *Ia ~ kesalahan itu pd temannja,* He threw the blame on his friend. 7 to subtract. *~ 5 dari 10* to subtract 5 from 10. **pen–** rejector. *~ bisa* antidote, antitoxin. **pen–an** 1 refusal, rejection. 2 combat, warding off, parrying. **–an** 1 rejection. 2 rejected. *barang* – rejected articles. 3 pushing. 4 parrying. 5 subtraction. *– –men–* 1 to parry e.o. 2 to push e.o. *– angsur* give and take (in bargaining). *– bala* warding off misfortune. *– bahar, – bara* ballast. *– belakang* taking leave of e.o. *– pinggang* with arms akimbo. *– raih* bargaining.

tolan comrade, friend.

toléh men– to turn, look around.

~ kekanan to look to the right. **men–kan** to turn o's head.

toleransi tolerance.

tolok 1 equal, match. 2 partner. *tidak ber–* peerless. **men–** 1 to compare. 2 to try. **pen–** 1 an equal. 2 standard.

tolol 1 stupid. *– benar kamu,* You're really stupid. 2 silly, foolish. **ke–an** 1 stupidity. 2 foolishness. *si–* moron.

tolong help. *Minta –,* Get help for me. *– minta tuan Rahmat datang sebentar,* Please ask Mr. Rahmat to come here a moment. **ber– –²an** to give mutual assistance. **ke–an** to be helped, aided. *Jg luka itu masih blm ~ ,* The wounded were still not being helped. **men–(i)** to help, aid, assist, s.o. **pen–** 1 helper, benefactor. 2 rescuer. **(per)–an** help, aid, assistance. *~ pertama dlm ketjelakaan* first aid. *– –men–* to give mutual aid. *tidak ter–* irretrievable, irrevocable.

tomat tomato.

tombak 1 spear, lance. 2 a linear measure (12 ft.) **men–(i)** to stab with a spear.

tombok men– 1 to pay extra, an additional fee. *Berapa kami harus ~ utk melandjutkan perdjalanan ini?* How much extra must we pay in order to continue this trip? 2 to pay to a dance-hall girl.

tombol 1 doorknob. 2 button. *Tekanlah – membunjikan bél,* Push the button to ring the bell.

tombong mortar (artillery).

tompang see TUMPANG.

ton 1 ton. 2 abbrev. for PELETON platoon.

tonase tonnage.

tondjol bump, lump. **ber–** to bulge, be lumpy. *Sakunja ~ penuh dgn uang,* His pocket was bulging with money. **ber– –²** bumpy. *djalan jg ~* a bumpy road. **kemen–an** 1 bulging. 2 protruding. 3 conspicuousness. **men–** 1 to bulge. *bungkusan jg ~ penuh berisi* a package with bulging contents. 2 to protrude, stick out. *Badannja ~ dari djendéla,* His body stuck out the window. 3 conspicuous, prominent. *kekajaannja jg ~* his conspicuous wealth. 4 disturbing. *tingkah lakunja jg amat ~* his very disturbing behavior. 5 obvious. *Hal ini ~ ,* This matter is obvious. **men–kan** 1 to stick s.t. out. *Ia ~ kepalanja dari djendéla,* He stuck his head out the window. *~ pistol* to stick out o's pistol. 2 to push, thrust forward. *~ diri* to thrust o.s. forward.

3 to show off, present. ~ *angka²nja* to show off o's grades. 4 to feature. *Kita -kan* ... We feature ... **ter-** 1 pushed, thrust forward. 2 bulging. *Sakunja ~ penuh dgn uang*, His pocket was bulging with money. 3 conspicuous. *Warna jg mérah ~ djelas*, The red was conspicuous. **-an** outstanding. *tokoh ~ minggu ini* this week's outstanding figure, man or woman of the week.

tong barrel, vat, cask. *se- bir* a barrel of beer. **-an** in barrels. *- sampah* trash bin.

tonggak 1 tree stump. 2 post, pole. 3 tree trunk. 4 pillar of a house. 5 1,500 meters. **men-** to drink from a bottle by holding it bottom up. *- gantungan* gallows.

tonggok heap, pile. **ber-** to stand upright. **men-** to pile up s.t. *~ batu bata* to pile up bricks. **se-** a pile (of papers, etc.).

tonggos large and prominent. *Giginja -*, He had buckteeth. **ber-** bucktoothed.

tongkang a barge.

tongkat 1 cane, walking stick. 2 crutch. 3 baton. 4 swagger stick. **ber-** to use as a cane. *Orang tua itu ~ besi*, The old man had an iron walking stick. *~ ketiak* to walk on crutches. *~ senduk* to be far along in years. **ber-kan** to rest on. *rumah jg ~ batu* a house resting on stones. **men-(kan)** 1 to hold up. *Apakah jg ~ dibawah tempat tidur?* What is holding it up under the bed? 2 to raise. *~ bantalnja dgn djas* to raise o's pillow by placing a jacket under it. *- ampai* divining rod. *- djalan* walking stick. *- ketiak* crutches.

tongkéng coccyx.

tongkol 1 tuna fish. 2 ear. *se- djagung* an ear of corn. 3 nugget, lump. *se- mas* a gold nugget. **ber-** like a lump.

tongkrong **men-** 1 to squat. 2 to lounge around, take it easy.

tongol **men-** to emerge, appear. *Kepalanja ~ dari djendéla*, Her head emerged from the window.

tongong nincompoop, blockhead.

tongtong signal drum made from a bamboo or hollowed-out log.

tonika tonic.

tonil 1 legitimate theater, the stage. 2 play, show. **men-kan** 1 to act, perform. 2 to dramatize, put into a play. *Meréka ~ bukunja*, They dramatized his book.

tonton **memper-kan**, **men-kan** 1 to show (off), exhibit. *~ kepandaiannja* to show off his cleverness. 2 to play,

perform. *Meréka ~ tari Djawa*, They performed Javanese dances. **men-** 1 to watch, note, observe, look at. *Ia ~ kesibukan dipasar*, He watched the hustle and bustle in the market place. 2 to go to the show, movies. *Mari kita ~* , Let's go to the movies. **men-i** to look at. *Kamu bisa makan tanpa di-i orang*, You can eat without being seen by anyone. **pen-** spectator, onlooker. **-an** 1 show, performance. 2 exhibition, presentation. 3 spectacle. *Nonton dimana?* 1 What's playing where? 2 To which show are you going?

topan typhoon, hurricane.

topang 1 prop, support. 2 gaff. **ber-** 1 to lean on, be supported on. *Rumah itu ~ pd batu besar*, The house was supported by a large stone. 2 to contradict. *Perkataannja ~ pd jg dikatakan semula*, His words contradicted what he had said previously. 3 to be in conflict. *Ia ~ dgn temannja dlm soal itu*, He was in conflict with his friend in that matter. *~ dagu* to sit with o's chin in o's hands. **men-** 1 to support. *~ kepala dgn tangannja* to support the head with the hands. 2 to contradict. *Ia ~ perkataan gurunja*, He contradicted his teacher's words. 3 to disagree. **pen-** support, prop. **per-an** 1 contradiction. 2 conflict, dispute. **-an** prop, support.

topdal ship's log.

topéng mask. *- gas* gas mask. **ber-** 1 to have or wear a mask. 2 to put on a front, cover up. *Ia selalu ~ djika berhadapan dgn orang*, He was always putting on a front when he met a person. **memper-** 1 to mask, hide, disguise. *~ kesusahannja* to disguise o's sorrow. 2 to wear as a mask. *Ia ~ rupa raksasa*, He put on a giant's mask.

topi hat (Western style). **ber-** to wear a hat. *- badja* steel helmet. *- djaksi* Panama hat. *- gabus* pith helmet. *- keselamatan* safety helmet. *- pandan, - rumput, - tikar* straw hat.

topo rag.

topong 1 a small basket. 2 conical.

torak bobbin holder. *-²* cylinder.

toréh **men-** to cut into, cut open. **-an** a notch, incision.

torék ear disease.

torés see TORÉH.

torné tour. **ber-** to make a tour.

toros see TURUS. *satu - sabun tjutji* a long piece of soap.

torpedir **ment-** to torpedo.

torpédo torpedo.

torsi torsion.

total total. **ke–an** totality. – *djéndral sum* total.
totalisator sweepstakes.
totalitér total. *peperangan* – total war.
totalitérisme totalitarianism.
totalitét totality.
toto see TOTALISATOR.
totok 1 full-blooded. *Belanda* – a full-blooded Dutchman. 2 newcomer. *Saja masih* – *disini,* I'm still a newcomer here. 3 see TUTUK.
tournooi tourney.
TPS [*Tempat Pemungutan Suara*] poll, voting place.
trachum trachoma.
tradisi tradition.
tragédi tragedy.
tragik tragedy.
tragis tragic.
trajék stretch, section.
traksi traction.
traktir **men–** to treat s.o. *Ia suka* ∼ *teman²nja,* He likes to treat his friends.
traktor tractor. **ment–i** to do work with a tractor. **pent–an** bulldozing.
trampil **ke–an** skill.
transaksi transaction.
transfusi transfusion.
Transkopemada [(*Départemén*) *Transmigrasi, Koperasi dan Pembangunan Masjarakat Désa*] Ministry of Resettlement, Co-operatives, and Village Development.
transmigran 1 settler. 2 migrant.
transmigrasi resettlement.
trasi see TERASI.
trasir **ment–** to trace.
trém streetcar, tram.
tresno fond. *Ia* – *kpd partai itu,* He's fond of that party.
tri three (commonly used in compounds).
tribulan quarterly.
tribune stand (part of stadium). – *barat* west stand. – *terbuka* bleachers, open stands.
Trikomando see KOMANDO RAKJAT.
Trikora [*Tri Komando Rakjat*] see KOMANDO RAKJAT.
trilipat in triplicate.
trimatra three-dimensional.
trimurti (Holy) Trinity.
trindil robbed, fleeced.
triplék see KAJU.
Triprogram a program consisting of three points.
tri-sila threefold. *sumpah* – threefold oath.
tritunggal trilogy.
triwarsa 3 years.
triwindu 24 years.
triwulan see TRIBULAN. **–an** quarterly.

trm. [*transmigrasi*] resettlement.
tromolpos P.O. box (portable). see TEROMOL.
trompét trumpet.
tropika tropics.
trotoir sidewalk.
truk truck.
tsb [*tersebut*] (above-)mentioned.
TSP [*toko sandang pangan*] government shop for basic necessities.
tst [*tahu sama tahu*] silent agreement between two persons participating in a mutually advantageous illegal deal.
t.t. 1 [*tertanda*] signed. 2 [*tertanggal*] dated.
TT [*Timur Tengah*] Middle East.
t.t.d. [*tertanda*] signed.
ttg 1 [*tentang*] about, concerning. 2 [*tertanggal*] dated.
ttgl [*tertanggal*] dated.
t.t(h). [*tanpa tahun*] no year.
tu 1 see ITU. 2 see SATU.
T.U. [*Tata Usaha*] administration.
tua 1 old. *Ia sdh* –, He's old. *Ia* – *5 bulan dari saja,* He was 5 months older than I. 2 dark of color. *mérah* – dark red. 3 pure. *mas* – pure gold. 4 head, chief. – *kampung* village elder. – *rumah* head of the family. 5 ripe. *Buahnja masih masam karena blm* –, The fruit is still sour because it isn't ripe yet. **ber–** –² 1 according to seniority. *Meréka berdjédjer* ∼ , They lined up according to seniority. 2 to grow old together. *Laki isteri* ∼ , Husband and wife grew old together. **ke–** see KETUA. **ke–an** too old. *Ia* ∼ , He's too old. **men–i** to head. *Ali* ∼ *rombongan itu,* Ali headed that group. **men–kan** 1 to let s.t. grow older, riper, etc. ∼ *buah dipohonnja* to let the fruit ripen on the tree. ∼ *mas* to make the gold purer. ∼ *warnanja* to let the color get deeper. 2 to marry s.o. off. 3 to make s.o. head. *Rapat* ∼ *Pak Karto,* The meeting made Pak Karto chairman. 4 to consider older. *Dlm pemilihan itu ia di–kan daripada saja,* In the elections he was thought older than I. **menge–i** see KETUA. **penge–** see KETUA. **ter–** oldest. **–²** 1 old age. 2 freckles. ∼ *keladi,* ∼ *kelapa* old and firm (said of s.o. still sexually attractive to the opposite sex). ∼ *terung asam* an old fellow who pretends to be young. **–an** older. – *bangka* very old, senile. – *bangkot* old in years but young in spirit. – *datuk* old and dignified. – *ganjut* trying to look younger than o's years. – *kutuk* old scoundrel. – *lara* a wretched old person. – *lélér* 1 run-down, dilapidated. 2 old, past o's prime. – *lontok*

senile. – *renta* 1 decrepit, in o's
dotage. 2 dilapidated. – *suntuk* old,
aged. – *tjatuk* feeble-minded from old
age. – *uzur* very old.
tuah 1 luck, fortune. 2 magic power.
3 respect, honor, prestige. – *seorang
pahlawan naik sesudah matinja*, A
hero's prestige increases after his
death. **ber-** 1 lucky, fortunate. *Ia* ~
menarik loteré, He was lucky to hit
the jackpot. 2 to bring good luck.
3 to have magic power. *makam jg* ~
a grave which has magic power.
ke--an 1 invulnerability. 2 lucky, fortunate. *Meréka* ~ *dgn datangnja
dinegeri itu*, They were very lucky
to come to that country. 3 to be
under magic influence. *Ia* ~ , She
was under magic influence.
tuai men- 1 to harvest rice by cutting each stalk individually close to
the ear with an *ani²*. 2 to reap. *Jg
membeli itu kelak jg* ~ , The buyer
is the o. who reaps later on. **pen-**
rice harvest knife. **pen-an** harvesting
of rice.
tuak 1 palm wine. 2 toddy.
tual a block of wood. **ber-** –² in
blocks.
tuala towel.
tualang wanderer, tramp. **ber-** 1
to wander, roam, tramp around.
2 to swarm (of bees). **pe-an** gadding
about. **pe(r)-** wanderer, tramp. **per-**
an adventure.
tuam hot compress. **ber-, men-** to
apply a hot compress. **men-i** to
treat with compresses.
tuan 1 Mr. – *Ali* Mr. Ali. 2 you
(form of address for Western adult
males but sometimes used to Indonesians). *Apa* – *suka ini?* Do you
like this? 3 sir. *Sdh*, –, Yes, sir.
4 master. *budak dan –nja* a slave
and his master. 5 lord. – *tanah*
landlord. *-ku* 1 Sire. 2 Your Majesty.
ber- 1 to act as boss. *Semeninggal
ajahnja ia* ~ *dirumahnja*, After the
death of his father he acted as boss
at home. 2 to serve as master. *Kpd
siapa meréka* ~? Whom do they
serve as master? 3 to have a master.
daérah tidak ~ no man's land.
4 to address as *tuan. Meréka selalu*
~ , They always use *tuan* to e.o.
memper-i to dominate, exercise control over. **memper-(kan)** 1 to respect. *Ia diper- oléh anak buahnja*,
He was respected by his crew. 2 to
address s.o. with *tuan. Jg Diper-
Agung* His Majesty. **per-an** 1 sovereignty, suzerainty. 2 ruling class,
upper class. 3 rule, government. ~
tanah landlordism, land ownership.

– *besar* 1 boss, head. 2 important
individual. – *pabrik* factory owner. –
puteri princess. – *rumah* 1 family
head. 2 host. – *tamu* host. – *tanah*
landholder, landlord.
tuang men- 1 to pour. ~ *kopi
ketjangkir* to pour coffee into a
cup. 2 to cast. ~ *besi* to cast iron.
men-i to pour into. ~ *tjangkir dgn
air panas* to pour hot water into a
cup. **men-kan** to pour out, empty.
~ *kopi ketjangkir* to pour coffee into
a cup. **-an** 1 a mold used in casting
a matrix. 2 shape, form. 3 pouring.
4 casting.
tuangku = TUANKU.
tuanku see TUAN.
tuarang dry period.
tuas lever. **men-** to lift, raise, s.t.
up.
tuba 1 stupefying drug used in fishing. 2 name of plants from which
such a drug is obtained. **men-(i)** to
catch fish by poisoning or drugging.
– *tikus* arsenic.
tuban² amnion.
tuberculosa tuberculosis.
tubi ber-(-) 1 persistently, repeatedly. ~ *andjing itu dipukul*,
The dog was beaten repeatedly.
Dibatjanja buku itu ~ , He read the
book repeatedly. 2 indefatigably, un-
tiringly. **memper-** –² to intensify.
Ia ~ *pukulannja*, He intensified his
blows. **men-** 1 to persevere in,
keep at. 2 to repeat. *Ia* ~ *pertanjaannja*, He repeated his question.
tubin the fourth day hence.
tubir ravine, gully. **men-** deep, steep.
tubruk ber-an to have a collision.
Mobil ~ *dgn truk*, The car collided
with a truck. **ke-** 1 to hit, strike.
Kepalanja ~ *témbok*, His head struck
a wall. 2 struck, run over. *Ada orang*
~ *mobil*, S.o. was hit by a car. **men-**
1 to collide with, run into. *Ia*
~ *témbok*, He ran into a wall. 2
to run over, hit, s.o. **-an** collision,
crash.
tubuh 1 body. 2 person. *menghadap*
– to appear in person. **berse-, menje-i**
to have sexual intercourse with. **men-**
kan 1 to realize, bring to realization.
~ *tjita²nja* to realize o's ideals.
2 to incorporate. 3 to shape, create.
per-an 1 organization. 2 corporation.
perse-an coitus, copulation. **se-** 1
in harmony. 2 coitus, copulation. *djas
bekas* – a worn-out jacket.
tuding sloping, at an angle. **men-**
to accuse.
tudjah men-(kan) to stab downward.
tudju the act of bewitching s.o. by
pointing at him. **ber-an** 1 to have a

purpose, an aim. *Kehidupannja tiada* ~, His life has no purpose. *katakerdja* ~ transitive verb. 2 to intend. *Saudara* ~ *kemana?* Where do you intend to go? *Ia* ~ *menjelesaikan pekerdjaannja*, He intends to finish his work. **berse-** 1 to have o. and the same aim or purpose. 2 to agree. ~ *dgn* in accordance with. ~ *dgn permintaan tuan* in accordance with your request. **ke-** agreed. ~ *hati* o's favorite, fondest, wish. **memperkan** to bring into line, co-ordinate. **menje-i** 1 to agree with. ~ *usul* to agree with a proposal. 2 to approve. ~ *belandja tahunan* to approve the annual budget. 3 to ratify. *Parlemén* ~ *tindakan pemerintah*, Parliament ratified the government's action. **men-(i)** 1 in the direction of. *Ia berangkat* ~ *Paris*, He headed for Paris. 2 to go toward. *Meréka* ~ *selatan*, They went southward. 3 to aim, strive, for. *Meréka giat berusaha* ~ *keamanan dunia*, They were striving hard for world peace. 4 to concern, be aimed at. *Sindiran itu* ~ *kamu*, Those hints were aimed at you. 5 to practice sorcery on s.o. *Ia sakit di- orang*, He was made ill by sorcery. **menje-kan** to bring into line. ~ *pengeluaran dgn pemasukan* to make both ends meet. **men-kan** 1 to point, aim. *Ia* ~ *pistolnja kpd saja*, He pointed his gun at me. 2 to direct, aim. *Ia* ~ *perahunja kepelabuhan*, He directed his boat toward the harbor. *Ia* ~ *sindirannja kpd saja*, He directed his hints at me. 3 to head, go. *Ia* ~ *langkahnja keselatan*, He headed south. **pen-** 1 agreed. 2 director, indicator. ~ *hati* to o's liking. *makanan* ~ *hati* o's favorite dish. **perse-an** 1 treaty, agreement. ~ *Versailles* Treaty of Versailles. 2 approval. ~ *parlémén* approval of parliament. 3 settlement, agreement. **se-** *(dgn, kpd)* 1 to agree (with). *Meréka* ~ *dgn usul*, They agreed with the proposal. *tanda tidak* ~*nja* a sign of disagreement. 2 to harmonize, agree with. *Warna témbok jg* ~ *dgn warna perkakas rumah*, The color of the wall harmonized with the furniture. 3 to like. *Ambillah kalau* ~ *dgn barang itu*, Take it if you like it. **se-an** 1 of o. purpose, aim. *Banjak djalan jg* ~ *maksudnja*, There are many roads with the same purpose. 2 having the same direction. *Kapal²itu berlajar* ~ , The ships sailed in the same direction. **-an** 1 aim, purpose, objective. *Apakah* ~ *saudara datang kemari?* What's your purpose

in coming here? *Apa* ~ *perkumpulan ini?* What's the aim of this organization? 2 direction. ~ *pesawat itu ke Birma*, The direction of the plane is toward Burma. 3 object (gram.). 4 object, party. – *penderita* the suffering party. 5 end. *guna* ~² *sendiri* for their own ends. 6 destination, goal. 7 target.

tudjuh 7. **ber-** to be 7. *Meréka* ~ *pergi kekota*, The 7 of them went to town. **men-** *(bulan, hari)* to commemorate the seventh month of pregnancy, seventh day of death. *Keluarganja* ~ *hari kematian ajahnja*, The family commemorated the seventh day of the father's death. – *belas* 17. – *puluh* 70.

tuduh men- to accuse. **men-kan** to accuse. *Ia* ~ *kegagalan itu kpd temannja*, He accused his friend of the failure. **pen-** 1 prosecutor. 2 accuser, plaintiff. **pen-an** accusation. **ter-** accused. *si*~ the accused. **-an** accusation, complaint, charge. *atas* ~ on a charge of. – **-men-** mutual recrimination.

tudung 1 veil, cover. 2 shade. – *lampu* lamp shade. 3 sun hat. **ber-** 1 to be covered. 2 to use a veil. **men-(i)** to cover s.t. up or over. **men-kan** to put s.t. as a cover. ~ *kain putih kpd médja* to cover a table with a white cloth. **pen-an** cover(ing). – *lingkup* veil used by Indonesian women in some areas of the country. – *muka* veil.

tugal dibble. **men-** to dibble, plant.

tugas 1 duty. 2 task, function. **ber-** to have the duty or task. *Ia pergi tiada* ~ , He left without an assignment. **men-kan** to charge s.o. with, give s.o. the task of. *Présidén* ~ *pembérésan keamanan didaérah itu kepadanja*, The president gave him the task of restoring security in that area. 2 to assign. – *kewadjiban* 1 duty. 2 task. 3 function. **pe-** 1 officer in charge. 2 jailer, guard. ~ *pesuratan* postman.

tugu 1 post, column, pillar. 2 monument. – *peringatan* memorial, monument.

Tuhan 1 God. 2 the Lord. **ber-** 1 to believe in God. *tidak* ~ atheistic. 2 to worship. *Meréka* ~ *kpd lembu*, They worship the cow. **berke-an** devout. **ke-an** 1 belief in God. 2 divinity, deity. 3 religious. 4 faith. **memper-(kan)** 1 to profess as God. 2 to worship s.t. as a deity. ~ *benda* to worship material objects as deities. – *Allah* God. – *jg Esa* the one God.

tuhfah 1 gift. 2 jewel.

tuil a jack, lever. **men–** to raise with a jack or lever.

tuk see DATUK.

tukai female sex organs.

tukak sore, ulcer. **men–** to fester.

tukal skein of yarn.

tukang 1 artisan. 2 workman, skilled laborer. 3 o. who does s.t. – *makan* eater. – *ngorok* snorer. – *tidur* sleeper. **ber–, men–** to be an artisan, skilled laborer. **ke–an** skill, craftsmanship. **men–i** 1 to work as a craftsman, make, construct. ~ *korsi* to make a chair. 2 to repair, work on s.t. ~ *korsi rusak* to repair a broken chair. ~ *kurung ajam* to work on a chicken coop. **per–an** 1 trade. *sekolah* ~ trade school. 2 handicraft. 3 craftsmanship. 4 craft, guild, association. – **-men–** to be jack-of-all-trades. – *air* water carrier. – *amin* a yes man. – *angon* shepherd. – *arlodji* watchmaker. – *azan* o. who summons to prayer. – *bakul* basket maker. – *banjol* a jokester. – *bantai* butcher. – *batu* bricklayer. – *bendé* public auctioneer. – *bengkong* o. who performs circumcisions. – *berkelahi* fighter. – *besi* blacksmith. – *bikin sadjak* composer of short verses. – *binatu* laundryman. – *bohong* liar. – *bontjéng* sponger, parasite. – *bubut* a fitter. – *chatan, – chitan* circumciser. – *daging* butcher. – *dansa* acrobat, entertainer. – *diko* car painter. – *djahit* tailor. – *djam* watch repairer. – *djentera* helmsman. – *djilid* bookbinder. – *djiplak* plagiarist, plagiarizer. – *dobi* laundryman. – *enggih* a yes man. – *gelap mata* conjurer, magician. – *genting* tilemaker. – *gerobak* wheelwright. – *gigi* dental technician (makes false teeth). – *gunting rambut* barber. – *ikan* fishmonger. – *intip* 1 peeping tom. 2 knot-hole watcher (at sports events). 3 spy. – *kaju* carpenter. – *kasut* shoemaker. – *katjau* agitator, troublemaker. – *kebun* gardener. – *kelontong* peddler, vendor. – *keréta* wheelwright. – *kuda* stableboy. – *kué* 1 baker. 2 breadseller. – *langsir* yardman. – *las* welder. – *lawak* joker, clown. – *léding* plumber. – *lélang* auctioneer. – *lepas uang* moneylender. – *listerik* electrician. – *loténg* roofer. – *lowa(k)* 1 secondhand dealer. 2 rag dealer, junkman. – *luak* junkman. – *mabuk* drunkard. – *madat* opium smoker. – *main biola* violinist. – *main piano* pianist. – *mas* goldsmith. – *masak* cook. – *melutju* comedian. – *mentjabut njawa* hired assassin. – *mind(e)ring* o. who sells on installment plan. – *ngarang buku* writer,

author. – *obat* druggist. – *pangkas* barber. – *pedati* wheelwright. – *pipa* pipe fitter, plumber. – *pos* postman. – *potong* butcher. – *potong rambut* barber. – *potrét* photographer. – *pukul* bodyguard. – *ramal* fortuneteller. – *rém* brakeman. – *rias* make-up artist. – *riba* usurer. – *rombéng(an)* secondhand, junk, dealer. – *roti* 1 baker. 2 breadman. – *rumah* mason. – *rumput* grasscutter. – *sajur* vegetable man. – *sampah* garbage man. – *sapu djalan* street sweeper. – *semir sepatu* bootblack. – *sepatu* shoemaker. – *serobot* pickpocket. – *sikut* deceiver, cheater. – *silap mata* conjurer, magician. – *suap* a briber. – *sunat* o. who performs circumcisions. – *sunglap* 1 juggler. 2 magician. – *susu* milkman. – *tadah* a fence. – *tambur* drummer. – *tandji* musician. – *tarohan* a bettor, gambler. – *télpon* telephone operator. – *tembaga* coppersmith. – *tembang* male crooner with gamelan orchestra. – *tenung, – tilik* fortuneteller. – *tera* inspector of weights and measures. – *tindju* boxer. – *tjakap perut* ventriloquist. – *tjap* printer. – *tjap batu* lithographer. – *tjat* painter. – *tjatut* ticket scalper. – *tjekék* thug. – *tjelep* dyer. – *tjeritera* skilled storyteller. – *tjét* painter. – *tjétak* printer. – *tjopét* pickpocket. – *tjukur* barber. – *tjuplik* plagiarist, plagiarizer. – *tjutji* laundryman. – *tundjuk* stoolpigeon. – *uang* 1 cashier. 2 purser. – *ukur* surveyor.

tukar ber– to change. *Malam* ~ *dgn siang,* Night has changed into day. ~ *pakaian* to change clothes. ~ *akal* to change o's mind. ~ *keréta* to change trains. ~ *warna* to change color. ~ *pikiran* 1 to change o's mind. 2 mad, crazy. 3 to differ, be different. ~ *dari jg sdh²* to be different from before. ~ *bulu* to molt. ~ *kapal* to transship. ~ *kulit* to molt, shed skin. **ber– –²** to keep changing. *Pikirannja selalu* ~ , She's always changing her mind. **ber– –²an** to exchange. *Banjak negeri* ~ *peladjar,* Many countries exchange students. **memper–kan** 1 to vary, alternate. 2 to exchange. **men–** 1 to change. ~ *ban* to change a tire. ~ *uang* to change money. 2 to exchange, barter, trade. **men–i** to exchange for. ~ *uang kertas dgn uang pérak* to exchange paper money for silver. **men–kan** 1 to change. *Ia* ~ *uangnja,* He changed his money. 2 to cash. ~ *tjék* to cash a check. **pen–** *uang* money-changer. **pen–an** 1 change, alteration. ~ *hawa* ventilation. ~ *iklim* change of climate. 2 interchange. ∼ *udara* ventilation. 3 exchange, trade. ∼ *barang* exchange of goods. ∼ *pikiran* exchange of ideas. 4 conversion. ∼ *agama* religious conversion. ∼ *uang* monetary conversion. ∼ *zat* metabolism. **per–an** exchange. – *djaga* changing of the guard. – *ganti* substitution. – *tjintjin* exchange of rings.

tukas 1 false accusation, aspersion. 2 rattan. **ber–** –² repeatedly. **men–** 1 to calumniate, accuse falsely. 2 to repeat. **–an** false accusation, slander.

tukik 1 notch, nick, indentation. 2 woodpecker. **men–** 1 to dive. 2 to make a notch. **men–kan** 1 to let dive, point s.t. downward. *Pandai benar ia ∼ pesawatnja*, He was very clever at letting his plane dive. 2 to focus. *Kita –kan perhatian kita kpd tjeramah itu*, We focus our attention on the lecture.

tukil see NUKIL.

tukuk 1 see TOKOK. 2 to beat, hammer.

tukul hammer. **men–** to hammer. **pen–** hammerer.

tulah 1 curse, malediction. 2 calamity, disaster, catastrophe. 3 wage increase. 4 tip, bonus. **ke–an** cursed. **men–i** to curse.

tulang bone. **ber–** bony. *daging tiada ∼* boneless meat. *tiada ∼* weak, spunkless. **ke–an** to have a fishbone stuck in the throat. **men–** to become bone. **men–i** to bone s.t. ∼ *ikan* to bone a fish. **ter–** to feel to the marrow. *sakitnja ∼* pained to the bone. **–²an** 1 skeleton. 2 carcass, frame. – *air mata* lachrymal. – *belakang* spine, backbone. – *belikat* shoulder blade. – *belulang* skin and bones. – *bertjagak* jawbone. – *betis* shinbone. – *dada* breastbone. – *daun* rib of leaf. – *halus* cartilage. – *hasta* ulna. – *insang* whalebone. – *kelangkang* sacrum. – *kering* shinbone. – *ketok djari* knuckle(s). – *ketul* cartilage. – *langit²* hard palate. – *lembusir* shoulder blade. – *muda* cartilage. – *papan* breastbone. – *pengumpil* radius. – *pipi* cheekbone. – *punggung* spinal column. – *rahang* jawbone. – *rawan* 1 cartilage. 2 sternum. – *rusuk* rib. – *selangka* collarbone. – *sendi* joint. – *tongkéng* coccyx. – *tundjang* 1 leg bone of fowls. 2 bony part of haunches. – *tungging* coccyx.

tular **ke–an** infected, contaminated. **men–** 1 contagious, infectious. *penjakit ∼* a contagious disease. 2 to infect, contaminate, spread. *Penjakit itu ∼ ke-mana²*, That disease spread everywhere. 3 to spread. *Pemogokan*

∼ *diseluruh negeri*, The strike spread over the entire nation. **men–i** to infect, contaminate. *Penjakit itu ∼ penduduk kota itu*, That disease has contaminated the town's population. **men–kan** 1 to carry a disease. 2 to spread. *Hawa jg panas ∼ penjakit*, Hot weather spreads the disease. **pen–** infecter. **pen–an** infection.

tulat within 3 days.

tulén pure, genuine. *mas* – pure gold. **ke–an** authenticity, genuineness.

tuli deaf. **men–kan** 1 to deafen. *Bunji itu ∼ telinga saja*, That sound deafened my ears. 2 deafening. –² a silver cord on a kris.

tulis **ber–** 1 inscribed. *batu ∼* an inscribed stone. 2 written on. *Kertas ini tidak ∼* , This sheet isn't written on. **men–** 1 to write. ∼ *surat* to write a letter. 2 to draw. ∼ *gambar* to draw a picture. **men–i** to write on s.t. ∼ *kertas putih* to write on white paper. **men–kan** 1 to write down. ∼ *pikirannja dikertas* to write down o's thoughts on paper. 2 to write with. ∼ *potlot pd papan* to write with a pencil on a board. **pen–** 1 writer (of a letter, etc.). 2 secretary (of an association). ∼ *tjepat* stenographer. **pen–an** writing. ∼ *kembali* rewriting. ∼ *sedjarah* historiography. **per–an** inscription. **ter–** written. *Suratnjapun blm ∼* , Even his letter hasn't been written yet. **–an** 1 writing(s). ∼ *tangan* handwriting. *dgn ∼* in writing. *Ia memasukkan kerésnja dgn ∼* , He handed him his request in writing. 2 manuscript. ∼ *tjepat* stenography. – **–men–** 1 correspondence. *Ia ada hubungan ∼* , He's in correspondence with me. 2 administrative. *Ia mendapat pekerdjaan ∼* , He got an administrative job.

tulung see TOLONG.

tulus honest, upright, sincere. **ke–an** *hati* honesty, sincerity, integrity. – *ichlas* honest and straightforward.

tuma louse.

tuman to be accustomed to. *Ia – pergi kesana*, He was accustomed to going there.

tumbak see TOMBAK.

tumbal antidote. **men–** to swallow hastily.

tumbang to crash, tumble down. *Kekuasaannja – sedjak perang itu*, Its power has declined since the war. *Pohon² besar – kena angin ribut*, Big trees were tumbled down by the storm. **men–kan** 1 to fell. ∼ *pohon* to fell a tree. 2 to slaughter (cattle, etc.). 3 to overthrow. 4 to destroy, annihilate. *Kekuasaannja di–kan dgn*

perang itu, Its power was destroyed by the war. 5 to lower, break. ∼ *rékor dunia* to break a world's record. **per–an** 1 destruction, annihilation. 2 overthrow.
tumbén how odd! how does it happen (that you are here, etc.)?
tumbu a small basket.
tumbuh 1 to grow. *Pohon ini dpt – di-mana²*, This tree can grow anywhere. 2 to develop, grow. 3 to come out. *Perusahaannja – dgn suburnja*, His business has developed rapidly. 4 to come out, appear. *Giginja –*, His teeth came out. 5 to arise, emerge, happen. *Disini – perselisihan*, Conflict arose here. 6 growth. **ber–** to grow. *Kelapa ∼ dihawa jg panas*, Coconuts grow in a warm climate. **ke–an** 1 growth, development. 2 grown over. *Halamannja ∼ tjendawan*, His yard was grown over with mushrooms. 3 smallpox. 4 skin eruption. **men–i** to grow over. *Lapangan itu di–i rumput*, The field was overgrown with grass. **men–kan** 1 to make s.t. grow. *obat utk ∼ rambut* medicine to make the hair grow. 2 to grow, raise. *Ia ∼ bunga²an dihalamannja*, She grows flowers in the yard. 3 to cause, incite, rouse. *Antjaman itu ∼ ketakutan*, The threat roused fear. **per–an** growth, development. **–an** 1 plant. 2 growth. **–²an** plants, vegetation, flora.
tumbuk ber– 1 to collide. *Mobil ∼ tjikar*, A car collided with a bullock cart. 2 to crash. *Kepalanja ∼ pd pal listrik*, His head crashed against a light pole. 3 to fight. *Ia ∼ dgn musuhnja*, He fought with his opponent. 4 to coincide, collide. *Perajaannja diundurkan karena ∼ dgn rapat umum*, The celebration was postponed because it coincided with the general meeting. 5 to run into, meet unexpectedly. *Siapa mengira bhw saja akan ∼ dia?* Whoever thought I'd run into him? **men–** 1 to pound, crush. *Ia ∼ kopi*, She pounded coffee. 2 to strike, deliver a blow. *Ia ∼ lawannja dimukanja*, He struck his opponent on the face. 3 to crash, collide with. *Mobil ∼ témbok*, A car crashed against a wall. **men–kan** 1 to smash, beat. *Ia ∼ kepalanja ketémbok*, He smashed his head against the wall. 2 to crush for s.o. *Ia ∼ ajahnja kopi*, She pounded coffee for her father. **pen–** crusher, pounder. **pen–an** 1 collision, crash. 2 blow, stroke. **ter–** 1 to collide with, strike against. *Badannja ∼ pohon*, Her body struck against a tree. 2

pounded, crushed. 3 to run into, meet. ∼ *akal* at the end of o's wits. **–an** 1 crash, collision. 2 blow, strike.
tumbung see TOMBONG.
tumbur ber–an to collide.
tumenggung see TEMENGGUNG.
tumis a dish of vegetables prepared in fat. **men–i** to cook s.t. in fat.
tumit heel. *– sepatu* shoe heel.
tumpah to spill. *Airnja –*, The water's spilled out. **ke–an** 1 spilled. 2 wet with. *Tangannja ∼ minjak*, His hand was wet from oil. **men–i** 1 to spill on s.t. *Air ∼ badjunja*, Water spilled on his clothes. 2 to cover with. **men–kan** 1 to shed, spill. ∼ *darah* to shed blood. ∼ *tinta* to spill ink. 2 to concentrate, devote. *Ia ∼ segala perhatiannja kpd pekerdjaannja*, He concentrated all his attention on his work. **pen–an** 1 spilling, shedding. ∼ *darah* bloodshed. 2 concentration, devotion. **per–an** *darah* shedding of blood. **ter–** 1 spilled, shed. *Airnja ∼* , The water's spilled. 2 to be concentrated on. *Segala tenaganja ∼ kpd tudjuannja itu*, All his strength was concentrated on his goal. **–an** *darah* the spilling of blood. ∼ *pikiran* concentration of o's thoughts. *– darah* to be born. *– ruah* 1 spilled, poured out everywhere. 2 filled to the brim.
tumpak 1 collection of wet rice fields. 2 place, spot. **ber–** in groups. *– tampak* field of vision.
tumpang ber– *tindih* piled up. **men–** 1 to ride in, go by. *Ia ∼ keréta api*, He rode in a train. *Ia pergi ∼ kapal*, He went by ship. 2 to join, go along with. *Ia pergi ∼ dgn temannja*, He went along with his friend. ∼ *makan* to eat with s.o. ∼ *tertawa* to laugh with s.o. 3 to hitchhike. 4 to stay, live with. *Ia ∼ dirumah pamannja*, He lived with his uncle. *Ia lebih suka ∼ dihotél*, He prefers to stay at a hotel. 5 to ask. ∼ *bertanja* to ask a question. *Ia ∼ bertanja kpd orang itu dimana rumah temannja*, He asked that man where his friend's home was. ∼ *djalan* excuse me (said when passing in front of or going around s.o.). ∼ *surat* to place a letter inside another for mailing. **men–i** 1 to ride in, be a passenger in. *Ia suka ∼ mobilnja*, He likes to ride in his car. 2 to live with. 3 to utilize, take advantage of s.t. **men–kan** 1 to let s.o. ride, go along. *Ia ∼ anaknja dimobil*, He let his child ride in the car. 2 to let stay, live. ∼ *tamu² dihotél* to let o's guests stay at the hotel. 3 to entrust. ∼ *anaknja pd*

temannja to entrust o's child with a friend. ~ *diri kpd* to entrust o.s. to. 4 to send along with. *Ia* ~ *surat kpd temannja*, He sent a letter (along with other letters) to his friend. **pen-** 1 passenger. 2 traveler. 3 boarder, hotel guest. **pen-an** 1 transportation. ~ *umum* public transportation. 2 lodging, shelter. **ter-**included. ~ *salam Trisno*, Trisno adds his greetings. **-an** 1 lodging. 2 fare, passenger, load. *Ia mentjari* ~ *buat mobilnja*, He's seeking passengers for his car. 3 cargo, load. 4 host, landlord. 5 ride, drive. 6 inclusion, addition. *dgn* ~ *salam Trisno* with the added greetings of Trisno. – *tindih* piling up unsystematically.

tumpas destroyed, annihilated, exterminated. **men-kan** to destroy, exterminate. **pen-an** annihilation, extermination. **-an** stain, spot. ~ *darah* bloodstain. – *langis* totally destroyed.

tumpat 1 stopped up, clogged up (of a drain, etc.). 2 crammed, solid. 3 to be at the end of o's rope. **men-kan** to cram, stuff. **ter-** crammed, stuffed.

tumpes see TUMPAS.

tumpil support. **men-** to support.

tumpu 1 footing. 2 foothold, support. 3 springboard. **ber-, men-** 1 to rest on. *Patung itu* ~ *pd batu besar*, The statue rests on a large stone. 2 to have support. *Kekuasaannja* ~ *pd kepopulérannja*, His power is supported by his popularity. 3 to border on, reach. *Negerinja tiada* ~ *laut*, His country does not border on the sea. 4 to concentrate o's efforts. 5 to push off from. *Ia* ~ *pd batu sebelum melompat*, He pushed off from a stone before leaping. **berse-** 1 to brace o.s. 2 to concentrate o's efforts. **men-kan** 1 to lean on. *Ia* ~ *tangannja pd médja*, He leaned on the table with his hands. 2 to support, sustain. *Batu besar* ~ *tangga kerumah*, A large stone supported the steps to the house. *Dialah jg* ~ *ibunja*, It was he who supported his mother. 3 to base on. *Témbok itu di-kan pd alasan jg kokoh*, The wall was based on a strong foundation. 4 to concentrate. ~ *segala perhatian kpd* to concentrate all o's attention on. ~ *segala usahanja* to concentrate all o's efforts. **pen-***kaki* footstool. **-an** 1 support, pillar, prop. 2 steppingstone. 3 focus, center (of interest).

tumpuk 1 heap, pile, stack. 2 group. **ber-(-)** 1 in piles, stacks. *Bukunja* ~ *dikamarnja*, His room was piled high with books. *Uangnja* ~ , He

has a lot of money. 2 in groups, in clusters. *Meréka datang* ~ , They came in groups. *pulau ketjil[2] jg* ~ tiny islands in clusters. 3 dense (of population). **ke-an** group. **men-(kan)** 1 to heap, pile up. ~ *batu bata* to pile up bricks. 2 to hoard, accumulate. *Orang dilarang* ~ *bahan makanan*, People are forbidden to hoard foodstuffs. **ter-** 1 piled up. 2 hoarded. **-an** 1 pile, stack. 2 group.

tumpul 1 dull, blunt. *pisau* – a blunt knife. 2 dull, stupid. *Pikirannja* –, He is dull. **ke-an** bluntness, dullness. **men-kan** to dull, blunt, s.t.

tumpur ruined, destroyed. **men-kan** to destroy.

tuna a wound, hurt. **ter-** hurt. *Kakinja* ~ , His foot was hurt. *Hatinja* ~ , His feelings were hurt. – *diri* self-inflicted wound.

tunai cash. *membajar* – to pay cash. **men-kan** 1 to pay cash. *Ia* ~ *pembelian itu*, He paid cash for that purchase. 2 to pay up, pay a bill. 3 to fulfill. ~ *perdjandjian* to fulfill a promise. 4 to carry out, accomplish. ~ *perintah* to carry out orders. ~ *tugas* to accomplish a task. 5 to cash. ~ *tjék* to cash a check. **pen-an, per-an** 1 (cash) payment. 2 settlement. 3 fulfillment.

tunakarja unemployment.

tunanétra juvenile delinquency.

tunang ber-(an) engaged, betrothed. *Lama meréka* ~ , They've been engaged for a long time. **memperkan, men-kan** to betroth. *Ia* ~ *anaknja*, He betrothed his daughter. **men-(i)** to be engaged to. *Anak saja* ~ *anaknja*, My son is engaged to his daughter. **pen-an, per-an** engagement, betrothal. **-an** fiancé(e).

tunas shoot, bud. **ber-** to sprout. **men-(i)** to prune. ~ *harapan* 1 ray of hope. 2 young bud(s).

tunasila 1 immorality. 2 prostitution.

tunawisma roofless, without housing.

tunda tow. **men-** to tow. ~ *mobil mogok* to tow a stalled car. **men-(kan)** 1 to postpone, delay. *Rapat di-*, The meeting was postponed. 2 to adjourn. 3 to push, shove, s.o. 4 to level s.t. off. **men-** tugboat. **pen-an** 1 postponement. 2 adjournment. 3 delay.

tundang see TUNANG.

tundjal men- to step off, jump off.

tundjam men-kan to stick s.t. *Ia* ~ *tongkatnja ditanah*, He stuck his cane in the ground.

tundjang leg. *Ia pandjang –nja*, He has long legs. **men-** 1 to support. *Besi pandjang* ~ *témbok itu*, An iron bar supported that wall. 2 to support financially. *Ia ~ ajahnja tiap bulan,* He gave his father financial support every month. 3 to collide with. **pen–** 1 supporter, fan, devotee. 2 supporting wall. **-an** 1 support, aid. 2 allowance, subsidy. *~ anak* dependent's allowance. *~ beladjar* subsidy for study, scholarship. *~ kemahalan* cost-of-living allowance. 3 alimony.

tundjuk index finger. **memper–kan** to show, exhibit. *Film itu tlh diperkan dikota ini,* That film has been shown in this town. **men–** 1 to point toward, indicate. *Ia ~ keselatan,* He pointed toward the south. 2 to show, indicate. *Papan ini ~ djalan keutara,* This sign indicates the road to the north. *Ia ~ halaman,* He showed the page. 3 to appoint. *Ia ~ temannja mewakili ia,* He appointed his friend to represent him. 4 to raise o's hand. *Jg blm dpt bagian harap ~ ,* Those who haven't received their share, please raise their hands. 5 with reference to (your letter). **men–i** to show s.t. to s.o. **men–kan** 1 to show. *Ia ~ tjara jg benar,* He showed the right way. 2 to indicate, prove. *Sikapnja itu ~ asalnja,* His attitude indicated where he came from. *~ bulu dulu* to be found out, to show o's real colors. **pe–an** appointment. **pen–** 1 indicator, pointer. 2 guide. 3 clock hand. *~ djalan* 1 signpost. 2 road sign. *~ angin* weather vane. *~ halaman* bookmark. **pen–an** 1 indication. 2 reference. *sumber ~* reference source. 3 appointment, assignment. **pe(r)–** 1 instruction, guidance. *Obat ini harus diminum menurut ~ dokter,* This medicine must be taken under a doctor's direction. 2 advice, guidance. *~² (dari) ajahnja* his father's advice. 3 indication, clue, hint. *~ ketjelakaan* an omen of disaster. *~ Tuhan* revelation. 4 directions. **per-an** 1 show, exhibition. 2 performance. *~ amal* charity performance. *~ pertama* première (of play or film). *– muka* to appear before.

tundjung lotus.

tunduk ke–an 1 submission. 2 loyalty, obedience. **men–** 1 to bow. *Ia ~ kepalanja,* He bowed his head. 2 to surrender, submit. *Musuhnja tlh ~ ,* The enemy surrendered. 3 to obey, bow, submit. *Ia ~ kpd gurunja,* He obeyed his teacher. **men–kan** 1 to bow. *Ia ~ kepalanja,* He bowed his head. 2 to have s.o. bow. *Ia ~ temannja,* He had his friend bow his head. 3 to conquer, overcome. *Ia ~*

musuhnja dgn mudah, He conquered his opponent with ease. **pen–an** submission, subjection. *– tengadah* 1 to ponder s.t. 2 to nod o's head.

tundun 1 female genitals. 2 bunch. *se– pisang* a bunch of bananas. 3 neck (of a horse, tiger).

tundung men– 1 to expel, exile. 2 to chase, drive away. *Ia di– oléh ajahnja,* He was chased away by his father. **-an** 1 exile. 2 exiled.

tungau a mite.

tunggak see TONGGAK. **men–** to be in arrears. *Ia ~ bulan ini,* He was in arrears this month. *Hutangnja di–,* The debt is not paid. **pe–** *padjak* tax delinquent. **-an** 1 arrears. 2 delinquent. *Banjak ~ bulan ini,* There were many delinquents this month. 3 remainder. *~ padjak* delinquent tax.

tunggal 1 single. *Ia masih –,* He's still single. *daun –* a single leaf. 2 sole, only. *anak –* an only child. 3 singular. *bukan madjemuk tetapi –* not plural but singular. 4 one. *berdiri berkaki –* to stand on o. foot. *Batara – o.* God. 5 simple. *kalimat –* a simple sentence. 6 whole, complete. *dgn hati – wholeheartedly.* 7 unconditional(ly). *Meréka menjerah –,* They surrendered unconditionally. **ke–an** 1 left alone. 2 singleness. 3 concentration of thought. **ke–nadaan** monotony. **men–** to be alone. *Lihat pesawat itu ~ ,* Look at that plane flying alone. **men–kan** to concentrate. **pen–** concentration. **se–** of o. kind or quality. *bapak dan anaknja ~* like father like son. *~ bandjar dgn* to be a neighbor of. *~ darah dgn* to be related to. *– berbéléng* quite alone. *– ika* one unit. *– nada* monotonous.

tunggang 1 upside down. 2 steep. *djalan jg amat –* a very steep road. **ber– -langgang** 1 to run head over heels. *Ia lari ~ -langgang,* He ran head over heels. 2 to dive, tumble head over heels. *Lihat pesawat itu ~ -langgang,* Look at that plane tumbling down. **memper–kan** to hold upside down. **men–** to turn upside down. **men– balikkan** to turn upside down. **men–(i)** to ride. *Ia ~ kuda 3 djam lamanja,* He rode horseback for 3 hours. **men–kan** to turn s.t. over. *Ia ~ pantji supaja isinja keluar,* She turned the pan over so its contents would run out. **men– -langgang-kan** 1 to let s.t. dive or tumble. 2 to cause to run helter-skelter. *Bunji pistol ~ musuhnja,* The sound of a pistol caused the enemy to run helter-skelter. **pen–** rider, passenger.

-an 1 mount, riding animal. 2 carriage, vehicle. – **-men-** head over heels. – *balik* head over heels. – *gunung* around sunset. – *hati* 1 keen about. 2 steadfast. – *langgang* head over heels. – *tunggik*, – *tunggit* to bob up and down, pitch.

tunggik see TUNGGANG.

tungging 1 with tail, rear end up. 2 four days from now. **men-** 1 to crawl with o's rear in the air. 2 to sink bow first. 3 to be upside down. *Botol* ∼ *dimédja*, The bottles stood upside down. 4 to dive. *Pesawat itu* ∼ *utk mendjatuhkan bom*, The plane dived to drop a bomb. 5 to bulge, protrude. *Sakunja* ∼ *penuh berisi*, His pocket protruded from the bulging contents. **men–kan** 1 to place upside down. *Botol di–kan diatas médja*, The bottle was placed upside down on the table. 2 to lift, raise. *Kuda itu* ∼ *ékornja*, The horse lifted its tail high. 3 to let dive. *Ia* ∼ *pesawatnja*, He put his plane into a dive. 4 to overthrow. ∼ *pemerintahan* to overthrow the government.

tunggit see TUNGGANG.

tunggu ber– to guard, keep watch. **me–n–²** to look forward to eagerly for some time. *Ia sdh lama* ∼ *kedatangan surat itu*, He'd been eagerly looking forward to that letter for a long time. **men–** 1 to wait for. *Ia* ∼ *ajahnja*, He waited for his father. – *sebentar*, Wait a moment. 2 to look forward. **men–i** 1 to watch over. ∼ *rumah kosong* to watch over an empty house. 2 to take care of, tend, nurse. ∼ *orang sakit* to nurse a sick person. 3 to dwell, watch over. *Ada djin* ∼ *sumur itu*, There's a genie watching over that well. 4 to look after, guard. *Meréka* ∼ *barang²nja disetasiun*, They were guarding their luggage at the station. **men–kan** 1 to wait for. *Ia* ∼ *ajahnja*, He waited for his father. 2 to expect. *Ia* ∼ *kedatangan ajahnja*, He was expecting his father's arrival. *Saja* ∼ *surat dari Djakarta*, I'm expecting a letter from Jakarta. 3 to watch over, look after. **pen–** 1 watchman, guard. 2 attendant. ∼ *orang sakit* hospital orderly. 3 spirit, genie. ∼ *pohon beringin* a genie inhabiting a banyan tree.

tunggul 1 tree trunk. 2 banner. **ke–an** *silsilah* 1 lineage. 2 dynasty.

tungku hearth, fireplace. – *arang* charcoal stove.

tungkul men– to submit, bow.

tungkup men– to lie prostrate. *Ia* ∼ *ditanah*, He lay prostrate on the ground. **men–kan** to place s.t. or

s.o. face downward. **men– -telentangkan** to consider s.t. from every angle. **ter–** prostrate.

tungkus parcel, package. – *lumus* overwhelmed (with debt, sorrow, burdens, etc.).

tuntun ber– guided, led. *Ia* ∼ *kpd petundjuk² temannja*, He was guided by his friend's instructions. *Ia berdjalan* ∼ *pd tongkatnja*, He walked along, guiding himself by his cane. **men–** 1 to guide, lead. *Ia* ∼ *orang buta*, He guided a blind person. 2 to cover the eyes. **pen–** 1 guide, leader. 2 manual, guide. **pen–an** example. **-an** guidance, leadership. *membeli kerbau ber–* to buy a pig in a poke.

tuntung 1 point (of a needle, etc.). 2 a small box or case. **men–** 1 to cut into tiny pieces. 2 to empty.

tuntut men– 1 to demand. *Ia* ∼ *supaja utangnja dibajar*, He demanded that the debt be paid. ∼ *haknja* to demand o's rights. 2 to prosecute. *Ia di– dimuka pengadilan*, He was summoned before the court. 3 to strive for. ∼ *kemenangan* to strive for victory. 4 to pursue, aspire to. ∼ *béla* to avenge s.o.'s death. ∼ *dakwa* to bring a charge (against s.o.). ∼ *ilmu* to pursue knowledge. ∼ *malu* to avenge o.s. **pen–** prosecutor. ∼ *djaksa umum* general prosecutor. ∼ *ilmu* scholar, student. **pen–an** 1 prosecution. 2 demand. 3 pursuit, study. **-an** 1 demand. 2 prosecution. 3 striving, pursuit. ∼ *darah* vendetta. ∼ *hukum* criminal procedure.

tunu men– to burn, be in flames. **men–kan** to burn s.t. **pen–** arsonist. **pen–an** burning, arson.

tupai squirrel. **-²** clamps on a boat. – *belang* striped squirrel. – *kerawak* large squirrel with reddish fur.

tupang see TOPANG.

tura ber– -² 1 to be delirious. 2 to talk in o's sleep.

turap plaster. **ber–** plastered.

turis tourist. **men–** to make a notch or scratch.

turisme tourism.

Turki 1 Turk, Turkish. 2 Turkey.

turnamén tournament.

turné see TORNÉ.

Tursina Sinai.

turun 1 to go down, descend. – *gunung* to go down a mountain. – *tachta* to descend from the throne, abdicate. 2 to come down. – *kedarat* to land. 3 to get into. – *kesampan* to get into a boat (from a landing). 4 to go. – *kesawah* to go to the rice field. 5 to get off. *Ia – dari sepédanja*, He got off his bicycle. 6 to get out of. – *mobil* to get out of a car. 7 to set, go down. *Matahari tlh –*, The sun's set. *matahari tengah –* about 3 P.M. in the tropics. 8 to descend, be inherited. *Penjakit bapaknja – kpd anaknja*, The father's disease was inherited by his son. 9 to decrease, go down, decline. *Penghasilannja –*, His income decreased. *Panasnja –*, His temperature went down. *Deradjatnja –*, His prestige declined. 10 to come down, fall. *Hudjan –*, It's raining. 11 to fall (in price). 12 to be demoted. – *pangkat* to be demoted in rank. 13 down. *dari jg tertinggi – kpd jg terendah* from the highest down to the lowest. 14 to leave, go. *Tamunja sdh –*, The guests have gone home. 15 to return from. – *dari Mekah* to return from Mecca. 16 to descend, land, hit. *Kemalangan – kepadanja*, Misfortune descended upon him. **ke–an** 1 possessed, seized. ∼ *orang halus* possessed by a spirit. 2 to inherit. *Ia* ∼ *penjakit orang tuanja*, He has inherited his parent's disease. 3 decline. ∼ *harga²* decline in prices. **men–** 1 to decrease, go down. *Harganja tidak* ∼ , The price didn't go down. 2 to decline, sink. *Kwalitétnja* ∼ , The quality declined. 3 to be hereditary. *Penjakit ini* ∼ , This disease is hereditary. 4 to slope downward. *Djalan ini* ∼ , This road slopes. 5 down, vertical (in crossword puzzles). **men–i** 1 to go down. ∼ *sungai* to go down to the river. 2 to go down, descend into. ∼ *sumur* to go down into a well. 3 to go down for, reach for. ∼ *bola jg djatuh dlm sumur* to go down for the ball which fell into the well. **men–kan** 1 to drop. ∼ *tentara pajung* to drop paratroopers. 2 to drop, throw. ∼ *sauh* to drop anchor. 3 to haul down. ∼ *bendéra* to haul down the flag. 4 to reduce, lower. ∼ *harga* to reduce the price. ∼ *kewaspadaannja* to lower o's guard. ∼ *pangkat* to demote. 5 to unload, discharge. ∼ *muatan* to unload a cargo. 6 to dismiss, cause to abdicate. 7 to drop off. *Ia* ∼ *temannja dimuka setasiun*, He dropped his friend off in front of the station. 8 to reveal. ∼ *Kitab Indjil* to reveal the New Testament. 9 to be the progenitors of. ∼ *radja² Perantjis* to beget a line of French kings. **men– -mandikan** to perform a bathing ceremony. **pen–an** 1 reduction, decline (of cost, prices, salary).

2 slope, descent. 3 discharge, unloading. **–an** 1 descendant. ∼ *radja²* descendant of kings. 2 generation. 3 copy. 4 etymology. 5 hereditary. *penjakit* ∼ hereditary disease. – *deradjat* demoted. – *keair* to bathe in the river. – *kebumi*, – *ketanah* ceremonial occasion of child's touching the earth for the first time. – *main* school recess. – *makan* lunch break. – *mandi* a child's first bath in the river. – *minum* rest period, time out (in sports, etc.). – *naik* to fluctuate. – *tangan* to meddle, interfere. – *tangga* 1 to descend steps or a ladder. 2 in staircase fashion. *Meréka berdjédjér – tangga*, They lined up in staircase fashion. – *temurun* 1 hereditary, from father to son. 2 from generation to generation.

turus 1 pillar, post. 2 style. – *lantjar* a fluent style. **men–** to rise up. *satu – rokok* a carton of cigarettes.

turut 1 to join in. – *makan* to join in eating. – *pergi* to go along with. 2 to follow. *sdr – sadja djalan ini*, You just follow this street. 3 obey. – *perintah* to obey orders. 4 to share. *Ia hrs – bertanggungdjawab*, He must share the responsibility. **ber–(–)** 1 in succession, successively. *Meréka berdjalan* ∼ , They walked in succession (o. after the other). 2 at a stretch. *tiga djam* ∼ three hours at a stretch. 3 continually. *Ia* ∼ *diminta pulang*, He was continually asked to go home. 4 continued. *tjerita* ∼ a continued story. **memper–kan** to follow, obey. ∼ *hati* to give way to o's emotions. **memper- -²kan** to have s.o. get involved. *Ia diper- -²kan dlm soal itu*, He was forced to become involved in that matter. **men–** 1 to follow. ∼ *djedjak pamannja* to follow in his uncle's footsteps. ∼ *perkabaran dgn teliti* to follow the news closely. 2 according to. ∼ *kata orang ia kaja*, According to what people say he's rich. 3 to imitate. *Ia ke-tawa²* ∼ *kakaknja*, He was laughing in imitation of his older brother. 4 to copy. ∼ *tjontoh dipapan* to copy an example on the board. 5 to obey, follow. *Ia* ∼ *kata ajahnja*, He obeyed his father's words. ∼ *akal* reasonable, rational. ∼ *waktu* chronological. **men–i** 1 to follow. ∼ *pentjuri jg lari* to follow the fleeing thief. 2 to grant. ∼ *permintaan* to grant a request. 3 to comply with. 4 to copy, imitate. **men–kan** 1 to obey, follow. *Ia* ∼ *perintah*, He obeyed the order. 2 to follow, copy, imitate. *Ia* ∼ *tingkah* *laku temannja,* He copied his friend's behavior. 3 to have join or follow. 4 to grant. ~ *permintaan* to grant a request. **pen–** follower, an obedient person. ~ *(kata)* to be obedient. **pen-an** 1 follower. 2 accommodating, easy to get along with. **se–** in accordance with. **-an** 1 guidance, example. 2 sequence, succession. 3 along with. **-²an** 1 accommodating, merely follows others. *Ia tak pernah ada pendapat sendiri; selalu ~ sadja,* He never has an opinion of his own; he just follows others. 2 guidance, example. – *menentukan* to have a share in deciding. – *serta* to go along with, participate in. – *tjampur* 1 to associate with. 2 to meddle, mix in.

tuslah 1 extra allowance. 2 excess fare, extra charge on tickets, surcharge.

tus(s)or k.o. material for men's suits.

tusuk 1 a pin. 2 stick, skewer. *dua – saté* two skewers of barbecued meat. **men–** 1 to stab s.o. 2 to prick, stick. ~ *dgn djarum* to prick with a needle. 3 to run pieces of meat on a skewer. 4 to hurt, prick. *Perkataan itu ~ hatinja,* Those words hurt his feelings. **men-kan** 1 to stab, jab s.t. (into s.o.). *Ia ~ pisau kpd musuhnja,* He jabbed a knife into his opponent. 2 to stick. ~ *djarum kedalam bantal* to stick a needle into a pillow. – *gigi* toothpick. – *kondé* hairpin.

tuter (auto) horn. **men–** to blow a horn.

tuts piano key.

tutuh men– to prune.

tutuk men– to tap, knock on.

tutul 1 pockmarked. *Mukanja –,* His face was pockmarked. 2 spotted, stained.

tutup 1 closed, shut. *Kantor sdh –,* The office is closed. 2 cover, lid, top. – *pantji* pan top. 3 complete, full. *setahun –* a full year. **ber–** to have covers, lids. *tjangkir ~* cup with cover. **men–** 1 to close, shut. ~ *buku* to close a book. 2 to close the books (end of fiscal year). ~ *kantor* to close the office. ~ *médja* to set the table. ~ *pintu*

to close or shut the door. – *mulut!* Shut up! *Rapat di– pd djam 12 malam,* The meeting was concluded at midnight. ~ *mata* to die. 3 to seal, close. *Kaléng² itu di– rapat,* The cans were sealed tightly. 4 to button. ~ *badju* to button up a jacket. 5 to cover. ~ *mesin tulis sesudah dipakai* to cover a typewriter after using it. ~ *muka* to cover the face. ~ *ongkos* to cover expenses. 6 to hide, conceal. ~ *maksud jg buruk* to hide o's bad intentions. 7 to fill in, cover over. ~ *selokan* to fill in a ditch. 8 to block. ~ *djalan* to block a road. 9 to fill. ~ *lowong(an)* to fill a gap, vacuum, vacancy. 10 to lock, shut up in jail. *Ia di– dlm pendjara,* He was locked up in jail. **men–i** 1 to cover (up). 2 to cover, close, shut repeatedly. **men-kan** 1 to cover with s.t. *Ia ~ topinja kpd muka anaknja,* He covered his child's face with his hat. 2 to close, shut, seal for. *Ia ~ ibunja surat itu,* He sealed the letter for his mother. **pen–** 1 cover, lid. ~ *botol* bottle cap. 2 shutter of camera. 3 closing. *sebagai ~* in closing (of letters or speeches). *utjapan ~* closing address. **pen-an** 1 covering. 2 closing, shutting. **ter–** 1 shut, closed. 2 locked, secured. **-an** cover, lid. – *buku* balanced (of books). – *djendéla* curtain. – *malu* a front for hiding s.t. – *tahun* annual balancing of books.

tutur ber– *(kata)* to talk, speak. *Ia ~ dlm bahasa asing,* He spoke in a foreign language. **ber– -²** to talk, converse. **men-kan** 1 to relate, narrate, tell about. *Ia ~ pengalamannja,* He related his experiences. 2 to pronounce, express. 3 to inform. 4 to announce. **pe-an** descendant. **pen-an** 1 discussion. 2 announcement. 3 information. 4 narrative. 5 lowest part of thatched roof. **per-an** 1 pronunciation. 2 conversation. 3 word, phrase. **-an** 1 story, narrative, account. 2 information. 3 announcement. – *kata* words, phrases, sayings, expressions. *mendjadi buah –* to be the talk of the town.

typis typical.

U

uak 1 uncle. 2 aunt. 3 see KUAK.
meng- 1 to moo, low (of buffaloes).
2 to croak (of frogs). 3 to quack.
4 to tear at.
uang money. **ber-** 1 to have money.
2 to bear interest. **ke-an** 1 financial.
2 finance. *kementerian* ~ ministry of
finance. **meng-i** to finance s.t. *Ia* ~
perusahaan anaknja, He financed his
son's business. **meng-kan** to cash. − −
kanlah poswésél ini se-lekas²nja, Please
cash this money order as soon as
possible. **per-an** 1 finance. 2 financial, monetary. **−²an** counterfeit
money. − *adat* lawsuit expenses. −
angus bridegroom's share in wedding
expenses. − *antaran* dowry. − *bandar*
stake (in gambling). − *bantuan* financial support, contribution. − *belandja*
1 shopping money. 2 salary. 3 budget. − *bolong* perforated coin (5 cents).
− *buta* 1 unemployment compensation. 2 official half pay. − *djadjan*
pocket money. − *djaga²* reserve fund.
− *djalan* 1 declaration of travel expenses. 2 travel expenses (for o's
driver, etc.). − *djamin(an)* financial
guarantee. − *djasa* 1 bonus. 2 honorarium. 3 pension. − *djerih* tip. −
djudjur(an) token sum of money. −
duduk attendance honorarium. − *entré*
admission fee. − *imbalan* fee, consideration. − *iuran* 1 contribution. 2
dues. − *kantjing* deposit. − *karun*
fabulous wealth. − *kembali* change.
− *kertas* paper money, bank note.
− *ketjil* small change. − *komisi* commission, fee. − *kontan* cash. − *kopi*
tip. − *kuliah* university tuition.
− *kuntji* key money. − *langganan*
subscription fee. − *lantjung* counterfeit money. − *lauk-pauk* military subsistence. − *lembur* overtime pay. −
logam coin. − *makan* official per diem.
− *méndréngan* a loan repaid in installments. − *muka* advance payment. − *panas* 1 loan at high interest
rate. 2 easy come, easy go. − *pangkal*
1 capital. 2 subscription. 3 deposit,
down payment. 4 registration fee. −
pantjang bribe. − *pas* exact amount.
− *persén* tip. − *petjah* small change. −
pintu, − *plétjét* hush money. − *pokok*

capital. − *rétjéh* small change. − *rokok*
tip. − *saksi* witness' fee. − *sangu* traveling money. − *sara* 1 maintenance. 2
pension. − *sekolah* school fee, tuition.
− *sembah* money given to girl's parents
after broken engagement. − *senin*
bribe. − *séwa* rent. − *sidang* pay to
members of council while in session.
− *sirih* tip. − *sogok,* − *sorok,* − *suap*
bribe. − *tagihan* claim, garnisheed
money. − *tali* 25-cent piece. − *tam-
bangan* passage, fare. − *taruhan* savings. − *téh* tip. − *tembaga* copper coin.
− *tempah* advance payments. − *terdjun*
extra pay for paratrooper. − *tikaman*
stake (in gambling). − *tjadangan* reserve fund. − *tjengkeram* advance payment as security. − *tjitjilan* installment payment. − *tjurai* loose cash.
− *tumpangan* 1 rent for lodgings. 2
entrusted money. − *tunai* cash. −
utangan borrowed money. *setali tiga*
− six of one and half a dozen of the
other.
uap steam, vapor. **ber-** to steam.
meng- 1 to steam, evaporate. 2 to
vaporize. 3 to yawn. **meng-i** 1 to
dry-clean. 2 to steam. *Ia* ~ *nasi,*
She steamed the rice. **meng-kan** 1
to steam. 2 to let evaporate. ~ *air
laut* to let sea water evaporate.
(peng)-an evaporation. − *air* steam,
vapor.
uba vessel for sago meal.
ubah difference. **ber-** 1 to change,
alter. *Bunga itu* ~ *warna,* The flower
changed its color. *Ia* ~ *hatinja,* She
changed her mind. 2 to shift (of the
wind). 3 to break, change (of the
weather). ~ *akal* 1 to lose o's head.
2 not be in o's right senses. 3 to
change o's mind. **ber-** **−²** fickle,
changeable. **memper-kan** *dgn* to discriminate against s.t. or s.o. ~ *anak
kaja daripada anak orang miskin*
to treat children of the wealthy differently from those of the poor.
meng- 1 to change, alter. ~ *sikapnja*
to change o's attitude. 2 to commute.
*Hukum mati di− mendjadi seumur
hidup,* The death sentence was com-
muted to life imprisonment. **meng-i**
1 to change, revise, modify s.t. 2 to

break a contract. **meng-kan** to cause
s.t. to change. **peng-** corrector. **peng-
an** correcting, altering. **per-an** 1
change, alteration. 2 shift. 3 transition. 4 variation. **ter-** changeable.
-an 1 variation. 2 change, alteration. 3 variety. *tak – dgn* similar to.
uban gray hair. **ber-** 1 graying (of
hair). 2 worn-out. *Ia sdh ∼ dlm pekerdjaan itu,* He has become old in
that job. *Ia tinggal disana dari ketjil
hingga ∼ ,* He stayed there from his
childhood till old age. *Ia masih muda
tetapi tlh ∼ ,* He was young and yet
gray. **meng-** 1 to be graying. 2 worn-
out. *Pakaiannja ∼ ,* His clothes were
worn out. **meng-i** to pull out o's
gray hairs. *Ia ∼ ajahnja,* She pulled
out her father's gray hairs. **-an**
gray-headed.
ubar dye, paint. **meng-** 1 to dye.
2 to paint. 3 to spread out s.t. that
is rolled up.
ubel² turban of a pilgrim to Mecca.
uber meng-(-) to chase, go after.
peng-an the chase, pursuit.
ubi 1 tuber. 2 sweet potato, yam. *–
djalar* sweet-potato plant. *– djawa*
sweet potato. *– kaju,* *– kaspé,* *–
perantjis* cassava. *– keledek* sweet potato. *– kentang* potato. *– rambat*
sweet potato.
ubin floor tile.
ubrak-abrik meng- to rummage in.
ubub(an) a pair of bellows.
ubun² 1 crown (of the head), fontanel. 2 nun.
ubur² jellyfish.
uchuwah association, organization.
udah see SUDAH.
udak meng- to chase, pursue.
udang shrimp. *– karang,* *– laut* lobster. *– kering* dried shrimp. *– dlm
tangguk* worried, uneasy. *– tak tahu
dibungkuknja* not to know o's defects.
Ada – dibalik batu, There is s.t.
behind it.
udap –²an salad made of all k.o.
vegetables; often bought as a tidbit
on the street.
udar reel. **meng-** 1 to reel, wind. 2
to disentangle. **meng-kan** to explain.
udara 1 air. 2 atmosphere. *– meling-
kungi bumi,* The atmosphere sur-
rounds the earth. *– politik* political
atmosphere. 3 sky. 4 weather.
ude(h) see SUDAH.
udet woman's belt.
udi accident, catastrophe.
udik 1 upper course of a river. *disungai* on the upper course of a river.
2 interior, inland country. 3 backward. **-an** o. raised in a rural area.
udjar phrase, expression. **meng-kan**

to say. **-nja** he says, said. *∼ bhw ia
akan datang nanti,* He said he'd come
later.
udji test, experiment. **ber-** to test,
have a test. *Meréka ∼ siapa jg lebih
kuat,* They were testing who was the
strongest. **ke-an** 1 found out, discovered. 2 tested, tried. **meng-** 1 to
test, examine. *Ia ∼ mas,* He tested
the gold. *Ia ∼ murid baru,* He tested
the new student. 2 to test, try.
Pengalaman itu ∼ kesabaran saja,
That experience tried my patience.
peng- examiner. **peng-an** test, trial.
-an 1 examination. 2 test, trial, experiment. 3 assay. *∼ lisan* oral
examination. *∼ masuk* entrance
examination. *∼ negeri* government
examination. *∼ penghabisan* final examination. *∼ persiapan* propaedeutic
examination at the end of first
university year. *∼ tulisan* written
examination. *∼ ulangan* re-examina-
tion. *Kedjudjurannja sedang dlm ∼ ,*
His honesty is being tested.
udjud see WUDJUD.
udjung end, tip, point, top. *– bulan
Djanuari* end of January. *– lidah*
1 tip of the tongue. 2 spokesman.
ber- 1 pointed. *besi jg ∼ tadjam* an
iron bar with a sharp point. 2 to
originate in. *Perundingan itu ∼ pd
persetudjuan,* The discussion origi-
nated in an agreement. *Tak tentu –
pangkalnja,* It makes no sense. **meng-**
1 to become sharp. 2 to sharpen. 3
to intensify. *Perselisihan tlh ∼ dan
mungkin perang akan meletus,* The
conflict has intensified and war will
probably break out. **peng-** extreme
end. *– djalan* end of the road. *– djari*
finger tip. *– hidung* tip of nose. *–
kota* suburbs, outskirts. *– mata* corner
of eye. *– pangkal* lower and upper
ends, beginning and end. *– susu*
nipple. *– tanah* cape. *– utara* North
Cape.
udjur see UZUR.
udu' 1 see WUDU'. 2 enemy. **ber-**
hostile.
uduh see ODOH.
uduk see NASI.
udut meng- to smoke. *Ia ∼ tjandu,*
He smokes opium. *Djangan ∼ pipa,*
Don't smoke a pipe. **peng-,** **-an** 1
smoker. 2 pipe.
ufuk horizon.
ugahari 1 frugal. 2 moderate, temperate. 3 average, medium. 4 equal.
teman jg – a friend on an equal social
footing.
ugal²an 1 mischievous, naughty. 2
reckless, inconsiderate.
ugama see AGAMA.

ugem meng–i to believe in. *Ia* ∼ *kekuasaan pemerintah*, He believes in the state's authority.

uger pillar, support. **-an** *hukum* rule of law.

U.G.M. [*Universita(s) Gadjah Mada*] Gadjah Mada University in Jogjakarta.

ugut meng– 1 to frighten, intimidate. 2 to threaten. 3 to bully. **peng–an** intimidation. **-an** 1 threat. 2 bluff.

UI [*Universita(s) Indonésia*] University of Indonesia in Jakarta.

uik meng– to quack.

uir[2] locust.

ukir ber– carved, engraved. *médja* ∼ carved table. **ber-** **-**[2] pockmarked. **meng–** to carve, engrave, chisel. **meng–kan** 1 to engrave, carve. *Ia* ∼ *namanja pd tjintjin*, He engraved her name on the ring. 2 to chisel. 3 to imprint, implant. *Ia* ∼ *peladjaran itu dlm hatinja*, He implanted that lesson on his mind. **peng–** engraver. **-an** 1 sculpture. 2 a carving. ∼ *kaju* a wood carving. **-meng–kaju** act of carving wood.

ukup 1 incense, perfume. 2 scent. **ber-** to be perfumed. **meng-** to perfume. **meng–i** to perfume with. **-an** 1 perfume. 2 scent. 3 censer. **per–an** censer.

ukur 1 measure. 2 measuring tape. **ber–an** to measure. *Peluru itu* ∼ *30 métér*, The missile measured 30 meters. meng– 1 to measure, survey. 2 to read a meter. ∼ *djalan* to stroll about. **peng–** meter. ∼ *api* pyrometer. ∼ *demam* clinical thermometer. ∼ *djarak* speedometer. ∼ *demam* clinical thermometer. ∼ *djarak* speedometer. ∼ *hudjan* rain gauge. ∼ *lengas* hygrometer. ∼ *suhu* clinical thermometer. ∼ *tjepat* speedometer. **-an** 1 measurement, measure. 2 size, dimension. 3 format. 4 norm, criterion. 5 measuring stick. 6 standard. ∼ *isi* cubic measure. ∼ *luas* square measure. ∼ *pandjang* linear measure. **se-** in agreement (with). ∼ *dgn* in conformity with. – *alit* rules and regulations. – *badju dibadan sendiri* to judge others by o.s. ∼ *djangka* fixed time.

ulah 1 manner, way. 2 see OLAH. meng– to prepare.

ulajat see WILAJAT.

ulak meng– to pulverize, grind. *Ia* ∼ *sambal itu*, She pulverized the spice. **-**[2] *pinggang* hollow above the hip.

ulam raw vegetable as side dish with rice. **ber-** 1 to have a vegetable as side dish. *Ia makan tidak* ∼ , He ate without any vegetables. 2 to take as a concubine. *Ia* ∼ *orang sana*, He had a woman from there as a concubine. **-**[2] concubine. – *mentjari sambal* a woman looking for a husband.

ulama Moslem scholar. – *pendjara* prison chaplain.

ulang frequent, repeatedly. **ber-** to repeat. ∼ *tahun* to have a birthday, anniversary, commemoration. **ber-** **-**[2](an) repeatedly. meng–(i) 1 to repeat. *Ia* ∼ *pertanjaannja*, He repeated his question. 2 to rehearse. *Meréka* ∼ *peladjaran utk bésok*, They rehearsed their studies for tomorrow. 3 to frequent, visit. **peng–** coach, tutor. **per–an** 1 repetition. 2 time of return. **-an** 1 repetition. 2 rehearsal. 3 refrain. 4 test. – *aling* to and fro. – *perang* battle, war maneuvers. – *tahun* anniversary.

ulap[2] meng– **-**[2]**kan** to beckon with. *Ia* ∼ *tangannja*, He beckoned with his hand.

ular 1 snake. 2 pennant. **-an,** **-**[2] rubber hose or tube. **-**[2]**an** 1 a cramp. 2 toy snake. – *danau* water snake. – *kepak* viper. – *mengiang* rainbow. – *naga* dragon. – *sawa* python. – *séndok* cobra. – *welang* a poisonous snake. – *bukan ikanpun bukan* neither fish nor fowl. – *kepala dua* uncertain attitude.

ulas 1 wrapper, covering. 2 pillowcase. 3 continuation. **ber-** 1 wrapped, covered. *Médja* ∼ , The table had a cover. ∼ *tangan* to have an assistant. *Tempat tidurnja tiada* ∼ , The bed has no sheet. 2 to be painted with. *Bibirnja* ∼ *mérah*, Her lips were painted red. meng– 1 to cover, wrap. 2 to line a nest. 3 to extend, continue, lengthen. 4 to analyze, review, comment on, explain. 5 to paint. ∼ *témbok* to paint a wall. – *njawa* to save o's life. ∼ *pembitjaraan* to continue the discussion. ∼ *tangan* to help, lend a hand, assist. meng–i 1 to put a cover on s.t. *Ia* ∼ *bukunja*, He put a cover on his book. 2 to paint again and again. **per–an** connected part. **se-** *djeruk* section of citrus fruit. **-an** 1 envelope, cover. 2 lining. 3 continuation, extension. 4 analysis, review, commentary. 5 remark. 6 painting. – *bantal* pillow. – *buku* 1 book jacket. 2 book review. – *kasur* bed sheet. – *médja* tablecloth. – *mulas* colic. – *surat* envelope. – *tangan* assistant.

ulat 1 caterpillar. 2 worm, insect. 3 tough. 4 persevering. **ber-** wormeaten. ∼ *mata melihat* to dislike.

ke-an perseverance, stamina. – *se-rangga* insects. – *sutera* silkworm.
ulek² crusher, masher. see ULAK.
ulem meng-i to invite. **-an,** **-²** invitation.
uler kambang leech. **ng-** *kambang* slowly.
ules meng- to pulverize.
ulet see ULAT. **meng-** to stretch (after sleeping).
uli meng- to knead dough.
ulia see AULIA.
ulik see ULIT. **meng-** to investigate. **peng-an** investigation.
ulir thread of a screw. **meng-** to put in a screw. – *sekerup* screw driver.
ulit meng-(i) to rock to sleep. **meng-kan** to sing to sleep. *Ia sedang* ∼ *anaknja*, She was singing her child to sleep. **peng-** 1 lullaby. 2 lullaby singer.
ulu see HULU.
ulubalang see HULUBALANG.
uluk salam to extend greetings.
ulung 1 excellent, superior. 2 capable, skilled. **ke-an** superiority.
ulur slave. **meng-** 1 to pay out. *Ia* ∼ *tali itu*, He paid out the rope. 2 to stretch, extend. 3 to make concessions. **meng-i** to hand over to s.o. *Ia* ∼ *saja buku*, He handed over a book to me. **meng-kan** to stretch, reach out, pass, extend. *Ia* ∼ *kertas itu pd saja*, He handed, passed, me the sheet of paper. *Ia* ∼ *lidah*, She put out her tongue. *Maskapai itu* ∼ *perdjandjian*, The company extended its contract. ∼ *bendéra* to put out the flag. ∼ *tangan* to extend a (helping) hand. **(peng)-an** 1 concession. 2 paying out (of rope). 3 contribution. 4 slackening. 5 assistance. **ter-** 1 protruding, projecting. 2 stretched out.
umang² 1 hermit crab. 2 o. who likes to dress in fine, but borrowed, clothes.
umat see UMMAT.
umbai dangling, swinging to and fro. **ber-** 1 fringed. 2 to swing, dangle. *Ranting* ∼ *dikawat télpon*, A branch was dangling on the telephone wire. **meng-** **-²kan** to swing, dangle s.t. **ter-** **-²** dangling, swinging. *Ia* ∼ *diantara langit dan bumi*, He was dangling between earth and sky.
umbalan passage, fare.
umban sling. **meng-** to throw away, sling. **peng-** missile, sling.
umbang ber- ambing to bob up and down, toss about. **meng-** to float. *Kaju* – *diair*, Wood floats on water. **meng-** ambingkan to drift to and fro, toss about. see OMBANG.
umbar meng- to free, let loose, set

free. *Kambingnja di-* *dihalaman*, The goat was let loose in the yard. ∼ *hawa nafsu* to give o's passion free rein.
umbi tuber, root. **ber-** rooted. *se-* one plant. – *akar* root tuber. **-²an** belonging to the tuber, yam group. – *dan akar* 1 to the very roots. 2 completely, drastically.
umbuk meng- 1 to swindle. 2 to persuade. 3 to appease. **peng-** swindler. – *umbai* swindle.
umbul hypertrophic. **meng-** to bubble up, rise rapidly. **-²** banner.
umbut edible palm pith. **meng-** to extract. ∼ *njawa* to take s.o.'s life.
ummat member of a religious community. – *Islam* Moslems. – *Keristen* the Christian world. – *Muhammad* followers of Mohammed.
ummi illiterate.
ump. [*umpamanja*] for example.
umpak 1 foot, step. 2 pedestal. **meng-** to extol a person to the skies. **-²an** praise, flattery.
umpama 1 example. *sebagai* – as an example. 2 like, as. **meng-kan** 1 to compare. *Ia* ∼ *kuda dgn kambing*, He compared a horse with a goat. 2 to follow in o's footsteps, imitate o's example. *Ia* ∼ *ajahnja dlm mendjalankan tugas itu*, He followed in his father's footsteps in carrying out the task. 3 to assume, suppose. *Kami* ∼ *kapal itu berdjalan*, We assumed the ship was moving. 4 to represent as. 5 to respect, treat well. *Ia tjukup di-kan dikota itu*, He was sufficiently respected in that city. **per-an** 1 proverb. 2 parable, metaphor. 3 aphorism. 4 resemblance. **se-** like, equal. **(se)-nja**, – *kata* for example.
umpan 1 bait, food. – *itik* duck food. – *pantjing* fish bait. 2 victim, prey. **meng-** to tempt, lure. **meng-i** 1 to feed. 2 to entice. *Ia* ∼ *temannja dgn utjapan² jg manis²*, He enticed his friend with sweet words. **meng-kan** to put out as bait. – *kera* to put a monkey out as bait. – *keris*, – *pisau* doomed to death. – *peluru* cannon fodder. – *tekak* appetizer.
umpat 1 slander. 2 reproach. 3 scandal. 4 grudge, resentment. **meng-** 1 to slander. 2 to abuse. **peng-** slanderer. **-an** 1 slander. 2 reproach.
umpet meng- to go hide, lie low. ∼ *rahasia* to keep a secret. **-²an** hide-and-seek.
umpil meng- 1 to lift, raise. 2 to row, scull. **peng-** lever, crowbar.
umpuk heap, pile. *se-* *batu* a pile of stones. **ber-** in a pile.

umrah visit to a holy place as part of a pilgrimage.

umuk to brag, boast.

umum 1 general. *rapat* – general (public) meeting. 2 public. *télpon* – public telephone. 3 the public. *tidak terbuka pd* – not open to the public. 4 commonly. *Kemédja ini sdh mulai – dipakai,* This shirt has begun to be commonly worn. **ke-an** generality. **meng-kan** 1 to announce, notify. 2 to publish. ~ *dgn keluhuran* to proclaim solemnly. **peng-an** 1 announcement, notification. 2 publication. 3 communication. 4 communiqué. ~ *perang* declaration of war. **per-an** 1 generalizing. 2 generalization. **se-nja** 1 generally. 2 in all, altogether. **-nja** 1 usually. ~ *ia bekerdja pd pagi hari,* Usually he works in the morning. 2 in general. *pd* ~ generally.

umur 1 age. *Berapa –nja?* How old is he? 2 life. *Kalau masih ada – pasti ia akan kemari,* If he were still alive, I'm certain he'd come here. **ber-** 1 to last. 2 to be old. *Ia* ~ *tiga tahun,* She's 3 years old. *Ia sdh* ~ , He's grown up, of age. *Orangnja tlh* ~ , He was an old man. **se-** of the same age. *Ia* ~ *dgn anak saja,* He's the same age as my child. ~ *hidup* 1 lifelong, for life. 2 life imprisonment. *dihukum* ~ *hidup* sentenced for life. *(di)bawah* – underage. – *balig* adult. *blm sampai* – underage. *sdh landjut –nja* advanced in years. *sdh sampai* – adult.

UnAir [*Universita(s) Airlangga*] Airlangga University in Surabaya.

unda ber- –² being in tow o. behind the other. **meng-** –² to tow o. behind the other.

undak ber- to find strong opposition. **ber-(-)** 1 to have stairs. *Rumahnja tidak* ~ , The house has no stairs. 2 to have stories. *Rumah itu* ~ *tiga,* That house has three stories. **meng-** 1 to fail to make headway (of a ship). 2 to obstruct. **-²an** stairs, steps.

undan ber- 1 protracted, drawn out. 2 to be hesitant, unwilling. *Anak itu* ~ *diair,* The child was unwilling to leave the water.

undang meng- to invite, summon. *Ia* ~ *temannja utk makan malam,* He invited his friend for dinner. **meng-kan** to proclaim, enact, establish by law. **peng-an** enactment. **per-** –²an legislation. **-an** 1 invitation. 2 invited guest. **-²** law, ordinance, act. ~ *darurat* emergency regulations. ~ *dasar* constitution. ~ *ketjelakaan* workmen's compensation act.

undi lot. **memper-kan** to raffle off.

meng- to draw lots. ~ *suara* to vote. **peng-an** lottery, raffle. ~ *suara* vote. **-an** 1 lottery. 2 test. ~ *suara* voting. ~ *uang* money lottery.

undjam meng-kan 1 to thrust into. 2 to drill, bore. 3 to plant. **peng-tenggala** plowshare. **ter-** vertical, perpendicular.

undjuk meng-(kan) 1 to hold out, extend. *Jg blm dpt bagian disuruh* ~ , Anyone who failed to get his share was asked to raise his hand. 2 to present, hand over, pass. *Ia* ~ *surat kpd ajahnja,* He handed the letter to his father. **meng-kan** 1 to indicate, point out, point. *Ia* ~ *kpd bulan,* He pointed at the moon. 2 to show. *Ia* ~ *gambar² perdjalanannja,* He showed pictures of his trip. **peng-an** 1 offer, presentation. 2 information, explanation. – *bertahu* to inform.

undjung see KUNDJUNG.

undjur extended, stretched out. **bel-** to sit with o's legs stretched out. *Ia duduk* ~ *ditanah,* He sat on the ground with his legs stretched out. **meng-** to stretch o.s. **meng-kan** 1 to stretch out. *Ia* ~ *kakinja,* He stretched out his legs. 2 to stretch s.o. out. *Ia* ~ *jg sakit itu ditempat tidur,* He stretched the patient out on the bed. **-an** foot of a bed.

undjut small bag, bundle tied at end with knots. **meng-** to wrap up in a bundle.

unduk² sea horse.

undung² veil thrown over the head. **ber-** –² to wear a veil over the head. **memper-kan, meng-(-)kan** to use as a head covering. *Ia* ~ *kain itu kpd kepalanja,* She used the cloth as a veil over her head.

undur 1 to back, withdraw. 2 to turn away. **meng-kan** 1 to drive back, make yield. *Ia* ~ *mobilnja,* He backed his car. 2 to postpone. *Ia* ~ *hari berangkatnja,* He postponed the day of departure. 3 to withdraw. *Ia* ~ *tentaranja,* He withdrew his troops. ~ *diri* 1 to withdraw, retire. 2 to retire. *Ia* ~ *diri dari pekerdjaannja,* He retired from his work. 3 to resign. 4 to set back. *Ia* ~ *djam,* He set the clock back. 5 to put s.t. back. **peng-an** 1 retreat, withdrawal. 2 postponement. 3 adjournment.

UnGam [*Universita(s) Gadjah Mada*] Gadjah Mada University in Jogjakarta.

ungap meng- to gasp for breath.

unggang-unggit to go up and down as of a seesaw or rocking chair.

unggas bird, fowl. per-an poultry husbandry.

unggat-unggit to move up and down.

unggis meng- to nibble, gnaw at.

ungguk heap, pile. -an pile.

unggul 1 superior, excellent, first-class, tops. kepandaian jg – superior ability. bibit – prime seed. 2 to prevail. ke-an 1 superiority, special quality. 2 lead, advantage. meng-i to surpass, exceed.

unggun 1 woodpile. 2 campfire. ber- (-) 1 in heaps. 2 to smoulder. 3 to make a campfire. Apinja masih ~, The fire was still smouldering. 4 to make a campfire. Meréka ~ didekat sungai, They made a campfire near the river. meng-kan to gather wood for making a fire. -an 1 campfire. 2 heap, pile. – -timbun pile, heap.

unggut ber- -²an tug of war. meng- to pull at, tug.

ungka gibbon.

ungkai meng- 1 to untie, undo, loosen. Ia ~ tali, He untied the rope. 2 to force open. 3 to undo, take off. Ia ~ badjunja, He took off his jacket. 4 to disclose. Ia ~ soal lama, He disclosed (dug up) an old matter.

ungkang-ungkit see UNGGANG-UNGGIT.

ungkap meng- 1 to gasp for breath. 2 to use sign language. 3 to catch o's breath. Bila kita ~ kembali ... When we catch our breath ... -an 1 gasping. 2 facial expression. 3 gesture. ~ pelembut euphemism. ~ pengeras hyperbole. ~ timbalan litotes. ter- -² gasping for breath. Ia ~ sesudah menaik tangga, He was gasping for breath after climbing the stairs.

ungkat meng- 1 to bring up an old matter. 2 to be an Indian giver.

ungkil meng- 1 to lift, pry up. 2 to pry loose. peng- lever.

ungkit meng- 1 to lift, raise. 2 to open old sores. meng- -² to bob up and down. peng- lever.

ungku see ENGKU.

ungkur ber- -²(an) scattered in all directions.

ungsi meng- 1 to flee. 2 to evacuate. meng-kan to evacuate s.o. peng- refugee, evacuee. peng-an 1 evacuation. 2 asylum, refuge.

ungu violet, purple.

UnHas [Universita(s) Hasanuddin] Hasanuddin University in Macassar.

uni 1 older sister. 2 union. 3 see HUNI.

Uni Afrika Selatan Union of South Africa.

unifikasi unification.

unik unique.

Uni Sovjét Soviet Union.

universil universal.

universita(s) university. ke-an university. kalangan ~ university circles.

universitér university. urusan – university affairs.

universitét university.

unjai softly, gently. ber- -² 1 softly, gently. 2 little by little. meng- to do s.t. slowly.

UnPad [Universita(s) Padjadjaran] Padjadjaran University in Bandung.

UNRA [Universita(s) Rakjat] People's University in Jakarta.

unsur element, substance. – pembangun constituent element.

unsuri 1 elementary. 2 elemental.

unta camel.

untai string, lace. ber-(an) 1 to hang loosely. 2 on a string. bidji ~ beads on a string. meng- 1 to dangle, hang down. 2 to string. Ia ~ bidji, She strung seeds. -an 1 series. 2 string, chain. se- kalung a necklace.

untal pill. meng- to roll pills.

untang-anting swinging to and fro.

until meng- 1 to dangle, hang down. 2 to roll a pill. se- 1 a pill, pellet. 2 a little bit.

unting strand, skein. meng- to sound, plumb. se- 1 a skein. ~ benang a skein of thread. 2 a handful. ~ djagung a handful of corn. -² plumb, plummet.

untjang traveling bag. – untjit 1 restless, unsettled. 2 by installments. Ia membajar – untjit, He pays on the installment plan.

untuk 1 for. Uang itu – membeli nasi, That money is for buying rice. 2 for, meant for. – siapa buku ini? For whom is this book? minjak – penggosok kulit oil for rubbing on the skin. 3 to, in order to. Ia pergi – menemui ajahnja, He went to meet his father. 4 by way of. 5 on behalf of. 6 for the benefit of. 7 as. Ia diterima – djurutulis, He was accepted as a clerk. 8 share, ration. memper-kan, meng-kan 1 to intend, destine for, earmark. Buku ini di-kan bagi peladjar, This book is intended for students. 2 to allot, allocate, assign. Ia ~ bahan makanan kpd pengungsi, He allocated foodstuffs to the evacuees. ter- intended, destined for. – mana for which.

untung 1 luck, fortune. 2 destiny, fate. 3 advantage. 4 profit. 5 interest. – lima ribu dolar $5,000 profit. ber- 1 lucky. Ia ~ mendapat rumah, He was lucky to get a house. 2 successful. Ia ~ dlm usahanja, He was successful in his efforts. 3 to make a profit. *Ia ~ 2 rupiah*, He made a profit of 2 rupiahs. **ke-an** 1 profit. 2 success. 3 luck. *~ besar baginja*, It was a big success for him. **keberan** luck, success. **meng-kan** 1 to favor, benefit. *Pendapat umum ~ negeri itu*, Public opinion favors that country. 2 favorable. *Itu peraturan jg ~ penduduk*, It was a regulation favorable to the people. *Kedjudjuran ~* , Honesty pays. **per-an** 1 fortune, fate. 2 profit, income. **–²an** at random. *~ sadja saja memilih dia*, I just voted for him, hoping for the best. **–lah** 1 fortunately, thank goodness. 2 it so happens that..., incidentally, coincidental. *– bersih* net profit. *– djahat* bad luck. *– malang* bad luck, fate, destiny. *– nasib* adventure(s). *– pegawai* bonus. *– séro* dividend.

untut elephantiasis.

u.p. [*untuk perhatian*] for the attention of.

upa a prefix meaning deputy, assistant. *– gurubesar* assistant professor.

upah 1 pay, wages. 2 fee, commission. 3 tip. **ber-** rewarded. *menolong orang dgn tiada ~* to help people without reward. **meng-(i)** to pay a salary, wages. *Ia ~ temannja mengambil surat*, He paid his friend for getting his letter for him. **meng-kan** to have s.t. done upon payment. *Ia ~ badjunja*, He had a suit made on advance payment. **per-an** wage matters. **–an** 1 wages. 2 wage earner. *– bulanan* monthly wage. *– djahit* charge for sewing. *– lembur* overtime pay. *– mengangkut barang* charge for transportation of goods. *– pokok* base pay. *– pokok terendah* minimum subsistence wage.

upaja means, expedient. **ber-** to do o's best, utmost. **meng-kan** to strive for, seek. *Ia ~ tertjapainja keamanan*, He strove to achieve peace.

upam polish. **meng-** to polish. *Ia ~ mas dan pérak*, She polished the gold and silver. **peng-** polisher. **-an** polish.

upama see UMPAMA.

upas 1 messenger, attendant. 2 policeman. 3 poison (on plants). *– pos* postman.

upatjara 1 ceremony. 2 honor, homage. 3 regalia. *– pelantikan* inaugural ceremony. *dgn –* official, solemn.

upet wick, fuse.

upeti tribute paid by subjects.

upik si– Miss So and So. *~ djantan* tomboy. *Blm tentu ~ sibujungnja*, The final decision was uncertain.

urah **meng-** 1 to demolish, tear down. *Ia ~ rumah tua*, He demolished an old house. 2 to relate. *Ia ~ pengalamannja dimasa Djepang*, He related his experience during the Japanese period.

urai apart. **ber-** 1 to come to pieces. *Karena ia lari gelungnja ~* , Because she was running, her hair bun came to pieces. 2 to scatter, disperse. *Penonton pasar malam ~ ketika hudjan turun*, The fairgoers dispersed when rain fell. *~ air mata* to shed tears. **meng-** to burst, open. **meng-kan** 1 to loosen. *Ia ~ rambutnja*, She loosened her hair. 2 to untie, open. *Ia ~ kantong*, She untied her bag. 3 to scatter. *Ia ~ tumpukan batu*, He scattered a heap of stones. 4 to explain. *Ia ~ tjara pemilihan*, He explained the system of election. 5 to analyze. *Tjoba –kan soal ini*, Please analyze this problem. 6 to disrupt. 7 to dislocate. **peng-** analyst. **per-an** dissociation. **ter-** loose, scattered. **-an** 1 analysis. 2 explanation. 3 digression. 4 issue, outcome. *– sendi* dislocation.

urap ointment, salve. **ber- –²an** to rub ointment on o.s. **meng-(i)** to rub with ointment. *Ia ~ badannja sebelum tidur*, She rubbed her body with ointment before going to sleep. **meng-kan** to apply s.t. to the body. *Ia ~ bedak wangi kpd badannja*, She applied scented powder to her body.

uras ointment, salve. **ber-** 1 anointed. *Badannja ~ balsem*, His body was anointed with balm. 2 embalmed. **meng-i** to smear, rub in. *Ia ~ badannja*, She rubbed ointment on her body. **meng-kan** to spread with. *Ia ~ minjak wangi kpd badannja*, She spread perfume over her body.

urat 1 tendon. 2 nerve. 3 vein. **ber-** muscular, sinewy. *Ia tiada ~* , He's weak. *~ berakar* deeply rooted. *Agama Islam ~ berakar pd orang Bantam*, The Islamic religion is deeply rooted in the people of Bantam. **meng-** 1 to be rooted. *Mentjuri ~ kepadanja*, Stealing is rooted in him. 2 to become tough. *– daging* muscle, sinew. *– darah* blood vessel. *– darah halus* vein. *– keting* Achilles' tendon. *– léhér* neck muscle. *– merih* jugular vein. *– nadi* radial artery. *– saraf* nerve.

urbanisasi urbanization.

URI [*Uang Républik Indonésia*] Republic of Indonesia money.

uri placenta, afterbirth. **meng-** to revolve rapidly.

urik meng– to pick, pluck.
uring philtrum. –²**an** 1 to grumble.
2 to be angry.
URSS [*Uni Républik Sosialis Sovjét*]
USSR.
uruk meng– 1 to bury. 2 to dig out
of the earth. 3 to fill in. ~ *bagian
ladang jg rendah* to fill in the lower
part of the field.
urung 1 failed, unsuccessful, misfired.
Ia – djadi duta besar di negeri itu,
He was unsuccessful in becoming
ambassador to that country. 2 not
take place. *Pertemuannja – karena
tak ada tempat utk bertemu,* The meeting did not take place because there
was no place to meet. meng–**kan** 1
to cause to fail. 2 to abandon, drop.
3 to cancel, postpone. *Udjiannja
di–kan karena gurunja sakit,* The examination was canceled because his
teacher was sick. *tak – for sure. Ia
tak – dinaikkan pangkat,* He was sure
to be promoted.
urup meng– 1 to barter, exchange.
Ia ~ barang itu, He exchanged the
goods. 2 to change money. peng–
money-changer. –**an** 1 the thing exchanged. 2 change (money).
urus ber–**an** 1 to get in touch with,
contact. *Kamu harus ~ dgn dia dlm
–an itu,* You must get in touch with
him on that matter. 2 to be concerned with. *Ia tidak ~ dgn perdagangan lagi,* He had nothing to do
with business any more. 3 to meddle.
*Rupanja ia mau ~ sendiri dgn soal
itu,* It seemed he wanted to meddle
in that problem himself. 4 to have
business with. *Ia sedang ~ dgn tuan
rumah,* He had business with his
landlord. ~ *kpd* 1 to apply to. 2 to
have connections with. *Anak²nja
tidak ~ sekolahnja,* His children's
schooling was being neglected. meng–
(**kan**) 1 to arrange. *Ia mau ~
perumahan,* He wants to arrange
housing. *Ia ~ ajahnja tempat tinggal,*
He arranged a place for his father to
stay. 2 to put in order. *Ia sdh ~
kamar tidur,* She has already put the
bedroom in order. 3 to take care of,
look after. *Ia tidak ~ keséhatannja,*
He didn't take care of his health.
4 to manage, conduct, run. ~ *perusahaan* to manage a business. 5 to
settle. *Biarlah dia jg ~nja; tuan tak
usah ikut tjampur,* Let him settle it;
you don't need to meddle. 6 to deal
with. *Polisi ~ pentjurian,* The police
dealt with the theft. peng– 1 board,
management. 2 manager. ~ *besar*
board of directors, executive board.

peng–an 1 management. 2 arrangement. –**an** 1 affair, matter. *Itu bukan
~ saja,* That's not my affair. (That's
none of my business.) ~ *agama* religious affairs. 2 arrangement, organization. ~*nja kurang baik,* It
wasn't too well arranged. ~ *kemasjarakatan* social affairs, problems. ~
keuangan financial matters. ~ *pegawai*
personnel affairs. ~ *rumahtangga*
household duties. –² laxative, purgative. *tidak* ke–**an**, *tidak* ter– neglected.
urut ber– –² consecutively, in succession. *Meréka keluar ~ dari rumah,*
They came out of the house in succession. meng– 1 to massage. *Ia ~
lengan adiknja,* He massaged his little
brother's arm. 2 to rub in, massage.
Ia ~ dgn balsem tjap matjan, She
rubbed with tiger balm. 3 to squeeze.
*Ia ~ telundjuk jg luka supaja keluar
darah,* He squeezed his hurt finger so
the blood would come out. 4 to
caress, stroke. *Ia ~ kepala adiknja
supaja berhenti menangis,* He caressed
his little brother's head so that he
would stop crying. –**an** order, sequence, succession. –²**an** consecutively, successively. – *tanggal* chronology.
US [*Uni Sovjét*] Soviet Union.
usah –**kan** 1 let alone, not to mention. 2 instead of. *tak(tidak) –* 1 un-
necessary, it's not necessary. *Tak –
kamu datang,* No need for you to
come. 2 don't. *Tak – kamu melarang
saja,* Don't stop me.
usaha 1 effort, exertion. 2 labor,
work. 3 initiative, action. 4 on the
part of. *Gagalnja – fakultét utk
mengangkat guru besar tetap bagi...*
The failure on the part of the faculty
to appoint permanent professors for...
– *pemerintah* government initiative.
ber– 1 to try, endeavor. 2 to exert,
do the utmost. *Meréka ~ se-baik²nja,*
They are making every effort. (They
are doing their utmost.) memper–**kan**
1 to carry on. *Ia ~ perdagangan,*
He is carrying on trade. 2 to cultivate, raise. meng–**kan** 1 to carry on.
Ia ~ pertanian, He's carrying on
farming. 2 to cultivate. *Ia ~ tanah,*
He cultivates the soil. 3 to make
an effort, try. *Pemerintah ~ penuru-
nan harga,* The government made
an effort to lower prices. 4 to organize. *Ia ~ rapat,* He organized a
meeting. ~ *diri* to exert o.s. *Ia ~
dirinja supaja lulus udjian,* He exerted
himself in order to pass the examination. ~ *kekuasaan* to employ force.
peng– 1 industrialist, entrepreneur. 2

employer. **peng–an** 1 effort, exertion.
2 trade, business. **per–an** 1 business,
enterprise, undertaking, concern. 2
effort, trouble. ∼ *air* waterworks.
∼ *Negara Arta Yasa* the state mint.
∼ *pelajaran* shipping firm. ∼ *tanah*
plantation, estate. ∼ *ternak* cattle
raising. – *bersama* mutual effort. –
melawan, – *menentang* reaction. –
sendiri personal effort. – *tamasja*
tourist service. – *tani* farm operations, enterprises. *atas* – at the instigation of.
usahawan 1 entrepreneur. 2 industrialist.
usai 1 finished, ready. 2 dispersed.
Pertemuan itu – *pd tengah malam,*
The meeting broke up at midnight.
meng– to break up, disperse. **meng–
kan** to break up, loosen.
usak to decrease, lessen. **meng–** to
ebb, decrease. *Air laut* ∼ , The sea
ebbs. **meng–i** to decrease s.t.
usam 1 dregs. 2 waste remaining
after the oil has been pressed from
coconut meat. 3 vague, dull (of
color).
usang 1 worn-out, decrepit. 2 dry,
barren, withered. **ke–an** 1 dryness.
2 decrepitude. **meng–** to dry up,
wither.
usap meng– 1 to stroke. *Ia* ∼ *dadanja,* He stroked his chest. 2 to wipe
off. *Ia* ∼ *keringatnja dgn saputangan,*
He wiped off the perspiration with a
handkerchief. 3 to caress, stroke. *Ia*
∼ *rambut anaknja,* He caressed his
child's hair.
USDEK [*Undang² dasar 1945;* So-
sialisme ala Indonésia; *Démokrasi
terpimpin;* *Ékonomi terpimpin;* *Kepribadian Indonésia*] 1945 Constitution; Socialism à la Indonesia; Guided
democracy; Guided economy; National identity.
usia age. **ber–** to be so and so old.
Ia ∼ *15 tahun,* He's a 15-year old.
usik meng– 1 to annoy, worry,
bother. 2 to touch on. *Ia* ∼ *soal lama,*
He touched on an old problem. 3 to
meddle in. *Ia* ∼ *dlm soal itu,* He
meddled in that matter. 4 to criticize. **peng–** disturber. **–an** 1 annoyance, disturbance. 2 meddling. 3
criticism.
usil annoying, troublesome. *Djangan
–!* Hands off! *Ia tidak – ttg itu,* He
didn't care about it.
usir ber– –²an to chase e.o. **meng–**
1 to chase away, drive away. *Ia* ∼
andjing dari dlm rumah, He chased
the dog out of the house. 2 to dismiss rudely, throw out. *Ia di– dari
kantornja karena sering terdapat mabok*

disana, He was thrown out of the
office because he often turned up
drunk there. **peng–an** 1 eviction. 2
exile. 3 pursuit. **–an** fugitive. **- -meng–**
to chase e.o.
uskup bishop. **ke–an** bishopric. –
agung archbishop.
Ustrali Australia.
Ustria Austria.
usuk rafter.
usul 1 proposal, suggestion. *Ia memadjukan – jg berikut,* He suggested
the following proposal. 2 nature,
characteristic. **meng–(i)** to examine
s.o. **meng–kan** 1 to propose, suggest.
2 to move. **peng–** proposer. **peng–an**
inquiry, examination. – *periksa* investigation. *Dia ditangkap dgn tiada
– periksa lagi,* He was arrested without due investigation. *asal* – origin.
– *balasan* counterproposal. – *perubahan* amendment. – *menundjukkan
asal,* Hereditary traits (manners)
betray descent. **–²** *perdamaian* peace
terms.
usung meng– to carry on the shoulders. *Meréka* ∼ *majat,* They carried
a corpse. **–an** stretcher, litter. ∼
majat bier.
usur tithe.
usus intestines, bowels. – *besar* large
intestine. – *buntut* appendix. – *halus*
small intestine. – *mulas* colic.
usut meng– 1 to feel all over, handle.
2 to examine. 3 to prosecute. *Perkara
itu di– oléh seorang djaksa,* The case
was prosecuted by a public prosecutor. **peng–** investigator. **peng–an**
examination, investigation.
utama 1 prominent, excellent, eminent. 2 staple, principal, main, prime.
Beras adalah hasil –, Rice is a staple
product. 3 important. **ke–an** 1 superiority, excellence. ∼ *kekuasaan
udara mendatangkan kemenangan,* Superiority of air power brought victory.
2 virtue, decency. **meng–kan** to emphasize, stress. *Meréka* ∼ *pembuatan
alat perang,* They emphasized the
production of war materials. **ter–** 1
superior, best. *Ia peladjar jg* ∼
dikelasnja, He was the best student
in his class. 2 especially, particularly.
Kesukaran ini ∼ *disebabkan oléh
perang,* This hardship was caused
especially by the war. 3 most important. *Sebab jg* ∼ *ialah kemiskinan,*
The most important cause was
poverty. *dgn –* chiefly.
utan see HUTAN.
utang 1 debt, obligation. 2 credit.
ber– to owe. *Ia* ∼ *$100,* She owes
$100. ∼ *budi* to be grateful. ∼ *njawa*
to owe o's life to. **memper–kan**

utar² — vulkanisir

1 to lend s.t. to s.o. 2 to borrow.
meng-i 1 to loan, lend. *Ia ~ temannja
5 rupiah,* He lent his friend 5 rupiahs.
2 to be indebted to. *Dia ~ saja,*
I am indebted to him. – *piutang* 1
debit and credit. 2 debtors and
creditors. – *emas dpt dibajar; – budi
dibawa mati,* A monetary debt can
be repaid; a debt of gratitude o.
takes to his grave. – *tiap helai bulu*
up to o's ears in debt.
utar² small round shield.
utara north. **meng-kan** 1 to explain,
expound. 2 to inform. 3 to stress,
emphasize. ~ *tjeramah* to deliver a
talk or lecture. **peng-an** 1 explanation. 2 communication. – *barat laut*
north-northwest. – *semata timur,* –
timur laut north-northeast. – *tepat*
due north.
Utarid Mercury (planet).
utas 1 skilled, capable. 2 cord,
string. 3 bundle. **ber-** *permata* with
a string of precious stones.
utik meng- –² to touch with the
finger.
utjap meng-(kan) 1 to express, utter.
Saja ~ terimakasih atas bantuanmu,
I thank you for your assistance.
2 to pronounce. *Ia ~ kata dgn
djelas,* He pronounced the word
clearly. ~ *do'a* to utter a prayer.

~ *pidato* to make a speech. ~ *selamat*
to congratulate. **-an** 1 utterance,
expression. 2 statement, communication. 3 pronunciation. ~ *selamat*
congratulation.
utjek meng-kan *mata* to rub o's eyes.
utjus see USUS.
utk [*untuk*] for, in order to.
utopi utopia.
utuh whole, sound, intact, unimpaired, undamaged. *Tradisi itu masih
hidup dgn –nja,* The tradition **lives**
on unimpaired. **ke-an** totality. **meng-
kan** to leave unimpaired.
utus meng-(kan) to send, delegate,
depute, s.o. **peng-an** mission. **per-an**
delegation, deputation. **-an** 1 messenger. 2 envoy. 3 delegate. ~
Allah God's messenger. ~ *indjil*
missionary.
U.U. [*Undang²*] law, decree.
U.U.D. [*Undang² Dasar*] the Constitution.
U.U.D.S. [*Undang² Dasar Sementara*]
provisional constitution.
uzur 1 weak, feeble, sickly (from old
age). *Ia –,* He was sickly. 2 hindrance, obstacle. **ke-an** 1 hindrance.
2 unable. 3 hindered, detained. *Ia ~
tak dpt datang,* He was hindered from
coming.

V

vak 1 subject of study. 2 profession, trade. *sekolah* – vocational
school.
valénsi valence.
valuta currency. – *asing* foreign currency.
varia 1 variety. 2 varied.
variasi variation.
véem wharfage and transport business. **per-an** wharfage business.
véntilasi ventilation.
ver- see PER-.
vérifikasi verification.
vernis see PERNIS.
verpléher male hospital attendant.
verpléhster nurse.
vérsi version.

versnéling gear. – *dua* second gear.
vértikal vertical.
véteran veteran.
véto veto. **memv-** to veto.
vilt felt.
vinjét vignette.
visa, visum visa.
vital vital. **ke-an** vitality.
vitalita vitality.
vitamine vitamin.
vokal vowel.
vonis see PONIS.
votum vote. – *kepertjajaan* vote of
confidence.
vulgarisasi vulgarization. **memv-** to
vulgarize.
vulkanisasi vulkanization.
vulkanisir memv- to vulcanize.

W

wa and.

wa'ad treaty, contract. **ber-** to conclude a treaty, contract.

wa'adat treaty, contract, covenant.

waba'dahu furthermore, moreover, next, now then (usual phrase to indicate the writer has finished his formal introduction and is now ready to take up his topic).

waba'du see WABA'DAHU.

wabah epidemic.

wadag 1 body. 2 physical.

wadah 1 bowl, receptacle, basin. 2 form. 3 place. - *gula* sugar bowl.

wadas stony ground.

wadat to live as a celibate.

wadja steel. see BADJA.

wadjah 1 countenance, face. 2 view, aspect. *Rupanja me- dimata saja*, I imagined how he looked.

wadjan frying pan (large).

wadjar 1 real, natural, true. 2 genuine. *Itu dianggap sesuatu jang -*, It's considered to be s.t. genuine. **ke-an** spontaneity. **kese-an** 1 genuineness. 2 naturalness. **se-nja** real, true, natural. *Mémang ~ dia naik pangkat*, It's natural that he should be promoted. *Dia tidak bekerdja sebagai ~* , He doesn't work the way he should.

wadjib 1 necessary, obligatory. *Tiap orang - membajar padjak*, Everyone is obliged to pay taxes. 2 duty, obligation. **ber(ke)-(an)** to be obliged to. *jg ~* the authorities. **ke-an** obligation, duty. *Djangan lupa ~* , Don't forget your duty. *~ beladjar, ~ bersekolah* compulsory education. **me-kan** to require, make compulsory. *Pemerintah ~ tiap anak bersekolah*, The government requires every child to go to school. *Buku² ini di-kan*, These books are compulsory. **pe-**s.o. who is liable. *~ daftar o.* who is liable for registration. - *latih* compulsory military training. - *padjak* taxpayer, o. who is liable for taxes. - *sumbang* compulsory contribution.

wadjik sweet sticky rice cake.

waduk 1 stomach, paunch. 2 rumen. - *air* 1 basin, pool. 2 reservoir. - *listerik* condensation.

wadul to tell on s.o., be a tattletale.

wadung ax.

wafat to pass away, depart this world. **ke-an** death, demise.

wah 1 why, well! you don't say! -*!* *Énak betul!* Say! This is delicious! -, *susah ini!* Doggone it! -*! Djahat ini!* dammit! 2 my goodness!

wahai 1 alas! 2 hello. -*! Mau kemana engkau?* Hey! Where're you going? 3 Oh!

waham 1 imagination. 2 distrust, suspicion. **me-kan** 1 to surmise. 2 to suspect.

wahid 1 one, unique (of God). 2 alone, without peer. *nomor -* first class.

wahju divine revelation, vision from God to man. **me-i** to inspire. **me-kan** to reveal.

wahon coach, car (of train).

wajang 1 puppet. 2 Javanese puppet show. **me-kan** 1 to act. 2 to perform. *dunia* **pe-an** world of the wayang. - *bébér* performance using a picture scroll. - *gambar, - gelap* movie. - *golék, - kelitik, - kerutjil* wooden puppet show. - *kulit* shadow play with leather puppets. - *orang* Javanese stage show. - *potéhi* Chinese puppet show. - *suluh* puppet show in the Indonesian language. - *wong* Javanese stage show.

wak see UAK.

waka [*wakil kepala*] deputy head.

wakaf 1 property donated for religious or community use. 2 religious institution. 3 pause in reading. **me-kan** to donate (property) to be used for religious or community use. *Orang kaja itu ~ tanahnja utk mesdjid*, The rich man donated his land as a site for a mosque.

wakil 1 deputy, agent, representative. 2 vice-, deputy. - *présidén* vice-president. - *gubernur* deputy governor. **ber-** to have as a representative. **me-i** to represent, look after o's interests. *Indonésia di-i oléh menteri dalam negeri*, Indonesia was represented by the minister of home affairs. **me-kan** to authorize. *Kepala désa di-kan bertindak*, The village

chief was authorized to act. **per–an**
1 delegation. 2 agency. ~ *mutlak,* ~
tunggal sole, exclusive, agency. 3
representation. *Déwan* ~ *Rakjat*
house of representatives, parliament.
~ *berimbang* proportional representation.
waktu 1 time. – *sdh habis,* The time
is up. *Sdh –nja berangkat,* It's time
to leave. 2 when (in the past).
– *saja pergi, temanku tiba,* When I
left, my friend came. 3 whenever.
di– hudjan litjin slippery when wet.
4 tense. – *lampau* past tense. **se–**
1 when. 2 then, at that time. **se–**
upon a time, once. **se– –²** 1 always.
2 at any time. – *djeda* break, pause,
recess, interval. – *hamil* pregnancy
period. – *istirahat* intermission, break,
recess. – *maghrib* time for sunset
prayer. – *pembajaran* due date. –
samar muka 1 late dusk. 2 dawn.
– *sekolah* school hours. – *senggang*
leisure (time). – *terluang* spare time.
dalam – jg singkat shortly. *pd – itu*
at that time. *beberapa – jg lalu* some
time ago. *pd –nja* in time, duly.
pd – disampaikan on presentation.
Wala [*Wadjib Latih*] conscript.
wal'afiat hale and hearty, in excellent
spirits. see SÉHAT.
walakin although.
Walama [*Wadjib Latih Mahasiswa*]
student conscript.
walang grasshopper, locust. – *hati*
anxious, concerned. – *sangat* rice pest.
walaupun (al)though. – *dia sakit,*
tetapi dia hendak pergi kebioskop,
Even though he is ill, he still intends
to go to the movies. – *demikian* 1
nevertheless, yet. 2 in spite of that.
walhasil with the result that...
wali 1 male relative legally responsible for bride under Moslem law,
normally her father. 2 high civil
servant. – *kota* mayor. – *negara* head
of state during the period of the
United States of Indonesia. 3 guardian, proxy. 4 religious leader. – *ullah*
a Moslem saint. **me(mper)–kan** 1 to
be guardian of. 2 to govern. 3 to
appoint s.o. to be guardian. **per–an**
1 guardianship. 2 trusteeship. – *geré-*
dja church head. – *negeri* 1 provincial
head. 2 governor. 3 former governor-
general.
waliullah see WALI.
wallahi I swear by God.
wallahu a'lam 1 God knows best. –
bisawab God knows the truth. 2
heaven knows (I don't), goodness
knows.
waluku plow.
Wamilda [*Wadjib Militér Darurat*]

emergency military obligation. **me–**
kan to engage in an emergency military obligation.
WAMPA [*Wakil Menteri Pertama*]
deputy chief minister.
wang see UANG.
wangi fragrant. **me–** 1 fragrant. 2
to scent, perfume. **me–kan** to perfume
s.t. **–an** 1 fragrance, scent. 2 perfume.
–²an perfumery.
wangsa ke–an kinship.
wanita 1 woman. 2 female, feminine,
womanly. **ke–an** 1 femininity. 2
womanhood. – *kudus* female saint.
– "*P*" prostitute.
wanti² repeatedly.
wapat see WAFAT.
wara 1 abstinence. 2 to abstain from.
warakat see WARKAT.
warangan arsenic.
waras healthy, recovered. **ke–an**
health, recovery. *kurang* – slightly
insane.
warawiri 1 hibiscus. 2 back and
forth. 3 fickle, unstable.
warga 1 accredited member of an
association. 2 caste. **ke–an** 1 membership. 2 citizenry. **ke–duniaan** 1 cos-
mopolitan. 2 cosmopolitanism. **ke–**
negaraan 1 citizenship. 2 civics. **pe–**
negaraan naturalization. – *dunia*
stateless. – *kota* city resident. –
negara citizen.
waringin banyan tree.
waris heir. **me–i** to inherit from.
Dia ~ *semua kekajaan pamannja,*
He inherits all his uncle's wealth.
me–kan to bequeath. *Dia* ~ *semuanja*
kpd anaknja, He bequeathed everything to his child. **pe–an** 1 inheriting.
2 inheritance. **–an** legacy, inheritance,
estate. – *asli* the actual heir (child).
– *sah* legal heir.
warkat 1 letter. – *pos* letter paper
which folds to form envelope (similar
to air letter). 2 records, files.
warna color. **ber–** colored. *bangsa* ~
colored people. **ber– –²** 1 various.
2 multicolored. *Dia suka pakaian*
~ , She likes multicolored clothes.
me–i to color, paint. *Pintu dan*
djendéla di–inja hidjau, He painted
the doors and windows green. *Ia* ~
Jefferson, He painted Jefferson. **me–**
kan to color, paint. – *bunji* timbre.
– *keramat* (Indonesian) national colors
(red and white). – *riang* bright col-
or(s). – *sari* anthology. – *tjokelat*
brown. – *warni* all kinds of, various.
– *warta* miscellany, all kinds of news.
warta 1 report, communication. 2
news. **me–kan** to report, inform.
pe– 1 correspondent, reporter. 2 news
bulletin. – *berita* news report. –

harian daily newspaper. – *sepekan* weekly news.

wartawan journalist, correspondent. **ke–an** journalism.

wartawati woman reporter.

warung small shop, stall. **ber–** to run a small shop. – *kopi* coffee shop. – *nasi* eating stall.

wasangka see SJAK.

wasi executor of a will.

wasiat 1 dying exhortation, last will and testament (spoken or written). 2 magic power (of an ancient heirloom). *lampu* – magic lamp. **ber–** to make o's will. **me–kan** to will, bequeath.

wasit 1 referee, umpire. 2 arbiter.

wasitah matchmaker, go-between.

waskom washbasin.

waspada cautious, alert, wary. –*lah*, Be vigilant. **ke–an** 1 vigilance, alertness. 2 caution. **me–i** to guard against.

wassalam 1 peace be with you! 2 (at end of letters) respectfully, yours truly, sincerely. see SALAM.

waswas 1 suspicion, anxiety. 2 evil thoughts. 3 doubt.

watak character, nature, disposition. **ber–** to have character. *Ia ~ djantan*, He's a man of character. **per–an** characterization.

watas border, boundary, frontier, limit. **ber–(an)** to border. *Kebunnja ~ dgn halaman kami*, His garden borders on our yard. **me–i** to limit, restrict, confine. *Pemerintah ~ pemakaian listrik*, The government limits the consumption of electricity. **per–an** 1 limitation, restriction. 2 border, frontier. see BATAS.

watermantel water-cooled machine gun.

wauwau k.o. monkey.

wawansantap friendly, informal meal or banquet.

wawantjara interview. *Dlm – singkat dgn Antara ia menerangkan ...* In a brief interview with Antara he stated ... **ber–** to hold an interview.

wawasan insight.

W.C. [*wésé*] water closet, toilet.

wedana district chief. **ke–an** 1 district. 2 residence of district chief.

wedar to disclose. **ter–** 1 disclosed. *Rahasia itu ~ ,* The secret was disclosed. 2 to be let down. *Rambutnja ~ ,* Her hair was let down.

wedel **me–** to dye. –*an* dyeing.

wedjang **di–** advised, instructed. **me–kan** to give advice or instructions. –*an* 1 instruction(s), teaching. 2 advice. 3 explanation.

weduk invulnerable. **ke–an** invulnerability.

wegah reluctant, unwilling. *Dia – pergi sebab hari hudjan*, He's unwilling to go because it's raining.

welang spotted, striped.

weling last will and testament.

welirang see BELÉRANG.

wenang entitled to, qualified. **ber–** to have jurisdiction. **berse–** –² 1 to act arbitrarily, at o's own discretion. 2 to act cruelly, despotically. **ke–an** competence. **ke–** –²**an** 1 arbitrariness. 2 despotism, tyranny. *~ meradjaléla*, Despotism prevails. **se–** –² 1 arbitrarily, at will. 2 despotic, cruel, tyrannical. *Tindakan jg ~ itu menjakiti hati penduduk*, The cruel actions hurt the feelings of the people.

wénang see WENANG.

wérak recruiter of laborers.

werdi 1 significance. 2 sense, meaning. 3 definition.

wésel 1 money order, draft. 2 railway switch. *salah* – 1 derailed. 2 misunderstood.

wétan east.

wewenang 1 competence. 2 right, authority. **ber–** to have the authority. *Siapa jg ~ disini?* Who has the authority here? see WENANG.

wibawa authority, power. **ber–** 1 prestigeful. 2 responsible. **ke–an** prestige, authority. *~ pemerintah pusat tidak diakui*, The authority of the central government was not acknowledged. –²**an** authority.

widjén sesame seed.

Wiéna Vienna.

wih exclamation to call attention.

wijaga Javanese gamelan player.

wijata education.

wiladah confinement, childbirth.

wilajah region, district, province.

Wina Vienna.

windu a cycle of 8 years in Javanese calendrical reckoning.

wira 1 man. 2 hero.

wirama see IRAMA.

wirawan 1 hero. 2 heroic, courageous.

wirjaan see HAL.

wiron pleat, fold. **ber–** pleated.

wiru pleat, fold. **ber–** –² pleated.

wisata a tour. **ber–** to tour.

wisatawan tourist.

wiski whisky.

wisma building. – *budaja* art gallery.

wk(l) [*wakil*] vice-, deputy, assistant.

WMP see WAMPA.

w.n. [*warga negara*] citizen.

WNA [*Warga Negara Asli*] citizen by birth.

WNI [*Warganegara Indonésia*] citizen of Indonesia.

wol wool.

wolanda see BELANDA.

wortel see BORTOL.

wss [*waktu Sumatera Selatan*] South Sumatran time.

wsu [*waktu Sumatera Utara*] North Sumatran time.

W'ton [*Washington*] Washington, D.C.

wudjud 1 existence, being. 2 intention, aim. **ber–** 1 to have the shape of. *Médja itu* ∼ *bundar*, The table is round. 2 perceptible, concrete, tangible. 3 to be composed of. *Kursus itu akan* ∼ *peladjaran tertulis*, The course will be composed of written lessons. **me–kan** 1 to give shape, create. 2 to realize. *Susah dia* ∼ *tjita²nja*, It's difficult for him to realize his ideals. **per–an** 1 shape, form. 2 realization, materialization. 3 phenomenon. **ter–** materialized, shaped.

wudu ritual ablution before prayers.

wuduk see NASI.

wutuh see UTUH.

wuwung 1 ceiling. 2 house ridge.

Z

zabardjah crystal.

zabib 1 raisins. 2 dried figs.

zabur psalm. see KITAB.

zahid of holy, ascetic life.

zahir see LAHIR.

zait(un) olive (tree, fruit, oil).

zakar penis.

zakat religious tax, k.o. tithe. **ber–** to pay the religious tax.

zalim despotic, tyrannical.

zaman period, epoch, time. – *Belanda* period of Dutch rule. – *depan* future. – *dulu* former times, past. – *kawi* ancient times. – *keemasan* golden age. – *madya* the Middle Ages. – *malaise*, – *melését* hard times, depression. – *muka* future. – *pertengahan* Middle Ages. – *sekarang* the present. *sampai achir* – forever. *sdh dimakan* – archaic, old, oldfashioned.

zamrud emerald.

zamzam 1 sacred well in Mecca. 2 holy water from Mecca's sacred well.

zanggi 1 Negro. 2 Ethiopian.

zarafah see ZURAPAH.

zar(r)ah 1 particle, crumb, matter. 2 atom. **se–** a bit. *petjah* **men–** pulverized.

zat 1 essence of God. 2 substance, matter. – *air* hydrogen. – *air belérang* hydrogen sulphide. – *anti* antimatter. – *arang* carbon. – *asam* oxygen. – *garam* salts. – *hidjau* chlorophyl. – *kapur* calcium. – *lemak* fats. – *maka-* *nan* calory, vitamin. – *padat* solid matter (in physics). – (*pe*)*lemas* nitrogen. – *pembakar* oxygen. – *pengenal* reagents. – *penularan* germ of infection. – *putih telur* albumen. – *sakar* glucose. – *sendawa* nitrogen. – *telur* protein, albumen.

zeni see DJENI.

ziarah visit to a sacred place (e.g. the hallowed grave of o's parents, ancestors, a saint). **ber–** to visit a sacred place. *Ia* ∼ *kemakam Pangéran Diponegoro*, He paid a visit to the grave of Prince Diponegoro. **men–i** to visit (a sacred place). see DJIARAH.

zikir 1 continuously repeated recitation of the first part of the Moslem confession of faith *la ilaha illa'llah*. 2 recollection, remembrance. 3 see DIKIR.

zina(h) adultery. **ber–** to commit adultery. **per–an** adultery.

Zohal Saturn.

Zohrah Venus.

zuadah see DJUADAH.

Zuhal see ZOHAL.

Zuhrah see ZOHRAH.

zuhur see LOHOR.

Zulhidjah twelfth month of the Moslem year.

Zulkaédah eleventh month of the Moslem year.

zurapah giraffe.